John Moir 30th Jan 1979.

THE CONTAINMENT OF URBAN ENGLAND

VOLUME ONE

URBAN AND METROPOLITAN GROWTH PROCESSES

or Megalopolis Denied

THE CONTAINMENT OF URBAN ENGLAND

BY

PETER HALL
HARRY GRACEY
ROY DREWETT
RAY THOMAS

ASSISTED BY
BOB PEACOCK, ANNE WHALLEY, CHRIS SMITH,
ANTHONY BECK AND WERNER HEIDEMANN

VOLUME ONE

URBAN AND METROPOLITAN GROWTH PROCESSES

or Megalopolis Denied

PEP
12 Upper Belgrave Street, London

London
GEORGE ALLEN & UNWIN LTD

Beverly Hills
SAGE PUBLICATIONS INC

First published in 1973

ISBN 0 04 352040 5 (George Allen & Unwin Ltd)
ISBN 0 8039 0245 X (Sage Publications Inc)

Library of Congress Catalog Card No. 73–77182

Printed in Great Britain
in 10 point Times Roman
by Alden & Mowbray Ltd
at the Alden Press, Oxford

To the memory of
John Madge

CONTENTS

VOLUME ONE URBAN AND METROPOLITAN GROWTH PROCESSES

CONTENTS

VOLUME TWO THE PLANNING SYSTEM: OBJECTIVES, OPERATIONS, IMPACTS

LIST OF TABLES (VOLUME ONE)

NOTE

The Tables for Volume Two are separately listed at the beginning of that Volume.

LIST OF FIGURES (VOLUME ONE)

LIST OF FIGURES

NOTE

The Figures for Volume Two are separately listed at the beginning of that Volume.

PREFACE

This present Volume may be read as a self-contained entity. But it also forms the first half of a larger work, *The Containment of Urban England*, which represents the output of a five-year study at Political and Economic Planning (PEP) into the processes of urban growth in England after the Second World War and the impact of the postwar British land-use planning system upon those processes. The two Volumes have different starting points and different foci of attention. But it is hoped that read together, they will illuminate and reinforce each other.

This first Volume has as its central focus the process of urban growth. It looks at definitions of urbanism and of urban growth, tries to devise new frameworks for the analysis of these phenomena, and presents a uniform statistical picture of growth and change in 100 major urban areas of England and Wales for the period from the early 1930s to the early 1970s. Then it turns to a detailed analysis of five extended areas of complex urban development, located within the most heavily urbanized belt of England: the area we call Megalopolis England, though this turns out to be more a useful framework of analysis than a real phenomenon in a physical sense. It studies changes within these areas in land use, in migration patterns and in socio-economic segregation. Finally, it recounts in detail the postwar history of development in each of these five zones and the impact of planning policies and planning controls upon it. In these later Chapters of the present Volume, the theme of planning is explicitly introduced. The final Chapter attempts to sum up the main conclusions that have been learned both from the overall statistical analysis and the detailed accounts.

In Volume Two, entitled *The Planning System: Objectives, Operations, Impacts*, the main focus is on the planning system and its interaction with other actors in the land development process. The Volume centrally tries to answer three questions. First, what were the objectives of the rather sophisticated system of urban and regional planning which was set up in Britain after the Second World War? Secondly, how in practice did the system operate, especially in so far as it involved complex interrelationships with developers and with clients such as industrialists and intending house owners? And thirdly, what have been some of the principal impacts of the system, intended and unintended: on the house building programme, on the housing and land markets, on patterns of journeys to work? What, specifically, has been the contribution of the new towns and expanding towns programmes to the total pattern of urban development since the Second World War? Finally, what sort of judgement can be reached on the system in comparison with what might have existed without it? What policy options exist for the future in the light of knowledge of the recent past?

Thus the stance of the two Volumes is different. Whereas the present Volume is concerned with urban development and urban growth, Volume

Two is centrally concerned with the processes that bring about that development and growth – above all the planning process. Whereas this Volume is concerned first with statistical analysis of trends and then with historical dissection of events, Volume Two is principally concerned with systematic deep probing of the forces which bring about urban growth, and of their interrelationships. Whereas the main input into Volume One is first geographical and then historical, the main inputs into Volume Two are sociological, political and economic. Whereas the present Volume will reach certain provisional conclusions about the ways the urban growth process has operated, it is left to the end of the second Volume to make a considered summing-up of the contribution of the British land-use planning system in comparison with what might have existed in its place.

A NOTE ON AUTHORSHIP

Both this Volume, and its companion, were produced by a team which worked for four years at Political and Economic Planning (PEP). Of this central team, one (Peter Hall) was part-time, the others (Ray Thomas, Harry Gracey and Roy Drewett) were full-time members. The team was assisted by a number of research assistants, the most important of whom are credited specifically on the title page and in the Acknowledgements of both Volumes.

The great bulk of both Volumes was drafted by individual team members, usually alone, occasionally in co-operation. In each case, the authorship is clearly shown in the contents list and at the beginning of each Chapter. These Chapters essentially represent the views of their authors, who bear responsibility for them individually. Certain of the concluding Chapters of Volume Two, however, were drafted collectively after intensive team discussion; and these can be regarded as the work of the whole team. Both Volumes were edited for final publication by Peter Hall.

PUBLICATIONS OF THE PEP URBAN GROWTH STUDY

As well as this two-volume work, the following PEP Broadsheets by Ray Thomas were produced as part of the study:

- No. 504, *Journeys to Work* (1968)
- No. 510, *London's New Towns: A Study of Self-Contained and Balanced Communities* (1969)
- No. 516, *Aycliffe to Cumbernauld: A Study of Seven New Towns in their Regions* (1969)

Certain mimeographed Working Papers (WPs), referred to in this work, are also available from PEP.

ACKNOWLEDGEMENTS

This five-year study (1966–71) would have been impossible without the help of two institutions which provided nearly all the necessary financial support. Resources for the Future, Inc., first provided a grant to initiate the study, simultaneously with the start of their own parallel study of suburban land conversion in the Northeastern Urban Complex of the United States; and they provided a one year supplementary grant to bring the study to a conclusion. The main finance was provided by the Leverhulme Trust. PEP is very grateful to both the Leverhulme Trust and Resources for the Future.

Dr Marion Clawson of Resources for the Future, who initiated and directed the parallel study, has been a constant source of advice and encouragement to us during the five-year period of both studies.

We owe a great debt to the advisory group of eminent individuals who gave so many hours to reading successive drafts of the manuscript and to regular meetings which discussed them, as well as to others who gave informal help in designing the research and in reading and commenting on the drafts. Many were central and local government officials who cannot be thanked by name. We are grateful to them all.

Our particular thanks go also to many individuals and institutions who gave without stint of their time and expertise to help us with difficult technical questions and to make material available to us. Particularly we want to thank Mr Pearson and Mr Rossi of the Ministry of Housing and Local Government (later Department of the Environment) Library, and Miss Whale and Mr Grove of the Ministry's Map Library, and Miss Munro who was instrumental in finding many other land use maps from Ministry files. Librarians at the British Museum and the London School of Economics Library also helped us by prompt and efficient service in our bibliographic explorations.

We owe a special debt to Dr Alice Coleman, Director of the Second Land Utilization Survey of Great Britain, for making freely available to us all published and unpublished sheets of the survey, and for giving research space to our assistants. Without her generous help the analysis of the survey would have been impossible. Similarly, we wish to express our thanks to county planning officers all over the country, who worked to make available the sheets of their original land use analyses made as part of the survey work for the first edition of the Development Plans for their areas. Their labours alone made it possible to reconstruct the land-use pattern of urban England at the time the 1947 Planning System was set up.

We owe another debt to the planning officers and their staffs for co-operating so freely in our survey of the planning system recorded in Volume Two of our study. Similarly, we wish to thank all the developers who took part in our survey of developers' decision-making processes.

One development company should be mentioned by name: Messrs. Wates Limited, who made a small supplementary grant to permit the exhaustive work of bibliographic preparation on the philosophy of the planning system, which was the basis of Chapter 7 of Volume Two of the study. We are indebted to them for this help.

The main research officers, who worked on the project during the whole or principal time of the study, are properly shown on the title page of this volume. Without their unstinting work, often involving tedious and repetitive calculations, much of the foundation of the study would have been lacking. Other research workers, who gave valuable help to the study for shorter periods, include: Jeannie Drake, Paddy Hughes, John MacMullen, Sylvia Kasch, Netta Bloom and Mike Bristow. A special debt is due to Mohammed Hegazi and Elizabeth Razowska, who performed much of the detailed analysis of land-use patterns.

The majority of the maps were drawn by Mrs Kathleen King, whose speed and accuracy, coupled with a rare ability to spot imperfections in original drafts and to suggest improvements, greatly eased our task. Mrs Eunice Wilson, of the London School of Economics drawing office, gave us many hours of help on the difficulties of interpreting the First Land Utilization Survey, on which she had worked. Mrs Wilson, and Mrs Jeanne Marie Stanton of the same office, also drew a whole series of supplementary maps for the study, which are incorporated in these volumes. We owe a great debt to all these valiant cartographic workers.

The secretarial team at PEP bore an exceptional burden during the five years of the study in typing and retyping manuscripts amounting in total to many millions of words, often under severe time constraints. They include Mrs Ann Eccles, Mrs Alex Morrison, Miss Elizabeth Green (to whom we owe a special debt), Mrs Elspeth Waddilove, Miss Stephanie Purcell and Miss Barbara Livermore. Their task, and ours, was greatly eased by the always efficient and helpful administrative staff at PEP.

Magda Hall and Francon Whelan were successively responsible for the exhausting work of checking and editing for press a manuscript of over half a million words. Sally Burningham undertook the equally daunting task of reading the whole work in proof. We wish to put on record our thanks for their meticulous care. The editor and authors, however, bear full responsibility for any errors.

Lastly the team, and PEP, have one sad debt to record. John Madge, who as Chief Consultant to PEP was convenor of the research team, died suddenly in 1968 in the middle of our work. We dedicate it to his memory as our only appropriate mark of his contribution.

PH

RT

HG

RD

THE STRUCTURE OF THIS WORK

The study has been written in two Volumes, each of which consists of four Parts. This first Volume concentrates on the actual processes of urban and metropolitan growth in England with which the planning system has had to contend since the Second World War. It deals incidentally with the planning system and its impacts. Its focus ranges from the Megalopolitan scale, through the metropolitan scale, to the local area scale, but with special emphasis on the first two. Much of it is descriptive, even in those places where it is heavily statistical. It aims to document what has happened, leaving detailed explanation and discussion to Volume Two. Volume Two then turns to focus on the planning system: its main objectives, the machinery and the people who operated it, the complex processes of interaction between the main agents of development, and the chief impacts. Much of its focus is either at a very particular or a very general scale. It is essentially concerned with exposition and explanation.

The first Part of Volume One is a geographical and historical introduction to the whole study. Chapter 1 is an overview of the world pattern of urban growth, and focuses on the concept of the super-urban-agglomeration, or Megalopolis. It tentatively identifies one such concentration in England, and discusses some problems of scale and definition that arise in analysing trends within it.

Chapter 2 describes the processes of urban growth in England from the Industrial Revolution to the Second World War, with particular reference to those features which contemporaries identified as calling for more effective planning: the crowded, unhealthy nineteenth-century city, the spreading suburbs of the interwar period, and the contrast between the prosperous South and Midlands, and the unprosperous North, in the 1930s.

Chapter 3 runs parallel with Chapter 2, and describes the evolution of the planning movement from its nineteenth-century origins to the report of the Barlow Commission in 1940, the subsequent wartime reports and plans, and the legislation which set up the postwar planning system between 1945 and 1952.

Part Two takes us into the heart of the study. Its main focus is a detailed account, mainly from statistics, of geographical changes in urban England in the period approximately from 1931–66, a period that includes the great urban spread of the 1930s, and the operation of the planning system after the Second World War. This type of analysis has been often and well done by American demographers and geographers,[1] but has been less common in

[1] Donald Bogue, *The Structure of the Metropolitan Community*. University of Michigan, Ann Arbor (1949). Donald Bogue, 'Urbanism in the United States, 1950', *American Journal of Sociology*, 60 (1955), pp. 471–86. Amos K. Hawley, *The Changing Shape of Metropolitan America: Deconcentration since 1920*. Free Press, Glencoe (1956).

Britain. It has three chief geographical frames of reference: 100 *metropolitan areas*, a functional concept of urbanization borrowed from the United States; *Megalopolis England*, a super-urban-agglomeration of sixty-three SMSAs; and five *study areas* within Megalopolis, composed of groups of metropolitan areas, for more detailed analysis of growth and change.

Chapter 4 is a purely technical chapter introducing some of these concepts, and discussing problems of measurement and analysis. The general reader may skip it, except for its conclusions.

Chapter 5 is in many ways the heart of Part Two. It is a detailed analysis, from Census statistics, of growth and change in the 100 metropolitan areas of England and Wales. These are urban areas functionally defined in terms of commuting patterns around major employment centres. The analysis demonstrates not merely a pronounced growth trend in most of these areas, but also a notable tendency to internal decentralization of residential population and, latterly, employment.

Chapter 6, building on Chapter 5, asks whether a Megalopolis can meaningfully be identified in England. It concludes that such an area, taking a notably linear form along the main urban and industrial axis of England from the Sussex coast to Lancashire and Yorkshire, is a meaningful and useful focus for the study of urban growth and the impact of planning, though in a physical sense the operation of the planning system has so contributed to the containment of urban spread that the existence of Megalopolis has been denied. It ends by isolating five areas within Megalopolis for more detailed study and analysing land-use changes within them.

Chapter 7 analyses patterns of migration and social segregation within these five chosen study areas. It is an essential preliminary to the detailed history of urban growth, and the impact of the planning system on that growth, in the five study areas, which forms the subject matter of Part Three of our study.

Part Three, therefore, focuses on the five study areas. For each, it presents a detailed history of urban growth since the 1930s, and of the impact of the planning system on that growth after the Second World War. As far as possible, this history is taken from official sources: the plans, reports and studies which form the plan-making activity in each area. A deeper analysis of attitudes, actors and interrelationships is reserved until Volume Two of the study, Part Two.

Chapter 8 describes London's western fringes: the western suburbs of Greater London, developed rapidly during the 1930s, and the adjacent home counties of Buckinghamshire, Berkshire, Surrey and eastern Hampshire, together with the County Borough of Reading. This has been an area of exceptionally rapid urban growth both in interwar and postwar times, and of strenuous attempts by planning authorities to control it since the Second World War.

Chapter 9 looks at another area of rapid growth, though on a smaller scale: South Hampshire, developed around the two cities of Southampton and Portsmouth.

Chapter 10 considers the impact of a major provincial conurbation, Birmingham and the West Midlands, and the neighbouring city of Coventry, one of the most rapidly-growing large cities of England in the twentieth century, upon the neighbouring counties of Worcestershire and Warwickshire.

Chapter 11, on Leicester and Leicestershire, in contrast recounts the history of a freestanding city of moderate size and its relationships to its surrounding county.

Chapter 12 returns to the impact of conurbation growth. In this case, North-West England, there are two major conurbations, with centres only thirty-five miles apart. They have had a profound impact upon the neighbouring counties of Lancashire and Cheshire.

Part Four consists only of Chapter 13. It tries to summarize some of the main conclusions of Volume One and to provide a link forward to the analytic studies of interrelationships within the planning process, which form a major theme of Volume Two.

In Volume Two there is a shift of focus to the planning system created between 1945 and 1952. Its object is a systematic analysis of the system in theory and in practice. It looks at the objectives of the system as conceived by those who set it up, and at the machinery created to serve the attainment of the objectives. It then shows how in practice the system worked as a complex series of interrelationships between different actors in the development process – planners of all kinds, developers, industrialists and home buyers. It then turns to look at some main effects of the system on land values, on house building, on commuting patterns, on social segregation, and on the creation of planned communities. Finally, in a series of three interlinked Chapters, it attempts to give a tentative verdict on the system and its results.

Part One is an introduction to the analysis. Its aim is to introduce and describe the system.

Chapter 1 examines the objectives of the system as they evolved in the minds of those who helped create it, over a long period from about 1898 – the date of Howard's classic *Garden Cities of Tomorrow* – to 1947, the date of the historic Town and Country Planning Act.

Chapter 2 describes the planning machinery set up under the 1947 Act and associated Acts. It looks at the operation of the local planning authority offices and at the interrelationships between different parts of the machinery. It acts as an introduction to the detailed studies of development control which follow in Part Two.

Part Two is one of the central sections of Volume Two. It describes and analyses the operation of the planning system in practice by successively focusing on the major agents or actors in what is, essentially, a complex process of interaction among planners of different kinds; developers of housing, and industrialists; and the clients who buy the houses in the new residential areas.

Chapter 3 is the first of two chapters on the role of the planner. Dealing with the control of new employment (especially manufacturing industry), it looks particularly at interrelationships between the industrialist and two sorts of planner – the central government planner concerned with administering the scheme of central control over factory location, and the local authority planner.

Chapter 4 deals with the parallel control over new residential development. It focuses on private developments by speculative builders for sale, and brings out the complex and delicate interrelationships between the local authority planners, the developers and their architects.

Chapter 5 introduces yet another agent in the system: the buyers of the new homes provided by the developers. From a sample survey, it considers their motives for moving and for their selection of their new home; their experiences there, their degree of satisfaction with the move, and their future aspirations.

Chapter 6, finally, focuses on the residential developer. It considers his land buying decisions and his subsequent construction processes. It brings out the fine financial calculations that he must make, and the critical role of land prices in the calculation. Thus it provides a direct bridge to Chapter 7.

Part Three moves towards the final conclusions of the study. It consists of a series of chapters which describe the main effects of the planning system on the pattern of urban growth and on related phenomena. Some of these chapters range outside Megalopolis to draw on additional experience in other urban areas of Britain.

Chapter 7 takes up a theme already identified at the end of Chapter 6; the remarkable rise in land values since the Second World War, especially during the second half of the 1960s. It considers how far the planning control system itself was responsible, and how far the Land Commission affected the trend during its brief life.

Chapter 8 logically takes up the pattern of housebuilding in relation to migration and household formation. It finds that the density of occupation, measured in persons per room, has fallen between the 1930s and the 1960s. But in the medium density ranges, this is due to falling size of household rather than rising size of dwelling. The chapter also supports the idea that rising land values have contributed to higher house prices.

Chapter 9 analyses the relationships between home and workplace. It shows that as population has decentralized faster than employment, the length of journeys to work has almost certainly increased.

Chapter 10 turns to the phenomenon of the comprehensively planned communities – the new and expanding towns. It concludes that the new towns have succeeded in being self-contained communities as their planners intended, though many of the expanding towns have not. But even the new towns have not achieved social balance: they have failed to cater for enough of the poorer unskilled workers' families who – as Chapter 7 of Volume One has shown – have remained behind in the urban cores.

Part Four, finally, contains the conclusions of the study. It is organized in three chapters.

Chapter 11 tries to summarize the essential functions of the planning system set up after the Second World War. It concludes that the most important of these was the control or guidance of social change.

Chapter 12 turns to some concrete results of the system. Based mainly on the findings of Chapters 7–10, it identifies some of the most important as physical urban containment; suburbanization, or the separation of home and workplace; and rising land values. It compares what might have occurred under possible alternative systems.

Chapter 13, finally, considers the relationships between planning policies and a wide variety of policies in closely related fields such as economic development, agriculture, housing and transport. It does so both for the recent past – the period from the Second World War to 1970 – and the immediate future of the 1970s and 1980s.

Our study ends without positive policy recommendations; for such have not been our aim. Rather, we have sought to clarify the objectives set by those who operated the system, and to see how far these have been attained in practice. We have been especially concerned to look beyond the surface language of policies, to see underlying objectives. We have been concerned, too, to analyse in detail the interactions between the objectives of the planning system and the reality of the world that was being planned – a world that often seemed to change faster than the planning system could adapt. From this analysis, finally, we have tried to evaluate – not in the form of a rigorously standardized cost-benefit analysis, but in a more general way – the effect of the whole system on the process and the form of urban growth. In this way, we hope that we shall give indirect guidelines to policy-makers and administrators in the future. For though the 1947 system of planning that we describe has technically been subsumed by the 1968 system, essentially its foundations remain the same; and the same agents, the same personalities, interact within it.

PART ONE

SETTING THE SCENE

This study is in two volumes. Volume One concentrates on the actual processes of urban and metropolitan growth and change in England with which the planning system has had to contend since the Second World War. It deals incidentally with the planning system and its impacts. Volume Two turns round to focus on the planning system: its main objectives, the machinery and the people who operate it, the complex processes of interaction between the main agents of development and the chief impacts of the planning system.

Volume One is in four parts. This first part is a geographical and historical introduction to the whole study.

Chapter One is an overview of the world pattern of urban growth: it focuses on the phenomenon of the super-urban-agglomeration, or Megalopolis, and tentatively identifies five of them in the world, including a Megalopolis England which will be a principal frame for the whole study. It discusses some problems of scale and definition in urban analysis.

Chapter Two describes the processes of urban growth in England from the Industrial Revolution to the Second World War, with particular reference to those features which contemporaries identified as calling for more effective planning: the crowded, unhealthy nineteenth-century city, the spreading suburbs of the interwar period, and the contrast between the prosperous South and Midlands, and the unprosperous North, in the 1930s.

Chapter Three runs parallel to Chapter Two, and describes the evolution of the planning movement from its nineteenth-century origins to the report of the Barlow Commission in 1940, the subsequent wartime reports and plans and the legislation which set up the postwar planning system between 1945 and 1952.

CHAPTER ONE

URBAN ENGLAND IN AN URBAN WORLD

This introductory chapter identifies the central themes of the book. The focus is on urban growth in Britain generally, but in particular on a central, highly urbanized area where (it is hypothesized) urban growth has impinged as a special problem: Megalopolis England. This is one of five great Megalopolitan regions which can be identified in the world today; another, the Northeastern Urban Complex of the United States, was first identified by Gottmann in his book Megalopolis *and is the subject of the parallel study to this one by Resources for the Future, in Washington.*

The chapter goes on to isolate the two chief themes or objectives of the book. First, to describe and analyse the facts of urban growth and change in contemporary England and Wales – the main theme of Volume One. Second, to look at the objectives of the post-1947 planning system in Britain and how far they have been realized – the subject matter of Volume Two. This is done through case studies of areas of urban change and by special studies of particular aspects, both within Megalopolis and outside it. Finally, the study attempts to bring these strands together in a verdict on the British planning system. How well has it served the interests and ideals of different sections of the public? What have been its failures and successes? And what are the lessons for the future?

This chapter was written by Peter Hall. The work on the definition of comparative world Megalopolises was done by Anne Whalley.

INTRODUCTION

In one way or another, urban growth obsesses most of us in Britain almost every day. Most of us are urbanites – 80 per cent of us officially so, more of us on any realistic definition – and we all experience some of the side effects of urbanization, good and bad. We nearly all enjoy very ready access to urban jobs, shops, schools and services – probably at least as good, in fact, as the people of any other nation in the world except the Crown Colony of Hong Kong. But in order to reach and enjoy these things, many of us suffer traffic congestion and air pollution and noise and long journeys. We are directly conscious that rapid population growth, in a highly urbanized nation like ours, causes more and more of the landscape to be covered by bricks and mortar and asphalt. We may feel an immediate effect as the commuter road into the town becomes more congested, or as our children come home from school to report crowded classes at the start of the new term, or as our favourite walk in the neighbouring wood disappears under the builder's bulldozer. From the mass media we hear threats that eventually London will join up with Birmingham, and Birmingham with Manchester, to form an horrendous sort of super-city hundreds of miles long: a Megalopolis. We read warnings that more and more of our most precious agricultural land or scenery is being consumed by urban development. And we listen to warnings from the ecologists and the biologists that the optimum population of Britain has already been exceeded.[1]

This book is about the phenomenon of urban growth in modern Britain. Its main focus is the growth of people and of employment in urban areas, their outward spread, and their consequent occupation of land that was previously rural. It is particularly concerned with the effect of the planning system on these processes since the Second World War. For as a result of fears about the consequences of unplanned and unrestrained urban growth in the 1930s, in the period 1945–52 Britain set up one of the most comprehensive and powerful planning systems in the world. The key to the system was that the right to develop land was in effect nationalized, with compensation to be paid for the lost development rights of landowners. Thereafter, the landowner's rights were restricted to his enjoyment of land and property in its existing use. If he wished to develop, in the form of new buildings or a change of land use, he could do so only after obtaining permission from a local planning authority, which would be given only if the proposal were in accordance with that authority's published plan. These plans were to be produced by every local planning authority, and revised every five years; both the original plan, and all revisions, were to be approved or modified by a central government planning ministry.The powers conveyed by the 1947 Act made it practicable, for the first time, to limit the physical growth of urban areas, through the use of green belts and other devices.

But at the same time, the planning system then created had a strong positive side. The New Towns Act of 1946 made it possible to build new towns through the agency of government-financed public Development Corporations; and a dozen such towns were started in England and Wales in the short period from 1946 to 1950. The National Parks and Access to the Countryside Act of 1949 made possible the designation of National Parks, as well as a number of other types of specially reserved areas where planning controls were to be applied with exceptional strictness in the interests of conservation. Behind these various pieces of machinery was the force of a visionary idea, first expressed by Ebenezer Howard in his celebrated book *Garden Cities of Tomorrow*, in 1898: the planned dispersal of thousands, even millions of people from the great urban agglomerations to new planned communities.

[1] L. R. Taylor (ed.), 'The Optimum Population for Britain', *Symposia of the Institute of Biology*, No. 19. Academic Press, London and New York (1970), p. 7.

It was an ambitious, even audacious idea, accompanied by radical and effective machinery. By the early 1970s, the resulting system had been in operation for a quarter of a century. Professionals, and others concerned with problems of urban growth all over the world, have been intrigued by it and have admired it. British green belts, and new towns, are quoted wherever planners meet, from San Diego to Irkutsk. It had survived in essence while undergoing progressive modification in detail, most particularly by the 1968 Planning Act, which created a quite fundamentally different system of development plan making, less rigid and less codified than the old, hopefully more flexible in its response to change. As this new system was being introduced progressively throughout the country it seemed an appropriate time to try to pass a verdict on the history of British planning in its first twenty-five years, to ask what were its basic objectives, and how far it had realized them.

Viewed more closely this study has therefore not one main focus but two, which are in effect different faces of the same phenomenon. One is the urban growth process; the other is the planning system which sought to control it but was, in turn, forced to respond to it. The structure of the resulting book reflects this. In Volume One the main focus is on urban growth processes, particularly in the first half, Parts One and Two, which form an historical introduction to the subject and which then concentrate on detailed statistical analysis of patterns of urban growth and change in postwar England and Wales. But in the second half of Volume One, Parts Three and Four, the operation of the planning system is introduced in the form of a series of historical chronicles which try to describe the reactions of the planners to unexpected facts of urban growth and change. Volume Two is centrally concerned with deeper analysis of the planning system and its results. Part One describes the objectives of the system and the machinery that was created to implement them; Part Two concentrates on the main actors in the system and their interactions; and Part Three describes some principal effects of the system in practice. Lastly, Part Four attempts to sum up some of the conclusions of the whole study. It asks what alternatives might have existed to the planning system, and how different their effects might have been. It looks at a whole range of alternative policies in related policy fields, like housing and transport, to see how these interact with the planning system itself. It asks finally which groups of people have been affected, and in what ways, by the system. Who have been the gainers, and who the losers? Is it possible to come to any more general verdict on behalf of British society as a whole, or is that too amorphous a concept to pass judgement on? These are some of the basic questions of the study.

The answers, it is hoped, will be useful to planners and policy makers as they think about the objectives of planning, and the machinery for their realization, in the next quarter century up to the year 2000. But for this purpose they are of greater value if compared directly with the experience of other countries where different systems of planning, and of land-use control, have operated. For this reason, the present study was set up from the very beginning to run in parallel with a study of urban growth in the postwar

United States, conducted by a team under Dr Marion Clawson at Resources for the Future, in Washington DC.[2] Throughout, the two teams have maintained the closest possible contact; the basic concepts and techniques of analysis have been compared and, as far as possible, standardized. The basic geographic areas for study have been chosen to be very closely comparable in matter of size and population and, on the conclusion of the two studies, their results have been compared in a volume written jointly by Dr Clawson and Professor Peter Hall.[3]

PROBLEMS OF SCALE AND DEFINITION

In both the British and American studies a recurrent theme has been the conceptual and technical problem of the right geographical grain to use in the analysis of urban growth. Whether the subject is population decentralization or changes in land use, important characteristics that appear at one scale may be obscured completely at another. It is critically important to establish the right scale for the analysis in hand; one sort of analysis may demand one scale, another will demand a different scale. Again, there are many different ways of defining an urban area: the administrative city, the physically built-up city, the commuting zone, the conurbation, the metropolitan area. We need to know which sort of definition is most useful for which type of analysis. We therefore need a preliminary set of distinctions and definitions. This will be a deck-clearing operation, basic to much of the analysis in this book.

DEFINITIONS OF URBANIZATION

First, an elementary verbal distinction: henceforth, *urbanization* will refer to the degree to which urban development has taken place (a static concept), while *urban growth* will refer to the process of change (a dynamic concept). Now both urbanization, and urban growth, can have at least three possible meanings. Not so long ago, the meanings coincided. But increasingly in modern times they do not, and that is the root of the problem.

The first is a purely *physical* meaning. That which is urban looks like a town. It has large numbers of buildings close together. They are functionally differentiated: some are designed for work, some for residence, some for shopping, some for recreation. The second is a *functional* meaning. That which is urban functions like a town. The economic functions of a town are manufacturing and the provision of services. The social functions are intercommunication and interaction on a large scale. People involved economically and socially in urban functions are urban. By extension, the area they live and work in is also urban. The third is a *political* definition. That which is urban is governed, as a town, by a town council.

[2] Marion Clawson, *Suburban Land Conversion in the United States: An Economic and Governmental Process*. Johns Hopkins U.P., Baltimore (1971).

[3] Marion Clawson and Peter Hall, *Planning and Urban Growth: An Anglo-American Comparison*. Johns Hopkins U.P., Baltimore (1973).

In ancient and medieval times, and indeed up to the mid-nineteenth century, none of these definitions would have given much trouble nor would they have exhibited much conflict. Towns were clearly differentiated in a physical sense from the countryside: the buildings huddled close together up to the boundary of the fields, and there they stopped. Similarly, towns were distinguished functionally from the countryside. Their inhabitants performed urban jobs and they lived in urban society, while people in the countryside did quite different jobs and obviously belonged to a different rural society. The political boundaries of the city corresponded to their physical and economic reality. There was hardly any ambiguity and everyone could say who, or what, was urban.

In the late-twentieth century it is all much more difficult. To take the physical distinction first: instead of stopping neatly, towns diffuse into the countryside at progressively lower densities. There are parts of Berkshire which most people would regard as urban, in that they show few traces of fields or of cultivation, but where densities of houses or people are lower than in some parts of peasant Europe, let alone South-East Asia. (And had we not had the postwar planning system we are here analysing this would have been even more marked in Britain, as it is today in North America.) This is complex enough, but the difficulties on the functional side are much greater. Economically, less than 5 per cent of the labour force in Britain was engaged in agriculture in the late 1960s. Even in the villages, in the vast majority of cases, the bulk of the labour force is now engaged in occupations which have traditionally been regarded as urban. Many of them indeed work in urban areas as defined in a physical sense, commuting back and forth between the country and the town. Socially, or culturally, distinctions have equally broken down. The remotest British farmer buys the same sorts of food and clothes, watches the same television programmes, and reads the same newspapers, as the inhabitant of the town. His car gives him an access to friends, or entertainments, far greater than many urbanites possessed at the beginning of the twentieth century. Many observers have concluded from this that the urban/rural distinction has quite broken down and that, in the words of Melvin Webber,[4] the urban place has been replaced by the nonplace urban realm, which is a state of cultural urbanization experienced everywhere in advanced countries. If this is true at all, it is certainly truer of Britain than of almost any other country in the world. For because of relatively small size and a tradition of centralization, as well as long exposure to urbanization, our degree of cultural homogenization is surely unique.

One important conclusion follows from this. It is that the simple accordance between the physical definition of urbanization, and the functional definition, has broken down; nor do either of these, as a rule, correspond to the political definition. Even though the physical city has become blurred at the edges, we

[4] Melvin Webber, 'The Urban Place and the Nonplace Urban Realm' in Webber *et al.*, *Explorations into Urban Structure*. University of Pennsylvania, Philadelphia (1964).

do not anywhere yet have the situation envisaged by the American architect Frank Lloyd Wright in his utopian vision of Broadacre City: a uniform low-density sprawl of the entire population over the entire land area, with several acres per person. To be sure, as average densities in suburban communities fall, over time we should need to redefine the boundary of what is physically urban and what is physically rural, for the standards of the 1870s would not do for the 1970s. But though there would be room for differences in interpretation, few would doubt that there is still a distinction. Not so, as we have noticed, for functional urbanization. When Brian Berry and his co-workers came to produce realistic definitions of functional urban areas for the United States Census, they included virtually the whole land area east of the Rockies and only the uninhabited mountains and deserts were outside the influence of the major urban centres.[5] When we came to apply the same definitions to England as part of this project, we found exactly the same.

This distinction between the physical and the functional is a basic theme running through this whole study. The essential feature of the post-Second World War planning system in England is that it can be seen as an attempt to impose physical constraints on urban growth in a country that was already almost fully urbanized in a functional sense. It has been largely successful in its own terms, but what it could not do was to impose a limit on functional urbanization. This has continued, and the effect has been to impinge on the countryside in a much more generalized way than before the Second World War. Small market towns and villages have become even more completely urban in an economic and a social sense, even though in physical appearance they may have barely altered. Apparently rural roads, running through the green belts preserved by the planners in the interests of protection of the countryside, are full of urban commuter traffic at the rush hours. And despite all the attempts of the planning system, functional urbanization invariably tends towards more pressure for physical urbanization to follow, even if in muted form. The more a village is occupied by commuting urbanites, the greater the pressure for new housing estates at its periphery.

Physical definitions of urbanization are invariably in terms of coverage, or density. The British *conurbation* is defined in terms of continuous built-up area, the American *urbanized area* is defined in terms of a certain density of population corresponding to a density of dwellings. Functional definitions in the modern world, though, are invariably – at least in part – in terms of flows, or interactions. *The Standard Metropolitan Statistical Area* (SMSA), which is a basic unit of statistical analysis in the United States Census, is a good example. It unites at least three concepts: an employment centre, or core, of given size; a commuting field all around it, in terms of flows of people to work; and an index of character of the local economy within the commuting field. The *catchment area of a central place* or shopping centre, much used in

[5] Brian J. L. Berry, *Functional Economic Areas and Consolidated Urban Regions of the United States: Final Report of the SSRC Study of Principles of Metropolitan Area Classification*. Mimeo, Chicago (1967).

geographical analysis, is another example. It utilizes at least two concepts: one, a concept of size or density of activity in the shopping centre, and two, an index of flows into that centre of shoppers or shopping expenditure. In both, the essential threads that bind the constituent parts together are interconnections, or flows; though indices of density, or economic character, also enter into the definition.

A look at different sorts of functional urban areas, as designed by statisticians or geographers or planners for their various purposes, suggests that common to all of them is a notion of hierarchy. The element of flow, or interaction, in all such definitions is flow or interaction for a purpose. It is possible (at least theoretically) to classify these interactions or flows into higher or lower orders, according to their commonness or rareness, or according to the value which people put on them. A good example of this is the work of the pioneer German geographer who developed central place analysis, Walter Christaller.[6] According to him, all goods or services provided in central places could be classified into orders. Higher-order goods had a greater range than lower-order goods, that is, people would travel farther to obtain them. Thus in order to get an adequate range of variety they had to go to more specialized centres to get them. Consequently, only higher-order centres supplied higher-order goods. This principle of hierarchy is now seen to apply very generally in geographical analysis.

This suggests a new approach to the study of urbanization. If we could classify all sorts of flows, or interactions, doubtless we should obtain a complete hierarchy, with very commonplace short-distance interactions at one end and very rare long-distance interactions at the other. (At one extreme we might have our neighbour taking the dog round the corner for a walk and at the other, two statesmen flying round the world to sign a treaty.) In this extended hierarchy, urban places would fit as they fitted into Christaller's more limited hierarchy of service provision. Lower-order places would serve all sorts of lower-order purposes and would attract mainly short-distance movement. Higher-order centres would provide lower-order functions for their own populations (that is the nature of higher-order centres) but would also provide more specialized services for people who come a long way. We know from experience that this is true. Fewer people come from a distance to visit Hinckley (Leicestershire) than London, and Hinckley has manifestly fewer functions than London, especially of the more specialized type.

Therefore, it is important to stress that all functional definitions of urbanization are in essence arbitrary; it all depends on what function one is considering. Most functional definitions of urbanization commonly found, like those used for the most part in this book, reflect very ordinary mass interconnections made very frequently and regularly, over short distances. Commuting fields are the classic example. By stressing rarer or more special functions, one would produce a completely different map of functional urban

[6] Walter Christaller, *Central Places in Southern Germany*, tr C. W. Baskin. Prentice Hall, Englewood Cliffs (1966).

regions. At the extreme, as for instance in an art dealer's map of the world, a few great international centres like London or Paris would command contacts scattered all over the world, and the entire globe would constitute one interactive region.

MEGALOPOLIS: ANALYTIC TOOL OR FUNCTIONAL REALITY?

Scale problems and boundary problems like these are particularly acute when trying to isolate an appropriate geographical framework for the whole study: an area where urban growth is already most evident and most problematic, and where pressures for further growth are most intense. The parallel American study naturally focuses on the 600 mile belt of intense urbanization and, particularly, suburbanization, which the geographer Jean Gottmann called Megalopolis: the urbanized Northeastern Seaboard of the United States,[7] and which Marion Clawson terms the Northeastern Urban Complex. We naturally sought to define a similar framework. But throughout, a central question for us has been: is such an area merely a convenient fiction, a tool of analysis, or has it a deeper functional or physical reality?

The word Megalopolis itself has gone through many meanings. To the ancient Greeks it was a large planned town. To Lewis Mumford in 1938 it was the great metropolitan city, whose growth had gone out of control.[8] To the geographer Jean Gottmann in 1960, it was yet something else.

> A remarkable development – an almost continuous stretch of urban and suburban areas from southern New Hampshire to northern Virginia and from the Atlantic shore to the Appalachian foothills. . . . No other section of the United States has such a large concentration of population, with such a high average density, spread over such a large area.[9]

Subsequently, Gottmann makes clear what are the essential features of this complex, to which he has applied an old name. It is first, 'an almost continuous system of deeply interwoven urban and suburban areas, with a total population of about 37 million people in 1960 . . .'.[10] It is an area where the suburban outgrowth from the cities has gone so far that most of the intervening countryside between one city and another is urbanized in the functional sense we have used here. It is an area which performs specialized services (those requiring the most distant interactions in our discussion above), for the whole of the United States: the Main Street of America. It is perhaps 'the cradle of a new order in the organization of inhabited space'.[11] It is above all an area where social and economic relationships are extremely complex and mutually entangled.

[7] Jean Gottmann, *Megalopolis: the Urbanized Northeastern Seaboard of the United States*. Twentieth Century Fund, New York (1961).

[8] Lewis Mumford, *The Culture of Cities*. Secker and Warburg, London (1940).

[9] Gottmann, op. cit., p. 3.

[10] Ibid., p. 7.

[11] Ibid., p. 9.

In the first chapter of *Megalopolis* Gottmann makes in effect a number of alternative definitions of Megalopolis. It is first defined in physical terms as a very high concentration of built structures on the earth's surface. But as Gottmann makes clear, by no means all that surface is covered by urbanization. His 'continuous stretch of urban and suburban areas' must therefore be a functional definition: Gottmann confirms it by defining a Megalopolis in terms of Standard Metropolitan Areas. A provisional definition of a Megalopolis is an area in which many contiguous commuting areas, or Standard Metropolitan Areas, run together: in it, no place is outside the range of influence of a city. But as we earlier saw by another, later definition, most of the continental United States would fall into this category. What seems essential to a Megalopolis, in addition, is two things. First, the commuting areas are not merely contiguous: they interact in complex ways, so that many areas are influenced by more than one city. And secondly, there is interaction at higher levels: a Megalopolis is bound together by many visible and invisible functional linkages. Scheduled air trips, car journeys, letters and parcels, and telephone messages connect major and minor centres, forming a network of interrelationships – an exchange of people, goods and information – without parallel in the United States and perhaps in the world. All these features, we may surmise, are essential characteristics of a Megalopolis which is the most complex urban form to appear in world history.

The difficulty is that most of them are not strictly measurable, even in a country like the United States where information is relatively plentiful and accurate. For all his brilliant evocation of a Megalopolis, Gottmann never succeeds in defining it as a unique entity, and so never proves that it exists. If one seeks to ask whether other such Megalopolises occur in other parts of the world, this difficulty is compounded. The difficulties of comparing urbanization and urban growth in various parts of the world are notorious. They arise especially from the varied quality of the statistical sources and the different definitions used in different countries. The United Nations have done a great deal in recent years to persuade Census authorities the world over to adopt common definitions, but there are still large differences.

There is one way out of these difficulties. It is to make a standard definition of an urban area, and then try to apply it uniformly across the world. Because of the poor quality of the statistics in many countries, the definition must be a fairly simple one. This was the approach used by International Population and Urban Research (IPUR), of Berkeley in California,[12] in their definitive study of the world's metropolitan areas. They took the Standard Metropolitan Area concept, as developed in the United States Census, and simplified it so as to make it generally applicable to the Census statistics of the world. To be included in a metropolitan area, a unit of territory had to fulfil three conditions: (i) it had to touch a principal city or territorial unit already included; (ii) it had to have at least 65 per cent of its economically active population

12 International Population and Urban Research, *The World's Metropolitan Areas*. California U.P., Berkeley and Los Angeles (1959).

engaged in non-agricultural industries; and (iii) it had to be close enough to the principal city to make commuting feasible. The resulting area had to contain at least 100,000 people to qualify.[13] On this basis, the Berkeley researchers defined some 1,064 metropolitan areas in the world in the mid 1950s and they managed to get reasonably adequate statistical data for just over four-fifths of them.[14]

The results of the IPUR research have been summarized and analysed by Jack Gibbs and Leo Schnore. They show that in 1940, some 21·4 per cent of the population of the world lived in those metropolitan areas for which figures could be supplied. From then on, the average annual rate of metropolitan growth was some 2 per cent per year, a rate which would take the proportion living in metropolitan areas to some 26 per cent in 1950 and some 32 per cent in 1960. But this percentage varied very greatly, of course, from one part of the world to another. In 1940 it was 51·6 per cent in North America but only 9 per cent in Africa. Those parts of the world that were less industrialized had low proportions of metropolitan population but high rates of metropolitan growth, and vice versa. But, as Gibbs and Schnore point out, that merely reflects the fact that the highly industrialized countries had very high proportions of their population in metropolitan areas already and they could not be expected to maintain such rates of metropolitan growth.[15]

Our interest focuses particularly on the greatest urban agglomerations of the world. Using the IPUR definitions but employing later data from the 1960–61 round of Censuses, Peter Hall identified twenty-four super metropolitan-areas with populations of over 3 million apiece: thirteen of these had over 5 million and four had over 10 million.[16] Some of these, including some of the greatest – New York, London, Paris – had grown outwards around one dominant centre. But others – Tokyo-Yokohama, the Randstad or Ring City of the Netherlands, and the Rhine-Ruhr district of Western Germany – took a very different form. Their growth had taken place simultaneously round a number of smaller, specialized, closely related centres. These polycentric urban regions have a particular interest for us for they illustrate in embryonic form the forces that work to form a Megalopolis. Indeed, some of the definitions used in *The World Cities*, which produced the 'polycentric' super metropolitan-areas and which were adapted from the IPUR definitions, might be questioned on the grounds of arbitrariness. The Dutch Randstad involved adding together seven contiguous metropolitan areas; the German Rhine-Ruhr area also involved adding together seven. But in Britain, because of the extremely dense and concentrated urbanization,

[13] Ibid., pp. 25–30. Jack P. Gibbs and Leo E. Schnore, 'Metropolitan Growth: An International Study', *American Journal of Sociology*, Vol. 66 (1960–61), p. 160.

[14] Gibbs and Schnore, op. cit., p. 161.

[15] Ibid., pp. 164–9.

[16] Peter Hall, *The World Cities*. World University Library, London and New York (1966), Table 1.

it would have been possible to add together some sixty-three Standard Metropolitan Areas in northern and midland England, plus industrial areas, to give a super metropolitan-area with a population of over 32 million in 1961.

MEGALOPOLIS: A WORLD-WIDE PHENOMENON?

In starting to look for evidence of Megalopolitan development in other parts of the world, one obvious starting point is to continue this argument to its conclusion. By mapping metropolitan areas, as Gottmann did in first defining his East Coast Megalopolis, one can define those parts of the world where dense urbanization produces very large numbers of contiguous metropolitan areas stretching over large tracts of land surface. When this is done, one finds the expected: that on this criterion, Megalopolitan development is only occurring in those continents and countries which are highly metropolitan, in the sense that a very high proportion of their populations live in metropolitan areas. We should not expect to find a Megalopolis in most of Africa, for instance.

For defining a Megalopolitan form of development some minimum cut off in terms of population is clearly necessary. IPUR used 100,000 as a minimum for a Standard Metropolitan Area. Bearing in mind that we wanted to distinguish something quite different from even the largest of Peter Hall's World Cities (which was New York-northeastern New Jersey, with 14,759,000 people in 1960)[17] we determined on a minimum of 20 million in the year 1960–61 as evidence of a Megalopolis. By any comparative standards this is a very large agglomeration of people to find in contiguous functional urban areas. Indeed, on this rigorous criterion only five examples of Megalopolis are to be found in the world. The first of these is Gottmann's original Megalopolis on the East Coast of North America, stretching from Boston through New York, Philadelphia and Baltimore to Washington and beyond. In Marion Clawson's redefinition of this area for his study of the Northeastern Urban Complex, companion to the present volume, it contained 34·2 million people in 1960. The second is a Megalopolis on the shores of the Great Lakes in mid-western North America embracing the great cities of Chicago, Detroit and Cleveland: it had 19·7 million people at the United States Census of 1960, and went over the 20 million level soon after. The third is a Japanese Megalopolis along the main urbanized axis of the island of Honshu, embracing Tokyo, Yokohama, Nagoya and Osaka-Kobe. Depending on the definition used, it contained up to 40·5 million people in 1960. Fourth is a great Megalopolis in the northwestern part of the European continent, stretching from the mouth of the Rhine up that river from the Netherlands into the industrial Ruhr and beyond it, all the way up the Neckar to Stuttgart and beyond. It takes in such great cities as Amsterdam, Rotterdam, Essen, Dortmund, Duisburg, Düsseldorf, Frankfurt, Mainz, Mannheim and Stuttgart, and numbered 29·2 million people in 1960–61.

[17] Ibid., Table 1.

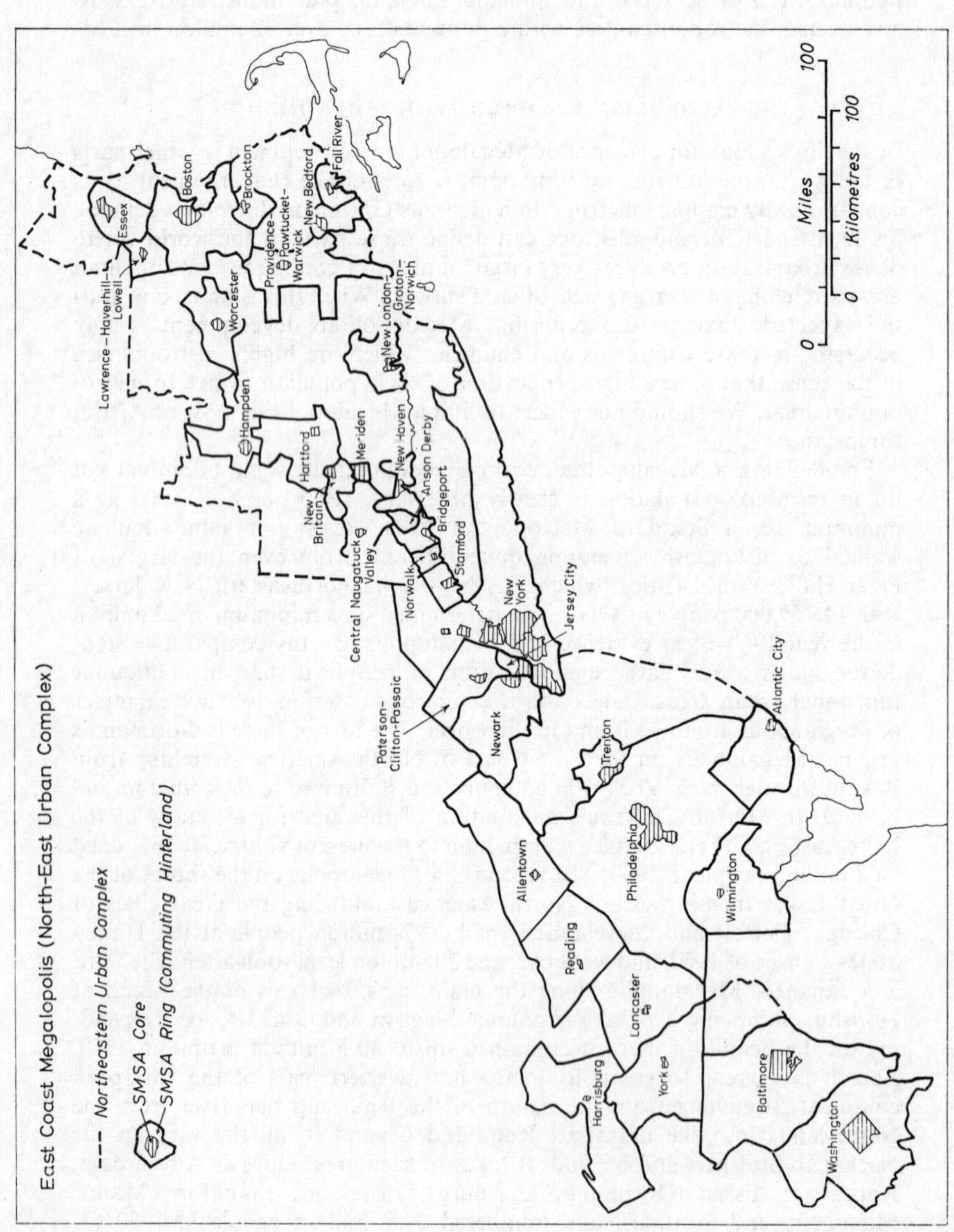
East Coast Megalopolis (North-East Urban Complex)
Northeastern Urban Complex
SMSA Core
SMSA Ring (Commuting Hinterland)
Miles
Kilometres
0
100
Lawrence – Haverhill – Lowell
Essex
Boston
Brockton
Worcester
Providence – Pawtucket – Warwick
New Bedford
Fall River
New London – Groton – Norwich
Hampden
Hartford
New Britain
Meriden
New Haven
Anson Derby
Central Naugatuck Valley
Bridgeport
Norwalk
Stamford
New York
Jersey City
Paterson – Clifton – Passaic
Newark
Atlantic City
Trenton
Allentown
Philadelphia
Wilmington
Reading
Lancaster
Harrisburg
York
Baltimore
Washington

Lastly there is the subject matter of this book, the area we have called Megalopolis England stretching from the south coast through London and the Midlands up to Lancashire and Yorkshire, and taking in many of the great cities of England: London, Birmingham, Manchester, Liverpool, Leeds, Bradford, Sheffield, Nottingham and Leicester to name only some. It had a population of 32·2 million in 1961.

As defined by Marion Clawson for his study of the Northeastern Urban Complex in postwar America, the East Coast Megalopolis of North America (Figure 1.1) incorporates thirty-four contiguous Standard Metropolitan Statistical Areas running from Lawrence-Haverhill (Massachusetts) in the north to Washington in the south, as well as seven counties not included in any SMSA which connect and round off the complex, and all remaining parts of any counties partly included in a metropolitan area: 78 counties, in fact, are included in all. This area, some 400 miles long and taking in 31,500 square miles, some 1 per cent of the national United States total, had some 34·2 million people at the Census of 1960, or 18 per cent of the national total, living at over 1,000 to the square mile. Of the total in Megalopolis, 31·7 million lived in urbanized areas (urbanized, that is, in a physical sense), with over 1,000 persons to the square mile.

The Great Lakes Megalopolis (Figure 1.2) is slightly bigger in extent than the East Coast Megalopolis; from Rockford in Illinois in the extreme west to Youngstown in Ohio in the extreme east it extends over 480 miles. It had a total 1960 population of 19·7 million, of whom all but 1·4 million were in twenty-three SMSAs. More than the East Coast Megalopolis, the Great Lakes complex proved to cohere into three distinct groups of metropolitan areas. The first consisted of seven SMSAs around Chicago and stretching north to Milwaukee, west to Rockford, Indiana (eighty miles from Chicago) and eastwards to South Bend, Indiana. It counted 8·7 million people in 1960, of whom nearly three-quarters were in the Chicago SMSA itself. The second group, over 200 miles to the east, is centred on Detroit and takes in a rather far flung group of metropolitan areas in the State westwards to Grand Rapids, Kalamazoo and Muskegon. South of Detroit it extends to Toledo in Ohio. The third group takes on from there, and includes five metropolitan areas along the south side of Lake Erie, extending inland as far as Youngstown: centred on Cleveland, this group included 3·4 million people at the 1960 Census.

In some ways the Japanese Megalopolis (Figure 1.3) is the hardest to define. It extends over some 300 miles from Tokyo in the east to Kobe in the west. It is dominated by five very large metropolitan areas, which fall into three groups quite separate from each other: Tokyo-Yokohama in the east, Nagoya in the centre and Osaka-Kyoto-Kobe in the west. Our definition includes all the prefectures or counties in which these SMSAs are situated, plus two intervening prefectures which contain a number of SMSAs identified in the IPUR study. In all, there are nineteen metropolitan areas in the Japanese Megalopolis, and it is estimated that they contained less than three-quarters of the total of the 40·5 million people in the whole area at the 1960 Census. Almost

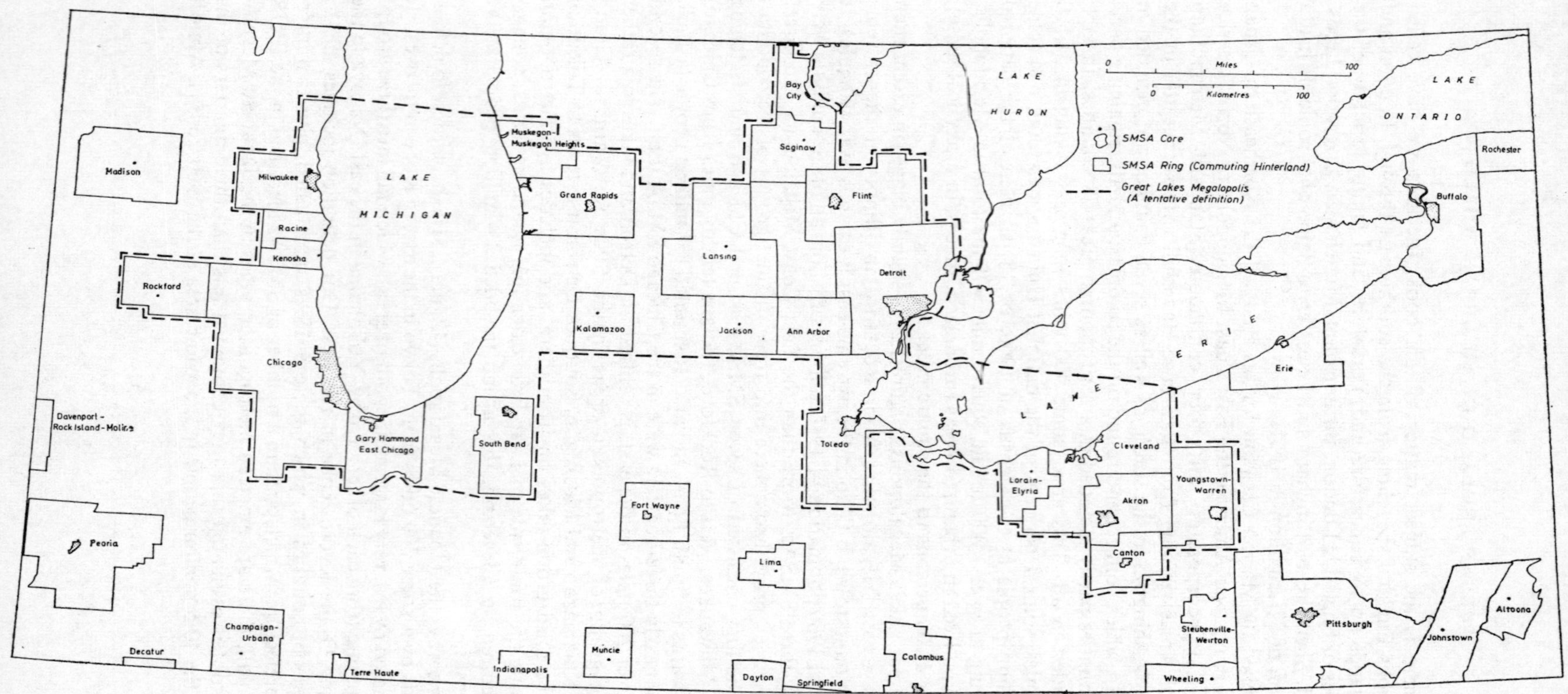

Figure 1.2 Great Lakes Megalopolis USA

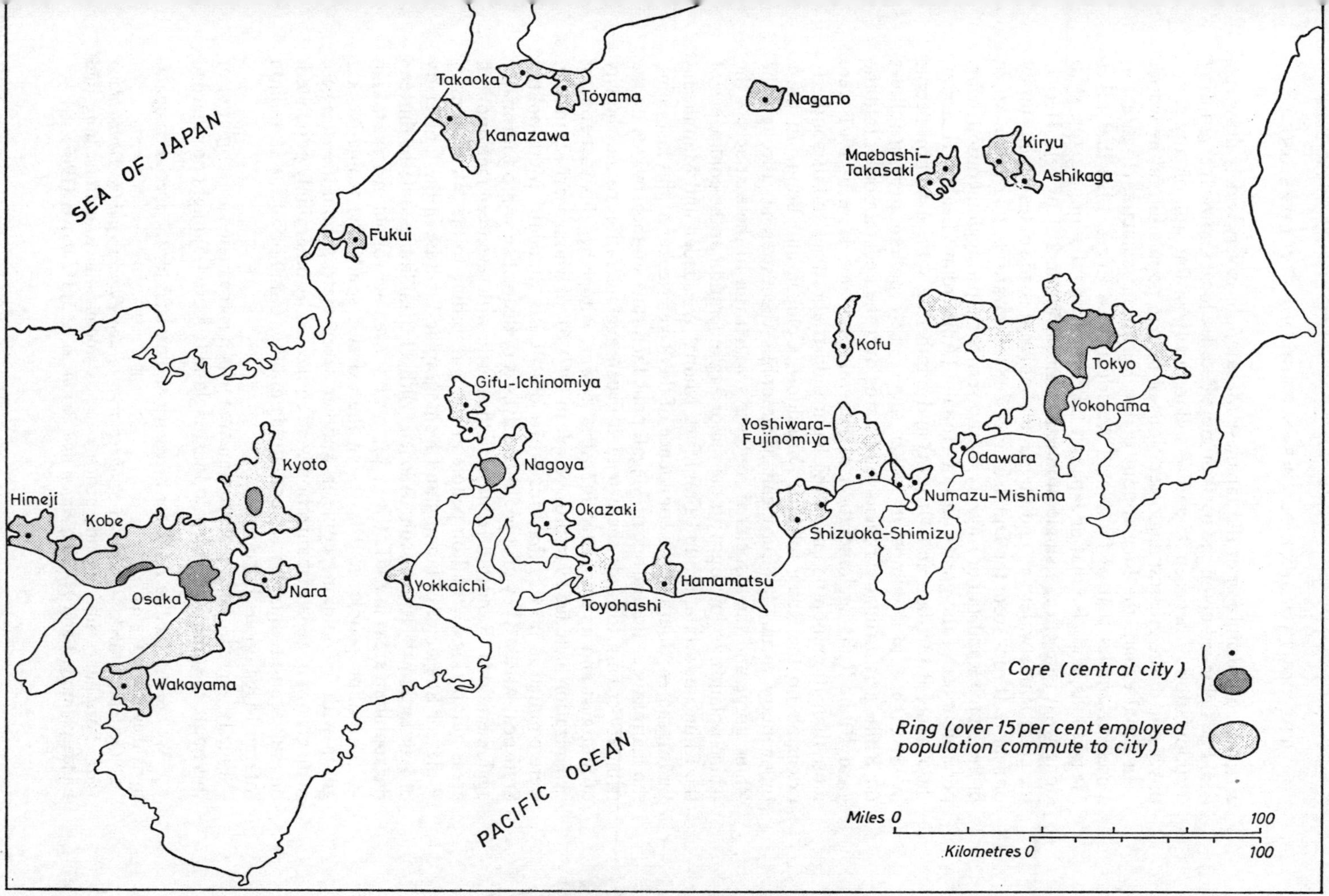

Figure 1.3 Japanese Megalopolis

certainly, our definition of the Japanese Megalopolis is very widely drawn; it could be tightened up on the basis of more detailed local knowledge, reducing its population to between 35 and 40 million in 1960. But still, on any count this is one of the greatest agglomerations of human population in the world.

In aerial extent, the Megalopolis of the European mainland (Figure 1.4) closely resembles that of the North American East Coast. Like that other Megalopolis, and also that of Japan, it takes the form of a long narrow strip along what is in effect a single dominant transportation axis or belt. Here is the great Rhine waterway and the parallel rail and road routes which run by or near it. It runs from the Dutch Zuider Zee southwards to take in the whole of the Dutch Randstad or ring city, the horseshoe shaped agglomeration incorporating most of the great cities of Holland (Amsterdam, Leiden, Haarlem, the Hague, Rotterdam and Utrecht) and numbering some 4 million people in 1960. Then, in an almost unbroken line of metropolitan areas, it follows the Rhine axis through Arnhem southwards over the Federal border into the great Rhine-Ruhr agglomeration of Federal Germany. Here in 1961 were more than 10 million people in the Ruhr industrial district and its southerly extension up the Rhine towards Düsseldorf, Cologne and Bonn. In more fragmentary form, the European Megalopolis then stretches through the Rhine gorge and the associated routeways which run to the east across the Rhine uplands, to join up with the major agglomeration at the confluence of the Rhine and Main, around Frankfurt, Mainz, Wiesbaden and Mannheim-Ludwigshafen. South of the confluence of the River Neckar at this last point, the main axis of the European Megalopolis then runs southeastwards up the tributary stream towards the extended urban agglomeration round the city of Stuttgart and its associated industrial towns. Altogether this vast zone of urbanization included 29 million people in 1960–61, of whom nearly 23 million were counted in no less than forty-two of IPUR's Standard Metropolitan Statistical Areas. They grouped themselves very distinctively into four major agglomerations: Randstad Holland in the north, with seventeen metropolitan areas numbering 5·2 million people in 1960, according to the calculations of Professor Steigenga's Planning and Demographic Institute in the University of Amsterdam;[18] Rhine-Ruhr-Aachen, with 11·3 million people in thirteen metropolitan areas in 1961; Rhine-Main with seven metropolitan areas taking in 3·6 million people; and lastly, in the extreme south, the Rhine-Neckar group with 2·7 million people in another seven metropolitan areas. These main groups of dense urbanization were connected by other thinly populated, but still semi-urbanized areas containing another 6 million of the 29 million total in Megalopolis Europe.[19]

Finally, there is the Megalopolitan area which is the main subject matter of this book. In some ways, Megalopolis England (Figure 1.5) might be regarded

[18] We are indebted to Professor Steigenga and his staff for the special computations they made for us.

[19] German SMSAs are from *Stadtregionen in der Bundesrepublik Deutschland 1961*. Forschungs und Sitzungsberichte der Akademie für Raumforschung und Landesplanung, Band XXXII, *Raum und Bevölkerung* 5, Hannover (1967).

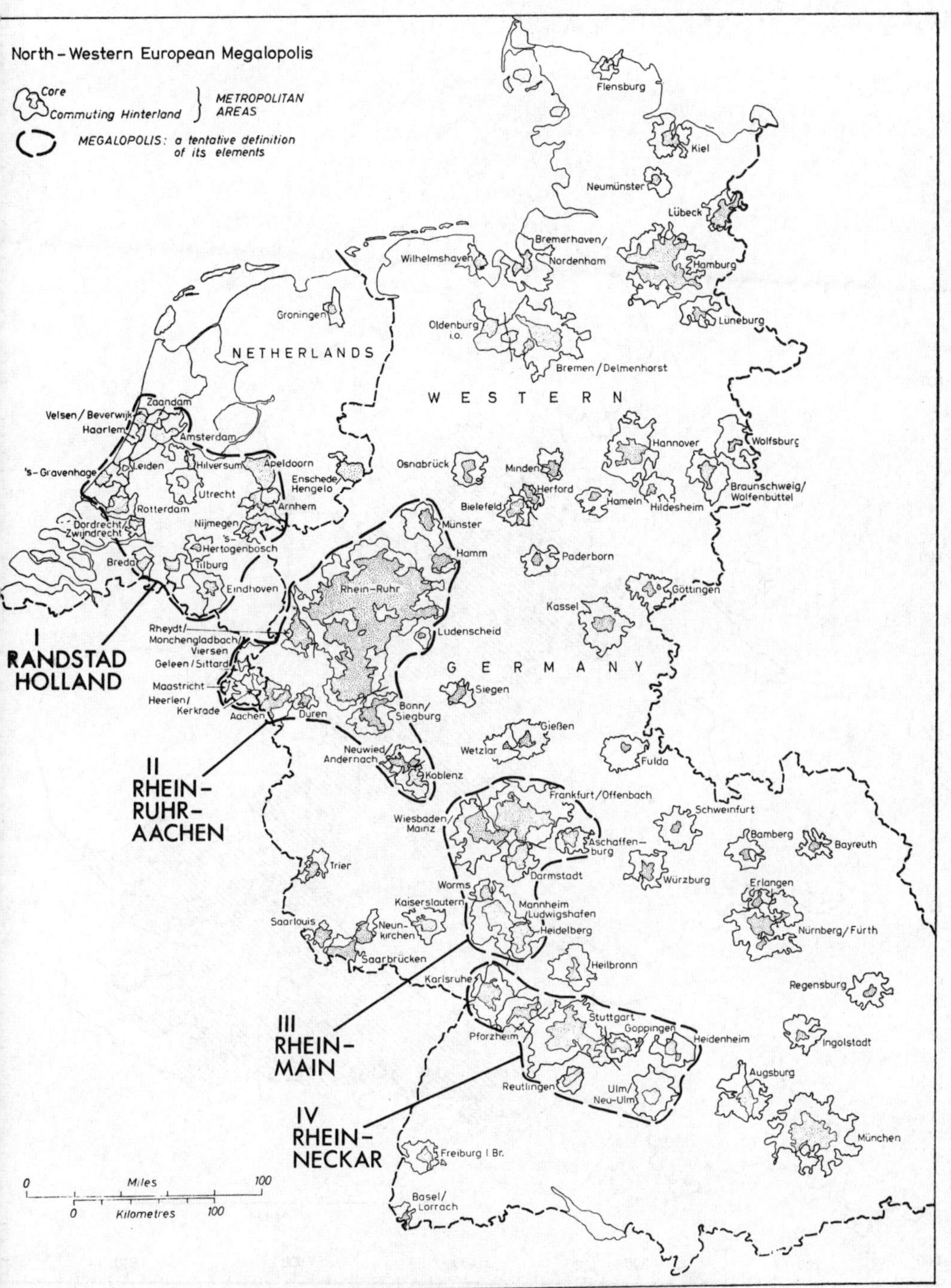

Figure 1.4 North-West European Megalopolis

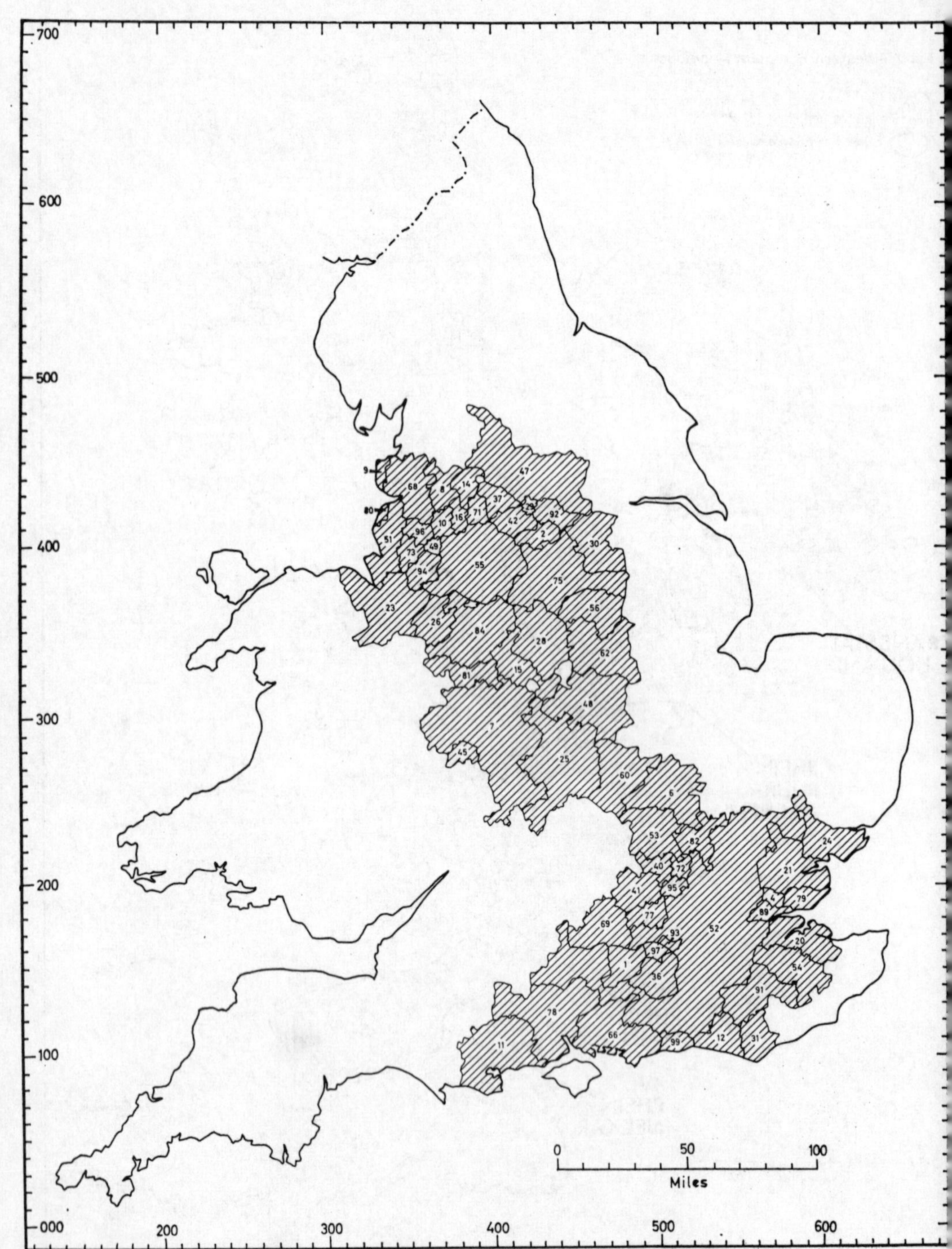

Figure 1.5 Megalopolis England (*for key see page 254–293*)

as an extension of the main Megalopolitan axis of the European mainland, broken from it by the 140 mile stretch of water between the Rhine estuary and the Thames estuary. At its greatest extent, Megalopolis England is one of the smallest of the massings of humanity we have identified here. It extends just over 250 miles from the coast of Sussex in the south to Preston in the north-west or York in the north-east. But, less bounded by physical restrictions than some other Megalopolitan areas, it also attains locally a considerable breadth, over 100 miles at its greatest extent, giving it a characteristic coffin shape which has been commented on by observers since the 1930s. It numbered 32·2 million people at the Census of 1961, of whom no less than 28·3 million lived in sixty-three metropolitan areas as specially defined for the present study. These metropolitan areas were mostly amassed into two groups, separated from each other by a narrow belt of non-metropolitan territory which seems certain to be closed in the 1970s, if not already by the 1971 Census. The first of these groups consists of London and a group of twenty-five metropolitan areas all around it, stretching down discontinuously to the south coast of England. It contained 12·6 million people in 1961. The second takes in no less than thirty-three contiguous metropolitan areas in the highly industrialized, densely populated areas of Lancashire, Yorkshire, the West Midlands and the East Midlands; it includes a very large number of the bigger provincial cities of Britain. This great urban tract, about 130 miles from north to south and over 100 miles across at its widest point, included 14·1 million people at the Census of 1961.[20] Altogether, despite its more restricted longitudinal extent, in population the English Megalopolis bears a very close resemblance to the Northeastern Urban Complex, or American Megalopolis, which Marion Clawson and his co-workers have studied in their parallel work on urban growth in the postwar United States.

Any reader with a critical faculty will notice that in the paragraphs above we have avoided the issue: in what sense can we call any of these areas a Megalopolis? The very limited statistics available to us for international comparison at least allow us to conclude that all these areas have at least one essential attribute of a Megalopolis: they are areas where urban regions, defined in a functional sense, impinge very closely on each other, and may even interpenetrate. They are therefore those areas which, in a largely urban society, are most intimately affected by the influence of major urban centres. We would therefore expect that in a physical sense, they are the areas of the world where urban growth presents the most complex and least tractable problems. The pressure on land from nearby cities, for different purposes, (residential development, transportation, water supply, recreation), is likely to be most intense in these areas of the world. The problems of organizing essential services, food supply (especially fresh foods), transportation, water and power, recreation, are likely to be most difficult here, and to compete with each other more in demands on scarce space. The spillover effects of development decisions, in terms of noise, pollution and general environmental

20 For a more detailed analysis, see Chap. 6, *passim*.

despoilation, are likely to impinge more on the average individual in such parts of the world. On the other hand, the benefits in terms of economic organization need stressing too. These areas provide uniquely large and concentrated consumer markets, pools of labour (specially skilled labour) and specialized services. They give a new meaning in a geographical context to the economist's economies of scale. And that is one good reason why they have grown to their present size and importance.

In this book, therefore, we shall look at one such area of the world, the area we have provisionally called Megalopolis England. In the course of our inquiry we shall define it more closely, and in doing so we shall ask whether it is more than just a convenient unit of analysis. In particular, we shall ask whether it is a meaningful unit of urbanization, in either a physical or a functional sense as we have used those terms. But at any rate, it is hoped to demonstrate its usefulness for our purposes of analysis.

Within the framework of Megalopolis our next focus will be at the metropolitan scale, the scale of the functional urban area, defined in terms of regular daily interactions. For it is within this framework that we should expect to find the most intense pressures for further urban growth. To isolate this growth, we shall have to focus on the physically urbanized areas within the Metropolitan Area framework, defined in terms of land uses or in terms of concentrations of resident population upon the ground. And lastly, for more detailed analysis with an explanatory content, we shall need to focus yet more finely on small areas or zones within the newly urbanized areas, where we can study the interactions of the different agents in the urban development process: the developers, the consumers and producers in the form of house buyers or industrialists, and the various agents who, at one level or another, play the roles of planners.

CHAPTER TWO

THE ORIGINS: URBAN GROWTH IN BRITAIN 1801–1939

This chapter introduces some of the main problems we shall meet in more detail in the rest of this book. Straightaway it poses the problem: what do we mean by urban? It looks at other people's answers to this question, starting with the pioneer work of Adna Ferrin Weber and coming down to contemporary researchers. The conclusion is that there is more than one sort of urbanization, and more than one definition of urban: the answer depends on the purpose one has in asking the question.

The chapter continues with an overview of the process of urban growth in England from the Industrial Revolution up to the outbreak of the Second World War, which helps to illustrate some of these critical distinctions. It illustrates the evolution of the idea of the conurbation, and later the idea of the axial belt or Megalopolis, from contemporary writings of the period 1910–30, ideas which were instrumental in the setting up of the Barlow Commission in 1937.

This chapter was researched and written by Peter Hall.

INTRODUCTION

The British are so conscious of being an urban nation that they treat the fact as self evident; it does not normally occur to them to question it, or to ask themselves what they mean by it. In this, as in other respects, they are not very interested in definitions. But we shall necessarily be involved in problems of definition throughout the whole of this book; indeed, we have already been led into the problems in Chapter One. So we can logically start, by looking at how other observers have categorized the English population into urban or rural.

The obvious starting point is Adna Ferrin Weber. A young American scholar, Weber in 1899 produced a book which is the true beginning of comparative urban analysis.[1] He was the first to document the fact that the British were the most urbanized nation in the world, and that they had been highly urbanized for a longer period than any other. In reaching this conclusion, he was also the first to treat comprehensively the problems of defining what an urban population was. He found that already in 1801, 16·9 per cent

[1] Adna Ferrin Weber, *The Growth of Cities in the Nineteenth Century*. Macmillan, New York (1899), Table 18, p. 46.

of the population of England and Wales lived in cities of 20,000 and more; by 1851 this figure was 35 per cent, and by 1891 it was 53·6 per cent. But this figure excluded the very large aggregate of population within the smaller urban settlements, and fuller figures, available only for the second half of the nineteenth century, showed that the entire urban population was already 50·1 per cent in 1851, and had reached 72·1 per cent in 1891.[2] No other nation, at that date, had anything like a comparable percentage. France had 37·4 per cent, Prussia 40·7 per cent, and the United States only 27·6 per cent.[3]

Since then the other countries have all caught up to a large degree, but England and Wales are remarkable for their degree of urbanization. The official Census statistics take up Weber's series, and show that the urban population was already 77·0 per cent of the whole in 1901. Thereafter it rose only marginally, to 80·8 per cent in 1951; and thence it fell, to 80 per cent in the 1961 census and to 78·3 per cent in 1971 (Table 2.1). Meanwhile, the urban percentage for Germany had risen to 76·8 per cent (in 1961), and in the United States to 69·9 per cent (in 1960).[4] In these countries, transfers of population from the countryside to the towns were still taking place as a result of the growing efficiency of agriculture and the continuing demands of the towns for manufacturing and servicing labour. But in Britain the process seems to have been about as complete, by the beginning of the twentieth century, as it could possibly be.

The difficulty with this analysis, and this conclusion, is that it is based on a very arbitrary definition of what is urban and what is not. According to the English Census an urban area is an administrative area described as urban; that is, a county borough, a municipal or metropolitan or London borough, or an urban district. These areas came into existence as the result of a series of local government reforms made between 1835 and 1901,[5] with an additional term, the London borough, introduced as late as 1963. They may bear only a very distant relationship to urban areas defined in other, narrower ways. Thus an urban district or a borough may be overbounded so that it contains large tracts of open farmland, occupied by a population engaged chiefly in farming and in providing services to farmers; most people would probably agree that this land was not urban in a meaningful sense. To take the opposite and perhaps commoner case, rural districts may be increasingly invaded by suburban development as the growth of towns washes across administrative boundaries. They may be covered largely by houses with gardens, and by services for these houses such as shops and schools, while the great majority of the inhabitants do not earn their living from agriculture or from services rendered to agriculturalists. Most people would probably agree that in some

[2] Ibid., Table 19, p. 47.

[3] Ibid., pp. 30, 68, 82.

[4] Peter Hall, *The World Cities*. World University Library, London (1966), Table 3, p. 18, quoting *United Nations Demographic Yearbook* (1960).

[5] For an account see V. D. Lipman, *Local Government Areas, 1834–1945*. Blackwell, Oxford (1949), *passim*; and T. W. Freeman, *Geography and Regional Administration*. Hutchinson, London (1968), Chap. 2, *passim*.

Table 2.1

THE URBAN POPULATION OF ENGLAND AND WALES, 1851–1971

Population, '000s

	1851	1861	1871	1881	1891	1901	1911	1921
Urban	8,990·9	10,961·0	14,041·4	17,636·6	20,895·5	25,058·4	28,162·9	30,035·4
Rural	8,936·8	9,105·2	8,670·9	8,337·8	8,107·0	7,469·5	7,907·6	7,851·3

	1931	1951	1961	1966	1971*
Urban	31,951·9	35,335·7	36,872·0	37,213·3	38,025·4
Rural	8,000·5	8,422·2	9,233·0	9,922·3	10,568·3

Percentages of total

	1851	1861	1871	1881	1891	1901	1911	1921
Urban	50·1	54·6	61·8	67·9	72·0	77·0	78·1	79·3
Rural	49·9	44·4	38·2	32·1	28·0	23·0	21·9	20·7

	1931	1951	1961	1966	1971*
Urban	80·0	80·8	80·0	78·9	78·3
Rural	20·0	19·2	20·0	21·1	21·7

Percentage growth

	1851–61	1861–71	1871–81	1881–91	1891–1901	1901–11	1911–21	1921–31
Urban	21·9	28·1	25·6	18·5	19·9	12·4	6·5	6·5
Rural	1·9	−5·9	−3·8	−2·8	−7·9	5·9	−0·7	1·9

	1931–51	1951–61	1961–66	1961–71*
Urban	15·2†	4·3	1·8†	2·4
Rural	2·6†	9·2	15·0†	18·0

Source: Adna F. Weber, *The Growth of Cities in the Nineteenth Century*, op. cit., Tables p. 44, 18 (p. 46), 19 (p. 47). Census 1951, *General Tables*, Tables 3 (p. 3), 4 (p. 5), 5 (p. 7). Census 1961, *General Tables*, Tables 3 (p. 3), 4 (p. 5), 5 (p. 7). Census 1966, unpublished data.

* Preliminary results.

† Per decade.

sense, this type of area would fall in the category of urban land. This indeed is the only possible explanation of a paradox: in the decade 1951–61, the rural districts of England and Wales were increasing in population more than twice as fast as the urban areas; in the decade 1961–71, they were increasing seven times as fast. Clearly, some more firmly based definition of an urban area is needed. What this might be is one of the central questions of this first section of the present book.

PEOPLE AND LAND: A BASIS FOR DEFINITION?

One elementary approach to this question is to say that urban areas are areas with a special relationship between people and land; in other words, to try to forge a *physical* definition of urbanization. This definition (and its alternative, the *functional* definition of urbanization) will have to be discussed and analysed in more detail in Chapter Four. But starting from here we can try to define urban areas physically, either in terms of a certain density of population per unit of land surface, or in terms of the proportion of the land surface which is occupied by land uses which we have decided to call urban. Clearly, both these definitions in turn raise many other problems of definition; what population density can be regarded as urban? What exactly is an urban land use? and so on. At this stage it will be enough to see what other authorities have done on this basis.

The Census authorities themselves, in 1951, attempted a precise definition on the basis of density. They took wards and civil parishes with an overall density of ten persons to the acre and more, and tried to group them into clusters of urban population. The result was a rather different breakdown of urban and rural population than the one set out in Table 2.1, as Table 2.2 shows. The urban population according to this definition numbered 31·5 million, or 72 per cent of the total population of England and Wales. As compared with Table 2.1, the main source of difference is the fact that the urban administrative areas contained no less than 4·4 million people who should have been categorized as non-urban. In contrast, the rural areas had only 585,000 who should have been classed as urban. No parallel analysis was produced for 1961 or 1966, but, in view of the rapid growth of rural population in the intervening years, it would undoubtedly show a big increase in the urban population living in rural administrative areas.

The 1951 Census also tried to grapple with the problem of defining meaningful urban clusters. Almost every Census, since the nineteenth century, has tried to give some analysis of the population according to the size of urban settlement. But since the late nineteenth century, as separate urban settlements have coalesced into agglomerations, these figures for separate administrative entities have become steadily less meaningful.

Patrick Geddes, in the year 1910, was probably the first to recognize this problem; in doing so, he gave the word conurbation to the English language.[6]

[6] Patrick Geddes, *Cities in Evolution*. Williams and Norgate, London (1915), pp. 40–1, describing the 'New Heptarchy'.

Table 2.2

DISTRIBUTION OF URBANIZED POPULATION, ENGLAND AND WALES, 1951

Region	Urbanized population			Non-urbanized population		
	In urban administrative areas	In rural administrative areas	Total	In urban administrative areas	In rural administrative areas	Total
	a	b	c	d	e	f
Northern	1,929,487	61,684	1,991,171	487,677	661,655	1,149,332
East and West Ridings	2,925,851	15,030	2,940,881	636,820	519,477	1,156,297
North-Western	5,440,822	85,632	5,526,454	488,100	432,224	920,324
North Midland	1,897,221	94,268	1,991,489	377,481	1,009,177	1,386,658
Midland	3,414,564	44,582	3,459,146	274,537	688,828	963,365
Eastern	1,517,122	72,390	1,589,512	429,062	1,079,553	1,508,615
London and South-Eastern	9,518,725	9,060	9,590,785	513,216	783,852	1,315,068
Southern	1,415,967	73,559	1,489,526	305,628	854,204	1,159,832
South-Western	1,530,144	34,916	1,565,060	339,226	1,116,472	1,455,698
Wales (including Monmouthshire)	1,281,212	94,065	1,375,277	531,859	691,539	1,223,398
England and Wales	30,934,115	585,186	31,519,301	4,401,606	7,836,981	12,238,587

Source: Census 1951, *England and Wales General Report*, Table 31 (p. 83).

Table 2.3

THE CONURBATIONS OF ENGLAND AND WALES, 1891–1971

Population, '000s

	1891	1901	1911	1921	1931	1951	1961	1966	1971‡
Six conurbations	**11,670·0**	**13,417·8**	**14,726·9**	**15,315·4**	**16,404·8**	**16,918·4**	**16,901·0**	**16,327·5***	**15,928·0***
Greater London	5,638·4	6,586·3	7,255·9	7,488·4	8,215·7	8,348·0	8,183·0	7,671·2*	7,379·0*
South-East Lancashire	1,893·6	2,116·8	2,328·0	2,361·2	2,426·9	2,422·7	2,428·0	2,404·1	2,386·8*
West Midlands	1,268·7	1,482·8	1,634·5	1,773·4	1,933·0	2,237·1	2,347·0	2,374·1*	2,369·2*
West Yorkshire	1,410·1	1,523·8	1,589·8	1,613·5	1,655·4	1,692·7	1,704·0	1,708·3	1,726·1*
Merseyside	908·3	1,030·2	1,157·2	1,263·3	1,346·7	1,382·4	1,384·0	1,337·5	1,262·5*
Tyneside	550·9	677·9	761·5	815·6	827·1	835·5	855·0	832·3	804·4*

Percentage total population

	1891	1901	1911	1921	1931	1951	1961	1966	1971‡
Six conurbations	**40·2**	**43·3**	**40·8**	**40·5**	**41·1**	**38·7**	**36·7**	**34·6***	**32·8***
Greater London	19·4	20·2	20·1	19·8	20·6	19·1	17·7	16·3*	15·2*
South-East Lancashire	6·5	8·5	6·5	6·2	6·1	5·5	5·3	5·1	4·9*
West Midlands	4·4	4·6	4·5	4·7	4·8	5·1	5·1	5·0*	4·9*
West Yorkshire	4·9	4·7	4·4	4·3	4·1	3·9	3·7	3·6	3·6*
Merseyside	3·1	3·2	3·2	3·3	3·4	3·2	3·0	2·8	2·6*
Tyneside	1·9	2·1	2·1	2·2	2·1	1·9	1·9	1·8	1·7*

Population growth

	1891–1901	1901–11	1911–21	1921–31	1931–51	1951–61	1961–66†	1961–71
Six conurbations	**15·0**	**9·8**	**4·0**	**7·1**	**3·1**	**−0·1**	**−3·4***	**−4·9***
Greater London	16·8	10·2	3·1	9·9	0·8	−2·0	−4·1*	−7·7*
South-East Lancashire	11·8	10·0	1·4	2·8	−0·1	0·2	−1·0	−1·7*
West Midlands	16·9	10·2	8·3	9·0	7·6	4·8	−0·2*	−0·4*
West Yorkshire	8·1	4·3	1·5	2·6	1·1	0·6	0·3	1·3*
Merseyside	13·4	12·3	9·0	6·7	1·3	−0·1	−3·4	−8·8*
Tyneside	23·1	12·3	7·0	1·4	0·5	2·3	−2·7	−6·0*

Source: Census 1951, *General Tables*, Tables 3 (p. 3), 4 (p. 5), 5 (p. 7). 1961 *General Tables*, *do.* 1966 *General Tables*. 1971 *Preliminary Report.*
* Boundary change. Growth figures based on adjusted 1961 totals.
† Decennial figure adjusted for boundary change.
‡ Preliminary figures.

For Geddes, a conurbation was a much bigger, looser urban region than later generations of demographers or geographers have been willing to accept. His Greater London, Lancaston, West Yorkshire, Midlandton, Waleston and Clyde-Forth regions embraced not only the tightly built-up, coalescent urban areas, but wide hinterlands around them. It was not Geddes, but the geographer C. B. Fawcett who in 1932 created the much narrower definition of conurbation that has survived: 'an area occupied by a continuous series of dwellings, factories, and other buildings, harbour and docks, urban parks and playing fields, etc., which are not separated from one another by rural land; though in many cases in this country such an urban area includes enclaves of rural land which is still in agricultural occupation'.[7] This was the definition adopted by the Census when, in 1951, they recognized the conurbations officially for the first time.[8] At that time, Greater London and five other conurbations constituted some 39 per cent of the total population of England and Wales. But significantly, even then the conurbations were showing slower rates of population growth than the country as a whole, and this differential has increased in the decades 1951–61 and 1961–71, during which the conurbations suffered population loss overall, as Table 2.3 shows. It is always possible, of course, that this represents reality. But in fact the evidence shows that the main population growth is taking place just outside the conurbations; that the conurbation boundaries, in other words, are too restrictively defined. Thus in the inter-censal decade 1951–61 Greater London lost population but the so called Outer Metropolitan Area, just beyond it, gained no less than 970,000 people; the West Midlands conurbation increased by 110,000, or 5 per cent, but the area roughly fifteen miles wide in all directions beyond it (but excluding Coventry) increased by 153,000 or 15 per cent; and the population of the Merseyside conurbation fell marginally, while the area fifteen miles around gained 96,000, or 25 per cent.[9] In other words, only ten years after they had been fixed, the conurbation boundaries look as if they were too restrictively defined.

A differently based definition was made in the 1951 Census of the populations in urban clusters of different sizes, and this gave a significantly different result. The major conurbations at that time (Table 2.3) contained 16,918,000 people, or 38·7 per cent of the population; the so-called urban clusters of over 500,000 people contained slightly less people, 16,214,000 (Table 2.4). Altogether, 24 million people, or over 57 per cent of the total population, lived in urban clusters of 100,000 people or more. And this, it should be remembered,

[7] C. B. Fawcett, 'Distribution of the Urban Population in Great Britain', *Geographical Journal*, Vol. 79 (1932), p. 100. Also see the discussion in T. W. Freeman, *The Conurbations of Great Britain.* Manchester University Press, Manchester (1966), Chap. 1, *passim.*

[8] Census of England and Wales 1951, *Report on Greater London, Five Other Conurbations.* HMSO, London (1956).

[9] Peter Hall, *London 2000.* Faber, London (1963), pp. 194–5; Figures revised on basis of Census final volumes.

Table 2.4

URBAN CLUSTERS BY SIZE, ENGLAND AND WALES, 1951

	Regions of England											
	Northern		East and West Ridings		North Western		North Midland		Midland		Eastern	
Type of Area	No. of clusters	Population	No. of clusters	Population	No. of clusters	Population	No. of clusters	Population	No. of clusters	Population	No. of clusters	Population
	a	b	c	d	e	f	g	h	j	k	l	m
Urban clusters wholly or mainly in the area, of:												
Over 500,000 population	1	817,318	2	1,156,017	2	3,585,680	—	—	1	2,228,702	—	—
100,000–499,999	2	501,842	5	1,109,092	6	819,696	6	1,258,369	2	625,915	5	647,528
25,000–99,999	10	476,387	9	479,450	17	909,761	9	432,869	9	402,779	9	442,690
10,000–24,999	12	179,310	13	195,603	13	184,653	16	275,322	11	173,968	12	197,174
5,000–9,999	1	5,235	4	32,959	3	25,424	1	7,680	4	28,963	4	31,975
2,000–4,999	1	4,834	—	—	1	4,413	—	—	—	—	2	6,605
All sizes	27	1,984,926	33	2,973,121	42	5,529,627	32	1,974,240	27	3,460,327	32	1,325,972
Add population within the area in clusters mainly situated outside it		6,245		—		971		26,205		—		272,696
Deduct population outside the area in clusters mainly situated inside it		—		32,240		4,144		8,956		1,181		9,156
All urbanized areas		1,991,171		2,940,881		5,526,454		1,991,489		3,459,146		1,589,512
Non-urbanized areas		1,149,332		1,156,297		920,324		1,386,658		963,365		1,508,615
Total population		3,140,503		4,097,178		6,446,778		3,378,147		4,422,511		3,098,127

	Regions of England—*continued*									
	London and South Eastern		Southern		South Western		Wales (including Monmouthshire)		England and Wales	
Type of Area	No. of clusters	Population	No. of clusters	Population	No. of clusters	Population	No. of clusters	Population	No. of clusters	Population
	n	o	p	q	r	s	t	u	v	w
Urban clusters wholly or mainly in the area, of:										
Over 500,000 population	1	8,426,087	—	—	—	—	—	—	7	16,213,804
100,000–499,999	3	519,541	5	978,262	2	717,133	4	613,145	40	7,790,523
25,000–99,999	13	589,551	6	274,678	9	549,631	10	370,199	101	4,927,995
10,000–24,999	17	292,126	12	198,071	12	202,513	18	272,843	136	2,171,583
5,000–9,999	4	35,805	2	15,846	12	91,316	14	108,158	49	383,361
2,000–4,999	—	—	1	4,928	1	4,467	2	6,788	8	32,035
All sizes	38	9,863,110	26	1,471,785	36	1,565,060	48	1,371,133	341	31,519,301
Add population within the area in clusters mainly situated outside it		9,156		17,741		—		4,144		
Deduct population outside the area in clusters mainly situated inside it		281,481		—		—		—		
All urbanized areas		9,590,785		1,489,526		1,565,060		1,375,277		31,519,301
Non-urbanized areas		1,315,068		1,159,832		1,455,698		1,223,398		12,238,587
Total population		10,905,853		2,649,358		3,020,758		2,598,675		43,757,888

Source: Census 1951, *General Report*, Table 32 (p. 84).

is a definition based on a fairly restrictive lower density limit of ten persons per acre over the whole administrative area concerned.

In these definitions we can see that the Census statisticians themselves have oscillated between two different sorts of physical definitions. The urban clusters are based on a density criterion. But the conurbations are essentially based on a bricks and mortar, or land use, criterion. In fact they were based on a close study of topographic maps. This is the simplest way of producing urban area definitions on a land use basis, and for much of modern history it is the only way because of the lack of accurate and reliable land use statistics. But it has two drawbacks. The information is not quantified, though this can be overcome by measuring from the map (a technique we discuss in Chapter Four). More seriously, the information is generally undifferentiated. We know that the map shows buildings of some sort, but often we do not know what sort, or what takes place inside them. Consequently, we are not always certain that the buildings are serving the urban population. In other words, the measurement from topographic maps gives a definition that is wholly physical; it does not, because it cannot, connect itself with activities or functions in any way.

The most important research work that has been done on the measurement of land use has in fact depended on other sources. One of these is the agricultural returns, which have been obtained from farmers each June since 1866. They were not reasonably complete before 1891, so that it is dangerous to draw conclusions from them before about the turn of the century. Even after that time it is known that their quality has increased steadily, so that comparisons over a long period of time have to incorporate an allowance for the fact. And they include a residual element of land not accounted for, which it is difficult to allocate with certainty to rural or urban use. Nevertheless, these are the only figures that can give any picture of land use changes over a long period.[10]

The second source is virtually unique to Britain: it consists of the two land use surveys of the country, made by voluntary workers under the direction of the late Sir Dudley Stamp in the early 1930s, and of Dr Alice Coleman in the early 1960s. The third source is closely related; it consists of the planning authorities' surveys made under the Town and Country Planning Act of 1947. These three direct Land Use Surveys constitute together an extraordinarily detailed record of land use in Britain, though not without great problems of comparability; they have been used as the basis of the analysis of land use change in this book.[11]

Up to now, the most extensive and careful work done on land use changes in Britain has come from Dr Robin Best, in an ongoing research project at

[10] For a fuller account, see J. T. Coppock, 'The Origin and Development of Agricultural Statistics' and 'The Accuracy and Comparability of the Agricultural Returns' in Robin H. Best and J. T. Coppock (eds), *The Changing Use of Land in Britain*. Faber, London (1962), Chaps 1 and 2, *passim*.

[11] They are described in detail, with references, in Chap. 4 below.

Wye College in the University of London. Best's starting point is an attempt to compare the reliability of the agricultural returns and the Land Use Surveys. Already in the 1930s two separate estimates of the urban acreage had been produced for Great Britain by Sir George Stapeldon, on the basis of the agricultural returns, and by Dudley Stamp, on the basis of his own survey. The discrepancy is very great; 4,685,000 acres in England and Wales according to Stapeldon, to 2,748,000 acres according to Stamp.[12] Best discovered from his analysis that the total urban acreage in England and Wales in 1950 was about 3,602,000 acres,[13] and bearing in mind the amount of urban growth that had taken place since the early 1930s, he concluded that the Stamp estimate was validated.

On this basis, Best could proceed with some confidence to analyse changes in time from the agricultural returns from 1900 onwards, correcting them by references to better sources wherever this proved possible. The main results are set out in Table 2.5. They show that in 1900 only 2 million acres, or just over 5 per cent of the total land area of Britain, could be regarded as urban; this figure advanced very slowly indeed to only 2·2 million acres, or 5·9 per cent, by 1920. But then, during the 1920s and 1930s, the urban acreage of Britain increased almost 50 per cent, to 3·2 million, or 8·6 per cent, in 1939. Since then the increase has been more modest, to a total of 4 million acres, or 10·8 per cent, in 1960. Best predicted that on the most realistic estimates of

Table 2.5

THE URBAN ACREAGE, ENGLAND AND WALES, 1900–1960, WITH PROJECTIONS TO 1980 AND 2000

Year	Population millions	Urban area million acres	Urban land provision acres per thousand population	Urban area as percentage of total land area
1900–1	32·5	2·0	61·5	5·4
1920–1	37·9	2·2	58·0	5·9
1930–1	40·0	2·6	65·0	7·0
1939	41·5	3·2	77·1	8·6
1950–1	43·8	3·6	82·2	9·7
1960–1	46·1	4·0	86·8	10·8
1970–1	50·1	4·4	87·8	11·9
1980–1	53·8	4·9	91·1	13·2
1990–1	58·2	5·4	92·8	14·5
2000–1	63·7	6·0	94·2	16·2

Source: Robin Best, *Town and Country Planning*, Vol. 32 (1964), Table 1 (p. 352).

[12] Robin Best, *The Major Land Uses of Great Britain*. Wye College, Wye (1959), Table 5, p. 30; Table 6, p. 32.

[13] Ibid., Table 8, p. 34.

likely planning policies for the future this figure would have increased to only 6 million acres, or 16·2 per cent of the total area, by the year 2000.[14]

In fact, Best demonstrates conclusively that the loss of land to urban uses was much greater between the two world wars, than after the Second World War (Table 2.6). The period 1927–34 witnessed the early growth of new suburbs around the nineteenth-century towns with the acceptance of higher space standards for housing, somewhat countered by economic depression, and the annual loss averaged 46,800 acres a year. Between 1934 and 1939,

Table 2.6

LOSSES OF AGRICULTURAL LAND TO URBAN AREAS, ENGLAND AND WALES, 1927–1965

Period	Average area transferred per year to		
	Building and general constructional development	Sports grounds	Total urban area
1927–8 – 1933–4	37,800	9,000	46,800
1934–5 – 1938–9	50,000	10,600	60,600
1950–1 – 1959–60	32,800	3,500	36,300
1960–1 – 1964–5	35,100	3,100	38,200

Source: Robin Best, *Geographical Journal*, Vol. 131 (1965), Table 1 (p. 3). Robin Best, *Urban Studies*, Vol. 5 (1968), Table 1 (p. 5).

when mass surburban development was coupled with economic revival, the annual rate of loss accelerated to 60,600 acres a year. In the decade 1950–60, in contrast, the annual loss averaged only 36,300 acres a year, a fact mainly ascribable to the more effective physical planning controls introduced by the 1947 Town and Country Planning Act.[15] This compares with an official estimate (recently disputed) of over 1 million acres a year loss in the United States of America.[16]

[14] Best has presented this analysis in various articles. The most convenient is probably Robin Best, 'The Future Urban Acreage', *Town and Country Planning*, Vol. 32 (1964), pp. 350–5.

[15] Again the estimate is available in various of Best's publications. This is from Robin Best, 'Recent Changes and Future Prospects of Land Use in England and Wales', *Geographical Journal*, Vol. 131 (1965), Table 1, p. 3, supplemented by Best, 'Extent of Urban Growth and Agricultural Displacement in Post-War Britain', *Urban Studies*, Vol. 5 (1968), Table 1, pp. 4–5.

[16] This estimate is from the United States Department of Agriculture. Marion Clawson's estimate was 660,000 acres. But of the U.S.D.A. estimates, 450,000 acres represent losses to roads, airports and other essentially rural facilities. Best, op. cit. (1968), p. 19. The reservation comes from John Fraser Hart, 'Loss and Abandonment of Cleared Farm Land in the Eastern United States', *Annals of the Association of American Geographers*, Vol. 58 (1968), pp. 426–7. Hart suggests that of the total area of cleared farm land lost in eastern states between 1910 and 1959, no more than one-third to one-fifth represented losses to urban growth.

This overall picture, though, conceals very great localized pressures in the major urban regions. Here, Best's closer analysis demonstrates that the main transfers of agricultural land to all other uses have taken place in a definite belt of the country, the area which used to be known in the 1930s as the coffin, later as the hourglass, and which is known throughout this book as Megalopolis England. Throughout this belt, in the period 1955–60, losses of 1 per cent or more of the rural area were common and in places, as in the Midlands and also west of London, the losses exceeded 1·5 per cent, compared with an average national loss of only 0·7 per cent (Table 2.7).[17] Indeed, Best's study shows that invariably the losses of land were greatest in the areas which are already heavily urbanized. Thus in the South-East, around London, more

Table 2.7

PERCENTAGE OF LAND LOST FROM AGRICULTURE TO OTHER USES, BY COUNTIES, 1955–1960

Group 1 Northern Counties		*Group 2 continued*	
Northumberland	1·5	Berkshire	0·8
Durham	1·2	Hampshire	0·9
Cumberland	1·1	Sussex West	1·2
		Essex	0·7
Group 2 Megalopolis		Surrey	1·8
Lancashire	1·3	Middlesex	1·6
West Riding	1·0	Hertfordshire	1·3
Cheshire	1·2		
Staffordshire	1·3	*Group 3 Wales*	
Derbyshire	0·9	Caernarvon	1·2
Nottinghamshire	1·0	Cardigan	2·3
Worcestershire	1·6	Montgomery	1·5
Warwickshire	0·9	Carmarthen	1·2
Leicestershire	0·8	Glamorgan	1·6
Rutland	1·9	Monmouth	1·3
Northamptonshire	0·9	Denbigh	0·8
Bedfordshire	2·0	Flint	0·9
Buckinghamshire	1·3		

Source: Robin Best, *Geographical Journal*, Vol. 131 (1965), Table 3 (pp. 8–9).

than one-third of the land is already urbanized and the rate of urbanization (considered as a percentage of the total regional area) is double the national average. However, in terms of the percentage growth of the urban area in relation to the 1951 urban area, the highly urbanized regions score rather low; this is because they have not got the room for rapid expansion. Here it is not surprising that the highest percentage rates of growth are marked up in regions with moderate degrees of urbanization, notably the Eastern region (25·9 per cent), Southern region (20·9 per cent), North Midland region (12·6

[17] Best, op. cit. (1965), Table 3, pp. 8–9.

Table 2.8

URBAN LAND USE, AND URBAN GROWTH, ENGLAND AND WALES, 1950–1960, BY OLD STANDARD REGIONS

Old standard region	Urban area as a percentage of regional total, 1960–61	Percentage rate of urban growth 1950–60	
		Percentage of total regional area	Percentage of 1951 urban area
London and South-Eastern	35·6	2·1	6·3
North-Western	28·7	1·8	6·4
East and West Ridings	14·2	0·9	6·5
Midland	12·7	1·4	12·4
Southern	9·7	1·6	20·9
North Midland	7·8	0·9	12·6
Eastern	6·9	1·4	25·9
Northern	5·9	0·5	8·5
South-Western	5·0	0·5	10·1
Wales	4·4	0·2	6·1
England and Wales	10·6	1·0	10·1

Source: Robin Best, *Geographical Journal*, Vol. 131 (1965), Table 4 (p. 11). Robin Best, *Urban Studies*, Vol. 5 (1968), Table 3 (p. 12).

Table 2.9

RATES OF RURAL-URBAN LAND CONVERSION, MAJOR REGIONS OF ENGLAND AND WALES, 1945–1965

Area	Five-year averages			
	1945–50	1950–55	1955–60	1960–65
Per cent conversion rate				
Central Urban Region	0·20	0·18	0·15	0·20
London Region	0·19	0·18	0·14	0·12
Rural Regions	0·06	0·04	0·03	0·05
England and Wales	0·12	0·10	0·08	0·10
Conversion Index				
Central Urban Region	172	183	183	196
London Region	163	176	169	125
Rural Regions	49	39	42	50
England and Wales	100	100	100	100

Source: R. H. Best and A. G. Champion, *Institute of British Geographers, Transactions*, Vol. 49 (1970), Table 1.

per cent) and Midlands region (12·4 per cent). These happen to be the parts of Megalopolis England, or the coffin, where land is still available (Table 2.8).

Subsequently, Best and Champion obtained more reliable official land use data which allowed them to make a detailed county by county study of

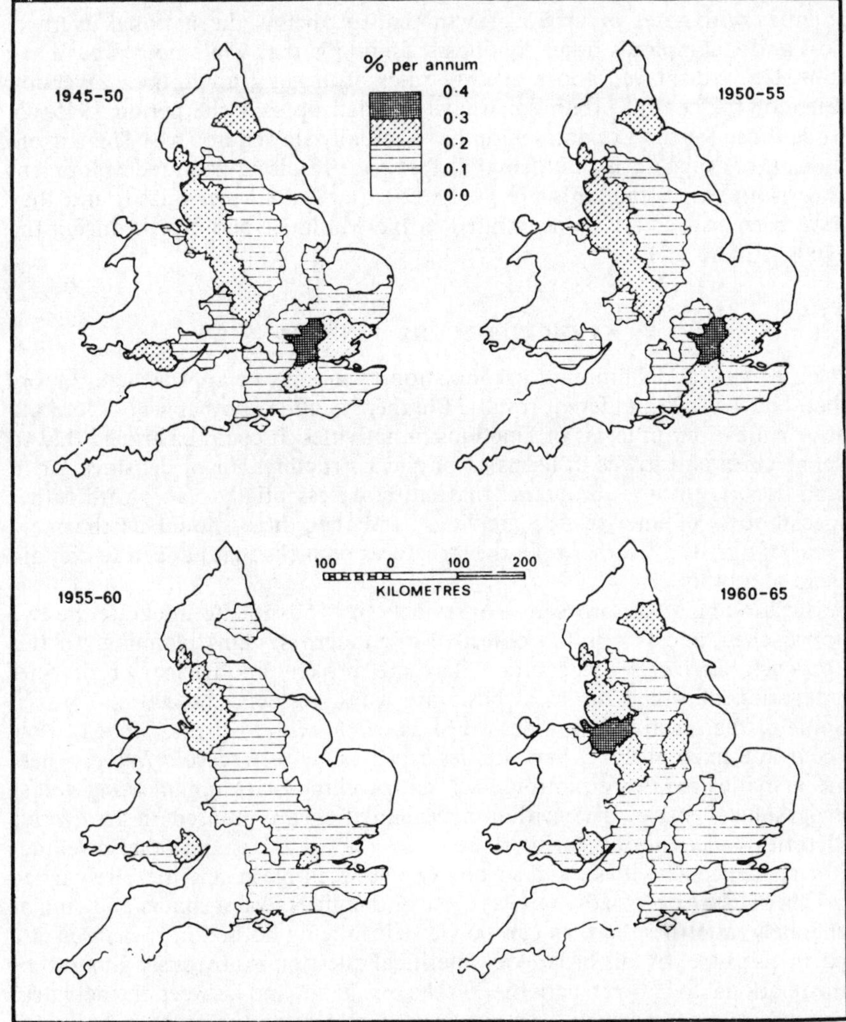

Figure 2.1 Land Conversions in Postwar England and Wales by Counties (after Robin Best and A. G. Champion)

urban growth in five-year periods since the Second World War (Table 2.9). Their analysis shows that urban growth between 1945 and 1965 was again concentrated along the main axial belt from London to Lancashire and

Yorkshire. However, the areas of most rapid transfer of land to urban use do not form a continuous zone. Rather, they form two clearly separated areas. One is around London; the other embraces the West and East Midlands, Lancashire and Yorkshire, and can be called for simplicity the central urban zone. Between these two areas runs a clear divide formed by rather rural counties with rates of urban growth that are below the national average. Best and Champion's other significant finding is that while both areas have consistently displayed above average rates of urban growth, the conversion rates for the central urban zone have speeded up over the period 1945–65, while those for the London region have actually slowed down.[18] The reason, the authors suggest, is that demands for space resulting from redevelopment and rising space standards are greater than are often recognized, and they have been particularly concentrated in the Midlands and North during the 1960s (Figure 2.1).

STRUCTURES AND FUNCTIONS

Even a physical definition of urbanization, then, may be approached in more than one way, with different results. But there is quite another way of looking at urbanization: in terms of functions or activities. It could be argued that to define cities and towns in terms of physical structures, or of densities, or of land uses, is to miss the point; that cities are essentially places with rather special sorts of inter-related activities, and that these should be the main focus of our study, rather than the structures or shells that happen to contain them at any time.

But looking at the problem more widely, it is possible to integrate the two approaches, and this is the objective of modern systems planning. In this approach, *activities* are central: they are broken up by coarser or finer categories, of which the most basic are work, residence, social and travel. Some of these activities are described as *within-place activities*: that is, they occur in a fixed place. Others are described as *between-place activities*: these are activities requiring motion, such as travelling or communicating across geographical space. The within-place activities are housed in *structures*: factories, offices, shops (for work activities), houses, flats and other dwellings (for residence activities), and so on. The between-place activities are carried on via *networks* of roads, railways, telephone lines, water mains and similar channels; and these in turn can be viewed as being housed in *structures* of a particular type. In this broad view a critical question is obviously going to be the relationship between activities on the one hand, and between the networks and structures (invariably of a physical character) on the other.

This analysis gives us several alternative ways of looking at cities and towns from a functional point of view. We have already seen that in a physical sense

[18] R. H. Best and A. G. Champion, 'Regional Conversions of Agricultural Land to Urban Use in England and Wales, 1945–67', *Institute of British Geographers, Transactions*, Vol. 49 (1970), pp. 15–32.

we could define urban areas in terms of densities of people or of structures (for instance houses) per unit of land area, or in terms of the coverage of land uses (representing coverage by certain sorts of structure, or the absence of structures). Similarly, in a functional sense we could define urban areas in terms of a certain density of a defined activity or activities per unit of land area: for instance, the density of industrial workers per square kilometre or square mile. Or we could define urbanization in terms of network linkages with activities: for instance, the percentage of residents who travel daily to work into areas that have already been defined as urban, on the basis of density of activities per unit of land area. All this depends of course, on the availability of reliable and fairly sophisticated statistics, which provides a major limitation until fairly recent times.

Without benefit of such statistics, we can make one generalization about the growth of urban areas in Britain since the Industrial Revolution. It is that over the course of time urban growth has been accompanied by increasing complexity of the urban structure, and in particular by growing complexity in the relationship between the physical definitions of urbanization and the functional ones. At the beginning of the nineteenth century, urban areas were compact and tightly packed; they ended sharply against open countryside. Physical definitions corresponded with functional ones: the town looked different from the countryside, and it performed different functions. Internally, the structure was also simple. Workplaces and residential areas tended to be intermingled, because of an almost total lack of mechanical transport for the journey to work. Where there was an element of differentiation, for instance in the formation of a central business district in the largest cities, residential areas gathered tightly round it, so as to minimize the walk to work.

The modern urban area presents just the opposite picture. More extremely so in North America or in Australia than in Britain or in Europe generally, the tidy division between town and country tends to disappear: suburban growth penetrates far into the countryside, sometimes leapfrogging open areas to land on others further from the city. Even when an attempt is made through planning to preserve a tidy physical demarcation, there is still an almost complete lack of relation between physical forms and functional realities: the old villages may be occupied almost completely by commuters to the city, and even the jobs performed in the countryside are likely to have little to do with agriculture, directly or indirectly. Within the urban areas as functionally defined, the patterns of within-place activities and between-place activities are extremely complex, with a wide scatter (modified by local concentration) of employment opportunities, and criss-cross patterns of movement in all directions between home and workplace.

In the paragraphs that follow we try to show schematically, and in summary, how this process of increasing complexity affected British cities between about 1800, the time of the early Industrial Revolution, and about 1939, when the continued growth of urban areas was just beginning to be viewed as a subject for public concern. The account essentially covers that period when cities and towns grew through unco-ordinated private actions, modified by elementary planning provisions of a local and regulatory kind, and in the case of some cities by broader co-ordinated action in the sphere of municipal housing and municipal transport. It is a period in which the broad philosophy of British town and country planning developed.

URBAN GROWTH IN ENGLAND, 1801–1939

Even up to the middle of the nineteenth century, it is a surprising fact that in England there were relatively few cities of any size; even they were relatively small in population by the standards we have become accustomed to in the twentieth century, and they were occupied at relatively high densities, so that by modern standards they occupied very small areas. In 1801 London had about a million people; no other town had as many as 100,000. The biggest were Liverpool with 82,000, Manchester with 75,000, Birmingham with 71,000, and Bristol with 61,000. By 1851 the population of London was up to 2,491,000 (or 2,685,000 if the area of Greater London is considered); three other great provincial cities had over 200,000: Liverpool with 376,000, Manchester with 303,000 and Birmingham with 233,000. Four other cities had more than 100,000: Leeds with 172,000, Bristol with 137,000, Sheffield with 135,000 and Bradford with 104,000.

Furthermore, these populations were often crowded on to very small areas. London provides the extreme example; because of its relatively large population, the lack of urban transportation caused extremely high densities close to the workplaces in the centre. In 1801, the most crowded districts of central London, totalling in all only 2,852 acres or 4½ square miles, held some 425,000 people (44 per cent of the total population of London) at an average density of 149 to the acre. By 1851, this most crowded area had extended somewhat, to include 5,797 acres (9 square miles); it then housed 945,000 people (40 per cent of the population of London) living at an average density of 165 to the acre. Statistics are not available on an equally fine grain for most provincial cities, but Manchester provides an illustration. In 1851, with 303,000 people, it was the third city of England. It had a roughly circular form with an average radius of about 2 miles from the centre; that is, an area of about 12 square miles. But five innermost statistical areas covering only 1,480 acres (2·5 square miles) contained 187,000 of these, or about 60 per cent of the total, at a density of 126 to the acre.[19] This was the typical situation in a city without any developed form of mass transportation; it reached its extreme point around 1851 or 1861.

Such a degree of crowding could be relieved only by cheap and efficient mass transportation; and this arrived only slowly, during the second half of the nineteenth century. Then the innermost areas, which had suffered the most

[19] Direct calculation from 1851 Census *Population Tables*. For a more detailed analysis of London population in the nineteenth century see Karl Gustav Grytzell, *County of London: Population Changes 1801–1901*. Lund Studies in Geography, Ser. B, No. 26. Gleerup, Lund (1969), *passim*.

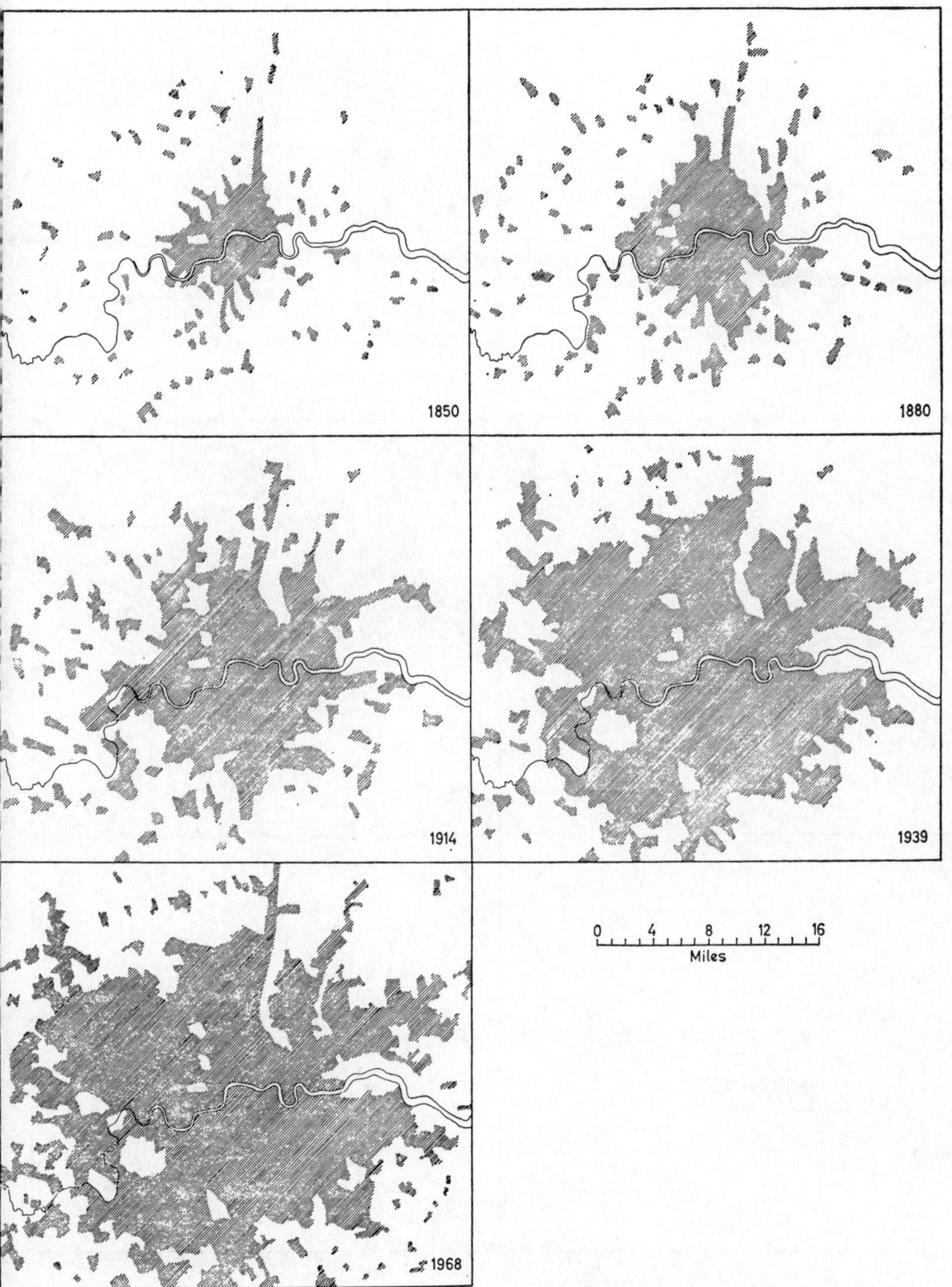

Figure 2.2 The Growth of London

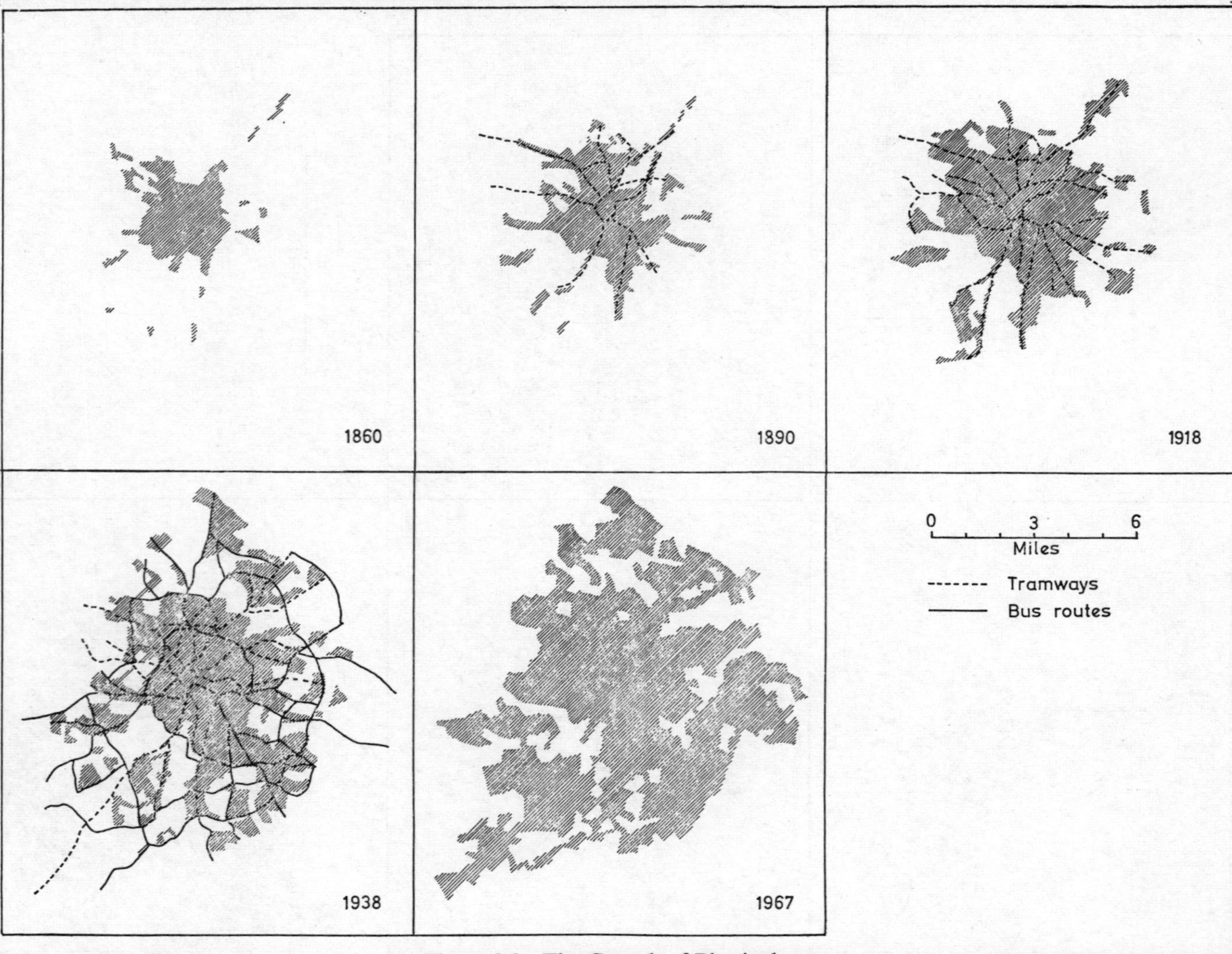

Figure 2.3 The Growth of Birmingham

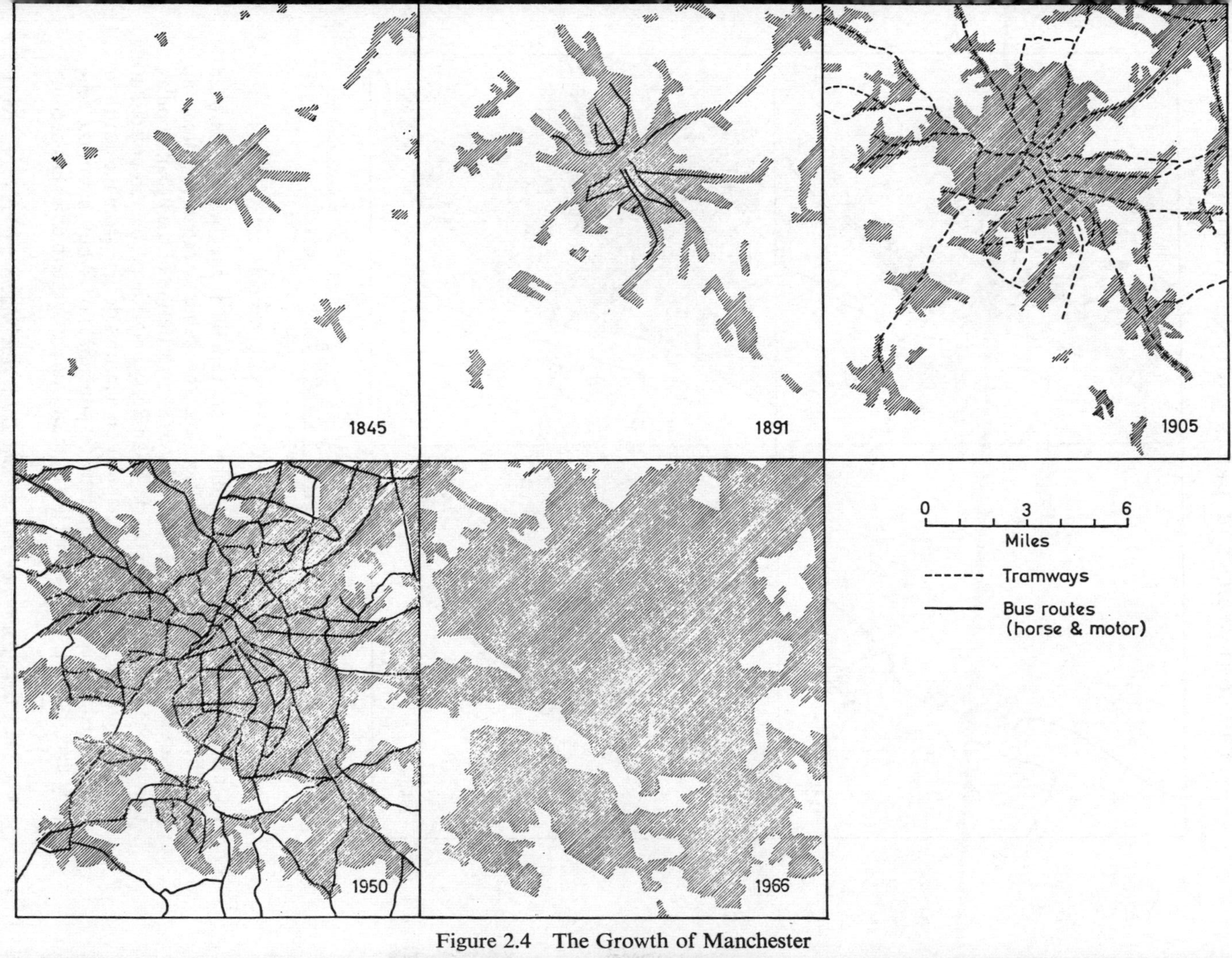

Figure 2.4 The Growth of Manchester

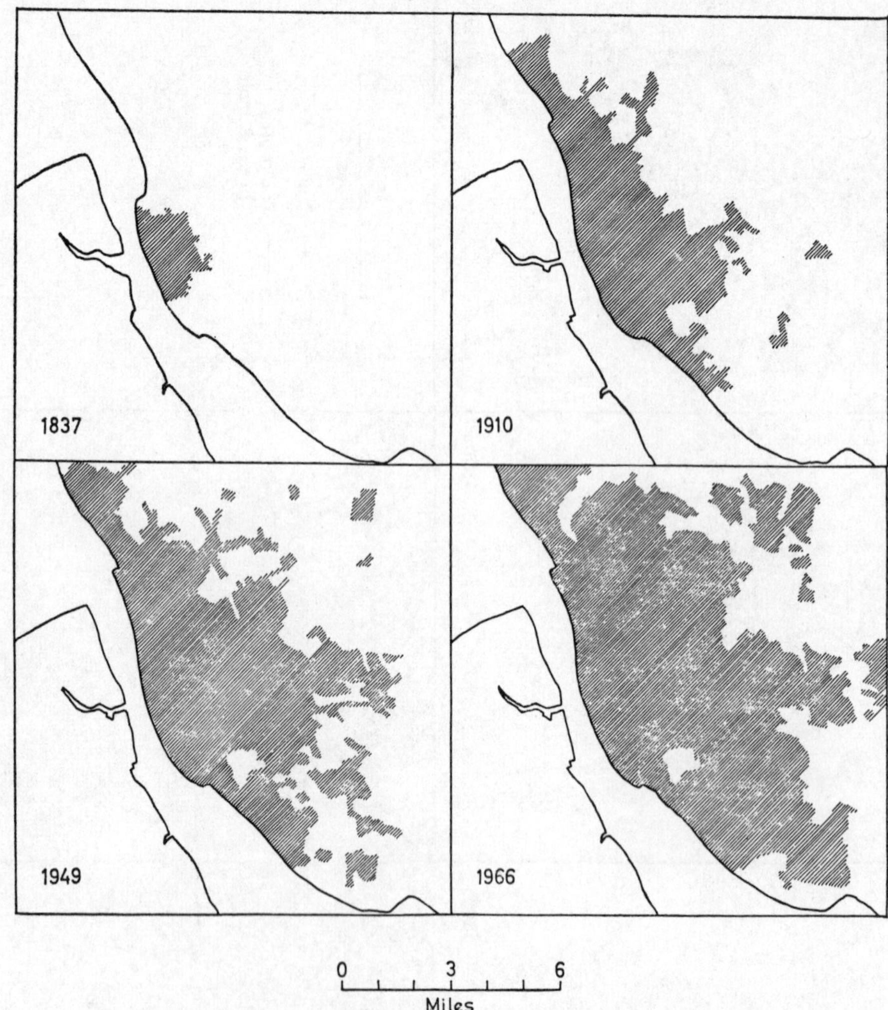

Figure 2.5 The Growth of Liverpool

intense overcrowding, lost population quite rapidly as they were taken over by offices, warehouses and factories, and the suburbs began to spread at moderate densities. As a result, the internal distribution of the urban population changed rapidly. Colin Clark, Brian Berry and others have observed that in almost all cities at all times, population densities decline from the centre to the rural edge according to a negative exponential law,[20] but that in the century since 1860 the slope of the line in the advanced Western cities has become

[20] Colin Clark, *Population Growth and Land Use*. Macmillan, London (1967), Chap. 8, *passim*. Colin Clark, 'Urban Population Densities', *Journal of the Royal*

steadily less steep, due to the liberating effects of urban mass-transportation. For London detailed statistics allow the process to be very precisely documented; it began after the 1861 Census, when cheap suburban trains allowed first the middle class, then the working class, to seek homes at progressively greater distances from the centre. By the end of the nineteenth century this had produced a radical change in the form of most British cities. The available forms of urban transportation, the steam train, or the electric tram, both

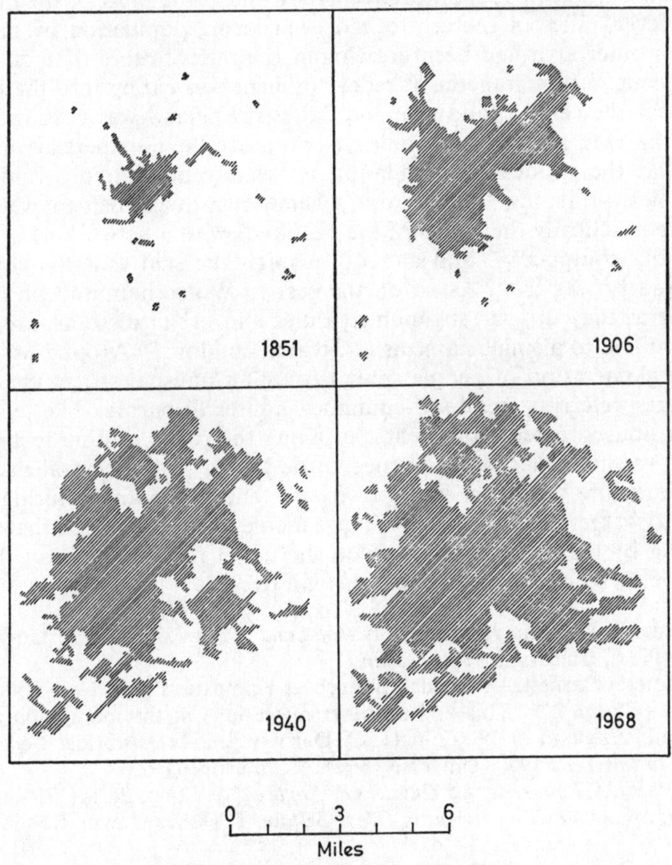

Figure 2.6 The Growth of Sheffield

demanded appreciable investment in basic infrastructure. They therefore tended to be concentrated along certain radial routes, and the growth of the

Statistical Society, A, Vol. 114 (1951), pp. 490–6. Colin Clark, 'Urban Population Densities', *Bulletin of the International Statistical Society*, Vol. 36 (1957), pp. 60–8; Brian J. L. Berry, James W. Simmons, Robert J. Tennant, 'Urban Population Densities: Structure and Change', *Geographical Review*, Vol. 53 (1963), pp. 389–405.

city tended to a tentacular form alongside these routes and within walking distance of them. Homer Hoyt, for Chicago in 1933, was probably the first to demonstrate this effect in detail;[21] it could be repeated for most British cities about 1900. Figures 2.2 to 2.6 show it for London, Birmingham, Manchester, Liverpool and Sheffield.

This process was recorded by contemporaries. 'Every year London grows, stretching out into the country long and generally unlovely arms', wrote Henrietta Barnett in 1905;[22] between 1881 and 1901, most of the inner area within seven miles of the centre had been losing population by migration, while an outer area had been growing at the rate of more than 50 per cent each decade.[23] Simultaneously, redevelopment was eating into the old slum areas near the centre; land near the Bank of England was costing up to £1 million an acre and, 'Even a mile or two away the commercial value is so great that the residential population is steadily and rapidly vanishing'.[24] In the West Midlands, 'A very large scheme is gradually being developed for covering practically the whole of the Midlands with a network of tram lines, electrically equipped',[25] and already 'it might be said that the continuous roads and houses from Aston on the east to Wolverhampton on the west, covering as they do, various municipalities and urban districts, are quite as much entitled to a single name as is Greater London'.[26] Around Manchester the 'conglomeration of people spreads over an unusual space, the working class here preferring small self-contained houses to barrack-like tenements', and the houses 'extend long tentacles along the roads leading to the neighbouring towns, which often seemed to be joined to the central mass'.[27] In West Yorkshire the towns had grown into 'one vast manufacturing hive, in which city verges on city, and one village merges into another, so that a person travelling by night from Kildwick on the north to Holmfirth on the south would never be out of sight of the gas lamps'.[28]

[21] Homer Hoyt, *One Hundred Years of Land Values in Chicago*. University of Chicago Press, Chicago (1933), *passim*.

[22] Henrietta Barnett, 'A Garden Suburb at Hampstead', *Contemporary Review*, Vol. 87 (1905), p. 231. This and all other quotations in this paragraph are from Peter Hall, 'England in 1900', in H. C. Darby (ed.), *An Historical Geography of England to the Year 1900*. University Press, Cambridge (1973).

[23] D. Pasquet, *Londres et les Ouvriers de Londres*. A. Colin, Paris (1914), pp. 23–4. A. Shaw, *Municipal Government in Great Britain*. T. Fisher Unwin, London (1895), p. 295.

[24] B. F. C. Costelloe, *The Housing Problem*. J. Heywood, Manchester (1899), p. 53.

[25] *Annual Report of the Chief Inspector of Factories and Workshops for the Year 1900*. B.P.P. (1901, 12), p. 245.

[26] Cornish's *Stranger's Guide Through Birmingham*. Cornish Brothers, Birmingham (1902), p. 17.

[27] A. R. Hope Moncrieff (ed.), *Black's Guide to Manchester*. A. and C. Black, London (1900), p. 3.

[28] British Association, *Handbook to Bradford and the Neighbourhood*. Bradford (1900).

This tentacular growth and coalescence of towns depended on the characteristics of the steam train and the electric tram. But already, in 1890, the first electric tube line in London had been opened; by 1907 the earlier Underground lines had been electrified and London had a dense network of new Tube lines; by 1908 the electrification of the surface lines south of the river was beginning to take place. In Manchester the line to Bury had been electrified in 1913–16 and the line to Altrincham was electrified in 1931; in Liverpool the Mersey Railway was electrified in 1903 and the line to Southport in 1904.[29] The number of electric trams continued to rise rapidly during the period up to the First World War, from 6,783 (in all Britain) in 1904 to 12,518 in 1914. Thence the total rose slowly to a peak of 14,413 in 1927. It fell slowly up to about 1935, then much more rapidly.[30]

Already, long before this time, new extensions of the urban network in many cities had been by bus; Sheffield contemplated this step in 1905, and opened its first bus service in 1913, though it was building new stretches of tramway as late as 1928.[31] Manchester from the start served its new housing estate in Wythenshawe by buses in the early 1930s,[32] and started abandoning trams after 1930.[33]

The result of this change is almost dramatically illustrated in the case of London. Between 1919 and 1939 Greater London expanded in population from 6 million to 8 million; but it expanded in area about five times (Figure 2.2). Furthermore, the form of the growth changed; the electric railway network, with its relatively frequent stops at half-mile intervals, and the new motor bus feeder services into the stations, permitted a much freer spread of development, which assumed a circular rather than a tentacular form. This is clearly seen in the contrast between the London of 1914 and the London of 1939 (Figure 2.2). It is almost certain that in the 1920s and 1930s the real cost of housing plus transportation in the London suburbs fell to an unprecedentedly low level.[34] The result was a much wider spread of rather low-density suburban housing, built at a generally uniform standard of about twelve to the net residential acre, than had ever been possible with previous transportation technologies. There was a parallel extension in the major provincial cities,

[29] H. W. A. Linecar, *British Electric Trains*. Ian Allen, London (1949), *passim*.

[30] British Road Federation, *Basic Road Statistics, 1969*, and information from BRF staff.

[31] Sheffield Transport Department, *The Tramway Era in Sheffield* (1960).

[32] A. Redford, *The History of Local Government in Manchester*, Vol. 3, *The Last Half Century*. Longmans, London (1940), p. 283.

[33] Ibid., p. 285.

[34] Mary Waugh, *The Suburban Development of North-West Kent 1861–1961*. Unpublished Ph.D. thesis, University of London (1968). In the 1930s, £800 houses could be bought around London for as little as £25 down, and then between 1931 and 1939 745,000 houses were built by private builders in the Home Counties, out of a total of 1,810,000 in all England and Wales. J. H. Johnson, 'The Suburban Expansion of London 1919–39', in J. T. Coppock and Hugh Prince (eds), *Greater London*. Faber, London (1964), pp. 156–7.

though in general it was less dramatic because of their lower total rate of growth in the interwar period, and in some of the northern cities, notably Manchester and Liverpool, the pattern of extensions was dominated to a much greater degree by local authority housing schemes.[35]

Between about 1880 and 1939, therefore, almost all major British urban areas witnessed a rapid and pronounced decentralization of their residential populations. But work activities showed a much greater inertia. It was about 1880 that the real growth of central business districts first came about in British cities. Sometimes this happened spontaneously, as in Manchester where warehouses gave way to offices in the 1880s; sometimes, as in Joseph Chamberlain's Birmingham, the process was accelerated and guided by the city itself. By the 1930s, all major British cities had well-differentiated central areas, which occupied an appreciable percentage of their entire employed population. Factory industry, in contrast, had shown a much greater willingness to disperse on its own initiative. Up to about 1880, in the bigger cities there was a characteristic belt or collar of small workshop industry just outside the central area; good examples are the furniture and clothing quarters of the East End of London, or the jewellery and gun quarters of Birmingham.[36] But between 1880 and 1914, there was a marked outward movement of bigger plants to green field sites in the suburbs of both cities: Cadbury at Bournville and General Electric at Witton Park in the case of Birmingham, Lebus and others in the Lea Valley in the case of London, and the whole Trafford Park development in Manchester. However, in this process factory industry still remained tightly concentrated in certain belts or zones. To its existing industrial areas in the East End and along the river, London added new zones in the Lea Valley and then in West Middlesex; to its older industrial quarters and the canal and railway-based industry of the inner suburbs, Birmingham added concentrations in places like Longbridge and the Tame Valley; soon after the coming of the Manchester Ship Canal made it a major port, Manchester built one of the greatest industrial concentrations in Europe at Trafford Park.[37]

[35] Between 1920 and 1938, the Manchester City Corporation built 27,447 houses while private enterprise built 8,315 houses with City assistance, and 15,845 houses unassisted. Redford, op. cit., Table following p. 246. Between 1919 and 1939 in Birmingham the totals were: 50,268 by the City, 54,536 by private enterprise. Asa Briggs, *The History of Birmingham*, Vol. 2, *Borough and City 1865–1938*. Oxford University Press, London (1952), p. 229.

[36] Peter Hall, *The Industries of London since 1861*. Hutchinson, London (1962), Chaps 4 and 5. J. E. Martin, *Greater London – An Industrial Geography*. Bell, London (1966), Chap. 1. M. J. Wise and P. O'N. Thorpe, 'The Growth of Birmingham 1800–1950', in *Birmingham and its Regional Setting: A Scientific Survey*. British Association for the Advancement of Science, Birmingham (1950), pp. 222–4. M. J. Wise, 'On the Evolution of the Jewellery and Gun Quarters in Birmingham', *Institute of British Geographers, Transactions and Papers*, Vol. 15 (1949), pp. 59–72.

[37] Hall, op. cit., Chaps 7–8. Wise and Thorpe, op. cit., p. 227. T. W. Freeman, 'The Manchester Conurbation', in *Manchester and its Region*. British Association for the Advancement of Science, Manchester (1962), pp. 56–7.

The result for transportation was interesting. To a large degree, up to 1939 mass transportation in most British cities remained largely radial. The Tube lines and Southern Electric lines in London, the bus routes in Birmingham and Manchester, ran from the city centres to the new housing estates and on their way they passed the factory zones. In the mornings they brought large flows of commuters into the centres; they took commuters in both directions to the industrial estates, outwards from the older areas of the city, inwards from the newer housing estates. In the evenings, the reverse happened. The public transport systems were efficient, and they were well adapted to the job they had to do; they attracted heavy flows of traffic, in an age when car ownership was still the privilege of the minority, and they thus managed to combine a high level of service with impressive financial results.[38]

For most municipal councillors, and most city treasurers, this seemed to be a beneficial and desirable form of development, which could long continue. They asked merely for freedom from economic depression for their city, coupled with sufficient prosperity in the country generally to keep their housing and slum clearance programmes rolling. But especially in relation to London, a growing vocal minority viewed the whole process with alarm, and in the aftermath of the Great Depression of 1929–32 their views began to command much respect.

THE AXIAL BELT

The Great Depression marked a fundamental divide. Up until then the few reformers who had been interested in city planning had mainly concerned themselves with the individual city; only a very few men of insight, like Howard and Geddes, had grasped the significance of the broader geographical patterns of urban growth. But in Britain, throughout the Great Depression and afterwards, there came the growing realization of strong and enduring regional differences between one industrial area and another. While areas like Central Scotland, the North-East and South Wales seemed to be unable to share in the gradual climb out of the trough, other areas like London, Birmingham and Leicester never seemed to have gone through it. Seeking to generalize about this distinction, the geographers and planners of the time seized on the notion of the axial belt. Under the alternative names of the hourglass and the coffin, it became a main theme of public controversy in the late 1930s. Under the title Megalopolis England it provides one main focus of the present book.

In a sense, the notion of the axial belt is implicit in Geddes' classic description of the conurbations, written as long ago as 1910. But it became explicit only in 1931, with Fawcett's redefinition of the conurbations. His map of the

38 Peter Hall, 'The Development of Communications', in J. T. Coppock and H. C. Prince (eds), *Greater London*. Faber, London (1964), pp. 52–76. Peter Hall, 'Transportation' in Peter Cowan (ed.), *Developing Patterns of Urbanisation*. Oliver and Boyd, Edinburgh (1970), pp. 130–56.

seven major conurbations, and thirty other minor ones, made it clear that the great majority (five out of the seven; fifteen out of the thirty) were concentrated into a single axial belt running from Lancashire and Yorkshire, down through the Midlands and London, to the south coast of Kent, Sussex and Hampshire (Figure 2.7a). Fawcett himself drew attention to the fact that:

> An observer in an airship hovering above one of these conurbations on a clear dark evening, when all its lamps are lit, would see beneath him a large area covered by a continuous network of lights, glowing here and there in brighter patches where the main roads meet in its nodal shopping districts and elsewhere shading into the darker patches of its less fully urbanized areas – parks, water surfaces, or enclaves of rural land. To such an observer the continuity of the conurbation would be the most salient fact about it. If he were high above the Pennines between Leeds and Manchester he could see at least four great conurbations. Near him to the north-east is the one formed by the confluent industrial towns of West Yorkshire; westward he would see the still larger one which is focussed on Manchester and beyond it the lights of the seaport on Merseyside; while to the south-east lies Sheffield. If he were at a sufficient height he might be able to see the haze of light over Birmingham, 75 miles to the south and over Tyneside, 90 miles away to the north. Amongst and around the nearer conurbations he would see the many smaller scattered patches of light which

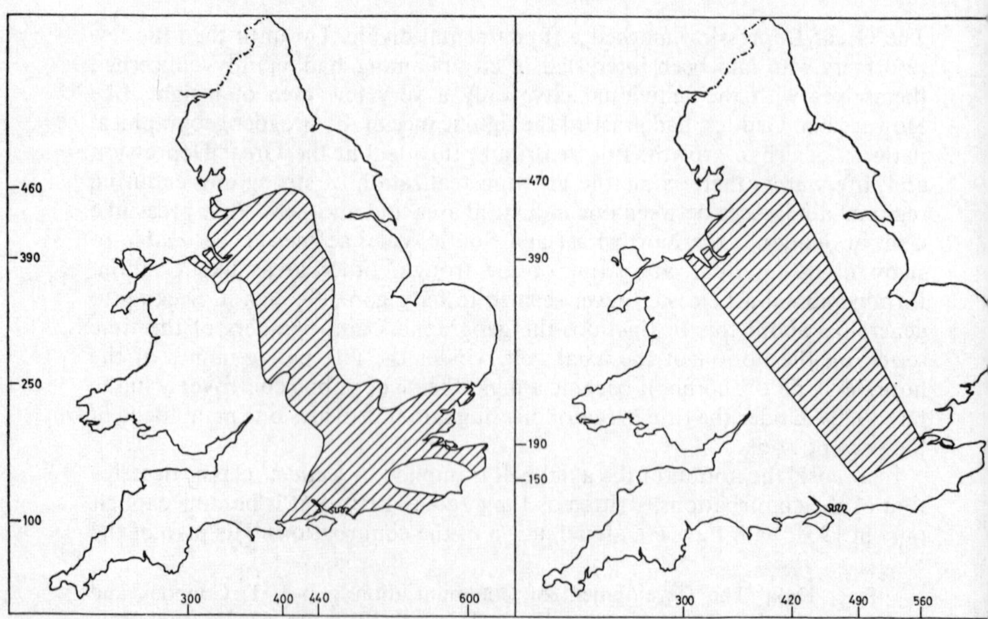

Figure 2.7 The Coffin or Axial Belt (a) as defined by C. B. Fawcett, (b) as defined by E. G. R. Taylor

mark the lesser towns. And it would be easy to imagine an outspreading of all these towards coalescence in one vast urban region covering the whole of this industrialized central area of Great Britain.[39]

Incipiently, then, Fawcett had recognized the idea of what came to be known as an axial belt of industry and people, or Megalopolis England. But he was careful to notice that the pattern of population growth gave a different picture: a concentration into two relatively small areas, one in the South-East, one in the Midlands. This difference was subsequently to be the source of much confusion and much controversy; and, as we shall see later, it still exists.

Fawcett wrote:

> There is an area of marked concentration of population in the form of a zone extending diagonally across England from south-east to north-west... In the last inter-Censal period (1921–31), three-fourths of the increase of population in Great Britain was in this zone ... This zone across England covers approximately 18,000 square miles, or about a fifth of the area of Great Britain. And it had in 1921, 56 per cent of the total population, a proportion which rose to 58 per cent in 1931, when its population numbered 25,805,915.[40]

But by this time, the notion was exciting politicians and administrators as well as geographers. In 1934 Sir Malcolm Stewart was appointed Special Commissioner for the Special Areas; these were the areas which had shown exceptionally high unemployment rates during the Great Depression, and exceptional difficulty in recovering subsequently. His second report, in 1936, made this comment on London.

> The macrocosm of London grows with a rapidity which is beginning to cause alarm ... There is a considerable portion of industrial production not dependent on considerations which are absolutely essential to its location in London. It is this part of the industrial flow which might reasonably be directed elsewhere.[41]

Stewart was criticized by some observers, but the point was a politically sensitive one; in 1937, the government set up the Royal Commission on the Geographical Distribution of the Industrial Population, under the chairmanship of Sir Anderson Montague-Barlow. Their terms of reference were threefold:

> To inquire into the causes which have influenced the present geographical distribution of the industrial population of Great Britain and the probable

39 Fawcett, op. cit. (1932), p. 101. In a modern jet airplane, of course, he would achieve the requisite height.

40 C. B. Fawcett, 'Areas of Concentration of Population in the English-Speaking Countries', *Population* (1934), p. 10. Also C. B. Fawcett, 'The Changing Distribution of Population', *Scottish Geographical Magazine*. Vol. 53 (1937), pp. 361–73.

41 *Third Report of the Commissioner for the Special Areas* (*England and Wales*), Cmd 5303, HMSO, London (1936), para. 21.

> direction of any change in that distribution in the future; to consider what social, economic or strategical disadvantages arise from the concentration of industries or of the industrial population in large towns or in particular areas of the country; and to report what remedial measures if any should be taken in the national interest.[42]

The geographers responded warmly to the Barlow Commission's call for expert evidence, and at a discussion at the Royal Geographical Society in May 1938, Professor E. G. R. Taylor further refined the notion of Megalopolis. In a discussion on the geographical location of industry she said:

> . . . there is a belt of such high concentration, following an axis aligned from south-east or north-west, and broadening as it gets farther from Greater London. At either extremity of this belt are the sea-entries which dominate England's external trade relations; the Port of London, and Liverpool-Manchester, together handling two-thirds of the total imports and exports. Southampton and Hull, though they exist mainly to serve this axial belt, are separated from it by forty to fifty miles of non-industrial farming country.[43]

As Baker and Gilbert noted in 1941,[44] there is a change in emphasis here; the south coast area disappears, and there is a suggestion that the area is dominated by areas of dense population, defined by the rather low minimum limit of 200 persons per square mile or roughly one-third of a person to each acre. Nevertheless, the notion of the axial belt was blessed by the Royal Geographical Society and was passed on in the form of a memorandum to the Royal Commission (Figure 2.7b). There, it is described as a belt covering approximately 14,500 square miles, or 39 per cent of the area of England and Wales, stretching from Greater London up to South Lancashire and the West Riding.[45] This evidence was referred to in the Barlow Commission report when it appeared in 1940,[46] and in the subsequent report of the Scott Committee on Land Use in Rural Areas.

After this general acceptance of the notion, in 1941, J. N. L. Baker and E. W. Gilbert delivered a weighty attack on it in a talk to the Royal Geographical Society.[47] They based their criticism on two main grounds: first, that there was no continuous belt of dense population from London up to the North, because the belt was in fact intersected at right angles by a low density from

[42] *Report of the Royal Commission on the Distribution of the Industrial Population*, Cmd 6153, HMSO, London (1940), pp. vii–viii.

[43] E. G. R. Taylor, 'Discussion on the Geographical Distribution of Industry', *Geographical Journal*, Vol. 92 (1938), p. 23.

[44] J. N. L. Baker and E. W. Gilbert, 'The Doctrine of an Axial Belt of Industry in England', *Geographical Journal*, Vol. 103 (1944), p. 51.

[45] 'Memorandum on the Geographical Factors Relevant to the Location of Industry', *Geographical Journal*, Vol. 92 (1938), p. 502.

[46] Royal Commission on the Industrial Population, op. cit., p. 152.

[47] Baker and Gilbert, op. cit.

the Severn to the Wash; secondly that in terms of population growth the real contrast was between the South and the Midlands on one hand, and the North on the other.[48] In fact, the Barlow Commission had already recognized this fact, by stressing the regional differences rather than the common identity of Megalopolis. Their analysis showed that while in England and Wales as a whole employment had risen by 22·3 per cent from 1923–37, for London

Table 2.10

THE DEVELOPMENT OF REGIONS OF THE AXIAL BELT AND REGIONS OUTSIDE IT, UP TO 1937

A *Percentage distribution of total population*

	1801	1901	1921	1931	1937
London and Home Counties	18·0	23·4	23·5	24·8	25·7
Lancashire	6·4	11·9	11·6	11·2	10·9
West Riding, Notts and Derbyshire	8·5	10·7	10·9	11·0	10·8
Midlands	8·1	9·2	9·5	9·6	9·7
Total axial belt	**41·0**	**55·2**	**55·5**	**56·6**	**57·1**
Northumberland and Durham	3·0	4·8	5·2	5·0	4·8
Mid-Scotland	3·7	6·2	6·2	5·9	6·0
Glamorgan and Monmouth	1·1	3·1	4·0	3·7	3·4
Peripheral industrial areas	**7·8**	**14·1**	**15·4**	**14·6**	**14·2**
Rest of Great Britain	**51·2**	**30·7**	**29·1**	**28·8**	**28·7**
Total Great Britain	100·0	100·0	100·0	100·0	100·0

B *Percentage distribution of the insured (employed) population*

	1923	1937
London and Home Counties	22·4	26·0
Lancashire	15·7	13·8
West Riding, Notts and Derbyshire	13·0	12·2
Midlands	11·2	11·7
Total axial belt	**62·3**	**63·7**
Northumberland and Durham	5·7	4·9
Mid-Scotland	7·3	6·6
Glamorgan and Monmouth	4·2	3·3
Peripheral industrial areas	**17·2**	**14·8**
Rest of Great Britain	**20·5**	**21·5**
Total Great Britain	100·0	100·0

[48] Robin Best's analysis, published twenty-six years later, supports the contention that Baker and Gilbert's analysis is still true; on the basis of urban growth, Best concludes, 'Megalopolis still does not exist as a single continuous area'. Cf. Best and Champion, op. cit. (1970), pp. 17–19, 26.

and Home Counties the figure was 42·7 per cent. The same figure, 42·7 per cent, represented the share of London and the Home Counties, in the national growth. At the same time, as Table 2.10 shows, other parts of Megalopolis were stagnant or in decline. The growth of London was the outstanding feature of the economic geography of Britain in the interwar years; and if anything, the concept of an axial belt only tended to obscure it.[49]

Therefore, though the Barlow Commission recognized the existence of the Megalopolis, they put the main weight of their analysis elsewhere.[50] First, they analysed the conurbations, and reached their celebrated conclusion:

> It is not possible from the evidence submitted to us to avoid the conclusion that the disadvantages in many, if not in most of the great industrial concentrations, alike on the strategical, the social, and the economic side, do constitute serious handicaps and even in some respects dangers to the nation's life and development, and we are of the opinion that definite action should be taken by the Government towards remedying them.[51]

Then they analysed the related problem: the growth of one of these great industrial concentrations, the London area. They concluded:

> The continued drift of the industrial population to London and the Home Counties constitutes a social, economic and strategical problem which demands immediate attention.[52]

These conclusions were backed by an impressive weight of evidence, much of it statistical, to the effect that industrial and urban areas suffered grave social and economic disadvantages including poor housing, overcrowding, poor public health (especially child health), high land and property values, long journeys to work, and traffic congestion; in addition there were strategic disadvantages (on which the Commission heard evidence in camera) through liability to mass destruction from the air. They culminated in recommendations for the state to take an active role in influencing the future distribution of industry. Here the Commission split, the majority recommending a fairly modest control on new industrial location in the London area, a minority (including the influential planner Patrick Abercrombie) preferring a comprehensive system of state control of industrial location. These arguments and these recommendations may be read in the pages of the report itself, and in many commentaries;[53] they need not be repeated again here. But it is important, as a basis for this study, to try to bring out some general points about the essential historical basis of the idea of the Barlow Commissioners and their contemporaries. This is the burden of Chapter Three.

[49] Royal Commission on the Industrial Population, op. cit.

[50] They advocated an attempt to drive the growth of activity in London into other parts of the belt. Ibid., para. 319.

[51] Ibid., para. 413.

[52] Ibid., para. 428.

[53] Cf. Peter Hall, *London 2000*. Faber, London (1963, 1969), Chap. 2, for a criticism of the arguments.

CHAPTER THREE

THE ORIGINS: EVOLUTION OF PLANNING FROM SOCIAL MOVEMENT TO SOCIAL POLICY

This chapter runs parallel to Chapter Two. It analyses the evolution of the central ideas of the planning system in response to the urban changes already described in the earlier chapter. It shows not only how a social movement evolved into a profession and an official activity, but also how it communicated the central ideas of the social movement to those professional and bureaucratic activities. It examines the central notion of the planning movement, which developed in response to the conditions of the early nineteenth-century city but was transferred intact into the twentieth century: the idea that change in the physical environment of urban life would solve social problems. It examines the embodiment of these ideas in legislation, culminating in the appointment of the Barlow Commission in 1937. It ends with an examination, to be taken up in greater detail in Chapter One at the start of Volume Two, of the central philosophical notions of the Barlow Report of 1940 and the various other reports which followed it and together constituted the basis of the postwar British planning system.

This chapter was written by Harry Gracey and Peter Hall. Harry Gracey contributed the analysis of the evolution of planning ideas up to Barlow. Peter Hall contributed the section on the central notions of Barlow and the related reports.

INTRODUCTION

The Barlow Report can be said to be the essential basis of the postwar British planning system. From its recommendations sprang the reports of the Uthwatt Committee on compensation and betterment and the Scott Report on rural land use, both of which can fairly be regarded as appendices to Barlow. From its minority report (one of whose signatories was Abercrombie) sprang the decision to set up comprehensive controls over the location of industry, which was embodied in the Distribution of Industry Act of 1945. From its comments on new towns came the appointment of Lord Reith's Committee in 1945, and then the New Towns Act of 1946 which carried the Reith proposals into action. Finally, from its insistence on comprehensive and effective land use planning came the great Town and Country Planning Act of 1947 which was the legislative basis, as Barlow was the philosophical basis, of the whole planning system whose impact on urban growth is the subject matter of this book.

But just as the Barlow Report was the origin of all that followed, so it represented the distilled and logical outcome of the history that had led up to it. It is essentially the manifesto of a social movement, which at this point in history happened to have its ideology accepted as the received view. This movement is the political, or ideological face, of town and country planning in Britain.

In fact planning in Britain has three such faces; that is, it can be studied from three points of view in its historical development and operational interrelationships. It is an activity of central and local governments carried on in bureaucracies with their hierarchies of officials, implementing the provisions of the various Town Planning Acts passed since the war. It is a profession whose practitioners have traditionally been trained in schools of architecture, design, planning or engineering at universities and have obtained professional qualifications, usually a pre-condition to employment and especially to advancement in the field. And it is a social movement, a loosely organized group of dedicated people with a mission to promote planning in general, and especially a threefold programme of physical containment of the large cities, preservation of the countryside and the construction of comprehensively-planned new communities to accommodate the growing urban population.

Historically, the social movement was the first of these three aspects of planning to develop. Growing out of the nineteenth-century agitation for social reform, in the face of the massive social problems of the urban Industrial Revolution, the planning movement was one of the contemporary expressions of the ethic of social responsibility which was to become institutionalized in the twentieth-century welfare state. The movement's goals were humanitarian and reformist; its basic assumption was environmental determinism of social life and individual character. Town planning as an activity of government was developed in the twentieth century in response to the recurrent national crises of wars and depression. A series of government planning acts gradually adopted the programme long advocated by the planning movement and incorporated procedures for the efficient planning of cities, which had been advocated by professionals in geology and geography beginning as early as 1840. The planning profession was established shortly after the first Town Planning Act was passed in 1909, in what seems to have been an effort by the established professions of architecture and engineering to control this new government activity, which was so close to their own professional domains.

The historical backdrop of modern town planning is to be found in the nineteenth-century processes of urbanization and industrialization, through which England was transformed from a prosperous agrarian society into an immensely rich and powerful urban-industrial nation. The industrialization of the economy, begun during the eighteenth century, was substantially completed by the end of the nineteenth. The activities of investment, manufacturing and trade, which constituted industrial capitalism, were the driving forces of social change in Britain for this century. The establishment by the 1830s of a machine tool industry and an engineering profession made the new industrial system technologically self-regenerating. One indication of the amount of growth and prosperity which the industrial system brought to nineteenth-century Britain is the sheer increase in the number of people supported. The British population increased threefold during the nineteenth century, from just under 9 million people in 1801 to 32·5 million in 1901. It had previously taken over 700 years for such a proportionate increase in population.[1] Recent estimates indicate that the material wealth of the country may have grown even faster during this period. The net national income is estimated to have almost trebled during the second half of the nineteenth century, growing from £636 million in 1855 to £1,727 million by 1901, at constant 1960 prices.[2] Since the population did not quite double in size during this half century, there was at least a statistical increase in *per capita* income for the century. There is no doubt that England became a rich nation by any historical or comparative standards during this epoch and it can be argued, according to the historian Walker, that the Industrial Revolution did not introduce a universal degrading of the conditions of the lower classes, but on the contrary made it possible for the new working class to improve their life conditions through co-ordinated action in the trade unions and in politics.[3]

The nineteenth century was very much a time of unfettered free enterprise, during which the government was made to remove legal obstacles to business and commercial activity generally, and the great goal of liberal economics, free trade, was achieved by the end of the century. The government was not simply freeing businessmen from legal restrictions on the pursuit of profit, but it was going much further in support of business to provide legal support for the factory industrial system, and when necessary, military support to help control the new industrial labour force. Private business, on the other hand, not only created the new production, financing and trade apparatus of the industrial revolution, but it built the infrastructure of an industrial society as well. In the eighteenth and nineteenth centuries private investment companies built the canals, trunk roads and railways which opened up most of the country for their economic activity and provided all the workers' housing and much of the other urban facilities in the new industrial cities.

Following from the process of industrialization, the nineteenth century was also the period of urbanization for Britain. As was earlier shown, most of the new economic activity and population growth took place in the cities, which grew at a far faster rate than the country as a whole, as the new industrial proletariat assembled in the country's manufacturing cities and towns. The metropolis of London, already the largest city in the world, increased its population from 1·1 million at the beginning of the century to 6·5 million by its close. The large cities of Britain increased their populations by seven or eight times during the course of the century: Liverpool grew from 82,000

[1] J. Walker, *British Economic and Social History 1700–1967*. Macdonald and Evans, London (1968), p. 8.

[2] B. R. Mitchell, *Abstract of British Historical Statistics*. University Press, Cambridge (1962), p. 367.

[3] Walker, op. cit., p. 11.

people in 1801 to 704,000 in 1901; Manchester grew from 75,000 to 645,000; and Birmingham from 71,000 to 523,000. The smaller cities, which were also experiencing industrialization, grew by similar magnitudes during the nineteenth century: for example, the population of Nottingham increased from 29,000 to 240,000; Leicester grew from 17,000 to 212,000; and Reading from 10,000 to 81,000.[4] The proportion of the national population which was classified as in urban residence rose from 20 per cent in 1801 to 60 per cent in 1901, and reached its peak of 80 per cent urban by the Census of 1931.

Modern town planning was first employed in the late eighteenth and early nineteenth centuries to build comprehensively designed residential neighbourhoods for the wealthy. The large urban land holdings of the aristocracy made it possible to develop sizable tracts of land for housing in the better districts of the cities. The upper classes began to use some of their new wealth to have the famous architects of the day, such as John Nash, design them attractive city neighbourhoods and pleasant seaside and country resorts. Part of the new wealth of industrial England was being used by the upper classes in the traditional way, for creating comfortable and impressive living environments, and these did provide the earliest models of comprehensive urban development on a neighbourhood scale in modern Britain, even if they contributed little to the solutions of the general urban problems of the time.

These original town planners were responsible for designing the fashionable Victorian and Georgian squares in large cities such as London, Edinburgh and Liverpool, and attractive resorts including Bath, Brighton, Leamington, Bournemouth and Scarborough. They planned the development of these areas by the neighbourhood, or the town, rather than house by house, and the results of their small scale comprehensive planning still bring forth admiration today. Ashworth, for example, says of the work of Thomas Cubitt, designer of 'probably the most fashionable district in London', Belgravia:

> All his work was characterized by broad and airy streets, spacious squares and formal design, with the use of a considerable number of trees, and contrasted markedly with much higgledy-piggledy development at the same time in other districts catering for less wealthy residents.[5]

J. H. Robertson described Birkenhead, where Hamilton Square had been built for the homes of the rich merchants of Liverpool in this way:

> . . . few towns in modern times have been built with such regard to sanatory regulations as Birkenhead; and in no instance has so much been done for the health, comfort and enjoyment of a people, as by those energetic individuals with whose names the rise and progress of Birkenhead are so intimately connected.[6]

[4] Mitchell, op. cit., Table 6, p. 19; Table 8, pp. 24–5.

[5] W. Ashworth, *The Genesis of Modern British Town Planning*. Routledge and Kegan Paul, London (1954), p. 38.

[6] Ibid., p. 40.

J. MacPherson, in an address to the National Association for the Promotion of Social Science in 1875, claimed that the seaside resorts for the wealthy in Britain were 'superior to all others in natural beauty, in ranges of magnificent houses, in piers and jetties, and very generally in bathing grounds.'[7]

As the commercial activity and wealth of the new industrial nation grew, living conditions in the major cities and towns deteriorated dramatically under the impact of uncontrolled industrialization and continued population growth from natural increase and migration. According to contemporary observers of all shades of opinion, these cities were suffering from congestion, overcrowding, the lack of sanitary provisions, high rates of disease and crime and great working-class poverty, as the new population packed into them. Successive governments could not, or would not, exercise any effective control over the industrial development or housing development. Ruth Glass has summarized the urban conditions observed during this period, saying:

> In the towns, certainly until the First World War – Britain's class structure was reduced to a frightening simplicity: here Disraeli's two nations met and then turned their backs upon one another; here wealth was manufactured and poverty accumulated. The cities were (called) 'the crowded nurseries of disease', 'the devil's hotbeds of evil and crime'. There was no means of escape from urban social problems; their solution, it seemed, was the key to universal social progress.[8]

Nineteenth-century revolutionaries in Britain saw the cities as arenas of class struggle and conflict, while the reformers saw them as a new 'universe for the collection of data demonstrating the need for social reform'[9] Both reformer and revolutionary assumed, as Mrs Glass goes on to point out, that perfection was attainable, for there was too much confidence, gained by spectacular success in some fields, for failure in others to be suffered gladly![10] The urban social problems of the nineteenth century were defined as failures of the society by those who became the social reformers and it was assumed implicitly that their solution was the key to universal social progress.

The interesting fact is that the middle-class reformers came to define the living and working conditions of the urban proletariat as societal failures and to demand action from the government to improve them throughout the country. It was the two new forms of social organization developed in the nineteenth century – the mechanized factory and the industrial city – which came to be defined as social problems by the reformers and were made the focus of their major efforts to bring about change in the conditions of the working class through government policy and private action. The long agitation for factory reform brought very gradual improvements in industrial working conditions including reducing hours of work, limiting the employment

[7] Ibid., p. 46.

[8] Ruth Glass, 'Urban Sociology in Great Britain: A Trend Report', *Current Sociolology*, Vol. 4 (1955), p. 9.

[9] Ibid., p. 6.

[10] Ibid., p. 9.

of women and children in factories and mines, and increasing requirements for machine safety and employee disability payments. Reforms in the cities, which had to do with sanitation, health, housing and congestion, and were the forerunners to the programmes developed in the planning movement, began to be implemented by the government in the 1840s in response to the cholera epidemics and on the advice of the reformers and various Royal Commissions of the time.

Living conditions were probably no worse for the masses of the poor in the newly industrializing cities than they had been for the poor in the countryside prior to industrialization. The massive migration to the cities from the countryside, which took place in the nineteenth century, and the growth of the national population can be cited as evidence that life was better for these people in the industrial towns and cities. It was probably this assembling of the poor in the crowded quarters of the urban slum and their natural increase there which, making poverty visible and even threatening to the other classes, led to these urban conditions being defined as a basic problem for society. As wealth and property increased through industrial economic activities, the contrast between the rich and the poor became vivid and readily observable and there seems to have been an escalation in standards of social welfare. The poverty of the urban masses was a visible and intolerable part of the new social scene, not invisible and therefore tolerable as the preceding rural poverty: it was a social problem which must be tackled and which could be solved by right action.

Most of the social conditions which were defined as problematic societal failures were particularly evident in the nineteenth-century cities, though they by no means occurred only in cities. Mines and mining villages, to take just one example, exhibited some of the worst working and living conditions in the country during the nineteenth century. But the problems of exploitation, poverty, disease, congestion and crime were most readily observable in the cities and came to be linked with urban living in the minds of the nineteenth-century reformers. The reports of observers across the political spectrum, from government officials to reformers and revolutionaries like Frederick Engels, depicted the same horrors of urban life for the labouring masses. Engels' vivid description of a working-class neighbourhood in Manchester of the 1840s, for example, illustrates what was being reported from many industrial cities at this time.

> The cottages are very small, old and dirty, while the streets are uneven, partly unpaved, not properly drained and full of ruts. Heaps of refuse, offal and sickening filth are everywhere, interspersed with pools of stagnant liquid. The atmosphere is polluted by the stench and is darkened by the thick smoke of a dozen factory chimneys. A horde of ragged women and children swarm about the streets and they are just as dirty as the pigs which wallow happily on the heaps of garbage and in the pools of filth.[11]

[11] Frederick Engels, *The Condition of the Working Class in England*, W. O. Henderson and W. H. Chaloner (trans and eds). Basil Blackwell, Oxford (1958), p. 71.

Ashworth in his history of town planning, on which this account draws heavily, cites a number of official government observations and reports which give a similar picture of urban living for the masses. He reports, for example, that a public health physician in London gave the following description of London's East End in 1840:

> Such is the filthy, close and unwashed state of the houses and the poisonous condition of the localities in which the greater part of the houses are situated, from the total want of drainage, and the masses of putrefying matters of all sorts which are allowed to remain and accumulate indefinitely, that during the last year [1839] in several of the parishes both relieving officers and medical men lost their lives, on consequence of the brief stay in those places which they were obliged to make in the performance of their duties.[12]

Ashworth also cites the melodramatic report by the Glasgow police chief describing the danger of these slums to the rest of the city:

> In these horrid dens the most abandoned characters of the city are collected, and from thence they nightly issue to disseminate disease, and to pour upon the town every species of crime and abomination.[13]

The nature of the problem was evidently the same to social reformers and revolutionaries alike: conditions of overcrowding, congestion, poverty, crime, ill health and heavy mortality characterized urban living for the masses of the industrial proletariat at this time. The reformers argued for change in government policy to meet the problems. They urged new housing and sanitary legislation, redevelopment of the congested parts of the old cities, and the construction of new, totally planned industrial communities. They saw the change of the working-class physical environment as the way of solving these major social problems. The reformers' arguments included appeals to conscience, doing the right thing for the poor, but they also stressed very conservative self-interest for the benefit of the powerful groups to whom they addressed their arguments. Congestion, they pointed out, made transportation and communication inefficient in the cities and therefore costly to business. They warned that the diseases endemic to the working-class quarters could easily spread to the rest of the city. They pointed out that the crime generated among the poor was a clear threat to the rest of the community. They argued, with supporting statistics of varying degrees of reliability, that the poor health and high mortality among the working classes (life expectancy was less than forty years in some urban slums) constituted a serious loss of man-power to industry and a heavy financial burden on city governments in the provision of hospital care and, it was even argued, burial expenses. Finally, the reformers warned of the danger to the wealth and power of the upper classes should the lower classes turn to revolution to better their lot.

[12] Ashworth, op. cit., p. 51.
[13] Ibid., p. 49.

THE MOVEMENT TOWARDS PLANNING

The arguments of the reformers were taken up by government bodies and found their way into official reports on urban reform. The 1840 Select Committee on the Health of Towns argued strongly for urban reconstruction, concluding that:

> some such measures are urgently called for, as claims of humanity and justice to great multitudes of our fellow men, and as necessary not less for the welfare of the poor than the safety of property and the security of the rich.[14]

The original advocacy of town planning as public policy was thus politically conservative in its social context. The reformers, who advocated planning, housing reform and sanitary measures to combat the period's urban problems, would modify the physical structure of the cities in order to preserve the social structure of society. By way of contrast, the radicals who advocated political revolution by an organized urban proletariat, would change the social structure, destroying the power of the ruling groups and redistributing the wealth of society, so that these social problems could no longer exist. The radicals' programme for change called for the revolutionary overthrow of the capitalist society, with its class structure, and the establishment of the communist utopia with its classless social equality. If there had ever been a serious possibility of revolutionary change in Britain, however, it died completely with the demise of Chartism in the middle of the nineteenth century, and the social problems of the Industrial Revolution came to be tackled as problems of housing, sanitation, and eventually, of planning.

It is evident that the terrible conditions of the slums for those who had to live in them, and the very real dangers they posed to the health and safety of the rest of society, were clearly recognized by reformers and some government officials by the 1830s as the major social problems of the time. The fact that these conditions were most evident in the cities led early to the conclusion, which rapidly became a conviction and a basic assumption of reform, that the way to solve the problems was to change the physical environment of the city. Environmental determinism became the keystone assumption of social reform, including the planning movement. A change of the physical environment, here the industrial city, was assumed to be an effective way of bringing about social and economic changes. Specifically, the reformers and planners came to believe that altering the physical environment of the working classes would alleviate the effects of poverty on their lives, and reduce the dangers of this poverty for social stability.

The reformers had a different dream from that of the radicals, but certainly also utopian at that time. They dreamed of a new society in which all the people enjoyed what was essentially a middle-class standard of living, with good comfortable housing, clean and attractive communities, sufficient food,

[14] Ibid., p. 54.

clothes and medicines to live a healthy life, and so on. This was a utopia which was made to seem a reasonable hope by the unprecedented growth of material wealth in nineteenth-century Britain. The reformers drew up programmes for new working-class housing in the cities, for the provision of sanitary and health services for all, and perhaps most ambitiously, those reformers who were associated with the planning movement gradually developed programmes for the reconstruction of the deteriorated parts of the old cities and even for the creation of new, totally planned industrial cities and towns to provide all the residents with decent working and living conditions. The planning reformers eventually developed their own utopian ideal, the garden city, a planned new industrial town which was to combine all the beneficial features of urban and rural life in one place, while also avoiding all the detrimental conditions then found in both environments.

However, the reformers' arguments and their activities, even with support from government commissions, were never enough in themselves to bring about new legislation for urban reforms. New programmes in sanitation or housing or town planning would involve additional public expenditure and a necessary infringement of property rights, and reform was resisted for these reasons. It took a vivid demonstration of the reformers' arguments in two cholera epidemics, one in London in the 1830s and one on a national scale in the 1840s, to induce the government to pass the first housing and health reform acts. These were mild measures even so, avoiding as much as possible any new form of public expenditure and infringing as little as possible on the property rights of builders and landowners.

The idea of comprehensive urban planning for Britain's cities was developed by the reformers in the late 1840s and early 1850s, by the time the fact of massive and seemingly permanent urban growth was evident to all. A few academics in the fields of geology and geography at this time proposed initiating comprehensive town planning in the large cities to rationalize their development and alleviate some of the worst living conditions in the working-class districts.[15] These men testified before government commissions on urban problems and proposed that professionals in their fields and in engineering undertake civic surveys to assess the needs for future development in the cities and draw up comprehensive plans to provide for this growth and regulate it in the best interests of the community as a whole. As Ashworth points out, most of the early city planning proposals were largely confined to civil engineering matters like the efficient movement of traffic and the effective provision of public services. However, the basic planning procedures of survey, analysis and plan making were also proposed and demonstrated by the reformers at this time.

According to Ashworth:

> The best idea of what was intended was probably given by Butler Williams, Professor of Geodesy at the College for Civil Engineers, Putney. He emphasized the importance of public surveys for each town, which should be used

[15] Ibid., pp. 24–6.

to guide future improvements. Such surveys should show the ground plan of the objects in the town, contour levels; geological formation; materials, character and use of public buildings and houses; the different construction of roads; the courses of existing sewer, gas and water pipes; the average amount of traffic; and statistical details of internal structural improvements.[16]

Professor Williams demonstrated the feasibility of part of his programme by using his students to prepare a survey of the City of London. Some professional reformers in 1845 had proposed that the city governments of Britain take on the responsibility for comprehensive development control and planning in their communities. This proposal was taken up as a plank in the platform of the planning movement towards the end of the nineteenth century. It was to be precisely one hundred years after its proposal that the programme of survey, analysis and plan would be incorporated into the government's programme for comprehensive town and country planning in Britain.

Another early progenitor of the town planning movement was the movement for urban sanitary reform, organized by another group of professionals including scientists, doctors and local health officials during the second half of the nineteenth century. These professionals also testified before the new government Commissions on the health of the towns, advocating the provision of adequate sanitary systems and public health services for the cities. Many cities had no general water or sewage systems at this time, and these reformers saw the provision of these and of more adequate public health programmes as the way to deal with most of the social problems of the time. The sanitary reform movement vigorously campaigned for the whole range of new urban health measures as the solution to the problems of poverty, as well as ill health in nineteenth-century Britain.

As part of its campaign the sanitary reform movement even produced a utopia, in the form of B. W. Richardson's Hygeia, the City of Health. Hygeia is a cultural forerunner of Ebenezer Howard's garden city, which became the planning movement's utopian community. Richardson first proposed Hygeia to the Social Science Congress in Brighton in 1875. In a programme which was to find direct development in the planning movement, Richardson advocated the building of new industrial cities in the countryside as the means of solving the problems of urban living. These problems Richardson defined to the Congress as health problems which must be solved through modern sanitary town design. Hygeia, therefore, would be scientifically designed so 'that in it the perfection of sanitary results will be approached if not actually realized in the co-existence of the lowest possible general mortality with the highest possible individual longevity'.[17] These new communities were conceived by Richardson as comprehensively planned and

[16] Ibid., p. 25.

[17] B. W. Richardson, *Hygeia, A City of Health*. Macmillan, London (1876), pp. 10–11.

developed cities of 100,000 people which would take population and industry from the slums of the existing cities and house them in an urban environment, scientifically designed and controlled to the highest possible sanitary standards. Each Hygeia, unlike the individual garden cities proposed by Howard, was conceived as being large enough to contain a cross section of the national population and a wide range of employment opportunities in industry, service trades, and even, like the garden city, agricultural enterprises in its rural hinterlands. Richardson's book lays heavy emphasis on the elaborate public health and sanitary measures in the new city, ranging from the design of the individual homes and gardens to the city-wide underground waste disposal and street cleansing systems. He also proposes a public health service which would record and investigate each and every illness in the community to discover and contain its source and provide a full range of health facilities absolutely free to the public.

Like others in the movement, Richardson's faith in the efficacy of sanitary reform seems to have been complete: all that was needed to solve the modern problems of urban living for the lower classes was clean houses in clean towns. He claimed, for instance, that 'gutter children are an impossibility in a place where there are no gutters for their innocent delectation' and in his ideal community, 'instead of the gutter, the poorest child has the garden, for the foul sight and smell of unwholesome garbage, he has flowers and green sward'.[18] Richardson even believed that these changes in the physical environment of urban man would eliminate poverty from society, for he proclaimed the naive faith of many of these reformers, 'poverty is the shadow of disease, and wealth the shadow of health'.[19] A social problem, poverty, was defined by these reformers as a physical problem, disease, and an alteration in the physical environment, the building of new cities, was proposed as its solution. The sanitary reformers shared the environmental determinist assumption of the later planning reformers.

The idea of the new industrial community, comprehensively planned and built from scratch in the countryside, became quite popular among reformers in the second half of the nineteenth century as a way of tackling the multifold problems which urbanization and industrialization had brought to the country. In 1883 a group of reformers and industrialists formed the Society for Promoting Industrial Villages to advocate solving Britain's urban problems by the construction of planned industrial villages throughout the country and the relocation of population and employment from the crowded cities to these new communities. The economist Alfred Marshall even gave his blessing to the idea, in an article published the following year in which he pointed out that such a programme would have the advantage of tackling the problems of urban overcrowding, unemployment, and rural depopulation all at once.[20]

[18] Ibid., p. 21.

[19] Ibid., p. 7.

[20] Alfred Marshall, 'The Housing of the London Poor', *Contemporary Review*, Vol. 45 (1884), pp. 224–31.

A few small comprehensively planned new industrial communities were actually constructed in the nineteenth century in Britain, though by socially conscious industrialists rather than public authorities. Cadbury's Bournville Village, Titus Salt's mill town of Saltaire, and Lever's Port Sunlight are perhaps the best known of these small industrial towns built in the second half of the century. Each of these towns was to house a single industry, its employees and their families, in what were considered the best possible physical and social conditions. These shrewd puritan industrialists considered that by providing their workers with good homes, healthy environments and public services and facilities far superior to anything available to the working class in the industrial cities, they would be assuring themselves of a reliable, healthy and highly motivated workforce. The community facilities which were provided in these towns were those which the industrialists felt the working people needed for wholesome living. There were schools, churches, playing fields, even libraries, baths and an art museum at Saltaire, but no pubs were built in most of them. The new industrial village was seen by some businessmen as a way of imposing a new middle-class puritan ethic on the workers, to the mutual benefit of worker and employer. There was a great deal of interest in these small, purpose-built industrial communities in the second half of the nineteenth century, as solutions to the problems and dangers of the overcrowded industrial cities.

Towards the end of the nineteenth century the reformer Ebenezer Howard proposed his now famous garden city as a 'peaceful path to real reform' of industrial society. The twin evils of modern society, according to Howard, were the simultaneous depopulation of the countryside, which he saw as man's natural habitat, and overcrowding in the new industrial cities. Howard in effect defined urbanization itself, as occurring in the nineteenth century, as the social problem and proposed that it be solved by building new industrial communities in the countryside to which the urban masses could be dispersed. The crux of Howard's argument was that planned towns of 30,000 people properly located in the countryside, comprehensively designed and carefully developed, could provide a new human environment which would combine all the advantages of city life, such as opportunities for work, socialization and creativity, with all the advantages of country life, including a healthy environment and opportunity for communion with nature, while at the same time exhibiting none of the disadvantages of contemporary town and country life. Howard's environmental determinist assumptions at the base of his work were quite clear. He wrote that:

> . . . the key to the problem how to restore the people to the land, that beautiful land of ours, with its canopy of sky, the air that blows upon it, the sun that warms it, the rain and dew that moisten it, the very embodiment of Divine love for man – is indeed a *Master-Key* [to the social problems of industrial society] . . . it is the key to a portal through which, even when scarce ajar, will be seen to pour a flood of light on the problems of intemperance, of excessive toil, of restless anxiety, of grinding poverty – the true

limits of Governmental interference, ay, and even the relations of man to the Supreme Power.[21]

It is no exaggeration to say that Howard claimed his new industrial communities would solve most of the social problems identified by the nineteenth-century reformers.

Each garden city was to have a population of 32,000 and Howard proposed they be developed in groups of six around a comprehensively planned central city of 58,000 to make totally planned urban units of 250,000 people. The garden city was a true utopia as Howard conceived of it, for all material, moral and spiritual values were to be possible of realization in it. Freedom and happiness would be found there as well as beauty, health, comfort, companionship and prosperity. Population would be attracted to the new cities, he felt, once their advantages over other environments became known: 'Each city may be regarded as a magnet' Howard said, 'each person as a needle; and so viewed, it is at once seen that nothing short of the discovery of a method for constructing magnets of yet greater power than our cities possess can be effective for redistributing the population in a spontaneous and healthy manner.'[22] The bulk of Howard's book is devoted to just these practical matters of how the new cities can be located, planned, built and governed, with special emphasis on financing. It is probably this eminently practical emphasis of Howard's presentation which made his idea so attractive to the planning movement.

In 1905 the planning reformers founded the Garden City Association to promote Howard's ideas. This group, renamed the Town Planning and Garden City Association, and eventually the Town and Country Planning Association, progressively widened its interests to include urban redevelopment and countryside preservation. It has remained the very active organized centre of the planning movement to this day.[23] Two garden cities, Letchworth and Welwyn, were built by the Association from 1901 and 1920 respectively and new towns built by the government after the Second World War took much of their original inspiration from the garden city idea.

The first Town Planning Act was passed by the government in 1909 and gave local authorities power to make comprehensive plans for the development of new suburbs on their periphery, after obtaining permission of the Ministry. The act was passed by Parliament after conscription for the South African War had provided statistical evidence on a national scale of the poor physical condition of recruits for the army and an investigating commission had attributed this to the unhealthy effects of city life, due, it thought, to overcrowding and pollution of the environment. The Commission's report pointed out specifically that the urban conditions thought to be so harmful to health

[21] Ebenezer Howard, *Tomorrow: A Peaceful Path to Real Reform*. Swan Sonnenschein, London (1898), p. 5. Republished in 1901 as *Garden Cities of Tomorrow*.

[22] Ibid., p. 6.

[23] See Donald Foley, 'Idea and Influence: The Town and Country Planning Association', *Journal of the American Institute of Planners*, Vol. 28 (1962), pp. 10–17.

were being recreated in the new urban growth occurring around all the major cities, and recommended comprehensive planning of new suburbs to create more healthy urban environments. Germany was frequently cited as an example of advanced town planning which ought to be emulated in Britain 'because Germany was the most formidable rival, commercially and militarily'.[24] One contemporary observer warned in 1908 that:

> Unless we begin at once at least to protect the health of our people by making the towns in which most of them now live more wholesome for body and mind, we may as well hand over our trade, our colonies, our whole influence in the world, to Germany without undergoing all the trouble of a struggle in which we condemn ourselves beforehand to certain failure.[25]

International politics and commerce had made town planning relevant to national policy in the first part of the twentieth century.

TWENTIETH-CENTURY LEGISLATION

The Housing, Town Planning and *etc.* Act of 1909 was a very limited first step towards the comprehensive, compulsory town planning which was to become law after the Second World War. Use of the power granted by the 1909 Act was voluntary for local authorities; they were not required to plan for their new suburbs. Those authorities who wanted to plan found themselves hemmed in by administrative procedures of the government when they sought to exercise the powers granted under the Act. It is as if the government was frightened by the 'radical' nature of this innovation in public policy, and expressed its timidity by hamstringing local authorities in a welter of administrative controls. The authorities who fought through this web of controls and planned their new suburbs universally adopted the physical plan of the garden city neighbourhood from Ebenezer Howard and laid out Garden Suburbs on their peripheries. The purists in the planning movement, however, considered this a debasement of their idea of the self-contained new city located in the country, and continued to call for the creation of real garden cities to solve the urban problem. Town Planning under the 1909 Act was more an extension of the principles of nineteenth-century urban neighbourhood design for the upper classes to the new suburban estates for middle and working-class families, than an application of Howard's idea for satellite cities.

The Town Planning Act of 1919 was generated by the difficulties found in implementing the provisions of the 1909 Act and eliminated much of the government red tape binding planning, including the requirement of prior permission before local authorities could even take up the task of city planning. This Act also made town planning obligatory for towns of more than

[24] Ashworth, op. cit., p. 178.

[25] T. C. Horsfall, *The Relation of Town Planning to the National Life*. Wolverhampton (1908), pp. 13–14, cited in Ashworth, op. cit., p. 169.

20,000 population, and even gave them some limited authority to plan for already built-up areas of the city. The 1919 Act also permitted adjacent local authorities to draw up joint development plans if they so desired. This seems to be the first official recognition of the fact that in regions of rapid population growth and economic development, the political boundaries of local authorities seldom coincided with the extent of the urbanized area, let alone the functional urban unit of city, suburb and rural hinterland. The Town Planning Act of 1932 sought to further encourage joint planning efforts by local authorities in the major urban regions and in 1935 the Restriction of Ribbon Development Act gave them specific power to limit ribbon development, or suburban spread, then taking place along the roads leading out of the major cities and towns. The people in the planning movement were rather upset that their ideas for self-contained new communities, built at carefully selected locations in the countryside, were not incorporated into these early planning Acts. A Committee of the Ministry of Health did propose in 1920 that the government build a ring of satellite garden cities around London as one measure for relieving congestion in the metropolis.

It is clear that the modern planning idea was an invention of the nineteenth-century social reformers who saw it as a means for curing the problems of crowding, disease and poverty in the growing industrial cities and towns. It is equally clear that the government adopted the planning programme as social policy when it was seen as relevant to the twentieth-century crises of war, international competition and economic depression. Perhaps social inventions, such as the planning idea, generally occur in response to conditions which have been defined as social problems, while purposive social change, such as new policy innovations, generally occur in response to social crises, that is to external threats to the existence of society. The history of planning, which we are developing here, may be seen as an example of such a general historical process whereby social problems are a stimulus to invention, while crises stimulate policy change. Inventions come as a response to perceived social problems on the part of reformers and revolutionaries, whereas innovations in government policy are made by powerful groups in society in response to dangerous social crises, such as epidemics, wars and depressions.

In the 1930s government interest in planning was further stimulated by the depression and the start of a new war in Europe. There was a new interest in regional economic planning to alleviate the effects of the depression, and in industrial dispersal from the cities to protect industry from possible enemy air attacks in a new European war which seemed to be brewing even by the early 1930s. The Depression had far less serious economic effects on Britain nationally than on most other Western countries, but internally it had the effect of accelerating the trends of economic decline in the old mining and manufacturing districts, mainly in the North of England, Central Scotland, and South Wales.[26] The effects of the Great Depression could therefore be

[26] See H. W. Richardson, 'The Economic Significance of the Depression in Britain', *Journal of Contemporary History*, Vol. 4 (1969), pp. 3–21.

tackled by the government as continuations of trends in the long-term economic decline of these older mining and manufacturing regions. It was this problem of continuing regional decline, as we have seen, that led directly to the appointment of the Barlow Commission in 1937. Though this Commission was created to find ways of dealing with the problems of unemployment in the depressed industrial areas of Britain, it was given the authority in its terms of reference to examine these problems in the context of the overall national distribution of employment and population. Instead of being asked to look simply at the economic problems of the chronically depressed regions, the Commission was asked specifically to look at the growth of the expanding and wealthy regions as well, including the spread of the large cities and conurbations within them. The underlying position was that the problems of the depressed areas ought to be considered in conjunction with the problems of the growth and spread of London and the other conurbations of Britain. The economic problem of accelerating regional decline was going to be used to provide an additional *raison d'être* for a national policy of urban dispersal, which had been advocated for so long by the reformers in the planning movement. By the time the Commission made its report, war was once again making planning relevant to national survival, for the danger of aerial bombardment of the cities made the dispersion of people and industry seem imperative to national survival. The Barlow Commission proposed a national strategy of policies including the decentralization and dispersal of industry and population from the large cities, the redevelopment of the congested centres of these cities, the attainment of a balance of industrial development in the different regions of Britain, and diversification of industry within each region.

THE PHILOSOPHICAL BASIS OF THE 1947 SYSTEM

It is only against this historical background that we can begin to understand not merely the Barlow Report but also the subsidiary reports that stemmed from it – the Scott Report on Rural Land Use of 1942, the Uthwatt Report on Compensation and Betterment in the same year, the Abercrombie Greater London Plan of 1944 and the Reith Reports on new towns in 1945–46. From these reports we can distinguish a number of basic postulates which came to be the philosophical foundations of postwar British planning. From Barlow came the notions of correcting regional imbalance of employment and of containing conurbation growth linked together as two parts of a single policy. From the Scott Report came the idea of conserving agricultural land as a priceless national asset. From the Reith Report, essentially, came the idea that planning has the right and the responsibility to try to shape the life of the community through good physical arrangements, as exemplified in the new towns.

Yet another postulate, most clearly illustrated in the Abercrombie regional plans such as the famous Greater London Plan of 1944, is the belief in a fixed, end-state master plan. Finally there is the distinction, implicit in all the legislation but especially in the great 1947 Act, between the normal process of local development control and the deliberate creation of new communities.

Each of these ideas is worth examining briefly in turn at this stage, in order fully to understand the history in later chapters of this Volume. At the start of Volume Two of this book we shall need to come back and examine some of the philosophical antecedents more thoroughly.

Of the two main ideas or concepts in the Barlow Report, one, the belief in urban containment, is much older. It goes back to the nineteenth century, even to Frederick Engels and Edwin Chadwick in the 1840s; its basis and its justification is the manifest list of disadvantages of life in many of Britain's industrialized urbanized areas. For that, Barlow could find plenty of statistical evidence in 1940 as could Engels and Chadwick almost exactly a century earlier; despite the achievements of the great cities in the interwar period, there was still a stubborn gap, as the report showed, between the housing and public health statistics of urban industrial England and the rest.[27]

If the analysis is essentially Chadwick's, the remedy is essentially Ebenezer Howard's. We have seen that forty years before Barlow, Howard had argued, in *Garden Cities of Tomorrow*, that in trying to remedy the evils of the nineteenth-century city, the twentieth century might add new evils of its own. Specifically, Howard and his fellow reformers in the planning movement argued against trying to cure the problem of the slums by suburbanization. Howard saw clearly the fundamental change that was being wrought in cities during the last years of the nineteenth century, when new forms of urban transportation were giving new and unparalleled possibilities of urban dispersal. A dispersal of people from the cities in continued suburbanization, without dispersal of jobs, would in the long run prove self-defeating, Howard claimed. It would lead to a cleaner, healthier version of the nineteenth-century city perhaps, but it would bring problems of its own, such as long journeys to work, high costs of housing and transportation, and loss of contact with the countryside. In Howard's famous concept of the three magnets, the garden city was the new, hybrid settlement which combined all the main advantages of urban and of rural living, without any of the attendant disadvantages then associated with both.[28] For four decades after Howard wrote, his ideas were little noticed by the powers in the land, and only two garden cities were actually started. But then, largely through the agency of the planner Patrick Abercrombie (who was a member of the Commission) Barlow rediscovered the notion, and gave it almost official blessing.

The other notion that is central to the Barlow Report is not essentially Howard's; it goes back in a different line, through Fawcett to Geddes. Particularly, it draws on Fawcett's notion of the axial belt, and on Geddes'

[27] The actual statistical evidence presented to the Barlow Commission, and analysed by them, did not fully justify the rather sweeping conclusions they drew. London in particular was even then about as healthy as the nation as a whole. The statement was truer of many northern industrial cities, some of which had been particularly hard hit by the depression, an effect which should have been separated from that of urbanization. For a criticism cf. Peter Hall, *London 2000*. Faber, London (1969), pp. 36–8.

[28] Howard, op. cit., pp. 6–11, 12–19.

notion of the new character of industry in the neotechnic age. As Barlow put it, it stated that there was a permanent imbalance in the rate of economic development between one part of Britain and another, and that left to itself this would continue and intensify. The southern and midland parts of the axial belt, corresponding to London and the home counties, the West Midlands and the East Midlands, had a built-in advantage because of their industrial structure, which was biased in the direction of those industries which were exhibiting rapid growth. Conversely, the northern and western periphery of the country suffered from a long-standing dependence on industries which were in decline. Since coal had ceased to be a critical factor of location, industry would be drawn to markets, to labour supplies and to specialized services; all these were available abundantly in London and in the West Midlands, and in these circumstances the decline would be continuous and accelerating, unless the government took deliberate action.[29]

Neither of the main strands in the argument of the Barlow Report, therefore, was original to it. What was original was their union: regional imbalance should be corrected by positive government interference, because of the manifest disadvantages of the conurbations. It might be argued that this juxtaposition was logically wrong: that the worst social indices, even in the 1930s, belonged not to the fastest growing conurbations but precisely to those stagnant or declining areas of the North and West, some of which were not even in conurbations at all. But this criticism is in a sense irrelevant. It was not apparently voiced in the 1930s, but it was axiomatically accepted that by restricting the growth of the conurbations – above all, Greater London and Greater Birmingham – one would simultaneously serve the best interests both of the people in those conurbations, and of the people in what were then still recognized as the depressed areas. The terms of reference almost instructed the Commission to return a verdict of guilty against the big cities, but to judge by the argument, they needed little encouragement. This was a rare opportunity to give the philosophy of containment an official stamp; it was eagerly seized.

From the analysis, a double set of policies necessarily springs. One is the attempt to divert economic activity, and above all growing lines of manufacturing industry, which were thought to be the mainspring of economic growth, out of the big conurbations and their fringe areas altogether, and into the depressed areas. The other, failing this, was the local decentralization of activity and people to self-contained communities of a garden city character, accompanied by physical containment of the conurbations. This would require a totally new and comprehensive apparatus of control: economic controls on the location of industry, over all or part of the country,

[29] Strictly, the question of the Special Areas was not within the Commission's terms of reference. The report recognizes this, but trusts that its proposal for a National Industrial Board would act to encourage 'a reasonable balance of industrial development, so far as possible, throughout the various divisions or regions of Great Britain . . .'. *Royal Commission on the Distribution of the Industrial Population, Report.* Cmd 6153, HMSO, London (1940).

on the one hand, and physical controls on the use of land development, on the other.

Barlow's was the greatest single contribution to the philosophy of postwar planning and, indeed, to the whole character of British society after the Second World War. But another critical contribution was made by the Scott Committee on Land Use in Rural Areas, which was set up on Barlow's recommendation and which reported in 1942.[30] Scott's contribution, which almost certainly originated mainly from the powerful voice of Sir Dudley Stamp, was to reinforce the Barlow conclusions on the physical control of urban growth, and indeed to put them in extreme form. The philosophical position of the report, which came in for strong criticism after the Second World War and was indeed never followed in its pure form, was that the community had overriding obligation to protect agriculture and the agricultural use of land. Impressed by the well-documented loss of the high quality market gardening tracts on the fertile Taplow terrace gravels west of London, or the Sussex plain behind Worthing, the Committee put forward a new planning principle, the *onus of proof*. In Professor Gerald Wibberley's words this stated:

> That the use and users of the land in its existing state have a prior claim and that the proposed new use and new users should prove that the community will benefit if the land in question is passed over to them.[31]

The land that most needed this protection was of good, but not outstanding quality; on the best land there was no question that the planning authority would refuse permission to develop. To the planners of the 1940s, in the middle of the great war drive to restore the English countryside to basic food production, the point needed no arguing. But after the pressure of the Second World War was over, the doctrine was never wholeheartedly applied. Yet it had indirect influence: two new town sites were rejected because they stood on good agricultural land, while others were reduced in size. Elsewhere, in producing its future development plan, the local authority has to consult the Ministry of Agriculture on the relative agricultural quality, but where there is no alternative site for any given use, the fact of agricultural quality appears to make no difference.

Yet another distinctive philosophical strain emerges in a whole series of documents towards the war's end: first in advisory regional plans like Abercrombie's for Greater London, and then in the important report of Lord Reith's Committee on the planning and organization of new towns.[32] The inspiration is again Howard's, though it is fortified by the contribution of

[30] *Report of the Committee on Land Utilisation in Rural Areas.* Cmd 6378, HMSO, London (1942).

[31] G. P. Wibberley, *Agriculture and Urban Growth.* Michael Joseph, London (1959), p. 73. In a minority report, Professor S. R. Dennison objected to the implicit assumption here that agriculture should be maintained at the wartime level.

[32] *Final Report of the New Towns Committee.* Cmd 6876, HMSO, London (1946).

some American planners of the interwar years, which had been learned and incorporated by the planner Barry Parker in his plan for the satellite town of Wythenshawe south of Manchester. It is the notion that the planner has the right and the responsibility to try to shape the life of the community through physical arrangements. In this view, which undoubtedly appealed to Reith as creator of the pre-war BBC, the informed professional had a sacred responsibility not merely to provide a level of material satisfaction corresponding to the felt needs of the public, but to provide a positive lead to that public by setting higher standards of consciousness or taste or social organization. Though in British planning this idea can be traced back to Howard, it readily fits within a more general paternalistic view of social planning, which can be well seen in that wing of early Fabianism represented by the Webbs. In the spirit of intense idealism which seized the country in the last years of the war, it found a ready response.

There is yet another specific strain to be distinguished in the philosophy of postwar planning as it developed during these critical wartime years. Its origins are less easy to pinpoint. It is that in reshaping and controlling urban areas, planning should aim at some desirable future end-state embodied in a physical form as a master plan. Such a conception of planning did not very easily accept a state of rapid growth or change. Indeed, as Abercrombie made it clear in his West Midlands Plan,[33] change could often be regarded as positively undesirable, since it led to rapid obsolescence and waste. The aim, if possible, was to provide for any desirable change, and then to try to freeze the pattern of development. A city would of course continue to grow after that, but since much of its natural propensity to grow would have been channelled elsewhere, into overspill developments, the whole process would be slow enough to allow the planner to deal with it. This static concept fitted well the circumstances of the time, for planners like Abercrombie had spent their whole professional lives in a world where change, whether in population or in economic activity, must have seemed so slow as to be imperceptible.

A last set of assumptions of the planning system created in the immediate postwar period can only be grasped by reading the voluminous materials in the regional planning reports such as Abercrombie on Greater London or Abercrombie and Jackson on the West Midlands. It concerns the role and the relationships of *plan making*, *development control* and the *creation of self contained and balanced communities*. Plan making, as we already saw, involved the creation of plans in the form of fixed end-state designs. Regional plans, which were more general and diagrammatic in character, would be produced by *ad hoc* teams since there was no formal place in the national or local government structure to house them. Blessed and perhaps modified by Whitehall, they would lay down guidelines for more local plans to be produced by counties and county boroughs, who received this responsibility under the

[33] Patrick Abercrombie and Herbert Jackson, *West Midlands Plan*, Interim Confidential Edition. Ministry of Town and Country Planning (1948), Vol. 4, para. 1, pp. 10–12.

Town and Country Planning Act of 1947. The local plan would then make orderly provision for the additional employment, population, homes and infrastructure of all kinds that detailed survey had shown to be necessary. It would set out the provision in some detail, in the form of a binding land use plan. Though under the Act this was to be revised every five years, plan making was seen as a well ordered, unhurried affair. Events would not move so quickly as to call for rapid or unexpected responses.

Under the 1947 Act, development control was linked with local plan-making. Counties and county boroughs were first to draw up plans (and then revise them every five years); they would then exercise planning control according to the plan. They were able to exercise effective control because the 1947 Act, which brought the new planning authorities into being, also nationalized development rights on land (not the property title to the enjoyment of the land in its existing use), and then transferred the rights to them. (Compensation for the lost development rights was to be paid out of a £300 million fund, which was supposed to represent the historic value of the rights in the country, scaled down to exclude double counting.) The process of control, like the process of plan making, could then take place in deliberate and orderly fashion. Since the plan itself would have correctly forecast the pace of change, within fairly narrow limits of error, the problem would merely be to guide intending private developers into those areas which the plan had indicated to be suitable for development, and away from other areas.

But here it is important to underline another feature which seems to have been central to the 1947 system as it was originally conceived. The basic assumption throughout seems to have been that private development would not be very important anyway. The Uthwatt Committee on Compensation and Betterment, reporting in 1942, had suggested that all development rights on land outside the urban areas should in effect be nationalized, and that they should actually be purchased by a state agency when needed for development. The 1947 Act rejected this solution; it extended the principle of nationalization of development rights to all land, but then proposed to deal with development values by taking them all for the state. In other words, the private land market was allowed to continue in existence but it lost virtually all incentive to go on working, since the financial provisions of the 1947 Act, as interpreted in the regulations, took all profit from development for the community. The assumption seems to have been that some builders would have been satisfied to make a profit from building while foregoing any profit from speculation and development; large-scale speculative development, as witnessed in the 1920s and 1930s around the major conurbations, was presumably ruled out. In the circumstances, it may well have been imagined, the new planning machinery could cope well enough with the limited development pressures which remained.

This would leave a gap, which would be filled by comprehensively-planned public development. Indeed, the central feature of the new system for contemporaries seems to have been that much of the new development in the countryside would take place outside the market system and therefore outside the normal scope of development control. Of the expected efflux of population from the conurbations and great cities, the great majority would go into schemes for comprehensively-planned new communities outside the existing urban areas, which would be both planned and built by public authorities. The regional plans would identify the locations and sizes of these new communities; thereafter, they would be developed in one of two ways. First, the New Towns Act of 1946 carried into law the recommendations of Lord Reith's Committee on New Towns: that these towns should be built by autonomous public Development Corporations, one for each town, drawing on direct Treasury finance and largely outside the existing local government structure. Since the responsibility to Parliament was restricted to an annual report, the constitutional position of these town development Corporations was analogous to the boards of the industries which were nationalized by the Labour Government of 1945–50. Then, the Town Development Act of 1952, an Act introduced by Labour but carried through by the Conservatives, provided for the expansion of existing small and medium-sized country towns through co-operation between exporting (or overspilling) authorities and receiving authorities, ,with central government aid for expensive public services. The 1952 Act provided machinery which was almost the opposite of the 1946 Act for a similar purpose; but the local circumstances would be different. New towns would be built mainly on green field sites, or on the basis of villages or small towns, where the existing local government structure could not meet the financial and organizational problems involved; towns to be expanded under the 1952 Act were assumed to have active and competent local governments capable of meeting the strain. At least this seems to have been the distinction that was intended.

The development of the new communities would be helped too, by more general measures. Central government, in the shape of the Board of Trade, had taken control over the location of new industry or the expansion of existing industry by the 1945 Distribution of Industry Act. As well as assisting the revival of the development areas, this control could be used to steer industry from the congested conurbations to the new and expanding towns, thus ensuring that employment would be decentralized in pace with population. The more general processes of development control, exercised by the local planning authorities, were necessary to maintain open land between the conurbations and the new communities that would be built to receive their overspill; only in this way could the ideal of physical self-containment be guaranteed.

Both the new towns and the expanded towns were already clearly conceived as parallel arms of regional policy in Abercrombie's Greater London Plan of 1944, even though it took eight years before the legislation was passed to bring the second arm into being. And it is clear, from the 1944 Plan, that there they are seen as the normal means of development in postwar Britain. In the plan, out of 1¼ million people to be overspilled from London in the postwar period (there is no fixed time given), no less than one million would be housed in such public developments, outside the normal operation of market forces. This, then, was to be the normal means of development, a point which explains the otherwise extraordinary decision of the Labour Government to take the whole of the private developer's profit for the state. Speculative building, which had been so characteristic of the interwar years, no longer had a significant place – as witness the fact that between 1945 and 1951, in a period of strict licensing of new building, it hardly received any resources at all.

It perhaps goes without saying that in actuality things worked out very differently, partly through unforeseen circumstances, partly through deliberate reversal of policies. A major theme of this Study is to trace how the ideal vision of the pioneers who created the 1947 system became transmuted into the very different reality of the 1947–70 period. This is done in two main ways. First, through a descriptive account of the events of this quarter century. This is the burden of the present Volume, and it will be done in two parallel streams: a statistical account of growth and change of population and employment in urban England and Wales, and a more detailed historical narrative of events in five specially chosen study areas. Secondly, through systematic analysis of different elements of the actual development process: the planning system, the objectives of the planners, the way they exercised control, the motivations of the client population which provided the market for the new homes, the developers themselves and the constraints on their actions. This, together with systematic studies of the housing and land markets, the patterns of home-workplace relationships, and the planned communities, is the major subject matter of Volume Two.

PART TWO

FROM METROPOLITAN AREA TO MEGALOPOLIS

This second part of Volume One takes us into the heart of the study. Its main focus is a detailed account, mainly based on official statistics, of geographical changes in urban England in the period from approximately 1931 to approximately 1966, a period that includes the great urban spread of the 1930s, and the operation of the planning system after the Second World War. It has three chief geographical frames of reference: 100 metropolitan areas, a functional concept of urbanization borrowed from the United States: Megalopolis England, a super urban-agglomeration of over sixty-three of these metropolitan areas; and five study areas within Megalopolis, composed of groups of metropolitan areas, for more detailed analysis of growth and change.

Chapter Four is a purely technical chapter introducing some of these concepts, and discussing problems of measurement and analysis. The general reader may skip it, except for its conclusions.

Chapter Five is in many ways the heart of Part Two. It is a detailed analysis, from Census statistics, of growth and change in 100 metropolitan areas of England and Wales. These are urban areas functionally defined in terms of commuting patterns around major employment centres. The analysis demonstrates not merely a pronounced growth trend in most of the areas, but also a notable tendency to internal decentralization of residential population and, latterly, employment.

Chapter Six, building on Chapter Five, asks whether a Megalopolis can meaningfully be identified in England. It concludes that such an area, taking a notably linear form along the main urban and industrial axis of England from the Sussex coast to Lancashire and Yorkshire, is a meaningful and useful focus for the study of urban growth and the impact of planning, although in a physical sense, no Megalopolis exists. It ends by isolating five areas within Megalopolis for more detailed study.

Chapter Seven analyses patterns of recent migration within these five study areas. It also specifically examines the statistical evidence for the increasing segregation of different socio-economic groups in the study areas. It is an essential preliminary to the detailed history of urban growth, and the impact of the planning system on that growth, in the five study areas, which forms the subject matter of Part Three of our study.

CHAPTER FOUR

BUILDING BLOCKS

This is a technical chapter which may not appeal to the general reader; he will find a summary of its conclusions at the end (see pages 138–140). It deals with the problems of measuring and analysing urbanization and urban growth. It develops a fundamental distinction between two possible definitions of an urban area: the physical definition in terms of bricks and mortar, and the functional definition in terms of activity patterns.

The functional definition must be based on available statistics of activity patterns or flows; among the most readily available are Census statistics data on residence, employment and journey to work. These make it possible to define areas similar in concept to the Standard Metropolitan Statistical Areas of the United States Census, used in the parallel Resources for the Future study of urban growth in the North American Northeastern Urban Complex.

Physical urbanization is most readily defined in terms of land use, taking account of the intensity as well as the category of the use; unfortunately these two characteristics often have to be measured from different sources. This chapter introduces Britain's unique source for recording land use: the three national surveys of the early 1930s, the late 1940s and the 1960s. It considers ways of measuring land uses from the original surveys. Lastly it develops a concept of urbanized area, almost identical with that used by the United States Census and by the parallel Resources for the Future study.

This chapter was written by Peter Hall. The early research on metropolitan area definition was done by Peter Hall and Roy Drewett. Anne Whalley did much of the subsequent development work. Roy Drewett did the ground work in developing techniques of measuring changes in land use.

INTRODUCTION

In Chapters One and Two, as soon as we wanted to discuss urban growth in any rigorous, exact way, we discovered problems of definition and measurement. We must now face these problems in detail. This chapter is concerned to define, and refine, the building blocks to be used in the rest of the analysis. Necessarily, it is technical in character. General readers who do not want this technical detail should skip this chapter, pausing only to take in the summary in the final section.[1]

There are two basic problems involved here. One is the question of what we want to measure: what exactly we mean by urban, urbanization or urban growth. The other is the scale at which we want to measure it. Naturally, the two problems are closely related.

SOME PRELIMINARY DEFINITIONS

In earlier chapters we have already seen that urbanization, or urban growth, can have at least two basic meanings. On the one hand, we can talk of urban growth in a *physical* sense. This is perhaps the more elementary and obvious meaning. It refers to the use of the land for urban purposes, begging for the moment the question of how to define an urban purpose. On the other hand, we can talk of urban growth in a *functional* sense. This focuses on people rather than on land or physical structures. It refers to the activities of the people (economic, social, and cultural), and seeks to determine whether in any area these are urban in character, or not.

Evidently, these two definitions of urbanization, or urban growth, may be in accord in any particular case, or they may not; there is no automatic reason why they should agree. Thus in southern Italy there are many settlements which are urban in a physical sense, because they consist of houses and other structures, juxtaposed closely on the ground, but which perform almost wholly agricultural functions. Conversely, in the agricultural zone of western Connecticut, thirty miles outside New York city, there is an area which physically appears quite rural, but is almost wholly occupied by middle-class professional workers who commute out every evening from their offices in the city. Indeed, in any analysis of contemporary urban growth, one focus will need to be on the complex relationships between physical urban growth, and functional urban growth. And this immediately introduces us to the other problem of scale.

Throughout this study there is a particular focus on particular sorts of area: areas where rapid physical urban growth is happening, in the sense of bricks and mortar being put on top of land that was previously open. (We are only indirectly interested in the phenomenon of change and redevelopment within existing built-up areas.) We shall be most interested in rapid physical growth, though, where it is somehow physically related to existing urban areas which are physically big enough to seem important, and where in consequence further urban growth may appear as a problem or a threat. And that, in turn, raises the question of the functional relationships between the new urban area and the existing urban area of which it will be a part in the future.

To see this more clearly, consider a typical example. New urban growth,

[1] Pages 138–140.

especially in England since 1945, often takes the form of relatively small clusters. Pockets of land are covered, fairly intensively, with buildings forming new estates or developments, but between each pocket and the next, tracts of open land will be left. So to study physical growth one needs a fairly small scale of analysis: the scale of the individual housing development or industrial estate. That is the ideal, if source materials allow it. But sometimes they may not: statistics of new housing are presented by local authority areas; statistics of people and of the stock of dwellings are presented in the published Census volumes by wards and parishes.[2] This smallest possible scale of analysis, which stresses the physical fact of new urban growth, we shall call the *micro* scale.

But next we need to set these pockets of growth in relation to existing urban areas, and other pockets of new growth elsewhere. These relationships will be both physical and functional. Physically we shall want to consider the relationship of a new housing estate, say, to a city, to the main employment areas within that city, and to the transport systems that connect them up. Functionally we shall want to consider the accessibility of the new estate to job opportunities, and to analyse the commuting flows that result. Similarly we shall need to consider the needs of the people in the new estates for all sorts of urban services at various levels – shopping, education, health and welfare services, entertainment, recreation. All this clearly must be done at a larger scale than the single cluster or clump of new housing: it will be the scale which describes the range of people's everyday movements between home and work, home services, and home and entertainment or recreation. This we can call the *intermediate or metropolitan* scale. Defined basically in functional terms (that is, in terms of relationships or flows), the metropolitan scale of analysis nevertheless contains physical elements, in the form of urban land uses, whose disposition on the ground will be an important area of study.

Lastly, we must set these metropolitan units of analysis within an even wider frame. We shall want to discover whether urban growth, and the resulting pressure on the land, show any clear geographical pattern at the national scale: whether, for instance, some regions are showing much faster urban growth than others, whether the pattern of most rapid growth shows any tendency to follow lines of communications, and whether it is clustered or dispersed. In particular, as one important objective of the first section of this study, we shall want to consider the evidence for or against the existence of an English Megalopolis. The third scale of analysis then is the *macro* or *national* scale, which includes a possible but unproven *Megalopolitan* scale.

Against this background of different scales of inquiry it is now possible to turn to the basic problem of this chapter: the problem of the two definitions of urbanization and of urban growth. We shall find it convenient first to discuss the functional meaning of urbanization, and then the physical.

[2] Unpublished data are available for smaller units, the enumeration districts. But they cannot be obtained for previous Censuses, so historical analysis is precluded.

FUNCTIONAL URBANIZATION

Earlier, in Chapter Two, we have already attempted a simple classification of human functions, whether in cities or anywhere else. We noticed that functions could be defined first *topically*, into residential, working, recreational, and so on, and second *geographically* into within-place functions and between-place functions. Between-place functions essentially consist of ways of travelling, or communicating, between within-place functions. They may connect two within-place functions of a similar type as, for instance, a telephone call or a journey made in the course of one's business day. Or, more commonly, they connect two different within-place functions, for instance, the journey between home and work, or between home and recreation. We need too to introduce another attribute, or dimension, of functions: this is *intensity*. Any given function may have an intensity, or density, usually expressed as a density in terms of units of ground area or of physical structure. Examples of the intensity of within-place activities are densities of workers or residential population per square mile or per square kilometre, or density of weekend visitors per mile of beach, or density of sales per foot unit of shop frontage. Examples of the intensity of between-place activities are traffic flows per route mile (expressed in terms of passengers, or ton-miles or ton-kilometres) or traffic flows per lane of road (expressed in terms of vehicles, or equivalent passenger car units, per lane per hour). All functions, urban or otherwise, are capable of being analysed and classified in these three ways.

This seems tidy. But in practice, it leaves open a number of questions. One, an obvious question, concerns the topical classification of activities that is to be used. Some activities, as for instance work, are capable of more minute classification than others, because more study has been made of their classification problems. (Work can be classified in two ways, industrially and occupationally, and then for each in varying degrees of fineness.)[3] In other fields, for instance leisure and recreation, much less work has been done.[4] We need not spend much time on this problem, because in practice we shall need only rather coarse and obvious topical classes of activity.

Another problem is more central and more serious. It concerns the definition of the terms within-place and between-place. These two terms are in reality arbitrary, for they depend on the grain of the analysis that is being conducted, and that in turn depends on the statistics that are available for the purpose. If we have only a handbook of international statistics referring to the nations of the world, all activity within any of those countries must be

[3] An industrial classification refers to the end product of the work, an occupational classification to the character of the work. The Standard Industrial Classification (S.I.C.) used in Britain in 1951 and 1961 has 24 Main Order headings, but these are broken down into over 200 Minimum List Headings.

[4] But cf. Marion Clawson, Arthur L. Moore and Ivan M. Lee, *Economic Studies of Outdoor Recreation*. Resources for the Future, Washington (1962); and Outdoor Recreation Resources Review Commission, O.R.R.C. Study Report No. 24.

regarded as within-place. But if we now obtain detailed statistics for administrative areas within that country, it is possible to disaggregate much of the analysis, and consider between-place relationships within that country. It is all a question of the level at which our statistics are aggregated.

Yet another fundamental question refers to the third dimension of functional urbanization: intensity. We can suppose that if we seek to distinguish an urban area from a rural area on functional grounds, one essential criterion will be a certain defined intensity of some function or another; thus we might say that an urban area is one with a certain minimum overall density of workers or resident population per acre, or with certain intensities of transportation or communication flows connecting it to another area. The question here, as with all quantitative measures, is the criterion of acceptance or rejection for inclusion. Most measures of this kind prove, when analysed, to exhibit to some extent the phenomenon of a continuum. One good example is a familiar measure of between-place activity: the journey to work, as recorded by Census data on commuting. Many studies show that when the percentages of the resident employed population commuting to an employment centre are correlated with distance of the journey, the result is a good linear regression, with a high coefficient of correlation.[5] Because the function is linear, it is difficult to define any cut-off point that is not arbitrary. The same problem occurs with within-place activity; here too, indices like the density of employment per square mile prove to vary very regularly, without any obvious break points which could be used as thresholds for inclusion or rejection.

From this discussion it is possible to see that to devise functional urban areas for analysis it is necessary to go through three processes. First, a *topical* classification of activities must be made, and certain functions chosen as key indicators. Second, a *geographical* scale must be chosen; this will determine what is regarded as within-place activity, and what as between-place activity. And third, significant levels of *intensity* must be defined. It is this last test which will usually determine whether an area is to be treated as functionally urban, or not.

In working through all these stages, the limitations of the data are critical. In England as almost everywhere else, the only reasonably standardized data for the whole country come from a limited number of official, national statistical sources such as the Census of Population, the Censuses of Production and of Distribution, and the local employment exchange records of the Department of Employment (DE). Though more detailed records may exist for certain areas (for instance, the transportation study data now available for most conurbations) they are not uniformly available and comparable

[5] For London, for instance, cf. Roger Leigh, *Regression Analysis of the Journey to Work to Central London, 1951*. London School of Economics Graduate School of Geography Discussion Paper No. 2 (1966); and Patricia Ellman, 'The Socio-Geographic Enquiry', in *Royal Commission on Local Government in England, Research Report No. 1, Local Government in South-East England*. Greater London Group, London School of Economics and Political Science, HMSO, London (1968).

across the whole country. Even with the standardized data, there are difficulties of comparison both as to the topical classifications used and as to the geographical classification of areas employed. For instance, both the Census of Population and the DE give employment figures for local areas classified according to the Standard Industrial Classification. But the criteria of inclusion differ as between the two sets of data in several ways, making it difficult to compare them at local area level; and while the Census figures relate to local authorities, the DE statistics relate to a quite different set of employment exchange areas. In practice, it is necessary to restrict the analysis to data which meet certain specifications. They should as far as possible relate to the same agreed set of conventional geographical areas. And they should be comparable in their topical classification, as far as possible, from one date to another. These specifications immediately suggest that the Census of Population, with its basis in administrative areas and its regular character over a long period, will be the most useful source.

In detail, the most important useful sources of data are few in number. For within-place activities, the Census of Population has statistics of residence, in considerable geographical detail (local authority, ward and civil parish, latterly also enumeration district) for every Census date. The data relate to population, its grouping into household units, and the housing structures which accommodate those units. For employment, the Census offers alternative topical classifications (occupational and industrial) at each Census since 1921; the geographical presentation has varied, but has commonly related to the local authority area. The DE figures on employment are available annually, but they exclude certain classes of worker (for instance, the self employed)[6] and the geographical framework is not used anywhere else. For retailing the Board of Trade Census of Retail Distribution gives considerable topical detail down to local authority area level, with central areas distinguished separately in more recent Censuses; the data are available only for 1950, 1961 and 1966, however. Between-place activities are even harder to analyse. The most finely documented activity is the journey to work, which is recorded in Census tabulations for 1921, 1951, 1961 and 1966; the published tabulations all relate to movements between local authority areas, and movements wholly within local authorities are not analysed separately.[7] There are, additionally, some *ad hoc* surveys which show patterns of communication between places: goods vehicle tonnage moved, letters or telephone messages conveyed, and so on. They are usually presented on a rather coarse geographical base, which does not relate to conventional areas, and is hence not comparable from one survey to another, so they are difficult to build into an integrated picture. Lastly the Census has details of migration since 1961, again basically at local authority level.

[6] For a comparison of the results of the two at national level, cf. Census England and Wales, 1961, *Industry Tables*, Part 1, Table 7. HMSO, London (1966).

[7] They are available as data for movements between enumeration districts, on an unpublished basis.

Because they are available over a long period in reasonably comparable form, the Census statistics on residence, employment and journey to work stand out in this list. Though they may be supplemented with other data, on shopping for instance, they form a uniquely valuable source. And there is a certain logic in relying upon them: together, they present an integrated picture of the two most important within-place activities in most people's lives, in terms of the time devoted to them,[8] together with a between-place function that relates them together.[9] More than this, they focus on those relationships likely to be of great importance in the study of urban growth processes: the job, the home, and the journey between the two. If one is seeking a logically based geographical framework for a functional urban area, within which to study the physical facts of urban growth, a metropolitan area defined in these terms seems the most promising one.

THE METROPOLITAN AREA CONCEPT

Curiously, despite the relative richness of the data on employment and commuting in the English census, relatively little work seems to have been done on such delimitation by British geographers or planners. There is Kate Liepmann's pioneer work on *Journey to Work*,[10] and some valuable analyses of census data by the geographer R. Lawton.[11] But British workers on urban delimitation, from A. E. Smailes in 1944 through F. H. W. Green and H. E. Bracey to W. I. Carruthers,[12] have proved to be much more interested in the delimitation of service hinterlands, based on indices of retailing and other

[8] Evidence is provided by the international studies of time budgets completed in recent years.

[9] There is justification for this in the fact that everywhere the journey to work remains the most important single journey purpose. For instance, in London the London Transportation Study showed that in 1962 work journeys represented 47·5 per cent of all journeys. Despite a big predicted increase in other journeys, because of rising car ownership, the expected proportion in 1981 was still 35·4 per cent. *London Traffic Survey Vol. 2*. Greater London Council, London (1966), Table 13.7, p. 51.

[10] Kate Liepmann, *The Journey to Work*. Kegan Paul, London (1944).

[11] R. Lawton, 'The Daily Journey to Work in England and Wales', *Town Planning Review*, Vol. 29 (1959), pp. 241–51. R. Lawton, 'The Journey to Work in England and Wales: Forty Years of Change', *Tijdschrift voor Economische en Sociale Geografie*, Vol. 54 (1963), pp. 61–9. R. Lawton, 'The Journey to Work in Britain: Some Trends and Problems', *Regional Studies*, Vol. 2 (1968), pp. 27–40.

[12] A. E. Smailes, 'The Urban Hierarchy in England and Wales', *Geography*, Vol. 29 (1944), pp. 41–51. A. E. Smailes, 'The Urban Mesh of England and Wales', *Transactions and Papers, Institute of British Geographers*, Vol. 11 (1946), pp. 87–101. F. H. W. Green, 'Urban Hinterlands in England and Wales: An Analysis of Bus Services', *Geographical Journal*, Vol. 116 (1950), pp. 64–8. W. I. Carruthers, 'Service Centres in Greater London', *Town Planning Review*, Vol. 33 (1962), pp. 5–31. W. I. Carruthers, 'Major Shopping Centres in England and Wales, 1961', *Regional Studies*, Vol. 1 (1967), pp. 65–81.

services. In the United States, however, starting with the Metropolitan Region of the 1940 Census and running through the Standard Metropolitan Area of 1950 to the Standard Metropolitan Statistical Area of 1960, there has been a determined and coherent attempt to define functional units on a basis of employment and the journey to work;[13] and this, despite the fact that American data on these matters has been consistently sparser than equivalent British data. Standard Metropolitan Statistical Areas (SMSAs)[14] are used extensively by most United States government departments for reporting statistics, including the Censuses of Population, Housing, Manufacture, Business and Government; and latterly, with the development of Federally induced planning programmes in the 1960s, they have become the units of organization for transportation and regional planning studies. The Resources for the Future study of the Northeastern Urban Complex, which is the parallel study to ours on the Eastern Seaboard of the United States, has defined its study area in terms of thirty-four contiguous SMSAs stretching from north of Boston to south of Washington, and has chosen some of them as basic units of analysis for detailed urban growth studies.[15] And it is significant that the most ambitious work on urban delimitation in Britain to date, that conducted by International Population and Urban Research, as part of their international study of metropolitan area definition, was done by Americans, on the basis of the American experience of Standard Metropolitan Areas.[16] On all these grounds, it seemed logical to start our own functional analysis of urban areas in terms of similar building blocks, by trying to create, if we could, a system of Standard Metropolitan Areas for Britain.

But it was important to do this in a critical spirit; and we started by a close look at the basis of the SMSA definition. The Standard Metropolitan Statistical Area is built up (except in New England) of counties, and these are units which in the eastern USA are smaller than their English equivalent but in the western USA are generally larger.[17] The definition then involves two considerations. First, there must be a city of some specified population to constitute a *central city*; the county containing this city is then described as the *central county*. Then, contiguous counties are defined which have *metropolitan character* and also have specific social and economic *metropolitan integration* with the central city or county. In more detail, the most basic criteria are:

[13] Henry S. Shryock, 'The Natural History of Standard Metropolitan Areas', *American Journal of Sociology*, vol. 63 (1957), pp. 163–70.

[14] Executive Office of the President, Bureau of the Budget, *Standard Metropolitan Statistical Areas*. Washington D.C. (1964).

[15] Marion Clawson, *Suburban Land Conversion in the United States, An Economic and Governmental Process*. Johns Hopkins U.P., Baltimore (1971).

[16] Kingsley Davis, *The World's Metropolitan Areas*. University of California Press, Berkeley and Los Angeles (1959). Leo F. Schnore, 'Metropolitan Development in the United Kingdom', *Economic Geography*, Vol. 38 (1962), pp. 215–33.

[17] San Bernardino County in California, which stretches from suburban southern California across 200 miles of uninhabited desert, is the extreme example.

(i) a county containing a legal (corporate) central city of at least 50,000 population, or twin cities totalling 50,000;
(ii) contiguous counties with a metropolitan character, in that 75 per cent of their labour force is non-agricultural and lives in contiguous minor civil divisions with a population density of at least 150 persons per square mile;
(iii) at least 15 per cent of the resident workers in each of these counties are commuters to the central city. They demonstrate metropolitan integration.

These criteria have been criticized within the United States, particularly in a recent research project by Brian J. L. Berry and his colleagues for the United States Social Science Research Council.[18] Their chief criticisms are that the definition of the central city in terms of its legal limits is arbitrary; that the minimum population criterion is also arbitrary; that the use of criteria of metropolitan character is irrelevant at a time when the great majority of society is culturally urbanized; and that the 15 per cent cut-off level for commuting to the central city is arbitrary, excluding many people in areas with close links to the central city.

Other workers have found, additionally, that there is great difficulty in applying the criteria to other countries where the data provided by the Census may be different in range or presentation from that of the United States. Kingsley Davis of International Population and Urban Research at Berkeley made the attempt at comparability on a world-wide basis in 1959,[19] but had to use a greatly simplified definition based mainly (for lack of internationally comparable commuting data) on criteria of metropolitan character:

> An area of 100,000 or more inhabitants, containing at least one city (or contiguous urban areas) with 50,000 or more inhabitants and those administrative divisions contiguous to the city (or to the contiguous urban area) which meet certain requirements as to metropolitan character. That is, with at least 65 per cent of the labour force working in economic activities other than agriculture, hunting, and fishing, or, failing the requisite figures on employment, an area, which meets certain requirements as to density of population in relation to areas nearer the central city of areas farther away.[20]

In the case of Britain, however, detailed commuting data permitted metropolitan areas to be defined which were very similar to their American counterparts.[21] There were fifty-seven of these and they accounted for 35,359,000

[18] Brian J. L. Berry, *Functional Economic Areas and Consolidated Urban Regions of the United States, Final Report of the SSRC Study of Metropolitan Area Classification*. Mimeo (1967). For a summary of this report and its recommendations see Karl A. Fox, 'Functional Economic Areas and Consolidated Urban Regions of the United States', *Statistical Reporter*, March (1968), pp. 145–8.

[19] Davis, op. cit.

[20] Ibid., pp. 27–30.

[21] Calculated from data in Leo F. Schnore, op. cit.

people, or 72 per cent of the total population of Britain at the 1951 Census.[22]

The starting point of our approach was the recent criticisms of the SMSA concept. To summarize, the most important criticisms seemed to be:

(i) the arbitrary definition of the central city;
(ii) the irrelevant criteria of metropolitan character;
(iii) the arbitrary cut-off limit of 15 per cent for commuting.

We therefore decided not to bring Davis' metropolitan areas up to date as they stood, but to start again.[23] First, we dropped the criteria of metropolitan character, which if anything are more completely irrelevant for Britain than for the United States; 95 per cent of all British workers are in non-agricultural occupations, and very few rural English districts anywhere near large or medium cities fail to reach the minimum population density of 150 persons per square mile (0·23 per acre).

Second, we looked more closely at the central city. Davis' British metropolitan areas certainly suffer from apparently arbitrary definitions; thus the London metropolitan area is based on a centre equivalent to the old London County Council, or inner London, while Birmingham is defined in terms of the whole West Midlands conurbation, and so on. It seemed to us that if the central city was essentially the chief centre for employment and inwards commuting, it ought logically to be defined in terms of levels of employment, and the best single index that could be used was the *density of employment per acre*. This does give a reasonably standard definition of a labour centre in conurbations and in certain of the large freestanding cities. But it fails with some medium-sized, free-standing towns, which may be very overbounded and so may fail to meet the criterion of workplace density. Among the major English cities, for example, the density of employment in 1961 varied only from 15·7 per acre in the case of Manchester and 14·4 in that of Liverpool through 12·8 in Birmingham to 6·7 in Leeds. Thus a standard definition of five persons per acre over the total area will include all the great cities of the conurbations and most freestanding big cities. But it still leaves out many important medium-sized towns, for instance Chesterfield (with an employment density of 4·1 per acre) Exeter (4·6) Rochdale (4·9) Southport (3·1) Peterborough (3·5) Shrewsbury (3·3) Halifax (3·6) and Rotherham (4·7). Therefore it was decided to allow an alternative criterion: an absolute lower level of employment in the case of freestanding towns, which was fixed at 20,000. The basic criterion for the definition of a central labour area was thus either an employment level of five persons per acre over the whole area, *or* an employment of 20,000 in the case of freestanding towns.

[22] Ibid., pp. 215–22.

[23] The work on metropolitan area definition was done by Peter Hall, Roy Drewett and Patricia Ellman. This section of the chapter is based on the detailed account in Roy Drewett, *The Definition of Standard Metropolitan Labour Areas*. WP/1 Urban Growth Study PEP London. March 1967. For an early use of the definition see Ellman, op cit. That study by the Greater London Group, made under the supervision of Peter Hall, served in effect as a pilot for the PEP study.

Next, we looked at criteria of integration. We were mindful that besides commuting, other possible criteria of integration existed, but we found none that could compare with it for relevance and availability of comparable data over a long period, as already argued above. The real question, therefore, was the level of integration which should be taken as the critical criterion for inclusion or exclusion. Was the 15 per cent level, used to define the limits of the United States Standard Metropolitan Area, and borrowed from it for Schnore's analysis of metropolitan areas in Britain, meaningful, or arbitrary? Should it be replaced by a higher or a lower level, or by alternative measurements?

On this question, we were compelled to recognize the force of Brian J. L. Berry's criticism of the 15 per cent level. By the use of detailed Census tract data, Berry was able to show conclusively that this level is often arbitrary and too narrowly exclusive. We recognized the alternative he puts forward, the *Functional Economic Area*, which includes all those areas sending more commuters to a particular central city than to any other, and extends as far as any commuters at all travelling to that city.[24] In particular we thought that the more important of these, described by Berry as *Metropolitan Economic Areas*,[25] might provide a useful alternative to the SMSA concept for the British study. These are Functional Economic Areas in which the population of the central city exceeds 50,000 and are thus similar, in terms of their central city definition, to the SMSAs. Berry includes also in his study Functional Economic Areas whose central cities do not reach this level, because he finds they have an importance in thinly-populated areas equal to that of the bigger centres in more densely-populated parts of the United States. This might well be true, too, of some parts of peripheral highland Britain. But as our focus is urbanization, we can safely ignore the smaller Functional Economic Areas for the sake of simplicity.

In favour of the Standard Metropolitan Area, on the other hand, there is the argument that it is old established and well understood, particularly in the United States but more generally among urban research workers everywhere. Its status in the United States is important, because the present study is intended specifically to be comparative with the Resources for the Future Study of the Eastern Seaboard, and because that study works throughout in terms of the SMSA as defined at the 1960 Census. But fortunately, we do not have to choose between the SMSA principle and the Functional Economic Area principle, since they can be defined in terms of a common core area, and throughout this study we can use both.

In the present study, therefore, there are two basic functional building blocks, both at the metropolitan scale.

(i) *The Standard Metropolitan Labour Area* (SMLA). We add the word Labour to indicate the importance of employment in defining the central core. The SMLA consists of:

[24] Berry, op. cit. (1967), p. 6.
[25] Ibid.

(*a*) a SMLA core consisting of an administrative area or a number of contiguous areas with a density of five workers and over per acre, or a single administrative area with 20,000 and more workers;
(*b*) a SMLA ring consisting of administrative areas contiguous to the core and sending 15 per cent of their resident employed population to that core.

To be regarded as a SMLA the whole group should have an enumerated population of 70,000 and more.*

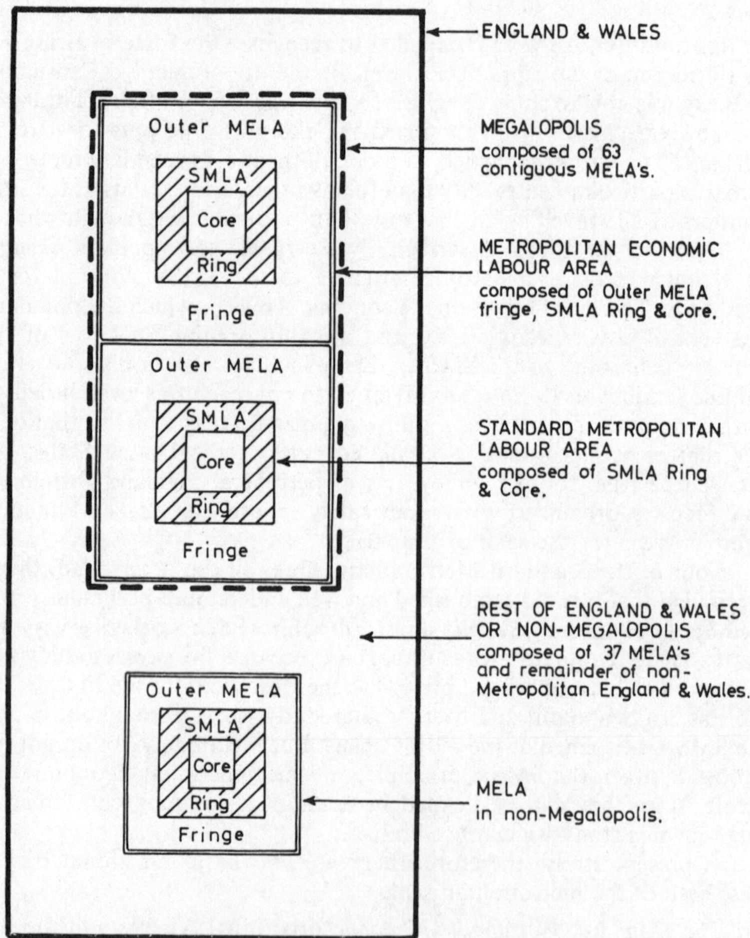

Figure 4.1 Schematic Diagram of the Standard Metropolitan Labour Area and Metropolitan Economic Labour Area

* An exception was made for Stafford which had 65,700 in 1961 but 70,900 by 1966.

(ii) *The Metropolitan Economic Labour Area* (MELA), which consists of:

(*a*) a SMLA core, identical to the above;
(*b*) a SMLA ring, identical to the above;
(*c*) the remainder of the MELA, which takes in all administrative areas not included in the SMLA core or SMLA ring, but contiguous with either, and sending more of their resident employed population to the SMLA core than to another SMLA core. Any area will be included here which sends *any* commuters to the SMLA core, always provided it does not send more commuters to another SMLA core.

An area is classed as a MELA only if the SMLA contained within it has an enumerated population of 70,000 or more.

Clearly the SMLA will always fit within the MELA, like one box fitting into another (Figure 4.1). There are a number of cases where the two are identical; many of them tend to be in heavily urbanized areas where the watershed between one commuting area and another tends to occur at the 15 per cent level. In three cases, indeed, there are SMLA–MELA units which consist of an SMLA core only, this meeting the 70,000 population criterion; they are Basildon, Rhondda and Southport. Many other problems occur in practice in the definition of SMLAs and MELAs, particularly in the treatment of areas which send almost equal numbers of commuters in two or more different directions. In order not to create extra complications, our study uses one simplification; unlike the American SMSA, our SMLAs and MELAs are defined in terms of commuting patterns at one point in time only, this being taken as 1961. Thus the definition of an SMLA does not 'float' from Census to Census, as it does in the United States.

PHYSICAL URBANIZATION

In starting our discussion of functional urbanization, we listed three dimensions: the topical, the geographical (within-place and between-place) and the intensity. Physical urbanization has the same three dimensions. We can talk of land being in an urban, rather than a rural use; that is the topical dimension, which raised the question of defining an urban land use. We can talk about within-place, or between-place, physical urban growth: a housing development or an industrial estate could be described as within-place, a new motorway as between-place. In practice, though, this is a rather theoretical distinction when applied to physical urbanization, and we do not use it much here. The third attribute or dimension, intensity, is however very important indeed when discussing land use of all kinds; we want to know not merely whether the land is covered by growing wheat or by newly built houses, but also the intensity of use in terms of bushels per acre or houses per acre. The following discussion, therefore, concentrates first on the topical classification problem, and then on intensity.

The classification of the land use is basic, for it will determine the nature of the unit whose intensity we will later measure, be this bushels per acre, or residential dwelling units per acre. But it immediately raises a very fundamental problem of definition. By physical urbanization, we mean the use of land for urban purposes; but what are urban purposes? Are allotment gardens on the fringe of a city urban, or rural? Is a tract of green belt, with mixed agriculture and recreation, perhaps even on the same field, which is used sometimes for grazing, sometimes for football, urban, or rural? What about a large village near a city which has almost ceased to perform any agricultural function, and is occupied almost completely by commuters and retired urbanites? These illustrations show that in many cases, to say that we will define urban land use in physical terms, is to beg the question: necessarily, we have to know the purpose, that is the function, of the land use. There is no easy way out of this paradox: it is necessary to draw lines, some of which will be arbitrary. To simplify, for instance, it is desirable to say that all clusters of buildings constitute urban development in a physical sense, as do open spaces surrounded wholly by buildings and used primarily for purposes other than agriculture or forestry, and all roads, railways and other transport land bordered by such buildings or open spaces. Agricultural land, on the other hand, will be rural even when worked by urbanites in their spare time (as in the case of the allotment gardens). This has the merit of being consistent, for it defines urbanization in terms of particular sorts of land use, and is uninfluenced by function as far as possible.

This leaves the question of intensity. If a tract of land is labelled physically urban, because it is wholly occupied by houses and private gardens for instance, it may still be occupied by one house, or by one hundred, just as a field can produce many bushels of crops, or support one cow. The chief problem with intensity is that different land uses each give their own, individual measure of intensity and it may be difficult to compare one with another. One cannot with meaning compare bushels per acre with cows per acre, or dwelling houses per acre with factories per acre. In an effort to find a common unit of intensity, many urban analysts use occupation by people, though this is not strictly a physical, but rather a functional, definition. Instead of measuring structures per acre, or even rooms per acre, they measure residential population or daytime working population per acre. Indeed, one of the best known physical definitions of urbanization, the United States Census Bureau's urbanized area, is based simply on density of residential population.

Even if this can be accepted, and if we concentrate on people per acre as a measure of residential land use, this apparently simple index has several meanings and several definitions of density are possible. Marion Clawson has distinguished six, of which four are strictly residential:[26]

(i) the ratio of total population to total land in a given statistical unit; for short, we call this the total density;

[26] Clawson, op. cit. (1971), p. 25.

(ii) the ratio of population to developed urban land of all sorts. This is what the British Department of the Environment call the overall residential density. It poses the problem of where exactly the boundary of urban areas can be said to be;

(iii) the ratio of population to the residential land uses, including local non-residential land uses which are ministering to the needs of the local population: local shops, schools and parks. This is what is known in British planning practice as gross residential density.

(iv) the ratio of population to the residential area in the strict sense, excluding all local facilities such as schools, parks, shops and the like. Street space on the wholly residential streets would have to come in though. This is the net residential density, in British terminology;

(v) the ratio of population to the actual lots on which the residences stand, excluding the local streets, but including private open space;

(vi) the ratio of population to the actual floor area of the buildings, that is excluding even the private open space round the buildings.

The exact relationships between these six definitions seem complex. Even the two best known of them, the net and the gross residential density, do not vary together in any very obvious way because of the fact that there is a fixed amount of space which must be provided for community facilities (schools, shops, parks) and which is related to the number of people. Thus in raising net residential densities from 136 to 200 persons per acre, the effect is to raise gross densities only from 71 to 87 persons per acre.[27] The saving of land is much greater if low densities are raised to medium densities. Thus, at an open space and community play standard of eight acres per thousand people, an increase in net density from 24 to 40 per acre saves 17 gross acres per thousand people, while an increase from 159 to 222 per acre would save only 1·8 acres per thousand people.[28] And much of the relationship between the different definitions depends on the way open space is used. Thus the old London County Council, in the famous Roehampton estate in south-west London, built at about 100 people per acre net, leaving the great bulk of the land in public open space, by the expedient of housing over 70 per cent in big blocks without private open space (except for balconies).[29] Here, there is an extreme difference between net and gross residential density. In this study, we shall use sometimes one definition of the people/land ratio, sometimes another. But mainly we shall use definitions (i) (total), (iii) (gross residential) and (iv) (net residential).

[27] This was first demonstrated in the *County of London Plan* (1943), pp. 81–2.

[28] Ministry of Housing and Local Government, *Residential Areas: Higher Densities*. HMSO, London (1962), p. 5.

[29] London County Council, *London Plan*, Administrative County of London Development Plan, First Review 1960, Vol. 1. The Council, London (1960), Figure 54, and para. 340.

MEASURING LAND USE

In this, we shall be constrained by the nature of the information available to us, and above all by the scale at which it is available. Our information about the use of land comes either from censuses of land use, whether conducted by government agencies (the Ministry of Agriculture) or private organizations (the two Land Utilization Surveys). The results may be presented as tabulated statistics (the Ministry of Agriculture returns) or as maps (the Land Utilization Surveys). The first suffers from the disadvantage that it is presented at only one level of aggregation, the parish. Thus it is not flexible in use. (It suffers also from the disadvantage of poor comparability over time, as discovered by Best and mentioned earlier in Chapter Two.) The second suffers from the disadvantage that it is not directly recorded in quantified form at all. However, if it could be analysed quantitatively, the resulting data could be obtained and presented at almost any scale of aggregation or disaggregation: a critical advantage for this present study. It also gives the possibility of a finer classification of urban land use than the Ministry of Agriculture returns. For this reason, the Land Utilization Surveys have been used as our basic source of land use information in this study.

We already noticed, in Chapter Two, that there are only three complete and uniform national Land Use Surveys. Fortunately, they were taken at particularly appropriate times, both from the viewpoint of comparability with other data and from the viewpoint of the history of urban development in modern Britain, so this is not a critical limitation. The main difficulty, since they are three independently conceived and organized surveys, is of co-ordinating them one with another.[30]

The First Land Utilization Survey of Great Britain was made between 1930 and 1934 under the direction of Sir Dudley Stamp.[31] Its basic survey work was performed remarkably quickly by teams of volunteers,[32] so that even despite the rapid urban growth of that time, the survey sheets give a reasonably comparable picture across the country at a particular point in time. And this timing was particularly fortunate: it coincides not only with the 1931 Census, but with the beginning of the most rapid period in urban growth (in a physical sense) that Britain ever experienced. Unfortunately its value to us is limited, since its main object was to study agricultural land. All agriculturally unproductive land is thrown into a single category; domestic gardens and public parks are thrown into another together with allotments, orchards, nurseries and low-density housing. There are inconsistencies in

30 The following section is based on Roy Drewett, *Sources of Land Use data in Britain*, WP/2; and *The Measurement of Changes in Land Use*, WP/3. PEP, London, 1968/9.

31 The best detailed introduction to the First Survey is by its Director: L. Dudley Stamp, *The Land of Britain: Its Use and Misuse*. Longmans, London (1948, revised 1962), Chaps 1 and 2.

32 Ninety per cent of the country, including virtually all the highly urbanized areas, was surveyed within four years, Aug. 1930–Aug. 1934. Ibid., p. 11.

survey between one sheet and another, which are not easy to trace without field checks.[33] All in all, the main effect of these limitations is to make the greater detail of the later surveys useless for comparative purposes.

The local authority Land Use Surveys were produced between 1947 and 1951 by the newly formed local planning authorities as part of their work of survey which had to precede the preparation of the Development Plan under the 1947 Act.[34] Some degree of consistency was secured between one authority and another by a Ministry circular, which gave guidance on survey and preparation.[35] The local authority surveys, again, are fortunately timed. They correspond closely to the 1951 Census, as did the Stamp Survey to the 1931 Census, and they illustrate the pattern of urban growth after the great explosion of the 1930s, but before the resurgence of private building in the 1950s. In effect, they show the pattern which British towns and cities had reached at the beginning of effective land use control.

The Second Land Utilization Survey of Britain has essentially the same organization which proved so efficacious in the case of the First. It has been organized by Dr Alice Coleman of King's College, University of London, and the survey has been carried out by volunteer teams. The time spread is rather greater than in the First Survey, but not significantly so as to cause concern. Like its predecessor this is primarily geared to a study of changes in rural land use, and the amount of detail it gives for urban areas (though considerably greater than the Stamp Survey) is limited by the need to present it within the framework of conventional maps, on a uniform scale, for the whole country.[36] Nevertheless, residential and commercial development is distinguished separately from industry, transport, derelict land and open space; while orchards and allotments are unambiguously separated.

33 Generally, houses at less than twelve to the acre net were supposed to go into the gardens, allotments, etc. category, but the surveyors were not given precise instructions. Also there is a confusion between new housing areas and new orchards in the area round London, where growth was particularly rapid at that time. The manuscript maps of the First Survey were destroyed by arson in 1970.

34 Unlike the statutory Development Plan itself, the Land Use Survey did not have to be submitted or published. But all authorities appear to have sent their survey maps to the Ministry, if only in manuscript form. Before this project, however, they do not appear to have been systematically collated. Particular thanks are due here to Miss Whale of the Department of the Environment map library, and to Mr Pearson and Mr Rossi of the Ministry library for their unfailing help and interest in finally collecting together the maps from the different departments of their Ministry. Cf. Drewett, op. cit.

35 Ministry of Town and Country Planning, *Reproduction of Survey and Development Plan Maps*. Circular 92, HMSO, London (1951).

36 The published scale of the Second Survey is 1 : 25,000 as compared with 1 : 10,560 in the case of urban areas and 1 : 63,360 in the case of rural areas for the local authority survey, and 1 : 63,360 throughout in the case of the First Survey. The field survey scale for all the surveys appears to have been the same, 1 : 10,560.

Table 4.1

CLASSIFICATIONS OF URBAN LAND USE IN THE THREE LAND USE SURVEYS

First land utilization survey (1930s)	Local authority land use surveys (1950s)	Second land utilization survey (1960s)	Aggregated category used in this study
	Shopping Business Civic Residential	Commercial and residential Newly built up	Residential (including commercial) land
	Industry Surface mineral Military land Water/Reservoirs Sewage disposal	Industry	Work land
Houses and gardens Land agriculturally unproductive Ponds and waterworks	Roads Car parks Railways Waterways Wharves Airfields	Transport	Transport
	Open space Public open space Large gardens Areas of landscape, historic, or scientific value	Open space	Open space
Orchards Nurseries	Agriculture (market gardens and allotments)	Market gardening Orchards	Specialized agriculture
Forest and woodland Heath and rough grazing Meadow and permanent pasture Arable	Remainder unclassified	Woodland Heath Grassland Arable	Other land (basically rural)

Source: The Land Use Surveys.

The critical problem is how far, and in what ways, these three surveys are comparable from the viewpoint of analysing urban growth. The First Survey is the least detailed, showing only undifferentiated land in the non-agriculturally productive category; for comparison with it, information from the other two surveys has to be aggregated to this level of coarseness. But the more detailed breakdown of the later surveys does permit a broad comparison between land use categories, as Table 4.1 shows. This means that between 1947–51 and 1961–64, it is possible to compare the distribution of residential/commercial land, work land (industry and transport, but excluding commerce which is inextricably mixed with residences), and the rural/urban fringe of market gardens and allotments.[37]

There is another difficulty with the Land Use Surveys. They tell us about one dimension of land use, the category, but little about the other dimension, the intensity. Intensity is measured in terms of units like dwellings, rooms, households, or people, per unit of area. The main source for all these will be statistical sources like the Census, which give information relating to aggregate geographical areas like enumeration districts, wards and parishes, and administrative areas. In general, for comparison of historical changes it is not possible to get figures for the smallest of these units, the enumeration districts and it is necessary to work with bigger aggregates, far bigger in fact than the individual land parcels for which land use can be measured. So one is faced with comparing data on two different geographical scales.

Usually, one can overcome this only by aggregating the fine grain data, the data on land use categories, to the coarser grain of the statistical sources. One illustration will show how much detail is lost here. Wokingham Rural District in Berkshire is on the east side of Reading, and in recent years has received most of the suburban population growth round that town. Indeed, between 1951 and 1961 it had one of the highest percentage rates of population growth of any local authority area in England, apart from the ones containing new towns: over 15,000 or slightly more than 42 per cent. It is divided into fifteen parishes, two of which, Earley, and Woodley and Sandford, took the brunt of this suburban growth. Yet measurement of the actual land use shows that even in 1961 only 20 per cent of the entire rural district could be classed as urban land, and even at the finer parish level, only 42·6 per cent of Earley, or 29·2 per cent of Woodley and Sandford, fell into the urban category. But this last is the finest level at which it is possible to measure changes in indices like population, households and dwellings.

There is no easy way round this. For the purpose of overview in this first section of the book, it is only possible to work at the aggregate parish level, classifying parishes according to a definite criterion as urban or rural. As elsewhere in this chapter and this book, for the sake of comparability we have

[37] There are other technical problems of comparison. Thus there are cartographic inaccuracies in the topographic base of the First Survey, which was on a different projection from the others. This restricts the validity of small area comparisons. Cf. Drewett, op. cit.

borrowed an American concept, much used in the parallel study of urban growth on the Northeastern Seaboard: the urbanized area. The official United States Census definition of urban area is any small unit (in the United States terminology, Census tract) with over 1,000 people per square mile, that is 1·56 people or more per acre. Our first reaction to this was that it would be too low to be realistic for British conditions. But sample comparisons of land use in some suburban fringe areas of Britain convinced us that in virtually every case this limit is successful in identifying those parishes with 30 per cent or more urban cover: a high figure for a rural parish, when one considers the way planning controls have operated to stop development from spilling across rural areas in the postwar period. So we have borrowed the American definition to give us one of our basic building blocks of statistical analysis. An urbanized area is that part of a Standard Metropolitan Area, as already defined earlier in this chapter, consisting of contiguous parishes, all of which have a density of 1·56 persons or more per acre.

For more detailed studies later on in the book, this will not suffice. There, it is necessary to devise a uniform, easily managed system of recording and measuring land use. The metric grid of the Ordnance Survey maps has an obvious advantage for this purpose. Because of its uniformity and its metric characteristics it allows data of all kinds (not merely land use data) to be easily recorded, stored and retrieved within a uniform set of cells; computations may then easily be performed with the use of simple geometry. Indeed, for the future, from the Census of 1971 onwards, it seems certain that much statistical data on intensity will be recorded in this way, so that the problem of comparing land use and other data may largely disappear. But this advantage, of course, was not available to us.[38]

Despite this lack of comparability in the past, it seemed advantageous and even necessary to measure land use by grid squares, at least for selected parts of the country. Technically, this might have been done by some sort of remote scanning, but after an exhaustive study of the possibilities, we chose a manual method based on sampling. Given this decision, there were various geographical sampling frames which may be used, based either on two dimensional shapes such as squares, or on lines;[39] we chose the squares of the metric grid. There are also various sorts of sample that can be used; we chose a well

[38] On the use of metric grid squares as the basis of a land use record system, cf. Owe Salomonsson, 'Data Banking Systems for Urban Planning', *Proceedings of the Conference on Information in Urban Planning*, CES–IP 8. Centre for Environmental Studies, London (1969), Mimeo. E. L. Cripps, 'A Comparative Study of Information Systems for Urban and Regional Planning: 1. Scandinavia', *Urban Systems Research Unit*, *Working Paper No. 7*. Department of Geography, University of Reading, Reading (1970), Mimeo, *passim*. Michael Stubbs, *Geographical Coordinate Data Referencing*. London (1969), Mimeo, *passim*.

[39] David Thomas has successfully used line sampling for measuring areas in the metropolitan green belt. Cf. *London's Green Belt*. Faber, London (1970), p. 125.

tested method, already used with success for measuring areas of flood plains.[40] It is called a stratified systematic unaligned sample; its essence is that starting from an origin at one corner of a map sheet (the north-west corner), it works systematically along both major axes of the map, eastwards and southwards, generating random sampling points.

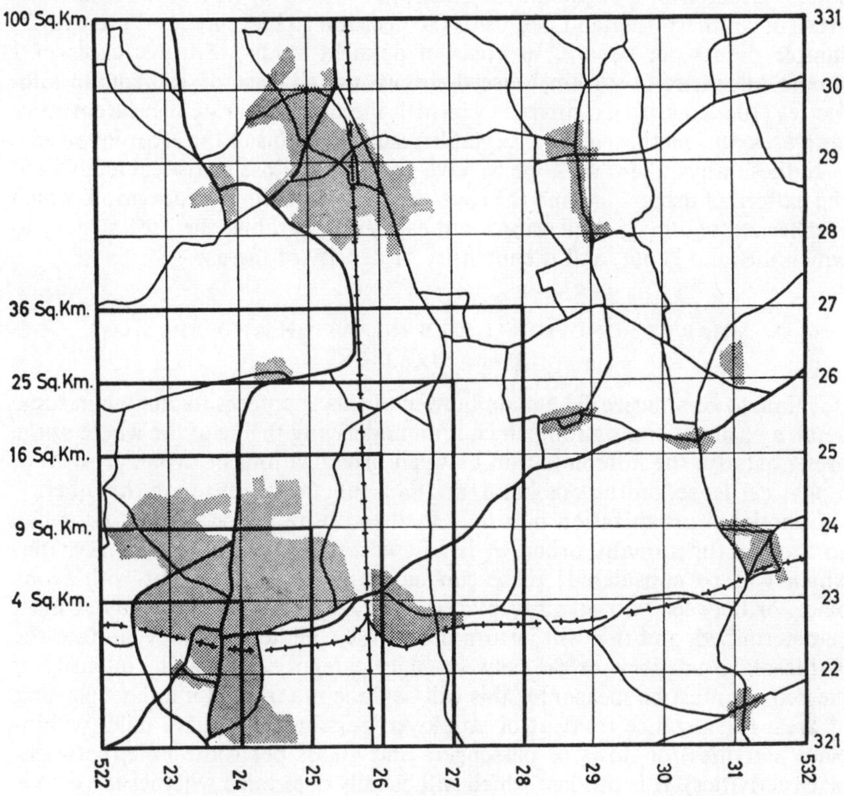

Figure 4.2 Metric Grid Squares and their Relationship to Distribution of Urban Land

There are many technical problems about taking such a sample, concerned with the acceptable size of error for the job in hand. This error is affected by

40 M. H. Quenouille, 'Problems in Plain Sampling', *Annals of Mathematical Statistics*, Vol. 20 (1949), pp. 355–75. Brian J. L. Berry, *Sampling, Coding and Storing Flood Plain Data*. U.S. Department of Agriculture, Agriculture Handbook 237, Government Printing Office, Washington D.C. (1962), *passim*. See also F. Yates, *Sampling Methods for Census and Surveys*. Griffin, London (1949); and W. G. Cochran, *Sampling Techniques*. John Wiley, New York, 2nd edn. (1963), especially Chap. 8.

the size of the grid square chosen, by the number of sampling points in the square, and by the percentage importance of the land use being measured. Broadly, if one wants to keep the same error at any scale of analysis the rule is to use the same number of sample points: 25 sample points on 1 square kilometre of the map will give the same error as 25 points applied to 100 square kilometres. Our preliminary tests, performed on typical suburban map areas in southern England, led us to the decision to measure land use with 25 sample points per square. In areas of detailed study we use squares of 1 square kilometre (1 × 1 km); elsewhere, we use squares of 100 square kilometres (10 × 10 km). Compared even with the most accurate measurement of land uses, this method gives acceptable results in terms of the error involved.

In these ways, then, we hope to have provided a close statistical analysis of the pattern of urban land and the changes in it over a thirty-year period, which emphasizes two main dimensions, not easily comparable: the use category to which the land is put, and the intensity or density of the use.

SUMMARY: FUNCTIONAL URBANIZATION AND PHYSICAL URBANIZATION

It is time to summarize. The main burden of this chapter is to analyse in some detail a basic differentiation, which is an underlying theme of the whole of the present study: the differentiation between urbanization (or urban growth) in a physical sense, on the one hand, and in a functional sense, on the other.

Functional urbanization naturally focuses on human activities. To define an area as functionally urban, it is first necessary to define those activities which will be considered; these can be activities which occur within one place, or between two or more places. Then, the scale of the analysis must be determined, and this will in turn determine whether activities fall into the within-place category, or the between-place category. Lastly, the intensity of the activity must be measured; this will be done in terms of numbers per unit of area, for instance resident or employed persons per square mile (within-place activities) or flows of passengers and goods per route mile (between-place activities). It is this last which will usually determine whether the area is to be regarded as functionally urbanized, or not.

Definitions of functional urbanization are heavily dependent on available data. The best broadly comparable data available for fairly small areas over a long period are the Census data of resident and employed population (within-place activity), and of journey to work (between place activity). They also happen to focus on those relationships likely to be of greatest importance in the urban growth process.

The Standard Metropolitan Area, a familiar concept in urban analysis developed by the United States Census, is based on a somewhat ambiguously-defined central county containing a central city (or cities) plus contiguous areas which satisfy criteria of metropolitan character (in terms of economic structure) and metropolitan integration (in terms of commuting ties with the central city). The concept has been criticized in the United States and is not fully relevant to British experience. But it is well known, and it is being used as the statistical basis of the parallel study of urban growth in the Northeastern Urban Complex of the United States, which has been conducted at Resources for the Future under the direction of Dr Marion Clawson. So it is adopted here as one statistical basis of the present study, in a modified version which is based on a more rigorous definition of the central city in terms of employment totals or density; it is called here the Standard Metropolitan Labour Area (SMLA). Recognizing current American criticisms, an alternative measure is also proposed, taking in the widest possible commuting area but using the same central city as base; this is known as the Metropolitan Economic Labour Area (MELA).

Urbanization in a physical sense naturally focuses on the use of land. It has two main dimensions: coverage, and intensity. Coverage refers to the land use category, and raises the basic problem of what categories are to be regarded as urban; for there are many fringe categories which are ambiguous, like allotment gardens and commuter villages. In this study we define urban land, on the whole, as clusters or groups of buildings, without regard to their purpose. Intensity is related to a given unit of land surface; it raises the problem that different intensity measures (bushes per acre, cows per acre, houses per acre) are not easily comparable each with the other. For urban analysis, the use of people per acre provides a way out; though it is not strictly a physical index, it is very commonly used as, for instance, in the well known concept of urbanized area used by the United States Census. Even then, there are several alternative measures of intensity or occupation by people depending on which part of the urban area is measured; the distinction between net density and gross density being the best known example. Any analysis of urban growth will need to use different measures at different times.

The study of physical urbanization entails measurement of land uses. For this, Britain has a uniquely useful source in three national Land Use Surveys, which date respectively from the early 1930s, the late 1940s and the early 1960s. They are so important that despite many technical difficulties in measuring and comparing land use patterns from them, they are used as the basic source of land use information in this study. They do not however give a picture of intensity.

When an overall measure of physical urbanization involving intensity is needed then the United States Census definition of urbanized area (UBZA) will serve well enough. It is adapted for use here by defining it as a group of wards or civil parishes with 1,000 persons per square mile or more, the same threshold as in the United States. When a finer-grain analysis is necessary, the land use is sampled directly from the survey sheets according to the grid squares of the Ordnance Survey National Grid. Two main scales are used: 100 square kilometres (10 × 10 km) for coarse-grain analysis and 1 square kilometre for fine grain analysis.

These then are our basic building blocks. In the rest of the overview of national and regional trends in Volume One, and in much of the more detailed analysis, the metropolitan areas are defined either as the Standard

Metropolitan Labour Area (SMLA) or the wider Metropolitan Economic Labour Area (MELA). Within that framework, physical urbanization is measured crudely by use of the concept of urbanized area (UBZA), and at a more fine grain by the analysis of land use and population at the 10 square kilometre and 1 square kilometre grid scale.

CHAPTER FIVE

THE ANATOMY OF METROPOLITAN ENGLAND

Chapter Five is the heart of this Second Part of the book. Using the statistical building blocks developed in Chapter Four it is essentially a detailed statistical analysis of the 100 Standard Metropolitan Areas which contain just over three-quarters of the population of England and Wales. It chronicles their growth (almost exactly in line with the general increase in the population) and their internal changes (with a pronounced tendency to decentralization of population and a less pronounced, more delayed tendency to decentralization of employment). Comparing these trends, it ends by trying to develop a very simple general model of urban development trends in modern Britain. According to this, decentralization of population will be followed by decentralization of employment, with the biggest metropolitan areas leading the way; and then eventually, perhaps, in the biggest metropolitan areas, by actual loss of people and employment to smaller, peripheral, metropolitan areas.

Chapter Five was written by Peter Hall. The early work on metropolitan area definition was done by Peter Hall and Roy Drewett. Roy Drewett produced the trend and shift analyses. Anne Whalley did nearly all the basic work of statistical analysis and checking.

INTRODUCTION

Chapter Four was a deck-clearing operation. It gave us the building blocks we need for a meaningful analysis of urban growth in modern England and Wales. This is the object of the present Chapter. We shall use the standardized units of Chapter Four, the metropolitan area and the urbanized area, to give a broad brush picture of the most important general trends in population and employment within urban England and Wales between the early 1930s and the late 1960s. The object in this chapter is always to look at general, comparative trends. We shall be concerned to ask: how similar are the urban areas of England and Wales? Insofar as their history seems to be different, how far can we explain the differences in a systematic way; in terms, for instance, of the different behaviour of different regions, or the different behaviour of large urban areas as compared with small ones? Necessarily, since we are concerned with generalization, our method will be statistical. We shall produce a great number of standardized statistical tables, of a fairly simple character, and comment on the trends they illustrate. This chapter then is the heart of the overview of urban growth, which forms Part Two of this work.

THE CENSUS: OUR MAIN SOURCE

Our main source for the analysis will be the decennial Census of population. It was taken in 1931, 1951 and 1961, with a gap in 1941 due to the war. In addition, there was the important 10 per cent sample Census of 1966, the first inter-Censal quinquennial count to be taken in Britain.

The main use of the Census in this chapter is to provide standardized, reliable, comparable figures of areas, populations, and employment totals. It does this job adequately, but sometimes far from ideally. The reliability of the Census is affected by the number of persons who are missing from the Census, or misclassified; and this, as a percentage of the total, is likely to alter from one part of the country to another. It is almost certain to be higher, for instance, in areas where there is a large transitory population, or where the population is of lower average educational-level, or where the population is apprehensive of the purposes of the inquiry; and unfortunately too often these features will coincide. Standardization and comparability are affected by differences in classification methods between one Census and another, both in terms of the categories which are counted and of the areas within which they are counted. Classifications of occupations and industries, for instance, are notoriously apt to change in detail from one Census to another. So are the boundaries of the adminstrative areas for which most Census data are presented. And though it is sometimes possible to correct earlier figures by detailed adjustments, sometimes it is not. (This is generally possible, for instance, with population figures but not with employment figures, although even the population figures for urbanized areas cannot be made strictly comparable for 1931–51–61 due to difficulties arising from boundary changes.)

Lastly, the degree of detail in the Census varies capriciously from year to year. For instance, the 1961 Census gave much less detail on the critical question of local industrial employment than the 1951. The 1931 Census classed this detail by area of residence rather than area of workplace, which was used in 1951 and 1961. The 1966 Census gives no published details for administrative areas of less than 15,000 people, and no figures whatsoever for wards of towns or civil parishes in rural areas. This last fact means that it is impossible to calculate urbanized area data for 1966. In all these ways, the Census record is incomplete. And sample biases give trouble in using certain data for 1961, and all data for 1966.

Most other official sources do not give the degree of local detail which our study needs, or give it according to geographical units which are difficult to compare with Census units; the Department of Employment figures of detailed local employment, which are presented by employment exchange areas, are perhaps the best example. In what follows, therefore, the main focus is on area, population and employment taken from the Census of Population. The analysis of land use sources, which demands different techniques of analysis, is reserved until Chapter Six. Throughout, in order to maintain comparability with the Resources for the Future study of the United States Northeastern Urban Complex, the analysis is conducted mainly in terms of Standard Metropolitan Labour Areas (SMLAs).

METROPOLITAN ENGLAND

Table 5.1 shows that in 1961 out of 46,104,548 people counted in the Census of England and Wales, 35,719,463 (77·5 per cent) lived in exactly 100 Standard Metropolitan Labour Areas as defined in Chapter Four, and as mapped in Figure 5.1. This proportion, furthermore, had changed hardly at all over the forty years 1931–71: it had been 77 per cent in 1931; it rose to 77·3 per cent in 1951 and 77·5 per cent in 1961, then falling marginally to 77·1 per cent in the sample Census of 1966 and to 76·3 per cent in the preliminary results of the 1971 Census. Because the metropolitan areas were gaining population at roughly the same rate as the country as a whole, they added 5·5 million to their populations between 1931 and 1971, growing from 30,757,549 to 37,087,272. Notably, though, their pace of development varied over this period. They added just over 3 million in the twenty years from 1931 to 1951, close on 1·9 million in the decade from 1951 to 1961, but only 1,368,000 from 1961 to 1971. This meant a percentage rate of growth which (standardized in decennial terms for easy comparison) rose from 5 per cent in the 1930s and 1940s, to 5·6 per cent in the 1950s, but then fell to 3·8 per cent in the 1960s. Partly this was in line with trends in the whole country; but in the SMLAs it was more extreme, so that the proportion of the population living in the SMLAs fell very marginally between 1961 and 1971, as already noticed.*

If now the area of analysis is extended outwards from the boundaries of the SMLAs, to take in the farthest boundaries of the commuting region of each major urban centre, the result is to put nearly nineteen out of every twenty people in England and Wales within the boundaries of what have often been called city regions.[1] 100 Metropolitan Economic Labour Areas (MELAs), based on exactly the same central cores as the SMLAs, contained 43,295,000 people or 93·9 per cent of the population in 1961 (Figure 5.2). This proportion, too, was roughly constant over a forty-year period: it had been 93·3 per cent at the Census of 1931 and 93·7 per cent at that of 1951; it was 93·9 per cent in 1966, the same as in 1961, and rose marginally to 94·0 per cent in 1971. The MELAs, like the SMLAs, had a faster percentage growth

* This is partly influenced by an important fact: unlike SMLAs in the United States Census, our SMLAs are based on a constant definition in terms of 1961 commuting patterns. See above, Chapter 4.

[1] Cf. Derek Senior (ed.), *The Regional City*. Longmans, London (1966); especially Senior's own contribution. And *Report of the Royal Commission on Local Government in England*. HMSO, London (1969), Vols. 1 and 3.

Table 5.1

ENGLAND AND WALES, METROPOLITAN ECONOMIC LABOUR AREAS, STANDARD METROPOLITAN LABOUR AREAS AND URBANIZED AREAS: SUMMARY: POPULATION, 1931–1971, AND EMPLOYMENT, 1951–1966

	Area		Population									
	'000s of acres 1961	Per cent of England and Wales area	1931 '000s	Per cent of England and Wales	1951 '000s	Per cent of England and Wales	1961 '000s	Per cent of England and Wales	1966 '000s	Per cent of England and Wales	1971* '000s	Per cent of England and Wales
England and Wales	37,342·4	100·0	39,952·4	100·0	43,757·9	100·0	46,104·5	100·0	47,135·5	100·0	48,593·7	100·0
MELAs	27,465·5	73·6	37,286·6	93·3	41,007·2	93·7	43,294·6	93·9	44,263·3	93·9	45,659·1	94·0
Outer MELA fringes	14,855·4	39·8	6,529·1	16·3	7,176·6	16·4	7,575·1	16·4	7,903·7	16·8	8,571·8	17·6
SMLAs	12,610·1	33·8	30,757·5	77·0	33,830·6	77·3	35,719·5	77·5	36,359·6	77·1	37,087·3	76·3
SMLA rings	11,098·1	29·8	8,786·4	22·0	11,714·7	26·8	13,449·1	29·2	14,572·9	30·9	15,175·7	31·2
SMLA cores	1,512·0	4·0	21,971·1	55·0	22,115·9	50·5	22,270·4	48·3	21,786·7	46·2	21,911·6	45·1
SMLA urbanized areas	3,312·1	8·9	26,896·6	67·3	29,865·8	68·3	31,929·1	69·3	n/a	n/a	n/a	n/a

	Population change											
	1931–51			1951–61			1961–66			1961–71*		
	Absolute change '000s	Per cent change	Per cent of England and Wales change	Absolute change '000s	Per cent change	Per cent of England and Wales change	Absolute change '000s	Per cent change	Per cent of England and Wales change	Absolute change '000s	Per cent change	Per cent of England and Wales change
England and Wales	3,805·5	9·5	100·0	2,346·6	5·4	100·0	1,031·0	2·2	100·0	2,489·2	5·4	100·0
MELAs	3,720·6	10·0	97·8	2,287·4	5·6	97·5	968·7	2·2	94·0	2,364·5	5·5	95·0
Outer MELA fringes	647·5	9·9	17·1	398·5	5·6	17·0	328·6	4·3	31·9	996·7	13·2	40·0
SMLAs	3,073·1	10·0	80·8	1,888·9	5·6	80·5	640·1	1·8	62·1	1,367·8	3·8	54·9
SMLA rings	2,938·3	33·3	77·0	1,734·4	14·8	73·9	1,123·8	8·4	109·0	1,726·6	12·8	69·4
SMLA cores	144·8	0·7	3·8	154·5	1·3	6·6	−483·7	−2·2	−46·9	−358·8	−1·6	−14·4
SMLA urbanized areas	2,969·2	11·0	78·0	2,063·3	6·9	87·9	n/a	n/a	n/a			

* Preliminary figures, not adjusted for boundary changes

Table 5.1 – *continued*

	Employment					
	1951 '000s	Per cent of England and Wales	1961 '000s	Per cent of England and Wales	1966* '000s	Per cent of England and Wales
England and Wales	19,940·0	100·0	21,081·7	100·0	21,921·4	100·0
MELAs	19,024·6	95·4	19,856·2	94·2	20,785·1	94·8
Outer MELA fringes	3,275·7	16·4	3,108·7	14·7	3,353·3	15·3
SMLAs	15,748·9	79·0	16,747·5	79·4	17,431·8	79·5
SMLA rings	4,127·2	20·7	4,460·1	21·1	4,987·6	22·8
SMLA cores	11,621·7	58·3	12,287·4	58·3	12,444·2	56·8
SMLA urbanized areas	n/a	n/a	n/a	n/a	n/a	n/a

* Not adjusted for boundary change 1961–66.

	Employment change					
	1951–61			1961–66*		
	Absolute change '000s	Per cent change	Per cent of England and Wales change	Absolute change '000s	Per cent change	Per cent of England and Wales change
England and Wales	1,141·7	5·7	100·0	839·7	3·9	100·0
MELAs	831·6	4·4	72·8	928·9	4·7	110·6
Outer MELA fringes	−167·0	−5·1	−14·6	244·6	7·8	29·1
SMLAs	998·6	6·3	87·5	684·3	4·1	81·5
SMLA rings	332·9	8·1	29·2	527·5	11·8	62·8
SMLA cores	665·7	5·7	58·3	156·8	1·3	18·7
SMLA urbanized areas	n/a	n/a	n/a	n/a	n/a	n/a

* Not adjusted for boundary changes 1961–66.

Source: Statistical Abstract A, *SMLA/MELA Population Data 1931–1966*. WP/9; Statistical Abstract B, *SMLA/MELA Population Change Data 1931–1966*; Statistical Abstract C, *SMLA/MELA Employment and Employment Change Data 1961–1966*. PEP, London, 1969 (mimeo).

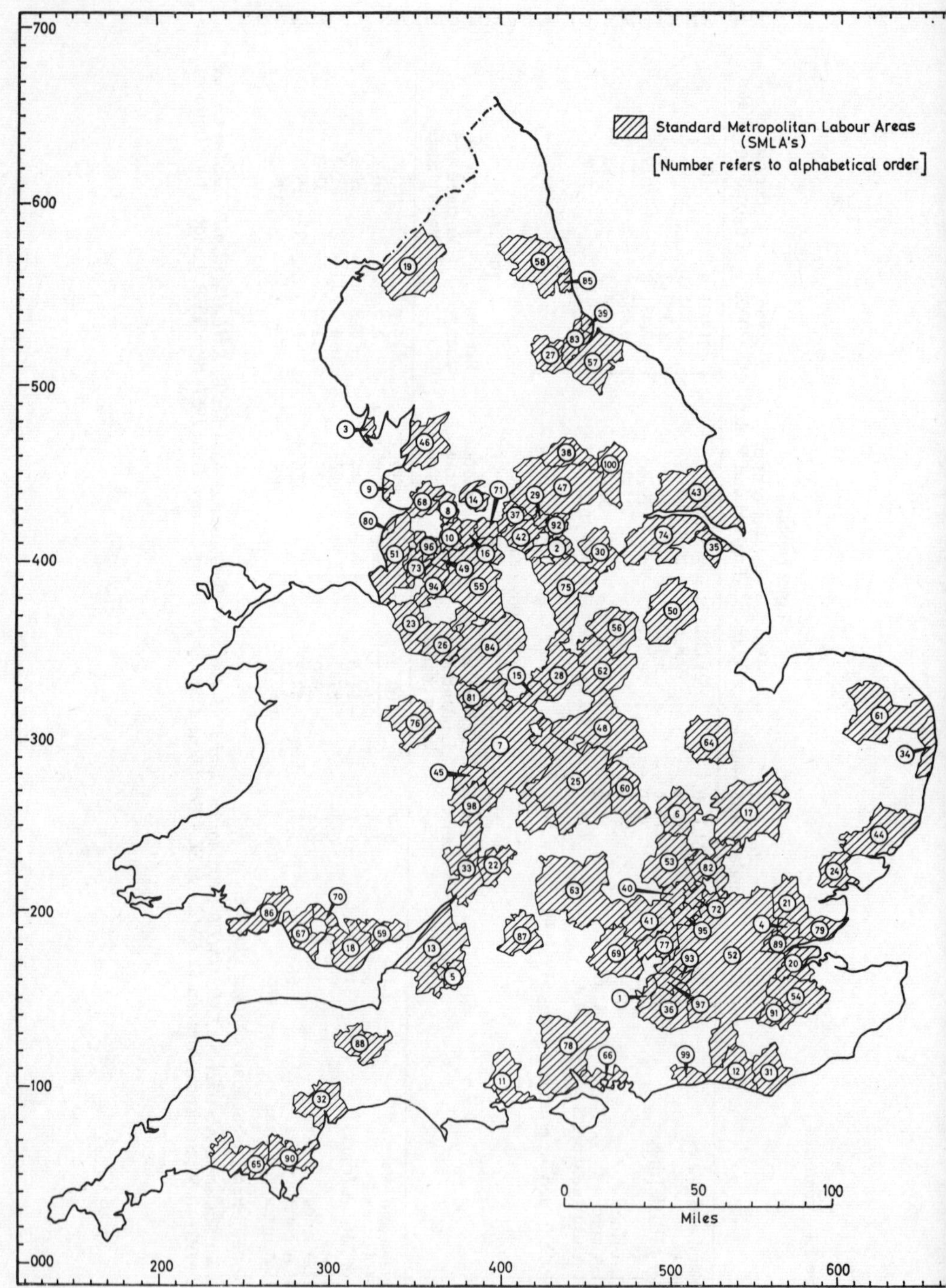

Figure 5.1 SMLAs, England and Wales, 1961
(*Key: pages 254–293*)

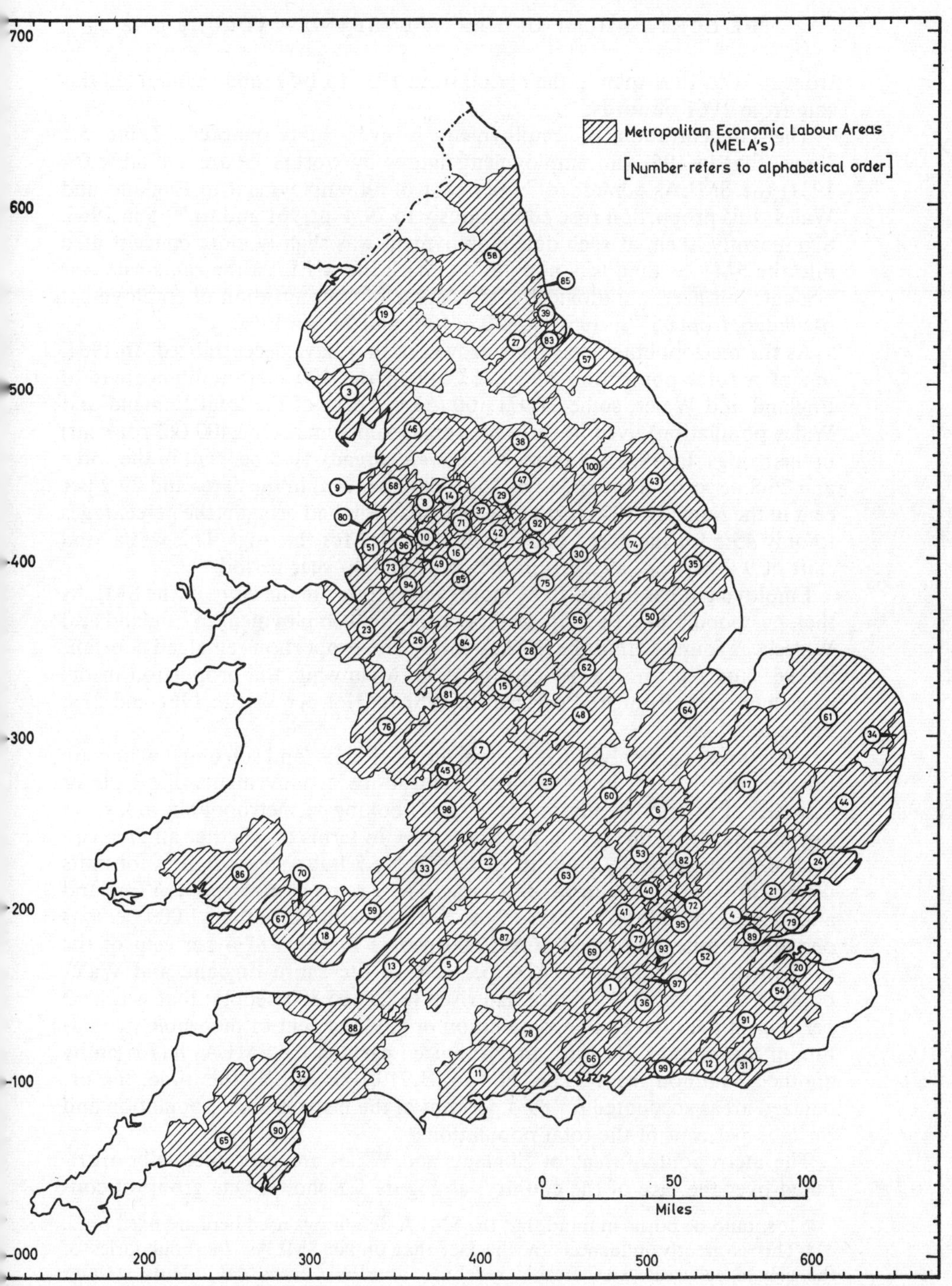

Figure 5.2 MELAs, England and Wales, 1961
(*Key: pages 254–293*)

from 1951 to 1961 than in the period from 1931 to 1951, and maintained this rate from 1961 onwards.

The concentration of employment is even more marked. Table 5.1 shows that in 1951 (no employment figures by workplace are available for 1931) the SMLAs contained 79 per cent of all employment in England and Wales; this proportion rose continuously to 79·4 in 1961 and to 79·5 in 1966. Significantly, then, at each date employment was slightly more concentrated into the SMLAs than was population. With the MELAs, the same rule was evident; but here, paradoxically, the degree of concentration of employment oscillated, from 95·4 in 1951 to 94·2 in 1961 and 94·8 in 1966.

As the metropolitan areas have grown, so they have decentralized. In 1931, out of a total population of 30,757,549 in the 100 metropolitan areas of England and Wales, some 21,971,100 (55 per cent of the total England and Wales population) lived in their core areas and some 8,786,400 (22 per cent) in their rings. By 1951 the proportions were already 50·5 per cent in the cores and 26·8 per cent in the rings; by 1961, 48·3 per cent in the cores and 29·2 per cent in the rings; by 1971 further decentralization had brought the percentages to only 45·1 for the cores, and as much as 31·2 for the rings. This was a total shift of 9·9 per cent away from the cores in a 40-year period.*

Employment has tended to be more concentrated in the cores of the SMLAs than has population. In 1951, 58·3 per cent of all employment in England and Wales was found within the SMLA cores. The proportion remained constant in 1961 and fell to 56·8 per cent in 1966. Meanwhile the proportion in the rings had risen, from 20·7 per cent in 1951 to 21·1 per cent in 1961 and 22·8 per cent in 1966.

Up to now, our analysis has been in terms of units (and sub units) which are functionally defined, in terms of concentrations or movements of people or activities. But another important way of looking at metropolitan areas, we saw in Chapter Four, is in a physical sense, in terms of whether an area can be said to be physically built-up, or not. Table 5.1 also shows figures for units defined in this way, the urbanized areas. These parts of metropolitan England and Wales, that is those parts of the SMLAs with more than 1,000 persons per square mile, contained 26,896,600 people in 1931: 87·4 per cent of the total SMLA population or 67·3 per cent of the entire England and Wales population. By 1951 the figure had risen to 29,865,800 people: that was 88·3 per cent of the total SMLA population or 68·3 per cent of the whole population of the country. By 1961, the urbanized parts of the SMLAs had risen by another 2 million from 29,865,800 to 31,919,100, and by this time, the urbanized areas accounted for 89·4 per cent of the metropolitan population and for 69·3 per cent of the total population.†

The metropolitan areas of England and Wales are very unequally distributed over the face of the country, as Figure 5.1 shows. One group of con-

* It should be borne in mind that the SMLA definitions used here are fixed ones.

† This is greatly influenced by the fact that unlike SMLAs, the boundaries of the urbanized areas were freshly redefined at each Census date. Thus at later dates, they include bigger areas.

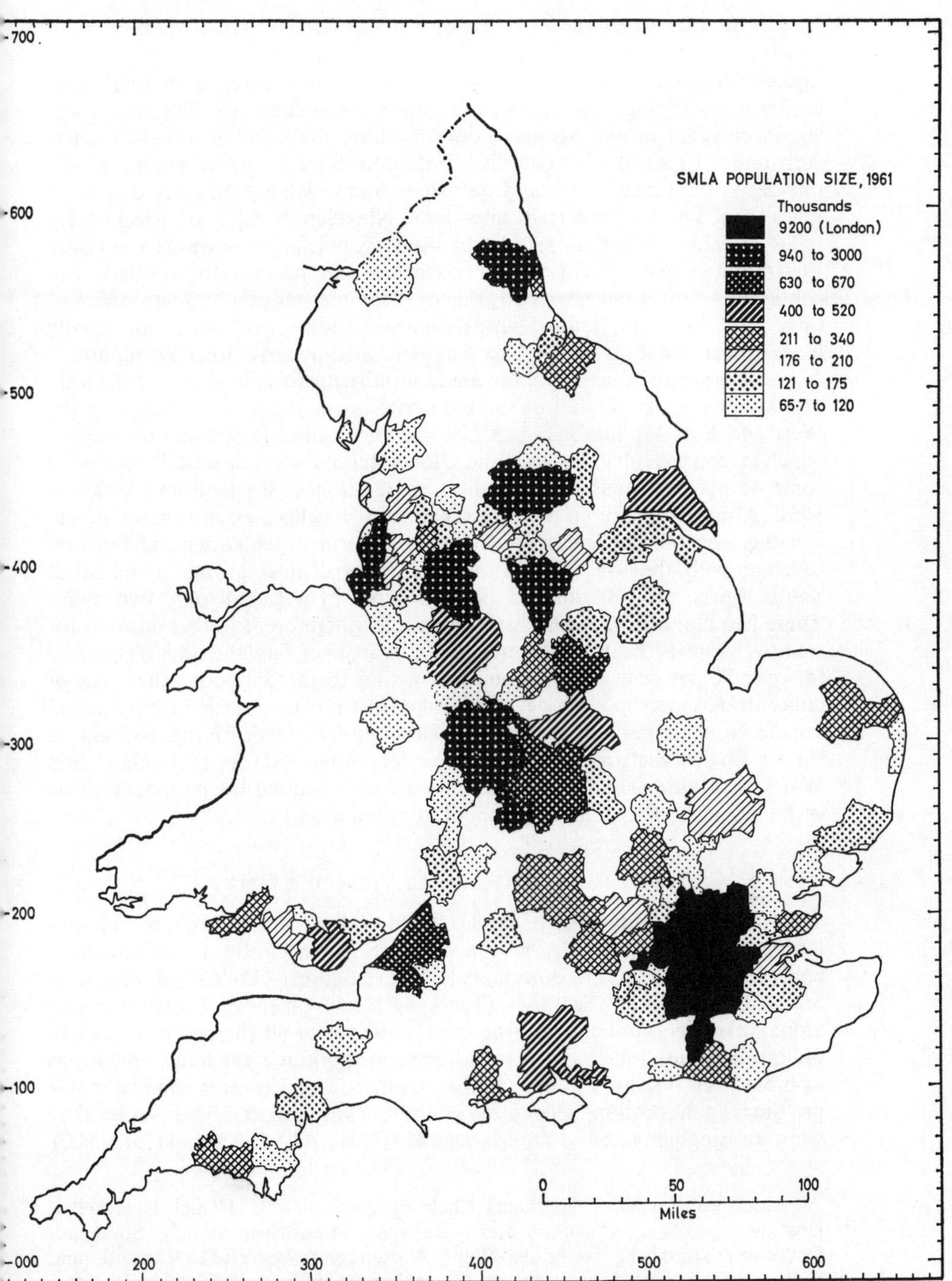

Figure 5.3 SMLAs, Population Size, 1961

tiguous SMLAs, numbering twenty-six (or over one-quarter of the total), and taking in more than one-fifth of the total metropolitan population in 1961, is concentrated in and around London. Here, the London SMLA itself is surrounded by a ring of twenty-five contiguous SMLAs, which are more than one deep on the east, north and west sides, and which extend more than sixty miles from London in certain directions. Nineteen of these are within forty miles of central London, and lie in the ring officially known as the Outer Metropolitan Area.[2] This major concentration has certain outliers, not contiguous with it but nearly so; one of these consists of a loose grouping of three SMLAs in the South Hampshire area, another consists of an equally loose group extending up the East Anglian coast towards Great Yarmouth.

Another group of metropolitan areas, numbering forty in all out of the total of 100, covers virtually all of the industrial heart of England, including the West and East Midlands, Lancashire and Yorkshire. It throws out tongues which extend to Hull in the east, and Gloucester in the south-west. It contained some 43 per cent of the metropolitan population of England and Wales in 1961. Almost contiguous with this belt, and in effect extensions of it, are isolated metropolitan areas like Blackpool, Burnley, Lancaster and Lincoln, together with the five SMLAs which form a distinct group in industrial South Wales, plus Bristol and Bath, isolated by a gap of only two miles. These two major groups and their extensions, therefore, together account for well over four-fifths of all the metropolitan areas of England and Wales, and for over 90 per cent of the population within them. Only one other area of concentrated metropolitan development exists; it is the North-East industrial area in Northumberland, County Durham and the North Riding, accounting for six further metropolitan areas. The remaining SMLAs of England and Wales, as Figure 5.1 shows, are scattered widely around the peripheral areas of the country; they tend to be small in population.

METROPOLITAN AREAS VIEWED BY SIZE

The 100 metropolitan areas of England and Wales, in 1961, had a total population of 35,719,500 people, or on average 357,200 each. But this mean figure concealed enormous variations in scale, from London (9,156,683) at one end to Stafford (65,736) at the other (Table 5.2 and Appendix Table). London alone, therefore, contained a little over a quarter of all the people in metropolitan England and Wales. Five other metropolitan areas had populations of more than one million apiece; they happened to represent the five major provincial conurbations recognized in the Census (Figure 5.3). In order they were Birmingham (2,693,100), Manchester (2,041,700), Liverpool (1,480,900),

[2] Aldershot, Basildon, Chatham, Chelmsford, Guildford, Hemel Hempstead, High Wycombe, Luton, Maidstone, Reading, St Albans, Slough, Southend, Stevenage, Thurrock, Tunbridge Wells, Walton and Weybridge, Watford, and Woking. Six others form a rather discontinuous outer ring 50–60 miles from London: Bedford, Brighton, Cambridge, Eastbourne, Oxford, and Worthing.

Table 5.2

STANDARD METROPOLITAN LABOUR AREAS, ENGLAND AND WALES, ARRAYED IN ORDER OF POPULATION 1961

SMLA	Population 1961	SMLA	Population 1961	SMLA	Population 1961	SMLA	Population 1961
1 London	9,156,683	26 Reading	241,705	51 Exeter	147,133	76 Stevenage	105,678
2 Birmingham	2,693,069	27 Swansea	235,678	52 York	146,932	77 Eastbourne	103,338
3 Manchester	2,041,694	28 Norwich	232,817	53 Stockton	145,919	78 Chester	102,089
4 Liverpool	1,480,930	29 Slough	231,493	54 Wakefield	139,922	79 Bath	101,209
5 Leeds	1,163,455	30 Sunderland	218,054	55 Maidstone	137,834	80 Carlisle	100,759
6 Newcastle	1,061,681	31 Chatham	200,597	56 Swindon	137,342	81 Rhondda	100,287
7 Sheffield	949,528	32 Preston	196,599	57 Aldershot	131,515	82 Colchester	98,611
8 Bristol	661,186	33 Doncaster	196,398	58 Mansfield	130,871	83 Chelmsford	98,012
9 Coventry	643,678	34 Huddersfield	193,809	59 Bury	130,431	84 Tunbridge Wells	96,560
10 Nottingham	634,683	35 Cambridge	190,384	60 Thurrock	129,868	85 West Hartlepool	94,710
11 Stoke-on-Trent	519,059	36 St Helens	189,943	61 Scunthorpe	127,733	86 Leigh	93,244
12 Leicester	456,551	37 Blackpool	186,559	62 Lincoln	126,826	87 Crewe	91,429
13 Cardiff	432,552	38 High Wycombe	183,548	63 Gloucester	124,840	88 St Albans	89,240
14 Hull	419,481	39 Port Talbot	181,641	64 Worthing	118,665	89 Basildon	88,524
15 Portsmouth	410,394	40 Wigan	180,080	65 Rochdale	116,140	90 Hemel Hempstead	87,995
16 Southampton	401,832	41 Ipswich	173,627	66 Torquay	115,342	91 Burton	87,929
17 Brighton	337,806	42 Watford	169,336	67 Lancaster	114,818	92 Walton and Weybridge	85,900
18 Derby	314,532	43 Warrington	168,425	68 Gt Yarmouth	114,734	93 Woking	83,699
19 Bournemouth	305,022	44 Blackburn	168,121	69 Worcester	114,019	94 Southport	82,004
20 Middlesbrough	289,450	45 Halifax	167,434	70 Burnley	113,511	95 Harrogate	80,396
21 Oxford	286,876	46 Barnsley	165,018	71 Dewsbury	113,315	96 Barrow-in-Furness	75,243
22 Plymouth	269,548	47 Guildford	159,168	72 Cheltenham	110,747	97 Shrewsbury	74,577
23 Luton	266,826	48 Newport	154,214	73 Darlington	110,127	98 Taunton	73,048
24 Bolton	249,708	49 Northampton	151,191	74 Peterborough	107,925	99 Kidderminster	70,406
25 Southend	246,838	50 Grimsby	147,181	75 Bedford	106,249	100 Stafford	65,736

Source: Statistical Abstract A, op. cit. For details of composition see *Constituent Authorities in SMLAs and MELAs in England and Wales* WP/12. PEP, London, 1969 (mimeo).

Table 5.3

SMLAs BY POPULATION SIZE, 1961, AND STANDARD REGION

(Population figures in thousands)

SMLA pop. size 1961		Standard region: South-East	South-West	East Anglia	West Midlands	East Midlands	North-West	Yorks. and Humberside	Northern	Wales and Monmouth	Total
Over 289·0	No. of SMLAs	5	1	0	3	3	2	3	2	1	20
	Total pop.	10,611·7	661·2	0·0	3,855·8	1,405·8	3,522·6	2,532·5	1,351·1	432·6	24,373·3
	Mean pop./SMLA	2,122·3	661·2	0·0	1,288·6	468·6	1,761·3	844·2	675·6	432·6	1,218·6
	Per cent national SMLA pop.	29·7	1·9	0·0	10·8	3·9	9·9	7·1	3·8	1·2	68·2
289·0 to 180·0	No. of SMLAs	7	1	2	0	0	5	2	1	2	20
	Total pop.	1,657·9	269·5	432·2	0·0	0·0	1,002·9	390·2	218·1	417·3	4,379·1
	Mean pop./SMLA	234·0	269·5	211·6	0·0	0·0	200·6	195·1	218·1	208·7	219·0
	Per cent national SMLA pop.	4·6	0·8	1·2	0·0	0·0	2·8	1·1	0·6	1·2	12·3
180·0 to 129·0	No. of SMLAs	5	2	1	0	2	3	5	1	1	20
	Total pop.	727·7	284·5	173·6	0·0	282·1	467·0	766·5	145·9	154·2	3,001·5
	Mean pop./SMLA	145·5	142·3	173·0	0·0	141·1	155·7	153·3	145·9	154·2	150·1
	Per cent national SMLA pop.	2·0	0·8	0·5	0·0	0·8	1·3	2·2	0·4	0·4	8·4
129·0 to 100·5	No. of SMLAs	4	4	2	1	1	4	2	2	0	20
	Total pop.	433·9	452·1	222·7	114·0	126·8	416·6	241·0	210·9	0·0	2,248·1
	Mean pop./SMLA	108·5	113·0	111·4	114·0	126·8	111·7	120·5	105·5	0·0	112·4
	Per cent national SMLA pop.	1·2	1·3	0·6	0·3	0·4	1·3	0·7	0·6	0·0	6·3
Under 100·5	No. of SMLAs	8	1	0	4	0	4	1	1	1	20
	Total pop.	729·5	73·0	0·0	298·6	0·0	341·9	80·4	94·7	100·3	1,718·4
	Mean pop./SMLA	91·2	73·0	0·0	74·7	0·0	85·5	80·4	94·7	100·3	85·9
	Per cent national SMLA pop.	2·0	0·2	0·0	0·8	0·0	1·0	0·2	0·3	0·3	4·8
Total	No. of SMLAs	29	9	5	8	6	18	13	7	5	100
	Total pop.	14,160·7	1,740·3	819·5	4,268·4	1,814·7	5,781·0	4,010·6	2,020·7	1,104·4	35,719·5
	Mean pop./SMLA	488·3	193·4	163·9	533·6	302·5	321·2	308·5	288·7	220·9	357·2
	Per cent national SMLA pop.	39·6	4·9	2·3	12·0	5·1	16·2	11·2	5·7	3·1	100·0

Leeds (1,163,500), and Newcastle upon Tyne (1,061,700). Together these six areas contained 17,597,600 people: almost exactly half the population of metropolitan England and Wales. At the other extreme, sixty-nine out of the 100 SMLAs contained less than 200,000 people apiece; and nineteen had less than 100,000.

If the metropolitan areas are divided into five equal groups in order of size, the same disproportion appears (Table 5.3). The twenty largest areas contained over 24,300,000 people, two-thirds of the total; at the other extreme, the twenty smallest, which were all on the 100,000 mark or lower, contributed a mere 1,718,000 to the aggregate.

Table 5.3 also shows the size distribution by standard regions. The metropolitan areas, as might be imagined, are heavily concentrated in the more highly-urbanized, industrialized regions of England and Wales. Twenty-nine out of the 100 are in the South-East, eighteen in the North-West, and thirteen in Yorkshire and Humberside. Together East Anglia, the East Midlands, and Wales contribute only sixteen to the total. Viewed in terms of their contribution to population, though, the regions emerge somewhat differently. The South-East again dominates, with 14,160,700 or nearly 40 per cent of the total; of this, of course, London contributes about two-thirds. The North-West contributes 5,781,000, the Yorkshire-Humberside region 4,010,600 and the West Midlands 4,268,400. This last total is concentrated in only eight metropolitan areas, with an average population of 533,600, the highest average of any standard region. The South-East, with the next highest average, has like the West Midlands, some very large metropolitan areas and some very small ones, with relatively fewer in the middle ranges. On the whole, as might be expected, the very rural regions (the South-West, East Anglia, North Wales) have the smallest metropolitan areas in population terms, on average. But they are not widely divergent from the North-West and Yorkshire-Humberside, which are distinguished by relatively large numbers of medium and small-sized metropolitan areas.

On the whole the size distribution of the Standard Metropolitan Areas in England and Wales does accord with the rank size rule, which Marion Clawson has shown to be approximately true for metropolitan areas in the Northeastern Urban Complex in the United States. That is to say, when the sizes of the metropolitan areas (in terms of population) are plotted against their rank order on double log graph paper, a straight-line distribution emerges, (Figure 5.4). Of course, the rule is not perfect. The English graph shows significant break points, or under-developed areas: between 700,000 and 900,000, between 520,000 and 630,000, between 340,000 and 400,000, and between 200,000 and 230,000. The assumption would seem to be that these sizes do not accord well with the demands of the urban population for certain levels of services, or of employers for labour; there is apparently a natural tendency for urban areas to grow beyond these points to the next level of the hierarchy.

There were great differences, in 1961, in the relationship between population and area in the different metropolitan areas of England and Wales. The

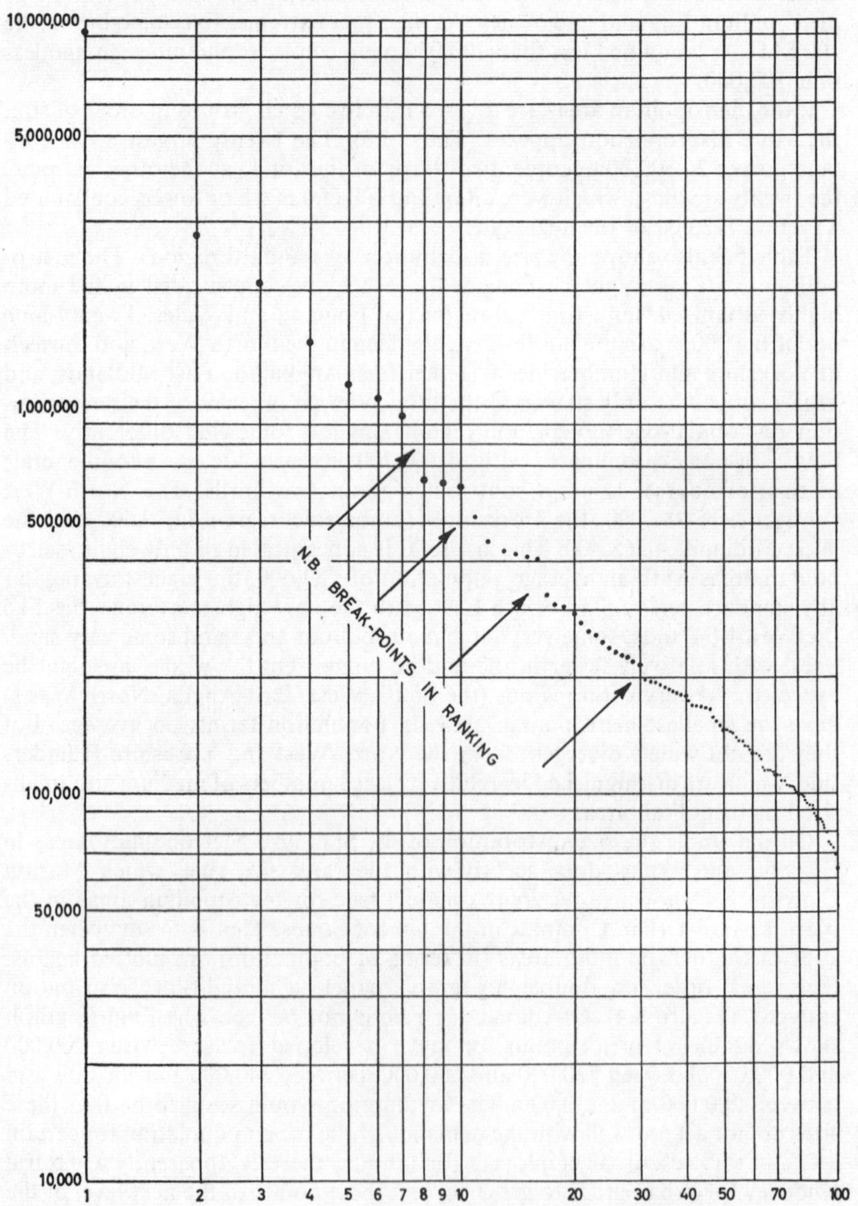

Figure 5.4 Rank Size Ordering of SMLAs, 1961

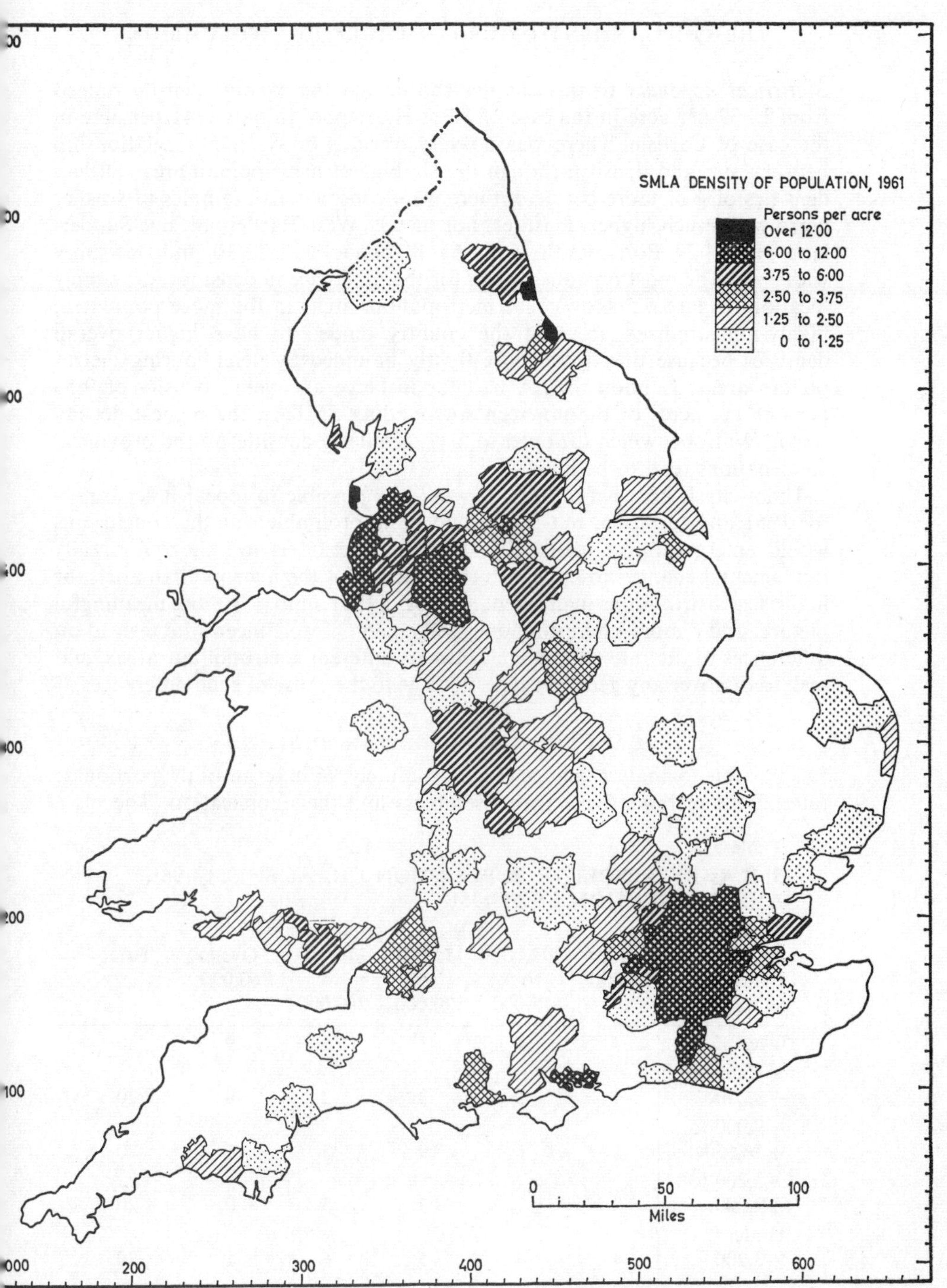

Figure 5.5 SMLAs, Density of Population, 1961

Statistical Appendix to this chapter shows that the average density ranged from 15·39 per acre in the case of West Hartlepool to only 0·41 per acre in the case of Carlisle. There was no very obvious or systematic relationship between size and density; though the six biggest metropolitan areas all had densities of 4 or more per acre, there were conspicuous examples of smaller areas with much higher densities, not merely West Hartlepool, but Sunderland with 14·27, Portsmouth with 8·65, Blackpool with 13·10, and Dewsbury with 7·42. The most obvious reason for the difference in densities was simply location. Figure 5.5 shows that metropolitan areas in the more populated, highly-industrialized areas of the country tended to have higher overall densities because they were more tightly bounded by neighbouring metropolitan areas. London SMLA had for instance an overall density of 9·55 persons per acre; of the nineteen surrounding SMLAs, the highest density was in Watford, which dropped to 5·11. Similarly densities in the provincial conurbations tend to be high.

The analysis here is for 1961. It would be possible to repeat it separately for 1951 and for 1966, but this would be unprofitable, for the conclusions would emerge almost identically. The time period is too short for really fundamental changes to appear in the ordering of the metropolitan areas, or in the size distributions in different regions of the country. A more meaningful picture, and a more interesting one, will emerge if we concentrate instead on differences in the rate of change between different metropolitan areas, and seek to discover any general suggestions as to the cause of such differences.

CHANGE IN METROPOLITAN ENGLAND

It is possible to analyse change either absolutely, or in terms of proportionate rates. Both methods have their usefulness and their application. The plain

Table 5.4

SMLAs BY ABSOLUTE POPULATION CHANGE, 1951–1961, AND POPULATION SIZE, 1951

Absolute population change 1951–61	SMLA population size 1951: Under 92,000	92,000 to 115,000	115,000 to 170,000	170,000 to 260,000	Over 260,000	Total
Over 33,100	3	1	1	6	9	20
+16,650 to +33,100	4	2	3	2	9	20
+9,000 to +16,650	1	6	9	3	1	20
+3,200 to +9,000	8	7	2	3	0	20
Under +3,200	4	4	5	6	1	20
Total	20	20	20	20	20	100

Table 5.5

SMLAs BY ABSOLUTE POPULATION CHANGE, 1951–1961, AND STANDARD REGION

(Population figures in thousands)

Abs. pop. change 1951–61		Standard region: South East	South-West	East Anglia	West Midlands	East Midlands	North-West	Yorks. and Humberside	Northern	Wales and Monmouth	Total
Over +33·10	No. of SMLAs	13	1	0	2	1	1	0	2	0	20
	Total abs. pop. change	561·6	44·1	0·0	294·2	41·8	53·2	0·0	70·0	0·0	1,064·9
	Average change/SMLA	43·2	44·1	0·0	147·1	41·8	53·2	0·0	35·0	0·0	53·2
	Per cent national SMLA growth	29·7	2·3	0·0	15·6	2·2	2·8	0·0	3·7	0·0	56·4
+33·10 to +16·65	No. of SMLAs	9	2	1	1	2	1	3	0	1	20
	Total abs. pop. change	203·5	50·9	23·5	16·7	41·0	29·3	75·1	0·0	32·2	472·2
	Average change/SMLA	22·6	25·5	23·5	16·7	20·5	29·3	25·0	0·0	32·2	23·6
	Per cent national SMLA growth	10·8	2·7	1·2	0·9	2·2	1·6	4·0	0·0	1·7	25·0
+16·65 to +9·00	No. of SMLAs	4	2	3	0	3	1	3	3	1	20
	Total abs. pop. change	57·0	23·8	41·7	0·0	32·7	16·3	42·1	38·1	14·6	266·3
	Average change/SMLA	14·3	11·9	13·9	0·0	10·9	16·3	14·0	12·7	14·6	13·3
	Per cent national SMLA growth	3·0	1·3	2·2	0·0	1·7	0·9	2·2	2·0	0·8	14·1
+9·00 to +3·20	No. of SMLAs	3	3	1	4	0	4	2	1	2	20
	Total abs. pop. change	24·9	15·4	6·1	24·9	0·0	21·1	15·2	4·8	11·0	123·4
	Average change/SMLA	8·3	5·1	6·1	6·2	0·0	5·3	7·6	4·8	5·5	6·2
	Per cent national SMLA growth	1·3	0·8	0·3	1·3	0·0	1·1	0·8	0·3	0·6	6·5
Under +3·20	No. of SMLAs	0	1	0	1	0	11	5	1	1	20
	Total abs. pop. change	0·0	−0·6	0·0	3·0	0·0	−28·7	−2·7	3·1	−11·1	−37·0
	Average change/SMLA	0·0	−0·6	0·0	3·0	0·0	−2·6	−0·5	3·1	−11·1	−1·9
	Per cent national SMLA growth	0·0	−0·03	0·0	0·2	0·0	−1·5	−0·1	0·2	−0·6	−2·0
Total	No. of SMLAs	29	9	5	8	6	18	13	7	5	100
	Total abs. pop. change	847·0	133·6	71·3	338·8	115·5	91·2	129·7	116·0	46·7	1,889·8
	Average change/SMLA	29·2	14·8	14·3	42·4	19·3	5·1	10·0	16·6	9·3	18·9
	Per cent national SMLA growth	44·8	7·1	3·8	17·9	6·1	4·8	6·9	6·1	2·5	100·0

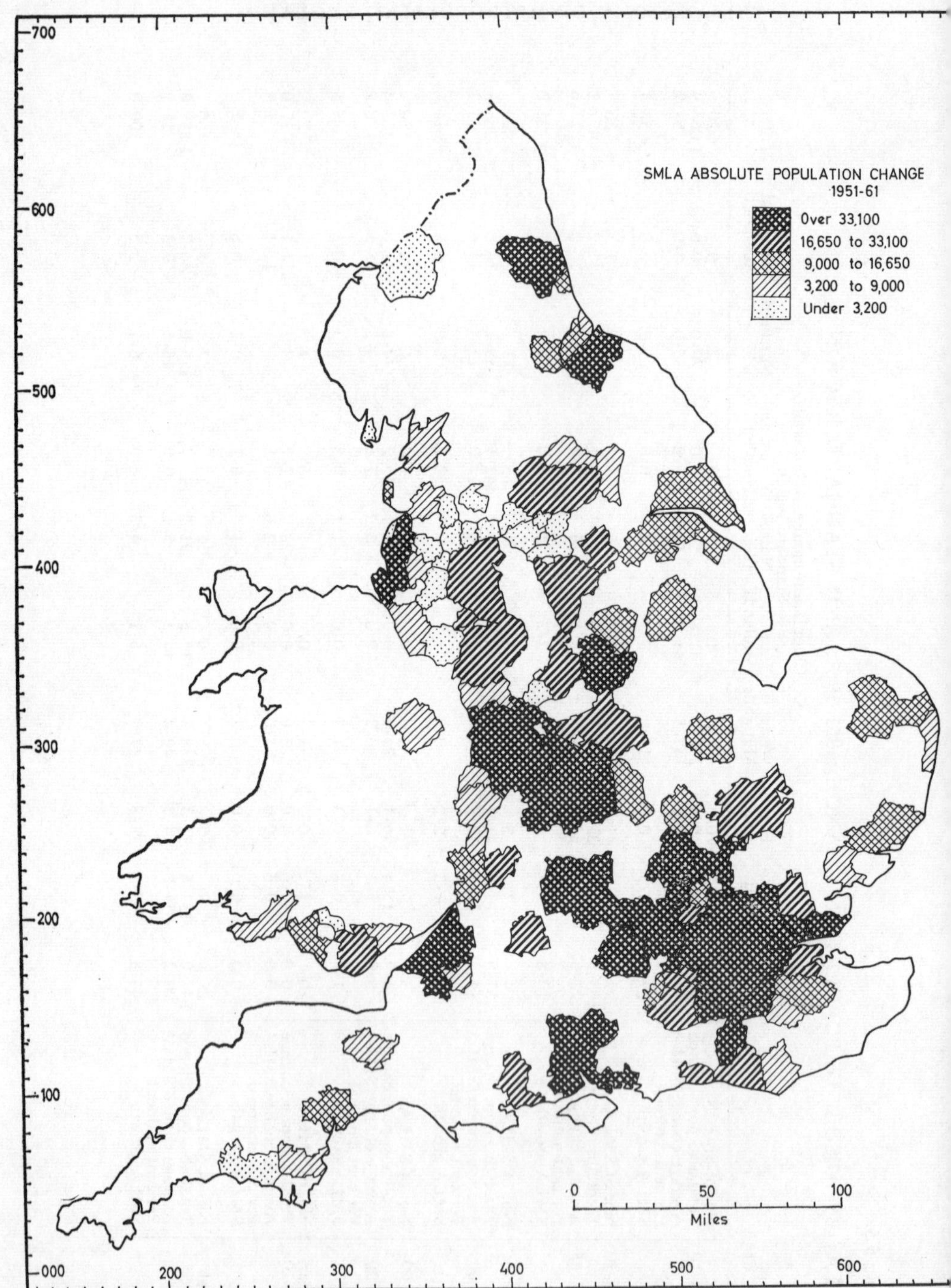

Figure 5.6 SMLAs, Absolute Population Change, 1951–1961

fact, as a study of the actual statistics amply shows, is that big areas tend to have big absolute additions to their populations. Even if they have low percentage rates of growth (as very often proves to be the case) it will still be true that they make a disproportionate contribution to the total growth of metropolitan England and Wales.

This is clearly seen from Table 5.4. Of the twenty biggest metropolitan areas in 1951, nine were counted among those making the biggest absolute gains during the subsequent decade, and another nine were in the category containing the next biggest gains. The relationship though was not quite systematic. Among the group of the twenty biggest metropolitan areas, some of the smallest were adding as many to their populations during the decade as some of the biggest ones. Thus Bournemouth, with only 274,000 people in 1951, added 30,700 during the next decade, more than Manchester with 2,012,400, and some of the biggest absolute gains among the 100 SMLAs were made by the metropolitan areas based on new towns like Stevenage, Basildon and Hemel Hempstead, which had very small populations at the beginning of the decade (Figure 5.6). Nevertheless, the general rule holds for those SMLAs that were increasing in population, though it should be noticed that some other medium and even large SMLAs were recording losses. In fact, looking at the group of declining SMLAs as a whole, it is clear that they include examples from every size category, from the biggest to the smallest.

In regional terms, the most conspicuous fact is that absolute growth in the decade 1951–61 was concentrated in the South-East and the Midlands (Table 5.5). Of the total addition to population within the metropolitan areas of 1,889,000, 847,000 or nearly one-half was in the South-East; another 338,000 was in the Midlands. Out of its twenty-nine SMLAs, the South-East had thirteen of the twenty highest absolute increases in England and Wales, and nine out of twenty in the next category of growth. Conversely, out of the twenty showing the poorest growth records (most of which were actually losing people) the North-West registered eleven and Yorkshire-Humberside five; the South-East had none and the West Midlands only one. Of the thirteen SMLAs actually making a loss, the North-West had nine, Yorkshire-Humberside two, the South-West and Wales one apiece.[3]

By the quinquennium 1961–66, the picture had become confused. Table 5.6 shows that there was a much less clear relationship between size and absolute growth. Some of the biggest metropolitan areas were actually losing population (London minus 266,000, Manchester minus 29,000, Liverpool minus 30,700), while many medium-sized areas (especially in the South-East) were making substantial gains (Luton plus 32,400, Reading plus 37,400, High Wycombe plus 31,800) (Figure 5.7.) But the regional distribution of growth and decline remained as striking as before (Table 5.7). Two out of the twenty highest growth areas were in the South-East, as well as ten out of the next

[3] In the North-West: Barrow, Blackburn, Bolton, Burnley, Bury, Rochdale, Southport, Warrington, and Wigan. In Yorkshire: Dewsbury, and Halifax. Also: Plymouth, and Rhondda.

twenty. Out of a total gain in population in metropolitan England and Wales of 640,000, 163,100 was in the South-East and another 128,600 in the West Midlands. The declining areas were again concentrated in the industrial North, though not to the same degree as in the 1950s: the list was not so dominated by the Lancashire cotton towns.[4]

Table 5.6

SMLAs BY ABSOLUTE POPULATION CHANGE, 1961–1966, AND POPULATION SIZE, 1961

Absolute population change 1961–66	SMLA population size 1961 Under 100,500	100,500 to 129,000	129,000 to 180,000	180,000 to 289,000	Over 289,000	Total
Over +14,400	2	0	3	7	8	20
+8,900 to +14,400	3	6	5	3	3	20
+5,400 to +8,900	3	7	4	3	3	20
+2,000 to +5,400	7	3	4	4	2	20
Under +2,000	5	4	4	3	4	20
Total	20	20	20	20	20	100

The real explanation of the process of change is that while growth in the South-East continued almost unabated, it transferred itself progressively from the biggest, central metropolitan areas to smaller metropolitan areas outside them; and this process was especially evident around London. Altogether, within approximately forty miles of central London, apart from the London metropolitan area itself, we have already noticed that nineteen separate and smaller areas can be distinguished: many of them are immediately contiguous to London; all of them lie within what is conventionally called the Outer Metropolitan Area. In 1951–61, London gained 44,300 people while the peripheral outer SMLAs gained 573,100; in 1961–66 London lost 266,000 people while the outer SMLAs gained 302,000. Thus what had been a relative decentralization of population in the 1950s turned into an absolute decentralization in the 1960s. Elsewhere, there was no real parallel to this process. The area of England most similar in metropolitan organization to London, South Lancashire, exhibited similar dynamics of large-scale metropolitan change, even though the amount and scale of change and the factors involved

[4] In the South-East: London, and (significantly) Watford. In the North-West: Barrow, Blackburn, Burnley, Liverpool, Manchester, and Southport. In Yorkshire: Halifax. Also: Plymouth, and Rhondda.

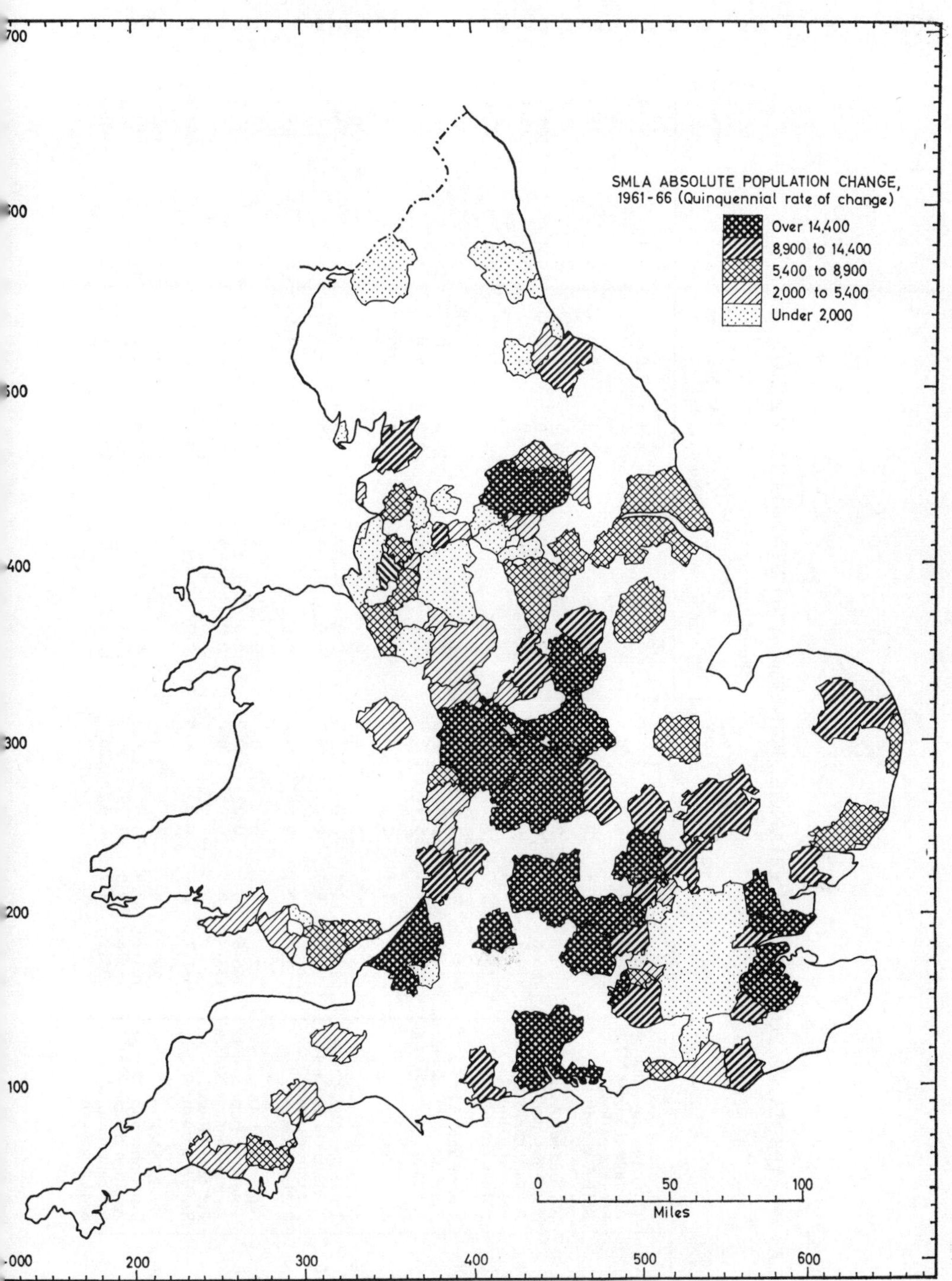

Figure 5.7 SMLAs, Absolute Population Change, 1961–1966

Table 5.7

SMLAs BY ABSOLUTE POPULATION CHANGE, 1961–1966, AND STANDARD REGION

(Population figures in thousands)

Abs. pop. change 1961–66		Standard region									
		South-East	South-West	East Anglia	West Midlands	East Midlands	North-West	Yorks. and Humberside	Northern	Wales and Monmouth	Total
Over +14·4	No. of SMLAs	12	2	0	2	2	1	1	0	0	20
	Total abs. pop. change	294·7	48·8	0·0	101·2	67·2	22·9	14·4	0·0	0·0	549·4
	Average change/SMLA	24·6	24·4	0·0	50·6	33·6	22·9	14·4	0·0	0·0	27·5
	Per cent national SMLA growth	46·1	7·6	0·0	15·8	10·5	3·6	2·3	0·0	0·0	85·8
+14·4 to +8·9	No. of SMLAs	10	2	2	0	3	2	0	1	0	20
	Total abs. pop. change	106·6	19·2	20·3	0·0	30·7	20·9	0·0	11·0	0·0	208·8
	Average change/SMLA	10·7	9·6	10·2	0·0	10·2	10·5	0·0	11·0	0·0	10·4
	Per cent national SMLA growth	16·7	3·0	3·2	0·0	4·8	3·3	0·0	1·7	0·0	32·6
+8·9 to +5·4	No. of SMLAs	2	1	3	1	1	4	6	0	2	20
	Total abs. pop. change	14·5	7·1	18·3	5·9	7·3	26·5	39·6	0·0	15·6	134·8
	Average change/SMLA	7·3	7·1	6·1	5·9	7·3	6·6	6·6	0·0	7·8	6·7
	Per cent national SMLA growth	2·3	1·1	2·9	0·9	1·1	4·1	6·2	0·0	2·4	21·1
+5·4 to +2·0	No. of SMLAs	3	3	0	5	0	3	3	1	2	20
	Total abs. pop. change	13·8	13·2	0·0	21·5	0·0	12·1	11·4	5·1	7·6	84·8
	Average change/SMLA	4·8	4·4	0·0	4·3	0·0	4·0	3·8	5·1	3·8	4·2
	Per cent national SMLA growth	2·2	2·1	0·0	3·4	0·0	1·9	1·8	0·8	1·2	13·2
Under +2·0	No. of SMLAs	2	1	0	0	0	8	3	5	1	20
	Total abs. pop. change	−266·6	−0·5	0·0	0·0	0·0	−65·2	2·1	−2·9	−4·6	−337·7
	Average change/SMLA	−133·3	−0·5	0·0	0·0	0·0	−8·2	0·7	−0·6	−4·6	−76·9
	Per cent national SMLA growth	−41·7	−0·1	0·0	0·0	0·0	−10·2	0·3	−0·5	−0·7	−52·8
Total	No. of SMLAs	29	9	5	8	6	18	13	7	5	100
	Total abs. pop. change	163·1	87·9	38·6	128·6	105·1	17·2	67·6	13·2	18·6	640·0
	Average change/SMLA	5·6	9·8	7·7	16·1	17·5	1·0	5·2	1·9	3·7	6·4
	Per cent national SMLA growth	25·5	13·7	6·0	20·1	16·4	2·7	10·6	2·1	2·9	100·3

were vastly different from those of the London area. The Manchester SMLA gained a modest 29,300 people during 1951–61, but then lost an equivalent number (minus 29,000) during 1961–66. The surrounding group of six closely linked metropolitan areas,[5] however, showed a reverse trend. They suffered a loss of 17,199 people during 1951–61, following the regional trend, but showed an overall gain of 35,162 over 1961–66. Thus, although the whole area only just managed to keep a fairly static population level (a reflection of the regional tendency to stagnation), internally it experienced a shift from the central, large congested SMLA to the surrounding smaller ones, a tendency rather like that in the South-East. In the Midlands there were different forces shaping the area, with the largest SMLAs (Birmingham and Coventry in the west, Derby, Leicester and Nottingham in the east) showing comfortable gains in both periods. Yet even here, Birmingham shows a much lower growth in the later period, presumably reflecting the general pattern of evolution for the largest metropolitan areas elsewhere.[6]

Moving from absolute to percentage rates of change, the pattern is a starkly simple one. Table 5.8 shows that of the twenty SMLAs showing the highest percentage rates of growth in the 1950s, seventeen were in the South-East. Topmost of all were certain SMLAs representing the London new towns: Basildon, Hemel Hempstead and Stevenage, all of which recorded increases of over 70 per cent in the decade. This, of course, was because they started with relatively small base populations in 1951. But only a little behind, in the next three positions in the list, were three SMLAs in the Outer Metropolitan Area which grew mainly through private enterprise building for sale: Thurrock (a growth of 39 per cent), Woking (36 per cent) and Slough (31 per cent). Conversely, of the twenty SMLAs with the poorest growth record (most of which were actually declining in the decade) no less than eleven were in the North-West and another six in Yorkshire and Humberside. (Figure 5.8). Put another way, out of the eighteen SMLAs in the North-West, eleven were in the poorest growth category and another six in the next poorest; out of thirteen in Yorkshire-Humberside, the figures were respectively six and two.[7] The three SMLAs outside these regions which came into the category of

[5] Bolton, Bury, Leigh, Rochdale, Warrington, and Wigan.

[6] As these figures show:

	1951–61	1961–66 (five-year rate)
Birmingham	204,963	57,051
Coventry	89,226	44,172
Derby	21,895	9,578
Leicester	19,072	46,989
Nottingham	41,816	20,187

[7] Those in the poorest growth category were, in the North-West: Manchester, Leigh (which were increasing slightly), Bolton, Bury, Wigan, Southport, Blackburn, Barrow, Rochdale, Warrington, and Burnley (in order of percentage decline). In Yorkshire the list was Leeds, Wakefield, Barnsley, Huddersfield (increasing marginally), Dewsbury, and Halifax (in order of decline).

Table 5.8

SMLAs BY PERCENTAGE POPULATION CHANGE, 1951–1961, AND STANDARD REGION

Per cent pop. change 1951–61		Standard region									
		South-East	South-West	East Anglia	West Midlands	East Midlands	North-West	Yorks. and Humberside	Northern	Wales and Monmouth	Total
Over +14·5	No. of SMLAs	17	2	0	1	0	0	0	0	0	20
	Average per cent change per SMLA*	26·9	25·8	0·0	16·1	0·0	0·0	0·0	0·0	0·0	24·8
+14·5 to +9·5	No. of SMLAs	7	1	3	2	1	0	3	3	0	20
	Average per cent change per SMLA*	11·8	11·5	12·5	10·9	10·6	0·0	11·7	12·4	0·0	11·9
+9·5 to +5·3	No. of SMLAs	4	3	2	2	4	1	2	0	2	20
	Average per cent change per SMLA*	8·3	7·4	5·7	8·2	7·4	9·6	6·7	0·0	8·3	7·8
+5·3 to +1·6	No. of SMLAs	0	2	0	3	1	6	2	4	2	20
	Average per cent change per SMLA*	0·0	4·3	0·0	3·7	4·4	3·7	3·8	3·9	2·9	3·8
Under +1·6	No. of SMLAs	1	1	0	0	0	11	6	0	1	20
	Average per cent change per SMLA*	0·5	−0·2	0·0	0·0	0·0	−0·1	1·0	0·0	−10·0	0·3
Total	No. of SMLAs	29	9	5	8	6	18	13	7	5	100
	Average per cent change per SMLA*	6·4	8·3	9·5	8·6	6·8	1·5	3·3	6·1	4·4	5·6

* Average per cent change per SMLA $= \frac{\text{Aggregate absolute change 1951–61}}{\text{Aggregate population 1951}}$.

Table 5.9

SMLAs BY PERCENTAGE POPULATION CHANGE, 1961–1966, AND STANDARD REGION

Per cent pop. change 1961–66		Standard region: South East	South-West	East Anglia	West Midlands	East Midlands	North-West	Yorks. and Humberside	Northern	Wales and Monmouth	Total
Over +8·53	No. of SMLAs	15	1	0	0	2	2	0	0	0	20
	Average per cent change per SMLA*	12·9	11·3	0·0	0·0	10·0	10·7	0·0	0·0	0·0	12·1
+8·53 to +5·23	No. of SMLAs	8	3	1	3	2	2	1	0	0	20
	Average per cent change per SMLA*	7·3	7·5	5·6	7·1	5·9	7·3	7·1	0·0	0·0	7·1
+5·23 to +3·55	No. of SMLAs	3	2	4	3	0	3	3	1	1	20
	Average per cent change per SMLA*	4·1	5·0	4·6	4·2	0·0	4·5	4·6	3·8	4·8	4·5
+3·55 to +1·05	No. of SMLAs	1	2	0	1	2	4	5	3	2	20
	Average per cent change per SMLA*	1·5	2·3	0·0	2·1	3·1	2·4	1·3	2·3	2·2	2·1
Under +1·05	No. of SMLAs	2	1	0	1	0	7	4	3	2	20
	Average per cent change per SMLA*	−2·9	−0·5	0·0	0·9	0·0	−1·6	0·6	−0·4	−0·6	−1·9
Total	No. of SMLAs	29	9	5	8	6	18	13	7	5	100
	Average per cent change per SMLA*	1·2	5·4	4·7	3·0	5·8	0·3	1·5	0·7	1·7	1·8

* Average per cent change per SMLA $= \dfrac{\text{Aggregate absolute change 1961–66}}{\text{Aggregate population 1961}}$.

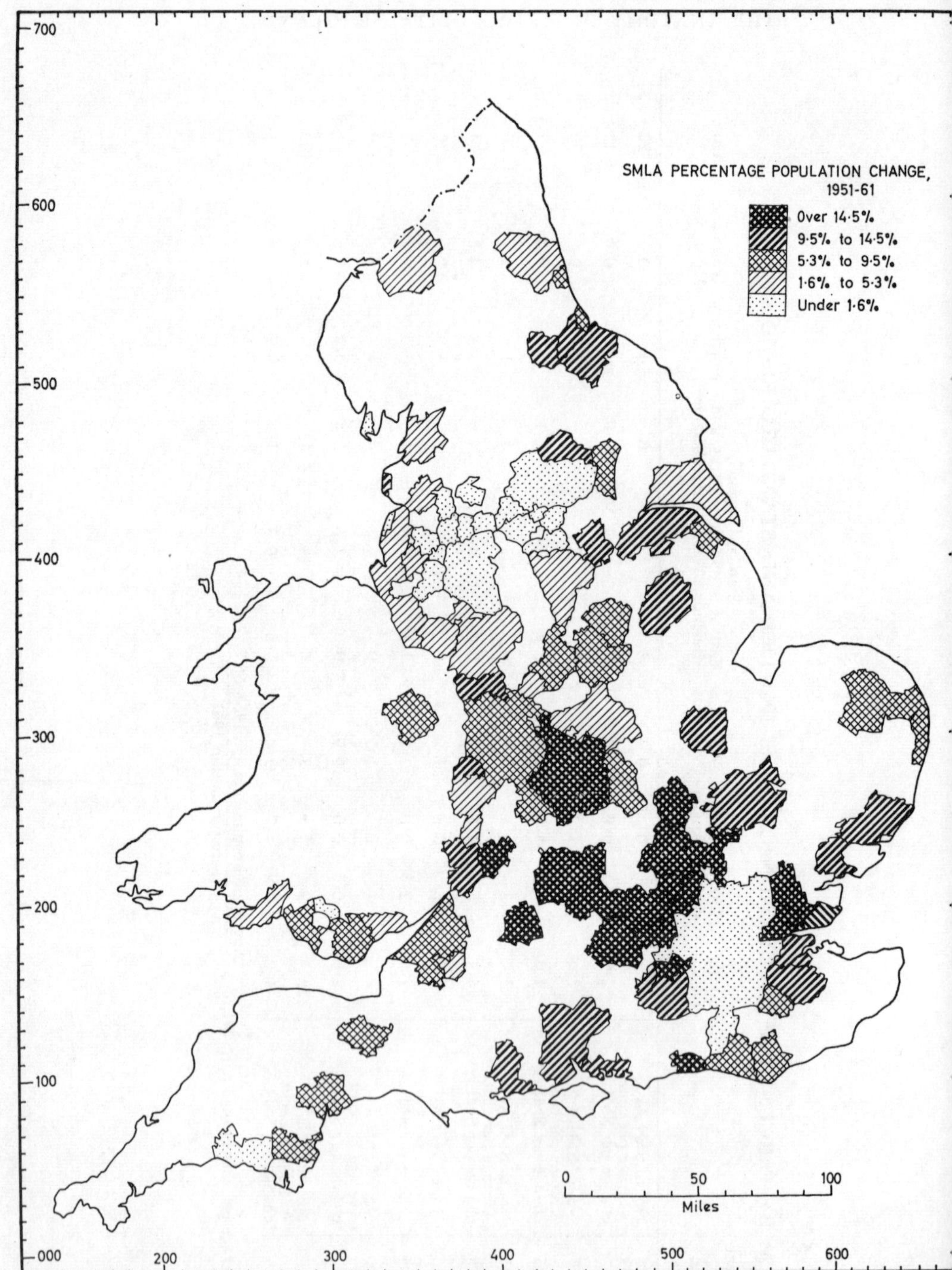

Figure 5.8 SMLAs, Percentage Population Change, 1951–1961

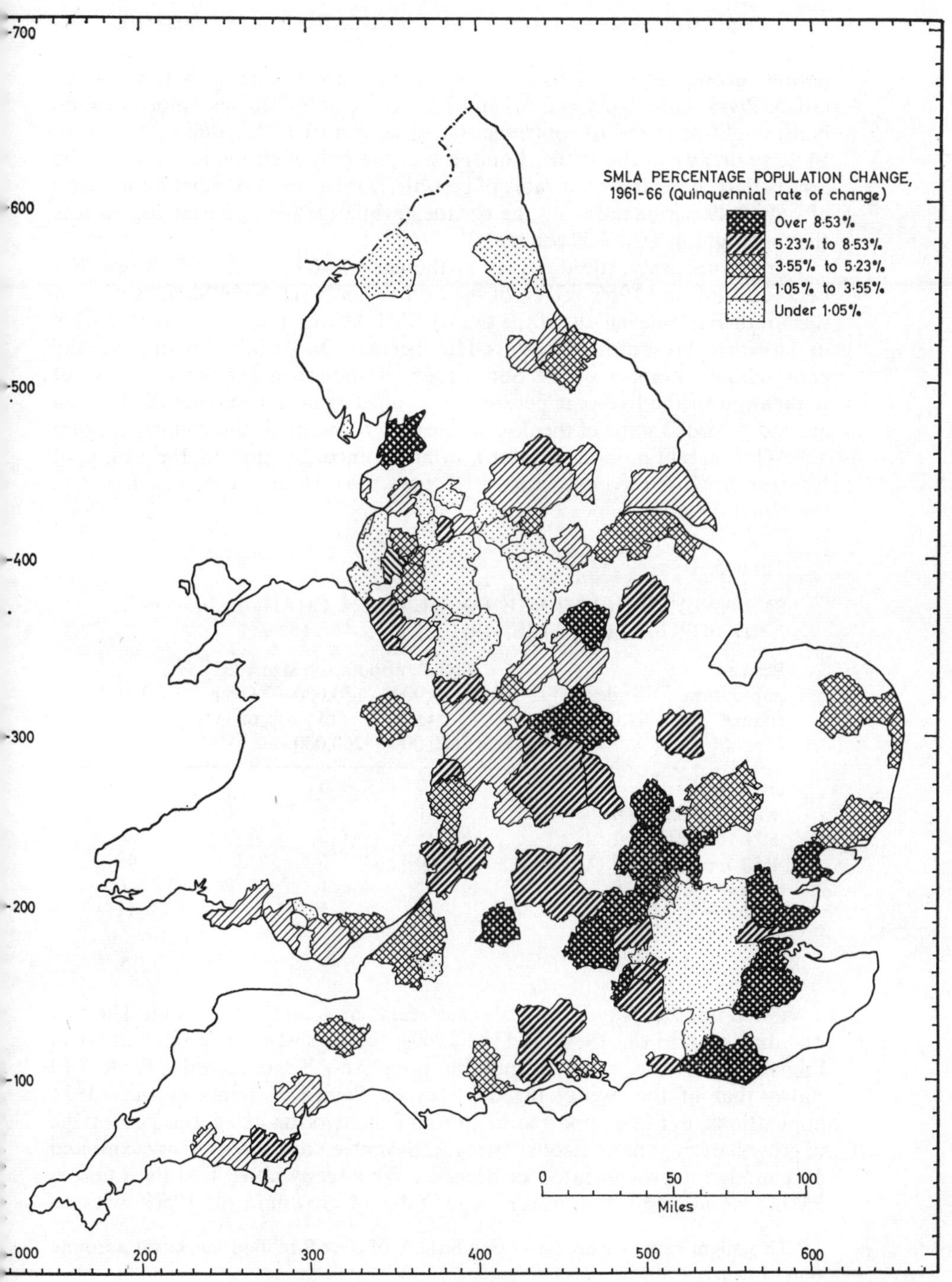

Figure 5.9 SMLAs, Percentage Population Change, 1961–1966

poorest growth show a striking contrast: they are Rhondda (bottom of the table), Plymouth (eighty-eighth) and London (eighty-fifth). No more striking index could be found to contradict the usual picture of London's dynamism. In fact, already in the 1950s, London was the only metropolitan area in the South-East to exhibit poor rates of growth; it recorded a population increase of only 0·49 per cent during the decade,[8] while the next poorest record was that of Brighton with 7·59 per cent.

The picture was little different in the early 1960s. Table 5.9 shows that between 1961 and 1966, fifteen of the twenty fastest growing SMLAs were in the South-East; eleven out of the twenty SMLAs with the poorest record were in the North-West or in Yorkshire-Humberside. Once again, London was the conspicuous anomaly in the South-East: it showed a 2·9 per cent loss of population in the five-year period, while once again the smaller SMLAs all around recorded some of the fastest rates of growth in all the country (Figure 5.9). One exception was Watford, which joined London in the group of fourteen SMLAs recording a loss. Of these SMLAs, six were to be found in the North-West.[9]

Table 5.10

SMLAs BY PERCENTAGE POPULATION CHANGE, 1951–1961, AND POPULATION SIZE, 1951

Per cent population change 1951–61	SMLA population size 1951					
	Under 92,000	92,000 to 115,000	115,000 to 170,000	170,000 to 260,000	Over 260,000	Total
Over +31	4	1	0	0	0	5
+21 to +31	4	1	1	3	0	9
+11 to +21	1	6	5	5	3	20
+1 to +11	9	9	10	6	15	49
−1 to +1	0	2	1	1	2	6
Under −1	2	1	3	5	0	11
Total	20	20	20	20	20	100

Viewed another way, London's case seems no longer anomalous. The fact was that both in the 1950s and the 1960s, the biggest metropolitan areas in England and Wales exhibited notably poor growth rate records. Table 5.10 shows that of the twenty biggest SMLAs classed in terms of their 1951 populations, not one appeared in either of the two top categories percentage of growth during the subsequent decade. Seventeen out of the twenty exhibited only moderate growth rates, or declines. We already noted that the London SMLA stood eighty-fifth in the league table of growth in the 1950s, with an

[8] This slight rate of increase in one SMLA of over 9 million marks an absolute gain of nearly 45,000.

[9] See p. 160 footnote 4 for a list.

increase of only 0·49 per cent. Manchester stood eighty-third (1·46 per cent), Leeds eighty-first (1·56 per cent), Newcastle seventy-second (3·57 per cent), and Liverpool seventieth (3·73 per cent). Only one of the six biggest SMLAs appeared in the top half of the growth league table: Birmingham, which with an 8·24 per cent increase stood forty-eighth. Conversely, it is evident that some of the smallest SMLAs showed the highest rates of growth; of the fourteen SMLAs showing the highest growth rates, ten were in the two smallest size categories in 1951. Three of these, of course, were the SMLAs based on the London new towns. All except Cheltenham and Swindon were in the Outer Metropolitan Area (Figure 5.8). Viewing all the small SMLAs as a whole, however, they exhibited very varying growth rates, from very good to very poor, with a tendency to cluster in the middle range. The fact is that the small SMLAs include some very varied cases, from the new towns at one extreme to the declining textile and mining areas of the North at the other.

Table 5.11

SMLAs BY PERCENTAGE POPULATION CHANGE, 1961–1966, AND POPULATION SIZE, 1961

Per cent population change 1961–66	SMLA population size 1961: Under 100,500	100,500 to 129,000	129,000 to 180,000	180,000 to 289,000	Over 289,000	Total
Over +15·5	2	0	0	1	0	3
+10·5 to +15·5	2	0	3	3	0	8
+5·5 to +10·5	6	11	5	4	3	29
+0·5 to +5·5	7	6	9	10	13	45
−0·5 to +0·5	0	2	1	2	1	6
Under −0·5	3	1	2	0	3	9
Total	20	20	20	20	20	100

Again, the same tendencies are visible in the 1960s (Table 5.11). Of the twenty biggest SMLAs, none appeared in the two top growth categories, while three appeared in the group of nine SMLAs constituting the poorest growth category, all of which in fact recorded declines. Four of the six biggest SMLAs were now actually recording declines during the quinquennium; London (minus 2·90 per cent) dropped to ninety-eighth in the growth league table, with only Burnley and Rhondda below;[10] Liverpool (minus

[10] And just as London's slight percentage growth during 1951–61 had represented a substantial absolute growth, so a 2·9 per cent decline concealed an absolute loss of over a quarter million.

2·08 per cent) stood next at ninety-seventh, Manchester (minus 1·42 per cent) was ninety-fifth and Newcastle (minus 0·50 per cent) was ninety-second. Thus, among the big SMLAs, only Birmingham and Leeds achieved even modest rates of growth. At the other extreme the smallest metropolitan areas once again showed a very mixed growth record, ranging from very good to very poor. Looking at it the other way round, it was notable that in this period the SMLAs with the best growth records were not by any means the smallest. Of the eleven with the best records of all (over 10·5 per cent growth in six years), no less than seven fell into the middle-size groups with between 129,000 and 289,000 people in 1961.[11] Of the three fastest-growing SMLAs in all England and Wales, all of which were in the South East, only one, Basildon, was a new town; the other two, Chelmsford and Reading, were both growing almost wholly through spontaneous migration to speculatively built housing for sale (Figure 5.9).

Summing up, it is clear that during the whole of the fifteen-year period from 1951 to 1966, two different tendencies were operating in SMLA growth in England and Wales. One was a *regional effect*: the dynamism of the South-East and the Midlands was causing a general growth of metropolitan areas in those regions, while the sluggish tendencies of the regional economies in Lancashire and Yorkshire were causing very poor rates of growth overall, with many individual cases of population loss. Tables 5·8 and 5·9 together show that the average rate of growth in the SMLAs of these two groups of regions were:

Area	1951–61	1961–66 (5 years)
South-East	6·4	2·8*
West Midlands	8·6	3·0
East Midlands	6·8	5·8
North-West	1·5	0·3
Yorkshire-Humberside	3·3	1·5

* Excluding London, the average growth for the SMLAs in the South-East during 1961–66 was 8·6 per cent.

The process is very graphically seen in Figures 5.8 and 5.9. The other trend, particularly striking in the South-East, was a *local decentralization effect*. The biggest SMLAs, which happened to sit in the centre of clusters of smaller SMLAs, tended to show growth records which were in general poorer than the regional average, and which became actual declines in many cases in the 1960s. Where the region was exhibiting general dynamism, this was accompanied by extraordinarily rapid growth of the peripheral SMLAs in the cluster around, as in the South-East around London or (on a more modest scale) in

[11] They were Luton, Reading, St Helens, High Wycombe, Maidstone, Swindon, and Aldershot. The other high growth-rate SMLAs, Chelmsford, Tunbridge Wells, Basildon, and Hemel Hempstead, were smaller.

the West Midlands around Birmingham. Where the region was exhibiting no dynamism at all, stagnation or decline at the centre was accompanied by similar stagnation or decline on the periphery, or by increases which approximately balanced the central decline.

REGIONAL TRENDS AND LOCAL RESIDUALS

These relationships between regional and local variations seem important enough for further analysis. Conventional maps are not easy to use for this. But it is possible to take the values of the data, locate them at the centres of gravity of the SMLAs to which they refer, and then produce by computer a smooth statistical surface which best fits them. From the map of the surface it is then possible to distinguish on the one hand the general regional *trend*, and on the other the unexplained *residuals*, or deviations from it, which are attributable to local variations.[12]

The map of percentage population trends during 1951–61 (Figure 5.10) shows a surface with a high point over London, dipping fairly regularly in all directions. Much of southern and midland England, and also Yorkshire, exhibits positive values; but there is a very pronounced zone of negative values centred on Lancashire, Cheshire and North Wales. In North Wales this can be explained by lack of data points, but for the North-West of England, where there are seventeen SMLAs in Lancashire alone, it represents the very poor growth performance of the region which has already been observed. The map of residuals (Figure 5.11) is dominated by quite small centres. London has a negative residual of over 10 per cent, but most other large cities have residuals which are much smaller than this; in other words they are near to the regional trend line. There are several positive residuals around London including a number of new and expanded towns; the older freestanding towns of the Outer Metropolitan Area, and the commuter settlements, mainly have negative residuals. In general, the northern half of the country shows far fewer residuals, indicating that many more places have values close to the regional trend.

The corresponding map for the quinquennium 1961–66 shows the values adjusted to a decennial rate for purposes of comparison and it has two interesting characteristics. First, figure 5.12 shows that though the high point of the trend surface remains fixed in the South-East, the slope downwards to the north and west has become more gentle, implying a reduction in the variation between regions. Second, Figure 5.13 reveals some interesting

[12] The system was first used widely in geological mapping. It is open to the objection that when it is based on an uneven distribution of data points there may not be a consistent separation between the regional and local component. But it has been shown experimentally that these effects are minimal when second or third order trend surfaces are used. Cf. J. R. Drewett and C. Smith, 'Variations in Curve-Fitting: Some Experiments with Trend Surface Analysis', *Seminar Proceedings: Trend Surface Analysis*. Planning and Transport Research and Computation Company, London (1969). This is available as: WP/4, PEP, London, 1969.

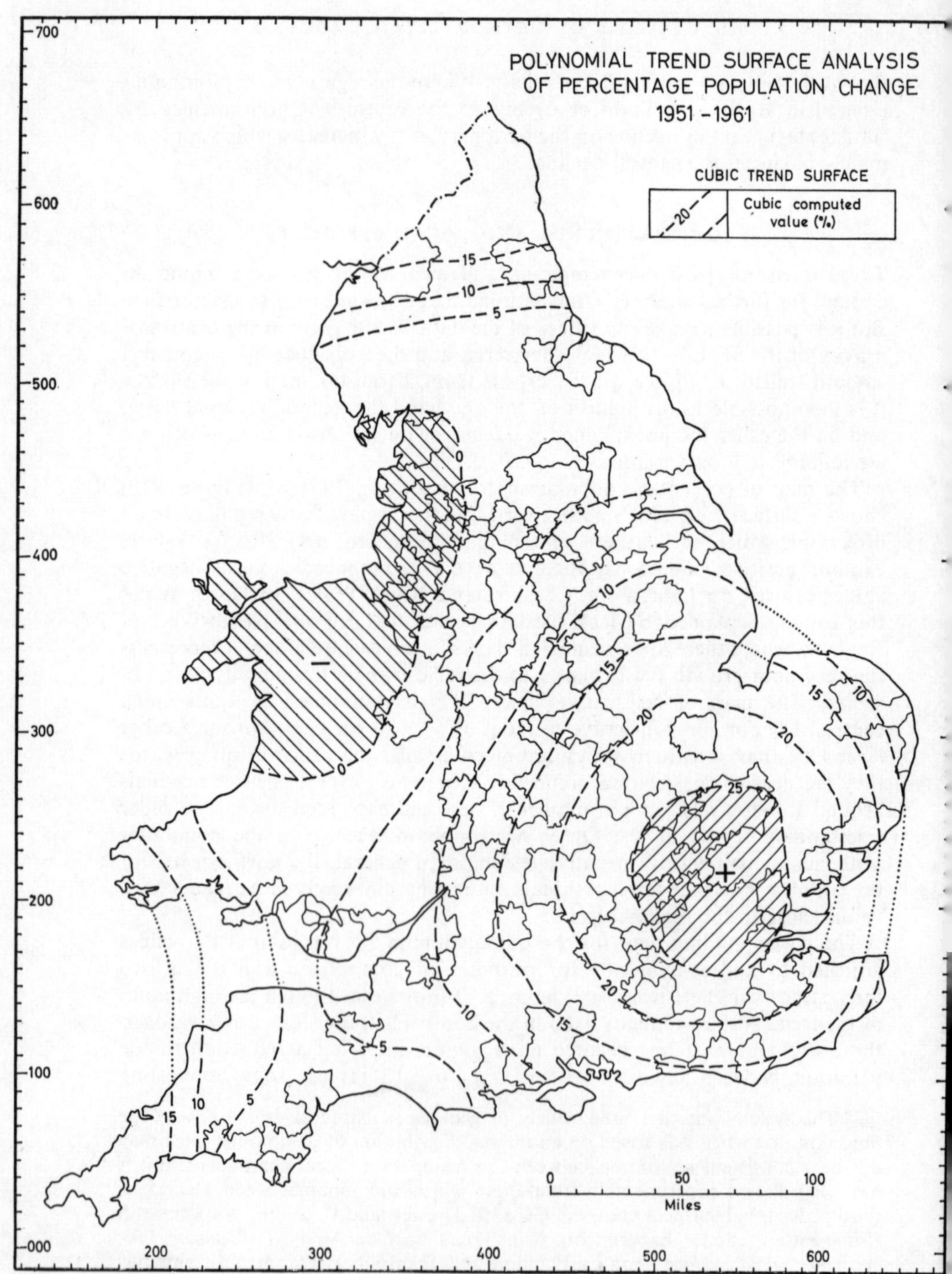

Figure 5.10 SMLAs, Polynomial Trend Surface of Percentage Population Change, 1951–1961

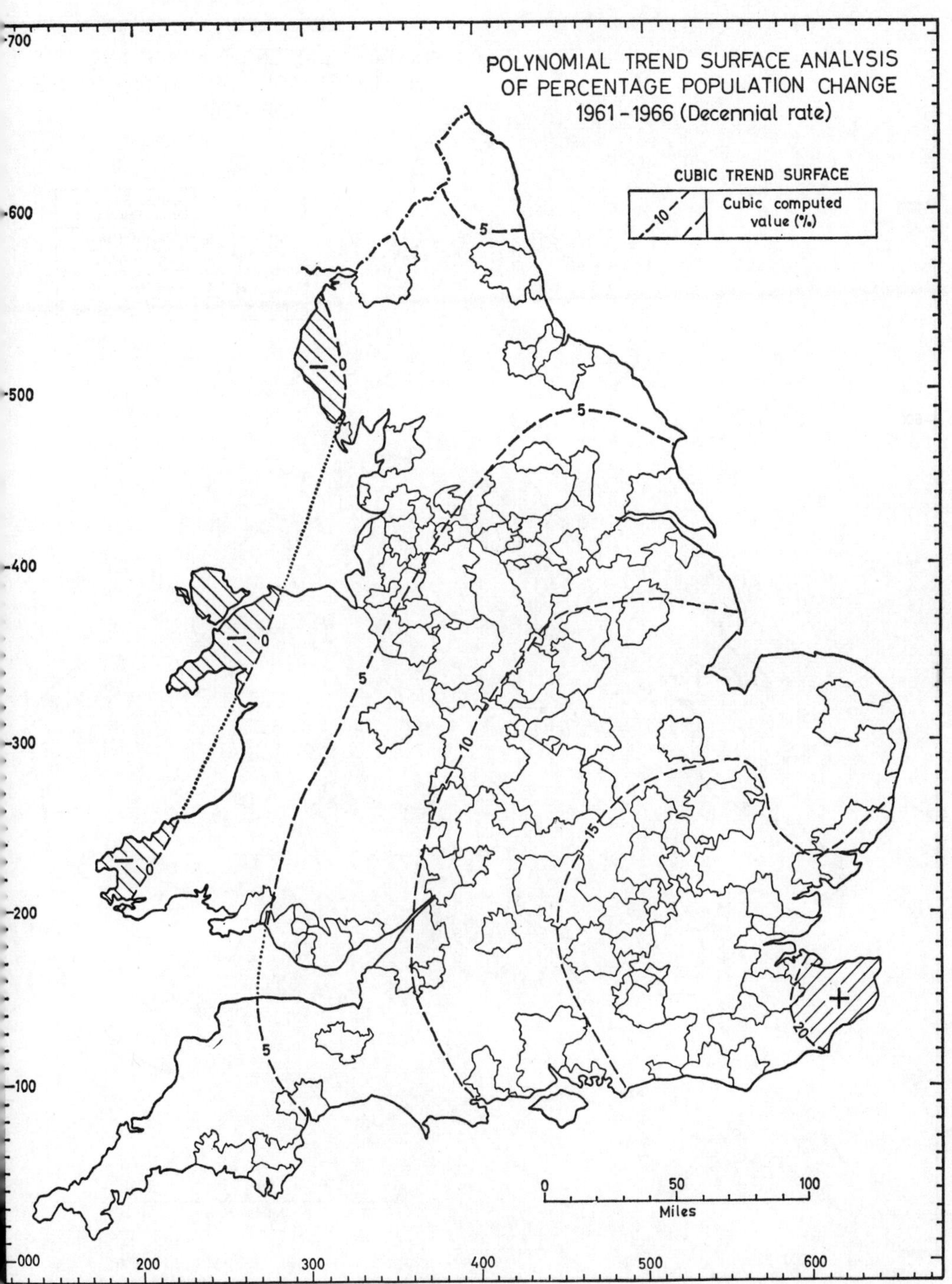

Figure 5.12 SMLAs, Polynomial Trend Surface Analysis of Percentage Population Change, 1961–1966

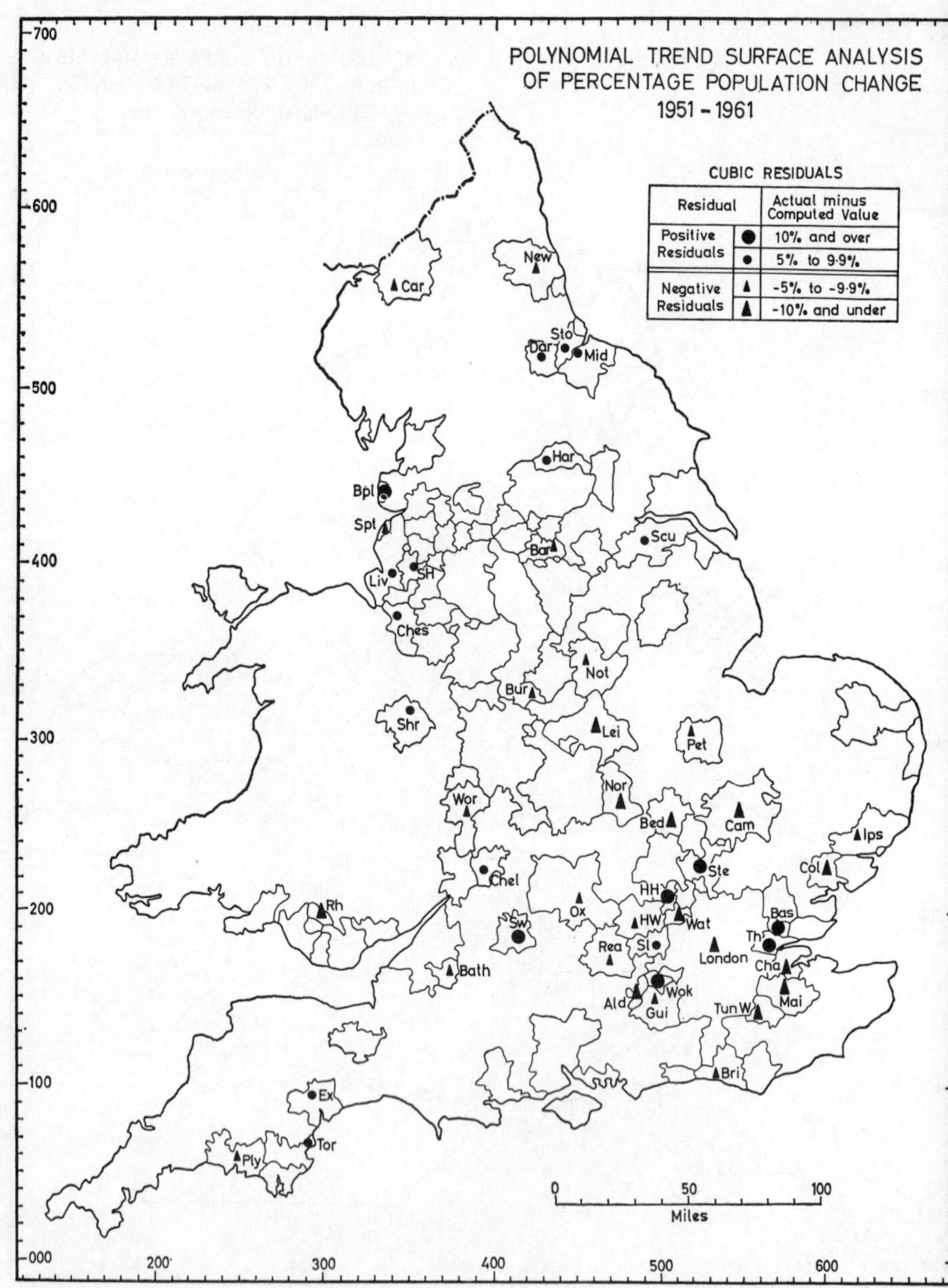

Figure 5.11 SMLAs, Residuals from Polynomial Trend Surface Analysis of Percentage Population Change, 1951–1961

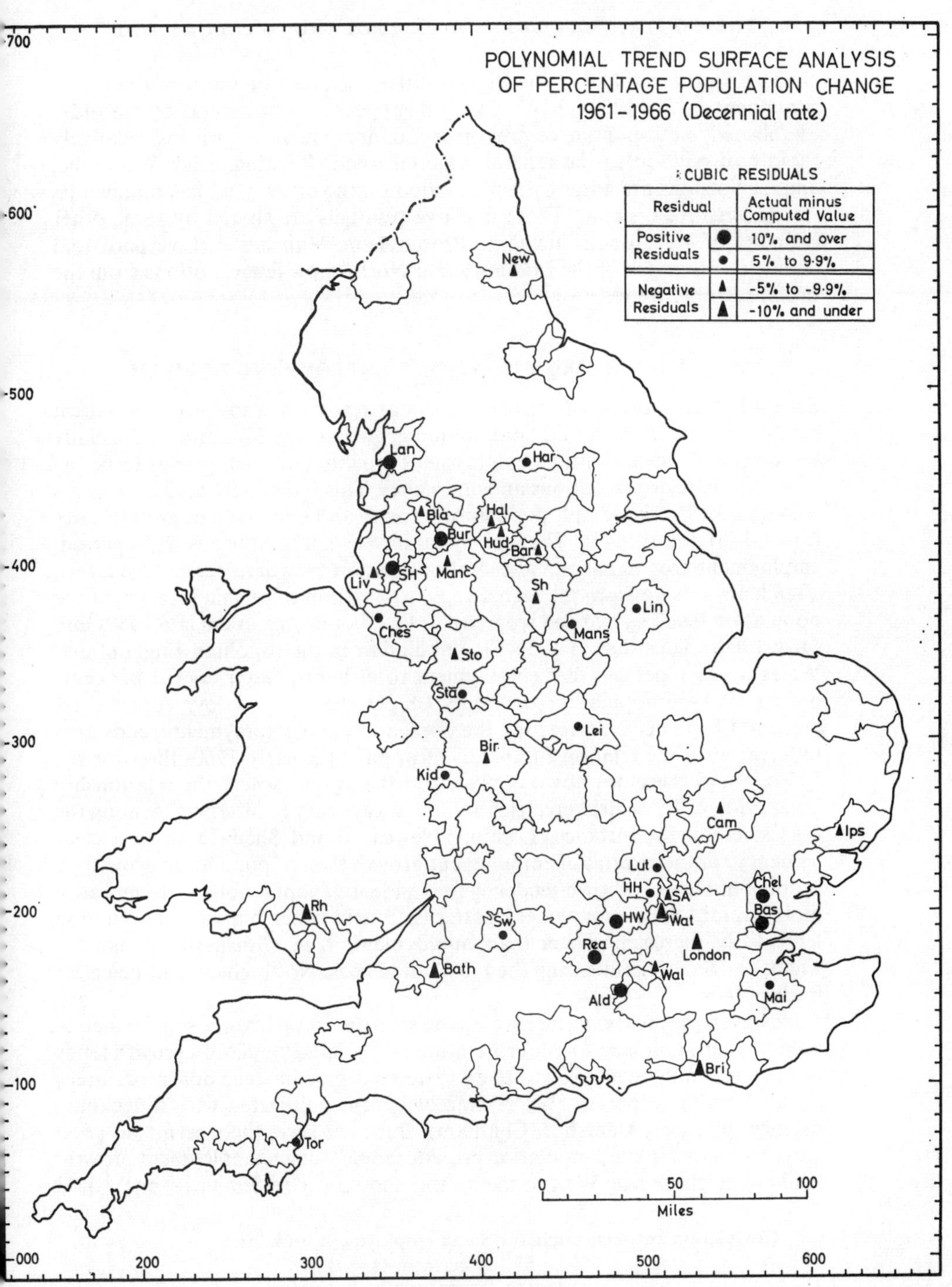

Figure 5.13 SMLAs, Residuals from Polynomial Trend Surface Analysis of Percentgea Population Change, 1961–1966

changes in the residuals. The high positive residuals of the new towns, so prominent in the 1950s, have mostly disappeared. But several of the older established metropolitan centres near London are now growing relatively rapidly in relation to the general regional trend: Reading, High Wycombe, and Chelmsford are among them. London on the other hand has retained its strong negative residual. These negative residuals are shared by some other big cities of Megalopolis including Birmingham, Manchester, Liverpool, and Sheffield. But much of the Midlands and North show few variations from the broad regional trends.

POPULATION GROWTH VERSUS EMPLOYMENT GROWTH

Except in a few special cases such as holiday resorts, spa towns or retirement centres, we would expect that population growth in any SMLA would usually be correlated closely with its employment growth, and such proves to be the case. But there are exceptions and anomalies. This is demonstrated by Figures 5.14 and 5.15 which graph population growth and employment growth rates for 1951–61 and 1961–66. They show that increasingly, in the post 1951 period, employment growth has run ahead of population growth in percentage terms, a tendency arising from the increasing participation of certain sections of the population (such as married women) in the labour force in the late 1950s and early 1960s. Thus during 1951–61, population in metropolitan England and Wales rose 5·6 per cent but employment rose slightly faster, by 6·3 per cent; during 1961–66 population grew only 1·8 per cent but employment rose 4·1 per cent (Table 5.1). Correlating the population and employment trends area by area, also, the relationship is less strong for the early 1960s than for the 1950s,[13] and there are obvious places on the graphs where the relationship breaks down. These discrepancies are not always easy to interpret. Among the biggest cities, for instance, London, Newcastle and Sheffield show a clear tendency for faster rates of employment growth than of population growth – a product of the well known tendency for residential populations to decentralize more rapidly than employment patterns. But in other big cities population tends to be increasing faster than employment, as in Manchester, Stoke-on-Trent, and Sunderland during the 1950s, and Leeds, Nottingham, and Leicester in the 1960s.

However, the most extreme discrepancies in the graph involve smaller metropolitan areas, and here too interpretation is difficult. Population growth tends to outrun employment growth to an extreme degree in some dormitory areas round London, especially where employment is associated with a declining defence function (Aldershot, Chatham). But even here, there seems no good reason why in Woking population growth should outrun employment growth, while in neighbouring Walton the reverse should occur. Similarly, one would

[13] Correlation between population and employment growth:
1951–61: 86 per cent (r = 0·93)
1961–66: 48 per cent (r = 0·69)

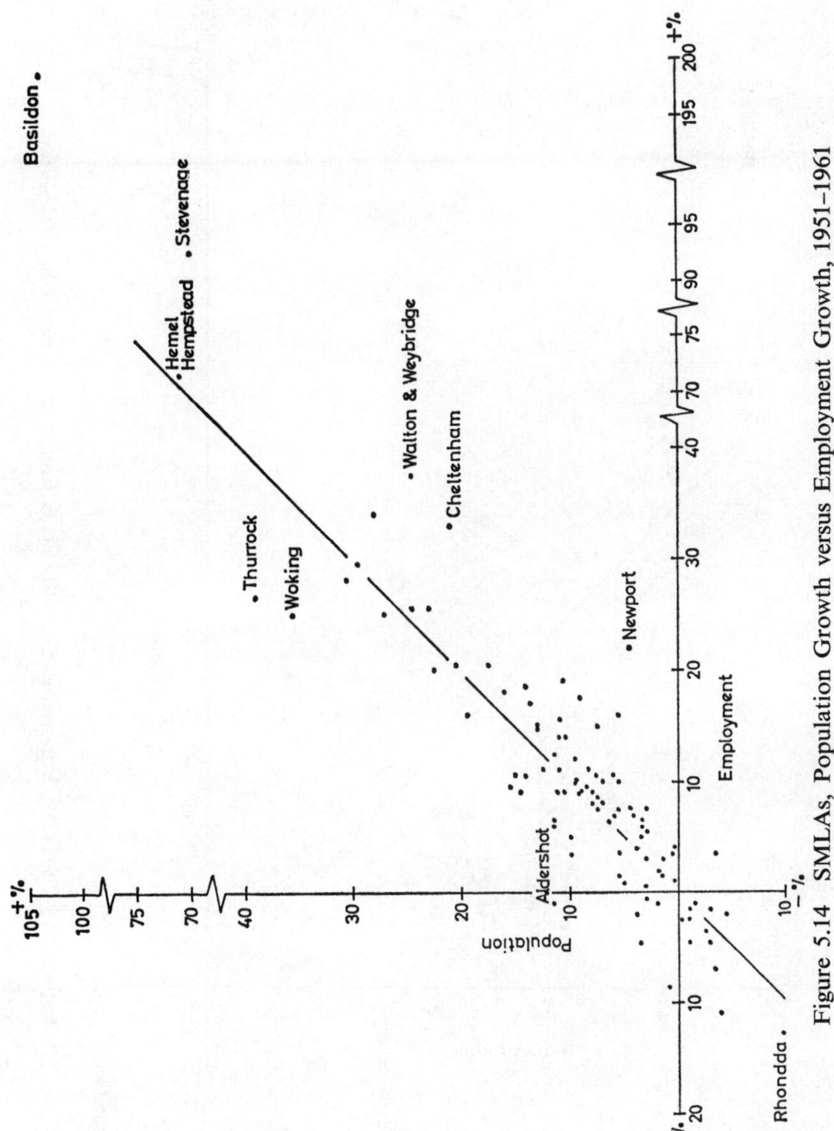

Figure 5.14 SMLAs, Population Growth versus Employment Growth, 1951–1961

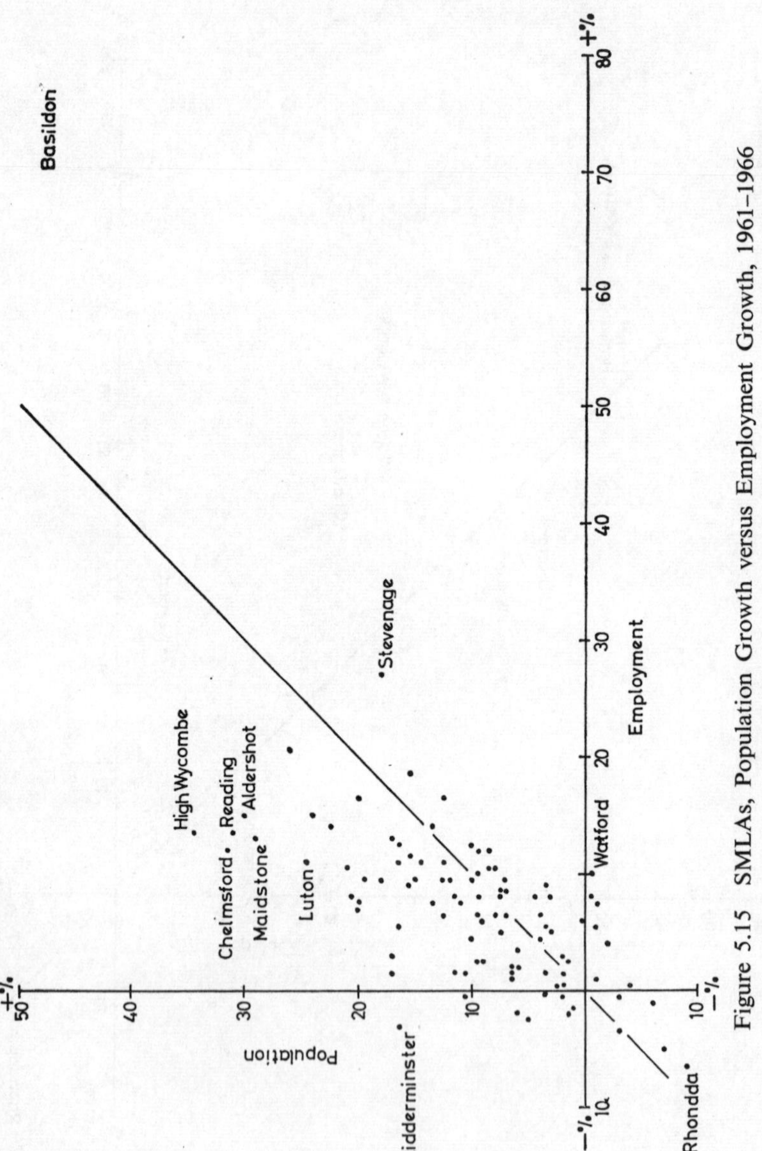

Figure 5.15 SMLAs, Population Growth versus Employment Growth, 1961–1966

expect population to increase faster than jobs in a seaside retirement centre like Worthing, except that the reverse occurs in nearby Brighton. Some county market towns (Ipswich, Gloucester, Oxford, Bedford) show a much faster rise of population than of jobs; other similar towns (Cheltenham, York) show the reverse. Almost the only clearly explicable features are the big excesses of new jobs at Newport and Port Talbot, which represent the building of new strip mills during the period under study.

NATIONAL AVERAGE AND LOCAL SHIFT

One particularly useful shorthand way of looking at these different trends in population and employment is in terms of their relationship to a national average. The method here is simple enough. First, areas suffering population or employment loss are separately treated, and are described as having an *absolute downward shift*. All areas with increases are then put on a scale, in which the national average increase is represented as zero. (Thus, if an area has a 10 per cent increase while the national increase is only 5 per cent, that area would have an *absolute upward shift* of 5 per cent. But if the area's increase was only 2 per cent, it would be recorded as having a *relative downward shift* of 3 per cent.) In other words, all areas experiencing *downward shifts* are either increasing less slowly than the average (*relative*) or are declining (*absolute*). The great advantage of such a device is in visual presentation, for it standardizes the pattern of each map in a way that makes for easy comparison between one and another.

The first pair of maps refer to 1951–61. Figure 5.16 refers to population and Figure 5.17 to employment. They show an extraordinarily close accordance throughout. In both, SMLAs with upward shifts were concentrated around London, in the Midlands and in parts of Yorkshire. In both, downward shifts were very largely restricted, one or two isolated peripheral areas and London apart, to Lancashire and the West Riding. But it was notable that both Lancashire and Yorkshire contained areas where population was continuing to rise, albeit more slowly than the national average, while employment was actually declining.

The second pair of maps refer to the quinquennium 1961–66. Figure 5.18 refers to population and Figure 5.19 to employment. They show a rather different picture. A great number of SMLAs in the South and Midlands, as before, have upward shifts in both population and employment. But there are now notable illustrations of SMLAs where the growth of employment is more pronounced than that of population. London and Liverpool had a relative downward shift in employment (i.e. jobs were increasing less rapidly than in the nation as a whole) but an absolute decline in population. Birmingham had a relative downward shift in population but an upward shift in employment. Manchester and several other areas in the North-West had absolute losses in both people and jobs. But this was quite a rare condition.

Finally, Figure 5.20 tries to bring all this information together, and also

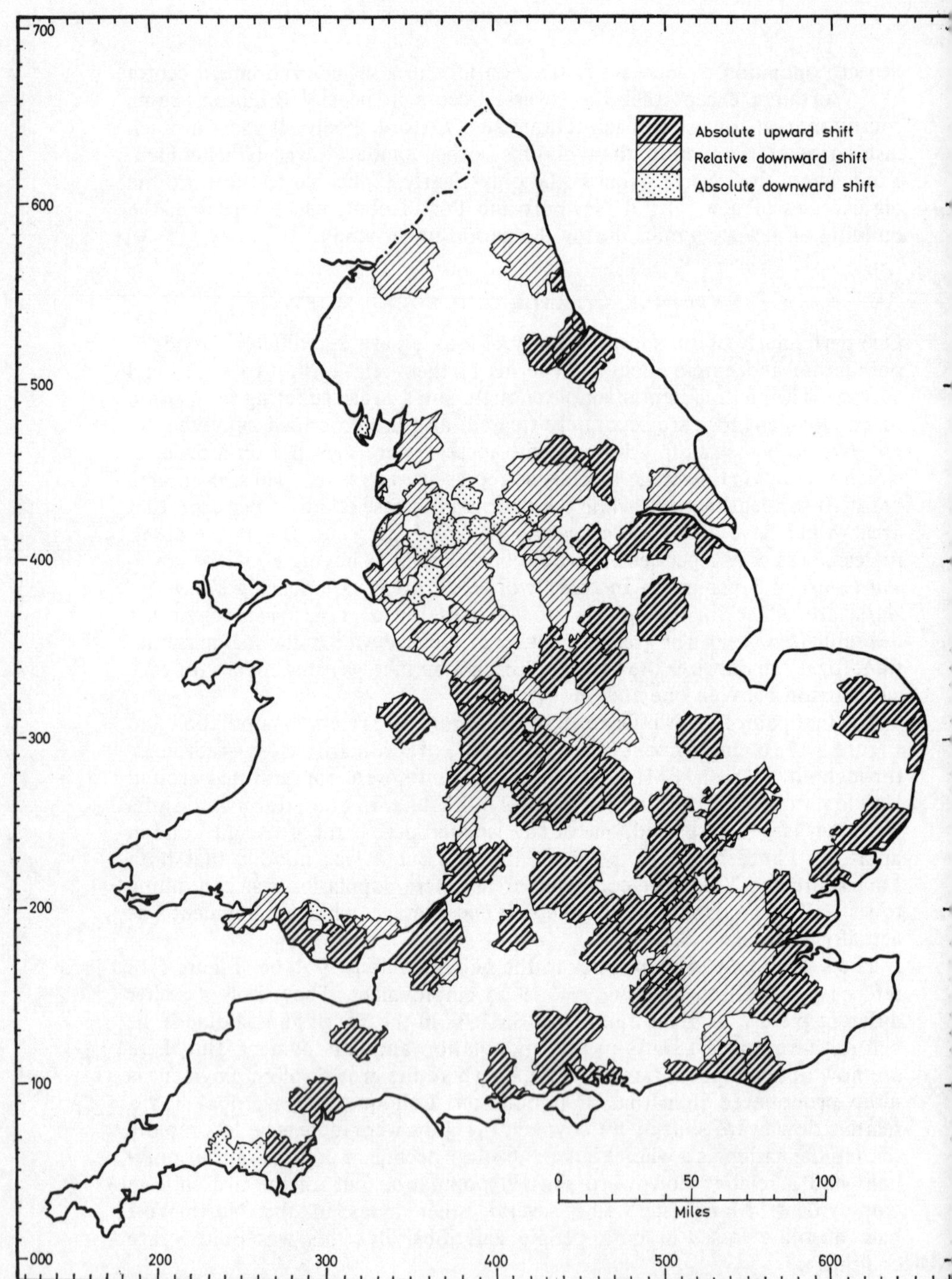

Figure 5.16 SMLAs, Population Shift Analysis, 1951–1961

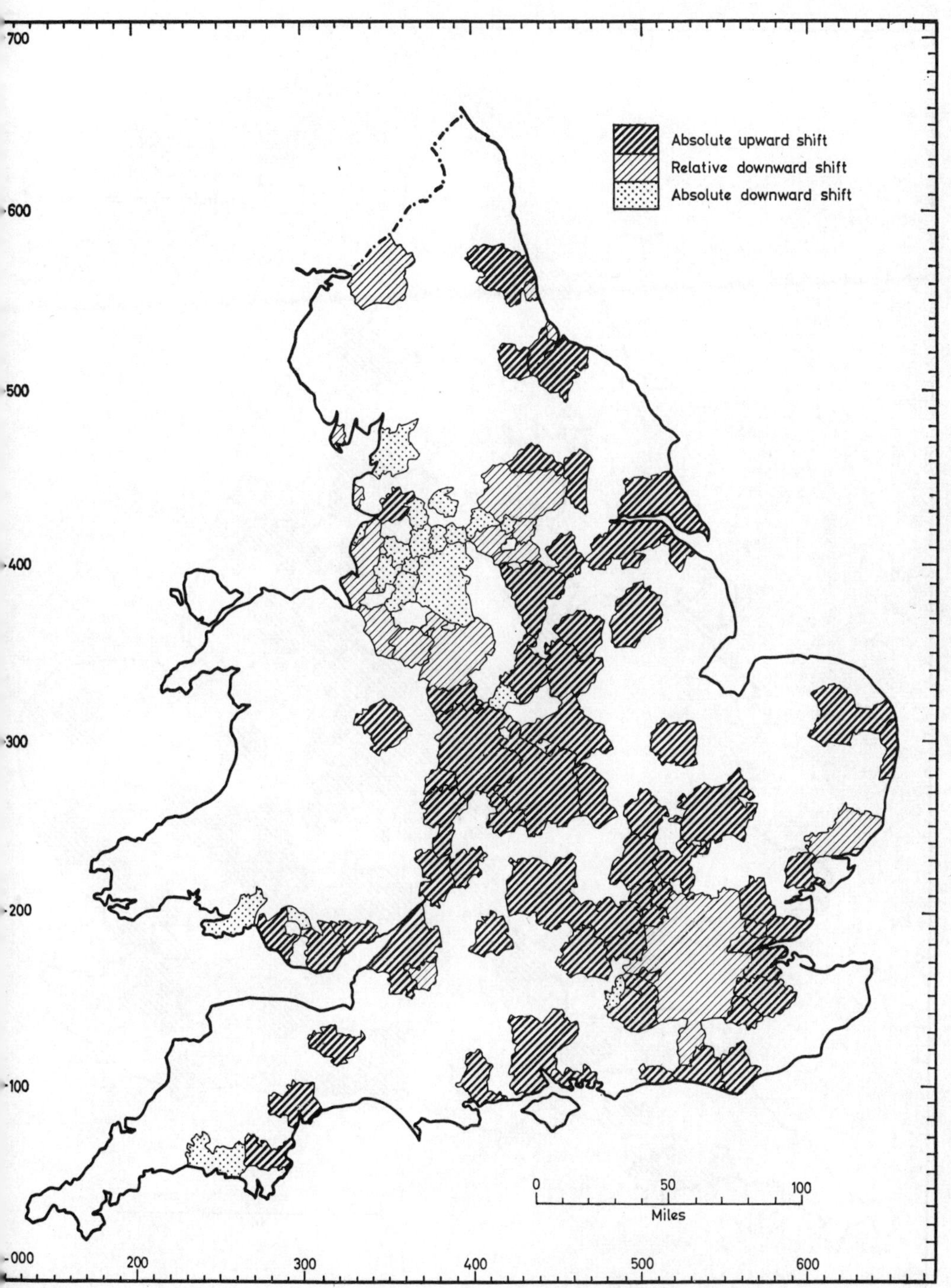

Figure 5.17 SMLAs, Employment Shift Analysis, 1951–1961

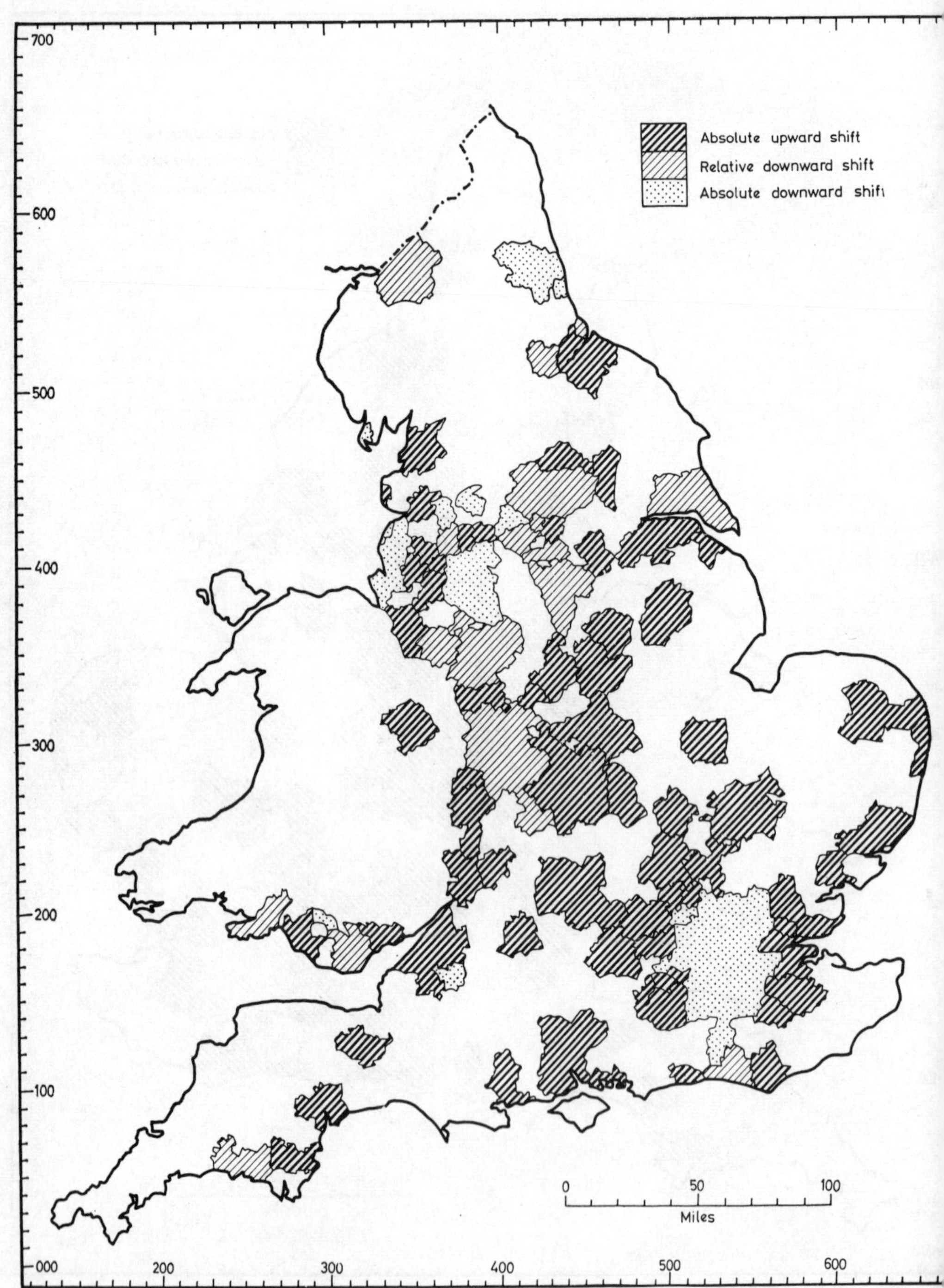

Figure 5.18 SMLAs, Population Shift Analysis, 1961–1966

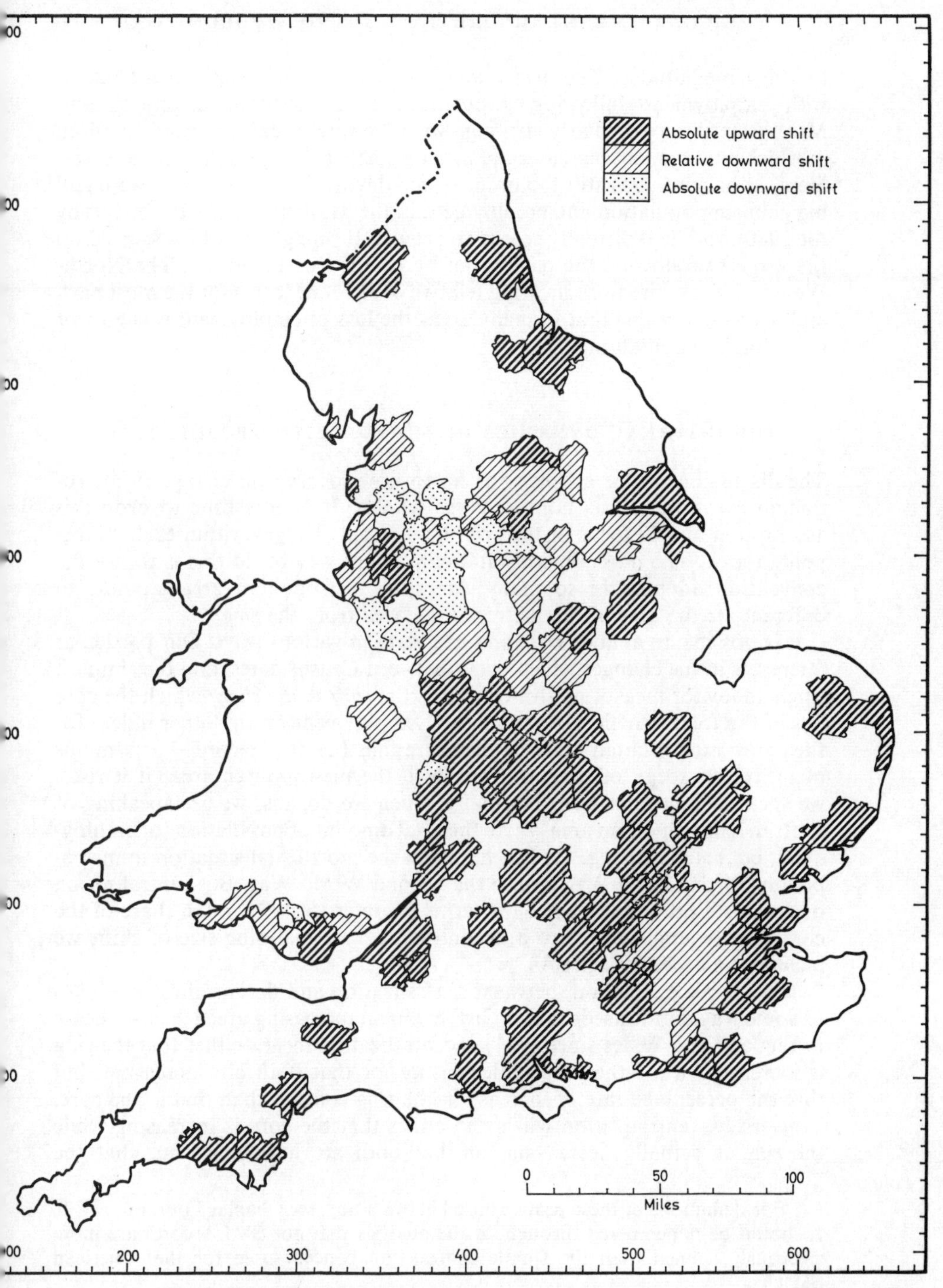

Figure 5.19 SMLAs, Employment Shift Analysis, 1961–1966

to show magnitudes. The accelerating population and employment losses, with employment following population, from London, Liverpool, and Manchester are particularly striking. So is the ring of gains around London, in which employment increases are usually smaller than population increases. Here, imbalance, was still the order of the day in the 1960s. There were still big gains in population and employment in the Midlands in the 1950s, but by the 1960s both had virtually ceased to grow in Birmingham, which seemed on the verge of following the pattern set by London or Liverpool. The North-West and Yorkshire were showing relative or absolute losses for the most part, and it was noticeable that in many areas the loss of employment was greater than that of population.

THE INTERNAL DYNAMICS OF METROPOLITAN POPULATION

The discussion in this chapter has up to now focused on change in metropolitan areas viewed as homogeneous wholes. It is now time to drop this assumption and to focus instead on the internal changes within each metropolitan area. The most obvious and convenient way to do this is to use the convention adopted in so many American metropolitan area studies: to differentiate the *core* of the metropolitan area from the *ring*.*

It is possible to analyse core and ring data in various ways. Our particular interest is in the changes which occur between Census dates, and the simplest single index for measuring this change is the *shift in the share* which the core has of the total (whether of population, employment or any other index) for the entire metropolitan area. If this share falls (i.e. it is recorded as a minus quantity) we speak of decentralization in the metropolitan area; if it rises, we speak of centralization. Normally, when we do this, we are speaking of shifts in a metropolitan area where the total amount of population (or employment, etc.) is increasing, for this has been the most usual situation in metropolitan England and Wales since the Second World War. But centralization or decentralization, as we use the terms (to refer to shifts in the share of the core) can be applied also to a declining area. In analysing size of shift, we include the declining SMLAs.

This simple distinction, between centralization and decentralization, takes us some way, but it needs taking further. In an increasing area (the usual case in England and Wales since 1931) decentralization means either that the ring is increasing while the core is decreasing, or that both are increasing, but that the percentage rate of increase in the ring is faster than that in the core. Conversely, centralization will mean either that the core is increasing while the ring is actually decreasing, or that both are increasing, but that the

* For definitions of these terms as used in this study, see Chapter Four, pp. 127–8. It should be remembered throughout the analysis that our SMLA cores are more rigorously defined than the simple central city concept used for the American SMLAs.

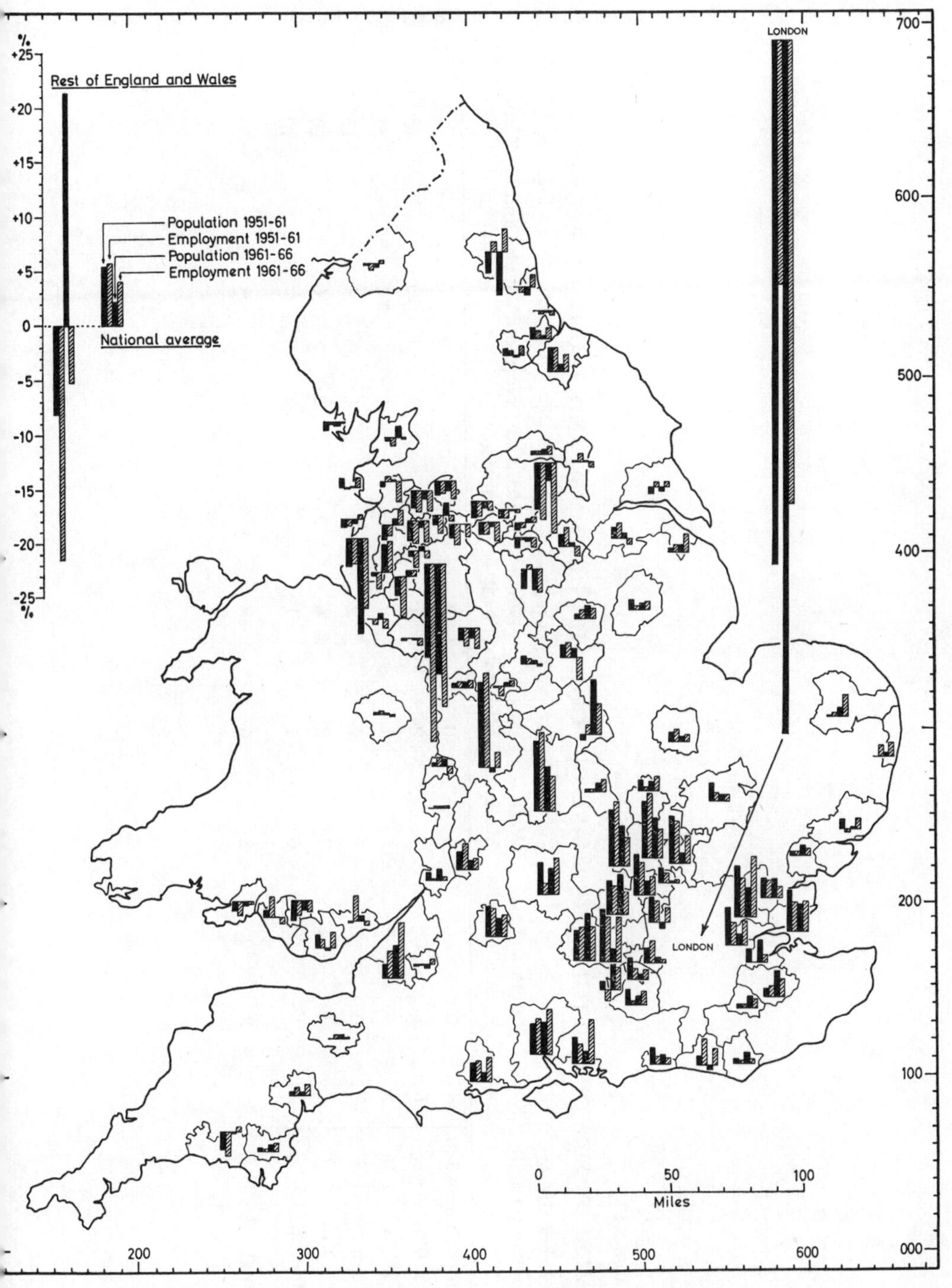

Figure 5.20 SMLAs, Population and Employment Shift Analysis Deviations from National Average, 1951–1961 and 1961–1966

Table 5.12

SMLAs BY SIZE OF SHIFT IN CORE SHARE OF POPULATION, 1951–1961, AND STANDARD REGION

Per cent size of population shift 1951–61	Standard region									
	South-East	South-West	East Anglia	West Midlands	East Midlands	North-West	Yorks. and Humberside	Northern	Wales and Monmouth	Total
More than +3·0	4	0	0	1	0	0	2	0	0	7
+1·0 to +3·0	6	1	2	1	0	1	1	1	2	15
−1·7 to +1·0	5	5	2	4	1	7	5	3	1	33
−3·0 to −1·7	7	0	0	0	2	2	2	0	1	15
−5·3 to −3·0	2	2	1	2	2	6	3	2	0	20
More than −5·3	5	1	0	0	1	1	0	1	1	10
Total	29	9	5	8	6	18	13	7	5	100

Table 5.13

SMLAs BY SIZE OF SHIFT IN CORE SHARE OF POPULATION, 1961–1966, AND STANDARD REGION

Per cent size of population shift 1961–66	Standard region									
	South-East	South-West	East Anglia	West Midlands	East Midlands	North-West	Yorks. and Humberside	Northern	Wales and Monmouth	Total
More than +0·50	3	0	0	0	0	0	0	0	0	3
−0·85 to +0·50	2	2	1	2	1	1	2	2	1	14
−1·50 to −0·85	4	2	0	2	0	2	4	1	1	16
−2·65 to −1·50	9	1	3	3	2	3	3	1	2	27
−3·75 to −2·65	4	1	0	1	1	9	1	3	0	20
More than −3·75	7	3	1	0	2	3	3	0	1	20
Total	29	9	5	8	6	18	13	7	5	100

percentage rate of increase in the core is faster than that in the ring.[14] From this it is possible to create a simple typology:

1 Decreasing areas:
  1a Centralizing (positive shift)
  1b Decentralizing (negative shift)

2 Increasing areas:
  2a Absolutely centralizing (positive shift) (Core increasing, ring decreasing)
  2b Relatively centralizing (positive shift) (Core and ring increasing, core relatively faster than ring)

[14] It is necessary to specify percentage rates of change here. In many cases, where the core has a very large share of the total SMLA population at the start of a period while the ring has a very small share, the absolute increase in the core in the subsequent period will often be greater than the absolute increase in the ring; the core will thereby take a large share of the total increase. But so long as the percentage rate of growth is greater in the ring, then the ring will record a larger percentage of the SMLA total at the end of the period than at the start, and this is what we mean by relative decentralization. The following cases will illustrate:

(1) Situation with a relative centralization of 1 per cent (positive shift + 1 per cent)

	1951		1951–61			1961	
	Amount '000s	Per cent total amount	Increase absolute '000s	Per cent	Per cent total increase	Amount '000s	Per cent total amount
Core	70	70	15	(21·4)	75	85	71
Ring	30	30	5	(16·7)	25	35	29
SMLA	100	100	20	(20·0)	100	120	100

(2) Situation with a relative decentralization of 2·5 per cent (negative shift −2·5 per cent)

	1951		1951–61			1961	
	Amount '000s	Per cent total amount	Increase absolute '000s	Per cent	Per cent total increase	Amount '000s	Per cent total amount
Core	90	90	15	(16·7)	75	105	87·5
Ring	10	10	5	(50·0)	25	15	12·5
SMLA	100	100	20	(20·0)	100	120	100

In both cases, the absolute increase is far greater in the core, and is in fact 75 per cent of total SMLA increase. The sole reason why in the first case there is centralization, and in the second decentralization, is that in the first the percentage rate of increase is greater in the core than in the ring, while in the second the reverse is true.

It follows from this analysis that while the size of shift analysis may include declining areas, the type of shift analysis used here only includes increasing areas. In the type of share tables, declining areas are shown therefore as a separate category.

2c Relatively decentralizing (negative shift) (Core and ring increasing, ring relatively faster than core)
2d Absolutely decentralizing (negative shift) (Core decreasing, ring increasing)

Notice that this classification says nothing about the actual *rates* of change involved, only about the relationship of those rates to each other. For some purposes it is useful to know about rates too. But for many purposes of analysis it is sufficient to fix first the general rate of growth of the metropolitan area as a whole, and then to treat the internal changes in terms solely of the relationship between changes in the core and in the ring. In the analysis that follows, we shall use first a 'size of shift' analysis and second a 'type of shift analysis'.

The great majority of SMLAs in England and Wales, both in the 1950s and the early 1960s, were decentralizing their populations. Sixty-eight out of 100 metropolitan areas in the decade 1951–61, no less than ninety-four out of 100 in the quinquennium 1961–66, recorded a negative shift of the core's share in the total SMLA population. And this process was becoming more pronounced. During 1951–61, thirty out of the sixty-eight decentralizing areas recorded negative shifts of 3 per cent or more but by 1961–66, no less than sixty-seven out of the ninety-four recorded shifts of more than 3 per cent (decennial rate) while fully twenty recorded shifts of over 7·5 per cent. Tables 5.12 and 5.13 and Figures 5.21 and 5.22 show that there was a certain tendency for the centralizing SMLAs to concentrate in the South-East in the 1950s, though this was much less marked in the 1960s. Curiously, though, the South-East also had a high concentration of the most rapidly decentralizing areas, both in the 1950s and the 1960s.[15]

More striking perhaps is the relationship between rates of decentralization and size of SMLA (Tables 5.14 and 5.15). The very big SMLAs, both in the 1950s and the 1960s, showed a very strong tendency to rapid decentralization; the moderately sized SMLAs tended to have moderate rates of decentralization, while most of the cases of marked centralization were among the smallest size group. This indicates that decentralization becomes necessary when an SMLA reaches a certain size. The smaller SMLAs which recorded centralization, it should be noticed, included several areas based on new towns, where the patterns of population growth were quite abnormal during both periods.

[15] The most extreme cases of centralization were temporary phenomena caused by the building up of the new towns, while the older-established centres often tended to show persistent and strong decentralization:

	Shift in share of core	
	1951–61	1961–66
Stevenage	29·09	8·16
Hemel Hempstead	17·24	1·71
Southend	−8·76	−5·40
Reading	−5·87	−4·34

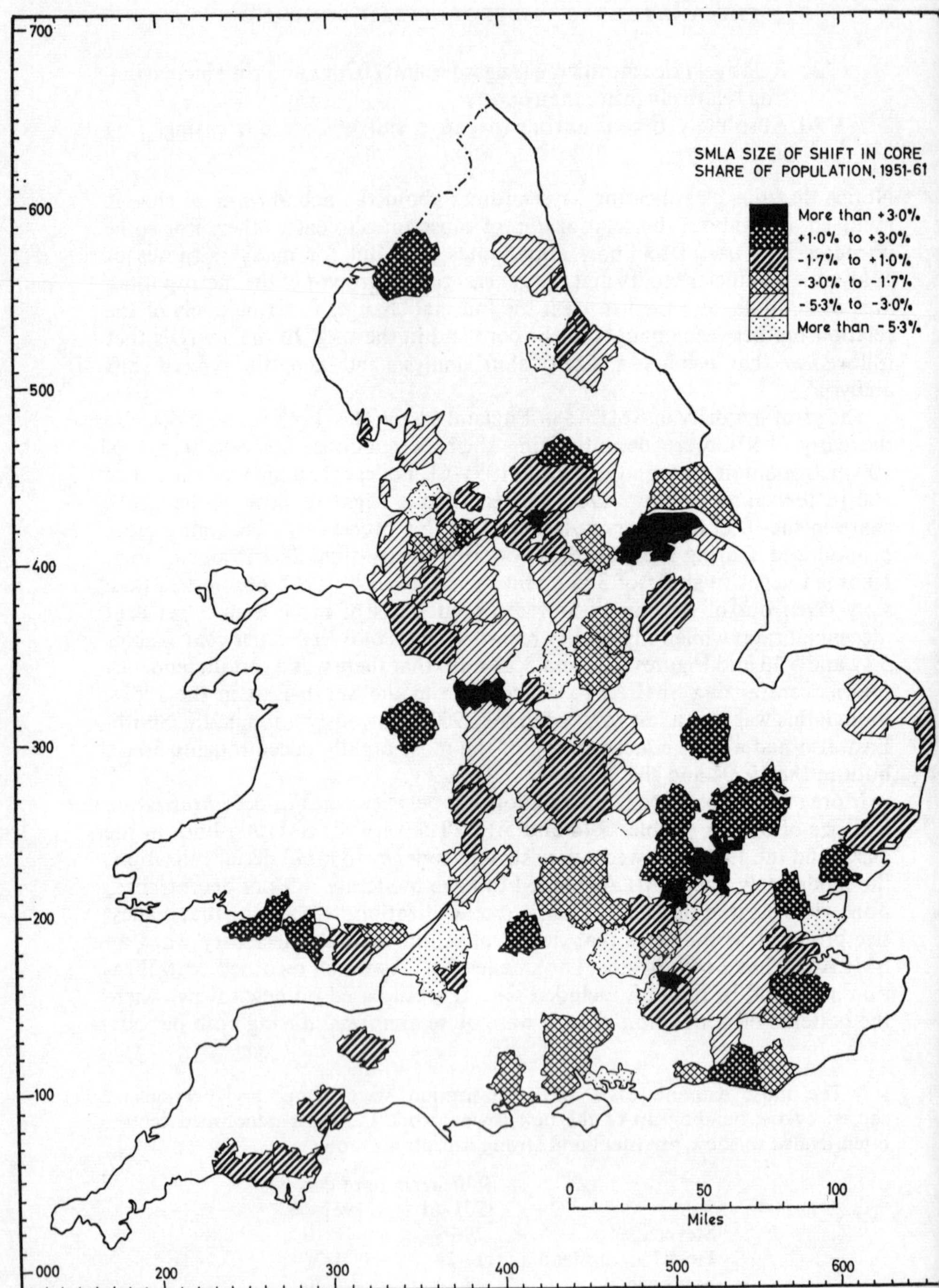

Figure 5.21 SMLAs, Size of Shift in Core Share of Population, 1951–1961

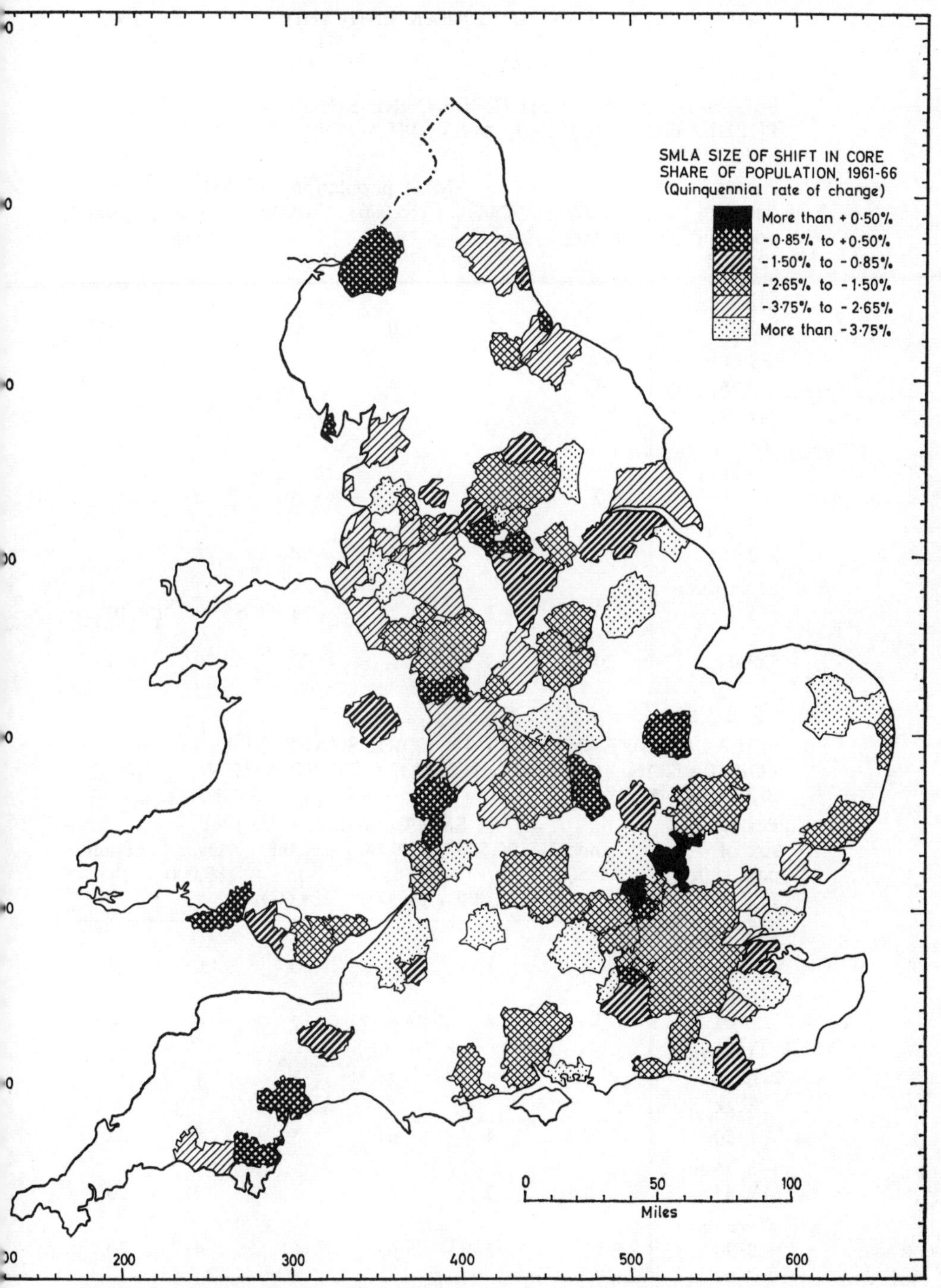

Figure 5.22 SMLAs, Size of Shift in Core Share of Population, 1961–1966

Table 5.14

SMLAs BY SIZE OF SHIFT IN CORE SHARE OF POPULATION, 1951–1961, AND SMLA POPULATION SIZE, 1951

Per cent size of pop. shift 1951–61	SMLA population size 1951: Under 92,000	92,000 to 115,000	115,000 to 170,000	170,000 to 260,000	Over 260,000	Total
More than +3·0	5	2	0	0	0	7
+1·0 to +3·0	4	4	4	2	1	15
−1·7 to +1·0	7	7	9	6	4	33
−3·0 to −1·7	2	2	2	5	4	15
−5·3 to −3·0	2	3	3	4	8	20
More than −5·3	0	2	2	3	3	10
Total	20	20	20	20	20	100

Table 5.15

SMLAs BY SIZE OF SHIFT IN CORE SHARE OF POPULATION, 1961–1966, AND SMLA POPULATION SIZE, 1961

Per cent size of pop. shift 1961–66	SMLA population size 1961: Under 100,500	100,500 to 129,000	129,000 to 180,000	180,000 to 289,000	Over 289,000	Total
More than +0·50	2	1	0	0	0	3
−0·85 to +0·05	4	4	4	2	0	14
−1·50 to −0·85	4	6	2	3	1	16
−2·65 to −1·50	4	4	6	5	8	27
−3·75 to −2·65	5	2	2	4	7	20
More than −3·75	1	3	6	6	4	20
Total	20	20	20	20	20	100

This last point also explains a striking feature in Tables 5.16 and 5.17, that most of the cases of centralization occured in SMLAs exhibiting exceptionally rapid growth, such as new towns. Strong decentralization, on the other hand, affected fast-growing and slow-growing SMLAs alike, though there was a striking tendency in the 1960s for some of the fastest-decentralizing areas to be also very fast-growing, almost a reversal of the tendency in the previous decade.

Table 5.16

SMLAs BY SIZE OF SHIFT IN CORE SHARE OF POPULATION, 1951–1961, AND SMLA PERCENTAGE POPULATION CHANGE, 1951–1961

	Per cent population change 1951–61					
Per cent size of population shift 1951–61	Under +1·6	+1·6 to +5·3	+5·3 to +9·5	+9·5 to +14·5	Over +14·5	Total
More than +3·0	1	0	0	2	4	7
+1·0 to +3·0	1	2	4	4	4	15
−1·7 to +1·0	11	8	4	6	4	33
−3·0 to −1·7	3	2	4	3	3	15
−5·3 to −3·0	3	7	6	2	2	20
More than −5·3	1	1	2	3	3	10
Total	20	20	20	20	20	100

Table 5.17

SMLAs BY SIZE OF SHIFT IN CORE SHARE OF POPULATION, 1961–1966, AND SMLA PERCENTAGE POPULATION CHANGE, 1961–1966

	Per cent population change 1961–66					
Per cent size of population shift 1961–66	Under +1·05	+1·05 to +3·55	+3·55 to +5·23	+5·23 to +8·53	Over +8·53	Total
More than +0·50	0	0	0	0	3	3
−0·85 to +0·50	6	2	1	5	0	14
−1·50 to −0·85	5	2	3	3	3	16
−2·65 to −1·50	3	6	8	8	2	27
−3·75 to −2·65	5	6	3	2	4	20
More than −3·75	1	4	5	2	8	20
Total	20	20	20	20	20	100

One obvious hypothesis about rates of decentralization is that they are related to the previously existing degree of concentration in the core: the greater the concentration, the greater the subsequent tendency to dispersion. However, Tables 5.18 and 5.19 show very conclusively that no general tendency of this kind existed in British SMLAs in these periods under consideration. Indeed, they show no general tendency at all. More fruitful is the hypothesis that rapid decentralization is associated with the higher-density

Table 5.18

SMLAs BY SIZE OF SHIFT IN CORE SHARE OF POPULATION, 1951–1961, AND CORE SHARE OF POPULATION, 1951

	Per cent core share of population 1951					
Per cent size of population shift 1951–61	Under 48·3	48·3 to 58·0	58·0 to 66·5	66·5 to 73·2	Over 73·2	Total
More than +3·0	3	1	0	2	1	7
+1·0 to +3·0	3	4	4	4	0	15
−1·7 to +1·0	6	8	6	5	8	33
−3·0 to −1·7	6	1	2	2	4	15
−5·3 to −3·0	1	3	6	6	4	20
More than −5·3	1	3	2	1	3	10
Total	20	20	20	20	20	100

Table 5.19

SMLAs BY SIZE OF SHIFT IN CORE SHARE OF POPULATION, 1961–1966, AND CORE SHARE OF POPULATION, 1961

	Per cent core share of population 1961					
Per cent size of population shift 1961–66	Under 48·10	48·10 to 57·75	57·75 to 66·10	66·10 to 71·10	Over 71·10	Total
More than +0·50	1	0	1	0	1	3
−0·85 to +0·50	2	1	2	4	5	14
−1·50 to −0·85	2	4	3	4	3	16
−2·65 to −1·50	8	7	5	4	3	27
−3·75 to −2·65	4	3	4	3	6	20
More than −3·75	3	5	5	5	2	20
Total	20	20	20	20	20	100

Table 5.20

SMLAs BY SIZE OF SHIFT IN CORE SHARE OF POPULATION, 1951–1961, AND CORE DENSITY OF POPULATION, 1951

	Core density of population 1951					
Per cent size of population shift 1951–61	Under 7·81 persons per acre (under 5,000 per sq. m.)	7·81 to 15·62 persons per acre (5,000 to 10,000 per sq. m.)	15·62 to 23·44 persons per acre (10,000 to 15,000 per sq. m.)	23·44 to 31·25 persons per acre (15,000 to 20,000 per sq. m.)	Over 31·25 persons per acre (over 20,000 per sq. m.)	Total
More than +3·0	5	2	0	0	0	7
+1·0 to +3·0	6	9	0	0	0	15
−1·7 to +1·0	7	22	4	0	0	33
−3·0 to −1·7	3	9	3	0	0	15
−5·3 to −3·0	1	10	7	1	1	20
More than −5·3	2	5	2	1	0	10
Total	24	57	16	2	1	100

Table 5.21

SMLAs BY SIZE OF SHIFT IN CORE SHARE OF POPULATION, 1961–1966, AND CORE DENSITY OF POPULATION, 1961

	Core density of population 1961				
Per cent size of population shift 1961–66	Under 7·81 persons per acre (under 5,000 per sq. m.)	7·81 to 15·62 persons per acre (5,000 to 10,000 per sq. m.)	15·62 to 23·44 persons per acre (10,000 to 15,000 per sq. m.)	Over 23·44 persons per acre (over 15,000 per sq. m.)	Total
More than +0·50	3	0	0	0	3
−0·85 to +0·50	5	7	2	0	14
−1·50 to −0·85	6	8	2	0	16
−2·65 to −1·50	3	21	2	1	27
−3·75 to −2·65	4	8	7	1	20
More than −3·75	2	11	7	0	20
Total	23	55	20	2	100

Table 5.22

SMLAs BY TYPE OF SHIFT IN CORE SHARE OF POPULATION, 1951–1961, AND STANDARD REGION

Type of population shift 1951–61	Standard region									
	South-East	South-West	East Anglia	West Midlands	East Midlands	North-West	Yorks. and Humberside	Northern	Wales and Monmouth	Total
Absolute centralization	1	0	0	1	0	0	1	1	1	5
Relative centralization	12	1	2	3	0	0	3	1	1	23
Relative decentralization	13	6	2	3	4	3	4	3	2	40
Absolute decentralization	3	1	1	1	2	6	3	2	0	19
Subtotal	29	8	5	8	6	9	11	7	4	87
Declining SMLA population	0	1	0	0	0	9	2	0	1	13
Total	29	9	5	8	6	18	13	7	5	100

Table 5.23

SMLAs BY TYPE OF SHIFT IN CORE SHARE OF POPULATION, 1961–1966, AND STANDARD REGION

Type of population shift 1961–66	Standard region									
	South-East	South-West	East Anglia	West Midlands	East Midlands	North-West	Yorks. and Humberside	Northern	Wales and Monmouth	Total
Absolute centralization	2	0	0	0	0	0	0	0	0	2
Relative centralization	1	0	0	1	0	0	0	1	0	3
Relative decentralization	22	6	3	5	2	4	2	0	2	46
Absolute decentralization	2	2	2	2	4	8	10	4	2	36
Subtotal	27	8	5	8	6	12	12	5	4	87
Declining SMLA population	2	1	0	0	0	6	1	2	1	13
Total	29	9	5	8	6	18	13	7	5	100

core. Although Tables 5.20 and 5.21 are somewhat distorted, with over 50 per cent of SMLA cores falling into the moderate-density category in both time periods, a fairly clear pattern emerges. The tables show that the SMLAs with lower-density cores are mostly centralizing or only minimally decentralizing SMLAs. This tendency can be seen in both the 1950s and the 1960s and is, if anything, more marked in the latter, within the general context of increasing decentralization indices. The Tables also show that most of this decentralization is relative, i.e. that the core is not in fact losing population. Thus, although the size of shift categories do show that decentralization has been increasing, in extent and intensity, there has in fact been a slight increase of cores in the higher-density categories.

TYPE OF POPULATION SHIFT

More significant, in many ways, is the precise type of shift which produced the patterns of centralization or decentralization. Table 5.22 shows that out of the 100 SMLAs in England and Wales, thirteen were actually losing population in the decade 1951–61.[16] Of the eighty-seven SMLAs which were increasing in population, twenty-eight were centralizing their populations (five of them absolutely), and fifty-nine were decentralizing (nineteen absolutely). Of the twenty-eight centralizing SMLAs thirteen, or nearly half, were found in the South-East region.[17] This region also had a slightly higher than proportionate concentration of SMLAs in the relatively decentralizing category. Among the group of absolutely decentralizing metropolitan areas, however, the northern industrial areas were dominant: six out of nineteen were in the North-West and another three were in Yorkshire and Humberside (Figure 5.23).[18]

By the 1960s there had been a notable change in patterns (Figure 5.24 and Table 5.23). Centralizing SMLAs were by then almost non-existent; they totalled a mere five out of the 100. Declining metropolitan areas numbered thirteen, as before. This left eighty-two out of the 100 SMLAs in the decentralizing category: thirty-six of them were decentralizing absolutely. The South-East had a more than proportionate share of the relatively decentralizing areas, as before; but again, the absolutely decentralizing group was dominated by the northern industrial areas, with exactly half (eighteen out

[16] A list is on p. 159, footnote 3.

[17] Bedford, Brighton, Chatham, Chelmsford, Colchester, Hemel Hempstead, Luton, Maidstone, Stevenage, Thurrock, Walton and Weybridge, and Woking, together with Basildon which had 100 per cent of its population in its core throughout. Three of these represented new town development. The other fifteen centralizing SMLAs were Cambridge, Carlisle, Harrogate, Huddersfield, Kidderminster, Peterborough, Port Talbot, Scunthorpe, Shrewsbury, Stafford, Swansea, Swindon, Wakefield, West Hartlepool, and Worcester.

[18] They were a mixed list, predominantly slow-growing with some big SMLAs (Manchester, Liverpool, Sheffield) as well as smaller manufacturing or mining SMLAs like St Helens, Leigh or Barnsley.

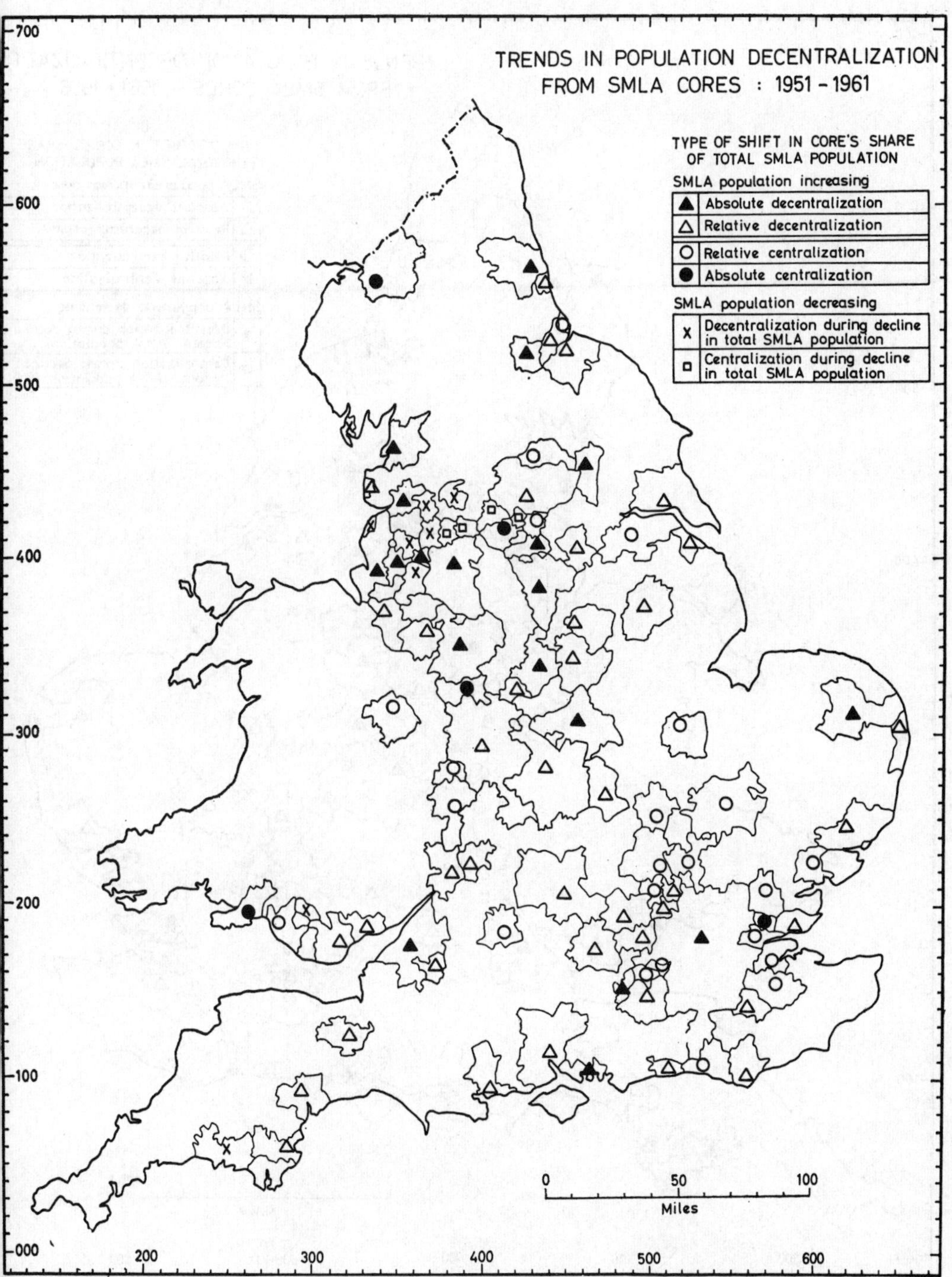

Figure 5.23 SMLAs, Type of Shift in Core Share of Population, 1951–1961

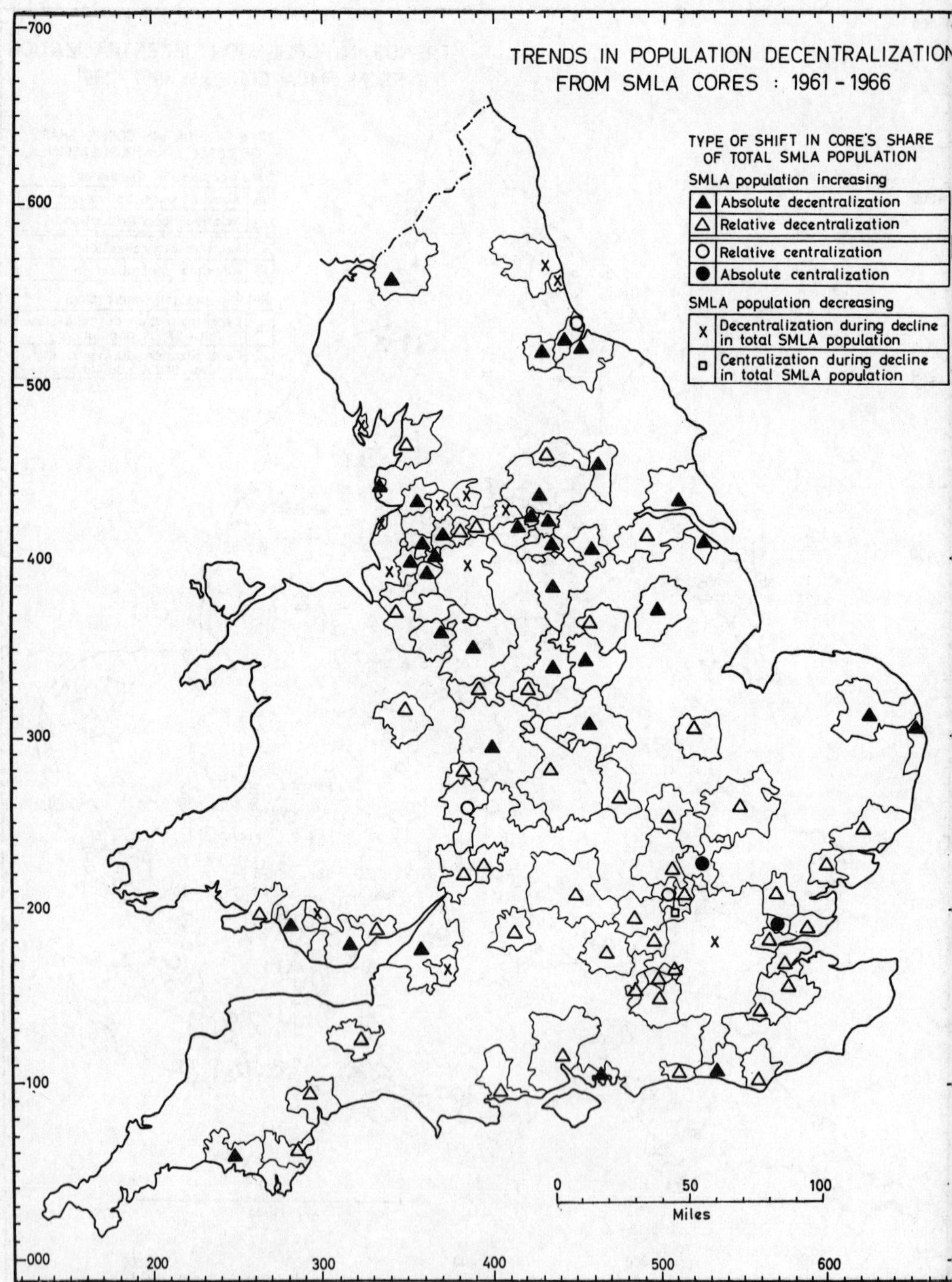

Figure 5.24 SMLAs, Type of Shift in Core Share of Population, 1961–1966

of thirty-six) in the North-West and Yorkshire-Humberside regions.[19]

This distinction would indicate a possible reason: the relatively decentralizing metropolitan areas were the faster-growing ones, especially in the South-East, while the absolutely decentralizing ones were the more slowly-growing (or even declining) areas of the North, where extensive redevelopment of the central cores, associated with massive slum-clearance programmes, was causing a rapid thinning out of population by the early 1960s. Tables 5.24 and 5.25 show this thesis to be broadly correct: nineteen out of forty of the relatively decentralizing SMLAs in 1951–61, thirty-four out of forty-six in 1961–66, were in the two top growth-rate categories. Conversely, twelve out of nineteen absolutely decentralizing SMLAs in 1951–61, and twenty-three out of thirty-six in 1961–66, were in the two categories of poorest growth record. Notable also from Table 5.24 is the fact that the category of relatively centralizing SMLAs (which almost disappeared after 1961) was dominated by fast-growing areas, sixteen out of twenty-three being in the top two growth categories. In fact close examination shows that many of these tended to be in the ring of SMLAs (including the new towns) round London.[20]

Because of this fact, as Table 5.26 shows, the centralizing metropolitan areas of the 1950s also tended to be small; sixteen out of twenty-three of the relatively centralizing SMLAs, and three out of five of the absolutely centralizing group, had less than 115,000 people each in 1951. In this decade, relative decentralization was not a phenomenon associated with any particular size group; it occurred impartially in all groups. Absolute decentralization, however, was strongly associated in this decade with the bigger metropolitan areas: thirteen out of nineteen SMLAs in this category had more than 170,000 people.

These tendencies continued into the 1960s. Table 5.27 shows that though relative decentralization affected all but the largest metropolitan areas impartially, twenty-three out of the thirty-six absolutely decentralizing SMLAs were in the categories with more than 180,000 people. And the process was very dramatically illustrated in the biggest metropolitan areas of all (Table 5.28). In some of these, a relative decentralization in the 1950s turned into an absolute decentralization in the 1960s: for instance Birmingham, Leeds, Nottingham or Cardiff. With many others, more advanced along what seems to be a cycle, absolute decentralization in the 1950s turned into decline of the whole SMLA in the 1960s, as the gain in the ring failed to make up for the increasingly massive losses in the core: thus London, Manchester, Liverpool, and Newcastle.

[19] They were mainly (though not exclusively) mining and manufacturing SMLAs on the coalfields, exhibiting slow growth. In the North-West: Blackpool, Bolton, Crewe, Leigh, Preston, St Helens, Warrington, and Wigan. In Yorkshire-Humberside: Barnsley, Dewsbury, Doncaster, Grimsby, Huddersfield, Leeds, Lincoln, Sheffield, Wakefield, and York.

[20] These were: Chatham, Chelmsford, Hemel Hempstead, Luton, Maidstone, Stevenage, Thurrock, Walton and Weybridge, and Woking, with Basildon also centralizing. Others relatively centralizing in the South-East were Bedford, Brighton, and Colchester.

Table 5.24

SMLAs BY TYPE OF SHIFT IN CORE SHARE OF POPULATION, 1951–1961, AND SMLA PERCENTAGE POPULATION CHANGE, 1951–1961

Type of population shift 1951–61	Per cent population change 1951–61: Under +1·6	+1·6 to +5·3	+5·3 to +9·5	+9·5 to +14·5	Over +14·5	Total
Absolute centralization	1	2	0	1	1	5
Relative centralization	1	2	4	7	9	23
Relative decentralization	1	8	12	9	10	40
Absolute decentralization	4	8	4	3	0	19
Subtotal	7	20	20	20	20	87
Declining SMLA population	13	0	0	0	0	13
Total	20	20	20	20	20	100

Table 5.25

SMLAs BY TYPE OF SHIFT IN CORE SHARE OF POPULATION, 1961–1966, AND SMLA PERCENTAGE POPULATION CHANGE, 1961–1966

Type of population shift 1961–66	Per cent population change 1961–66: Under +1·05	+1·05 to +3·55	+3·55 to +5·23	+5·23 to +8·53	Over +8·53	Total
Absolute centralization	0	0	0	0	2	2
Relative centralization	0	1	1	0	1	3
Relative decentralization	1	2	9	19	15	46
Absolute decentralization	6	17	10	1	2	36
Subtotal	7	20	20	20	20	87
Declining SMLA population	13	0	0	0	0	13
Total	20	20	20	20	20	100

Table 5.26

SMLAs BY TYPE OF SHIFT IN CORE SHARE OF POPULATION, 1951–1961, AND SMLA POPULATION SIZE, 1951

	SMLA population size 1951					
Type of population shift 1951–61	Under 92,000	92,000 to 115,000	115,000 to 170,000	170,000 to 260,000	Over 260,000	Total
Absolute centralization	2	1	0	2	0	5
Relative centralization	10	6	4	2	1	23
Relative decentralization	6	8	10	8	8	40
Absolute decentralization	0	3	3	3	10	19
Subtotal	18	18	17	15	19	87
Declining SMLA population	2	2	3	5	1	13
Total	20	20	20	20	20	100

Table 5.27

SMLAs BY TYPE OF SHIFT IN CORE SHARE OF POPULATION, 1961–1966, AND SMLA POPULATION, SIZE 1961

	SMLA population size 1961					
Type of population shift 1961–66	Under 100,500	100,500 to 129,000	129,000 to 180,000	180,000 to 289,000	Over 289,000	Total
Absolute centralization	1	1	0	0	0	2
Relative centralization	2	1	0	0	0	3
Relative decentralization	12	11	11	9	3	46
Absolute decentralization	2	5	6	10	13	36
Subtotal	17	18	17	19	16	87
Declining SMLA population	3	2	3	1	4	13
Total	20	20	20	20	20	100

As with rate of shift, so with type of shift. Tables 5.29 and 5.30 demonstrate that there was no definite association with the share of population in the core at the beginning of the period. This indeed proved to be an indicator of almost no significance at all.

Table 5.28

PATTERN OF POPULATION CHANGE IN LARGE SMLAs, 1951–1961 AND 1961–1966

	1951–61			1961–66 (decennial)		
	Core	Ring	Net	Core	Ring	Net
	'000s			'000s		
Birmingham	+47·4	+324·9	RD	−73·4	+78·8	AD
Leeds	+5·4	+16·9	RD	−25·1	+54·0	AD
Nottingham	+10·2	+31·6	RD	−5·8	+46·2	AD
Cardiff	+13·0	+19·3	RD	−5·3	+21·8	AD
London	−280·6	+324·9	AD	−610·7	+78·8	Dec
Manchester	−74·1	+103·4	AD	−187·5	+129·4	Dec
Liverpool	−38·0	+91·2	AD	−124·4	+63·0	Dec
Newcastle	−24·3	+60·9	AD	−65·3	+54·6	Dec

RD: Relative decentralization.
AD: Absolute decentralization.
Dec: Decline of SMLA.

Table 5.29

SMLAs BY TYPE OF SHIFT IN CORE SHARE OF POPULATION, 1951–1961, AND CORE SHARE OF POPULATION, 1951

	Per cent core share of population 1951					
Type of population shift 1961–61	Under 48·3	48·3 to 58·0	58·0 to 66·5	66·5 to 73·2	Over 73·2	Total
Absolute centralization	0	0	0	4	1	5
Relative centralization	5	8	5	3	2	23
Relative decentralization	8	7	8	8	9	40
Absolute decentralization	3	4	6	4	2	19
Subtotal	16	19	19	19	14	87
Declining SMLA population	4	1	1	1	6	13
Total	20	20	20	20	20	100

The relationship between core density and type of shift is examined in Tables 5.31 and 5.32. Again dominated by the category of SMLAs with moderate core-densities, these tables show that the pattern of type of shift is related to the density of the core: the higher this density, the stronger the tendency to decentralization and even absolute decentralization. Further, this pattern is more marked in the 1960s than in the 1950s. Taking into account the uneven distribution of core-densities, the 1960s show a sharp increase in the numbers of relatively decentralizing SMLAs with quite low core-densities, and an equally sharp increase in the numbers of absolutely decentralizing SMLAs with relatively high core-densities. The first group is a mixed one, but notably includes some of the rapidly-growing, small to medium sized SMLAs in the South-East;[21] the latter includes some of the large metropolitan centres.[22]

The internal dynamics of population in the SMLAs, then, may be fairly concisely summarized. Both in the 1950s and the 1960s the dominant trend was towards decentralization of population from the core to the ring. A small but distinct group of relatively centralizing SMLAs was noticeable up

Table 5.30

SMLAs BY TYPE OF SHIFT IN CORE SHARE OF POPULATION, 1961–1966, AND CORE SHARE OF POPULATION, 1961

Type of population shift 1961–66	Per cent core share of population 1961: Under 48·10	48·10 to 57·75	57·75 to 66·10	66·10 to 71·10	Over 71·10	Total
Absolute centralization	1	0	0	0	1	2
Relative centralization	0	0	2	0	1	3
Relative decentralization	10	12	8	10	6	46
Absolute decentralization	8	7	6	8	7	36
Subtotal	19	19	16	18	15	87
Declining SMLA population	1	1	4	2	5	13
Total	20	20	20	20	20	100

[21] For instance, High Wycombe, Guildford, Eastbourne, and Tunbridge Wells, in 1951, plus Thurrock and Colchester, in 1961.

[22] Including Manchester, Newcastle, Leicester, and Derby in 1951, and, in addition, Birmingham, Bristol, Leicester, Cardiff, Hull, Portsmouth, and Middlesbrough, in 1961.

to 1961, but thenceforth disappeared; it was associated particularly with the rapid building-up of new towns and the spontaneous growth of older towns in the ring around London. These metropolitan areas typically tended to be small, with low population densities in their cores. Among big SMLAs there seemed to be a cycle of progress from relative decentralization to absolute decentralization to decline.

THE OUTWARD PUSH OF JOBS

The internal changes in employment patterns within each SMLA can be measured in precisely the same way as can population shifts. When this is done, however, the resulting pattern is more complex than the pattern of population changes.

The most important difference is that with jobs the tendency has by no means been one of simple decentralization. In 1951–61, in fact, fifty-eight out of 100 SMLAs recorded centralization of their employment patterns in

Table 5.31

SMLAs BY TYPE OF SHIFT IN CORE SHARE OF POPULATION, 1951–1961, AND CORE DENSITY OF POPULATION, 1951

Type of population shift 1951–61	Core density of population 1951					
	Under 7·81 persons per acre (under 5,000 per sq. m.)	7·81 to 15·62 persons per acre (5,000 to 10,000 per sq. m.)	15·62 to 23·44 persons per acre (10,000 to 15,000 per sq. m.)	23·44 to 31·25 persons per acre (15,000 to 20,000 per sq. m.)	Over 31·25 persons per acre (over 20,000 per sq. m.)	Total
Absolute centralization	2	3	0	0	0	5
Relative centralization	11	12	0	0	0	23
Relative decentralization	6	26	8	0	0	40
Absolute decentralization	2	9	5	2	1	19
Subtotal	21	50	13	2	1	87
Declining SMLA population	3	7	3	0	0	13
Total	24	57	16	2	1	100

terms of the shift in the share of the core. And no less than thirty-nine of these recorded decisive centralization tendencies of 2·5 per cent or more over the decade. There were no strongly-marked regional differences in this pattern. But by the 1960s, a most striking change had occurred. In the quinquennium 1961–66 the percentage of centralizing SMLAs had dropped to thirty-eight and over one half of all SMLAs were recording decentralization of 1·5 per cent or more over the quinquennium, or 3 per cent or more projected over the decade. Again, as Tables 5.33 and 5.34 show, no conspicuous regional distinctions are to be observed in this pattern. Figures 5.25 and 5.26 demonstrate this graphically.

Table 5.32

SMLAs BY TYPE OF SHIFT IN CORE SHARE OF POPULATION, 1961–1966, AND CORE DENSITY OF POPULATION, 1961

	Core density of population 1961				
Type of population shift 1961–66	Under 7·81 persons per acre (under 5,000 per sq. m.)	7·81 to 15·62 persons per acre (5,000 to 10,000 per sq. m.)	15·62 to 23·44 persons per acre (10,000 to 15,000 per sq. m.)	Over 23·44 persons per acre (over 15,000 per sq. m.)	Total
Absolute centralization	2	0	0	0	2
Relative centralization	1	1	1	0	3
Relative decentralization	15	28	3	0	46
Absolute decentralization	2	22	12	0	36
Subtotal	20	51	16	0	87
Declining SMLA population	3	4	4	2	13
Total	23	55	20	2	100

A much clearer relationship appears, though, when the patterns of employment change are compared with the size of the metropolitan area, defined in terms of the concentration of employment. Even in the 1950s it was evident that strong centralizing tendencies were chiefly found in the smaller metropolitan areas. The largest SMLAs (those with employment totals of 118,000 or more in 1951), tended to be centralizing moderately or decentralizing moderately (Table 5.35). By the 1960s, however, a clear distinction had emerged. Centralization now tended to be restricted to the smaller SMLAs, and

Table 5.33

SMLAs BY SIZE OF SHIFT IN CORE SHARE OF EMPLOYMENT, 1951–1961, AND STANDARD REGION

Per cent size of employment shift 1951–61	Standard region									
	South-East	South-West	East Anglia	West Midlands	East Midlands	North-West	Yorks. and Humberside	Northern	Wales and Monmouth	Total
More than +10·0	3	0	0	0	0	0	0	0	0	3
+2·5 to +10·0	9	3	4	5	1	7	3	2	2	36
0·0 to +2·5	5	2	0	1	1	3	4	1	1	19
−1·5 to 0·0	3	1	1	0	3	5	4	1	0	18
−3·0 to −1·5	6	2	0	2	1	2	1	2	0	16
More than −3·0	3	0	0	0	0	1	1	1	2	8
Total	29	9	5	8	6	18	13	7	5	100

Table 5.34

SMLAs BY SIZE OF SHIFT IN CORE SHARE OF EMPLOYMENT, 1961–1966, AND STANDARD REGION

Per cent size of employment shift 1961–66	Standard region									
	South-East	South-West	East Anglia	West Midlands	East Midlands	North-West	Yorks. and Humberside	Northern	Wales and Monmouth	Total
More than +3·0	3	0	1	1	1	1	0	0	1	8
+1·5 to +3·0	3	1	0	3	0	1	1	1	0	10
−0·5 to +1·5	3	4	3	2	2	4	5	2	2	27
−1·5 to −0·5	6	1	0	0	0	3	2	1	0	13
−2·5 to −1·5	7	1	0	2	1	4	5	1	0	21
More than −2·5	7	2	1	0	2	5	0	2	2	21
Total	29	9	5	8	6	18	13	7	5	100

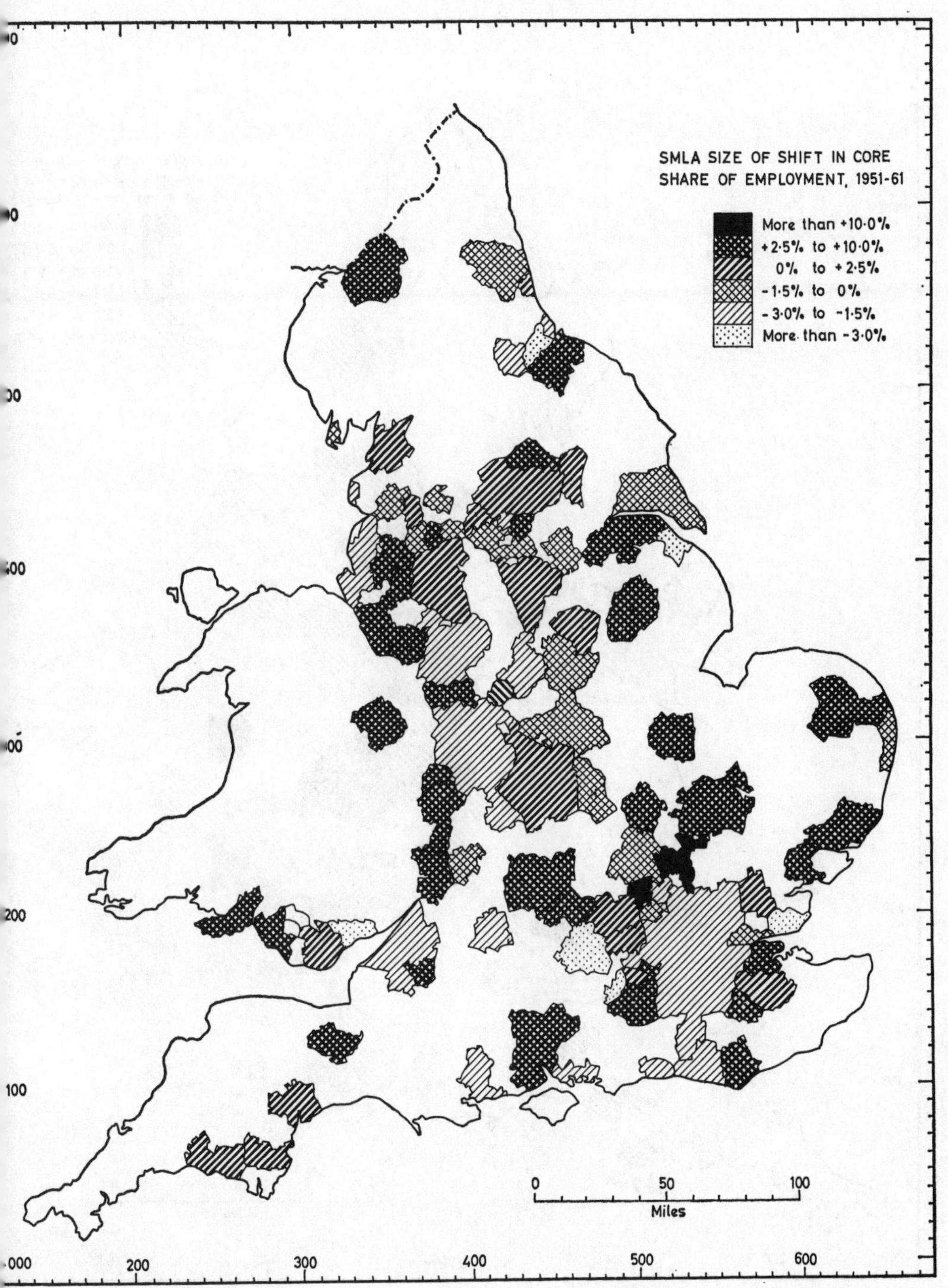

Figure 5.25 SMLAs, Size of Shift in Core Share of Employment, 1951–1961

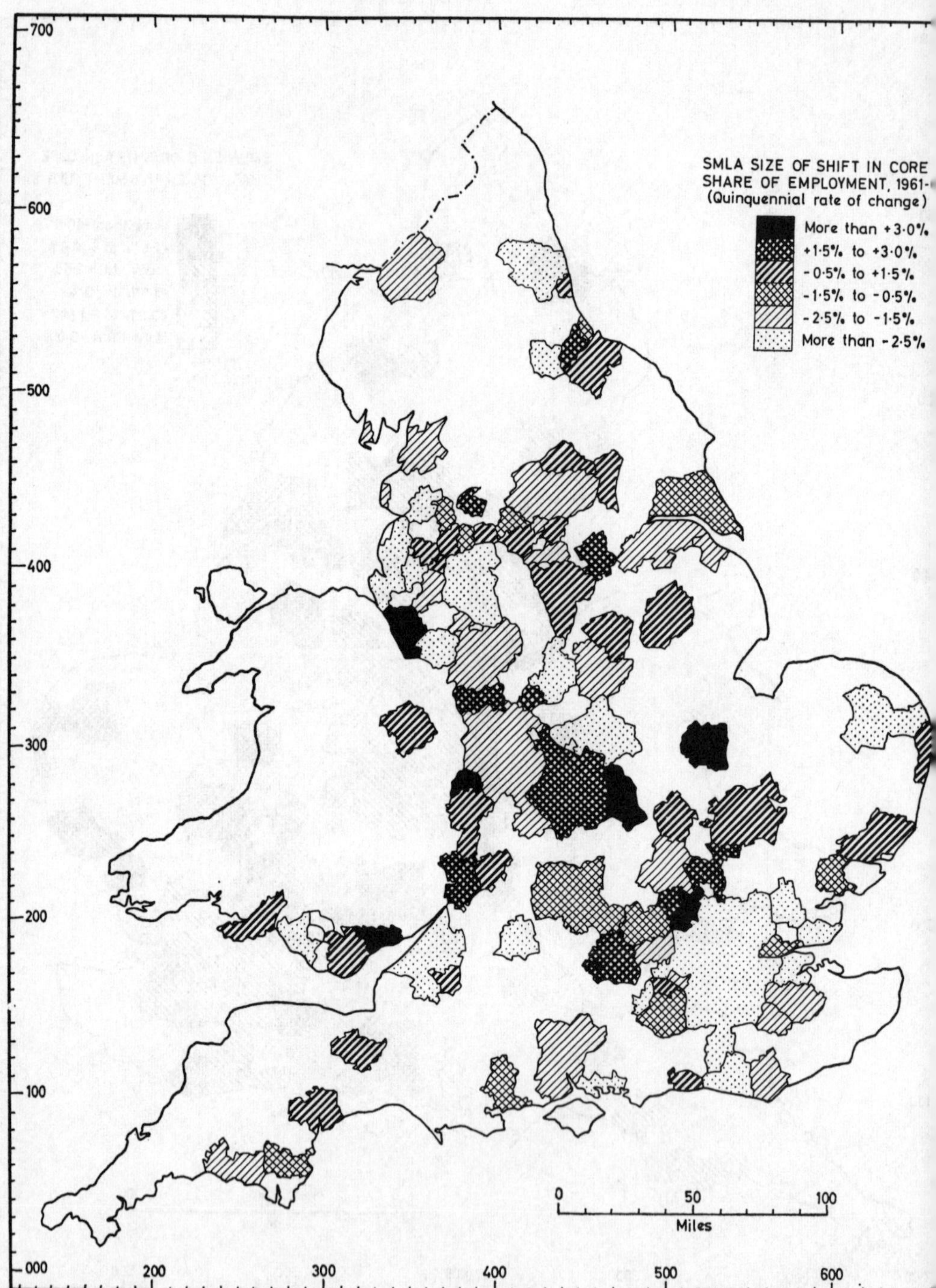

Figure 5.26 SMLAs, Size of Shift in Core Share of Employment, 1961–1966

the group of largest SMLAs (over 120,000) were exhibiting strong tendencies to decentralize. Of these twenty SMLAs, nine had a shift from the core of more than 2·5 per cent, while none had an equivalent shift to the core. The decentralization trend, however, was so strong by this quinquennium that it affected all size groups (Table 5.36).

Table 5.35

SMLAs BY SIZE OF SHIFT IN CORE SHARE OF EMPLOYMENT, 1951–1961, AND SMLA EMPLOYMENT SIZE, 1951

Per cent size of employment shift 1951–61	SMLA employment size 1951 Under 38,000	38,000 to 53,000	53,000 to 69,700	69,700 to 118,000	Over 118,000	Total
More than +10·0	3	0	0	0	0	3
+2·5 to +10·0	8	12	5	9	2	36
0·0 to +2·5	2	3	4	4	6	19
−1·5 to 0·0	2	2	5	4	5	18
−3·0 to −1·5	3	3	1	2	7	16
More than −3·0	2	0	5	1	0	8
Total	20	20	20	20	20	100

Table 5.36

SMLAs BY SIZE OF SHIFT IN CORE SHARE OF EMPLOYMENT, 1961–1966, AND SMLA EMPLOYMENT SIZE 1961

Per cent size of employment shift 1961–66	SMLA employment size 1961 Under 42,080	42,080 to 59,600	59,600 to 77,000	77,000 to 120,000	Over 120,000	Total
More than +3·0	3	2	3	0	0	8
+1·5 to +3·0	3	3	1	2	1	10
−0·5 to +1·5	5	8	5	6	3	27
−1·5 to −0·5	3	1	5	2	2	13
−2·5 to −1·5	3	5	4	4	5	21
More than −2·5	3	1	2	6	9	21
Total	20	20	20	20	20	100

In fact, what seems to have happened is that the trend towards decentralization has progressively spread from the bigger SMLAs to the smaller. Even in the 1950s the biggest metropolitan areas were already exhibiting the trend, with one or two exceptions; by 1961–66 it became almost universal among this group, as Table 5.36 shows. Among the smallest metropolitan areas, on the other hand, there are many examples where a centralizing trend in the 1950s was replaced by a decentralizing trend in the 1960s, as the selected examples in Table 5.37 show.

Table 5.37

SHIFTS IN EMPLOYMENT, 1951–1961 AND 1961–1966, IN SELECTED SMLAs

	1951–61	1961–66
(*a*) Selected large SMLAs	Shift in share of core	
London	−2·21	−2·74
Birmingham	−1·74	−2·35
Manchester	0·37	−3·70
Liverpool	−2·42	−3·51
Leeds	1·15	−1·90
Newcastle	−1·28	−3·16
Sheffield	0·36	−0·28
Bristol	−2·24	−2·81
Coventry	0·31	1 82
Nottingham	−0·64	−1·96
(*b*) Selected small SMLAs		
Colchester	3·91	−1·36
Chelmsford	1·54	−3·69
Tunbridge Wells	3·34	−2·08
Crewe	3·18	−4·23
Hemel Hempstead	16·10	2·09
Walton and Weybridge	6·57	−1·86

One obvious hypothesis is that decentralization is related to pressure of employment at the centre: a very heavy concentration of employment there, coupled with a rapid increase of employment in the metropolitan area, would be likely to lead to rapid decentralization. Tables 5.38 and 5.39 examine this theory in relation to the share of core employment, Tables 5.40 and 5.41 do the same in relation to the density of employment there, and lastly Tables 5.42 and 5.43 relate centralization or decentralization to the rate of growth of employment in the metropolitan area. They show a certain tendency, though not a very strong one, for decentralization to occur particularly in those SMLAs which had a high proportion of employment in their cores; a tendency which was more marked in the 1950s than in the 1960s. But there was very little discernible relationship in either of these two periods between decentralization and high density of employment in the core; although with increasing densities over time, by the 1960s the higher-density cores began to

Table 5.38

SMLAs BY SIZE OF SHIFT IN CORE SHARE OF EMPLOYMENT, 1951–1961, AND CORE SHARE OF EMPLOYMENT, 1951

Per cent size of employment shift 1951–61	Per cent core share of employment 1951					
	Under 55·0	55·0 to 66·5	66·5 to 73·0	73·0 to 78·0	Over 78·0	Total
More than +10·0	2	0	0	0	1	3
+2·5 to +10·0	10	15	7	3	1	36
0·0 to +2·5	5	1	3	5	5	19
−1·5 to 0·0	1	2	4	7	4	18
−3·0 to −1·5	1	1	5	3	6	16
More than −3·0	1	1	1	2	3	8
Total	20	20	20	20	20	100

Table 5.39

SMLAs BY SIZE OF SHIFT IN CORE SHARE OF EMPLOYMENT, 1961–1966, AND CORE SHARE OF EMPLOYMENT, 1961

Per cent size of employment shift 1961–66	Per cent core share of employment 1961					
	Under 56·8	56·8 to 68·7	68·7 to 73·5	73·5 to 79·0	Over 79·0	Total
More than +3·0	0	5	1	0	2	8
+1·5 to +3·0	4	2	2	1	1	10
−0·5 to +1·5	4	4	7	6	6	27
−1·5 to −0·5	3	2	1	3	4	13
−2·5 to −1·5	8	1	6	2	4	21
More than −2·5	1	6	3	8	3	21
Total	20	20	20	20	20	100

Table 5.40

SMLAs BY SIZE OF SHIFT IN CORE SHARE OF EMPLOYMENT, 1951–1961, AND CORE DENSITY OF EMPLOYMENT, 1951

	Core density of employment 1951					
Per cent size of employment shift 1951–61	Under 3·28 workers per acre	3·28 to 4·85 workers per acre	4·85 to 6·00 workers per acre	6·00 to 7·50 workers per acre	Over 7·50 workers per acre	Total
More than +10·0	3	0	0	0	0	3
+2·5 to +10·0	9	8	8	9	2	36
0·0 to +2·5	3	4	4	2	6	19
−1·5 to 0·0	2	1	6	2	7	18
−3·0 to −1·5	2	3	1	5	5	16
More than −3·0	1	4	1	2	0	8
Total	20	20	20	20	20	100

Table 5.41

SMLAs BY SIZE OF SHIFT IN CORE SHARE OF EMPLOYMENT, 1961–1966, AND CORE DENSITY OF EMPLOYMENT, 1961

	Core density of employment 1961					
Per cent size of employment shift 1951–66	Under 3·60 workers per acre	3·60 to 5·30 workers per acre	5·30 to 6·67 workers per acre	6·67 to 8·70 workers per acre	Over 8·70 workers per acre	Total
More than +3·0	2	2	0	2	2	8
+1·5 to +3·0	1	2	5	1	1	10
−0·5 to +1·5	5	7	7	5	3	27
−1·5 to −0·5	5	4	1	2	1	13
−2·5 to −1·5	5	4	2	6	4	21
More than −2·5	2	1	5	4	9	21
Total	20	20	20	20	20	100

dominate the categories which were decentralizing most rapidly or between decentralization and rapid employment growth. There is a rather better relationship, in fact, though not an overwhelmingly strong one, between decentralization and high densities of residential population in the core. This would indicate that one main pressure towards decentralization was not pressure of employment in the centre, but sheer pressure of people (Tables 5.44 and 5.45).

Table 5.42

SMLAs BY SIZE OF SHIFT IN CORE SHARE OF EMPLOYMENT, 1951–1961, AND SMLA PERCENTAGE EMPLOYMENT CHANGE, 1951–1961

Per cent size of employment shift 1951–61	Per cent employment change 1951–61: Under +0·50	+0·50 to +6·25	+6·25 to +10·10	+10·10 to +17·00	Over +17·00	Total
More than +10·0	0	0	0	0	3	3
+2·5 to +10·0	8	7	10	8	3	36
0·0 to +2·5	5	3	2	4	5	19
−1·5 to 0·0	3	5	4	2	4	18
−3·0 to −1·5	1	5	4	4	2	16
More than −3·0	3	0	0	2	3	8
Total	20	20	20	20	20	100

Table 5.43

SMLAs BY SIZE OF SHIFT IN CORE SHARE OF EMPLOYMENT, 1961–1966, AND SMLA PERCENTAGE EMPLOYMENT CHANGE, 1961–1966

Per cent size of employment shift 1961–66	Per cent employment change 1961–66: Under +1·25	+1·25 to +5·60	+5·60 to +8·25	+8·25 to +11·50	Over +11·50	Total
More than +3·0	2	1	2	2	1	8
+1·5 to +3·0	2	0	3	2	3	10
−0·5 to +1·5	4	6	7	7	3	27
−1·5 to −0·5	4	2	0	4	3	13
−2·5 to −1·5	2	8	5	2	4	21
More than −2·5	6	3	3	3	6	21
Total	20	20	20	20	20	100

Table 5.44
SMLAs BY SIZE OF SHIFT IN CORE SHARE OF EMPLOYMENT, 1951–1961, AND CORE DENSITY OF POPULATION, 1951

Per cent size of employment shift 1951–61	Core density of population 1951: Under 7·81 persons per acre	7·81 to 15·62 persons per acre	15·62 to 23·44 persons per acre	23·44 to 31·25 persons per acre	Over 31·25 persons per acre	Total
More than +10·0	3	0	0	0	0	3
+2·5 to +10·0	12	21	3	0	0	36
0·0 to +2·5	5	11	3	0	0	19
−1·5 to 0·0	2	10	6	0	1	18
−3·0 to −1·5	0	10	3	2	0	16
More than −3·0	2	5	1	0	0	8
Total	24	57	16	2	1	100

Table 5.45
SMLAs BY SIZE OF SHIFT IN CORE SHARE OF EMPLOYMENT, 1961–1966, AND CORE DENSITY OF POPULATION, 1961

Per cent size of employment shift 1961–66	Core density of population 1961: Under 7·81 persons per acre	7·81 to 15·62 persons per acre	15·62 to 23·44 persons per acre	Over 23·44 persons per acre	Total
More than +3·0	2	5	1	0	8
+1·5 to +3·0	2	7	1	0	10
−0·5 to +1·5	6	18	3	0	27
−1·5 to −0·5	6	5	2	0	13
−2·5 to −1·5	4	12	5	0	21
More than −2·5	3	8	8	2	21
Total	23	55	20	2	100

TYPE OF EMPLOYMENT SHIFT

The results of these comparisons, evidently, are very inconclusive. But as we have already noticed for population, simple shifts in the share of employment do not give anything like a complete picture of the dynamics of metropolitan growth and change. For this, it is necessary to go to the more detailed typology, which considers absolute and relative changes. Table 5.46 shows that in the decade 1951–61, eighty-one out of 100 metropolitan areas were recording

Table 5.46

SMLAs BY TYPE OF SHIFT IN CORE SHARE OF EMPLOYMENT, 1951–1961, AND STANDARD REGION

Type of employment shift 1951–61	Standard region									
	South-East	South-West	East Anglia	West Midlands	East Midlands	North-West	Yorks. and Humberside	Northern	Wales and Monmouth	Total
Absolute centralization	6	3	3	3	1	2	4	3	0	25
Relative centralization	11	2	1	2	1	0	2	0	2	21
Relative decentralization	11	3	1	1	4	4	5	3	1	33
Absolute decentralization	0	0	0	1	0	0	0	1	0	2
Subtotal	28	8	5	7	6	6	11	7	3	81
Declining SMLA employment	1	1	0	1	0	12	2	0	2	19
Total	29	9	5	8	6	18	13	7	5	100

Table 5.47

SMLAs BY TYPE OF SHIFT IN CORE SHARE OF EMPLOYMENT, 1961–1966, AND STANDARD REGION

Type of employment shift 1961–66	Standard region									
	South-East	South-West	East Anglia	West Midlands	East Midlands	North-West	Yorks. and Humberside	Northern	Wales and Monmouth	Total
Absolute centralization	3	0	1	3	1	0	2	1	2	13
Relative centralization	5	4	2	2	2	1	1	1	1	19
Relative decentralization	20	5	2	1	1	4	4	4	0	41
Absolute decentralization	1	0	0	1	2	3	4	1	1	13
Subtotal	29	9	5	7	6	8	11	7	4	86
Declining SMLA employment	0	0	0	1	0	10	2	0	1	14
Total	29	9	5	8	6	18	13	7	5	100

gains in employment, and that out of this total forty-six were experiencing employment centralization (twenty-five of them absolutely); of the thirty-five decentralizing SMLAs, only two were recording absolute decentralization of jobs, that is, an absolute decline of jobs in the core area. By 1961–66, a notable change had taken place (Table 5.47). Only fourteen out of the 100 metropolitan areas were by this time recording actual declines in employment. Of the eighty-six reporting increases, thirty-two reported centralization (only two of these centralizing absolutely), and fifty-four recorded decentralization (thirteen absolutely). There was, therefore, a much stronger tendency to decentralization of jobs, including absolute decentralization, in the 1960s than in the 1950s. This change was to some extent concealed in the previous analysis, because it treated increasing and declining SMLAs without differentiation.

Tables 5.46 and 5.47, together with Figures 5.27 and 5.28, also bring out some regional differences of emphasis in these patterns. The SMLAs where employment was declining, both in the 1950s and the 1960s, were almost all concentrated in the industrial north, in the North-West and Yorkshire-Humberside.[23] There was a certain tendency for relatively decentralizing areas to be concentrated in the more heavily urbanized and industrialized areas such as the South-East and the industrial north during the 1950s; by the 1960s, such areas are found almost wholly in the South-East.[24] There was a certain tendency to centralization in the West Midlands in both periods.[25]

There is a much more evident relationship between type of shift and the size of the metropolitan areas (Tables 5.48 and 5.49). In both periods, the

23 Fourteen out of nineteen in the 1950s; twelve out of fourteen in the 1960s. In increasing order of percentage decline they were (SMLAs outside these two regions in brackets): 1951–61, Lancaster, Wigan, (Aldershot), (Swansea), Manchester, Halifax, Dewsbury, St Helens, Burnley, Bolton, (Plymouth), Southport, Blackburn, (Burton), Bury, Rochdale, Leigh, Warrington, and (Rhondda); 1961–66, Crewe, Barnsley, Manchester, Southport, Leigh, Bolton, Chester, Huddersfield, Preston, Rochdale, (Kidderminster), Blackburn, Burnley, and (Rhondda).

24 The tendency in the 1950s was not a very striking one. Out of thirty-three relatively decentralizing SMLAs, eleven were in the South-East (Bournemouth, Brighton, London, Luton, Portsmouth, Reading, St Albans, Southend, Thurrock, Watford, and Worthing) and another nine in the North-West and Yorkshire-Humberside (Barnsley, Barrow, Blackpool, Doncaster, Grimsby, Huddersfield, Hull, Liverpool, and Preston). But the tendency in the 1960s was very strong, with twenty out of forty-one in the South-East: Aldershot, Bedford, Bournemouth, Brighton, Chatham, Chelmsford, Colchester, Eastbourne, High Wycombe, Guildford, Luton, Maidstone, Oxford, Portsmouth, Slough, Southampton, Southend, Thurrock, Tunbridge Wells, and Walton and Weybridge.

25 Out of the eight West Midland SMLAs, five reported centralization of employment in the 1950s: Shrewsbury, Stafford, and Worcester absolutely, Coventry and Kidderminster relatively. In the 1960s the proportion was again five, this time Coventry, Shrewsbury, and Stafford absolutely, and Burton and Worcester relatively.

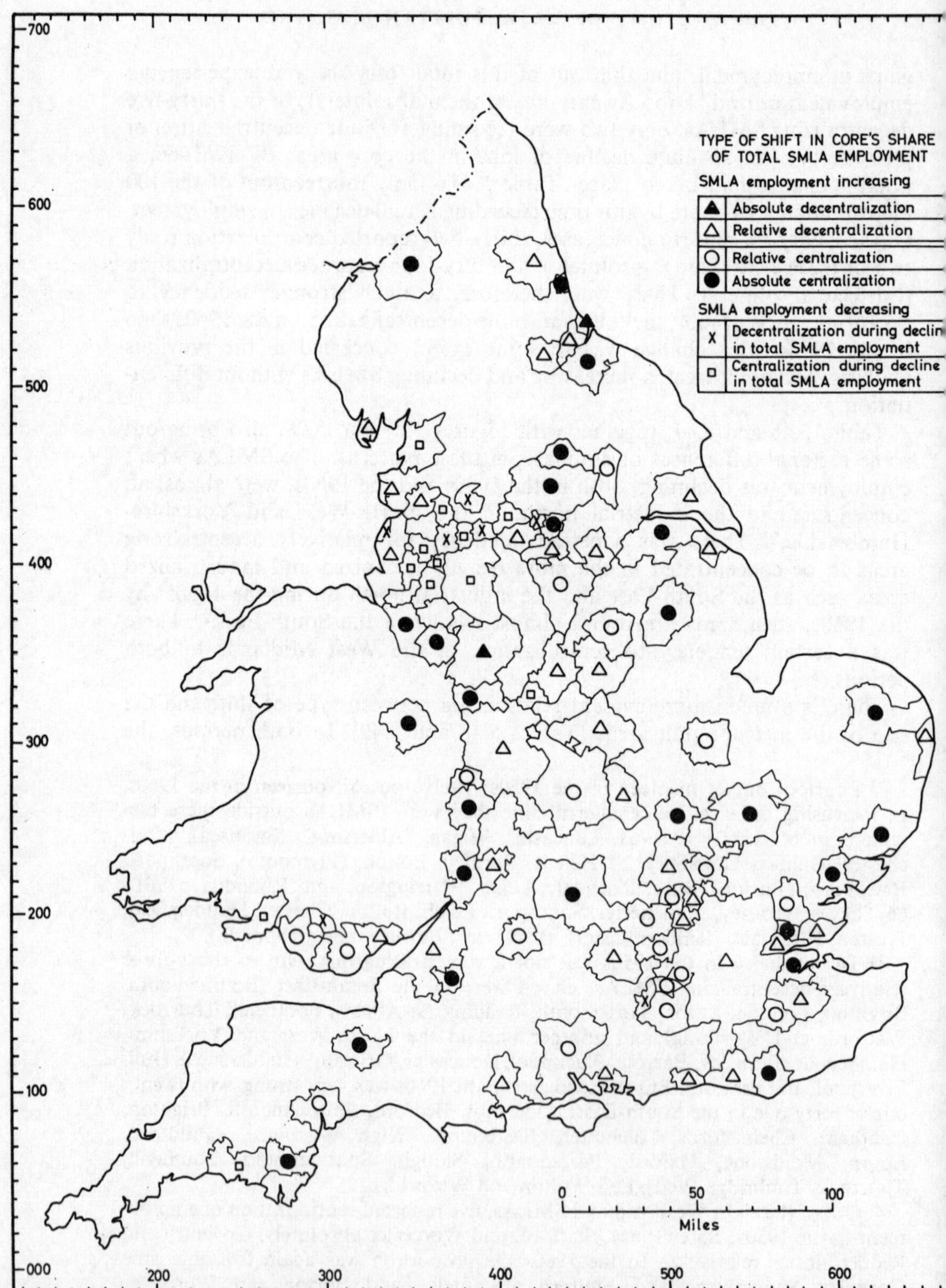

Figure 5.27 SMLAs, Type of Shift in Core Share of Employment, 1951–1961

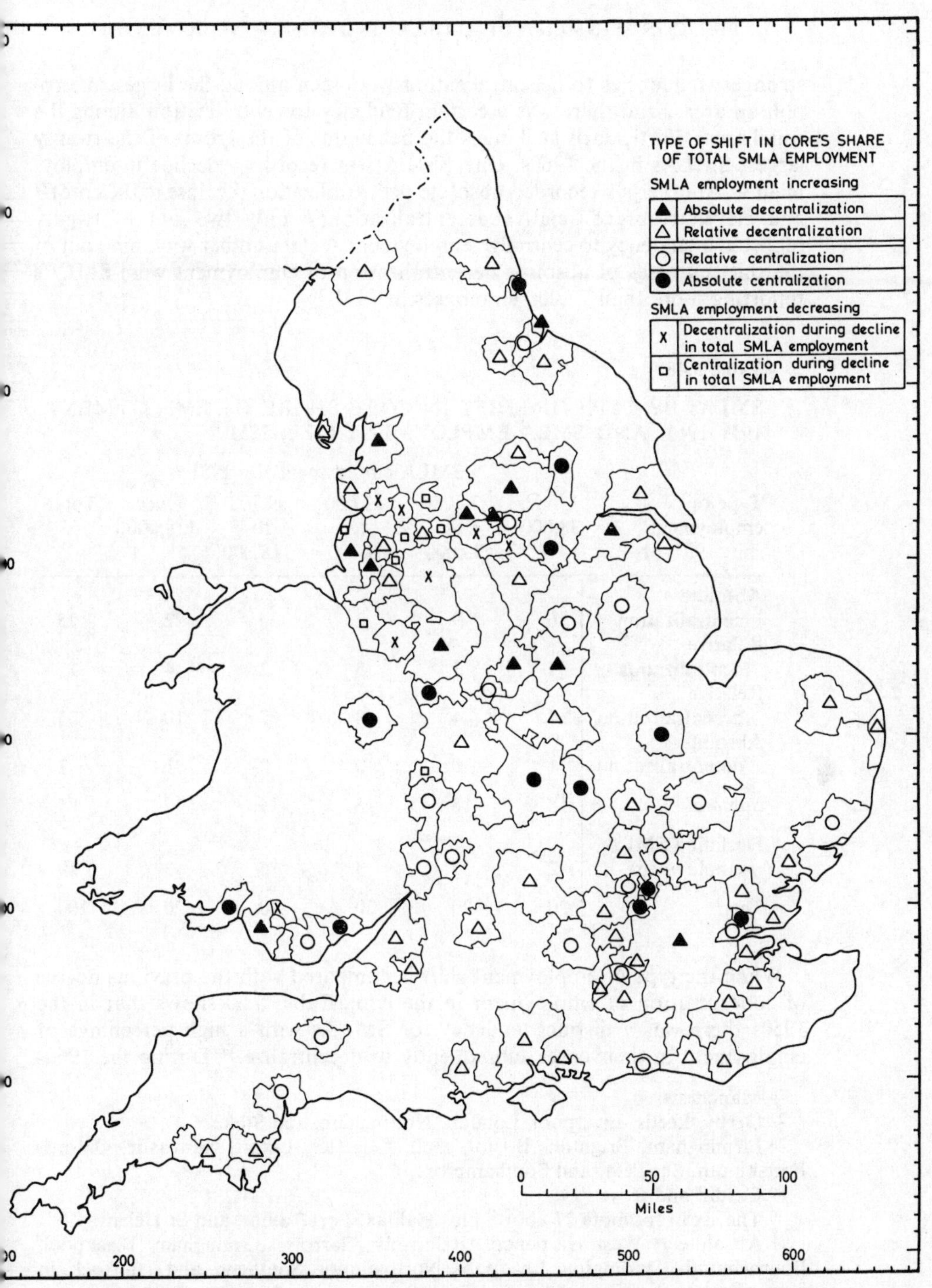

Figure 5.28 SMLAs, Type of Shift in Core Share of Employment, 1961–1966

strongest tendencies to decentralization were seen among the largest metropolitan areas, and there was a certain tendency to centralization among the small areas. Particularly striking is the behaviour of the group of the twenty largest SMLAs in the 1960s. One SMLA was recording decline in employment.[26] Another six recorded absolute decentralization (i.e. loss in the core)[27] and eleven recorded relative decentralization;[28] only two out of twenty reported a tendency to centralize employment.[29] Put another way, nine out of the thirteen cases of absolute decentralization of employment were SMLAs reporting more than 77,000 employees in 1961.[30]

Table 5.48

SMLAs BY TYPE OF SHIFT IN CORE SHARE OF EMPLOYMENT, 1951–1961, AND SMLA EMPLOYMENT SIZE, 1951

Type of employment shift 1951–61	SMLA employment size 1951: Under 38,000	38,000 to 53,000	53,000 to 69,700	69,700 to 118,000	Over 118,000	Total
Absolute centralization	6	9	2	6	2	25
Relative centralization	7	3	5	2	4	21
Relative decentralization	4	4	8	7	10	33
Absolute decentralization	1	0	0	0	1	2
Subtotal	18	16	15	15	17	81
Declining SMLA employment	2	4	5	5	3	19
Total	20	20	20	20	20	100

When the type of employment shift is compared with the previous degree of concentration of employment in the core, Table 5.50 shows that in the 1950s there was a distinct tendency for SMLAs with a high percentage of employment in their cores subsequently to decentralize.[31] During the 1960s

26 Manchester.

27 Derby, Leeds, Liverpool, London, Nottingham, and Stoke.

28 Birmingham, Brighton, Bristol, Hull, Leicester, Luton, Newcastle, Oxford, Portsmouth, Sheffield, and Southampton.

29 Cardiff and Coventry.

30 The six in footnote 27 above, plus Halifax, Port Talbot, and St Helens.

31 Absolutely: West Hartlepool. Relatively: Barrow, Birmingham, Blackpool, Bournemouth, Darlington, Liverpool, Northampton, Southend, and Thurrock, in every respect a heterogeneous group.

the picture altered in several ways (Table 5.51). More SMLAs were decentralizing employment, but this tendency was no longer confined to those with a high percentage of employment in the core as at the beginning of the period.

Table 5.49

SMLAs BY TYPE OF SHIFT IN CORE SHARE OF EMPLOYMENT, 1961–1966, AND SMLA EMPLOYMENT SIZE, 1961

Type of employment shift 1961–66	SMLA employment size 1961					
	Under 42,080	42,080 to 59,600	59,600 to 77,000	77,000 to 120,000	Over 120,000	Total
Absolute centralization	4	1	3	4	1	13
Relative centralization	6	4	6	2	1	19
Relative decentralization	6	8	9	7	11	41
Absolute decentralization	1	3	0	3	6	13
Subtotal	17	16	18	16	19	86
Declining SMLA employment	3	4	2	4	1	14
Total	20	20	20	20	20	100

Table 5.50

SMLAs BY TYPE OF SHIFT IN CORE SHARE OF EMPLOYMENT, 1951–1961, AND CORE SHARE OF EMPLOYMENT, 1951

Type of employment shift 1951–61	Per cent core share of employment 1951					
	Under 55·0	55·0 to 66·5	66·5 to 73·0	73·0 to 78·4	Over 78·4	Total
Absolute centralization	2	10	6	5	2	25
Relative centralization	10	3	2	2	4	21
Relative decentralization	2	3	8	11	9	33
Absolute decentralization	0	1	0	0	1	2
Subtotal	14	17	16	18	16	81
Declining SMLA employment	6	3	4	2	4	19
Total	20	20	20	20	20	100

Table 5.51

SMLAs BY TYPE OF SHIFT IN CORE SHARE OF EMPLOYMENT, 1961–1966, AND CORE SHARE OF EMPLOYMENT, 1961

Type of employment shift 1961–66	Per cent core share of employment 1961					
	Under 56·8	56·8 to 68·7	68·7 to 73·5	73·5 to 79·0	Over 79·0	Total
Absolute centralization	1	4	1	3	5	13
Relative centralization	6	5	7	0	1	19
Relative decentralization	9	5	7	11	9	41
Absolute decentralization	3	4	2	2	2	13
Subtotal	19	17	17	16	17	86
Declining SMLA employment	1	3	3	4	3	14
Total	20	20	20	20	20	100

Table 5.52

SMLAs BY TYPE OF SHIFT IN CORE SHARE OF EMPLOYMENT, 1951–1961, AND CORE DENSITY OF EMPLOYMENT, 1951

Type of employment shift 1951–61	Core density of employment 1951					
	Under 3·28 workers per acre	3·28 to 4·85 workers per acre	4·85 to 6·00 workers per acre	6·00 to 7·50 workers per acre	Over 7·50 workers per acre	Total
Absolute centralization	6	4	6	7	2	25
Relative centralization	8	5	4	2	2	21
Relative decentralization	4	5	6	7	11	33
Absolute decentralization	0	0	0	2	0	2
Subtotal	18	14	16	18	15	81
Declining SMLA employment	2	6	4	2	5	19
Total	20	20	20	20	20	100

In fact twelve out of the twenty with the lowest share in the core were now recording decentralization,[32] while eight of the thirteen SMLAs centralizing absolutely were to be found in the two categories having over 73·5 per cent of employment in the cores,[33] and another seven SMLAs from these categories were losing employment. However, the majority of those relatively centralizing were still in the low-share categories, and the majority of those relatively decentralizing were in the high-share categories.

A comparison with the density of employment in the core shows a more stable position. Thus in the 1950s (Table 5.52), of the twenty SMLAs with the highest densities of core employment, five recorded declines and eleven decentralization of jobs (all relatively);[34] in the 1960s (Table 5.53) the figures were respectively three declines and twelve cases of decentralization, of which

Table 5.53

SMLAs BY TYPE OF SHIFT IN CORE SHARE OF EMPLOYMENT, 1961–1966, AND CORE DENSITY OF EMPLOYMENT, 1961

Type of employment shift 1961–66	Core density of employment 1961: Under 3·60 workers per acre	3·60 to 5·30 workers per acre	5·30 to 6·67 workers per acre	6·67 to 8·70 workers per acre	Over 8·70 workers per acre	Total
Absolute centralization	4	1	3	1	4	13
Relative centralization	3	6	5	4	1	19
Relative decentralization	9	5	8	10	9	41
Absolute decentralization	2	3	3	2	3	13
Subtotal	18	15	19	17	17	86
Declining SMLA employment	2	5	1	3	3	14
Total	20	20	20	20	20	100

[32] Absolutely: Dewsbury, Lancaster, and Port Talbot. Relatively: Bury, Great Yarmouth, Guildford, High Wycombe, Maidstone, Slough, Southampton, Tunbridge Wells, and Warrington.

[33] Basildon, Coventry, Northampton, Shrewsbury, Stafford, Sunderland, Swansea, and York.

[34] Five declines: Blackburn, Burnley, Manchester, Plymouth, and Warrington. Eleven cases of relative decentralization: Birmingham, Derby, Hull, Leicester, Liverpool, London, Newcastle, Northampton, Nottingham, Portsmouth, and Preston. A significant proportion of these are very big SMLAs.

three were absolute.[35] The thirteen SMLAs which were decentralizing absolutely in the 1960s were spread evenly through all employment densities.

Lastly, Tables 5.54 and 5.55 compare the type of shift with the growth rate of employment in each SMLA. It might be hypothesized here that the faster-growing areas showed the greatest tendency to decentralize. The Tables show that this was not so in the 1950s, when eleven out of the twenty fastest-growing

Table 5.54

SMLAs BY TYPE OF SHIFT IN CORE SHARE OF EMPLOYMENT, 1951–1961, AND SMLA PERCENTAGE EMPLOYMENT CHANGE, 1951–1961

Type of employment shift 1951–61	Per cent employment change 1951–61: Under +0·50	+0·50 to +6·25	+6·25 to +10·10	+10·10 to +17·00	Over +17·00	Total
Absolute centralization	1	8	9	5	2	25
Relative centralization	0	2	3	7	9	21
Relative decentralization	0	8	8	8	9	33
Absolute decentralization	0	2	0	0	0	2
Subtotal	1	20	20	20	20	81
Declining SMLA employment	19	0	0	0	0	19
Total	20	20	20	20	20	100

areas were actually recording centralization of employment.[36] Indeed, the striking feature of this table is that there was almost no association between the growth of the metropolitan area employment and any tendency to centralize or decentralize. In the 1960s however (Table 5.55), only five of the twenty fastest-growing SMLAs were centralizing[37] and three of these were connected with London's new towns. Fourteen out of these twenty were

[35] Declines: Burnley, Manchester, and Preston. Absolute decentralization: Derby, Liverpool, and London. Relative decentralization: Birmingham, Hull, Leicester, Luton, Newcastle, Norwich, Portsmouth, Slough, and Warrington.

[36] Absolute: Scunthorpe plus Basildon (100 per cent in core). Relative: Chelmsford, Coventry, Hemel Hempstead, High Wycombe, Kidderminster, Port Talbot, Slough, Stevenage, and Woking, a list dominated by the fast growing, centralizing SMLAs of the Outer Metropolitan Area.

[37] Basildon (100 per cent in core, thus registering increase as absolute centralization); and Hemel Hempstead, Reading, Stevenage, and Woking, relatively centralizing.

relatively decentralizing, and also showing this tendency was a majority of the next fastest-growing group. In those SMLAs which were growing very slowly, on the other hand, absolute decentralization was taking place.[38] Trends were thus still very slight even in the 1960s.

The conclusion that emerges from this analysis, therefore, merely confirms the results of the earlier study of the rate of shift. There is very little evidence at all, in metropolitan England and Wales during the 1950s and early 1960s,

Table 5.55

SMLAs BY TYPE OF SHIFT IN CORE SHARE OF EMPLOYMENT, 1961–1966, AND SMLA PERCENTAGE EMPLOYMENT CHANGE, 1961–1966

Type of employment shift 1961–66	Per cent employment change 1961–66 Under +1·25	+1·25 to +5·60	+5·60 to +8·25	+8·25 to +11·50	Over +11·50	Total
Absolute centralization	1	4	4	3	1	13
Relative centralization	0	2	6	7	4	19
Relative decentralization	0	7	10	10	14	41
Absolute decentralization	5	7	0	0	1	13
Subtotal	6	20	20	20	20	86
Declining SMLA employment	14	0	0	0	0	14
Total	20	20	20	20	20	100

of any clear relationship between patterns of centralization or decentralization of employment on the one hand, and factors like growth rates, or concentration of employment on the other. There does seem however to be a clear and increasingly striking association with size. The larger metropolitan areas have begun to show a strong tendency to decentralize employment as well as population from their central cores and into their suburbs, a tendency which became more striking after 1961.

SHIFTS IN POPULATION AND SHIFTS IN EMPLOYMENT

The critical last point in this whole analysis must be to try to relate the internal shifts in employment within each SMLA to the internal shifts in population. It is clear, from the whole of the analysis in this chapter, that the tendency to

38 Halifax, Leeds, Liverpool, London, and West Hartlepool.

decentralize population is much longer established, and much more universal, than the tendency to decentralize jobs. The question is whether there is any clear relationship between the two tendencies, in time or in space or perhaps in both. Unfortunately it is very difficult to derive a satisfactory index to measure this relationship, because of the fact that trends are often working in different directions (e.g. centralization of employment accompanying decentralization of population). In order to overcome this difficulty, Tables 5.56 and 5.57 compare the trends in a visual way, in the form of a simple matrix of types of change in population and employment.

The matrix for the decade 1951–61 (Table 5.56) reveals a straightforward and largely regular pattern. The tendency to decentralize was stronger for population than for employment, so that eighty-seven of the 100 entries appear either on the diagonal of the matrix, or in the lower left corner. There is a strong tendency for the entries to cluster either on the diagonal or immediately below it to the left, indicating that decentralization of population was only a little more marked than decentralization of employment. Sixty-three of the eighty-seven cases of population increase involve relative changes (either centralization or decentralization) alone; twenty-four cases involve absolute changes only. The general picture can be summed up:

Relative centralization of population associated with absolute or relative centralization of employment (eighteen cases).

Relative decentralization of population associated with absolute centralization, or relative centralization, or relative decentralization of employment (thirty-nine cases).

Absolute decentralization of population associated with relative decentralization of employment (ten cases).

Decline in population associated with decline in employment (twelve cases).

so that of 100 entries in 25 possible cells in the matrix, seventy-nine appear in only 7 cells.

For 1961–66 (Table 5.57) the picture is similar, but the weight of the matrix has fallen down and to the right, and the entries are rather more spread out, indicating first that centralization either of people or of jobs has ceased to occur, and second that there is less relationship between the tendencies in population and in employment. Again, only thirteen of 100 entries occur above and to the right of the diagonal. Most of these, however, do not indicate that jobs are decentralizing faster than population, which still occurs in only four cases; they indicate declines in employment associated with rises in population, and they number nine, six of which are also losing population from the core. There are also eight cases where the employment increase is associated with population decline, and five more cases losing both population and employment. Disregarding these twenty-two entries, of the seventy-eight remaining, where both population and employment are increasing,

Table 5.56

TYPE OF SHIFT IN CORE SHARE OF POPULATION VERSUS TYPE OF SHIFT IN CORE SHARE OF EMPLOYMENT, 1951–1961

			Employment				
			Absolute centralization	Relative centralization	Relative decentralization	Absolute decentralization	Declining employment
	All SMLAs	100	25	21	33	2	19
Population	Absolute centralization	5	**3**	0	1	0	1
	Relative centralization	23	9	**9**	4	1	0
	Relative decentralization	40	12	10	**17**	0	1
	Absolute decentralization	19	1	2	10	**1**	5
	Declining population	13	0	0	1	0	**12**

Table 5.57

TYPE OF SHIFT IN CORE SHARE OF POPULATION VERSUS TYPE OF SHIFT IN CORE SHARE OF EMPLOYMENT, 1961–1966

			Employment				
			Absolute centralization	Relative centralization	Relative decentralization	Absolute decentralization	Declining employment
	All SMLAs	100	13	19	41	13	14
Population	Absolute centralization	2	**1**	1	0	0	0
	Relative centralization	3	0	**2**	0	1	0
	Relative decentralization	46	8	11	**22**	2	3
	Absolute decentralization	36	2	5	16	**7**	6
	Declining population	13	2	0	3	3	**5**

thirty-two are found on the diagonal, and forty-two below and to the left of it. The general picture can be summed up:

Relative decentralization of population associated with absolute centralization of employment (eight cases), relative centralization (eleven cases) and relative decentralization (twenty-two cases).

Absolute decentralization of population associated with relative decentralization of employment (sixteen cases), with absolute decentralization of employment (seven cases), and employment decline (six cases).

Decline of population associated with employment decline (five cases).

so that of 100 entries in 25 possible cells, seventy-five occur in only 7 cells.

In general, therefore, in this later period it can still be said that in the great majority of cases population was still decentralizing in the same way as, or even more markedly than, employment.

THE PATTERN OF JOURNEY TO WORK

These changes in living patterns and work patterns must be reflected in the patterns of journey to work. Thus if population decentralizes out of the metropolitan area cores faster than employment, the result must be an increase in work journeys from ring to core. And if, at a later stage, employment begins to follow residential population into the rings, we should expect to find an accompanying increase in wholly suburban journeys made within the ring. Such changes are inevitable results of the changing patterns we have already described, so there is no point in conducting an elaborate general analysis. But it is instructive, perhaps, to consider some contrasted type cases, and to follow the changes through.

To this end, we have chosen nine representative metropolitan areas from the ring around London, from the West and East Midlands, from Lancashire and from Yorkshire. They represent not merely a wide spread of geographical regions, but of size (from Birmingham down to Stevenage and Tunbridge Wells) and population and employment change (from Stevenage at one extreme to Halifax and Burnley at the other). They also contain a large number of areas that are exhibiting decentralization of population as well as one or two that are exhibiting centralization. In short, they have been deliberately selected to illustrate most of the typical variations in metropolitan area change during the 1950s. Journey to work figures for the nine areas are summarized in Table 5.58.

Table 5.58

WORK JOURNEYS IN SELECTED SMLAs, 1951, 1961 AND 1966

1 Reading SMLA

1951 From/To	Core %	Ring %	Other %	Total journeys	Of which crossing journeys
Core %	45	5	4	52,604	8,318
Ring %	8	28	5	40,692	15,455
Other %	2	4	—	5,875	5,875
Total journeys	53,702	36,612	8,857	99,171	
Of which crossing journeys	9,416	11,375	8,857		29,648 (30 per cent of total)

1961 From/To	Core %	Ring %	Other %	Total journeys	Of which crossing journeys
Core %	37	6	4	56,200	11,450
Ring %	10	26	8	53,380	25,270
Other %	3	7	—	11,510	11,510
Total journeys	60,130	46,980	13,980	121,090	
Of which crossing journeys	15,380	18,870	13,980		48,230 (40 per cent of total)

1966 From/To	Core %	Ring %	Other %	Total journeys	Of which crossing journeys
Core %	34	5	4	60,930	12,450
Ring %	12	26	10	68,760	37,430
Other %	3	5	—	12,000	12,000
Total journeys	69,690	51,740	20,260	141,690	
Of which crossing journeys	21,210	20,410	20,260		61,880 (44 per cent of total)

2 Southend SMLA

1951 From/To	Core %	Ring %	Other %	Total journeys	Of which crossing journeys
Core %	52	2	20	63,215	19,176
Ring %	5	11	7	19,491	10,787
Other %	2	1	—	2,332	2,332
Total journeys	49,345	12,392	23,301	85,038	
Of which crossing journeys	5,306	3,688	23,301		32,295 (38 per cent of total)

1961 From/To	Core %	Ring %	Other %	Total journeys	Of which crossing journeys
Core %	43	4	17	68,060	22,190
Ring %	7	11	14	34,650	23,650
Other %	2	2	—	4,090	4,090
Total journeys	55,350	17,880	33,570	106,800	
Of which crossing journeys	9,480	6,880	33,570		49,930 (47 per cent of total)

1966 From/To	Core %	Ring %	Other %	Total journeys	Of which crossing journeys
Core %	40	5	15	73,740	24,550
Ring %	7	13	16	44,900	30,940
Other %	2	2	—	5,000	5,000
Total journeys	60,940	24,030	38,670	123,640	
Of which crossing journeys	11,750	10,070	38,670		60,490 (49 per cent of total)

3 **Tunbridge Wells SMLA**

1951 From/To	Core %	Ring %	Other %	Total journeys	Of which crossing journeys
Core %	32	3	4	16,171	3,077
Ring %	7	40	6	21,442	6,998
Other %	4	3	—	2,823	2,823
Total journeys	17,271	18,912	4,253	40,436	
Of which crossing journeys	4,177	4,468	4,253		12,898 (32 per cent of total)

1961 From/To	Core %	Ring %	Other %	Total journeys	Of which crossing journeys
Core %	29	3	5	17,330	3,980
Ring %	8	34	10	23,890	9,590
Other %	6	4	—	4,720	4,720
Total journeys	19,850	18,950	7,140	45,940	
Of which crossing journeys	6,500	4,650	7,140		18,290 (40 per cent of total)

1966 From/To	Core %	Ring %	Other %	Total journeys	Of which crossing journeys
Core %	26	4	5	18,600	4,710
Ring %	8	33	14	29,100	13,900
Other %	6	5	—	5,470	5,470
Total journeys	20,940	21,700	10,530	53,170	
Of which crossing journeys	7,050	6,500	10,530		24,080 (45 per cent of total)

4 Stevenage SMLA

1951 From/To	Core %	Ring %	Other %	Total journeys	Of which crossing journeys
Core %	7	1	2	2,997	901
Ring %	4	48	27	22,660	10,085
Other %	2	8	—	3,083	3,083
Total journeys	3,879	16,672	8,189	28,740	
Of which crossing journeys	1,785	4,097	8,189		14,069 (49 per cent of total)

1961 From/To	Core %	Ring %	Other %	Total journeys	Of which crossing journeys
Core %	33	2	4	19,460	2,710
Ring %	5	26	20	10,310	14,350
Other %	5	6	—	5,690	5,690
Total journeys	22,110	17,160	12,230	51,500	
Of which crossing journeys	5,360	5,160	12,230		22,750 (44 per cent of total)

1966 From/To	Core %	Ring %	Other %	Total journeys	Of which crossing journeys
Core %	35	2	4	26,140	3,930
Ring %	5	23	17	28,550	15,220
Other %	6	8	—	8,870	8,870
Total journeys	29,160	20,790	13,610	63,560	
Of which crossing journeys	6,950	7,460	13,610		28,020 (44 per cent of total)

5 Birmingham SMLA

1951 From/To	Core %	Ring %	Other %	Total journeys	Of which crossing journeys
Core %	71	2	1	930,120	156,590
Ring %	8	15	2	311,520	158,140
Other %	1	1	—	26,600	26,600
Total journeys	1,012,330	225,740	30,170	1,268,240	
Of which crossing journeys	238,800	72,360	30,170		341,330 (27 per cent of total)

1961 From/To	Core %	Ring %	Other %	Total journeys	Of which crossing journeys
Core %	64	3	1	934,510	190,360
Ring %	11	16	2	403,520	229,460
Other %	1	1	—	38,250	38,250
Total journeys	1,064,150	272,690	39,440	1,376,280	
Of which crossing journeys	320,000	98,630	39,440		458,070 (33 per cent of total)

1966 From/To	Core %	Ring %	Other %	Total journeys	Of which crossing journeys
Core %	63	3	0·3	936,850	149,360
Ring %	11	15	2	403,680	216,570
Other %	3	1	—	54,470	54,470
Total journeys	1,073,850	282,410	38,740	1,395,000	
Of which crossing journeys	286,360	95,300	38,740		420,400 (30 per cent of total)

6 Northampton SMLA

1951 From/To	Core %	Ring %	Other %	Total journeys	Of which crossing journeys
Core %	65	5	2	51,633	5,325
Ring %	8	12	2	15,818	7,303
Other %	3	1	—	3,461	3,461
Total journeys	54,281	13,563	3,068	70,912	
Of which crossing journeys	7,973	5,048	3,068		16,089 (23 per cent of total)

1961 From/To	Core %	Ring %	Other %	Total journeys	Of which crossing journeys
Core %	58	6	3	51,010	6,640
Ring %	12	12	3	20,290	11,480
Other %	5	1	—	4,550	4,550
Total journeys	56,720	14,960	4,170	75,850	
Of which crossing journeys	12,350	6,150	4,170		22,670 (30 per cent of total)

1966 From/To	Core %	Ring %	Other %	Total journeys	Of which crossing journeys
Core %	67	3	4	60,460	5,140
Ring %	8	9	2	16,120	8,640
Other %	6	1	—	6,460	6,460
Total journeys	67,180	10,970	4,890	83,040	
Of which crossing journeys	11,860	3,490	4,890		20,240 (24 per cent of total)

7 Leicester SMLA

1951 From/To	Core %	Ring %	Other %	Total journeys	Of which crossing journeys
Core %	61	2	1	147,750	7,748
Ring %	11	17	3	71,850	34,004
Other %	2	2	—	9,330	9,330
Total journeys	168,455	49,898	10,577	228,930	
Of which crossing journeys	28,453	12,052	10,577		51,082 (22 per cent of total)

1961 From/To	Core %	Ring %	Other %	Total journeys	Of which crossing journeys
Core %	53	3	1	140,350	10,260
Ring %	17	18	4	94,720	55,360
Other %	2	2	—	10,520	10,520
Total journeys	176,950	56,390	12,250	245,590	
Of which crossing journeys	46,860	17,030	12,250		76,140 (31 per cent of total)

1966 From/To	Core %	Ring %	Other %	Total journeys	Of which crossing journeys
Core %	50	4	1	143,530	12,690
Ring %	16	19	5	103,450	57,920
Other %	3	3	—	16,490	16,490
Total journeys	180,400	68,270	14,800	263,470	
Of which crossing journeys	49,560	22,740	14,800		87,100 (33 per cent of total)

8 **Burnley SMLA**

1951 From/To	Core %	Ring %	Other %	Total journeys	Of which crossing journeys
Core %	57	5	5	45,710	6,538
Ring %	5	16	5	17,562	7,681
Other %	4	4	—	5,225	5,225
Total journeys	45,188	16,882	6,427	68,497	
Of which crossing journeys	6,016	7,001	6,427		19,444 (23 per cent of total)

1961 From/To	Core %	Ring %	Other %	Total journeys	Of which crossing journeys
Core %	52	6	4	41,040	6,800
Ring %	6	13	6	16,840	9,600
Other %	7	6	—	8,440	8,440
Total journeys	42,810	16,800	6,710	66,320	
Of which crossing journeys	8,570	9,560	6,710		24,840 (37 per cent of total)

1966 From/To	Core %	Ring %	Other %	Total journeys	Of which crossing journeys
Core %	51	5	5	39,080	6,570
Ring %	8	12	6	16,730	10,040
Other %	8	5	—	8,230	8,230
Total journeys	42,150	14,540	7,350	64,040	
Of which crossing journeys	9,640	7,850	7,350		24,840 (39 per cent of total)

9 Halifax SMLA

1951 From/To	Core %	Ring %	Other %	Total journeys	Of which crossing journeys
Core %	45	4	2	49,360	5,510
Ring %	5	28	4	35,931	10,531
Other %	3	10	—	12,976	12,976
Total journeys	51,781	40,895	5,591	98,267	
Of which crossing journeys	7,931	15,495	5,591		29,017 (30 per cent of total)

1961 From/To	Core %	Ring %	Other %	Total journeys	Of which crossing journeys
Core %	46	4	3	48,510	6,200
Ring %	6	27	5	35,310	12,210
Other %	4	5	—	8,170	8,170
Total journeys	51,770	33,170	7,050	91,990	
Of which crossing journeys	9,460	10,070	7,050		26,580 (29 per cent of total)

1966 From/To	Core %	Ring %	Other %	Total journeys	Of which crossing journeys
Core %	43	5	3	46,980	6,810
Ring %	7	27	5	35,660	13,080
Other %	5	5	—	9,890	9,890
Total journeys	51,370	34,340	6,820	92,530	
Of which crossing journeys	11,200	11,760	6,820		29,780 (32 per cent of total)

Four of the nine SMLAs are chosen from the ring of rapidly growing metropolitan areas around London. Two of them, Reading and Southend, are at first sight similar: they are high growth areas with strong concentrations of employment in their core towns, and with rapid decentralization of population. But they differ in one important respect: historically Southend has always been more dependent on London for jobs, and this dependence has continued despite a substantial increase in jobs in the SMLA itself and particularly within its core. Total work journeys into and out of, and within the Reading SMLA, rose from 99,000 to 121,000 from 1951 to 1961, and then to 142,000 in 1966. There was an even more rapid increase in journeys crossing local authority boundaries, from 30 per cent to 40 per cent and then to 44 per cent of the total. Originating journeys (residents in employment) within the SMLA rose from 93,000 to 110,000 and then to 129,000. Arriving journeys (i.e. jobs) rose from 90,000 to 107,000 and then to 121,000, so that a slight job deficiency continued for the SMLA as a whole, increasing notably after 1961. Journeys to the core increased from 54,000 to 70,000 over the period, but fell as a proportion of the whole from 55 to 49 per cent. There was a sharp fall in the proportion of journeys wholly within the core, representing a static total from 1951–61; thenceforth the total rose somewhat but the percentage fell. Ring to core journeys rose steadily from 7,500 to 17,000 in 1966 (from 8 to 12 per cent of the total); reverse journeys from core to ring rose and then fell, keeping roughly the same percentage of the total.

The Reading SMLA is distinguished by a large number of ring to ring journeys within its suburbs, and these rose from 28,000 to 37,000 over the period, though their percentage share of the total fell marginally from 28 to 26 per cent. Significantly, journeys from the ring to other metropolitan areas (mainly London) rose absolutely and relatively during the period, from 5,000 to nearly 15,000 and from 5 to 10 per cent of the total. Journeys in the reverse direction, from other areas into the ring, rose from 1951 to 1961 but thereafter declined. Reading then is an example of a decentralized employment pattern where, by the early 1960s, more than half the workers had jobs outside the core. But the main reason for this was the sharp rise in journeys out of the metropolitan area altogether, and the ring had only a marginally higher share of SMLA employment in 1966 than in 1951. In 1951, out of 93,000 resident employed, 9,000 left the area. The figures for 1966 were 129,000 and 20,000.

In the Southend SMLA total journeys in, out and within the area showed similarly big increases, from 85,000 in 1951 to 124,000 in 1966. Crossing journeys rose even faster, from 38 per cent to 49 per cent of the total, though this increase was faster up to 1961 than after it. Within the SMLA, originating work journeys rose steadily from 83,000 to 119,000; arriving work journeys (jobs) rose from 62,000 in 1951 to 73,000 in 1961 and then to no less than 85,000 in 1966. The deficiency of jobs in the metropolitan area was therefore more pronounced at the end of the period than at the beginning, despite a big creation of new jobs. The share of total employment in the core fell despite an actual increase in numbers, and core to core journeys fell noticeably as a proportion of the total, from 52 to 40 per cent, though the actual total rose slightly. Ring to core journeys rose slightly as a proportion of all journeys, while there was a spectacular increase in core to ring journeys from a small base. But the two distinctive features of the Southend SMLA both became more marked during the period. They were the high and rising numbers of ring to ring work journeys (increasing from 11 to 13 per cent of all journeys) and the high proportion of journeys made from the ring to other metropolitan areas, which almost quadrupled in number and rose from 7 to 16 per cent of the total. There was also a large number of core to other SMLA journeys, but this remained constant in numbers and declined as a proportion of the total. Altogether, the most remarkable feature of the entire Southend SMLA was its dependence on employment elsewhere. Of a workforce of 83,000 in 1951, 23,000 left the SMLA for work; by 1966 the corresponding figures were 119,000 and 39,000. Even more than Reading, the Southend SMLA is marked by an extraordinary degree of dependency on employment elsewhere, above all in London.

The Tunbridge Wells SMLA had a more modest gain in total work journeys, from 40,000 to 53,000 between 1951 and 1966. Crossing journeys rose rapidly from 32 to 45 per cent of the total. Journeys with core destinations were a minority even in 1951, and the proportion fell slightly between 1961 and 1966, from 43 to 39 per cent. Most of these were core to core journeys, which formed a constant total but a falling proportion of all journeys. Ring to ring journeys were a more important category in Tunbridge Wells, even in 1951, but here also the share in total journeys fell. As in Reading and Southend there was a noticeable dependence on outside metropolitan areas for work. Out of 38,000 originating work trips in 1951, 4,300 were bound outside the metropolitan area; the corresponding figures in 1966 were 48,000 and 10,500, representing a spectacular increase in the proportion. Tunbridge Wells therefore was not immune from the general tendency in the metropolitan areas around London. While its total originating journeys (resident employed) rose from 38,000 to 48,000 in the period, its total arriving journeys (jobs) rose only from 36,000 to 43,000; the deficiency of jobs in the metropolitan area, here as at Reading and Southend, grew slightly over the period.

The last of the four metropolitan areas from the ring around London examined here, Stevenage SMLA, is in many ways a special case. Because of the development of the new town it was one of the fastest-growing SMLAs in England and Wales during the 1950s and (at a slower pace) the early 1960s. Total work journeys rose from 29,000 to 51,000 between 1951 and 1961, and thence to 64,000 by 1966. Originating journeys within the SMLA increased from 25,000 to 55,000 over the fifteen-year period; arriving journeys (i.e. jobs) rose from 21,000 to 50,000. Most of the people and the jobs were concentrated in the new town, and a notable feature is the high proportion of journeys made within the core; only 7 per cent of all journeys in 1951, such trips accounted for 33 per cent in 1961 and for 35 per cent in 1966. The next biggest group, ring to ring journeys, increased marginally in total over the period, but for obvious reasons fell sharply as a percentage of all journeys. Most interesting of all, with a new town such as this, is the dependence of the metropolitan area on outside employment. In 1951, out of a total resident workforce of 25,000, 8,000 left the SMLA for work. By 1966, out of a total of 55,000, 14,000 left. But most of this increase was accounted for by the ring of the SMLA, including some outer suburban dormitories. Out of the 3,000 resident workers of the core in 1951, 500 left; out of the 26,000 in 1966, 3,000 left. The new town had thus proved relatively successful in providing jobs for its own residents. But interestingly, it had not been conspicuously more successful than Southend in providing employment for the metropolitan area of which it formed the core, and had been actually less successful than Reading. Every day in 1966 nearly 25 per cent of the SMLA workforce left the Stevenage area for work, compared with some 15 per cent in Reading.

The largest SMLA outside London, Birmingham, could not present a greater contrast. This is an extreme case of highly-centralized employment patterns, for 80 per cent of all journeys into, out of, or within the SMLA in 1951, and 77 per cent in 1961 and 1966, were made into a large core which included not merely Birmingham itself but many Black Country towns. Jobs rose modestly from 1,012,000 to 1,074,000 between 1951 and 1966; in the ring they rose from 226,000 to 282,000, most of the increases occurring before 1961. Residents in employment in the core remained almost static at 930,000 to 940,000 over the whole period while the number in the ring rose rapidly from 312,000 to 404,000 between 1961 and 1966, thereafter remaining almost constant. The most striking feature of the area is the large proportion of all journeys which both begin and end in the core: the total fell only from 895,000 to 885,000 over the period. Ring to core commuters rose from 104,000 to 156,000 during the 1950s, but again remained almost static afterwards; the same was true of ring to ring commuters. A significant feature was the marked increase in long-distance commuters from outside the SMLA altogether, particularly into the core, after 1961. This total nearly trebled, from 13,000 to 35,000 between 1951 and 1966. But it was not enough to affect the general picture: in this large metropolitan area, journeys into or out of the area altogether were relatively insignificant, and crossing journeys as a whole remained a relatively small proportion of total journeys, partly due to the influence of Birmingham, the largest undivided local authority area in England.

Though it is far smaller, the Northampton metropolitan area shares some of the features of Birmingham. It is an SMLA with centralized employment (accounting for 77 per cent of all journeys made to the core in 1951, 75 per cent in 1961, and 81 per cent after a boundary extension in 1966), with relatively few crossing journeys (23 per cent in 1951, 30 per cent in 1961, and 24 per cent after the extension of the central core in 1966), and with a high proportion of all journeys made completely within the core (65 per cent in 1951, 58 per cent a decade later, 67 per cent in 1966). Between 1951 and 1961, when the definitions of core and ring remained constant, journeys originating within the ring rose from 22 to 27 per cent, and ring to core trips rose from 5,500 to 8,800, or from 8 to 12 per cent of the total; after the boundary change, between 1961 and 1966, these trends were reversed. Doubtless, were it not for the accident of the boundary extension, Northampton during the early 1960s would have revealed the same trends as in the 1950s: modest decentralization of population, rather faster than the decentralization of jobs, against a base of a highly centralized distribution of both.

Leicester SMLA is a less extreme example of these same trends. Its employment is highly concentrated in the core though the percentage is falling (168,000 out of 218,000 in 1951, 180,000 out of 249,000 in 1966), but the active resident population in the core fell over the same period from 148,000 to 144,000, despite a small boundary extension. The proportion of core to core journeys fell quite sharply over the period, from 61 to 50 per cent of all work journeys into, out of, or within the SMLA, representing a fall in numbers from 140,000 to 130,000. Ring to core journeys rose from 21,000 to 41,000 and from 11 to 16 per cent of the total. Leicester SMLA was therefore another metropolitan area with a sharp increase in the proportion of crossing journeys (from 22 to 33 per cent of the total); but as with other Midland metropolitan areas, the proportion of journeys into or out of the SMLA remained a very small part of the whole.

Lastly, our analysis includes two metropolitan areas in the North which have experienced actual declines in population and economic activity in the period since 1951. Burnley is a metropolitan area where historically both population and employment have been highly concentrated in the core. 67 per cent of all work journeys into, out of, or within the metropolitan area in 1951, and 61 per cent in 1966 began there; 66 per cent, both in 1951 and 1966, ended there. Core to core journeys therefore dominated the commuting picture, accounting for 57 per cent of all journeys in 1951 and for 51 per cent in 1966. But this total was declining absolutely as well as relatively. Ring to ring journeys also fell both absolutely and relatively, from 16 per cent of total journeys in 1951 to 12 per cent in 1966. Perhaps the most notable trend was the increasing proportion of journeys which began or ended outside the metropolitan area altogether, a product of high densities of population and employment in neighbouring metropolitan areas only a few miles distant. Journeys into the metropolitan area rose from 8 to 13 per cent of total journeys during the fifteen-year period; journeys in the reverse direction rose more modestly from 10 to 11 per cent. These helped to swell the proportion of journeys which crossed local authority boundaries from 23 per cent at the beginning of the period to 39 per cent at the end of it.

The last of our sample of SMLAs, Halifax, is an old-established industrial area with a much weaker degree of centralization of people and jobs compared with Burnley. Alike in 1951, 1961 and 1966, the core accounted for only about half the originating work trips into, out of or within the SMLA and for about half the arriving ones. The total number of journeys declined somewhat from 1951 to 1961 and thereafter remained constant. Particularly notable is the very high proportion of journeys bound for work destinations in the ring (42 per cent in 1951, 37 per cent in 1966), a product of high employment opportunities in some of the small towns and industrial villages in the ring. Halifax is curiously like Stevenage, if in no other respect, in its high proportion of ring to ring journeys, which, at 28 per cent in 1951 and 27 per cent in 1966, are not far behind the proportion of core to core journeys (45 per cent and 43 per cent respectively). And as at Burnley, there is a high proportion of journeys which cross the boundaries of the metropolitan area altogether; 13 per cent in 1951 and 10 per cent in 1966 came in, while 6 per cent in 1951 and 8 per cent in 1966 went out. But because of the high proportion of ring to ring journeys, the total crossing journeys form only a small part of the whole: 30 per cent in 1951 and 32 per cent in 1966.

All in all, it is difficult to generalize from such varied instances. But that is probably because they have been deliberately chosen for their variation. The most typical English SMLA, in the 1950s and 1960s, was a small- or medium-sized metropolitan area with rather centralized employment beginning to decentralize, and with decentralizing population, resulting in a fall in core to core journeys and a rise in ring to core journeys. But in all cases, the proportion of work journeys ending in the ring was either static or rising, and in some typical medium-sized SMLAs there was a particularly noticeable increase in the proportion of these journeys made to suburban workplaces.

The significance of this lies in the type of journey that is made and the way it is made. The old core to core journey, within the central city or town, was characteristically made by public transport: a dense population gave the possibility of a good public transport service, and traffic congestion made the use of the private car more difficult here. The same is likely to occur with ring to core journeys, where the limitation on car use will still be the congestion at the city end. But the ring to ring journey (or the rarer core to ring journey) does not suffer the same limitations, and may be made by private car.

For the first time, the 1966 Census provided information that threw some light on this point. Unfortunately it does not allow an elaborate cross classification of all these types of journey in terms of the mode of transport used. But the published data do allow us to divide all journeys beginning in cores and rings of SMLAs, and all journeys arriving in the same cores and rings, according to the means of transport used. Figures 5.29 and 5.30 map journeys by private mode (including car, van, motor bicycle or pedal cycle) as a percentage of all originating journeys, and all arriving journeys, respectively. Figure 5.30 is particularly interesting, because it would be thought that the pattern of arriving work journeys was particularly related to conditions of congestion at the work end. Studies in North America, particularly by W. Owen, show clearly that private modes account for a much larger proportion of all arriving journeys in rings than in cores of metropolitan areas, except in some western cities which have from the start been developed round the car. They show that the suburban rings everywhere have a high proportion of private travel, but that the central cores have a varying proportion depending principally on the age of development of the city; east coast cities have much lower proportions than west coast cities. Figure 5.30 however shows that this clear pattern is not observable in Britain. For many small and medium-sized metropolitan areas, the proportions travelling by private modes are very

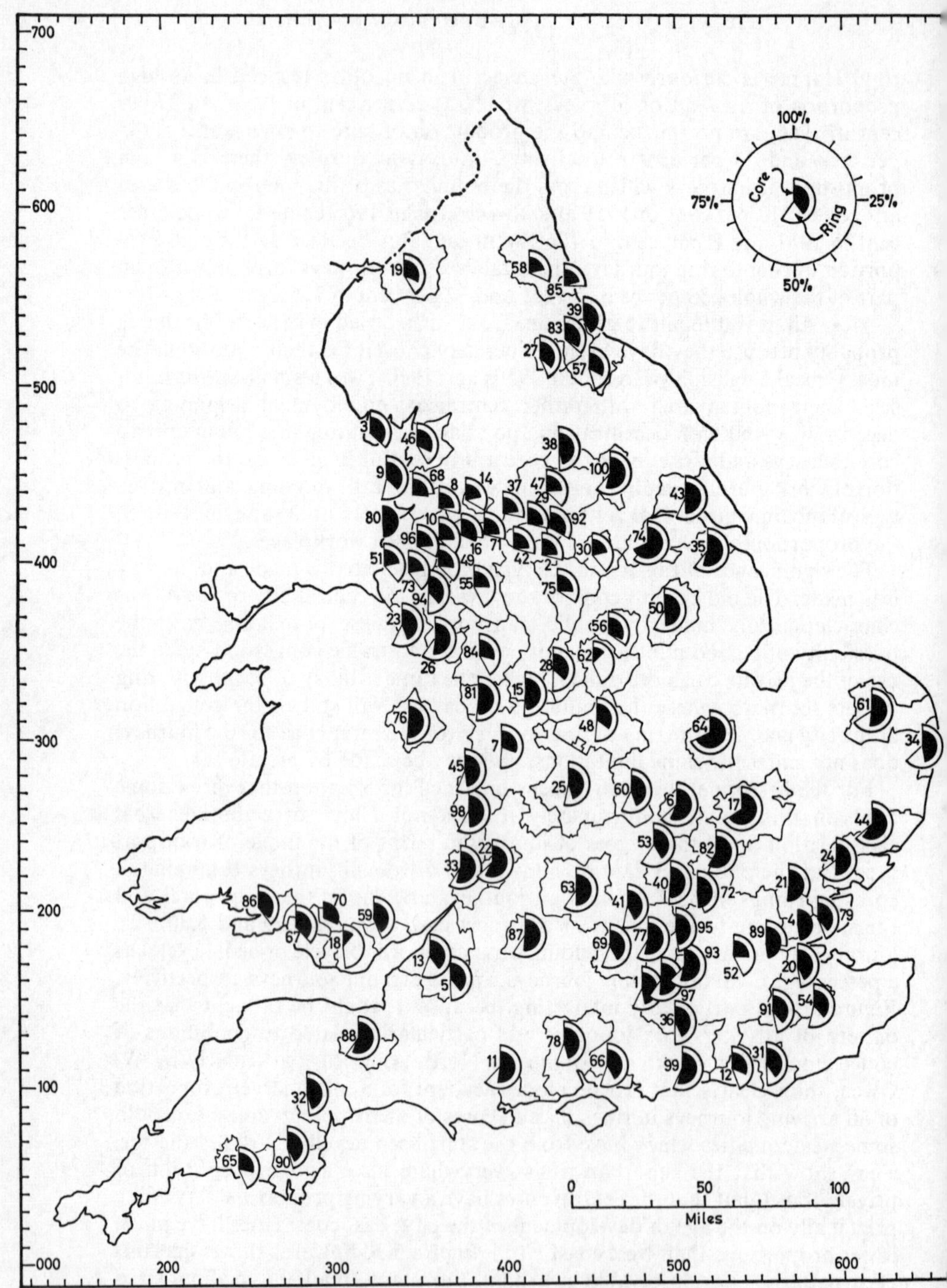

Figure 5.29 Originating Journeys to Work: Proportion by Private Transport, in SMLAs, 1966 (*Key: pages 254–292*)

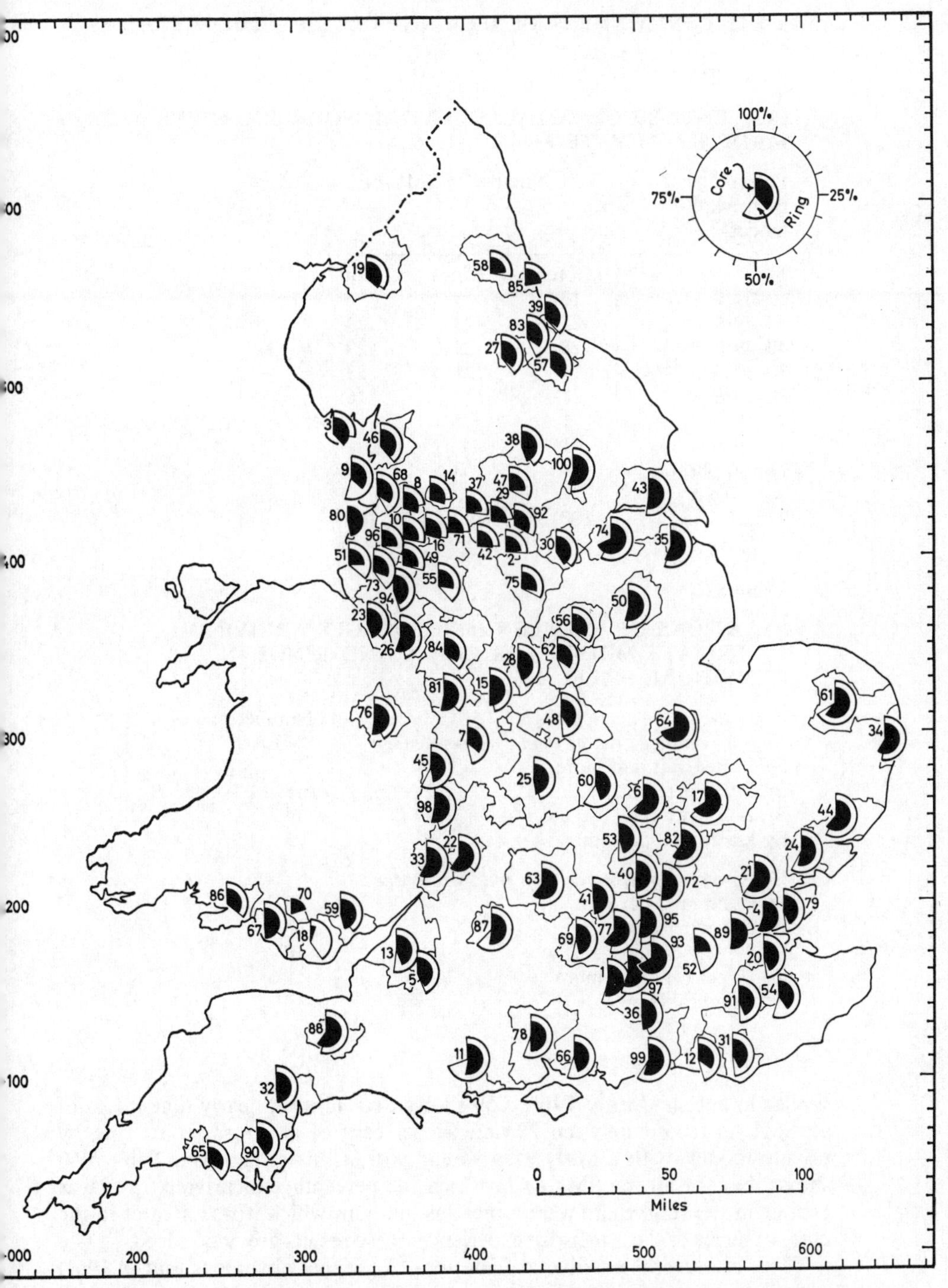

Figure 5.30 Arriving Journeys to Work: Proportion by Private Transport, in SMLAs, 1966 (*Key: pages 254–292*)

Table 5.59

PERCENTAGE OF TOTAL ARRIVING WORK JOURNEYS MADE BY PRIVATE MODES, 1966

Percentage by private modes	Number of SMLAs		
	Cores	Rings	Total
60–69·9	10	8	6
50–59·9	22	25	24
40–49·9	28	29	29
30–39·9	17	21	23
20–29·9	21	13	16
10–19·9	1	1	2
0– 9·9	1	—	—
Not applicable	—	3	—
Total	100	100	100

Table 5.60

RELATIONSHIP BETWEEN PERCENTAGES ARRIVING BY PRIVATE MODES, FOR CORES AND RINGS IN INDIVIDUAL SMLAs, 1966

	Number of SMLAs	
Ring percentage greater than core percentage		
By 10 per cent and more	11	51
By 5–9·9 per cent	18	
By 2–4·9 per cent	14	
By less than 2 per cent	8	
Core percentage greater than ring percentage		
By less than 2 per cent	12	46
By 2–4·9 per cent	16	
By 5–9·9 per cent	10	
By 10 per cent and more	8	
Not applicable	3	
Total	100	

similar in core and ring. Table 5.59 shows that in both, nearly nine in ten of all SMLAs record between 20 and 60 per cent of all journeys arriving by private modes, with a fairly even spread within this range. And Table 5.60 shows that for all the SMLAs in which the percentage of private travel was greater in the ring, there were almost as many in which it was greater in the core. In terms of the American experience, these results are odd indeed.

There are several possible explanations. The most obvious is that in 1966, overall car ownership in England and Wales, at about 46 per cent of all households, was much lower than in North America, and constraints on car usage correspondingly less severe. There appears to be a close relationship indeed between the pattern of car ownership and the percentage of private travel in the arriving work journeys. Another point is that income distribution is probably more even, between cores and rings of SMLAs, than in the United States. Insofar as there are differences, they are quite likely to favour the core where many of the well paid factory and office jobs are, rather than the agricultural hinterland. What is significant is that the larger SMLAs almost without exception demonstrated the North American pattern, with much higher proportions of private modes in the suburbs. In Table 5.60, Birmingham, Cardiff, Liverpool, London, and Manchester all appeared in the group where the percentage was 10 per cent or more higher in the ring than in the core; Bristol, Leeds, Leicester, and Nottingham appeared in the 5–10 per cent group, Newcastle and Sheffield in the 2–5 per cent group. These SMLAs stand out in Figure 5.30 and they probably represent a pattern which will spread to smaller metropolitan areas as the pressure of car traffic intensifies.

SOME CONCLUSIONS

It is now possible to see, in a way that would not have been possible without the use of metropolitan area analysis, some of the main trends in the urban growth patterns of England and Wales in the 35-year period from 1931 to 1966 – a period that covered the urban spread of the 1930s, the halt to urban development of the war years, and the resumption of urban growth and spread in the 1950s and early 1960s.

The first conclusion concerns the absolute dominance of metropolitan England and Wales within the national society and the national economy. Standard Metropolitan Areas, defined according to broadly the same principles as the Standard Metropolitan Areas of the United States Census, have accounted for an almost constant 77–78 per cent of the population counted at home, and 79–80 per cent of the employment counted at place of work. A more generous definition of the sphere of urban influence, the Metropolitan Economic Labour Area, takes in all those areas contributing commuters to major employment centres; such areas account for a steady 93–94 per cent of the national population, and for 94–96 per cent of national employment, over the period 1931–66. Whatever the definition used, it can broadly be said that the growth of population and employment in the metropolitan areas has marched in line with that in the country generally. Viewed on the map, however, such metropolitan areas are by no means evenly spread over the face of the country. One quarter of them, accounting for about one-fifth of the total metroplitan population, are found in and around London. Another two-fifths of all metropolitan areas, accounting for as much as 50 per cent of the total metropolitan population, are found in a solid mass extending from the West and East Midlands up to Lancashire and Yorkshire, including projections northeastwards towards Humberside and southwestwards towards Severnside and South Wales. Altogether then, 90 per cent of the metropolitan population of England and Wales is concentrated in these two great zones based on London and the Midlands-Lancashire-Yorkshire axis. A mere glance at the map is enough to suggest that here, perhaps, is reason to believe in the existence of an English Megalopolis. This is a proposition which we shall have to examine more rigorously in the chapter that follows.

The second important conclusion concerns the dynamics of change in metropolitan England and Wales. Though as a whole the metropolitan areas have kept pace with the general growth of population in the country as a whole, the growth has been by no means even. Whether one measures gains or losses in absolute terms (that is, in terms of actual people or workers gained or lost) or in relative terms (that is, in terms of percentages), there is a clear regional pattern; metropolitan areas in the South-East and the Midlands have broadly tended to gain, while those in the North-West and in Yorkshire have tended to stagnate or even (especially after 1961) to lose. Otherwise, in terms of size, the pattern is less clear. If big metropolitan areas gain at all, they may tend to have big gains in an absolute sense, even if in percentage terms the gain would seem small. Such big absolute gains, which appeared small when put into percentage terms, were typical of some of the biggest metropolitan areas, broadly constituting the conurbations and the zones round the biggest free-standing cities, in the 1950s. But since 1961 some of the biggest metropolitan areas have actually experienced loss. Conversely, some of the biggest gainers, even in absolute, but above all in percentage terms, have been relatively small metropolitan areas in the faster-growing regions, like the ring of standard metropolitan areas round London; though in regions showing poor general growth, these smaller metropolitan areas might stagnate or even decline. Putting together the regional trend and the size trend, one can distinguish a general effect. By and large, the biggest metropolitan areas seem to have come to a period of stagnation and even decline, which is evident in the slow-growing and the fast-growing regions alike. But in fast-growing regions, this is accompanied by extremely rapid growth of smaller, peripheral metropolitan areas, a trend best of all marked around London. When however regional dynamism is weak, losses in the big central metropolitan area may be accompanied by only modest gains in the smaller areas on the periphery, and the overall effect will be one of stagnation at best. This is an important conclusion, which we shall need to follow through in detail in some of our case studies which form Part Two of this work.

Our third conclusion concerns the internal dynamics of centralization and decentralization within each metropolitan area. Here, the tendency is clear: population has shown a marked tendency to decentralize from the core to the ring, while employment has shown a remarkable stability in its patterns, at least until recently. Of the total metropolitan population of England and Wales, 71 per cent was found in metropolitan cores in 1931; this proportion had fallen to 60 per cent by 1966. Conversely, the proportion of the total population in the rings had risen from 29 to 40 per cent in the same period. Yet between 1951 and 1966, the proportion of employment fell only very marginally from 74 to 71 per cent in the cores, rising from 26 to 29 per cent in the rings. At first sight then, it appears as if population is leaving the central cities while employment is remaining relatively immobile, a situation which can only lead to increased length of journey to work with all the attendant problems that it may bring.

Examined in more detail, the great majority of metropolitan areas in the 1950s and the 1960s were decentralizing their populations, whatever measure one uses to analyse this process. In particular the larger metropolitan areas, based on the conurbations and the large freestanding cities, were tending to decentralize earliest and fastest. And some of the most important of these tended actually to be losing populations from their cores in an absolute sense by the 1960s; London, Manchester, Liverpool, and Newcastle were all among such cases of absolute decentralization in the period 1961–66. Conversely, the case of centralization tended to occur among the smaller metropolitan areas which were experiencing rapid growth, such as some of those in the ring of growth round London. Even there, centralization tended to disappear as a phenomenon after 1961; by then, the tendency to decentralize population had spread from the larger authorities until it was fairly general.

In one sense, however, decentralization of population did not take place. Even if they moved in an absolute or a relative sense from central city to suburb, the populations of metropolitan England and Wales tended to remain in built-up areas, which could be called urbanized in a physical sense. The proportion of the total England and Wales population which lived in so called urbanized areas remained constant at 67–68 per cent over the whole period 1931–66. To put it another way, throughout the whole period around nine in ten of all the inhabitants of metropolitan areas lived in their urbanized parts.

Employment, we have said, apparently showed much less tendency to migrate from the central cities. But a closer look shows that the larger metropolitan areas had begun to show a distinct tendency to decentralize jobs as well as people – at any rate, in a relative sense – even by the 1950s. By the 1960s this trend was more distinct, and some of these larger areas were actually recording absolute losses of jobs in their cores coupled with increases in their suburban rings. It is clear that the outward movement of people is older and more strongly rooted than the outward movement of jobs, and this was certainly the pattern of the 1950s. But since 1961 the pattern has become more complex.

The conclusion to be drawn from this analysis seems inescapable. It takes the form of a very simple model of urban development. Most urban areas in England and Wales are still in the earlier stages of evolution of this model, but a few of the biggest metropolitan areas have reached the later stages.

The *first stage* takes place long before the time of the analysis in this book. For most urban areas it is probably true of the nineteenth-century situation, though after 1880 some of the biggest metropolitan areas were undoubtedly moving out of it. In this stage, both people and jobs tend to centralize in the core of the metropolitan area; in fact the ring still remains rural, in both a physical and a functional sense, and it probably loses population and employment to the town.

The *second stage* is typical of many urban areas in England and Wales from 1900 up to 1950, and even beyond that in the case of many smaller metropolitan areas. In this stage, due to the liberating influence of new forms of urban transportation and the spread of owner occupiership, population begins to migrate from the core of the metropolitan area to the suburban periphery, a process which we have already described historically in Chapter Two. Generally, natural increase is sufficient to keep the population of the central core rising rapidly, despite the out-migration; thus decentralization is relative rather than absolute, in the sense we have used in the type of shift analysis in this chapter. But in the biggest cities, even before 1939, slum clearance might contribute to absolute decentralization of population. Invariably, however, increasing office and retail employment at the centre is more rapid than new factory building at the periphery, in the suburban ring; so centralization of employment, usually of a relative kind, is the general rule at this stage.

The *third stage* is typical of larger metropolitan areas in this country since 1951 but above all since 1961; it may gradually be expected to extend to smaller metropolitan areas. In it, redevelopment of the inner city, both for commercial purposes at the centre, and for slum-clearance purposes around the centre, causes a massive and sudden drop in population. Much of the overspilled population passes directly into the suburban ring, and the result is marked absolute decentralization of population. At the same time, the scale of the redevelopment programme may even bite on employment. Though there are continued increases in office and other service employment in the core of the city, these are out-weighed by the effect of redevelopment and above all by the rapid growth of local service employment (plus perhaps some decentralized factory employment) in the suburbs. The result is relative – much more rarely, absolute – decentralization of employment.

The *fourth stage* has so far only been reached by London, and perhaps by Manchester, in the 1960s; necessarily, it applies only to very large metropolitan areas. In this stage, the process of decentralization, both of people and jobs, continues a stage further; the result is that the metropolitan areas as a whole begins to lose people and jobs. This is invariably accompanied by a rapid increase of both populations and employment in a ring of smaller metropolitan areas around the central declining area – which will be the more rapid, the greater the general regional dynamism of the area. London and the ring of metropolitan areas in the so called Outer Metropolitan Area[39] are undoubtedly the clearest case. One might perhaps expect that in time, other large metropolitan areas – Birmingham, Manchester, Liverpool, Leeds – would exhibit the same tendency. But here one must enter a word of warning. Each of these major metropolitan areas has very distinctive characteristics, characteristics which do not emerge at all from the very generalized statistical analysis that has been the task of this chapter. It will be the object of Part

[39] The term Outer Metropolitan Area is of course used officially in a sense quite different from Metropolitan area as used in this book.

Three of this book to examine in detail these special characteristics, which can easily make nonsense of any facile generalization.

But one conclusion can safely be drawn from this whole analysis. It hinges on the vital question of scale in urban analysis – a question we have constantly reiterated in the course of this book. In popular discussion, it is characteristic to think of the major urban areas of Britain growing through constant accretion at the expense of the rest of the country. The analysis shows that this is far from being the case; proportionately, the biggest urban areas tend to grow more slowly, in fact. More important is that as urban areas grow, they decentralize. First, as most people recognize from their everyday experience, they disperse people into suburban homes. Then, they disperse jobs into suburban factories, offices, shops and schools. This is a trend which most British people still think characteristic of North America, not of Britain. Our analysis shows that after a due time-lag, the process has set in here too. Furthermore, it contains a built in self-reinforcing mechanism, for much of the suburban growth in employment consists of local services which are directly tied to the earlier growth in local population. Therefore, we should expect both decentralizing trends, in population and in employment, to reinforce each other, and to intensify, in the years to come. Finally, though at this stage this is a mere speculation, a number of larger metropolitan areas may follow the path of London: their growth may reach a point where both people and jobs decentralize altogether out of the metropolitan area, into peripheral complexes of living and working, based on smaller employment centres. This would represent an advanced stage in a process which can be traced back to the nineteenth century at least: the suburbanization of the English people.

			Land area 1961 ('000 acres)	Population ('000s)					Population density (persons per acre)				Labour force working in area ('000s)		
				1931	1951	1961	1966	1971*	1931	1951	1961	1966	1951	1961	1966
1. Aldershot	MELA		116·6	131·1	160·4	177·3	206·2	253·5	1·12	1·38	1·52	1·77	77·8	79·9	90·2
	SMLA		29·5	97·2	117·7	131·5	151·3	171·9	3·29	4·00	4·47	5·13	63·4	62·8	72·2
	Core		9·0	53·8	64·4	63·1	66·8	74·5	5·98	7·19	7·05	7·42	42·8	36·6	39·7
	UBZA	MELA	34·6	107·2	124·8	143·5	—	—	—	—	—	—	—	—	—
		SMLA	29·5	97·2	117·7	131·5	—	—	—	3·99	4·46	—	—	—	—
2. Barnsley	MELA		63·4	171·9	180·2	180·7	182·5	185·1	2·71	2·84	2·85	2·88	62·5	64·5	44·5
	SMLA		61·4	156·6	164·5	165·0	166·7	169·3	2·55	2·68	2·69	2·71	57·4	59·7	59·5
	Core		7·8	73·9	75·6	74·7	74·2	75·3	9·47	9·68	9·56	9·51	32·2	33·2	31·8
	UBZA	MELA	28·8	150·6	166·3	169·6	—	—	—	—	—	—	—	—	—
		SMLA	26·8	135·3	150·6	153·8	—	—	—	5·62	5·74	—	—	—	—
3. Barrow-in-Furness	MELA		161·1	118·6	118·7	117·4	116·5	118·0	0·74	0·74	0·73	0·72	45·9	47·4	49·2
	SMLA		19·0	76·7	77·9	75·2	74·5	75·2	4·04	4·09	3·96	3·92	31·9	32·9	34·2
	Core		11·0	66·2	67·5	64·9	63·9	64·0	6·02	6·13	5·90	5·81	30·2	31·0	31·4
	UBZA	MELA	16·4	87·6	91·3	93·6	—	—	—	—	—	—	—	—	—
		SMLA	13·2	73·1	74·5	72·1	—	—	—	5·64	5·46	—	—	—	—
4. Basildon	MELA		27·1	27·5	43·4	88·5	110·0	129·1	1·01	1·60	3·27	4·06	8·4	25·2	44·5
	SMLA		27·1	27·5	43·4	88·5	110·0	129·1	1·01	1·60	3·26	4·06	8·4	25·2	44·5
	Core		27·1	27·5	43·4	88·5	110·0	129·1	1·01	1·60	3·26	4·06	8·4	25·2	44·5
	UBZA	MELA	21·7	4·0	18·3	81·6	—	—	—	—	—	—	—	—	—
		SMLA	21·7	4·0	18·3	81·6	—	—	—	0·84	3·76	—	—	—	—
5. Bath	MELA		223·6	177·9	210·9	234·6	241·3	254·6	0·80	0·94	1·05	1·08	104·6	107·9	109·9
	SMLA		46·3	84·8	97·9	101·2	100·7	102·8	1·83	2·12	2·19	2·17	40·1	42·1	45·1
	Core		6·3	73·7	79·3	80·9	79·6	84·5	11·70	12·63	12·89	12·63	34·5	37·7	40·4
	UBZA	MELA	23·1	126·0	153·9	160·1	—	—	—	—	—	—	—	—	—
		SMLA	10·0	70·2	83·9	89·8	—	—	—	8·39	8·98	—	—	—	—

Note: The sources for this Appendix are: Statistical Abstract A, *SMLA/MELA Population Data 1931–1966*, WP/9. PEP, London, 1969; Statistical Abstract B, *SMLA/MELA Population Change Data 1931–1966*, WP/10. PEP, London, 1969; Statistical Abstract C, *SMLA/MELA* [illegible]

		Population change ('000s)								Employment change ('000s)			
		1931–51		1951–61		1961–66		1961–71		1951–61		1961–66	
Aldershot	SMLA	Absolute 20,540	*per cent 10·6	Absolute 13,816	per cent 11·7	Absolute 19,825	*per cent 30·1	Absolute 40,350	per cent 30·7	Absolute −581	per cent −0·9	Absolute 9,360	*per cent 29·8
	Core	Share at start 55·4	*Shift in share −0·4	Share at start 54·7	Shift in share −6·7	Share at start 48·0	*Shift in share −7·8	Share at start 48·0	Shift in share −4·6	Share at start 67·5	Shift in share −9·3	Share at start 58·3	*Shift in share −6·6
Barnsley	SMLA	Absolute 7,838	*per cent 2·5	Absolute 5·49	per cent 0·3	Absolute 1,722	*per cent 2·1	Absolute 4,299	per cent 2·6	Absolute 2,292	per cent 4·0	Absolute −160	*per cent −0·5
	Core	Share at start 47·2	*Shift in share −0·6	Share at start 46·0	Shift in share −0·7	Share at start 45·3	*Shift in share −1·6	Share at start 45·3	Shift in share −0·8	Share at start 56·1	Shift in share −0·5	Share at start 55·6	*Shift in share −4·4
Barrow-in-Furness	SMLA	Absolute 1,183	*per cent 0·8	Absolute −2,631	per cent −3·4	Absolute −703	*per cent −1·9	Absolute −28	per cent 0·0	Absolute 1,080	per cent 3·4	Absolute 1,240	*per cent 7·5
	Core	Share at start 86·3	*Shift in share 0·2	Share at start 86·7	Shift in share −0·4	Share at start 86·3	*Shift in share −1·2	Share at start 86·3	Shift in share −1·2	Share at start 94·9	Shift in share −0·8	Share at start 94·0	*Shift in share −4·7
Basildon	SMLA	Absolute 15,926	*per cent 29·0	Absolute 45,144	per cent 104·1	Absolute 21,516	*per cent 48·6	Absolute 40,549	per cent 45·8	Absolute 16,730	per cent 198·7	Absolute 19,310	*per cent 153·5
	Core	Share at start 100·0	*Shift in share —	Share at start 100·0	Shift in share —	Share at start 100·0	*Shift in share —	Share at start 100·0	Shift in share 0·0	Share at start 100·0	Shift in share —	Share at start 100·0	*Shift in share —
Bath	SMLA	Absolute 13,065	*per cent 7·7	Absolute 3,323	per cent 3·4	Absolute −479	*per cent −0·9	Absolute 1,581	per cent 1·6	Absolute 1,925	per cent 4·8	Absolute 3,070	*per cent 14·6
	Core	Share at start 86·9	*Shift in share −2·9	Share at start 81·0	Shift in share −1·1	Share at start 79·9	*Shift in share −1·8	Share at start 79·9	Shift in share +2·4	Share at start 86·0	Shift in share 3·7	Share at start 89·7	*Shift in share −0·4

* Decennial rate.

		Land area 1961 ('000 acres)	Population ('000s)					Population density (persons per acre)				Labour force working in area ('000s)		
			1931	1951	1961	1966	1971*	1931	1951	1961	1966	1951	1961	1966
6. Bedford	MELA	265·2	131·6	165·4	183·1	198·3	236·2	0·50	0·62	0·62	0·75	76·1	80·9	93·8
	SMLA	118·9	70·3	92·4	106·2	115·4	124·3	0·59	0·78	0·89	0·97	43·7	48·2	54·5
	Core	5·0	42·6	53·1	63·3	67·4	73·1	8·52	10·67	12·74	13·48	26·0	33·1	37·4
	UBZA MELA	17·1	66·7	100·3	109·6	—	—	—	—	—	—	—	—	—
	SMLA	6·3	48·1	61·7	72·5	—	—	—	9·79	11·51	—	—	—	—
7. Birmingham	MELA	850·8	2,258·0	2,623·6	2,841·3	2,920·6	3,003·0	2·63	3·08	3·34	3·43	1,292·6	1,390·3	1,451·0
	SMLA	578·1	2,147·8	2,488·1	2,693·1	2,750·1	2,818·0	3·72	4·66	4·30	4·76	1,218·7	1,326·5	1,384·1
	Core	102·9	1,660·7	1,823·2	1,870·6	1,833·9	1,796·8	16·14	17·73	18·19	17·82	995·4	1,060·4	1,073·9
	UBZA MELA	213·7	2,063·2	2,024·3	2,308·1	—	—	—	—	—	—	—	—	—
	SMLA	200·5	2,027·0	1,962·8	2,231·3	—	—	—	9·79	11·13	—	—	—	—
8. Blackburn	MELA	84·7	281·3	257·4	251·3	239·2	253·5	3·32	3·04	2·96	2·82	131·1	123·7	122·3
	SMLA	41·3	190·8	173·2	168·1	165·8	170·9	4·62	4·19	4·07	4·01	88·2	84·3	81·6
	Core	8·1	122·8	111·2	106·2	100·9	101·7	15·16	13·75	13·14	12·46	61·4	59·3	56·4
	UBZA MELA	32·4	263·0	241·3	234·3	—	—	—	—	—	—	—	—	—
	SMLA	19·6	177·1	162·0	156·1	—	—	—	8·27	7·96	—	—	—	—
9. Blackpool	MELA	25·9	122·3	230·4	252·8	258·2	267·3	6·65	8·90	9·76	9·97	91·5	95·3	103·5
	SMLA	14·2	121·5	170·3	186·6	190·9	194·6	8·56	11·96	13·10	13·44	67·4	70·7	76·4
	Core	8·6	106·0	147·3	153·2	150·6	151·3	12·33	17·11	17·79	17·51	57·4	58·9	62·0
	UBZA MELA	22·6	168·5	228·2	250·4	—	—	—	—	—	—	—	—	—
	SMLA	14·2	119·7	170·3	186·6	—	—	—	11·99	13·14	—	—	—	—
10. Bolton	MELA	45·5	265·7	252·7	249·7	250·8	256·8	5·84	5·56	5·49	5·51	119·9	117·1	115·5
	SMLA	45·5	265·7	252·7	249·7	250·8	256·8	5·84	5·56	5·49	5·51	119·9	117·1	115·5
	Core	16·8	206·0	195·8	188·3	181·3	180·8	12·26	11·66	11·22	10·79	97·7	94·5	94·2
	UBZA MELA	29·7	257·8	243·1	243·0	—	—	—	—	—	—	—	—	—
	SMLA	29·7	257·8	243·1	243·0	—	—	—	8·19	8·18	—	—	—	—

*Provisional

		Population change ('000s)								Employment change ('000s)			
		1931–51		1951–61		1961–66		1961–71		1951–61		1961–66	
Bedford	SMLA	Absolute 22,135	*per cent 15·7	Absolute 13,816	per cent 15·0	Absolute 9,111	*per cent 17·2	Absolute 18,051	per cent 17·0	Absolute 4,490	per cent 10·3	Absolute 6,270	*per cent 26·0
	Core	Share at start 60·6	*Shift in share −1·6	Share at start 57·4	Shift in share 2·19	Share at start 59·6	*Shift in share −2·4	Share at start 59·6	Shift in share −1·3	Share at start 59·6	Shift in share 9·14	Share at start 68·7	*Shift in share −0·1
Birmingham	SMLA	Absolute 340,297	*per cent 7·9	Absolute 204,963	per cent 8·2	Absolute 57,051	per cent 4·2	Absolute 124,953	per cent 4·6	Absolute 107,850	*per cent 8·9	Absolute 57,600	*per cent 8·7
	Core	Share at start 77·3	*Shift in share −2·0	Share at start 73·3	Shift in share −3·8	Share at start 69·5	*Shift in share −5·6	Share at start 69·5	Shift in share −0·7	Share at start 81·67	Shift in share −1·7	Share at start 79·93	*Shift in share −4·7
Blackburn	SMLA	Absolute 17,602	*per cent −4·6	Absolute −5,093	per cent −2·9	Absolute −2,331	*per cent −2·8	Absolute 2,788	per cent 1·7	Absolute −3,903	per cent −4·4	Absolute −2,770	*per cent −6·6
	Core	Share at start 64·4	*Shift in share −0·1	Share at start 64·2	Shift in share −1·0	Share at start 63·2	*Shift in share −4·6	Share at start 63·2	Shift in share −3·7	Share at start 69·6	Shift in share 0·8	Share at start 70·3	*Shift in share −2·4
Blackpool	SMLA	Absolute 48,788	*per cent 20·1	Absolute 16,256	per cent 9·6	Absolute 4,301	*per cent 4·6	Absolute 8,022	per cent 4·3	Absolute 3,253	per cent 4·8	Absolute 5,710	*per cent 16·2
	Core	Share at start 87·3	*Shift in share −0·4	Share at start 86·5	Shift in share −4·4	Share at start 82·1	*Shift in share −6·5	Share at start 82·1	Shift in share −3·3	Share at start 85·2	Shift in share −1·8	Share at start 83·4	*Shift in share −4·5
Bolton	SMLA	Absolute −12,995	*per cent −2·4	Absolute −2,965	per cent −1·2	Absolute 1,122	*per cent 0·9	Absolute 7,139	per cent 2·9	Absolute −2,765	per cent −2·31	Absolute −1,680	*per cent −2.86
	Core	Share at start 77·5	*Shift in share −0·0	Share at start 77·5	Shift in share −2·1	Share at start 75·4	*Shift in share −6·3	Share at start 75·4	Shift in share −4·0	Share at start 81·5	Shift in share −0·9	Share at start 80·7	*Shift in share 1·9

* Decennial rate.

		Land area 1961 ('000 acres)	Population ('000s)					Population density (persons per acre)				Labour force working in area ('000s)		
			1931	1951	1961	1966	1971*	1931	1951	1961	1966	1951	1961	1966
11. Bournemouth	MELA	379·6	278·3	365·8	406·7	424·8	459·1	0·73	0·96	1·07	1·12	140·6	159·1	174·9
	SMLA	113·5	209·1	274·3	305·0	317·7	338·9	1·84	2·42	2·67	2·80	102·3	116·4	128·5
	Core	27·2	177·0	227·9	246·4	251·5	260·1	6·51	8·37	9·06	9·25	86·5	96·5	105·8
	UBZA MELA	45·1	203·6	258·9	305·9	—	—	—	—	—	—	—	—	—
	UBZA SMLA	33·8	184·4	243·8	278·9	—	—	—	7·21	8·25	—	—	—	—
12. Brighton	MELA	96·7	268·3	314·0	337·8	342·8	359·2	2·77	3·25	3·49	3·45	116·5	133·8	144·2
	SMLA	96·7	268·3	314·0	337·8	342·8	359·2	2·77	3·25	3·49	3·45	116·5	133·8	144·2
	Core	18·3	202·9	227·6	236·1	232·1	238·7	11·09	12·44	12·91	12·68	88·1	97·9	101·5
	UBZA MELA	35·0	238·9	297·1	322·6	—	—	—	—	—	—	—	—	—
	UBZA SMLA	35·0	238·9	297·1	322·6	—	—	—	8·49	9·22	—	—	—	—
13. Bristol	MELA	384·2	608·2	709·3	763·1	762·7	840·2	1·58	1·85	1·99	1·99	300·8	331·1	362·6
	SMLA	227·9	532·0	617·1	661·2	694·5	718·1	2·33	2·71	2·90	3·05	266·9	293·1	321·3
	Core	26·4	405·9	443·0	473·0	432·0	425·2	15·88	16·81	16·59	16·36	195·6	208·2	219·3
	UBZA MELA	64·1	497·9	583·6	636·9	—	—	—	—	—	—	—	—	—
	UBZA SMLA	54·2	453·2	528·2	573·1	—	—	—	9·75	10·57	—	—	—	—
14. Burnley	MELA	66·6	231·1	204·1	193·8	187·8	188·9	3·47	3·06	2·91	2·82	108·4	97·7	94·6
	SMLA	46·3	135·0	118·8	113·5	109·6	112·3	2·92	2·57	2·45	2·37	60·9	59·6	56·7
	Core	4·7	98·3	85·0	80·6	76·3	76·5	20·91	18·14	17·19	16·23	44·2	42·8	42·2
	UBZA MELA	17·6	219·2	177·4	168·8	—	—	—	—	—	—	—	—	—
	UBZA SMLA	6·5	117·6	102·0	97·5	—	—	—	15·69	15·00	—	—	—	—
15. Burton	MELA	76·4	103·7	132·1	112·3	115·8	120·9	1·36	1·73	1·47	1·52	51·6	49·2	53·1
	SMLA	39·7	80·5	84·9	87·9	92·0	94·9	2·03	2·14	2·22	2·32	40·5	38·7	41·9
	Core	4·2	49·5	49·2	50·8	50·9	50·2	11·79	11·65	12·03	2·12	25·3	26·2	29·3
	UBZA MELA	12·8	73·2	77·4	80·2	—	—	—	—	—	—	—	—	—
	UBZA SMLA	10·3	70·1	72·4	74·5	—	—	—	7·03	7·23	—	—	—	—

		Population change ('000s)								Employment change ('000s)			
		1931–51		1951–61		1961–66		1961–71		1951–61		1961–66	
Bournemouth	SMLA	Absolute 65,169	*per cent 15·6	Absolute 30,763	per cent 11·2	Absolute 12,698	*per cent 8·3	Absolute 33,861	per cent 11·1	Absolute 14,145	per cent 13·81	Absolute 12,050	*per cent 20·7
	Core	Share at start 84·7	*Shift in share −0·8	Share at start 83·08	Shift in share −2·3	Share at start 80·8	*Shift in share −3·3	Share at start 80·8	Shift in share −4·0	Share at start 84·6	Shift in share −1·69	Share at start 82·9	*Shift in share −1·1
Brighton	SMLA	Absolute 45,665	*per cent 8·6	Absolute 23,818	per cent 7·6	Absolute 4,994	*per cent 3·0	Absolute 21,433	per cent 6·3	Absolute 17,284	per cent 14·8	Absolute 10,370	*per cent 15·5
	Core	Share at start 75·6	*Shift in share −1·6	Share at start 72·5	Shift in share 1·7	Share at start 74·2	*Shift in share −12·9	Share at start 74·2	Shift in share −7·7	Share at start 75·7	Shift in share −2·5	Share at start 73·2	*Shift in share −5·6
Bristol	SMLA	Absolute 85,086	*per cent 8·0	Absolute 44,121	per cent 7·2	Absolute 33,294	*per cent 10·1	Absolute 56,922	per cent 8·6	Absolute 26,185	per cent 9·8	Absolute 28,280	*per cent 9·7
	Core	Share at start 76·3	*Shift in share −2·3	Share at start 71·8	Shift in share −5·7	Share at start 66·1	*Shift in share −7·8	Share at start 66·1	Shift in share −6·9	Share at start 73·3	Shift in share −2·2	Share at start 71·0	*Shift in share −5·6
Burnley	SMLA	Absolute −16,200	*per cent −6·0	Absolute −5,297	per cent −4·5	Absolute −3,881	*per cent −6·8	Absolute −1,204	per cent −1·1	Absolute −1,331	per cent −2·2	Absolute −2,890	*per cent −9·7
	Core	Share at start 72·8	*Shift in share −0·6	Share at start 71·5	Shift in share −0·6	Share at start 71·0	*Shift in share −2·7	Share at start 71·0	Shift in share −2·9	Share at start 72·6	Shift in share −0·8	Share at start 71·8	*Shift in share 5·1
Burton	SMLA	Absolute 4,424	*per cent 2·8	Absolute 3,016	per cent 3·6	Absolute 4,071	*per cent 9·3	Absolute 6,949	per cent 7·9	Absolute −1,816	per cent −4·48	Absolute 3,180	*per cent 16·42
	Core	Share at start 61·5	*Shift in share −1·8	Share at start 57·9	Shift in share −0·2	Share at start 57·7	*Shift in share −4·9	Share at start 57·7	Shift in share −4·8	Share at start 62·4	Shift in share 5·3	Share at start 67·6	*Shift in share 4·7

* Decennial rate.

		Land area 1961 ('000 acres)	Population ('000s)					Population density (persons per acre)				Labour force working in area ('000s)		
			1931	1951	1961	1966	1971*	1931	1951	1961	1966	1951	1961	1966
16. Bury	MELA	41·2	151·1	146·5	144·8	155·6	168·1	3·67	3·56	3·51	3·78	76·7	74·4	75·1
	SMLA	33·0	134·5	132·0	130·4	141·5	153·1	4·08	4·00	3·95	4·29	69·6	66·4	67·4
	Core	7·4	58·3	58·8	60·2	62·8	67·8	7·88	7·92	8·09	8·49	30·3	32·5	32·5
	UBZA MELA	21·4	126·4	140·6	138·3	—	—	—	—	—	—	—	—	—
	SMLA	20·9	122·9	126·1	123·9	—	—	—	6·03	5·93	—	—	—	—
17. Cambridge	MELA	840·8	272·2	325·8	359·4	378·4	415·9	0·32	0·39	0·43	0·45	150·1	157·1	169·4
	SMLA	315·2	140·0	166·9	190·4	199·4	212·6	0·44	0·53	0·60	0·63	74·9	82·6	87·8
	Core	10·1	70·2	81·5	95·5	95·9	98·5	6·95	8·10	9·50	9·50	42·0	51·2	55·5
	UBZA MELA	28·0	99·8	120·4	157·2	—	—	—	—	—	—	—	—	—
	SMLA	17·8	68·3	81·5	109·0	—	—	—	4·58	6·12	—	—	—	—
18. Carlisle	MELA	1,135·9	196·0	212·5	208·4	213·3	213·1	0·17	0·19	0·18	0·19	92·6	87·8	92·3
	SMLA	255·0	83·4	97·6	100·8	100·9	100·7	0·33	0·40	0·41	0·40	46·6	46·8	49·5
	Core	6·1	57·3	67·8	71·1	70·6	71·5	9·39	11·67	12·21	11·57	31·9	33·5	34·4
	UBZA MELA	18·1	87·9	99·5	110·3	—	—	—	—	—	—	—	—	—
	SMLA	6·1	57·3	67·8	71·1	—	—	—	11·11	11·66	—	—	—	—
19. Cardiff	MELA	189·2	648·8	657·5	677·6	680·9	694·5	3·48	3·48	3·58	3·60	253·0	281·5	292·7
	SMLA	113·4	37·4	400·3	432·6	440·8	455·0	0·33	4·07	4·40	3·89	173·1	186·7	198·8
	Core	15·1	226·9	243·6	256·6	253·9	278·2	15·03	16·15	17·01	16·81	120·8	133·0	141·8
	UBZA MELA	109·2	605·9	579·8	615·0	—	—	—	—	—	—	—	—	—
	SMLA	53·6	354·4	358·2	406·9	—	—	—	6·68	7·59	—	—	—	—
20. Chatham	MELA	173·8	258·7	298·0	325·8	359·2	392·4	1·49	1·71	1·87	2·07	119·4	122·1	133·6
	SMLA	65·2	154·6	179·9	200·6	220·9	241·1	2·37	2·76	3·07	3·39	77·1	81·7	87·6
	Core	8·4	75·4	88·4	98·9	106·4	112·4	8·98	10·59	11·85	12·67	46·0	54·7	56·3
	UBZA MELA	31·1	207·6	238·8	262·5	—	—	—	—	—	—	—	—	—
	SMLA	19·4	134·0	159·0	177·1	—	—	—	8·20	9·13	—	—	—	—

		Population change ('000s)								Employment change ('000s)			
		1931–51		1951–61		1961–66		1961–71		1951–61		1961–66	
Bury	SMLA	Absolute −22,443	*per cent −0·9	Absolute −1,577	per cent −1·2	Absolute 11,109	*per cent 17·0	Absolute 22,695	per cent 17·4	Absolute −3,198	per cent −4·6	Absolute 1,000	*per cent 3·0
	Core	Share at start 43·5	*Shift in share 0·6	Share at start 44·6	Shift in share 1·6	Share at start 46·1	*Shift in share −3·6	Share at start 46·1	Shift in share −1·8	Share at start 43·6	Shift in share 5·4	Share at start 48·9	*Shift in share 1·4
Cambridge	SMLA	Absolute 26,883	*per cent 9·61	Absolute 23,497	per cent 14·1	Absolute 8,976	*per cent 9·4	Absolute 22,166	per cent 11·6	Absolute 7,720	per cent 10·3	Absolute 5,200	*per cent 12·6
	Core	Share at start 50·1	*Shift in share −0·6	Share at start 48·8	Shift in share 1·3	Share at start 50·2	*Shift in share −4·2	Share at start 50·2	Shift in share −3·8	Share at start 56·1	Shift in share 5·9	Share at start 62·0	*Shift in share 2·3
Carlisle	SMLA	Absolute 14,290	*per cent 7·8	Absolute 3,116	per cent 3·2	Absolute 111	*per cent 0·2	Absolute −10	per cent 0·0	Absolute 206	per cent 0·4	Absolute 2,730	*per cent 5·8
	Core	Share at start 68·8	*Shift in share 0·3	Share at start 69·4	Shift in share 1·2	Share at start 70·6	*Shift in share −1·2	Share at start 70·6	Shift in share 0·4	Share at start 68·5	Shift in share 3·1	Share at start 71·6	*Shift in share 4·2
Cardiff	SMLA	Absolute 26,026	*per cent 3·5	Absolute 32,210	per cent 8·0	Absolute 8,218	*per cent 3·8	Absolute 22,416	per cent 5·2	Absolute 13,626	per cent 7·9	Absolute 12,100	*per cent 6·5
	Core	Share at start 60·6	*Shift in share 0·1	Share at start 60·7	Shift in share −1·5	Share at start 59·3	*Shift in share −3·4	Share at start 59·3	Shift in share 1·9	Share at start 69·8	Shift in share 1·4	Share at start 71·2	*Shift in share 0·2
Chatham	SMLA	Absolute 25,318	*per cent 8·2	Absolute 20,719	per cent 11·5	Absolute 20,273	*per cent 20·2	Absolute 40,521	per cent 20·2	Absolute 4,593	per cent 5·9	Absolute 5,810	*per cent 7·1
	Core	Share at start 48·8	*Shift in share 0·2	Share at start 49·1	Shift in share 0·2	Share at start 49·3	*Shift in share −2·3	Share at start 49·3	Shift in share −2·7	Share at start 59·6	Shift in share 7·4	Share at start 66·9	*Shift in share 5·4

* Decennial rate.

		Land area 1961 ('000 acres)	Population ('000s)					Population density (persons per acre)				Labour force working in area ('000s)		
			1931	1951	1961	1966	1971*	1931	1951	1961	1966	1951	1961	1966
21. Chelmsford	MELA	296·3	117·3	159·9	180·7	205·2	235·2	0·40	0·54	0·61	0·69	37·1	78·9	88·6
	SMLA	134·3	55·3	77·2	98·0	113·3	128·8	0·41	0·57	0·73	0·84	37·1	46·4	51·9
	Core	4·8	27·5	37·9	49·9	53·9	58·1	5·73	7·94	10·46	11·23	27·5	35·1	37·3
	UBZA MELA	17·3	48·7	70·9	92·9	—	—	—	—	—	—	—	—	—
	SMLA	10·3	27·5	44·5	63·4	—	—	—	4·32	6·16	—	—	—	—
22. Cheltenham	MELA	295·7	104·8	134·8	151·8	161·0	172·1	0·35	0·46	0·51	0·54	54·1	67·3	71·2
	SMLA	90·5	70·8	91·4	110·7	119·8	120·4	0·78	1·01	1·22	1·32	37·5	49·9	55·4
	Core	5·2	50·2	62·9	75·2	72·4	69·7	9·65	12·18	13·98	13·92	26·3	34·8	38·8
	UBZA MELA	16·8	56·1	79·8	99·0	—	—	—	—	—	—	—	—	—
	SMLA	12·8	50·2	71·1	89·5	—	—	—	5·55	6·99	—	—	—	—
23. Chester	MELA	321·8	284·0	339·3	364·5	380·2	448·8	0·88	1·05	1·13	1·18	150·9	164·1	199·1
	SMLA	111·4	80·5	97·1	102·1	107·9	115·4	0·72	0·87	0·92	0·97	49·1	49·7	48·9
	Core	4·7	51·6	57·0	59·3	59·8	62·7	10·98	12·22	12·72	12·72	29·7	33·4	34·6
	UBZA MELA	55·2	174·3	229·2	290·8	—	—	—	—	—	—	—	—	—
	SMLA	7·1	50·3	70·5	72·8	—	—	—	9·93	10·25	—	—	—	—
24. Colchester	MELA	213·4	146·9	174·0	187·5	209·0	239·7	0·69	0·82	0·88	0·98	68·7	73·2	81·7
	SMLA	85·6	77·0	90·0	98·6	108·3	124·2	0·90	1·05	1·15	1·27	39·7	43·7	47·8
	Core	12·0	49·1	57·4	65·1	68·3	76·1	4·09	4·78	5·42	5·69	29·7	34·4	37·0
	UBZA MELA	26·8	80·6	109·4	148·9	—	—	—	—	—	—	—	—	—
	SMLA	16·4	45·6	64·3	72·6	—	—	—	3·92	4·43	—	—	—	—
25. Coventry	MELA	475·1	458·4	610·2	702·8	740·7	800·0	0·96	1·28	1·48	1·56	293·5	341·5	365·9
	SMLA	409·9	421·7	554·5	643·7	687·9	741·6	1·03	1·35	1·57	1·68	268·5	316·3	339·5
	Core	40·8	288·7	394·4	457·2	476·8	506·2	7·08	9·68	11·21	11·69	205·0	242·5	266·5
	UBZA MELA	83·9	353·6	489·6	589·8	—	—	—	—	—	—	—	—	—
	SMLA	70·8	328·1	450·5	548·2	—	—	—	6·36	7·74	—	—	—	—

* Provisional.

		Population change ('000s)								Employment change ('000s)			
		1931–51		1951–61		1961–66		1961–71		1951–61		1961–66	
Chelmsford	SMLA	Absolute 21,859	*per cent 19·8	Absolute 20,860	per cent 27·0	Absolute 15,328	*per cent 31·3	Absolute 30,817	per cent 31·4	Absolute 9,295	per cent 25·0	Absolute 5,460	per cent 23·5
	Core	Share at start 49·7	*Shift in share −0·3	Share at start 49·1	Shift in share 1·8	Share at start 50·9	Shift in share −6·8	Share at start 50·9	Shift in share −5·9	Share at start 73·1	Shift in share 1·5	Share at start 75·7	*Shift in share −7·4
Cheltenham	SMLA	Absolute 20,607	*per cent 14·6	Absolute 19,378	per cent 21·2	Absolute 9,063	*per cent 16·4	Absolute 9,607	per cent 8·7	Absolute 12,333	per cent 32·9	Absolute 5,540	*per cent 22·2
	Core	Share at start 70·9	*Shift in share −1·1	Share at start 68·8	Shift in share −3·6	Share at start 65·1	*Shift in share −9·5	Share at start 65·1	Shift in share −7·4	Share at start 70·1	Shift in share −0·4	Share at start 69·7	*Shift in share 0·8
Chester	SMLA	Absolute 16,553	*per cent 10·3	Absolute 4,991	per cent 5·1	Absolute 5,771	*per cent 11·3	Absolute 13,347	per cent 13·1	Absolute 553	per cent 1·1	Absolute −800	*per cent −3·2
	Core	Share at start 64·1	*Shift in share −2·7	Share at start 58·6	Shift in share −0·6	Share at start 58·1	*Shift in share −7·3	Share at start 58·1	Shift in share −3·8	Share at start 60·4	Shift in share 6·9	Share at start 67·3	*Shift in share 6·9
Colchester	SMLA	Absolute 13,046	*per cent 8·5	Absolute 8,609	per cent 9·6	Absolute 9,699	*per cent 19·7	Absolute 25,587	per cent 25·9	Absolute 3,997	per cent 10·1	Absolute 4,050	*per cent 18·5
	Core	Share at start 63·8	*Shift in share −0·0	Share at start 63·8	Shift in share 2·2	Share at start 66·0	*Shift in share −5·9	Share at start 66·0	Shift in share −4·7	Share at start 74·8	Shift in share 3·9	Share at start 78·7	*Shift in share −2·7
Coventry	SMLA	Absolute 132,788	*per cent 15·7	Absolute 89,226	per cent 16·1	Absolute 44,172	*per cent 13·7	Absolute 97,906	per cent 15·2	Absolute 47,852	per cent 17·8	Absolute 23,160	*per cent 14·6
	Core	Share at start 61·7	*Shift in share 4·7	Share at start 71·1	Shift in share −0·1	Share at start 71·0	*Shift in share −3·4	Share at start 71·0	Shift in share −2·7	Share at start 76·4	Shift in share 0·3	Share at start 76·7	*Shift in share 3·6

* Decennial rate.

		Land area 1961 ('000 acres)	Population ('000s)					Population density (persons per acre)				Labour force working in area ('000s)		
			1931	1951	1961	1966	1971*	1931	1951	1961	1966	1951	1961	1966
26. Crewe	MELA	138·2	115·0	131·5	134·0	141·4	186·1	0·83	0·95	0·97	1·02	60·2	60·0	62·6
	SMLA	106·4	80·8	88·9	91·4	93·1	97·0	0·76	0·84	0·86	0·88	41·6	43·8	43·7
	Core	4·4	48·3	52·4	53·2	52·0	51·3	10·98	11·95	12·13	11·82	28·6	31·5	29·6
	UBZA MELA	19·5	83·1	98·4	109·4	—	—	—	—	—	—	—	—	—
	SMLA	8·5	60·2	68·9	72·0	—	—	—	8·11	8·47	—	—	—	—
27. Darlington	MELA	407·0	282·0	306·7	304·1	302·5	313·5	0·69	0·75	0·75	0·74	139·7	131·2	134·9
	SMLA	71·7	83·5	99·2	110·1	111·9	119·8	1·16	1·38	1·54	1·56	48·4	52·8	57·6
	Core	6·5	72·1	84·9	84·2	83·3	85·9	11·09	13·12	13·01	12·82	39·5	41·8	42·9
	UBZA MELA	47·4	201·9	227·8	217·2	—	—	—	—	—	—	—	—	—
	SMLA	9·0	72·1	84·9	97·1	—	—	—	9·43	10·79	—	—	—	—
28. Derby	MELA	288·8	325·8	374·3	395·5	404·8	414·8	1·13	1·30	1·37	1·40	178·4	190·5	197·7
	SMLA	170·3	248·0	292·6	314·5	324·1	333·1	1·46	1·72	1·85	1·90	144·8	155·5	160·9
	Core	8·1	142·5	141·3	132·4	125·9	219·3	17·59	17·41	16·31	15·54	99·7	104·3	101·4
	UBZA MELA	54·6	242·9	288·2	317·0	—	—	—	—	—	—	—	—	—
	SMLA	40·1	192·6	241·8	263·1	—	—	—	6·03	6·56	—	—	—	—
29. Dewsbury	MELA	15·3	117·2	114·2	113·3	115·4	119·5	7·66	7·48	7·42	7·54	49·0	48·2	49·0
	SMLA	15·3	117·2	114·2	113·3	115·4	119·5	7·66	7·48	7·42	7·54	49·0	48·2	49·0
	Core	6·7	54·3	53·5	53·0	50·9	51·3	8·10	7·96	7·88	7·60	24·7	23·3	22·8
	UBZA MELA	13·8	117·2	112·0	111·4	—	—	—	—	—	—	—	—	—
	SMLA	13·8	117·2	112·0	111·4	—	—	—	8·12	8·07	—	—	—	—
30. Doncaster	MELA	177·4	217·2	244·6	269·0	279·5	307·6	1·22	1·38	1·52	1·58	11·41	115·4	118·9
	SMLA	97·6	150·8	176·6	196·4	202·9	206·5	1·55	1·81	2·01	2·08	79·9	92·2	92·9
	Core	8·4	64·7	82·1	86·3	84·1	82·5	7·70	9·80	10·31	10·01	46·2	52·2	54·3
	UBZA MELA	35·5	155·3	189·2	206·9	—	—	—	—	—	—	—	—	—
	SMLA	27·7	129·4	158·0	173·6	—	—	—	5·70	6·27	—	—	—	—

* Provisional.

		Population change ('000s)								Employment change ('000s)			
		1931–51		1951–61		1961–66		1961–71		1951–61		1961–66	
Crewe	SMLA	Absolute 8,070	*per cent 5·0	Absolute 2,530	per cent 2·8	Absolute 1,621	*per cent 3·5	Absolute 5,594	per cent 6·1	Absolute 2,207	per cent 5·3	Absolute −70	*per cent −0·3
	Core	Share at start 59·8	*Shift in share −0·4	Share at start 59·0	Shift in share −0·8	Share at start 58·2	*Shift in share −4·5	Share at start 58·2	Shift in share −5·3	Share at start 68·8	Shift in share 3·2	Share at start 72·0	*Shift in share −8·5
Darlington	SMLA	Absolute 15,757	*per cent 9·4	Absolute 10,923	per cent 11·0	Absolute 1,813	*per cent 3·3	Absolute 9,712	per cent 8·8	Absolute 4,405	per cent 9·1	Absolute 4,750	*per cent 18·0
	Core	Share at start 86·4	*Shift in share −0·4	Share at start 85·6	Shift in share −9·1	Share at start 76·4	*Shift in share −4·0	Share at start 76·4	Shift in share −4·7	Share at start 81·6	Shift in share −2·5	Share at start 79·2	*Shift in share −9·3
Derby	SMLA	Absolute 44,661	*per cent 9·0	Absolute 21,895	per cent 7·5	Absolute 9,578	*per cent 6·1	Absolute 18,593	per cent 5·9	Absolute 10,731	per cent 7·4	Absolute 5,410	*per cent 7·9
	Core	Share at start 57·5	*Shift in share −4·6	Share at start 48·3	Shift in share −6·2	Share at start 42·1	*Shift in share −6·5	Share at start 42·1	Shift in share 23·7	Share at start 68·9	Shift in share −1·8	Share at start 67·1	*Shift in share −8·1
Dewsbury	SMLA	Absolute −2,961	*per cent −1·3	Absolute −908	per cent −0·8	Absolute 2,065	*per cent 3·6	Absolute 6,231	per cent 5·5	Absolute −853	per cent −1·7	Absolute 780	*per cent 1·6
	Core	Share at start 46·3	*Shift in share 0·2	Share at start 46·8	Shift in share 3·7	Share at start 50·5	*Shift in share −12·8	Share at start 50·5	Shift in share −7·6	Share at start 50·4	Shift in share −2·0	Share at start 48·4	*Shift in share −3·8
Doncaster	SMLA	Absolute 25,797	*per cent 8·6	Absolute 19,798	per cent 11·2	Absolute 6,522	*per cent 6·6	Absolute 10,122	per cent 5·2	Absolute 12,342	per cent 15·4	Absolute 650	*per cent 1·4
	Core	Share at start 42·9	*Shift in share 1·8	Share at start 46·5	Shift in share −2·5	Share at start 44·0	*Shift in share −5·0	Share at start 44·0	Shift in share −4·0	Share at start 57·9	Shift in share −1·3	Share at start 56·6	*Shift in share 3·8

* Decennial rate.

		Land area 1961 ('000 acres)	Population ('000s)					Population density (persons per acre)				Labour force working in area ('000s)		
			1931	1951	1961	1966	1971*	1931	1951	1961	1966	1951	1961	1966
31. Eastbourne	MELA	120·9	172·4	186·1	198·8	215·3	229·0	1·43	1·54	1·64	1·78	66·5	70·1	77·9
	SMLA	105·6	87·6	94·9	103·3	113·1	124·0	0·83	0·90	0·98	1·07	35·8	39·1	41·9
	Core	11·0	58·5	57·8	60·9	65·1	70·5	5·32	5·28	5·56	5·92	24·2	27·5	28·9
	UBZA MELA	21·2	142·7	151·2	155·3	—	—	—	—	—	—	—	—	—
	SMLA	10·0	58·5	63·9	65·3	—	—	—	6·39	6·53	—	—	—	—
32. Exeter	MELA	635·5	224·1	252·2	266·3	294·6	296·3	0·35	0·40	0·42	0·46	99·3	105·0	116·6
	SMLA	134·6	117·7	136·2	147·1	152·3	163·8	0·87	1·01	1·09	1·13	55·3	61·4	67·1
	Core	9·0	67·6	75·5	80·3	82·5	95·6	7·51	8·36	8·89	9·17	36·8	42·0	46·7
	UBZA MELA	33·0	100·7	137·2	160·6	—	—	—	—	—	—	—	—	—
	SMLA	20·4	81·2	104·6	119·4	—	—	—	5·13	5·85	—	—	—	—
33. Gloucester	MELA	360·8	210·0	250·7	267·4	283·8	293·6	0·58	0·69	0·74	0·79	114·6	119·0	127·7
	SMLA	117·0	85·5	112·0	124·8	135·0	136·8	0·73	0·96	1·07	1·15	58·4	62·2	65·7
	Core	5·3	55·6	67·3	69·8	71·9	90·1	10·49	12·71	13·18	13·57	32·9	37·9	41·1
	UBZA MELA	33·7	93·3	146·3	166·0	—	—	—	—	—	—	—	—	—
	SMLA	13·8	55·9	83·5	98·7	—	—	—	6·05	7·15	—	—	—	—
34. Great Yarmouth	MELA	53·2	114·6	108·7	114·7	120·3	124·8	2·15	2·04	2·16	2·26	42·5	49·3	55·2
	SMLA	53·2	114·6	108·7	114·7	120·3	124·8	2·15	2·04	2·16	2·26	42·5	49·3	55·2
	Core	3·7	56·8	51·1	53·0	52·4	50·2	15·35	13·85	14·36	14·16	21·8	24·9	27·8
	UBZA MELA	8·5	100·8	93·9	98·7	—	—	—	—	—	—	—	—	—
	SMLA	8·5	100·8	93·9	98·7	—	—	—	11·05	11·61	—	—	—	—
35. Grimsby	MELA	203·3	158·2	166·8	176·4	184·0	192·8	0·78	0·82	0·87	0·91	78·1	73·8	80·9
	SMLA	47·4	131·8	137·0	147·2	154·7	162·3	2·78	2·89	3·11	3·26	55·8	61·7	69·5
	Core	5·9	92·5	94·6	96·7	95·0	95·7	15·68	16·08	16·44	16·10	42·5	44·2	48·7
	UBZA MELA	13·4	130·8	135·2	145·7	—	—	—	—	—	—	—	—	—
	SMLA	10·6	121·1	124·1	134·1	—	—	—	11·71	12·65	—	—	—	—

		Population change ('000s)								Employment change ('000s)			
		1931–51		1951–61		1961–66		1961–71		1951–61		1961–66	
Eastbourne	SMLA	Absolute 7,231	*per cent 4·1	Absolute 8,459	per cent 8·9	Absolute 9,752	*per cent 19·9	Absolute 20,659	per cent 20·0	Absolute 3,278	per cent 9·2	Absolute 2,890	*per cent 14·8
	Core	Share at start 66·7	*Shift in share −2·9	Share at start 60·9	Shift in share −2·0	Share at start 58·9	*Shift in share −2·8	Share at start 58·9	Shift in share −2·0	Share at start 67·6	Shift in share 2·9	Share at start 70·5	*Shift in share −3·3
Exeter	SMLA	Absolute 18,466	*per cent 7·8	Absolute 10,956	per cent 8·0	Absolute 5,177	*per cent 7·0	Absolute 16,680	per cent 11·3	Absolute 6,146	per cent 11·1	Absolute 5,740	*per cent 18·7
	Core	Share at start 57·4	*Shift in share −1·0	Share at start 55·4	Shift in share −0·9	Share at start 54·6	*Shift in share −0·8	Share at start 54·6	Shift in share 3·8	Share at start 66·6	Shift in share 1·7	Share at start 68·3	*Shift in share 2·3
Gloucester	SMLA	Absolute 26,435	*per cent 15·4	Absolute 12,861	per cent 11·5	Absolute 10,180	*per cent 16·3	Absolute 11,936	per cent 9·6	Absolute 3,771	per cent 6·4	Absolute 3,540	*per cent 11·4
	Core	Share at start 66·2	*Shift in share −3·1	Share at start 60·1	Shift in share −4·2	Share at start 55·9	*Shift in share −5·3	Share at start 55·9	Shift in share 10·0	Share at start 56·3	Shift in share 4·6	Share at start 60·9	*Shift in share 3·1
Great Yarmouth	SMLA	Absolute −5,896	*per cent −2·6	Absolute 6,079	per cent 5·6	Absolute 5,566	*per cent 9·7	Absolute 10,060	per cent 8·8	Absolute 6,791	per cent 16·0	Absolute 5,890	*per cent 23·9
	Core	Share at start 49·6	*Shift in share −1·3	Share at start 47·0	Shift in share −0·9	Share at start 46·2	*Shift in share −5·3	Share at start 46·2	Shift in share −6·0	Share at start 51·3	Shift in share −0·8	Share at start 50·5	*Shift in share −0·2
Grimsby	SMLA	Absolute 5,162	*per cent 2·0	Absolute 10,195	per cent 7·4	Absolute 7,539	*per cent 10·2	Absolute 15,138	per cent 10·3	Absolute 5,843	per cent 10·5	Absolute 7,840	*per cent 25·4
	Core	Share at start 70·1	*Shift in share −0·6	Share at start 69·0	Shift in share −3·3	Share at start 65·7	*Shift in share −8·6	Share at start 65·7	Shift in share −6·8	Share at start 76·1	Shift in share −4·4	Share at start 71·7	*Shift in share −3·4

* Decennial rate.

		Land area 1961 ('000 acres)	Population ('000s)					Population density (persons per acre)				Labour force working in area ('000s)		
			1931	1951	1961	1966	1971*	1931	1951	1961	1966	1951	1961	1966
36. Guildford	MELA	137·5	101·7	139·1	159·2	169·0	177·6	0·74	1·01	1·16	1·23	55·0	60·0	66·6
	SMLA	137·5	101·7	139·1	159·2	169·0	177·6	0·74	1·01	1·16	1·23	55·0	60·0	66·6
	Core	7·3	34·2	48·0	54·0	55·0	56·9	4·68	6·56	7·37	7·53	24·3	28·4	31·0
	UBZA MELA	16·6	47·9	73·9	88·0	—	—	—	—	—	—	—	—	—
	SMLA	16·6	47·9	73·9	88·0	—	—	—	4·45	5·30	—	—	—	—
37. Halifax	MELA	70·0	189·6	186·6	180·5	179·5	176·1	2·71	2·67	2·58	2·56	93·7	91·6	92·9
	SMLA	41·2	174·0	172·3	167·4	166·6	164·1	4·22	3·67	3·57	4·04	86·2	84·8	85·7
	Core	14·1	98·1	98·4	96·1	94·1	91·2	6·96	6·99	6·83	6·67	51·3	51·7	51·4
	UBZA MELA	31·8	157·5	160·5	158·4	—	—	—	—	—	—	—	—	—
	SMLA	31·3	151·2	155·2	153·7	—	—	—	4·96	4·91	—	—	—	—
38. Harrogate	MELA	212·5	837·6	96·8	103·5	109·1	114·8	0·39	0·46	0·49	0·51	42·1	44·5	48·3
	SMLA	85·8	62·8	73·4	80·4	86·1	90·5	0·73	0·85	0·94	1·00	31·8	35·0	38·8
	Core	8·3	43·8	50·5	56·3	59·2	62·3	5·28	6·07	6·77	7·13	22·9	26·7	29·5
	UBZA MELA	13·3	59·0	70·4	77·2	—	—	—	—	—	—	—	—	—
	SMLA	10·8	50·4	58·9	65·7	—	—	—	5·45	6·08	—	—	—	—
39. Hemel Hempstead	MELA	51·4	37·3	56·4	94·1	107·1	115·7	0·79	1·10	1·83	2·11	21·9	36·7	44·6
	SMLA	47·0	37·3	51·4	88·0	99·3	106·5	0·79	1·09	1·87	2·11	20·3	34·8	41·9
	Core	7·2	16·1	23·4	55·3	64·1	69·4	2·24	3·26	7·68	8·90	11·0	24·5	30·4
	UBZA MELA	11·2	25·2	37·9	72·6	—	—	—	—	—	—	—	—	—
	SMLA	11·2	25·2	37·9	72·6	—	—	—	3·38	6·48	—	—	—	—
40. High Wycombe	MELA	135·0	106·4	147·3	183·5	215·3	236·6	0·79	1·09	1·36	1·59	58·9	73·9	83·8
	SMLA	135·0	106·4	147·3	183·5	215·3	236·6	0·79	1·09	1·36	1·59	58·9	73·9	83·8
	Core	7·1	29·6	40·7	50·0	53·9	59·3	4·17	5·74	7·05	7·59	23·2	30·5	34·0
	UBZA MELA	41·2	50·7	95·0	145·9	—	—	—	—	—	—	—	—	—
	SMLA	41·2	50·7	95·0	145·9	—	—	—	2·31	3·54	—	—	—	—

		Population change ('000s)								Employment change ('000s)			
		1931–51		1951–61		1961–66		1961–66		1951–61		1961–66	
Guildford	SMLA	Absolute 37,429	*per cent 18·4	Absolute 20,089	per cent 14·4	Absolute 9,812	*per cent 12·3	Absolute 18,440	per cent 11·6	Absolute 5,059	per cent 9·2	Absolute 6,560	*per cent 21·8
	Core	Share at start 33·7	*Shift in share 0·4	Share at start 34·5	Shift in share −0·6	Share at start 33·9	*Shift in share −3·8	Share at start 33·9	Shift in share −1·9	Share at start 44·1	Shift in share 3·1	Share at start 47·3	*Shift in share −1·4
Halifax	SMLA	Absolute −1,698	*per cent −0·5	Absolute −4,827	per cent −2·8	Absolute −874	*per cent −1·0	Absolute −3,293	per cent −20·6	Absolute −1,358	per cent −1·6	Absolute 890	*per cent 2·1
	Core	Share at start 56·4	*Shift in share 0·4	Share at start 57·1	Shift in share 0·3	Share at start 57·4	*Shift in share −1·8	Share at start 57·4	Shift in share −1·9	Share at start 59·5	Shift in share 1·5	Share at start 60·9	*Shift in share −2·0
Harrogate	SMLA	Absolute 10,552	*per cent 8·4	Absolute 7,022	per cent 9·6	Absolute 5,734	*per cent 14·3	Absolute 10,079	per cent 12·5	Absolute 7,237	per cent 10·2	Absolute 3,780	*per cent 21·6
	Core	Share at start 69·6	*Shift in share −0·4	Share at start 68·8	Shift in share 1·3	Share at start 70·1	*Shift in share −2·8	Share at start 68·8	Shift in share −1·3	Share at start 72·1	Shift in share 4·0	Share at start 76·1	*Shift in share −0·4
Hemel Hempstead	SMLA	Absolute 14,168	*per cent 19·0	Absolute 36,566	per cent 71·1	Absolute 11,345	*per cent 25·8	Absolute 18,508	per cent 21·0	Absolute 14,518	per cent 71·7	Absolute 7,090	*per cent −40·8
	Core	Share at start 43·3	*Shift in share 1·1	Share at start 45·6	Shift in share 17·2	Share at start 62·8	*Shift in share 3·4	Share at start 62·8	Shift in share 2·3	Share at start 54·3	Shift in share 16·1	Share at start 70·4	*Shift in share 4·2
High Wycombe	SMLA	Absolute 40,968	*per cent 19·2	Absolute 36,207	per cent 24·6	Absolute 31,792	*per cent 34·6	Absolute 53,076	per cent 28·9	Absolute 15,029	per cent 25·5	Absolute 9,890	*per cent 26·7
	Core	Share at start 27·8	*Shift in share −0·1	Share at start 27·6	Shift in share −0·4	Share at start 27·2	*Shift in share −4·4	Share at start 27·2	Shift in share −2·1	Share at start 39·5	Shift in share 1·8	Share at start 41·2	*Shift in share −1·4

* Decennial rate.

		Land area 1961 ('000 acres)	Population ('000s)					Population density (persons per acre)				Labour force working in area ('000s)		
			1931	1951	1961	1966	1971*	1931	1951	1961	1966	1951	1961	1966
41. Huddersfield	MELA	77·8	201·7	203·1	203·2	205·4	208·7	2·59	2·61	2·61	2·64	102·9	103·8	102·1
	SMLA	67·6	191·2	193·4	193·8	195·1	197·6	2·83	2·86	2·87	2·89	98·6	99·4	97·6
	Core	14·1	123·0	129·0	130·7	130·2	131·0	8·72	9·12	9·24	9·23	72·7	73·2	71·5
	UBZA MELA	25·1	162·0	132·6	165·8	—	—	—	—	—	—	—	—	—
	SMLA	24·0	156·5	129·0	161·4	—	—	—	5·38	6·73	—	—	—	—
42. Hull	MELA	422·0	414·6	433·0	449·3	455·0	456·9	0·98	1·03	1·06	1·08	179·1	191·0	198·8
	SMLA	251·3	386·8	403·1	419·5	425·8	426·6	1·54	1·60	1·67	1·69	167·2	179·2	188·0
	Core	14·4	313·6	299·1	303·3	295·3	285·5	21·78	20·74	21·03	20·51	131·0	138·4	143·3
	UBZA MELA	35·6	346·1	371·3	387·5	—	—	—	—	—	—	—	—	—
	SMLA	33·1	340·1	364·3	380·6	—	—	—	11·01	11·50	—	—	—	—
43. Ipswich	MELA	509·5	228·6	254·9	272·1	282·2	296·7	0·45	0·50	0·53	0·55	110·6	113·7	122·0
	SMLA	169·7	133·5	157·4	173·6	180·3	191·2	0·79	0·93	1·02	1·06	74·0	76·7	83·1
	Core	10·0	88·2	107·4	117·4	118·7	122·8	8·82	10·79	11·79	11·87	46·3	54·3	58·9
	UBZA MELA	19·5	112·2	140·0	156·1	—	—	—	—	—	—	—	—	—
	SMLA	13·3	92·3	116·0	129·3	—	—	—	8·72	9·72	—	—	—	—
44. Kidder-minster	MELA	48·4	49·1	63·9	70·4	76·3	84·9	1·01	1·32	1·46	1·58	26·8	31·9	30·9
	SMLA	48·4	49·1	63·9	70·4	76·3	84·9	1·01	1·32	1·46	1·58	26·8	31·9	30·9
	Core	4·7	29·5	37·4	41·7	44·2	47·3	6·28	7·97	8·88	9·40	16·8	21·8	23·9
	UBZA MELA	7·9	38·2	49·9	53·4	—	—	—	—	—	—	—	—	—
	SMLA	7·9	38·2	49·9	53·4	—	—	—	6·32	6·76	—	—	—	—
45. Lancaster	MELA	446·4	136·0	165·1	166·1	176·8	179·6	0·30	0·37	0·37	0·40	70·3	70·5	73·6
	SMLA	139·7	87·4	114·5	114·8	124·6	123·5	0·63	0·80	0·82	0·89	47·9	47·8	49·3
	Core	4·9	43·6	51·7	48·2	48·6	49·5	8·90	10·39	9·70	9·92	24·7	25·7	25·6
	UBZA MELA	16·6	87·7	110·6	115·7	—	—	—	—	—	—	—	—	—
	SMLA	12·0	71·4	92·1	95·5	—	—	—	7·68	7·97	—	—	—	—

* Provisional.

		Population change ('000s)								Employment change ('000s)			
		1931–51		1951–61		1961–66		1961–71		1o51–61		1961–66	
Huddersfield	SMLA	Absolute 2,203	*per cent 0·6	Absolute 449	per cent 0·2	Absolute 1,271	*per cent 1·3	Absolute 3,777	per cent 1·9	Absolute 856	per cent 0·9	Absolute −1,840	*per cent −3·7
	Core	Share at start 64·4	*Shift in share 1·2	Share at start 66·7	Shift in share 0·7	Share at start 67·4	*Shift in share −1·3	Share at start 67·4	Shift in share −1·1	Share at start 73·7	Shift in share −0·1	Share at start 73·6	*Shift in share −0·6
Hull	SMLA	Absolute 16,953	*per cent 2·2	Absolute 16,375	per cent 4·1	Absolute 6,349	*per cent 3·0	Absolute 7,116	per cent 1·7	Absolute 11,975	per cent 7·2	Absolute 8,800	*per cent 9·8
	Core	Share at start 81·1	*Shift in share −3·4	Share at start 74·2	Shift in share −1·9	Share at start 72·3	*Shift in share −5·9	Share at start 72·3	Shift in share −5·4	Share at start 78·3	Shift in share −1·1	Share at start 77·3	*Shift in share −2·0
Ipswich	SMLA	Absolute 23,890	*per cent 8·9	Absolute 16,214	per cent 10·3	Absolute 6,713	*per cent 7·7	Absolute 17,602	per cent 10·1	Absolute 2,711	per cent 3·7	Absolute 6,390	*per cent 16·7
	Core	Share at start 66·0	*Shift in share 1·1	Share at start 68·2	Shift in share −0·6	Share at start 67·6	*Shift in share −3·5	Share at start 67·6	Shift in share −3·4	Share at start 62·6	Shift in share 8·2	Share at start 70·8	*Shift in share 0·1
Kidderminster	SMLA	Absolute 14,713	*per cent 15·0	Absolute 6,549	per cent 10·3	Absolute 5,884	*per cent 16·7	Absolute 14,490	per cent 20·6	Absolute 5,111	per cent 19·1	Absolute −980	*per cent −6·1
	Core	Share at start 60·1	*Shift in share −0·7	Share at start 58·6	Shift in share 0·6	Share at start 59·2	*Shift in share −2·4	Share at start 59·2	Shift in share −3·5	Share at start 62·7	Shift in share 5·7	Share at start 68·4	*Shift in share 17·9
Lancaster	SMLA	Absolute 24,068	*per cent 13·8	Absolute 3,355	per cent 3·0	Absolute 9,802	*per cent 17·1	Absolute 8,658	per cent 7·5	Absolute −162	per cent −0·3	Absolute 1,520	*per cent 6·4
	Core	Share at start 49·9	*Shift in share −1·8	Share at start 46·3	Shift in share −4·3	Share at start 42·0	*Shift in share −6·0	Share at start 42·0	Shift in share −1·9	Share at start 51·6	Shift in share 2·2	Share at start 53·8	*Shift in share −3·8

* Decennial rate.

		Land area 1961 ('000 acres)	Population ('000s)					Population density (persons per acre)				Labour force working in area ('000s)		
			1931	1951	1961	1966	1971*	1931	1951	1961	1966	1951	1961	1966
46. Leeds	MELA	500·6	1,228·2	1,324·9	1,347·5	1,366·6	1,399·4	2·45	2·65	2·69	2·73	649·6	658·5	667·8
	SMLA	273·6	1,051·1	1,141·2	1,163·5	1,177·9	1,204·7	3·84	4·17	4·25	4·31	565·2	574·3	575·6
	Core	68·3	811·9	831·0	836·4	823·8	817·2	11·89	12·16	12·24	12·06	437·8	451·6	441·6
	UBZA MELA	169·7	933·0	1,227·3	1,247·0	—	—	—	—	—	—	—	—	—
	SMLA	141·8	803·0	1,089·5	1,103·5	—	—	—	7·68	7·78	—	—	—	—
47. Leicester	MELA	356·8	461·9	538·0	565·3	620·7	669·8	1·29	1·51	1·58	1·74	265·2	286·8	312·4
	SMLA	269·7	373·8	437·5	456·6	503·5	533·8	1·39	4·17	4·25	1·87	216·6	232·7	251·2
	Core	17·0	257·7	285·2	273·5	268·3	283·6	15·16	12·24	12·16	15·78	167·1	176·5	180·4
	UBZA MELA	75·4	375·4	444·1	499·2	—	—	—	—	—	—	—	—	—
	SMLA	47·7	311·8	367·7	411·0	—	—	—	7·71	8·62	—	—	—	—
48. Leigh	MELA	18·2	85·7	92·5	93·2	98·1	102·5	4·71	5·01	5·13	5·39	47·7	43·6	43·3
	SMLA	18·2	85·7	92·5	93·2	98·1	102·5	4·71	5·01	5·13	5·39	47·7	43·6	43·3
	Core	6·4	45·3	48·7	46·2	45·6	46·1	7·08	7·66	7·26	7·13	26·0	26·1	26·0
	UBZA MELA	15·8	81·9	86·9	90·9	—	—	—	—	—	—	—	—	—
	SMLA	15·8	81·9	86·9	90·9	—	—	—	5·50	5·75	—	—	—	—
49. Lincoln	MELA	458·7	143·8	169·4	179·2	189·0	206·5	0·31	0·37	0·39	0·41	75·6	78·1	83·7
	SMLA	192·0	97·0	114·6	126·8	134·1	140·9	0·51	0·60	0·66	0·70	52·1	56·7	61·1
	Core	7·5	66·0	70·3	77·1	75·6	74·2	8·83	9·36	10·25	10·08	34·4	39·8	43·1
	UBZA MELA	12·7	73·1	83·1	92·2	—	—	—	—	—	—	—	—	—
	SMLA	10·3	68·2	76·1	85·3	—	—	—	7·39	8·28	—	—	—	—
50. Liverpool	MELA	172·8	1,375·8	1,427·7	1,480·9	1,450·2	1,383·1	7·96	8·26	8·57	8·39	604·6	629·0	632·7
	SMLA	172·8	1,375·8	1,427·7	1,480·9	1,450·2	1,383·1	7·96	8·26	8·57	8·39	604·6	629·0	632·7
	Core	39·5	1,085·7	1,008·3	970·3	908·1	818·8	27·49	25·54	24·57	22·99	494·7	499·4	480·2
	UBZA MELA	91·5	1,318·8	2,043·3	2,068·6	—	—	—	—	—	—	—	—	—
	SMLA	91·5	1,318·8	1,380·5	1,437·4	—	—	—	15·09	15·71	—	—	—	—

* Provisional.

		Population change ('000s)								Employment change ('000s)			
		1931–51		1951–61		1961–66		1961–71		1951–61		1961–66	
Leeds	SMLA	Absolute 90,105	*per cent 4·3	Absolute 22,284	per cent 1·6	Absolute 14,485	*per cent 2·5	Absolute 41,290	per cent 3·5	Absolute 9,120	per cent 1·6	Absolute 1,320	*per cent 0·4
	Core	Share at start 77·2	*Shift in share −2·2	Share at start 72·8	Shift in share −0·9	Share at start 71·9	*Shift in share −3·9	Share at start 71·9	Shift in share −4·1	Share at start 77·5	Shift in share 1·1	Share at start 78·6	*Shift in share −3·8
Leicester	SMLA	Absolute 63,644	*per cent 8·5	Absolute 19,072	per cent 4·7	Absolute 46,989	*per cent 20·6	Absolute 77,236	per cent 16·9	Absolute 16,070	per cent 7·4	Absolute 18,510	*per cent 15·9
	Core	Share at start 68·9	*Shift in share −1·9	Share at start 65·2	Shift in share −5·3	Share at start 59·9	*Shift in share −13·2	Share at start 59·9	Shift in share −6·8	Share at start 77·1	Shift in share −1·3	Share at start 75·9	*Shift in share −8·1
Leigh	SMLA	Absolute 6,760	*per cent 3·9	Absolute 758	per cent 0·8	Absolute 4,856	*per cent 10·4	Absolute 9,281	per cent 10·0	Absolute −4,097	per cent −8·6	Absolute −310	*per cent −1·4
	Core	Share at start 52·9	*Shift in share −0·1	Share at start 52·7	Shift in share −3·2	Share at start 49·5	*Shift in share −6·1	Share at start 49·5	Shift in share −4·5	Share at start 54·5	Shift in share 5·4	Share at start 59·9	*Shift in share 0·4
Lincoln	SMLA	Absolute 17,629	*per cent 9·1	Absolute 12,183	per cent 10·6	Absolute 7,254	*per cent 11·4	Absolute 14,123	per cent 11·1	Absolute 4,588	per cent 8·8	Absolute 4,440	*per cent 15·7
	Core	Share at start 68·3	*Shift in share −3·5	Share at start 61·3	Shift in share −0·6	Share at start 60·8	*Shift in share −8·8	Share at start 60·8	Shift in share −8·2	Share at start 66·0	Shift in share 4·2	Share at start 70·2	*Shift in share 0·6
Liverpool	SMLA	Absolute 51,875	*per cent 1·9	Absolute 53,208	per cent 3·7	Absolute −30,730	*per cent −4·2	Absolute −97,872	per cent −6·6	Absolute 24,363	per cent 4·0	Absolute 3,740	*per cent 1·2
	Core	Share at start 78·9	*Shift in share −4·1	Share at start 70·6	Shift in share −5·1	Share at start 65·5	*Shift in share −5·8	Share at start 65·5	Shift in share −6·3	Share at start 81·8	Shift in share −2·4	Share at start 79·4	*Shift in share −7·0

* Decennial rate.

		Land area 1961 ('000 acres)	Population ('000s)					Population density (persons per acre)				Labour force working in area ('000s)		
			1931	1951	1961	1966	1971*	1931	1951	1961	1966	1951	1961	1966
51. London	MELA	1,895·0	8,949·3	10,007·4	10,242·0	9,538·0	9,411·4	4·72	5·28	5·40	5·03	4,727·3	4,940·6	5,041·0
	SMLA	959·3	8,627·6	9,112·4	9,156·7	8,890·7	8,634·2	8·99	9·55	9·50	8·99	4,553·5	4,713·7	4,760·6
	Core	183·2	6,683·0	5,917·3	5,636·7	5,331·3	5,036·0	36·48	32·29	30·76	29·10	3,538·9	3,559·3	3,464·7
	UBZA MELA	649·8	8,643·8	8,867·5	9,090·9	—	—	—	—	—	—	—	—	—
	SMLA	587·9	8,537·0	8,714·6	8,765·1	—	—	—	14·82	14·91	—	—	—	—
52. Luton	MELA	210·5	168·7	244·1	308·8	348·2	392·9	0·80	1·16	1·47	1·65	110·1	143·6	161·7
	SMLA	167·1	139·2	208·5	266·8	299·3	326·3	0·83	1·25	1·60	1·79	93·3	125·1	138·6
	Core	10·9	80·3	127·6	157·2	174·0	193·0	7·37	11·74	14·47	15·96	71·7	96·0	103·6
	UBZA MELA	32·5	86·4	170·2	229·2	—	—	—	—	—	—	—	—	—
	SMLA	25·6	69·1	145·1	201·8	—	—	—	0·57	0·79	—	—	—	—
53. Maidstone	MELA	188·2	134·1	159·8	176·6	211·1	226·6	0·71	0·85	0·94	1·12	72·6	82·5	93·7
	SMLA	143·1	103·7	125·0	137·8	157·7	175·0	0·72	0·87	0·95	1·10	56·3	64·2	72·5
	Core	6·2	44·9	54·0	59·8	64·7	70·9	7·24	8·73	9·66	10·44	28·0	32·1	34·9
	UBZA MELA	21·6	76·2	94·6	111·1	—	—	—	—	—	—	—	—	—
	SMLA	15·9	54·1	69·8	83·1	—	—	—	4·39	5·23	—	—	—	—
54. Manchester	MELA	475·1	2,146·0	2,172·0	2,201·3	2,185·7	2,203·4	4·52	4·57	4·63	4·60	1,101·5	1,082·6	1,082·0
	SMLA	291·5	1,988·7	2,012·4	2,041·7	2,012·7	1,991·3	6·82	7·01	6·91	6·90	1,021·9	1,007·5	1,004·1
	Core	71·2	1,539·9	1,462·0	1,387·9	1,294·2	1,219·4	21·63	19·51	20·55	18·18	800·1	792·5	752·8
	UBZA MELA	179·2	2,036·6	2,043·3	2,068·6	—	—	—	—	—	—	—	—	—
	SMLA	152·7	1,932·1	1,933·5	1,952·1	—	—	—	12·66	12·78	—	—	—	—
55. Mansfield	MELA	184·0	196·8	212·0	224·1	236·4	257·2	1·07	1·15	1·22	1·28	85·6	97·5	105·1
	SMLA	137·6	107·1	119·8	130·9	142·8	152·8	0·78	0·87	0·95	1·04	52·3	58·7	64·3
	Core	7·0	46·1	51·4	53·2	55·6	57·6	6·59	7·33	7·59	7·94	22·9	27·1	30·3
	UBZA MELA	33·2	133·2	137·0	162·6	—	—	—	—	—	—	—	—	—
	SMLA	15·2	63·7	73·1	93·3	—	—	—	4·81	6·14	—	—	—	—

* Provisional

		Population change (000's)								Employment change ('000s)			
		1931–51		1961–61		1961–66		1961–71		1951–61		1961–66	
London	SMLA	Absolute 484,827	*per cent 2·9	Absolute 44,294	per cent 0·5	Absolute −265,963	per cent −5·8	Absolute −522,495	*per cent −5·7	Absolute 160,199	per cent 3·5	Absolute 46,940	*per cent 2·0
	Core	Share at start 77·5	*Shift in share −6·3	Share at start 64·9	Shift in share −3·4	Share at start 61·6	Shift in share −3·2	Share at start 61·6	*Shift in share −3·3	Share at start 77·7	Shift in share −2·2	Share at start 75·5	*Shift in share −5·5
Luton	SMLA	Absolute 69,365	*per cent 24·9	Absolute 58,286	per cent 27·9	Absolute 32,434	per cent 24·3	Absolute 59,515	*per cent 22·3	Absolute 31,751	per cent 34·0	Absolute 13,480	*per cent 21·5
	Core	Share at start 57·7	*Shift in share 1·7	Share at start 61·2	Shift in share 2·1	Share at start 63·3	Shift in share −10·2	Share at start 63·3	*Shift in share −4·2	Share at start 76·8	Shift in share −0·1	Share at start 76·7	*Shift in share −4·0
Maidstone	SMLA	Absolute 21,321	*per cent 10·3	Absolute 12,821	per cent 10·3	Absolute 19,886	per cent 28·9	Absolute 37,139	*per cent 26·9	Absolute 7,833	per cent 13·9	Absolute 8,310	*per cent 25·9
	Core	Share at start 43·3	*Shift in share −0·0	Share at start 43·2	Shift in share 2·1	Share at start 45·4	Shift in share −8·8	Share at start 45·4	*Shift in share −4·9	Share at start 49·6	Shift in share 0·4	Share at start 50·0	*Shift in share −3·9
Manchester	SMLA	Absolute 23,658	*per cent 0·6	Absolute 29,319	per cent 1·5	Absolute −29,034	per cent −2·8	Absolute −50,422	*per cent −2·5	Absolute −14,408	per cent −1·4	Absolute −3,340	*per cent −0·7
	Core	Share at start 77·4	*Shift in share −2·4	Share at start 72·6	Shift in share −4·7	Share at start 68·0	Shift in share −7·4	Share at start 68·0	*Shift in share −6·8	Share at start 78·3	Shift in share 0·4	Share at start 78·7	*Shift in share −7·4
Mansfield	SMLA	Absolute 12,692	*per cent 5·9	Absolute 11,089	per cent 9·3	Absolute 11,929	per cent 18·2	Absolute 21,915	*per cent 16·7	Absolute 6,353	per cent 12·1	Absolute 5,560	*per cent 19·9
	Core	Share at start 43·0	*Shift in share −0·1	Share at start 42·9	Shift in share −2·2	Share at start 40·7	Shift in share −3·4	Share at start 40·7	*Shift in share −3·0	Share at start 43·7	Shift in share 2·4	Share at start 46·1	*Shift in share 12·0

* Decennial rate.

		Land area 1961 ('000 acres)	Population ('000s)					Population density (persons per acre)				Labour force working in area ('000s)		
			1931	1951	1961	1966	1971*	1931	1951	1961	1966	1951	1961	1966
56. Middlesbrough	MELA	270·8	265·9	287·1	320·8	332·5	495·5	0·98	1·06	1·18	1·23	114·0	128·6	138·8
	SMLA	144·5	233·9	256·1	289·6	300·5	463·3	1·62	1·77	2·00	2·08	102·3	117·7	127·4
	Core	12·3	170·3	180·6	194·6	191·2	395·5	13·85	14·68	15·82	15·54	76·9	95·2	102·7
	UBZA MELA	34·6	220·3	238·4	278·6	—	—	—	—	—	—	—	—	—
	SMLA	31·8	206·9	226·5	265·2	—	—	—	7·12	8·34	—	—	—	—
57. Newcastle	MELA	896·3	1,387·1	1,391·9	1,429·5	1,405·8	1,408·0	1·55	1·55	1·59	1·57	569·3	600·2	615·0
	SMLA	209·6	1,021·3	1,025·1	1,061·7	1,056·4	1,046·1	4·87	4·89	5·07	5·04	424·0	452·4	477·4
	Core	31·9	694·4	680·4	656·1	623·5	584·2	21·77	21·33	20·56	19·55	325·6	341·5	345·4
	UBZA MELA	157·6	1,252·1	1,254·5	1,270·1	—	—	—	—	—	—	—	—	—
	SMLA	90·0	976·0	981·2	995·4	—	—	—	10·90	11·06	—	—	—	—
58. Newport	MELA	245·0	301·8	304·9	327·4	340·7	338·5	1·23	1·24	1·34	1·39	129·2	147·0	151·8
	SMLA	64·5	139·2	147·7	154·2	161·6	166·4	2·18	2·29	2·39	2·51	63·4	77·2	79·1
	Core	7·7	99·2	106·4	108·1	110·1	112·0	12·88	13·83	14·05	14·30	47·4	53·6	61·8
	UBZA MELA	61·5	261·3	260·8	278·5	—	—	—	—	—	—	—	—	—
	SMLA	17·0	127·0	133·3	136·1	—	—	—	7·84	8·01	—	—	—	—
59. Northampton	MELA	274·9	214·3	240·3	255·1	270·7	299·3	0·78	0·87	0·93	0·98	109·8	118·1	125·7
	SMLA	139·2	125·9	141·7	151·2	160·4	167·4	0·90	1·02	1·09	1·15	67·0	71·5	78·2
	Core	6·2	96·5	104·4	105·4	111·0	126·6	15·56	16·84	17·00	17·90	53·7	56·6	67·2
	UBZA MELA	18·8	147·0	164·9	180·4	—	—	—	—	—	—	—	—	—
	SMLA	9·1	96·5	73·1	93·3	—	—	—	8·03	10·25	—	—	—	—
60. Norwich	MELA	959·3	359·8	400·9	407·5	420·1	454·6	0·38	0·42	0·42	0·44	173·5	164·1	182·1
	SMLA	256·6	200·1	220·0	232·8	244·1	267·7	0·78	0·86	0·91	0·95	95·4	102·0	112·4
	Core	8·1	126·2	121·2	120·1	116·4	121·7	15·58	14·89	14·75	14·37	66·2	75·5	78·5
	UBZA MELA	26·1	145·5	167·2	187·1	—	—	—	—	—	—	—	—	—
	SMLA	18·8	130·6	146·5	164·0	—	—	—	7·79	8·72	—	—	—	—

* Provisional.

		Population change ('000s)								Employment change ('000s)			
		1931–51		1951–61		1961–66		1961–71		1951–61		1961–66	
Middlesbrough	SMLA	Absolute 22,119	*per cent 4·7	Absolute 33,388	per cent 13·0	Absolute 11,040	*per cent 7·6	Absolute 173,844	per cent 60·1	Absolute 15,393	per cent 15·0	Absolute 9,620	*per cent 16·3
	Core	Share at start 72·8	*Shift in share −1·1	Share at start 70·5	Shift in share −3·3	Share at start 67·2	*Shift in share −7·3	Share at start 67·2	Shift in share 18·2	Share at start 75·1	Shift in share 5·8	Share at start 80·9	*Shift in share −0·4
Newcastle	SMLA	Absolute 3,756	*per cent 0·2	Absolute 36,581	per cent 3·6	Absolute −5,331	*per cent −1·0	Absolute −15,597	per cent −1·5	Absolute 28,333	per cent 6·7	Absolute 25,040	*per cent 11·1
	Core	Share at start 68·0	*Shift in share −0·8	Share at start 66·4	Shift in share −4·6	Share at start 61·8	*Shift in share −5·6	Share at start 61·8	Shift in share −6·0	Share at start 76·8	Shift in share −1·3	Share at start 75·5	*Shift in share −6·3
Newport	SMLA	Absolute 8,417	*per cent 3·0	Absolute 6,552	per cent 4·4	Absolute 7,336	*per cent 9·5	Absolute 12,214	per cent 7·9	Absolute 13,804	per cent 21·8	Absolute 1,880	*per cent 4·9
	Core	Share at start 71·2	*Shift in share 0·4	Share at start 72·1	Shift in share −2·0	Share at start 70·1	*Shift in share −3·9	Share at start 70·1	Shift in share −2·8	Share at start 74·8	Shift in share −5·4	Share at start 69·4	*Shift in share 17·5
Northampton	SMLA	Absolute 15,781	*per cent 6·3	Absolute 9,470	per cent 6·7	Absolute 9,199	*per cent 12·2	Absolute 16,189	per cent 10·7	Absolute 4,500	per cent 6·7	Absolute 6,640	*per cent 18·6
	Core	Share at start 76·7	*Shift in share −1·5	Share at start 73·7	Shift in share −3·8	Share at start 69·9	*Shift in share −1·5	Share at start 69·9	Shift in share 5·7	Share at start 80·1	Shift in share −1·0	Share at start 79·1	*Shift in share 13·7
Norwich	SMLA	Absolute 19,872	*per cent 5·0	Absolute 12,798	per cent 5·8	Absolute 11,323	*per cent 19·4	Absolute 34,840	per cent 15·0	Absolute 6,604	per cent 6·9	Absolute 10,410	*per cent 20·4
	Core	Share at start 63·1	*Shift in share −4·0	Share at start 55·1	Shift in share −3·5	Share at start 51·6	*Shift in share −7·8	Share at start 51·6	Shift in share −6·1	Share at start 69·4	Shift in share 4·6	Share at start 74·0	*Shift in share −8·4

* Decennial rate.

		Land area 1961 ('000 acres)	Population ('000s)					Population density (persons per acre)				Labour force working in area ('000s)		
			1931	1951	1961	1966	1971*	1931	1951	1961	1966	1951	1961	1966
61. Nottingham	MELA	276·5	576·7	685·2	731·4	753·2	793·1	2·09	2·48	2·65	2·72	323·8	347·5	353·7
	SMLA	184·4	494·7	592·9	634·7	654·9	673·9	2·68	3·21	3·44	3·55	284·3	306·5	312·0
	Core	24·8	304·3	357·7	367·9	365·0	363·3	12·27	14·40	14·81	14·72	200·0	213·7	211·4
	UBZA MELA	79·8	496·9	623·0	653·6	—	—	—	—	—	—	—	—	—
	SMLA	65·0	450·7	545·6	572·8	—	—	—	8·39	8·81	—	—	—	—
62. Oxford	MELA	780·6	294·7	396·6	457·8	504·7	563·5	0·38	0·51	0·59	0·65	188·4	209·7	238·1
	SMLA	404·3	180·9	248·1	286·9	310·7	343·8	0·45	0·61	0·71	0·77	119·4	130·7	146·9
	Core	8·8	80·5	98·7	106·3	108·8	108·6	9·09	11·24	12·10	12·36	60·7	74·2	81·8
	UBZA MELA	46·5	137·7	208·4	258·4	—	—	—	—	—	—	—	—	—
	SMLA	31·1	100·3	147·8	181·1	—	—	—	4·75	5·82	—	—	—	—
63. Peterborough	MELA	737·7	265·7	294·6	315·4	333·0	352·7	0·36	0·40	0·43	0·45	132·2	142·8	157·5
	SMLA	138·2	79·4	95·2	107·9	114·0	124·2	0·57	0·69	0·78	0·82	45·3	52·9	56·9
	Core	10·0	43·6	53·4	62·3	65·4	70·0	4·36	5·33	6·22	6·54	29·2	35·7	40·7
	UBZA MELA	30·4	100·2	132·5	146·0	—	—	—	—	—	—	—	—	—
	SMLA	13·4	51·0	66·6	78·1	—	—	—	5·12	5·83	—	—	—	—
64. Plymouth	MELA	470·2	321·5	332·4	330·7	310·8	350·9	0·68	0·71	0·70	0·66	140·8	136·3	144·0
	SMLA	134·7	263·1	270·1	269·5	274·0	283·6	1·95	2·00	2·00	2·03	118·5	115·4	121·7
	Core	13·1	214·9	208·0	204·3	199·9	239·3	16·40	15·55	15·27	15·26	98·5	97·5	100·3
	UBZA MELA	28·2	250·7	246·1	248·6	—	—	—	—	—	—	—	—	—
	SMLA	18·6	232·9	226·3	226·9	—	—	—	12·17	12·20	—	—	—	—
65. Portsmouth	MELA	276·5	433·2	505·1	560·0	592·1	642·7	1·57	1·83	2·03	2·14	205·3	222·6	249·4
	SMLA	47·5	335·2	369·8	410·4	427·5	462·2	7·06	7·79	8·65	9·00	153·2	169·8	189·8
	Core	9·2	252·4	233·5	215·1	201·4	197·0	27·43	25·25	23·25	21·89	106·8	113·9	114·5
	UBZA MELA	53·5	348·8	416·8	465·6	—	—	—	—	—	—	—	—	—
	SMLA	42·9	311·7	362·3	405·5	—	—	—	8·45	9·45	—	—	—	—

		Population change ('000s)								Employment change ('000s)			
		1931–51		1951–61		1961–66		1961–71		1951–61		1961–66	
Nottingham	SMLA	Absolute 98,170	*per cent 9·9	Absolute 41,816	per cent 7·0	Absolute 20,187	*per cent 6·4	Absolute 39,231	per cent 6·2	Absolute 22,252	per cent 7·8	Absolute 5,500	*per cent 3·6
	Core	Share at start 61·5	*Shift in share −0·6	Share at start 60·3	Shift in share −2·4	Share at start 58·0	*Shift in share −4·5	Share at start 58·0	Shift in share −4·1	Share at start 70·3	Shift in share −0·6	Share at start 69·7	*Shift in share 3·9
Oxford	SMLA	Absolute 67,224	*per cent 18·6	Absolute 38,740	per cent 15·6	Absolute 23,834	*per cent 16·6	Absolute 56,882	per cent 19·8	Absolute 11,293	per cent 9·5	Absolute 16,270	*per cent 24·9
	Core	Share at start 44·5	*Shift in share −2·4	Share at start 39·8	Shift in share −2·7	Share at start 37·0	*Shift in share −4·1	Share at start 37·1	Shift in share −0·5	Share at start 50·8	Shift in share 6·0	Share at start 56·8	*Shift in share −2·3
Peterborough	SMLA	Absolute 15,768	*per cent 9·9	Absolute 12,723	per cent 13·4	Absolute 6,065	*per cent 11·2	Absolute 16,266	per cent 15·1	Absolute 7,623	per cent 16·8	Absolute 4,020	*per cent 15·2
	Core	Share at start 54·8	*Shift in share 0·6	Share at start 56·1	Shift in share 1·6	Share at start 57·8	*Shift in share −0·8	Share at start 57·8	Shift in share −1·4	Share at start 64·6	Shift in share 2·9	Share at start 67·5	*Shift in share 8·0
Plymouth	SMLA	Absolute 7,064	*per cent 1·3	Absolute −575	per cent −0·2	Absolute 4,452	*per cent 3·3	Absolute 14,080	per cent 5·2	Absolute −3,167	per cent −2·7	Absolute 6,270	*per cent 10·9
	Core	Share at start 81·7	*Shift in share −2·3	Share at start 77·0	Shift in share −1·2	Share at start 75·8	*Shift in share −5·7	Share at start 75·8	Shift in share −8·6	Share at start 83·1	Shift in share 1·4	Share at start 84·5	*Shift in share −4·1
Portsmouth	SMLA	Absolute 34,584	*per cent 5·2	Absolute 40,634	per cent 11·0	Absolute 17,106	*per cent 8·3	Absolute 51,821	per cent 12·6	Absolute 16,530	per cent 10·8	Absolute 20,010	*per cent 23·6
	Core	Share at start 75·3	*Shift in share −6·1	Share at start 63·2	Shift in share −10·7	Share at start 52·4	*Shift in share −10·6	Share at start 52·4	Shift in share −5·8	Share at start 69·7	Shift in share −2·6	Share at start 67·1	*Shift in share −13·5

* Decennial rate.

		Land area 1961 ('000 acres)	Population ('000s)					Population density (persons per acre)				Labour force working in area ('000s)		
			1931	1951	1961	1966	1971*	1931	1951	1961	1966	1951	1961	1966
66. Port Talbot	MELA	164·2	222·2	231·2	243·5	246·8	252·1	1·35	1·41	1·48	1·50	104·5	113·0	111·8
	SMLA	94·3	155·5	167·0	181·6	186·8	191·9	1·65	1·77	1·93	1·98	70·0	83·3	84·6
	Core	23·4	40·7	44·1	51·3	50·7	50·7	1·74	1·88	2·19	2·17	25·2	34·0	31·3
	UBZA MELA	40·6	148·9	156·4	167·4	—	—	—	—	—	—	—	—	—
	SMLA	31·5	122·1	137·9	148·4	—	—	—	4·38	4·71	—	—	—	—
67. Preston	MELA	165·3	266·3	304·6	315·3	328·7	347·0	1·61	1·84	1·92	1·99	159·0	164·7	160·6
	SMLA	20·2	173·0	191·2	196·6	202·2	205·1	8·56	9·46	9·72	10·01	91·3	98·1	96·2
	Core	6·4	119·7	121·4	113·3	106·1	97·4	18·70	19·09	17·83	16·58	68·7	72·9	68·4
	UBZA MELA	34·4	199·4	223·6	238·7	—	—	—	—	—	—	—	—	—
	SMLA	21·1	146·8	161·6	171·8	—	—	—	7·66	8·14	—	—	—	—
68. Reading	MELA	184·4	180·4	230·7	271·9	316·5	362·3	0·98	1·25	1·47	1·72	103·7	121·3	137·6
	SMLA	161·0	160·6	205·8	241·7	279·1	313·6	1·00	1·29	1·50	1·73	88·7	107·1	121·5
	Core	9·1	97·1	114·2	119·9	126·4	132·0	10·67	12·54	13·17	13·89	52·7	59·8	69·8
	UBZA MELA	26·3	127·2	165·5	193·1	—	—	—	—	—	—	—	—	—
	SMLA	23·7	112·9	147·7	172·7	—	—	—	6·23	7·29	—	—	—	—
69. Rhondda	MELA	23·9	141·3	111·4	100·3	95·7	88·9	5·91	4·66	4·20	4·00	34·3	29·8	27·9
	SMLA	23·9	141·3	111·4	100·3	95·7	88·9	5·91	4·66	4·20	4·00	34·3	29·8	27·9
	Core	23·9	141·3	111·4	100·3	95·7	88·9	5·91	4·66	4·20	4·00	34·3	29·8	27·9
	UBZA MELA	23·9	141·3	111·4	100·3	—	—	—	—	—	—	—	—	—
	SMLA	23·9	141·3	111·4	100·3	—	—	—	4·66	4·20	—	—	—	—
70. Rochdale	MELA	49·2	172·2	157·7	150·8	151·3	156·7	3·50	3·21	3·07	3·08	85·0	77·6	74·1
	SMLA	30·3	129·3	120·3	116·1	119·1	126·4	4·27	3·97	3·84	3·93	66·4	61·7	60·2
	Core	9·6	95·5	88·4	85·8	86·9	91·3	9·95	9·21	8·94	9·05	50·7	46·9	46·2
	UBZA MELA	20·0	148·6	130·8	123·7	—	—	—	—	—	—	—	—	—
	SMLA	12·3	116·3	105·2	99·7	—	—	—	8·55	8·11	—	—	—	—

* Provisional.

		Population change ('000s)								Employment change (000's)			
		1931–51		1951–61		1961–66		1961–71		1951–61		1961–66	
Port Talbot	SMLA	Absolute 11,555	*per cent 3·7	Absolute 14,610	per cent 8·7	Absolute 5,109	*per cent 5·6	Absolute 10,226	per cent 5·6	Absolute 12,402	per cent 17·7	Absolute 1,320	*per cent 3·2
	Core	Share at start 26·2	*Shift in share 0·1	Share at start 26·4	Shift in share 1·8	Share at start 28·2	*Shift in share −2·2	Share at start 28·3	Shift in share −1·9	Share at start 36·1	Shift in share 4·8	Share at start 40·9	*Shift in share −7·7
Preston	SMLA	Absolute 18,191	*per cent 5·3	Absolute 5,410	per cent 2·8	Absolute 6,581	*per cent 6·2	Absolute 8,515	per cent 4·3	Absolute 6,865	per cent 7·5	Absolute −1,970	*per cent −4·0
	Core	Share at start 69·2	*Shift in share −2·8	Share at start 63·5	Shift in share −5·8	Share at start 57·6	*Shift in share −10·3	Share at start 57·7	Shift in share −10·2	Share at start 75·3	Shift in share −1·0	Share at start 74·2	*Shift in share −6·2
Reading	SMLA	Absolute 45,189	*per cent 14·1	Absolute 35,893	per cent 17·4	Absolute 37,355	*per cent 30·9	Absolute 71,919	per cent 29·8	Absolute 18,322	per cent 20·6	Absolute 14,480	*per cent 27·0
	Core	Share at start 60·5	*Shift in share −2·5	Share at start 55·5	Shift in share −5·9	Share at start 49·6	*Shift in share −8·7	Share at start 49·6	Shift in share −7·5	Share at start 59·4	Shift in share −3·6	Share at start 55·8	*Shift in share 3·2
Rhondda	SMLA	Absolute −29,957	*per cent −10·6	Absolute −11,102	per cent −10·0	Absolute −4,607	*per cent −9·2	Absolute 11,363	per cent 11·3	Absolute −4,443	per cent −13·0	Absolute −1,980	*per cent −13·3
	Core	Share at start 100·0	*Shift in share —	Share at start 100·0	Shift in share —	Share at start 100·0	*Shift in share —	Share at start 100·0	Shift in share 0·0	Share at start 100·0	Shift in share —	Share at start 100·0	*Shift in share —
Rochdale	SMLA	Absolute −8,993	*per cent −3·5	Absolute −4,198	per cent −3·5	Absolute 2,930	*per cent 5·0	Absolute 10,271	per cent 8·8	Absolute −4,701	per cent −7·1	Absolute −1,510	*per cent −4·9
	Core	Share at start 73·9	*Shift in share −0·2	Share at start 73·5	Shift in share 0·4	Share at start 73·9	*Shift in share −1·8	Share at start 73·9	Shift in share −1·6	Share at start 76·3	Shift in share −0·3	Share at start 76·0	*Shift in share 1·5

* Decennial rate.

		Land area 1961 ('000 acres)	Population ('000s)					Population density (persons per acre)				Labour force working in area ('000s)		
			1931	1951	1961	1966	1971*	1931	1951	1961	1966	1951	1961	1966
71. St. Albans	MELA	36·9	46·5	72·7	89·2	92·9	97·4	1·26	1·97	2·42	2·52	27·4	32·9	35·1
	SMLA	36·9	46·6	72·7	89·2	92·9	97·4	1·26	1·97	2·42	2·52	27·4	32·9	35·1
	Core	5·1	30·7	44·1	50·3	50·7	52·1	6·02	8·65	9·81	9·94	19·1	22·4	25·4
	UBZA MELA	18·0	34·6	51·8	80·1	—	—	—	—	—	—	—	—	—
	SMLA	18·0	34·6	51·8	80·1	—	—	—	2·88	4·45	—	—	—	—
72. St. Helens	MELA	46·4	155·3	182·6	189·9	212·9	236·3	3·35	3·94	4·09	4·59	85·8	84·0	96·7
	SMLA	46·4	155·3	182·6	189·9	212·9	236·3	3·35	3·94	4·09	4·59	85·8	84·0	96·7
	Core	8·9	108·5	112·5	108·7	102·0	104·2	12·19	12·69	12·26	11·46	48·6	54·8	53·5
	UBZA MELA	21·9	136·8	164·0	170·4	—	—	—	—	—	—	—	—	—
	SMLA	21·9	136·8	164·0	170·4	—	—	—	7·49	7·78	—	—	—	—
73. Scunthorpe	MELA	443·1	160·6	187·2	201·2	207·9	218·2	0·36	0·42	0·45	0·47	80·8	87·7	88·1
	SMLA	203·1	88·0	112·2	127·2	134·4	143·2	0·43	0·55	0·63	0·66	48·9	57·9	58·7
	Core	7·9	33·8	54·3	67·3	69·2	70·9	4·28	6·87	8·53	8·76	29·5	39·9	39·4
	UBZA MELA	15·3	78·9	98·6	113·8	—	—	—	—	—	—	—	—	—
	SMLA	10·7	37·9	59·8	75·4	—	—	—	5·59	7·05	—	—	—	—
74. Sheffield	MELA	438·9	102·0	1,082·3	1,123·2	1,132·3	1,148·1	2·32	2·47	2·56	2·56	484·8	520·5	534·4
	SMLA	243·7	867·0	916·5	949·5	956·3	958·3	3·56	3·76	3·90	3·92	417·9	443·7	454·2
	Core	57·3	657·6	663·7	647·7	640·0	674·5	11·48	11·58	11·30	11·17	327·9	349·7	356·7
	UBZA MELA	145·6	439·5	957·3	1012·7	1,012·7	—	—	—	—	—	—	—	—
	SMLA	115·1	338·1	848·1	891·5	—	—	—	7·37	7·75	—	—	—	—
75. Shrewsbury	MELA	447·9	105·6	118·1	122·1	129·1	170·9	0·24	0·26	0·27	0·29	50·5	52·4	60·2
	SMLA	148·8	58·7	68·8	74·6	77·9	82·3	0·39	0·46	0·51	0·52	31·4	34·4	35·2
	Core	8·1	36·7	44·9	49·6	50·9	56·1	4·53	5·53	6·11	6·28	22·7	26·8	27·8
	UBZA MELA	14·6	51·9	63·2	70·3	—	—	—	—	—	—	—	—	—
	SMLA	9·1	38·4	46·2	51·7	—	—	—	5·08	5·68	—	—	—	—

* Provisional.

		Population change ('000s)								Employment change ('000s)			
		1931–51		1951–61		1961–66		1961–71		1951–61		1961–66	
St. Albans	SMLA	Absolute 26,173	*per cent 28·1	Absolute 16,534	per cent 22·7	Absolute 3,460	*per cent 7·8	Absolute 8,132	per cent 9·1	Absolute 5,499	per cent 20·1	Absolute 2,200	*per cent 13·4
	Core	Share at start 66·0	*Shift in share −2·7	Share at start 60·6	Shift in share −4·3	Share at start 56·4	*Shift in share −3·5	Share at start 56·4	Shift in share −0·9	Share at start 69·8	Shift in share −1·7	Share at start 68·1	*Shift in share 8·4
St. Helens	SMLA	Absolute 27,255	*per cent 8·8	Absolute 7,382	per cent 4·0	Absolute 22,937	*per cent 24·2	Absolute 46,318	per cent 24·4	Absolute −1,846	per cent −2·1	Absolute 12,750	*per cent 30·4
	Core	Share at start 69·9	*Shift in share −4·1	Share at start 61·6	Shift in share −4·4	Share at start 67·2	*Shift in share −18·6	Share at start 67·2	Shift in share −23·1	Share at start 56·7	Shift in share 8·5	Share at start 65·2	*Shift in share −19·8
Scunthorpe	SMLA	Absolute 24,230	*per cent 13·8	Absolute 15,543	per cent 13·8	Absolute 6,627	*per cent 10·4	Absolute 15,491	per cent 12·1	Absolute 8,952	per cent 18·3	Absolute 780	*per cent 2·7
	Core	Share at start 38·4	*Shift in share 5·0	Share at start 48·4	Shift in share 4·3	Share at start 52·7	*Shift in share −2·4	Share at start 52·7	Shift in share −3·2	Share at start 60·2	Shift in share 8·6	Share at start 68·8	*Shift in share −3·4
Sheffield	SMLA	Absolute 49,474	*per cent 2·8	Absolute 33,054	per cent 3·6	Absolute 6,812	*per cent 1·4	Absolute 8,797	per cent 0·9	Absolute 25,804	per cent 6·2	Absolute 10,470	*per cent 4·7
	Core	Share at start 75·8	*Shift in share −1·7	Share at start 72·4	Shift in share −4·2	Share at start 68·2	*Shift in share −2·6	Share at start 68·2	Shift in share 2·2	Share at start 78·4	Shift in share 0·4	Share at start 78·8	*Shift in share −0·6
Shrewsbury	SMLA	Absolute 10,058	*per cent 8·6	Absolute 5,813	per cent 8·4	Absolute 3,333	*per cent 8·9	Absolute 7,752	perc ent 10·4	Absolute 3,049	per cent 9·7	Absolute 810	*per cent 4·7
	Core	Share at start 62·6	*Shift in share 1·4	Share at start 65·3	Shift in share 1·1	Share at start 66·5	*Shift in share −2·2	Share at start 66·5	Shift in share 1·7	Share at start 72·5	Shift in share 5·3	Share at start 77·8	*Shift in share 2·2

* Decennial rate.

			Land area 1961 ('000 acres)	Population ('000s)					Population density (persons per acre)				Labour force working in area ('000s)		
				1931	1951	1961	1966	1971*	1931	1951	1961	1966	1951	1961	1966
76. Slough	MELA		77·3	118·4	177·2	231·5	245·8	257·1	1·53	2·29	3·00	3·18	83·5	106·7	124·4
	SMLA		77·3	118·4	177·2	231·5	245·8	257·1	1·53	2·29	3·00	3·18	83·5	106·7	124·4
	Core		6·2	33·6	66·5	80·8	82·0	86·8	5·42	10·72	13·02	13·23	41·3	54·5	61·5
	UBZA	MELA	45·3	61·2	139·3	210·3	—	—	—	—	—	—	—	—	—
		SMLA	45·3	61·2	139·3	210·3	—	—	—	3·08	4·64	—	—	—	—
77. Southampton	MELA		423·8	352·1	410·3	459·7	491·2	522·8	0·83	0·97	1·08	1·16	177·1	202·4	224·2
	SMLA		310·1	307·7	356·5	401·8	432·8	461·0	0·99	1·15	1·30	1·40	154·1	177·6	198·4
	Core		11·5	178·3	189·8	204·8	210·3	214·8	15·50	16·44	17·74	18·29	81·2	99·9	107·1
	UBZA	MELA	39·2	270·6	314·8	359·2	—	—	—	—	—	—	—	—	—
		SMLA	35·5	244·2	281·7	323·7	—	—	—	7·94	9·12	—	—	—	—
78. Southend	MELA		58·5	162·3	200·7	246·8	271·2	278·5	2·77	3·43	4·22	4·64	58·2	72·9	85·0
	SMLA		58·5	162·3	200·7	246·8	271·2	278·5	2·77	3·43	4·22	4·64	58·2	72·9	85·0
	Core		10·3	129·8	151·8	165·1	166·8	162·3	12·60	14·76	16·05	16·19	46·7	55·1	60·9
	UBZA	MELA	27·2	145·5	188·4	235·7	—	—	—	—	—	—	—	—	—
		SMLA	27·2	145·5	188·4	235·7	—	—	—	6·93	8·67	—	—	—	—
79. Southport	MELA		9·7	78·9	84·0	82·0	80·7	84·3	8·13	1·30	1·15	8·32	31·6	30·5	30·5
	SMLA		9·7	78·9	84·0	82·0	80·7	84·3	8·13	1·30	1·15	8·32	31·6	30·5	30·4
	Core		9·7	78·9	84·0	82·0	80·7	84·3	8·13	16·44	17·74	8·32	31·6	30·5	30·4
	UBZA	MELA	9·7	78·9	84·0	82·0	—	—	—	—	—	—	—	—	—
		SMLA	9·7	78·9	84·0	82·0	—	—	—	8·66	8·45	—	—	—	—
80. Stafford	MELA		177·2	78·2	99·4	112·1	106·0	143·5	0·44	0·56	0·63	0·60	51·3	56·9	65·4
	SMLA		85·3	43·7	58·9	65·7	70·9	77·8	0·51	0·69	0·77	0·83	33·0	37·3	40·6
	Core		5·1	30·9	40·3	47·8	51·5	54·9	6·06	7·91	9·39	10·06	24·9	30·4	34·0
	UBZA	MELA	13·3	50·5	88·7	79·2	—	—	—	—	—	—	—	—	—
		SMLA	9·1	28·9	40·3	47·8	—	—	—	4·43	5·25	—	—	—	—

* Provisional.

		Population change ('000s)								Employment change ('000s)			
		1931–51		1951–61		1961–66		1961–71		1951–61		1961–66	
Slough	SMLA	Absolute 58,804	*per cent 24·8	Absolute 54,269	per cent 30·6	Absolute 14,307	*per cent 12·4	Absolute 25,572	per cent 11·0	Absolute 23,180	per cent 27·8	Absolute 17,700	*per cent 33·2
	Core	Share at start 28·4	*Shift in share 4·6	Share at start 37·5	Shift in share −2·6	Share at start 34·9	*Shift in share −3·1	Share at start 34·9	Shift in share 1·7	Share at start 49·4	Shift in share 1·6	Share at start 51·0	*Shift in share −3·3
Southampton	SMLA	Absolute 48,797	*per cent 7·9	Absolute 45,307	per cent 12·7	Absolute 31,008	*per cent 15·4	Absolute 58,665	per cent 14·5	Absolute 23,457	per cent 15·2	Absolute 20,840	*per cent 23·5
	Core	Share at start 57·9	*Shift in share −2·3	Share at start 53·2	Shift in share −2·3	Share at start 51·0	*Shift in share −4·8	Share at start 51·0	Shift in share −4·3	Share at start 52·7	Shift in share 3·5	Share at start 56·2	*Shift in share −4·5
Southend	SMLA	Absolute 38,435	*per cent 11·8	Absolute 46,153	per cent 23·0	Absolute 24,382	*per cent 19·8	Absolute 31,679	per cent 12·8	Absolute 14,760	per cent 25·4	Absolute 12,030	*per cent 33·0
	Core	Share at start 80·0	*Shift in share −2·2	Share at start 75·6	Shift in share −8·8	Share at start 66·9	Shift in share −10·8	Share at start 66·9	Shift in share −8·3	Share at start 80·2	Shift in share −4·6	Share at start 75·6	*Shift in share −7·6
Southport	SMLA	Absolute 5,114	*per cent 3·2	Absolute −2,035	per cent −2·4	Absolute −1,304	*per cent −3·2	Absolute 2,345	per cent 2·9	Absolute −1,072	per cent −3·4	Absolute −170	*per cent −1·1
	Core	Share at start 100·0	*Shift in share —	Share at start 100·0	Shift in share —	Share at start 100·0	*Shift in share —	Share at start 100·0	Shift in share —	Share at start 100·0	Shift in share —	Share at start 100·0	*Shift in share —
Stafford	SMLA	Absolute 15,131	*per cent 17·3	Absolute 6,859	per cent 11·6	Absolute 5,134	*per cent 15·6	Absolute 12,112	per cent 18·4	Absolute 4,206	per cent 12·7	Absolute 3,350	*per cent 18·0
	Core	Share at start 70·5	*Shift in share −1·1	Share at start 68·4	Shift in share 4·3	Share at start 72·7	*Shift in share −0·2	Share at start 72·7	Shift in share −2·2	Share at start 75·3	Shift in share 6·4	Share at start 81·6	*Shift in share 4·3

* Decennial rate.

		Land area 1961 ('000 acres)	Population ('000s)					Population density (persons per acre)				Labour force working in area ('000s)		
			1931	1951	1961	1966	1971*	1931	1951	1961	1966	1951	1961	1966
81. Stevenage	MELA	128·3	63·3	88·4	118·0	148·7	170·3	0·49	0·69	0·92	1·16	37·0	59·8	73·2
	SMLA	122·8	45·4	62·1	105·7	115·2	133·1	0·37	0·51	0·86	0·94	20·4	39·3	50·0
	Core	5·9	5·8	7·2	43·0	56·2	66·9	0·98	1·21	7·28	9·53	3·8	22·3	29·2
	UBZA MELA	15·2	30·3	52·5	99·5	—	—	—	—	—	—	—	—	—
	SMLA	9·8	14·5	26·2	67·2	—	—	—	2·71	6·86	—	—	—	—
82. Stockton	MELA	55·9	116·1	130·0	145·9	151·1	+	2·08	2·13	2·61	2·70	64·6	71·6	77·8
	SMLA	55·9	116·1	130·0	145·9	151·1	+	2·08	2·33	2·61	2·70	64·6	71·6	77·8
	Core	6·0	67·7	74·2	81·3	79·6	+	11·27	12·40	13·57	13·27	27·3	27·7	31·8
	UBZA MELA	14·8	106·3	119·5	136·2	—	+	—	—	—	—	—	—	—
	SMLA	14·8	106·3	119·5	136·2	—	+	—	8·07	9·20	—	—	—	—
83. Stoke-on-Trent	MELA	316·1	470·2	507·7	523·8	526·7	554·1	1·49	1·61	1·66	1·67	240·3	262·8	247·1
	SMLA	289·1	466·2	502·4	519·1	523·8	537·3	1·61	1·74	1·80	1·81	237·4	243·9	247·1
	Core	21·2	276·6	275·1	265·3	257·1	265·2	13·05	12·97	12·51	12·13	155·1	155·1	153·0
	UBZA MELA	56·2	383·0	403·4	431·8	—	—	—	—	—	—	—	—	—
	SMLA	56·2	383·0	403·4	431·8	—	—	—	7·18	7·68	—	—	—	—
84. Sunderland	MELA	27·3	288·6	282·1	292·2	291·1	289·8	10·57	10·33	10·70	10·66	110·6	113·4	122·1
	SMLA	15·3	210·5	206·8	218·1	217·5	216·9	13·76	13·53	14·27	14·22	86·1	88·9	96·2
	Core	8·6	185·9	181·5	189·7	186·8	216·9	21·62	21·17	22·12	21·72	76·8	80·4	88·0
	UBZA MELA	24·4	287·1	277·8	289·6	—	—	—	—	—	—	—	—	—
	SMLA	14·1	209·0	205·1	217·9	—	—	—	14·55	15·45	—	—	—	—
85. Swansea	MELA	640·9	415·7	405·4	405·8	402·5	408·8	0·65	0·63	0·63	0·63	159·5	156·4	157·0
	SMLA	113·3	237·7	231·2	235·7	238·2	245·3	2·10	2·04	2·08	2·10	89·4	88·5	91·1
	Core	21·6	164·8	161·0	167·3	168·8	172·6	7·63	7·45	7·75	7·81	63·3	66·5	69·3
	UBZA MELA	36·8	263·5	247·1	242·4	—	—	—	—	—	—	—	—	—
	SMLA	26·2	199·8	181·4	180·8	—	—	—	6·82	6·90	—	—	—	—

*Provisional

		Population change ('000s)								Employment change ('000s)			
		1931–51		1951–61		1961–66		1961–71		1951–61		1961–66	
Stevenage	SMLA	Absolute 16,674	*per cent 18·3	Absolute 43,557	per cent 70·1	Absolute 9,532	*per cent 18·0	Absolute 27,457	per cent 26·0	Absolute 18,862	per cent 92·4	Absolute 10,670	*per cent 54·3
	Core	Share at start 12·7	*Shift in share −0·5	Share at start 11·6	Shift in share 29·1	Share at start 40·7	*Shift in share 16·3	Share at start 40·7	Shift in share 9·6	Share at start 18·7	Shift in share 38·0	Share at start 56·7	*Shift in share 3·2
Stockton	SMLA	Absolute 13,933	*per cent 6·0	Absolute 15,932	per cent 12·3	Absolute 5,141	*per cent 7·0	Absolute abolished	per cent	Absolute 6,985	per cent 10·8	Absolute 6,200	*per cent 17·3
	Core	Share at start 58·3	*Shift in share −0·6	Share at start 57·1	Shift in share −1·4	Share at start 55·7	*Shift in share −6·0	Share at start abolished	Shift in share	Share at start 42·3	Shift in share −3·7	Share at start 38·6	*Shift in share 4·5
Stoke-on-Trent	SMLA	Absolute 36,158	*per cent 3·9	Absolute 16,670	per cent 3·3	Absolute 4,771	*per cent 1·8	Absolute 18,254	per cent 3·5	Absolute 6,445	per cent 2·7	Absolute 3,260	*per cent 2·7
	Core	Share at start 59·3	*Shift in share −2·3	Share at start 54·8	Shift in share −3·6	Share at start 51·1	*Shift in share −4·1	Share at start 51·1	Shift in share −1·8	Share at start 65·3	Shift in share −1·7	Share at start 63·6	*Shift in share −3·4
Sunderland	SMLA	Absolute −3,638	*per cent −0·9	Absolute 11,237	per cent 5·4	Absolute −524	*per cent −0·5	Absolute −1,162	per cent −0·5	Absolute 2,828	per cent 3·3	Absolute 7,260	*per cent 16·3
	Core	Share at start 88·3	*Shift in share −0·3	Share at start 87·8	Shift in share −0·8	Share at start 87·0	*Shift in share −2·2	Share at start 87·0	Shift in share 13·0	Share at start 89·2	Shift in share 1·2	Share at start 90·4	*Shift in share 2·2
Swansea	SMLA	Absolute −6,474	*per cent −1·4	Absolute 4,484	per cent 1·9	Absolute 2,502	*per cent 2·1	Absolute 9,582	per cent 4·1	Absolute −896	per cent −1·0	Absolute 2,620	*per cent 5·9
	Core	Share at start 69·3	*Shift in share 0·1	Share at start 69·6	Shift in share 1·4	Share at start 71·0	*Shift in share −0·3	Share at start 71·0	Shift in share −0·6	Share at start 70·8	Shift in share 4·3	Share at start 75·1	*Shift in share 1·8

* Decennial rate.

			Land area 1961 ('000 acres)	Population ('000s)					Population density (persons per acre)				Labour force working in area ('000s)		
				1931	1951	1961	1966	1971*	1931	1951	1961	1966	1951	1961	1966
86. Swindon	MELA		433·6	152·4	183·7	214·9	232·6	256·8	0·35	0·42	0·50	0·54	82·3	93·5	104·1
	SMLA		100·7	89·2	105·9	137·3	152·9	161·6	0·89	1·05	1·36	1·52	48·1	62·3	71·0
	Core		6·4	62·4	69·0	91·7	94·5	90·8	9·75	10·86	14·43	14·77	33·9	42·4	45·6
	UBZA	MELA	15·9	81·1	95·1	122·2	—	—	—	—	—	—	—	—	—
		SMLA	8·6	66·8	76·7	102·9	—	—	—	8·92	11·97	—	—	—	—
87. Taunton	MELA		419·2	145·8	172·2	183·0	191·0	205·5	0·35	0·41	0·44	0·46	73·8	78·8	84·1
	SMLA		113·2	56·4	69·2	73·0	76·6	82·0	0·50	0·61	0·65	0·68	31·9	35·0	36·6
	Core		2·6	25·4	33·6	35·2	35·9	37·4	9·77	13·06	13·67	13·81	18·3	21·5	22·8
	UBZA	MELA	13·4	70·0	87·3	93·3	—	—	—	—	—	—	—	—	—
		SMLA	5·0	33·3	42·1	43·9	—	—	—	8·42	8·78	—	—	—	—
88. Thurrock	MELA		45·0	65·4	93·4	129·9	140·0	151·1	1·46	2·08	2·89	3·11	42·8	54·2	64·2
	SMLA		45·0	65·4	93·4	129·9	140·0	151·1	1·46	2·08	2·89	3·11	42·8	54·2	64·2
	Core		40·6	61·9	82·1	114·3	119·2	124·7	1·52	2·02	2·82	2·94	40·9	51·2	60·0
	UBZA	MELA	111·8	50·0	70·7	111·8	—	—	—	—	—	—	—	—	—
		SMLA	21·4	50·0	70·7	111·8	—	—	—	3·30	5·22	—	—	—	—
89. Torquay	MELA		204·4	130·5	154·5	164·6	174·7	185·8	0·64	0·76	0·81	0·85	58·1	61·7	68·1
	SMLA		99·4	89·8	107·1	115·3	122·5	129·8	0·90	1·09	1·17	1·23	38·8	42·1	46·1
	Core		11·4	64·8	78·8	84·2	88·7	108·9	5·68	6·92	7·40	7·78	28·7	32·0	34·7
	UBZA	MELA	19·4	89·5	110·5	118·9	—	—	—	—	—	—	—	—	—
		SMLA	13·9	73·2	91·5	98·3	—	—	—	6·58	7·07	—	—	—	—
90. Tunbridge Wells	MELA		225·7	160·3	180·6	189·7	203·8	224·6	0·49	0·55	0·58	0·63	69·9	70·5	75·8
	SMLA		54·1	78·1	88·8	96·6	106·7	116·1	1·44	1·64	1·79	1·97	35·4	38·6	42·6
	Core		6·0	35·8	38·4	39·9	40·8	44·5	5·97	6·36	6·61	6·80	16·9	19·8	20·9
	UBZA	MELA	17·8	70·1	77·4	85·5	—	—	—	—	—	—	—	—	—
		SMLA	12·4	56·3	66·5	72·9	—	—	—	5·36	5·88	—	—	—	—

* Provisional.

		Population change ('000s)								Employment change ('000s)			
		1931–51		1951–61		1961–66		1961–71		1951–61		1961–66	
Swindon	SMLA	Absolute 16,616	*per cent 9·3	Absolute 31,479	per cent 29·7	Absolute 15,508	*per cent 22·6	Absolute 24,236	per cent 17·6	Absolute 14,190	per cent 29·5	Absolute 8,690	*per cent 27·9
	Core	Share at start 69·9	*Shift in share −2·4	Share at start 65·2	Shift in share 1·6	Share at start 66·8	*Shift in share −9·9	Share at start 66·8	Shift in share −10·6	Share at start 70·5	Shift in share −2·4	Share at start 68·1	*Shift in share 7·6
Taunton	SMLA	Absolute 12,805	*per cent 11·3	Absolute 3,806	per cent 5·5	Absolute 3,572	*per cent 9·8	Absolute 8,902	per cent 12·2	Absolute 3,116	per cent 9·76	Absolute 1,550	*per cent 8·8
	Core	Share at start 45·0	*Shift in share 1·8	Share at start 48·6	Shift in share −0·4	Share at start 48·2	*Shift in share −2·8	Share at start 48·2	Shift in share −2·6	Share at start 57·2	Shift in share 4·3	Share at start 61·5	*Shift in share 1·6
Thurrock	SMLA	Absolute 27,946	*per cent 21·4	Absolute 36,502	per cent 39·1	Absolute 10,152	*per cent 15·6	Absolute 21,276	per cent 16·4	Absolute 11,437	per cent 26·8	Absolute 9,930	*per cent 36·6
	Core	Share at start 94·1	*Shift in share −3·3	Share at start 87·9	Shift in share 0·0	Share at start 88·0	*Shift in share −5·7	Share at start 88·0	Shift in shase −5·5	Share at start 95·5	Shift in share −1·2	Share at start 94·3	*Shift in share −1·6
Torquay	SMLA	Absolute 17,255	*per cent 9·6	Absolute 8,288	per cent 7·7	Absolute 7,148	*per cent 12·4	Absolute 14,441	per cent 12·5	Absolute 3,299	per cent 8·5	Absolute 4,040	*per cent 19·1
	Core	Share at start 72·1	*Shift in share 0·8	Share at start 73·6	Shift in share −0·6	Share at start 73·0	*Shift in share −1·1	Share at start 73·0	Shift in share 10·9	Share at start 73·9	Shift in share 2·2	Share at start 76·1	*Shift in share −1·8
Tunbridge Wells	SMLA	Absolute 10,657	*per cent 6·8	Absolute 7,798	per cent 8·8	Absolute 10,180	*per cent 21·1	Absolute 19,545	per cent 20·2	Absolute 3,239	per cent 9·2	Absolute 4,030	*per cent 20·9
	Core	Share at start 45·9	*Shift in share −1·3	Share at start 43·3	Shift in share −2·0	Share at start 41·3	*Shift in share −6·2	Share at start 41·3	Shift in share −3·0	Share at start 47·8	Shift in share 3·3	Share at start 51·2	*Shift in share −4·2

* Decennial rate.

		Land area 1961 ('000 acres)	Population ('000s)					Population density (persons per acre)				Labour force working in area ('000s)		
			1931	1951	1961	1966	1971*	1931	1951	1961	1966	1951	1961	1966
91. Wakefield	MELA	77·3	211·4	213·9	220·6	226·5	228·8	2·73	2·77	2·85	2·93	95·0	82·0	95·5
	SMLA	39·7	136·8	137·9	139·9	145·0	147·9	3·45	3·47	3·53	3·65	63·4	65·2	69·6
	Core	5·8	59·3	60·4	61·3	59·8	59·7	10·22	10·41	10·57	10·31	32·0	36·7	39·2
	UBZA MELA	40·8	193·9	188·8	196·2	—	—	—	—	—	—	—	—	—
	SMLA	23·7	129·0	127·7	131·5	—	—	—	5·39	5·55	—	—	—	—
92. Walton and Weybridge	MELA	19·0	42·6	69·0	85·9	91·3	95·9	2·24	3·63	4·52	4·81	28·8	39·6	42·2
	SMLA	19·0	42·6	69·0	85·9	91·3	95·9	2·24	3·63	4·52	4·81	28·8	39·6	42·2
	Core	9·0	26·6	38·1	45·5	48·8	51·0	2·96	4·21	5·03	5·42	18·0	27·3	28·3
	UBZA MELA	14·5	32·6	60·9	80·0	—	—	—	—	—	—	—	—	—
	SMLA	14·5	32·6	60·9	80·0	—	—	—	4·20	5·52	—	—	—	—
93. Warrington	MELA	84·4	207·4	247·3	246·6	256·1	278·0	2·46	2·93	2·92	3·03	129·0	117·1	124·4
	SMLA	75·5	144·2	174·9	168·4	176·2	185·4	1·91	2·32	2·23	2·33	95·2	84·7	89·9
	Core	4·5	81·6	80·7	76·0	72·4	68·3	18·13	17·86	16·81	16·09	47·0	46·6	47·4
	UBZA MELA	29·7	173·2	219·9	218·8	—	—	—	—	—	—	—	—	—
	SMLA	20·9	110·0	147·4	140·5	—	—	—	7·05	6·72	—	—	—	—
94. Watford	MELA	33·2	88·2	140·4	169·3	168·7	170·0	2·66	4·23	5·11	5·08	57·3	68·9	75·9
	SMLA	33·2	88·2	140·4	169·3	168·7	170·0	2·66	4·23	5·11	5·08	57·3	68·9	75·9
	Core	5·3	58·5	73·1	75·6	76·0	78·1	11·04	13·81	14·28	14·34	38·9	46·7	54·5
	UBZA MELA	25·5	70·2	147·4	140·5	—	—	—	—	—	—	—	—	—
	SMLA	26·5	70·2	147·4	140·5	—	—	—	5·56	5·30	—	—	—	—
95. West Hartlepool	MELA	40·8	169·3	172·1	179·9	181·1	182·3	4·15	4·22	4·41	4·44	63·8	63·1	62·4
	SMLA	6·2	90·1	89·9	94·7	95·7	97·0	14·53	14·61	15·39	15·44	34·0	34·5	34·6
	Core	4·7	69·5	76·7	77·0	78·0	97·0	14·79	15·53	16·46	16·60	28·2	27·7	27·4
	UBZA MELA	24·4	166·2	166·5	168·5	—	—	—	—	—	—	—	—	—
	SMLA	6·2	90·1	89·8	94·7	—	—	—	14·48	15·27	—	—	—	—

		Population change ('000s)								Employment change (000's)			
		1931–51		1951–61		1961–66		1961–71		1951–61		1961–66	
Wakefield	SMLA	Absolute 1,056	*per cent 0·4	Absolute 2,038	per cent 1·5	Absolute 5,038	*per cent 7·2	Absolute 7,999	per cent 5·7	Absolute 1,804	per cent 2·8	Absolute 4,380	*per cent 13·4
	Core	Share at start 43·3	*Shift in share 0·2	Share at start 43·8	Shift in share 0·0	Share at start 43·8	*Shift in share −5·1	Share at start 43·8	Shift in share −3·5	Share at start 50·5	Shift in share 5·7	Share at start 56·2	*Shift in share 0·1
Walton and Weybridge	SMLA	Absolute 26,318	*per cent 30·8	Absolute 16,936	per cent 24·6	Absolute 5,380	*per cent 12·5	Absolute −10	per cent 0·0	Absolute 10,780	per cent 37·4	Absolute 2,640	*per cent 13·3
	Core	Share at start 60·2	*Shift in share −2·5	Share at start 55·3	Shift in share 0·7	Share at start 56·0	*Shift in share −5·0	Share at start 56·0	Shift in share −2·8	Share at start 62·3	Shift in share 6·6	Share at start 68·9	*Shift in share −3·7
Warrington	SMLA	Absolute 30,713	*per cent 10·6	Absolute −6,490	per cent −3·7	Absolute 7,775	*per cent 9·2	Absolute 16,928	per cent 10·1	Absolute −10,508	per cent −11·0	Absolute 5,120	*per cent 12·1
	Core	Share at start 56·6	*Shift in share −5·2	Share at start 46·2	Shift in share −1·1	Share at start 45·1	*Shift in share −8·1	Share at start 45·1	Shift in share −8·3	Share at start 49·4	Shift in share 5·6	Share at start 55·0	*Shift in share −4·5
Watford	SMLA	Absolute 52,218	*per cent 29·6	Absolute 28,951	per cent 20·6	Absolute −606	*per cent −0·7	Absolute 650	per cent 0·4	Absolute 11,623	per cent 20·3	Absolute 7,010	*per cent 20·3
	Core	Share at start 66·4	*Shift in share −7·1	Share at start 52·1	Shift in share −7·4	Share at start 44·6	*Shift in share 0·7	Share at start 44·6	Shift in share 1·4	Share at start 67·9	Shift in share −0·1	Share at start 67·8	*Shift in share 8·1
West Hartlepool	SMLA	Absolute −19·6	*per cent −0·1	Absolute 4,818	per cent 5·4	Absolute 1,010	*per cent 2·1	Absolute 2,188	per cent 2·3	Absolute 467	per cent 1·4	Absolute 160	*per cent 0·9
	Core	Share at start 77·1	*Shift in share 1·9	Share at start 80·8	Shift in share 0·5	Share at start 81·3	*Shift in share 0·4	Share at start 81·3	Shift in share 18·7	Share at start 82·9	Shift in share −2·5	Share at start 80·4	*Shift in share −2·8

* Decennial rate.

			Land area 1961 ('000 acres)	Population ('000s)					Population density (persons per acre)				Labour force working in area ('000s)		
				1931	1951	1961	1966	1971*	1931	1951	1961	1966	1951	1961	1966
96. Wigan	MELA		41·4	188·6	184·0	186·4	194·7	223·9	4·56	4·44	4·54	4·70	68·0	67·7	76·5
	SMLA		39·5	182·4	182·8	180·1	187·5	223·9	4·62	4·63	4·56	4·75	66·5	66·0	72·8
	Core		5·1	85·4	84·6	78·7	76·4	81·3	16·75	16·64	15·48	14·98	35·3	37·1	41·2
	UBZA	MELA	25·9	178·5	176·4	175·4	—	—	—	—	—	—	—	—	—
		SMLA	23·9	172·3	170·2	169·1	—	—	—	7·12	7·08	—	—	—	—
97. Woking	MELA		31·9	47·0	61·7	83·7	89·3	97·0	1·47	1·93	2·62	2·80	23·0	28·8	32·9
	SMLA		31·9	47·0	61·7	83·7	89·3	97·0	1·47	1·93	2·62	2·80	23·0	28·8	32·9
	Core		15·7	36·0	47·6	67·5	71·7	75·8	2·29	3·03	4·30	4·57	19·0	24·5	28·1
	UBZA	MELA	15·7	32·1	46·9	67·5	—	—	—	—	—	—	—	—	—
		SMLA	15·7	32·1	46·9	67·5	—	—	—	2·99	4·30	—	—	—	—
98. Worcester	MELA		317·6	144·3	171·4	181·3	188·3	212·3	0·45	0·54	0·57	0·59	79·6	84·1	89·5
	SMLA		162·1	90·1	108·3	114·0	118·2	129·3	0·56	0·67	0·70	0·73	51·6	55·5	58·4
	Core		6·1	51·9	62·1	65·9	68·7	73·4	8·51	10·16	10·78	11·26	32·8	38·9	41·5
	UBZA	MELA	17·5	79·8	99·1	156·8	—	—	—	—	—	—	—	—	—
		SMLA	7·8	56·5	68·5	73·9	—	—	—	8·78	9·47	—	—	—	—
99. Worthing	MELA		360·8	71·0	113·2	134·4	145·7	157·2	0·20	0·16	0·19	0·40	36·1	42·2	46·5
	SMLA		117·0	60·6	99·3	118·7	127·6	138·6	0·52	0·85	1·01	1·09	31·8	36·9	40·3
	Core		5·3	46·6	69·4	80·2	83·9	88·2	8·79	15·09	15·13	15·83	23·1	26·1	28·9
	UBZA	MELA	17·6	63·2	104·2	126·5	—	—	—	—	—	—	—	—	—
		SMLA	15·1	63·2	90·2	112·6	—	—	—	5·97	7·46	—	—	—	—
100. York	MELA		437·3	182·0	209·9	217·3	223·9	233·7	0·42	0·48	0·50	0·51	96·6	102·6	106·0
	SMLA		98·1	117·5	158·7	146·9	151·2	155·2	1·20	1·41	1·50	1·54	65·8	72·8	74·2
	Core		6·9	94·1	105·4	104·4	101·6	104·5	13·64	15·20	15·06	16·93	54·5	60·8	62·8
	UBZA	MELA	19·3	106·3	129·6	141·4	—	—	—	—	—	—	—	—	—
		SMLA	14·3	96·0	115·5	126·8	—	—	—	8·08	8·87	—	—	—	—

* Provisional.

		Population change ('000s)								Employment change ('000s)			
		1931–51		1951–61		1961–66		1961–71		1951–61		1961–66	
Wigan	SMLA	Absolute 386	*per cent 0·1	Absolute −2,736	per cent −1·5	Absolute 7,370	*per cent 8·2	Absolute 43,792	per cent 24·3	Absolute −584	per cent −0·9	Absolute 6,860	*per cent 20·8
	Core	Share at start 46·8	*Shift in share −0·3	Share at start 46·2	Shift in share −2·5	Share at start 43·7	*Shift in share −5·9	Share at start 43·7	Shift in share −7·4	Share at start 53·0	Shift in share 3·2	Share at start 56·2	*Shift in share 0·9
Woking	SMLA	Absolute 14,625	*per cent 15·5	Absolute 21,994	per cent 35·6	Absolute 5,601	*per cent 13·4	Absolute 13,093	per cent 15·6	Absolute 5,804	per cent 25·2	Absolute 4,070	*per cent 28·2
	Core	Share at start 76·5	*Shift in share −1·7	Share at start 73·1	Shift in share 7·5	Share at start 80·7	*Shift in share 0·7	Share at start 80·7	Shift in share −2·4	Share at start 82·6	Shift in share 2·3	Share at start 84·9	*Shift in share 1·2
Worcester	SMLA	Absolute 18,271	*per cent 10·1	Absolute 5,698	per cent 5·3	Absolute 4,191	*per cent 7·4	Absolute 15,287	per cent 13·4	Absolute 3,955	per cent 7·7	Absolute 2,850	*per cent 10·3
	Core	Share at start 57·6	*Shift in share −0·2	Share at start 57·3	Shift in share 0·5	Share at start 57·8	*Shift in share 0·5	Share at start 57·8	Shift in share −1·0	Share at start 63·7	Shift in share 6·5	Share at start 70·1	*Shift in share 1·9
Worthing	SMLA	Absolute 38,788	*per cent 32·0	Absolute 19,320	per cent 19·4	Absolute 8,885	*per cent 15·0	Absolute 19,929	per cent 16·8	Absolute 5,033	per cent 15·8	Absolute 3,430	*per cent 18·6
	Core	Share at start 76·9	*Shift in share −3·5	Share at start 69·9	Shift in share −2·3	Share at start 67·6	*Shift in share −3·7	Share at start 67·6	Shift in share −4·0	Share at start 72·6	Shift in share −1·9	Share at start 70·8	*Shift in share 1·7
York	SMLA	Absolute 21,237	*per cent 9·0	Absolute 8,199	per cent 5·9	Absolute 4,278	*per cent 5·8	Absolute 8,268	per cent 5·6	Absolute 7,028	per cent 10·7	Absolute 1,390	*per cent 3·8
	Core	Share at start 80·1	*Shift in share −2·0	Share at start 76·0	Shift in share −4·9	Share at start 71·0	*Shift in share −7·8	Share at start 71·0	Shift in share −3·7	Share at start 83·0	Shift in share 0·6	Share at start 83·5	*Shift in share 2·3

* Decennial rate.

CHAPTER SIX

MEGALOPOLIS ENGLAND: THE PATTERN OF URBAN GROWTH

This chapter analyses in more detail the pattern of urban concentration in England and Wales. It asks: is there such a thing in England as a Megalopolis: a super urban area, embracing many metropolitan areas? To answer this question it looks particularly at four features. The first is contact (or coalescence, or overlap) of neighbouring urban areas. The chapter finds that there is such contact in England, though it is not complete. The second is interaction, especially in an economic sense, between the constituent metropolitan areas of England and Wales. The analysis shows that there are indeed very strong linkages within the area provisionally mapped out on the basis of contact. A third analysis shows that Megalopolis accounts for a disproportionate part of national growth. The fourth analysis, of physical growth in terms of land use, shows a striking concentration of the process within the familiar coffin shaped area running from London to Lancashire and Yorkshire. On the basis of this analysis, the chapter concludes that it is after all legitimate to talk of Megalopolis England.

From this conclusion, the main bulk of the chapter goes on to isolate some of the areas of greatest growth and stress within the Megalopolis, as a basis for choosing the detailed study areas which are the subject matter of Parts Two and Three of this book. It identifies five zones of exceptionally rapid growth in the post-1945 period: the western fringes of London, stretching as far as Basingstoke and Reading; the South Hampshire coast; the southern fringes of Birmingham and Coventry; Leicester and Leicestershire; and the southern fringes of the Merseyside and South-East Lancashire conurbations. It analyses the main details of population and employment change in these five areas, and for three of them it also considers the physical impact of urban development in terms of land use patterns.

This chapter was written by Peter Hall; Anne Whalley did most of the computations. Roy Drewett analysed and wrote the sections on detailed population and employment changes. Chris Smith analysed the data on interactions.

INTRODUCTION

In Chapter Five we tried comprehensively to dissect the anatomy of modern metropolitan Britain. But in this process it was abundantly clear that the 100 metropolitan areas occupied a limited, and highly selective, part of the total land surface of England and Wales. Out of a total of 37,342,000 acres of land and inland water in England and Wales, the metropolitan areas as defined here occupied only 12,610,000 acres – less than 34 per cent. Furthermore, large tracts of the country are almost free from metropolitan influence. A great belt of Wessex, embracing the chalk lands of the Marlborough Downs and Salisbury Plain and stretching down to the Dorset coast; the whole of North Devon and North Cornwall; all of Wales except the southern coalfield; the thinly populated heart of East Anglia and the coasts of North Norfolk and of Lincolnshire; the rural East Riding of Yorkshire, and the whole of the northern Pennines and the Lake District, fall outside the orbit of the Standard Metropolitan Labour Areas (Figure 5.1).

Conversely, as we already saw in Chapter Five, the SMLAs are concentrated to an extraordinary degree in certain limited parts of the country; they group themselves into two major concentrations, and half-a-dozen minor ones. The first major concentration consists of London and twenty-five contiguous SMLAs, nineteen of them concentrated within forty miles of Piccadilly Circus, the other six forming a more scattered group up to sixty and more miles away. It contained in 1961 36·8 per cent of the population of the entire country, living on only 9·5 per cent of the land area, The second concentration is even bigger: a continuous block of forty SMLAs occupies the whole of the industrial East and West Midlands, Lancashire and the West Riding. With only a small empty block in the Derbyshire Pennines, it assembled together 43·2 per cent of the population of metropolitan England and Wales in 1961, or 33·4 per cent of the population of the country, living on only 14·2 per cent of its land area. It extends in long tongues to Gloucester in the south-west and to Hull in the north-east. Only the narrowest break, along the line of the Cotswold belt, separates it from the other great conglomeration around London. Defined rigorously in this way, the coffin of the 1930s appears almost a reality. But significantly, the break in it still occurs where (as we saw in Chapter 2) the critics of the theory, Baker and Gilbert, said it did. By 1990, however, the growth of the great new city of Milton Keynes, and of the new town attached to Northampton, will have closed this gap; there will be an unbroken stretch of metropolitan areas stretching from Beachy Head in Sussex to Garstang in Lancashire, a distance of 270 miles.

The minor groupings, for the most part, can be seen almost as isolated extensions, or outliers, of the major concentrations. One, composed of Portsmouth, Southampton, and Bournemouth, clusters along the Hampshire coast; another, composed of Colchester and Ipswich with another isolated outlier in Norwich and Great Yarmouth, makes a straggling belt of metropolitan influence along the East Anglian coast. Blackpool, Burnley, and Lancaster should properly be treated as extensions of the great metropolitan cluster of the Midlands and North, from which they are excluded by only a few miles; as are Bristol and Bath to the south, and Lincoln on the east. The North-East industrial area consists of two separate groups, separated from each other only by a few miles, and containing together six metropolitan areas. Five other SMLAs cluster on the South Wales coast and coalfield, and form in effect an extension of the Midlands corridor running from Birmingham to Bristol. Another cluster of metropolitan areas occurs on the South Devon coast. Only a handful of SMLAs (Taunton, Peterborough, Shrewsbury, Barrow, and Carlisle) are truly isolated; and with some of these, the isolation may not persist for many more decades.

So strong is the overall picture in Figure 5.1, indeed, that we can legitimately ask whether Megalopolis England is not already a reality. The word *Megalopolis*, of course, has meant different things to different people. To the Greeks it was simply a city, which was planned as the biggest in the world. To Lewis Mumford, writing in the 1930s, it was an overgrown urban agglomeration containing several millions of people, but still recognizably based on one centre: London, Paris, above all New York. To the geographer Jean Gottmann, writing his definitive work on Megalopolis in 1960, it was:

> an almost continuous stretch of urban and suburban areas from southern New Hampshire to northern Virginia and from the Atlantic shore to the Appalachian foothills.[1]

In a physical sense, this statement is patently untrue; Gottmann's own analysis, later in his book, shows that. In fact, Gottmann soon makes clear that though he does not define Megalopolis precisely, he has in mind not a physical definition, but what we have called a functional definition, of urbanization and urban growth. Early in the book, he defines his Megalopolis in terms of Standard Metropolitan Areas, though he questions the definitions of some of these areas as given in the United States Census. And Marion Clawson, in his study of the Northeastern Urban Complex, defines his area in terms of thirty-four Standard Metropolitan Statistical Areas, taken from the 1960 Census, which stretch from just north of Boston to just south of Washington, together with all more or less directly intervening rural areas, where functional urbanization may spread in the next few decades. The area is far from including all the places influenced by the major urban centres of the region. Indeed, as Clawson points out, some of these areas of influence extend across the world. But, as Clawson says:

> The concern of this book is with land use, and definitions of the regions and ways of using data are evaluated in terms of their effect upon the description of land use within the region.[2]

This is the essential objective in defining an area for the study of urban growth, which is why it has been our starting point, as it has Clawson's. The aim is specifically to look at those areas which, falling under the influence of the major cities and towns in a functional sense, are then susceptible to

[1] Jean Gottmann, *Megalopolis: The Urbanised Northeastern Seaboard of the United States*. Twentieth Century Fund, New York (1961), p. 1.

[2] Marion Clawson, *Suburban Land Conversion in the United States: An Economic and Governmental Process*. Johns Hopkins U.P., Baltimore (1971), p. 195.

urban growth in a physical sense. It is this relationship, between the shadow cast by the city in a functional sense and the fact of physical land conversion from rural to urban use, which is central to both studies. So it is logical to start by defining functional areas in terms of commuting patterns and by looking at the growth of physically urbanized areas within them, as we have done in Chapters Four and Five. It is equally logical now to try to define a wider area, where these separate buildings blocks make contact, coalesce and even overlap, for it is here that the pressures for physical development are likely to be greatest, and here that the satisfaction of the pressures is likely to lead to most complex problems. Hence the need to define as a study area a group of metropolitan areas, which together form an urban complex, or Megalopolis.

Megalopolis, it is clear, is an even harder concept to define rigorously than most units of urban analysis, for of all these units, it is the most complex. One essential element is a notion of *contact*, or coalescence, or overlap, among neighbouring functional urban areas. A second element is a high degree of functional *interaction* between these separate units. Yet a third, and absolutely critical element is *growth* in a functional sense; one main reason why we are interested in Megalopolis is because of the problems which arise when commuting fields interact and overlap. Fourth, and relatedly, we are concerned with growths in a *physical* sense. We should expect to find that Megalopolis is an area where, to an extreme degree, the growth of neighbouring towns impinges each on the other through physical demands on land. It is now worth examining each of those attributes in detail.

DEFINING MEGALOPOLIS: THE CRITERION OF CONTACT

Our first concern in delineating a study area, then, is to define a set of functional urban areas, which should be continuous, and which should contain the greatest possible concentration of urban population in England and Wales. But as compared with the American study, the problem for us is somewhat complicated by the smaller size of our basic building blocks. Our Standard Metropolitan Labour Areas were consciously based on cores which were not too restrictively defined; yet nevertheless, the SMLAs that emerge prove to occupy a much more restricted area than the equivalent American SMSAs. Table 6.1 shows a comparison of areas and populations for a selection of SMLAs and SMSAs, chosen so as to match up in population; though in some cases the areas are also fairly equivalent, in the great majority the American examples are bigger, in some cases much bigger. This is partly due to a bigger average size of building block (the American county, basis of the SMSA definition except in New England, is larger on average than the English rural district), and partly perhaps to greater mobility, which extends the commuting fields more widely.

The effect of this is that while in most cases the American SMSAs form a contiguous set of areas along the Northeastern Seaboard, giving an easily defined Northeastern Urban Complex for purpose of study (Figure 1.1), the

Table 6.1

SAMPLE STANDARD METROPOLITAN LABOUR AREAS AND SAMPLE METROPOLITAN STATISTICAL AREAS: POPULATIONS AND AREAS, 1960–1961

		Area	Population
		Square miles	Thousands
1	London SMLA	1,499	9,157
	New York SMSA	2,149	10,695
2	Birmingham SMLA	903	2,693
	Boston SMSA	969	2,589
3	Manchester SMLA	455	2,042
	Washington SMSA	1,485	2,003
4	Stoke-on-Trent SMLA	452	519
	Hartford SMSA	514	525
5	Brighton SMLA	151	338
	Bridgeport SMSA	161	335
6	Luton SMLA	261	267
	Trenton SMSA	228	266
7	Bolton SMLA	71	250
	York SMSA	911	238
8	Wakefield SMLA	62	140
	Fall River SMSA	144	138

Source: Census, England and Wales, 1961. Census, United States, 1960.

English SMLAs do not. The two main groupings of SMLAs, one around London, the other around the Midlands and stretching up to Lancashire and Yorkshire, do not quite join up, and they leave some ragged interstitial areas. On the other hand, it is clear that together these two groups, perhaps with some neighbouring minor concentrations which in effect form extensions of them, constitute an approximate definition of our study area. In terms of the contiguity principle, something very near to a Megalopolis England exists; it is merely necessary, for the sake of precision, to give it a definition.

This we did, by using the Metropolitan Economic Labour Areas as building blocks. The central characteristic of these units, most useful for this purpose, is that they exhaust the whole area of the territory they cover, so long as there is any recorded commuting movement to a SMLA core. We accordingly took the 100 Metropolitan Economic Labour Areas of England and Wales, defined in terms of their 1961 Census populations, and arrayed them in a particular way: we expressed each MELA in terms of its percentage share of the population of England and Wales, and then in terms of its percentage share in the area, and arrayed all MELAs in terms of the size of the difference between these two measures (Figure 6.1). The effect is to

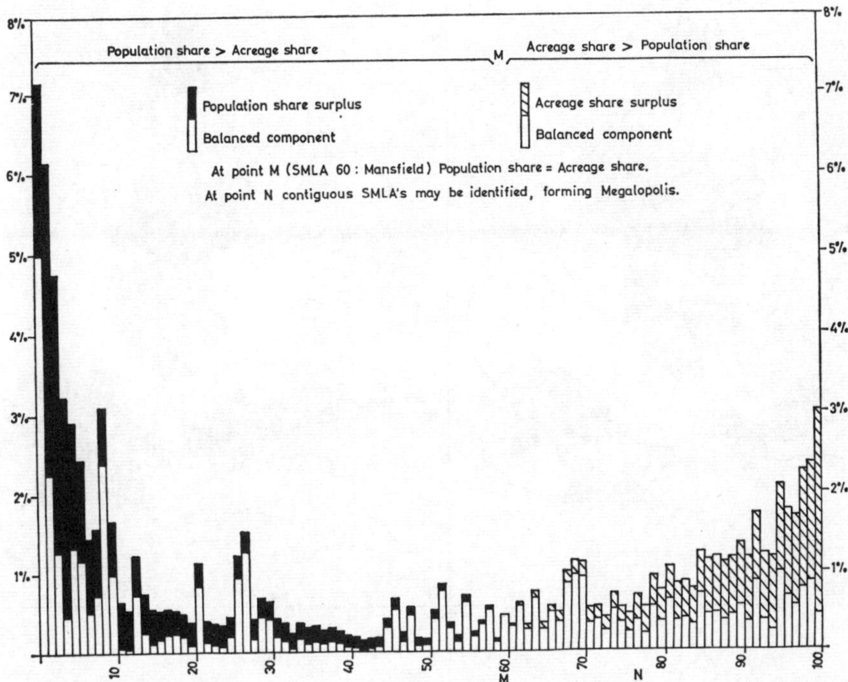

Figure 6.1 MELAs ranked by Share in England and Wales Population and Area, 1961

achieve what we want here: to obtain a set of contiguous areas, which at any point will give the maximum possible concentration of people on area.

The effect of this process, as with the smaller Standard Metropolitan Labour Areas, is again to identify two major groupings, and two minor ones (Severnside-South Wales and the North-East); these, which appear early in the grouping process (Figure 6.2a) represent the basic elements in the metropolitan geography of England and Wales. As the grouping process continues, these areas persist, extend and thicken up (Figure 6.2b); but until very late in the process, they do not coalesce (Figure 6.2c).[3] In particular, the great Midlands-Northern group is divided from the great London group by the narrow strip of territory, which Baker and Gilbert first noticed in the 1940s, dividing Coventry and Leicester on one side from Bedford and Luton on the other (Figure 6.2b). By the time this gap is bridged, according to the

[3] At point 77 (Figure 6.2(c)) a continuous Megalopolis of sixty-one MELAs is formed. Included in the final Megalopolis are two more MELAs (Chelmsford and Maidstone) which are tied strongly to the London centre in terms of their commuting patterns and could be regarded, in effect, as constituents of the London MELA.

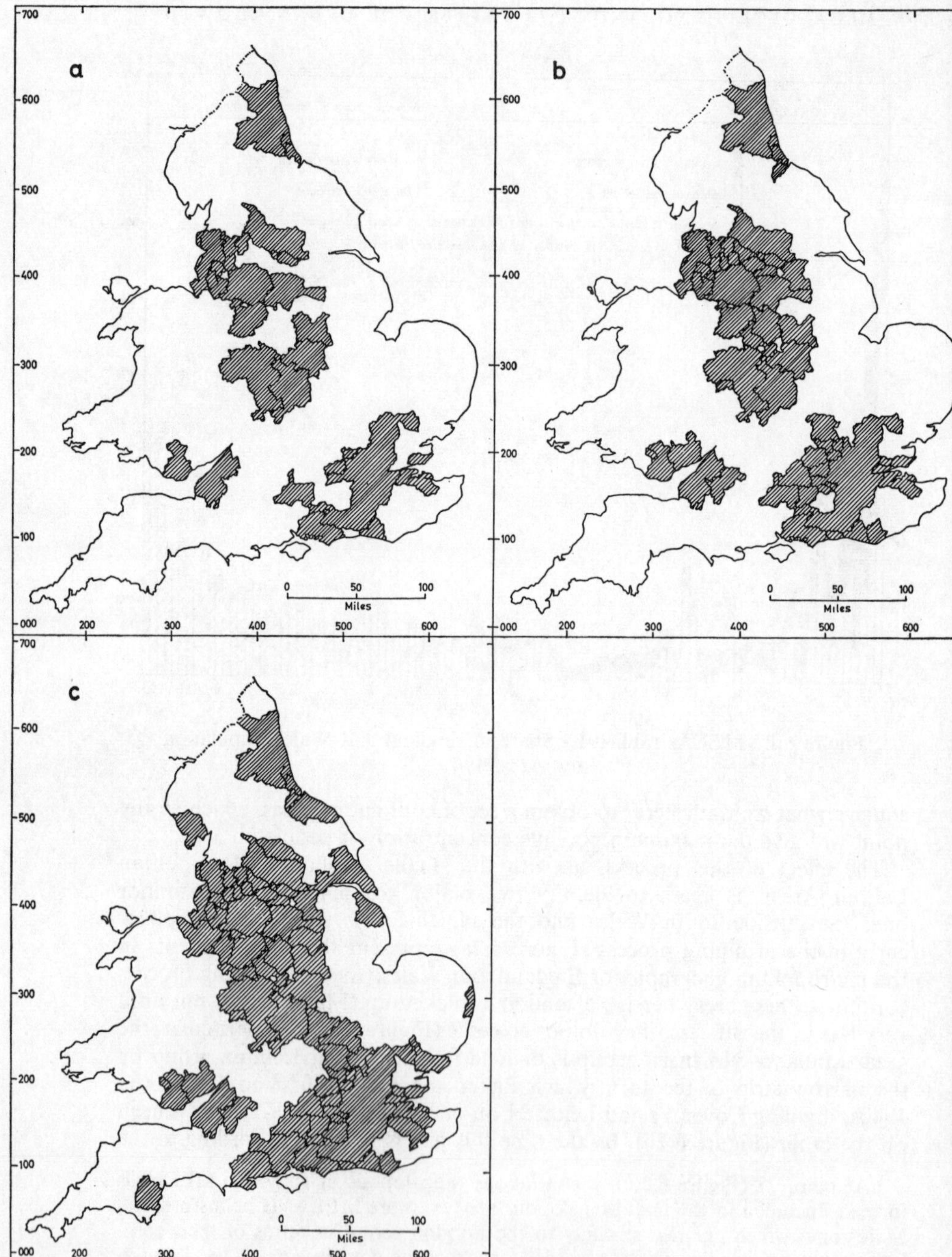

Figure 6.2 The Building Up of Megalopolis: (a) Stage 30, (b) Stage 59, (c) Stage 77

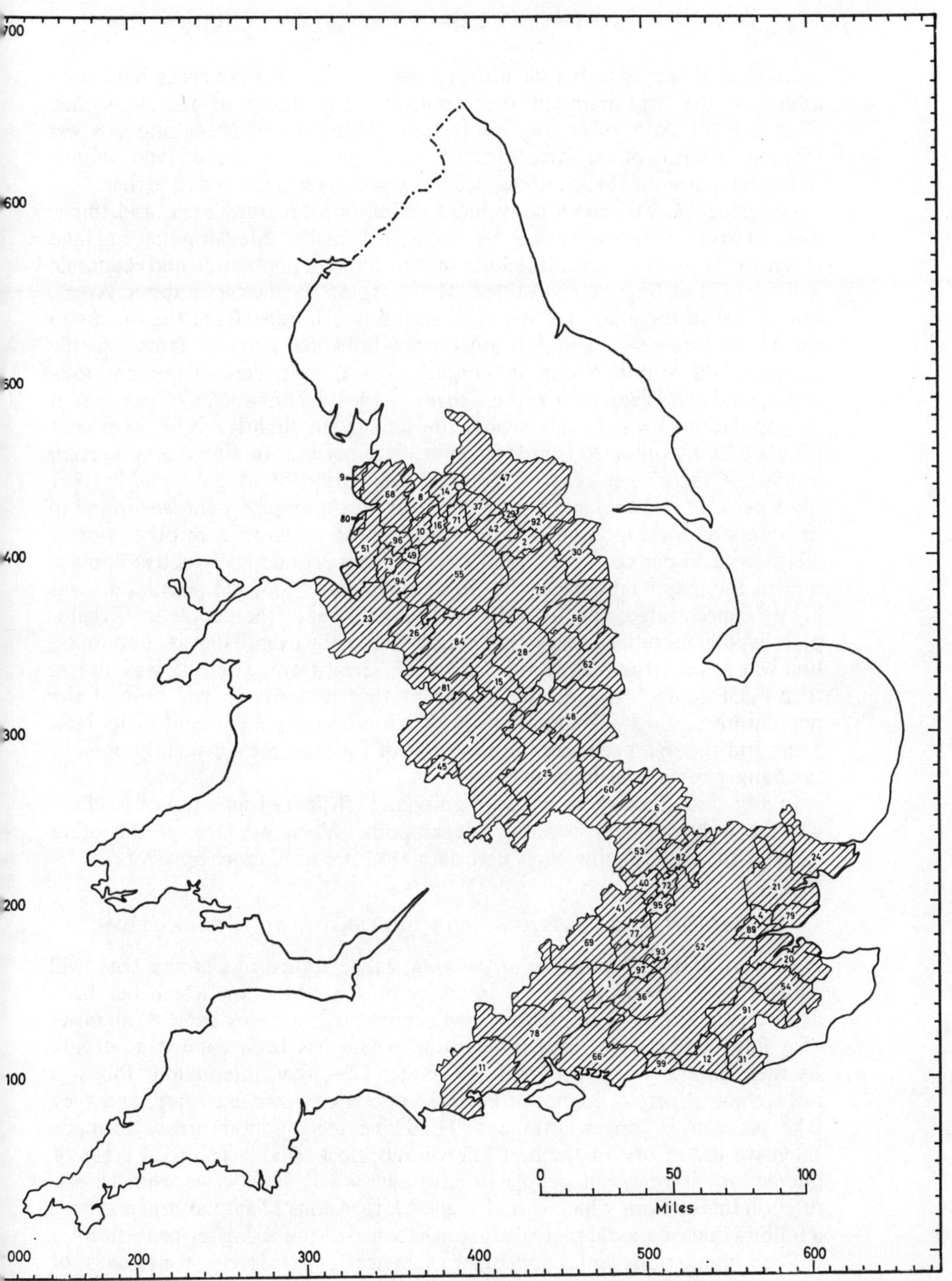

Figure 6.3 Megalopolis England (*Key: pages 254–292*)

method used here, nearly four-fifths of the 100 metropolitan areas have been added to the list, many of them outside Megalopolis as finally defined (Figure 6.2c). And, of course, the resulting definition of Megalopolis is less efficient in terms of the concentration of people on an area of land, than it might have been if the grouping process could have been ended earlier.

Nevertheless, we need a convenient definition of a study area, and this is one. Despite the reservation we have just made, Megalopolis England (Figure 6.3) does have a remarkable concentration of population and economic activity. Consisting of sixty-three Metropolitan Economic Labour Areas, out of 100 in England and Wales, it stretches 270 miles from the Sussex to the Lancashire coast, and 180 miles from Lulworth Cove in Dorset to the mouth of the Suffolk Stour. It occupies only 33·5 per cent of the land area of England and Wales; but at the Census of 1961, it contained 69·9 per cent of its population. By 1971 this proportion had fallen slightly, to 69·6 per cent (Table 6.2). It contained, similarly, some 71·6 per cent of all the employment in 1961. Over 87 per cent of the total population of Megalopolis in 1961 (86·3 per cent in 1971) and over 89 per cent of the employment was found in its Standard Metropolitan Labour Areas: those parts of it, in other words, which send 15 per cent or more of their resident economically-active population to the major labour centres. In another sense, too, the population was highly concentrated, for in 1961 some 87 per cent of the people in Megalopolis lived in urbanized areas, that is areas where the overall density of population was at least 1,000 to each square mile. Their average density was no less than 6,336 to each square mile. It meant that in 1961, 56 per cent of the population of England and Wales was living on only 7 per cent of its land area; and this, be it recalled, on that part of England most evidently open to the danger of suburban sprawl.

In any case, the criteria of contiguity and efficient occupation of land are not the only ones for defining Megalopolis. When we look at the other criteria, the case for this particular definition becomes more positive.

DEFINING MEGALOPOLIS: THE CRITERION OF INTERACTION

A functional definition of an urban area, as we argued in Chapter One, will depend on a certain degree of intensity of some function which has been defined as urban; and commonly it will consist of a certain degree of intensity of a flow, or between-place interaction, which has been defined as urban. By their nature, we also argued in Chapter One, such interactions follow a hierarchial principle; higher-order interactions or flows are rarer, and they take place over longer distances. To define metropolitan areas, we made extensive use of one of the best known and most reliably recorded types of interaction: journeys of people to and from work. If now we want to distinguish interactions which would suggest larger units of spatial organization, it follows that we should try to distinguish longer-distance, higher-order flows.

Such interactions could consist of exchanges of goods, or of messages, or of people. Exchanges of goods of all kinds would measure the degree of

Table 6.2

MEGALOPOLIS: POPULATION, 1931–1971; EMPLOYMENT, 1951–1966

	Area		Population ('000s)										Employment ('000s)					
	1961 '000*s* of *acres*	*% of all Mega-lopolis*	1931	*% of Mega-lopolis* 1931	1951	*% of Mega-lopolis* 1951	1961	*% of Mega-lopolis* 1961	1966	*% of Mega-lopolis* 1966	1971*	*% of Mega-lopolis* 1971	1951	*% of Mega-lopolis employ-ment* 1951	1961	*% of Mega-lopolis employ-ment* 1961	1966	*% of Mega-lopolis employ-ment* 1966
Megalopolis	12,520·5	100·0	27,595·4	100·0	30,498·9	100·0	32,241·9	100·0	32,864·5	100·0	33,839·3	100·0	14,262·8	100·0	15,103·5	100·0	15,780·9	100·0
Outer MELAs in Megalopolis	4,826·3	38·6	3,149·2	11·4	3,579·1	11·7	3,921·5	12·2	4,140·6	12·6	4,648·5	13·7	1,481·5	10·4	1,637·7	10·8	1,820·8	11·5
SMLAs in Megalopolis	7,694·3	61·5	24,446·2	88·6	26,919·8	88·3	28,320·4	87·8	28,724·0	87·4	29,190·8	86·3	12,781·3	89·6	13,465·8	89·2	13,960·1	88·5
Rings	6,567·3	52·5	6,793·6	24·6	9,342·6	30·6	10,731·6	33·3	11,572·3	35·2	12,181·9	36·0	3,254·0	22·8	3,513·6	23·3	3,946·4	25·0
Cores	1,126·9	9·0	17,652·6	64·0	17,577·2	57·6	17,588·8	54·6	17,151·6	52·2	17,008·8	50·3	9,527·4	66·8	9,952·2	65·9	10,013·7	63·5
Their UBZAs	2,595·8	20·7	21,701·0	78·6	24,128·6	79·1	25,715·2	79·8	—	—	—	—	—	—	—	—	—	—

	Population change ('000s)								Employment change ('000s)			
	Net change 1931–51	*% change* 1931–51	*Net change* 1951–61	*% change* 1951–61	*Net change* 1961–66	*% change* 1961–66	*Net change* 1961–71	*% change* 1961–71	*Net change* 1951–61	*% change* 1951–61	*Net change* 1961–66	*% change* 1961–66
Megalopolis	2,903·5	10·5	1,743·0	5·7	622·6	1·9	1,597·4	5·0	840·7	5·9	677·4	4·5
Outer MELAs in Megalopolis	429·9	13·7	342·4	9·6	219·1	5·6	727·0	18·5	156·2	10·5	183·1	11·2
SMLAs in Megalopolis	2,473·6	10·1	1,400·6	5·2	403·6	1·4	870·4	3·1	684·5	5·4	494·3	3·4
Rings	2,549·0	37·5	1,389·0	14·9	840·7	7·8	1,450·3	13·5	259·6	8·0	432·8	12·3
Cores	−75·4	−0·4	11·6	0·1	−437·2	−2·5	−580·0	−3·3	424·8	4·5	61·5	0·6
Their UBZAs	2,427·6	11·2	1,586·6	6·4	—	—	—	—	—	—	—	—

* Provisional figures.

interaction in the economy; if the types of goods could be disaggregated, then it would be possible to distinguish interactions in particular sectors of the economy, the manufacturing sector for instance. Exchanges of messages, on the other hand, reflect flows of intelligence or information; they are therefore particularly likely to represent interaction in those parts of the economy which rely on exchanges of such information, particularly the specialized decision-making functions that Jean Gottmann has called the quaternary sector. Finally, physical exchanges of people may take place for many purposes, many of them not economic at all. But insofar as some personal journeys are made in course of work, then they represent essentially an alternative way of transmitting information, sometimes coupled with possession of a manual skill. In part, therefore, personal journeys too are a measure of interaction in the economy.

Perhaps none of the higher-order, longer-distance types of movement are as well documented as the daily commuter movement which we used as the basis for our metropolitan area definitions. But information is more readily available than many geographers have realized. Exchanges of goods by road have been very completely analysed by fairly small zones, by means of a Ministry of Transport sample census, in 1964–5. Some information is available also on transfers of goods by rail. Again, letter and parcel post movements are well documented in Post Office records. Records of telephone calls have paradoxically suffered from automation, since subscriber trunk dialled calls are not automatically monitored as to origin and destination. So it is necessary to rely on data from 1958, the last pre-automation year. Passenger movements by train have been recorded by British Rail, but the records appear to be incomplete. Perhaps the biggest difficulty in making a comprehensive comparison is that each survey has its own geographical data base, and that it proves quite impossible to collapse these into one common scheme of areas for analysis.

Some of these records are being examined in detail in order to build up a picture of the geographical structure of the British economy, which may eventually go a long way to remedying the gap in our knowledge about inter-regional commodity flows. We could not attempt to replicate any such study in what was, after all, a strictly subsidiary exercise for us. But we did make a simple graphical and statistical analysis of some of the more manageable data on interactions.

The first of these dealt with road and rail freight (Figure 6.4). Our analysis isolated as worthy of consideration any individual flow of over 2,000 units. Such flows gave an aggregate total for England and Wales, during the sample period, of 12,826,615 units. Of this total, no less than 57·8 per cent, or some 7,418,765 units, consisted of interactions entirely within (i.e. both originating and destinating in) a single area unit. Of the sixty-seven areas in England and Wales used in this analysis, forty-one are within Megalopolis as it has been defined earlier; and 8,388,243 journeys, or 68·9 per cent of all those journeys in England and Wales which were above the level of significance for the analysis, both began and ended in Megalopolis. Adding journeys which

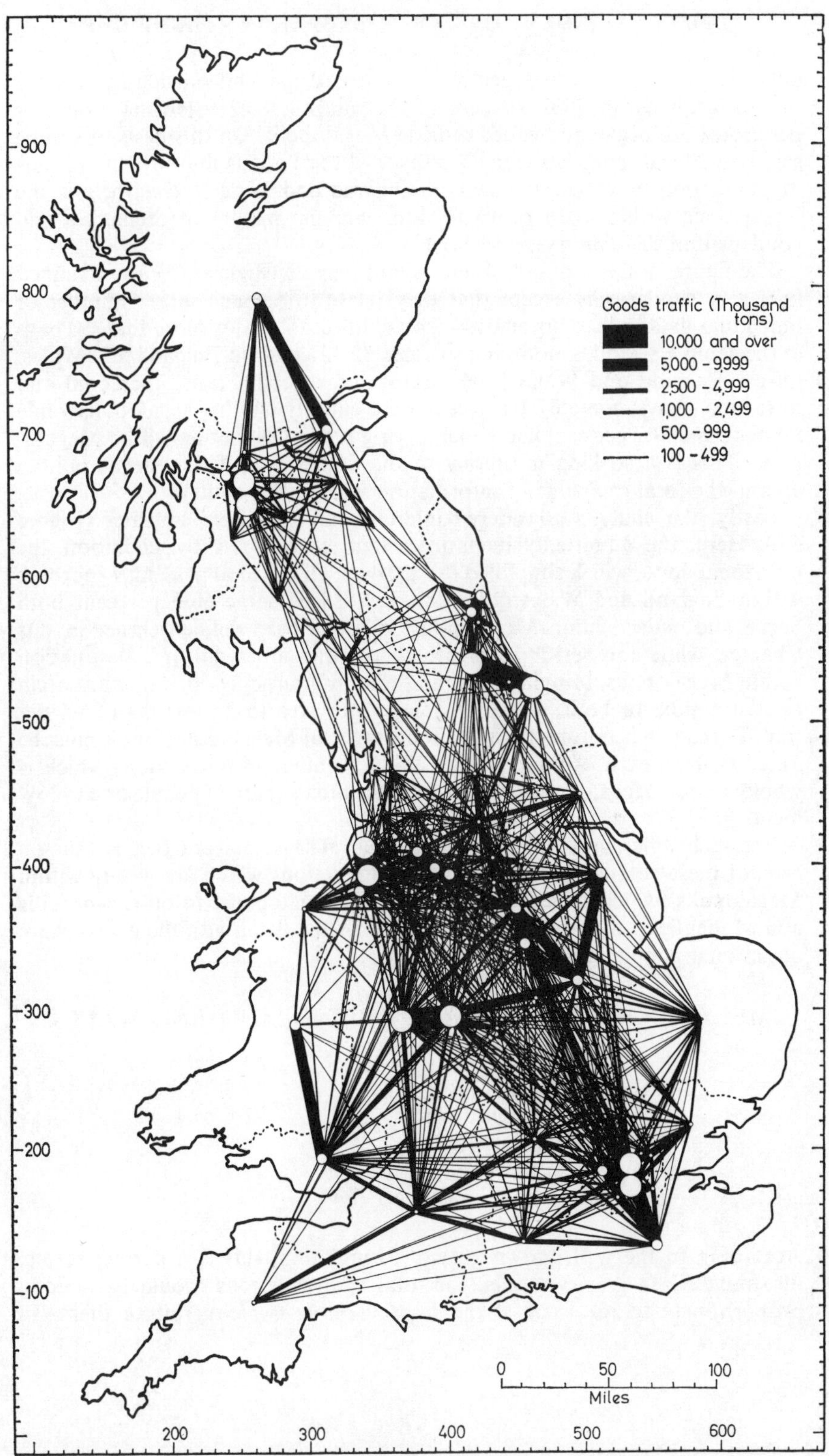

Figure 6.4 Goods Traffic by Road and Rail, 1964

either began or ended in Megalopolis, but had one end outside it, brought this to 9,439,896 or 73·6 per cent of the total. 3,386,719 journeys, or 26·4 per cent, both began and ended outside Megalopolis. On this basis, it can be said that Megalopolis has a smaller share of total goods journeys than it has of population or of employment in England and Wales. Nevertheless, the interactions within it do prove to dominate the picture of exchanges and goods within the country as a whole.

The figures for exchanges of letters and parcels (Figure 6.5) are arranged in a very similar way except that they relate to a much larger number of individual data units. Our analysis isolated those flows of more than 50 bags in the sample period, amounting to some 32,121 bags in England and Wales. Of the England and Wales total, taking into account both interzonal and intrazonal flows, some 67·1 per cent were entirely within Megalopolis while no less than 90·7 per cent had either an origin or a destination within Megalopolis. This is a striking testimony to the dominance of the Megalopolitan area in the total exchange of information within the country.

Lastly, the analysis considered intercity rail passenger statistics (Figure 6.6). Here, the admittedly incomplete figures excluded by definition the intrazonal flows, which simplified the analysis. Of the total passenger journeys within England and Wales (186,058), 123,818 or some 66·6 per cent both began and ended within Megalopolis as it has been defined earlier in this Chapter, while another 29·8 per cent had either an origin or a destination within Megalopolis, bringing the grand total of journeys with either an origin or destination, or both, in the Megalopolitan area to no less than 96·4 per cent. This again is testimony to the importance of Megalopolis. But it must be noted that on each of these counts, the percentage of interactions which is wholly within Megalopolis is lower than the area's share of people or employment.

Yet such differences are highly marginal. The significant fact is that on each of these counts, the percentage of interactions which are *wholly* within Megalopolis (which have both ends within Megalopolis, in other words) is almost identical, within the limits of error of the data, with the area's share of national population or employment:

MEGALOPOLIS PERCENTAGE OF ENGLAND AND WALES

	per cent
Population (1961)	69·9
Employment (1961)	71·6
Freight flows (1964)	68·9
Postal flows	67·1
Intercity rail passenger flows	66·6

According to the well known gravity formulation, this is a correct result; in a normalized gravity model, the total of interactions should be directly proportionate to the total of the mass variables which produce them. In

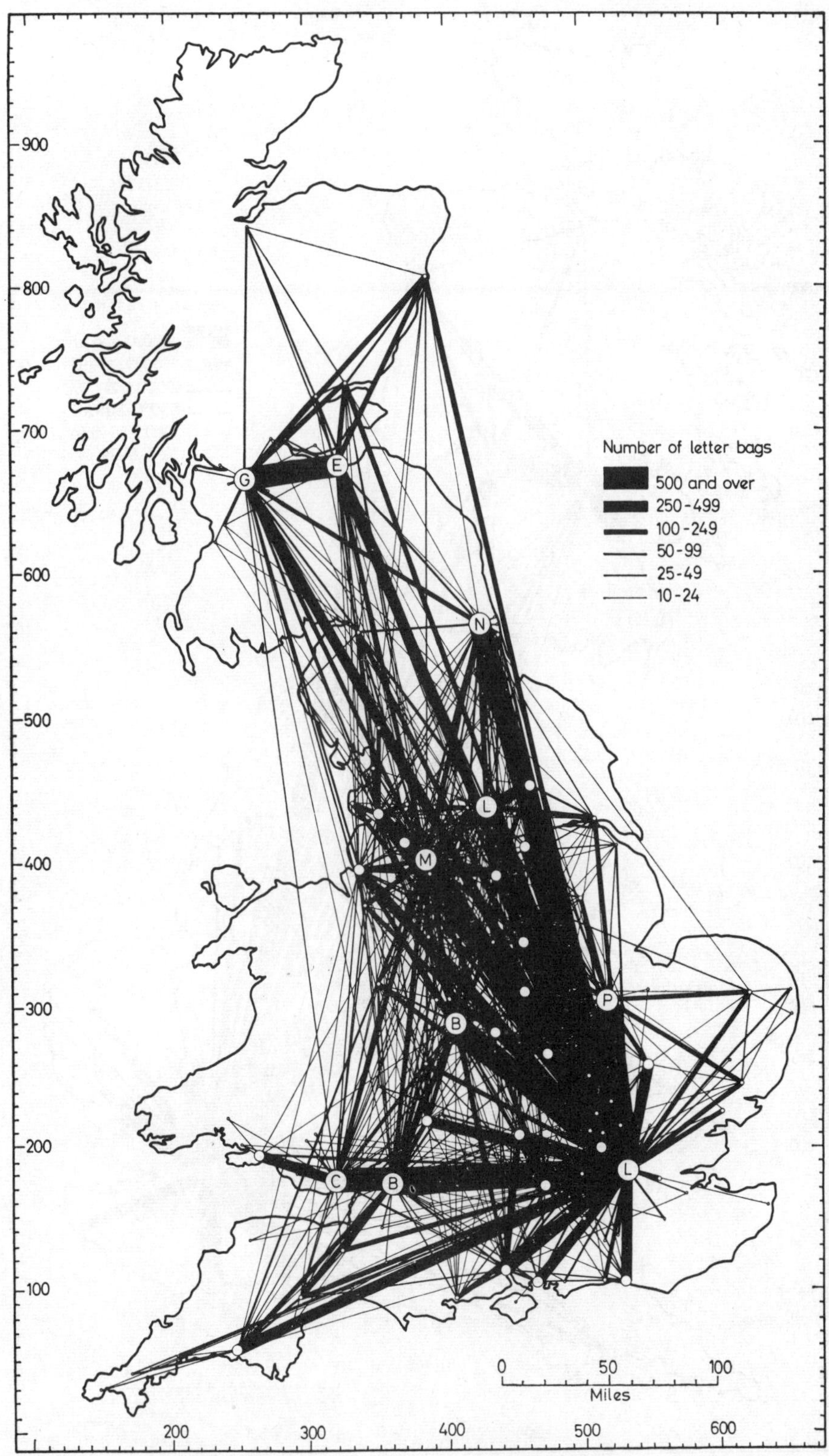

Figure 6.5 Post Office Letter Traffic, 1965

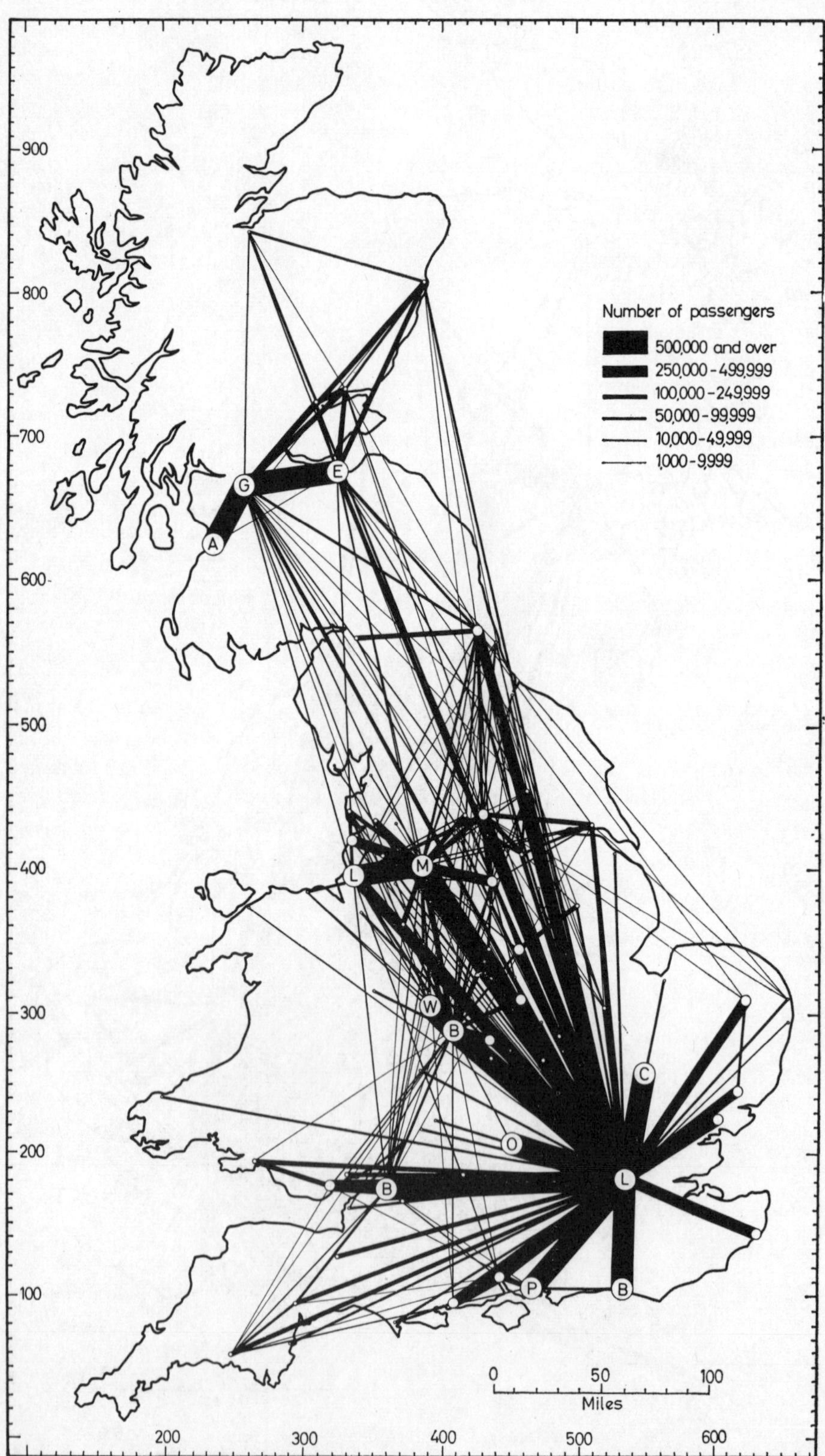

Figure 6.6 Passenger Traffic by British Rail, 1965

other words, the pattern of interaction within the British economy faithfully mirrors the pattern of activities which produces the interaction. Megalopolis dominates the pattern of flows of people, messages and goods, as it dominates the pattern of population and of economic activity within the country.

DEFINING MEGALOPOLIS: THE CRITERION OF GROWTH

The third and quite critical criterion in defining the study area is the fact of growth. Even if Megalopolis England were proved to exist in terms of contiguity and interaction, it would have no interest for the present study if it were not experiencing rapid and increasingly complex growth.

This growth, as we know, can apply either in a functional or a physical sense, or both. Thus the impact of commuting can extend to include more and more people; the percentage of the total area that is urbanized can grow; and the percentage of total land area in urban uses can likewise grow. We are especially concerned to find out those areas in which all these things are happening.

For the first, the sixty-three Metropolitan Economic Labour Areas which constitute Megalopolis have accounted for a steadily increasing proportion of the population in England and Wales. In 1931, 69·1 per cent of the population of the country lived in Megalopolis, an area accounting for only 33·5 per cent of the area of England and Wales. By 1951 the proportion was 69·7 per cent, by 1961 70·0 per cent and by 1966 71·3 per cent. Of this total, though, it was notable that a slightly decreasing proportion at each date was accounted for by the SMLAs (Table 6.2); an increasing proportion of the population in Megalopolis was going to the outermost fringes of the commuting area.

If the population was dispersing in this functional sense, it was concentrating in a physical sense. In 1931, Table 6.2 shows that 79 per cent of the population of Megalopolis lived in those parts of it defined as urbanized in a physical sense, that is in wards or civil parishes within SMLAs and with more than 1,000 people per square mile. The proportion was 79 per cent in 1951, and nearly 80 per cent in 1961; no figures are available in the 1966 Census. And since this figure excluded areas outside SMLAs, it did not provide the full measure of the urbanization of the population of Megalopolis. In 1961, in fact, 87 per cent of the people in Megalopolis lived in minor civil divisions recording more than 1,000 people per square mile.

DEFINING MEGALOPOLIS: THE CRITERION OF PHYSICAL IMPACT

The last of the four criteria, by which it may be possible to justify the choice of Megalopolis England as a distinctive study area, is that of physical impact: the total amount and proportion of land affected by physical urban development. Almost certainly this is the criterion which professional planners, or interested members of the general public, would consider most important.

Their concern is that the physical spread of cities and conurbations, in this most heavily industrialized and heavily populated belt of Great Britain, has already reached such proportions that there is a serious danger of physical merger within the foreseeable future.

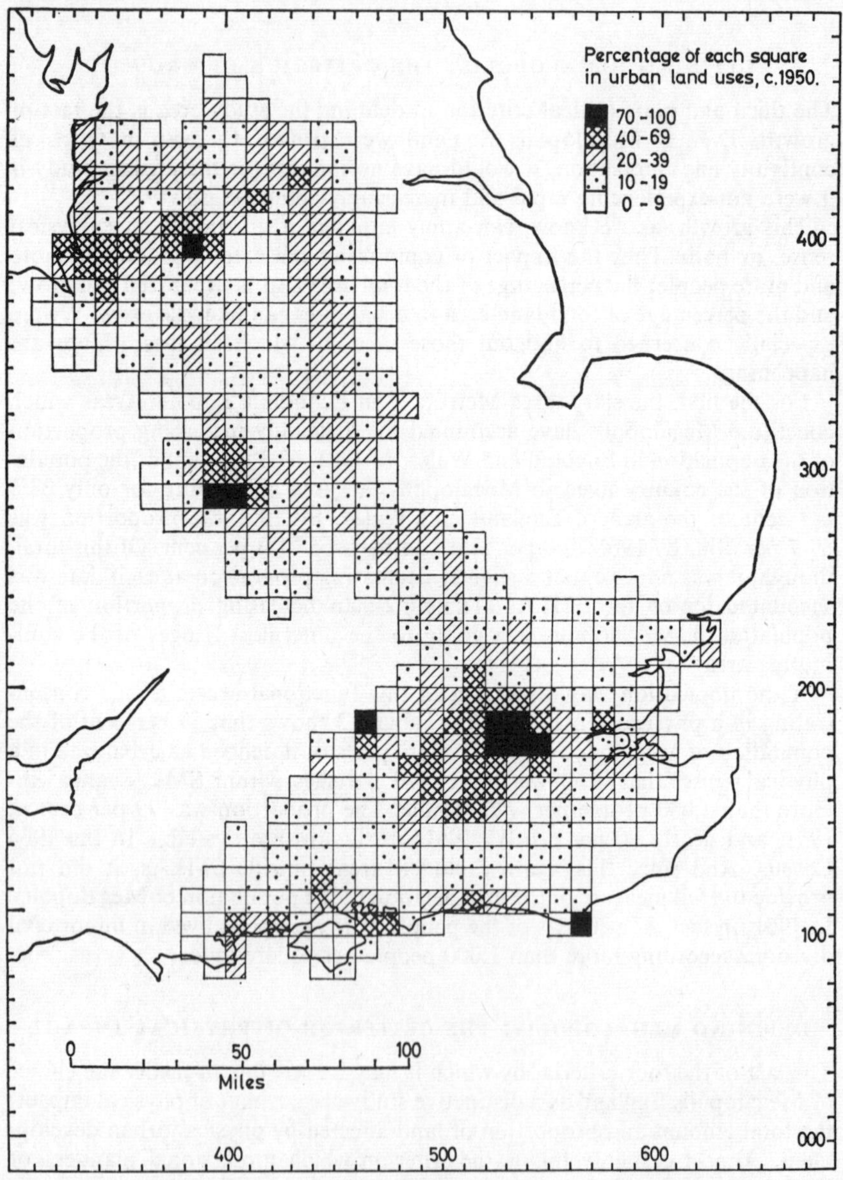

Figure 6.7 Megalopolis: Land Use, showing Degree of Urbanization, *circa* 1950

It was for this reason that the study of land use patterns, and of changes in those patterns, was made a central feature of our study. The plan, as outlined in Chapter Four, was an ambitious one, involving the comparison of three separate national land use studies. But in the event, unforeseen technical troubles prevented the satisfactory completion of the analysis of the first of these studies, the First Land Utilization Survey, in time for the publication of this book. The second survey, in chronological order of production (that made by the Local Planning Offices about the year 1950), was completely and satisfactorily analysed, but despite every attempt to ensure comparability between the classification of land uses in this survey and in the succeeding Second Land Utilization Survey, it soon became clear – both from general and from detailed comparison – that discrepancies existed.

Table 6.3

THE DEVELOPED AREA OF MEGALOPOLIS ENGLAND, CIRCA 1950

Major division	Total area	Developed area	Developed area as percentage of total area
	Square miles		
1 London and the South-East	7,413	1,584	21·4
2 South Coast	2,741	453	16·5
3 West Midlands	2,973	591	19·9
4 East Midlands	2,239	410	18·3
5 North-West	3,166	709	22·4
6 Yorkshire West Riding	2,317	409	17·7
Megalopolis	20,849	4,156	19·9

Source: Local Planning Authority Land Use Surveys.

Since we are confident that the Second Land Utilization Survey is highly accurate, we place our main reliance on it. It gives a picture of land use in Megalopolis at an important date for our purposes, shortly after the 1961 Census on which much of our previous statistical analysis, both in this chapter and the last, has been based. In comparison, it is clear that the Local Planning Authorities' survey overestimates the amount of urban development at the beginning of the 1950s. Overall, it indicates that just under 20 per cent of the area of Megalopolis was covered by various forms of urban land use at that time, as compared with less than 18 per cent just over a decade later. Making all possible allowance for clearance of wartime defence installations during the intervening period, and for slum clearance in large cities after 1955, this is not reasonable and does not accord with other estimates such as those of Robin Best; it indicates that the classification used in 1950 overstated

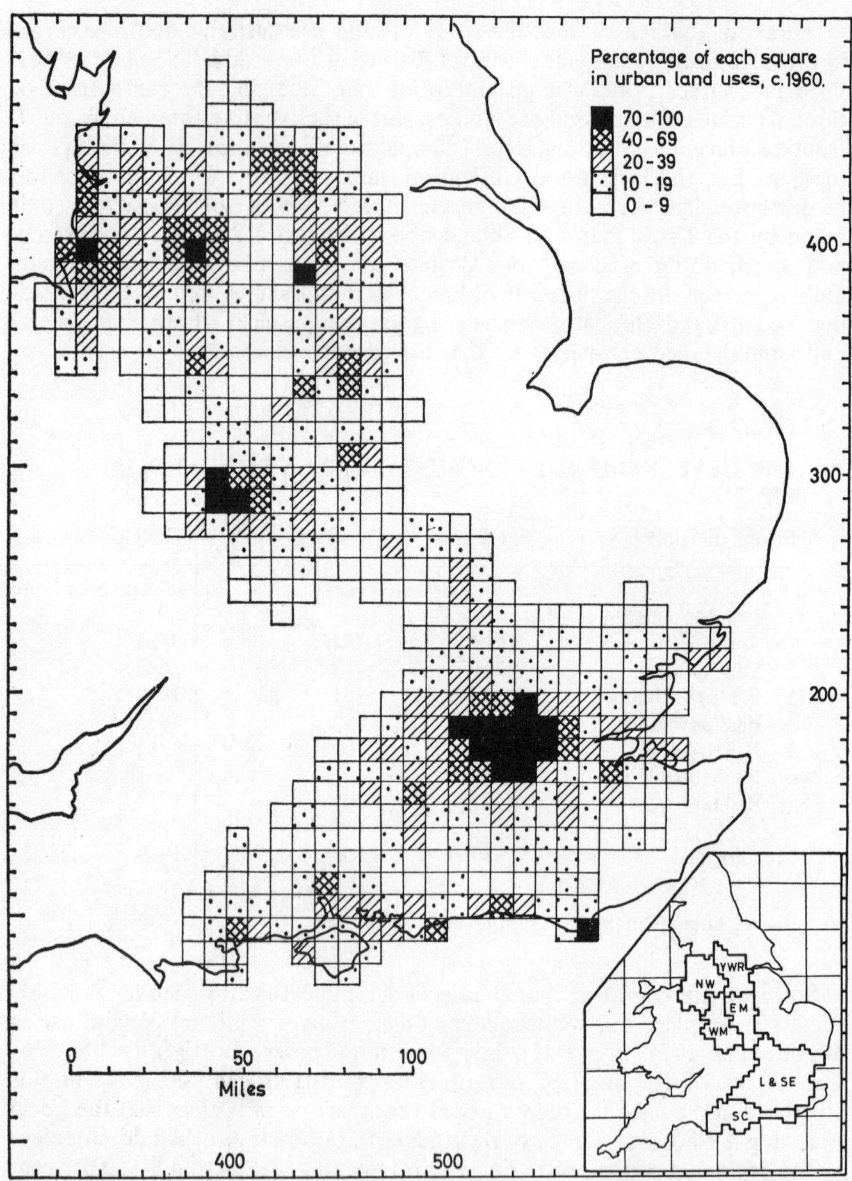

Figure 6.8 Megalopolis: Land Use, showing Degree of Urbanization, *circa* 1960

urban development in some systematic way, and detailed comparison of individual squares confirms that this is the case. Of the 540 squares, each 100 square kilometres in extent, used to analyse the data for Megalopolis, no fewer than three-fifths recorded a greater degree of urban development in the period about 1950 than in the early 1960s. The degree of discrepancy varies from square to square. Though there are some extreme cases, some of which may represent genuine losses of developed area, such as the closure of defence

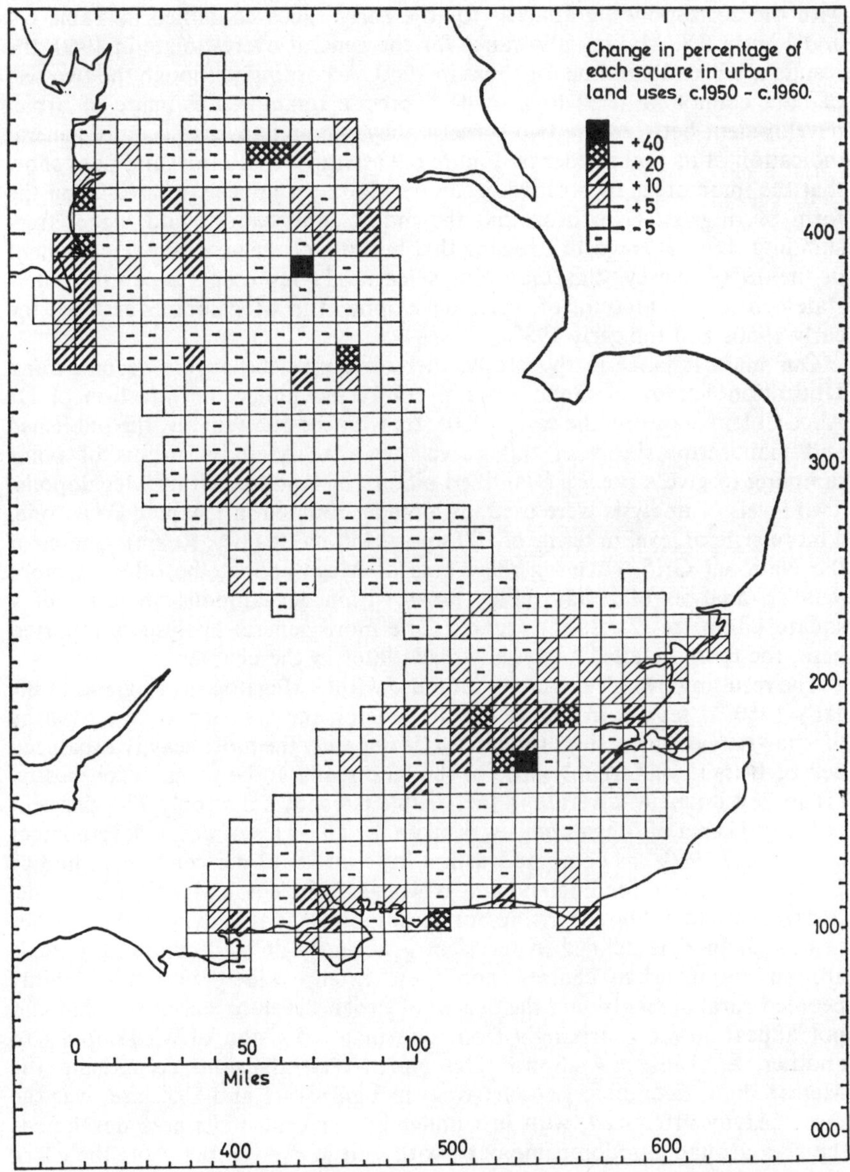

Figure 6.9 Megalopolis: Land Use Changes, showing Degree of Urban Development, *circa* 1950–*circa* 1960

installations, these are a minority, and in general the tendency to systematic overstatement of the urban area is confirmed by the detailed analysis.

The use that can be made of the 1950 analysis, therefore, is limited. Table 6.3 and Figure 6.7 present the results, which may be compared directly with the corresponding analysis for the early 1960s contained in Table 6.4 and Figure 6.8. Making allowance for the general overestimate in 1950, the results are broadly in line for those in 1960. Accordingly, though the two sets of data cannot be used to provide a precise quantified estimate of urban development between the two surveys, they can perhaps give a more general indication of its real incidence. Figure 6.9 attempts to do this, and does show that the main areas of positive urban development appear to have taken the form of rings of growth around the major conurbations and bigger free-standing cities. It is worth stressing that because of the general overstatement in the 1950s survey, this map almost certainly represents a severe understatement of the amount of urban development in Megalopolis between the early 1950s and the early 1960s.

Our main reliance in this study, therefore, must be on the Second Land Utilization Survey of Great Britain, conducted under the direction of Dr Alice Coleman during the early 1960s. As with the 1950 survey, the published and manuscript sheets of this survey were analysed by means of point sampling to give a precise quantified picture of land use within Megalopolis. Two levels of analysis were used, as already outlined in Chapter Four: one, a more general level in terms of 100 square kilometre (10 × 10 km) squares of the National Grid, covering the whole of Megalopolis; the other, a more detailed analysis of certain study areas within Megalopolis, in terms of 4 square kilometre (2 × 2 km) squares. The more general analysis is reported here; the more detailed analysis is made later in the chapter.

The resulting overall picture of land use within Megalopolis England in the early 1960s is set out in Figure 6.8. In general, the first impression given by the map may be surprising: though this is certainly the most heavily urbanized belt of Britain, remarkably little of the land seems to be actually covered by urban development. Overall, in fact, Table 6.4 shows that only 17·8 per cent of the total area of Megalopolis was taken for all forms of urban development in the early 1960s, as compared with a little under 12 per cent, according to Dr Best's analysis, for England and Wales as a whole at about the same time. But this should not be surprising, for Megalopolis, as already described earlier in this chapter, is defined in terms of generously defined commuting fields around major urban centres, and these extend widely into quite thinly peopled rural areas. In fact the degree of urban development at this date did not appear to vary strikingly from one major division of Megalopolis to another, as Table 6.4 shows. The North-West division, comprising the Metropolitan Economic Labour Areas in Lancashire and Cheshire, was the most heavily urbanized, with just under 22 per cent of its area developed; the area around London came next, with a little over 20 per cent; the other divisions had between 12 and 19 per cent of their land areas developed for urban purposes.

Table 6.4

THE DEVELOPED AREA OF MEGALOPOLIS ENGLAND, CIRCA 1960–1965

Major division	Total area	Developed area	As per cent total area	Residential area	as per cent total area	as per cent developed area
	square miles	square miles	per cent	square miles	per cent	per cent
1 London and the South-East	7,413	1,515	20·4	870	11·7	57·4
2 South Coast	2,741	374	13·6	229	8·4	61·3
3 West Midlands	2,973	450	15·1	164	5·5	36·4
4 East Midlands	2,239	262	11·7	111	5·0	42·4
5 North-West	3,166	688	21·7	317	10·0	46·0
6 Yorkshire West Riding	2,317	429	18·5	205	8·8	47·8
Megalopolis	20,849	3,718	17·8	1,896	9·1	51·0

Source: Second Land Utilization Survey of Great Britain.

Of the developed urban area within Megalopolis, by far the most important individual component is residential land. It took up about 51 per cent of the total developed area, or about 9 per cent of the entire land area of Megalopolis, in the early 1960s. But the proportion of residential area to total developed area varied quite considerably from one main division of Megalopolis to another, as Table 6.4. shows. In the southern part of Megalopolis, where industrial and other uses are more limited and residential space standards have tended to be more generous, some 50–60 per cent of the total developed area is used for housing; but in the more heavily industrialized areas of the North this proportion falls below 50 per cent, or even, in the West Midlands, as low as 36 per cent. Altogether, though, the most striking fact to emerge from this analysis is perhaps the statistic that of a total area in Megalopolis of some 20,000 square miles, housing and immediately associated land uses occupy less than 2,000 square miles. As Dr Best has emphasized, for the whole of England and Wales differences in the density of development in the future could hardly have any great effect on the overall picture of land use in Megalopolis for a long time to come.

The picture that emerges, then, is one of a very economical use of land; and this is fully confirmed when the land use data are compared with those for population within the major divisions of Megalopolis England. This comparison involves some small degree of inaccuracy, since the land use data are recorded in terms of 100 square kilometre squares while the population data relate to irregularly shaped administrative areas; thus the land use data relate to a total area of 20,758 square miles or 13,343,000 acres, while the total area to which population data relate is only 12,520,000 acres (Table 6.2).[4] The anomaly, which is most serious in the North-West, means that the recorded densities in Table 6.5 are slight underestimates; but in terms of the developed area and the residential area, the degree of distortion is undoubtedly very slight indeed.

Bearing this in mind, the comparison shows that in terms of total population/total area, the population of Megalopolis England lived at a density of round about 1,600 per square mile (2·4 per acre) in the early 1960s; this is almost certainly a slight underestimate. Taking into account just the developed area, this proportion rises to about 8,700 per square mile or 14 per acre. And taking just the residential area, the density rises to about 17,000 per square mile or about 27 to the acre. This last proportion shows quite considerable variation from one part of Megalopolis to another: it was as high as 41 to the acre in the West Midlands and as low as 14 to the acre in the South Coast

[4] There are several reasons for this discrepancy. The definition of Megalopolis in terms of 100 square kilometre units was deliberately inclusive rather than exclusive; it tended to include a square if a part of it fell within Megalopolis. The population figures are aggregates of metropolitan areas; they do not include certain thinly-populated interstitial areas which are not part of any Metropolitan Economic Labour Area. Overall, the difference is composed almost exclusively of rather thinly populated rural areas, so that the figures for developed or residential areas are hardly affected.

Table 6.5

POPULATION DENSITIES IN MEGALOPOLIS ENGLAND, CIRCA 1960–1965

Major division	Population density					
	Persons per total area		Persons per developed area		Persons per residential area	
	Per square mile	Per acre	Per square mile	Per acre	Per square mile	Per acre
1 London and the South-East	1,870	2·9	9,151	14·3	15,936	24·9
2 South Coast	765	1·2	5,608	8·8	9,159	14·3
3 West Midlands	1,462	2·3	9,661	15·1	26,507	41·4
4 East Midlands	953	1·5	8,149	12·7	19,234	30·1
5 North-West	2,040	3·2	9,387	14·6	20,373	31·8
6 Yorkshire West Riding	1,561	2·4	8,429	13·1	17,639	27·6
Megalopolis	1,560	2·4	8,746	13·7	17,151	26·8

Source: Census 1961. Second Land Utilization Survey of Great Britain.

Table 6.6

FREQUENCY DISTRIBUTION OF 100 SQUARE KILOMETRE SQUARES, BY DEGREE OF DEVELOPMENT, IN MEGALOPOLIS ENGLAND, CIRCA 1960–1965

Major division		Number and percentage of 100 square kilometre squares with:					
		0–10	10–20	20–40	40–70	70–100	Total squares
		Per cent of area developed					
1 London and the South East	Number	70	61	43	6	12	192
	per cent	36	32	22	3	6	100
2 South Coast	Number	27	29	10	4	1	71
	per cent	38	41	14	6	1	100
3 West Midlands	Number	36	24	10	4	3	77
	per cent	47	32	13	5	4	100
4 East Midlands	Number	35	13	6	4	—	58
	per cent	60	22	10	7	0	100
5 North-West	Number	23	23	22	12	2	82
	per cent	28	28	27	15	2	100
6 Yorkshire West Riding	Number	21	20	13	5	1	60
	per cent	35	33	15	8	1	100
Megalopolis	Number	212	170	104	35	19	540
	per cent	39	31	19	6	4	100

Source: Second Land Utilization Survey of Great Britain.

area, ranging elsewhere between 25 and 32 to the acre. Of course, these overall proportions include all the land classed as residential by the Second Land Utilization Survey, including older, higher-density residential areas as well as newer, lower-density areas. Because of the systematic overestimates of the urban area in the earlier Local Authority Land Use Survey, it is regrettably not possible to arrive at any reasonably accurate estimate of the residential density at which the additional population was housed between this and the later Second Land Utilization Survey. Nevertheless, it can be concluded that the population of Megalopolis seems to have been remarkably economical in its use of land.

Such overall figures, it may be argued, do not give a complete picture of the impact of urban development in Megalopolis. The impact of urbanization, according to this argument, is not merely a function of the percentage of the land that is developed, but also of the degree of compactness or scatter of that development: the 18 per cent of the land area of Megalopolis, which was recorded as under urban development in the early 1960s, might be highly concentrated in a few areas, or scattered among many. In fact, as the frequency distribution of urban development (Table 6.6) shows, urban development in Megalopolis England is not merely limited; it is quite highly concentrated. Of the 540 squares, each 100 square kilometres in extent, which constitute Megalopolis, no less than 39 per cent had less than 10 per cent developed. Since virtually all the countryside, even in quite thinly populated areas, has some development in the form of isolated farms or small hamlets, such areas can safely be regarded as completely rural. Additionally, another 31 per cent of all squares had between 10 and 20 per cent development; such a pattern could easily arise in a rural area with nucleated settlement in the form of substantial villages, so that these areas could be described as more thickly settled rural. In other words, no less than 70 per cent of the total area of Megalopolis consisted of areas which the observer would think of as rural. A further 19 per cent of squares were lightly influenced by urban development, with between 20 and 40 per cent of their areas covered by developed land uses; 6 per cent were heavily influenced, with between 40 and 70 per cent developed; and a mere 4 per cent were more or less completely urbanized, with 70 per cent or more developed. Figure 6.8 shows, moreover, that these highly developed squares, and even a substantial part of the more lightly developed ones, were concentrated together in certain parts of Megalopolis, particularly in and around the great conurbations. But because all the individual divisions of Megalopolis had one or more considerable urban areas of this kind, a remarkable feature of the analysis in Table 6.6 is that the proportions of urban development did not vary much from one major division to another. As might be expected, the areas where urban development impinged the least were the East and West Midlands and the South Coast, with between 79 and 82 per cent of their constituent squares having less than 20 per cent development; the most heavily influenced was the North-West, with only 56 per cent. The South-East, often quoted as the area most heavily threatened by rapid urban growth, was close to the average for all Megalopolis with 68 per cent of its squares having 20 per cent development or less.

The analysis at this scale does not tell the whole story, of course; for the impact of urban development on a region is critically dependent on the precise degree of grouping or compaction of the developed areas. For this reason, the analysis in a later section of this chapter takes a finer-grained look at local patterns of development within certain heavily urbanized study areas of Megalopolis England. But at this stage, it can be concluded that the greater part of Megalopolis is free of urban development; four-fifths of the whole 20,000 square-mile area, in the early 1960s, were still rural on any reasonable criterion. Megalopolis England is, therefore, a functional rather than a physical reality. Just like the comparable Northeastern Urban Complex of the United States – Gottmann's Megalopolis – it is a giant urban area only in the sense that here is a large tract of the earth's surface where the great majority of people depend on urban jobs and urban services; and where the impact of these jobs and services, in terms of measurements like commuter zones, service areas and the exchange of goods and information, expands to involve each part of the area in a complex series of interactions with other parts. It is not, and does not conceivably seem likely to be, a giant urban area in the sense that the physical growth of its parts will gradually coalesce into continuous sprawl from London to Birmingham to Manchester. That is a nightmare that has no foundation whatsoever in reality.

Thus there will always be room for argument about whether such a thing as a Megalopolis exists in England, and about what the term precisely means. And even if agreement is reached on those related points, there is still room for controversy about the precise definition of the area; it could be argued, in particular, that the area could have been more narrowly defined than it has here, so as to concentrate more closely on the areas of greatest pressure of urban growth. This however would not be a matter of objective fact, so much as of value judgement.

Our argument for retaining the concept, and the title, is that Megalopolis proves to be a convenient unit for isolating the areas of greatest pressure for urban growth in contemporary Britain. It is the zone where functional urban areas, in terms of commuting fields or urban service areas, grow and merge and overlap in increasing ways. It is the area where the physical forces of urban growth, though never actually threatening to cause the coalescence of major urban areas, nevertheless pose greatest problems for physical planners in accommodating the different and strident claims of different land uses, and of different groups of the population for living space. It thus provided a convenient framework of search for the detailed study areas where so much of our work, described in the remaining chapters of this volume and in the next, was focused. And lastly, Megalopolis England as a working unit had one particular advantage; as Table 6.7 amply demonstrates, it is very close in certain important respects to the definition of the Northeastern Urban Complex, which was used by Dr Marion Clawson in his parallel study at Resources for the Future on urban growth processes in the contemporary

Table 6.7

STUDY AREAS COMPARED

	Area (million acres) (1960–61)		Population (millions)					
	England	U.S.A.	England			U.S.A.		
			1971*	1961	1951	1970	1960	1950
The whole country (England and Wales/U.S.A.)	37·3	1,904·0	48·6	46·1	43·8	202·1	180·7	150·7
Megalopolis/Northeastern Urban Complex	12·5	20·2	34·5	32·2	30·5	38·9	34·2	29·3
SMSAs/SMLAs within	7·7	13·8	29·2	28·3	26·9	—	31·7	26·9
Their urbanized areas	3·3	3·5	—	25·7	24·1	—	28·5	24·0

Source: Table 6.2; Marion Clawson, *Suburban Land Conversion in the United States: An Economic and Governmental Process*. Baltimore (1971).

* Provisional figures.

United States.[5] Since both that study, and our own, were intended from the beginning to fit into a subsequent comparative study of urban growth in the two countries since the Second World War,[6] that was a more than incidental advantage.

Megalopolis England, then, is in our view both a meaningful concept and a helpful working framework of analysis. But it is important to keep in mind what it is, and what it is not. As we have already seen in Chapters Two and Three, it was largely the fear of uncontrolled urban growth – fear, in fact, of an incipient physical Megalopolis – that inspired the creation of the highly effective postwar British physical planning machinery; and since the Second World War, that machinery has worked fairly faithfully to operate the policies of containment, which were set out in the 1950 Barlow Report. Thus, if there ever really was a danger of the development of a Megalopolis in this physical sense, the containment policy has certainly averted it: Megalopolis, in the popular sense, has been denied. It is the main object of the book and its companion volume to consider why this was done, how it was done, and what some of the main results have been for the people who were being planned for.

A BRIEF ANATOMY OF MEGALOPOLIS

Not only are the fact of urbanization, and the process of urban growth, highly concentrated within Megalopolis; they are highly concentrated within certain parts of it. To a large degree this must already have been apparent from the long statistical analysis in Chapter Five; for, purporting to be an analysis of metropolitan England and Wales, the study was very much dominated by those SMLAs, sixty-three out of 100, which are located in Megalopolis. So it is unnecessary to repeat that analysis here for Megalopolis alone. But it is necessary to look more closely within Megalopolis, to see the very different forces of urbanization and urban growth which operate in different portions of it.

Table 6.8 shows that of the sixty-three SMLAs in Megalopolis, all are within six of the ten standard regions of England and Wales. Though Megalopolis as defined extends marginally into the South-West, East Anglian and Welsh regions, it includes no SMLAs in those areas or in Wales, and twenty-eight of the sixty-three are in fact in the South-East, six in the West Midlands, five in the East Midlands, sixteen in the North-West, and eight in Yorkshire. In terms of population, the distribution is equally distorted. Nearly half the total population within the SMLAs of Megalopolis, 13,900,000 out of 28,300,000, is found in the South-East; one-seventh, or 3,100,000, in the West Midlands; a little over one-twentieth, 1,700,000, in the East Midlands; about one-fifth, 5,600,000, in the North-West; and just under

[5] Clawson, op. cit.

[6] Marion Clawson and Peter Hall, *Planning and Urban Growth: An Anglo-American Comparison*. Johns Hopkins U.P., Baltimore (1973).

Table 6.8

MEGALOPOLIS SMLAs BY POPULATION SIZE, 1961, AND NEW STANDARD REGION

Population size 1961		New standard region (Population figures in '000s)									
		South-East	South-West	East Anglia	West Midlands	East Midlands	North-West	Yorks. and Humberside	Northern	Wales and Monmouth	Total
9,200·0	No. of SMLAs	5	..	..	3	3	2	2	..	..	15
to	Total SMLA pop.	10,620·7	..	..	3,855·9	1,405·8	3,522·6	2,112·0	..	..	21,517·0
287·0	Mean SMLA pop.	2,124·1	..	..	1,285·3	468·6	1,761·3	1,056·0	..	..	1,434·5
	Per cent national SMLA pop.	29·7	..	..	10·8	3·9	9·9	5·9	..	..	60·2
287·0	No. of SMLAs	6	..	..	0	0	5	2	..	..	13
to	Total SMLA pop.	1,370·9	..	..	0·0	0·0	1,002·9	390·2	..	..	2,764·0
179·0	Mean SMLA pop.	228·5	..	..	0·0	0·0	200·6	195·2	..	..	212·6
	Per cent national SMLA pop.	3·8	..	..	0·0	0·0	2·8	1·1	..	..	7·7
179·0	No. of SMLAs	5	..	..	0	2	3	3	..	..	13
to	Total SMLA pop.	727·7	..	..	0·0	282·1	466·9	472·3	..	..	1,949·0
128·0	Mean SMLA pop.	145·5	..	..	0·0	141·1	1,556·0	157·4	..	..	149·9
	Per cent national SMLA pop.	2·0	..	..	0·0	0·8	1·3	1·3	..	..	5·5
128·0	No. of SMLAs	4	..	..	0	0	3	1	..	..	8
to	Total SMLA pop.	433·9	..	..	0·0	0·0	331·7	113·3	..	..	878·9
100·4	Mean SMLA pop.	108·5	..	..	0·0	0·0	110·6	113·3	..	..	109·9
	Per cent national SMLA pop.	1·2	..	..	0·0	0·0	0·9	0·3	..	..	2·5
100·4	No. of SMLAs	8	..	..	3	0	3	0	..	..	14
to	Total SMLA pop.	728·5	..	..	223·0	0·0	266·6	0·0	..	..	1,218·1
65·0	Mean SMLA pop.	91·1	..	..	74·3	0·0	88·9	0·0	..	..	87·0
	Per cent national SMLA pop.	2·0	..	..	0·6	0·0	0·7	0·0	..	..	3·4
Total	No. of SMLAs	28	..	..	6	5	16	8	..	..	63
	Total SMLA pop.	13,881·7	..	..	4,078·9	1,687·9	5,590·7	3,087·8	..	..	28,327·0
	Mean SMLA pop.	495·8	..	..	679·8	337·6	349·4	386·0	..	..	449·6
	Per cent national SMLA pop.	38·9	..	..	11·4	4·7	15·7	8·6	..	..	79·3

Source: Census.

Table 6.9

MEGALOPOLIS SMLAs BY ABSOLUTE POPULATION CHANGE, 1951–1961, AND NEW STANDARD REGION

Population change 1951–61		South-East	South-West	East Anglia	West Midlands	East Midlands	North-West	Yorks. and Humberside	Northern	Wales and Monmouth	Total
		New standard region (Population figures in '000s)									
205·0	No. of SMLAs	12	..	..	2	1	1	0	..	..	16
to	Total pop. change	522·9	..	..	294·2	41·8	53·2	0·0	..	..	912·1
33·0	Mean change/SMLA	43·6	..	..	147·1	41·8	53·2	0·0	..	..	57·0
	Per cent nat. SMLA growth	27·7	..	..	15·6	2·2	2·8	0·0	..	..	48·3
33·0	No. of SMLAs	9	..	..	1	2	1	3	..	..	16
to	Total pop. change	203·5	..	..	16·7	41·0	29·3	75·1	..	..	365·6
16·6	Mean change/SMLA	22·6	..	..	16·7	20·5	29·3	25·0	..	..	22·9
	Per cent nat. SMLA growth	10·8	..	..	0·9	2·2	1·6	4·0	..	..	19·4
16·6	No. of SMLAs	4	..	..	0	2	1	0	..	..	7
to	Total pop. change	57·0	..	..	0·0	20·5	16·3	0·0	..	..	93·8
8·9	Mean change/SMLA	14·3	..	..	0·0	10·3	16·3	0·0	..	..	13·4
	Per cent nat. SMLA growth	3·0	..	..	0·0	1·1	0·9	0·0	..	..	5·0
8·9	No. of SMLAs	3	..	..	2	0	3	0	..	..	16
to	Total pop. change	24·9	..	..	13·4	0·0	17·8	0·0	..	..	−25·8
3·2	Mean change/SMLA	8·3	..	..	6·7	0·0	5·9	0·0	..	..	−1·6
	Per cent nat. SMLA growth	1·3	..	..	0·7	0·0	0·9.	0·0	..	..	−1·4
3·2	No. of SMLAs	0	..	..	1	0	10	5	..	..	16
to	Total pop. change	0·0	..	..	3·0	0·0	−26·1	−2·7	..	..	−25·8
−11·5	Mean change/SMLA	0·0	..	..	3·0	0·0	2·6	−0·5	..	..	−1·6
	Per cent nat. SMLA growth	0·0	..	..	0·2	0·0	−1·4	−0·1	..	..	−1·4
Total	No. of SMLAs	28	..	..	6	5	16	9	..	..	63
	Total pop. change	808·3	..	..	327·3	103·3	90·5	72·4	..	..	1,401·8
	Mean change/SMLA	28·9	..	..	54·6	20·7	5·7	8·0	..	..	22·3
	Per cent nat. SMLA growth	42·8	..	..	17·3	5·5	4·8	3·8	..	..	74·2

Source: Census.

one-ninth, 3,100,000, in Yorkshire and Humberside. As with the country as a whole, the biggest SMLAs of Megalopolis on average are found in the West Midlands; the South-East is next.

In terms of the existing pressure of population, then, the map of Megalopolis (Figure 6.3) gives the right impression; it is dumb-bell shaped, with heavy southern and northern ends and a thin middle. But when we turn to the dynamics of population change (and of population pressure) within Megalopolis, the weighting is completely different. Tables 6.9 and 6.10 show absolute change for the 1950s and for the early 1960s respectively. Out of a total addition to population in the sixty-three SMLAs of over 1,400,000, well over half (808,300) was in the twenty-eight SMLAs of the South-East; nearly one-quarter (327,300) was in the West Midlands and another 103,300 was in the East Midlands. Thus, nearly 90 per cent of the total growth in the SMLAs of Megalopolis occurred within the southern and midland parts of it together, and the North-West and Yorkshire-Humberside mustered a total growth between them of only 163,000 people. Table 6.9 and Table 6.10 show that the situation hardly changed by the early 1960s. Of the SMLAs within Megalopolis which had the biggest absolute additions to their populations, twelve out of sixteen in the earlier period, and eleven out of seventeen in the latter period, were actually concentrated within the South-East.

In terms of percentage change, the disproportion is even more pronounced (Tables 6.11 and 6.12). Sixteen out of seventeen of the fastest growing metropolitan areas in the 1950s, fifteen out of eighteen in the early 1960s, were in the South-East; of the group with the poorest record, sixteen out of seventeen in the earlier period and ten out of thirteen in the latter period were in the North-West and Yorkshire-Humberside regions.

MEGALOPOLIS: AREAS OF PRESSURE AND AREAS OF STRESS

We have chosen to take Megalopolis England as a broad framework for study because it is that part of England where the fact of urban growth has most impact now, and is likely to have most impact in the immediate future. But we cannot escape the fact that viewed closely, Megalopolis is an amalgam of very different parts, united only in the fact of their urban character. That fact emerged clearly enough from the analysis we have just made, which demonstrates just how much patterns of urban growth were differing from one region in Megalopolis to another. In this last part of the chapter we take this analysis further, and look as closely as we can at what is happening in different parts of our 19,600 square mile area. This is interesting for its own sake, for it tells us as much about local detail as we can handle at this scale of analysis. But we have to do it, too, in order to provide detailed local knowledge, to allow us to make a rational choice of areas for more detailed study.

The first and obvious criterion, in this selection process, is to isolate the areas that have experienced most rapid urban growth, in the physical sense, during the period from the late 1940s to the mid 1960s. Beyond this one necessary principle, we want to find as much variation as possible in the conditions of growth.

Table 6.10

MEGALOPOLIS SMLAs BY ABSOLUTE POPULATION CHANGE, 1961–1966, AND NEW STANDARD REGION

Population change 1961–66		New standard region (Population figures in '000s) South-East	South-West	East Anglia	West Midlands	East Midlands	North-West	Yorks. and Humberside	Northern	Wales and Monmouth	Total
Over 14·4	No. of SMLAs	11	..	..	2	2	1	1	..	..	17
	Total pop. change	270·9	..	..	101·2	67·2	22·9	14·5	..	..	476·7
	Mean change/SMLA	24·6	..	..	50·6	33·6	22·9	14·5	..	..	28·0
	Per cent nat. SMLA growth	42·3	..	..	15·8	10·5	3·6	2·3	..	..	74·5
14·4 to 8·9	No. of SMLAs	10	..	..	0	3	1	0	..	..	14
	Total pop. change	106·6	..	..	0·0	30·7	11·1	0·0	..	..	148·4
	Mean change/SMLA	10·7	..	..	0·0	10·2	11·1	0·0	..	..	10·6
	Per cent nat. SMLA growth	16·7	..	..	0·0	4·8	1·7	0·0	..	..	23·2
8·9 to 5·4	No. of SMLAs	2	..	..	1	0	4	2	..	..	9
	Total pop. change	14·5	..	..	5·9	0·0	26·5	13·3	..	..	60·2
	Mean change/SMLA	7·2	..	..	5·9	0·0	6·6	6·7	..	..	6·7
	Per cent nat. SMLA growth	2·3	..	..	0·9	0·0	4·1	2·1	..	..	9·4
5·4 to 2·0	No. of SMLAs	3	..	..	3	0	3	2	..	..	11
	Total pop. change	13·8	..	..	14·0	0·0	12·1	7·1	..	..	47·0
	Mean change/SMLA	4·6	..	..	4·7	0·0	4·0	3·6	..	..	4·3
	Per cent nat. SMLA growth	2·2	..	..	2·1	0·0	1·9	1·1	..	..	7·3
Under 2·0	No. of SMLAs	2	..	..	0	0	7	3	..	..	12
	Total pop. change	−266·6	..	..	0·0	0·0	−64·5	2·1	..	..	−329·0
	Mean change/SMLA	−133·3	..	..	0·0	0·0	−9·2	0·7	..	..	−27·4
	Per cent nat. SMLA growth	−41·7	..	..	0·0	0·0	−10·1	0·3	..	..	−51·4
Total	No. of SMLAs	28	..	..	6	5	16	8	..	..	63
	Total pop. change	139·2	..	..	121·1	97·9	8·1	37·0	..	..	403·3
	Mean change/SMLA	5·0	..	..	20·2	19·6	0·5	4·6	..	..	6·4
	Per cent nat. SMLA growth	21·8	..	..	18·9	15·3	1·3	5·8	..	..	63·0

Source: Census.

Table 6.11

MEGALOPOLIS SMLAs BY PERCENTAGE POPULATION CHANGE, 1951–1961, AND NEW STANDARD REGION

Per cent Population change 1951–61		New standard region									
		South-East	South-West	East Anglia	West Midlands	East Midlands	North-West	Yorks. and Humberside	Northern	Wales and Monmouth	Total
5·0 to 14·5	No. of SMLAs	16	..	..	1	0	0	0	..	..	17
	Average per cent change/SMLA*	28·38	..	..	16·09	0·00	0·00	0·00	..	..	25·65
14·5 to 9·5	No. of SMLAs	7	..	..	2	0	0	1	..	..	10
	Average per cent change/SMLA*	11·79	..	..	10·92	0·00	0·00	11·21	..	..	11·68
9·5 to 5·3	No. of SMLAs	4	..	..	1	4	1	0	..	..	10
	Average per cent change/SMLA*	8·28	..	..	8·24	7·35	9·55	0·00	..	..	8·06
5·3 to 1·6	No. of SMLAs	0	..	..	2	1	5	1	..	..	9
	Average per cent change/SMLA*	0·00	..	..	3·60	4·36	3·70	3·61	..	..	3·72
1·6 to −10·0	No. of SMLAs	1	..	..	0	0	10	6	..	..	17
	Average per cent change/SMLA*	0·49	..	..	0·00	0·00	−0·01	1·02	..	..	0·44
Total	No. of SMLAs	28	..	..	6	5	16	8	..	..	63
	Average per cent change/SMLA*	6·27	..	..	8·25	6·52	1·63	2·40	..	..	5·23

* Average per cent change/SMLA = $\frac{\text{Total SMLA change 1951–61}}{\text{Total SMLA population 1951}}$.

Source: Census.

Table 6.12

MEGALOPOLIS SMLAs BY PERCENTAGE POPULATION CHANGE, 1961–1966, AND NEW STANDARD REGION

Per cent population change 1961–66		New standard region									
		South-East	South-West	East Anglia	West Midlands	East Midlands	North-West	Yorks. and Humberside	Northern	Wales and Monmouth	Total
Over 8·53	No. of SMLAs	15	..	..	0	2	1	0	..	..	18
	Average per cent change/SMLA*	12·87	..	..	0·00	10·03	12·08	0·00	..	..	12·27
8·53 to 5·23	No. of SMLAs	7	..	..	3	1	2	0	..	..	13
	Average per cent change/SMLA*	7·03	..	..	7·08	6·08	7·26	0·00	..	..	7·01
5·23 to 3·55	No. of SMLAs	3	..	..	1	0	3	1	..	..	8
	Average per cent change/SMLA*	4·13	..	..	4·63	0·00	4·53	3·60	..	..	4·23
3·55 to 1·05	No. of SMLAs	1	..	..	1	2	4	3	..	..	11
	Average per cent change/SMLA*	1·48	..	..	2·12	3·14	2·44	1·57	..	..	2·14
Under +1·05	No. of SMLAs	2	..	..	1	0	6	4	..	..	13
	Average per cent change/SMLA*	−2·86	..	..	0·92	0·00	−1·60	0·61	..	..	−2·06
Total	No. of SMLAs	28	..	..	6	5	16	8	..	..	63
	Average per cent change/SMLA*	1·01	..	..	2·97	5·80	0·14	1·20	..	..	1·42

* Average per cent change/SMLA $= \frac{\text{Total SMLA change 1961–66}}{\text{Total SMLA population 1961}}$.

Source: Census.

One important type of difference is in the *form of physical growth*. There are at least these variations:

i simple peripheral growth in freestanding towns;
ii simple peripheral growth round conurbations;
iii expansion of villages in green belts;
iv expansion of villages and small towns beyond green belts;
v expansion of large towns, beyond the green belts around the largest conurbations, by the normal processes of development control;
vi planned expansions of towns, whether small or large, beyond the green belts, through the Town Development Act;
vii new towns.

Associated with this is a difference in the *character of the agency* that initiates the development process. We can isolate these agents:

i local authorities building within their own boundaries in freestanding towns or conurbations;
ii private builders, and housing associations;
iii new town corporations;
iv local authorities building outside their borders, through overspill agreements under the Town Development Act.

In principle, we are interested in the fact of urban growth, whoever initiates it. The process of decision making that leads to the fact of development is interesting to us, whoever are the agents of development. Nevertheless, there will be a certain inevitable bias, in most of the study, towards the study of development in the private sector.[7] This is because such development is less well documented, and more complex as a decision process, than development in the public sector; we want to see how the private builders, and their potential buyers, and the planners, have reacted together. Thus, while some of our studies of the planners' decision processes in the selected study areas will relate to the public sector, logically our studies of private individuals' residential choices will be located wholly within the private owner-occupier sector. This bias will react backwards upon the sorts of area we choose for study; they will have to be areas associated with extensive house building in the private sector.

Also very important are the *functional relationships*, within which physical development occurs. We need to know how the fact of development in one place, rather than in another place, will affect the patterns of people's everyday lives, and in particular their patterns of everyday movement. It would be possible to list all sorts of relationships, some more or less obscure, some more or less ill documented. But one type of movement in particular, is neither obscure nor ill documented; it is the daily movement to work. This is the

[7] Later in the book (Chap. 10, Vol. II) we examine specifically the contribution of the new towns and of town development to the urban growth process. For the sake of comprehensive treatment, this account is not limited to Megalopolis.

movement we have used to define our basic pattern of SMLAs and MELAs; and it means we shall have to look at the way physical urbanization relates to the boundaries of these metropolitan areas. On that basis, we can define these possibilities:

i development in the cores of Standard Metropolitan Areas, close to the greatest concentrations of workplaces; resulting in short journeys and perhaps outward as well as inward commuting;

ii development in the rings of Standard Metropolitan Labour Areas; leading to considerable commuting into the cores;

iii development in the outer fringes of Metropolitan Economic Labour Areas. By definition this is associated with a small minority of workers commuting into the cores of the SMLAs, and with a great deal of fragmented commuting into small local concentrations of employment. In some of these areas, there may be very complex patterns of movement, with some workers travelling considerable distances to a number of different labour centres.

We shall want to get a good balance between these different types of situation, though it may not always be possible. Thus, it is a truism that the cores of metropolitan areas are now in general fully developed, so that new urbanization in them is a very infrequent phenomenon. And there are quite considerable areas of Megalopolis, Lancashire and the West Riding for instance, where little growth is happening in the rings either, so that it is difficult to get any sample of development of any sort.

With this in mind, we can focus on the main elements of Megalopolis. For this purpose, we want a finer and a less arbitrary grouping than that provided by the new standard (or economic planning) regions used earlier,[8] for it is evident that any planning region is far from homogeneous. It may contain elements of growth and elements of decline, different economic bases, and entirely different patterns of urban settlement, which need separate analysis. The only way to produce a better framework for analysis is to look at the evidence and make one's own (Table 6.13).

LONDON AND ITS PERIPHERAL SMLAS

If we do this, the first outstanding element in the geography of Megalopolis undoubtedly consists of the London SMLA and the ring of small SMLAs around it (Table 6.14). Here immediately is a striking contrast. The London SMLA is immeasurably the largest in the country, though it is not nearly as big as the 'Metropolitan Area' which has often been distinguished in official planning studies; indeed, with a 1961 population of 9,157,000 it is only a million or so bigger than the conurbation. It happened to have one of the lowest

[8] With small anomalies in detail, the new standard regions are the same as the economic planning regions.

Table 6.13

POPULATION GROWTH FOR VARIOUS GROUPS OF SMLAs IN MEGALOPOLIS, 1951–1961 AND 1961–1966
(Figures to nearest thousand)

SMLA grouping	Population 1961	Net change 1951–61	Net change 1961–66	Per cent of all Megalopolis growth 1951–61	Per cent of all Megalopolis growth 1961–66
Megalopolis SMLAs	28,327,000	1,402,000	403,000	100·0	100·0
1 London and ring of SMLAs	11,993,000	618,000	33,000	44·0	8·2
2 South Coast	1,676,000	168,000	84,000	11·9	20·9
3 West Midlands	3,561,000	311,000	116,000	22·2	28·8
4 East Midlands	1,688,000	103,000	96,000	7·4	23·8
5 Manchester and textile towns	3,290,000	14,000	−2,000	1·0	−0·5
6 Liverpool and region	2,032,000	56,000	4,000	3·9	1·1
7 Yorkshire woollen towns	1,777,000	19,000	22,000	1·4	5·5
8 South Yorkshire	1,311,000	53,000	15,000	3·8	4·7

Note: Not all SMLAs in Megalopolis are included in the above groupings: there are several free-standing SMLAs, such as Blackpool and Colchester.
Source: Census.

rates of growth of any metropolitan area during the 1960s, with a percentage increase of only 0·49; a fact which may prove surprising to those impressed by propaganda about London's continued growth. The fact is that by the 1950s, and to some extent before, London's growth had been transmuted into something else: the growth of the whole South-East complex. Surrounding the London metropolitan area is a series of no less than nineteen separate small metropolitan areas, part of a Megalopolis, all of which have their centres between fifteen and forty miles from central London. The biggest of these, Luton, had in 1961 a population of 267,000; the smallest, Woking, numbered only 84,000. They numbered some of the fastest-growing metropolitan areas in the country in the 1950s and 1960s, in terms of both popula-population and employment. Some of them, such as Stevenage and Hemel Hempstead, are based on new towns, whose rapid growth is predictable, but most are centred on very old-established towns, which have been caught up in the general export of population and employment from London. As a group London and its ring accounted for no less than 44 per cent of the total growth of the SMLAs of Megalopolis during the 1950s; 618,000. London SMLA contributed only 44,000, or about 7 per cent. From 1961–66 the group gained only 33,000; London lost.

This phenomenon needs some stressing. Since the SMLAs are defined in terms of commuting fields, this means that the population growth in the south-

Table 6.14

LONDON AND ITS RING OF SMLAs: POPULATION CHANGE AND EMPLOYMENT CHANGE, 1951–1961, AND 1961–1966

SMLA	Population change					Employment change				
	Population 1961	Net change 1951–61	Per cent change 1951–61	Net change 1961–66	Per cent change 1961–66	Employment 1961	Net change 1951–61	Per cent change 1951–61	Net change 1961–66	Per cent change 1961–66
1 London	9,156,683	44,294	0·49	–265,963	–2·90	4,713,660	160,199	3·52	46,940	0·99
2 Luton	266,826	58,286	27·95	32,434	12·16	125,090	31,751	34·02	13,480	10·77
3 Southend	246,838	46,153	22·99	24,382	9·88	72,940	14,760	25·37	12,030	16·49
4 Reading	241,705	35,893	17·44	37,355	15·45	107,050	18,322	20·65	14,480	13·52
5 Slough	231,493	54,269	30·62	14,307	6·18	106,670	23,180	27·76	17,700	16·59
6 Chatham	200,597	20,719	11·52	20,273	10·11	81,740	4,593	5·95	5,810	7·10
7 High Wycombe	183,548	36,207	24·57	31,793	17·32	73,930	15,029	25·52	9,890	13·37
8 Watford	169,336	28,951	20·62	–606	–0·36	68,880	11,623	20·30	7,010	10·17
9 Guildford	159,168	20,089	14·44	9,812	6·16	60,030	5,059	9·20	6,560	10·92
10 Maidstone	137,834	12,821	10·28	19,886	14·43	64,180	7,833	13·90	8,310	12·94
11 Aldershot	131,515	13,816	11·74	19,825	15·07	62,810	–581	–0·92	9,360	14·90
12 Thurrock	129,868	36,502	39·10	10,152	7·82	54,230	11,437	26·73	9,930	18·31
13 Stevenage	105,678	43,557	70·12	9,532	9·02	39,280	18,862	92·38	10,670	27·61
14 Chelmsford	98,012	20,860	27·04	15,328	15·64	46,410	9,295	25·04	5,460	11·76
15 Tunbridge Wells	96,560	7,798	8·79	10,180	10·54	38,610	3,239	9·16	4,030	10·43
16 St Albans	89,240	16,534	22·74	3,460	3·88	32,880	5,499	20·08	2,200	6·69
17 Basildon	88,524	45,144	104·07	21,516	24·31	25,150	16,730	198·69	19,310	76·77
18 Hemel Hempstead	87,995	36,566	71·10	11,345	12·89	34,770	14,518	71·69	7,090	20·39
19 Walton and Weybridge	85,900	16,936	24·56	5,380	6·26	39,570	10,780	37·44	2,640	6·67
20 Woking	83,699	21,994	35·64	5,601	6·69	28,840	5,804	25·20	4,070	14·11

Source: Census.

east corner of Megalopolis, by far the fastest growing part of Megalopolis, has been diverted almost entirely out of London and into areas where the characteristic feature is short-distance commuting into a large number of rather small employment centres. A few of these are new towns; the great majority are old market towns, in some cases county towns, located at distances between twenty and forty miles from central London. It is true that long-distance commuting, back into the core of the London SMLA, can still occur in these areas; but by definition, it does not affect more than a small minority of the resident workforce. Actually, as later detailed studies will show, a remarkable feature about this whole ring round London is the fact that in general the boundaries of the SMLAs do not show much overlap, either with each other or with the outer boundary of the London SMLA; in other words, as defined by the SMLA standard of 15 per cent of workers commuting into a centre, clear cut patterns of movement emerge.

Table 6.15

LONDON AND ITS RING OF SMLAs: RELATIVE DECENTRALIZATION OF POPULATION AND EMPLOYMENT, 1931–1966

SMLA	Per cent shift in core share of population			Per cent shift in employment	
	1931–51	1951–61	1961–66	1951–61	1961–66
London	−6·26	−3·38	−3·18	−2·21	−5·48
Luton	1·74	2·10	−10·24	−0·07	−4·00
Southend	−2·18	−8·76	−10·80	−4·60	−7·62
Reading	−2·50	−5·87	−8·68	−3·58	3·20
Slough	4·57	−2·61	−2·90	1·60	−3·26
Chatham	0·18	0·20	−2·26	7·36	−5·36
High Wycombe	−0·12	−0·39	−4·38	1·78	−1·44
Watford	−7·15	−7·44	0·74	−0·09	8·10
Guildford	0·44	−0·64	−2·76	3·13	−0·14
Maidstone	−0·03	2·15	−8·76	0·40	−3·92
Aldershot	−0·35	−6·68	−7·76	−9·26	−6·60
Thurrock	−3·33	0·04	−5·70	−1·21	−1·56
Stevenage	−0·54	29·09	16·32	38·05	3·24
Chelmsford	−0·28	1·81	−6·76	1·54	−7·38
Tunbridge Wells	−1·32	−1·97	−6·22	3·34	−4·16
St Albans	−2·69	−4·29	−3·48	−1·75	8·38
Basildon	—	—	—	—	—
Hemel Hempstead	1·11	17·24	3·42	16·10	4·18
Walton and Weybridge	−2·46	0·72	4·98	6·57	−3·72
Woking	−1·67	7·54	−0·72	2·31	1·18

Note: Shifts for 1931–51 and 1961–66 are given as decennial rates: actual shifts are obtained by doubling and halving respectively the figures above.

Source: Census.

In terms of the internal pattern of change within each metropolitan area, the pattern around London is very confused. Some areas, in particular those based on new towns, show a very violent and untypical centralization in population trends in the 1950s; Stevenage and Hemel Hempstead are the classic cases. Some of the bigger, older-established towns on the other hand showed rapid decentralization; Southend, Reading, Watford, and Aldershot for instance. Almost certainly, this means that the core cities have become physically saturated. Significantly, in most of these cases the tendency to decentralization has accelerated strongly in the 1951–66 period, as compared with 1931–51 (Table 6.15).

In most cases, the tendency was towards modest decentralization of people, And in nearly every case, people were decentralizing their homes out of the cores faster than employers were decentralizing jobs. This was the situation not only in London itself, but in the major peripheral SMLAs like Luton, Reading, Watford, and Southend. In some cases indeed, population showed modest decentralization while employment showed relative concentration: Slough, Wycombe, Guildford and above all Maidstone came into this category in the 1950s. This was bound to mean some increase in the average length of the commuter journey. But since the average SMLA in the outer part of the London region was relatively small, this was perhaps of little real consequence.

The peripheral SMLAs form a sort of loose ring around London, except on the south side where they have failed to develop, and where as a result the outer boundary of the London SMLA expands farthest to fill the vacuum. But viewed more closely, they tend to cluster in three rather well defined groups, plus a minor group. These groups occur west, north and east of London, and they are clearly related to the pattern of main routes out of the metropolis, which tend to bunch rather closely together in these areas, giving excellent communications either into London or outwards into other parts of England. The group *west* of London contains seven contiguous SMLAs (Wycombe, Slough, Reading, Aldershot, Guildford, Woking, and Walton) astride the four main radial highways formed by the A40 (in course of being superseded by the M40), A4-M4, A30 (superseded by the M3 during 1971) and A3. It is also served by three main rail routes: Paddington-Birmingham, London-Bristol and London-Southampton (or Portsmouth). Including as it does the Chiltern Hills, Thames Valley and the heathlands around Bagshot and Camberley, it was attracting the more prosperous commuters as early as the 1920s, and in the 1930s, much of this area was attracting sporadic pepperpot development. The area has been subject to extremely strong planning controls in the postwar period, including the metropolitan green belt and its extensions, local green belts like the Reading Blue Line, and control in places like the Chilterns, which have been designated an area of outstanding natural beauty. Nevertheless this area had the greatest population growth in aggregate, during the postwar period, of any part of the ring round London. These seven metropolitan areas added no less than 199,200 people during the inter-Censal period 1951–61; an increase of 21·7 per cent.

Not far behind, in terms of total growth, is the wider sector *north* and *north-west of London*, which is contiguous with the western sector at its inner end, around Rickmansworth and Denham. It includes three SMLAs based on important old market towns, now become industrial centres: Watford, St. Albans, and Luton. Already growing rapidly in the 1930s due to the development of the engineering and motor trades, these towns have continued to attract a large share of the total growth of this zone in the 1950s, though some of those nearest London showed a marked slowing down of growth after 1961. But in addition, this is the zone of greatest concentration for new towns. It contains no fewer than four, all in Hertfordshire: Hemel Hempstead, Hatfield, Welwyn, and Stevenage. The first and last of these were important enough by 1961 to constitute the cores of separate Standard Metropolitan Labour Areas. In turn the three older centres all also formed the basis of SMLAs. Together these five experienced a total growth during the period 1951–61 of 184,000 people, a growth rate of 34·4 per cent.

To the *east* of London, along the north bank of the Thames and extending away from the river as far as Chelmsford, is a third zone of SMLAs which experienced very rapid growth during the 1950s and early 1960s. These SMLAs, however, are of very varied character. Thurrock is the centre of the new, downstream development of the Port of London, twenty-five miles below Tower Bridge. Basildon is basically the new town, biggest in population of all the London new towns by 1961; it is significant that this is one of the very rare SMLAs in all England to have no metropolitan ring. Southend was formerly a dormitory, seaside and local shopping centre which has received a great variety of light industry (especially electronics) and decentralized London office work in the postwar period. Further inland, Chelmsford is an old market town on the main A12 and London-Ipswich rail line, electrified as far as Colchester since 1947; it also has attracted a great expansion of light industry during the 1950s and 1960s. Together, these four SMLAs experienced a population growth of 149,000, or 36 per cent, between 1951 and 1961.

In addition to these three great zones of growth, there was more modest growth in the south-east sector around London, where three SMLAs (Chatham-Rochester, Maidstone, and Tunbridge Wells) together accounted for a 42,000 growth of population (10·7 per cent) during the 1950s. But it is clear that for a study of the patterns of metropolitan growth, the choice must be made among the three major growth sectors. Our choice was determined by the fact that we wished to concentrate, in our study of the private residential decision-making process, on the private sector of development. This made it seem more relevant to look at the pattern of growth west of London, where the pressures for private development for owner-occupiership were probably the most intense in all England, than north of London in Hertfordshire, where the picture was dominated to a far greater degree by the growth of the new towns. Our search therefore was concentrated upon the seven Standard Metropolitan Labour Areas in the sector between High Wycombe and Guildford. To round off this area of search, we added a London MELA

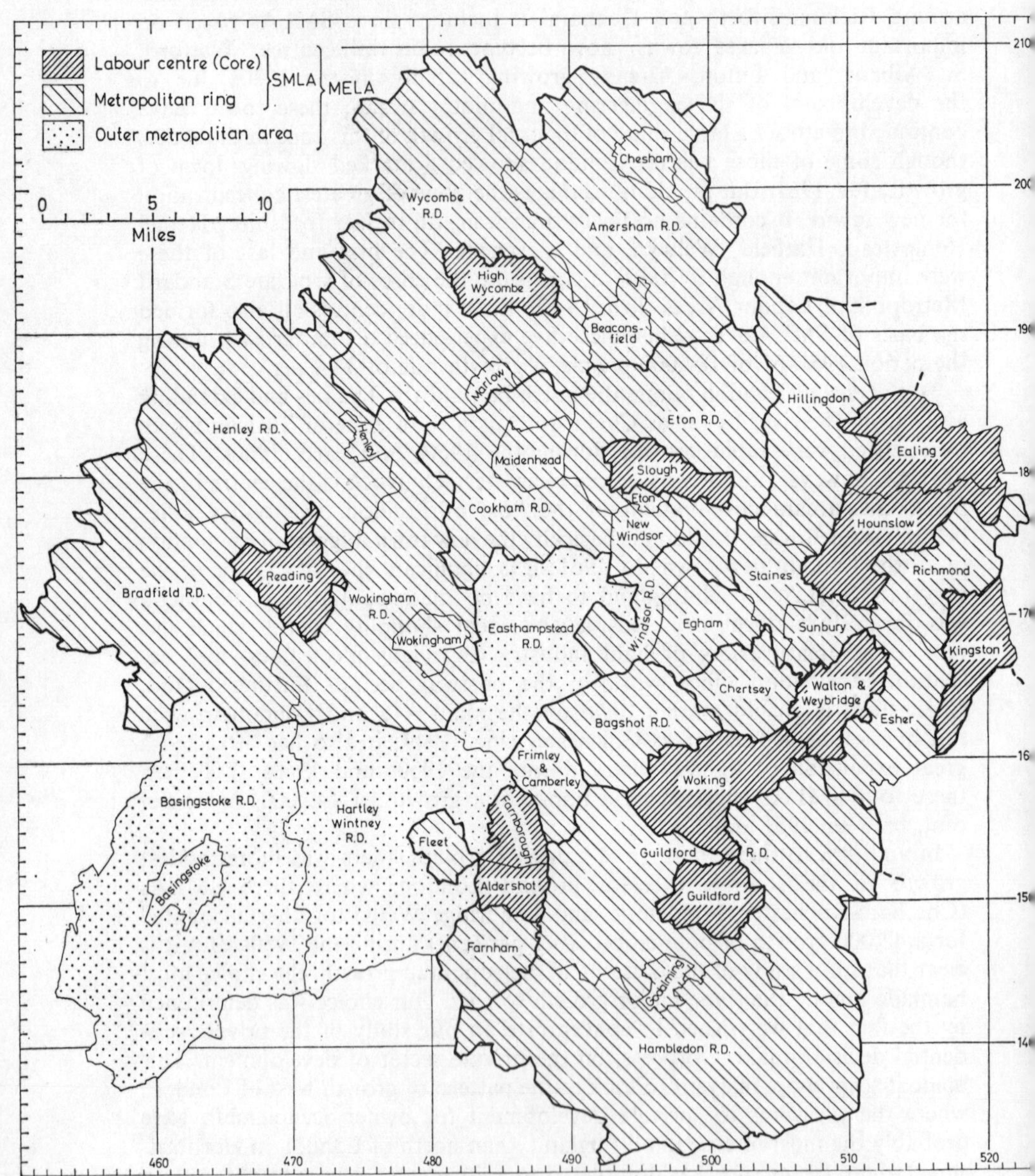

Figure 6.10 London West Metropolitan Sector: Constituent Areas

zone not in any peripheral SMLA as defined in 1961, but likely to qualify for SMLA status during the 1960s by reason of its rapid expansion: the area round Basingstoke, which is being expanded from a population of about 26,000 to 80,000 between 1961 and 1981 under a Town Development Act agreement between London, Hampshire and the town itself. The area thus chosen for study is shown in Figure 6.10 as defined in terms of the SMLA-MELA units we have used in this and in previous chapters.

Because this area forms the subject of a detailed historical study in Chapter Eight it is worthwhile to develop our analysis of postwar population and employment changes in greater local detail. Within the area, the most striking demographic change over the period is the persistent loss of population from the whole London core (Tables 6.16(a) and 6.16(b)). The whole core declined by 280,583 between 1951 and 1961, and by 305,344 in the five years 1961–66. This latter figure may slightly exaggerate the loss, as underenumeration of about 1·7 per cent in the 1966 Sample Census is suspected for central cities, especially large ones. If the London core figures are adjusted for this possible error, the loss still remains at 300,153. In other words, the London core has lost *at least* 580,736 people during the past fifteen years. The three London boroughs included in the study area, out of the total of thirty-two London boroughs, reflect this overall trend, losing 33,070 during the same period.

This apparent decentralization of population from the core has mainly been directed into three types of areas: the London ring, the peripheral SMLA cores, and the peripheral SMLA rings. Growth in these latter three areas has also been reinforced by inter-regional migration. The London ring has continued to absorb population throughout the period; the whole ring increased by 324,877 during 1951–61 but this declined to an increase of only 39,381 during 1961–66. This balance between London's core and ring resulted in the whole London SMLA having a population increase of 44,294 during 1951–61, but since 1961 the whole metropolitan area population has declined substantially overall by 265,963. In the latter period the London ring has therefore failed to compensate for the declining core and the London SMLA is now losing population in absolute terms for the first time. The London core (part) and ring (part) of the West London Metropolitan Sector reflect these overall trends. The core declined by 11,821 during 1951–61 and by a further 21,259 in 1961–66. The ring meanwhile compensated for these losses during 1951–61 with a population increase of 49,723; but it failed to offset the core losses during 1961–66 with an increase of only 5,007.

In contrast, the whole London core increased in employment during 1951–61 by 20,395 jobs while the ring gained 139,804 jobs. But by 1961–66 the changing distribution of employment was strikingly similar to that of population change in the 1950s: a declining core and growing ring. The London core lost 94,680 jobs during the five years while the ring gained 141,620 (equivalent to double the rate of increase achieved in the previous decennium). Considered as a whole, the London SMLA gained 160,199 jobs during 1951–66 but only 46,940 during 1961–66. The relative decentralization of employment from the core to the ring which characterized the 1950s has become an absolute decentralization in the 1960s with the London ring just able to compensate for core losses, as it did for population in the 1951–61 period. If this trend in employment change follows that of population one can predict an absolute decline in the London SMLA employment during the 1966–71 period and beyond.

The pattern of employment change in the West London Metropolitan Sector is similar. The core (part) increased during 1951–61 by over 34,775 jobs (actually more than the whole core) and the ring (part) by over 25,000. However, the 1961–66 period followed the trend of the whole core with a decline in employment by 1,250 while the ring increased by 28,550 (more than double the rate of the previous ten years).

This feature of decentralization into peripheral satellite cities is peculiar to the London metropolitan area. Other major centres of population in this country seem to decentralize into the immediate peripheral ring. The stage of metropolitan evolution in the London case would appear to have reached a threshold where peripheral cities and towns act as true satellites or sub-dominants in an interdependent metropolitan space-economy.

The changes in population and employment in the peripheral cores and rings are all positive; the rings have absorbed more population during both time periods and during 1961–66 the rings received a larger share of the growth (80·9 per cent) as against 69·2 per cent for 1951–61. Trends in employment location are similar although less pronounced. Employment continues to increase in both the cores and the rings but whereas the cores received 2,893 more jobs than the ring during 1951–61 the position was reversed after 1961 with the rings increasing by 2,820 more jobs than the cores.

Absolute decentralization of population and employment has therefore been reached in these satellite metropolitan communities after 1961. However, unlike their London counterpart the satellite cores were still attracting population and jobs. The outer MELAs have increased in population and employment during both time periods and at a more rapid rate during the past five years. There was an increase of 33,000 people and 9,697 jobs during 1951–61; and a 23,628 increase in population and 11,690 in jobs during 1961–66. The growth rates of these fringe areas, where less than 15 per cent of the local labour force commute to a SMLA core, is one of the most significant trends of the post-1961 period.

Having considered in detail the growth and change in each area we can now examine the relative performance of these areas as a part of the whole West London Metropolitan Sector. The measure used is the percentage share of sector growth in population and in employment (Tables 6.16(a) and 6.16(b)).

The London core (part) received a declining share of population growth during the two time periods while the ring also declined in share from 18·4 per cent to 3·8 per cent. The peripheral cores and rings received the bulk of the area growth during both periods, the shares being 73·7 per cent and 94·4 per cent respectively. The peripheral cores declined slightly after 1961 as land within the cores became scarce, while the suburbanization of peripheral rings accelerated considerably. This transfer of population out of the London

Table 6.16(a)

POPULATION AND EMPLOYMENT CHANGE: WEST LONDON METROPOLITAN SECTOR, 1951–1961

	Population				Employment			
	Population 1961	Net change 1951–61	Per cent change 1951–61	Per cent sector growth 1951–61	Employment 1961	Net change 1951–61	Per cent change 1951–61	Per cent sector growth 1951–61
1 London core (part)	656,549	−11,821	−1·77	−4·38	340,570	34,775	11·41	23·59
2 Urbanized London ring (part)	605,739	47,122	8·44	17·44	234,690	25,574	12·23	17·35
3 Non-urbanized London ring (part)	5,344	2,601	94·82	0·96				
4 Peripheral SMLA cores	480,840	61,345	14·62	22·71	261,410	40,143	18·14	27·23
5 Urbanized SMLA rings	415,071	126,896	44·04	46·97	217,490	37,250	17·75	25·26
6 Non-urbanized SMLA rings	221,117	10,963	5·22	4·06				
7 Urbanized MELAs (part)	62,116	27,512	79·20	10·18	45,000	9,697	27·47	6·58
8 Non-urbanized MELAs (part)	50,536	5,530	12·34	2·05				
Total	2,497,312	270,148	12·13	100·00	1,099,160	147,439	15·49	100·00
London core	5,636,674	−280,583	−4·74	—	3,559,330	20,395	0·58	—
London ring	3,520,009	324,877	10·17	—	1,154,330	139,804	13·78	—
London SMLA total	9,156,683	44,294	0·49	—	4,713,660	160,199	3·52	—

Source: Census.

Table 6.16(b)

POPULATION AND EMPLOYMENT CHANGE: WEST LONDON METROPOLITAN SECTOR, 1961–1966

	Population				Employment			
	Population 1966	Net change 1961–66	Per cent change 1961–66	Per cent sector growth 1961–66	Employment 1966	Net change 1961–66	Per cent change 1961–66	Per cent sector growth 1961–66
1 London core (part)	635,290	–21,259	–3·24	–16·17	339,320	–1,250	–0·37	–1·21
2 London ring (part)	616,050	5,007	0·82	3·81	263,240	28,550	12·17	27·53
3 Peripheral SMLA cores	504,580	23,740	4·97	18·06	292,350	30,940	11·84	29·84
4 Peripheral SMLA rings	736,520	100,332	15·77	76·33	251,250	33,760	15·23	32·56
5 MELAs (part)	136,280	23,628	20·97	17·98	56,690	11,690	25·98	11·27
Total	2,628,720	131,448	4·18	100·00	1,202,850	103,690	9·43	100·00
London core	5,331,330	–305,344	–5·42	—	3,464,650	–94,680	–2·66	—
London ring	3,559,390	39,381	1·11	—	1,295,950	141,620	12·27	—
London SMLA total	8,890,720	–265,963	–2·91	—	4,760,600	46,940	0·99	—

Source: Census.

core and ring to centres beyond the green belt suggests that development control policies in the London ring really began to take effect after 1961.

The outward wave of employment decentralization is less pronounced, although the trends are similar. During 1951–61 employment growth in all sectors, except the outer MELAs, was fairly constant, being between 17·4 per cent and 27·2 per cent. However, after 1961 the London core started to export jobs and the main growth in employment occurred in the London ring and in the peripheral SMLA cores and rings. In contrast to population, the London ring remained a major reception area for new jobs. The 28,000 new jobs in the ring were equivalent to more than double the rate of the previous ten years. Thus the wave of employment decentralization has lagged behind population but it has clearly gathered momentum, particularly since 1961.

The relationship between population and employment growth by sectors is listed in Table 6.17. Here population-employment index is derived by dividing the population change by employment change. This gives an indication of whether the two distributions are in or out of phase. Assuming that a population to employment ratio of roughly 2·5:1 is balanced it would appear that the peripheral rings and the MELAs are in phase or lacking in new jobs. Elsewhere the jobs are increasing faster than the equivalent population change can support; this is particularly the case in the London core at both periods, and the London ring and peripheral cores after 1961. In other words, there is insufficient population growth in these latter three areas to match the increase in the number of jobs. This clearly implies a wider separation of some places of work and places of residence. If the peripheral cores and rings are considered together as one functional daily urban system it appears that during both the 1951–61 and 1961–66 periods the ratio of population to employment growth was roughly balanced, being 2·6 and 2·0 respectively. The main imbalance occurred in the London core and ring.

One further characteristic of the changing distribution of population is the concentration of growth into *urbanized areas.* These areas are defined as parishes and wards with a population density of over 1,000 persons per square mile (1·56 persons per acre). Data on this trend are only available for 1951–61 (Table 6.16a). During that time span some 95 per cent of the population growth in the London ring took place in urbanized areas; in the peripheral SMLA rings the proportion was over 92 per cent and in the outer MELAs it reached 84 per cent.

THE SOUTH COAST

The second well differentiated group of SMLAs which contributed substantially to urban growth in Megalopolis in the postwar period, is strung out in a loose chain along the south coast of England, over a distance of some eighty miles from west of Bournemouth to east of Eastbourne. In the west, the three of these which occur in the county of Hampshire (the westernmost of which, Bournemouth-Poole, extends into Dorset) are relatively large in area, and two of them (Southampton and Portsmouth)

Table 6.17

RATIO OF POPULATION CHANGE TO EMPLOYMENT CHANGE, WEST LONDON METROPOLITAN SECTOR, 1951–1961, AND 1961–1966

	1951–61			1961–66		
	Population change	Employment change	Population employment ratio	Population change	Employment change	Population employment ratio
London core (part)	−11,821	34,775	−0·34	−21,259	−1,250	17·01
London ring (part)	47,700	25,574	1·94	5,007	28,550	0·18
Peripheral cores	61,345	40,143	1·53	23,740	30,940	0·76
Peripheral rings	137,000	37,250	3·68	100,332	33,760	2·97
MELAs (part)	33,000	9,697	3·40	23,628	11,690	2·02

Source: Census.

Table 6.18

THE SOUTH COAST: POPULATION CHANGE AND EMPLOYMENT CHANGE, 1951–1961, AND 1961–1966

	Population change					Employment change				
SMLA	Population 1961	Net change 1951–61	Per cent change 1951–61	Net change 1961–66	Per cent change 1961–66	Employment 1961	Net change 1951–61	Per cent change 1951–61	Net change 1961–66	Per cent change 1961–66
Portsmouth	410,394	40,634	10·99	17,106	4·17	169,770	16,530	10·79	20,010	11·78
Southampton	401,832	45,307	12·71	31,008	7·72	177,580	23,457	15·22	20,840	11·73
Brighton	337,806	23,818	7·59	4,994	1·48	133,800	17,284	14·83	10,370	7·75
Bournemouth	305,022	30,763	11·22	12,698	4·16	116,420	14,145	13·83	12,050	10·35
Worthing	118,665	19,320	19·45	8,885	7·49	36,880	5,033	15·80	3,430	9·30
Eastbourne	103,338	8,459	8·92	9,752	9·44	39,050	3,278	9·16	2,890	7·40

Source: Census.

are contiguous with each other; this is largely a result of the very large rural districts which form their rings. In contrast the three SMLAs along the Sussex coast (Worthing, Brighton, and Eastbourne) are rather tightly bounded by the facts of relief and administrative geography; they are contiguous with each other along the coast, but are quite distinctly separated from the three SMLAs of the Solent-Hampshire coast region.

This group of only six SMLAs made a substantial contribution to the total growth of Megalopolis during the 1950s, with a population increase of 168,300 (12 per cent of the total for the Megalopolis SMLAs) and an employment increase of 79,727 (12 per cent of the total Megalopolis SMLA increase). During the 1960s the pattern continued, with a total growth of 84,000 people in only five years, 20 per cent of the total for the SMLAs of Megalopolis. There are two good reasons for this very special rapid increase: one is the growth of employment opportunities in a wide range of electrical, electronic and general engineering industries in the Solent (Southampton-Portsmouth) urban region, which is now the second major zone of population and industrial concentration in south-east England, the other is the continued migration of retired people to the South Coast resorts. The one primarily affects Southampton and Portsmouth SMLAs, the other the other four SMLAs. From the statistics, there seems no doubt that the first of these is the dominant trend. During the 1950s, out of the net growth of population along the South Coast SMLAs of 168,300, Portsmouth contributed 40,600 and Southampton 45,300. During the 1960s the trend continued: out of an 84,400 total growth

Table 6.19

THE SOUTH COAST: RELATIVE DECENTRALIZATION OF POPULATION AND EMPLOYMENT, 1931–1966

SMLA	Per cent shift in core share of population			Per cent shift in employment	
	1931–51	1951–61	1961–66	1951–61	1961–66
Portsmouth	−6·08	−10·75	−10·60	−2·62	−13·54
Southampton	−2·35	−2·27	−4·78	+3·54	−4·50
Bournemouth	−1·56	+1·69	−12·90	−2·48	−5·62
Brighton	−0·79	−2·30	−3·26	−1·69	−1·11
Worthing	−3·49	−2·27	−3·68	−1·87	+1·74
Eastbourne	−2·87	−1·99	−2·84	+2·87	−3·28

Note: Shifts for 1931–51 and 1961–66 are decennial rates. Actual shifts are obtained by doubling and halving respectively the figures above.

Source: Census.

over the five-year period 1961–66, Portsmouth contributed 17,100, Southampton 31,000. The dominance of these two areas in employment growth was of course even more striking (Tables 6.18 and 6.19). Therefore, we were left in little doubt that the Southampton-Portsmouth zone should be our second area of detailed study (Figure 6.11).

A distinct contrast existed in the pattern of the population changes for the two metropolitan areas of Southampton and Portsmouth (Tables 6.20(a) and 6.20(b)). While the Southampton core continued to absorb population over the whole period, with a slower rate during 1961–66 (reflecting slower national growth rates), the Portsmouth core, constricted by its island location, declined by 18,468 between 1951–66. It fared even worse after 1961, losing

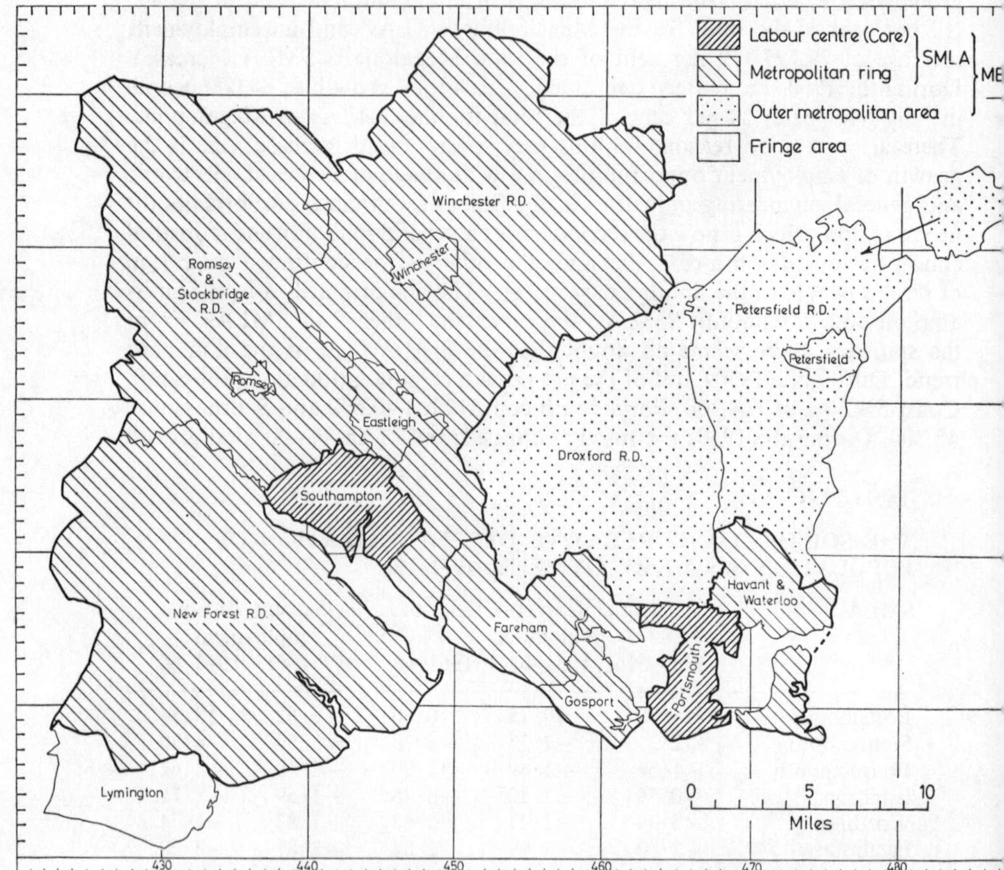

Figure 6.11 South Hampshire: Constituent Areas

13,677 people in only five years. These trends in the core are offset by the population changes in the rings. Although the Portsmouth ring is considerably smaller than the Southampton ring (38,208 acres compared with 298,532 acres), the growth of population in the former has been greater. The decentralization of population into the Portsmouth ring was virtually the same for both the 1951–61 period and 1961–61 (using decennial equivalents). In

Table 6.20(a)

POPULATION AND EMPLOYMENT CHANGE, SOUTHAMPTON-PORTSMOUTH SMLAs, 1951–1961

Area	Population				Employment			
	Population 1961	Net change 1951–61	Per cent change 1951–61	Per cent sector growth 1951–61	Employment 1961	Net change 1951–61	Per cent change 1951–61	Per cent sector growth 1951–61
Southampton core	204,822	15,001	7·90	16·46	99,860	18,649	22·96	48·81
Southampton ring	197,010	30,306	18·18	33·26	77,720	4,808	6·59	12·58
Portsmouth core	215,077	−18,468	−7·91	−20·27	113,880	7,071	6·62	18·51
Portsmouth ring	195,317	59,102	43·39	64·86	55,890	9,459	20·37	24·76
MELAs	52,066	5,185	11·06	5·69	16,740	−1,779	−10·63	−4·66
Total	864,292	91,126	11·79	100·00	364,090	38,208	11·72	100·00

Source: Census.

Table 6.20(b)

POPULATION AND EMPLOYMENT CHANGE, SOUTHAMPTON-PORTSMOUTH SMLAs, 1961–1966

Area	Population				Employment			
	Population 1966	Net change 1961–66	Per cent change 1961–66	Per cent sector growth 1961–66	Employ-ment 1966	Net change 1961–66	Per cent change 1961–66	Per cent sector growth 1961–66
Southampton core	210,260	5,438	2·65	10·04	101,860	2,000	2·80	10·50
Southampton ring	222,580	25,570	12·98	47·23	85,950	8,230	10·59	43·22
Portsmouth core	201,400	– 13,677	–6·36	–25·26	109,580	–4,300	–3·78	–22·58
Portsmouth ring	226,100	30,783	15·76	56·86	69,410	13,520	24·19	71·01
MELAs	58,090	6,024	11·57	11·13	16,330	–410	–2·51	–2·15
Total	918,430	54,138	5·89	100·00	383,130	19,040	5·23	100·00

Source: Census.

contrast the rates for Southampton doubled in the second period. In other words, the transfer of people from the Southampton core and the growth in the ring has been much slower than the rate for Portsmouth but did gather momentum after 1961.

A comparison of the trends for employment shows much less divergence. Both cores increased in employment during 1951–61, with Southampton gaining more than Portsmouth (18,649 against 7,071). Between 1961 and 1966 both cores experienced negative shifts; Southampton gained only 2,000 jobs while Portsmouth showed a decline of 4,300. These core trends imply a decentralization of employment and this is reflected by the growth of employment in both SMLA rings. In fact, both rings increased in employment by more during the 1961–66 period than in the previous decennium.

The relative performance of each sector is summarized in Table 6.20, the measure being the percentage share of growth for the whole area. Here the population growth by sector for 1951–61 and 1961–66 are of similar proportions. The Portsmouth ring absorbs a greater proportion of population during both periods and the Southampton ring approaches similar proportion after 1961. Both cores decline in share during the second period but while Southampton's share is declining (16·46 per cent to 10·04 per cent), the core does have positive growth. Portsmouth, on the other hand, has both a declining share (−20·27 per cent to −25·26 per cent) and obviously an absolute decline as well.

For employment, the changes in share are different. Both cores had a decline in share and Portsmouth declined absolutely as well. The Southampton core share dropped by 38 per cent and Portsmouth by 41 per cent. In comparison, the increase in employment share was considerable in both rings. Portsmouth consistently received the most employment of the two; 24 per cent and 71 per cent for the two periods, while Southampton's share was 13 per cent and 43 per cent.

The employment in the MELA continued to decline over the two periods. Employment was therefore centralizing regionally but decentralizing locally. For population however, the MELA trends were quite the reverse, with an increasing share from 6 per cent to 11 per cent.

The relationship between population and employment changes by sectors is listed in Table 6.21. The regional ratio between the two was 2·38 in 1951–61 and increased slightly by 1961–66. When the SMLA is considered as a single unit, for 1951–61 the ratio for Southampton was 2·88 and that for Portsmouth 2·85. For 1961–66 these ratios increased to 3·03 and 4·82 respectively. This apparent equilibrium is disturbed if the cores and rings are measured separately. Clearly both cores during 1951–61 received more employment than the equivalent population could support. This is offset by the rings having high ratios, an indicator of the increasing interdependence of town and country. However, these disequilibria disappear during 1961–66 with massive employment increases in both rings. Despite large population increases in the MELA, employment declined during both periods.

Table 6.21

RATIO OF POPULATION CHANGE TO EMPLOYMENT CHANGE, SOUTHAMPTON-PORTSMOUTH SMLAs, 1951–1961, AND 1961–1966

	1951–61			1961–66		
	Population change	Employment change	Population-Employment ratio	Population change	Employment change	Population-Employment ratio
Southampton core	15,001	18,649	0·80	5,438	2,000	2·72
Portsmouth core	−18,468	4,808	−3·84	−13,677	−4,300	3·18
Southampton ring	30,306	7,071	4·29	25,570	8,230	3·11
Portsmouth ring	59,102	9,459	6·25	30,783	13,520	2·28
MELAs	5,185	−1,779	−2·91	6,024	−410	−14·69
Total	91,126	38,208	2·38	54,138	19,040	2·84

Source: Census.

One striking feature is again the trend of population growth to occur in urbanized areas. The Southampton and Portsmouth SMLAs urbanized rings accounted for over 98 per cent of the population growth of South Hampshire between 1951–61.

Overall, therefore, as was usual in most fast growing areas of England in the postwar period, both the Southampton and Portsmouth SMLAs were experiencing rapid decentralization of population during the 1950s and 1960s. Indeed, in Portsmouth, where the core city is constricted by its island location, the process achieved unprecedented proportions in the 1950s; between 1951 and 1961 the core lost 18,500 people, between 1961 and 1966 no less than 13,000. The ring is contrast gained 59,100 and 30,800 in the corresponding periods, giving a shift in the share of the core of −10·7 in 1951–61, and −5·30 in 1961–66. So violent is this shift, so rapid the growth of the ring in the mainland zone, that we decided our second study area should focus on this section.

THE WEST MIDLANDS AND THE BIRMINGHAM-COVENTRY BELT

The third outstanding zone of urban growth within Megalopolis England, in the postwar period, has without doubt been the West Midlands. Here, during the inter-Censal period 1951–61, five SMLAs recorded a population increase of 310,600, or over 22 per cent of the net growth of all the SMLAs of Megalopolis in that period (Table 6.22). The increase in employment, in an area with abundant opportunity, was even more striking: 163,203 or 24 per cent. From 1961 to 1966 the same story continued, but with some slowing down of the rate of growth after the Commonwealth Immigration Act of 1962: the population increase over the five years was 116,300, accounting for some 29 per cent of the net growth of the SMLAs of Megalopolis.

But the pattern of growth in the West Midlands, inspected more closely, proves very different from anything we have seen in the south. Three of our five SMLAs, Burton, Kidderminster, and Stafford, are among the smallest of the English SMLAs, with populations in 1961 that ranged from 88,000 down to 66,000. The two others on the other hand are giants: Birmingham with 2,693,100 at the Census of 1961, and Coventry with 643,700. In the West Midlands, population and industry, and the growth in both of these, are concentrated to quite extraordinary degree into large commuting zones, one centred upon a conurbation consisting of one major city (Coventry) together with four other medium-sized centres of employment, the other forming a complex multi-core SMLA. Of the total population growth of 310,600 during the 1950s, 205,000 occurred in the Birmingham SMLA, another 89,200 in the Coventry SMLA. The other three SMLAs contributed a derisory 16,300 growth. The same pattern is repeated for the early 1960s.

Our attention naturally focused therefore on these two giant SMLAs, whose growth in the postwar period is based on the solid achievement of the vehicle, engineering and electrical industries. Looked at more closely, their internal pattern of growth is also very distinctive. Like the great majority

Table 6.22

THE WEST MIDLANDS: POPULATION CHANGE AND EMPLOYMENT CHANGE, 1951–1961, AND 1961–1966

SMLA	Population change					Employment change				
	Population 1961	Net change 1951–61	Per cent change 1951–61	Net change 1961–66	Per cent change 1961–66	Employment 1961	Net change 1951–61	Per cent change 1951–61	Net change 1961–66	Per cent change 1961–66
Birmingham	2,693,069	204,963	8·24	57,051	2·12	1,326,540	107,850	8·85	57,600	4·34
Coventry	643,678	89,226	16·09	44,172	6·86	316,320	47,852	17·82	23,160	7·32
Burton	87,929	3,016	3·55	4,071	4·63	38,720	−1,816	−4·48	3,180	8·21
Kidderminster	70,406	6,549	10·26	5,884	8·36	31,900	5,111	19·08	−980	−3·07
Stafford	65,736	6,859	11·65	5,134	7·81	37,250	4,206	12·73	3,350	8·99

Source: Census.

of SMLAs in England, Birmingham is experiencing relative decentralization of people (Table 6.23). Its core, consisting of Birmingham and the other

Table 6.23

THE WEST MIDLANDS: RELATIVE DECENTRALIZATION OF POPULATION AND EMPLOYMENT, 1931–1966

SMLA	Per cent shift in core share of population			Per cent shift in employment	
	1931–51	1951–61	1961–66	1951–61	1961–66
Birmingham	−2·02	−3·82	−5·56	−1·74	−4·70
Coventry	4·74	−0·12	−3·42	0·31	3·64
Burton	−1·82	−0·18	−4·86	5·16	4·68
Kidderminster	−0·75	0·61	−2·42	5·14	17·86
Stafford	−1·07	4·34	−0·16	6·38	4·34

Note: Shifts for 1931–51 and 1961–66 are given as decennial rates: actual shifts are obtained by doubling and halving respectively the figures above.

Source: Census.

major towns of the conurbation,[9] gained 47,400 people during 1951–61; but its ring, which stretches far out beyond the green belt into Shropshire on the west, beyond Stratford-on-Avon on the south-east, gained 157,600. In the early 1960s, with urban renewal and the filling up of the empty spaces in the conurbation, relative decentralization became absolute decentralization. The core lost 36,700 people from 1961 to 1966, while the ring gained the unprecedented total of 93,700. In contrast to London, therefore, where the pattern of growth is passing out of the central SMLA ring and into a series of peripheral SMLAs, Birmingham is at an earlier and simpler stage of evolution; massive growth is now taking place in its SMLA ring.

But this pattern has to be seen in parallel with the growth of employment. Here too, Birmingham is distinctive; for it is showing only a very modest tendency to decentralization. In the period 1951–61, its core gained close on 65,000 workers, its ring 42,900; expressed in terms of the share of the core, this signified a relative decentralization of only 1·74, a remarkably low index for such a large and apparently congested conurbation. Furthermore, this still left a very large proportion concentrated in Birmingham's core: close on 80 per cent in 1961, a figure which is paralleled closely by other major provincial concentrations of industry like Manchester and Liverpool. As compared with London, it is clear that up to this time, employment had not felt the need, or the pressure, to decentralize out of the provincial metropolitan core to the same extent, even over the relatively short distances to the ring of the same SMLA. But during 1961–66, there was a much stronger decentralization trend, with an actual decline in employment in the SMLA core.

[9] Birmingham C.B., Walsall C.B., Warley C.B., West Bromwich C.B., and Wolverhampton C.B.

Table 6.24(a)

POPULATION AND EMPLOYMENT CHANGE: BIRMINGHAM-COVENTRY SMLAs, 1951–1961

Area	Population				Employment			
	Population 1961	Net change 1951–1961	Per cent change 1961–1966	Per cent sector growth 1951–61	Employment 1961	Net change 1951–61	Per cent change 1951–61	Per cent sector growth 1951–61
1 Birmingham core (part)	1,107,187	−5,498	−4·88	−4·64	655,080	30,860	4·28	32·41
2 Urbanized Birmingham ring (part)	113,633	24,142	26·98	20·36	60,460 (rows 2–3)	16,516 (rows 2–3)	37·58 (rows 2–3)	17·34 (rows 2–3)
3 Non-urbanized Birmingham ring (part)	62,671	10,710	20·61	9·03				
4 Coventry core	305,521	47,279	18·31	39·87	169,990	28,095	19·79	29·50
5 Peripheral SMLA cores	151,636	15,457	11·35	13·04	72,530	9,424	14·93	9·8
6 Urbanized SMLA rings	91,011	20,094	28·33	16·95	66,330 (rows 6–7)	10,333 (rows 6–7)	18·45 (rows 6–7)	10·85 (rows 6–7)
7 Non-urbanized SMLA rings	95,510	6,396	7·18	5·39				
Total	1,945,169	118,580	6·56	100·00	1,024,390	95,228	10·24	100·00

Source: Census.

Table 6.24(b)

POPULATION AND EMPLOYMENT CHANGE: BIRMINGHAM-COVENTRY SMLAs, 1961–1966

Area	Population				Employment			
	Population 1966	Net change 1961–66	Per cent change 1961–66	Per cent sector growth 1961–66	Employment 1966	Net change 1961–66	Per cent change 1961–66	Per cent sector growth 1961–66
1 Birmingham core (part)	1,064,220	−46,463	−4·18	−387·97	625,860	−29,220	−4·46	−842·07
2 Birmingham ring (part)	202,450	13,897	7·37	116·04	65,790	5,330	8·81	153·60
3 Coventry core	328,980	12,351	3·90	103·13	185,980	15,990	9·41	460·81
4 Peripheral SMLA core	159,210	7,575	4·76	63·25	73,630	1,100	1·52	31·70
5 Peripheral SMLA rings	212,340	24,616	13·11	205·54	69,660	3,330	5·02	95·96
Total	1,967,200	11,976	0·61	100·00	1,020,920	3,470	0·39	100·00

Source: Census.

The situation in the Coventry SMLA was somewhat different. During the period 1931–51 it had been almost unique among English SMLAs in showing a strong centralization of population. This tendency disappeared after 1961, the proportion of SMLA population in the core areas (71 per cent) remaining fairly constant until 1961. During this decade, both core and ring authorities recorded substantial growth, the four cities making up the core gaining 62,700 people and the ring gaining 26,400. After 1961, the ring increased in population faster than the core, gaining 24,600 people as against the core's 19,600 during the quinquennium 1961–66, an increase making for a shift to the ring of 3·4 per cent. Employment likewise showed a relative increase in the core areas during the 1950s and this tendency was actually reinforced during the five years 1961–66.[10] Although the core in this case included four distinct cities, the trends do not vary between them to any great extent. Surprisingly, the one which is showing the most centralization is Coventry itself, the largest city, accounting for over 40 per cent of the SMLA population and over 50 per cent of its employment.

These trends are set out in detail in Table 6.24, which shows the strong tendency during the 1950s (equivalent data are not available for the early 1960s) for the decentralization of population to be concentrated in urbanized areas as they have been defined in this study. Table 6.25 compares ratios of population change and employment change, and shows that the 1951–61 period was characterized by a rapid growth of jobs in relation to population in both the Birmingham and Coventry areas; in contrast during 1961–66 population and employment were more evenly balanced except in Coventry.

On the basis of these analyses, for the detailed study of planning decisions we considered a wide rectangle of territory, stretching from the southern suburbs of Birmingham southwards and eastwards to embrace Coventry itself, Rugby, Nuneaton, Leamington Spa, and Stratford-upon-Avon, and including the whole of the complex Coventry-Nuneaton SMLA plus the southeastern sector of the Birmingham SMLA. The metropolitan complex selected for detailed study therefore included the Birmingham core, the south-west part of the Birmingham ring and the complete Coventry SMLA which includes the towns of Rugby, Nuneaton, and Leamington Spa. It is shown in Figure 6.12.

THE EAST MIDLANDS CITIES

Our area of detailed study in the Birmingham-Coventry zone abuts directly, in its east side, against another important zone of postwar growth in the English Megalopolis: the East Midlands. Really, in fact, the distinction between west and east is difficult to make here, between Nuneaton and Leicester; but the critical boundary, where the Coventry-Nuneaton SMLA abuts for over ten miles against the Leicester SMLA, still follows the ancient

[10] This may in part be accounted for by boundary extensions to Coventry C.B. in the 1960s.

Table 6.25

RATIO OF POPULATION CHANGE TO EMPLOYMENT CHANGE, BIRMINGHAM-COVENTRY SMLAs, 1951–1961, AND 1961–1966

	1951–61			1961–66		
	Population change	Employment change	Population-Employment ratio	Population change	Employment change	Population-Employment ratio
Birmingham core (part)	−5,498	30,860	0·78	−46,463	−29,220	1·59
Birmingham ring (part)	34,852	16,516	2·11	13,897	5,330	2·61
Coventry core	47,279	28,095	1·68	12,351	15,990	0·77
Peripheral cores	15,457	9,424	1·64	7,575	1,100	6·88
Peripheral rings	26,490	10,333	2·56	24,616	3,330	7·39
Total	118,580	95,228	1·24	11,976	3,470	3·45

Source: Census.

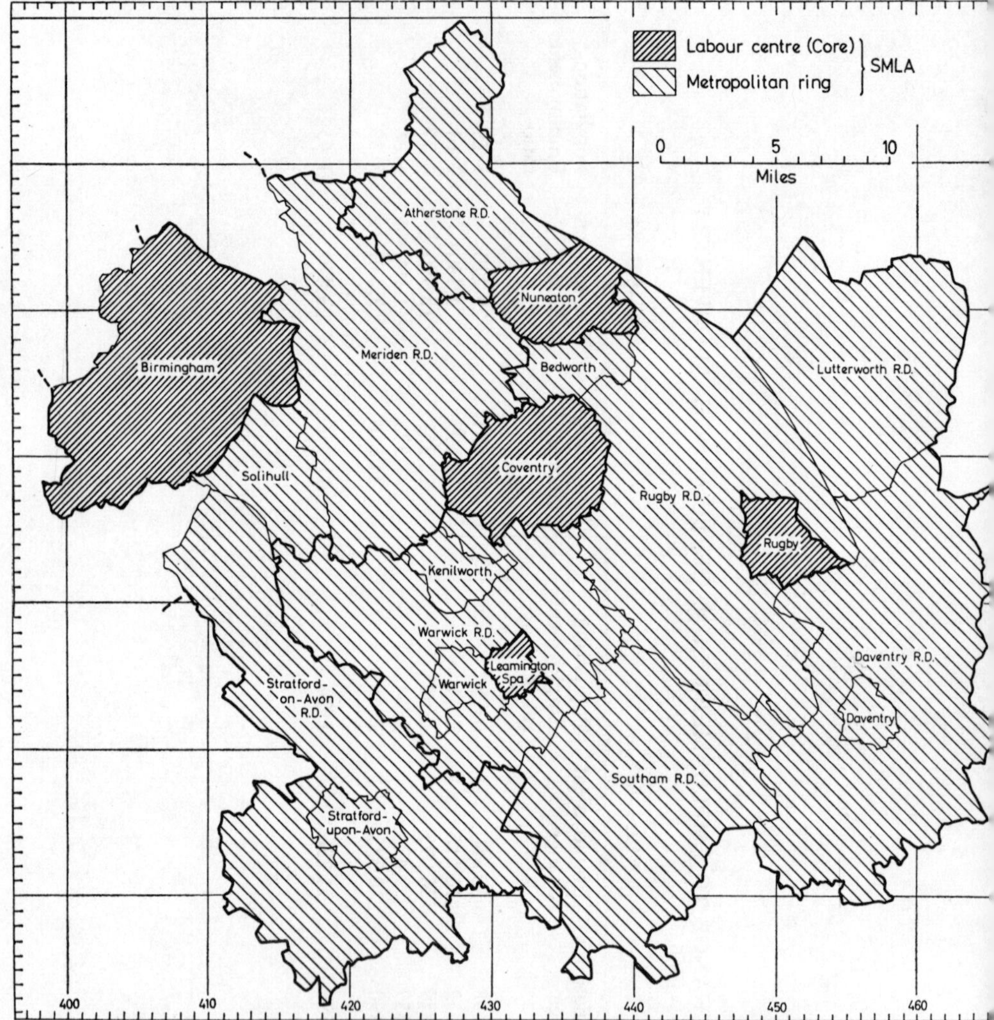

Figure 6.12 Birmingham-Coventry: Constituent Areas

Roman Watling Street, which in the ninth century marked the boundary of the Dane law against Alfred's English kingdom. The character of urbanization in the East Midlands, as all students of geography know, is heavily influenced by the boroughs which the Danes founded at that time, which later became the great county cities and the natural locations for a wide range of industries. When the industrial revolution arrived in the nineteenth century, apart from the opening up of the Nottinghamshire coalfield and the development of factory industry in the old knitting villages of Western Leicestershire,

Table 6.26

THE EAST MIDLANDS: POPULATION CHANGE AND EMPLOYMENT CHANGE, 1951–1961, AND 1961–1966

		Population change				Employment change				
SMLA	Population 1961	Net change 1951–61	Per cent change 1951–61	Net change 1961–66	Per cent change 1961–66	Employment 1961	Net change 1951–61	Per cent change 1951–61	Net change 1961–66	Per cent change 1961–66
Nottingham	634,683	41,816	7·05	20,187	3·18	306,540	22,252	7·83	5,500	1·79
Derby	314,532	21,875	7·48	7,578	3·05	155,510	16,731	7·41	5,410	3·47
Leicester	456,551	19,072	4·36	46,989	10·29	232,690	16,070	7·42	18,510	7·95
Northampton	151,191	9,470	6·68	9,199	6·08	71,510	4,500	6·72	6,640	9·28
Mansfield	130,871	11,087	9·28	11,929	9·12	58,700	6,353	12·14	5,560	9·47

Source: Census.

the new industry naturally went into the existing cities. The coming of the Midland railway, which linked them with each other and with London and the coalfield, completed and fortified this process. Lastly, between 1959 and 1965 the completion of England's main spinal motorway, the M1, gave further recognition to the point. It passes three miles west of Northampton, four miles west of Leicester, five miles west of Nottingham and six miles east of Derby, putting each of these cities within an hour's drive at most of any of the others, and linking them even more effectively into the home market which their industries are geared to serve.

The continued prosperity and growth of these industries (shoes, knitwear, and a wide range of light engineering) has been the basic reason for the growth of the East Midlands cities in the postwar geography of Megalopolis. During the 1950s five SMLAs strung up what was to be the line of the M1, added over 103,300 to their combined population, thus accounting for nearly 8 per cent of the total population growth of all the SMLAs in Megalopolis (Table 6.26). In the short period 1961–66, their rate of growth has been even more outstanding: nearly 96,000 or no less than 24 per cent of the net growth of the SMLAs in English Megalopolis in this most recent period. This fact fully

Table 6.27

THE EAST MIDLANDS: RELATIVE DECENTRALIZATION OF POPULATION AND EMPLOYMENT, 1931–1966

	Per cent shift in core share of population			Per cent shift in employment	
	1931–51	1951–61	1961–66	1951–61	1961–66
Nottingham	−0·59	−2·37	−4·46	−0·64	−3·92
Derby	−4·60	−6·17	−11·54	−1·80	−8·08
Leicester	−1·97	−5·29	−13·22	−1·28	−8·10
Northampton	−1·49	−3·76	−1·50	−0·97	13·70
Mansfield	−0·08	−2·21	−3·44	2·36	1·96

Note: Shifts for 1931–51 and 1961–66 are given as decennial rates: actual shifts are obtained by doubling and halving respectively the figures above.

Source: Census.

justified us in choosing a detailed study zone within one of these SMLAs, and for a number of reasons we chose to look at Leicester. First, its recent growth has been particularly dramatic; while between 1951 and 1961 its 19,000 increase was modest compared with that of Nottingham (19,100 against 41,800), since 1961 it has far overhauled its rival (1961–66: 47,000 against 20,200). Second, it illustrates very well a simpler pattern of growth than we have been able to find earlier in our bigger metropolitan complexes, a pattern based on peripheral urbanization of the inner part of the metropolitan ring, all round the core. Third, Leicester, as the county town and major supply centre for its subregion as well as a considerable industrial centre,

Table 6.28(a)

POPULATION AND EMPLOYMENT CHANGE: LEICESTER SMLA, 1951–1961

	Population			Employment		
Area	1961	Net change 1951–61	Per cent change 1951–61	1961	Net change 1951–61	Per cent change 1951–61
Leicester core	273,470	−11,711	−4·11	176,520	9,413	5·63
Leicester ring	183,081	30,783	20·21	56,170	6,657	13·44
Total	456,551	19,072	4·36	232,690	16,070	7·42

Table 6.28(b)

POPULATION AND EMPLOYMENT CHANGE: LEICESTER SMLA, 1961–1966

	Population			Employment		
Area	1966	Net change 1961–66	Per cent change 1961–66	1966	Net change 1961–66	Per cent change 1961–66
Leicester core	268,340	−5,130	−1·88	180,400	3,880	2·19
Leicester ring	235,200	52,119	28·47	70,800	14,630	26·04
Total	503,540	46,989	10·29	251,200	18,510	7·95

Source: Census.

Table 6.29

RATIO OF POPULATION CHANGE TO EMPLOYMENT CHANGE, LEICESTER SMLA, 1951–1961, AND 1961–1966

	1951–61			1961–66		
	Population change	Employment change	Population-Employment ratio	Population change	Employment change	Population-Employment ratio
Leicester core	–11,711	9,413	–1·24	–5,130	3,880	–1·32
Leicester ring	30,783	6,657	4·62	52,119	14,630	3·56
Total	19,072	16,070	1·19	46,989	18,510	2·54

Source: Census.

demonstrates in a very classical way the dichotomy between rapid decentralization of population and less rapid decentralization of employment (Table 6.27). In the period 1931–51, it already demonstrated relative decentralization of people, and by the 1950s this had become absolute; its core lost 11,700 people, its ring gained 30,800. In the early 1960s the process simply continued: the core lost 5,130 from 1961 to 1966, the ring gained no less than 52,119. But at the same time, the parallel decentralization of jobs was a much slower affair. In a relative sense decentralization of jobs was happening during the 1950s to a modest degree, but even so the absolute growth of jobs in the core was 9,413, against only 6,657 for the ring. In the 1960s the core began to lose jobs (minus 3,880 during 1961–66) while in the same period the ring gained rapidly (plus 14,630) (Tables 6.28(a) and (b) and 6.29).

Our fourth area for detailed study, therefore, consists simply of the Leicester Standard Metropolitan Labour Area. It embraces the city of Leicester, forming the core, together with a ring of urban districts and rural districts occupying an area which stretches on average, ten to twelve miles from the centre of the city (Figure 6.13). Within this area, by the 1950s, it had already become difficult to discover where the precise physical limits of the city lay. Suburban growth had overrun the administrative boundaries, passing into two small urban districts (Wigston and Oadby) to the south of the city and into three rural districts (Barrow-upon-Soar, Billesdon, and Blaby) respectively north, east and south-west of the city.

SOUTH LANCASHIRE – NORTH CHESHIRE

When we pass across the Trent into the northern half of Megalopolis, it is still true, as it was true in the thirties, that we pass into a zone of much less dynamic growth and less urgent pressure for urbanization. That is clear from the most cursory inspection of the statistics in the Census volumes. But it becomes clearer within the framework of the SMLA analysis, because the SMLA concept allows us to see that not merely are the densely built-up cores of these areas declining (as is true, indeed, of many dynamic areas in the Midlands and South), but that in fact whole SMLAs are stagnant or even, in many cases, in a state of actual decline. The Manchester SMLA, together with a well marked group of SMLAs, forming a great arc west and north of Manchester and identifiable as centred upon the cotton towns, registered an aggregate population growth during the 1950s of only 13,621 people, a mere one per cent of the net growth of all the SMLAs in Megalopolis (Table 6.30). In the succeeding period 1961–66, they registered an aggregate decline of population of just over 1,000. The fortunes of individual SMLAs were mostly reversed: in the 1950s Manchester gained people while the peripheral SMLAs all lost, in the 1960s Manchester lost while several peripheral SMLAs showed slight increases. When taken together, though, these increases were not quite large enough to off-set declines in the Manchester and the two most peripheral SMLAs.

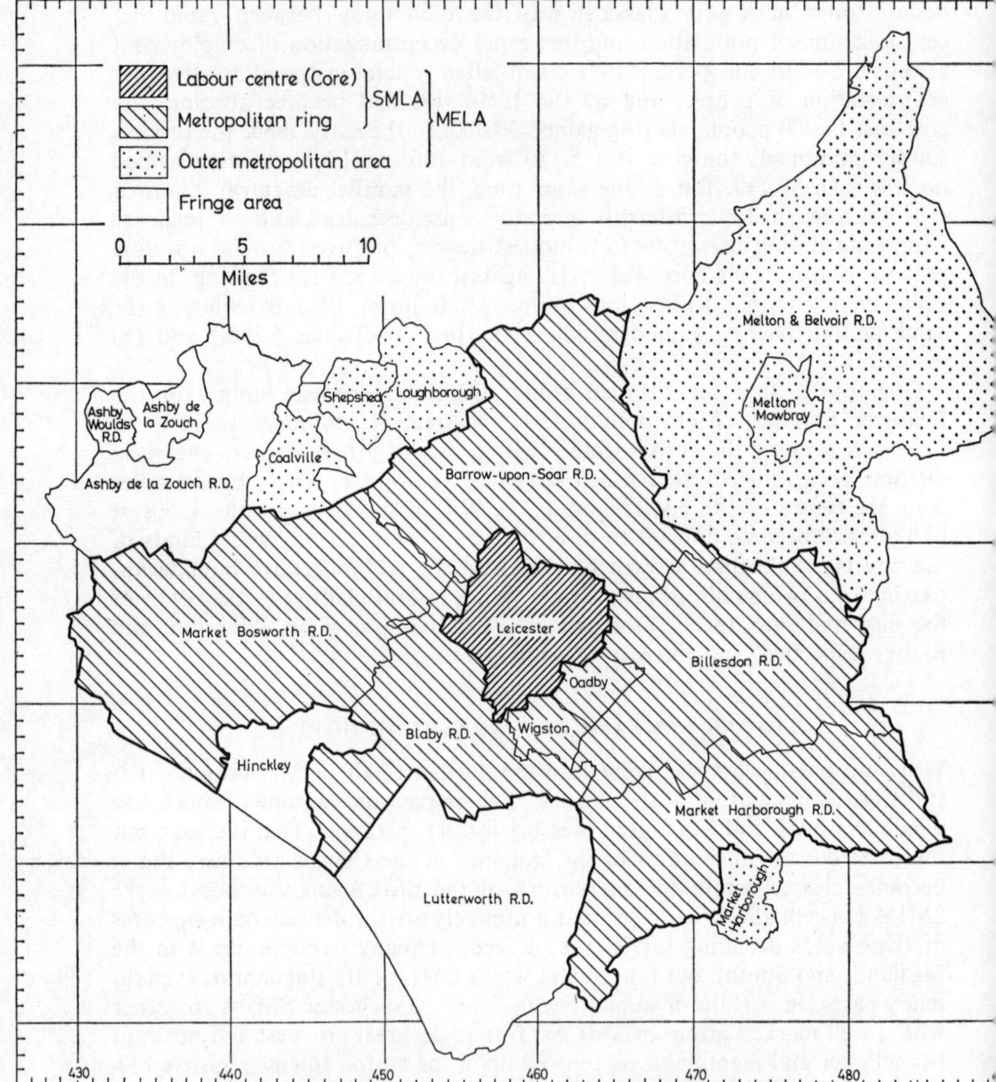

Figure 6.13 Leicester-Leicestershire: Constituent Areas

In effect, this means that population loss in the cores of the northern towns – a natural result of the destruction of the slum housing, coupled with renewal at a rather lower density – is not being compensated by gains in the rings (Table 6.31). This is seen particularly clearly in the Manchester SMLA. During the period 1931–51, and even more powerfully during 1951–61, it was showing marked decentralization of population; during the latter period

Table 6.30

MANCHESTER AND THE COTTON TOWNS: POPULATION CHANGE AND EMPLOYMENT CHANGE, 1951–1961, AND 1961–1966

	Population change					Employment change				
SMLA	Population 1961	Net change 1951–61	Per cent change 1951–61	Net change 1961–66	Per cent change 1961–66	Employment 1961	Net change 1951–61	Per cent change 1951–61	Net change 1961–66	Per cent change 1961–66
Manchester	2,041,694	29,319	1·46	−29,034	−1·42	1,007,470	−14,408	−1·41	−3,340	−0·33
Bolton	249,708	−2,965	−1·17	1,122	0·45	117,140	−2,765	−2·31	−1,680	−1·43
Preston	196,599	5,410	2·82	5,581	2·84	98,120	6,865	7·52	−1,970	−2·00
Wigan	180,080	−2,736	−1·50	7,370	4·09	65,960	−584	−0·88	6,860	10·40
Blackburn	168,121	−5,093	−2·94	−2,331	−1·39	84,340	−3,903	−4·42	−2,770	−3·28
Bury	130,431	−1,577	−1·19	11,109	8·52	66,390	−3,198	−4·60	1,000	1·50
Rochdale	116,140	−4,198	−3·49	2,930	2·52	61,700	−4,701	−7·08	−1,510	−2·44
Burnley	113,511	−5,297	−4·46	−3,881	−3·42	59,580	−1,331	−2·19	−2,890	−4·85
Leigh	93,244	758	0·82	4,856	5·27	43,590	−4,097	−8·59	−310	−0·71

Source: Census.

its core lost 74,100 people while its ring gained 103,400, chiefly on the previously undeveloped farmlands south of the city in the county of Cheshire. But in the period 1961–66, while the population of its core fell even more catastrophically as a result of urban renewal by 93,700, its ring gained only 64,700; the ring was failing to take up the loss in the core, which was passing out of the metropolitan area, and even out of the north-west region, altogether.

Table 6.31

MANCHESTER AND THE COTTON TOWNS: RELATIVE DECENTRALIZATION OF POPULATION AND EMPLOYMENT, 1931–1966

SMLA	Per cent shift in core share of population			Per cent shift in employment	
	1931–51	1951–61	1961–66	1951–61	1961–66
Manchester	−2·39	−4·67	−7·36	0·37	−7·40
Bolton	−0·03	−2·08	−6·28	−0·85	1·86
Preston	−2·85	−5·83	−10·32	−1·02	−6·20
Wigan	−0·23	−2·55	−5·86	3·22	0·86
Blackburn	−0·07	−1·02	−4·64	0·75	−2·36
Bury	0·54	1·55	−3·58	5·35	−1·42
Rochdale	−0·19	0·39	−1·78	−0·32	1·48
Burnley	−0·63	−0·56	−2·70	−0·80	5·10
Leigh	−0·09	−3·17	−6·08	5·41	0·36

Note: Shifts for 1931–51 and 1961–66 are given as decennial rates: actual shifts are obtained by doubling and halving respectively the figures above.

Source: Census.

As in the case of Birmingham, but even more remarkably, Manchester has continued to keep its employment concentrated in its central core, consisting of twelve administrative areas centred upon the twin cities of Manchester and Salford. Both the core and the ring actually lost employment marginally during the 1950s, but the loss in the ring was slightly greater, leading to a slight relative centralization; still, in 1961, nearly 79 per cent of all jobs in the SMLA were concentrated in the core area compared with only 62 per cent of the population. In Manchester, then, urban renewal and decentralization of people are without doubt leading to lengthened work journeys back into the core and out again every day.

Very much the same tendencies are observable in the smaller complex of SMLAs around the Mersey estuary (Table 6.32). Here Liverpool plus four other SMLAs (St Helens and Warrington in the middle Mersey glass and chemical region, Chester, and Southport), gained 57,000 people in the 1950s, or just under 4 per cent of the net metropolitan area growth of the English Megalopolis. By the early 1960s, as with Manchester, even this modest rate of growth has slowed catastrophically: the gain was a mere 4,500 people.

Table 6.32

LIVERPOOL AND ITS REGION: POPULATION CHANGE AND EMPLOYMENT CHANGE, 1951–1961, AND 1961–1966

		Population change				Employment change				
SMLA	Population 1961	Net change 1951–61	Per cent change 1951–61	Net change 1961–66	Per cent change 1961–66	Employment 1961	Net change 1951–61	Per cent change 1951–61	Net change 1961–66	Per cent change 1961–66
Liverpool	1,480,930	53,208	3·73	−30,730	−2·08	628,970	24,363	4·03	3,740	0·59
St Helens	189,943	7,382	4·04	22,937	12·08	83,980	−1,846	−2·15	12,570	15·18
Warrington	168,425	−6,490	−3·71	7,775	4·62	84,730	−10,508	−11·03	5,120	6·04
Chester	102,209	4,991	5·14	5,771	5·65	49,660	553	1·13	−800	−1·61
Southport	82,004	−2,035	−2·42	−1,304	−1·59	30,540	−1,072	−3·39	−170	−0·55

Source: Census.

What had happened, again, was a massive loss from the core of the major SMLA, coupled with a failure on the part of the ring to compensate. In the 1950s, Warrington and Southport SMLAs had both recorded small losses,

Table 6.33

LIVERPOOL AND ITS REGION: RELATIVE DECENTRALIZATION OF POPULATION AND EMPLOYMENT, 1931–1966

SMLA	Per cent shift in core share of population			Per cent employment shift	
	1931–51	1951–61	1961–66	1951–61	1961–66
Liverpool	−4·15	−5·10	−5·80	−2·42	−7·02
St Helens	−4·11	−4·42	−18·62	8·54	−19·82
Warrington	−5·20	−1·06	−8·06	5·64	−4·48
Chester	−2·73	−0·59	−7·30	6·87	6·94

Southport (SMLA has no ring: 100 per cent population and employment in core)

Note: Shifts for 1931–51 and 1961–66 are given as decennial rates: actual shifts are obtained by doubling and halving respectively the figures above.

Source: Census.

St Helens and Chester small gains; but all these were overshadowed by the growth of Liverpool. Here, a net gain of 53,200 was made up of a loss in the core of 38,000, balanced by a gain in the ring of 91,200. By the 1961–66 period, an accelerated loss from the core (62,200 in only five years, the product of a very rapid urban renewal programme) was accompanied by a gain of only 31,500 in the ring. At the same time, as elsewhere in the big provincial SMLAs, Liverpool has kept a very high proportion of its total employment in its core: 79·4 per cent in 1961, representing a modest relative decentralization during the 1950s (Table 6.33).

Taking the whole complex of SMLAs between Merseyside and Manchester, the detailed analysis in Table 6.34 shows that when increases in population did occur they were concentrated in the urbanized rings of the SMLAs, particularly in Manchester and Liverpool where over 178,000 people were added to the rings during 1951–61. The peripheral SMLAs also expanded population into their urbanized rings but this did not offset losses in the cores. The trends during the period 1961–66 were completely reversed. Manchester and Liverpool failed to offset core losses in their rings as they had done in the 1950s. The peripheral SMLA cores again lost population, but increases in the rings more than compensated for this. The ratio of population change to employment change (Table 6.35) illustrates the confusing trends in the 1950s when the relationship between population and employment changes was frequently an inverse one. After 1961, the peripheral cores were clearly centralizing employment while decentralizing population, while Manchester

Table 6.34(a)

POPULATION AND EMPLOYMENT CHANGE, SOUTH LANCASHIRE-NORTH CHESHIRE, 1951–1961

Area	Population				Employment			
	1961	Net change 1951–61	Per cent change 1951–61	Per cent sector growth 1951–61	1961	Net change 1951–61	Per cent change 1951–61	Per cent sector decline 1951–61
1 Manchester core	1,387,891	−74,101	−5·07	−83·93	792,470	−7,608	−0·95	53·20
2 Urbanized Manchester ring	564,197	90,521	19·11	102·53	215,000	−6,800	−3·07	47·55
3 Non-urbanized Manchester ring	89,606	12,829	16·71	14·53				
4 Liverpool core	970,336	−37,980	−3·77	−43·02	499,390	4,727	0·96	−33·06
5 Urbanized Liverpool ring	467,020	88,544	23·39	100·29	129,580	19,636	17·86	−137·31
6 Non-urbanized Liverpool ring	43,574	2,644	6·46	2·99				
7 Peripheral SMLA cores	725,733	−27,900	−3·70	−31·60	368,990	1,762	0·48	−12·32
8 Urbanized SMLA rings	398,114	21,560	5·73	24·42	185,040	−30,533	−14·16	213·52
9 Non-urbanized SMLA rings	86,126	−5,523	−6·03	−6·26				
10 Outer MELAs (part)	129,211	17,626	15·80	19·96	59,630	4,516	8·19	−31·58
Totals	4,861,778	88,220	1·85	100·00	2,250,100	−14,300	−0·63	100·00

Source: Census.

Table 6.34(b)

POPULATION AND EMPLOYMENT CHANGE, SOUTH LANCASHIRE-NORTH CHESHIRE, 1961–1966

Area	Population				Employment			
	1966	Net change 1961–66	Per cent change 1961–66	Per cent sector growth 1961–66	1966	Net change 1961–66	Per cent change 1961–66	Per cent sector decline 1961–66
1 Manchester core	1,294,150	−93,741	−6·75	−1,574·95	727,060	−65,410	−8·25	787·12
2 Manchester ring	718,510	64,707	9·90	1,087·15	217,050	2,050	0·95	−24·67
3 Liverpool core	908,120	−62,216	−6·41	−1,045·30	463,270	−36,120	−7·23	434·66
4 Liverpool ring	542,080	31,486	6·17	529·00	141,590	12,010	9·27	−144·52
5 Peripheral cores	707,950	−17,783	−2·45	−298·77	428,470	59,480	16·12	−715·76
6 Peripheral rings	558,820	74,578	15·40	1,252·99	194,310	9,270	5·01	−111·55
7 Outer MELAs (part)	138,100	8,889	6·88	149·34	70,040	10,410	17·46	−125·27
Totals	4,867,730	5,952	0·12	100·00	2,241,790	−8,310	−0·37	100·00

Source: Census.

experienced the curious trend of decentralizing population to the ring without a compensating increase in jobs.

In the North-West, clearly, it takes a longer search to identify areas of really rapid growth than in the southern half of Megalopolis. The small SMLAs around the manufacturing towns of the coalfield are so stagnant, or actually in decline, that they have little interest for the purposes of studying residential mobility; the only areas where there is room for large-scale growth are on the Cheshire side of the river Mersey, immediately adjacent to the southern sides of the region's two great conurbations. Accordingly, we concentrated our search into a broad strip across this zone, running from the Wirral across to the foothills of the Cheshire Pennines (Figure 6.14).

THE WEST RIDING AND THE SOUTH YORKSHIRE COMPLEX

Lastly, we have identified two other logical groupings of SMLAs on the opposite side of the Pennines. Neither of them contributed at all substantially to the urban growth process in Megalopolis in the postwar period. A group of five Yorkshire woollen towns (Leeds, Huddersfield, Halifax, Wakefield, and Dewsbury) contributed a mere 19,000 to the net growth of the metropolitan areas of Megalopolis in the 1950s, and another 22,000 in the early 1960s. Further south, the Sheffield-Doncaster-Barnsley complex did rather better with a growth of 53,000 in the period 1951–61, but then relapsed heavily with a net addition of only 15,000 from 1961 to 1966. Neither of these two areas, however, contributes anything unusual or substantial to our understanding of the way the process of urbanization is taking place in Megalopolis in the postwar period. Since our object is to concentrate on growth, we therefore have concentrated our detailed studies on the areas where growth was happening, in the southern and midland parts of Megalopis (Figure 6.15).

LAND USE PATTERNS IN THREE STUDY AREAS: URBAN GROWTH AND CONTAINMENT

Our tour across Megalopolis has sought to concentrate on the broad features of growth; more detail will follow in the next main part of this book, when we come to concentrate on our local study areas. These areas, the first west of London, the second on the Solent, the third in the belt between Birmingham and Coventry, the fourth on the periphery of Leicester, the fifth in the North Cheshire plain south of Liverpool and Manchester, are we think entirely representative of the great explosion of suburban privately built housing, which occurred in Megalopolis England in the period between 1951 and 1966. Accordingly, the next major section of our study, Chapters Seven to Twelve, focuses on them. But first, it is useful to take a more detailed look at the physical expression of urban development in some of these areas.

Earlier in this chapter, we analysed the degree of urban development, and its spatial distribution, within Megalopolis England during the postwar

Table 6.35

RATIO OF POPULATION CHANGE TO EMPLOYMENT CHANGE, SOUTH LANCASHIRE-NORTH CHESHIRE, 1951–1961, AND 1961–1966

	1951–61			1961–66		
	Population change	Employment change	Population-Employment ratio	Population change	Employment change	Population-Employment ratio
Manchester core	– 74,101	– 7,608	9·73	– 93,741	– 65,410	1·43
Manchester ring	103,350	– 6,800	– 15·19	64,707	2,050	31·56
Liverpool core	– 37,980	4,727	– 8·03	– 62,216	– 36,120	1·72
Liverpool ring	91,188	19,636	4·64	31,486	12,010	2·62
Peripheral cores	– 27,900	1,762	– 15·83	– 17,783	59,480	– 0·29
Peripheral rings	16,037	– 30,533	– 0·53	74,578	9,270	8·04
Outer MELAs	17,626	4,516	3·90	8,889	10,410	0·85
Total	88,220	– 14,300	– 6·17	5,952	– 8,310	– 0·72

Source: Census.

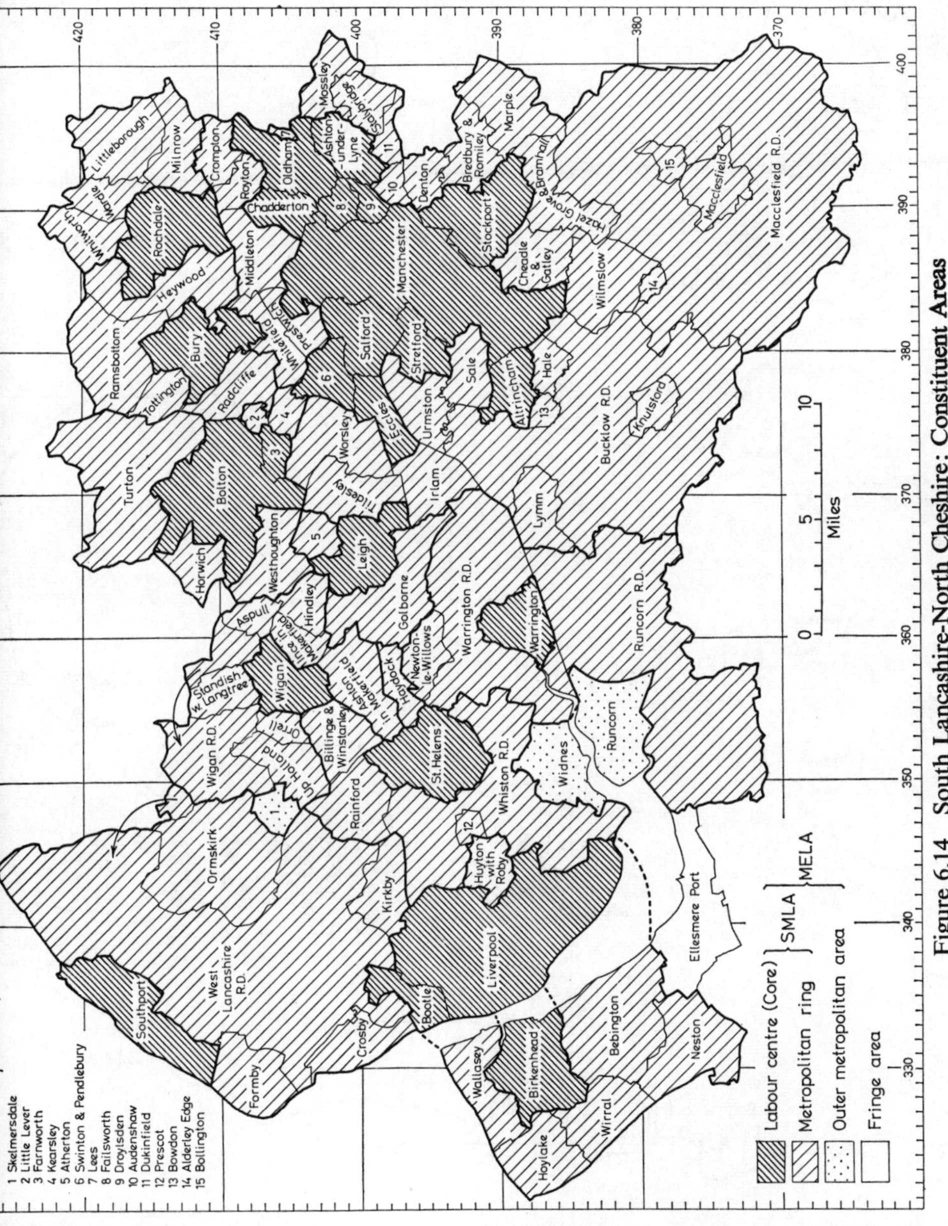

Figure 6.14 South Lancashire-North Cheshire: Constituent Areas

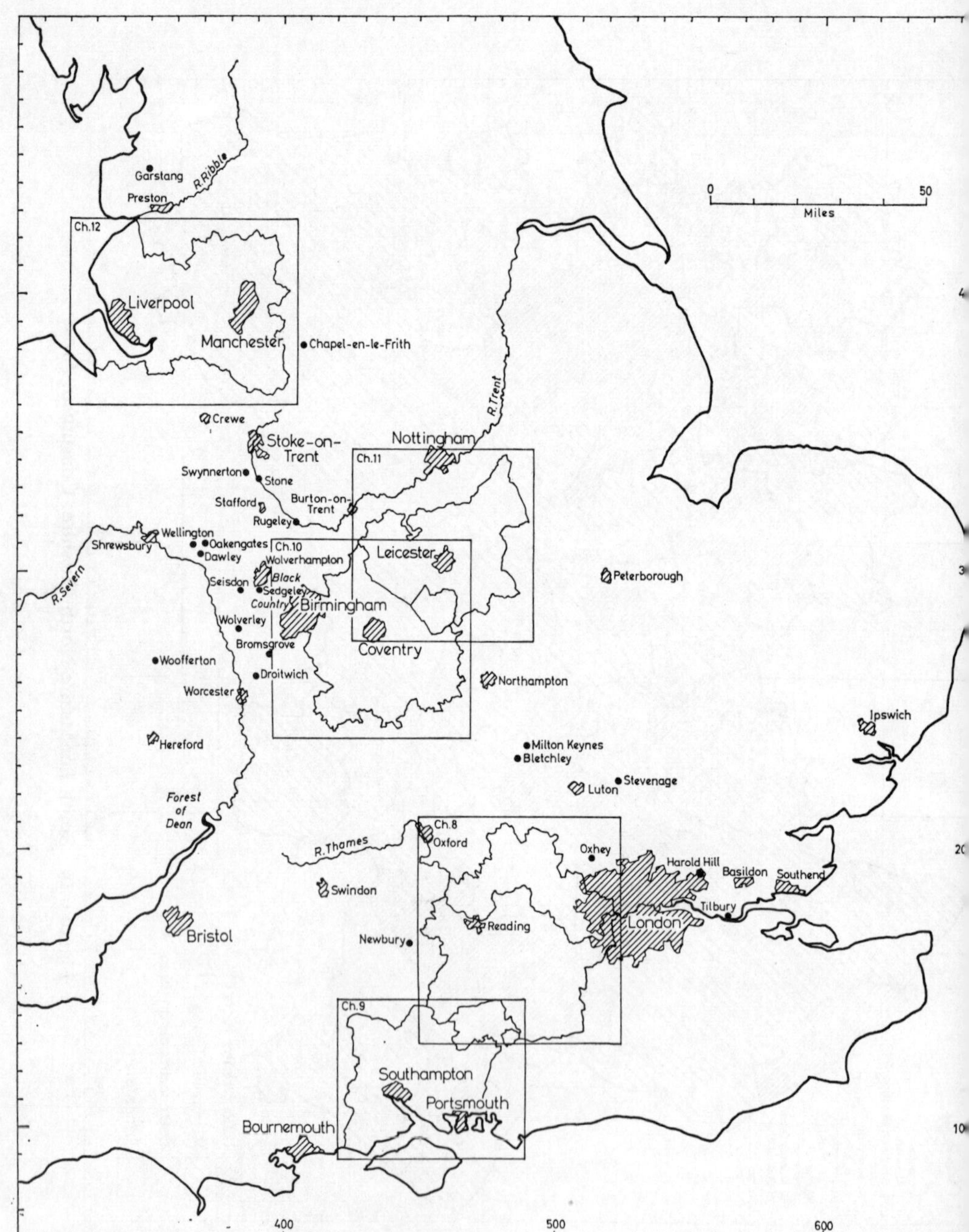

Figure 6.15 The Five Study Areas

period. Our tool for this purpose consisted of the two national surveys of land utilization, one conducted about 1950 by the newly-created County and County Borough Planning Offices as part of the process of preparing their development plans, the other organized shortly after 1960 under the direction of Dr Alice Coleman. For the overall look at land use patterns across the whole of Megalopolis, we used a framework of rather large squares, based on the Ordnance Survey national metric grid: the whole of the Megalopolis area, or a slightly simplified version of it, was broken down into a series of 540 squares, each 100 square kilometres (10 × 10 km) in extent. Now, in contrast, we want to take a closer look at land use patterns in some of the local areas within Megalopolis, which we have just identified as zones of rapid urban growth in the period since the Second World War. For that purpose, we obviously need a finer mesh of squares. Ideally, they should be very small, but there are limits set by the nature of the point sampling method that has been used to analyse each square. For the detailed analysis of land use in the local study areas, therefore, we use a mesh of squares each 4 square kilometres (2 × 2 km) in extent. Such squares, each a little more than 1 square mile in size, are sufficiently small to catch the local nuances of urban growth patterns, including the critical effects of postwar planning policies, which it is our particular aim to consider.

The scope of the analysis had to be limited by the resources available. Of all the pieces of research carried out within the PEP urban growth project, this was by far the most labour-intensive; the laborious work of point sampling involved many months of detailed and tedious analysis. It was, unhappily, accompanied by many unforeseen technical problems, which led to delay in completion of the entire study. Subsequent sample checks showed that a part of the work, that involving the First Land Utilization Survey of Britain (the Dudley Stamp Survey, in the early 1930s), was too unreliable to use; this was due to inaccuracies in the analysis, and the work could not be repeated. Consequently, one of the chief original aims of the analysis, to compare the patterns of urban growth in the later 1930s with those of the 1950s, was never achieved. Certain other parts of the analysis, involving the detailed study area west of London, suffered from non-availability of materials, and could not be completed in time for the publication of the entire report. It is hoped that this analysis will be completed and published separately elsewhere. Meanwhile, the present analysis concentrates upon three of the study areas whose history is recounted in the next immediately following chapters of this volume: the Birmingham-Coventry area, the Leicester area, and the South Lancashire-North Cheshire area. For purposes of convenience, since they are contiguous, the first two of these areas are analysed as a single unit in what follows.

The problem of analysis, however, did not end there. It soon became evident that despite the attempt to obtain comparability between the land use classifications used in the 1950 and the 1960 surveys, large and irreconcilable differences remained. In particular, the County Planning Office Surveys tended to indicate multiple uses for rural land in such a way that it would be classed as in a developed, or urban, use while the Coleman Survey used a much stricter definition which put all agricultural land into the undeveloped category. Hence, when the two are compared, the paradoxical effect is that many individual squares, an actual majority in the case of the West Midlands-Leicestershire area, show apparent decreases in the degree of urban development between about 1950 and the early 1960s: a result which we know, from other evidence, to be wrong. Admittedly, as the separate analyses of Dr Robin Best show, there was still by 1950 a considerable area of defence land uses in many areas, much of which was returned to civilian uses, generally agriculture, in the succeeding decade, but it does not at all explain the full extent of the anomaly. Because of the very great number of cases in which the anomaly occurs, it is simply impossible to try to make detailed corrections from local evidence. In order to make any comparison at all, therefore, it is simply

Table 6.36

WEST MIDLANDS-LEICESTER AND SOUTH LANCASHIRE-NORTH CHESHIRE: ANALYSIS OF LAND USE CHANGES, CIRCA 1950–CIRCA 1960

Change in percentage of each 2 × 2 km square in developed land use	Number of 2 × 2 km squares in each group in: West Midlands and Leicestershire	South Lancashire and North Cheshire
+90– +100	—	—
+80– +90	—	—
+70– +80	—	—
+60– +70	4	1
+50– +60	7	1
+40– +50	13	2
+30– +40	17	9
+20– +30	21	15
+10– +20	77	37
0– +10	345	124
0– −10	363	67
−10– −20	156	32
−20– −30	41	7
−30– −40	11	5
−40– −50	6	—
−50– −60	4	—
−60– −70	1	—
−70– −80	2	—
−80– −90	—	—
−90– −100	2	—
Total squares	1,070	300

Source: County Planning Office, Land Use Surveys. Second Land Utilization Survey of Great Britain.

necessary to accept that the comparison of the two surveys involves a massive distortion. Almost certainly, a very large proportion of the apparent decreases should be ignored, but we are unable to say what proportion, or in what particular case this is so.

In the analysis that follows, therefore, we are forced simply to disregard these cases, and to concentrate on the squares which record positive changes in urban development. But because of the distortions which are clearly present, as well as the problem of sample error, we concentrate even further, on those squares where a very considerable degree of urban development (positive change) was recorded. Analysis of Table 6.36 shows clearly that only a small proportion of all squares (62 out of 1,070 in the Midlands, 28 out of 300 in Lancashire-Cheshire), recorded positive changes of 20 per cent or more between the two surveys. We concluded therefore that these should be the squares subjected to intensive analysis.

Our prime objective, in this analysis, was to consider the possible effect of planning policies. We wanted particularly to discover whether physical urban growth had been diverted systematically away from the larger urban masses, in pursuance of the objective of urban containment. Therefore, we needed a way of classifying urban masses by size. To do this, we first analysed the degree of development within each square at the beginning of the period, about 1950. The County Planning Office Surveys show that at this time, a large proportion of all squares in the two study areas (703 out of 1,070 squares or about two-thirds of all squares in the Midlands, 137 out of 300 or a little less than one-half of those in the more intensely built up North-West), were

Table 6.37

WEST MIDLANDS-LEICESTER AND SOUTH LANCASHIRE-NORTH CHESHIRE: ANALYSIS OF LAND USE, CIRCA 1950

Percentage of each 2 × 2 km square in developed land uses	Number of 2 × 2 km squares in each group in: West Midlands and Leicestershire	South Lancashire and North Cheshire
0–9	467	100
10–19	236	37
20–29	137	51
30–39	78	20
40–49	42	29
50–59	30	14
60–69	20	12
70–79	18	7
80–89	24	14
90–100	18	16
Total	1,070	300

Source: County Planning Office Land Use Surveys

Table 6.38

WEST MIDLANDS AND LEICESTER: ANALYSIS OF LAND USE, CIRCA 1950

	Numbers of 2 × 2 km squares having:				
	0–19 per cent	20–39 per cent	40–69 per cent	70 per cent and over	Total 20 per cent and over
	developed as urban land uses:				
Large urban areas*					
West Midlands conurbation (part)	—	40	33	38	111
Leicester-Loughborough	—	31	18	10	59
Coventry-Kenilworth	—	20	11	7	38
Nuneaton	—	9	7	1	17
Rugby	—	11	3	1	15
Warwick-Leamington	—	4	6	—	10
Small urban areas (16)	—	31	14	3	48
Isolated developments without urban nuclei†	—	69	—	—	69
Total 'developed' (20 per cent and more) squares	—	215	92	60	367
Undeveloped squares‡	703	—	—	—	—
Total squares	703	215	92	60	1,070

* 10 or more developed squares contiguous to each other and with some squares having 40 per cent or more development.

† One or more squares 20–39 per cent without contiguous development at 40 per cent or more.

‡ Includes 1 undeveloped square completely contained within West Midlands conurbation area.

Source: County Planning Office Land Use Surveys.

recorded as having less than 20 per cent development at this time; and, as already observed, this was almost certainly an underestimate of the true situation (Table 6.37). The analysis therefore concentrated on the squares recording 20 per cent or more or urban type development at this time, and classified them broadly into three groups: lightly developed (20–39 per cent), moderately developed (40–69 per cent), and heavily developed (70 and more per cent). Figures 6.10 and 6.11 show the pattern of physical development at this time according to these three categories.

The next stage was to analyse the distribution and the grouping of the developed squares. Tables 6.38 and 6.39 do this for the Midlands and the North-West study areas respectively. They show that in both areas, a very high proportion of the developed squares were in fact concentrated in substantial urban areas, that is, areas containing at least 10 (and sometimes very many more) contiguous developed squares. Thus, of the 367 developed squares in the Midlands area, 111 or nearly one-third were in the section of

Table 6.39

SOUTH LANCASHIRE-NORTH CHESHIRE: ANALYSIS OF LAND USE, CIRCA 1950

	Numbers of 2 × 2 km squares having:				
	0–19 per cent	20–39 per cent	40–69 per cent	70 per cent and over	Total 20 per cent and over
	developed as urban land uses:				
Large urban areas*					
SELNEC (South East Lancashire-North East Cheshire) conurbation (part)	—	32	38	34	104
Wigan-Warrington-Widnes (part)	—	18	7	3	28
Northwich area	—	6	6	—	12
Macclesfield	—	7	3	—	10
Small urban area (Knutsford)	—	2	1	—	3
Isolated developments without urban nuclei†	—	6	—	—	6
Total developed (20 per cent and more) squares	—	71	55	37	163
Undeveloped squares‡	137	—	—	—	—
Total squares	137	71	55	37	300

* 10 or more developed squares contiguous to each other and with some squares having 40 per cent or more development.

† One or more squares 20–39 per cent without contiguous development at 40 per cent or more.

‡ Includes 4 undeveloped squares completely contained within SELNEC area.

Source: County Planning Office Land Use Surveys.

the West Midlands conurbation area which appears on the west side of the study area; 59 more were in the Leicester-Loughborough area and another 38 in the Coventry area; 42 more were in three smaller urban conglomerations. Another 48 developed squares occurred in what are here described as small urban areas: that is, areas with less than 10 contiguous urban squares but with at least one square having 40 per cent or more development. Finally, 69 squares of light development (20–39 per cent) occurred in isolated form, either singly or in small groups, but not attached to any more intensively developed squares; these can invariably be regarded as very small towns or large village developments in the open countryside. Thus 250 out of 367 developed squares in the West Midlands were in urban agglomerations of at least 40 square kilometres extent; 298 out of 367 were in urban agglomerations of one sort or another.

In the North-West study area (Table 6.39) the degree of agglomeration of the development was if anything even more extreme. Out of a total of 163 developed squares, 104 or nearly two-thirds were in that part of the SELNEC (South-East Lancashire – North-East Cheshire, or Greater Manchester) conurbation which appears in the area; 50 or more were in smaller but still substantial urban areas; 3 were in one small urban area of less than 10 contiguous developed squares. Only 6 squares, out of a total of 163, were recorded as isolated and without a more intensively developed urban nucleus. In fact, the true degree of concentration is greater even than this, for the

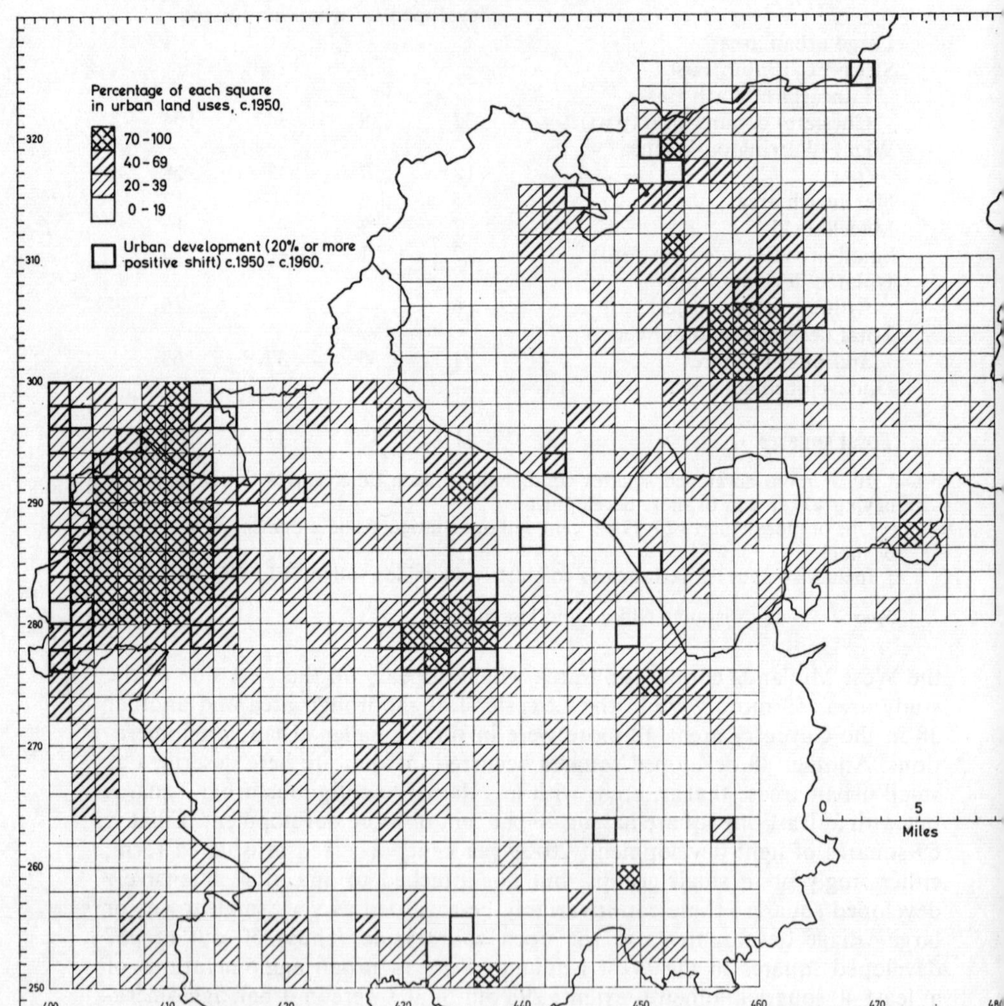

Figure 6.16 Birmingham-Coventry-Leicester: Urban Development, *circa* 1950–*circa* 1960, related to Degree of Urbanization, *circa* 1950

SELNEC concentration is joined continuously to the second largest urban agglomeration (Wigan-Warrington-Widnes), so that 132 out of 163 developed squares occurred in a single mass at the north border of the study area.

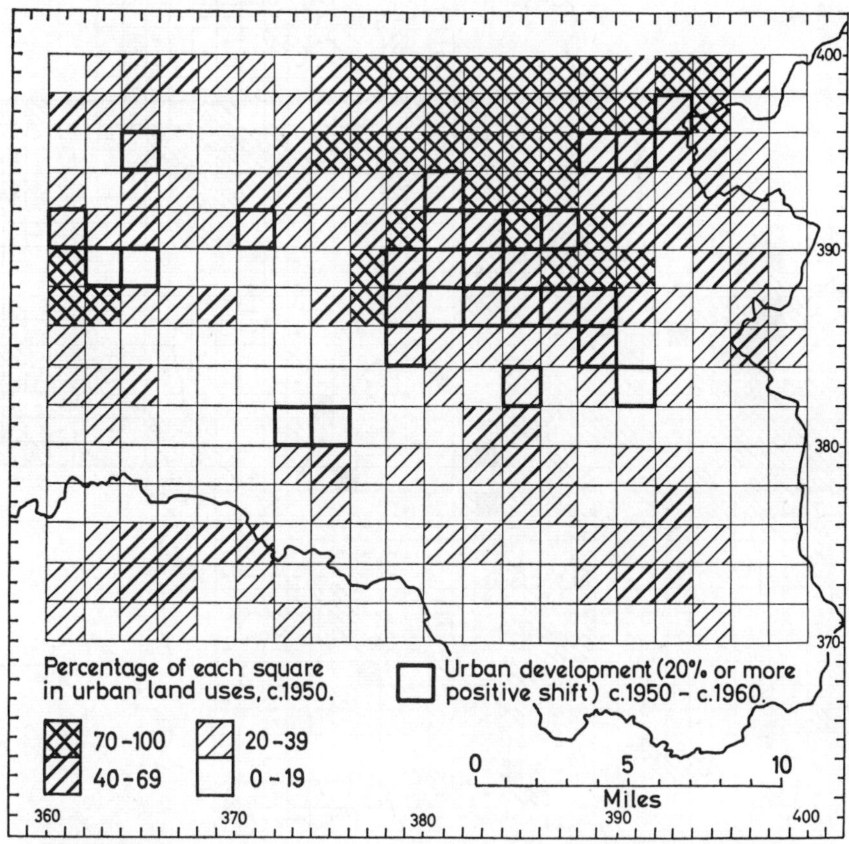

Figure 6.17 South Lancashire-North Cheshire: Urban Development, *circa* 1950–*circa* 1960, related to Degree of Urbanization, *circa* 1950

The simple classification just used, which classifies developed squares into three types of grouping (large urban, small urban, and isolated low intensity) forms a convenient basis for the analysis of subsequent urban development. We already argued that urban development, in the study period between the two land use analyses, should be defined in terms of a 20 per cent or greater positive change in the percentage of urban land use in any square. Figure 6.16 and Figure 6.17 show developing squares, on this criterion, against the background of classification of urban areas which has just been outlined, for

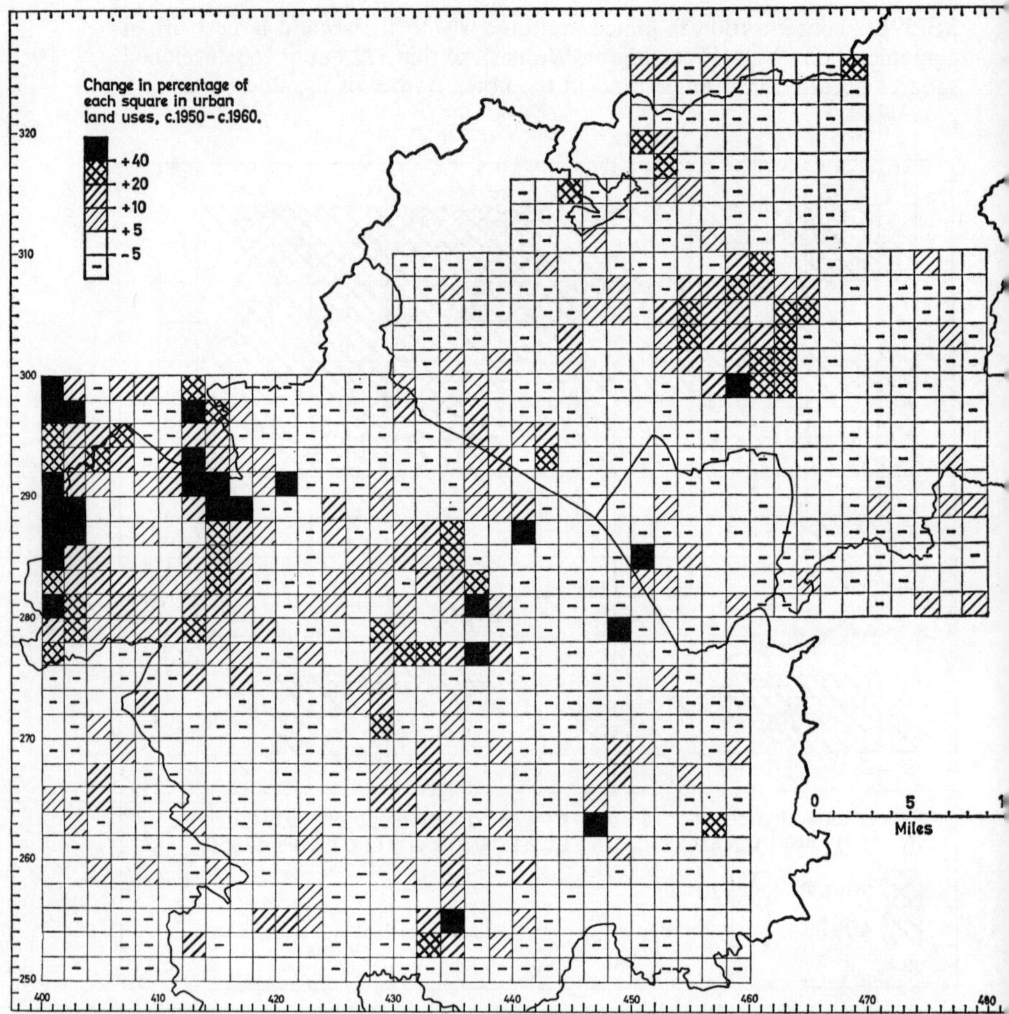

Figure 6.18 Birmingham-Coventry-Leicester: Degree of Urban Development, *circa* 1950–*circa* 1960

the Midlands and North-West areas respectively. Figures 6.18 and 6.19 show the pattern of developing squares in finer detail.

For further analysis, one additional simple scheme of classification is needed. The impact of urban development, as defined here, on any particular square will obviously depend on the amount of previous urban development. There is a great difference, for instance, between a 20 per cent addition to urban development applied to a square where previously there was only 5 per cent of such development, and the same percentage applied to a square

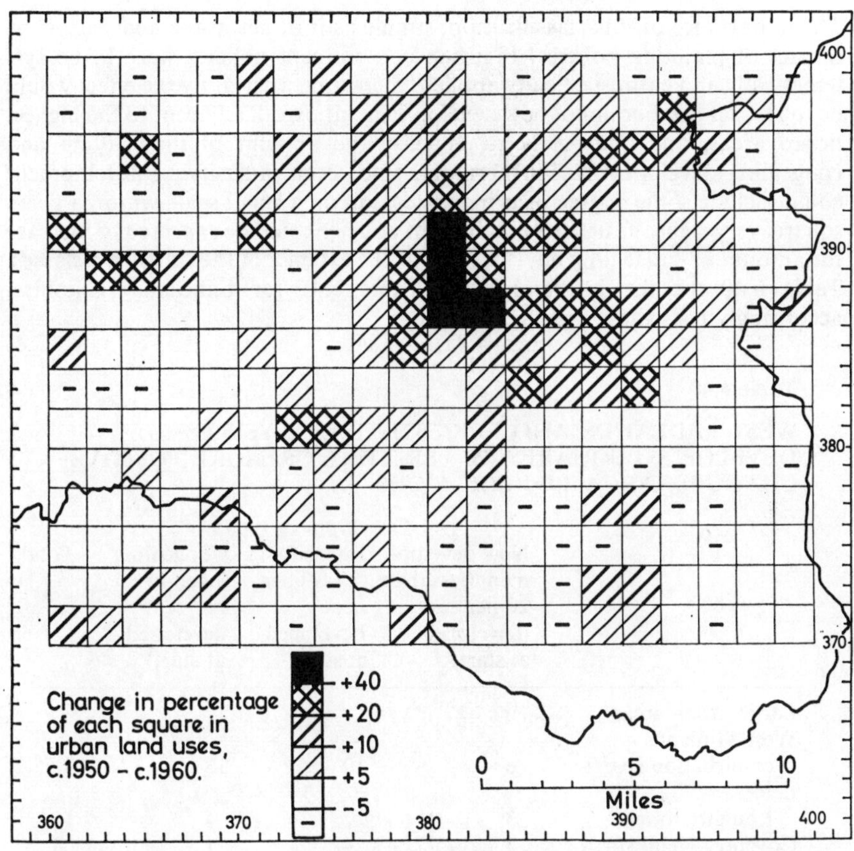

Figure 6.19 South Lancashire-North Cheshire: Degree of Urban Development, *circa* 1950–*circa* 1960

with 75 per cent of development. Using the simple classification suggested earlier, we can relate the change to the degree of previous development by means of this terminology:

Previous degree of development	Type of development in this period	Minimum degree of development at end of period per cent
None (i.e. less than 20 per cent)	New	20
Light (i.e. 20–39 per cent)	Intensifying	40
Moderate (i.e. 40–69 per cent)	Congealing	60
Heavy (i.e. 70 per cent and more)	Congealing (very rare)	90

The importance of this classification, simple as it is, lies in the analysis of the impact of planning policies. If urban containment policies were to be systematically and enthusiastically applied, then almost certainly the effect would be to restrict the amount of new development, above all adjacent to the biggest urban areas, and conversely to increase the amount of intensifying and congealing development. Furthermore, since even intensifying development could include some degree of urban extension on a small scale within a given square, very rigorous urban containment policies could be expected to increase the amount of congealing development at the expense of the other two classes. Table 6.40 for the Midlands, and Table 6.41 for Lancashire-Cheshire, accordingly tests these hypotheses.

Table 6.40

WEST MIDLANDS AND LEICESTER: ANALYSIS OF DEVELOPING SQUARES (20 PER CENT OR MORE POSITIVE CHANGE), CIRCA 1950–CIRCA 1960

	Development type:			
	New development (less than 20 per cent (developed at start)	Intensifying (20–39 per cent developed at start)	Congealing (over 40 per cent developed at start)	Total
Large urban areas				
West Midlands conurbation (part)	6	10	15	31
Leicester-Loughborough	3	7	4	14
Coventry-Kenilworth	3	4	1	8
Small urban areas (4)	3	—	1	4
Isolated developments without urban nuclei	—	1	—	1
Not attached to previous development	4	—	—	4
Total squares developed	19	22	21	62

Source: County Planning Office Land Use Surveys. Second Land Utilization Survey of Britain.

In the Midlands, Table 6.40 shows that the amount of new development has been restricted, especially around the conurbation, though it has not been entirely inhibited. 19 squares have been newly developed according to the criterion used, but 7, or over one-third, are isolated developments in the countryside, either completely on their own, or attached to existing low density developments. 3 more are attached to small urban areas, 3 each to the Leicester and Coventry areas, and only 6 in all to the West Midlands

Table 6.41

SOUTH LANCASHIRE-NORTH CHESHIRE: ANALYSIS OF DEVELOPING SQUARES (20 PER CENT OR MORE POSITIVE CHANGE), CIRCA 1950–CIRCA 1960

	Development type:			
	New development (less than 20 per cent developed at start)	Intensifying (20–39 per cent developed at start)	Congealing (over 40 per cent developed at start)	Total
Large urban areas				
SELNEC (South-East Lancashire-North-East Cheshire) conurbation (part)	2	7	13	22
Wigan-Warrington-Widnes (part)	2	2	—	4
Small urban area (Knutsford)	2	—	—	2
Isolated developments without urban nuclei	—	—	—	—
Not attached to previous development	—	—	—	—
Total squares developed	6	9	13	28

Source: County Planning Office Land Use Surveys. Second Land Utilization Survey of Britain.

conurbation – a very restricted total, when it is remembered that this agglomeration included 111 developed squares at the beginning of the period. Conversely, it is evident that this area has adapted to the situation by developing more intensively within its own urban fence: 10 out of 22 intensifying squares, and no less than 15 out of 21 congealing squares, are to be found here, while nearly all the other squares in these categories are in the next two biggest urban areas of Leicester-Loughborough and Coventry-Kenilworth. The ratio which the three categories of development bear to each other, indeed, does not vary significantly as between these three biggest urban areas.

In the North-West (Table 6.41) the impact of containment has been even more drastic. Only 6 squares, out of 28 developing squares, can be classed as newly developing; and two of these are attached to a single small urban area, Knutsford in Cheshire. The Greater Manchester conurbation, with 104 developed squares inside the study area at the start of the period, numbers only two newly developing squares. In comparison, 7 squares can be described as intensifying and no less than 13 as congealing: a most remarkable case of a major urban area developing almost entirely in the form of greater intensity within its own boundaries.

Despite all the weaknesses in the comparison, then, it does point to a clear and consistent conclusion. The policy of urban containment has been applied enthusiastically by the local planning authorities bordering the main urban areas, particularly the major conurbations, and it has had a clear physical impact. During the 1950s and the beginning of the 1960s, the period between the two land use analyses, these urban areas were increasingly forced to house their surplus populations within their own built-up areas. How this situation developed, and how the city and conurbation authorities responded, is traced out in detail, for these and other study areas, in Chapters Eight to Twelve inclusive; and Chapter Thirteen tries to sum up generally on the experience. But before this, in Chapter Seven, it is useful to make a more detailed analysis of migration patterns and of social changes in the five study areas than was possible in this necessarily general chapter.

CHAPTER SEVEN

MIGRATION AND SOCIAL POLARIZATION: A STUDY IN FIVE AREAS OF MEGALOPOLIS

This chapter takes up where Chapter Six left off, and goes into a more detailed analysis of migration and social change in the five detailed study areas identified there. First, it analyses migration movements in the year 1960–61. It shows that there is a very general trend for long-distance migration into the cores of Standard Metropolitan Areas, paralleled by shorter distance migration from the cores to immediately contiguous areas or just beyond. There are however some differences in pattern between the study areas; thus in London's western fringes there is a marked movement from Greater London to the core areas of SMLAs at (or just beyond) the edge of the London commuting area, while in the North-West the pattern is complicated by the general out-movement from the area.

Secondly, the chapter seeks to discover whether social polarization, in the sense of increasing segregation of different socio-economic groups, is occurring in the study areas. Using data on socio-economic groups and on housing tenure from 1961 and 1966, it concludes that there is some evidence of segregation of different groups: white-collar groups, and more skilled blue-collar workers, are migrating from the cores to the rings, leaving the less skilled manual workers behind. But this is not accompanied, apparently, by segregation of different types of housing tenure as between cores and rings.

Roy Drewett wrote the section on migration, Werner Heidemann the section on social polarization. Peter Hall edited the whole chapter.

INTRODUCTION

In the second half of Chapter Six we have identified five areas of rapid postwar growth and change in Megalopolis England: London's western fringes, South Hampshire, the Birmingham-Coventry belt, Leicester and Leicestershire, and South Lancashire-North Cheshire, and have made a detailed analysis of population and employment changes within each of them. We have concluded that though there is a general and a marked tendency to decentralization of people and jobs in all areas, the precise expression of the trend differs from area to area. While the usual case is decentralization of people from cores to rings within the metropolitan areas, followed after a time by decentralization of employment, in London there has been a tendency to decentralize to quite separate metropolitan areas at the edge of the London commuting zone and beyond, while in the North-West decentralization has to be seen against a background of overall out-movement from the region.

This overall tendency to decentralization is however an oversimplification of the actual process of movement. In this chapter, therefore, we take the analysis deeper, in two ways. First, we analyse the patterns of migration in our five study areas in more detail, considering not merely the net changes in population, but the gross flows that produce them. And secondly, we look at changes in the overall socio-economic composition within the metropolitan areas that make up our chosen study areas, together with changes in the patterns of housing tenure within them. These two parallel analyses are necessarily both technical in character, and detailed. But together, they throw important light on the process of social change within some of the most rapidly-growing urban areas in postwar Britain, which it is necessary to understand in order to appreciate the full effect of the planning policies whose history is recounted in Chapters Eight to Twelve.

MIGRATION IN THE FIVE STUDY AREAS: LONDON'S WESTERN FRINGES

Detailed and reliable information on migration patterns in Britain only became available for the first time in the 1960s; both the 1961 and the 1966

Table 7.1

MIGRATION ANALYSIS, WEST LONDON METROPOLITAN SECTOR, 1960–1961

(a) CORES

In-Migration

	SMLA core reception						
Source Area	Walton and Weybridge U.D.	Woking U.D.	Slough M.B.	Guildford M.B.	Reading C.B.	High Wycombe M.B.	Aldershot M.B.
				Total numbers			
Peripheral	410	100	470	370	1,200	580	100
Local	520	1,810	760	1,220	1,180	420	640
Greater London	1,020	1,810	2,555	590	1,210	1,000	230
Rest of Britain	740	990	1,390	920	1,850	960	1,030
Abroad	590	760	290	220	580	440	350
Total	3,280	5,740	5,460	3,920	6,020	3,400	2,350
				Percentages			
Peripheral	12·5	1·8	8·6	11·1	19·6	17·1	4·3
Local	15·9	33·1	13·9	36·7	19·6	12·3	27·2
Greater London	31·1	33·1	46·7	17·8	20·1	29·4	9·8
Rest of Britain	22·6	18·1	25·5	27·7	30·7	28·2	43·8
Abroad	17·9	13·9	5·3	6·6	9·6	12·9	14·9
Total	100·0	100·0	100·0	100·0	100·0	100·0	100·0

Out-Migration

Reception area	SMLA core source Walton and Weybridge U.D.	Woking U.D.	Slough M.B.	Guildford M.B.	Reading C.B.	High Wycombe M.B.	Aldershot M.B.
	Total numbers						
Peripheral	310	280	780	410	1,920	570	350
Local	1,110	2,140	1,410	1,080	1,460	500	1,670
Greater London	620	690	800	200	890	290	310
Rest of Britain	660	1,160	1,420	1,110	1,710	860	1,380
Abroad	—	—	—	—	—	—	—
Total	2,700	4,270	4,410	2,800	5,980	2,220	3,710
	Percentages						
Peripheral	11·5	6·6	17·7	14·6	32·1	25·7	9·4
Local	41·1	50·1	31·9	38·6	24·4	22·5	45·0
Greater London	22·9	16·2	18·1	7·1	14·9	13·1	8·4
Rest of Britain	24·4	27·2	32·2	39·6	28·6	38·7	37·2
Abroad	—	—	—	—	—	—	—
Total	100·0	100·0	100·0	100·0	100·0	100·0	100·0

Migration Balance

Area of exchange	SMLA core area Walton and Weybridge U.D.	Woking U.D.	Slough M.B.	Guildford M.B.	Reading C.B.	High Wycombe M.B.	Aldershot M.B.
	Total numbers						
Peripheral	+100	−180	−310	−40	−720	+10	−250
Local	−590	−330	−650	+140	−280	−80	−1,030
Greater London	+400	+1,120	+1,750	+390	+320	+710	−80
Rest of Britain	+580	−170	−30	−190	+140	+100	−350
Abroad	+90	+760	+290	+220	+580	+440	+350
Total	+580	+1,200	+1,050	+520	+40	+1,180	−1,360

(b) RINGS

In-Migration

Source area	SMLA ring reception Sunbury on Thames U.D.	Staines U.D.	Eton R.D.	Wokingham R.D.	Easthampstead R.D.	Bradfield R.D.
	Total numbers					
Peripheral	640	1,440	1,060	1,470	540	1,290
Local	460	670	720	980	360	570
Greater London	290	570	2,040	1,650	2,830	660
Rest of Britain	720	790	1,020	1,520	1,500	800
Abroad	120	280	740	250	350	180
Total	2,230	3,750	5,580	5,870	5,580	3,500
	Percentages					
Peripheral	28·7	38·4	18·9	25·0	9·7	36·9
Local	20·6	17·9	12·9	16·7	6·5	16·3
Greater London	13·0	15·2	36·6	28·1	50·7	18·9
Rest of Britain	32·3	21·1	18·3	25·9	26·9	22·9
Abroad	5·4	7·6	13·3	4·3	6·3	5·1
Total	100·0	100·0	100·0	100·0	100·0	100·0

Out-Migration

Reception area	SMLA ring source					
	Sunbury on Thames U.D.	Staines U.D.	Eton R.D.	Wokingham R.D.	Easthampstead R.D.	Bradfield R.D.
			Total numbers			
Peripheral	840	730	960	800	750	500
Local	910	1,040	530	570	270	440
Greater London	240	190	1,050	110	660	—
Rest of Britain	600	1,000	990	790	780	650
Abroad	—	—	—	—	—	—
Total	2,590	2,960	3,530	2,270	2,460	1,590
			Percentages			
Peripheral	32·4	24·7	27·2	35·2	30·5	31·5
Local	35·1	35·1	15·0	25·1	10·9	27·7
Greater London	9·3	6·4	29·7	4·8	26·8	—
Rest of Britain	23·2	33·8	28·0	34·8	31·7	40·9
Abroad	—	—	—	—	—	—
Total	100·0	100·0	100·0	100·0	100·0	100·0

Migration Balance

Area of exchange	SMLA ring area					
	Sunbury on Thames U.D.	Staines U.D.	Eton R.D.	Wokingham R.D.	Easthampstead R.D.	Bradfield R.D.
			Total numbers			
Peripheral	−200	+710	+100	+670	−210	+790
Local	−450	−370	+190	+410	+90	+130
Greater London	+50	+380	+990	+1,540	+2,170	+660
Rest of Britain	+120	−210	+30	+730	+720	+150
Abroad	+120	+280	+740	+250	+350	+180
Total	−360	+790	+2,050	+3,600	+3,120	+1910

Source: Census 1961, England and Wales, *Migration Tables.*

Censuses contained detailed tabulations of migration between local authority areas over one year and five year periods preceding the Census date. The analysis in this chapter relates to the migration patterns in the single year 1960–61, as recorded in the Census of 1961. Throughout, a standardized grouping of local authorities is used for the purpose of simplicity:

peripheral, i.e. immediately contiguous local authorities;
local, i.e. non-contiguous local authorities and adjoining counties;
Greater London, i.e. the conurbation as defined in 1961;
the rest of Great Britain; and
abroad; by definition, figures of migration are available for in-migration from abroad only.

The analysis for the first detailed study area, comprising the western section of the London SMLA and the adjacent SMLAs to the west of it, is

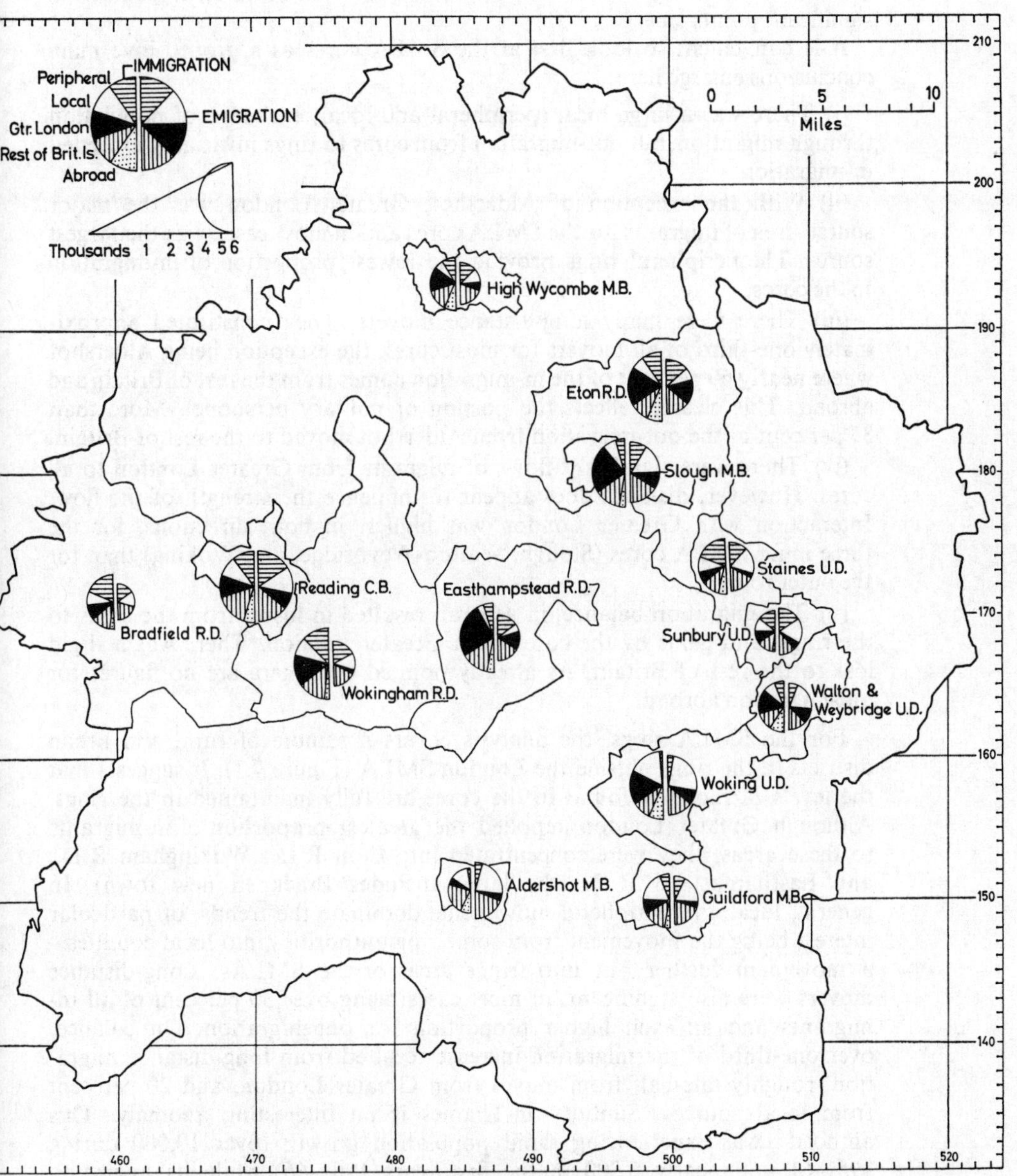

Figure 7.1 London West Metropolitan Sector: Migration Patterns, 1960–1961

set out in Table 7.1 and is mapped in Figure 7.1. From it, a number of significant points emerge.

It is convenient to look first at the SMLA cores as a group. Five main conclusions emerge here:

(i) There was a large local (peripheral and local) exchange of population through migration, but out-migration from cores to rings invariably exceeded in-migration.

(ii) With the exception of Aldershot, Greater London was the major source-area of migrants for the SMLA cores and in most cases was the largest source. The peripheral rings provide the lowest proportion of in-migration to the cores.

(iii) There were many long-distance movers. They constituted approximately one-third of all movers for most cores, the exception being Aldershot where nearly 60 per cent of the in-migration comes from the rest of Britain and abroad. This clearly reflects the posting of military personnel. More than 37 per cent of the out-migration from Aldershot moved to the rest of Britain.

(iv) There were significant flows of migrants from Greater London to all cores. However, distance does appear to influence the strength of the flow. Interaction with Greater London was higher, in both directions, for the three inner SMLA cores (Slough, Walton-Weybridge, and Woking) than for the outer four.

(v) The migration balance, in general, resulted in losses from the cores to the rings, and gains by the cores from Greater London. There was a slight loss to the rest of Britain. As already pointed out, there are no figures for out-migration abroad.

For the SMLA rings, the analysis covers a sample of rural and urban districts in the rings outside the London SMLA (Figure 7.1). It suggests that the levels of mobility found in the cores are fully maintained in the rings. Although Greater London supplied the greatest proportion of in-migrants to these areas, they were concentrated into Eton R.D., Wokingham R.D., and Easthampstead R.D. (the latter includes Bracknell new town). In general, local and peripheral movements dominate the trends, of particular interest being the movement from some ring authorities into local counties – a movement further out into fringe areas of the SMLAs. Long-distance movers were also significant, in most cases being over 30 per cent of all in-migrants and an even higher proportion for out-migration. On balance, over one-third of the migration increase resulted from long-distance migration, roughly one-half from moves from Greater London, and 20 per cent from local sources. Sunbury-on-Thames is an interesting anomaly. This authority was experiencing rapid population growth (over 10,000 during 1951–61 and nearly 6,000 in the five years 1961–66) while its migration balance was negative during 1960–61. On balance the rings were gaining from the cores, Greater London and the rest of Britain. With the exception of Easthampstead and Eton there was little reverse migration to Greater London.

Table 7.2

MIGRATION ANALYSIS, SOUTH HAMPSHIRE, 1960–1961

(a) CORES

	SMLA core source		SMLA core reception		SMLA core area	
	In-Migration		Out-Migration		Migration balance	
Area of exchange	Southampton C.B.	Portsmouth C.B.	Southampton C.B.	Portsmouth C.B.	Southampton C.B.	Portsmouth C.B.
			Total numbers			
Peripheral	1,710	1,840	2,860	4,240	−1,150	−2,300
Local	1,870	2,220	2,040	2,190	−170	430
Greater London	740	1,280	750	1,390	−10	−110
Rest of Britain	2,360	3,800	1,910	2,630	450	1,270
Abroad	1,190	2,030	—	—	1,190	2,020
Total	7,870	11,360	7,560	10,450	310	910
			Percentages			
Peripheral	21·7	17·1	37·8	40·6	—	—
Local	23·8	19·5	27·0	21·0	—	—
Greater London	9·4	11·3	9·9	13·3	—	—
Rest of Britain	30·0	34·3	25·3	25·1	—	—
Abroad	15·1	17·8	—	—	—	—
Total	100·0	100·0	100·0	100·0	—	—

(b) RINGS

In-Migration

Source area	SMLA ring reception New Forest R.D.	Eastleigh R.D.	Winchester M.B.	Winchester R.D.	Droxford R.D.	Fareham R.D.	Havant and Waterloo U.D.	Gosport M.B.
	Total numbers							
Peripheral	1,260	500	310	1,710	440	1,760	3,010	940
Local	710	600	700	1,170	740	980	1,980	610
Greater London	530	130	430	300	120	780	1,130	740
Rest of Britain	1,460	890	580	1,240	820	1,820	1,560	2,330
Abroad	360	160	260	320	250	510	690	1,060
Total	4,320	2,080	2,280	4,740	2,370	5,600	8,370	9,680
	Percentages							
Peripheral	29·2	24·0	13·6	36·0	18·6	32·0	36·0	16·6
Local	16·4	28·8	30·7	24·7	31·2	17·8	23·7	10·7
Greater London	12·3	6·3	18·9	6·3	5·1	13·3	13·5	13·0
Rest of Britain	33·8	33·2	25·4	26·2	34·6	27·6	18·6	41·0
Abroad	8·3	7·7	11·4	6·8	10·5	9·3	8·2	18·7
Total	100·0	100·0	100·0	100·0	100·0	100·0	100·0	100·0

Out-Migration

	SMLA ring source							
Reception area	New Forest R.D.	Eastleigh R.D.	Winchester M.B.	Winchester R.D.	Droxford R.D.	Fareham R.D.	Havant and Waterloo U.D.	Gosport M.B.
				Total numbers				
Peripheral	860	680	260	1,010	—	800	1,430	1,370
Local	320	630	740	900	—	960	980	1,090
Greater London	—	—	120	—	—	240	340	230
Rest of Britain	1,180	770	720	1,020	—	1,000	1,060	2,110
Abroad	—	—	—	—	—	—	—	—
Total	2,860	2,030	1,840	2,930	—	3,000	3,790	4,800
				Percentages				
Peripheral	36·4	31·0	14·1	34·5	—	26·7	37·7	28·5
Local	13·6	31·0	40·2	30·7	—	32·0	25·3	22·7
Greater London	—	—	6·6	—	—	8·0	9·0	4·8
Rest of Britain	50·0	38·0	39·1	34·8	—	33·3	28·0	44·0
Abroad	—	—	—	—	—	—	—	—
Total	100·0	100·0	100·0	100·0	—	100·0	100·0	100·0

Migration balance

	SMLA ring area							
Area of exchange	New Forest R.D.	Eastleigh R.D.	Winchester M.B.	Winchester R.D.	Droxford R.D.	Fareham R.D.	Havant and Waterloo U.D.	Gosport M.B.
				Total numbers				
Peripheral	+400	−130	+50	+700	—	+960	+1,580	−430
Local	+390	−30	−40	+270	—	+20	+1,020	−480
Greater London	+530	+130	+310	+300	—	+490	+790	+510
Rest of Britain	+29	−80	−140	+220	—	+520	+550	+220
Abroad	+350	+160	+260	+320	—	+510	+690	+1,060
Total	+1,960	+50	+440	+1,810	—	+2,500	+4,480	+4,880

Source: Census 1961, England and Wales, *Migration Tables.*

When the relationship between the cores and the rings is examined we find that in most cases more people moved *out* of the cores to local areas than moved *in* from local areas. These two trends are consistent with the hypothesis that people who migrate long distances initially locate near or in large centres of population (the cores) because they have low levels of information concerning the choice of house that is available (housing markets are notoriously parochial). As time elapses some of these people re-locate locally to a more suitable residence, the choice reflecting higher levels of information which have been assimilated with time. Other local moves can be explained by changes in income and stages in the life cycle as the requirements for space fluctuate. For the long-distance migrant the SMLA cores may act as a staging post or springboard for a second but much shorter move. It is known that people who have already made one move have a high propensity to make a second. This hypothesis is impossible to test rigorously from the census data used here for the migration analysis. We return to it in the detailed study of movers made specially as part of our programme, which is reported in Chapter Five (Volume Two) of this study.

MIGRATION IN SOUTH HAMPSHIRE

The in-migration and out-migration pattern for the local authorities in the Southampton and Portsmouth SMLAs is shown in Table 7.2 and mapped in Figure 7.2. The classification of origins and destinations is the same as for the London sector (see page 388). Again, it is convenient to treat cores and rings separately.

For the two cores, the following trends emerge:

(i) Although Portsmouth experienced more immigration and emigration than did Southampton, the proportional flows to and from each core were very similar. The rest of Britain provided the bulk of the in-migration.

(ii) There were large peripheral and local exchanges in both directions, but out-migration was dominant and these out-flows went mainly to peripheral authorities, closely followed by local areas and the rest of Britain. This pattern then was very similar to that of west London.

(iii) As one would expect, the influence of London has diminished in comparison to the previous region discussed. The flows to and from London were roughly equal.

(iv) Many long-distance movers entered or left the region. Over 45 per cent of the immigrants to Southampton and over 51 per cent to Portsmouth originated from the rest of Britain or abroad. Approximately 25 per cent of all people leaving the core left the region for the rest of Britain (excluding Greater London).

(v) In both cities, the losses from the cores to nearby authorities were compensated for by the volume of long-distance migration. Both cores gained on balance from migration during the period.

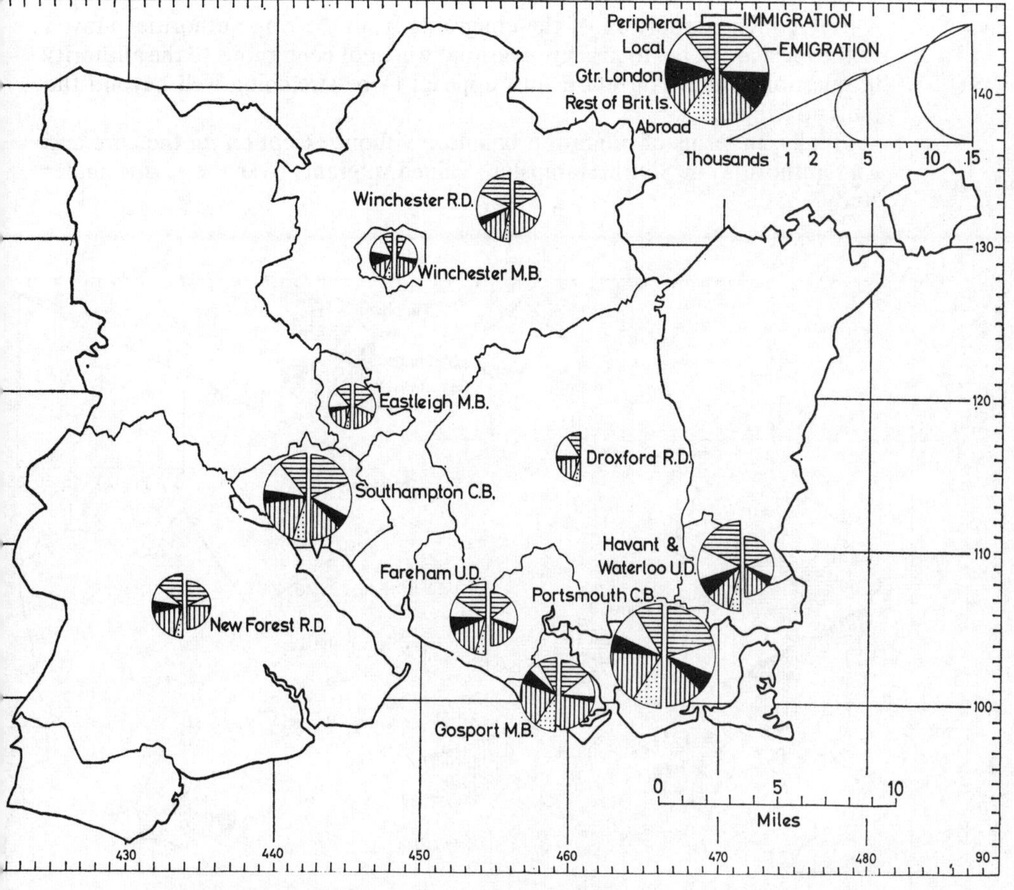

Figure 7.2 South Hampshire: Migration Patterns, 1960–1961

For the sample of ring authorities, the following trends emerge:

(i) Long-distance migration again dominated the pattern. With the exception of Havant and Waterloo, the long-distance mover made up over 30 per cent of all immigrants; and for all authorities, over 30 per cent of emigrants moved outside the region.

(ii) Once again, there was considerable movement between the peripheral and local areas; in many cases over 60 per cent of moves both in and out were in this category. In most areas there was more peripheral movement out of the authority than back again.

(iii) As a source area, Greater London was of greater significance for the rings than for the cores. All ring authorities received migrants from London and these flows were consistently higher than the return flows to London; in fact, return flows were only recorded for half of the authorities investigated.

(iv) A high proportion of the emigrants from the ring authorities moved to the local areas, i.e. to nearby areas that were not contiguous to the authority in question. Suburbanization thus appears to be stretching well beyond the built up fringes.

Finally, in terms of migration balance, without exception *all* the core and ring authorities in South Hampshire gained migrants over the period under study.

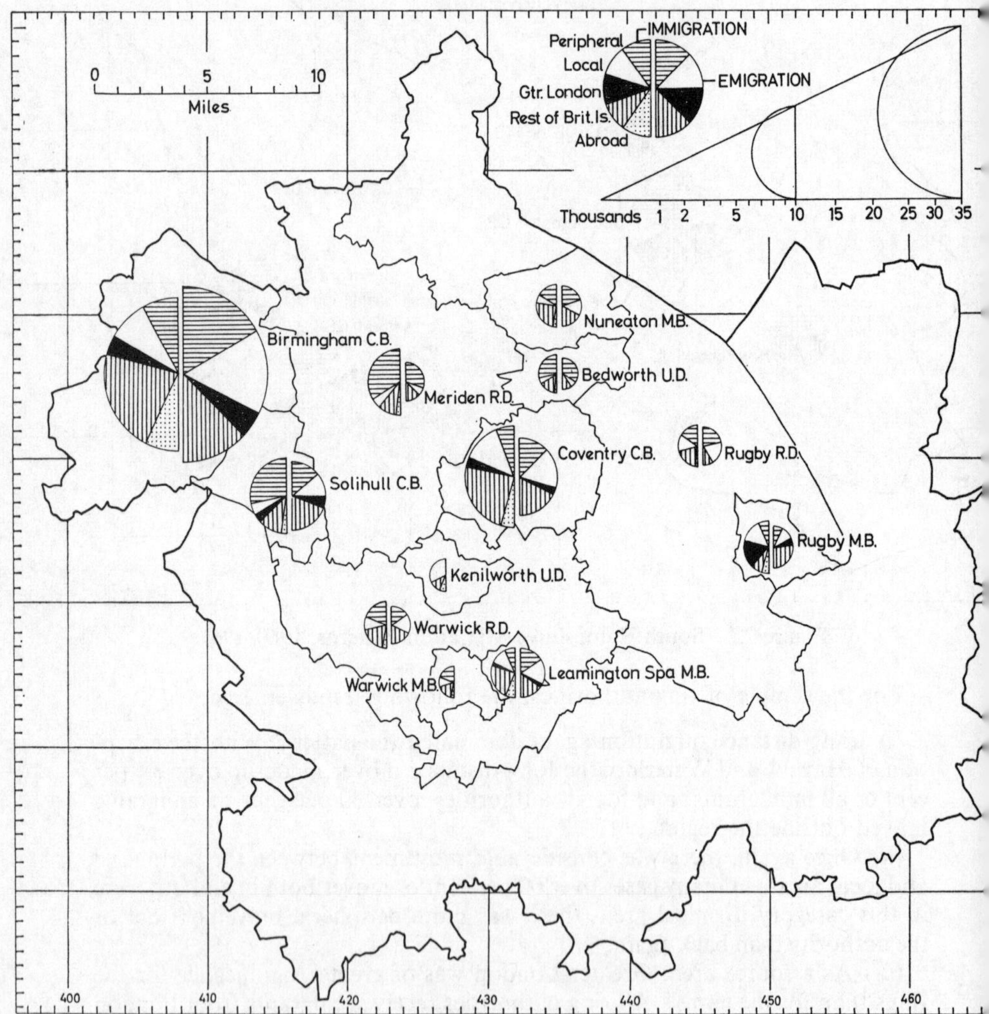

Figure 7.3 West Midlands: Migration Patterns, 1960–1961

Table 7.3

MIGRATION ANALYSIS, BIRMINGHAM-COVENTRY AREA, 1960–1961

(a) CORES

In-Migration

Source area	SMLA core reception: Birmingham C.B.	Coventry C.B.	Rugby M.B.	Royal Leamington Spa M.B.	Nuneaton M.B.
			Total numbers		
Peripheral	4,110	1,400	410	870	690
Local	4,600	8,000	880	620	510
Greater London	2,240	780	110	130	—
Rest of Britain	11,650	6,670	450	1,310	820
Abroad	8,850	1,090	290	850	110
Total	26,460	11,890	8,140	2,780	2,130
			Percentages		
Peripheral	15·5	11·8	19·2	13·3	32·4
Local	17·4	25·2	41·1	22·3	23·9
Greater London	8·5	6·1	5·1	4·7	—
Rest of Britain	44·1	47·7	21·0	47·1	38·5
Abroad	14·5	9·2	13·6	12·6	5·2
Total	100·0	100·0	100·0	100·0	100·0

Out-Migration

Reception area	SMLA core source: Birmingham C.B.	Coventry C.B.	Rugby M.B.	Royal Leamington Spa M.B.	Nuneaton M.B.
			Total numbers		
Peripheral	12,110	1,710	290	820	750
Local	10,740	2,340	420	890	490
Greater London	8,620	460	240	100	—
Rest of Britain	8,850	2,430	1,090	800	640
Abroad	—	—	—	—	—
Total	35,320	6,930	2,040	2,610	1,880
			Percentages		
Peripheral	34·3	24·7	14·2	31·4	39·9
Local	30·4	33·8	20·6	34·1	26·1
Greater London	10·2	6·5	11·8	3·8	—
Rest of Britain	25·1	35·0	53·4	30·7	34·0
Abroad	—	—	—	—	—
Total	100·0	100·0	100·0	100·0	100·0

Migration Balance

Area of exchange	SMLA core area: Birmingham C.B.	Coventry C.B.	Rugby M.B.	Royal Leamington Spa M.B.	Nuneaton M.B.
			Total numbers		
Peripheral	−8,000	−310	+120	−450	−60
Local	−6,140	+660	+460	−270	+20
Greater London	−1,380	+280	−130	−130	—
Rest of Britain	+2,800	+3,240	−640	+510	+180
Abroad	+8,850	+1,090	+290	+350	+110
Total	−8,970	+4,950	+1,100	+170	+250

(b) RINGS

In-Migration

Source area	SMLA ring reception						
	Solihull C.B.	Bedworth U.D.	Kenilworth U.D.	Warwick M.B.	Warwick R.D.	Rugby R.D.	Meriden R.D.
				Total numbers			
Peripheral	3,850	980	—	410	960	600	3,440
Local	700	160	790	1220	480	520	530
Greater London	430	—	—	—	—	—	—
Rest of Britain	1,460	610	290	380	960	770	980
Abroad	280	40	160	70	130	60	200
Total	6,720	1,640	1,240	1,080	2,530	1,950	5,120
				Percentages			
Peripheral	57·3	56·7	—	37·9	37·9	30·8	67·2
Local	10·4	9·8	63·7	20·4	19·0	26·6	10·3
Greater London	6·4	—	—	—	—	—	—
Rest of Britain	21·7	31·1	23·4	35·2	37·9	39·5	18·6
Abroad	4·2	2·4	12·9	6·5	5·2	3·1	3·9
Total	100·0	100·0	100·0	100·0	100·0	100·0	100·0

Out-Migration

Reception area	SMLA ring source						
	Solihull C.B.	Bedworth U.D.	Kenilworth U.D.	Warwick M.B.	Warwick R.D.	Rugby R.D.	Meriden R.D.
				Total numbers			
Peripheral	1,470	750	—	—	500	740	1,100
Local	1,250	140	—	—	530	660	260
Greater London	570	—	—	—	—	—	—
Rest of Britain	2,040	210	—	—	590	280	440
Abroad	—	—	—	—	—	—	—
Total	5,330	1,100	—	—	1,620	1,680	1,800
				Percentages			
Peripheral	27·6	68·2	—	—	30·9	44·0	61·1
Local	23·5	12·7	—	—	32·7	39·3	14·4
Greater London	10·7	—	—	—	—	—	—
Rest of Britain	38·2	19·1	—	—	36·4	16·7	24·5
Abroad	—	—	—	—	—	—	—
Total	100·0	100·0	—	—	100·0	100·0	100·0

Migration Balance

Area of exchange	SMLA ring area						
	Solihull C.B.	Bedworth U.D.	Kenilworth U.D.	Warwick M.B.	Warwick R.D.	Rugby R.D.	Meriden R.D.
				Total numbers			
Peripheral	+2,380	+180	—	—	+460	−140	+2,340
Local	−550	+20	—	—	−50	−140	+270
Greater London	−140	—	—	—	—	—	—
Rest of Britain	−580	+300	—	—	+370	+490	+510
Abroad	+280	+40	—	—	+180	+60	+200
Total	+1,390	+540	—	—	+910	+270	+3,320

Source: Census 1961, England and Wales, *Migration Tables.*

MIGRATION IN THE BIRMINGHAM-COVENTRY AREA

The main trends are summarized in Table 7.3 and Figure 7.3. Of all the individual local authorities analysed in this study area, Birmingham C.B. was the only authority to experience a migration balance deficit. All the other authorities gained in population through migration. With the exception of Rugby, the in-migration to cores was dominated by flows from the rest of Britain. For these cores the strength of the flows accounted for between 38 and 47 per cent of the immigration. If overseas immigration is included the totals were even higher. The proportion of migrants from overseas was similar to the proportions in the cores in the West London Metropolitan Sector and South Hampshire (between 5 and 14 per cent).

The in-migration from the periphery to the cores was again low; it was considerably less than the proportions emigrating from the cores to local and peripheral areas. The only exception to this trend was Rugby, where peripheral immigration outnumbers the emigration. Coventry and Rugby also gained from local migration.

For the ring authorities the values for overseas in-migration were much lower than for the cores. The proportion coming from the rest of Britain was also lower, while the influence of Greater London was of little significance in either direction, except in Solihull which is physically contiguous with the Birmingham C.B. Migration in the ring was completely dominated by the massive exchanges with peripheral and local (non-contiguous) areas. The in-migration was dominated by peripheral movement while the emigration was characterized by a longer move to nearby counties.

Table 7.4
MIGRATION ANALYSIS, LEICESTER-LEICESTERSHIRE, 1960–1961
(a) CORE

	In-Migration	Out-Migration	Migration balance
		SMLA core area	
Area of exchange	Leicester C.B.	Leicester C.B.	Leicester C.B.
		Total numbers	
Peripheral	1,470	6,350	−4,880
Local	1,560	2,520	−960
Greater London	1,110	1,050	+60
Rest of Britain	3,070	2,840	+230
Abroad	1,060	—	+1,030
Total	8,270	12,760	−4,490
		Percentages	
Peripheral	17·8	49·8	—
Local	18·9	19·7	—
Greater London	13·4	8·2	—
Rest of Britain	37·1	22·3	—
Abroad	12·8	—	—
Total	100·0	100·0	—

(b) RING

In-Migration

Source area	Oadby U.D.	Wigston U.D.	Market Bosworth R.D.	Barrow upon Soar R.D.	Billesdon R.D.	Blaby R.D.
	SMLA ring reception					
	Total numbers					
Peripheral	490	970	—	1,660	880	3,380
Local	240	180	—	550	290	1,000
Greater London	—	—	—	—	—	110
Rest of Britain	530	390	—	1,160	450	1,080
Abroad	50	60	—	150	—	100
Total	1,310	1,550	—	3,520	1,620	5,570
	Percentages					
Peripheral	37·4	62·6	—	47·2	54·3	59·8
Local	18·3	8·4	—	15·6	17·9	18·0
Greater London	—	—	—	—	—	2·0
Rest of Britain	40·5	25·2	—	33·0	27·8	18·4
Abroad	3·8	3·8	—	4·2	—	1·8
Total	100·0	100·0	—	100·0	100·0	100·0

Out-Migration

Reception area	Oadby U.D.	Wigston U.D.	Market Bosworth U.D.	Barrow upon Soar R.D.	Billesdon R.D.	Blaby R.D.
	SMLA ring source					
	Total numbers					
Peripheral	—	—	450	590	400	580
Local	—	—	430	520	490	390
Greater London	—	—	—	—	—	—
Rest of Britain	—	—	300	660	120	460
Abroad	—	—	—	—	—	—
Total	—	—	1,180	1,770	1,010	1,430
	Percentages					
Peripheral	—	—	38·2	33·3	39·6	40·6
Local	—	—	36·4	29·4	48·5	27·2
Greater London	—	—	—	—	—	—
Rest of Britain	—	—	25·4	37·3	11·9	32·2
Abroad	—	—	—	—	—	—
Total	—	—	100·0	100·0	100·0	100·0

Migration Balance

Area of exchange	Oadby U.D.	Wigston U.D.	Market Bosworth R.D.	Barrow upon Soar R.D.	Billesdon R.D.	Blaby R.D.
	SMLA ring area					
	Total numbers					
Peripheral	—	—	—	+1,070	+480	+2,750
Local	—	—	—	+30	−200	+610
Greater London	—	—	—	—	—	+110
Rest of Britain	—	—	—	+500	+330	+570
Abroad	—	—	—	+150	—	+100
Total	—	—	—	+1,750	+610	+4,440

Source: Census 1961, England and Wales, *Migration Tables.*

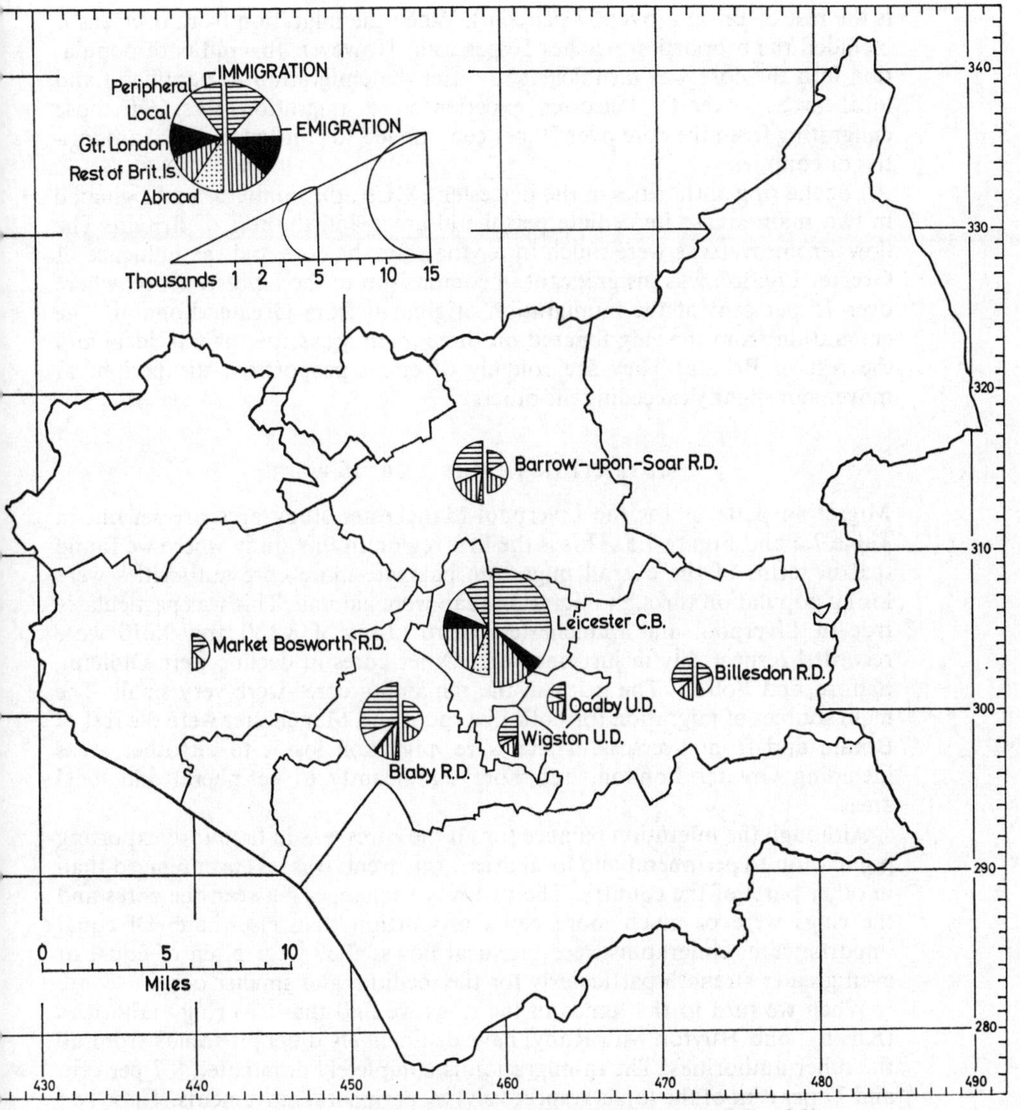

Figure 7.4 Leicester-Leicestershire: Migration Patterns, 1960–1961

MIGRATION IN THE LEICESTER SMLA

The movements in this study area are set out in Table 7.4 and Figure 7.4. This is the only SMLA in the five study areas which is not part of a conurbation or in close proximity to other SMLAs. This freestanding SMLA, however, still exhibits many of the characteristics that we have found in the other areas. The dominant source of migrants coming to the Leicester core is the rest of Britain (over 37 per cent). When the migration from overseas is included the proportion reaches 50 per cent. However, this influx of population into the core was insufficient to offset the emigration to peripheral and local areas; overall, Leicester experienced a migration loss. Of those emigrating from the core over 70 per cent moved to contiguous local authorities or counties.

For the ring authorities in the Leicester SMLA, the immigration originated in two main areas; immediate peripheral areas and the rest of Britain. The flows from overseas were much lower than for the core and the influence of Greater London was insignificant in comparison to the Leicester core, where over 15 per cent of the immigration originated from Greater London. The emigration from the ring focused on three main areas; peripheral, local and the rest of Britain. They are roughly of equal proportion, the peripheral movement slightly exceeding the others.

MIGRATION IN THE NORTH-WEST

Migration patterns for the Liverpool-Manchester study area are set out in Table 7.5 and Figure 7.5. This is the first region in this study where we found that in terms of the overall migration balance, more core authorities were losing population through migration than were gaining. This was particularly true of Liverpool and Manchester where losses of 8,130 and 9,210 were recorded respectively in just one year. Other cores in decline were Oldham, Salford and Bolton. The gains in the remaining cores were very small. The main sources of migration for both Liverpool and Manchester were the rest of Britain and from overseas. There were migration losses to all other areas including Greater London, but more significantly to peripheral and local areas.

Although the migration balance for all the cores was in favour of exporting population to peripheral and local areas, this trend was less pronounced than in other parts of the country. The two-way exchanges between the cores and the rings were of much more equal proportion than elsewhere. Of equal importance in emigration were the local flows; they were often of equal or even greater strength particularly for the medium and smaller cores.

When we turn to the trends in the rings we find that two ring authorities (Kirkby, and Huyton with Roby) have distinctively different trends from all the other authorities. The in-migration is completely dominated (87 per cent and 77 per cent of the totals respectively) by peripheral movements. These two authorities are essentially overspill towns with a high proportion of public housing and they would appear to be fulfilling their objective. The remaining ring authorities tend to follow the national pattern with immigration dominated by local and national movement, and a very low proportion coming from overseas. The bulk of emigrants did not fall into a distinctive pattern. There were no recorded flows to Greater London, and Kirkby, as one would expect, had a very low flow to the rest of Britain. The remaining ring authorities had a higher level of interaction with the rest of Britain but the emigration was

Table 7.5

MIGRATION ANALYSIS, SOUTH LANCASHIRE-NORTH CHESHIRE, 1960–1961

(a) CORES

In-Migration

	SMLA core reception									
Source area	Liverpool C.B.	Birkenhead C.B.	Manchester C.B.	Altrincham M.B.	Oldham C.B.	Salford C.B.	Stockport C.B.	Stretford M.B.	Bolton C.B.	St. Helens C.B.
	Total numbers									
Peripheral	5,400	2,290	6,880	700	760	8,660	8,560	1,870	930	140
Local	2,880	840	4,320	640	1,180	1,880	1,210	710	2,000	690
Greater London	880	—	1,060	—	—	—	—	100	—	—
Rest of Britain	3,970	1,020	5,400	580	600	1,070	800	900	800	870
Abroad	1,420	350	2,110	50	260	500	360	220	260	140
Total	14,500	4,500	19,270	1,970	2,890	5,610	4,920	3,800	3,710	1,340
	Percentages									
Peripheral	37·2	50·9	33·1	35·5	26·3	47·4	52·0	49·2	17·5	10·4
Local	19·5	18·7	22·4	32·5	40·8	24·6	24·6	18·7	53·9	51·5
Greater London	6·1	—	5·5	—	—	—	—	2·6	—	—
Rest of Britain	27·4	22·7	28·0	29·4	23·9	19·1	16·3	23·7	21·6	27·6
Abroad	9·8	7·7	11·0	2·6	9·0	8·9	7·1	5·8	7·0	10·4
Total	100·0	100·0	100·0	100·0	100·0	100·0	100·0	100·0	100·0	100·0

Out-Migration

Source area	SMLA core source									
	Liverpool C.B.	Birkenhead C.B.	Manchester C.B.	Altrincham M.B.	Oldham C.B.	Salford C.B.	Stockport C.B.	Stretford M.B.	Bolton C.B.	St. Helens C.B.
	Total numbers									
Peripheral	10,810	2,200	14,210	570	1,360	2,870	1,660	1,800	1,440	410
Local	6,310	1,060	8,960	810	2,390	8,150	1,870	1,240	1,970	1,870
Greater London	1,740	—	1,610	—	—	100	100	—	480	—
Rest of Britain	3,770	1,050	3,750	590	790	780	1,250	660	1,000	520
Abroad	—	—	—	—	—	—	—	—	—	—
Total	22,630	4,310	28,510	1,970	4,530	6,900	4,880	3,700	4,640	2,800
	Percentages									
Peripheral	47·8	51·0	49·8	28·9	29·8	41·6	34·0	48·6	31·0	14·6
Local	27·8	24·6	31·4	41·2	52·8	45·7	38·3	33·6	38·1	66·8
Greater London	7·7	—	5·6	—	—	1·4	2·1	—	9·3	—
Rest of Britain	16·7	24·4	13·2	29·9	17·4	11·3	25·6	17·8	21·6	18·6
Abroad	—	—	—	—	—	—	—	—	—	—
Total	100·0	100·0	100·0	100·0	100·0	100·0	100·0	100·0	100·0	100·0

Migration balance

Area of exchange	SMLA core area									
	Liverpool C.B.	Birkenhead C.B.	Manchester C.B.	Altrincham M.B.	Oldham C.B.	Salford C.B.	Stockport C.B.	Stretford M.B.	Bolton C.B.	St. Helens C.B.
	Total numbers									
Peripheral	−5,410	+90	−7,830	+130	−590	−210	+900	+70	−790	−270
Local	−3,480	−220	−4,640	−170	−1,210	−1,770	−660	−530	+230	−1,180
Greater London	−860	—	−580	—	—	−100	−100	+100	−430	—
Rest of Britain	+200	− 30	+1,670	−10	−100	+290	−450	+240	−290	−150
Abroad	+1,420	+350	+2,110	+50	+260	+500	+350	+220	+260	+140
Total	−8,130	+190	−9,240	—	−1,640	−1,290	+40	+100	−930	−1,460

(b) RINGS

In-Migration

Source area	SMLA ring reception						
	Kirkby U.D.	Wilmslow U.D.	Wirral U.D.	Huyton with Roby U.D.	Macclesfield R.D.	Bucklow R.D.	Whiston R.D.
				Total numbers			
Peripheral	2,080	360	290	2,570	490	1,770	1,810
Local	180	900	870	400	900	750	850
Greater London	—	200	—	—	—	—	—
Rest of Britain	150	530	440	250	420	300	470
Abroad	30	90	90	90	140	50	180
Total	2,890	2,080	1,690	3,310	1,950	2,870	2,760
				Percentages			
Peripheral	87·0	17·3	17·2	77·6	25·1	61·7	47·3
Local	5·4	43·3	51·5	12·1	46·2	26·1	30·8
Greater London	—	9·6	—	—	—	—	—
Rest of Britain	6·3	25·5	26·0	7·6	21·5	10·5	17·0
Abroad	1·3	4·3	5·3	2·7	7·2	1·7	4·7
Total	100·0	100·0	100·0	100·0	100·0	100·0	100·0

Out-Migration

	SMLA ring source						
Reception area	Kirkby U.D.	Wilmslow U.D.	Wirral U.D.	Huyton with Roby U.D.	Macclesfield R.D.	Bucklow R.D.	Whiston R.D.
				Total numbers			
Peripheral	1,920	260	310	1,880	—	—	390
Local	480	650	600	1,150	—	—	440
Greater London	—	—	—	—	—	—	—
Rest of Britain	170	710	360	370	—	—	290
Abroad	—	—	—	—	—	—	—
Total	2,570	1,620	1,270	2,900	—	—	1,120
				Percentages			
Peripheral	74·7	16·0	24·4	47·5	—	—	34·8
Local	18·7	40·2	47·3	39·7	—	—	39·3
Greater London	—	—	—	—	—	—	—
Rest of Britain	6·6	43·8	28·3	12·8	—	—	25·9
Abroad	—	—	—	—	—	—	—
Total	100·0	100·0	100·0	100·0	—	—	100·0

Migration balance

	SMLA ring area						
Area of exchange	Kirkby U.D.	Wilmslow U.D.	Wirral U.D.	Huyton with Roby U.D.	Macclesfield R.D.	Bucklow R.D.	Whiston R.D.
				Total numbers			
Peripheral	+160	+100	−20	+1,190	—	—	+920
Local	−350	+250	+270	−750	—	—	+410
Greater London	—	+200	—	—	—	—	—
Rest of Britain	−20	−180	+80	−120	—	—	+180
Abroad	+80	+90	+90	+90	—	—	+130
Total	−180	+460	+480	+410	—	—	+1,640

Source: Census 1961, England and Wales, *Migration Tables.*

dominated by flows to peripheral and local (non-contiguous) areas. With the exception of Kirkby, all the ring authorities had a positive migration balance.

MIGRATION: THE GENERAL TRENDS

This analysis of migration in the five study areas has focused upon changes in the cores and rings and with the rest of the country. The rates of change in migration varied according to the size of the metropolitan area and the region in which it is situated, and in particular one interesting difference emerged. Most of the large city cores analysed, including Birmingham, Leicester, Liverpool and Manchester, all experienced a net migration loss; and several smaller cores in the North-West were similarly placed. In contrast, there were several large metropolitan cores that gained through migration, including Southampton, Portsmouth, and Coventry; many of the smaller cores in the West London Metropolitan Sector also gained.

Against this background of central city gains and losses through migration, one characteristic emerges which is common to all the study areas: there were complex two-way exchanges of population between all cores and rings, but the movements from the core to the ring dominated the out-migration. The major flows of people from central cities were thus short-distance movers; the majority moved to peripheral areas, defined in this study as contiguous local authorities (commonly rural districts). In essence this is a measure of the strength of the suburbanization trend towards new residential development at the edge of the city but beyond the political limits of the city. As many other studies and reports have shown, most British cities are characteristically under-bounded.

Although the overall migration balance was negative in many of the cores, the losses to the ring were partially or completely offset by another trend common to all cores. There was a consistent migration gain by immigration from outside the metropolitan area concerned. In London's western fringes the source area was London itself and the rest of the country; for the remaining areas the main source was the rest of Britain. Immigration to the cores was therefore characteristically a long-distance move. This in-migration trend to central cities was accentuated by the migration from overseas; overseas migration was consistently greater to core areas than to the rings.

For ring authorities the main immigration sources were the central cities as outlined above, together with long-distance movers from the rest of Britain. Migration from overseas was minimal. The emigration totals for the rings include some who moved back to the city, but by far the largest majority moved within to peripheral (contiguous) areas or, more significantly, to local non-contiguous areas. This is clearly not a suburbanization trend on the normal model but a decentralization into rural areas, nearby villages and small towns.

We can thus develop a simple model of central cities losing population to the rings, the balance being met in part or in full by long-distance movers from other parts of the country or from overseas. In the suburban areas

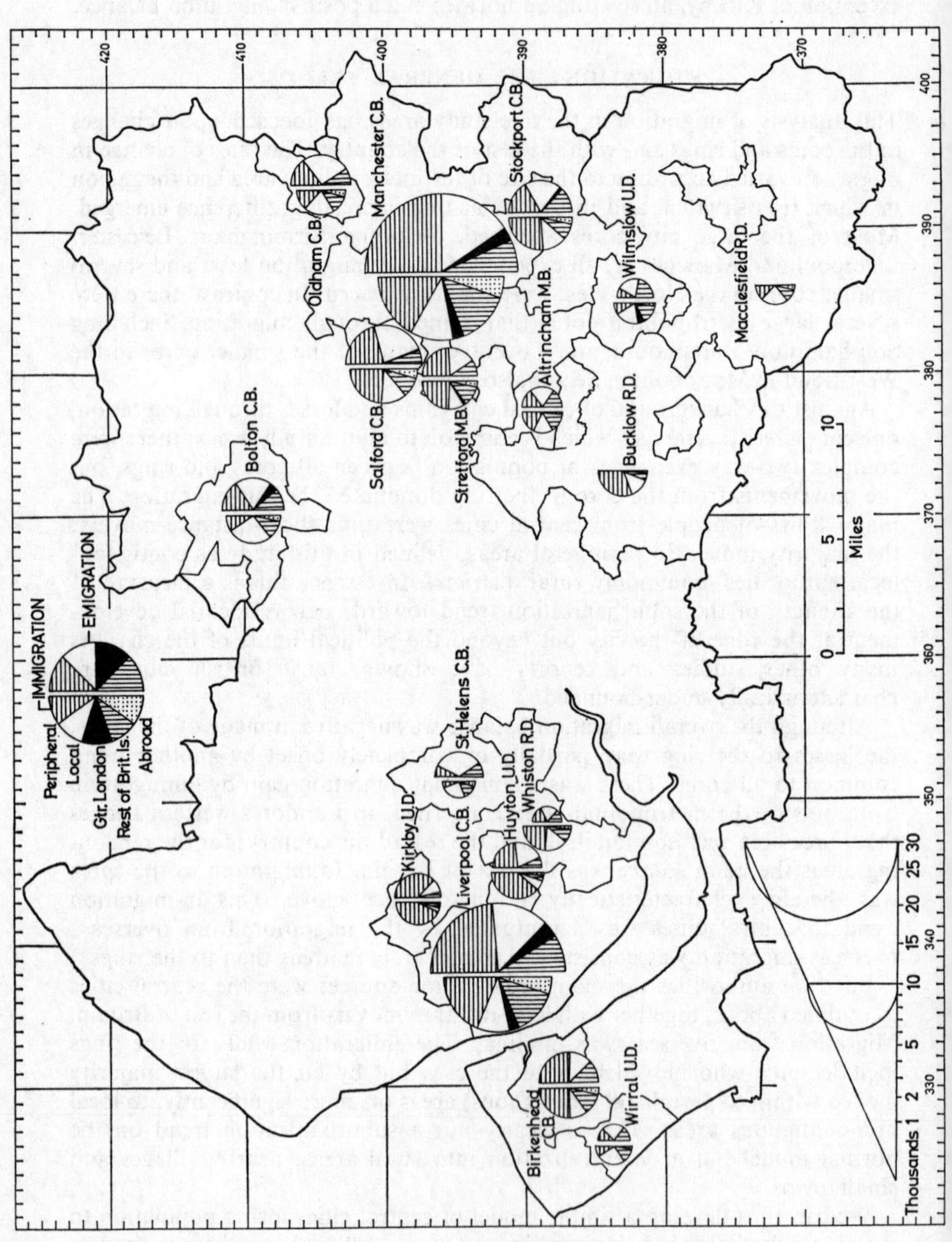
IMMIGRATION
EMIGRATION
Peripheral
Local
Gtr. London
Rest of Brit.Is.
Abroad
Bolton C.B.
Oldham C.B.
Manchester C.B.
Stockport C.B.
Salford C.B.
Stretford M.B.
Altrincham M.B.
Wilmslow U.D.
Macclesfield R.D.
Bucklow R.D.
St.Helens C.B.
Whiston R.D.
Huyton U.D.
Kirkby U.D.
Liverpool C.B.
Birkenhead C.B.
Wirral U.D.
Miles
0 5 10
Thousands 1 2 5 10 15 20 25 30

further decentralization was occurring to even more distant parts of the metropolitan rings. With our knowledge of rising land costs and transport costs and the propensity for most private residential development to occur on green field sites at the periphery, it seems certain that those most able to benefit from (and afford) this type of residential location were those in the private sector. The migration trends thus seem likely, unless corrected, to lead to social polarization of different types of housing and of different socio-economic groups. For this reason we turn in the next section to a detailed analysis of the changing patterns of socio-economic composition and housing tenures.

SOCIAL POLARIZATION: AN INTRODUCTION

Social polarization is a major concern of much writing in urban sociology in the period since the Second World War. Broadly, the thesis of this literature is that different socio-economic groups are becoming increasingly segregated from each other in geographical terms. As urban areas grow, the more affluent groups, particularly the white-collar middle class, tend to move out of the inner urban areas into the newer suburbs where newer, better housing is available. The less affluent groups, in particular the less skilled blue-collar workers, tend to remain disproportionately behind, in the older urban areas where housing conditions are generally poorer. A number of mutually reinforcing explanations can be produced for this trend. New private housing for sale will tend to be more expensive, and so only available for the more privileged groups; the new suburbs are not well served by public transport, and depend on car ownership, even multi-car ownership within the single family; there may be racial barriers to the movement of some less affluent groups; the low-paid service jobs, which employ these less affluent groups, may remain behind in the central city while other groups leave; urban renewal and public housing programmes are concentrated in the older urban areas, and so on.

It is no surprise that much of the literature of polarization comes from the United States. Indeed the first mentions of the phenomenon may be traced in the very origins of American urban sociology: in the writings of the Chicago school of human ecology, which was derived from the German concept of ecology.[1, 2, 3, 4] The original thesis, contained in Burgess' classic paper, was that polarization in urban areas took place in the form of concentric rings of the city, each with a distinctive sort of population and housing; later analyses suggested alternative distributions, either around

[1] A comprehensive reader was compiled by G. A. Theodorson, *Studies in Human Ecology*. Evanston, Ill./Elmsford, New York (1961), with original articles.

[2] H. H. Barrows, 'Geography as Human Ecology', *Annals of the Association of American Geographers*, 13 (1923), pp. 1–14.

[3] E. Häckel, *Natürliche Schöpfungs-Geschichte*. G. Reimer, Berlin (1866).

[4] R. E. Park et al., *The City*. University of Chicago Press, Chicago (1967).

separate nuclei within the city[5] or in the form of sectors radiating from the centre.[6] After the Second World War more sophisticated statistical techniques of social area analysis came to be widely applied.[7, 8] At the same time, other sociologists were investigating the concept of social mobility[9] which, it came to be realized, has a close possible connection with geographical mobility within the urban area.

The problem, essentially, is whether a hypothesis developed within an American context can be applied within a European one. As R. E. Pahl has pointed out:

> unlike American cities, European cities have grown or developed from medieval origins and this has important implications for the socio-economic pattern today.[10]

Therefore, though the techniques of analysis may be usefully borrowed from the Americans,[11] we should bear in mind that the conclusions may well be different. Our purpose in this chapter is to investigate how far people's preferences in choosing their area of residence within any given urban area[12] can be assessed with the aid of the available Census data. We concentrate primarily on the most immediately relevant data: that on socio-economic groupings, which are derived directly from the Census figures of occupation, classified according to place of residence. But we then try to relate this data to information on housing tenure. In this way we seek to throw light on a parallel question: if the existence of polarization can be demonstrated, how far is this reflected in, or even perhaps caused by, increasing geographical segregation of the public and private housing sector building programmes?

Increasing convenience of public transport facilities in interwar England and, as a postwar development, private car ownership has been the main means of achieving a potential desire for segregation,[13] contributing in turn partly to the urban growth. This is as true for the horse-drawn tram as for the M4 linkage between London and the Western Metropolitan Sector, and there is much evidence for the phenomenon in other areas as well. Living in a society where separation is not achieved any longer in terms of 'bricks and mortar',

[5] M. R. Davie, 'The Pattern of Urban Growth', in *Studies in the Sciences of Society*. New Haven, Conn. (1937).

[6] H. Hoyt, *The Structure and Growth of Residential Neighbourhoods in American Cities*. Washington, D.C. (1939).

[7] E. Shevky and W. Bell, *Social Area Analysis*. Stanford University Press (1955).

[8] D. T. Herbert, 'Social Area Analysis: A British Study', *Urban Studies*, 4 (1967), pp. 41–60.

[9] P. A. Sorokin, *Social and Cultural Mobility*. Free Press, Glencoe, Ill. (1959).

[10] R. E. Pahl, *Patterns of Urban Life*. Longmans, London (1970), p. 38.

[11] For a detailed description of the techniques and operational definitions employed in the paper, see the later paragraphs of this section.

[12] P. Hall, *London 2000*. Faber and Faber, London (1969), pp. 248–9.

[13] In the literature the term segregation is used in a more specific sense, referring only to ethnic or foreign-born groups.

it seems that areas of open space and road structure may be substituted. This appears to be a clear tendency:

> 'as social mobility increases, so place of residence becomes increasingly important as a means of buying and establishing a position in society.'[14]

That is why the question of this section must be: is there segregation on a larger regional scale? How far can we confirm the fact of socio-spatial segregation within our Standard Metropolitan Labour Areas?[15] By definition, these are not continuous built-up areas. The literature on the social composition of commuter flows, however, tends to support a pattern of socio-economic characteristics in terms of a core/ring structure. We wish to test two hypotheses. First, whether, with increasing social differentiation of the inhabitants, one will find spatial differentiation by residential area as well. And second, whether segregation by socio-economic groups within the SMLA has any effects on the pattern of housing tenures. The assumption to be tested here would be that there is a different percentage change in the core/ring distribution for the owner-occupied sector, as compared with publicly renting households.

It seems appropriate, in any event, to look at the phenomenon of spatial separation of residents by analysing Census figures for socio-economic groups and private housing tenureship. Data for these items are now published for 1961 or 1966 for reasonably disaggregated areas, enabling us to come to a valid conclusion about the hypotheses to be tested.[16] The areas are not as disaggregated as one would ideally like, and aggregating them into the cores and rings of SMLAs introduces a further element of arbitrariness. We shall consider later how serious this is.

For purposes of analysis, some simplification of the Census Socio-Economic Groups (SEG) categories is needed. The main criteria for clustering the fifteen SEGs came from consideration of car-ownership figures for Great Britain during the 1960s. This also correlates with the grouping used in some Census publications for the summary tables. The resulting clusters, referred to in the remainder of this section, are:

Clusters	Numbers of SEGs combined[17]	Appelation
I	1 2 3 4 13	High-income non-manual workers
II	5 6	Low-income non-manual workers
III	8 9 12 14	High-income manual workers
IV	7 10 11 15	Low-income manual workers

[14] Pahl, op. cit. (1970), p. 41.

[15] This analysis implicitly assumes, for the sake of argument, that the SMLA concept is valid as a framework for analysing socio-economic differences.

[16] There are no adequate data for 1951, when social class data were not readily comparable.

[17] For further references see *Classification of Occupations*. HMSO (1966).

The name given to each cluster is a short description of the SEGs included in it, in terms of wages and type of activity. SEGs 16 and 17 are not included in any cluster. This is because we want to investigate whether there is an increasing segregation by SEG of residents between core and ring, and how far this is reflected by the housing tenureship. Any changes in either of these groups would not be significant in this respect.[18]

For the analysis of housing tenure patterns, published figures extend only down to the 15,000 population level.[19] These units appear to be adequate for our approach, which does not need elaborate spatial disaggregation.

Unfortunately the Census figures for tenureship by SEG of the chief economic supporter are not broken down further than regions. The situation in individual local authorities, therefore, can only be assessed by the analogous figures for economically active males by SEG and the regional figures.[20] In all Tables we distinguish by three columns between (*a*) owner-occupied, (*b*) local authority and new town corporation rented, and (*c*) private, etc. rented households.

Looking at areas of such a size, one has to be clear about the extent of the statistical validity and reliability of Census data for small area units. Many of the 1961 data, and all the 1966 data, are based on a 10 per cent sample. As a result, changes based on less than fifteen cases are subject to a large sample error. Therefore, changes within such a small sample should not be

[18] Members of the armed forces, SEG 16, are certainly directed in their choice of a place of residence. There are unfortunately no data available to distinguish within this group, e.g. marital status. These figures, therefore, do not show any personal decision.

Great changes also occur in the 1966 Census compared with 1961 for the SEG 17: 'Indefinite: persons with inadequately stated occupation'. This is due to a better response rate to the 1966 Census, particularly on the employment question. It is difficult to decide to which group (or groups) these changes are applicable. Direct data on this issue are not available, because the 1961 post-enumeration material which might have been used for comparison is no longer in existence.

Some hints are given by the 1961 Census, *General Report – Comparison of Census with Post-Enumeration Survey*. HMSO, London (1966), Table 45. In these tables, the level of agreement for men was generally high, the lowest proportion being 89 per cent for farmers, employers and managers, SEG 13, and 91 per cent for unskilled manual workers, SEG 11. The area of greatest variation appears to be in SEGs 9 to 11, i.e. mainly cluster I which represents manual workers of semiskilled and unskilled groups (advice from Mr A. T. Blundell, of the Registrar General's office).

One can assume from this comparison that a great deal of these numerical changes took place in groups of poor education, mostly manual workers. In this case the small number of indefinite persons would not make much difference to the tendency within the groups. If the changes occur in a small unit of a single SMLA core or ring, it would have the most serious effect on the regional interpretation of the data

[19] Tables 7.8 and 7.11, where some figures for the rings are incomplete.

[20] Thereby, however, we have to be aware of a spurious correlation when correlating both sets of data.

used for reliable inferences about trends in the population.[21] On the one side, one cannot expect any spectacular change in our variables over a five-year interval. So conclusions must be rather broad. On the other hand, the literature gives hints that in the U.S.A. these changes are increasing in scale.

For comparison over time we also have to bear in mind boundary changes, which influence percentage changes for any individual SMLA. In these cases, inferences based on smaller modifications or changes in a single group have to be very carefully treated and can only be seen as marginal arguments. On the other hand, these hazards may be lessened by the process of grouping the districts to form a ring. Boundary changes within SMLAs are likely to benefit the cores, and this obviously makes any increase over time in a cluster for the adjacent ring even more valid.

In the late sixties, C. B. Hall and R. A. Smith did a study of the socio-economic pattern for England and Wales on a more aggregated level of clusters with 1961 figures.[22] Although our approach differs to a considerable extent, the map published in that paper will be a useful reference for the wider framework. As in that study, here we cannot claim to look at homogeneous units.[23] The structures of individual SMLA rings are by no means everywhere homogeneous, a fact we have to bear in mind in the following sections. Derived as they are from administrative units, the rings contain pockets of residential areas which should be viewed as outskirts of the core, though with perhaps fringe-type residents.

ANALYSIS OF THE SELECTED AREAS AS A WHOLE

This chapter is mainly concerned with five particular study areas, which have already been identified in Chapter Six:

1 West London Metropolitan Sector
2 South Hampshire
3 West Midlands (part)
4 Leicester-Leicestershire
5 South Lancashire-North Cheshire

Before looking at each of these parts of urbanized Britain in more detail, we shall first test our hypotheses, as already stated, by using aggregate data for the areas as a whole, bearing always in mind the composition of the data. Starting from the most aggregate level, we first look at the total figures given in Table 7.6. Comparing these with Table 7.7, we can at least roughly assess differences in the pattern of general change as it takes place on a smaller regional level as well as in parts of the regions.

[21] The term population is to be interpreted in its statistical sense as a number of distributed objects.

[22] C. B. Hall and R. A. Smith, 'Socio-Economic Pattern of England and Wales', *Urban Studies*, vol. 5 (1968), pp. 58–66.

[23] Some more individual variations will be demonstrated for Reading sub-region in a later section of this chapter.

Table 7.6

SOCIO-ECONOMIC PATTERN IN THE FIVE STUDY AREAS, 1961 AND 1966

1 WEST LONDON (SMLAs 1, 36, 41, 52, 69, 77, 93, 97)

(a) CORES

Cluster	Economically active males		Change	Per cent change	Per cent total	Per cent total
	1961	1966	1961–66	1961–66	1961	1966
I	55,290	69,560	14,270	25·8	16·2	18·6
II	72,690	80,380	7,690	10·6	21·2	21·6
III	126,470	136,900	10,430	8·3	36·9	36·7
IV	71,270	76,540	5,270	7·4	20·8	20·5
16 and 17	16,890	9,810	−7,080	−41·9	4·9	2·6
Total	342,610	373,190	30,580	8·9	100·0	100·0

(b) RINGS

Cluster	Economically active males		Change	Per cent change	Per cent total	Per cent total
	1961	1966	1961–66	1961–66	1961	1966
I	91,090	105,870	14,780	16·2	22·7	25·3
II	82,890	89,520	6,630	8·0	20·7	21·3
III	132,840	137,010	4,170	3·1	33·1	32·7
IV	74,760	73,690	−1,070	−1·4	18·7	17·6
16 and 17	19,380	13,030	−6,350	−32·8	4·8	3·1
Total	400,960	419,120	18,160	4·5	100·0	100·0

2 SOUTH HAMPSHIRE (SMLAs 66, 78)

(a) CORES

Cluster	Economically active males		Change	Per cent change	Per cent total	Per cent total
	1961	1966	1961–66	1961–66	1961	1966
I	14,130	14,630	500	3·5	10·5	11·3
II	21,650	23,010	1,360	6·3	16·2	17·8
III	51,030	49,520	−1,510	−3·0	38·1	38·2
IV	34,310	31,320	−2,990	−8·7	25·6	24·2
16 and 17	12,800	11,010	−1,790	−14·0	9·6	8·5
Total	133,920	129,490	−4,430	−3·3	100·0	100·0

(b) RINGS

Cluster	Economically active males		Change	Per cent change	Per cent total	Per cent total
	1961	1966	1961–66	1961–66	1961	1966
I	16,980	20,910	3,930	23·1	14·1	15·6
II	18,930	22,700	3,770	19·9	15·8	17·0
III	42,760	47,810	5,050	11·8	35·6	35·7
IV	28,280	28,570	290	1·0	23·5	21·4
16 and 17	13,250	13,850	600	4·5	11·0	10·3
Total	120,200	133,840	13,640	11·4	100·0	100·0

3 WEST MIDLANDS (SMLAs 7, 25)

(a) CORES

Cluster	Economically active males		Change	Per cent change	Per cent total	Per cent total
	1961	1966	1961–66	1961–66	1961	1966
I	53,450	54,980	1,530	2·9	10·3	10·9
II	74,410	75,450	1,040	1·4	14·3	15·0
III	236,260	224,700	−11,560	−4·9	45·5	44·6
IV	141,630	145,070	3,440	2·4	27·3	28·8
16 and 17	13,310	3,670	−9,640	−72·4	2·6	0·7
Total	519,060	503,870	−15,190	−2·9	100·0	100·0

(b) RINGS

Cluster	Economically active males		Change	Per cent change	Per cent total	Per cent total
	1961	1966	1961–66	1961–66	1961	1966
I	25,000	28,720	3,720	14·9	19·9	21·5
II	19,280	21,780	2,500	12·9	15·4	16·3
III	47,240	51,580	4,340	9·2	37·7	38·6
IV	27,190	29,220	2,030	7·5	21·7	21·9
16 and 17	6,680	2,340	−4,340	−65·0	5·3	1·7
Total	125,390	133,640	8,250	6·6	100·0	100·0

4 LEICESTER-LEICESTERSHIRE (SMLA 48)

(a) CORES

Cluster	Economically active males		Change	Per cent change	Per cent total	Per cent total
	1961	1966	1961–66	1961–66	1961	1966
I	10,550	10,240	−310	−2·9	12·0	11·7
II	13,760	13,020	−740	−5·4	15·7	14·9
III	41,110	40,650	−460	−1·1	46·9	46·5
IV	20,830	23,220	2,390	11·5	23·7	26·5
16 and 17	1,500	340	−1,160	−77·3	1·7	0·4
Total	87,750	87,470	−280	−0·3	100·0	100·0

(b) RINGS

Cluster	Economically active males		Change	Per cent change	Per cent total	Per cent total
	1961	1966	1961–66	1961–66	1961	1966
I	11,860	14,590	2,730	23·0	18·4	20·9
II	10,160	12,480	2,320	22·8	15·8	17·9
III	27,760	28,840	1,080	3·9	43·1	41·3
IV	13,090	13,370	280	2·1	20·3	19·2
16 and 17	1,510	460	−1,050	−69·5	2·4	0·7
Total	64,380	69,740	5,360	8·3	100·0	100·0

5 NORTH CHESHIRE-SOUTH LANCASHIRE

(SMLAs 10, 16, 49, 51, 55, 71, 73, 80, 94, 96)

(a) CORES

Cluster	Economically active males		Change	Per cent change	Per cent total	Per cent total
	1961	1966	1961–66	1961–66	1961	1966
I	93,070	90,030	−304	−3·3	9·9	10·5
II	148,650	137,860	−1,079	−7·3	15·8	16·1
III	389,390	355,430	−3,396	−8·7	41·3	41·6
IV	294,720	265,380	−2,934	−10·0	31·2	31·0
16 and 17	17,270	6,410	−1,086	−62·9	1·8	0·8
Total	943,100	855,110	−8,799	−9·3	100·0	100·0

(b) RINGS

Cluster	Economically active males		Change	Per cent change	Per cent total	Per cent total
	1961	1966	1961–66	1961–66	1961	1966
I	91,330	105,000	1,367	15·0	17·8	19·2
II	94,710	104,430	972	10·3	18·5	19·1
III	195,180	209,930	1,475	7·5	38·1	38·3
IV	123,600	125,070	147	1·2	24·1	22·8
16 and 17	7,660	3,080	−458	−59·8	1·5	0·5
Total	512,480	547,510	3,503	6·8	100·0	100·0

Source: Censuses.

Already at this large scale one can see a significant difference between the West London Metropolitan Sector and the four other areas. The importance of the non-manual cluster in the London zone is fairly obvious. The variations among the individual SMLAs, however, are not sufficiently demonstrated by Table 7.6. The unique character of this area will become more apparent in the part dealing with the individual areas. In some cases the influence of Greater London appears to interfere with the core/ring distinction. In the South Hampshire segment the differences are not very clear, because of the large element of armed forces personnel which causes all percentages in the

Table 7.7

ECONOMICALLY ACTIVE MALES BY S.E.G. STANDARD REGIONS, 1961 AND 1966

(a) England and Wales

Cluster	Economically active males		Change	Per cent change	Per cent total	Per cent total
	1961	1966	1961–66	1961–66	1961	1966
I	2,088,430	2,223,570	135,140	6·5	14·3	15·4
II	2,415,790	2,497,310	81,520	3·4	16·5	17·2
III	5,757,560	5,714,790	−42,770	−7·4	39·3	39·4
IV	3,846,770	3,753,850	−92,920	−2·4	26·2	25·9
16 and 17	540,530	301,020	−239,510	−44·3	3·7	2·1
Total	14,649,080	14,490,540	−158,540	−10·8	100	100

(b) South-East Region

Cluster	Economically active males		Change	Per cent change	Per cent total	Per cent total
	1961	1966	1961–66	1961–66	1961	1966
I	925,240	956,740	31,500	3·4	16·7	18·5
II	1,140,310	1,089,990	−50,320	−4·4	20·5	21·1
III	1,968,350	1,834,200	−134,150	−6·8	35·4	35·6
IV	1,298,600	1,154,190	−144,410	−11·1	23·4	22·4
16 and 17	220,310	122,850	−97,460	−44·2	4·0	2·4
Total	5,552,810	5,157,970	−394,840	−7·1	100	100

(c) South-East Region without G.L.C.*

Cluster	Economically active males		Change	Per cent change	Per cent total	Per cent total
	1961	1966	1961–66	1961–66	1961	1966
I	472,810	519,530	46,720	9·9	16·6	19·3
II	520,760	510,120	−10,640	−2·0	18·2	19·0
III	1,029,790	969,510	−60,280	−5·9	36·1	36·0
IV	683,570	599,290	−84,280	−12·3	23·9	22·3
16 and 17	149,480	91,220	−58,260	−38·0	5·2	3·4
Total	2,856,410	2,689,670	−166,740	−5·8	100	100

(d) West Midland Region

Cluster	Economically active males		Change	Per cent change	Per cent total	Per cent total
	1961	1966	1961–66	1961–66	1961	1966
I	200,530	217,770	17,240	8·6	12·7	13·7
II	214,520	227,250	12,730	5·9	13·6	14·3
III	703,610	696,330	−7,280	−1·0	44·7	44·0
IV	411,400	422,760	11,360	2·8	26·2	26·7
16 and 17	44,330	19,860	−24,470	−55·2	2·8	1·3
Total	1,574,390	1,583,970	9,580	0·6	100	100

(e) North-West Region

Cluster	Economically active males		Change	Per cent change	Per cent total	Per cent total
	1961	1966	1961–66	1961–66	1961	1966
I	265,170	279,450	14,280	5·4	12·9	14·1
II	332,060	335,470	3,410	1·0	16·2	16·9
III	831,730	810,680	−21,050	−2·5	40·6	40·8
IV	578,690	547,130	−31,560	−5·5	28·3	27·5
16 and 17	40,120	15,080	−25,040	−62·4	2·0	0·7
Total	2,047,770	1,987,810	−59,960	−29·3	100	100

* Boundary changes are ignored.

Source: Census.

other SEGs to be correspondingly reduced. The pattern here is however easier to compare with that of the northern zone than with the nearby West London Metropolitan Sector. The comparison of these two areas illustrates how much conditions may vary within standard regions.

For the three Midlands and Northern areas the pattern appears to be very similar. But one has to be aware of the different degree of aggregation of those areas; for their internal differentiation and structure is closely related to their size, a point which was recently made again by F. Lancaster Jones.[24] This is suggested even by very small deviations in the zones. Nonetheless it is interesting to notice the degree of conformity in the data despite the great variation in extent of the five study areas. It will be a task of the later detailed analysis to point out the differences in size which characterize each zone.

A comparison of cores and rings of the selected areas seems to suggest a clear preference of high-income non-manual workers to live in the fringe of the SMLAs. This also appears to be true for their low-income non-manual colleagues, but to a less extent.

These main distinctions are emphasized by the 1961–66 percentage changes. Here we have an absolute decrease in the cores, and a significant increase in the rings, in two of the zones, for these non-manual groups. In two other areas, the important differences in the rates of increase between cores and rings can be regarded as further verification of our hypothetical assumption of an increasing polarization in terms of a core/ring pattern. Yet the West London Metropolitan Sector shows a contrary development (Table 7.6(1)). This again emphasizes the special situation in this area, which presumably is to be seen as part of a wider ring for the Greater London area.

But what about the manual worker? Cluster III includes by definition the bulk of all active males. There are signs of a diminishing concentration in the core; thus there is a slight increase in the rings, e.g. in the West Midlands (Table 7.6(3)). But a clearer picture occurs for the low-income manual worker, cluster IV. The fact that he is also most important in the core, like his high-income manual-worker colleague, can be seen in all area aggregates. But while the cluster III share appears to converge for core and ring over time, the low-income manual worker seems to concentrate, in a relative sense, in the core.

These movements are less obvious than they might be, because there is a general decrease in both clusters, for the country as well as for most regions, as is shown in Table 7.7. Therefore, areas where this factor does not occur to such an extent show a clearer pattern: the West Midlands, for instance (Table 7.6(3))[25]. In the other zones these changes are only moderate or manifest themselves in the form of stagnation.

[24] F. Lancaster Jones, 'Social Analysis: Some Theoretical and Methodological Comments Illustrated with Australian Data', *British Journal of Sociology*, vol. 5 (1968), p. 427.

[25] See also Hall and Smith, op. cit., p. 60.

Table 7.8

PRIVATE HOUSEHOLDS BY TENURE: AVERAGES FOR THE FIVE STUDY AREAS, 1961 AND 1966

Area	1961 Owner-occupied	1961 Local authority New town corporation	1961 Private, etc.	1961 Total	1966 Owner-occupied	1966 Local authority New town corporation	1966 Private, etc.	1966 Total
	percentages of total				percentages of total			
Cores								
West London	47·6	22·8	29·6	100·0	52·4	22·5	25·1	100·0
South Hampshire	45·1	21·0	33·9	100·0	46·8	23·7	29·5	100·0
West Midlands	44·1	28·8	27·1	100·0	47·5	30·6	21·9	100·0
Leicestershire	44·3	23·2	32·5	100·0	43·7	27·5	28·8	100·0
Lancashire-Cheshire	41·8	24·4	33·8	100·0	45·6	26·8	27·6	100·0
Rings								
West London	55·6	17·2	27·2	100·0	60·3	17·3	22·4	100·0
South Hampshire	51·1	23·9	25·0	100·0	56·0	23·5	20·5	100·0
West Midlands	53·5	19·6	26·9	100·0	58·3	20·3	21·4	100·0
Leicestershire	57·3	19·5	23·2	100·0	67·6	14·2	18·2	100·0
Lancashire-Cheshire	49·8	23·7	26·5	100·0	55·7	25·3	19·0	100·0

Source: Census.

Table 7.9

PRIVATE HOUSEHOLDS BY S.E.G. OF CHIEF ECONOMIC SUPPORTER, BY TENURE, ENGLAND AND WALES, 1961 AND 1966, AND STANDARD REGIONS, 1966

(a) England and Wales

Tenure cluster	1961 Owner-occupied	1961 Local authority New town corporation	1961 Private, etc.	1961 Total	1966 Owner-occupied	1966 Local authority New town corporation	1966 Private, etc.	1966 Total
	percentages of total				percentages of total			
I	24·0	4·4	12·1	15·4	24·7	4·4	12·3	16·1
	67·3	6·8	25·9	100	72·3	7·1	20·6	100
II	23·5	12·1	18·2	19·0	23·8	12·5	19·4	19·7
	53·4	15·3	31·2	100	57·0	16·5	26·5	100
III	33·8	44·4	34·2	36·5	33·7	43·5	32·4	35·9
	40·0	29·3	30·7	100	44·3	31·4	24·3	100
IV	15·9	36·5	30·6	25·6	16·2	38·1	31·8	26·0
	26·7	34·2	39·1	100	29·1	37·9	33·0	100
16 and 17	2·8	2·6	4·9	3·5	1·6	1·5	4·0	2·3
	35·0	18·6	46·4	100	35·3	16·8	47·9	100
Total	100	100	100	100	100	100	100	100
	43·1	24·6	32·8	100	47·2	26·0	26·8	100

Note: The following figures for the region refer to 1966, as no equivalent for 1961 are published.

(b) South-East region (without Greater London)

Tenure cluster	1966 Owner-occupied	Local authority New town corporation	Private, etc.	Total
	percentages of total			
I	29·7	6·2	14·8	20·7
	76·4	6·9	16·7	100
II	26·2	13·7	20·0	21·9
	64·0	14·5	21·5	100
III	28·5	44·2	29·1	32·3
	47·2	31·6	21·2	100
IV	13·0	34·4	29·5	21·8
	31·7	36·5	31·8	100
16 and 17	2·6	1·5	6·6	3·3
	42·0	10·9	47·1	100
Total	100	100	100	100
	53·4	23·1	23·5	100

(c) West Midland region

Tenure cluster	1966 Owner-occupied	Local authority New town corporation	Private, etc.	Total
	percentages of total			
I	22·9	3·6	12·5	14·6
	73·8	7·8	18·4	100
II	20·5	9·8	16·0	16·1
	59·6	19·1	21·3	100
III	38·6	47·9	36·4	41·1
	44·1	36·9	19·0	100
IV	16·9	37·4	32·4	26·7
	29·7	44·2	26·1	100
16 and 17	1·1	1·3	2·7	1·5
	33·1	27·9	40·0	100
Total	100	100	100	100
	46·9	31·6	21·5	100

(d) North-West region

Tenure cluster	1966 Owner-occupied	Local authority New town corporation	Private, etc.	Total
	percentages of total			
I	21·6	3·9	9·6	14·2
	76·7	6·7	16·6	100
II	22·6	12·9	17·5	19·0
	60·5	16·7	22·8	100
III	36·1	40·5	34·9	36·9
	49·7	27·0	23·3	100
IV	18·6	41·3	36·0	28·5
	33·2	35·6	31·2	100
16 and 17	1·1	1·4	2·0	1·4
	40·5	24·5	35·0	100
Total	100	100	100	100
	50·8	24·6	24·6	100

Read: The figures in the table say: e.g. $\frac{24\cdot 0}{67\cdot 3}$ that is, in 24·0 per cent of all owner-occupied private households in England and Wales the chief economic supporter belongs to SEG cluster I; while 67·3 per cent of all chief economic supporters belonging to SEG cluster I occupy their home as owner, etc.

Note: The right marginal total cannot be compared with those given in Table 7.7, which only include *males.*

Source: Censuses.

How far does this picture correlate with the housing tables (Tables 7.8 and 7.9) for the same areas? Considering average data for the five areas, we do not find our hypothetical assumption of a polarization in tenureship by core and ring confirmed as clearly as when we compare SEG patterns. The only significant difference between cores and rings is in owner-occupied households. Their geographical patterns indeed seem to become more distinctive over time since they increase more rapidly in the rings. But the same cannot be said as emphatically for the local authority and new town corporation rented households. In all SMLAs these figures do not change so much over time at all. Notable increases can be seen only in the cores. But the apparent decrease in the rings is far from great. Here again we have to refer to our detailed section below, since these figures are by definition very sensitive to the fact of whether there is a new town in the ring or not. The reasons for the more general changes are to be seen as a counterpart to the significant decline in the privately rented sector.

Is there any accord between the pattern of SEGs and the pattern of tenure? Can we allocate a certain type of tenureship to each of our clusters? Again, the aggregative level of the data constrains the depths of our analysis. One might be surprised by the fairly uniform proportions for different kinds of tenureship in cluster IV for England and Wales (Table 7.9). A significant variation only occurs in the West Midlands, where the private sector is the lowest of all regions.[26] This at least contradicts the assumption that there is a barrier to owner-occupation among low-income manual workers. But the public sector nevertheless provides the main resource of accommodation for these people, and they are still relatively excluded from owner-occupation with its requirements of long-term investment. Yet there is no simple and clear association between the distribution patterns of socio-economic groups and the distribution patterns of housing tenure.

CHARACTERISTICS OF THE INDIVIDUAL AREAS: LONDON'S WESTERN FRINGES

In a more specific analysis of the variations within the three largest study areas, we shall now follow the same approach. Bearing in mind the general structure, we shall take account of the local variations and try to explain them within the regional framework. We have to be aware of overvaluing insignificant variations as well as of explaining trends based on small samples. But one can assume that the aggregation of several SEGs and less detailed conclusions on the local level may also obscure the effect of any biased figure within the tables. The numbers and nature of cases, stated below, are distinct enough to suggest that the pattern is not caused randomly. We have already mentioned the distinctive character of the West London Metropolitan Sector in comparison to the other zones. But it also appears to be outstandingly distinctive among the major divisions of the South-East region.[27] The

[26] This is shown by the marginal figures at the bottom of Table 7.9(c).
[27] This is proved by a comparison of Tables 7.6(1) and 7.7(b) and (c).

Table 7.10

SOCIO-ECONOMIC PATTERN IN THE WEST LONDON METROPOLITAN SECTOR (SINGLE SMLAs), 1961 AND 1966

HIGH WYCOMBE

(a) CORE

Cluster	Economically active males		Change	Per cent change	Per cent total	Per cent total
	1961	1966	1961–66	1961–66	1961	1966
I	2,130	2,440	310	14·6	12·8	13·7
II	2,320	2,710	390	16·8	13·9	15·3
III	7,800	8,190	390	5·0	46·8	46·2
IV	3,180	3,970	790	24·8	19·1	22·4
16 and 17	1,230	430	−800	−65·0	7·4	2·4
Total	16,660	17,740	1,080	6·5	100·0	100·0

(b) RING

Cluster	Economically active males		Change	Per cent change	Per cent total	Per cent total
	1961	1966	1961–66	1961–66	1961	1966
I	10,950	14,560	3,610	33·0	24·1	29·2
II	7,910	8,640	730	9·2	17·4	17·3
III	15,990	17,350	1,360	8·5	35·2	34·7
IV	7,980	7,760	−220	−2·8	17·5	15·5
16 and 17	2,630	1,640	−990	−37·6	5·8	3·3
Total	45,460	49,950	4,490	9·9	100·0	100·0

SLOUGH

(a) CORE

Cluster	Economically active males		Change	Per cent change	Per cent total	Per cent total
	1961	1966	1961–66	1961–66	1961	1966
I	3,510	3,790	280	8·0	13·0	13·5
II	4,220	4,420	200	4·7	15·6	15·8
III	11,060	11,100	40	0·4	40·0	39·5
IV	7,400	8,510	1,110	15·0	27·3	30·3
16 and 17	880	250	−630	−71·6	3·2	0·9
Total	27,070	28,070	1,000	3·7	100·0	100·0

(b) RING

Cluster	Economically active males		Change	Per cent change	Per cent total	Per cent total
	1961	1966	1961–66	1961–66	1961	1966
I	11,940	12,240	300	2·5	25·1	25·1
II	8,620	9,090	470	5·5	18·2	18·7
III	15,200	16,480	1,280	8·4	32·0	33·8
IV	9,240	10,210	970	10·5	19·4	21·0
16 and 17	2,500	700	−1,800	−72·0	5·3	1·4
Total	47,500	48,720	1,220	2·6	100·0	100·0

LONDON (part)

(a) CORE

Cluster	Economically active males		Change	Per cent change	Per cent total	Per cent total
	1961	1966	1961–66	1961–66	1961	1966
I	29,780	39,950	10,170	34·2	16·1	18·9
II	42,490	49,380	6,890	16·2	22·9	23·4
III	70,230	77,640	7,410	10·6	37·9	36·8
IV	38,280	41,860	3,580	9·4	20·6	19·8
16 and 17	4,590	2,200	−2,390	−52·1	2·5	1·1
Total	185,370	211,030	25,660	13·8	100·0	100·0

(b) RING

Cluster	Economically active males		Change	Per cent change	Per cent total	Per cent total
	1961	1966	1961–66	1961–66	1961	1966
I	44,060	47,970	3,910	8·9	22·3	24·7
II	45,830	45,960	130	0·3	23·2	23·7
III	66,360	63,510	−2,850	−4·3	33·7	32·7
IV	35,330	32,960	−2,370	−6·7	17·9	17·0
16 and 17	5,700	3,700	−2,000	−35·1	2·9	1·9
Total	197,280	194,100	−3,180	−1·6	100·0	100·0

WALTON AND WEYBRIDGE

(a) CORE

Cluster	Economically active males		Change	Per cent change	Per cent total	Per cent total
	1961	1966	1961–66	1961–66	1961	1966
I	3,920	4,940	1,020	26·0	27·7	32·3
II	3,380	3,400	20	0·6	23·8	22·3
III	4,430	4,560	130	2·9	31·2	29·9
IV	2,230	2,240	10	0·5	15·7	14·7
16 and 17	230	120	−110	−47·8	1·6	0·8
Total	14,190	15,260	1,070	7·5	100·0	100·0

(b) RING

Cluster	Economically active males		Change	Per cent change	Per cent total	Per cent total
	1961	1966	1961–66	1961–66	1961	1966
I	2,460	2,700	240	9·8	19·3	19·8
II	2,330	2,670	340	14·6	18·2	19·5
III	5,170	5,520	350	6·8	40·5	40·4
IV	2,600	2,640	40	1·5	20·4	19·3
16 and 17	200	140	−60	−30·0	1·6	1·0
Total	12,760	13,670	910	7·1	100·0	100·0

WOKING

(a) CORE

Cluster	Economically active males		Change	Per cent change	Per cent total	Per cent total
	1961	1966	1961–66	1961–66	1961	1966
I	4,880	6,250	1,370	28·1	23·6	28·8
II	5,010	4,360	−650	−13·0	24·2	20·1
III	6,240	6,740	500	8·0	30·1	31·0
IV	3,780	3,840	60	1·6	18·2	17·7
16 and 17	800	520	−280	−35·0	3·9	2·4
Total	20,710	21,710	1,000	4·8	100·0	100·0

(b) RING

Cluster	Economically active males		Change	Per cent change	Per cent total	Per cent total
	1961	1966	1961–66	1961–66	1961	1966
I	1,110	1,440	330	29·7	22·4	26·4
II	740	910	170	23·0	15·0	16·7
III	1,650	1,740	90	5·5	33·3	31·9
IV	1,250	1,290	40	3·2	25·3	23·7
16 and 17	200	70	−130	−65·0	4·0	1·3
Total	4,950	5,450	500	10·1	100·0	100·0

GUILDFORD

(a) CORE

Cluster	Economically active males		Change	Per cent change	Per cent total	Per cent total
	1961	1966	1961–66	1961–66	1961	1966
I	3,150	3,640	490	15·6	19·8	22·4
II	3,910	4,070	160	4·1	24·5	25·1
III	5,390	5,510	120	2·2	33·8	34·0
IV	3,060	2,830	−230	−7·5	19·2	17·5
16 and 17	430	160	−270	−62·8	2·7	1·0
Total	15,940	16,210	270	1·7	100·0	100·0

(b) RING

Cluster	Economically active males		Change	Per cent change	Per cent total	Per cent total
	1961	1966	1961–66	1961–66	1961	1966
I	7,990	8,860	870	10·9	24·1	25·6
II	5,420	6,230	810	14·9	16·4	18·0
III	9,970	10,420	450	4·5	30·1	30·2
IV	7,100	6,950	−150	−2·1	21·5	20·1
16 and 17	2,600	2,090	−510	−19·6	7·9	6·1
Total	33,080	34,550	1,470	4·4	100·0	100·0

ALDERSHOT

(a) CORE

Cluster	Economically active males		Change	Per cent change	Per cent total	Per cent total
	1961	1966	1961–66	1961–66	1961	1966
I	2,490	2,840	350	14·1	10·5	12·1
II	3,760	4,250	490	13·0	15·9	18·0
III	6,210	7,030	820	13·2	26·2	29·8
IV	3,670	3,780	110	3·0	15·5	16·0
16 and 17	7,570	5,680	−1,890	−25·0	31·9	24·1
Total	23,700	23,580	−120	−0·5	100·0	100·0

(b) RING

Cluster	Economically active males		Change	Per cent change	Per cent total	Per cent total
	1961	1966	1961–66	1961–66	1961	1966
I	4,380	6,710	2,330	53·2	20·1	26·3
II	4,250	5,150	900	21·2	19·5	20·2
III	7,110	7,620	510	7·2	32·7	29·9
IV	3,550	3,850	300	8·5	16·3	15·1
16 and 17	2,470	2,150	−320	−13·0	11·4	8·5
Total	21,760	25,480	3,720	17·1	100·0	100·0

READING

(a) CORE

Cluster	Economically active males		Change	Per cent change	Per cent total	Per cent total
	1961	1966	1961–66	1961–66	1961	1966
I	5,430	5,710	280	5·2	13·9	14·4
II	7,600	7,790	190	2·5	19·5	19·7
III	15,110	16,130	1,020	6·8	38·8	40·7
IV	9,670	9,510	−160	−1·7	24·8	24·0
16 and 17	1,160	450	−710	−61·2	3·0	1·2
Total	38,970	39,590	620	1·6	100·0	100·0

(b) RING

Cluster	Economically active males		Change	Per cent change	Per cent total	Per cent total
	1961	1966	1961–66	1961–66	1961	1966
I	8,200	11,390	3,190	38·9	21·5	24·1
II	7,790	10,870	3,080	39·5	20·4	23·0
III	11,390	14,370	2,980	26·2	29·8	30·5
IV	7,710	8,030	320	4·2	20·2	17·0
16 and 17	3,080	2,540	−540	−17·5	8·1	5·4
Total	38,170	47,200	9,030	23·7	100·0	100·0

Source: Censuses.

considerably higher share of non-manual workers is a peculiarity of the whole region, which is exceptionally well illustrated in this particular sector. But even here one of the main distinctions in our analysis, the polarization between core and ring, is proved for cluster I, the high-income non-manual workers. The mean difference of approximately 5 per cent in a rather similar change of about 2·5 per cent in the importance of these groups, however, is the result of adding up more or less contrary trends in two of the SMLAs. This becomes clear from Table 7.10.

Here, examining percentage changes, one finds that SMLAs like High Wycombe, Reading, and Aldershot show clear indications of a trend which may be defined as decentralization of high-income, non-manual workers towards the rings. Slough belongs to this group too, although it shows no significant increase in the polarization of the first cluster between 1961 and 1966. But not all segments of the zone are in accordance with this general tendency. The London part is rather difficult to assess because of its composition. There are also some notable exceptions to the south-south-west of London: Walton and Weybridge, Woking, and even to a lesser extent Guildford. It is noteworthy that all these exceptions show little deviation from the usual pattern in their rings. Only the cores present significant differences from the general trends, in that they have a higher proportion in cluster I. This has been particularly intensified by a notable increase in the relevant SEGs, especially employers and managers, in the time interval considered here.

This pattern expresses the complexity of the changes, particularly their root causes.[28] While the core areas of some of these SMLAs can be regarded as countryside for the core of Greater London, the rural districts of the same SMLAs may serve equally the core of the SMLA or both. Even living in a core does not necessarily imply working there. This appears to be more obvious if there is a dominant centre like London nearby, conveniently accessible by one means of transport or another.

At this point it may be useful to look in more detail at the other clusters, especially the high-income manual workers. These SEGs appear to be linked with the core, although to a lesser extent than the analogous non-manual cluster is tied to the ring. This turns out to be a stable situation though we find a considerably higher change in time in the rings for some SMLAs.[29] It should be noted that the share of this cluster is nearly equal in core and ring for the exceptional SMLAs which we have mentioned above. Difficulties arise when looking at the low-income manual workers. Within this group, changes are fundamentally affected by the overall decrease. This occurs especially in the rings; we therefore find an apparent relative concentration towards the cores.

[28] It is justifiable to explain this special pattern in part by the numerical composition of two SMLAs, which only consist of one authority in their rings: but this would not apply to Guildford. Therefore, we would suggest the following interpretation.

[29] But that does not notably modify the differences, as cluster III is more important in the cores – in 1961 on average by 4 per cent; therefore, an increase has greater effects with regard to the percentage of that cluster in 1966.

Table 7.11

PRIVATE HOUSEHOLDS BY TENURE, SINGLE SMLAs IN THE FIVE STUDY AREAS, 1961 AND 1966 CORES

SMLA	1961				1966			
	Owner-occupied	Local authority New town corporation	Private, etc.	Total	Owner-occupied	Local authority New town corporation	Private, etc.	Total
	percentages of total				percentages of total			
High Wycombe	48·3	29·9	21·8	100	51·2	29·5	19·3	100
Slough	44·2	33·2	22·6	100	46·2	34·8	19·0	100
London (part)	50·1	14·2	35·7	100	51·8	15·7	32·5	100
Walton and Weybridge	55·1	16·0	28·9	100	61·0	14·9	24·1	100
Woking	55·4	20·9	23·7	100	60·6	20·5	18·9	100
Guildford	45·0	25·1	29·9	100	49·7	25·1	25·2	100
Aldershot	38·3	21·1	40·6	100	45·6	21·9	32·5	100
Reading	44·1	21·8	34·1	100	53·0	17·6	29·4	100
Southampton	41·1	27·7	31·2	100	42·4	30·1	27·5	100
Portsmouth	49·0	14·3	36·7	100	51·1	17·3	31·6	100
Birmingham (part)	35·1	35·0	29·9	100	37·7	38·5	23·8	100
Coventry	53·0	22·6	24·4	100	57·2	22·8	20·0	100
Leicester	44·3	23·2	32·5	100	43·7	27·5	28·8	100
Manchester	37·3	21·3	41·4	100	40·8	25·4	33·8	100
Rochdale	41·2	25·1	33·7	100	45·6	27·5	26·9	100
Bury	53·6	24·1	22·3	100	60·2	22·8	17·0	100
Bolton	55·5	23·0	21·5	100	57·5	24·5	18·0	100
Leigh	44·0	32·8	23·2	100	47·3	33·7	19·0	100
Wigan	37·6	25·9	36·5	100	41·9	32·6	25·5	100
Warrington	32·4	30·3	37·3	100	34·9	34·6	30·5	100
Liverpool	25·5	27·9	46·6	100	29·3	30·5	40·2	100
St. Helens	33·4	27·6	39·0	100	36·8	30·0	33·2	100
Southport	57·1	6·5	36·4	100	61·8	6·8	31·4	100

RINGS

SMLA	1961 Owner-occupied	1961 Local authority New town corporation	1961 Private, etc.	1961 Total	1966 Owner-occupied	1966 Local authority New town corporation	1966 Private, etc.	1966 Total
	percentages of total				percentages of total			
High Wycombe (i)	57·2	18·0	24·8	100	62·5	16·4	21·1	100
Slough (ii)	50·5	22·1	27·4	100	54·4	23·3	22·3	100
London (part)	53·7	16·9	29·4	100	57·0	17·5	25·4	100
Walton and Weybridge	61·9	15·2	22·9	100	65·9	16·7	17·4	100
Woking	55·6	16·2	28·2	100	59·4	15·4	25·2	100
Guildford	54·1	17·1	28·8	100	58·3	17·7	24·0	100
Aldershot	53·2	18·5	28·3	100	58·8	18·5	22·7	100
Reading (iii)	58·3	13·7	28·0	100	66·0	13·0	21·0	100
Southampton	48·9	21·4	29·7	100	54·3	21·2	24·5	100
Portsmouth	53·2	26·4	20·4	100	57·7	25·7	16·6	100
Birmingham (part)	61·5	15·1	23·4	100	63·5	16·8	19·7	100
Coventry (iv)	45·5	24·1	30·4	100	53·0	23·8	23·2	100
Leicester (v)	57·3	19·5	23·2	100	67·6	14·2	18·2	100
Manchester (vi)	55·3	22·5	22·2	100	59·8	24·8	16·4	100
Rochdale	34·7	23·6	41·7	100		not available		
Bury (vii)	47·4	23·1	29·5	100	48·0	31·4	20·6	100
Bolton (viii)	60·8	18·3	20·9	100	68·0	17·2	14·8	100
Leigh (ix)	45·0	32·1	22·9	100	52·0	33·4	14·6	100
Wigan (x)	41·5	22·5	36·0	100	50·4	24·4	25·2	100
Warrington (xi)	51·0	22·3	26·7	100	60·7	19·7	19·6	100
Liverpool	47·5	25·4	27·1	100	51·7	26·2	22·1	100
St. Helens	45·8	30·7	23·5	100		not available		
Southport		No ring						

(i) without Beaconsfield U.D., Marlow U.D.
(ii) without Eton U.D.
(iii) without Henley U.D.
(iv) without Daventry M.B., Lutterworth R.D.
(v) without Market Harborough R.D.
(vi) without Mossley M.B., Audenshaw U.D., Alderley Edge U.D., Crompton U.D., Knutsford U.D., Lees U.D., Lymm U.D., Bollington U.D.
(vii) without Ramsbottom U.D., Tottington U.D.
(viii) without Kearsley U.D., Little Lever U.D.
(ix) without Abram U.D.
(x) without Apsul U.D., Orrel U.D., Standish with Langtree U.D., Up Holland U.D., Wigan R.D.
(xi) without Runcorn R.D.

Do the housing tables (Tables 7.8 and 7.11) confirm this apparent tendency for non-manual high-income workers to move to the rings? As expected, the owner-occupied proportions are distinctively high for these SMLAs, with an average of 52·4 per cent for the cores and 60·3 per cent for the rings in 1966. Again the greatest anomalies in the cores are found in Walton and Weybridge, and Woking. Corresponding to their distinctive social structure, these SMLA cores have also numerical values near and above the average for their rings.

In general the major changes are taking place as between the owner-occupied and the privately rented sector, while the figures in the public sector remain rather stagnant. Only in a place like Slough, where the social structure is characterized by the predominance of manufacturing industry,[30] does this sector become important; here the local authority and new town corporation-rented sector rose to 34·2 per cent of the whole in 1966. The ring of this SMLA, however, also has the greatest amount in the public sector for the zone, with a percentage of 23·3 per cent in 1966.

Within the individual SMLAs in the London segment, the Reading SMLA has a quite distinct core/ring polarization. In 1961 about equal numbers of people lived in core and ring. While no significant increase is shown for the core between 1961 and 1966, the substantial increase of 23·7 per cent during the five-year interval in the ring is clearly dominated by both non-manual clusters.[31]

A SURVEY OF ATTITUDES

To analyse the reasons for this segregation, it is useful to enlarge the area by adding Easthampstead (with Bracknell new town) and Basingstoke M.B. with its surrounding Rural District. We refer to this enlarged area as the Reading sub-region, since previous discussions have proved Reading to be a more distinct sub-centre than any other SMLA west of London.

Without any claim for representativeness, a household survey was done in September to October 1970 in villages south of Reading,[32] lying within the ring of the SMLA. All settlements belong to those villages in the county for which it was resolved by the County Planning Committee that Village Plans be prepared 'as there was an urgent need for a comprehensive analysis of the situation and a detailed policy for the future'.[33] It is significant, perhaps,

30 Hall and Smith, op. cit. (1968), pp. 64–6.

31 Table 7.10, Reading SMLA.

32 The survey by questionnaire in Spencers Wood (Berkshire) was a 10 per cent sample survey, chosen by selecting every tenth household in the village from the electoral register, 1969. Thus 46 households were contacted of which 36 (78·4 per cent) responded. We asked the husband and his wife to complete separate sheets which gave us 68 answers to the crucial questions. The survey in Burghfield Common was made by contacting every tenth household for particular areas by chance of visit; so was the procedure in Sherborne St. John (north-west of Basingstoke M.B., Hants). Therefore, we shall use those results more illustratively.

33 Preamble in 12 village plans for Berkshire C.C.

that consultation with members of the Village Plan team of the counties revealed that no social survey had been made, nor was any likely to be done.[34] The plans emphasized that proper means of development are infilling and rounding off, as they 'will not materially alter the physical, social or visual character of the settlement'. Therefore, no attention was paid to social changes which are the inevitable concomitant of any demographic alteration, particularly in small population units. As the preservation of identity, shape and form, etc. appeared to be the major objective, the proposals were based principally on the recommendation of a village envelope as the basis of planning decisions over the next ten years.

We clustered the households responding to our questionnaire by our two main occupational categories,[35] manual and non-manual, distinguished in our Census statistics. In the village of Spencers Wood, the bulk (80·5 per cent) allocated themselves to white-collar groups, such as professional and supervisory, only 13·9 per cent were classified as manual (skilled and unskilled), while two heads of the household were retired. Only a minority of the non-manual group had their employment locally (20·7 per cent) compared with 34·5 per cent mentioning Reading as place of work. There was a significant divergence among the rest; while three (10·3 per cent) commuted to London, the same percentage as stated the labour centre (i.e. Reading) mentioned other towns as the place of their employment. This diffused pattern of home and workplace separation became even more apparent in the smaller sample for Burghfield Common, which was also dominated by non-manual workers, 79 per cent versus 21 per cent manual. Only seven of the nineteen heads of the households interviewed were employed locally or within adjacent villages, as compared with four in Reading, and twice as many in London (four) and other places (four). It is noteworthy that in Spencers Wood more than one-third of the wives of those heads of the households classified as non-manual were at least part-time employed, stating most often clerical-supervisory as their occupational group. In the Burghfield Common sample this correlation became less evident.

When asked to rank the reasons for coming to live in the village,[36] most of the non-manual males mentioned work reasons in the first place. At the first sight this appears to be a little illogical, as most of them were employed at other places than the village. The motivation was clarified, however, when taking into account the other rankings, e.g. those given to the environmental and/or housing reasons. 'Living in the countryside' etc., were the reasons most often given in the first or second place, while place of work came in third place, after the housing reasons; a distribution which was even more distinct in the answers stated by the women.

[34] Partly because of lack of staff, rather than lack of interest.

[35] In the questionnaire, groups were given as: professional/managerial, clerical/supervisory, skilled manual, unskilled manual.

[36] More than half of the non-manual households did not live in Spencers Wood six years ago, while only nine (31 per cent) were residents for more than eleven years.

Questions were asked about people's perception of their environment. More than two-thirds of the non-manual households considered that they lived in a village – although their 'ideal village' was most definitely different from Spencers Wood. The interests, however, were mainly home based, and were more likely to increase there or even outside the village, while the wives' activities appeared to be more equally distributed, although not primarily tied to the village.[37] Naturally, certain of the village societies catered mainly for women, both facts supporting evidence that participation in village life is predominantly a function of time spent in the place.[38] On the other hand, one would suggest that these different interests are considerably affected by lack of mobility, as the car available for the household is used for commuting and the wife has to rely on an insufficient public transport system.[39]

Even though there was no particular question whether people intended to move on in the near future, the impression was often gained that Spencers Wood was merely an intermediate location, temporarily satisfying particular needs.[40] Asked about their idea of a village community, different people responded quite differently. Those giving negatively accentuated answers, such as 'groups meeting specifically for a purpose', seemed to feel that reality had been obscured by false expectations,[41] while others, who were members for

[37] Three categories were distinguished for those questions.

Affirmative answers	Home based	Village based	Outside the village
Present leisure patterns:			
Non-manual males	17	6	13
Wives of non-manual males	12	11*	15
Increasing leisure spent by:			
males	8	2	12
wives	8	4*	12

* Thirteen of the twenty-six wives in the non-manual household group were members of a local society.

[38] Although the absolute figures will not give statistical proof, it should be admitted that three of the seven non-manual males belonging to a local society did commute to other places than Reading. Membership of village organizations was also uncorrelated with length of residence.

[39] In Spencers Wood, eighteen (50 per cent) households had one car, eight families had none or two cars, while two households had three cars at their disposal. The bus service was thought to be poor here as in Burghfield Common.

[40] While most of the non-manual households interviewed were happy with the present residential development (21 out of 29), they would not like to see further extensions of the built up area – not to become even more an out-of-town place with regards to Reading.

[41] In those cases we often found statements like 'you have to go to Devon to come upon real village life'; whereby ten out of seventeen non-manual heads of the households correlated physical/environmental features to the village as against six social and one miscellaneous issues. Those settlements were often envisaged as places for retirement.

example of the local tennis club, seemed to·be quite satisfied with their way of life in the village.

South-east of Reading, and just outside the area of the SMLA, we find Bracknell, one of the eight London new towns, which were designated in the years 1946–49 to become 'self-contained and balanced' communities. While the social segregation within a new town, as well as for all London new towns,[42] is sufficiently documented, less is known about the differences between the towns and their surrounding districts.[43] In the case of Bracknell, using the Census data for 1961 and 1966, the statement can be made: there is a high proportion of non-manual workers in the new town, but there is also an increasing difference between Bracknell and its adjacent rural district. It is difficult to argue a causal explanation for this polarization, but some figures may help to illustrate the basic pattern. Analysing their records and interviewing fifty households which intended to move out in 1963 (May to September) the Development Corporation found that two-thirds of those were non-manual occupants. But the structure of this mobility became even more distinct when isolating the twenty-two of the heads of those households intending to keep their present jobs in the town. Those moving home, but retaining Bracknell jobs, were largely non-manual employees,[44] who were found to be moving to places within a few miles of the town, as to parishes like Crowthorne, Binfield and Wokingham M.B. The Development Corporation report goes on to emphasize that 52 per cent of those visited were leaving to buy a house. Yet owner-occupation is also available for Corporation houses in the new town itself. As has been stated by the recent reports for most new towns, there is, however, no demand to buy Corporation houses.[45] We may, therefore, suggest that in cases like Bracknell, even new towns are sometimes transitional links in a chain leading families from the centre of the urban region to its more rural fringe parts, a movement which is obviously differentiated by socio-economic characteristics of the families to a considerable extent. The increasing success of private development, even in otherwise chiefly public sponsored enterprises, can be taken as a further indication of changes in demand.

The other London branch in the Reading sub-region, though outside the SMLA, is Basingstoke. Ten years after the agreement between the former

[42] B. J. Heraud, 'Social Class and the New Towns', *Urban Studies*, vol. 5 (1968), pp. 33–58; R. Thomas, *London's New Towns*, P.E.P. (1969), p. 416. The evidence from R. Thomas is summarized in Vol. 2, Chap. 10.

[43] L. Bolwell, B. Clarke and D. Stoppard, 'Social Class in a New Town: A Comment', *Urban Studies*, 6 (1969), pp. 93–6. The authors published as a part of the analysis of the shopping patterns a table (Table 1, p. 95) of the SEGs in Crawley and its hinterland.

[44] Bracknell Development Corporation, *Tenants leaving Bracknell*, Oct.–Sept. (1963), p. 2; Similar movements are now reported for Crawley by Bolwell, Clarke and Stoppard, op. cit. (1969), pp. 95–6.

[45] HMSO, *Reports of the Development Corporation*, (1970); BBC 13 Oct. 1970. Bolwell, Clarke and Stoppard, op. cit. (1969), p. 96, go as far as to suggest that a development of owner-occupied housing would approach a social balance.

London County Council and the local authorities responsible for the market town, the development is imposing all types of influence over the surrounding districts. The Development Group is very much engaged in achieving a target of 1,000 houses per annum with all the infrastructural accessories. It is claimed that people are happy within their environment.[46] There has been a reasonable amount of private development, as in similar undertakings all over the country, and more mixed development is proposed. Residents of the surrounding villages have articulated their feelings about a further expansion of the built-up area[47] – proposed by the planners to accommodate another 26,000 residents[48] and to cope with the increasing demand for floorspace per household.

These parishes fear for their rural calm as 'the Town' goes on creeping towards them with every new estate. One such village, Sherborne St. John, where we conducted a survey, actually seems unlikely to be increased because the agricultural land in the area is of high quality,[49] and because the Village Plan, dated January 1965, contains the credo of British rural planning: 'This village lies within the "white" area of the Basingstoke Town Map and one of the objects of this map is to preserve the rural character of Sherborne St. John and maintain a rural area between it and the town'.[50] There has been substantial additional private development since this was written. From the answers given by twenty-two out of the thirty-two residents,[51] though, we have to assume that this is regarded as in keeping with village character, as called for by the plan. The majority (63·6 per cent) of the villagers would disapprove of any further development and only 36·4 per cent were so realistic as to allow limited development, secluded to maintain the character of the existing village. There were good reasons for the majority[52] to dislike any development: more than one-third came to the place primarily because of environmental reasons (e.g. countryside, peace and quiet, etc.) in the first place, while two-thirds in all mentioned this as one reason for arrival. This, however, would be destroyed by further housing expansion, as was stated by these people seeking attractive countryside.

Nearly half of the residents interviewed had lived in the village less than six years. Their main place of work was Basingstoke (almost exclusively for the males) where most of the shopping was also done. Only a few residents characterized their further activities as village based, while fifteen (i.e. two-thirds of those responding to this question at all) emphasized home based activities. The next most important group of activities was oriented to a

[46] Basingstoke B.C., *Expanding Basingstoke*. Bulletin No. 13, April (1971).

[47] *Evening Post*, Reading, 26 June, 1970.

[48] Hampshire C.C., *Basingstoke: Further Growth*. June (1970).

[49] Ibid., Map 1.

[50] Hampshire C.C., *Sherborne St John Village Plan*. Jan. (1965).

[51] In this survey 17 households were visited getting response from 32 persons in the core of the civic parish, for which the plan gave a population of 800 in 1965.

[52] Those answering the occupations questions were 61·5 per cent non-manual, which was less than in the other villages surveyed.

greater degree outside the village, where the majority were likely to spend any increase in leisure time.

What kind of general conclusions can be drawn from this survey[53] in terms of the main issues in this chapter? Although non-manual residents dominated in all examples, there were some variations in the distribution of socio-economic groups. Neither those villages nor the whole ring of the SMLA are homogeneous units in terms of demographic characteristics: there are, however, certain similarities, and sometimes differences are greater within than among villages. Even people's motivations were shown to fall into defined general categories. The desire for a place in the country was heavily correlated with other variables, particularly car ownership, given the poor public transport system outside the urban areas. People's perceptions of the rural scene, however, were negatively correlated with the use they made of it. On the other side it is clear that for those who lived in a village which owed its character to the county planning office, but which was essentially part of a metropolitan area, people's aspirations were increasingly being disappointed.

As regards housing tenureship, we found that substantial public housing in the ring can be explained by the need to accommodate people affected by slum clearance or the like in other parts of the county, rather than by the exercise of free choice. Those areas have a definite negative influence on the value of nearby land. On the other side, planning policy has clearly favoured affluent groups more than it has promoted social balance, whatever advantages might lie in social diversity.

DETAILED VARIATIONS IN THE WEST MIDLANDS AND NORTH-WEST

With the West Midlands we come to a part of Britain which differs to a considerable extent from the rest of the country. Comparing the different sections in Table 7.7 one will notice a definite tendency for growth in the region as a whole, which indicates its strong position in the national economy.

This tendency, somewhat modified, is also evident in the segment of the area which is analysed here (Tables 7.6 and 7.12). Within this segment, there are notable differences between the Birmingham SMLA (part) and the Coventry SMLA, especially in the degree of segregation in the non-manual workers' cluster. Considering the shape of the segments and the composition of the figures there seems to be a more complex pattern of segregation here. It is less based on a core/ring structure, as distinguished in the SMLA concept, than on the relationship to the larger area of the conurbation with its high quality residential parts at the fringe, that is in and beyond the green belt.[54] The figures suggest that segregation appears to be related to population density, an impression which is strengthened by the housing figures (Table 7.11), where there is a remarkable differentiation in the Birmingham SMLA, but not for the Coventry SMLA.

[53] The survey was done in settlements commonly called villages, and therefore has no definite relation to what is happening in the urban districts of the rings.

[54] Thus there is only a slight decrease in cluster III as between core and ring, while we can set aside changes in S.E.G.s 16 and 17.

Table 7.12

SOCIO-ECONOMIC PATTERN IN THE WEST MIDLANDS (SINGLE SMLAs), 1961 AND 1966

BIRMINGHAM

(a) CORE

Cluster	Economically active males		Change	Per cent change	Per cent total	Per cent total
	1961	1966	1961–66	1961–66	1961	1966
I	35,530	35,080	−450	−1·3	9·7	10·2
II	51,530	50,850	−680	−1·3	14·2	14·8
III	166,410	154,210	−12,200	−7·3	45·7	44·8
IV	99,410	101,430	2,020	2·0	27·3	29·4
16 and 17	11,360	2,740	−8,620	−75·9	3·1	0·8
Total	364,240	344,310	−19,930	−5·5	100·0	100·0

(b) RING

Cluster	Economically active males		Change	Per cent change	Per cent total	Per cent total
	1961	1966	1961–66	1961–66	1961	1966
I	15,990	17,740	1,750	10·9	25·4	27·4
II	11,940	12,820	880	7·4	18·9	19·8
III	21,890	22,510	620	2·8	34·8	34·8
IV	10,690	10,970	280	2·6	17·0	17·0
16 and 17	2,460	620	−1,840	−74·8	3·9	1·0
Total	62,970	64,660	1,690	2·7	100·0	100·0

COVENTRY

(a) CORE

Cluster	Economically active males		Change	Per cent change	Per cent total	Per cent total
	1961	1966	1961–66	1961–66	1961	1966
I	17,920	19,900	1,980	11·1	11·6	12·5
II	22,880	24,600	1,720	7·5	14·8	15·4
III	69,850	70,490	640	0·9	45·1	44·2
IV	42,220	43,640	1,420	3·4	27·3	27·3
16 and 17	1,950	930	−1,020	−52·3	1·2	0·6
Total	154,820	159,560	4,740	3·1	100·0	100·0

(b) RING

Cluster	Economically active males		Change	Per cent change	Per cent total	Per cent total
	1961	1966	1961–66	1961–66	1961	1966
I	9,010	10,980	1,970	21·9	14·4	15·9
II	7,340	8,960	1,620	22·1	11·8	13·0
III	25,350	29,070	3,720	14·7	40·6	42·1
IV	16,500	18,250	1,750	10·6	26·4	26·5
16 and 17	4,220	1,720	−2,500	−59·2	6·8	2·5
Total	62,420	68,980	6,560	10·5	100·0	100·0

Source: Censuses.

Table 7.13

SOCIO-ECONOMIC PATTERN IN SOUTH LANCASHIRE AND NORTH CHESHIRE (SINGLE SMLAs), 1961 AND 1966

MANCHESTER

(a) CORE

Cluster	Economically active males		Change	Per cent change	Per cent total	Per cent total
	1961	1966	1961–66	1961–66	1961	1966
I	45,410	4,434	−107	−2·4	10·2	11·2
II	75,769	6,790	−786	−10·4	17·1	17·2
III	190,710	16,968	−2,103	−11·0	43·0	42·8
IV	124,481	11,119	−1,329	−10·7	28·1	28·0
16 and 17	6,910	291	−400	−57·0	1·6	0·7
Total	443,270	39,602	−4,725	−10·7	100·0	100·0

(b) RING

Cluster	Economically active males		Change	Per cent change	Per cent total	Per cent total
	1961	1966	1961–66	1961–66	1961	1966
I	44,730	4,947	474	10·6	21·6	22·4
II	41,900	4,520	330	7·9	20·3	20·5
III	75,570	8,258	701	9·3	36·6	37·4
IV	41,530	4,236	83	2·0	20·1	19·2
16 and 17	2,960	113	−183	−61·8	1·4	0·5
Total	206,690	22,074	1,405	6·8	100·00	100·0

ROCHDALE

(a) CORE

Cluster	Economically active males		Change	Per cent change	Per cent total	Per cent total
	1961	1966	1961–66	1961–66	1961	1966
I	3,140	380	66	21·0	11·6	14·0
II	3,630	374	11	3·0	13·5	13·7
III	11,210	1,122	1	0·1	41·5	41·3
IV	8,390	828	−11	−1·3	31·1	30·5
16 and 17	610	14	−47	−77·1	2·3	0·5
Total	26,980	2,718	20	0·7	100·0	100·0

(b) RING

Cluster	Economically active males		Change	Per cent change	Per cent total	Per cent total
	1961	1966	1961–66	1961–66	1961	1966
I	1,280	1,230	−50	−3·9	12·9	12·6
II	1,070	1,400	330	30·8	10·8	14·3
III	4,640	4,500	−140	−3·0	46·8	46·0
IV	2,740	2,510	−230	−8·4	27·6	25·7
16 and 17	190	140	−50	−26·3	1·9	1·4
Total	9,920	9,780	−140	−1·4	100·0	100·0

BURY

(a) CORE

Cluster	Economically active males		Change	Per cent change	Per cent total	Per cent total
	1961	1966	1961–66	1961–66	1961	1966
I	2,510	2,920	410	16·3	13·2	14·6
II	2,640	3,430	790	29·9	13·8	17·2
III	8,270	8,600	330	4·0	43·4	43·1
IV	5,250	4,900	−350	−6·7	27·6	24·6
16 and 17	380	90	−290	−76·3	2·0	0·5
Total	19,050	19,940	890	4·7	100·0	100·0

(b) RING

Cluster	Economically active males		Change	Per cent change	Per cent total	Per cent total
	1961	1966	1961–66	1961–66	1961	1966
I	2,710	3,290	580	21·4	11·8	13·5
II	3,200	3,710	510	15·9	13·9	15·3
III	10,480	10,780	300	2·9	45·6	44·3
IV	6,340	6,410	70	1·1	27·5	26·4
16 and 17	270	120	−150	−55·6	1·1	0·5
Total	23,000	24,310	1,310	5·7	100·0	100·0

BOLTON

(a) CORE

Cluster	Economically active males		Change	Per cent change	Per cent total	Per cent total
	1961	1966	1961–66	1961–66	1961	1966
I	6,190	6,940	750	12·1	10·5	12·4
II	8,100	8,110	10	0·1	13·8	14·5
III	25,590	24,630	−960	−3·8	43·5	44·0
IV	18,360	16,150	−2,210	−12·0	31·2	28·8
16 and 17	610	150	−460	−75·4	1·0	0·3
Total	58,850	55,980	−2,870	−4·9	100·0	100·0

(b) RING

Cluster	Economically active males		Change	Per cent change	Per cent total	Per cent total
	1961	1966	1961–66	1961–66	1961	1966
I	2,620	3,770	1,150	43·9	13·3	17·3
II	2,970	3,790	820	27·6	15·0	17·4
III	8,860	9,350	490	5·5	44·9	42·9
IV	5,190	4,810	−380	−7·3	26·3	22·0
16 and 17	100	90	−10	−10·0	0·5	0·4
Total	19,740	21,810	2,070	10·5	100·0	100·0

LEIGH

(a) CORE

Cluster	Economically active males		Change	Per cent change	Per cent total	Per cent total
	1961	1966	1961–66	1961–66	1961	1966
I	1,080	1,140	60	5·6	7·1	8·2
II	1,740	1,670	−70	−4·0	11·4	12·0
III	6,200	5,900	−300	−4·8	40·7	42·4
IV	5,970	5,100	−870	−14·6	39·2	36·7
16 and 17	250	100	−150	−60·0	1·6	0·7
Total	15,240	13,910	−1,330	−8·7	100·0	100·0

(b) RING

Cluster	Economically active males		Change	Per cent change	Per cent total	Per cent total
	1961	1966	1961–66	1961–66	1961	1966
I	1,750	2,140	390	22·3	11·7	13·3
II	1,650	2,480	830	50·3	11·0	15·4
III	6,250	6,660	410	6·6	41·8	41·3
IV	5,050	4,780	−270	−5·4	33·7	29·7
16 and 17	270	50	−220	−81·5	1·8	0·3
Total	14,970	16,110	1,140	7·6	100·0	100·0

WIGAN

(a) CORE

Cluster	Economically active males		Change	Per cent change	Per cent total	Per cent total
	1961	1966	1961–66	1961–66	1961	1966
I	2,220	2,470	250	11·3	8·8	10·6
II	2,820	2,810	−10	−0·4	11·2	12·1
III	10,520	10,110	—410	−3·9	41·7	43·4
IV	9,350	7,760	−1,590	−17·0	37·0	33·3
16 and 17	320	130	−190	−59·4	1·3	0·6
Total	25,230	23,280	−1,950	−7·7	100·0	100·0

(b) RING

Cluster	Economically active males		Change	Per cent change	Per cent total	Per cent total
	1961	1966	1961–66	1961–66	1961	1966
I	2,910	3,730	820	28·2	8·9	10·5
II	3,250	4,720	1,470	45·2	9·9	13·4
III	14,520	14,460	940	6·5	44·2	43·8
IV	11,750	11,090	−660	−5·6	35·8	31·4
16 and 17	410	310	−100	−24·4	1·2	0·9
Total	32,840	35,310	2,470	7·5	100·0	100·0

WARRINGTON

(a) CORE

Cluster	Economically active males		Change	Per cent change	Per cent total	Per cent total
	1961	1966	1961–66	1961–66	1961	1966
I	1,500	1,380	−120	−8·0	5·8	6·0
II	3,220	2,900	−320	−9·9	12·6	12·6
III	11,620	10,970	−650	−5·6	45·3	47·8
IV	8,830	7,610	−1,220	−13·8	34·5	33·2
16 and 17	460	100	−360	−78·3	1·8	0·4
Total	25,630	22,960	−2,670	−10·4	100·0	100·0

(b) RING

Cluster	Economically active males		Change	Per cent change	Per cent total	Per cent total
	1961	1966	1961–66	1961–66	1961	1966
I	5,360	6,090	730	13·6	18·3	19·3
II	5,250	5,610	360	6·9	17·9	17·8
III	11,810	13,080	1,270	10·8	40·3	41·6
IV	6,450	6,570	120	1·9	22·0	20·9
16 and 17	430	120	−310	−72·1	1·5	0·4
Total	29,300	31,470	2,170	7·4	100·0	100·0

LIVERPOOL

(a) CORE

Cluster	Economically active males		Change	Per cent change	Per cent total	Per cent total
	1961	1966	1961–66	1961–66	1961	1966
I	28,930	25,170	−3,760	−13·0	9·8	9·5
II	46,840	43,890	−2,950	−6·3	15·9	16·6
III	109,090	99,880	−9,210	−8·4	37·1	37·7
IV	102,320	93,550	−8,770	−8·5	34·7	35·3
16 and 17	7,230	2,530	−4,700	−65·0	2·5	0·9
Total	294,410	265,020	−29,390	−10·0	100·0	100·0

(b) RING

Cluster	Economically active males		Change	Per cent change	Per cent total	Per cent total
	1961	1966	1961–66	1961–66	1961	1966
I	26,550	30,850	4,300	16·2	17·7	19·8
II	31,420	32,300	880	2·8	20·9	20·7
III	52,230	54,180	1,950	3·7	34·8	34·8
IV	37,250	37,560	310	0·8	24·8	24·1
16 and 17	2,680	1,000	−1,680	−62·7	1·8	0·6
Total	150,130	155,890	5,760	3·8	100·0	100·0

ST. HELENS

(a) CORE

Cluster	Economically active males		Change	Per cent change	Per cent total	Per cent total
	1961	1966	1961–66	1961–66	1961	1966
I	2,090	1,870	−220	−10·5	6·1	6·1
II	3,900	3,410	−490	−12·6	11·3	11·1
III	16,180	14,440	−1,740	−10·8	47·0	46·8
IV	11,770	10,840	−930	−7·9	34·2	35·2
16 and 17	500	260	−240	−48·0	1·4	0·8
Total	34,440	30,820	−3,620	−10·5	100·0	100·0

(b) RING

Cluster	Economically active males		Change	Per cent change	Per cent total	Per cent total
	1961	1966	1961–66	1961–66	1961	1966
I	3,420	4,430	1,010	29·5	13·2	13·8
II	4,000	5,220	1,220	30·5	15·4	16·3
III	10,820	13,340	2,520	23·3	41·8	41·6
IV	7,300	8,980	1,680	23·0	28·2	28·0
16 and 17	350	120	−230	−65·7	1·4	0·3
Total	25,890	32,090	6,200	24·0	100·0	100·0

SOUTHPORT

(a) CORE

Cluster	Economically active males		Change	Per cent change	Per cent total	Per cent total
	1961	1966	1961–66	1961–66	1961	1966
I	5,480	5,280	−200	−3·7	24·0	24·3
II	4,850	4,480	−370	−7·6	21·2	20·6
III	8,140	7,600	−540	−6·6	35·6	34·9
IV	4,170	4,320	150	3·6	18·2	19·9
16 and 17	230	60	−170	−73·9	1·0	0·3
Total	22,870	21,740	−1,130	−4·9	100·0	100·0

(b) (NO RING)

The ring of the Coventry SMLA has a considerable share of manual workers; with 68·6 per cent of the total it is an index of the industrial character of this area. Although called rural districts, a number of these local authorities are no longer truly rural. As the high proportion of clusters III and IV shows, overspill from the neighbouring towns and the location of industry have transformed their function. Therefore, one would expect that here the favoured residential areas would occur in the wider fringe, rather than adjacent to the town nuclei.

A broad glance at the map (Fig. 6.14) for our part of the North-West region indicates the complexity of the structure. We need to discover in what ways the zone is influenced by its two potential foci, Manchester and Liverpool-Birkenhead.

Examining first the figures of distribution by SEGs in Table 7.7 we find that the region as a whole is more in line with national trends than, for example, the West Midlands. The share of high-income manual workers is lower than for the West Midlands. In this connection the importance of cluster IV, the low-income manual worker, mainly unskilled, is above all due to the domination of stagnant or declining industry in this particular part of the country.

The two big centres show clear evidence of polarization. Even the two smaller SMLAs between them, St. Helens and Warrington, and perhaps less clearly Leigh, show the same pattern. This indicates that the rings represent parts of the more favoured residential areas in and around the conurbation. Living here, one has the additional advantage of good accessibility to the labour centres. The substantially lower share of high-income non-manual workers for those intermediate SMLAs may again indicate a wider-meshed pattern of segregation.

Far more than could be deduced for London, and even for the West Midlands, Manchester appears to influence the development of the SMLAs north and north-west of it. Rochdale, Bury, Bolton, and Wigan all show a rather similar SEG structure in core and ring. On the other hand, it is very difficult to assess to what extent this balance is caused by other reasons. This would require a social survey, since the Census figures lose their validity when further broken down. But even the available data, as listed in Table 7.13, seem to suggest that there is no point in distinguishing between core and ring in the northern part of the zone. C. B. Hall and R. A. Smith also give some evidence on this point as far as social differentiation of people by area of residence is concerned. They publish percentage figures for their class 1 (our cluster I) showing the dominance of these SEGs in some local authorities south of Manchester.[55] The rings here have long since lost their function as dormitory areas for people in clusters I and II. As against this, cluster III has higher importance in the rings than in the corresponding cores. This does not occur as a characteristic within the other segments of this area, but we found a similar situation in the eastern sector of the West Midlands.

Summarizing the general pattern we have to emphasize again to what a considerable extent movements within the region and in some particular SMLAs are influenced by socio-economic factors. This is stressed by a study of K. G. Pickett for slightly different area sections. She compares the pattern of gross migration with proportion in SEG cluster I, showing 'that generally speaking, areas of high mobility are those with a high proportion of men in these groups and vice versa'.[56] Assuming that this correlation with the social structure is not merely a statistical accident, it would certainly support the hypothesis of an increasing core/ring polarization of certain socio-economic groups.

[55] Hall and Smith, op. cit. (1968), p. 61.

[56] K. G. Pickett, 'Aspects of Migration in North-West England', *Town Planning Review*, 38 (1967–68), p. 242.

As in other areas, we tried to compare the social pattern with that of the housing tenure. In doing this, we have to bear in mind that Table 7.9(d) gives evidence of a very equal share of tenureship groupings in cores and rings for cluster IV in the North-West region. In this area, the housing pattern is far from being as distinct as in the Midlands. This is suggested even by the average figures for private households by tenure in Table 7.8 and 7.11, especially for the local authority and new town corporation-rented houses. As already mentioned, the distinction used here (owner-occupied, public sector and private, etc. rented) turns out to be very susceptible to the presence of new-town development as well as slum clearance. This is proved by the high proportion of public rented households, often above 30 per cent; this average is somewhat falsified by the case of Southport with only 6·8 per cent in local authority and new-town housing in 1966.

CONCLUSIONS AND FURTHER THOUGHTS

Though we had to take into account that most of the figures used here are derived from a 10 per cent sample, the analysis of the data draws attention to several significant items in the distribution of residents of certain SEGs within selected metropolitan areas. The most important is that there is fairly clear verification of our hypothesis that there is polarization of the non-manual workers as between cores and rings. In the case of cluster I this is particularly pronounced in some areas. By definition the lower status households were more concentrated in the labour centres. But we could prove a significant deviation between the trends for clusters III and IV: while the high-income manual worker appeared to tend towards some degree of equilibrium within most SMLAs, the purely numerical values for his low-income colleague increased in the cores, which is logical as a result of the contrary movement in the other three clusters.

We infer that this is a reflection of the conflict between economic interest and social symbolism which determines the use of land by different groups. But we were unable to draw firm conclusions as to motivation. We had to be tentative on other fundamental constraints, like stages in the family cycle and type of social network, which are all much interlinked to the other factors. Some ideas were put forward, however, based on survey findings in one part of a SMLA.

We could not prove a similar strong correlation for the housing pattern by core and ring. The attitude towards moving is certainly influenced by the structure of the household as a whole, which unfortunately cannot be clearly established from the available data. High-income households tend to consist of more than one wage earner. The situation therefore is that internal variations in the different categories obscure the pattern.

Since the polarization based on the housing tenureship was not as clear as expected in most areas, we should look at it from another angle. Given that in the mid 1960s there was still a shortage of dwellings, one can ask: to what extent might this limit the tendency towards more extensive segregation?

According to American experience a surplus of at least 8 per cent of suitable dwellings is needed to keep a mobility cycle going. P. Collison commented on this demand for separation: 'If attempts are made to mix the social classes in close proximity it seems likely that these attempts will be resisted and as more dwellings become available, increasingly ineffective',[57] a statement which could be confirmed by our analysis of the planned resettlement in the West London Sector.

How far is segregation an inevitable and continuing trend?[58] On the very local scale, R. E. Pahl, reviewing the literature, concludes that people 'who are sure of their position in society may be less afraid to live near those of lower status'.[59] One would add that this is so if the environment guarantees a certain amount of privacy, which in any event will cause the high-status groups to leave the urban core. This being so, the daily commuting distance to the core is a significant criterion for higher socio-economic classes in choosing their place of residence in a given sphere of urban influence. At the first glance the economic disadvantage of locating on the fringe seems to be large. But we must consider the changes in the distribution of activities as well as the means of transportation. Doing so one will see that the locational patterns of land use within the urbanized area of the SMLA still result from basic economic forces. But there are changes in emphasis, between work and leisure for instance, so that the concept of accessibility has to be constantly redefined. One should for instance bear in mind H. B. Rodgers' finding that the more affluent socio-economic groups engage more in various forms of leisure activity,[60] or the finding of C. B. Hall and R. A. Smith, that retired people tended to be drawn to homes near to areas of outstanding natural beauty.[61] This, however, is about as far as we are able to go by way of causal inference.

We can be reasonably sure that individual behaviour will differ from one part of the country to another, even though there are some reassuring similarities in our statistical results, which indicate a certain degree of conformity. The same statistical results, measured in percentages, may have very different explanations in different areas: the social structure of individual sub-cultures in different parts of the country is undoubtedly different and will affect the spatial patterns. But going into greater depth, again, would demand more elaborate social research based on structural concepts. What is clear from our statistical analysis is that there are distinctive economic contrasts between the different areas. The North with its predominance of manufacturing industry shows a higher proportion in cluster IV and even cluster II. The South, in contrast, has a concentration in the professional and service

[57] P. Collison, 'Neighbourhood and Class', *Town and Country Planning* (1955), p. 337.

[58] Heraud, op. cit., p. 53.

[59] Pahl, op. cit. (1970), p. 41.

[60] H. B. Rodgers, 'Leisure and Recreation', *Urban Studies*, vol. 5 (1969), pp. 368–84.

[61] Hall and Smith, op. cit. (1968), p. 61.

trades, indicated by a relatively high share of non-manual, especially high-income non-manual, (cluster I), workers.

One important result of our study is that the rings of the Standard Metropolitan Areas sometimes appear far from homogeneous. This especially appears to be the case on the fringes of the big conurbations, where there may be complex overlapping influences of a number of separate urban cores. Here it is possible to find greater differences between neighbouring SMLAs than within them. Where these features are strongly marked it is difficult to deduce a distinctive type of core/ring polarization within any individual metropolitan area. Rather, it seemed that the whole zone could be regarded as part of a core/ring structure on a larger scale, which took in several neighbouring metropolitan areas. It proved impossible to analyse this interesting thesis in any more detail. It does, however, reinforce a thesis we have developed in other sections of this chapter: that in the zones of urban growth around the biggest conurbations, a system of urban dominance and sub-dominance may be developing over time.

PART THREE

FIVE CASE STUDIES: A HISTORY

Part Three of our study now focuses on the five study areas of Megalopolis, which were isolated at the end of Part Two. For each, it presents a detailed history of urban growth since the 1930s and of the impact of the planning system on that growth after the Second World War. As far as possible, this history is taken from the official sources: the plans, reports and studies which form the plan-making activity in each area. A deeper analysis of attitudes, actors, and inter-relationships in these same five areas is reserved until Part Two, Volume Two of the study.

Chapter Eight describes London's western fringes: the western suburbs of Greater London, developed rapidly during the 1930s, and the adjacent home counties in Buckinghamshire, Berkshire, Surrey and eastern Hampshire, together with the County Borough of Reading. This has been an area of exceptionally rapid urban growth both in interwar and postwar times – and of strenuous attempts by planning authorities to control it since the Second World War.

Chapter Nine looks at another area of very rapid growth, though on a smaller scale: South Hampshire, developed around the two cities of Southampton and Portsmouth.

Chapter Ten considers the impact of a major provincial conurbation, Birmingham and the West Midlands, and the neighbouring city of Coventry, one of the most rapidly growing large cities of England in the twentieth century, upon the neighbouring counties of Worcestershire and Warwickshire.

Chapter Eleven, on Leicester and Leicestershire, in contrast recounts the history of a freestanding city of moderate size and its relationships to its surrounding county.

Chapter Twelve returns to the impact of the growth of the conurbations. In this case, North-West England, there is not one but two major conurbations, whose centres are only thirty-five miles apart. They have had a profound impact upon the neighbouring counties of Lancashire and Cheshire.

CHAPTER EIGHT

LONDON'S WESTERN FRINGES

This is the first of our detailed histories of urban development, and planning problems, in our five selected case study areas within megalopolis. In many ways, it is the most complex; because of the great size of London and its commuting field, we have to consider a sector of it only. With it, we consider some of the metropolitan areas of London's outer fringes, which have grown so rapidly in the period since the Second World War: areas like Reading, Slough, and Aldershot.

This was the area par excellence where unplanned urban growth in the 1930s alerted public concern and led to the creation of the post-1945 system of planning controls. The chapter describes the developments between the wars, the creation of the postwar machinery and the original development plans with their heavy emphasis on control and containment. It describes the slow awakening to the changed facts of rapid population growth during the 1950s, and the return to regional planning in the 1960s. It ends by looking at the problems of organizing regional planning in an area as large as this.

This chapter was researched and written by Peter Hall.

INTRODUCTION

The area we shall investigate in this chapter is well known to most Londoners, and to a good many non-Londoners who have flown out of London Heathrow airport in a westerly direction. It sits astride the main radial routes westwards from London, both by road and rail. The discerning air traveller might see simultaneously three main rail routes, Waterloo to Southampton, Paddington to Bristol, and Paddington to Birmingham, as well as three radial motorways completed or under construction in 1970, the M3 London-Southampton, the M4 London-Bristol and the M40 London-Oxford. These lines of the main radial routeways are followed by straggling lines of urban growth for many miles, broken only by the effect of postwar planning controls and above all by the impact of London's green belt. In Reading the area has one town with well over 100,000 people, in Slough another with 90,000 in 1970; in Bracknell it has a rapidly growing new town, and in Basingstoke a town expansion scheme developed under the 1952 Town Development Act, which bids to rival the new town in rapidity of growth.

Figure 8.1 London's Western Fringes: Key Map

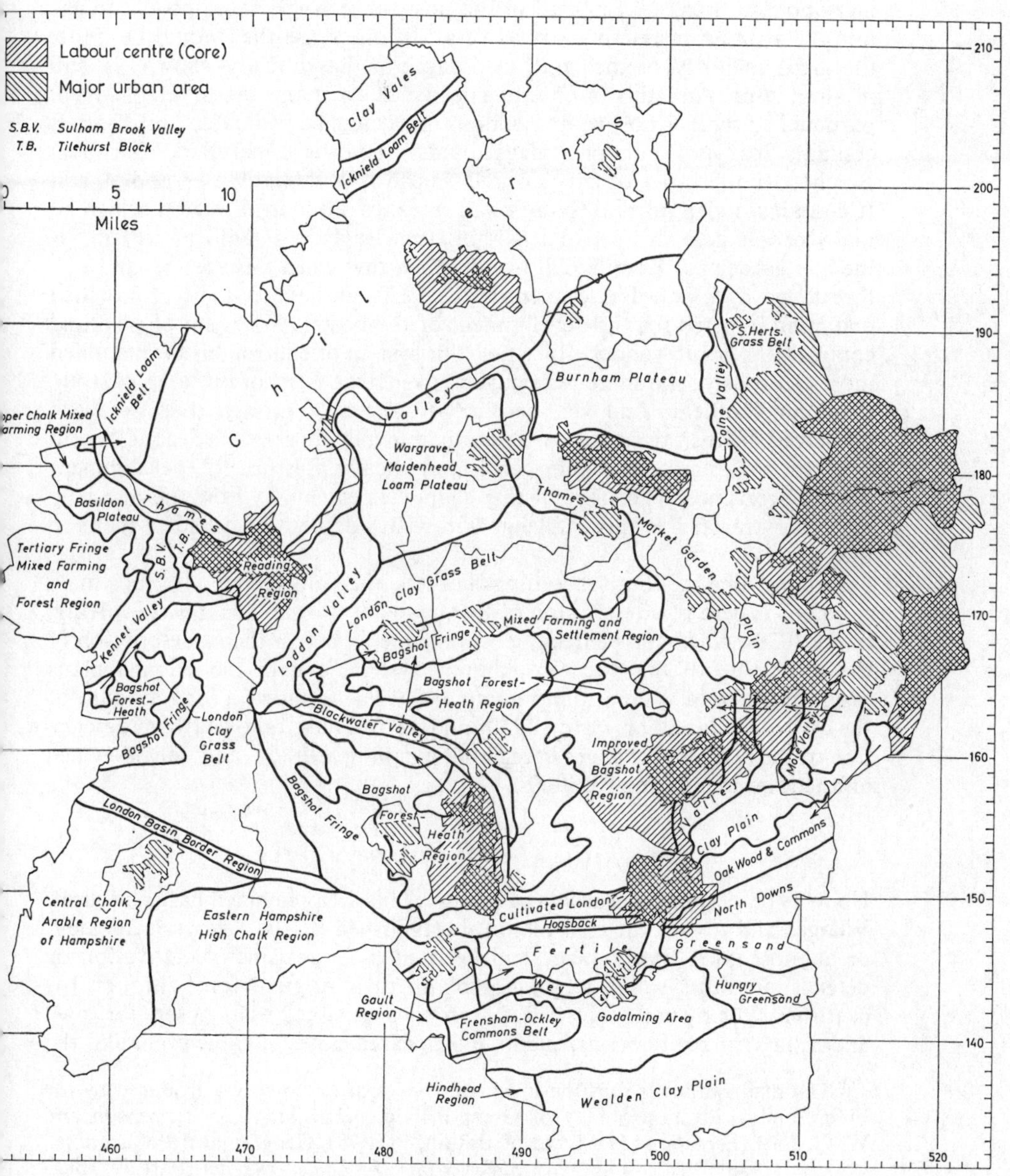

Figure 8.2 London's Western Fringes: Land Use Regions

Yet for all these signs of urban development, which is only too evident also from a statistical analysis (the area had some of the fastest-growing metropolitan areas of England in the postwar period), most people might think of it in an instinctive way as rural. In one sense they would be right: the great majority of the land, as Chapter 6 has already shown, is still in rural uses. And this is countryside which to many urban Englishmen, particularly those who live in London, is particularly valuable and dear. It contains many of London's playgrounds: Windsor Great Park, Burnham Beeches, the Thames at Henley and Marlow, Virginia Water and Ascot. It contains above all the Thames valley above London, a region which to many people is as distinctive a part of rural England as Salisbury Plain, or the hop gardens of Kent. Small wonder then that when this area began to be threatened by urban development in the 1920s and 1930s, the fact provided one main impetus for the development of the post-1945 system of planning control. It is small wonder either that this system of control has been applied more rigorously, and more restrictively, over large parts of our area of study than many others. And yet, because of forces of growth that were not conceived of when the system was set up immediately after the Second World War, the area has come under consistently heavy pressure for development almost ever since. The story of this chapter is essentially how the planning machinery reacted to this challenge and what adaptations it had to make in the process.

Broadly, like the four succeeding chapters, this falls readily into four main divisions. There is a description of the area as it was, and as it was evolving, in the 1930s, chiefly taken from prewar sources. There is then a description of the setting up of the postwar planning system, and of the original plans produced by that system round about 1950. Then follows a long account of the crisis of adaptation in the 1950s and early 1960s, followed by a description of the profound changes in regional planning attitudes and policies which affected the area during the 1960s.

THE ORIGINAL SETTLEMENT PATTERN[1]

Up to 1918, despite its nearness to London, this area remained basically rural. Villages and towns, the vast majority established by the Saxons, stagnated, or at most grew slowly. They had been sited for reasons of cultivation or defence or trade, which might not retain their original force through the centuries. Yet by and large well chosen sites remained well chosen, for town and village alike. Few settlements disappeared, save in cataclysms like the

[1] The main source here is the invaluable series of monographs produced by the First Land Utilization Survey of Great Britain, particularly: J. Stephenson and W. G. East, *Berkshire* (The Land of Britain, Part 78), Geographical Publications, London (1936); E. C. Willatts, *Middlesex and the London Region* (Part 79, ibid., 1937); D. Fryer, *Buckinghamshire* (Part 54, ibid., 1942); F. H. W. Green, *Hampshire* (Part 89, ibid., 1940); and L. D. Stamp and E. C. Willatts, *Surrey* (Part 81, ibid., 1942).

Black Death of the fourteenth century; only a few new settlements appeared, reflecting new location forces.

Thus the settlement pattern of 1918 was readily related on the one hand to patterns of agricultural potential, on the other to considerations of defence or administration or trade. The importance is that this pattern provided a set of fixed points, to which subsequent history must relate. If the old patterns had been in some way different, so would the new. In the spontaneous, unplanned growth of the 1930s, and in the planned development of the 1950s and 1960s, the original settlement pattern provided a set of nuclei. It is worthwhile, at the outset, to look at this essential basis.

In the very north of the area, the dip slope of the Chiltern Hills descends southwards, from the scarp top, down into the London basin. Based on chalk, this slope has an extensive covering of clays which greatly alter its character, producing a thick beechwood cover in many places. Together with the steep slopes produced by local dissection, this has somewhat inhibited clearance for farming; yet once the land is cleared, it produces good mixed farming as a rule. Settlement in the countryside tends to be scattered, with hamlets and isolated farms. And because of the relief, location of major towns has been difficult. The biggest town in the Southern Chilterns, High Wycombe, grew in a remarkable ribbon until it was six miles long, along the old London-Oxford road in the bottom of the valley of the river Wye. By 1939, it had already sent subsidiary ribbons of housing up the valley sides towards the plateau of the back slope itself. This was a product not so much of London commuters, as of the growth of the town's own industries; the old furniture trade, originally a domestic industry in the Chiltern beechwoods, was turning into a factory industry during this time.

The southern edge of this Chiltern dip slope is followed roughly by the Thames, which cuts a deep valley into the chalk rock in many places, especially between Henley and Maidenhead. In its meandering course the river has left extensive tracts of very similar country on both north and south banks. This borderland country rests always on the chalk platform, but there is an extensive cover of newer, tertiary rocks. In some places the terrain is dominated by gravels, which are covered in forest and heath; the biggest tract is Burnham Beeches in south Buckinghamshire. Westwards, and thus on the opposite bank of the river (for here, the Thames flows north-south), the Maidenhead-Wargrave loam plateau carries a mixture of soils including some of the heavier London clay, as well as the lighter Reading beds. Though these are good soils, settlements had remained sparse and population densities low. Even after the railway arrived in the nineteenth century, this area, some thirty miles from London, remained outside the metropolitan orbit up to 1918, and even up to 1939.

Urban settlement tended to cling to the river itself, where it tended to take the form of twin bridgepoint towns, one of them much more important than the other: Windsor-Eton, Maidenhead-Taplow, Reading-Caversham. Because the Thames is a county boundary upstream from London to Oxford, these pairs of towns were invariably in different counties. Rural settlement along the river, on the other hand, was inhibited by the flood danger in the wide alluvial valley bottoms, and by steep slopes up on to the chalk platform in which the river is incised.

There were, though, two exceptions to this rule about the Thames. The Reading beds, which lie on the chalk platform around the town which gives them their name, produce very fertile, warm soils which have been intensively cultivated. Reading itself, on an important site at the confluence of the Thames and the Kennet, was a Saxon foundation. It was restricted in its growth first by the wide, flood-prone valley bottoms, and secondly by a ring of large country parks all around. To avoid the floodlands it grew principally west and east, on the Reading beds. By 1918 it had already incorporated some of the parks in its structure, and the entire urban area numbered 95,000 people, most of them within the borough boundaries. By 1939 the population was up to 114,000, and there had been very rapid growth during the 1930s in suburbs outside the borough, like Tilehurst to the west or Woodley-Earley to the east.[2] The remaining nursery and orchard land was threatened; so were some of the remaining country parks, such as Whiteknights, Caversham and Bulmershe Court. Contemporary observers thought that they would all soon be swallowed, and regretted the fact.[3]

Eastwards, where the Thames Valley opens out east of Slough-Windsor, it is the same story. Here, the gravel terraces of the Thames itself, especially the wide Taplow terrace, north of the river, provided some of the most fertile soil for intensive cultivation in all England: a deep, rich loam. For centuries this land had been London's garden, though the actual market gardening area migrated westwards in front of the developing spread of London. The difficulty, though, was precisely that this land was good for almost any purpose one might name. It was so flat that it had been chosen, in 1784, for the first base line of the British topographic mapping service. Railways were easily run across it in the early nineteenth century; the engineer Brunel chose it, logically, for the direct east-west route of his main Great Western rail line from Ealing through Hayes and Southall to Maidenhead. The main coach road had followed a slightly more southerly course across the gravel belt. Water supplies were excellent and cesspits were easily dug, so the need for expensive main drainage could be postponed; thus the village of Ashford in Middlesex, with some 9,000 people, received main drainage only in 1934. By 1937, Willatts could write:

> The result is that today the eastern or Londonward end of the region is almost completely obliterated by a series of towns which merge into one another, while further out there are rapidly growing towns, which are frequently increasing in area as well as in population.[4]

These developments followed very closely the main radial transportation lines from London, both by rail and road. The most remarkable case was

[2] Berkshire Development Plan, *Review of the Reading Area*. Reading (1957), p. 5.

[3] Stephenson and East, op. cit., p. 36.

[4] Willatts, op. cit., p. 194.

Slough, which was located astride both the main Bath road and the Great Western Railway: started as a transport depot by the War Office in the First World War, the site was developed as an industrial trading estate by private enterprise after the war, and the result was an unplanned new town that grew from 27,000 people in 1921 to 63,000 by 1939.[5] Areas not so well served, like that between the main Great West Road, and the Staines road to the south, were much less affected; Windsor, which falls in this sector and is not on a main rail line, almost stagnated in the 1920s and actually lost people in the 1930s.[6] Thus the result, by 1939, was a marked clustering of urban growth along the main radial road and rail lines.

South of the critical transition zone of the Thames valley, the thick heavy London clay crops out. It gives characteristically heavy soils, very wet and intractable in winter, very dry in summer. In the early and Middle Ages, people had tended to avoid it; it stayed in forest for a long time. In the nineteenth century it became grassland. Small hamlets and isolated farms were the characteristic mode of settlement, and towns did not develop. To this day, it forms a very obvious and characteristically empty area on the map of this zone. Only where soils were mixed with Reading beds or valley gravels, as along the valley of the Loddon (a north-flowing Thames tributary) a few miles east of Reading, would villages tend to occur.

This rather negative zone gives way southward to another important transitional belt: the border of the heavy London clay against the extremely light Bagshot sands. This forms a narrow belt, usually about two miles wide, following the road from Reading via Wokingham and Bracknell to Ascot; then, further east towards Egham, it drops into the Thames valley. The soils in this belt are characteristically very mixed and the land uses are correspondingly varied. This was attractive terrain for settlement, and villages abound: Winnersh, Arborfield, Swallowfield, Mortimer and Burghfield form a half ring around Reading to the south. And since the main east-west road naturally follows the belt to avoid the difficult country to the north and south, naturally small market towns like Wokingham and Bracknell[7] also developed. Already, by 1939, the main importance of this belt was as a residential area. Well-drained land, good scenery, and easy road and rail communications were attracting the more adventurous London commuter out here in large numbers. The result was a rather loose string of settlements following the main road and electric railway from Egham via Virginia Water, Ascot, Bracknell, Wokingham, and Winnersh to Reading. All the time, during the 1930s, this still rather open pattern was tending to thicken up.[8]

Further south again comes a sudden change. The tertiary sands of the Bagshot and Bracklesham series form a flat-topped plateau rising sharply above the London clay land to the north to an average height of between

[5] Buckinghamshire Development Plan, *Slough and District Town Map, Report and Analysis of the Survey*. Aylesbury (1951), p. 6.

[6] Berkshire Development Plan, *Report of Survey*. Reading (1951), p. 5.

[7] Strictly, Bracknell was little more than a village, though it had a market.

[8] Stephenson, op. cit., p. 100.

350 and 420 feet above sea level. For centuries this was a vast, almost uninhabited waste. In the nineteenth century, enclosure and then extensive afforestation changed its outward appearance. But it remained true that this is an area almost without any old tradition of settlement. The places that do occur, therefore, are almost all a creation of the period since 1800. They take two main forms: towns like Woking, Fleet or Aldershot, or dispersed rural settlements like the houses strung out along the remarkable Nine Mile Ride between Crowthorne and Arborfield.

Nevertheless, where the circumstances were right, settlements could grow quickly and formlessly in this zone. The impetus was a double one: residential growth for commuting or retirement, and military needs. Woking, twenty-six miles south-west of London, was a mere group of cottages until the arrival of the main London-Southampton railway in 1838; then a new nucleus developed two miles to the north on open heath around the station, and low-density settlement spread steadily, eventually embodying some neighbouring villages between the two world wars. The town grew from 31,000 people in 1921 to 41,000 in 1939, with a heavy element of immigration in the 1930s.[9] Further to the west across the Hampshire border, Aldershot was developed deliberately by the War Office during the Crimean War of 1854, when it was decided to establish a permanent base for a regular home army; later the Royal Aircraft Establishment was developed nearby at Farnborough. Both Farnborough and Fleet developed as high-class residential areas in the late nineteenth century; they were attractive both to retired military families, and to commuters who used the stations on the main London-Southampton railway.[10] The Bagshot country, therefore, had developed a very characteristic settlement pattern by 1939; sprawling, low-density residential towns along the main railway line, garrisons and extensive training areas on the heathlands, occasional straggling rural settlements at very low densities along the forest roads.

In the south-east and south-west corners of this great heath and forest tract, though, there is a critical difference. On both sides of the Blackwater valley which forms the Surrey-Hampshire border, and in the area round Basingstoke, the Bagshots form lower, more dissected land at 150–200 feet, which has been systematically improved by fertilization. Market gardening is the characteristic activity here, and it divides the heathland into a large number of small, attractive commons which have drawn much low-density residential development with big gardens. The Blackwater valley itself intrudes into this pattern in the south-east: it forms a wide band of coarse alluvium, a major barrier to communications and to settlement, with a characteristically loose, sprawling pattern of urban communities on either side. In the south-west, Basingstoke forms a very different sort of urban focus: a traditional corn and cattle market

[9] Surrey Development Plan, *Report and Analysis of Survey, The Town Maps (5) Woking and District*. Kingston (1953), paras 5, 48–56, *passim*.

[10] Hampshire Development Plan, *Analysis of the Survey; Aldershot, Farnham and Fleet Town Map*. Winchester (1953), pp. 1, 12, 21–2.

town, whose status was enhanced by a canal in 1800 and by the main London-Southampton railway in the 1840s. But up to 1939, standing as it did over forty miles from London, it was really outside the metropolitan orbit.

Southward again, the chalk finally reappears from under the cover of newer rocks which fill the London basin. But in contrast to the northern rim of the basin, where the Chilterns have a long, gentle back-slope, here pressures in the earth's crust produced intense folding. The result is that the chalk forms a narrow, upstanding ridge, the famous Hog's Back between Guildford and Farnham. It forms a barrier to settlement between the Bagshot fringe country to the north and the heathlands of the western Weald to the south. Where the river Wey breaks through to the chalk ridge, Guildford was founded before the Norman conquest: a classic textbook example, for any schoolchild, of the river gap-town. Up to 1939, a little nearer London than Basingstoke, it had performed very much the same range of functions: local market town, home of local industries beginning to serve a national market, and only to a very limited degree a dormitory for London.

The process of urban growth in this whole area, up to 1939, can be easily summarized. Up to 1918, it was virtually outside the influence of London, and of London's growth. Only in a few favoured places along the commuter rail lines, as at Maidenhead or Woking or Fleet, did a small pioneering minority of London workers settle, generally in very exclusive low-density settlements; for after all, people who would live that far from London were clearly looking for space and rural tranquility. This situation had changed completely by 1939. The whole zone around London, up to a distance of about forty miles, shared in the general growth of the metropolitan area; for between 1923 and 1937, London and the home counties took some 42·7 per cent of the net growth of the employed population.[11] Stephenson, writing on land use in Berkshire in 1936, made the critical distinction between the east of the county, where settlement had dispersed because of metropolitan influence, and the still rural west, where a declining population was still in process of centralization and consolidation.[12]

However, within the zone of metropolitan shadow, there were still clear distinctions to be made. Willatts in 1937 made one of the most important:

> Within a circle with a diameter of approximately twenty-five miles the land is almost completely developed by building. Beyond this somewhat irregular main mass stretch extensions along certain well defined routes showing tailing lines of suburbs reaching for many more miles. . . . The traveller by railway and even more by road frequently obtains an exaggerated impression of the actual extent of building development since this is often of a ribbon nature, flanking the roads.[13]

[11] Report of *The Royal Commission on the Distribution of the Industrial Population.* HMSO, London (1940), p. 37.

[12] Stephenson, op. cit., p. 70.

[13] Willatts, op. cit., p. 164.

This distinction, between continuous built up mass and ribbon extensions, concealed a more basic, structural distinction. Willatts warned that:

> . . . it should not be thought that there had been merely a steady outward movement of London's fringe. The suburban growth has been a spontaneous movement, and many of the more distant towns have grown even more rapidly than the immediate suburbs of the metropolis. In many cases there has been a gradual expansion and transformation of an old nucleus, in some cases entirely new towns have arisen within the present century as a result of a new railway. . . . People increasingly take a pride in living, as they say "beyond the suburbs", thereby creating fresh suburbs even further out.[14]

This process, beyond the continuous built-up area, was an irregular one. Between the lines of most rapid urban growth along the main roads and railways, whole rural sectors might be preserved. Furthermore, Willatts stressed, different types of terrain could produce very different patterns of urban settlement: generalization was dangerous. The London clay, both north of the river in Middlesex and south of it in Surrey, tended to produce large compact estates, because of the need for drainage. The Bagshot heathlands of Berkshire and Surrey, in contrast, tended to generate a pattern of large houses standing in big grounds, because of the cheapness of land there.

Writing just before the Second World War, Willatts did not see this process of rapid growth as an unmitigated evil. On the one hand, the urban invasion of the villages would inevitably lead to a demand for urban services, with the result that rural rates would rise to pay for services which the original inhabitants might neither desire nor appreciate. On the other hand, an expanding local market for fresh milk and vegetables was an asset, especially for the smallholders on the poorer soils. Perhaps the most serious problem, Willatts thought, was that the prospect of continued disturbance for building brought a fatalistic outlook to the whole countryside.

> There are too many boards proclaiming land "ripe for development", "this desirable freehold building site for sale" and similar signs that there is no expectation of a rural future. There is little inducement to maintain the best traditions of good farming and estate management when there is small hope of another generation being able to enjoy the privilege of obtaining a living from the soil and when the best rural workers are continually being tempted to the towns.[15]

Willatts concluded, hopelessly:

> It is too late to speculate on what might have happened if some coordinated plan had guided the growth of London.[16]

[14] Ibid., p. 166.
[15] Ibid., p. 167.
[16] Ibid., p. 168.

It was against this background that we must view the Barlow Report, the Abercrombie Greater London Plan, and the whole attempt to set up effective land use planning in the period after 1947.

THE GREATER LONDON PLAN AND AFTER

The general philosophy of the Barlow Report, and of the Abercrombie Plan which followed it, have already been described in Chapter Three. The American observer, Donald Foley, has given a reminder of its impact on contemporaries:

> Nor should we overlook the appeal of the Greater London Plan and its companion County of London Plan on ideological and aesthetic grounds. The plans contained an adroit mixture respecting the traditional and taming the unwanted. . . . British citizens were offered the reassuring impression that the best features of London as they knew them could be maintained while forces at work to change the London they revered could be brought under control. This was a welcome and hopeful message.[17]

Abercrombie, in other words, shared the ideology of the British governing class who had appointed him. There can be no doubt, from the many official pronouncements of that time, that Foley's analysis of that ideology is correct. On the one hand, there was the good London: this was the old, fairly compact, highly-centralized London which had existed up to the end of the nineteenth century. This must be preserved, and given new strength. On the other, there was a bad London: the interwar London of the sprawling suburbs, which had been built by small builders, mainly for lower middle-class buyers, between 1918 and 1939. The governing class, who in no sense could be described as lower middle-class, were profoundly shocked by this evidence of the mass democracy of the market-place in action. An important minority of them resolved that positive action by the state was needed to stop it. And during the Second World War, after publication of the Barlow Report, the minority view became the received view of the majority.

The basic features of the 1944 Abercrombie Plan, then, as Foley has said, were strongly social in their motivation.[18] The community must act to provide the best possible living conditions, inside an orderly and workable physical plan for the whole region, and within a framework of full employment. Ideologically, as we saw in Chapter Three, these are basic views of moderate social reformers in England at least since the beginning of the twentieth century; but the plan at last made them look like a practical reality. It did so, in Foley's words, by providing a heavily *unitary* plan: that is, a concrete, single vision of the desired end-form for the city.[19] This puts it firmly within

[17] Donald Foley, *Controlling London's Growth: Planning the Great Wen 1940–1960*. University of California Press, Berkeley and Los Angeles (1963), p. 45.

[18] Ibid., pp. 32–3.

[19] Ibid., p. 56.

the tradition of architect plans which go back to the beginnings of the garden city movement.

Given the hindsight of history, Abercrombie's belief in his own ability to control a complex physical entity seems astoundingly self assured. But it must be remembered always that he produced his plan against the background of stagnation which was characteristic of Britain between the two world wars. Population, gross national product, disposable wealth, grew so slowly that it was easier to think of controlling the result. Abercrombie, like any planner, depended on his demographic advisers. They, like him, had embodied in themselves the pessimism of a whole age, and everywhere, the experts proved incapable of forecasting the changes to come.

Applied in detail to the study area, Abercrombie's Plan meant a green belt, starting at the edge of the built-up London of 1938, and extending roughly five miles to the west. Within it, there were some important towns: Staines at the busy Thames crossing, and Uxbridge in the Colne valley. These towns would have to be strictly limited in their future growth:

> ... the green belt ring, with its open lands and running streams used for recreative purposes, and acting as a barrier to the continuous expansion of London, should not provide, even in its inhabited parts, for the large scale building which, as described later on, will be necessary in connection with decentralization. If, due to the urgency of the immediate postwar period, exceptions have to be made, they should be few.[20]

Beyond this came the outer country ring, where the bulk of the overspill population, displaced from London by slum clearance and other redevelopment schemes, was to find new homes. But, 'Not by any means is the surplus population of the metropolis to be broadcast at random over its surface'. The essential strategy was seen essentially in terms of a single, once-for-all mass movement from London:

> ... by a series of carefully graded additions to the inhabited places, more generously measured than in the green belt ring, and by a series of new towns limited in number and in size, the decentralization of London will be largely accomplished, and still the characteristic farming pursuits will proceed uninterrupted over almost the whole of this area.[21]

For each part of the area, the implications were spelt out in detail. But sometimes, without any very specific remedy: logically, Abercrombie was much more specific about those places destined for specific planned overspill schemes, than about the middle-class areas which might grow slowly through spontaneous migration.

In the north of the area, at Wycombe, the emphasis at first should be 'on reconstruction and bettering the present community rather than on expansion';[22] but later on, the town might house 14,000 overspilled

[20] Patrick Abercrombie, *Greater London Plan 1944*. HMSO, London (1944), p. 26.
[21] Ibid., p. 26.
[22] Ibid., p. 127.

Londoners. Further eastwards, towards London, the emphasis was all on restriction. Beaconsfield had been carefully developed, and on the east and north sides it was clearly defined against the countryside; this feature should be preserved. On the west there was 'cheaper sprawling development' and all attempts to develop industry here should be thwarted.[23] At Gerrards Cross, prewar development should not be allowed to continue, and the eastern side towards London should be part of the green belt; Denham, within the green belt, should be stopped from growing.[24]

A little further south, Slough should be a priority town for receiving London industry; then, when the local labour supply was fully absorbed, people could come from London also, and eventually about 41,000 Londoners might be absorbed.[25] Windsor, on the other hand, had 'medieval charm' and little further expansion should be contemplated.[26] The most important development in Berkshire would be a totally new town, one of the eight proposed for the ring around London, at White Waltham west of Maidenhead. This was an 'excellent flat site', well served by the main railway and the proposed South Wales motorway. It should prove a popular site for manufacturing industry, and basic services could be easily provided.[27]

Further south still, on the middle-class landscapes of the Bagshot sands, Abercrombie's policy was characteristically less well defined. In the Bagshot area itself, the villages needed 'careful treatment' as part of green belt policy; they should be rounded off without further major growth, to keep as much open land between them as possible.[28] A little further out, in the Ascot-Sunninghill-Sunningdale area, the villages had 'an air of neglect and poverty and appear to lack any community of interest with their well-to-do neighbouring residents'; though there was no specific proposal to deal with this problem.[29] Just across the Surrey border in the Frimley-Camberley area, Abercrombie found Camberley 'featureless and rather dull', but restricted his proposals to a diversion of the main A30 road round the Camberley shopping area. Farther out, Basingstoke was a 'thriving market and shopping centre' with some expanding industries; there was no specific planning proposal.[30]

In May 1946 Lewis Silkin, Minister of Housing and Local Government, accepted on behalf of the government the main features of the Abercrombie Plan, though reserving judgement on details, notably, the location of the new towns.[31] This happened only after a thorough vetting of the plan, first by an interdepartmental committee of civil servants, and secondly by an advisory committee of local government representatives, who in fact leant

[23] Ibid., p. 126.
[24] Ibid., pp. 126–7.
[25] Ibid., p. 128.
[26] Ibid., p. 125.
[27] Ibid., p. 161.
[28] Ibid., p. 149.
[29] Ibid., p. 125.
[30] Ibid., p. 165.
[31] Foley, op. cit., pp. 31–2.

heavily on a technical subcommittee of officials. This latter group wished to introduce some important changes of emphasis: in particular, they proposed that new towns should house only 171,000 people as against Abercrombie's target of 402,000, placing the emphasis instead on expansions of existing towns (with a target of 821,000 against Abercrombie's 475,000). They also wished to house a rather greater proportion of the total increase in the green belt ring.[32] The Minister's answer, which appeared in 1947, accepted neither of these modifications. But it did agree to abandon the proposal for a new town at White Waltham west of Maidenhead, on the ground that it would promote continuous development between London and Reading. It left open the question of expanding Basingstoke, which had been suggested by the interdepartmental committee.[33]

THE PLANNING AUTHORITIES TAKE OVER: POLICIES IN THE 1950s

About the time of the Minister's reply, the historic Town and Country Planning Act provided the means of implementing Abercrombie. With one critical limitation, though: since all efforts to reform the structure of local government finally proved abortive at that time, the responsibility for producing and enforcing the plans was divided among a host of local county and county borough planning authorities, whose boundaries often reflected the accidents of history in Anglo-Saxon times. In the area west of London, these boundaries were if anything even more anomalous than in, say, the Midlands, because they tended to follow the river Thames, which in fact tended to provide town sites which have become the focus of the modern commuting and shopping regions. Donald Foley's comment is apposite:

> A vivid contrast emerges. On the one hand, a single strong, competent town planner, Patrick Abercrombie, was commissioned by the government to prepare a plan for metropolitan London. On the other, divers responsibilities were assigned to nine local planning authorities, to a Ministry committed to reviewing local plans and planning-control decisions but cool to national or strong regional planning, and to a multiplicity of sundry governmental authorities, some decidedly powerful in their own right. Serious splits in planning and development initiative and responsibility have followed. It is little wonder that, in such circumstances, the Greater London Plan proved able, at best, to provide ideas and grand policy but did not become the nucleus of the vital, comprehensive planning many desired.[34]

[32] Advisory Committee for London Regional Planning, *Report to the Minister of Town and Country Planning, Report of the Technical Sub-Committee*. HMSO, London (1946); proposals summarized in table on p. 21.

[33] *Greater London Plan: Memorandum by the Ministry of Town and Country Planning on the Report of the Advisory Committee for London Regional Planning*. HMSO, London (1947), pp. 5–7.

[34] Foley, op. cit., p. 79.

The local planning authorities were therefore left to interpret Abercrombie's prescription in their own way, subject to such pressures as the Ministry of Housing and Board of Trade might manage to impose. Their original Reports of Survey, prepared as essential background to the policy decisions embodied in their original County Development Plans of the 1948–52 period,[35] demonstrate these individual interpretations.

Basic to this work was the question of employment. For the planners at that time, the clear objective was to reduce the burden of long journeys to work. Therefore, almost axiomatically, those areas which were to receive extra people should receive extra jobs too. But here, the Board of Trade exercised a decisive influence. Again and again, the Reports of Survey revealed that in practice, the local planning authorities took the Board's policy pronouncements as immutable guidelines.

Thus in Buckinghamshire, the 1951 Report of Survey quotes the Board's policy: not to allow factory building in the county if it could be operated as economically in the Development Areas. There were exceptions: planned decantation of population under the Abercrombie Plan, redevelopment of obsolete or congested factories, or where a local firm had an 'irresistible' case.[36] Thus at High Wycombe, there was a labour shortage and no case for much new industry, though there would be much redevelopment of old premises, especially in the furniture industry. But at Slough, provision must be made for a planned influx of 22,000 Londoners, while local firms might make a vigorous case for expansion, which would be difficult to resist. Therefore, on the Board's own recommendation, land should be reserved for up to 4,000 extra factory workers, mainly on the trading estate.[37]

In Berkshire, the Board of Trade's view was that there was no reserve of labour: the only expansion on any scale should be as part of planned decantation schemes. By 1950 there was an acute shortage, both of male and female workers, in the Reading area and also in the Maidenhead-Windsor area. The county accepted the force of this argument in general, but with reservations about the journey to work involved for Berkshire workers to a centre like Slough; by that time, the county reported, both Slough and Reading had commuter catchment areas of up to ten miles. With this exception, 'it does seem that the Board of Trade policy of restricting future industrialization to expansion of existing concerns is realistic'.[38] The main problem, in the county planner's view, was not in East Berkshire but in the western part of the county (outside the present study area), where agricultural

[35] These were not parts of the Statutory Development Plan, but were submitted together with it to the Minister. They are filed in the Department of the Environment Library.

[36] Buckinghamshire Development Plan, *Report and Analysis of the Survey*. Aylesbury (1951).

[37] Ibid., p. 26.

[38] Berkshire Development Plan, *Report and Analysis of Survey and Plan*. Reading (1951), p. 57.

employment was shrinking and long journeys to isolated industrial centres were common.

No change in this view came during the 1950s. In 1950 and 1953, the Board of Trade confirmed and reinforced their original views of 1948 on employment in the Reading area: that labour shortage was rife and that there was no need to provide any extra employment to meet the needs of the existing population. This view the county accepted.[39] The county planners noticed that, in contrast to the interwar experience, after 1948 employment in this area had been growing more slowly than population. But, they observed:

> Although travel to work over substantial distances occurs, there is little indication that this is other than by choice. The assumption that the provision of new employment adjacent to new housing areas will eradicate daily travel is likely to prove fallacious.[40]

This, written in 1957, represents perhaps a new gloss on the situation; but it is used to support a continuation of what was, in essence, the Abercrombie policy.

In Surrey, the Report of the Survey was quite plain: the Board of Trade had set up interdepartmental panels of civil servants to determine the proper regional distribution of industry, and the county would follow their policies explicitly. Around London as a whole, the Board had defined three types of area, forming concentric rings: first, nearest London, *contraction* areas, where the industrial capacity was too great for the population that was proposed (in Surrey this included most authorities in the conurbation, and Chertsey); second, *neutral* areas where the capacity should be kept roughly constant because it was well balanced with the existing or planned population (in Surrey this zone included Guildford Borough and Rural District, Esher, and Bagshot Rural District – mainly, that is, the green belt); and third, outer *reception* areas capable of receiving more employment (here including Woking, and Frimley and Camberley, both of which were proposed centres for receiving GLC overspill).[41] With these defined exceptions:

> The survey shows that there are more opportunities for industrial employment than are required for the existing population, and that these opportunities will probably be sufficient for the estimated population. The County Development Plan is, therefore, based primarily on the government's policy that the overall growth of industry and employment in the county should be restrained.[42]

39 Berkshire Development Plan, *Review of the Reading Area*. Reading (1957), p. 9.

40 Ibid.

41 Surrey Development Plan, *Report of Survey, Part 1: The County Map*. Kingston (1953), para. 266.

42 Surrey, *Report of Survey*, op. cit., para 360.

The Hampshire analysis was less specific on employment; but it, too, followed in detail the lines laid down by the government. In the Aldershot-Farnham-Fleet town map there were very limited additional plans for industrial land; but at Basingstoke, following the idea of planned expansion, no less than 140 additional acres were provided.[43]

Essentially, therefore, the counties' policy was founded on a very selective growth of employment in a few carefully chosen centres, which were to receive a planned influx of Londoners. The most important were High Wycombe; Slough; the new town of Bracknell, which eventually (in 1949) replaced the White Waltham proposal; Wokingham and Frimley and Camberley. Later on, the proposal to expand Wokingham did not come to fruition, while the London County Council idea of a new town at Hook was replaced by the decision to expand Basingstoke. Apart from these centres, there was no encouragement of new factory industry. Local firms would be allowed to rebuild, and even expand to a limited degree, if they could make a good case on the availability of labour. In all the analysis, as in the Abercrombie Plan itself, the emphasis is almost wholly on restraining, or redistributing, factory jobs. Only very occasionally, as in the Surrey Development Plan at Woking,[44] is there mention of the possibilities of decentralizing office jobs from London for the very largely middle-class, white-collar residents of many of these areas. The reason is almost certainly that consciously or unconsciously, the planners saw their task largely as the planned movement of Londoners to publicly-provided housing schemes, whether in new towns or expanded towns; such people, the implicit argument must have run, were likely in the main to be factory workers. This idea was never supported by evidence; in fact, even at that time, it must have been far from true. But elsewhere, the middle-class dormitory areas would continue to be middle-class dormitory areas. This becomes clearer when we study the plans for the physical growth of settlements.

These plans can be summarized simply. There was to be a virtual ban on further growth in the green belt (save where immediate needs made it imperative, as at Slough); very modest expansion of places further out, to provide for an equally modest natural growth of the population; and highly selective expansion of one or two places on a much larger scale, to cater for the planned 'decantation', (the phrase seems originally to have been Abercrombie's)[45] from the great London redevelopment schemes.

Thus in Buckinghamshire, the Development Plan envisaged a population growth of 105,700, from 366,400 in 1947 to 472,100 in 1971. But of this, it was thought that the planned expansion of Slough would account for nearly 31,000 (from 75,400 to 106,300) and that of High Wycombe for another

[43] Hampshire Development Plan, *Analysis of Survey*, *Aldershot*, *Farnborough and Fleet Town Map*. Winchester (1952), p. 6.

[44] Surrey Development Plan, *Report and Analysis of Survey*, *Part 2*, *The Town Maps* (5) *Woking and District*. Kingston (1953), para. 79.

[45] In reference to High Wycombe: Abercrombie, op. cit., p. 127.

13,000 (from 50,000 to 63,000).[46] In Berkshire, the 1951 Development Plan could optimistically say:

> The postwar trend appears to have been a greater rate of growth than in England and Wales, but there are signs that this rate is now levelling off to something approaching the normal rate for the country.[47]

But, the plan added in what proved a considerable understatement:

> It should be appreciated that the forecasting of future population is at best a hazardous undertaking.[48]

The total growth population in the county for the period 1948–71 was forecast at 85,160, of which 'decantation' would account for nearly two-thirds. Of the remaining third, roughly equal parts would be contributed by natural increase, and by spontaneous migration.[49] Decantation would be particularly important in the east of the county, at Wokingham and perhaps in a new town which might replace the abandoned proposal for White Waltham. At Wokingham, the Development Plan envisaged an additional 5,516 people on top of the existing 8,234.[50] Elsewhere in East Berkshire, as at Maidenhead and Windsor, the proposals were deliberately very restrictive. The original Windsor town map provided for an increase of only 1,760 people, from 21,820 to 23,580;[51] that for Maidenhead for an increase of only 1,225 (26,820 to 28,045).[52]

Perhaps the major problem for the Berkshire planners at that time, as for their colleagues in Oxfordshire and in Reading, was Reading's own overspill. The population of the entire Reading area had been about 95,000 at the end of the First World War and about 114,000 at the end of the Second World War; it was estimated at 128,500 in 1947.[53] At that time the general assumption, based on Abercrombie, was that Reading should not grow, but that the town had a local overspill problem due to the need for redevelopment within the borough boundaries. A joint advisory committee was set up, including Reading, Berkshire, Oxfordshire, and some of the local borough and district councils in the area. When Reading tried to press its claim for a boundary extension to deal with its overspill problems, it finally agreed in October 1949 not to press its claims if the counties would zone some of their land to deal with the problem of Reading's housing list. In October 1950, 143 acres in Berkshire and 130 acres in Oxfordshire were accepted as suitable for this

[46] Buckinghamshire, *Report and Analysis of Survey*, op. cit., p. 17; *Slough and District Town Map, Report of Survey*, p. 6, *High Wycombe and District Town Map, Report of Survey*, p. 10.

[47] Berkshire, *Report and Analysis*, op. cit., p. 28.

[48] Ibid., p. 31.

[49] Ibid.

[50] Berkshire Development Plan, *Wokingham Town Map*. Reading (1951), Table 4.

[51] Ibid., *Windsor Town Map*, Table 4.

[52] Ibid., *Maidenhead Town Map*, Table 4.

[53] Berkshire Development Plan, *Review of the Reading Area*. Reading (1957), p. 5.

purpose. Yet arguments about overspill continued, in particular about the right way to develop the sites. Finally, it was agreed that the land should be transferred to Reading Corporation. The Oxfordshire Development Plan, submitted in November 1952 and approved in 1954, allocated 188 acres in the Caversham Park area on the Reading fringe, to house a total of 4,420 people; of this, 130 acres was earmarked specifically for the Reading housing list.[54]

Meanwhile, the three planning authorities had become increasingly conscious of the need for an agreed planning policy in the Reading area; they were urged on by the Ministry, which took the lead in formulating a positive suggestion. The Blue Line policy, which was essentially a limit to urban development for the whole area, was formulated in 1950, was agreed by the Joint Planning Committee in September 1951, and was rapidly incorporated into both the Berkshire and Oxfordshire Development Plans, which were submitted respectively in July 1951 and November 1952.[55]

By 1958, when Berkshire submitted its town map for the Woodley and Earley area east of Reading, the anticipation was that the population of the entire Reading area would rise from 137,300 (in 1956) to 160,000 by 1973; only 116,000 of them could be housed in the Borough itself.[56] By that time, the county planners were already recognizing a changed situation: the population of the urban area had grown by 8,000 between 1947 and 1956, and, as the Woodley-Earley analysis rather acidly commented, 'National policy has been to allow the full development of areas like Woodley-Earley'.[57] Nevertheless, the Blue Line policy would continue to be maintained, with detailed modifications. Within it, on the Woodley-Earley side of Reading, provision could be made for an extra 14,000 people, taking the population from 18,000 in 1955 to 32,500 in 1973. This allowed for a net immigration of 10,000, both from Reading and other areas. Woodley and Earley, then, became the biggest area of planned population growth in any town map area in Berkshire; it compared with an estimate of 25,000 growth for the new town at Bracknell.[58]

On the other, western, side of Reading, the county prepared its town map for Tilehurst at the same time. Here, the increase was more modest: 4,500 (1956) to 13,200 (1973), a net growth of 8,700.[59] Thus Berkshire's contribution to the growth of the Reading urban area was some 23,000, which was equal to the total expected increase.[60]

[54] Ibid., pp. 19–20, tells this story in detail.

[55] Ibid., p. 21.

[56] Ibid., p. 7 (as amended in manuscript after the approval of the Reading Borough Plan).

[57] Berkshire Development Plan, *Woodley and Earley Town Map, Report of Survey*. Reading (1958), p. 4.

[58] Ibid., pp. 3–4.

[59] Berkshire Development Plan, *Tilehurst Town Map*. Reading (1959), Table A.

[60] Berkshire, *Review of the Reading Area*, op. cit., p. 7.

Most of this great development, both in Tilehurst and in Woodley-Earley, was to be provided at high or moderately high densities.[61] The original densities in Woodley-Earley, up to 1950, had been low, with an average of fifteen per acre of residential land, and three-fifths of the total area having less than fifteen per acre. This had been related to the lack of a comprehensive sewer system. Since 1950 however there had been a distinct trend to higher densities, which the plan proposed to continue. Consent had already been given for low-density development on plots of half an acre to one acre at North Lake: and this, the planners thought, should satisfy all the potential demand for housing of this type. Despite the distinct tendency towards higher density, the overall effect would not be great because of the large areas of existing low-density development.[62]

Berkshire's policies were very different in another nearby area where major pressures emerged in the 1950s: eastern Berkshire, near the Surrey border. Much of this area is on the Bagshot sands, and had been developed in the very distinctive, low-density style already described. Because the agricultural land values were low and because there were no obvious village boundaries in the traditional sense, it proved hard to develop coherent planning policies. In the four square-mile Ascot town map area, the planners said in presenting their town map in 1957:

> There is a distinct threat that a policy of regarding the area as generally open to residential development would result in a complete change of character from rural to urban or suburban.[63]

An increasing demand for subdivision and infilling of the large house plots could easily alter the rural character, which the planners thought should be retained. Additionally, there was already provision at Bracknell and elsewhere for local population increases, which would be accompanied by jobs and services. Any extensive development in the Ascot area, on the other hand, would either call for an 'unrealistic' introduction of new activity and other employment, or alternatively aggravate what the planners confidently called the 'problems' of journeys to work.[64]

Therefore, for the county the policy was clear. It was to define the extent of existing settlements; land outside these limits should be part of a green belt linking the London and Bracknell green belts.[65] This last arm of the policy received formal embodiment in 1960 in the revision of the County Development Plan, when Berkshire recommended the creation of an 'East Berkshire green belt' linking the London and Bracknell green belts and

[61] Berkshire, *Woodley-Earley Town Map*, op. cit., Table A.

[62] Ibid., pp. 9–11.

[63] Berkshire Development Plan, *Ascot Town Map*, *Report of Survey*, Reading (1957), p. 2.

[64] Ibid., p. 3.

[65] Ibid., p. 3. Berkshire Development Plan, *Development Plan Revision*, *County Map Written Statement*. Reading (1960), p. 18.

extending westwards into the Finchampstead-Wokingham areas. The creation of this new green belt was recommended for 'checking the spread of Greater London into Berkshire, and . . . preventing neighbouring towns and villages in the area from merging into one another'.[66]

Within the envelope thus provided, the Ascot town map specified not merely overall gross densities, as was usual practice in all town maps, but also types of 'appropriate' development. Over a very large part of the total area, there would be very little increase in gross densities indeed. A few areas were indicated for 'relatively high-density' estates including local authority housing (at up to twelve houses to the acre), others for 'small estate developments at moderate densities' (say four to eight houses per acre), others for individual house plots and/or low-density developments, yet others for high-value residential areas. The permitted development would take place at densities similar to adjoining properties, and would be regarded as dormitory settlement for commuters, or for the retired. Thus an increased population would be accommodated mainly through a very large increase in the developed acreage, 433 acres in all.[67]

The policy of allowing large-scale, low-density development might seem an odd one in the general context of population pressure in the south-east and the constant calls to economize on land. The Berkshire planners were quite clear in their determination to preserve the existing character of this area:

> The preponderance of higher-rated residences in certain localities indicates the high residential amenities of those areas and is a factor to be considered in determining the type of new development appropriate to the district. A considerable proportion of the rates derived from residential properties in the area come from the highly rated properties. New development should not be allowed to affect this asset.[68]

In the neighbouring town map area of Sandhurst-Crowthorne, which also falls within the general area of the East Berkshire green belt, the policy was almost exactly the same. Here the existing net density, at the time of the 1958 Report of Survey, was only three dwellings per acre. The town map proposed the 'crystallization' of the planning policies as they had evolved here. The existing population of 11,500 would rise to a total of over 16,000 by 1973. Development would be confined to a definite area, but even so the developed area would rise by 50 per cent. Residential development would take place through private enterprise at densities comparable with those existing, and newcomers would fit themselves into the existing pattern of employment provided by local establishments (plus the projected transfer of the Road Research Laboratory to the area, which took place later), and by surrounding

66 Berkshire Plan Revision, op. cit., p. 18.
67 Berkshire, *Ascot Town Map*, op. cit., pp. 3–4.
68 Ibid., p. 14.

towns. 'In this way', the planners said, 'it is expected to maintain the character and amenity of the area.'[69]

Berkshire's policies, then, were explicit; they were intended to preserve and reinforce the different character of different areas. Large-scale public housing at high densities was to be provided in Bracknell new town and on the outskirts of Reading. Medium-density private enterprise housing was the rule in most of the Reading fringe, and at Wokingham. In the exclusive cocktail belt country on the Bagshot heathlands, the unique character of low-density houses, standing in their own grounds, would be maintained. But in their emphasis on preserving and extending the green belt, and in defining the physical separateness of settlements, the Berkshire planners followed the pure gospel according to Abercrombie. This was evident for instance in the revised Maidenhead and Windsor town map plans of 1959–60, with the emphasis on restricting new building to small-scale developments for the needs of the existing population; specifically migration into these areas would be discouraged by all means possible.[70]

Across the county boundary into Surrey and Hampshire, there were complications. At Frimley and Camberley there was the commitment to take more than 4,000 Londoners under the 1952 Town Development Act. Spontaneous migration was becoming difficult and hazardous to forecast by 1958, when the Surrey planners were drawing up the town map for this area, but it was hoped to provide for an increase of 21,700 in 1958, to as much as 36,000 by 1971.[71] There was a much greater emphasis on medium and even higher density here than in neighbouring areas of Berkshire like Sandhurst-Crowthorne. Westwards into Hampshire, the position in Aldershot-Farnborough-Fleet was complicated by the great amount of land (two-thirds of the total for the town map area) held by the War Department. In drawing up the town map as early as 1953, the Hampshire planners expected a population increase in this area from 57,300 to 67,500 between 1947 and 1971. Since it was possible to find land for only 62,950, some local overspill seemed inevitable.[72]

This account of planning policies in the 1950s has concentrated on the areas where important questions of principle arose. In many other parts of the home counties west of London, the simple assumption of the post-1947 period was that little growth would take place so that there was no need to provide extensive tracts of land for urbanization. With the exception of Slough and a small LCC estate at Woking, this was true for instance of the whole of the green belt ring between fifteen and twenty miles from London. Even beyond

[69] Berkshire Development Plan, *Sandhurst-Crowthorne Town Map Area, Report of Survey*. Reading (1958), p. 5.

[70] Berkshire Development Plan, *Windsor Town Map Revision*. Reading (1959). *Maidenhead Town Map Revision*. Reading (1960).

[71] Surrey Development Plan, *Frimley-Camberley Town Map, Report and Analysis of Survey*. Kingston (1961), Table A.

[72] Hampshire Development Plan, *Aldershot, Farnborough and Fleet Town Map, Report of Survey*. Winchester (1952), p. 31.

this, development would be selective and would emphasize the big schemes of 'decantation', with their emphasis on public housing. And this in turn reflected the general policy emphasis of that period. There would be some private-enterprise housing effort for middle-class buyers at lower densities, but it would represent a small part of the whole programme. Such a small part, perhaps, that no one in the county planning offices seemed to worry that it would increase journeys to work (which was being condemned everywhere else), or that it represented a fairly complete and rigid form of geographical class segregation.

THE GROWING PRESSURE OF POPULATION

The irony was that even while the county planners were preparing the first quinquennial reviews of their development plans, or producing detailed town map plans within the framework of the original county policies, planners in Whitehall were recognizing that the whole framework of planning in the south-east was changing. Thus as early as 1960, drawing on data up to 1958, a Ministry of Housing and Local Government planner was drawing public attention to the fact that in the South East Region, population and employment growth were far outrunning the estimates on which the plans had been based. In his paper called *The Recent Development of Greater London*,[73] Geoffrey Powell for the first time identified an important fact that had escaped public notice: that while the Greater London population had stagnated in the 1950s, the area all around it and extending up to forty or fifty miles from central London, had become the fastest-growing zone in all Britain. In fact, during the 1950s about one-third of the net population growth of all Britain took place in this ring. Powell argued that effectively this Outer Metropolitan Area was now part of a wider London, a functional London region far exceeding in area the physical conurbation whose growth Abercrombie had tried to halt.

It was shortly after publication of this paper that the government, impressed by the force of the facts, agreed to a major planning study of the region. Because no regional agency existed outside the Standing Conference of Planning Authorities, it was decided that this study should be conducted by central government officials from the Ministry of Housing and Local Government, and Powell himself took a major part. Meanwhile, the general public became increasingly conscious of the population explosion in the South-East, especially after the recession of 1962–63 drew attention to the continuing gap between a prosperous South and a less prosperous North. Still, when the *South-East Study*[74] was published in March 1964, it managed to cause a shock with its central premise: that in the twenty years from 1961–81

[73] A. G. Powell, 'The Recent Development of Greater London', *Advancement of Science*, vol. 17 (1960), pp. 76–86.

[74] *The South-East Study 1961–81.* HMSO, London (1964), pp. 83–5.

the South-East region would have to house some 3½ million extra people, of which 2½ million would represent the region's own natural increase of population. Twenty years after publication of the Abercrombie Plan, this new study spelt the end of an era.

Part of this growth, in particular that part which represented planned overspill from London, could be housed in distant counter-magnets sixty or more miles from London. The essential principle was to develop these new communities well beyond the range of the London commuter; in fact one of the proposals, for a new town at Newbury, was later dropped (and replaced by a proposal for a bigger expansion at Swindon) precisely because of a consultant's recommendation that Newbury seemed to be falling within the London orbit. There was one green field new town at Bletchley (later called Milton Keynes); there were also proposals for new towns attached to quite small towns, as at Newbury and Ashford (which latter was also dropped). But in other places, at Northampton and Peterborough and Ipswich, the study proposed the then revolutionary notion of new towns attached to existing towns and cities. And in the South Hampshire area, it proposed in effect the linking of Southampton and Portsmouth by means of a planned conurbation, eventually containing over a million people.

But even if these and other planned developments could provide for between 1¼ and 1½ million, that still left more than 2 million to be housed by what the study called the normal planning processes. One element here, the biggest, was the natural increase of population; this occurred all over the region roughly in relation to the distribution of the existing population. Another element, migration for retirement, affected especially the South Coast; it would not easily be stemmed unless and until house prices rose very greatly in competition with sites outside the region in places like Torquay or Scarborough. A third element, voluntary migration of working population from London, would affect especially the inner parts of the home counties adjoining the conurbation, areas like the sector considered in this chapter. Here, the allocations would need to take special account of transportation, especially routes where share capacity was available. And it would need to contain a contingency allowance for unexpected possibilities.

The study translated these ideas into concrete form, by means of a Table making a provisional allocation of land, to be dealt with in normal development plan reviews by each county of the region. This Table distinguished between natural increase and all other causes, including voluntary migration from London, retirement and the contingency allowance. Unfortunately, it lumped together data for county boroughs with that of neighbouring counties; and it nowhere subdivided counties, except to split the allocations for the Outer Metropolitan Area from those for the rest of the South-East. So it is impossible to give an accurate picture of the increase which the authors of the study had in mind for the sector we are considering, but some idea can be obtained from Table 8.1.

Many of the areas where this increase might have to be housed, the study admitted, were subject to applications by the counties for extensions of the

Table 8.1

POPULATION PROVISION IN THE SOUTH-EAST STUDY, 1964

	1961 population	Change 1961–81 Total	Natural increase	Other causes
	(all figures in thousands)			
Berkshire	226·9	96	57	22
Reading	120·4		17	
Surrey	645·1	252	99	153
Hampshire	93·1	50	29	21
Buckinghamshire	431·2	139	97	42
Oxfordshire	31·5	10	4	6

Source: South-East Study, Table 6, p. 86.

London green belt.[75] On this, the study was adamant: there was a danger of spreading these extensions too far afield and of drawing them too tightly round existing development, so that eventually population pressure would make it impossible to hold the line. The rule, the study said clearly, must be: first locate the land for the necessary development, and only then consider the desirable and feasibie extent of any green belt extension.[76]

But apart from this advice to the county planners, the study is conspicuously silent on detail. Whether it ever contained a more positive strategy or not, the published version very positively leaves the task of implementation to the local planning authorities; it does not attempt to impinge on their rights. This in fact is the keynote of the study. Since many of the authorities of the Outer Metropolitan Area were highly resistant to the ideal of further planned overspill, that element was transferred very firmly elsewhere; it has been calculated that out of a population increase of 1,600,000 in the Outer Metropolitan Areas between 1961 and 1981, only 200,000 would have represented planned overspill schemes. The rest, amounting to 1,400,000, would be housed by the normal processes of development planning, which it was the duty of the counties and country boroughs to do; they should get on with the job.[77] This, essentially, was the philosophy of the South-East Study.

The incoming Labour Government, in October 1964, did not accept the study's figures of population increase; a review of the study was therefore urgently set in hand, and published in early 1966.[78] Essentially the review

[75] Ibid., p. 93.

[76] Ibid., p. 96. The review emerged with the same forecast of population growth, but natural increase represented a much larger part of the total.

[77] Calculated by the author of this chapter in P. Hall, *London 2000*. Revised edition. Faber, London (1969), p. 184.

[78] The conclusions of the review are set out in the Ministry of Housing and Local Government, *Circular 5/66*. For a useful summary see Standing Conference on London and South-East Regional Planning, LRP 600, 9 March 1966.

comes to the paradoxical conclusion that though the estimate of net migration into the region made in the original study was too high, the projection of natural increase was too low, so that the total to be provided for is roughly the same. In the South-East planning region (a region smaller than the South-East of the original study, since it excluded East Anglia) the expected population growth between 1961 and 1981 would be 2,910,000 as opposed to the 2,995,000 of the original study; of this revised total, almost exactly half (1,561,000) would occur in the Outer Metropolitan Area.[79] Of this total, the suggested target populations for the counties in the London West Sector are set out in Table 8.2. As with the original study, it is impossible to give figures in any more precise geographical detail than this.

Table 8.2

POPULATION PROVISION, REVIEW OF THE SOUTH-EAST STUDY, 1966

Outer Metropolitan area	1964 population	Change 1964–81		
		Total	Natural increase	Other causes
		all figures in thousands		
Berkshire	259	98 (Berkshire and Reading)	48	33 (Berkshire and Reading)
Reading	123		17	
Surrey	950	178	107	71
Hampshire	107	50	26	24
Bucks	467	108	85	23
Oxfordshire	34	9	3	6

Source: Ministry of Housing and Local Government, *Circular* 5/66, p. 4.

As compared with the original South East Study projections, therefore, the projections in the review (which were for a period three years shorter than the originals) showed some decreases overall.

The review was no more specific than the Study had been about the location of this growth; that, clearly, was to be the preoccupation of the local planning authorities. Accordingly, some of the more progressive authorities began to work on new-style structure plans for the more important growth areas which were under the heaviest pressure. These broad diagrammatic plans had been recommended by the Planning Advisory Group report in 1965 and were made into a fundamental part of the plan-making process by the 1968 Planning Act. But only just after passage of this Act, Hampshire in December 1968 were already publishing their structure plan for their part of the Blackwater valley area.[80] It dealt deftly with the conflicting pressures in the area (for new homes, preservation of agricultural land and for holding of defence

[79] Hall, op. cit., Table 23, p. 121.

[80] Hampshire County Council, *North-East Hampshire Urban Plan*. The Council, Winchester (1968).

lands) by adding modest additional areas to those already zoned for development in existing town maps: 305 acres in all, at Minley, Church Crookham in Fleet, and in Crookham Village. These would add another 19,000 people to the 32,000 already accommodated in town map proposals, taking the population from 98,000 in 1964 to 150,000 by the early 1980s. They provided for precisely the amount of growth that was called for in the review of the study up to the early 1980s. But they were thus essentially a holding operation and their appearance, at a time when work on a new regional strategy for the whole South-East was just starting, illustrates just how difficult it is in a fast-growing region to produce an orderly sequence of plans for the region down to the sub-region and then to the locality.

FROM THE 1967 STRATEGY TO THE 1970 STRATEGIC PLAN

Still wanting, at the time when the Blackwater report appeared, was any agreed long-term strategic plan for the development of the South-East region and of the sub-regions within it. As we have seen, both the 1964 Study and the 1966 Review had carefully refrained from producing anything like such a strategy for the area within forty or fifty miles of London; and there was no formal planning machinery for the preparation of a strategy. Instead, by 1966 and 1967, there were two separate bodies having a strong interest in producing one, but for different reasons lacking effective power to do so. One of these was the Standing Conference on London and South-East Regional Planning. Embracing all the planning authorities of the region in a voluntary union for the purpose of considering broad strategic problems, the Conference was served by an able technical panel which for several years had been labouring to produce the essential statistical and documentary basis for the preparation of a strategy. In 1966 the panel had advanced so far that they were able to produce an important document as a basis for policy decisions, *The Conference Area in the Long Term*.[81] This argued that there would be long-term advantages in establishing axes of urban development along rail and road corridors. Such axial growth already in fact existed in many parts of the region among which, of course, the London West Sector was an obvious example. Despite this obvious lead from the technical officials, the thinking of the Conference then went in an entirely different direction; its next major statement, in August 1967,[82] showed three alternative strategies, none of which represented the corridor or axis principle of growth in any very obvious way. All three strategies incorporated the principle of accommodating most of the growth in a few specially selected areas, each with a considerable population. Such a solution, the Conference argued, would have certain advantages: it would promote industrial efficiency, would cater for the increasing scale of social

[81] Standing Conference on London and South-East Regional Planning, *The Conference Area in the Long Term*. LRP 680, 20 July and 23 November 1966, especially para. 13.

[82] Standing Conference on London and South-East Regional Planning, *Planning London and the South-East up to 2000 AD*. Press release, 25 April. 1967.

organization, would help preserve agriculture and open countryside, and would cut commuter journeys to a minimum. All three strategies prepared by the technical panel show a substantial concentration of growth in the west sector, between the M4 and the A3 radial highways, and centred roughly on the proposed M3 motorway in the Blackwater valley area; though with different scale and massing. All strategies, the Conference decided in 1967, had certain unsatisfactory features: the technical panel should try again.

Meanwhile, the other body responsible for planning in the South-East region, the Regional Economic Planning Council, set up early in 1966 as an advisory body to the First Secretary of State for Economic Affairs, had begun work on its own strategy for regional development, which was published in November 1967, called *A Strategy for the South-East*.[83] The thinking in this strategy drew on the initial 1966 analysis by the Standing Conference, as well as on an analysis of metropolitan area plans in Europe and elsewhere. Essentially, it proposed that development in the South-East should be concentrated into a series of sectors radiating out from London along major lines of communication, both rail and road. Generally, in each quarter of the compass from London, there would be a major sector leading to a planned counter magnet located at a considerable distance from London as proposed in the 1964 South-East Study, paralleled by a minor centre leading out towards a smaller (but still considerable) counter magnet. Thus in the London West Sector, the major sector of development would follow the London-Southampton rail line and the proposed M3 towards Southampton, while the minor sector would follow the Bristol rail line and the M4 towards Swindon. On either side of the pair of sectors would be wide green sectors, deliberately kept free of development as far as possible; they would embody country zones which were to have a specially protected status. In the case of the London West Sector, one such zone would embrace the Chiltern Hills, another the western end of the Weald of Sussex. Between the major and the minor sectors, also, land would be kept open to provide regional open space, easily accessible to the population within the sector. And lastly, it was never intended that the sectors should consist of continuous ribbon development on a vast scale. Rather, each sector should be viewed as beads of various sizes along a string; the development would consist of existing and new towns, existing villages and even new villages, all within a green setting.

The Strategy of the Planning Council fully accepted the principle of the South-East Study and the Review: that an increased part of the future population growth in the South-East should be steered beyond the boundaries of the metropolitan area, through the development of counter magnets more than fifty miles from London. But at the same time, it recognized that a strategy was needed above all to deal with the housing of those people who must be expected in the Outer Metropolitan Area. To this end, it identified key areas of likely population pressure, where more detailed study was

[83] South-East Economic Planning Council, *A Strategy for the South-East*. HMSO, London (1967), Chap. 3, *passim*.

recommended of the ways of housing the expected growth. Such study was particularly vital in those areas, about 30–40 miles from London, where major sectors closely paralleled minor sectors, and where, in consequence, the risk of poorly planned development would be most serious. The whole area within the quadrilateral Reading-Basingstoke-Aldershot-Bracknell, and centred on the Blackwater valley, was one of the most obvious candidates for such special study, which the Strategy recommended should be made by local authorities and central government in partnership.

In the event, the government did not accept the Council's strategy, even as a basis for further study, without qualification. Instead it announced in March 1968 that a further study would be undertaken by a team under the direction of Dr Wilfred Burns, Chief Planner at the Ministry of Housing and Local Government, in co-operation with both the Council and the Standing Conference. (The study was formally commissioned by the two bodies in May.) Meanwhile, the government announced, planning decisions would continue to be taken in the light of the 1966 Review; while the Ministry of Housing and Local Government would ask local authorities' co-operation in finding sites for 35,000 private houses a year in the Outer Metropolitan Area.[84] This last was necessary because studies had indicated that building land in this area was becoming harder to find. The Ministry themselves suggested that suitable sites might exist near manufacturing towns where labour demand was high, or where London rail links were available, and where the possibility existed of infilling and rounding off existing communities. Reading would seem to fall firmly into the right category on all three counts; the Blackwater valley towns would presumably qualify also, although that area was somewhat deficient in manufacturing employment.[85]

At the very start of the work of the new study team, in August 1968, the Town and Country Planning Association made a decisive intervention by proposing publicly that future development should be concentrated not in the more distant counter-magnets towards the periphery of the region, but in the Outer Metropolitan Area. Here existing centres should be developed using a modified type of new town development corporation machinery, and giving priority to circular or orbital rather than radial communication linkages. Though the existing green belt should be preserved, the Association stated, it should not be extended. New towns and cities situated beyond the limits of the Outer Metropolitan Area, the Association declared flatly, were not well sited. By this statement, the Association were bringing out into the open a deliberate alternative to the policies which had first received expression in the South-East Study four years before.

In the event, this alternative was heeded. The interim report of the South-East Joint Planning Team, published in December 1969 after a year and a

84 Ministry of Housing and Local Government press release, 21 March 1968.

85 This fact emerged subsequently, in an analysis published by the South-East Economic Planning Council, *South-East: Study of Sub-Divisions*. The Council (1969).

half's work,[86] showed two alternative strategies for the region in the year 1991, both of them compatible with the likely development up to 1981 which must be regarded as largely committed already. The first of these, labelled Strategy A, was deliberately set up to represent the strategy of the Planning Council. But it placed a very great emphasis, greater almost certainly than the Council had in mind at the time, on development of the distant counter-magnets as well as on development in the Outer Metropolitan Area south of London, in the Gatwick-Crawley area. Conversely, it placed less emphasis than the Council seems to have intended on certain of the study areas in the 1967 Strategy, including Aldershot-Basingstoke and Luton-Stevenage. The paradox was that these areas received full weight in the alternative Strategy B, which was supposed to represent a form of development radically different from that proposed by the Council. Here, the emphasis was all on big clusters of development in the Outer Metropolitan Area as advocated by the Town and Country Planning Association, particularly in the Reading-Basingstoke-Aldershot, Luton-Stevenage and Tilbury-Basildon-Southend areas. Perhaps the most obvious lesson that emerges from a look at these two strategies is the very large degree of constraint that operated on strategic planning in the region. Though the emphasis could be shifted from one part of the map to another, by and large all feasible strategies perhaps look more similar than dissimilar.

The eventual strategy, published in the team's final report of 1970,[87] differed in detail from both the strategies published in the interim report; it arose from an evaluation of both of them, and took features from each. The Strategic Plan was intended to be flexible in response to changing circumstances, while being firm enough to provide guidelines for local structure plans and for investment decisions by central and local government as well as the private sector.

It was based on three main objectives, which in fact dominated the choice of the final strategy. The first was the need to match population and employment growth, by making the maximum provision for mobile industry of all kinds to move from London. If this failed to happen, the certain outcome was a big increase in long-distance commuting to Greater London, which would involve problems of cost.[88] But, the team discovered, there was a limit to the mobility of much London industry and especially of office developments: they might move up to forty or fifty miles from London, not more. In other words, they would need to be accommodated in the Outer Metropolitan Area.

The second was the desirability of planning new growth in the form of large concentrations of people and employment, offering large labour markets, a variety of jobs and easy possibility of changing them, scope for social and economic policies aimed at improving life chances for the less

[86] South-East Joint Planning Team, *Interim Report* (1969).

[87] *Strategic Plan for the South-East: Report by the South-East Joint Planning Team.* HMSO, London (1970).

[88] Ibid., para. 9.26, p. 77.

privileged members of society, and a variety of life styles (and social and cultural provision generally) for a wide cross-section of the population. Coupled with the first objective, this suggested the building up of big centres in the Outer Metropolitan Area, not more than about fifty miles from London and desirably nearer even than that. Major new city regions at this distance from London would be more likely to be relatively independent of London than would smaller scale developments, thus reducing the pressure of long-distance commuting.[89]

The third principle was the need to make the best use of the countryside by protecting large areas from urban intrusion, with special attention to the preservation of a number of large areas for fine landscape and pleasant country towns and villages, and further promotion of agricultural productivity. This again fitted with the idea of concentrating future urban growth into a limited number of city regions.[90]

From these three main principles, the selection of major growth areas must have been fairly automatic. Along the main lines of communication leading radially from London, there were a limited number of areas which already had substantial urban development and which had demonstrated their capacity for rapid growth; they had already been distinguished in the 1967 Planning Council's Strategy. Five of them became major growth areas in the 1970 Strategic Plan:

First, and most distant from London, the South Hampshire area (70–80 miles from London) was expected to have a population towards the end of the century of up to 1·4 million. This area is fully discussed in Chapter Nine.

Second, north-west of London, the Milton Keynes-Northampton-Wellingborough area (50–70 miles from London) would have an end-century population of about 0·8 million.

Third would be the central part of the area considered in this chapter: the Reading-Wokingham-Aldershot-Basingstoke quadrilateral. Standing some 30–50 miles west and south-west of London, it might have a population of about 1·0 to 1·2 million by the end of the twentieth century.

Fourth would be an almost precisely complementary area on the east side of London, about 30–45 miles distant: South Essex, incorporating Southend and Basildon, with about 1 million people at the century's end.

Lastly, the Crawley-Gatwick area some 25–35 miles south of London would be further expanded to take about half a million people by the end of the century.[91]

These proposals had a neat and effective symmetry. They gave major population groupings at four points of the compass, with two west and south-west of London, separated from each other by wide areas of attractive country, and connected by existing and projected new lines of communication. In addition,

[89] Ibid., para. 9.27, p. 77 and para. 10.5, p. 80.

[90] Ibid., para. 10.4, p. 79.

[91] Ibid., para. 10.11, p. 81.

areas for more modest growth would be located in the intervening spaces, partly to provide a sort of safety valve in the event that any of the proposed major developments failed to grow at the expected rate: they included Maidstone-Medway, Ashford, Eastbourne-Hastings, Bournemouth-Poole, Aylesbury, Bishop's Stortford-Harlow, and Chelmsford.[92]

The new patterns of living and working in the South-East would not represent any radical break with the old; the basis of the future growth patterns was already clear in the early 1970s. But the period from 1970 to 2000 would see a profound shift in scale and emphasis. In an area such as Reading-Wokingham-Aldershot-Basingstoke, the separate towns and villages (while remaining physically distinct, in all probability) would functionally coalesce into a multicentred city region twenty or more miles across, with easy interaction for work, shopping, education and recreation; with a million people or more, such a city region could easily provide for most of the needs of its inhabitants whether for employment, shopping or entertainment. And in turn each of these city regions would be readily accessible to the others for business, professional and social purposes. The South-East, once dominated by London, would become much more multicentred, with the new city regions providing counter magnets to the central concentration.

In this particular city region, the consequences were certain to be profound. For of the major growth zones, the amount of expansion proposed for Reading-Wokingham-Aldershot-Basingstoke was by far the largest; of a total regional growth of rather more than 4·5 million between 1966 and 2001, it was proposed that this city region should take some 703,000 or between 15 and 16 per cent of the total. It has been calculated that on the basis of national calculations of the relationship between population growth and physical urban growth, estimated by Best and Stone, such a population growth would require between eighty and one-hundred and ten square miles of land in the Reading-Wokingham-Aldershot-Basingstoke area: rather more than one-third of the total area, in addition to that part which is already developed.[93]

The need for a positive plan then is obvious; and the Strategic Plan makes it clear that a broad structure plan for the whole area should be prepared fairly soon. In particular, a programme of investment in infrastructure, including roads and drainage, needed to be drawn up so as to:

> alleviate present problems, and provide a basis for rapid further growth. The appropriate urban form may well consist of a cluster of towns, some more closely related than others, perhaps in due course with a major new centre including offices, and with a wide range of cultural and community facilities.[94]

92 Ibid.

93 Peter Hall, 'Introductory Address' in Landscape Research Group (ed. J. B. Whittow), *Land Use and Landscape Quality*. Mimeo., Reading (1971), pp. 1.1–1.2.

94 Strategic Plan, op. cit., p. 101.

Defence lands provide a particular problem in parts of the area, and the plan provides a warning:

> It would clearly be undesirable if the urban form were largely determined by defence lands and in consequence failed to realize the full potential of the area unless it can be shown that retention of substantial parts of the area for defence purposes is essential in the national interest and that no suitable alternatives can be found.[95]

After extensive consultations, the government announced general approval of the plan in 1971. But, as in other areas of the South-East, the urgent need for a structure plan accorded ill with the realities of the existing local government structure. No less than five separate planning authorities would have been involved: one county borough (Reading) and four counties (Berkshire, Oxfordshire, Hampshire, and Surrey). Even under the proposals of the Redcliffe Maud Commission on Local Government in 1969, which were accepted by the Labour Government in January 1970, the responsibility for a structure plan would have been divided among two areas: a new Berkshire authority which was extended to include Basingstoke, and West Surrey.[96] And in the revised map accompanying the White Paper of the Conservative Government in 1971, it was even further divided among three authorities: the new Berkshire based on Reading, the new West Surrey based on Guildford (which acquired the whole of the important Blackwater valley area) and the existing county of Hampshire (which had minor boundary changes including the loss of the Blackwater valley).[97] Indeed it seemed likely that an important part of the new development would lie directly astraddle the new county boundaries. It seemed, indeed, like a complete contradiction of the essential concept of the city region, on which the whole movement for fundamental local government reform had been based.

SOME LESSONS OF PLANNING HISTORY IN THE SOUTH-EAST

The first, and overwhelmingly the most important, conclusion which emerges from this long chronicle is the lack of an agreed regional strategy, and the evident difficulty of producing one. Abercrombie managed to produce such a strategy, and a very detailed one, in the form of an ideal and static blueprint, in 1944. But that was in the middle of a major war, before local planning authorities as we know them were introduced in the 1947 Town and Country

95 Ibid.

96 *Reform of Local Government in England.* Cmnd 4276, HMSO, London (1970), para. 39, pp. 13–14, and end map.

97 Department of the Environment, *Circular 8/71, Local Government Reorganisation in England: Proposed New Areas.* HMSO, London (1971), pp. 19–20 and accompanying loose map. Later the Hampshire-Surrey boundary was moved back to its old position; but this still made three authorities responsible for the structure plan for the area.

Planning Act. A strategy as detailed as that would not, any more, be considered possible or realistic by most planners. They would call instead for a flexible plan which monitored and guided the development of the region, adjusting constantly and sensitively to changed circumstances. Detail would not be a concern of such a regional plan; that could be left to the local planning authorities, working within a general framework laid down by the regional plan, and producing plans for sub-regions which represented real functional units. This is the essential pattern foreseen by the Planning Advisory Group in 1965; it presupposes, of course, the fundamental reform of local government so that planning authorities can produce plans for realistic working areas. But however fundamental and enlightened the reform of local government areas, local planners must have a starting point, and this can only be a broad, agreed, strategy for the whole planning region.

Unfortunately, this is just where difficulty enters in. We have seen that for twenty years after Abercrombie, successive governments made no attempt to reform local government structure, or to produce an updated regional plan for the South-East themselves. When central government was at last forced by pressure of events to produce such regional guidelines, in the 1964 study, they were left as vague as possible in the area where the greatest pressures were being felt; and the 1966 Review was little more specific. The attempt to produce a strategy through voluntary co-operation among planning authorities was a failure; the sketch strategy produced by an advisory planning council was not acceptable to these same authorities; so the government was left to try again with an odd formula, involving the co-operation of central and local officials within a single team. Finally, it is significant that in accepting the proposals of the Redcliffe Maud Commission on Local Government, for a reformed system of local government based on unitary authorities for cities and their hinterlands, the Labour Government in January 1970 proposed no action on the recommendation for indirectly elected provincial planning authorities at the level of the economic planning region;[98] this was left to await the conclusions of the Crowther Commission on the Constitution, which were expected in 1973. There was thus no body formally capable of creating regional plans; the job was left to the *ad hoc* initiative of central government.

Why should this apparently intractable difficulty persist? In fact, it should not surprise anyone. Even the broadest, most flexible regional plan is exceedingly difficult to achieve, for a simple reason: no regional strategy is worth the paper it is written on, unless it makes some positive proposals that affect real people in real places. It is certainly not necessary or desirable for a regional strategic plan to make a detailed land allocation for every small housing-development; but it is most necessary and desirable that it shows in general terms where urban development should occur and where it should not. Again, it is not necessary or desirable for a regional strategy to establish the precise line of a new motorway; but it is most necessary that the plan

98 *Reform of Local Government in England*, op. cit., p. 7.

shows which towns the motorway shall connect, and even whether it passes to the north of them or to the south of them. Without this degree of specificity, the plan will fail in its central job of co-ordinating major proposals and providing a framework for more detailed planning exercises at the sub-regional and then the local level. But once a plan becomes even as specific as this, then it is a matter for local concern and local political action. If a plan is to be more than anodyne, it must contain the sort of proposals that will stimulate protest and public inquiry. It will affect local interests, which will organize themselves within the framework of local government and local politics.

Regional planners working at the scale of a province as large as the South-East, then, will essentially be holding the balance between many conflicting local or sub-regional interests. The interests of the London slum dweller will not be the same as the interests of a Berkshire middle-class cottage owner. The interests of a conurbation resident, who commutes out by car into Buckinghamshire, will be different from those of the Buckinghamshire farmer who is fighting the proposed line of the M40 motorway across his land. The interests of the shopper in a village outside Guildford, who would like to see a new out of town shopping centre where she could shop without congestion, are different from those of shopkeepers in Guildford High Street. Where they are sufficiently local (as in the last instance), there is some hope that these conflicts of interest could be resolved by bigger units of local government, on the Redcliffe Maud Plan. But where they are essentially conflicts between different parts of the region, then they can be resolved only by a provincial authority wielding sufficient power, or by central government.

One of the most important of these conflicts, actually and potentially, is simply between existing residents and possible new residents. Especially in the countryside, the existing resident may frequently prefer the *status quo*. He is not worried by land shortages; indeed they keep up the resale value of his property. Providing local services are adequate, he has no reason to see them expanded for the sake of newcomers, while there is always the risk that newcomers will simply put a bigger strain on the existing stock of public and private services, whether these be telephones or schools or shops. Change in general will not be welcome; it will be tolerated insofar as it seems to be minimal in terms of disturbance or distortion of the existing style of life. A few newcomers, especially if they have the same accents and clothes and life styles, may be absorbed and even welcomed; a mass incursion, especially of people regarded as coming from a different class or culture, will be resisted. In such circumstances, the local political system may work to minimize change, and in particular to ensure that any changes are as small and as unobtrusive as possible.

The most important effect of this is that it inhibits all major initiatives in planning. The incremental approach, even if it means minor inconveniences and perhaps an imperceptible worsening environment, will always be preferred. Thus a new close of bungalows at the end of the village will be preferred to a new village; a new town, especially if it threatens the arrival of people with life styles thought to be different from those of the existing population, will be rejected at all costs. In the County Development Plans, perhaps the most conspicuous feature is the determination to preserve the character of each area as it is now. Here, the planner's desire for containment and for conservation joins with the politician's wish to minimize the impact of change. Unfortunately, these ideas accord ill with the reality of a rapidly changing region.

The political realities, therefore, express themselves immediately as a conflict between local authorities. Until the reform of London government in 1963–65, the curious situation existed that the Outer Metropolitan Area was well organized politically for the expression of its views and interests, while London was extremely fragmented; the old London County Council represented the views of only 3 million inner Londoners, while many of the 5 million outer Londoners were governed by county authorities which also had the task of representing the interests of the inhabitants of the Outer Metropolitan Area. Since 1965, the situation has at least been tidier. A single conurbation authority represents the interests of Londoners, though it has soon found that the interests of inner Londoners may not agree with those of outer Londoners. And counties like Surrey, stripped of their conurbation populations, appear to represent a more cohesive and recognisable set of interests. The important point is that these conflicts would not have been removed by the Redcliffe Maud reforms; rather, with London ringed by a number of extremely large and powerful unitary authorities, they would be intensified.

But insofar as central government is left with the role of arbiter in the absence of provincial authorities, there is a potential conflict between it and the conservatively minded local authorities. This is because in some sensitive areas of policy, the central government is likely to be in effect the only agency capable of taking positive initiatives. Only central government, for instance, is likely to initiate major overspill programmes on a large scale (though individual authorities like the LCC and GLC have shown themselves capable of reaching individual agreements); only central government will build motorways or, through its appointed British Airports Authority, major civil airports. There is a major danger, in such a situation, that increasingly central government will come to be seen as a threat to the values and the life styles of the countryside, as the guardian of the urban against the rural interest. In the nature of things, given the pressure of a population that is 80 per cent urban, this is hardly to be avoided.

In a situation where there are many such conflicts, it is natural for central government to seek to reduce them. Given that it must sometimes find itself in opposition with local authorities on matters like roads or airports, ministers and Whitehall officials will tend to avoid conflict on what are formally local government matters like development plans. At most, they will try to steer local authority policies, through their power to accept or reject development plans. They may prefer to work through quasi-independent agencies, such as the British Airports Authority or the Land Commission, so that in the event of a fundamental clash they can fall back on their traditional function of arbiter. It is easier politically, one imagines, for a Minister to make his final decision on an inspector's report as between an agency and local objectors, than it is when his own ministry is one of the interested parties.

Whether central government works directly or through an agency, it still faces a fundamental dilemma. It can prohibit, by its final negative power to stop a proposed development after a public enquiry. But if (as is common) it wants to initiate, it has a limited and invidious choice. It can support a local authority wishing to take positive action against one wishing to stop it (as the government failed to do when it withdrew support from the Hook new town proposal in Hampshire); it can do the same thing in respect of a new town (as in the setting up of Bracknell). But it cannot compel local authorities to develop if they are firmly committed against development. And often, in the nature of things, they will be. In the case of the area west of London, the lesson is that where problems of urban growth extend over this scale they cannot be resolved by the expedient of bigger local government units. The dilemma of opposed interests will remain; and either a central government, or a new provincial scale government, will be faced with its resolution.

CHAPTER NINE
SOUTH HAMPSHIRE

This chapter deals with an altogether smaller and simpler area than the last. Nevertheless, it has been one of the most rapidly growing in all England in the period since the Second World War, a product of a fundamentally favourable economic structure as well as an attractive environment. Much of the history concerns the attempts of the planning authorities to come to terms with the forces of change, forces not fully appreciated at the close of the Second World War. As in Chapter Eight, a concluding theme is the search for a new and more effective regional planning system for the area.

This chapter was researched and written by Peter Hall.

INTRODUCTION

Between the extreme south-western fringe of the area treated in the last chapter, and the extreme north-eastern fringe of the area treated in this, there is a gap consisting of only about twelve to fifteen miles of open chalk downland. This area, like the last, is an exceptionally fast-growing part of a fast-growing region: the South-East. Yet in many respects, it is different from the area we investigated in Chapter Eight. For one thing, it is dominated by the sea and by inlets of the sea. This has influenced and even distorted its patterns of growth to a very great extent, as can clearly be seen in the shapes of its two leading cities, Southampton and Portsmouth. And for another thing, up to 1970 the area has remained almost completely outside the commuting or service-providing influence of the capital city. Seventy miles and more from London, the two chief cities have kept a remarkable independence from it; as witness the fact that though only twenty miles apart, they remain the two biggest and most important cities in the whole of the South-East outside the capital.

To an only slightly less extent than London's western fringes, this area contains some favourite pieces of English soil; the New Forest, the Solent, Hamble River, Buckler's Hard and Beaulieu. The potential of its fine landscapes is increasingly being exploited by tourism. Again, therefore, this makes for an acute conflict between the dynamic economy of the major towns, which had already caused suburban growth to wash over their boundaries by 1939, and the need to protect land and landscape. Again, it leads to a story very similar to that in the area west of London: the need of the new planning machine to react very rapidly to changes and challenges which were unforeseen just after the Second World War. Consequently, this chapter takes a form very like that of the last. It describes the situation in the 1930s, the creation of the machine, the original plans and their adaptation. Lastly it describes the profound changes that have come over the planning region in the 1960s due to the impact of new regional policies.

THE ORIGINAL SETTLEMENT PATTERN

In the early 1960s, the Hampshire basin contained 56 per cent of the population of Hampshire on only 32 per cent of the county area.[1] But in reality the concentration was greater even than this, because of the very great degree of physical constraint on the pattern of settlement. To the west, the New Forest extends almost to Southampton Water next to the Fawley oil refinery and the Marchwood power station.[2] To the north, the western end of the South Downs forms an upstanding chalk ridge, rather like the Hog's Back near Guildford; it forms a conspicuous barrier to the extension of settlement on the mainland north of Portsmouth, where it is known as Portsdown. To a very great extent therefore, the population of South Hampshire is confined into a corridor between the chalk ridge and the sea, bounded to the west by the edge of the New Forest and to the east, somewhat arbitrarily, by the narrowing of the coastal strip at the Sussex border.

Within this coastal strip, there have been two critical physical influences on settlement, each of which has had both positive and negative effects on urban growth. One is the presence of the sea; the other the character of the land.

The sea is important because it has invaded the land, producing a characteristic drowned coastline with the long, broad estuary of Southampton Water and the great, complex harbours of Portsmouth, Langstone and Chichester. Positively this has produced Southampton Water: a large stretch of deep water, with double tides, ideal for port development; it also presented the opportunity to develop a major naval dockyard at Portsmouth, and produced areas attractive for recreation. Negatively it has distorted the pattern of land transportation along the coast, causing the two major port cities to develop on sites which are ideal for access by water but poorer for access by land: Southampton on a peninsula between the Test and Itchen rivers, Portsmouth on the island of Portsea. One important result is that both city centres have difficult communications with some of their suburbs and hinterlands. Southampton is connected with some of its eastern suburbs by a floating bridge; Portsmouth is linked to the mainland by two bridges, and with Gosport by a ferry. Apart from the two port cities, the smaller market towns

[1] A. D. G. Smart in *A Survey of Southampton and its Region*. British Association for the Advancement of Science, Southampton (1964), p. 153.

[2] Ibid., pp. 153–4.

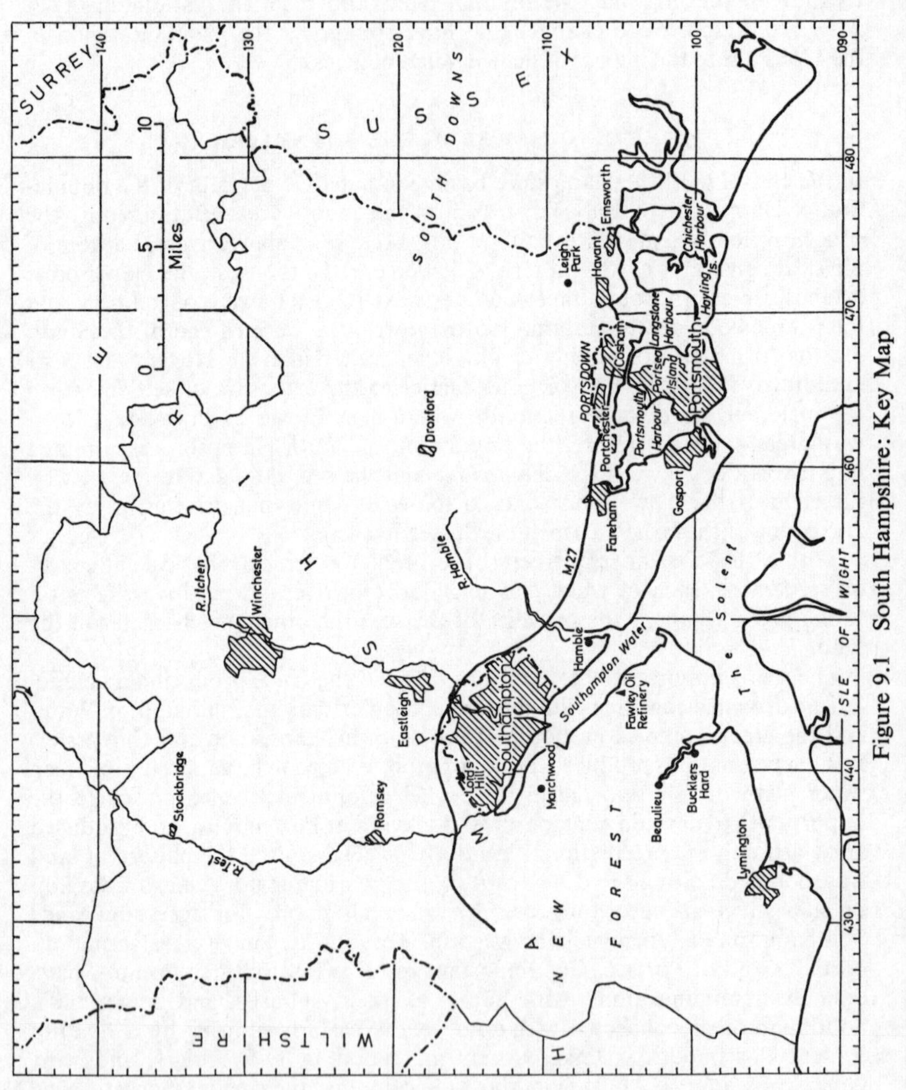

Figure 9.1 South Hampshire: Key Map

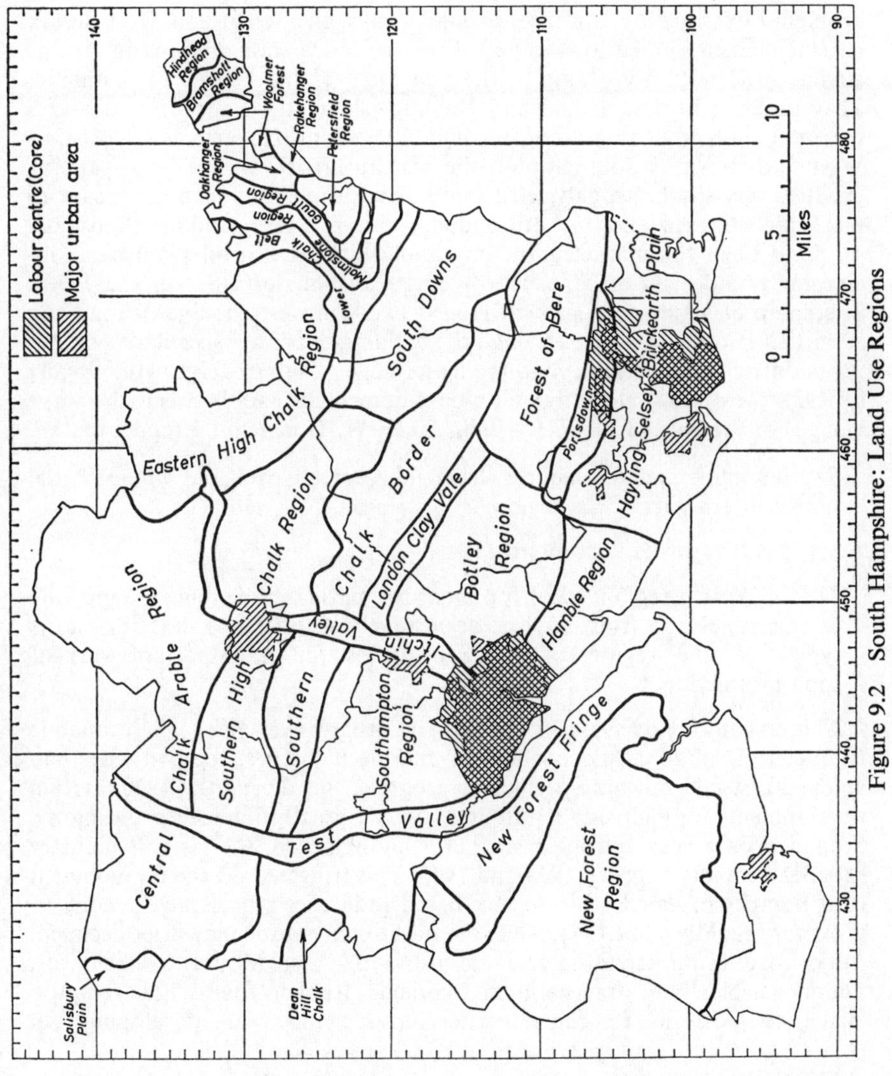

Figure 9.2 South Hampshire: Land Use Regions

of the plain developed inland, where communication lines could be more direct. Emsworth, Havant, Fareham, Romsey are all on convenient bridge-point sites. Eastleigh, a modern town created by the railway in the late nineteenth century, occupies a similar position.

The character of the land is important because its very richness presents a problem of competing land use. In many ways, the Solent and West Sussex coastal plain is similar to the gravel terrace lands west of London. It has similar brickearth soils, akin to the rich loess of the European mainland. They underlie Portsea Island and Hayling Island, the Gosport area and a narrow mainland strip passing through Emsworth, Havant, and Cosham.[3] Westwards towards Southampton the plateau gravels with a loam capping produce very similar, highly fertile soil.[4] The problem of such land, as with the Taplow terrace land west of London, is that it is very good for almost any purpose. Ideal for market gardening and fruit, the coastal plain came increasingly under the urban shadow of the two major cities in the 1930s. Southampton's suburban growth lapped over the western edge of the plain from 1920 onwards, largely through the building of private speculative estates for middle-class buyers; beyond the major edge of suburban growth, already by 1939 there was much straggling development in and between the large villages of the coastal plain. By 1940, F. H. W. Green could report that:

> Southampton and its suburbs have now spread over the whole of the northwestern part of the region.[5]

Further east towards Portsmouth:

> The brickearth region, ideal for intensive market gardening, the growing of vegetables and fruit, has . . . been largely sacrificed to industry and is typical of other regions of Britain being lost for the important work of food production.[6]

This expansion was associated with a progressive change in economic character. Traditionally dependent on marine industries, the two cities had enjoyed a steady but not spectacular progress. But during the 1930s certain developments were already in progress, which greatly intensified during the Second World War and afterwards. In Southampton, the aircraft industry expanded rapidly between 1939 and 1945. This triggered off the development of a number of small scale science-based industries which have tended to grow very rapidly since 1945, while the traditional marine industries declined. Major space using, capital-intensive industries like Esso, Monsanto Chemicals, Union Carbide and International Synthetic Rubber found Southampton Water an ideal site for the tidewater industry they were developing. Oil

[3] F. H. W. Green, *Hampshire* (The Land of Britain, Part 89). Geographical Publications, London (1940), p. 37.

[4] Ibid., p. 364.

[5] Ibid., p. 366.

[6] Ibid., p. 368.

refining, motor engineering and aircraft have been among Southampton's major growth industries since 1945, and the proportion of the labour force in fast-growing industries is much higher than the national average.[7]

THE 1947 PLANNING SYSTEM AND ITS OBJECTIVES

Under the 1947 Act, responsibility for planning in this area was divided between the Southampton and Portsmouth County Borough Councils and the Hampshire County Council. Since the growth of both cities had gone beyond their boundaries even before 1939, this was bound to mean divided responsibility in some of the areas of greatest pressure. And so this has proved. The areas of highest population growth in South Hampshire, and indeed among the highest in England, during 1951–66 have been some of the urban and rural districts adjacent to the County Boroughs, and have thus been the responsibility of the County Council.

Here the planners pursued an active if conventional enough policy. Without an effective regional plan to guide them as in the case of London, they have nevertheless managed to base their policies on premises of impeccable orthodoxy. A critical document was the town map for the southern parishes of Winchester Rural District, which appeared as one of the first submitted parts of the Hampshire Development Plan in 1952. Commenting on the scattered, haphazard development which had taken place between the two wars, the planners presented and justified the town map on four grounds: first, to prevent a repetition of the same pattern of growth; second, to protect the high grade agricultural land of the area; third, to provide for the growth which would take place next to Southampton; and fourth, to provide for a certain amount of development in the villages, mainly through infilling within the existing village envelope, but with some extensions. The plan provided for a considerable growth in population, in line with inter-war and wartime experience. Against a 29 per cent growth from 1931–39, and a 17 per cent growth between 1939 and 1947, it anticipated nearly a doubling of population between 1949 and 1971, from 18,908 to 36,020. Additional land was also reserved for industry, mainly at Hamble where there was an existing concentration of aircraft, marine industries and oil refining.[8]

To the east, across the Hamble river, the plan for Fareham was submitted to the Minister at the same time. The population growth here was more modest: it was calculated as about 25 per cent between 1949 and 1971 (from 40,180 to 50,000) which was considerably less than in the interwar period. The main reason was a big reduction in planned migration in the area, to approximately one-eighth the average rate of the 1930s, because alternative sites would be provided in the Havant area for the receipt of Portsmouth

[7] G. R. Denton and C. J. Thomas in *A Survey of Southampton and Its Region*, op. cit., pp. 259–63.

[8] Hampshire Development plan, *Written Analysis of Survey: Southern Parishes of Winchester R.D.C. Town Map*. Winchester (1952), Tables 4, 5.

overspill. This relatively modest growth could be accommodated within Fareham by developing the interstices between the ribbon growth which had taken place along the main radial roads during the 1930s.[9] Similarly, to the south in Gosport, the planned growth of 25 per cent (49,690 to 62,200) was intended mainly to cater for the expected natural increase; migration was assumed to run at only one-seventh the average for the 1930s.[10] Much of the Portsmouth overspill was to be housed in Havant and Waterloo Urban District, just as much of Southampton's overspill was to go to parts of Eastleigh and certain of the southern parishes of Winchester Rural District (Table 9.1).

Table 9.1

SOUTH HAMPSHIRE: POPULATION TARGETS, 1953 AND 1961

	1949 actual	1971 (original plan)	1959 actual	1981 (revised plan)
Eastleigh	29,980	34,000	36,300	54,500
Winchester	26,990	30,000	26,780	32,400
New Forest R.D.	41,480	54,000	51,670	70,100
Romsey and Stockbridge R.D.	24,250	37,500	20,660	23,500
Winchester R.D.	39,340	56,500	43,180	60,500
Fareham	40,180	50,500	54,610	81,100
Gosport	49,690	62,200	58,840	76,200
Havant and Waterloo	30,800	71,000	68,120	99,000
Petersfield	6,770	7,500	7,230	7,500
Droxford R.D.	19,310	19,500	21,250	23,900
Petersfield R.D.	18,620	18,500	22,080	26,300

Sources: Hampshire Development Plan, *Analysis of Survey* (1952), 4–5; *First Review, Report of Survey* (1961), Tables 1 and 3.

THE GROWTH OF POPULATION

The Hampshire Development Plan, including the necessary associated town maps for the urban areas of the South Hampshire corridor, was prepared between 1948 and 1951, submitted in June 1952, and was approved with some modifications in June 1955. Because of the date, like all the Development Plans of that period, it failed to anticipate the full scale of the postwar population growth. It assumed a growth in the South Hampshire area of only 7,600 a year, against an actual growth of 8,000 a year during 1931–39.[11] Virtually all this was natural increase, plus the planned overspill development from Southampton and Portsmouth. The firm assumption was that:

[9] Hampshire Development Plan, *Written Analysis of Survey: Fareham Town Map*. Winchester (1952), p. 7.

[10] Hampshire Development Plan, *Written Analysis of Survey: Gosport Town Map*. Winchester (1952), p. 2.

[11] Smart, op. cit., p. 154.

> The bulk of house building at that time was . . . being carried out by local authorities, who could restrict occupation to those with local qualifications, and largely expected to do so; it was assumed that this would continue to be the case throughout the plan period to 1971.[12]

In fact, during the period 1949–59, the growth was no less than 152,000 – a product of the rise in birthrates, plus renewed migration into new privately-built homes after building licences were abolished in 1954.[13] By 1954 in fact private builders already built as many houses as the public authorities; by 1961 they were completing seven times as many.[14] The result, in the words of Hampshire's Planning Officer, was that:

> By the mid-fifties, it was clear . . . that the pressures that had been operative in the years before 1939 had largely reasserted themselves and that, despite the best endeavour of the local planning authority, there was a distinct danger that the whole of the coastal belt, with the exception of the New Forest, would become a continuous sprawl of urban development unless strong counter measures were taken.[15]

This danger existed not so much in the town map areas themselves, though even there, in places, the urban areas were bursting at the seams, as on the so called 'white land' immediately outside.

The County Council's reaction was exactly the same as that of Berkshire's, faced with the continued outgrowth of the London area at the same time: the creation of a new green belt. Hampshire's proposed coastal green belt, submitted to the Minister of Housing in November 1958, was intended not so much to arrest development pressures, as to slow down growth rates and direct the process of dispersion into other areas. Basically, it aimed to keep apart the separate urban areas of Bournemouth, Southampton and Portsmouth, while leaving flexibility through room for expansion in some towns. It was based on the assumption that migration into the area would be countered by migration out of it – still perhaps a reasonable assumption at that time, in the absence of detailed and reliable migration figures for the mid 1950s, but soon to be proved massively wrong. Hampshire's current Planning Officer, Gerald Smart, has conceded that it is perhaps 'providential' that the proposal was not approved before the South-East Study was published with its proposal to house an extra 250,000 people in the area.[16] In the event, after objections and a public inquiry in 1959, the Minister announced in November 1960 his intention of approving the proposal with minor amendments; but this approval never materialized.

[12] Smart, op. cit., p. 154.
[13] Ibid., pp. 154–6.
[14] Ibid., p. 156.
[15] Ibid., p. 156.
[16] Gerald Smart, 'Green Belts: Is the Concept out of Date?', *Town and Country Planning*, Vol. 33 (1965), p. 376.

Yet in the lack of any overriding strategy for the area, development has of necessity been controlled in accordance with the green belt policy. The effect has been a complete halt in the growth of many villages, save for very limited 'infilling'. In others, some extension of building was allowed to limits specified on the plans. Provision was made, within the town map and also inside certain places in the green belt, for an additional population of 195,000.[17]

The First Review of the County Development Plan, produced about the same time as the green belt proposal, provided for greatly increased populations in many places in the coastal corridor (Table 9.1). If there was a total increase of about 145,000 between 1959 and 1981, Fareham was to accommodate 26,500; Havant and Waterloo another 30,900 and Gosport 17,400; at the other end of the corridor Eastleigh would house 18,200 and Winchester Rural District 17,300. No firm agreement had been reached at that time about the size of the Portsmouth and Southampton planned overspill problem. For Portsmouth, a reservation had already been made for 5,000 people at Leigh Park in Havant. The plan provided additionally for a 5,500 Portsmouth overspill in Havant and Waterloo (3,990), Fareham (560) and Droxford Rural District (950): and for a 7,090 Southampton overspill in Romsey (780), Eastleigh (2,110), New Forest Rural District (800), Romsey and Stockbridge Rural District (1,510) and Winchester Rural District (1,890). This land was to be developed for planned overspill only, as and when the need was established.[18] In the event this was not proceeded with, and the Lords Hill area of Southampton was developed instead.

THE SOUTH-EAST STUDY

Up until the beginning of the 1960s, then, the planning of South Hampshire had proceeded under two comfortable assumptions: first, that the net migration into the area was effectively nil and would continue to be nil; and second, associated with the first, that the future of the area was quite unconnected with the problems of the rest of the South-East region, particularly the overspill from the London conurbation. The first of these assumptions was shattered by the publication of the detailed results of the 1961 Census, which showed a rate of growth for the region about double that of the country as a whole, and a continuing heavy net in-migration.[19] The second was similarly shattered by the deliberations of the Whitehall officials who, between 1961 and 1964, were drafting the South-East Study. According to the calculations published for the first time in the study (themselves dependent on the new assumptions about natural increase of the population, which stemmed from the realization of the trends demonstrated by the 1961 Census) it would

[17] Ibid., pp. 376–7.

[18] Hampshire Development Plan, *First Review, Report of Survey*. Winchester (1961), pp. 6–7.

[19] The detailed figures are set out below, Table 9.3.

be necessary to plan for continued overspill from London, to the extent of between one million and 1¼ million over the twenty-year period 1961–81. The study proposed that a large part of this planned provision should take place in large schemes well away from the metropolis, beyond the boundaries of the Outer Metropolitan Area. This need for bigness arose from a general sense (there seemed to be little research on the point) that industrialists would profit from a large labour pool and workers, conversely, would benefit from varied employment opportunities; additionally, big centres could provide a wider range of social and recreational opportunities for a youthful population. This suggested towns much bigger than the 60,000 target of the original postwar new towns: a quarter of a million was suggested as the size to aim for. Furthermore, it would be easier to plan for rapid growth if there were a substantial nucleus of population in the area to start with; this would guarantee a certain number of economic and social opportunities in the early stages of growth, which had been conspicuously lacking in the early new towns. The new areas for development, the study suggested, should also be carefully sited in relation to communications, and should be based on areas with a proved capacity for growth. On all these grounds the Southampton-Portsmouth area was almost ideal. It already had a three-quarters of a million people, with strong growth, and considerable economic potential based on port facilities; it had good links with London by road and rail, and both towns were the strongest in their region outside London in terms of shopping, offices and commerce generally. Clearly, whether or not there was planned development, the area was destined for rapid growth; the study proposed to exploit this potential by encouraging planned migration from London on a large scale. Room could easily be found, the South-East Study argued, in the belt running north of the two cities and between them, for an eventual 250,000 people in addition to the region's own natural growth. Up to 1981, in addition to a forecast natural increase of 144,000, the study looked to a planned intake of no less than 150,000 people.[20]

THE BUCHANAN STUDY AND BEYOND

Immediately following the South-East Study's publication, the government commissioned Colin Buchanan and Partners to report on the physical suitability and potential of the Southampton-Portsmouth region for development, the feasibility of accommodating there the increase suggested in the South-East Study, and the form and phasing of such an expansion; they were also to comment on conservation, employment and communications aspects of the proposals. Following the study's framework, the precise brief was to consider accommodating a total growth of 300,000 by 1981, of which 150,000 would represent planned intake; as well as a planned intake of 100,000 after

[20] Ministry of Housing and Local Government, *The South-East Study 1961–1981*. HMSO, London (1964), pp. 72–3.

1981, together with natural increase. The consultants' report, together with supplementary detailed studies, was published in July 1966.[21]

The main conclusion of the Buchanan Study seems to have caught everyone, including the government, by surprise. It was that population growth in the region was running at such a high rate that it alone would give very nearly the totals proposed in the terms of reference, without any provision for planned intake. To be precise, the 1961 population figure, already 773,000, would be supplemented by a *spontaneous* net in-migration of 130,000 by 1981 if present trends continued, almost as many as the 150,000 planned intake specified in the terms of reference.[22] If therefore the area was to make the expected contribution to the solution of regional planning problems, then a much bigger total population would have to be planned for. The consultants therefore decided not to plan to any fixed total, but to consider the capacity of the area for expansion.[23]

To this end, they considered the effect of different rates of natural increase and of net migration into the areas, which gave resultant populations for the year 2001 ranging from 1,236,000 (an increase of nearly half a million over the 1961 total) to 1,793,000 (an increase of over a million, much more than had been suggested by the terms of reference).[24] They considered that a rather high rate of growth was almost inevitable given the high rate of natural increase (a product of a young population) and the spontaneous character of the migration into the area, even in periods of stringent restriction of expansion in the South-East. Therefore, the area's capacity to help London's overspill problem would depend on a rapid rate of growth, unless some steps could be taken to damp down the spontaneous immigration. But the highest growth rates would result in heavy burdens in providing certain services, for instance education and hospitals.[25] Nevertheless, the area had the physical capacity to take up to 1·7 million, and such an expansion would not present insuperable problems of conservation in areas like the New Forest, the Downs and the Solent.[26] Furthermore, the existing structure of manufacturing industry could provide much of the growth potential necessary to support the rapid employment expansion that would be necessary; new industry on a substantial scale would be needed only to support the higher rates of population growth suggested. Even this would not mean inducements to industry, or the introduction of industry into the South-East from elsewhere; it would mean expansion in this area rather than outside the South-East.[27]

Considering the form of expansion in more detail against the physical background of the area and the existing distribution of activities and com-

[21] Ministry of Housing and Local Government, *South Hampshire Study*, main report with two supplementary volumes. HMSO, London (1966).

[22] Ibid., p. 7.

[23] Ibid.

[24] Ibid., p. 31.

[25] Ibid., p. 88.

[26] Ibid., p. 88.

[27] Ibid., p. 47.

munications, the consultants' team concluded that development should take place in a corridor between the coast and the chalk, twenty-five miles long from east to west and about one to twelve miles wide from north to south.[28] Mainly flat in character and with few physical barriers to development, this corridor was bounded at either end by the two major cities of the area. To give flexible adaptation to an uncertain rate of population growth, the consultants suggested a development based on a directional grid of roads, with the main emphasis along the east–west grain, and with service centres free to develop in different ways and at different speeds according to circumstances over the forty-year period of growth.

On purely logical grounds, the Buchanan Report gave the government the clearest possible justification for action in implementing the recommendation in the South-East Study – especially since the South-East Planning Council, in its comments on the Buchanan Plan and again subsequently in the Strategy for the South-East, urged the government to make South Hampshire a top priority development within any plan for the South-East. But there were obvious political difficulties in dealing with such large and powerful planning authorities as the County of Hampshire and the County Boroughs of Southampton and Portsmouth, the two largest independent cities in the region outside London. In the circumstances, to create a new town development corporation of the traditional type was not easily contemplated, even though the government succeeded in doing this for the expansion of the towns of Peterborough and Northampton, which had also been proposals in the South-East Study. Finally, after a considerable delay, the Minister of Housing announced in July 1968 that the three local planning authorities had agreed with the government to set up a technical unit to draw up a master plan and detailed local plans.[29] This would be guided in policy matters by a steering committee of members and officers from the three local authorities, with a chairman nominated by the Minister of Housing. Since the local authorities would co-operate in this way, the Minister argued, to set up a Development Corporation would not be very appropriate. He assured the Commons that the development would take place largely on the basis of existing industry (or industry tied to the South-East) plus office development; the government did not intend to attract industry or offices which might be suitable for the development areas. Nevertheless, the Minister said, he accepted the feasibility of major growth here and the idea that South Hampshire should provide a major counter-magnet in the South-East.[30]

The critical and highly fraught question concerned London overspill. Local authorities in the area, and the local population generally, were willing

[28] Ibid., pp. 14–15.

[29] In this, they unwittingly anticipated a subsequent government decision. In January 1970, the White Paper on Local Government Reform proposed a metropolitan authority for South Hampshire (an area larger than that on which the study team were working) instead of the two unitary authorities proposed by the Royal Commission. See later, p. 501.

[30] Ministry of Housing and Local Government press release, 10 July 1968.

to accept the prospect of rapid growth; they were not easily reconciled to the prospect of housing 150,000 Londoners in planned developments on top of a rapid rate of spontaneous migration. The South-East Planning Council had suggested 60,000 as a possible figure to aim for; the Steering Group and the Technical Unit received a remit to study the possibility of a planned intake but no figure was given. Ironically a proposal that had started life as an urgent priority for solving the problems of London, ended as something else altogether.

Table 9.2

SOUTH HAMPSHIRE: POPULATION INCREASE 1931–1968

	Estimated resident population of development plan area, '000s	Average annual per cent change	Ratio to Great Britain change
1931	610·2		
1951	688·6	0·60	1·33 (1931–51)
1961	787·0	1·33	2·71 (1951–61)
1966	848·4	1·53	2·12 (1961–66)
1968	873·6	1·40	2·92 (1966–68)

Source: South Hampshire Plan Advisory Committee, *Study Report*, *Group D*, *People*, *Activities and Housing*, *No.* 1 *Population*, Table 1., p. 4.

The early reports of the Technical Unit made no mention of London overspill. Their analysis of population showed that the rate of growth within the area was actually accelerating in the 1960s; it had been 0·60 per cent between 1931 and 1951, rose to 1·33 per cent between 1951 and 1961, rose again to 1·53 per cent from then to 1966; and then dropped marginally to 1·40 per cent from 1966 to 1968. Having risen from 610,000 in 1931 to 689,000 in 1951 and then to 787,000 in 1968, the population of the study area was already 874,000 by 1968, an increase of 11 per cent in seven years since 1961[31] (Table 9.2). The study team forecast of future population, based on a complex model which took account of natural increase, the structure of the workforce and migration patterns, suggested an increase from 818,000 in 1966 to 887,000 in 1971, 1,014,000 in 1981, and 1,161,000 in 1991, to 1,333,000 in the year 2001,[32] a figure near the lower end of the Buchanan team projection but subject to a possible range of variation from –70,000 to +95,000[33] (Table 9.3). Still even this would represent an addition to the 1966 population of 515,000, an increase of 63 per cent in less than forty years.[34]

31 South Hampshire Plan Advisory Committee, South Hampshire Plan, *Study Report*, *Group D*, *People*, *Activities and Housing*, *No.* 1 *Population*. Winchester, pp. 3–4.

32 Ibid., p. 41.

33 Ibid.

34 *The Strategic Plan for the South-East*, published in summer 1970, gave very similar figures for an identical area in confirming its status as a major growth

Table 9.3

PROJECTED POPULATION INCREASES IN SOUTH HAMPSHIRE

(i) South Hampshire Study, 1966

	Total population ('000s) on assumptions of:			
	High natural increase		Low natural increase	
	Fast/fast immigration	Slow/slow immigration	Fast/fast immigration	Slow/slow immigration
1961	864	864	864	864
1971	892	892	876	876
1981	1,141	1,048	1,074	986
1991	1,436	1,223	1,294	1,106
2001	1,793	1,461	1,535	1,236

(ii) South Hampshire Plan Team, 1968

	Total population	Extreme values	Increase from 1966
	'000s	'000s	(mean) '000s
1966	818		
1971	887	−8 to +12	69
1981	1,014	−29 to +40	196
1991	1,161	−57 to +78	343
2001	1,333	−70 to +95	515

Source: South Hampshire Study. HMSO (1966), p. 31.
South Hampshire Plan Advisory Committee, South Hampshire Plan, *Study Report, Group D, People, Activities and Housing, No.* 1 *Population* (no date), p. 41.

Thus the surprising fact which emerged was that the normal growth of the area, quite apart from any question of housing overspill, was on a scale that would have been unimaginable a decade before. While previous policies had been based on very limited allocations of land for industry and commerce to provide for modest growth of population, the new projections of employment, even assuming continued strict government control on new jobs, suggested that normal employment growth could produce 122,000 extra jobs by the year 1991 with a large proportion in offices and in the electronics industry. This could entail providing 1,750 acres of industrial land and eight million square feet of office space by 1991. If this new employment was concentrated in or near the existing city centres, as had been the case in the past, the result could be massive congestion and a need for extensive redevelopment; the need was to locate new jobs and activities where congestion

zone: 836,000 (1966), 1,000,000 (1981), 1,210,000 (1991) and 1,400,000 (2001). Thus as compared with the South Hampshire team it assumed slightly higher growth rates in the period 1981–2001. *Strategic Plan for the South-East*, report by the South-East Joint Planning Team. London, HMSO (1970), Appendix D, Table 1, p. 95.

would be lessened, journeys to work minimized, and the movement of people and goods carried out economically and efficiently.

Summarizing these and other trends, the First Interim Report of the plan team, published in March 1970, isolated the critical issues in the choice of a plan for the area. Fundamentally the challenge was one of continued growth. Changes in economic structure, with the emergence of new growth industries well represented in the area (electronics, electrical goods and engineering, plus offices) together with recreational outlets and an excellent physical environment, all worked to encourage continued growth. But the growth brought problems in train, already evident but likely to loom larger: traffic congestion, especially on the approaches to the two major cities; increasingly long and complex journeys to work and to shop; crowding of beaches and parts of the countryside at holidays and weekends; increasing shortage of available land for new housing, schools, industry and open space; shortage of skilled labour for industry; overcrowding and overstrain of public services as varied as schools and sewage treatment plants. Above all, the Interim Report stressed:

> Despite the emergence of new employment centres no major changes in the historical nature of growth have emerged. Indeed, even rapid expansion of recent years has tended to reinforce the historical pattern, with the injection of new jobs and shops in the traditional centres. It is this continued concentration of activities, especially in the city and town centres and the built up areas that has done so much to create the present complicated traffic movement, consequent road congestion coupled with the fall in the use of public transport, and declining environmental standards for the housing and shopping areas.[35]

Against this background, the Interim Report discussed alternative futures for the region. Growth could be allowed to continue or, perhaps, it might be controlled by more rigid policies on industrial and commercial expansion. Within the area, growth might be channelled as before into the existing settlements, with the penalties in congestion and poor environment that would follow; or the attempt could be made to develop new patterns of development and transport which avoided the mistakes of the past.

In turn, these alternatives needed to be judged against certain criteria or broad objectives. The Interim Report set down eight. *A high-quality physical environment* was one of the area's chief assets and a plan should preserve and enhance it. *Wise use of economic resources* was essential, particularly in providing public services like transport and main drainage. *Conservation of physical resources*, ranging from agricultural land to the quality of the landscape and townscape, was yet another criterion. *Freedom of choice* in respect of jobs, housing, shopping, recreation and social activities for the individual and in the choice of industrial and commercial sites for the developer, was another central feature that the plan should guarantee. Yet another aim was

[35] South Hampshire Plan Advisory Committee, *First Interim Report on the South Hampshire Plan*. Winchester (1970), p. 111.

to provide a *clear identifiable form* for the area. *Mobility* must be provided for with a choice of public and private transport and with a minimum of congestion and restraint. The plan must have *flexibility* in coping with new and unexpected circumstances; and it must be capable of *implementation*.[36]

The statement of aims and choices in the Interim Plan provided the basis for the next stage: the formulation of actual alternative strategies in outline form, developed to the point where it was possible to appreciate at least some of their consequences. In August 1970, the Advisory Committee published four such strategies for public discussion in the area. The first was based on a distinctive new area of development, growing eventually to 200,000 people and set almost midway between Southampton and Portsmouth. The second consisted of the creation of several new satellite towns of 50,000 to 60,000 people, some linked closely to existing towns and cities which would also grow a little. The third consisted of new major extensions of the existing cities and towns, particularly Southampton and Portsmouth. The fourth was based on a series of new townships established near the new M27 motorway joining Portsmouth and Southampton, with their main jobs and shopping facilities alongside the major routeways.[37] The report spelt out some of the main consequences of each strategy for job patterns, transport patterns, recreation and patterns of life. It showed too how each strategy could be adapted to faster or slower rates of growth. The discussion document ended by asking people to rank in importance each of the eight main aims of the plan, and to say which of the four alternative strategies best suited the aims. At the same time, the report said, the team would continue its work on calculating some of the quantifiable consequences, on costs of public services, on traffic flows, on the life of existing communities, on physical resources and on the landscape of the area. From all this information, a preferred strategy would be chosen early in 1971. But before it was submitted to Whitehall for approval, the public statement promised, it would be further discussed and criticized within the region.

The final draft document, published in September 1972, concentrated upon a preferred strategy which emerged from a close consideration of alternative levels of use of public transport. Given the fact that only limited investment funds were likely to be available, this strategy was based on the maximum realistic use of public transport. Up to 1981, because of existing commitments and limitations in drainage and in road capacity, there would need to be continuing growth of population and employment around the existing urban centres. Beyond that, development should be concentrated in six principal growth sectors: west of Totton; west of Chandler's Ford; south of Horton Heath; north of Park Gate; in the western wards of Fareham; and west of Waterlooville. Two of these, Horton Heath and Waterlooville, would be served by possible new rapid transit systems. During the 1970s the two

[36] Ibid., pp. 115–19.

[37] South Hampshire Plan Advisory Committee, *South Hampshire Plan: Four Possibilities for the Future*. Winchester (1970).

major cities would develop further as major centres for employment, shopping and education; but beyond that, the growth sectors would begin to take much of the growth both in people and in jobs. The plan provided for growth down to 1991; but after that most of the growth sectors would be capable of further expansion if required, leaving considerable freedom of choice for the future. Thus overall the strategy put virtually all the net population growth and over four fifths of the employment growth outside the two cities; but interestingly, these cities took about two fifths of the projected growth in retail sales. As compared with the earlier strategies which were evaluated, this final choice put a decided emphasis on the cities – and on their central areas – for the performance of the higher order shopping and other service functions.

Meanwhile, in 1970 in London, the Strategic Plan for the South-East was published. Reporting that close liaison had been maintained with the South Hampshire Advisory Plan Committee, especially on the question of growth rates,[38] the report proposed that South Hampshire be treated as one of five major growth areas in the South-East during the period to the end of the century, with a total growth of population of about 560,000 between 1966 and 2001, an increase of over 69 per cent in thirty-five years. It was particularly suitable for this status, the South-East Strategic Plan team concluded, because local employment was growing rapidly enough to ensure that the area could take a major population increase without making much demand on the relatively scarce supplies of mobile industry elsewhere within the region. And though heavy investment in infrastructure would be needed, particularly for roads and sewerage, much would have been needed anyway, on the prevailing growth rates. The Strategic Plan for the South-East and the South Hampshire team proposals were compatible, the report concluded.[39] Paradoxically, therefore, the South Hampshire proposal survived with little change from the 1964 Study to the 1970 Strategic Plan; but in the course of those years, it changed from a plan with a large element of London overspill, to one whose main merit was its own self sustaining growth.

The South Hampshire Development Plan, then, is an outstanding example of a plan for major urban growth, involving radical change in the functional geography of a large urban area, which was produced by co-operation among three sovereign and equal planning authorities. For the future, though, the need for continued monitoring and updating of the plan would suggest a more formal reorganization of local government structure. Indeed, it was precisely for cases such as these that the need for a reformed local government system, based on the city region as the natural planning unit, was first mooted at the time the Redcliffe Maud Commission on Local Government in England was set up in 1966. For South Hampshire the critical question was not so much the need for a wider-based local government unit (that soon came to be

[38] For a comparison of the figures, cf. p. 496 (footnote 34).

[39] South-East Joint Planning Team, *Strategic Plan for the South-East*, op. cit., p. 107.

accepted) but rather how far this wider-based unit should stretch. Broadly there were three possible solutions: to adopt the city regional idea literally, and base two units on Southampton and Portsmouth respectively; to create a unit based on the conurbation of South Hampshire, with abolition or demotion of the County Boroughs; and to retain the entire county roughly on its present lines, again either with abolition or with demotion of the County Boroughs. The original Royal Commission report of 1969 plumped for the first solution of two authorities; it was heavily criticized on the grounds that South Hampshire needed a single planning authority. Consequently the first White Paper, issued by the Labour Government in 1970, proposed Hampshire as a metropolitan authority, which would allow the County Boroughs to exercise substantial powers as metropolitan area authorities. The second White Paper, emanating from the Conservatives in 1971, reversed this solution: it proposed that Hampshire should continue as a county authority, with Southampton and Portsmouth demoted to non-metropolitan district authorities retaining a limited number of powers within it. In all three cases, the county authority would retain the plan-making powers, but under the 1971 White Paper the district authorities (even outside the metropolitan areas) would exercise development control powers.

In few other areas of England are the arguments on local government reform, as they apply to planning, so finely balanced. The need is generally admitted for a broad-based structure plan covering at least the South Hampshire plan area; but if then the rest of Hampshire is detached, it forms an awkward rump area with insufficient population or rateable value to justify separate planning authority status. Equally, the need to involve the two major cities in the planning process is evident; but at the same time there is a need to avoid purely parochial decisions, involving maintenance of the existing *status quo*, in an area where such rapid and large-scale development is bound to occur in the medium term – a problem underlined, if it needed underlining, in the publications of the Advisory Committee. Any reform, then, must involve a certain tension between the interests of the cities, and the overriding need to take a broad look at the region as a whole. But there, it is relevant that out of a total population of 1,330,000 in the new Hampshire authority in 1970, about 880,000 lived in the South Hampshire plan area; over 410,000 in the two cities alone. The views of South Hampshire, and of the cities, will not go unheard in the new authority.

SOME CONCLUSIONS

Clearly, South Hampshire does not merely represent a different scale of problem compared with the situation in the Outer Metropolitan Area. It represents also a different kind of problem. This, after all, is an area where local planning authorities could agree spontaneously to come together to formulate basic planning strategies, and take major planning decisions, in concert; where these same authorities have accepted in principle the notion that they must plan for rapid growth of population including a high rate of migration into the area. Admittedly, it can be argued that the authorities agreed in the knowledge that the central government might have appointed an autonomous development corporation, with compulsory purchase powers, had they not agreed. Admittedly, too, there is genuine alarm in the area at some of the consequences of rapid growth. But making all allowances, it is difficult to conceive of the same degree of concord in the Outer Metropolitan Area. Though local authorities there have set up joint liaison committees, they have not been asked to produce plans for rapid growth. And they have conspicuously failed to agree on a policy for the region as a whole which, in practical terms, means that they have failed to agree on a policy for the Outer Metropolitan Area. Where does the difference stem?

The most obvious possible reason is simply the different scale. One effect of this is that the so-called overspill from the two major cities is strictly local movement; it has usually gone into immediately adjacent local authorities. Perhaps the area is fortunate here in that it has two cities rather than one; the result has been a spreading, and a dilution, of the overspill problem. Yet another critical aspect of scale is that the resulting problems of spillover must be met by only one county planning authority. There is no possibility of internecine warfare, of trying to pass an unwelcome problem next door. Had the county boundary of Hampshire stopped immediately west of Southampton or immediately east of Portsmouth, for instance, the situation might have been rather different.

But the most profound effect of scale may be purely psychological. The area has met its problems as it came to them, because they never appeared too large or too remote. Overspilled citizens of Southampton or Portsmouth did not appear as a major threat in Winchester Rural District or in Havant, in the same way that overspilled Londoners appeared as a threat in Berkshire. This perhaps is a function of the absolute scale of the overspill problem and of the distance separating the source of overspill from its possible reception area. It is notable that when at last South Hampshire was faced with the London overspill problem, after the 1964 South-East Study, it reacted in the same way as the home counties had earlier: with guarded hostility. As a result, the whole overspill development seems gradually to have disappeared from the structure planning process. The joint team are preparing a South Hampshire Development Plan for South Hampshire people; that presented no threat.

But one should not underrate the magnitude of the achievement. Though South Hampshire was not the first of the new style sub-regional structure planning exercises of the late 1960s (that distinction belongs to Leicester-Leicestershire), nor the first to suggest a growth zone away from existing major urban areas (that occurred in the Notts.-Derby study), it was the first to face the consequence of growth on such a large scale. Thus it was forced to reopen the whole complex of issues which Abercrombie and his generation faced a quarter century before in a much more comfortable, more static context: the problem of massive planned decentralization of people, jobs and services out of the existing, established centres. Furthermore, it was compelled to do so within a co-operative local government structure when the interests of the two major cities were bound to intrude themselves on the technical team's consciousness. Even to set up and face the alternative futures for the region head on, as the team did, was therefore a considerable achievement of courage and diplomacy.

Perhaps, then, above all South Hampshire illustrates that new structures for planning do bring new and freer styles of thought. When old divisions between town and country are broken down, both at the level of the technical officers in their everyday work, and at the level of political consideration by committee, the injection of new and even heretical ideas is easier. At least, it is not impossible. The question then is: can this happy relationship work at any scale and in any geographical circumstances? If the answer is yes, then new local government structures plus new planning procedures might in themselves achieve the object of loosening up the planning process; of posing fresh questions, of setting up very different alternatives, of evaluating and choosing in an open minded way. To see whether this is likely, we should consider a very different case where the conflicts between city and country have been long, bitter, and institutionalized.

CHAPTER TEN

THE WEST MIDLANDS: BIRMINGHAM, COVENTRY AND THE COUNTIES

This chapter recounts the complex history of urban growth and planning in one of the problematic urban areas of postwar England. Population and economic growth have intensified the redevelopment problems of Birmingham, Britain's biggest and most powerful provincial city. Changing national policies attempting to deal with overspill, coupled with the operation of national location of industry policies and suspicion and resentment among local authorities, have acted as a brake on the evolution of an effective strategy for the development of the region. Since 1965 there has been an awakened interest in regional planning and the beginnings of a strategy. But the problem remains of finding enough mobile industry to provide the employment to man up distant new towns and town expansions.

This chapter was researched and written by Peter Hall.

INTRODUCTION

Our third detailed study looks at an area very different from those so far considered. It presents a striking contrast; on the one hand, Birmingham and the Black Country, together forming a conurbation of two and one-third million people – an urban growth mainly of the nineteenth and twentieth centuries, occupying an area which was a poorly populated borderland in the Middle Ages, with pressing problems of congestion, obsolescence and dereliction arising from its history, yet with a markedly favourable industrial structure which has contributed to rapid economic growth and in-migration since the Second World War, thus intensifying an already serious problem of planning for overspill; on the other hand, Warwickshire and Worcestershire south of the conurbation – ancient English counties based on river basins (Warwick on the Avon, Worcester on the Severn), from where they are still administered through their ancient county towns by authorities conscious of their responsibility to protect and conserve their landscapes. It is a built in recipe for conflict and muddle; and so it has proved. Lastly, there is one anomalous additional element: Coventry, a medieval Avon valley town that outgrew its neighbours and became an industrial power in its own right, but without some of the attendant industrial problems that perplexed Birmingham.

The character of the different local authorities is particularly important here. Birmingham is a local government unit without parallel in England. The largest county borough in England for over half a century, Birmingham early developed a spirit of aggressive civic enterprise. It has always regarded itself as a special case among local authorities; supremely efficient and competent, wanting no advice from anybody, well able to manage its own affairs, resisting any attempt at change or at limitations of its powers. And, it seems, its neighbours – whether the smaller county boroughs in the conurbation to the north, or the counties to the south – were generally willing to recognize and respect this position: they harboured no aggressive designs on the city in the hope that it in turn would harbour no designs on them. But in the nature of things, Birmingham's expansion has been so great that it is bound to have an impact somewhere. This is the central story of the present chapter.

Like previous chapters, it follows as far as possible a chronological sequence. It starts by outlining the growth of the conurbation and the point it had reached in the 1930s; then outlines the impact of postwar plans on the region; looks at the changed situation created by rapid growth in the 1950s, and in particular at Birmingham's increasingly desperate efforts to house its overspill; and lastly chronicles the development of regional planning since 1965. Throughout, while the chapter tries to treat of the conurbation as a whole, the special emphasis is on Birmingham and its relations with its two neighbouring county authorities to the south.

THE BACKGROUND: BIRMINGHAM'S GROWTH

In the popular mind, Birmingham and the Black Country merge imperceptibly into each other; they are two sides of the same coin. Locals do not make that mistake. They will concede that Birmingham and the Black Country towns occupy the same area of Britain and that they are engaged in metals and engineering. But there the similarity ends. The two are physically different: Birmingham is a great city that has grown by peripheral additions; the Black Country towns and villages have joined up along the routeways connecting them to form a true conurbation. They are also economically different: Birmingham historically concentrated on jewellery and guns and small arms, now on cars; while the Black Country makes a great variety of metal wares ranging from locks to chains. This section of the book is principally about Birmingham and its pressures for expansion into the countryside south and east of the city. It is therefore concerned with the relationship between the city itself and the neighbouring administrative county of Warwickshire.

Birmingham is a classic case of a latecomer among British towns. The county market towns of the Midlands were located in the centres of river basins, and in the centres of their shires: Warwick on the Avon, Worcester and Shrewsbury on the Severn (separated by the Severn Gorge, which effectively created two separate basins), Stafford and Nottingham on the Trent.

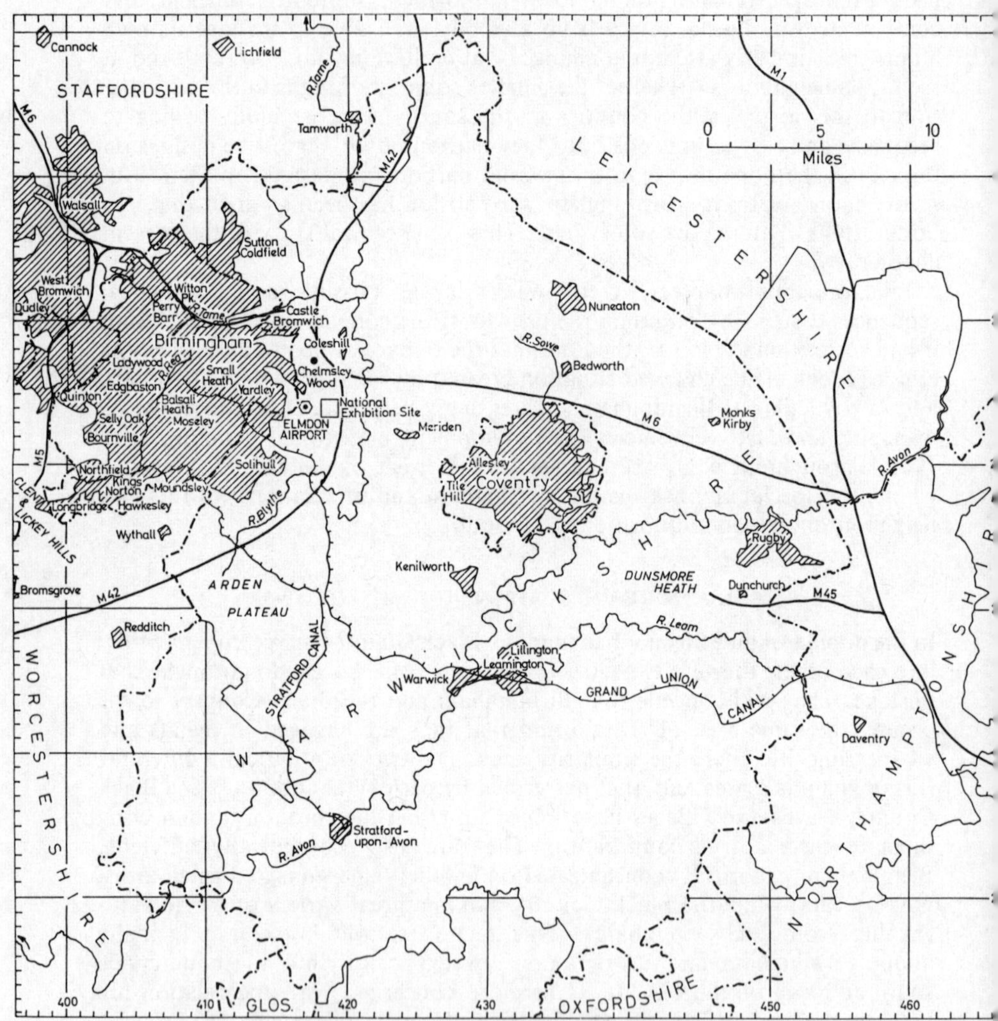

Figure 10.1 West Midlands: Key Map

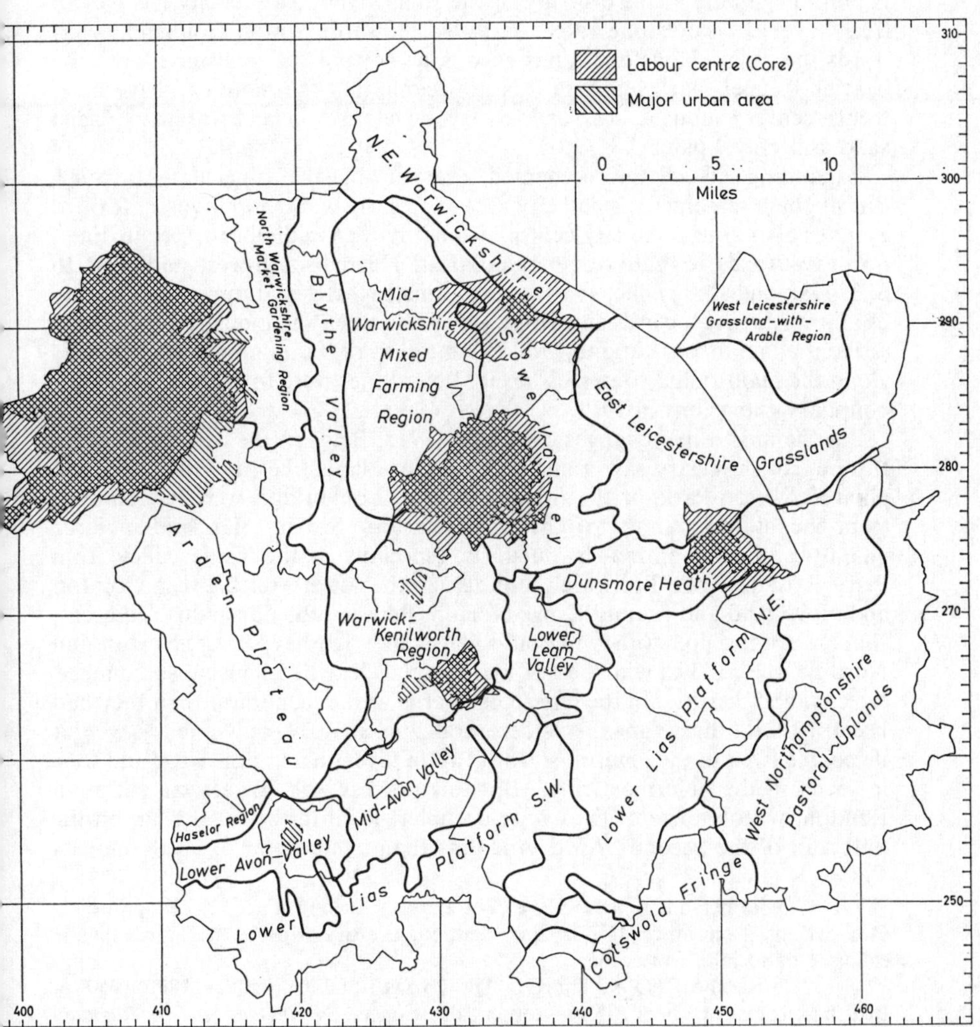

Figure 10.2 West Midlands: Land Use Regions

Birmingham in contrast is sited near the main water parting of England, between the North Sea and the Irish Sea; this is formed hereabouts by the ridge of Keuper sandstone, which runs from north to south separating the basin of the Severn in the west from that of the Trent in the north and east. From a beginning at the crossing of the small river Rea, the city has spread freely over the sandstone ridge, eastwards towards Sutton Coldfield, westwards towards Edgbaston. It has even gone beyond the sandstone, onto the heavier Keuper marl, but here it is noticeable that the more exclusive nineteenth-century suburbs, such as Moseley, developed on better-drained glacial sand and gravel patches.[1]

Expanding at an unprecedented rate during the nineteenth century, Birmingham remained a small city area. The early workshop industry formed a tight collar round the city centre, extending then radially in certain lines, northwestwards to Ladywood and Balsall Heath, south-west and west to Selly Oak and Bournville, south-east to Small Heath, and, most importantly of all, north-east towards the Tame valley. Between the industrial belts, new residential suburbs sprang up, following radial rail lines, and tramway lines along the main radial routes.[2] The city boundaries were formalized by major boundary extensions in 1911.

But the most rapid changes came after 1918. Between the two world wars, Birmingham industry saw a change of scale. Plants like the GEC electrical plant at Witton Park, or the Austin works at Longbridge, were far removed from the old workshops of the small masters. Seeking flat land in large quantities, they colonized the outskirts, especially in the Tame valley from Perry Barr to Castle Bromwich, but also in the south-west between Quinton and Northfield and around Kings Norton. Between the new industrial areas, suburbs sprang up, swallowing old villages like Yardley, Kings Norton and Northfield. By 1939 a wide belt of mainly semi-detached housing surrounded the city, and densities in the innermost wards were much lower than they had been in 1921.[3] Birmingham was decentralizing. In 1938, only one in seven of its people lived in the innermost ring; two in seven in a middle ring; and four in seven in the outermost ring.[4] But this process was not associated, as in London, with the rise of the owner-occupier. Even in the outer ring, on the outbreak of the Second World War, less than one-quarter of all the houses

[1] A. W. McPherson, *Warwickshire* (The Land of Britain, Part 62). Geographical Publications, London (1946). In the twentieth century Moseley became a classic example of social obsolescence.

[2] M. J. Wise and P. O'N. Thorpe, 'The Growth of Birmingham, 1800–1950' in British Association for the Advancement of Science, *Birmingham and Its Regional Setting: A Scientific Survey*. The Association, Birmingham (1950), pp. 223–4. C. R. Erlington and P. M. Tillot, 'The Growth of the City' in W. B. Stephens (ed.), *Victoria County History of Warwickshire*. Oxford U.P., London (1964), Vol. 7, pp. 17–25.

[3] Wise and Thorpe, op. cit., pp. 227–8.

[4] Asa Briggs, *History of Birmingham*, Vol. 2: *Borough and City, 1865–1938*. Oxford U.P., London (1952), pp. 305–6.

were owner-occupied; and of those that were, a majority of owners paid weekly mortgage payments similar to rent.[5]

The process was unlike London's in another way too. Birmingham people, traditionally, need not and generally did not, travel very far to their work. True, habits were changing: on municipal estates in the 1930s, more than half the principal wage earners travelled more than two miles to work, and at Longbridge more than 1,000 travelled more than ten miles.[6] But a survey in the west of Birmingham showed that only 15·9 per cent of the working-class population spent more than 3s. (15p) per week on travel, and only 3·3 per cent spent more than 5s. (25p).[7] Though large areas of the outer ring were little more than suburban dormitories, and though one-third of the total employment was still concentrated in the belt round the city's heart,[8] the economic effect on the average Birmingham citizen was not very profound. There was little commuting across the centre, and little reverse commuting from the centre to the edge, though some commuters travelled round the periphery from suburban housing estates to suburban industrial areas.

It was small wonder, then, that few people in Birmingham viewed the growth of their city, or the conurbation, with much alarm. Ironically, the one citizen of the city who was most concerned was also the most influential: as a subsequent chapter shows, Neville Chamberlain was a persistent advocate of satellite towns and garden cities throughout his political career, and the decision to appoint the Barlow Commission in 1937 was substantially his. But Chamberlain was clearly an untypical offshoot of the Birmingham political tree; and the Commission he brought into being soon found itself having difficulties of communication with the city's representatives. The city's memorandum argued that it would:

> view with serious alarm any measures which had for its object the diversion from Birmingham of industries which by their nature would seek a location in that area . . . the first consideration in industrial location must be one of simple economics, and any material departure from that principle, such as, for example, an extension of the financial facilities available to manufacturers establishing works in the special areas, would seriously disturb the economic equilibrium of the country.[9]

The 'prevalent dislike' of the growth of conurbations arose from errors in town planning, which Birmingham had managed to avoid;[10] Birmingham was not in the same boat as London.[11] Therefore, the right way for the city

[5] Ibid., p. 310.

[6] Ibid., pp. 311–12.

[7] Ibid., p. 311. This, though, meant a journey of 6–7 miles at that time.

[8] Ibid., p. 312.

[9] *Royal Commission on the Geographical Distribution of the Industrial Population, Minutes of Evidence*, 22nd Day, 19 May 1938. Memorandum of evidence by Birmingham, paras 54, 58. HMSO, London (1938).

[10] Ibid., para. 60.

[11] Ibid., Evidence of Alderman H. Roberts, Q.6016.

to expand was exactly as in the past: through peripheral suburban additions. There was no case for a green belt between these suburbs and the city; a green belt was something that should happen much farther out.[12] The Barlow Commission, of course, did not accept Birmingham's arguments; but as subsequent history showed, Birmingham never accepted the Barlow Commission's arguments either.

THE OTHER WARWICKSHIRE TOWNS

During the whole of this time, Birmingham's growth, and to a lesser extent that of Coventry, was increasingly dominating the map of Warwickshire. Between 1841 and 1931 Birmingham increased its share of the total population of the county (the administrative county plus the county boroughs) from 45·5 to 65·3 per cent; Coventry increased its share from 7·7 to 10·9 per cent.[13] While both these cities increased more than fivefold in the period, the smaller towns had a much more modest growth: Warwick grew a mere 38 per cent, Leamington 131 per cent, and Kenilworth 141 per cent over the ninety-year period. The only ones to grow rapidly among the smaller towns were two isolated industrial towns on the extreme east of the county, Nuneaton and Rugby, and two virtual suburbs of Birmingham, Solihull and Sutton Coldfield. They increased about six times in the ninety-year period.[14]

Of these towns, Sutton Coldfield was in many ways similar in medieval origins to Birmingham; it shared a site on the Keuper sandstone ridge, which exerted an almost magnetic effect on settlement in the Midlands, and it had been an old market centre half way between Birmingham and Lichfield. In the twentieth century its greatest expansion had been along the ridge itself, and towards Birmingham. Eastwards, on the less hospitable heavy Keuper marls, it has shown much less tendency to growth.[15]

Similar again, in many ways, was Solihull. Lying south of Birmingham in the marl belt, it had a strategic site on a patch of glacial sand and gravel, and had been an old market town. It too had grown as a dormitory in the twentieth century, mainly towards Birmingham. Since its growth had occupied land of indifferent agricultural quality, contemporary observers did not view the process with any great alarm.[16]

Several of the smaller towns of Warwickshire, together with Coventry, formed a well marked line along or near the line of the river Avon. Coventry had grown rapidly while the others had not, partly because of its situation at the southern end of the Warwickshire coalfield. Its growth during the nineteenth century, and up to the Second World War, was mainly in the direction of the coalfield. But by 1939, there were clear indications of growth towards the west, in the direction of Allesley and Tile Hill; if it continued,

[12] Ibid., Q.6017.
[13] McPherson, op. cit., p. 747.
[14] Ibid., p. 747.
[15] Ibid., pp. 753–5.
[16] Ibid., p. 755.

this development could threaten some of the richest agricultural soils of the Midlands, which formed a relatively narrow belt between Coventry and Birmingham.[17]

Kenilworth occupied a site of strategic importance, halfway between Coventry and Warwick in the Avon valley. In the modern period it attracted less industry than any other Avon valley town, and so experienced less residential growth also. To some degree it became a residential area for Coventry, which led to development in that direction between the wars. But it never achieved the same importance in this respect as Solihull or Sutton Coldfield did in relation to Birmingham; Coventry at that time was still too small, and had plenty of building land within its own boundaries,[18] and also it did not possess the same middle-class populations looking for suburban homes.

Further downstream, Warwick and Leamington formed a pair, on either side of the Avon-Leam confluence. Leamington, upstream, was a mere hamlet until its development as a spa, about 1790. From then on, the new residential town developed north of the river Leam; since this was the Birmingham side of the town, the main residential development continued to take place there in the twentieth century, enveloping the village of Lillington. But between the wars, population growth was slower than in the nineteenth century. The older town on the south bank of the Leam, which was served by the railway in the nineteenth century, became a minor industrial area.[19]

Below the confluence, Warwick in many ways resembled Kenilworth: a easily defended bridgepoint, site, it became the county town, but then experienced slow population growth in the modern age, due to its lack of industry. Such expansion as did occur was mainly to the north along the Grand Union Canal; the valuable Avon terrace lands were little affected.[20]

Stratford was the last of this series of Avon valley towns within Warwickshire's boundaries. Like the others, its site united the advantages of light, easily worked soils, good drainage and water supply, together with a sheltered climate. Again, like all its neighbours save Coventry, it is essentially a bridgepoint market town which has kept its character since the Industrial Revolution. Perhaps because of its canal and rail links with Birmingham it attracted some industry, and a higher rate of population growth, than either Leamington or Warwick. But it showed none of the urban sprawl that Coventry exhibited in the interwar period,[21] and it was still smaller than Warwick in 1931.

Of all the smaller Avon valley towns, the only one to show growth was Rugby in the extreme east. A market town like its neighbours, Rugby developed rapidly when it became a canal town after 1810 and a railway

[17] Ibid., pp. 755–7.
[18] Ibid., p. 763.
[19] Ibid., p. 762.
[20] Ibid., pp. 760–2.
[21] Ibid., pp. 759–60.

junction in the 1830s, but kept its former character too. By 1939, it had an important industrial base, with half its factory workers employed in electrical engineering. The town had grown north towards the railways, which were constricted in the narrow Avon valley itself, and also over the plateau lands towards the south. Up to the outbreak of the Second World War, this growth had not menaced any high-grade agricultural land. But there was a possible threat to the good soils around Dunchurch to the south, which exercised some observers at the time.[22]

The Avon valley and its borderlands, then, were little affected by large-scale urban growth up to the Second World War. Birmingham was growing north-east to envelop Sutton Coldfield, and south-east to join up with Solihull; but essentially, this was peripheral growth, which did not affect the towns and villages further south. Coventry's major development had been away from the Avon valley, towards the north. Contemporary conservationists were worried by the pressure being exerted between Birmingham and Coventry, on the fine soils of the Keele series; but this was about all.

Elsewhere, Warwickshire remained predominantly a green county. Overall, there was hardly an area of the county where the proportion of land in grass fell much below 70 per cent. This was a reflection not so much of climate, for much of Warwickshire had been corn country in the Middle Ages, as of the heavy marl soils, which became increasingly unprofitable to farm for crops after the advent of cheap foreign wheat in the 1870s and 1880s. The Arden plateau, McPherson described in his land use memorandum, had tended to 'tumble down' to low grade grass;[23] and the lower Leam valley was not very favourable land, and about three-quarters was in grass;[24] the mixed farming region between Warwick and Kenilworth had more prosperous agriculture on its varied soils, but even here about three-quarters was grass;[25] further east, the Sowe valley and the Monks Kirby region both had about 80 per cent in permanent grass, with a tendency to practice stock rearing on large holdings:[26] Dunsmore Heath had a little more in arable.[27] Only a few areas provided any exceptions or surprises. In the extreme north of the county, on both sides of the Tame valley around Castle Bromwich and Coleshill, a prosperous market gardening industry raised the proportion of cropland to one-third, the highest in the county;[28] in the Blythe valley to the south, smallholders concentrated on producing fluid milk for the Birmingham market;[29] and on the fine Keele complex soils between Birmingham and Coventry there was a similar concentration on smallholdings, with a high

[22] Ibid., pp. 762–3.
[23] Ibid., pp. 786, 791.
[24] Ibid., p. 803.
[25] Ibid., pp. 804–5.
[26] Ibid., pp. 823–4.
[27] Ibid., p. 827.
[28] Ibid., p. 814.
[29] Ibid., pp. 810–11.

proportion in grass (three-quarters), again representing the influence of the Birmingham milk market.[30]

The fact then was that most of the Avon valley land was not very high quality land. When the West Midland Group on Postwar Reconstruction considered the problem of land classification in 1948, with the aid of the classification produced by Dudley Stamp and his co-workers during the Second World War, they concluded that category I land should stay in agriculture as far as possible; category II land, which was only of slightly less importance, would not be subject to major development without a careful consideration of the agricultural possibilities.[31] But in central Warwickshire, the only land classed as category I ('highly productive under good management') was on the Keele beds between Birmingham and Coventry.[32] Even the more extensive category of mixed class I and class II land did not take in any areas in this zone, though it did include an area over the Worcestershire border between Wolverley and Bromsgrove.[33]

Just over the border to the west, in Worcestershire, the landscape showed some changes. In the extreme north it included part of the upturned southern lip of the Midland plateau, on which the Black Country proper developed. Here the ridge of the Clent and Lickey hills ran from north-west to south-east, rising to 1,000 feet and more against the Triassic lowland to the west. Bleak agriculturally, this area provided fine upland scenery, and had naturally become Birmingham's playground in an age when many citizens were limited in their weekend opportunities to the range of a tram ride.[34] The more affluent citizens of Birmingham were, however, colonizing the area, as Buchanan recorded in his land use memorandum in 1944:

> Sporadic weekend bungalows intrude a jarring tone into the scenery of the Clents while to the south the Lickeys have tended to become, as the many pleasant garden-girdled villas show, one of the more popular and desirable suburbs of Birmingham.[35]

This process would however be limited; for most of the Lickeys, and much of the Clent hills, were already in the ownership of the National Trust, or in covenant with it.[36]

Southwards from the hills, the Keuper marl lowlands were occupied by grass to the extent of 90 per cent, mainly for dairying. But because of its nearness to Birmingham, the area was already under the city's influence, as

30 Ibid., p. 807.

31 West Midland Group on Post-War Reconstruction and Planning, *Conurbation*. The Architectural Press, London (1948), pp. 190–1.

32 Ibid., pp. 188, 191.

33 Ibid., p. 192.

34 K. M. Buchanan, *Worcestershire* (The Land of Britain, Part 68). Geographical Publications, London (1944), p. 539.

35 Ibid., p. 539.

36 Ibid.

was evident from the ribbon development along the Birmingham-Redditch road or the accretions to villages like Wythall. Buchanan wrote of 'the almost general deterioration in farming with increasing proximity to the city' due to rises in rents, difficulties of housing and shortage of labour, coupled with discontent among farm workers because of the competition of high urban wages.[37] On these heavy, indifferent soils perhaps that could be viewed with equanimity. But further west, on the market gardening area based on the sandstones round Bromsgrove, the impact was more serious; here, an area equal to a good-sized town was already more or less suburbanized.[38]

BASIS OF POSTWAR PLANNING

As in the other major conurbations of Greater London, Merseyside and South-East Lancashire, postwar planning in the West Midlands first needed a definite statement of policies for the entire region. In the West Midlands, as in Greater London, this job was entrusted to Patrick Abercrombie, here working in collaboration with Herbert Jackson. Their West Midlands Plan, which appeared as a document for restricted circulation in 1948,[39] was produced largely in independence of the basic survey work done by a group of academics and planners calling themselves the West Midlands Group on Postwar Reconstruction. This report, *Conurbation*, also appeared in 1948[40] and in effect formed a unified whole with the Abercrombie-Jackson Plan. Like the London plans, both *Conurbation* and the Abercrombie-Jackson Plan start from a survey of past and predicted trends, and on this basis go on to set out principles which should guide planning policies. Again like the London plans, the West Midlands Plans proved in part faulty in their predictions, and this gravely affected the validity of the principles.

The most important of the survey assumptions concerned population. National projections at that time indicated an increase in the population of Great Britain from 46·6 million in 1941 to only 47·5 million in 1951; thenceforth population would actually decline, to 47·2 million in 1961 and 46 million in 1971.[41] In the West Midlands, the *Conurbation* group expected natural increase to be higher than the national average; and net migration might continue to be inward, as in the 1930s. Unless migration were controlled, the Group warned, there might be an increase of 300,000 in the regional population by 1970. If there were no increase due to migration, growth might be held to about 10,000 a year.[42] In addition, housing would be needed to meet population increase which had already occurred during

[37] Ibid., p. 561.

[38] Ibid., p. 657.

[39] Patrick Abercrombie and Herbert Jackson, *West Midlands Plan*, Interim Confidential Edition, 5 vols. Ministry of Town and Country Planning, Mimeo.

[40] West Midlands Group, op. cit.

[41] Ibid., p. 78.

[42] Ibid., pp. 85, 137.

the war, to repair enemy destruction, and to replace slums already earmarked for immediate demolition: a total of perhaps 128,000 houses was needed as soon as possible.[43]

The West Midlands Group were confident that this could easily be achieved on available land within the conurbation. Since more than half the land in the conurbation was actually unused, there could be no case for general dispersion.[44] Instead, the main task of planning was to create an acceptable urban form *within* the conurbation, with islands of settlement standing out of a sea of green space. Existing derelict and unused land would progressively be transformed into green strips and wedges, separating and articulating the major urban areas. These strips and wedges would coalesce, at the outer edge of the conurbation, into a continuous green setting (not a mere green belt) whose inner limits would be so drawn as to allow plenty of room for expansion to meet all anticipated needs.[45] The better category I and category II lands outside the conurbation, representing respectively 12·3 and 16·3 per cent of the total area surveyed, should be protected by strong discouragement, and even prohibition, of development; broadly it was undesirable to continue development south-west, north-west or north-east of the conurbation, while the area of very fertile Keele bed soils between Birmingham and Coventry should be specially safeguarded. Permissible areas of development, on land of lower agricultural value, were west of Sedgeley, south of Birmingham, north of Wolverhampton and north-west of Walsall.[46]

Abercrombie and Jackson began their report by accepting in principle the findings of the West Midlands Group; the differences were those of detail only. In particular, Abercrombie and Jackson were in no doubt of the planner's capacity to predict and to plan:

> As a result of much research during recent years, we now know with greater accuracy than hitherto the spaces necessary for urban population. This knowledge is the town planner's basic stock-in-trade. He is now able to say to the economist: "The exploitation of this or that resource will entail so much urban expansion here and that much congestion there, the former absorbing this much agricultural land, the latter costing so much in terms of urban butchery to relieve", and to the agriculturalist, "Deny me this land for urban expansion and the cost will be that much in uneconomical building elsewhere", and so on.[47]

On this basis, the authors could confidently say:

> The capacity of the conurbation has been calculated in relation to a given spread. The numbers of people that can be accommodated within certain limits are now displayed with a reasonable measure of accuracy. Beyond

[43] Ibid., p. 98.
[44] Ibid., pp. 200, 204.
[45] Ibid., pp. 200, 210.
[46] Ibid., pp. 194–5.
[47] Abercrombie and Jackson, op. cit., Vol. 1, Foreword.

these amounts it is a question of either development well away from the conurbation, peripheral spread about the existing built-up areas or higher densities within them. We adduce powerful arguments against the two latter and urge the former.[48]

However, the two inferior solutions might become necessary because of unknown factors in the planning equation; economic conditions, export drive, or policy of full employment.

Though unnecessary in the light of present knowledge, the pressure may come and have to be met.[49]

The 'powerful arguments' for controlled growth are contained in the heart of the report, and they are particularly interesting as a statement of the philosophy of the immediate postwar generation of regional planners. Urban growth, the authors state, is very like the rippling process when a stone is thrown into a pond: '. . . the growth of a town if allowed to take place in the ordinary course of events involves a considerable measure of change all round'.[50] This change affected the whole urban area, including the successive rings developed at previous periods. Where the physical structures could not be put to the new uses that this process involved, this meant structural obsolescence: 'The obsolete property is therefore often left to decay or given some inferior use.'[51] To some extent of course this was the price of progress:

It is inevitable that some changes will take place if progress is to be made, so that it is very much our business to see how the impact of necessary changes can be softened to minimize the effect of creating obsolescence.[52]

This could be done by preventing *obsolescence of land use*, which in turn would go a long way to eliminating *structural obsolescence*. In other words, by limiting the continued growth of urban areas, the planner could create a static situation, as nearly as was ever possible. The existing pattern of land uses and activities would remain the same for very long periods:

Let us assume . . . that a maximum population has been decided for a town, arrived at after consideration of all the factors appearing to be relevant. . . . Allowance has been made for proper space for all conceivable purposes in the light of present facts and the town planner's experience and imagination.

Accordingly, an envelope or green belt has been prescribed, outside which the land uses will be those involving little in the way of resident population. The town planner is now in the happy position for the first time of knowing

48 Ibid.
49 Ibid.
50 Abercrombie and Jackson, op. cit., Vol. 4, para. 4.1(10).
51 Ibid., para. 4.1(10).
52 Ibid., para. 4.1(12).

the limits of his problem. He is able to address himself to the design of the whole and the parts in the light of a basic overall figure for population. This process will be difficult enough in itself, but at least he starts with one fact to reassure him.[53]

The point here is a central one: the planner needed stability, for otherwise the situation was too complex for him to control. And even in a period where population growth was expected to be modest, there were difficulties enough in trying to achieve stability. If the planner were wise enough to leave enough room to ensure generous space standards, as he should, and if the town were attractive on account of its employment structure, more people would pour in and the situation would become unstable again. The only way the planner could act in this situation was by positive planning, to ensure that other places were at least as attractive as the place then under consideration.[54] This would be easier to achieve, Abercrombie and Jackson recognized, in a period of general shortage where building licences, or housing allocations, could be made a tool of planning policy.[55]

This had a particular relevance for the West Midlands. It was not possible to halt migration into the region, all at once. Abercrombie and Jackson assumed that over the whole period 1948–62, the net inward migration might equal the total for the years 1935–39. This would mean an extra 250,000 people to be housed, unless some of those already in the area could be induced to move away.[56] To house these people, and to redevelop the inner areas at a lower density, would demand urban growth somewhere, unless the community could accept a substandard and extravagant solution of high-density development.[57] To house the extra population by peripheral spread, on the other hand, would bring different evils: rapid obsolescence of buildings and infrastructure, extra transportation problems, isolation of city dwellers from the open country.[58] The clinching argument, for Abercrombie and Jackson, was that peripheral building would: 'lead towards conditions which are known to call for drastic action in the case of London'.[59]

If high density and peripheral spread were rejected, the corollary was development away from the conurbation to house the resulting overspill: a problem that the authors of *Conurbation* had not explicitly faced. Abercrombie and Jackson provisionally estimated the size of this overspill as 130–140,000 between 1948 and 1962.[60] The research officers of the Ministry of Town and Country Planning, in a note inserted into the report itself,

[53] Ibid., para. 4.1(15).
[54] Ibid., para. 4.1(16).
[55] Ibid., para. 4.1(17).
[56] Ibid., Vol. 1, para. 13.
[57] Ibid., Vol. 4, para. 4.3(1).
[58] Ibid., Vol. 1, para. 15.
[59] Ibid.
[60] Ibid.

estimated more precisely in January 1949 that about 96,700 could be accommodated by infilling and rounding off at the conurbation fringes without damage to the Abercrombie-Jackson principles, in places like Bromsgrove Urban District (21,200), Bromsgrove Rural District (19,500), Meriden Rural District (15,500), Cannock Rural District (17,800) and Seisdon Rural District (15,200). This would leave about 151,000 to be housed in more distant overspill developments such as Coventry (37,000), Tamworth (10,000) and a great number of rather small-scale expansions. The total thus housed was 247,000, which accorded closely enough with an estimated conurbation overspill of 252,100.[61] Appropriate totals of jobs were suggested to match the population, so as to minimize the risk of long-distance commuting from these more distant overspill sites.[62]

In total contradistinction to his policy for London, therefore, Abercrombie proposed no new towns to deal with the West Midlands overspill problem. Of the two places which were to be designated as new towns in later years, Redditch was marked for expansion, while Dawley was outside the region for which the plan was prepared.[63] But the authors were in no doubt about the need for a vigorous planned overspill policy:

> It is of the utmost importance . . . that the counties should appreciate the heavy responsibilities imposed on them, as it will not be sufficient merely to give support to positive policy by sterilizing from development areas of land about the conurbation, they must additionally help in creating the counter attractions elsewhere.[64]

The net result of the Abercrombie-Jackson policy, then, would be a powerful and rapid decentralization of the West Midlands population. The conurbation itself would lose some 252,100 people in about fourteen years – 220,800 from Birmingham alone.[65] The ring immediately around the conurbation, and including Lichfield, Cannock, Rugeley and Bromsgrove, would gain 115,600.[66] The outermost parts of the region which Abercrombie and Jackson considered, including zones in east and north Warwickshire, south Warwickshire, Worcestershire and mid Staffordshire, would gain a total of 136,100.[67] This would be achieved by a positive policy of urban limitation, which was seen as more than the creation of a mere green belt; though the report recommended creating such a belt, it was to be a temporary measure until it was possible, through detailed survey and supporting

[61] Note by research officer, Ministry of Town and Country Planning, 4 Jan. 1949; inserted into copy of Abercrombie and Jackson, op. cit., copy in Department of the Environment Library, Vol. 1, at para. 16.

[62] Abercrombie and Jackson, op. cit., Vol. 4, para. 4.3(24).

[63] Ibid., Vol. 4, paras 5.6(27)–(28).

[64] Ibid., Vol. 4, para. 4.7(7).

[65] Ibid., Tables 1 and 2 (follow para. 4.3(3)).

[66] Ibid., Table 2.

[67] Ibid.

organization, to keep clearly under review the effectiveness of an urban limitation policy.[68]

The Abercrombie-Jackson Plan appeared in 1948. It took two years of consultations with local planning authorities and government departments before a memorandum from the Minister of Housing and Local Government gave general blessing to the plan.[69] The recommendations in it, the Minister said, should be accepted as indications of population factors which planning authorities should bear in mind. Overspill should take the form of decentralized communities, united as far as possible with existing communities beyond the green belt, which would be maintained. Some of these would need extra industry as well as people: thus Droitwich, Redditch, Cannock Rural District, Lichfield Urban District, Tamworth Urban District and Rural District. Some already had enough industry to deal with the needs of newcomers: they included Leamington, Rugby, Coventry and Stafford.[70]

In a few points of detail and in one important point of principle, the Minister differed both from Abercrombie and Jackson, and the authors of *Conurbation*. From the experience of the years 1946–48, he concluded that net migration had ceased to be a factor of any importance in the growth of the region's population; it could therefore be disregarded.[71] So the population forecasts for the whole region were somewhat reduced in consequence. More people were predicted in the conurbation, fewer just around it; the totals for the outer areas were either reduced somewhat, or stayed the same (Table 10.1).

In the same memorandum, the Minister decisively rejected the idea of a single planning authority for the region. The government at that time had

Table 10.1

THE MINISTER'S MEMORANDUM ON THE WEST MIDLANDS PLAN: MAIN PROPOSALS

		Plan populations in '000s		
	1947 Actual	Registrar-General's projection	West Midlands plan	Minister's memorandum
Conurbation	2,173·3	2,380·5	2,176·0	2,209·0
Rest of central area	244·4	270·6	390·0	339·0
Warwickshire Coalfield and industrial area	371·3	415·3	563·0	463·0
Mid-Staffordshire	131·0	140·1	166·0	158·0
Warwickshire rural	202·8	219·2	277·0	272·0
Worcestershire rural	261·4	274·3	313·0	293·0

Source: Ministry Memorandum on the West Midlands Plan (1950).

68 Ibid., para. 4.7(2).

69 Ministry of Town and Country Planning, West Midlands Plan, *Memorandum by the Ministry of Town and Country Planning*. Mimeo. (1950).

70 Ibid., pp. 11–12.

71 Ibid., p. 8.

raised the spectre of local government reform, but had then suppressed it again. So the local authorities, the Minister declared, should co-operate in setting up a technical committee which could work closely with the Ministry. The Abercrombie Plan, as modified, was somehow to be implemented by no less than ten interested local planning authorities, consisting of six county boroughs (five, Birmingham, Wolverhampton, Walsall, West Bromwich and Dudley within the conurbation, and a sixth, Coventry, outside it) and four counties (three, Warwickshire, Worcestershire and Staffordshire, both inside and outside the conurbation and one, Shropshire, wholly outside it). It was not an obvious recipe for effective implementation.

ACTION ON THE PLAN: THE 1950s

Thus, by 1950, the way was clear for implementation of the regional plan. As Abercrombie and Jackson stressed, this would demand close and sympathetic co-operation between the overspilling authorities of the conurbation, (especially Birmingham, which had by far the biggest overspill problem), and the receiving counties around them. The counties, in particular, had to play a difficult double role, both positive and negative. On the one hand, under the plan, they must create a positive 'green setting' in which development would not normally be allowed. On the other hand, they must work in conjunction with their second-tier county district authorities to provide plans for the reception of overspill, especially in the areas more than twenty miles from the conurbation where the overspill programme was to be especially concentrated. The account from now on concentrates on the city of Birmingham and its relations with the counties that border it, especially Warwickshire, its southerly and easterly neighbour.

In 1952 Birmingham published the Report of Survey for its Development Plan. This took as basis a population projection from the Registrar General, endorsed by the Ministry of Housing, which stated that the population of Birmingham (estimated at 1,083,940 in 1947) would rise to 1,227,900 in 1971.[72] There was no estimate for net migration in this projection, though experience between 1947 and 1950 showed that even then, the population was growing by more than just natural increase. As against a target population for Birmingham of 900,000 in the Abercrombie-Jackson Plan and of 1,000,000 in the Ministry memorandum, the City Council had approved a target of 1,081,000 as the true capacity of the city within its present limits. (The report said that the city thought there should be no boundary extensions, but that it reserved the right to reconsider this position.) This capacity was calculated on the basis of redevelopment at between 75 and 120 persons per acre in the inner zone, and 50 in the outer parts of the city.[73]

The Report of Survey gave a range of estimates for the possible scale of overspill. At the low extreme, redevelopment might have displaced 60,000

[72] City of Birmingham Development Plan, *Report on the Survey*. (1952), p. 15.
[73] Ibid., pp. 16, 35.

for whom homes could not be found within the city boundaries. At the other, there were also housing register applications and people who might move from industrial areas; all of these, amounting to another 135,000, might move voluntarily. So the overspill might vary between 60,000 and 190,000 in the period up to 1961. On the basis of the higher extreme overspill estimate, the city's population would then be only 1,032,000. After 1971, the city planners thought there might be a further displacement of 101,000 from the inner city due to redevelopment schemes, but also a bonus of homes for 150,000 in the outer zone due to redevelopment at higher densities. On this rather rough and ready basis, the ultimate population emerged at 1,081,000: the figure approved by the City Council.[74]

On this basis, the council determined that there was evidently an overspill problem and that it would be desirable to come together with other authorities to see best how to provide for it. This demanded a look at employment policies, since without movement of jobs, movement of people from the conurbation was not likely to be feasible. Already in 1948, the government's White Paper on the Distribution of Industry had laid down the policy: that in Greater Birmingham as in Greater London, industrialists should have permission to build or extend only if it was uneconomic for them to go elsewhere and if their production was in the national interest.[75] In the event, the labour shortage in the West Midlands conurbation proved so acute that the Board of Trade felt fully justified in operating a tough policy. The Board recognized, though, that the industries which provided the bulk of Birmingham's jobs might not be able to move far. There was therefore a case for trying to relocate these industries in overspill towns ten to twenty miles away, if the necessary housing could be provided elsewhere.[76]

The city's official public pronouncement on the subject, even at this early date, was studiously cautious:

> Bearing in mind the importance to its workers of the maintenance of opportunities of employment, the key position of the city's industries from a national point of view, and the inherent danger of a disturbance of the balance of the city's industries leading to a retrogression, the city council feel that the question of dispersal of industry is one that should be approached with caution.[77]

The City Council summarized their policy under four heads: first, to safeguard the city's industrial virility; second, to ensure the full use and the orderly development of all land which could properly be made available for industry; third, to relieve industrial congestion, particularly in the city centre, and to provide land elsewhere for this purpose; and fourth, to approve the principle of dispersal of industry, subject to these other considerations.[78]

74 Ibid., pp. 37–8.
75 Ibid., p. 25.
76 Ibid., p. 26.
77 Ibid.
78 Ibid.

Quite clearly, this policy represented a complex juggling between alternatives, in which dispersal came as a rather lower priority than internal resorting of the city's own industrial pattern.

Meanwhile, the Report of Survey for the Warwickshire Development Plan had appeared as early as 1951, only a year after the Ministry's memorandum on the Abercrombie-Jackson Plan. It accepted that provision must be made for the acceptance of the broad conclusions in the memorandum. This would be done by appropriate allowances in the various town maps, some of which were submitted then with a promise of more later.[79] At the same time, the negative aspects of the policy were also stressed. In particular:

> Development control must be carefully exercised to ensure that there is complete separation between Rugby and Coventry and between Solihull and Coventry where already there are signs of excessive growth.[80]

In the written statement, forming part of the Statutory Plan, there was the same objective:

> Notwithstanding the pressure of land for housing and other purposes, encroachment into the proposed green belt and green wedges should be prevented. Special attention should be given to the need of preventing the coalescence of Birmingham and Coventry and the need for definition of a green belt around Coventry.[81]

Between 1951 and 1971, the population of the administrative county was expected to rise from 490,740 to 621,000. Of this growth 36,650 would represent natural increase and 93,610 net migration, including the overspill element.[82] The increase would be accommodated for the most part either on the fringes of Birmingham, in Coleshill, Castle Bromwich, Solihull, and Sutton Coldfield, where a certain amount of judicious rounding-off would be allowed, or in the principal freestanding towns of the county, most of them in a wide arc of the Avon valley from Nuneaton to Warwick.[83] Within the rural areas any development would be guided to established village settlements, in order to prevent encroachment on the land and the tendency for the Warwickshire coalfield, Birmingham and Coventry to coalesce.[84]

The precise population targets for the main town map areas are set out fully in Table 10.2. In effect, out of a total population increase for the administrative county of 130,000, approximately 78,200 would be housed

[79] Warwickshire Development Plan, *Report of the Survey and Statement of Proposals*. (1951), p. 33.

[80] Ibid., p. 12.

[81] Warwickshire Development Plan, *County Map Area, Written Statement*. (1951, approved 1956), para. 1, p. i.

[82] Ibid., para. 2, p. i.

[83] Ibid., para. 3, p. i.

[84] Ibid, para. 4, p. i.

on the conurbation fringes, in Coleshill and Castle Bromwich, Sutton Coldfield and Solihull. Of the remaining 52,000, about 40,800 would go into the arc of towns in the east and south of the county, though even here there were variations. Warwick and Stratford for instance would be severely restricted; towns with greater industrial potential, like Rugby or Leamington, were programmed for bigger increases.

Table 10.2
WARWICKSHIRE: PLANNED POPULATION INCREASES IN TOWN MAP AREAS

	1951 Actual	1971 Planned	Planned increase
Administrative county	490,740	621,000	130,260
Coleshill and Castle Bromwich	14,665	26,962	12,297
Sutton Coldfield	47,440	73,399	25,959
Solihull	63,200	103,250	40,050
Nuneaton	49,628	56,216	6,588
Bedworth	23,460	28,500	5,040
Rugby	45,490	55,107	9,617
Kenilworth	8,931	14,882	5,951
Royal Leamington Spa	40,041	48,156	8,115
Warwick	15,170	17,898	2,728
Stratford upon Avon	14,100	16,871	2,771

Source: Warwickshire Development Plan. *Written Statement* (as approved by Minister), 1956. Figures taken from each seperate Town Map volume.

As a separate county borough, Coventry submitted its own Development Plan in 1952.[85] This was prepared against the background of a prewar population growth almost unprecedented among major British cities: from 148,000 in 1921 to 220,000 by 1939 and an estimated 257,000 in 1950. The Registrar General's official projection, communicated by the Ministry of Town and Country Planning, was 285,000 by 1971. Coventry accepted in principle the case for a planned Birmingham overspill of 40,000, plus attendant industry. With further unplanned migration, this gave a probable 1971 population (including adjacent areas just outside the city boundary) of 340,000. While accepting overspill in principle, Coventry stressed that social problems – a housing shortage in the city, a lack of social facilities – needed to be solved first. Discussions on the problem between the two cities took place during 1956. Coventry by this time was not enthusiastic, insisting on sufficient industry being introduced to match the population increase, and on financial assistance from Birmingham, which Birmingham was apparently reluctant to provide. In the event, population in Coventry was already

[85] City of Coventry Development Plan, *Written Analysis* (incorporating Report of Survey). (1952), pp. 7–11.

beginning to rise much more rapidly than the original Development Plan had assumed, both by natural increase and by spontaneous migration. By the early 1960s, the increase was reaching 7,000 a year.[86]

THE CREATION OF THE GREEN BELT

Curiously, the original Development Plan proposals did not contain positive proposals for the creation of green belts around either Birmingham or Coventry, though local authorities had agreed on the need for a green belt as early as 1937 and there had been active consideration of the question during the Second World War, well before the Abercrombie-Jackson Plan. After hearing local authority views on that plan, the Minister had suggested that its proposed green belt should provide the basis for their own plan submissions. But there were no statutory means to do this, and Worcestershire was left with the expedient of defining the land as an area of landscape value; while several permissions for housing had to be granted after submission of the Development Plan in 1952. Basically, both in the Warwickshire Development Plan submitted in 1952 and in the Worcestershire Development Plan submitted in 1953, the green belt was shown as White Land. It was not until the request by Duncan Sandys as Housing Minister, in the famous Circular 42 of 1955, that the counties could produce sketch plans for their proposed green belts; Warwickshire, Worcestershire, and Staffordshire all acted quickly, and advised Birmingham to this effect in 1955. The Ministry observed that the Minister was in general agreement with the proposals and advised that they be embodied in amendments to the Development Plan. But as the plans were actually under consideration by the Minister at that time, this was inevitably delayed. Birmingham meanwhile was preparing its own rather different proposals, which allowed for considerably more overspill to be accommodated by peripheral extensions; it submitted these in 1957, and then in an amended form in 1958.[87]

The green belt as proposed by the counties was a substantial affair – wider than the one Abercrombie proposed for London, for instance, in his 1944 Greater London Plan. In Worcestershire, for instance, it covered some 145 square miles – nearly one-fifth of the area of the county; it was designed to be at least ten miles wide, and more generally fifteen, with its greatest width along the radial roads where the need for protection was greatest. Some of it, notably in the Clent and Lickey hills, was already in public ownership or management to provide open space for the people of the conurbation; of this, nearly one square mile in the Lickey hills was owned by the city of

[86] Joyce Long, *The Wythall Inquiry*. The Estates Gazette Ltd., London (1961), pp. 90–1.

[87] Long, op. cit., p. 56. B. L. L. Stephenson, 'Planning of the Birmingham-Coventry Green Belt', *Journal of the Institution of Municipal Engineers*, Vol. 86 (1959), p. 239. H. M. Watson, 'The West Midlands Green Belt', *Journal of the Town Planning Institute*, Vol. 46 (1960), p. 58.

Birmingham.[88] There is no doubt that pressure on the belt was intense. The Warwickshire County Planning Officer revealed in 1958 that since 1948 over 550 applications had been refused for development in the green belt in his county. These, including unsuccessful objections at the Development Plan inquiry, covered an area of 6,870 acres or over ten square miles – enough to accommodate some 46,000 houses.[89]

BIRMINGHAM OVERSPILL IN THE 1950S: THE WYTHALL INQUIRY

The original Development Plans, both for the cities and the county, were therefore ready in 1952; they were approved, usually without substantial modification, by the Ministry between 1956 and 1960. From then on, the story of Birmingham's overspill is best told by the protagonists in a celebrated planning inquiry: Wythall in 1959. This concerned an area of approximately two square miles, some one-quarter of which was in the Borough of Solihull in Warwickshire and three-quarters in Bromsgrove Rural District in Worcestershire, about seven miles south of Birmingham. Birmingham proposed to develop it to house 54,000 people, including 8,000 people already living in the area. There were many objections from landowners and from organizations of farmers and residents, and the case was referred to the Minister for decision, so becoming the subject of a public inquiry which provided the source for an important planning study.[90]

Birmingham's argument at the inquiry was that it had two sorts of overspill. One was 'planning' overspill, caused by the general growth of population and by pressures of redevelopment generally; this of course would be accommodated by the sorts of overspill schemes envisaged in the West Midlands Plan. But in addition there was 'statutory' overspill, representing families displaced by the Corporation's own redevelopment schemes, families in temporary buildings which would need clearance, families displaced by road schemes, and families on the Birmingham city housing list including an estimate for additional families which were expected to join that list. All these, Sir Herbert Manzoni explained on behalf of the Corporation, were groups which the city had a duty to rehouse as part of its own population; that was why the city needed the land at Wythall, adjacent to the city boundaries.[91] The opponents of the scheme, including the counties of Warwickshire and Worcestershire, found this distinction hard to understand, let alone accept.

The Wythall inquiry produced much evidence from Birmingham about the city's efforts to provide for what it called 'planning' overspill. Though the

[88] Watson, op. cit., pp. 58–60.

[89] T. R. Richardson, 'Green Belts, Past, Present and Future', *Journal of the Institution of Municipal Engineers*, Vol. 86 (1959), p. 289. J. J. Brooks, 'The Threat of Development in a Green Belt Area', *County Councils Gazette*, Vol. 51 (1958), p. 60.

[90] Long, op. cit.; this Wythall inquiry was actually one of a series of six, fought over essentially the same ground.

[91] Long, op. cit., pp. 7–8, 17, 30.

Abercrombie-Jackson Plan never specifically mentioned new towns, it was clear that planned overspill schemes on this scale could be carried through only in two ways: either through the new town mechanism, with a development corporation, or through some other machinery provided by agreement between the exporting authority and the importing authority. About the time of the Birmingham Development Plan, the 1952 Town Development Act did provide this second possibility. Birmingham gave serious thought to a new town, and the Council approved the idea in principle in July 1956.[92] But at subsequent discussions with the Minister of Housing in 1956 and 1957, he refused to provide any central government funds: Birmingham would have to build the town itself.[93] Coupled with doubts in Birmingham's mind about the mobility of its industrialists,[94] this set the seal on a new town for some years.

This left the Town Development Act. Birmingham in fact had begun negotiations with the three surrounding counties as early as 1952, and agreed a financial formula in principle in 1955. It secured eleven agreements in Staffordshire, providing for 7,710 houses, but no agreements at all in either Worcestershire or Warwickshire. By 1959 it had entered negotiations with a hundred local authorities in England and Wales, and had concluded fourteen agreements in addition to the Staffordshire ones. But up to June 1959, they had provided only 731 houses, none of them on the open land to the south of the city.[95]

The biggest failure was at Droitwich. Here, Worcestershire took the initiative in preparing a scheme for raising the population rapidly from 9,000 to 30,000 under the Town Development Act. With good services and easy access to the proposed M5 Birmingham-Bristol motorway, this was clearly a better site than Wythall. But Birmingham argued that it would not provide enough relief, since half the additional population would come from sources other than Birmingham. In any event, a letter from the Ministry in July 1959 indicated that there might be difficulties in providing grants for water supply and sewers; and in 1960, the inhabitants of Droitwich rejected the whole plan in a town poll.[96] North of Birmingham in Staffordshire, a site had been suggested on the old Royal Ordnance Depot site at Swynnerton. But the local authority, Stone Rural District Council, proved unenthusiastic; and according to Birmingham, the existing structure there was too big for the sort of industry that might be attracted.[97] At the Wythall Inquiry, Birmingham's representative was frankly sceptical of any possibilities there.

There seems no doubt, then, that Birmingham experienced considerable frustration in its efforts under the Act. The financial negotiations were long protracted and often broke down; high interest rates proved a discentive to

[92] Ibid., p. 85
[93] Ibid.
[94] Ibid., p. 86.
[95] Ibid., p. 76.
[96] Ibid., p. 84.
[97] Ibid., p. 92.

proceed.[98] On the other hand, many of the objectors at Wythall clearly believed that Birmingham could have done more if it had really tried. They pointed to the fact that Birmingham's own Development Plan provided for an increase of no less than 23·8 per cent in the area of land in the city zoned for industry; Worcestershire claimed that the Minister himself had specifically criticized this aspect of the plan in 1955 and again in 1958.[99] The Birmingham representatives were unrepentant about this, and about the fact that between 1956 and 1958 they had actually given permission for 4½ million square feet of extra industrial space,[100] Alderman Watton, leader of the Council, specifically said that: 'Birmingham people were entitled to remain in Birmingham if they wished'.[101] On the other hand, Sir Herbert Manzoni claimed that in the same period firms owning 1¼ million square feet of floor space had moved, or had agreed to move.[102] The fact was, as he said, that if a firm had a Board of Trade Industrial Development Certificate, then the Birmingham Corporation could not be expected to stop it redeveloping unless there were a good physical planning reason.[103] At that time, it was Board of Trade policy to grant IDCs freely; and in the circumstances, Birmingham could hardly have intervened.[104]

Birmingham's case at Wythall, therefore, really rested on several foundations, all of them fairly explicitly stated. One was that it was no longer government policy seriously to limit industrial growth in areas like Birmingham. Therefore, as long as space was available, Birmingham would not hinder the expansion of employment within the city. Second, many firms and many families had close links with the city, and would find it a hardship to move; this had to be reckoned against the pure planning theory that urban growth should be stopped. Third, there were certain sorts of people for which the city had to take a direct housing responsibility, and for which distant overspill might be unsuitable; again, here, the case was a humanitarian one. And fourth, that the attempt to make overspill agreements had very largely proved a failure up to the time of the inquiry in 1959, due in large measure to lack of government support.

Birmingham lost the Wythall Inquiry; though much later, in 1964, after another inquiry, it gained a consolation prize in the right to develop a housing scheme of about equivalent size, in the green belt at Chelmsley Wood to the east of the city. Reading the detailed account, one cannot help echoing Peter Self's statement of a 'measure of sympathy' with the city's case. Birmingham, like many great Midlands and northern cities, had a special problem due to the scale of its redevelopment programme. It had been faced with what Self

98 Ibid.
99 Ibid., pp. 35–6.
100 Ibid., p. 40.
101 Ibid., p. 41.
102 Ibid., p. 42.
103 Ibid., p. 43.
104 Ibid., p. 45. This is Joyce Long's own editorial comment.

called 'green belt politics', which were inevitably bound up with the fear of boundary extensions:

> The emphasis upon the restrictive or negative aspects of town and country planning had become dangerously strong, a situation for which large cities must take part of the blame.[105]

But even if more help had been forthcoming from the counties of Warwickshire and Worcestershire in the provision of overspill sites beyond the green belt, the fact was that Birmingham's problem (like that of Manchester or Liverpool or Glasgow) was special: the people being displaced by its slum clearance programme were not those most likely to go to a distant new town or expanded town. A very special type of operation, involving central and local government co-ordination, would have been necessary. And, Self concludes, looking at the history of Hook and of Lymm, Birmingham in the late 1950s cannot have been sanguine about its prospects in this direction. It probably seemed easier to fight the counties over Wythall.[106]

A CHANGING SITUATION

Soon after the inquiry, it became evident that the whole situation in the West Midlands was changing in a way that the original Development Plans had never foreseen, and that in effect rendered obsolete many of the plan proposals. The first statements to recognize this came not from an official body but from a remarkable voluntary body; the West Midlands New Towns Society, which included such redoubtable academic figures as P. Sargant Florence and David Eversley as well as notable industrialists such as Paul Cadbury, and which acted as a combined research and propaganda group in favour of a new towns policy for the Midlands. In the new situation then arising, it found a ready case.

What is most significant about the Society's work is that within a very short time, as new data became available, its estimates of the size of the overspill problem had to be rapidly upgraded. Thus in 1958, Eversley and his colleagues estimated the total scale of the problem as 80,000 houses to be built outside the conurbation, of which 18,000 were being negotiated by Birmingham with Warwickshire and another 16,600 were being negotiated with other counties, leaving a deficit of 46,000.[107] This, it was argued, was far too big a problem to be met by the Town Development Act through small scale town expansions; the only realistic solution was to provide new towns, two of them with about 23,000 houses and about 60,000 people apiece.[108] But by 1961, in an important policy statement which the Society issued with the Town and Country

[105] P. Self in Long, op. cit., p. xix.

[106] Ibid., p. xx.

[107] D. E. C. Eversley, D. M. R. Keate and Valerie Shaw, *The Overspill Problem in the West Midlands* (Studies in the Problems of Housing and Industrial Location No. 1). The Midlands New Towns Society (1958), pp. 11–13, 53–5, 57.

[108] Ibid., p. 57.

Planning Association, the size of the total overspill already had to be recalculated at 100,000 houses, or more than 300,000 people, in the period up to 1981.[109] Even if 150,000 of these people could be catered for in a string of smaller developments under the 1952 Town Development Act, plus a few bigger expansions at places like Worcester, Redditch, and Daventry, it still left a need for at least two new towns. These should be outside the conurbation commuting limits, but not so far as to discourage industrial mobility; a critical balance had to be maintained, and Dawley in Shropshire, plus Woofferton on the A49 between Shrewsbury and Hereford, were suggested.[110] (The government accepted the argument for Dawley in 1963, and designated it as a new town – the West Midlands' first, seventeen years after the first in the South-East.) But even two such towns would cater for only about 100,000 and there would be a need for special development schemes at greater distances, in areas like the Forest of Dean, north Staffordshire and north Shropshire.[111]

The 1961 report was based on preliminary figures from the Census of that year. But as the definite figures appeared, they showed a more serious problem than anyone had realized. In a 1965 report, published about the same time as the official West Midlands Study but prepared independently, Eversley and his co-workers therefore made a further and more definitive calculation. They showed that during the 1950s and early 1960s, the population growth in the conurbation had been rapidly accelerating; though Birmingham and the older parts of the conurbation were losing people by migration, the newer parts of the conurbation were gaining rapidly by the same means. But while before 1956 the losses in the one had exceeded the gains in the other, afterwards the situation was reversed.[112] Just outside the conurbation, the green belt ring gained 86,000 people by migration over the whole period 1951–63, a figure greatly in excess of the 24,000 loss from the conurbation.[113]

In fact, what had happened in the West Midlands since the Abercrombie Plan was that the conurbation authorities had constantly increased their planned target populations, so that overspill from the conurbation, estimated in the Abercrombie-Jackson Plan as 252,000 by the year 1962, had been completely absorbed by the conurbation itself, through changes in zoning, excursions into so-called White Land, and a general increase in densities. And there was still, in 1965, room left in the conurbation for about 50,000

109 Town and Country Planning Association and The Midlands New Towns Society, *The Future Development of the West Midlands Region*. Birmingham (1961), paras 9–10.

110 Ibid., paras 12, 13, 15, 18.

111 Ibid., para. 20.

112 D. E. C. Eversley, Valerie Jackson (née Shaw) and G. M. Lomas, *Population Growth and Planning Policy: An Analysis of Social and Economic Factors Affecting Housing and Employment Location in the West Midlands*. Frank Cass, London and Birmingham (1965), pp. 1–3.

113 Ibid., pp. 3–4.

houses or about 148,000 people. But, Eversley and his co-authors pointed out, the process must have its limits.[114]

For the future, assuming no net migration into the West Midlands – which, the report admitted, was quite unrealistic – the 1965 Report reached the staggering conclusion that between 1964 and 1986, the total overspill problem was of the order of 300,000 to 400,000 houses, compared with the 80,000 to 100,000 which the same team had been estimating in the period 1958–61.[115] The explanation lay not only in population growth, which was estimated at 622,000 between 1961 and 1986 for the conurbation alone, but in the tendency of the population to divide into more and more households needing separate homes, and in the need to keep up the clearance programme of obsolescent housing. The precise composition of the demand is set out in Table 10.3, where it is seen that of a total demand for 611,000 housing units in the so-called extended conurbation (including the green belt) in 1961, population growth accounted for 227,000, household fission for 125,000, overcrowding for 60,000 and clearance of obsolescent housing for 165,000.[116] Interestingly, the conurbation fringe, which up to then had been a reception area for overspill, was expected to contribute round about one-sixth of the deficiency, or 107,000, up to the mid 1980s.[117]

The critical question for Eversley and his co-workers was where the housing need could be met. Of the 611,000 deficiency in the conurbation and its fringe in 1961, new construction (minus demolition) up to 1965 had contributed 46,000 net additional units, bringing the need down to 565,000 units. Of this latter total, it was estimated that 120,000 could be met within the conurbation (40,000 in Birmingham), or 135,000 when Birmingham's Chelmsley Wood scheme was taken into account. Existing overspill agreements would reduce the deficit by about 55,000. This left a shortfall of no less than 374,000 housing units. Unknown factors might reduce this or (much more probably) increase it; hence the round total of 300,000 to 400,000 which emerged as the scale of the overspill problem.[118]

The existing mechanism for dealing with overspill, Eversley and his team made clear, was quite inadequate for dealing with a problem of this order; between 1958 and 1964 it had provided the derisory total of less than 3,000 new houses.[119] So the migration from the conurbation was almost wholly of a spontaneous character into the green belt and beyond, leading to an increase in commuter traffic. If this process continued, the team warned:

> . . . local authorities will simply build in green belt areas on their periphery, and private enterprise will invade ever more distant rural communities as it did the regions around London over the last 100 years. If this is allowed

[114] Ibid., p. 46.
[115] Ibid., pp. 84–5.
[116] Ibid., Table X.
[117] Ibid.
[118] Ibid., p. 46.
[119] Ibid., p. 48.

Table 10.3

TOTAL HOUSING DEMAND AND NECESSARY BUILDING RATES, 1961–1986, WEST MIDLANDS

	Birmingham	Rest of conurbation	Conurbation fringe	Total 'extended' conurbation	Rest of region	Midlands region
Natural increase	96,100	80,900	49,900	226,900	146,800	373,700
Household fission	33,800	57,000	34,600	125,400	101,700	227,100
Overcrowding	30,000	25,000	5,000	60,000	17,000	77,000
Realistic replacement	66,200	44,300	14,100	124,600	78,000	202,600
Extra desirable replacement	15,200	22,500	3,300	41,000	6,400	47,400
Immigration	—	—	—	33,000	27,000	60,000
Total demand	**241,300**	**229,700**	**106,900**	**610,900**	**376,900**	**987,800**
Net additions to stock, 1961–64	—	—	—	45,800	33,300	79,100
Remaining demand, 1964	—	—	—	**565,100**	**343,600**	**908,700**

Source: D. E. C. Eversley, V. Jackson and G. M. Lomas, *Population Growth and Planning Policy: An Analysis of Social and Economic Factors Affecting Housing and Employment Location in the West Midlands*. Frank Cass, London and Birmingham (1965), Table X.

> to happen, the West Midlands conurbation will grow until it stretches from Stafford to Worcester, and from Shrewsbury to Rugby, in an irregular but unbroken mass . . . if workplaces continue to grow, but the population capacity (of the area) remains more or less static, it is easy to calculate that by 1986 something approaching half a million people would have to travel daily into the centre from the unplanned overspill areas. We do not believe that this is desirable, nor, given the road and rail system as at present planned, is it feasible.[120]

The only alternative, Eversley's team were arguing in 1965 as they had argued in 1958 and again in 1961, was a coherent programme of major schemes of a new town character, with industrial and commercial jobs provided on the spot, and with sufficiently good communications to make them attractive to the industrialists, and the families, which had made the move. A delicate balance must be obtained in siting these developments: they must be far enough from the conurbation to be outside mass commuting range, but not so far as to discourage industry from moving out of the conurbation. There would need to be a deliberate policy of steering these conurbation firms into the new communities, which axiomatically meant modifying the policy of giving first priority to the Development Areas. This, in sum, amounted to a call for a major shift of policy by both central and local government, so as to effect a complete change in the basic patterns of growth of the region's economy.

THE CENTRAL PROBLEM OF EMPLOYMENT

How difficult this might be was partly grasped by Eversley and his co-workers, but emerged fully only as a result of work done in the team by Lomas and Wood after 1965.[121] The plain fact was that the growth of employment in the region remained stubbornly concentrated within the conurbation and in the ring just outside it, incorporating the green belt and the nearest overspill towns like Lichfield, Rugeley, Stafford, Nuneaton, Leamington, Warwick, and Redditch.[122] In percentage terms the most rapid growth was in this peripheral ring; but in absolute terms, between 1951 and 1963 some 53 per cent of the total employment growth went to the conurbation proper, a figure not far below the conurbation's 62 per cent share of regional employment at the start of the period.[123] Decentralization of employment then was very limited, and above all short-distance.

Of the additional jobs created in the conurbation, many were taken by new commuters who lived in or just beyond the green belt, for the increase in employment there was far bigger than was necessary for the increased

[120] Ibid., p. 85.

[121] G. M. Lomas and P. A. Wood, *Employment Location in Regional Economic Planning: A Case Study of the West Midlands*. Frank Cass, London (1970).

[122] Ibid., p. 16.

[123] Ibid., pp. 16–17.

working population within the conurbation itself. Thus Birmingham had a net increase of employment between 1951 and 1961 of 37,800 or 6 per cent, only 1 per cent of which was needed for additional working residents. To man the jobs, 15,000 extra commuters came in from Solihull and Sutton Coldfield, 11,000 from green belt villages and a further 3,520 from green belt towns; only 8,290 jobs were taken by shorter-distance commuters from within the conurbation itself.[124] The pattern was roughly similar in the Black Country, with differences in geographical emphasis: 51,500 extra jobs, a growth of 12 per cent, and 29,200 extra commuters. Here though, 16,200 of the new commuters, or well over half, came from other parts of the conurbation including Birmingham, while only 7,740 came from green belt villages and 3,410 from green belt towns.[125] There was a sharp increase in commuting, during the 1950s, out of the rural green belt, from 37,300 to 65,400; nearly all of it went to the conurbation.[126]

To put it in its simplest terms, then, employment growth in the region was still fundamentally concentrated where it had always been concentrated: within the conurbation, and even within the core of the conurbation represented by Birmingham and the Black Country. At most, a slight dispersal was taking place over very short distances across the green belt into the nearest towns beyond. There was no evidence of a fundamental longer-distance shift of employment; Lomas and Wood describe the process as expansion of the conurbation, rather than as decentralization from it.[127] And this was a continuation of a long observed tradition. Postwar official policies for dispersal of jobs, apparently, had had little effect on deep-seated trends in this region.

To this simple statement, one rider needs to be added. Outside the conurbation, and well away from it, certain independent centres had an economic life of their own, with independent and well-marked commuter hinterlands. Coventry was the most obvious, but Stafford and Worcester came into the same category. It was clear that the relative independence of a place, in terms of its economic relationship with the conurbation, depended on a number of factors: its size, its employment structure (which affected the choice of available jobs), and its degree of geographical isolation from the conurbation.[128] Places like Coventry and Stafford and Worcester, which had the size and the economic structure and the degree of isolation necessary, had somewhat strengthened their position between 1951 and 1961, enlarging, though not fundamentally altering, their commuter hinterlands.[129] Lomas and Wood concluded that their region had an enduring economic structure, which planning policies could not radically alter: Birmingham, the conurbation and Coventry would continue to dominate the region, with Worcester

124 Ibid., pp. 26–7.
125 Ibid., p. 27.
126 Ibid., p. 28.
127 Ibid., pp. 148–9.
128 Ibid., p. 32.
129 Ibid., p. 34.

and Stafford as subdominants capable of independent growth.[130] Inevitably, a great part of the continued growth of the region would continue to be related to the economic opportunities in the conurbation: it would take determined action even to shift a part of the growth to independent settlements of a new town character.

THE NEED FOR ACTION

To effect any change, urgent action on a large scale was needed; the present administrative organization was not capable of achieving it. This was the essential message in the reports from Eversley and his team. It found confirmation in the actual policies of planning authorities during that period of the early 1960s, which showed a marked failure to agree on a coherent strategy. Coventry City Planning Department drew attention in 1963 to the existence of a Coventry city region with some 601,000 people, only half of whom lived within the city boundaries; buoyant economic growth would take the population up to 830,000 by 1981, but after 1975 the city would be full up, and there was no provision for growth of this order in the Development Plans of either the city or neighbouring Warwickshire.[131] Coventry called for a 'radical solution' in the form of a sub-regional plan in which the county of Warwickshire must be involved. The city planners warned:

> If provision is not made, it does not follow that the problem will solve itself. The area will continue to be attractive to migrants, and natural increase cannot be halted. Pressure will build up which will either destroy the green belt, or force people to travel many miles to work.[132]

But at this time, in its quinquennial reviews of the town maps in its own development plan, Warwickshire showed little sign of the need for a radical new strategy; it merely continued the policies of the West Midlands Plan, adjusting them to accept the *fait accompli* of rapid population growth. In Solihull, more than two-thirds of the growth envisaged up to 1971 had taken place by 1961, at which rate the town would reach its 1971 target in 1964. But the target of 103,000 was retained unchanged from the original plan, on the ground that Solihull's policies should not be changed just as the town was becoming an independent county borough; and even more oddly, the same plan was approved in 1965 by the Minister as a Solihull County Borough Plan, though the 1966 Census showed that the population was already above 99,000.[133] In nearby Sutton Coldfield, the Warwickshire authorities revised

[130] Ibid.

[131] City of Coventry, First Quinquennial Review of the Development Plan, *Coventry City Region*. Coventry (1963), pp. 8–9, 11, 18, 20.

[132] Ibid., p. 20. After the West Midlands Study had repeated it in 1965, this argument was accepted; the government encouraged Coventry, Solihull and Warwickshire to set up a joint sub-regional planning study, in 1966. Cf. p. 544.

[133] Warwickshire Development Plan, First Quinquennial Review, *Solihull Town Map Area, Report of the Survey*. (1963), pp. 1–2.

the 1971 target from 73,000, a figure nearly reached by 1961, to 80,000;[134] eastwards, at Coleshill and Castle Bromwich, the 1971 target of 27,000 was already passed by 1963 and was revised upwards to 34,000;[135] next to Coventry at Bedworth, where the 1971 target of 29,000 was already well exceeded by 1963, a figure of 39,000 was substituted;[136] on the other side of Coventry at Kenilworth, where the 1971 target of 15,000 was well exceeded by 1963, the revised figure was 21,000, which was all that the proposed green belt would allow.[137] Elsewhere too the targets had to be revised, albeit sometimes modestly: at Rugby from 55,000 to 70,000,[138] at Leamington from 52,000 to 63,000,[139] at Warwick from 18,000 to 20,000[140] and at Stratford from 17,000 to 22,000.[141]

From these Warwickshire analyses of the period 1963–66, it is clear that nothing like a regional strategy existed. The Abercrombie-Jackson Plan, then a decade and a half old and hopelessly outdated by events, was still providing the only rule book for the local planners of the region; for the green belt policies had been based on it, and the only possible response was to cut back further growth as far as possible within the inner limits of the green belt, hoping somehow to contain the uncontainable. In all the statements on the town maps there is no indication of a long-term, considered policy of housing the population growth in relation to the growth in employment and the pattern of communications. This was evidently the job of regional planning; but for that, no authority was formally responsible. The only hint had been the designation of new towns at Dawley in Shropshire in 1963 and at Redditch in 1964. Finally, the central government had to take the initiative.

THE WEST MIDLANDS STUDY

The West Midlands Study, prepared by a central government team between 1963 and 1965 and issued by the Department of Economic Affairs in the

[134] Warwickshire Development Plan, First Quinquennial Review, *Sutton Coldfield Town Map Area, Report of the Survey*. (1963), pp. 1–2.

[135] Warwickshire Development Plan, First Quinquennial Review, *Coleshill and Castle Bromwich Town Map Area, Report of the Survey*. (1963), pp. 1–2.

[136] Warwickshire Development Plan, First Quinquennial Review, *Bedworth Town Map Area, Report of the Survey*. (1963), pp. 1–2.

[137] Warwickshire Development Plan, First Quinquennial Review, *Kenilworth Town Map Area, Report of the Survey*. (1966), pp. 1–2.

[138] Warwickshire Development Plan, First Quinquennial Review, *Rugby Town Map Area, Report of the Survey*. (1963), pp. 1–2.

[139] Warwickshire Development Plan, First Quinquennial Review, *Leamington Spa Town Map Area, Report of the Survey*. (1964), pp. 1–2.

[140] Warwickshire Development Plan, First Quinquennial Review, *Warwick Town Map Area, Report of the Survey*. (1964), pp. 1–2.

[141] Warwickshire Development Plan, First Quinquennial Review, *Stratford Town Map Area, Report of the Survey*. (1964), pp. 1–2.

summer of 1965,[142] was effectively a government attempt to provide a new regional strategy for the West Midlands, to replace the outdated Abercrombie-Jackson strategy of seventeen years before. It thus paralleled the South-East Study, which a year earlier had performed the same function in relation to Abercrombie's Greater London Plan of 1944. It analysed the problem, and it arrived at a solution in some ways like that of the 1961 statement of the West Midlands New Towns Society, a solution which marked a certain break with the policies of the Abercrombie-Jackson Plan.

The West Midlands Study started by summarizing the facts. Population growth in the West Midlands, during the 1950s, had been more rapid than in any other region save Northern Ireland.[143] An increasing proportion of the region's population was being concentrated in its central division, not so much in the heart of the conurbation as at its edges and in freestanding towns a little way away; in contrast, the rural fringes of the region had grown only slowly.[144] The study commented on:

> . . . a retentive and pulling power in the big industrial centres, a resultant tendency to congestion and complexity inside those centres, and a consequent heavy pressure from within them for expansion of their built up areas. Where any of the urban centres concerned is already big, congested, still much in need of physical renewal, and bounded by countryside widely thought to be worth keeping open, there are the makings of a frustrating and even explosive situation.[145]

There was no sign that the pressures would relent in the future. Even if migration were ignored – a big assumption, since it had been a significant element in growth over the whole period since 1931 – natural increase of a young population would give an 800,000 increase by 1981, taking the population to 5·7 million.[146] In addition, there should be at least a contingency allowance for migration. Estimates based on trends over different recent periods varied from 95,000 to 270,000; the study plumped for an average figure of 150,000 for which provision should be made 'if need be'.[147]

Population growth, however, was not the end of the story. It would mean 275,000 extra dwellings (on a basis of no migration) or 325,000 (on the basis of 150,000 migrants).[148] But on top of this, there was a need to replace existing outworn dwellings, especially in the conurbation (estimated by the authors of the study at 250,000 for the region)[149] and to meet existing

[142] Department of Economic Affairs, *The West Midlands: A Regional Study*. HMSO, London (1965).

[143] Department of Economic Affairs, op. cit., p. 5.

[144] Ibid.

[145] Ibid., p. 7.

[146] Ibid., p. 34.

[147] Ibid., p. 36.

[148] Ibid., p. 39.

[149] Ibid., p. 40.

shortages and overcrowding, estimated at 75,000 dwellings.[150] Together they gave a grand total of 600,000 extra dwellings, 340,000 generated by needs in the conurbation alone.[151]

This was a fairly staggering total for a time span of only sixteen years, albeit comparable with the estimates of the Eversley team. It raised immediately the critical question which the local authorities had tended to avoid: that of location.

> The special problem of the West Midlands is in deciding where the houses are to be built, in the public and the private sectors alike. Since houses must be related to jobs, and both to a total social organization, this means considering the region's whole future pattern of land use. And especially in relation to the Birmingham conurbation, since it is there that lie both the major economic cause of the region's future growth of population and the major physical element in its backlog of need of dwellings for even the existing population.[152]

Within the conurbation, space was scarce and it was badly used. Slum areas would have to be redeveloped at lower densities, yet there was a need for new space-consuming infrastructure, while private firms jealously retained spare land for possible expansion, and much derelict land remained. At the same time, the whole area was surrounded by a green belt, with a total lack of extra provision to take the overspill beyond it. In the rural zone outside the green belt there was much land prized for its amenity; the towns and villages had already experienced some population growth, and were reluctant to take more.[153] And there was pressure from the conurbation itself, as well as from Coventry, to resist any plan which met the land needs too far from where these needs were generated, despite the obvious difficulties in finding the required land any nearer. These were the reasons why, in fact, the local authorities had not been able to agree on a realistic development strategy for any period ahead at all.[154] Nevertheless, the authors of the West Midlands Study pointed out, there was a stark choice: either allocations of land beyond the green belt, at a place or places where development could be carried out 'successfully and suitably'; or incursions into the proposed green belt.[155] The authorities could not have it both ways.

To put it more precisely, the West Midlands Study offered three possibilities. Peripheral expansion, which might nibble into the green belt, had the disadvantage that by putting extra pressures on the conurbation it would hinder its internal restructuring, and would accelerate the pressures in the labour market there, making it even more difficult to decentralize jobs.[156] Near-in satellites, just beyond the green belt, had certain advantages: they were quick

150 Ibid., p. 41.
151 Ibid.
152 Ibid., p. 43.
153 Ibid., pp. 43–4.
154 Ibid.
155 Ibid., p. 44.
156 Ibid., pp. 63–4.

to build, they were part of the city region of which the conurbation was heart (and thus they did not involve extensive transfers of jobs), they were less disruptive of people's lives, and they did not need sizeable public projects. The study suggested that 50,000 could be housed in further Town Development Act growth at Stafford, Lichfield and Tamworth,[157] and thickening up of the settlement pattern all round the green belt could provide for an additional 140,000. But there was a certain limit to what could be done there, and it left an irreducible shortfall of about 50,000 homes; the equivalent of 150,000 people.

This left the third possibility of additional projects, farther out from the conurbation. These would have to be independent centres, well beyond commuting range of the conurbation, which suggested that they should be quite sizeable. Because of the existing clusters of development along the main Megalopolitan axis to the north and again to the south-east of the conurbation, the study suggested an emphasis on development to the west.[158] Worcester city should be expanded by 50,000 people, to reach about 120,000; Wellington and Oakengates should receive a similar number, in addition to the neighbouring Dawley new town development. Lastly, one development on the main axis could be countenanced: a site at Swynnerton, between Stafford and Stoke-on-Trent, should take between 50,000 and 60,000 people.[159] All these sites, the study suggested, were reasonably near the conurbation; all should be attractive to industry; all were on good communication lines either existing or needed. They should cater for the bulk of the 150,000 shortfall up to 1981, and might take even more if migration proved to be an important element, or if natural increase proved bigger than expected.

The net effect of these recommendations would be a profound reordering of the population patterns of the region within a relatively short time-span. While the conurbation would continue to be contained as Abercrombie and Jackson had argued, and inner areas of the region stagnate, the outer areas would grow rapidly; there would be a marked process of decentralization, more like the pattern seen in the London region after 1945 than anything so far witnessed in the West Midlands. While the conurbation would remain roughly static in population, south and west Warwickshire would gain 76,000; the Coventry belt, 103,000; Worcestershire, 163,000; eastern Shropshire, 140,000 (the greatest proportional growth of any of the sub-divisions) and South Staffordshire, including Burton on Trent, 203,000.[160] At last, it seemed the West Midlands had a strategic plan.

THE PLANNING COUNCIL'S CALCULATIONS AND THE GOVERNMENT'S RESPONSE

Even before publication in 1965 of the West Midlands Study as an independent exercise by the Department of Economic Affairs, the West Midlands

[157] Ibid., p. 66.
[158] Ibid.
[159] Ibid., pp. 67–8.
[160] Ibid., pp. 71–3.

Regional Economic Planning Council had been appointed by the government. It was natural that the new Council should turn their attention first to the West Midlands Study and to the policy implications in it. By early 1967 their first major report, *The West Midlands: Patterns of Growth*, had revised the study's estimates of future population growth. The Council allowed for some continuing net migration into the region after 1964 (a possibility excluded, as a basis for calculation, by the study) and arrived at a population increase between 1964 and 1981 of 875,000, or 80,000 more than the minimum in the study.[161] It updated the calculations of housing need accordingly, while retaining the same assumptions about replacement and household fissioning as the authors of the West Midlands Study; as a result, it emerged with a total housing demand for the conurbation of 355,000 additional units between 1964 and 1971, a figure remarkably close to the calculations of Eversley and his co-authors in their 1965 report.

Table 10.4
HOUSING REQUIREMENTS 1963–1982, WEST MIDLANDS
Dwellings required, 1963–81 (thousands)

	To remedy existing shortages	For replacement needs	For new household formation	Totals
Conurbation	62	130	163	355
Rest of region	13	120	142	275
Total	75	250	305	630

Source: West Midlands: Patterns of Growth, p. 21.

As to how this need should be catered for, the Planning Council retained their initial view that the study had been right in calling for the containment of the conurbation. A containment policy, the Council said, would reduce 'the social and economic threat' of a growing conurbation, as well as giving the population better opportunities for getting into the countryside.[162] This meant that the population in the continuously built-up area would actually fall, due to redevelopment; neither high-density redevelopment nor the use of derelict land, the Council concluded, could fundamentally alter this fact. On this basis, of the conurbation's need for 355,000 extra dwellings, 185,000 were still unprovided for either by redevelopment or by new development – or, taking Chelmsley Wood into account, 165,000. This was equivalent to an overspill of 500,000 within fourteen years, for which no provision was yet made.[163] Considering that only 25,000 people had actually moved in planned overspill schemes between 1945 and 1965, the Planning Council seems to

[161] West Midlands Economic Planning Council, *The West Midlands: Patterns of Growth*. HMSO, London (1967), pp. 18–19.

[162] Ibid., pp. 22–3.

[163] Ibid., pp. 23–4.

have been justified in calling this an 'unprecedented figure'.[164] It might mean that the overspill programme would have to be increased tenfold during the late 1960s and the 1970s. It would mean outward movement of jobs together with the population, on a scale larger even than that of London in the postwar period, with a generous IDC policy, and even incentives to industrialists to move. As Lomas and Wood put it in their later study, this question of job mobility was a 'formidable hurdle'[165]; a hurdle on which all previous attempts at decentralization had fallen. Their calculation was that the medium and longer-range overspill schemes in the West Midlands Study, including the new and expanded towns, would need 170,000 jobs, of which 90,000 would be in manufacturing; the growth closer to the conurbation would entail the creation of 25,000 jobs, of which half would be in factories.[166] If these jobs were not provided locally, commuting or the failure of the project would be the inevitable result. Small wonder, therefore, that the Planning Council approached some of the longer-distance schemes in the study with a degree of scepticism.

Therefore the need to make a realistic ordering of priorities was urgent. The Planning Council considered five possible main directions of development, or 'corridors of growth', outwards from the conurbation. To the north-west, they suggested that Wellington-Oakengates should be developed as rapidly as possible in association with Dawley; this should take priority over any early development farther out at Shrewsbury, such as the study had tentatively suggested. To the north, they urged the possibilities of developing in north Staffordshire and at Swynnerton. To the north-east, they thought that Burton-on-Trent should be investigated as a possible site for 40,000 overspill by 1981. To the south, they suggested the possible expansion of the new town of Redditch. To the south-west, they were considering the wisdom of a recent Ministry suggestion that Worcestershire and Birmingham should jointly consider the possibility of expansion to provide rapidly for 70,000 additional people in short distance schemes; they thought that the proposal to expand the city of Worcester by 50,000 was too great, and suggested 25,000 by 1981.[167]

By this time, in fact, events were rapidly overtaking the possibility of an orderly long-distance overspill programme. Already, in July 1967, the then Chief Planner at the Ministry of Housing, J. R. James, publicly dismissed the green belt policies, as employed round London, as 'unworkable', and suggested instead salients of development outward from the West Midlands conurbation following the main lines of communication.[168] In January 1968 this idea received concrete expression: the government rejected the Planning Council's suggestion that industry should receive financial incentives to move to overspill sites in the region outside the conurbation, because it would

164 Ibid., p. 24.

165 Lomas and Wood, op. cit., p. 140.

166 Ibid.

167 *The West Midlands: Patterns of Growth*, op. cit.

168 The *Guardian*, 14 July 1967; quoted *The Planning Bulletin*, 29/67.

interfere with the policy of steering industry to the Development Areas. It rejected also the Council's suggestions for substantial overspill schemes in North Staffordshire and at Burton. Going further, it publicly admitted that full reliance could not be placed on planned overspill for dealing with problems arising from population growth and from displacement due to redevelopment within the West Midlands conurbation. It concluded emphatically:

> This means that many more people will almost certainly have to be accommodated within commuting distance from their work in the conurbation and further study of urban development along these lines is required.[169]

In other words, the proposal for rapid growth just outside the conurbation, which the Council had promised to consider the previous summer, would almost certainly go ahead. This, *The Times* commented, was a major setback to the Planning Council and to all those in the region who had long argued for a planned overspill solution to the problems of the conurbation.[170] It appeared indeed as an encouragement to all those who argued that the only solution was to build large numbers of new houses in the countryside just outside the Birmingham city boundary.

Birmingham was quick to act on this lead. By June 1968 it had applied to Worcestershire to build at Wythall and at Bromsgrove in order to prevent its housing programme coming to a halt for lack of building land.[171] A month later came announcement of agreement between the two authorities on two sites to provide 11,000 houses for 35,000 people between Hawkesley and Moundsley not far away, on the east side of the Longbridge motor works. Worcestershire declared that the sites would present no insurmountable engineering or planning problems and that they would allow the city to maintain its building programme of 5,000 houses a year. It had originally opposed the city's proposal to build at Bromsgrove, but had become convinced that government policy was in fact to accept commuter development because the necessary industry could not be moved out fast enough; hence its counter proposals which had been accepted by Birmingham.[172]

Some consolation came for the proponents of a new town policy in the autumn; in October 1968, the government announced that 10,000 acres of land in and around Wellington and Oakengates would be added to the existing 9,000 acres of Dawley new town, to provide a much extended new city for 100,000 overspill by the middle or late 1980s. This, together with the existing population in the area and natural increase, would give an eventual total of about 220,000 people. The new city, the Minister announced, would be called Telford in memory of the great engineer who had done so much of his best

[169] *The Times*, 3 Jan. 1968; quoted *The Planning Bulletin*, 2/68.
[170] Ibid.
[171] The *Sunday Times*, 2 June 1968; quoted *The Planning Bulletin*, 23/68.
[172] The *Guardian*, 9 July 1968; quoted *The Planning Bulletin*, 29/68.

work in the area. This decision meant that at least one of the major long-distance overspill proposals in the 1964 study, warmly commended by the Planning Council, had been accepted.[173] But for the West Midlands New Town Society and for its allies on the Planning Council, it could barely sugar the pill. The government had conspicuously and deliberately decided that a wholehearted policy of dispersing West Midlands overspill was a non-starter. Years of campaigning by devoted individuals and organizations had, apparently, gone in vain.

THE SIGNIFICANCE OF LOCAL GOVERNMENT REFORM

The new emphasis on short-distance overspill schemes gave added point to the debate on local government reform, which gained a new focus after the publication of the Royal Commission report in the summer of 1969. All the central government departments appearing before the Commission, and virtually all private experts, had long agreed on the rightness of a so called city region solution to the problem everywhere in the country. The critical problem was the interpretation of the phrase in different regional circumstances. In the particular case of the West Midlands, it was possible to argue that because of its great size and its domination of the region of which it formed a part, the physically built-up conurbation itself was the appropriate unit; such a solution had been applied to the reform of London local government in the Act of 1963. But on the other hand it was arguable that certain areas outside the conurbation, within and beyond the green belt, had such close functional links with it, in the form of journeys to work or to shop, that they should be united within the conurbation in a single unit. And it was even possible to go further, as Derek Senior did in his memorandum of dissent to the Commission's report, and argue that the city region essentially was the area which needed to be planned as a whole; such an area might go well beyond the present commuter limits, to take in areas which were receiving overspill from the conurbation or might do so in the future.[174]

In the event, the Royal Commission recommendations of 1969 took a moderate course. A two-tier system of metropolitan government was to be set up for the major conurbations: the Birmingham metropolitan council would extend outside the physical conurbation to take in areas up to twenty miles from central Birmingham, including Stafford to the north, Bromsgrove and Redditch to the south. But it would not extend to take in all the major overspill areas for the conurbation; this, the Commission pointed out, would bring in Telford, and without Telford the well defined Shropshire county unit would be seriously weakened.[175] Nevertheless, the Redcliffe

173 *The Times*, 24 Oct. 1968; quoted *The Planning Bulletin*, 44/68.

174 Royal Commission on Local Government in England, 1966–69, *Memorandum of Dissent by Mr. D. Senior*. Cmnd 4040-I, HMSO, London (1969), paras 30–1, p. 8.

175 Royal Commission on Local Government in England, 1966–69, *Report*. Cmnd 4040, HMSO, London (1969), Annex I, p. 239.

Maud proposals, which were accepted by the Labour Government in their White Paper early in 1970,[176] essentially gave to the conurbation authority control over wide areas in Staffordshire, which was abolished, and Warwickshire and Worcestershire. It was a solution which was bound to be unpopular with the rural interests, who fought back on the grounds of the right to self determination.

The incoming Conservative Government of 1970 recognized these pleas. Their White Paper, early in 1971, announced a substantially different map of local government reform.[177] Everywhere, instead of the single-tier system proposed by Redcliffe Maud for the areas outside the conurbations, there was to be a two-tier system, with counties and county districts. Furthermore, the historic counties won back the disputed rural acres from the metropolitan authorities. The West Midlands metropolitan county, as it was now to be known, was cut back to the physical limits of the conurbation, with one curious exception. Contrary to everyone's expectations, Coventry was included in the metropolitan authority, together with the intervening green belt in the rural district of Meriden which separated the two urban areas.[178] On every criterion of social geography, the resulting map made virtual nonsense. Areas like Bromsgrove, which had very close links with the conurbation, were excluded from the metropolitan authority.[179] But Coventry, a largely self-contained city which sent few commuters into the conurbation, was included. Coventry's own suburbs, which in some cases were physically contiguous with it (Bedworth on the north, Kenilworth on the south), were cut off and put into Warwickshire, which became a curious sausage-shaped county almost cut in half by Coventry. The map made more sense in political terms. For the inclusion of Coventry in the metropolitan area gave it the status of a metropolitan district, and thus considerably greater powers than if it had remained in Warwickshire. Furthermore, cynics were not slow to point out, the metropolitan authority was given the Meriden green belt into which Birmingham had tried to make so many incursions in the past. More Chelmsley Woods, and a ready approval for the proposed National Exhibition Centre near the airport, the M6 motorway and the proposed orbital M42 motorway, would be feasible in the future as perhaps they were not in the past.

The official defence of the proposals was that, on balance, rural counties like Warwick and Worcester were better guardians of good planning principles than the metropolitan authority would be. And for that, there was some justification: David Gregory's study of development control in the West Midlands green belt, published a few months earlier, showed conclusively that

176 *Reform of Local Government in England.* Cmnd 4276, HMSO, London (1970).

177 *Local Government in England: Government Proposals for Reorganisation.* Cmnd 4584, HMSO, London (1969).

178 Department of the Environment, Circular 8/71, *Local Government Reorganisation in England: Proposed New Areas.* HMSO, London (1971), pp. 14–16.

179 Peter Hall, 'Commuting Across the New Boundaries', *New Society*, 25 Feb. 1971, p. 314.

after certain tracts had been turned over to urban authorities in a local government reform of 1965, the result had been new development on green areas where previously it had been controlled.[180] But on that argument, there was surely no case for allowing Birmingham's interest in the Meriden green belt. Meanwhile, in a planning decision shortly after the new map was published, the Minister actually allowed a limited amount of development by Birmingham in the Worcestershire green belt near Wythall in order to keep up the momentum of the city's housing programme.[181]

Here, as in the tract west of London, it seems likely that even after the fundamental reform of local government, it will still prove necessary for the new authorities to come together to produce the critical structure plans for growth around the conurbations; an outcome that few reformers can have believed possible in 1965 or 1966. The difficulty is that there may still remain a fundamental difference of outlook between the conurbation authority and the surrounding counties over questions of overspill. But there were at least two promising indications in the first half of 1971 that, at long last, it was proving possible for the urban authorities and the counties to work together and to reach agreement. The first was publication of the joint strategic study by Warwickshire, Coventry and Solihull for the area around Coventry and between that city and the conurbation, an area including the controversial Meriden green belt. The three authorities succeeded in recommending an agreed pattern of future development for this area, sufficient to house a likely growth of 340,000 people between 1970 and 1991. Nearly three-quarters of this growth, according to the recommendations, would be housed adjacent to the existing urban concentrations: both north and south of Coventry, in the Bedworth-Nuneaton zone and around Kenilworth; around Warwick and Leamington Spa; and on the edge of the conurbation, near Solihull and Sutton Coldfield. The pressures on the narrow Meriden green belt, it was significant, were kept to a minimum.[182]

Meanwhile, on an even larger scale the central government and all the local planning authorities of the region had been working to finalize an agreed regional strategy for the whole of the planning region, an area that stretched westwards to the Welsh border, southwards nearly to Gloucester, and northwards beyond Stoke-on-Trent. The sub-regional and the regional studies were complementary, and both teams maintained regular contact. For the main aim of both was the same: to discover whether, at last, the

[180] David Gregory, *Green Belts and Development Control*, University of Birmingham (Centre for Urban and Regional Studies, Birmingham, Occasional Paper No. 12, 1970), pp. 40–1, 46–7.

[181] The area is at Frankley. Development was also allowed at Hawksley, within the Birmingham city boundary and outside the green belt. Department of the Environment Press Notice, No. 52, 10 Mar. 1971.

[182] *Coventry-Solihull-Warwickshire: A Strategy for the Sub-Region*. Coventry City Council, Solihull County Borough Council, Warwickshire County Council (1971), *passim*.

different authorities could agree on plans for housing the developments that arose from the continued growth of the Birmingham conurbation.

In September 1971 this group reported. *Framework for the Future 1971–2001* did for the West Midlands what the Strategic Plan for the South-East had done the year before, with one difference: that here, the representatives of the different local planning authorities managed by themselves to agree on a regional strategy, without the necessity to bring in central government officials. The background to the report was the familiar one: the pressure of continued population growth. Within the study area (embracing the whole of the five counties of Worcestershire, Warwickshire, Staffordshire, Shropshire, and Herefordshire) a population increase of 1½ million within the thirty-year period was expected. The great bulk of this would consist of natural increase of the region's own population, with a birth rate that remained steadily above national average and an average family size that was the highest of any region in the country.

The critical question, of course, was the distribution of this growth within the region. While 48 per cent of the total regional population lived within the central conurbation in 1966, this proportion was falling; close on two-thirds of the expected growth up to the end of the century (900,000) would need to be housed outside the conurbation. But in addition, many more new homes would be needed to meet existing shortages and keep pace with obsolescence. In all, the report calculated, nearly 900,000 new homes would be needed during the thirty-year period, 726,000 of them on new sites. And given the shortage of building land within the conurbation, this in effect meant sites beyond the green belt.

Here was the central problem. For, as the report emphasized, it was useless to provide homes too far from jobs. And the study team's own special survey confirmed the general impression: that in the West Midlands, the supply of mobile industry in the conurbation was notoriously limited because of the strength of linkages between the many small industrial plants. Further, even though the region's traditional dependence on factory jobs would be modified by the more rapid growth of service occupations, the evidence was that many of these also would seek a base in the conurbation. Since the population of the conurbation would be thinning out because of urban renewal and spontaneous outward migration in search of space, the problem for the planners was to restrict the growth of long-distance commuting, which would place a severe strain on the region's transport services.

These thoughts dominated the choice of strategy that finally emerged after various alternatives had been considered. Sites for jobs would be reserved in five main factory zones around the edge of the conurbation, as near as possible to the new homes which would be built on both sides of the conurbation green belt. But, with the exception of the longer-distance new town at Telford, which would take 143,000 people, most of the new residential areas would be within commuting distance of the conurbation. The strategy thus resolved itself into a series of new housing areas in a broad arc mainly east and south of the conurbation, related to the planned M42 motorway which would form part of a giant ring road encircling the conurbation itself. Some of the most important would be south-west of Solihull, in the Earlswood area; north-east of Birmingham, in the area north of Minworth; major expansions in the Coventry belt, as forecast in the Coventry-Solihull-Warwickshire plan; and, most dramatic of all, a proposal for a national growth area eventually embracing some 400,000 people, in the Lichfield-Tamworth-Burton-on-Trent triangle. The first two of these would lie quite close to the conurbation but would be separated from it by distinct green areas; they would cater especially for shorter-term growth before 1981, though the clear hope was that eventually the more distant schemes would take the bulk of the population increase, together with decentralized jobs.

But, in the short term, it seemed clear that the proposals must lead to an increase of radial commuting into the conurbation. To deal with this, the framework report proposed major developments of the region's rail system, a system less exploited for commuting purposes than in any other major British urban area. The difficulty would however remain that the pattern of employment in the conurbation, with scattered factory zones and a relatively weak central business district, did not favour intensively-used public transport. At most, the aim would be to step up dependence on public transport for day-time travel to 20 per cent, or 30 per cent in the heart of the conurbation, with higher percentages at peak times; while the mileage travelled by people in cars would nearly double by the end of the century.

Thus the 1971 regional report, which was submitted to the Standing Conference of West Midland Planning Authorities for approval, underlined the essential point about urban development in the region which is the central theme of this chapter: the apparent impossibility of achieving the sort of long term, long distance, co-ordinated out-movement of people and jobs that London achieved after the Second World War, as the idealists in the West Midlands New Towns Society had advocated. The consequences, in terms of traffic congestion and long commuter journeys, looked like being serious. But at least, after many years of controversy, the planning authorities of the region seemed at last to have agreed on a formula for large-scale urban growth.

THE WEST MIDLANDS EXPERIENCE: A VERDICT

Visiting England in 1835, de Tocqueville commented on the fact that 'hardly any likeness' existed between Birmingham and London society. 'These folks' he commented on the citizens of Birmingham, 'never have a minute to themselves. They work as if they must get rich in the evening and die the next day.'[183] And more recent observers have commented on the frenetic pace of work in the West Midlands car factories. All in all, as compared with London, it may be suggested that the West Midlands shows a curiously American

183 Quoted by Asa Briggs in *Victoria County History of Warwickshire*. Oxford U.P., London (1964), Vol. 7, p. 223.

ethos. There is a similar emphasis on work and on leaving industry free to deliver the goods. It is however modified by a powerful social concern to alleviate poor housing conditions, a movement in which Birmingham took the lead in the late nineteenth century. What is conspicuously lacking, as compared with the prevailing method of London and the home counties, is a stress on conservation and preservation. Nor is there the same fear of urban growth; provided it continues to be well administered by councillors and officials who have Birmingham's interests at heart.

This difference, even opposition, in views already appeared quite clearly at the time of the Barlow Commission sittings in the late 1930s. We have already observed that the Commission did not accept Birmingham's arguments; but it is clear that Birmingham never accepted Barlow's. The result after the Second World War was that outside planners like Abercrombie and Jackson, and academics like Florence and Eversley, as well as the reformers of the West Midlands New Towns Society, were preaching a southern English gospel to an audience that espoused quite a different religion. Birmingham's case before the Wythall inquiry in 1960 is almost indistinguishable from its case before the Barlow Commission in 1938, except that in one or two places it is more circumspect; the fundamental principle was that enunciated by Alderman Watton:

> Birmingham people were entitled to remain in Birmingham if they wished.[184]

In fairness, it must be remembered that objectively the cases were different. Greater London by 1938 was a conurbation numbering over 8 million people on 700 square miles of land, with a pronounced centralization of employment that led to long work journeys and traffic congestion. Greater Birmingham was a much smaller conurbation with just over 2 million people on an area of about 270 square miles. Furthermore, its entire pattern of economic activity was different. The conurbation had developed not just in concentric circles round one core, as in London, but from a score of different centres. Instead of the concentrated service employment at the centre of the conurbations, the West Midlands had factory employment which was dispersed within the conurbation, but not outside it to any great extent. And Birmingham's role as a provider of the higher, more specialized functions was much weaker than London's. The 1961 Census, the first to record accurate figures on the subject, showed that the concentration of workers in the central business district of Birmingham was less than one-tenth of that found in the central business district of London. As a result, journeys in the West Midlands were shorter and less onerous, though traffic congestion became serious in the 1960s due to the rise in car ownership and greater dependence on the car for work journeys, even to the centre, than in London. Many people in the West Midlands conurbation found both jobs and homes within the conurbation but outside its centre. They were also nearer to open space because of

[184] Cf. *supra*, p. 527.

the much smaller area of the conurbation. Perhaps some point would come when Birmingham's problems approached London's in scale; Birmingham's answer would be that this was some considerable time in the future.[185]

Perhaps more fundamentally, the attitude of Birmingham and the other authorities was different. And here, it is perhaps not Birmingham, but London, which was the odd man out. The whole tenor of the London County Council's evidence to Barlow was that London's growth and by extension that of the conurbations generally, had gone too far and too fast, and might now safely be restricted.[186] This was an altruistic attitude seldom found; for it is the nature of local authorities to wish to expand. But the LCC's attitude was special. It did not represent the whole of the conurbation, but only the inner part of it. It had experienced no boundary change of substance since it came into being, and neither expected nor asked for any. (Indeed, subsequently, in the hearings of the Herbert Commission on London government in 1957–60, the LCC was one of the main opponents of any conurbation-wide system of government.) There were good party political reasons for this, in the 1930s as in the 1950s; but it did mean that the LCC's attitude was greatly coloured by the political fortunes of the majority party. Birmingham's position in contrast was much more open. The politicians of the major parties were agreed that the city was great and should become greater. Though Birmingham's representative could say to the Barlow Commissioners that he did not wish to see further boundary extensions and that he believed a majority of the councillors would agree, there was no notable conviction about the statement. Birmingham's position in other words was an entirely natural, even naive one: as the city prospered, so would it grow.

The attitude of the other local authorities of the conurbation, in essence, was no different from Birmingham's. Even if they harboured no aggressive boundary designs, they were in practice determined to keep as much economic activity within their borders as possible, for that represented rateable value. Lomas and Wood have summarized their attitude:

> Although, in the conurbation, they protest their endeavours to encourage firms to move out of their areas to the newer world of the overspill estates, our impression is that in practice they seem to say; "We will urge industry to move out, provided this does not conflict with our other aim of keeping as much as we can".[187]

There were no less than twenty-eight industrial estates being actively developed within the conurbation in the late 1960s; the Industrial Bureau, set up in 1957 to promote decentralization, had no staff of its own and achieved very little – in fact, after 1963, no concrete results in planning applications at all.[188]

[185] The author is indebted to Ruth Young for her enlightening comments on the differences between the London and West Midlands regions.

[186] Ibid., 14th Day (2 Mar. 1938), *Evidence of LCC*, para. 127, p. 421.

[187] Lomas and Wood, op. cit., p. 144.

[188] Ibid., pp. 143–4.

The attitude of the surrounding counties, on the other hand, seems to have been very like that of the home counties around London. Staffordshire was willing to conclude overspill agreements on a limited scale, some of them little more than peripheral extensions of the conurbation; Warwickshire and Worcestershire showed little enthusiasm throughout the 1950s and early 1960s, and their position was only strengthened by the famous Circular 42/55 on green belt policy. Essentially, like the home counties, they seem to have seen overspill, and above all planned overspill, as a threat. It had all the character of unfamiliarity and of social disruption, which seems to have struck alarm into the counties round London; but in addition, it carried with it the direct political threat of loss of territory through boundary extensions. The counties may well have concluded that their best strategy lay in inaction.[189]

Thus there was virtual deadlock between three sets of local interests: the conurbation authorities bent on keeping as much economic activity and rateable value as they could, a proud city which shared this attitude but which called additionally for *Lebensraum* for its citizens, and a set of county authorities determined to resist these demands. No one of the actors in this contest was in any way committed to the classic solution of the distant new town, providing homes and jobs outside commuting range of the conurbation; that was a solution argued only by a few academic and industrial idealists, imbued with the spirit of Ebenezer Howard. Yet if their solution was not adopted, the idealists argued, the region and its people would pay a heavy price: growing and finally irresistible pressure to build in the green belt, plus increasingly long commuter journeys for growing numbers of people into the conurbation.

A vital role thus passed to central government; only it could resolve the dilemma. In London after the Second World War, it had intervened decisively to impose a new towns solution, though its resolve weakened somewhat in the 1950s. In the West Midlands, however, the job seemed largely beyond its capacity. A critical reason, especially before 1950 and after 1960, was that the Board of Trade had to choose in effect between the interests of planned Midlands overspill, and the interests of the Development Areas. Not unnaturally, it put the Development Areas first. It divided West Midlands industry into two groups: the mobile, or divertible, and the non-mobile.

[189] This emerges particularly clearly from the evidence submitted to the Royal Commission on Local Government in England, published in 1968. Birmingham claimed that it should continue to exist as before, but thought there was no reason why its area should not be extended to take in areas where there was an identity of interest. Warwickshire proposed a two-tier solution with the county as top tier, and made it clear that Birmingham was too large to fit into such a unit; a 'city region' solution applied to the area would mean either Warwickshire's being swallowed in a Greater Birmingham, or its dismemberment. Worcestershire was not convinced of the need for change, but preferred a system based on the existing county boundaries. Royal Commission on Local Government in England, *Written Evidence of County Councils*. HMSO, London (1968), pp. 317–19, 329.

The first group, if it applied for Industrial Development Certificates, was encouraged to move to Development Areas. The second was allowed to stay in the conurbation, on the ground that its links with other conurbation industry were too strong to move it at all. Logically, this left nothing for overspill. It also happened to accord with the interests of the conurbation authorities, who were happy enough to provide factory space, much of it on former derelict land, to accommodate the non-mobile element. As employment grew, then, the dominance of the conurbation was maintained; and the development of commuter dormitories, in or just beyond the green belt, became inevitable.

In the event, then, the government's 1968 solution was a deliberate compromise, perhaps the best that could be achieved against the background of previous history. On the one hand, large peripheral development for commuters in Warwickshire would provide a breathing space and allow the Birmingham redevelopment programme to continue. On the other, Telford and Redditch could be built up, developing a new tradition for the region of medium to long-distance movement of people and jobs. Necessarily, this would mean some compromise on the policy of giving first priority to Development Areas; but the two new town sites had been carefully chosen and should be able themselves to generate a large proportion of the industrial capacity needed to provide employment for the new population. Essentially, after all, this was the same process of evolution as in the London region during the years 1945–50, when the government countenanced quasi-satellites at the periphery of the conurbation (such as Harold Hill and Oxhey) while starting the new towns farther out. It could be argued then that the West Midlands have lagged twenty years behind London in their history: a delay that can be ascribed partly to the different size and character of the region, partly to the different attitudes this provoked among local authorities.

Finally, though, successive governments cannot be entirely acquitted of a failure of logic. Especially during the 1950s, they accepted the central notion of containing the conurbation in its negative aspects, through encouraging the counties in their green belt policies; yet they failed to give the necessary impetus to a radical change in trends on the positive side, by neglecting to designate any new towns until 1963, and by relying on the inadequate mechanism of the Town Development Act. It may be that in essence, the notion containing the conurbation was unrealistic because too much of the region's capacity for economic growth was too firmly rooted within it; but again, the central government made all too little attempt, for a long time, to consider the implications of this argument. The men who had laid the foundation of regional planning for the West Midlands, Abercrombie and Jackson, had been at pains to stress the need for continuous work on the regional plan, based on better understanding of its economic and social requirements.[190] That was left undone, both by the central government and the local authorities; and the region paid a heavy price in indecision and muddle.

190 Lomas and Wood, op. cit., pp. 4–5.

CHAPTER ELEVEN

LEICESTER AND LEICESTERSHIRE

This chapter examines postwar planning experience in another smaller, less problematic region resembling South Hampshire: urban growth, though rapid, has not led to the acute overspill problems of London or Birmingham. In advance of local government reform it also took the lead in creating machinery which could eventually lead to the formulation of an agreed sub-regional plan.

This chapter was researched and written by Peter Hall.

INTRODUCTION

Leicester is as typically East Midland as Birmingham is dominantly West Midland. Instead of the travails of a great city and a complex conurbation, wrestling with problems of obsolescence and overspill, we find a prosperous city with conspicuously few problems; indeed, every writer on Leicester seems to conclude by stressing its unproblematic character. This, indeed, was one good reason for choosing it as one of our five study areas. The city has a favourable industrial structure, and a good record of growth; it has only a modest slum problem, very little land that could be called derelict, and even a remarkably low level of congestion for a city where economic activity patterns are so centralized. It sits almost in the geographic centre of an ancient county of the same name, and the county administration (in conspicuous contrast to the West Midlands) logically is sited in the city. Because the city's growth has outrun the speed of boundary extensions, its population has actually fallen in postwar years, while in a ring of continuous suburbs under county administration population has mushroomed. But as the following pages show, that has not brought any dramatic battles between city and country. Indeed, this area proves to have been one of the first in England to experiment with a new form of city-county planning co-operation, well in advance of a fundamental reform of local government.

As in previous chapters, the story of planning in Leicester and Leicestershire will be told as far as possible in simple chronological sequence from the interwar years down to the experiments in sub-regional planning of the late 1960s.

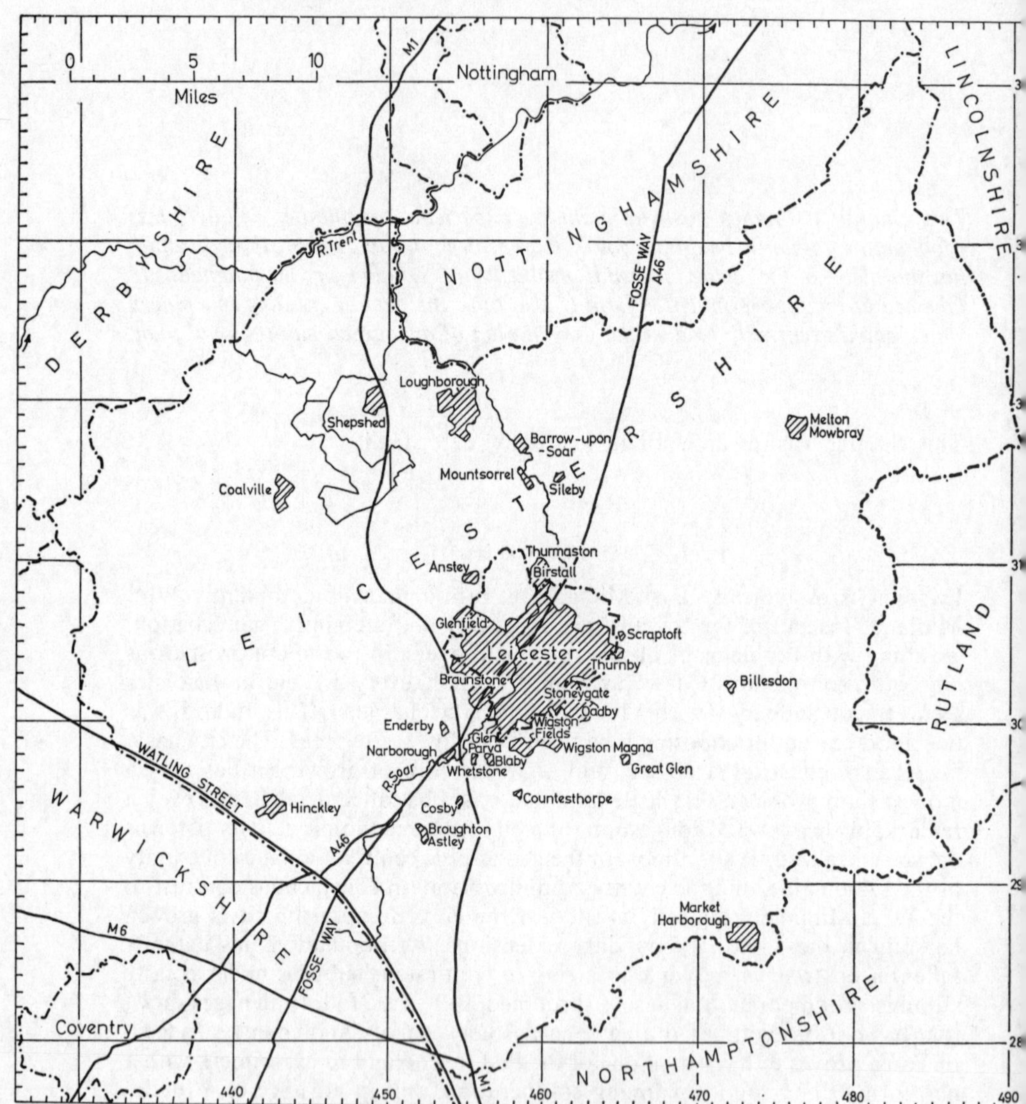

Figure 11.1 Leicester and Leicestershire: Key Map

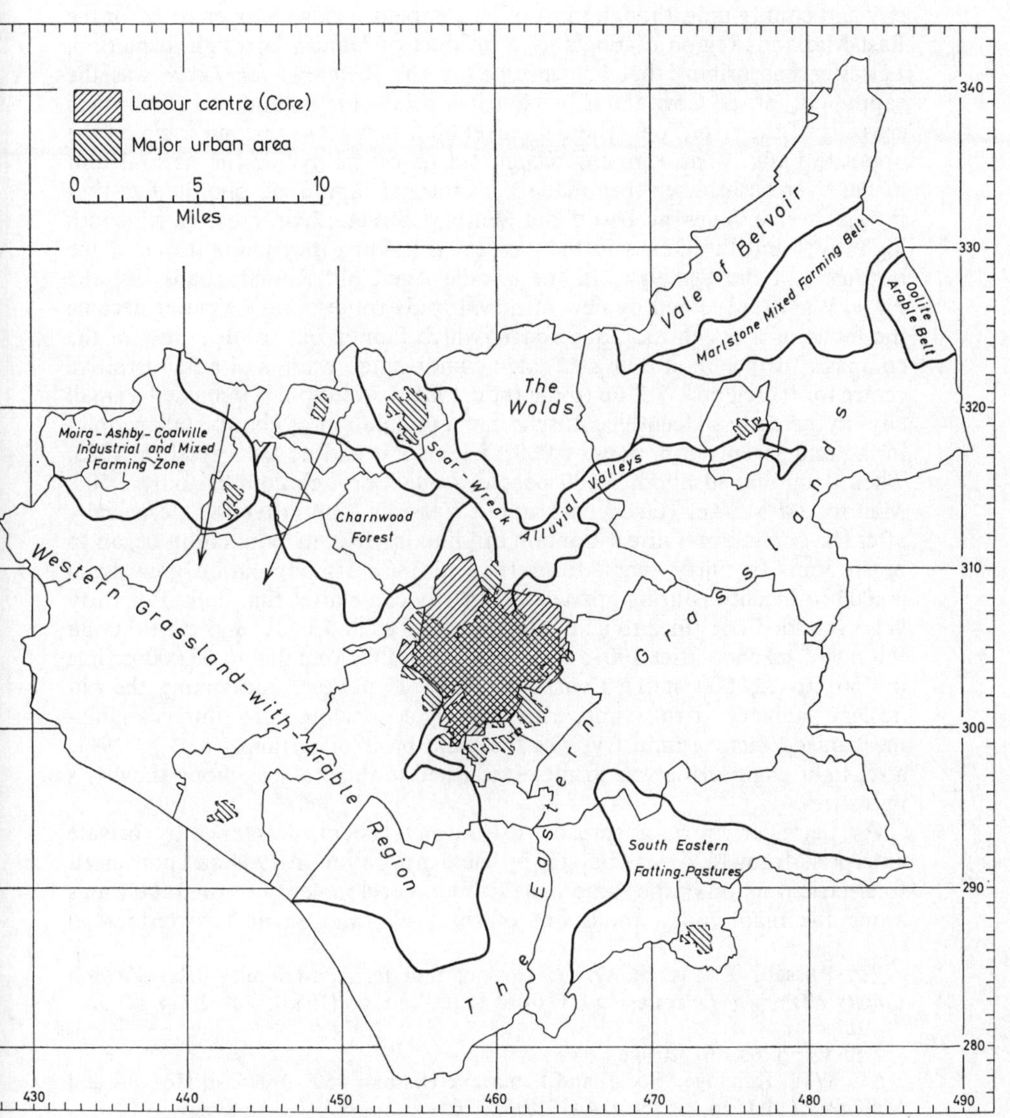

Fignre 11.2 Leicester and Leicestershire: Land Use Regions

THE HISTORICAL BASIS

Leicester must be one of the purest cases in England of the city region, or city and county unit, though most of its competitors also happen to be in the East Midlands region of England, a product of Danish borough formation. Leicester has origins that go back before the Romans: for *Ratae* was the capital city of the Coritani, a Belgic tribe, occupying a good site at a critical crossing of the river Soar where a gravel bluff faced a sandstone scarp on the opposite bank.[1] The Romans recognized its centrality for the natural unit of the river basin when they made it a cantonal capital, despite the fact that it was twelve miles at best from Watling Street, their great north-south highway;[2] and the Danes further respected it when they made it one of the boroughs of the Danelaw. In the Middle Ages, old Roman roads like the Fosse Way were joined by new medieval trade routes, and Leicester became the focus of a dozen radiating roads, which fanned out to all points of the compass, further reinforcing its role as undisputed trade and administrative centre for its region.[3] Yet up to the Industrial Revolution, it remained a small city. In the early sixteenth century it had a population of about 3,000 people; in the mid seventeenth, about 5,000.[4] Even so, it had no local rival: in 1563, when it numbered about 3,500 people, Loughborough counted only 1,500, Melton and Market Harborough about 500 each.[5] But after 1800, especially after the coming of a direct London rail link in 1840, its population began to mushroom. In thirty years, from 1831 to 1861, its population grew from 40,000 to 68,000.[6] But its greatest prosperity came after that date. For forty years it added one-third to its population total each decade; and even though the rate slackened after 1901, the city went in fifty years from 68,000 people in 1861 to 227,000 at the Census of 1911.[7] Footwear, outflanking the old hosiery industry at this time, after rapidly converting itself into a highly-mechanized factory industry, was the main basis of advance; and by 1911, also, light engineering was firmly established in third place among the city's industries.

As Leicester grew, it spread. A tramway system, developed by private enterprise from 1874, was bought by the Corporation in 1904 and converted to electric traction in the same year. Ribbon development followed the trams along the main radial roads out of the town, and whole new residential

[1] P. Russell, 'Roads', in W. G. Hoskins and R. A. McKinley (eds), *Victoria County History of Leicestershire*. Oxford U.P., London (1955), Vol. 3, pp. 62–3.

[2] Ibid.

[3] Ibid., pp. 63–76, *passim*.

[4] E. W. J. Kerridge, 'Social and Economic History, 1509–1660', in Hoskins and McKinley (eds), op. cit., Vol. 4 (1958), p. 76.

[5] Calculated from figures in W. G. Hoskins, *Leicestershire* (The Making of the English Landscape). Collins, London (1957), p. 67.

[6] R. A. McKinley and C. T. Smith, 'The City of Leicester: Social and Administrative History since 1835', in Hoskins and McKinley (eds), op. cit., Vol. 4, p. 260.

[7] Ibid., pp. 275–6.

suburbs were developed for the wealthy, especially at Stoneygate, south-east of the old town.[8]

Between the wars, though it grew more slowly than in the decades up to 1900, Leicester was notably more prosperous than many of the old established industrial areas of England. Its population grew from 245,000 at the end of the First World War to 261,000 in 1935.[9] Hosiery and footwear continued to dominate the industrial pattern, but engineering continued to increase its share of total employment, as before. A vigorous slum clearance and municipal housebuilding programme gave the city 4,500 new council houses between 1919 and 1929 (together with 2,000 more built by private enterprise with a state subsidy) and another 400 (with 900 subsidized private houses) between 1929 and 1939. The physical result was the growth of new municipal and private estates to the south and south-east of the city,[10] causing the built up area to join up with the villages of Wigston Magna and Oadby.

The surrounding countryside, which was gradually consumed by this continued growth, is easily described. Leicester sits astride the alluvial meadowlands of the Soar, which flows from the south towards the confluence with the Trent to the north, and cuts the county into two halves. Immediately to the east of Leicester, a readily distinguished eastern grassland region recorded nearly 100 per cent under grass before the Second World War. Developed on heavy boulder clay over a Lias clay cover, it supported sheep and cattle in almost equal proportions. This was handsome land, but there was a great deal of it and it could not be said to be of the first agricultural importance.[11]

The Soar terraces, northwards from Leicester to Loughborough, were a different matter. They were light lands, easily settled, where villages followed each other in quick succession. The soils were prized for market gardening.[12] But, Auty noted in his land use memorandum of 1943:

> The recent activities of speculative ribbon builders to the north and north-east of Leicester have resulted in further wasteful and less forgivable encroachments on the valuable soils, and much land which might otherwise have been highly productive of market gardening crops is now covered with suburban housing.[13]

West of Leicester itself, soils were a little lighter than to the east. Based on the Triassic Keuper marl, they were sandy clays or loams, of moderate and often variable quality. The Land Utilization Monograph distinguished this area from the eastern grasslands, though it was a matter of degree: even here, three-quarters of the acreage was in grass, and there was a heavy emphasis

[8] Ibid., pp. 296–300.
[9] Ibid., p. 300.
[10] Ibid., p. 297.
[11] D. M. Auty, *Leicestershire* (The Land of Britain, Part 57). Geographical Publications, London (1943), pp. 295–6.
[12] Ibid., p. 307.
[13] Ibid.

on dairying for the nearby industrial markets, fresh milk production having largely taken the place of the traditional Leicester cheese-making industry. The land was in poor condition by the 1930s.[14]

Over the whole county, nearly four-fifths of the land was still in grass on the eve of the Second World War.[15] By its end, there had been a revolution: under the influence of war conditions, by 1943–44 there was actually more arable than grass, a remarkable throw-back to the conditions of the Middle Ages.[16] At the war's end, of course, there was reconversion; but it did not restore the prewar *status quo*, and since the Second World War there has been twice the arable acreage of the interwar years.[17]

Apart from the clear concentration along the Soar valley, the nucleated villages of Leicestershire lie apparently scattered across the landscape. Only close inspection, as Hoskins has revealed, shows that their location is invariably logical and rational; water supply is the key, and it occurs in glacial sands or gravels which form islands, having the additional advantages of being easily cleared of woodland, within the heavier Triassic or glacial clays.[18] In the Middle Ages, these villages were denser in the east, reflecting better water supplies and higher fertility; consequently rural population densities had been higher here too.[19] But since the eighteenth century two factors had worked to reverse this situation: first, the almost complete turning-over of the eastern lands to grass; second, and more importantly, the development first of domestic industry and then of factory industry in the western villages, which greatly augmented their population.[20] Certain groups of villages were particularly affected by the rise of the hosiery industry, and some of these were within ten miles of the city of Leicester. One followed the Soar valley via Thurmaston, Mountsorrel, Sileby and Barrow-upon-Soar to Loughborough. Another was grouped south-west of the city; it included Enderby, Narborough, Whetstone, Cosby, Blaby, Countesthorpe, Broughton and Astley. A third ran from Wigston Magna, via Oadby towards Great Glen and Market Harborough.[21] The result of this was that at the beginning of the twentieth century much of the countryside round Leicester was not quite ordinary countryside; a viable and even flourishing hosiery industry helped offset the effects of agrarian depression. A sole exception was the countryside in a wide arc to the east, between the A6 road to the north of the city and the same road south-east of it, where industrialization had not taken place.

[14] Ibid., pp. 308–9.

[15] Hoskins, op. cit., *Leicestershire* (The Making of the English Landscape), p. 119.

[16] Ibid.

[17] Ibid. Cf. G. H. Dury, *The East Midlands and the Peak*. Nelson, London and Edinburgh (1963), p. 152.

[18] Hoskins, op. cit., p. 4.

[19] Auty, op. cit., p. 259.

[20] Ibid.

[21] L. A. Parker, 'Hosiery', in Hoskins and McKinley (eds), op. cit., Vol. 3, p. 3.

Not only hosiery production, but also footwear, was widely decentralized throughout the county by 1939. Nearly half the total county production of boots and shoes was concentrated in Hickley and its neighbouring villages, but there was a wide scatter across the county.[22] Engineering on the other hand was a larger-scale industry, which had tended to concentrate in the city itself, particularly in the boom period of the Second World War and after.[23]

THE DEVELOPMENT PLANS

It is clear that the urban growth process was a very different phenomenon in Leicestershire as compared with any of the great conurbations. Leicester had grown very rapidly in the century up to 1950; from a small city of 60,000 people to a major city of 285,000. This was actually a greater rate of growth than Greater London had experienced in a similar period. Yet to the people in the county, it did not appear a threat in the same way that the growth of London appeared to Berkshire or the growth of Birmingham to Warwickshire. That threat was clearly a mattter of absolute size as much as of rate of growth. In any case, it might be said that Leicester was not an ordinary agrarian county; it had been too much influenced by the nineteenth-century industrialization of many of its villages, to take up traditional county attitudes. Perhaps it helped too that Leicester was indisputably the county town, the centre for shopping and entertainment and administration, the seat of the county as well as of the city government. It was a city without the massive problems, and the accompanying reputation, of a Birmingham or a Manchester.

Whatever the reason, the original Development Plans of city and county show little hint of a conflict of interest. The Analysis of Survey for the city Development Plan, published in 1952, estimated that between 1951 and 1971 there would be an increase due to natural causes (estimated by the Registrar General) of 17,000; additionally there might be a net migration of 22,500, taking the population from 291,000 to 330,500. But of this the city would accommodate only 270,000: there would be an overspill of no less than 60,500 people.[24] This overspill, the City Planning Officer said, should be accommodated on the fringes of the Leicester urban area by 'infilling' and 'rounding off' the fringe areas already partly developed near the city boundary,[25] without allowing that boundary to influence the plan:

> Broadly, the planning objective is to secure by these means a satisfactorily terminated and rounded off urban area based on the present city, which

[22] W. G. Hoskins, 'Footwear', in Hoskins and McKinley (eds), op. cit., Vol. 3, p. 25.

[23] P. Russell, 'Engineering and Metal Working', in ibid., pp. 25–30.

[24] Leicester City Development Plan, *Written Analysis.* (1952), pp. 66–7, 71, 131.

[25] Ibid., p. 67.

would be interspersed with green wedges and surrounded by an adequate green belt where possible.[26]

Development at Scraptoft, already taking place, was the first step here. Glen Parva (not yet finally agreed with the county) would be the second, with Braunstone, Glenfield, and Wigston Fields to follow.[27]

The Development Plan for the city produced a separate estimate of industrial demands. Various estimates were made, one based on employment trends, one on the projected rise in population, one on a questionnaire to industrialists about their expected space needs. Taking the population method and the questionnaire method, which showed most agreement, and adding a 50 per cent safety margin, the city proposed a gross addition to floorspace of 959 acres, sufficient to cater for a 1971 population of the whole urban zone of just over 400,000; a very generous safety margin indeed.[28]

The County Development Plan, appearing a year earlier, was curiously non-committal on the question. It stated merely that in a large number of town map areas round the city (Anstey, the Birstall group, the Blaby group, Wigston, Oadby, the Braunstone group, Enderby, and Narborough) there was not enough information then available of an accurate, realistic kind to provide a sound basis for a twenty-year plan.[29] In the event the county map, submitted in 1951, was not approved by the Ministry until 1959; and none of the promised town maps had been submitted by the county down to 1970. This is all the more surprising, since most of the projected growth of population in the county was even then expected to be concentrated in the town map areas, of which a significant proportion are in the ring around Leicester. So during a period of extremely rapid growth all around the city, no detailed plans existed. In the event, after the lifting of building licensing in 1954, the growth was more rapid than anyone expected.

THE HISTORY OF GROWTH: 1951–1966

The first published report of the newly formed East Midlands Regional Economic Planning Council, The East Midlands Study, appeared in 1966. It provides a sort of historical epilogue to the period of rapid growth in the region of the late 1950s and early 1960s. In a detailed analysis of change in the sub-regions, it shows that the Leicester sub-region, basically Leicester and its suburbs,[30] had shown marginally faster increase even than the relatively rapid growth of the East Midlands as a whole. Though two-thirds of this growth represented natural increase of the area's own population, Greater Leicester's differentially high growth rate was due to a high level of inward

[26] Ibid., p. 68.

[27] Ibid.

[28] Ibid., pp. 117, 123.

[29] Leicestershire Development Plan, *Analysis of Survey*. (1951), p. 3.

[30] Leicester plus Oadby U.D., Wigston U.D., Shepshed U.D., Barrow R.D., Billesdon R.D., Blaby R.D., plus Loughborough. This was bigger than the Greater Leicester area in the 1969 sub-regional study.

migration: 18,000 people in the fourteen years 1951–65, more than twice that of Greater Nottingham. Altogether the sub-region had added over 60,000 people in a decade and a half.[31] Interestingly, the most rapid period of growth

Table 11.1
GROWTH OF THE LEICESTER SUB REGION, 1951–1965

1951	1951–65	1965
441,500 (15·3 per cent regional total)	plus 63,600 (plus 14.4 per cent) Natural increase plus 41,400 Armed Forces rundown plus, 3,700 Net migration plus 18,400	505,100 (15·5 per cent regional total)

Source: East Midlands Study, Appendix 7a, p. 117.

(accounting for 29,500 people, or 12,500 of the net inward migration) had been in the years 1951–61, when the removal of building licences had caused a big expansion of private building and when industrial firms had expanded freely; after that, the pace of growth had slackened.[32]

The growth of the sub-region had been based on a fundamentally favourable industrial structure. As in the West Midlands, a much higher proportion of workers than the national average were in manufacturing: 53·4 per cent against 43·5 per cent. Conversely, the service sector was under-represented, despite Leicester's obvious importance as a high-level central place for the surrounding region. Engineering, other manufacturing, professional and scientific services, and miscellaneous services, had shown the biggest increases between 1959 and 1963; though one of the sub-region's basic industries, clothing and footwear, recorded a drop in employment, this was probably due to increased efficiency.[33]

The conclusion of the East Midlands Study about the sub-region was that though it had local planning problems, these were not much to worry about.

> The problems arising from the existing size of Leicester make it unlikely that the area will be seriously considered as a reception area for planned overspill from elsewhere. Conversely, conditions do not warrant exporting population from the Leicester area under planned overspill arrangements. An appreciable increase in population can be accommodated within the city boundaries whilst the surrounding urbanized areas can probably take

[31] East Midlands Economic Planning Council, *The East Midlands Study*. HMSO, London (1966), pp. 17, 117. In the East Midlands the Study thus appeared after the Planning Council came into being, under its imprint.

[32] Ibid., p. 17.

[33] Ibid., Appendices 25–6, pp. 154–5.

care of expected increases in population for the rest of the century. The real obstacle is congestion.[34]

Clearly, the type and the scale of the problems could be well dealt with locally; and the Planning Council welcomed the idea of a sub-regional study, then just announced.[35] As a preliminary suggestion, it proposed the notion of development in a north-west thrust from the city towards Coalville, exploiting the line of the M1 motorway and the developing University of Loughborough. Most of the remaining land, the study suggested, would be reasonable and desirable to keep as open country.[36]

CITY AND COUNTY: CONFLICT AND CO-OPERATION

Almost all observers have agreed on the point made at the beginning of this chapter: that the city and county of Leicester together constitute a classic case of the city region, a functional region composed of the dominant city performing central place functions for a wide hinterland, both urban and rural. Clearly, too, as we have seen, in a physical sense Leicester's growth had lapped over the city boundaries to a considerable degree by the end of the 1950s, so that neighbouring parishes within the county had become to all intents and purposes part of the city itself. One critical question for planning, therefore, was: what was the right unit for planning in Leicestershire? Given that to some degree the distinction between city and county was artificial, was the right solution a physical one, to extend the city's limits to take in the continuously built-up area outside? Or was it a functional solution, to create a new planning unit based on recognition of the city region idea, and taking in both the city and its whole sphere of influence (rural as well as urban) over a wide area outside?

The government in 1958 had essentially taken the first view. It had recognized the pressing need for local government reform, but had then set up a Local Government Commission with very limited terms of reference. In effect, by the critical paragraph of these terms of reference, in most of England it was allowed to recommend boundary extensions for county boroughs (such as Leicester) only if it was convinced that the relevant areas were physically an extension of the city or town proper.[37] In the case of Leicester it found a city which had expanded very rapidly from 142,000 people in 1888 (when the County Borough had been created) to just over 273,000 in 1960. The rate of growth was slowing down; the cause was no failing in dynamism,

[34] Ibid., p. 92.

[35] Published 1969 as *Leicester and Leicestershire Sub-Regional Planning Study*, Vol. 1 *Report and Recommendations*, Vol. 2 *Technical Appendices*. Leicester City Council and Leicestershire County Council, Mar. (1969).

[36] East Midlands Study, op. cit., p. 92.

[37] Local Government Commission for England, *Report No. 3, Report and Proposals for the East Midlands General Review Area*. HMSO, London (1961), pp. 77, 82.

but simply the fact that the city had outgrown its allotted area. There had been large out-movements both to city housing schemes built by agreement outside the city boundaries, and to private estates.[38] The city proposed to recognize this by taking in parts of Oadby and Wigston Urban Districts and Barrow-on-Soar, Billesdon, and Blaby Rural Districts, a total of over 6,400 acres and 31,000 people.[39] It argued that these areas were properly part of the city; that they had lost their character as individual villages, and had become the dormitory suburbs for people who looked to the city for work, shipping, entertainment, business and even some of the higher-education functions. Over 8,600 of the people concerned were actually on city estates outside its boundaries, and another estate currently being developed would house 5,000 more. The proposal was opposed by the County Council, by District Councils in the main, and by a large body of local residents, especially after the Commission's draft proposals had been published. Essentially the residents argued that inside the city their rates would be higher, their returns poorer and their representation less.[40]

Nevertheless, in its final proposals the Commission stuck basically to its original suggestion: that the city should be extended to take in the built-up areas of Billesdon and Blaby Rural Districts, consisting essentially of the suburban areas of Scraptoft, Glen Parva, Braunstone, Glenfields, and some of Thurnaby. In return, Birstall was to be transferred from the city to the county. The Commission argued that these areas were continuously on a broad front with development in the city, and in their judgement had close and more special links with the city than arose from mere proximity.[41] The city had not asked for inclusion of the bulk of Oadby and Wigston Urban Districts, but nevertheless the Commission had considered the case for including them (as it was entitled to do under its terms of reference). But it had decided that Wigston had a long independent history; and since, together with Oadby it made up a strong unit for providing county services, especially education, it recommended against including them.[42]

In the event, the Commission's proposals were never implemented; published in 1961, they were overtaken by events in 1965, when Richard Crossman as Minister of Housing and Local Government decided to dismantle the Commission itself and to replace it by a more thoroughgoing investigation of local government reform through a new Royal Commission. In effect, of course, Crossman's decision meant the abandonment of a solution (here as elsewhere) based on a physical view of planning, and its replacement by a larger functional region. But the history does illustrate some of the basic difficulties that arise in a region like this. Essentially, any expanding city was bound to make recurrent requests for boundary extensions: Leicester had twice expanded before its application to the Commission, in 1891 and again

[38] Ibid., p. 75.
[39] Ibid.
[40] Ibid., p. 79.
[41] Ibid., p. 82.
[42] Ibid.

in 1935. Doubtless, if the extension had been made, Leicester in due course would have had to ask for yet another extension, and so on. The difficulty about this course of action was its effect on the county, which would have lost 30,000 population and £310,000 of rateable value in the process.[43] This, doubtless, was one of the points which caused Crossman to resolve on the more radical course of trying to secure a solution based on the effective union of the city and the county. It is significant perhaps that when the Royal Commission reported in 1969, Leicester was one of the few areas in the country where the solution proposed by the majority was in complete agreement with that proposed in Mr Derek Senior's memorandum of dissent; the case here seems to have been overwhelming for a unit of government based on the city plus the county. And in its 1971 White Paper on local government reorganization, the Conservative Government made no change in the size of this unit.

Meanwhile, despite the conflict of city and county over the boundary proposals, the two authorities were managing *ad hoc* co-operation in certain fields. One of the most important early fruits was the Leicester Traffic Plan, produced in 1964, after research and survey work over the two previous years.[44] A city document, it involved a considerable degree of help from county officials and its proposals had considerable implications for the county areas immediately outside the city. Starting from an expected population increase in Greater Leicester from 453,000 to 640,000 between 1961 and 1991,[45] the plan was based consciously on the development of the city and its centre as a strong concentration of urban activities serving the whole sub-region; necessarily therefore it had to cater for a very big increase in future radial journeys into and out of the centre. Rejecting a plan for full motorization as too expensive and too destructive of the environment, it nevertheless was led to recommend a total expenditure of £135 million over the period 1961–91 on primary roads and parking provision in the city.[46] The plan was never accepted in full by the City Council, and seems unlikely to be implemented as it stands on the basis of current Ministry projections of future investment. Nevertheless, it was significant as one of the first attempts outside London to produce a transport analysis and plan for a sub-region which overran existing local authority boundaries.

The subsequent venture was however bigger, both in geographical area and in scope. Officially called the Leicester and Leicestershire Sub-Regional Planning Study, it was commissioned jointly by the city and the county in 1966; it began work in January 1967 and produced its definitive report with recommendations in the summer of 1969. It happened to be the first, in point of time, of a series of such studies (shortly afterwards, others were announced for Nottingham-Derby-Nottinghamshire-Derbyshire and Coventry-Solihull-Warwickshire), based on a new concept of voluntary co-operation among

[43] Ibid., p. 83.

[44] Leicester City Council, *Leicester Traffic Plan*. Leicester (1964).

[45] Ibid., p. 11.

[46] Ibid., pp. 79–80.

neighbouring authorities. All of them owed their existence basically to Richard Crossman, who as Housing Minister advocated the concept to a number of neighbouring local authorities during 1965. He in turn was led to the conclusion from his study of the problem of local government reform and from his reading of the report of the Planning Advisory Group, then just published. The first indicated that tinkering with boundary details, on the lines of the Local Government Commission, would not do; wholesale reform was indicated. This was fortified by the second, which called for a completely new system of broad structure planning, and necessarily implied local authorities covering broad areas which straddled town and country. In the longer term, these considerations led Crossman to conclude that fundamental change could not be avoided: this was why he scrapped the existing Commission and replaced it by a new Royal Commission with wider terms of reference. But this would take time to bring results: in the interim, Crossman was convinced of the need for an *ad hoc* solution in quickly-growing areas like Greater Leicester, wherever neighbouring authorities could be persuaded to co-operate. Leicester and Leicestershire, in fact, provided a classic instance of the problems which were arising, as their recent history amply indicated.

The Leicester and Leicestershire Sub-Regional Planning Study, however, took in a much larger area than the earlier Traffic Plan; while the Traffic Plan had concentrated on the city and its contiguous built-up suburbs forming Greater Leicester, the Planning Study took in the whole functional city region of the city and the county,[47] a roughly circular area of average diameter of about thirty miles centred on the city. Its population in 1961 was 683,000, of which 390,000 or 57 per cent lived in Greater Leicester, a region defined in a more restrictive way than in the East Midlands Study or the Leicester Traffic Plan. Greater Leicester was expanding even more rapidly than the sub-region as a whole; but within Greater Leicester, the city itself

Table 11.2
LEICESTER-LEICESTERSHIRE AND GREATER LEICESTER: POPULATION, 1951, 1961 AND 1966

	Leicester-Leicestershire sub-region	Greater Leicester Total	City	Suburbs
1951	630,000 approx.	362,000	285,000	77,000
1961	682,000	390,000	273,500	116,500
1966	720,000	406,000	264,000	142,000

Source: Leicester and Leicestershire Sub-Regional Planning Study.[48]

47 Certain areas in the extreme north-east of the county were excluded while Brixworth R.D. (Northamptonshire) was included. Leicester Study, op. cit., Vol. 1, p. 6.

48 Calculated from text references and tables. The 1951 sub-regional total is inferred.

was continuing to decline in population in the early 1960s, while the contiguous suburbs continued to gain very rapidly indeed, as Table 11.2 shows.

For the future, the objective was how best to accommodate an expected increase of about 67,000 jobs and over 200,000 people in the period 1966–91.[49] Such a large increase was produced by a careful projection of recent trends in employment, natural increase of population and migration, and took account of the sub-region's economic dynamism with the heavy concentration of employment into the growth sectors of engineering and electrical goods, other manufacturing and services.[50] After considering a number of alternative strategies for accommodating the future expected growth, the Planning Study opted for a policy of concentrating growth in and immediately around Greater Leicester. In the earlier stages, up to 1981, the concentration would be on Greater Leicester itself (Table 11.3); then, from 1981 to 1991, emphasis would shift to the development of two main growth corridors, one north-westwards from the city along the line of the A50 Ashby road, the other south-westwards from the city along the line of the A46 Coventry road and the parallel projected Coventry motorway.[51] This alternative was preferred to all others considered, for ten main reasons which are worth setting out in full here because they illustrate so well the considerations that must enter into planning a city region such as this.

First, it fitted past trends and patterns of growth. The plan for the future could grow out of these trends through extensions and modifications rather than through dramatic innovations. Second, and relatedly, it fitted the current policies of the planning authorities, especially the employment distributions

Table 11.3

LEICESTER-LEICESTERSHIRE AND GREATER LEICESTER: PROJECTED POPULATION ON PREFERRED STRATEGY, 1966, 1971, 1981 AND 1991

	Leicester-Leicestershire sub-region	Greater Leicester Total	City	Suburbs
1966	720,000	406,000	264,000	142,000
1971	752,600	423,200	277,100	146,100
1981	833,900	492,400	293,300	199,100
1991	927,000	537,600	300,300	237,300

Source: Leicester and Leicestershire Sub-Regional Planning Study.[52]

proposed in the Leicester Traffic Plan, and the county's policies for village development. Third, the chosen strategy built on the economic dynamism of Greater Leicester while recognizing the special development needs of the

49 Study, op. cit., Vol. 1, p. 29.
50 Ibid., p. 24.
51 Study, ibid., Vol. 1, p. 85.
52 Ibid., Table 11.3, p. 92.

north-west corner of the county (and, to a lesser extent the south-west corner). Fourth, by concentrating on Greater Leicester the strategy offered people more choice in terms of work, entertainment, shopping, housing, transport and most other aspects of life. Fifth, it concentrated on actual and planned investment in the M1 and other main roads. Sixth, by concentrating on Greater Leicester it offered the best possible conditions for public transport. Seventh, it conserved agricultural productivity on the best land to the greatest possible extent. Eighth, it created attractive environments for work, living and recreation; ninth, it had a high degree of flexibility, necessary in a strategy with a time span of twenty-five years; and tenth and last, it built the bridge between regional and local planning proposals, as well as the framework for co-ordination among authorities, which the terms of reference required.[53]

SOME CONCLUSIONS FROM LEICESTERSHIRE

The Leicester and Leicestershire Planning Study is an example of the type of planning report which will become general as soon as the 1968 Planning Act is implemented in one area after the other, and in particular after a wholesale reform of local government along the lines of the structure in the 1972 Local Government Act. It is perhaps significant that in this tour across Megalopolis, we have found so far three areas where this type of work is being done: South Hampshire, Coventry-Solihull-Warwickshire and now Leicester-Leicestershire. The pattern in each case is similar: one or more medium-sized county boroughs with physical spread into new suburbs beyond the formal limits, and with a much wider sphere of influence for shopping, work and entertainment over the surrounding countryside; some localized history of dispute over boundary extensions here and there, but nothing like the gladitorial combat that has distinguished, for instance, the relationship of Birmingham with its neighbours. This illustrates simply a conclusion that has already been pointed up in South Hampshire. The problems of urban growth in contemporary England are simpler, and the more easily resolvable, in those urban regions where the problems of slum clearance and overspill are less daunting, and where in consequence relationships with the neighbouring county are less soured by past disputes. They are probably eased even further when, as at Leicester, the county administration is itself housed in the central city, with all the close informal proximity of individuals and elected members that entails. Leicester, in other words, as all observers seem to agree, is distinguished in our study of Megalopolis as the urban area without major problems. To complete our tour, therefore, it is only right to turn now to an urban region centred upon large conurbations, where the problems have been long-standing and extremely intractable.

[53] Ibid., pp. 85–7.

CHAPTER TWELVE

THE NORTH-WEST: LIVERPOOL, MANCHESTER AND NORTH CHESHIRE

This last synoptic chapter recounts the postwar experience in another large, complex region of urban growth. This has been one of the less dynamic parts of Megalopolis economically. But natural increase of population and a major slum clearance problem in Liverpool and Manchester – greater than in any other cities of England and Wales – have generated a very large total of overspill to be housed outside the cities and even outside the conurbations. Vacillations in government policy, plus disagreements and misunderstandings between authorities, delayed the formulation of a strategy for the region until the mid 1960s. By the end of that decade a policy for accommodating overspill was in existence but there was a doubt whether some of the elements in the policy were well conceived.

This chapter was researched and written by Peter Hall.

INTRODUCTION

Our final study area has obvious similarities, at first glance, to the West Midlands. There is the same sharp contrast. On the one hand, not one but two major conurbations: one with 2⅓ million people (almost exactly the same size as the West Midlands conurbation), based on Manchester; the other with 1¾ million people, based on Liverpool; both with gigantic problems of slum clearance and general obsolescence at the end of the war, even more daunting than Birmingham's, and leading to calculated overspill needs of hundreds of thousands of people. On the other hand, bordering both conurbations on the south side of the line of industry that marks the river Mersey and the Manchester Ship Canal, the county of Cheshire: like Warwickshire or Worcestershire in the Midlands an ancient county (a county palatine in fact), governed from an ancient medieval county town sitting in its river basin, and affected seriously by the outgrowth of the cities only in the last hundred years. Once again, there is the same obvious potential for conflict between the interests of the people of the big cities – especially their more unfortunate ones, suffering the worst housing conditions – and the interests of the rural populations bent on preserving a traditional way of life.

But we shall find that there are differences. The attitude of the two great cities has never been as proud or intransigent as that of Birmingham. Though there has been conflict, sometimes acute conflict, it has not reached the acrimony of the struggle in the West Midlands. There have been misunderstandings and errors, to be sure. But there are distinct signs that after a long period of prevarication, the region by 1973 is in sight of a solution to its problems.

Essentially the form of the chapter resembles that of the previous four. It starts with a general view of the conurbations and the county in the 1930s; describes in detail the ambitious regional advisory plans drawn up at the end of the war, and the county plans produced in the light of their advice; recounts the story of the failure to find solutions to the overspill problem during the 1950s; and lastly follows the complex story of the development of more effective regional planning since 1965.

THE PHYSIOGNOMY OF THE AREA

In North Cheshire we find an area very similar, in many ways, to south Warwickshire: an area of largely rural land, even in 1972 mainly under grass, lying immediately to the south of a conurbation with acute growing pains, and administered by a county authority that acts to guard the interests of its inhabitants. But there is one critical difference: the strip of land we are about to examine, some forty miles broad from east to west and some twenty miles deep from north to south, lies south of two major conurbations, whose centres are thirty miles apart and are separated by a number of significantly large freestanding industrial towns.

One of these two conurbations, known officially as SELNEC (South-East Lancashire and North-East Cheshire), and unofficially sometimes as Greater Manchester, has some obvious resemblances to the West Midlands conurbation; the other, Merseyside, has very few. As the geographer Wilfred Smith pointed out in 1953, the twin cities of Manchester and Salford, forming together a single urban mass, are surrounded by a whole constellation of towns ranging in size from 10,000 to 200,000. Particularly evident in a wide arc west and north of Manchester, from Leigh in the west to Ashton-under-Lyne in the north-east, these towns can most accurately be described as semi-freestanding: they merge into each other and into an intervening countryside occupied by small-scale dairying.[1] Smith summarized the character of Greater Manchester thus:

> While Merseyside is foreign to and has been superimposed on the rural landscape of South-West Lancashire and Wirral, Greater Manchester is autochthonous and has its roots deep into the soil of South-East Lancashire.[2]

In contrast to this loose, complex urban form, Merseyside is compact. It is dominated by the river axis of the Mersey which dominates its layout,

[1] W. Smith, 'Merseyside and the Merseyside District', in W. Smith (ed.), *A Scientific Survey of Merseyside*. University Press, Liverpool (1953), p. 2.

[2] Ibid.

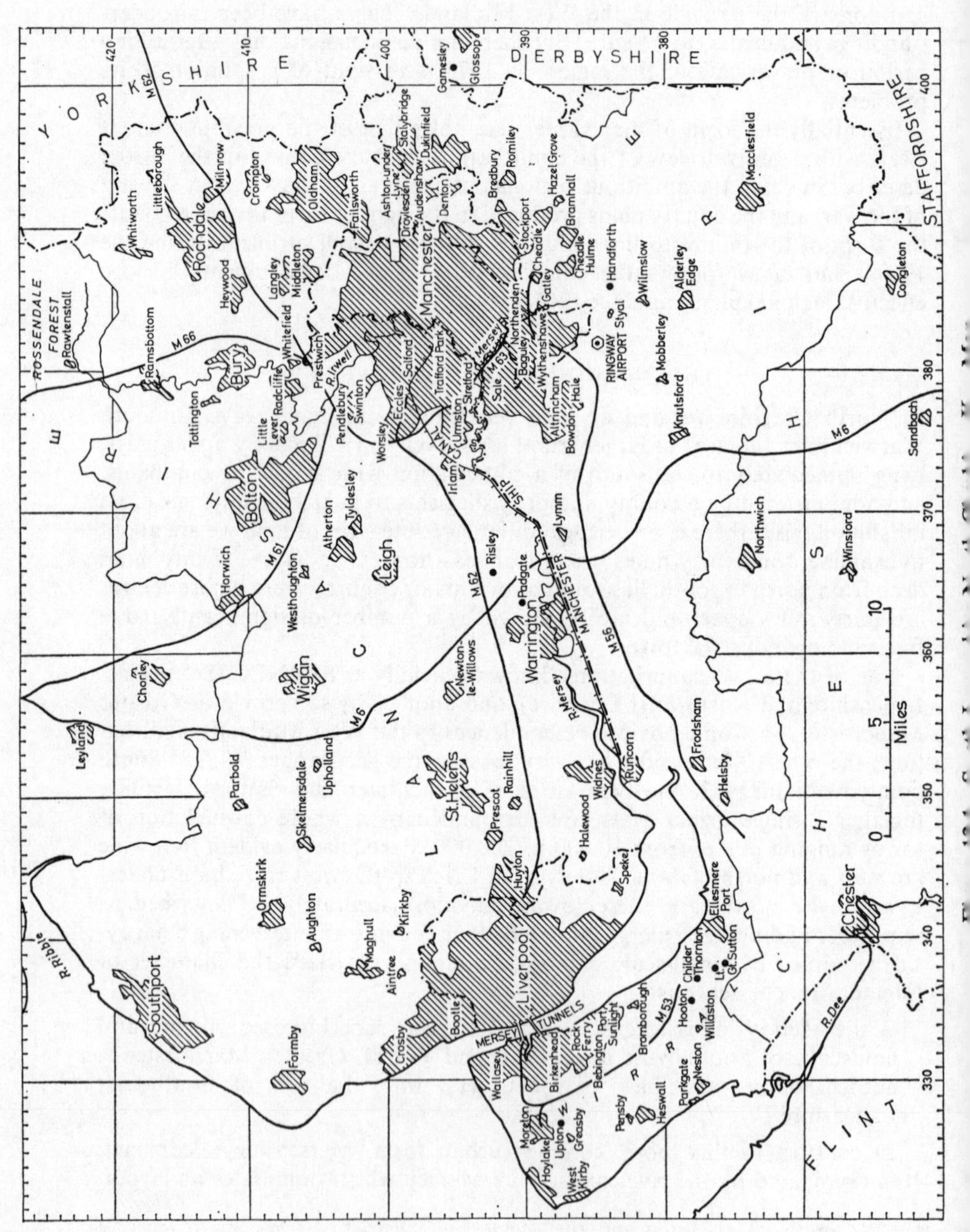
YORKSHIRE
DERBYSHIRE
STAFFORDSHIRE
LANCASHIRE
CHESHIRE
FLINT
ROSSENDALE FOREST
Rawtenstall
Whitworth
Littleborough
Milnrow
Rochdale
Crompton
Oldham
Failsworth
Ashton-under-Lyne
Stalybridge
Dukinfield
Droylesden
Audenshaw
Denton
Gamesley
Glossop
Bredbury
Romiley
Hazel Grove
Stockport
Bramhall
Cheadle
Cheadle Hulme
Handforth
Wilmslow
Alderley Edge
Macclesfield
Congleton
Heywood
Langley
Middleton
Manchester
Ramsbottom
Bury
Radcliffe
Whitefield
Prestwich
R. Irwell
Salford
Trafford Park
Stretford
Urmston
Eccles
Swinton
Pendlebury
Worsley
Irlam
Sale
Mersey
Northenden
Gatley
Baguley
Wythenshawe
Altrincham
Hale
Bowdon
RINGWAY AIRPORT
Styal
Mobberley
Knutsford
Sandbach
Tottington
Little Lever
Bolton
Tyldesley
Atherton
Leigh
Westhoughton
Horwich
Chorley
Leyland
Wigan
Newton-le-Willows
Risley
Padgate
Warrington
Lymm
MANCHESTER SHIP CANAL
Northwich
Winsford
Parbold
Skelmersdale
Upholland
St. Helens
Prescot
Rainhill
Widnes
Runcorn
Frodsham
Helsby
Halewood
Speke
Huyton
Kirkby
Ormskirk
Aughton
Maghull
Aintree
Liverpool
Bootle
Crosby
Formby
Southport
R. Ribble
MERSEY TUNNELS
Wallasey
Birkenhead
Rock Ferry
Port Sunlight
Bebington
Bromborough
Ellesmere Port
Childer Thornton
Lt. Sutton
Gt. Sutton
Hooton
Willaston
Neston
Parkgate
Heswall
Pensby
Greasby
Upton
Moreton
Hoylake
West Kirby
Chester
R. Dee
R. Mersey
M6
M61
M62
M63
M66
M53
M56
0
5
10
Miles
420
410
400
390
380
370
360
350
340
330

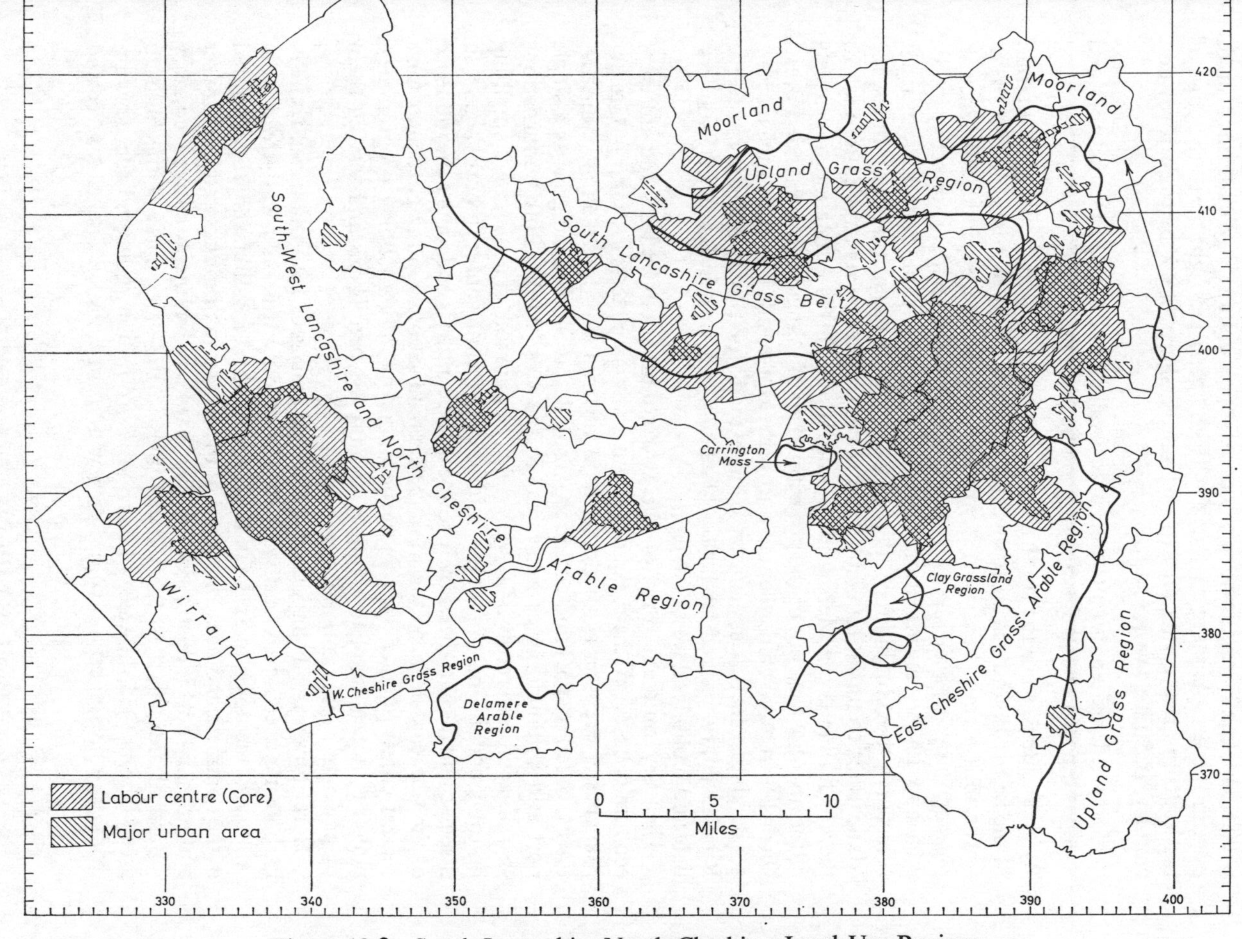

Figure 12.2 South Lancashire-North Cheshire: Land Use Regions

giving a symmetrical development outwards from the parallel axes along each bank, in the form of successive belts or concentric circles of development which end finally and suddenly against open country.[3] Well-farmed land, even in the pre-planning days of the 1930s, persisted right up to the edge of the built-up area, giving an extraordinarily sharp break between town and country. In Smith's words:

> Merseyside is an urban and industrial island created by the port and superimposed on a landscape of good husbandry.[4]

By an accident, since the south Lancashire coalfield does not extend south of Manchester, the industrial towns did not arise there to complete the arc of towns into a ring: Stockport is an anomaly. So the essential difference of physiognomy between the two conurbations is less evident, directly, in the area now under consideration than to the north, in the Lancashire fringes. It has an important indirect effect however; for it means that at all times, the Manchester conurbation is much more constrained in its physical growth to the north than is the Merseyside conurbation. This is a function not merely of the arc of towns, but of the projecting belt of highland (Rossendale Forest) which lies in turn behind them to the north. Merseyside knows no such barrier: a flat, almost featureless coastal plain extends for twenty-miles north to the Ribble estuary, backed by the low plateau of coal measures around Skelmersdale and Upholland west of Wigan.

The very different form of the two conurbations reflects the different economic bases of their rapid growth in the nineteenth century. Greater Manchester grew as a conglomeration of originally freestanding industrial towns, based on coal and cotton; Liverpool and Birkenhead grew as a single port and shipbuilding complex tied to the river banks. Both conurbations shared acute overcrowding, very high population densities and appalling housing conditions up to the middle nineteenth century; both began to disperse and decentralize slowly towards the century's end, under the influence of the tramcar. Between the wars, both conurbations (and in particular their central cities) pursued very energetic municipal housebuilding programmes, building thousands of new homes around the peripheries and serving them by new municipal tram and bus routes.

Here, however, an important difference emerged. Liverpool could satisfy its housing needs quite easily, by extending outwards on a wide front from Aintree in the north to Speke in the south.[5] Jobs were still firmly concentrated in the commercial offices and shops of the centre, in the docks and warehouses and primary port industries of the river bank, and in the extensive secondary industrial areas next to the railway lines in the older parts of the built-up area.[6] From 1936, however, Liverpool Corporation pioneered the development of industrial estates within its new housing areas, at Speke, Aintree and

[3] Ibid.

[4] Ibid.

[5] R. Lawton, 'Genesis of Population', in Smith (ed.), op. cit., p. 127.

[6] W. Smith, 'Location of Industry', in Smith (ed.), op. cit., pp. 177–9.

Kirkby.[7] They served the twin aims of helping new industry come to a depressed area, and of providing employment opportunities in the new housing areas so as to reduce the time and money burden of the journey to work. But up to 1939 this had a limited effect; and the Corporation were bound to be constrained by this when they considered the location of future housing estates.

Development on the Cheshire or Wirral side, on the other hand, was bound to be limited by the area's relative remoteness. True, there were employment opportunities here, in the shipyards of Birkenhead and in the chemical complex of Ellesmere Port and Port Sunlight; but these did not compare with the concentration of employment on the Lancashire shore. True too, regular river crossings had been developed since the first ferries in the early nineteenth century, but the railway under the river did not arrive until 1885; it was not electrified until 1903 (and not to the western Wirral resorts of Hoylake and West Kirby until 1938); and until the completion of the first Mersey road tunnel in 1934, the only other means of crossing were the river ferries.[8] In 1921, for instance, the Census showed that a significantly higher percentage of Wallasey residents commuted to Liverpool than of West Kirby residents: a contemporary writer ascribed this to the 'less frequent, slow and unsatisfactory service of trains for West Kirby and district'.[9]

Nevertheless, even by the 1920s a distinction was emerging between the eastern and the western Wirral. On the eastern side were a string of riverside settlements: the conglomeration of villages forming Wallasey on the north, then Birkenhead, Rock Ferry, Bromborough, and Ellesmere Port. All except Wallasey were fundamentally industrial rather than dormitory towns, exporting relatively few workers to Liverpool, and therefore largely self contained in their economy.[10] On the western side, and separated from the eastern settlements by a wide belt of still open country, were the small resort communities of West Kirby, Hoylake, and Neston-Parkgate: all cut off to some degree (the last almost completely so) from the influences of the central conurbation.[11] Still, there were already boundary disputes between Birkenhead and Wallasey on the one hand, Wirral Rural District on the other, as the towns spread into the Wirral countryside.[12] And in 1927, a contemporary observer could say:

> As the number of such units in a district increases, however, there seems to be an inevitable demand for urban services, paving, lighting, sewerage and transport, which tends to the filling up of the then unprofitable open

[7] W. Robertson, 'The Merseyside Development Area', in Smith (ed.), op. cit., p. 182.

[8] T. W. Freeman, *The Conurbations of Great Britain*. University Press, Manchester, 2nd edn (1966), pp. 104–6.

[9] E. H. Rideout, *The Growth of Wirral*. E. A. Bryant, Liverpool (1927), pp. 53–4.

[10] Ibid., *passim*.

[11] Ibid., pp. 52–4, 66, 77–9.

[12] Ibid., p. 93.

> areas and the production of a town more economic perhaps, but infinitely less healthful and less desirable for human residence. So, too, in rural districts in modern Wirral, we see the dreaded ribbon development of houses spreading along lines of communication, the country roads, usually bus routes, until we are threatened by a continuous town from the Dee to the Mersey.[13]

The same writer concluded:

> There would appear to be but one solution to the problem of Wirral's future and to that of many another area situated on the verge of a rapidly expanding city. Some units must be taken, ideally a geographical, economic and social unit, and out of the welter of conflicting interests, an administrative authority constituted which shall have larger powers of local jurisdiction than any existing unit, being subservient only to the central government.[14]

The Merseyside suburbs were advancing into Wirral, therefore; but they represented spontaneous migration out of the inner parts of the conurbation, and the whole process was on a modest scale. The results can well be seen in the population statistics. Considering for the sake of convenience the four decades 1911–51, and taking 1911 to represent a base index of 100, by 1951 the innermost zone of the conurbation stood as low as 70 (a product of interwar commercial growth and slum clearance); the middle zone stood where it had in 1911, at 100; while the outermost zone registered 400. But whereas the two sections comprising the Lancashire outer zone registered 526 and 423, the corresponding sections on the Wirral side registered only 295 and 317.[15]

Manchester's situation was very different. To the west it was completely hemmed in by Salford, to the north there was almost complete development along the main roads to Bolton and Bury and Rochdale and Oldham, to the east again the city merged imperceptibly into Ashton-under-Lyne. To the south, however, there was the one obvious escape route. Stretford lay to the south-west, an industrial enclave associated with the industrial estate of Trafford Park, developed by the side of the Manchester Ship Canal docks after the opening of the canal in 1894; Stockport, another industrial enclave, stood to the south-east; but between them was open land. Furthermore, the Mersey here was no barrier, but a fairly narrow stream with a floodplain about half a mile wide. Up to 1930, the river itself was the southern boundary of the city against Cheshire.

Already, on its own territory north of the river, Manchester had begun a major municipal housebuilding programme soon after the end of the war. By the middle 1920s, development had advanced south to the river. Land in the

13 Ibid., p. 75.

14 Ibid., p. 94.

15 W. Smith, 'Present Distribution of Population', in Smith (ed.), op. cit., pp. 132–5.

city was almost running out, and was fetching up to £400 an acre. Agricultural land in Cheshire on the other hand was easily acquired, at £80 an acre.[16] On it, there was the chance of building a real community, and of allowing the working class of Manchester to follow the middle-class route into green surroundings.[17]

Manchester, impelled by social vision as well as good hard sense, had only a little hesitation in seizing this chance. It bought land south of the river at Wythenshawe in 1926 for housing. After it became evident that the local rural district council could not supply the necessary services, Manchester proposed to annex the site. It took a parliamentary battle, but in 1930 Manchester incorporated the parishes of Baguley, Newton Etchells and Northenden into the city.[18] The history left a legacy of suspicion in Cheshire, a legacy which was to have unhappy consequences after the Second World War.

Meanwhile, spontaneous middle-class movement into Cheshire continued apace, with less publicity and less complaint. Cheshire exerted a rare magnetism on any Mancunian willing to move, for obvious reasons: the attraction of open countryside, the relatively dry climate (only thirty inches of rain a year against forty-five inches on the northern side of the city), the relative freedom from air pollution (important in prewar times) and a good train service from Altrincham electrified in 1929.[19] In the process Altrincham and Sale were completely swallowed up in the flood of housing; villages like Gatley, Cheadle, Cheadle Hulme and Handforth and Styal became suburban adjuncts to Manchester, and the suburban influence extended even as far as the old town of Wilmslow, twelve miles from central Manchester.[20] Between the 1931 and 1951 Censuses, the Cheshire part of the Manchester conurbation, excluding Wythenshawe, grew by 100,000 people; and this, despite the fact that in the extreme east, industrial towns like Dukinfield and Stalybridge actually lost people. Some urban districts actually doubled in size between 1931 and 1951.[21]

All this, whether in the Wirral or around Altrincham, was relatively innocent of any positive planning; Wythenshawe, where the master plan was laid down by the associate of Raymond Unwin and disciple of Ebenezer Howard, Barry Parker, was of course the striking exception.[22] Around

16 Arthur Redford, *The History of Local Government in Manchester*, Vol. 3: *The Last Half Century*. Longmans, London (1940), p. 248.

17 Ibid., p. 247.

18 Ibid., p. 253. T. W. Freeman, 'The Manchester Conurbation', in British Association for the Advancement of Science, *Manchester and Its Region*. University Press, Manchester (1962), p. 57.

19 T. W. Freeman, op. cit. (1966), pp. 44–5.

20 Ibid., p. 58.

21 Freeman, op. cit. (1962), p. 58.

22 Nikolaus Pevsner, *The Buildings of England: South Lancashire*. Penguin Books, Harmondsworth (1969), pp. 340–1. Walter L. Creese, *The Search for Environment*. Yale University Press, New Haven and London (1966), Chap. 11, *passim*.

Manchester, the local authorities had banded together to found the Manchester and District Joint Planning Advisory Committee as early as 1920; it covered an area of 1,142 square miles from Rawtenstall in the north to the Staffordshire border in the south, and from near Runcorn in the west to Chapel en le Frith in the east – the whole basin of the Mersey and its tributary, the Irwell, in fact, except for the estuary.[23] The Committee was renamed the South Lancashire and North Cheshire Advisory Committee in 1925, and worked through seventeen local joint executive planning committees, a model of early co-operation in regional planning for the textbooks; but it produced no plans up to the Second World War. The same applied to the local executive committees. Presumably the most important of them, because the largest and most central, was the Manchester and District Regional Planning Committee, which in 1945 comprised fourteen local authorities, all on the Lancashire side of the conurbation, together with the Lancashire County Council. There were similar advisory arrangements around Liverpool, but they were as totally ineffectual up to 1945.

The countryside affected by this urban growth was, in effect, an extension of the great lowland plain of midland England. Geologically, physiographically and economically, the Cheshire plain resembled nothing so much as the Warwickshire plain. Here as there, the basis was Keuper sandstone and marl, with a variable but often thick plastering of boulder clay from the last glaciation. The less permeable clays tended to be in grass; where there is sand or gravel mixture, coupled with lower rainfall, the proportion of arable was higher. Near the conurbations, market gardening vied with milk production to serve the needs of the city population. But both were facing competition of a different sort. In the Wirral, as the Land Utilization Survey of the 1930s put it:

> The big towns which demand farm produce are busy swallowing up the land which supplies it. . . . As soon as landlords see a prospect of realizing high prices for their land in building purposes, their interest in farming flags; as soon as this happens the tenant's position becomes insecure and his interest also flags. Neither landlord nor farmer is prepared to spend money for the future and the standard of farming goes steadily down.[24]

Perhaps the most striking case of competition for the use of the land, however, was in the eastern part of the plain, close to Manchester, where light soils and lower rainfall had produced intensive arable cultivation together with nurseries and market gardens. But because of this same climatic factor, and the relative freedom from air pollution, it proved attractive to the speculative

[23] J. B. Cullingworth, *Housing Needs and Planning Policy*. Routledge, London (1960), p. 115. R. Nicholas and M. J. Hellier (for South Lancashire and North Cheshire Advisory Planning Committee), *An Advisory Plan*. Richard Bates, Manchester (1947), pp. 3–7.

[24] E. P. Boon, *Cheshire* (The Land of Britain, Part 65). Geographical Publications, London (1941), p. 179.

builder. At the end of the 1930s, the suburban frontier had temporarily reached the village of Hale, and only a few were penetrating beyond to Wilmslow, Knutsford and Alderley Edge. But, the memorandum commented: 'Manchester is advancing steadily on rural Cheshire.'[25] The same was true further east, south of Stockport, around Wilmslow and Alderley Edge.[26]

The urban pressure of the 1930s chiefly affected the Wirral on the one hand, the land within fifteen miles of central Manchester on the other. It so happened that nearly all of it was good farmland, partly due to facts of physiography and climate, but mainly due to the deliberate development of specialized forms of farming in response to the needs of the urban populations. The same was true to some degree north of the Mersey in Lancashire, in the distinctive south-west Lancashire coastal plain.[27] This characteristic was enough to make the land worth defending. Cheshire's experience with Wythenshawe made it more likely that when the era of postwar planning began, defence would be forthcoming.

THE POSTWAR PLANS

As with London and the West Midlands, so with Greater Manchester and Merseyside, this postwar era was ushered in by regional advisory plans, which were intended to provide broad guidelines to the counties and country boroughs in their detailed work of plan making and plan implementation under the 1947 Act. In all postwar planning around the conurbations, one major theme is the relationship, or the lack of relationship, between these broad, often utopian blueprints and the daily grind of development control that they were supposed to influence and guide.

The two conurbations in the North-West had their regional plans prepared in very different ways. In Greater Manchester, the means existed in abundance in the form of joint committees. Logically, the plans which were produced went chronologically from the small scale to the large. A City of Manchester Plan emerged in 1945[28] and was followed in the same year by the Manchester Regional Plan, which was prepared by the Manchester and District Regional Planning Committee.[29] Then, in 1947, the Advisory Plan for South Lancashire and North Cheshire appeared, drawn up on behalf of the wider South Lancashire and North Cheshire Advisory Planning Committee.[30] In all three

[25] Ibid., p. 159.

[26] Ibid., p. 171.

[27] Wilfred Smith, *Lancashire* (The Land of Britain, Part 45). Geographical Publications, London (1941), p. 68.

[28] R. J. Nicholas, *City of Manchester Plan*. Jarrold, Norwich and London (1945).

[29] R. J. Nicholas (for the Manchester and District Regional Planning Committee), *Report on the Tentative Regional Planning Proposals*. Jarrold, Norwich and London (1945), paras 1 and 6.

[30] R. Nicholas and M. J. Hellier (for South Lancashire and North Cheshire Advisory Planning Committee), *An Advisory Plan*. Richard Bates, Manchester (1947), pp. 3–7.

documents the name of R. J. Nicholas, City Surveyor and Planning Officer for Manchester, appears prominently as author; he, if anyone, must be regarded as the architect of postwar regional policies in the Greater Manchester area.

Merseyside had no such elaborate hierarchy of joint bodies. The solution here was the same as in Greater London and Greater Birmingham: the central government called in a consultant, F. Longstreth Thompson, who was helped by a technical committee including representatives of both central and local government; they approved his main proposals before publication. The Merseyside Plan was published by HMSO, and thus with the imprint of central government, in 1945.[31] Together, in effect, the Thompson Plan for Merseyside and the South Lancashire-North Cheshire Plan fully cover the whole of south Lancashire and north Cheshire; since the first covers an area stretching from Preston to Chester, and from the coast to the future M6, while the second covers the whole basin of the Mersey except the lower estuarine reaches.

Very soon, the overspill problem emerged as a central theme of these plans. The 1945 Manchester Regional Plan, covering broadly the area of the conurbation, started from the assumption that all housing development at more than twenty-four houses to the acre would ultimately be re-developed at lower densities.[32] On this basis, it defined three types of area in the region. First were Manchester, Salford and Stretford, the core areas of the region, which could not hope to accommodate their population on redevelopment:[33] they essentially represented the overspill problem of the region, which was calculated to amount to 217,000 people (Table 12.1). Second there were areas which could provide for their own redevelopment needs, but could not take other people's overspill: they included Eccles, Prestwich, Swinton and

Table 12.1

MANCHESTER CONURBATION: OVERSPILL, 1945

	Overspill houses	Overspill population (at 3·25 per house)
Manchester	42,718	138,800
Salford	22,831	74,200
Stretford	1,231	4,000
Total	66,780	217,600

Source: Manchester Regional Plan, 1946.[34]

[31] F. Longstreth Thompson, *Merseyside Plan 1944*, A report prepared in consultation with a technical committee of the Merseyside Advisory Joint Planning Committee at the request of the Minister of Town and Country Planning. HMSO, London (1945).

[32] Nicholas (for Regional Planning Committee), op. cit., para. 169.

[33] Ibid, para. 170.

[34] Ibid., Table 7, p. 32.

Pendlebury, Audenshaw, Failsworth and Droylesden.[35] And third, there were areas on the fringe of the region that could take overspill: Middleton, Denton, Irlam, Urmston, and Worsley.[36] The plan estimated that these areas could accommodate some 19,750 houses in all, equivalent to close on 67,000 people. Certain adjustments within the areas might however contribute room for another 4,500 houses, giving a total contribution of 24,250.[37] Against the total of 66,780 dwellings which was the estimate of the scale of the problem, this left a shortfall of 42,500 dwellings which must be provided outside the limits of the Manchester Regional Plan area, equivalent to between 150,000 and 200,000 people.[38] These conclusions could not be final, though, till detailed planning was complete. They might be upset in detail by an increase in voluntary migration out of the region altogether, by variations in birth rate, or by the effects of national location of industry policy.[39] But whatever the detailed changes, it was fairly apparent that the problem could not be solved within the range of the Manchester region – that is, within the ring of local authorities surrounding Manchester and Salford to the west and north, on the Lancashire side of the conurbation. Longer-distance overspill would be necessary, entailing movement of jobs as well as people. On this, the report was clear:

> Every effort must be made . . . to encourage the dispersal of those industries which are not tied to their present sites by economic conditions.[40]

At this stage, the Regional Plan was still open as to the forms of decentralization. Proposals for garden cities, garden suburbs, satellite towns (i.e. new towns) and expansion of small towns were being discussed with Lancashire and Cheshire County Councils. It looked as if one or more new towns would be needed in addition to a programme of expansion.[41] They would need careful siting in relation to the communications pattern, the physical suitability of the land, the possibility of service provision, the agricultural land category, the effect on the general economic and social character of the area, and the suitability of the site for industrial development.[42] But, the report stressed, there could be no attempt to coerce people to move in any one direction.[43]

Clearly, a larger scale of planning was needed: a region which embraced all the possible sites for overspill development in Lancashire. The North Cheshire Advisory Committee was clearly the right framework, and it was logical that the Advisory Plan should appear from the Advisory Committee

35 Ibid., para. 172.
36 Ibid., para. 171.
37 Ibid., para. 178.
38 Ibid., para. 179.
39 Ibid., para. 181.
40 Ibid., para. 354.
41 Ibid., para. 186.
42 Ibid., para. 187.
43 Ibid., para. 186.

two years later, in 1947, under the authorship of R. J. Nicholas and M. J. Hellier.[44]

This report starts from the overspill estimates of the earlier Regional Plan, superimposed on an assumption which must have seemed reasonable enough at the time: that in the wider region as a whole, there would be a marginal natural *decrease* of the population, from 3,472,000 in 1941 to about 3,200,000 in 1971.[45] Since there would be little net immigration into the area considered as a whole, the sole problem was to cater for the internal decentralization of the population from the overcrowded central areas of the conurbation. On the scale of the overspill problem, the report accepted the estimate of the Manchester Regional Plan: between 150,000 and 250,000 to be rehoused from the inner part of the conurbation.[46] This, the report warned the peripheral authorities, was something that was in everyone's interest to plan:

> In the Advisory Area it is evident that if sporadic and ribbon building continues as before the war, the coalescence of district with district will quickly destroy the individuality of the existing towns, while the gradual spread of bricks and mortar will obscure any impression of open country from Wilmslow in the south to Littleborough and Chorley in the north, and from Glossop in the east to Newton-in-Makerfield in the west.[47]

In such a plan, the report argued, there would be four elements. First, in all the towns of the region there would be very local decongestion of any area that happened to be too densely developed, through dispersal into new or expanded neighbourhoods. Second, there would be a continuation of the process which had been so marked between the wars: those elements of the population which had economic freedom of choice would continue to move out into the more attractive residential districts. Third, after the war the controlled redistribution of industry would indirectly bring a movement of people in its train, perhaps from one region into another. And fourth, there would be an organized dispersal on both a small and a large scale.[48]

Clearly, it was this organized dispersal that provided the critical problem of the Advisory Plan. Two sites near the conurbation were suggested, following the earlier Manchester Regional Plan: at Middleton and at Worsley. Middleton's population would rise from 29,000 to nearly 51,000 between 1941 and 1970, largely due to planned intake; Worsley's population would increase from 25,000 to nearly 61,000 in the same period.[49] Further away from the conurbation, the Advisory Plan put forward two possible sites for major new town developments, both in Cheshire: at Lymm, which would expand from under 6,000 people to 50,000 by 1970; and at Mobberley in

[44] Nicholas and Hellier (for Advisory Planning Committee), op. cit.
[45] Ibid., pp. 28–9.
[46] Ibid., p. 81.
[47] Ibid., p. 70.
[48] Ibid., p. 81.
[49] Ibid., p. 84.

Bucklow Rural District, which would go up from 9,000 to 56,000.[50] The Mobberley proposal was not however firm, because it was not known whether subsidence made the ground unfit to build on.[51]

Other sites in Cheshire would play their part too. Most of them were near the conurbation fringes at the northern edge of the county, especially south of Manchester: Hazel Grove and Bramhall, Wilmslow and Alderley Edge, and Hale would between them take over 60,000 extra people, while further west the area south of Warrington was also to be developed. More distant expansions were proposed for Sandbach, Congleton, and Macclesfield.[52] Outside these areas, the regional planners agree with the views of Cheshire's Advisory Plan Committee: residential building should be restricted to existing villages or small towns, which might be expanded by a very small amount.[53]

Over on Merseyside, Thompson's Merseyside Plan of 1945 found an overspill problem rivalling that of Greater Manchester; over 190,000 people from the Lancashire side (of whom close on 148,000 were from Liverpool, and 35,000 from Bootle) and another 67,500 from the Cheshire side (of whom Birkenhead accounted for 38,000) – a grand total of just over 258,000 people to be rehoused elsewhere,[54] assuming that the redevelopment of older urban areas was to be carried out to approved standards (Table 12.2). Thompson proposed that a little under two-thirds should be accommodated on the Lancashire side and the rest on the Cheshire side.[55]

It would be possible to provide for this to happen in various ways; Thompson considered peripheral expansion, satellite towns and radial expansion between open wedges. He concluded that peripheral expansion no longer proved satisfactory for an agglomeration as big as Merseyside.[56] He went on to argue that in general, satellites had many advantages, but that in the special case of Merseyside they had disadvantages: there were few possible sites for them, involving a loss of valuable agricultural land, industry here was immobile as compared with other conurbations, and new industries were needed to help remedy a certain industrial imbalance within the conurbation itself.[57] Therefore, Thompson recommended a solution using radial spurs and green wedges, which would make full use of available infrastructure including transport lines.[58]

On the Lancashire side of the Mersey, the 8,000 acres needed for development could all be provided inside the boundaries of land which had already been developed in part, within four radial spurs: Speke, Halewood, Huyton,

50 Ibid., p. 86.
51 Ibid., pp. 81–2.
52 Ibid., pp. 82–6 and endpaper map.
53 Ibid., p. 75.
54 Longstreth Thompson, op. cit., para. 75.
55 Ibid., para. 79.
56 Ibid., para. 16.
57 Ibid., para. 17.
58 Ibid., para. 18.

Table 12.2

MERSEYSIDE: SUMMARY OF PROPOSALS IN THE THOMPSON PLAN, 1945

A Sources of overspill

	Population	Equivalent acreage
Lancashire side	190,534	6,085
Liverpool	147,834	4,743
Bootle	35,000	1,050
Cheshire side	67,550	2,032
Birkenhead	38,000	1,270
Total both sides	258,084	8,117
Add: Extra families		3,300
More open development		1,370
Total estimated needs		12,787

B Proposed sites

Lancashire acres		Cheshire acres	
Central Merseyside	6,530	Central Merseyside	2,235
Formby	740	Hoylake-West Kirby	550
Aughton	170	Greasby	240
Prescot-Rainhill	610	Heswall-Pensby	885
		Neston	345
Total	8,050	Childer Thornton	265
(*Estimated needs:*	8,000)	Great-Little Sutton	350
		Willaston	100
		Total	4,970
		(*Estimated needs:*	5,000)

Source: F. Longstreth Thompson, *Merseyside Plan*, 1944.

Kirkby and Maghull (Table 12.2).[59] On the Cheshire side, land was available within the existing urban fence at Wallasey, Birkenhead and Bebington. It would also be possible to round off and develop some outer Wirral suburbs: Moreton, Upton and Greasby. Lastly, there would need to be expansion of certain communities in western and southern Wirral to form a curving radial spur: West Kirby, Heswall, Neston, Willaston, Hooton, Childer Thornton, Great and Little Sutton.[60]

Interestingly, therefore, the philosophy of Thompson's Merseyside Plan was quite different from the advisory planners on the opposite side of Cheshire. South of Manchester, the emphasis was on expansion of a number of carefully selected communities up to thirty miles from the conurbation, plus two communities which were in effect new towns. South of Merseyside, Thompson's plan specifically rejected this type of solution on the grounds that it was ill-suited to the specific conditions of Merseyside, and proposed instead a strategy based on quite short radial spurs from the conurbation, not

[59] Ibid., paras 79, 80.

[60] Ibid., para. 81.

usually more than ten or twelve miles long. It is significant that Thompson rejected both of the places which, in the event, were later chosen as satellites for Merseyside: at Skelmersdale, he thought that construction costs on the subsidence-prone ground would be so high as to justify running the settlement down,[61] while Runcorn was seen as justifying a small new development to cater for a purely local overspill problem within the town itself.[62]

THE COUNTIES TAKE CHARGE

A critical question in the early postwar years was how the counties would react to these regional advisory plans and interpret them. Until 1947, the urban and rural district councils had formally been the planning authorities; it was they who had banded together in the local committees, and who had received the South Cheshire-North Cheshire Plan. But on the passage of the 1947 Act, powers passed to the county and county borough councils. South of the Mersey this meant that apart from the county boroughs of Wallasey and Birkenhead on Merseyside, and Stockport in the Greater Manchester conurbation (as well as the freestanding city of Chester), Cheshire was sole authority for a wide stretch of land, including nearly all the areas threatened by urban growth. To the north, the administrative county of Lancashire was more punctured by county borough authorities than any other in England.[63] But even it was broadly responsible for the further implications of the outgrowth of Merseyside northwards, and, to a much more limited extent, for those of Greater Manchester's expansion in the same direction.

The job of laying the foundations of county planning policies, in both cases, lay with the authors of advisory plan reports, which the counties prepared in advance of their Statutory Development Plans under the 1947 Act. That for Cheshire was prepared by a consultant, W. Dobson Chapman, and in first draft was submitted to the County Council as early as 1946; it was published with the authority of the Council in 1948.[64] That for Lancashire was actually prepared by the County Planning Officer, G. Sutton Brown, and was published as *A Preliminary Plan for Lancashire* in 1951,[65] shortly before the Statutory Development Plan which in main lines follows it. By being an advisory plan, though, it manages to escape the limitations of the administrative county boundaries and to consider the problems of county and county boroughs within a single framework.

61 Ibid., para. 116.

62 Ibid., paras 132–3.

63 Within the South-East Lancashire conurbation, by Bolton, Bury, Manchester, Oldham, Rochdale, and Salford. Within Merseyside, by Bootle. Outside the conurbation, by Barrow, Blackburn, Blackpool, Burnley, Preston, St Helens, Southport, Warrington, and Wigan.

64 W. Dobson Chapman, *County Palatine: A Plan for Cheshire*. Country Life, London (1948).

65 G. Sutton Brown, *A Preliminary Plan for Lancashire*. Lancashire County Council, Preston (1951).

The Chapman Plan for Cheshire represented the pure orthodoxy of immediate postwar thinking about urban growth; its avowed intention was:

> to demonstrate how the national planning policy with regard to the dispersal of industry and the revival of agriculture, as envisaged by the [Barlow and Scott] reports, might best be applied to the county of Cheshire.[66]

Uncontrolled urban growth, Chapman accepted, led to disadvantages which were economic (wasteful travel both for people and goods), sociological (lack of community spirit and hostility between different income groups) and political (apathy in local government).[67] But planned growth, Chapman was at pains to insist, was beneficial to Cheshire as well as to those who came to live there:

> Cheshire is willing and able to accommodate and adopt the industry and industrial population displaced from (the conurbations). Such a policy is not entirely disinterested. Cheshire can well do with further industrial growth provided that necessary precautions are taken to safeguard the primarily agricultural character of the county.[68]

As to the precise means, Chapman was strongly in favour of town expansion schemes rather than completely new towns or satellites close to the conurbations. Compared with new towns, they would bite less into agricultural land, would use an existing framework of services, and would have an old-established tradition to start with.[69] Compared with near-in satellites, they would have an independent community life of their own, as the Reith Committee had advocated.[70] Therefore, the essential job for Cheshire as Chapman saw it was to choose certain towns for rapid expansion; the bulk, he agreed with the regional planners, would need to be within a reasonable distance, say twenty miles, of the parent conurbations. Selected small towns would take the biggest expansion; larger towns, by definition, were suitable only for more modest growth. In all cases, the aim would be to diversify the town's economic and social structure; to make it more self dependent in terms of available jobs and services; and at the same time allow it to serve more effectively the rural hinterland around.[71]

Applied in detail, this philosophy meant a considerable scatter of the overspill into a number of quite small-scale expansions within twenty miles of the conurbations: the western and southern Wirral,[72] the middle Mersey region around Frodsham, Helsby, and Lymm[73] and, in the east of the county,

[66] Chapman, op. cit., p. 83.
[67] Ibid., p. 3.
[68] Ibid., p. 83.
[69] Ibid., pp. 84–6.
[70] Ibid.
[71] Ibid., pp. 84–9.
[72] Ibid., pp. 146, 161, 165–6, 173.
[73] Ibid., pp. 169, 176.

places like Bowdon, Cheadle and Gatley, Hale, Hazel Grove and Bramhall, and Knutsford and Mobberley.[74] Only a very few of the proposals were farther away from the two great conurbations; the Chapman Plan, like the Abercrombie-Jackson Plan for the West Midlands, is fundamentally a plan for short-distance dispersal. Indeed, even at that time, most of the suggested sites would have been within commuting distance of one or other of the conurbations for a reasonably affluent member of the population.

Brown's 1951 advisory plan for Lancashire is notable for a definitive statement of the overspill problem of the county, including the associated county boroughs, as it appeared at that time. Indeed, over 90 per cent of the problem originated in the county boroughs;[75] and the great bulk of that was in the two great conurbations. In the Oldham-Manchester area, which was roughly synonymous with the South-East Lancashire conurbation, the total overspill was 304,000, with Manchester contributing 193,000 and Salford 62,000.[76] On Merseyside it was nearly 186,000, of which Liverpool contributed 145,000 and Bootle 28,000.[77]

Brown's answer to this problem was in two parts. Immediately, there would have to be a concentration on short-distance schemes which did not depend on long-distance moves by industry. In the Manchester conurbation these moves, nearly all of them within the conurbation itself, could house only 86,000 out of the total of 304,200, leaving 217,600 to be accommodated in longer-distance schemes.[78] Liverpool and Bootle could house 100,800 within the conurbation or just outside within travelling distance, leaving nearly 85,000 to be housed in longer-distance schemes.[79] These more distant schemes would depend heavily on Board of Trade policies for guiding industry and on the possibility of building up adequate building labour forces. Brown suggested three possible candidates within Lancashire for new towns, at Parbold, west of Wigan; Leyland, between Wigan and Preston; and Garstang, between Preston and Lancaster.[80] On the last, Brown recommended no action until Cheshire's contribution was known, and a foreword to the published plan recorded that the idea had been abandoned for the present. Similarly the Leyland project was abandoned as a new town, though joint action between the county and the Urban District Council was suggested instead. Parbold too was abandoned, but the adjacent Skelmersdale site was proposed instead; this idea came to reality only a decade later, in 1961, when Skelmersdale was designated as the first new town in England for twelve years.[81]

Taken together, the Chapman and Brown Reports give a reasonably consistent picture. For a few years, until the momentum of industrial

[74] Ibid., pp. 158, 160, 164, 167, 182.
[75] Brown, op. cit., p. 36.
[76] Ibid., p. 38.
[77] Ibid., p. 39.
[78] Ibid., p. 9.
[79] Ibid.
[80] Ibid., pp. 41–2.
[81] Ibid., p. viii.

decentralization could be built up, the emphasis would have to be on short-distance overspill within the conurbations, or within two or three miles of their boundaries: the sort of development which in Abercrombie's London plan was labelled quasi-satellite. But this was regarded as a device to gain breathing space, and it was particularly disliked by Cheshire. Even in the longer run, industry and people would move to town expansions, or, in Lancashire's case, a new town, within twenty miles of the conurbations; it was unreasonable to expect people or industry to move much further, and it was for this reason particularly that the new town plan for Garstang found so little favour. The main pressure of overspill, however much Cheshire's plans diffused it, would fall on a well-defined belt of land within easy access of the conurbations. And in the nature of things, it was to be expected that this belt would contain land of some value, even high value, for agriculture. Thus the seeds of future conflict were sown.

THE 1950s: CONFLICT IN CHESHIRE

The definitive basis of planning policy was provided by the two County Development Plans. Lancashire's was published in 1951[82] and Cheshire's in 1952;[83] they were approved by the Minister only after a long delay, Lancashire's in 1956, Cheshire's in 1958. Both were based firmly on the analysis in the earlier advisory reports, with only minor changes of emphasis.

The Lancashire Development Plan made minor revisions in the overspill calculations of the earlier report, and additionally calculated the amount of overspill which was expected to be housed by 1971. Thus the total of overspill for South-East Lancashire was raised slightly from 304,000 to 317,000, of which rather more than one-third (117,000) would be rehoused by 1971. The proportion that could be housed in short-distance schemes remained unchanged, at 87,000: 31,000 would go to Worsley, Middleton, and Whitefield, 24,500 to the Bury area, and 20,600 (from Salford) to Westhoughton just outside the western boundary of the conurbation. And even taking into account the longer distance proposal for a new town at Skelmersdale west of Wigan, Lancashire could be expected to supply only 117,000 places: a little over one-third of the ultimate total and 50,000 short of the immediate twenty-year total of 167,000. But, the plan stated confidently, it was known that Cheshire would make a substantial contribution, which would go far to housing the 50,000 shortfall in the immediate period.[84]

On Merseyside the total overspill was also recalculated; it dropped marginally from 186,000 in the earlier report to 179,000, of which three-quarters (138,000) was to be accommodated in the plan period. Of this total, 109,000 (as against only 87,000 in the earlier report) could be housed in short-distance schemes, of which 19,000 would be in peripheral extensions of the

[82] Lancashire Development Plan, *Written Analysis*. Preston (1951).

[83] Cheshire Development Plan, *Report and Analysis of County Survey*. Chester (1952).

[84] Lancashire, op. cit., pp. 165–71.

conurbations at Speke and Halewood, and no less than 90,000 in self-contained units just beyond, separated from each other (according to the principles of the 1945 Thompson Plan) by green wedges: at Kirkby, Aintree and Maghull, Crosby and possibly at Widnes. Lastly, the Skelmersdale new town proposal would house 45,000 Merseysiders.[85] In the tradition of earlier documents, the plan stressed that the short-distance schemes were stopgap expedients, to fill the space before the longer-distance scheme got underway. In the event, when the Ministry approved the plan in 1956, it excluded the new town proposals though it left open the possibility of action at Skelmersdale under the Town Development Act. This decision was to be reversed only five years later, when Skelmersdale was designated a new town; but in all, that meant a delay of a decade from publication of the plan.[86]

As everyone accepted, then, the Lancashire Development Plan left a substantial total of overspill to be housed in Cheshire. Cheshire's firm proposals for dealing with the problem came in its definitive Development Plan, in 1952. The essential calculations there broadly agree with those in the Lancashire plan, with marginal differences. Cheshire assumed that South-East Lancashire would generate an ultimate overspill of 346,000 (Lancashire's calculation had been 317,000) of which Cheshire would need to house no less than 211,000 (Lancashire calculated 200,000). On Merseyside, Cheshire calculated the gross overspill at 172,000 (against Lancashire's 179,000) of which Cheshire would need to house only 22,999 (Lancashire had calculated 25,000).[87] Broadly, therefore, the essential situation was that Lancashire could deal with the vast bulk of the Merseyside overspill on the fairly open land of south-west Lancashire; but that because of the topographical and urban barriers to the north, a large part of the Manchester conurbation's overspill problem would necessarily have to be met by Cheshire. There was also a very minor overspill from Warrington, which could be housed locally on the south bank of the Manchester Ship Canal. Lastly, there was bound to be a large element of voluntary or spontaneous overspill from the two conurbations into Cheshire, as in the past: this was difficult to calculate, but Cheshire allowed for a total of 55,000 from Greater Manchester and 71,500 from Merseyside, of which an unknown total would come south into Cheshire.[88]

Cheshire's essential strategy for dealing with the planned overspill recognized the same essential fact that previous plans had faced: even longer distance overspill schemes would have to be within reasonable distance of the conurbations, otherwise they would have no chance of success. As it was, only 11 per cent of the county's area was urbanized, and 60 per cent of its population lived in a narrow belt, not usually more than five miles wide, along the northern border and joining the two conurbations; another 20 per

[85] Ibid., p. 173.

[86] J. B. Cullingworth, *Housing Needs and Planning Policy*. Routledge and Kegan Paul, London (1960), p. 118.

[87] Cheshire, op. cit., pp. 42–4.

[88] Ibid., pp. 42–3.

cent lived in two north-south axes running at right angles to this belt, one down from Runcorn to Crewe, another down from Manchester to Congleton.[89] Put another way, 51 per cent of the total lived in the conurbations and their fringes: 35 per cent in Greater Manchester and 16 per cent in Merseyside.[90] Recognizing these essential geographical facts, the plan proposed that of the total increase of population in the county during the plan period up to 1971, an almost equivalent proportion, 49 per cent, was to be housed in the conurbations or their fringes.[91] Of.a total increase for the county of 258,000, 57,000 were to be housed in the Wirral, 29,000 around Altrincham, and 41,000 on the Stockport fringe; 13,000 in addition would be housed in the central part of the northern belt between the two conurbations, at Runcorn.[92]

In detail, the separate town maps published as part of the Cheshire Development Plan reflect the same basic philosophy as the Chapman Report of 1946: dispersal of the overspill population into a whole series of small or medium-sized expansions, based on existing communities, within striking distance of the conurbations. In the eastern Wirral Bebington was to take 11,000 people in the plan period up to 1971, and Ellesmere Port 26,000, with another 9,500 a little further out in Chester's rural fringe; detailed plans were not prepared at that time for the resort towns of the western Wirral, which might be expected to come under pressure for voluntary movers out of Merseyside.[93] But the biggest provision, amounting to no less than one-sixth of the total increase in the whole county, was in the east, close to the Manchester conurbation. Sale, Altrincham, Hale and Bowdon were to take 14,000; Wilmslow and Alderley Edge 7,000; Bredbury and Romiley 15,000; and Cheadle, Gatley, Hazel Grove and Bramhall 22,000.[94] There was hardly any specific mention of overspill industry in these areas; clearly, the plan expected most of the working-age population to be commuters, apart from a minority employed in local services.

Essentially, then, the whole emphasis in the Cheshire Development Plan is on very short-distance overspill schemes. There were only two exceptions to this. One was small scale, and obviously tentative: 5,000 extra people, with attendant industry, were proposed for Macclesfield, eighteen miles south of Manchester, though even at this distance, the plan recognized that there might be difficulties in getting industry to move. But the other exception was much more significant: it was a proposal for a new town at Congleton, twenty-four miles south of Manchester and eight miles south-west of the Macclesfield expansion. When the Cheshire Development Plan appeared in 1952, this already had a long and tortuous history. As early as 1946 Manchester had proposed to build a new town itself at Mobberley, only

[89] Ibid., p. 18.
[90] Ibid.
[91] Ibid., p. 63.
[92] Ibid.
[93] *Cheshire Development Plan, Written Statement*. Chester (1952), pp. 4, 11–12.
[94] Ibid., pp. 4, 14–16.

about fourteen miles to the south; it dropped its own proposal when it realized the New Towns Act would offer a better procedure. The Nicholas-Hellier Advisory Plan proposed both Mobberley and Lymm, fifteen miles south-west of Manchester, as new town sites; the Chapman Plan proposed only modest expansion at both places. The Minister decided to develop at Mobberley in 1946, reversed his decision on the grounds of subsidence at the end of the year, again reintroduced the proposal in 1947 and yet again rescinded it in 1948 on geological grounds. He rejected the Lymm idea both in 1947 and in August 1948 on the grounds that it was too near the conurbation. Cheshire had proposed Congleton as a new town site in 1947, and the Minister agreed in 1948 that it was the best possibility. Manchester again returned in 1949 with a proposal for more limited development at Lymm and Mobberley; the Minister agreed to the Mobberley proposal, but it failed to get the necessary approval in a Manchester town poll. In September 1951, the Ministry again proposed discussions on Congleton; Manchester agreed reluctantly, though it thought it was too far from the conurbation to persuade industry to move on any scale. This was the situation when Cheshire published its plan including the Congleton proposal. But then, in June 1952, the incoming Conservative Minister (Harold Macmillan) decided that Congleton should go ahead not as a new town, but as an expansion agreed between Manchester and the local council under the Town Development Act which had just been passed.[95]

Both the Lancashire and the Cheshire Development Plans, therefore, were fairly clear and consistent about the scale of the problem and about the broad strategy needed to deal with it. Both proposed a two-staged attack, the first based on short-distance overspill to the periphery of the conurbation or just beyond, the second to take both industry and people a greater distance, though still within reasonable access of their parent conurbations. Clearly, the second stage presented the greater potential political and technical difficulties, and was bound to take longer. In fact, it took longer than anyone would have dared to think; for two main reasons. The first, was a basic difference between Manchester and Cheshire about the right location for a new town. In the case of Merseyside, Lancashire had finally proposed Skelmersdale, only sixteen miles from Liverpool, as a new town site, and had rejected more distant proposals as unrealistic. Manchester wanted similar sites for itself: Lymm fifteen miles distant, and Mobberley fourteen miles distant. Cheshire rejected both of these, partly on geological grounds in the case of Mobberley, mainly on agricultural grounds in the case of Lymm. It proposed instead Congleton, twenty-four miles from the city. Manchester held that such a distance was too great to tempt industry, and argued that a new town in such a location was bound to fail. The result was virtual deadlock.

95 *Lymm: Proceedings at a Public Local Inquiry into the Requirements of Manchester Corporation . . . for Permission to Develop . . . in the Urban District of Lymm.* Mimeo (1958), Day 1, pp. 16, 25–32.

This deadlock, in the early months of 1952, might have been resolved. But it was then further compounded by a shift in government policy. The Town Development Act of 1952 had been introduced before the 1951 election by the Labour Government, and was the logical complement to the 1946 new towns policy, as Abercrombie had recommended in his 1944 Greater London Plan. But under the incoming Conservative Minister, Harold Macmillan, and his successors, it became for a time an alternative to a new towns policy. Ideologically, the Conservatives wanted a retreat from state interference and state planning; they preferred the concept that overspill problems could be dealt with by agreement among local authorities without much interference from Whitehall, but with central government aid in the form of subsidy for essential infrastructure. Perhaps this hope was naive in any event. But as it happened, it was coupled with inadequacies in the subsidy structure, inadequacies which were discovered only belatedly, several years later, when it became clear to all that the Act was not producing much result. In the event, neither the Congleton nor the Skelmersdale proposal went ahead as a new town. Both conurbations were left to deal with the problem with the inadequate 1952 Act.

PLANNING CONFLICTS IN THE 1950s: THE LYMM INQUIRY

These changes, then, frustrated the clear intention of the original Lancashire and Cheshire Development Plans: that there should be a balance between short-distance migration within travelling distance of conurbation jobs, and longer-distance movement of industry and people to developments of a new town character. In fact, during the 1950s virtually the whole of the development related to the conurbations was at their immediate peripheries.

This was more serious for Manchester than for Liverpool. In Merseyside, from the Thompson Plan onwards, the successive plans had recognized that short-distance movement could and would deal adequately with a large part of the total problem. The conurbation was compact, much of its industry was relatively immobile, there were sites available at places like Kirkby and Halewood. But in Greater Manchester, it was not at all so easy. There, both the Lancashire and the Cheshire plans had recognized the unique problems: the scale of the overspill, the difficulty and even the impossibility of accommodating much of it in or near the conurbation, the scarcity of either short- or medium-distance sites within striking distance of the conurbation on the Lancashire side. Therefore everything depended on getting sites for developments of new town character within Cheshire, at most within about twenty-five miles of the centre of Manchester, and preferably nearer if possible. And this, we have already seen, was already becoming a difficult problem by 1952.

When the Ministry rejected the Congleton new town proposal in that year, and proposed action under the Town Development Act instead, Manchester's scepticism increased. It retaliated by fresh applications at Mobberley and Lymm, which the Minister called in for decision and then rejected in October 1954, on the grounds of their agricultural value and their position in a natural green belt around the conurbation, a formal green belt not then having been designated. Mobberley, the Minister declared, was too near the conurbation and would have been a dormitory suburb. He would have agreed to Lymm had no alternatives been forthcoming; but they were in the form of full use of redevelopment possibilities within the city and in alternative sites in Cheshire, Lancashire and Derbyshire.[96]

The same arguments were repeated by a new Minister, Duncan Sandys, when a deputation visited him in 1955 to point out the shortage of building sites in Manchester.[97] Finally, in July 1957, the Minister told the interested authorities (Manchester, Cheshire, Lancashire, Derbyshire) that if Manchester applied to develop Lymm he would again call in the application and hold an inquiry. Due to the long-continued controversy over the site, however, he proposed that such an inquiry should be held by an independent inspector, not associated with his Ministry; and he proposed that the report should be published. Manchester, predictably, filed their application within hours.[98]

This was the origin of one of the most important and interesting planning inquiries under the 1947 Act. It is comparable, more closely than might at first appear, with the inquiry on Birmingham's application to develop at Wythall half a year later. For while Birmingham's application was nominally to build a peripheral housing estate on pre-1939 lines, and Manchester's was to build a new town, the two sites were not strikingly different in their location. The point about Lymm, as about Mobberley, was that it was very near its parent conurbation: there were only three miles between it and Altrincham, and the building of the new town would cut the distance to two and a quarter miles.[99] One central issue of the inquiry, in fact, was why Manchester had to find a site so near the city. On this, Manchester's representative was quite specific: in the early period, 'before the slower movement of industry had caught up with the movement of the people',[100] people in the new town would have to be able to commute into the city for work. The new town would ideally therefore be about twelve miles from the city; it could on no account be more than twenty miles distant.[101]

Manchester wanted this site to deal with a serious and persistent housing shortage. How serious, the representatives of Cheshire were at pains to question, as they had in the 1953 inquiry. Manchester's own estimate was that they needed sites for 83,000 dwellings in the long run, made up as follows: unfit houses, 62,000; natural growth of the city's population, making allowance for migration, 10,000; families in lodgings needing separate accommodation,

[96] Lymm Inquiry, op. cit., Day 1, p. 37.

[97] Ibid., Day 1, pp. 38–42.

[98] Ministry of Housing and Local Government, *Report of Inquiry into the Proposed Development of Land at Lymm for Manchester overspill*. HMSO, London (1958), p. 4.

[99] Lymm Inquiry Proceedings, op. cit., Day 1, p. 58.

[100] Ibid., Day 1, p. 48.

[101] Ibid.

9,000; and other redevelopment needs, 2,000.[102] All these estimates were questioned, but particularly that for unfit housing. It was alleged that this was a vague figure not based on detailed survey and that it had survived without revision for many years, ever since 1922. The Inspector, too, had some doubts about the figure but thought that it could not be much less than 60,000. He would not question the estimates for lodgings and for other redevelopment, but he disallowed the estimate for natural increase because it ignored out-migration that had been taking place and which could be expected to continue. His final estimate then was that Manchester's ultimate housing need was not 83,000 dwellings, but 71,000: still an awe-inspiring total.[103]

More immediately relevant was the question of the city's short-term needs, up to the end of the then current Development Plan period: that is, up to 1971. The critical point of controversy here was the building rate the city could achieve, given the land; Manchester claimed it could build 3,000 a year, the critics uncharitably pointed out that it was then building at half that rate or less. The Inspector settled for a rate of 2,500 a year, which was considerably better than Manchester's recent performance; it gave a total of 33,000 sites to be found, against the city's estimate of 42,000.[104] Taken against the fact that 26,000 sites were definitely available either in the city or in schemes agreed outside, this gave a deficit of 7,750 dwellings.[105] The critical question was whether all these sites should be found by a decision to develop Lymm, or whether they should be provided in a variety of other ways: either within the city, or in other areas outside it.

On the first of these possibilities, controversy again centred upon Manchester's redevelopment policies. Manchester steadfastly based its redevelopment plans on a density of 90 habitable rooms per net acre, which allowed it to build 60 per cent of its redevelopments in the form of house-type dwellings (that is with doors on the ground floor) and only 40 per cent in multi-storey flats.[106] This policy, which applied uniformly throughout the city, was in sharp contrast to the policies of other major cities, and even to Manchester's own neighbour Salford. In the years 1945–53, for instance, Manchester had built 77 per cent of its new buildings in the form of houses; the corresponding figure for the London County Council was 7·6 per cent.[107] The policy had been adopted as long ago as 1943, on a recommendation of the Medical Officer of Health to the Health Committee; and the city had upheld it, despite plain indications from successive Ministers of Housing that it should raise densities in order to accommodate more of the displaced slum populations within the city. Manchester's reply, which was repeated again at the inquiry, was that by raising the standards from 90 to 120 habitable

102 Lymm Inquiry Report, op. cit., p. 5.
103 Ibid., p. 7.
104 Ibid., p. 8.
105 Ibid.
106 Ibid., p. 9.
107 Ibid.

rooms per acre, the net gain in all the redevelopment areas up to the end of the plan period in 1971 would be only 1,620 dwellings: a derisory total to weigh against the social loss involved in building 60 per cent of new housing units in the form of flats.[108] The gain would be larger if the standard could be raised still further to 160 rooms per acre; but this, Manchester claimed, would be unacceptable on grounds of cost quite as much as on grounds of good planning.[109] The Inspector seems to have been at a loss to resolve the question, which is understandable as he was a lawyer, not a planner; but he was inclined to think that with careful design, rebuilding at 120 to the acre could yield as many as 2,000 dwellings towards closing the 7,500 gap.[110]

Whether or not this could be done, the next question involved alternative sites outside the city. Of the sites suggested beyond commuting distance, the Inspector thought that Congleton and Macclesfield were unlikely to yield results. Crewe on the other hand had offered to build up to 3,500 houses, and the proposal had been welcomed by Manchester; possibilities existed both at Leyland and Chorley for big schemes. Among short-distance sites, some were clearly unsuitable on environmental grounds or because they were too far from the conurbation. The Inspector was extremely definite about Risley, east of Warrington:

> The future of the site presents an acute planning problem and I do not think it provides any solution on which Manchester could be expected to rely. The only possible significance of Risley to the problem of "overspill" seems to me to be the extent to which industrial concerns might wish to take advantage of existing substantial buildings at Risley rather than build elsewhere.[111]

Similarly, sites at Tyldesley and Tottington were unsuitable; Glossop and Stalybridge were doubtful starters. But three sites, Westhoughton, Little Lever (near Bolton) and Ramsbottom, were completely suitable on every ground. They could yield something like 10,000 dwellings.[112]

At the end of his report, the Inspector was forced to sum up on a question that had perhaps no good answer. He made a summary which was fair, which seemed reasonable in all probability, and which in the event proved largely wrong. This was that adding together all the possibilities of developing alternatives, the case for Lymm could not be proved. Of course, the trouble was that none of them were certain.

> There was, therefore, shown to be a large potential to satisfy Manchester's housing needs well past 1971 but the availability of the sites for Manchester are (sic) all subject to one or more difficulties, the solution of which is beyond the corporation's control.[113]

108 Ibid.
109 Ibid.
110 Ibid.
111 Ibid.
112 Ibid., pp. 12–13.
113 Ibid., p. 15.

In particular, then, if Manchester could be assured of Little Lever and Westhoughton quickly, this would allow Manchester to maintain its maximum housing output, while postponing or even removing forever the need to take good agricultural land. If Ramsbottom also proved to be available, that would reinforce the position. Before the situation then had to be reviewed, round about 1971, there should be firm decisions at Crewe, Leyland, Chorley and Glossop.[114]

Probably this decision was almost inevitable within the Inspector's terms of reference. He was asked to consider the fullest extent to which Manchester could meet its own housing within its borders, and also the need to avoid or postpone the use of good agricultural land. There was then a *prima facie* case that the need to hold good agricultural land was an overriding one. This became most evident when the city of Manchester produced Dr (later Professor) Gerald Wibberley. Wibberley's evidence, which he defended staunchly in cross examination and later summarized in a book, consisted of a calculation of the true value of the Lymm land in agriculture. It came to the startling conclusion that this was only about £750,000–£840,000 (depending on the rate of discount); this being the maximum sum that it would be worth the community's while to pay to save the land for agriculture.[115] The difficulty was that because of the terms of reference the argument was almost irrelevant, as the Inspector recognized in his report:

> This argument will, no doubt, be considered by those qualified to assess its validity in the present context together with the opposed argument of the National Farmers' Union that it is basically fallacious. It must assume that to save or postpone the taking of good agricultural land from building is at least as important as the maintenance by Manchester of a steady and adequate rate of house building.[116]

It was hardly surprising, in the circumstances, that the Minister should once again refuse Manchester's application. But significantly, his decision letter does not mention the question of Manchester's redevelopment densities. He stated simply that in his view Lymm was superior to the other overspill sites, but that these other overspill sites appeared to be available and that Manchester should use them first.[117] In the event, as will be seen, one of the most important of these sites failed to materialize.

GREEN BELTS, EXPANDED TOWNS AND NEW TOWNS

Meanwhile, Manchester struggled on as best it could with the 1952 Town Development Act. By 1956, Lancashire Planning and Development Committee

[114] Ibid., pp. 15–16.

[115] Lymm Inquiry Proceedings, op. cit., Day 1, p. 7; Evidence of Wibberley, pp. 46–7. (The figure of £6½ million, on page 46, is clearly a misprint for £½ million.) G. P. Wibberley, *Agriculture and Urban Growth*. Michael Joseph, London (1959), p. 212.

[116] Lymm Inquiry Report, op. cit., p. 15.

[117] Cullingworth, op. cit., p. 133.

could already report that it had successfully sponsored schemes which had built more than 10,000 houses, accommodating more than 40,000 families, in the administrative county. Worsley, which had been started even before the passage of the Act, had already housed 5,700 people from Salford, and was well on the way to its target of 18,000 by 1962; Middleton had housed more than 13,000 people from Manchester, about three-quarters of the planned total; nearby, plans at Whitworth and Heywood, to house 7,000 and 6,000 respectively, were still under discussion.[118] This was despite considerable difficulties with the financial provisions for help from central government under the Act, which had proved slow and capricious; these however had been largely ironed out by 1955.[119]

At about this time, though, another complicating factor entered the situation. As in the other major urban areas of the country, in about 1955 the Ministry began to urge local authorities to delimit green belts in order to define the conurbations, and to prevent them growing to link with peripheral towns and with each other. The result was a ready response in three green belt proposals, closely linked with each other, which were approved in July 1956 in the form of sketch plans for interim development control. That for Merseyside and South-East Lancashire, in which Lancashire took the initiative, was meant to control and define the two conurbations on their northern flanks; the two separate proposals for North Cheshire and West Cheshire were intended to do the same thing for each of the two conurbations on their Cheshire side.[120] In the event, though formal submissions were made in 1960–61, only one inquiry was ever held (into the Merseyside and South-East Lancashire proposal, in summer 1961), the other two inquiries having been postponed; and no firm decision to confirm these green belts has even been made.[121] Here, again, is a case of planning decisions being overtaken by events; for the green belts only make sense in relation to a firm policy of long-distance decentralization of people and industry beyond them, and this has clashed with Board of Trade policy on putting the Development Areas first.[122] By 1965 in fact, even the official North-West Study was declaring:

> Decisions on these green belt proposals cannot be deferred indefinitely; otherwise neither the public nor the local authorities in the North-West

118 Lancashire County Council, Planning and Development Committee, *Reception of Overspill Families in the Administrative County – Progress Report*, 8 June 1956, pp. 1–3.

119 Lancashire County Council, *Report of the Parliamentary Committee*, Agendum No. 12 (July 1955), Appendix A, pp. 12–13.

120 Department of Economic Affairs, *The North-West: A Regional Study*. HMSO, London (1965), p. 89.

121 Ibid.

122 Merseyside was a Development Area from 1945 to 1960 when the concept was abandoned; and again after 1966, when it was reintroduced. Overspill schemes for Merseyside also qualified for Development Area aid.

will know to what extent they can be relied on as a basis for future planning and action.[123]

Yet, the study concluded in the next paragraph, it would be premature to come to such a final decision until a full strategy for the region's development was produced.[124]

Meanwhile, all the efforts of the local authorities represented a pathetically small attack on an immense problem. Most surprising, as Cullingworth pointed out in 1960, virtually the whole development up to the end of the 1950s had been in the conurbations. This was contrary to stated planning policies, and contrary also to the intentions of the Town Development Act, which had been specifically supposed to promote longer-distance overspill schemes.[125] According to Cullingworth's calculations, whereas the conurbation authorities had proposed that 74,000 out of the 182,000 total overspill up to 1971 should be long-distance, up to 1959 only 1,500 out of 37,500 had actually gone outside the conurbation.[126] Not only had total progress been slow, Cullingworth concluded; houses had been built in precisely the wrong places, too near the conurbation but too far from conurbation jobs, thus leading to long commuter journeys which, as Cullingworth's own social survey showed, people greatly disliked. Cullingworth castigated the Ministry for its lack of positive policies:

> . . . large-scale redevelopment cannot take place without large-scale overspill. This necessitates development of new town character. Successive Ministries have refused to provide a new town and the local authorities have been left to grapple with the problem as best they can.[127]

Progress under the Act was not much better in the 1960s. By 1968, Manchester had succeeded in developing twenty-two piecemeal overspill sites ranging from Langley in Lancashire to Sale and Handforth in Cheshire and Gamesley in the Pennine foothills of Derbyshire; it had just succeeded, despite much local opposition, in reaching its first agreement with a county borough, at Bury.[128] The biggest failure had come at Westhoughton, a medium-distance overspill scheme (fifteen miles from Manchester) which had been suggested as an alternative at the Lymm inquiry. Manchester accepted it as an alternative, if the badly run down colliery village could be redeveloped at a high standard, comprehensively. But after successive negotiations, the orders made for the site excluded ribbons of existing property which criss-crossed the site; and despite a great deal of effort by the city and the county, the proposal was finally abandoned.[129] As for longer-distance schemes under

[123] North-West Study, op. cit., p. 90.
[124] Ibid.
[125] Cullingworth, op. cit., p. 133.
[126] Ibid., p. 134.
[127] Ibid., p. 136.
[128] J. S. Millar, 'Manchester City Region – Review and Prospect', *Town and Country Summer School*. Manchester (1968), p. 3.
[129] Ibid.

the Act in Cheshire, by 1968 less than 1,000 houses had actually been built at Winsford, Crewe, and Macclesfield; discussions were still taking place elsewhere, but the overwhelming difficulty was to attract industry without offering special incentives.[130] The major development at Winsford, envisaged as a scheme for Manchester, was actually transferred under Liverpool's umbrella because of that city's cherished Development Area status. Overall, the history of Manchester overspill justifies the verdict of Professor H. Myles Wright: 'the effort has been immense and the results very poor'.[131]

How poor, began to emerge clearly about the beginning of the 1960s. At this point, the slum clearance programme of 1955 had already been running more than half a decade and was beginning to yield impressive results. While the emphasis was on quick clearance, as Manchester's Planning Officer pointed out, there was a certain logic in concentrating on the short-distance schemes: as street after street was stripped and cleared, movement to a peripheral estate was quicker than industrial or tenant selection schemes. But as the back of this programme was broken, and as emphasis moved instead to development for growth, there must be a shift to a broader strategic view.[132]

This may have been the main reason for a fundamental shift in government policy, soon after 1960. In 1961 came the first new town designation in England for twelve years, at Skelmersdale – first proposed in the Lancashire Development Plan a whole decade earlier. Designed to take Liverpool overspill, it was well sited only fifteen miles north-east of the city. It had produced 1,500 houses by 1968, and development was continuing apace.[133] Runcorn, also designed to cope with Merseyside overspill, was designated in 1964; both towns were designed to receive eventual additional populations of 70,000,[134] taking Skelmersdale's eventual population to 80,000 and Runcorn's to 100,000.

Still, however, up to the mid 1960s there was no sign of any major relief for Manchester. The proposal to develop at Risley, roundly condemned by the Inspector at the 1958 Lymm inquiry, was resurrected and transformed into a proposal to create a new town by additions to (and redevelopment of) the existing town of Warrington; and consultants were asked to investigate the idea, reporting in 1966. An industrial town of 120,000 people in the mid 1960s, with pressing problems of poor housing and generally bad environment, Warrington is bordered eastwards by extensive tracts of land abandoned by defence agencies: the former Padgate RAF camp and the Admiralty centre at Risley.[135] Standing on flat, treeless land by the Manchester Ship Canal, with high pollution levels from neighbouring industry, the sites offer land but

130 Ibid.

131 Ibid.

132 Ibid.

133 Ibid., p. 5.

134 Ibid.

135 Ibid. Cf. Ministry of Housing and Local Government, *Expansion of Warrington: Consultants' Proposals for Designation.* HMSO, London (1966), *passim.*

little else; the development consultants did their best with unpromising materials. Eventually, in 1968, the Minister designated the site for a new town. At this time, too, the proposal was first floated for a much more ambitious new town development: a central Lancashire new city, which would eventually unite Leyland, Chorley and Preston into a polynuclear urban region, and which would eventually provide homes for 250,000 South Lancastrians.[136] After considerable investigation of the question, this area was finally designated as a new town in March 1970.

Table 12.3

THE SCALE OF THE HOUSING PROBLEM, SOUTH-EAST LANCASHIRE AND MERSEYSIDE, 1964–1981

	South-East Lancashire	Merseyside
A Demand for additional dwellings		
Existing shortage, 1964	26,910	40,140
Slum clearance and other redevelopment needs	222,900	124,850
Natural increase in number of households	105,940	90,950
Continuation of trends in voluntary migration (1956–64)	42,400	36,500
Total demand, assuming an end to voluntary migration trend	355,750	255,990
Total demand, assuming continuation of voluntary migration trend	313,350	219,490
B Sites for new dwellings		
In new areas	153,980	93,600
In redevelopment areas	111,570	67,320
Total within the area	265,550	160,920
Overspill sites (agreed)	45,100	29,210
Total sites available	310,650	190,130
C Surplus of deficit		
Assuming an end to voluntary migration trend	45,100	65,860
Assuming continuation of voluntary migration trend	2,700	29,360

Source: The North West Study, 1965.

THE NORTH-WEST STUDY AND AFTER

These were *ad hoc* adjustments to a rapidly changing situation; they badly needed to be fitted into a coherent strategy for the development of the region, which (despite the efforts of the immediate postwar years) the North-West as a whole had never had. In 1965 the newly formed Department of Economic

[136] Ministry of Housing and Local Government, *Central Lancashire: Study for a City*. HMSO, London (1967).

Affairs published the North-West Study, the first approach to a regional plan for the area in nearly twenty years.[137] It contained important detailed calculations of the scale of the overspill problem in the region's two major conurbations. Table 12.3 sets out these calculations, and Table 12.4 shows how the problem was distributed within the constituent sub-regions of each area. Together they provide a critically important picture of the scale of overspill as it appeared in the middle of the 1960s, which can act as a yardstick in measuring progress in new and expanded town policy.

Table 12.4

THE SCALE OF THE HOUSING PROBLEM, SUB-REGIONS OF SOUTH-EAST LANCASHIRE AND MERSEYSIDE, 1964–1981

Sub-regions	Deficit: Assuming an end to voluntary migration trend		Assuming continuation of voluntary migration trend	
South-East Lancashire	45,100		2,670	
Manchester	51,930		1,700	surplus
Outer Lancashire	1,300	surplus	19,800	surplus
Stalybridge and High Peak	7,090	surplus	9,790	surplus
Stockport and Altrincham	1,560		33,960	
Merseyside	65,860		29,360	
North Merseyside	69,030		27,330	
South Merseyside	3,170	surplus	2,030	

Source: The North West Study, 1965.

The first element in this calculation was the existing shortage of dwellings in 1964, calculated in two ways: first, by examining local authorities' waiting lists, and second, by comparing estimates of households needing separate accommodation with the numbers of dwellings actually occupied in 1964.[138] From this the remarkable fact emerged: that nearly half the shortage in the whole North-West region was concentrated on Merseyside. When South-East Lancashire was counted in, over four-fifths of the total shortage of dwellings occurred in the two subdivisions which represented the conurbations.[139]

Second, there was slum clearance together with renewal needs of other sorts. The estimates here were special ones prepared by local authorities for the study. But since they depend very largely on local authorities' own definitions of what was fit for human habitation, they were to some extent

137 Department of Economic Affairs, op. cit. Much of the work had been done before creation of the DEA by a team from the Ministry of Housing and Local Government; it passed to DEA when that body was set up and was given responsibility for regional planning.

138 Ibid.

139 Ibid.

arbitrary.[140] Again, the problem of renewal in the North-West was concentrated in the two conurbations, and the great majority of it represented slum clearance. Out of a total for the region of 480,000 dwellings needing clearance (440,000 of which were slums), 223,000 or nearly one-half were in the Manchester sub-division; 124,000 or one-quarter were in the Merseyside sub-division.[141] In both these divisions 30 per cent of the total housing stock was said to be in need of clearance.[142]

Lastly, the North-West Study had to estimate the future of population and its implications for housing need. Here, a great deal depended on assumptions about future migration, and in particular (since overspill movements were in the planner's control) voluntary or spontaneous migration. Such migration had two effects: it reduced the population estimates for the region as a whole, since the net movement of people was out of the region, and it resorted the region's population internally, with losses in the central urban parts and gains in the suburban parts. So a great deal depended on whether the estimate assumed that migration would continue as in the recent past, or not. Therefore two estimates were taken. One assumed that migration trends would continue as in the period 1956–64. The other assumed that all net migration movements, both as between the region and other regions, and internally within the region, would cease entirely. For the region as a whole, it was estimated that if migration trends continued, natural increases minus migration would create a demand for 227,000 dwellings; but if migration were to cease, the demand would rise to 281,600 dwellings.[143]

The study then went on to look at available building sites, based on returns sent in from local authorities. Within each area, separate estimates were made of virgin land (zoned for development, or thought suitable for development and outside the proposed green belts), and of land for redevelopment in slum clearance and other redevelopment areas. Lastly, an estimate was made of capacity in all overspill schemes relevant to each area. Putting demand and supply estimates together, the study concluded that if migration trends continued, in the South-East Lancashire area demand and supply would roughly balance; on Merseyside there would be a shortage of 29,360 dwellings. If out-migration were halted, on the other had, the situation would be much more acute: South-East Lancashire's need would rise to 45,100 and Merseyside's to 65,860 dwellings within the relatively short period up to 1981.[144]

The low estimates, it must be said, were probably more realistic, even if they did not satisfy the region's aspiration to prove attractive again to industry and people. From them, it would appear that the housing and land situation in the North-West was well under control, except on Merseyside.

140 Ibid., p. 73.
141 Ibid., pp. 76, 172–3 (Table 39).
142 Ibid., p. 76.
143 Ibid., pp. 176–7 (Table 41, on which Table 12.3 of this book is based).
144 Ibid.

But the more detailed breakdown in Table 12.4 shows that acute local shortages would develop. In South-East Lancashire, though there might be a surplus of sites on the less attractive Lancashire side of the conurbation, there would be an acute shortage on the more attractive Cheshire side.[145] Indeed it was estimated that building land would run out in the Stockport area around 1971 and in the Altrincham area around 1973.[146] Around Merseyside, land would run out on the Lancashire side about 1977.[147]

For the period up to 1981, the study concluded that: 'Shortage of land is likely to be almost entirely a problem affecting the Manchester and Merseyside conurbations'.[148] Even there, the four schemes proposed under the New Towns Act, plus a number of smaller developments, should meet the demand at least until the mid 1970s on Merseyside and up to 1981 in the Manchester area, though there might be a need in that latter case to designate some more land to cope with voluntary migration south of the conurbation.[149] This gave some time to do what was really necessary: prepare a long-term strategy for the future development of the whole North-West region, which would serve the twin aims of promoting economic growth and giving better living conditions to the people of the region. A special aim here should be to devote resources to the rapid renewal of some of the older towns.[150]

Clearly, the North-West Study authors thought, the decision to build a new town at Leyland-Chorley was an excellent one in relation to the aims of a strategy: for it would house people from the conurbations (up to 150,000), it was well placed to generate economic growth, and it would aid in the regeneration of existing towns.[151] Given this and the other commitments, it hardly seemed possible to think of another new town development at a great distance from the conurbations, at any rate for some years. Ideas for a new town in South Cheshire or in North Lancashire, for instance, would have to wait until later.[152]

Nevertheless, it would be necessary to think of other ways of housing the inevitable population increase from the conurbations, especially from Merseyside. Here, the study accepted the need for more developments at short distances, within daily travelling distance of the conurbations. One possibility was still North Cheshire, though the study recognized the special difficulties here.[153] Another was to regenerate the towns north of Manchester, though it was recognized that some of these places suffered from such disadvantages

[145] Ibid., pp. 84–5.
[146] Ibid., p. 85.
[147] Ibid., p. 86.
[148] Ibid., p. 109.
[149] Ibid., p. 110.
[150] Ibid.
[151] Ibid., pp. 110–11.
[152] Ibid., p. 111.
[153] Ibid.

that it was difficult to imagine reversing a long-continued trend of out-migration.[154] Yet another idea, a particularly attractive one, was the possibility of development on the North Wales coast in connection with a proposal for a Dee Barrage.[155] Lastly there was the notion of yet more development in the land between the two conurbations, where the new town developments at Runcorn and Warrington were already going ahead. There were difficulties here, but development in this zone would recognize its evident magnetism and its centrality within the region's communications network.[156]

THE PLANNING COUNCIL STARTS WORK

The North-West Economic Planning Council had already come into being, under the aegis of the Department of Economic Affairs, shortly before the North-West Study was published in July 1965. Automatically, therefore, the Study, provided a statistical basis, and some provisional policy conclusions,

Table 12.5

THE OVERSPILL PROBLEM, SOUTH-EAST LANCASHIRE AND MERSEYSIDE, 1964–1981, AS CALCULATED IN 1968

	South-East Lancashire	Merseyside
A Demand for additional dwellings		
Existing shortages, 1964	25,000	42,000
Slum clearance displacement	200,000	131,000 (slum clearance and other displacement combined)
Other displacement	11,000	
Natural increase in number of households	74,000	76,000
Continuation of trends in voluntary migration (1956–64)	31,000	33,000
Total demand, assuming an end to voluntary migration trend	310,000	249,000
Total demand, assuming continuation of voluntary migration trend	279,000	216,000
B Sites for new dwellings		
Sites earmarked in conurbation subdivisions	252,000	197,000
Sites earmarked elsewhere	35,000	10,000
Total sites available	287,000	207,000
C Surplus or deficit		
Assuming an end to voluntary migration trend	Deficit 23,000	Deficit 42,000
Assuming continuation of voluntary migration trend	Surplus 8,000	Deficit 9,000

Source: Strategy II, North-West Economic Planning Council, 1968.

[154] Ibid.
[155] Ibid.
[156] Ibid., p. 112.

for the Council's work. Thus, as in the West Midlands and the South-East, the Planning Council in the North-West had the benefit of at least a year's start because of the preliminary work that had been done within the government machine. Already, in February 1966, the Council was able to produce a tentative strategy, later known for clarity as Strategy I. It was supplemented and superseded by Strategy II, the Council's definitive policy proposals for the future development of the region, in 1968.[157]

An obvious first priority for the Council was to update the overspill calculations of the North West Study. The conclusions, as set out in Strategy II, are shown in Table 12.5. They can be compared with the study's estimates in Table 12.3 above. For South-East Lancashire the study had given a deficit of 45,100 houses if the out-migration trend ceased, and of 2,700 houses if the trend continued as in the early 1960s; the Council reduced the need to 23,000 if the migration ceased, and calculated a surplus of 8,000 houses if it continued. For Merseyside the study had given a deficit of 65,860 if migration ceased and of 29,360 if it continued; the Council's revised estimates reduced the deficit to 42,000 and 9,000 respectively. The main reason for the difference was the Registrar General's forecasts of future natural increase of the population, which had been reduced following the decline in the national birth rate after 1964.

This striking change, coming as it did within a very short period from 1965 to 1968, caused the Council to look again at the proposals in the North-West Study, and in its own Strategy I, for receiving overspill. The nearer-in developments, which were either started or in active preparation, should get first priority, the Council thought: they included the Skelmersdale and Runcorn new towns and the Winsford town expansion for Merseyside, and the Warrington new town plus the proposed Central Lancashire new town for South-East Lancashire.[158] Important here was the fact that because the supply of footloose industry was limited, a great deal of employment growth had taken place, and would continue to take place, on the periphery of the conurbation; on Merseyside, for instance, industrial development had been concentrated in locations like Ellesmere Port, Runcorn, Speke, Kirkby, Widnes, and Skelmersdale.[159] Some of these sites had excellent links with the nearer-in overspill schemes, better indeed, in some cases, than with the conurbation itself. But developments further out would not have the same easy accessibility to jobs. The Council therefore recognized that there was no longer the former urgency about two schemes in Strategy I: first, a proposal for development in the Lancaster-Garstang area of North Lancashire, that might have provided for an eventual total population of 130,000–190,000;[160] second, a proposal from Cheshire for development of a mid Cheshire axial town, running from north to south to include Northwich, Winsford, and

157 North West Economic Planning Council, *Strategy II: The North-West of the 1970s*. HMSO, London (1968).

158 Ibid., p. 41.

159 Ibid., pp. 41–2, 51.

160 Ibid., p. 54.

Crewe.[161] These should be kept under review and (in the Cheshire case), actively investigated, for extra new cities would be needed somewhere by the end of the century; but, the Council decided, they would be schemes of the 1980s and 1990s rather than the 1970s. Thus Strategy II confirmed the views of the North-West Study authors on this critical point.

A DISAPPEARING OVERSPILL PROBLEM?

The North-West Planning Council's Strategy II, produced in 1968 from analyses conducted in 1967, concluded that the overspill problem seemed to be marginally diminishing. A little over a year later, in the autumn of 1969, some observers in the region were beginning to wonder whether the problem was not disappearing altogether. The immediate cause was a report submitted to Liverpool City Council's Policy and Finance Committee, which indicated that the city might have to abandon a large part of its total overspill problem.[162] Behind this dramatic change in viewpoint, several important factors were operating.

The first has already been noted; it was the falling rate of natural increase of population in the region, which was leading to radical revisions of the total future population to be housed. The 1966-based projections for the region produced a 1981 population (allowing for migration) of 7,401,000; the corresponding 1968-based figure had fallen to only 7,115,000.[163] The second and third factors on the other hand represented new housing policies which the Ministry of Housing and Local Government had themselves developed and then encouraged local authorities to adopt. For good local reasons, they seem to have had most immediate effect on the great cities of the North-West. But it may well be that the effect will be felt more generally, throughout Megalopolis, in years to come. For this reason, they are of great importance.

One of these new policies was the emphasis on rehabilitation of existing housing rather than on demolition, which appeared in the 1968 White Paper *Old Houses into New Homes*[164] and was carried into law in the Housing Act of 1969. Since 1955, local authorities in the North-West had been outstandingly successful in clearing the hard core of slums; between 1955 and 1969, indeed, they cleared over 187,000, or 21·7 per cent of all the slums cleared in England and Wales, and after 1965 the proportion rose as high as 26·5.[165] But necessarily, this process has an end. Unfit houses were constantly

[161] Ibid., p. 53. See also *The Guardian*, 23 Jan. 1968, quoted in *Town and Country Planning Association Planning Bulletin*, 5/68. Cheshire had urged high priority for its scheme. See *Daily Telegraph*, 23 Dec. 1966, quoted in *Town and Country Planning Association Planning Bulletin*, 1/67.

[162] Cf. *The Guardian*, 29 Oct. 1969.

[163] Personal communication from Mr Kenneth O. Male, Cheshire County Planning Officer. The revised figure reflected both a reduced rate of natural growth and improved computation.

[164] *Old Houses into New Homes*. Cmnd 3602, HMSO, London (1967).

[165] North-West Economic Planning Council, *Housing in the North-West Region*. Mimeo (1970), p. 3.

being added to the list, but an increasing proportion of these would be capable of the rehabilitation treatment proposed in the 1968 White Paper. And while demolition and redevelopment automatically meant a big fall in population in most cases, the rehabilitation policy probably does not.

More fundamental, perhaps, was the combined application of two other policies, which was already appearing by 1969. On the one hand, local authorities were now enjoined to build to the standards recommended in the Parker Morris report, giving a standard of housing that must have seemed positively luxurious to many families in the North-West. Private builders were not placed under these obligations, and in the North-West they were constantly tempted to cut standards in order to keep costs down. A typical new three-bedroom house in the region, which in 1958 would have had 1,000 or 1,050 square feet, was by 1970 down to 800–850 feet. Such a house on a cheap site might cost only just above £3,000 to buy, which would involve a mortgage of £23·44 per month (or only £19·61 on the government's option mortgage scheme).[166] Yet on the other hand, local authorities were being encouraged to operate rent rebate schemes which meant that for those tenants able to pay, municipal rents might rise close to levels comparable with mortgages on the cheapest owner-occupied property. Faced then with the choice between a high-rent, Parker Morris-standard flat on a cleared inner city site and a cheap, minimum-standard house on cheap land outside the city, increasing numbers of people in the North-West began to choose the owner-occupied alternative. To some extent, this corrected an imbalance; for historically, the North-West had a smaller proportion of private building for owner-occupation than the country as a whole. And it can be argued that it was a perfectly natural and healthy trend; it produced some sort of equilibrium between the private and the public housing markets, and between in-city and out-city housing, so that people had a greater measure of choice to get the sort of housing, in the sort of location, they preferred. Nevertheless, it had extremely serious short-term consequences.

The most immediate was that Liverpool, and possibly other northern authorities, began to find that the demand for municipal property was sagging. They discovered that they could re-house a much greater proportion of their general waiting list, and even slum clearance cases, in existing council property which was falling vacant (the so called re-lets). Their need for overspill housing sites therefore fell correspondingly. Liverpool feared that if it continued with its present housing policies, it might actually have over 20,000 vacant houses by the end of the 1970s.[167]

Of course the important point is that the total overspill from Manchester and Liverpool was not really being reduced. Indeed J. S. Millar, Manchester's Planning Officer, calculated in 1968 that the total deficit of building sites in the two-city region, up to the end of the century, might amount to 600,000 even if Warrington and Central Lancashire new towns between them provided

[166] Ibid., p. 8.

[167] *The Guardian*, 6 Nov. 1969.

100,000 sites; a little over half the total deficit was in the Manchester area, the rest on Merseyside[168] (Table 12.6). What was happening in the late 1960s was a big increase in spontaneous migration into the surrounding country areas (Liverpool calculated that voluntary migration rose from 6,000 in 1968 to 16,000 in 1969),[169] with a corresponding reduction in the amount of

Table 12.6

ESTIMATED HOUSING NEEDS, MANCHESTER AND LIVERPOOL CITY REGIONS, 1964–2000

	Manchester city region	Merseyside city region
A Needs	Number of dwellings needed	
Existing shortages	29,500	44,950
Slum clearance, other redevelopment	294,700	145,400
Natural increase (to 1981)	118,750	114,450
Sub-total	442,950	304,800
Natural increase (1981–2000)	240,000	270,000
Allow 3 per cent vacancy	20,500	17,250
Total	703,500	592,250
	1,295,750	
B Available sites		
Local (including redevelopment)	314,000	250,500
Long distance	3,000*	29,350†
Total	317,500	280,000
Deficit	386,000	312,000
	700,000	
Warrington, Central Lancashire	100,000	
Final deficit	600,000	

* Town Development Act schemes.
† Skelmersdale, Runcorn, Widnes, Winsford.
Source: J. S. Millar, 1968, based on the *North-West Study*, 1965.

planned overspill for which provision was needed, either in new towns or in town expansions. The difficulty was that a great deal of public capital had been tied up in these schemes, in the expectation that overspill would be forthcoming. Cheshire, where several expansions and one new town were located, reacted immediately and sharply to the report of Liverpool's fundamental reappraisal of its housing policies.[170]

168 Millar, op. cit., p. 61.
169 *The Guardian*, 29 Oct. 1969.
170 *The Guardian*, 1 Nov. 1969.

Yet there are good grounds for thinking that the changed situation may persist throughout the 1970s. For one thing, future population estimates continue to fall, while it has long been known that there would be a slowing-down in the new household formation during the early 1970s, a product of a drop in birth rates during the early 1950s. For another, rising incomes and possibly lower interest rates are bound to encourage a greater proportion of people, in the North-West as elsewhere, to seek the tax advantages and the capital gains which come from owner occupiership. The result may well be that not merely Liverpool, but a number of northern cities and towns, have an actual surplus of municipal housing by the mid 1970s.[171]

VERDICT ON THE NORTH-WEST EXPERIENCE

This long account fortifies one conclusion, which our extended comparison of urban growth in Megalopolis had already shown: the history of urban development, and of the planning problems that arise from urban development, is very different in the major urban areas of Megalopolis. At first sight, this might seem surprising. After all, Megalopolis is only just over 200 miles long; its major urban areas grew up at about the same time, and they developed in what might seem superficially very similar ways; the history of housing and planning policies, as they have been applied from the national level downwards, has theoretically been the same. Yet in practice, the North-West displays such individuality as to seem in many ways unique.

The North-West's first distinctive feature is the sheer scale of the accumulated housing problem which the region faced in the period after the Second World War. Other parts of Megalopolis had inherited their share of slums from the Industrial Revolution; but no other cities had the 88,000 slums listed in Liverpool, or the 68,000 counted in Manchester, when the slum clearance programme began in earnest in 1955. To this must be added a buoyant birth-rate, which constantly exceeded the national average rate in its fluctuations upwards and downwards; this was a product of complex social and economic features in the region, but above all of the high proportion of Roman Catholics in the two major conurbations of Merseyside and South-East Lancashire. Consequently, though London's overspill problem was doubtless greater in absolute terms, the combined problem in Greater Manchester and on Merseyside must be counted the greater in relation to the size of the population involved.

A second distinctive feature, which was examined in detail in the first part of this chapter, is the region's distinctive physiognomy. Few other conurbations of Britain are quite as confined by the facts of physical and human geography as is South-East Lancashire on its northern and eastern sides. Merseyside does not have the same restrictions; but it is bounded by the sea on its whole west side and by first-class agricultural land on the north. As a

171 *The Guardian*, 1 Nov. 1969, quoted the fact that Salford had decided that it could maintain its clearance programme without the need for overspill.

whole, the North-West is not short of land, even though Robin Best's calculations show that it is one of the most highly-urbanized regions of Britain in terms of land use. The trouble is that the available land is mainly far from the conurbations, while land within twenty or thirty miles tends to be scarce.

The result is to make it more difficult to produce short-distance overspill schemes; and that in turn raises the question of the mobility of people and of industry. If many people are to move to overspill schemes far from the conurbations, that will mean that people will have to uproot themselves from relatives, friends, social, educational, recreational and purely sentimental ties and familiar backgrounds. And industry will have to detach itself from the complex interactions and economies which offer themselves in the familiar locations within the conurbation. In the North-West, there are good reasons for thinking that this will be exceptionally difficult. Socially, this is an old-established industrial community; the Industrial Revolution occurred here first, before any other region of Britain. The scheme of social and familial ties in the cities is exceptionally strong, extending as it has over many generations of urban life. Economically, of all the major urban areas we have examined in this chapter, the North-West has proved the least economically dynamic since the Second World War. One basic industry, cotton, has declined very rapidly, without adequate replacement, in many of the towns of South-East Lancashire. Other industries, like the Port in Liverpool, are not mobile – at least over any appreciable distance; as in this example, they may be manned by an old-established, well organized and somewhat conservative labour force. As compared with either London or Birmingham, it can be argued that the North-West has a smaller pool of industry which would be theoretically capable of moving out of the conurbations to distant overspill schemes.

There is a last difference, which is profound but which is extremely difficult to isolate or to prove. This is the character of local politics, and in particular the relationship between one local authority and its neighbour. We have already seen in other regions how much this may alter as between one authority and another. Birmingham's difficult relations with its neighbours, for instance, represent perhaps an extreme case. We do not find the same extreme in the North-West. Neither Manchester nor Liverpool, for instance, ever seem to have exhibited the same pride, or independence of spirit, as Birmingham. Neither would have ventured to say that nothing was wrong either with their city or with their past legacy of town planning, which Birmingham was always prepared to say with every impression of confidence in its case. It is surely significant that in giving evidence to the Royal Commission on Local Government in England in the late 1960s, both Manchester and Liverpool admitted the need for reform and proposed a two-tier system of metropolitan government very close to the one which the Commission eventually proposed (and the government accepted) for the major conurbations. Birmingham on the other hand refused to accept that anything was wrong with the local government system in Birmingham; whatever might be at fault with local government elsewhere, it stated in its evidence, Birmingham's was as good as could be obtained, and the only possible improvement would be to extend boundaries to give more people the chance of sharing in its excellence. Hence it goes without saying that the relations of Liverpool and Manchester with their neighbouring county authorities were more normal, and more neighbourly, than were Birmingham's with either Warwickshire or Worcestershire. Nevertheless, conflicts arose, particularly, as we have seen, between Manchester and Cheshire.

Essentially, these conflicts centred on two different concepts of overspill. As in Birmingham, though not to the same extreme degree, Manchester wanted short-distance overspill which would allow some workers to continue commuting into the conurbation, at least for a time; Cheshire wanted the pure version of overspill according to Howard and Abercrombie, with communities just far enough from the conurbation to be self-contained entities. Strangely, it seemed that Liverpool stood for the same conception of short-distance overspill, but that no one really opposed it, even in Cheshire: both of Liverpool's new towns, and some of the major town expansion schemes like Ellesmere Port, were essentially near to the parent conurbation. Part of the explanation may be the surviving history of bitterness between Manchester and Cheshire over the Wythenshawe takeover. More fundamental, undoubtedly, is that the character of the surrounding land was different, both physically and socially. Merseyside found reasonable amounts of land available in neighbouring Cheshire; Manchester did not. On the Cheshire side of Liverpool, there was suitable land alongside the Mersey, which no one was prepared to fight over; south of Manchester, where the land had acquired a very definite social character before the Second World War, the local interest was very much prepared to fight, either through the county council or (as at Wilmslow) on its own.

This gives extra point to the question of local government boundaries. Ever since the 1930s, Cheshire has feared depredations from Manchester; that undoubtedly explains in part its sensitivity over short-distance overspill. The Royal Commission on Local Government report, in 1969, advocated a metropolitan area based on Manchester, which would extend far into the tendentious area of North Cheshire; another proposed authority, based on Merseyside, took in the whole of the Wirral and an area as far as Chester and beyond.[172] This was precisely the solution advocated by Liverpool and Manchester themselves to the Commission[173] and it was endorsed by the Labour Government in the White Paper of 1970. Undoubtedly, it would mean a drastic resolution of future urban-county conflicts in favour of the urban interest; and it is significant that immediately after the Government had endorsed the main lines of the Redcliffe Maud proposals, the Conservative Party announced that if returned to power they would introduce a

[172] Royal Commission on Local Government in England, Vol. 1, *Report*. HMSO, London (1969), pp. 76–7.

[173] Royal Commission on Local Government in England, *Written Evidence of County Borough Councils*. HMSO, London (1968), pp. 92, 100–11.

quite different reform based on a two-tier system, as advocated by Cheshire and other counties.[174] While still in opposition Mr Peter Walker, who became Minister of Housing and Local Government and then Secretary for the Environment in 1970, was quite specific about one of the important reasons for this decision:

> The danger of drawing a metropolitan area as widely as some of these metropolitan areas have been drawn, is a relatively small rural area within a metropolitan area will be dominated by the major cities and towns, with the almost certainty (*sic*) – an understandable certainty – that these new metropolitan areas will make planning decisions to solve their housing problems by utilizing areas of rural land. I am not sure that this is good overall planning for the country.[175]

The right planning solution, he argued, would often be a new town at a greater distance from the conurbation. And that suggested that the boundaries of the conurbation authority should be more tightly drawn.

Elected in 1970, the Conservative Party made precisely the change they had promised. Their own White Paper on Local Government Reform,[176] published in February 1971, announced that the metropolitan area solution, with an upper level authority for plan making and transport planning and with most other powers reserved to metropolitan area authorities, would be retained for the conurbations. But in the accompanying circular and map, the boundaries of these metropolitan areas were cut back. In the case of the two Northwestern authorities, the new boundaries corresponded accurately to the boundaries of the continuously built-up conurbations; the green belts were returned to the counties of Lancashire and Cheshire, which were revived. Greater Manchester thus lost the farmlands of North Cheshire; Merseyside lost rural Wirral, the Chester area and Southport. Though the Merseyside new town of Skelmersdale was included within the Merseyside area, (a concession, presumably because of its nearness to the parent conurbation) the other Merseyside new town Runcorn, returned to Cheshire; while Warrington new town was included with Cheshire, where it had never belonged, instead of with Greater Manchester, for whose overspill it was intended. With more logic, the proposed Central Lancashire new town – which Mr Walker reconfirmed at almost the same time as the White Paper – became the logical centre of the new residual Lancashire authority.

Dropped from the 1971 White Paper, as from the earlier 1970 one, was any mention of a region-wide authority for planning purposes. On this point, both governments preferred to wait for the Crowther Commission on the Constitution, whose report was expected in 1973. Yet the revised metropolitan boundaries made the need for such a region-wide strategy all the more urgent.

[174] Ibid., *Written Evidence of County Councils*. HMSO, London (1968), pp. 8–15. Peter Walker, *Hansard*, 18 Feb. 1970, Col. 454–5.

[175] Ibid., Col. 451.

[176] *Local Government in England: Government Proposals for Reorganisation*. Cmnd. 4584. HMSO, London (1971).

One good argument of the Redcliffe Maud Commission for a widely drawn metropolitan authority was that it could take rational decisions about regional development without feeling too constrained to develop near the conurbations; but to do this, as the Commission recognized, it had to be very widely drawn. Having rejected this argument on the grounds that the counties were best guardians of the countryside, the new government had logically to provide some apparatus for resolving conflicts that might arise and for providing an overall strategy. This, they made clear in the White Paper, would best be provided by repeating the formula that had produced a successful result in the South-East; a joint planning team supported by the local authorities in concert, by the Regional Economic Planning Council, and by the central government. In February 1971, at a conference in Wigan, the decision was taken in principle to set up such a team for the North-West; and a month later Mr A. G. Powell, deputy director of the South-East Study, was appointed its director.

By the beginning of the 1970s, it might seem that some of the great planning conflicts of the postwar period in the region really had been buried in the past. The new towns programme, completed with the designation of Central Lancashire in 1970 and its confirmation by the new government in 1971, appeared to be more than ample to deal with any public sector housing overspill from the two major conurbations, without the need for a continuing programme of additional new town designations throughout the 1970s. If natural growth of population continued to fall, or even if it stabilized, and if the trend to private owner-occupiership continued, the whole programme of public overspill housing might indeed be reduced and cities would find it feasible to house a considerable part of their slum clearance populations within their own boundaries; though this depended on the future of differential subsidies for building densely on expensive inner-city land. At the same time, the tight conurbation boundaries announced in 1971 made it clear that the conurbations would get no easy relief by building in their green belts; public overspill would be rehoused in new and expanding towns which, in the case of Central Lancashire, might be as distant as thirty miles from the parent conurbation. That in turn raised the problem of attracting new industry to match population growth; and here the government made it clear that they had no intention of giving special help to the Central Lancashire town, though they had inherited the previous government's policy of helping the two Merseyside towns as if they were part of the Merseyside development area itself.

The major change that seems likely to come over the region is an increase in private migration from the conurbations into the county areas outside. Here, as elsewhere in the country, the question is whether the counties can make enough land available for the purposes without the risk of land shortage and escalating prices. And it may be that the new towns, especially those within easy striking distance of the conurbation, may be able to offer land on such terms that they can achieve the aim of building half their houses for sale. The difficulty may be to do that while still maintaining the good building standards and urban design qualities for which the new towns will want to be known. It seems clear that the trend to owner occupation in the region has been accompanied by a high proportion of very cheap houses; and these are not likely to be of a standard that the new towns would welcome.

PART FOUR

LOOKING BACK AND FORWARD

This Part consists of a single chapter – Chapter Thirteen. It tries to summarize some of the main conclusions of Volume One and to provide a link forward to the analysis studies of inter-relationships within the planning process, which form a major focus of Volume Two.

CHAPTER THIRTEEN

THE URBAN GROWTH PROCESS: A SUMMARY AND A COMPARISON

This chapter tries to draw together some of the main threads running through Volume One of the study. It starts by stressing the basic element of change in postwar Britain – population and economic growth, decentralization of people and then of jobs from the cities to their surrounding metropolitan rings, greater mobility – for which the planning system, set up to deal with a simpler, more static world, was ill prepared. Then it considers the conflict between city and countryside which developed in the 1950s, after the uneasy compromise between radical planners and rural conservationists had broken down and after a return to market forces in 1951–55. It shows how the 1960s marked a return to a search for more adequate planning at the regional and sub-regional scales, but how at the beginning of the 1970s, after a period of bewildering change, large question marks still existed about the future resolution of conflicts on land use. Finally it tries to emphasize the essential conflict between change and conservation in postwar Britain, and the way in which the planning of urban growth has in practice sought to resolve the conflict in the interests of the status quo; an assertion that awaits detailed documentation in Volume Two.

This chapter was written by Peter Hall.

INTRODUCTION

It is time to sum up. First through a detailed statistical analysis at different scales, then through an historical account of the planning problems and conflicts in five areas of major urban growth, this Volume has tried to present an anatomy of urban growth in England since the Second World War. The task now is to distil the important lessons. In particular, we need to identify the main features that have been more or less common to all parts of England's heavily urbanized main industrial axis; and then to distinguish those features which are special to one part of it as against another. A special aim is to identify those features of the urban growth and urban planning processes which need further, systematic study in depth – the objective of Volume Two of this study.

THE BACKGROUND OF CHANGE

The first conclusion must be so familiar, by this stage, that it hardly seems to bear repetition. But it is basic to an understanding of all that has happened. It is that the pace of change has been unprecedently rapid. Despite frequent complaints from critics about our sluggish pace of economic growth, urban England has witnessed a rate of change unparalleled in any era since the early Industrial Revolution; in absolute terms, of course, the additions both to population and national wealth have been much greater than then. The population of England and Wales rose by 9·5 per cent between 1931 and 1951, a period that included the sluggish growth of the 1930s, the delay in births occasioned by the war, and the postwar baby boom. Between 1951 and 1961, a period which included the short-lived downturn in births of the early 1950s and then the consistent rise in birth rate after 1955, it rose by 5·4 per cent in a decade. From 1961 to 1966, a period which witnessed first the continuation of the rise in births and then, after 1964, the beginnings of a fall, it rose 2·2 per cent. The pace of growth of urban England and Wales, if we adopt the most generous definition in terms of Metropolitan Economic Labour Areas, rose almost exactly in line with the growth of the population as a whole: an unsurprising fact when it is realized that these 100 areas contained between 93 and 94 per cent of the population during the period under consideration. Even the more tightly-bounded Standard Metropolitan Labour Areas, which grew more modestly than the population as a whole after 1961, added some 5½ million people to their populations between 1931 and 1966, 2½ million in the fifteen years 1951–66 alone. Consistently, over the whole 35-year period, the 100 Standard Metropolitan Labour Areas have retained between 77 and 78 per cent of the total population of England and Wales; with only some evidence of slippage in the 1960s, they have kept a constant share of the total growth of the population. And in terms of concentration of employment, the SMLAs have managed to gain a slightly larger share of the total over the whole period.

This growth has of course been by no means evenly spread across the country. Just over a quarter of the 100 SMLAs of England and Wales are found in and around London: forty more are found in a great conglomeration extending over much of the Midlands, the North-West and Yorkshire. During the 1950s, about two-thirds of the entire growth of population in the 100 SMLAs was concentrated either in the London group or in the Midlands at the southern end of the Midlands-Northern group; in the early 1960s the proportion was just under one-half. Seventeen out of twenty of the fastest-growing SMLAs in the period 1951–61, and fifteen out of twenty during 1961–66, were in the South-East. In contrast the metropolitan areas with the poorest growth records, both in the 1950s and early 1960s, were mainly in the North-West and Yorkshire. There was, then, a strong regional differential in the distribution of urban growth. But another important factor was size. The biggest metropolitan areas tended to have poor growth rates of population; and by the early 1960s, some of the biggest recorded actual declines.

It would be surprising if there were not a strong relationship between population growth and physical growth. New urban development, on previously unbuilt-on land, tends to reflect local population pressures. But population growth is not the only factor; especially after the slum clearance programme restarted in earnest in the late 1950s, urban renewal has been an important factor too. Its importance is that while population pressures have tended to be greatest in the South and Midlands, urban renewal, because of the distribution of the worst urban slums, has tended to be concentrated in the North. For this reason, the urban areas of the North have tended to have a much higher rate of physical urban growth, during the 1950s and 1960s, than their population growth record would suggest. Overall, however, the physical growth of the conurbations and cities within Megalopolis does not yet impinge very greatly on the rural background; for in the early 1960s, according to the Second Land Utilization Survey of Great Britain, less than 18 per cent of the total area of Megalopolis was developed while no less than 70 per cent of the 40-square-mile units making it up could fairly be regarded as almost untouched by urban development. This containment of urban growth is of course partly deliberate; it results from the conscious operation of planning policies since the Second World War.

Nevertheless, pressures for physical growth are real enough. Population growth in some areas, urban renewal in others and, in a few places, both operating simultaneously; rising standards of living and rising social expectations: all have contributed to continuing pressures for new homes requiring the development of land, at the edges of the existing urban area and beyond. It follows that the other characteristic feature of change in urban England, in the post-1945 period, has been a profound tendency towards decentralization in most urban areas. This made itself felt in terms of population earlier than in terms of economic activity; it made itself felt in larger urban areas earlier than in smaller ones. During the 1950s most of the Standard Metropolitan Areas were tending to decentralize people. But in most cases this was relative: both the central core area and the peripheral suburbs were gaining people, though the suburbs were gaining more rapidly. Absolute decentralization, marked by an actual fall in central core population, tended to be restricted to the big metropolitan areas of the North, where slum clearance was already starting to reduce the population of the inner urban areas. A minority of centralizing SMLAs was still to be observed, mainly in the ring around London; they tended to be very rapidly-growing areas, some of them based on new towns. By the 1960s decentralization was the general rule almost everywhere, and there were notable cases of absolute decentralization in the bigger northern SMLAs, where the slum-clearance programme was proceeding apace. Again, however, the typical SMLA was undergoing relative, not absolute, decentralization of people.

The pattern of employment change has been different: the decentralization trend set in later. During the 1950s, of those metropolitan areas which were gaining employment, a substantial majority were demonstrating actual centralization – rather over half of them absolutely, in the sense that employment was actually declining in the suburbs. But the early 1960s recorded a profound change: by then, the great majority of SMLAs which recorded growth in employment were decentralizing. It is safe then to generalize and say that while the tendency to decentralize population was already general by the 1950s, the tendency to decentralize employment only became general between 1961 and 1966. And from the detailed records, it is clear that the biggest metropolitan areas tended to decentralize employment earliest just as, by the 1960s, they were leading the way in experiencing absolute loss of population and, in some cases, employment. The largest metropolitan area of all, London, was already manifesting another trend by the early 1960s: its losses in population and in jobs were being balanced by rapid gains in a ring of separate peripheral SMLAs, contiguous to London in an almost unbroken ring around the capital.

It is necessary to emphasize these trends, because as yet they are not fully appreciated, either by policy makers or by the general informed public. They seem to show that with a fairly short time-lag, urban England is following the tendencies already so clearly manifested, and so well documented, in the United States. Rapid growth is accompanied by an outward push, both of people and of jobs. Partly, indeed, the decentralization of jobs is a lagged response to the decentralization of people; in an affluent society, decentralized residential population will in time generate local service jobs, tied with varying degrees of closeness to the residential population.

These overall trends result from large and complex movements. Overall, the pattern in many metropolitan areas of England's Megalopolis is a fairly clear one: longer-distance movements bring people into the cores of these areas, while shorter-distance flows take people out of these same cores into the suburban rings all around. These latter movements, in particular, seem to be leading to a greater social segregation of the population, since the white-collar workers – and increasingly the skilled blue-collar workers – find it easier to move out into the suburbs than do the less skilled blue-collar groups.

In the early 1970s, these changes are still working themselves out. We have not attempted in this first Volume to predict what future form and scale they will assume. But it seems certain that there will be continued and even increased pressure on space for suburban development. Even if future population projections have eased since the mid 1960s, the evidence is that household space standards are rising. As living standards increase, families are willing to pay more for houseroom. They find they need more room to accommodate bulky possessions. And because of changes in the life cycle (the migration of young people to higher education for part of the year, for instance) families find that they need a generous excess of houseroom, at least at certain times. At the same time, rising car ownership implies rising space demands for many of the local service activities in the residential areas, whether shops, schools, factories or clinics. The land use/transportation studies, in course of completion for major British urban areas during the late 1960s and early 1970s, have made it clear that by the 1980s, car ownership levels in suburban areas are likely to rise to the levels typical of North America in the early 1960s – that is, near universal car ownership. This will bring with it a profound reorientation in the pattern of people's activities, which will only begin to show as car ownership becomes a majority phenomenon in the course of the 1970s.

THE EVOLUTION OF PLANNING: FROM THE 1950s TO THE 1970s

These are the most important changes in the system of activities and land uses with which the planning system has to deal. The second set of conclusions concerns this planning system itself. It was set up at the end of the war in circumstances which suggested a very different environment from the one which actually manifested itself. The pace of change – demographic, social, economic – was expected to be slow. Change was regarded, in general, as a challenge to be resisted. The basic values were those of conservation of the existing order. Once-for-all changes were in order, but once they were completed the whole system would settle down in a steady state. The twenty-year history of planning, from the 1947 Planning Act to the 1968 one, is one of slow and sometimes agonized adjustment to a different order.

The adjustment was not made any easier by the politics of local government. Planning, in 1947, was set up within a framework which virtually guaranteed that town would be set up against country. This had already been a fairly explicit conflict in the 1930s, as rural land was threatened by the suburban tide. The system as created gave very considerable weight to the interests of the rural *status quo*. Plans were made by County Planning Offices in rural county towns, under the eye of planning committees representing the existing balance of interests in the county. They were implemented either by the same committees, or by delegated powers to local committees which were likely to be even more concerned to protect the existing order. There was always the right of appeal through the inspectors to the Minister. But the inspectors themselves were deeply imbued with the same values of conservation, which indeed were stressed in every official pronouncement.

It would not be fair to say that this was the sole strand in British planning philosophy during this period. There was another strand, which made itself powerfully felt in the late 1940s; the idealistic strand of socially inspired planning, best represented by the Town and Country Planning Association with its elaborate and well detailed schemes for planned urban dispersion. For a brief wartime and immediate postwar period, beginning with the publication of the Barlow Report and culminating in the legislation of 1945–47,[1] this strand of policy became allied with the conservative strand in a powerful double policy of rural conservation and planned urban dispersal. But the motives and the philosophies of the two allies were too disparate for this to survive. Planners and administrators of a radical persuasion, like Abercrombie or Reith or Osborn, were looking to a quite different political order after the war: an order in which the forces of the market would not merely be restrained, but in many cases completely superseded, by comprehensive planning. They saw a state of affairs in which the location of industry

[1] Chapter Three, *supra*.

would be determined completely by government controls, so that virtually all new industrial growth in the major conurbations would be diverted away to new communities; and in which the activities of the private speculative builder were subsumed, in the great majority of cases, by public Development Corporations and local authority enterprise. The Labour Government, during 1945–50, moved a long way in accepting this basic philosophy and in trying to implement it in legislation. But even it drew back at certain critical points: in particular, in its refusal to implement the radical land-management proposals of the Uthwatt report. And after 1951, the Conservative Government returned to power, determined to reverse the whole direction of this policy.

During the 1950s, therefore, an anomalous situation obtained. The Conservative Government, though elected on an anti-planning platform in 1951, proved by no means hostile to much of the 1947 legislation; apart from the financial provisions it did nothing to dismantle it, and in practice it sought to use it to implement certain policies. But noticeably, these were conservationist in character; the stress was on the negative powers, which the 1947 Act had given the counties. What was tacitly abandoned, in practice, was the radical attempt to by-pass the market. Political philosophy was obviously relevant here; but the unexpected rise in population due to the increase in the birth rate, which began in 1955 and continued until 1964, undoubtedly helped. Where this was accompanied by strong migratory gains, the result in certain cases was an unprecedented rise in population – over 1·1 million in the South-East and 440,000 in the West Midlands from 1951–61 – with which it would perhaps have been difficult to cope on the basis of carefully planned new communities. The private developer was brought in to fill the gap. He was released from the rigid limitations of building licensing; after the 1947 financial provisions were scrapped in 1953, he was free to make speculative gains on the land involved in development. At the same time the new towns programme was virtually abandoned; though the existing new towns designated between 1945 and 1950 were allowed to continue growing, no further new towns were designated in England between 1950 and 1961, and in 1957 the government went so far as to say no more would be designated. Trust was placed instead in the 1952 Town Development Act, which provided for voluntary agreements between exporting and importing authorities to expand small and medium-sized towns; but down to the end of the 1950s, the programme produced very few houses. Regional offices of the Ministry of Housing and Local Government were deliberately closed; no attempt was made to update regional plans.

Because of this very abrupt shift back to the market as a means of development, coupled with the absolute increase in the total output of housing, the production of new housing by the private builder rapidly rose. Though during the 1950s as a whole he provided a minority of all new housing in England and Wales (Table 13.1), by the end of that decade he was the main agent of new provision. This, in turn meant that the process of development control became overwhelmed by a pressure that had never been contemplated. Land allocations in the original development plans might be exhausted by the end of the 1950s or the beginning of the 1960s: in ten years instead of twenty. Land itself became a valuable commodity, to be traded – and hoarded. A system intended to deal with a minority of new development became responsible for the great majority of it, and this at a time when all the encouragement from the centre was for conservative holding processes against urban development. Small wonder then that the system nearly broke under the strain.

This strain in the system manifested itself dramatically, at the end of the 1950s, in such epic planning battles as that between Manchester and Cheshire over Lymm, in 1958, or the whole series of contests between Birmingham on the one hand, Worcestershire and Warwickshire on the other over Wythall. The cities were encouraged to build high and dense, though an increasing volume of research evidence showed that this was a highly uneconomic policy for the community as a whole. Nevertheless, they found it difficult to find land either within their boundaries, or through Town Development Act schemes, to maintain the momentum of their slum clearance and rehousing schemes, which they had embarked on in earnest with government encouragement after 1955.

The situation could not continue; and the beginning of the 1960s saw a pronounced break with the policies of the 1950s. In several different but interlinked ways, the search of successive governments throughout the 1960s was towards a more effective system of planning for conurbations, and for the larger freestanding cities, and their surrounding rural spheres of influence: the scale that has come to be known, popularly, as the city region. First there has been a whole series of attempts to provide overall regional frameworks for spatial planning for each of the major regions of the country, the scale which is now recognized as that of the economic planning region, or province. The series of *ad hoc* regional studies, published for regions like the North-East, the South-East, the West Midlands and the North-West between 1963 and 1965, was a first attempt in this direction. Then came a flood of studies and later strategies from the Regional Economic Planning Councils, between 1965 and 1969. Lastly, and perhaps marking a significant watershed, was the South-East Strategic Plan of 1970, which was the first plan produced jointly by a team of central and local authority officials and commissioned both by a standing conference of local authority councillors and by the Regional Economic Planning Council. This formula was emulated by the North-West in a study set up in 1971, and the government at almost the same time announced that it would be the general formula for studies of this kind in the future.

The second major trend of the 1960s, which also marked a pronounced break with the past, was the attempt to provide broad-based city region plans within the general framework of the regional studies and strategies. For this two things were necessary: first a change in the content of development plans, which would permit overall structure plans concentrating on broad strategies and omitting details, and second a change in the geographical scale at which such plans were produced. The first was provided by the recommendations of the Planning Advisory Group in 1965 and by their implementation in the Planning Act of 1968; but for the new plans to be effective, the change in geographical scale was also critical. As an interim measure the government encouraged the formation of *ad hoc* advisory plan groups, through co-operation among neighbouring local authorities; early examples, which have been mentioned in the preceding chapters, include Leicester-Leicestershire, Coventry-Solihull-Warwickshire and South Hampshire. Then it announced formally, in 1970, that in future such joint structure plans could be submitted directly for approval by the Minister. But this was essentially a second-best interim measure pending the complete reform of local government: a nettle first grasped by the Labour Government when the Royal Commission on Local Government in England was appointed in 1966, and

Table 13.1
HOUSEBUILDING, BY PUBLIC AND PRIVATE SECTORS, NEW TOWNS AND EXPANDED TOWNS, ENGLAND AND WALES, 1945–1969

	Public sector		Private sector		Total number
	number	per cent	number	per cent	
1945–50	577,864	79·1	152,757	20·9	730,621
1951–60	1,562,732	61·3	987,164	38·7	2,549,896
1961–69	1,210,715	41·6	1,699,394	58·4	2,910,109
1945–69	3,351,311	54·1	2,839,315	45·9	6,190,626

	New towns		Expanded towns	
	number	per cent	number	per cent
Date of designation – 1969	164,332*	2·7*	62,628	1·0

* Building by *all* sources in new towns including private building.

Source: Department of the Environment, *Housing Statistics*, November 1970. *Town and Country Planning*, January 1970.

culminating in that Body's report of 1969, its acceptance (in broad principle and in most details) by the Labour Government in a White Paper of 1970 and its modification in the Conservative Government's White Paper of February 1971.

Thus the broad trend of the 1960s was the reverse of that of the 1950s: it marked a return to positive planning for conurbations, large cities and their surrounding areas. But neither, it must be noted, did the 1960s represent a return to the principles of the late 1940s. The attempt to by-pass the market, and to carry through the great bulk of development in the form of comprehensively planned, publicly-executed projects, was not resuscitated. Indeed, overall the proportion of new housing provided by the public sector actually fell in the 1960s, as compared with the 1950s, as Table 13.1 shows. The result has been that instead of the great bulk of new development being carried out in new and expanding towns by public authorities, as the 1945 Government and planners like Abercrombie seemed to have assumed, in fact over the whole quarter century following the Second World War, the split between

Table 13.2

HOUSEBUILDING, PRIVATE AND PUBLIC SECTORS, BY REGIONS, 1945–1969

Region		Percentage of total housebuilding in:		
		Public sector	Of which new towns*	Private sector
South-East	1945–60	60·0	5·4	40·0
	1961–65	36·4	3·8	63·7
	1966–69	46·2	2·9	53·8
West Midlands	1945–50	64·3	—	35·7
	1961–65	40·5	—	59·6
	1966–69	49·3	1·7	50·7
East Midlands	1945–60	65·7	1·4	34·3
	1961–65	31·7	1·9	68·3
	1966–69	32·6	1·5	67·4
North-West	1945–60	65·9	—	34·1
	1961–65	41·1	0·1	58·9
	1966–69	46·2	2·1	53·8
Yorks.-Humberside	1945–60	70·5	—	29·5
	1961–65	43·0	—	57·0
	1966–69	48·5	—	51·5
Northern	1945–60	78·7	2·8	21·3
	1961–65	52·1	2·8	47·9
	1966–69	56·6	2·8	43·4
South-West	1945–60	63·1	—	36·9
	1961–65	28·8	—	71·2
	1966–69	31·0	—	69·0
East Anglia	1945–60	63·6	—	36·4
	1961–65	31·4	—	68·6
	1966–69	49·3	—	50·7
Wales	1945–60	76·4	2·6	23·6
	1961–65	48·5	1·9	51·5
	1966–69	49·9	2·1	50·1
England and Wales	1945–60	65·3	2·4	34·7
	1961–65	38·6	1·7	61·4
	1966–69	44·8	1·8	55·2

* Building by New Town Development Corporations only.

Source: Department of the Environment, *Housing Statistics*, November 1970.

public and private housebuilding was 54:46; while during the 1960s it was 42:58. Only during the period 1945–50, then, did public building truly dominate the picture. Furthermore, at no time did the new and expanding towns programme account for a substantial share of the total. Over the whole quarter century, indeed, the two programmes together contributed only 3·7 per cent of the new housing units built in England and Wales (Table 13.1). Though there were of course regional variations in the picture, as there were variations over time, it is notable that not even in the regions with the biggest overspill problems did the new towns programme loom very large. In the South-East it accounted for over 5 per cent of new units built between 1945 and 1960, but afterwards for less than 4 per cent; in the West Midlands it accounted for nothing at all up to 1965, and then for less than 2 per cent during the later 1960s; in the North-West it accounted for nothing up to 1960, for a mere 0·1 per cent in the early 1960s and for 2·1 per cent in the late 1960s (Table 13.2). These tables of course are related to totals which include urban renewal as well as new housebuilding on previously undeveloped land; and renewal, especially in the great Midlands and northern cities, became very important during the late 1950s and most of the 1960s as the slum-clearance programme gained momentum. But it must be evident that even in the case of new building, neither the new towns programme nor the expanding towns programme achieved the role which the planners of 1945 seem to have intended. This is an important conclusion from Volume One of this study, and in Volume Two, especially in Chapter Ten on the planned communities and Chapter Eleven on alternatives for urban development, we shall return to it in more detail.

We can therefore distinguish three quite distinct periods in the evolution of urban growth policy in England after the Second World War. First, the short period of belief in publicly controlled comprehensively-planned development, from approximately 1945 to 1951; second, the abrupt return to a free-market solution, from about 1951 to 1961; and third, the swing back to greater, positive planning-intervention at the scale of the city region, dating from approximately 1961 and extending up to the time of writing this chapter in 1970–71. Together, the initiatives of the middle and late 1960s have interacted to produce what promises to be a coherent and, hopefully, a workable formula for development in the 1970s and the 1980s.

SOME REGIONAL DIFFERENCES

Looking back at the history of these three periods in Chapters Eight to Twelve, it is possible to see that the application of the 1947 planning system, and the resulting balance of effects, have varied quite substantially from area to area within Megalopolis England. First, there were differences in the operation of physical containment. Around London, there seems no doubt that the original intention was to carry through a fairly thoroughgoing, comprehensively-planned solution: containment was to be accompanied by a radical policy of creating new communities. But that was compromised by unexpected population growth and by changing political philosophies during the 1950s; and the result may best be described as a mixture of a new towns solution and of peripheral growth of medium and small-sized towns around the conurbation. Around Birmingham and the Black Country, there was never the same wholehearted belief in the virtues of a comprehensively planned policy, at least in relation to new towns; Abercrombie himself did not originally propose new towns in his regional plan there. The resulting pattern has a considerable element of peripheral growth in the conurbation and, still more, infilling within it, with a belated and limited injection of new town planning in the wider region around it. Around Manchester and Salford, the result up to the mid 1960s could best be described as a continuation of inter-war trends: most of the growth of the conurbation had been absorbed within its own boundaries or by peripheral additions; there had been only a modest growth of freestanding towns, and no new towns had been started at all. After 1965 the designation of two new towns to take the Manchester and Salford overspill, at Warrington and Central Lancashire, brought an element of comprehensive planning to this area also, but in 1970 it was too early to see many results on the ground. The growth of Merseyside, on the other hand, contains diverse elements: peripheral extensions to the conurbation at places like Speke and Kirkby, the planned outgrowth of freestanding towns like Ellesmere Port, and comprehensive new town planning at Skelmersdale and Runcorn, designated respectively in 1961 and 1964. Outside these major conurbations, the larger and medium sized freestanding cities of Megalopolis England grew mainly by peripheral extension, though with green belt limitations which did not appear particularly restrictive in most cases; perhaps it would be true to say that here, planning orthodoxy did not seem to suggest the development of more distant freestanding towns as they did around London and, to a more limited degree, around Birmingham and Liverpool.

The solutions varied from area to area, too, in their location of new employment and hence in the patterns of commuting. Around Greater London in the 1950s, while some new jobs were created in the conurbation, the growth of employment was more rapid in the ring of freestanding towns around; after 1961, employment in the conurbation fell while the growth in the surrounding towns continued unabated. But around Birmingham, Manchester and Liverpool the pattern was rather different. Here, around 1959, many new jobs were created in the conurbations themselves, and there was particularly rapid growth at the periphery of the physically developed area (which might be outside the core of the Standard Metropolitan Area). Since 1961, the cores have tended to lose employment. But the resulting decentralization has not led to the creation of separate commuting systems outside the central metropolitan area as it has in the case of London. Whereas the archetype for the London region is a town like Reading or Southend or Luton, with large additions to employment created both by factories on the periphery and by increasing service jobs at the centre, the archetype for the Birmingham region is a town like Solihull, where a rapid population growth has given rise to some expansion of local service employment, but where a large proportion of the workforce commute to jobs in neighbouring parts of the conurbation. Except for Stafford, and to some degree Worcester in the West Midlands, and Chester in North Cheshire, the big provincial conurbations lack the equivalents of Reading or Southend: that is, they lack medium-sized, rapidly expanding freestanding towns which take a substantial part of the regional employment growth and form separate, largely self-contained commuting zones. While the development of South-East England is taking a polycentric, metropolitan form, the development of these other areas is still a simple process of suburbanization around a single urban core. And finally, the growth of employment around freestanding cities like Southampton, Portsmouth or Leicester even more strikingly follow this simple suburban model. Here, indeed, the tendency to decentralization of employment is weaker or, perhaps, more belated, than in the big conurbations. As in the freestanding towns around London, employment has been tending to grow in the cores of these metropolitan areas as well as in the suburban rings.

The result of all these differences, as between one area and another, is that it is very difficult to generalize simply about the operation of the 1947 planning system in actual practice. Round London, the system has put hundreds of thousands of people into suburban extensions of freestanding towns thirty, forty and fifty miles from the metropolis. Most of the breadwinners in these families work locally, commuting only short distances to the centre of the towns or to a peripheral factory estate or research establishment. Of the minority, often a very small minority, who commute longer distances, only a part go to London (mainly by train), the archetypal image of the long-distance, white-collar commuter. A bigger proportion go in a variety of different directions, generally in their own cars, travelling from one town to another within the Outer Metropolitan Area. In buying their houses, these people have experienced the effect of the land shortage in the home counties. They have paid more for an equivalent amount of houseroom than people in other parts of the country, and because of the scarcity of land, they find themselves occupying smaller house plots than their equivalents would have occupied ten years before. If they do commute by rail to London they will find that the cost of their season ticket has increased faster than the general level of prices and incomes during the 1960s, but if they commute by car to destinations in the Outer Metropolitan Areas, they will have found the reverse. And, when all this is said, it must be remembered that something like it would have happened anyway, plan or no plan. The living patterns and to some extent the job patterns would have occurred without a 1947 planning system at all.

Round Birmingham, the pattern has some similarities but many differences. The suburban estates are far closer to the periphery of the conurbation, sometimes even at the periphery, because the jobs are in the conurbation and the tradition of long-distance commuting is lacking, even for the middle class. The Longbridge draughtsmen or Birmingham schoolteacher commutes in from Solihull; the blue-collar worker at Fort Dunlop finds a Birmingham corporation flat in nearby Chelmsley Wood, an estate that invades the green belt. Only in the north, around Cannock and Stafford and Lichfield, is there a pattern which, in embryo, resembles that round London; and even there, the pattern is dominated by short-distance commuter moves into the adjacent conurbation. But the land shortage, and the rising prices, and the tendency for the speculatively-built housing to huddle together ever more closely on to each acre of building ground, are observable here as in the South-East. The real difference of interests, between suburbanite and ruralite (or exurbanite) is as great in Warwickshire as in Berkshire; it has been resolved in the same way.

Round Manchester and Liverpool, again, there are many differences. The geographical patterns of living, working and travelling resemble those of Birmingham rather than those of London. The pressure of population growth has been less; but it has been counteracted by the effects of massive urban renewal and slum clearance in the fifteen years from 1955 to 1970, so that the rate of occupation of the land has been even faster here than around London during the 1960s. Because this pressure came later than in the case of London, the necessary new town provision also came later. As a result these cities tended to run into conflict with neighbouring counties on the overspill issue during the 1950s, as also did Birmingham, which had a similarly large slum-clearance programme. The resulting difficulties have forced the major cities – even Manchester, which was most reluctant – to countenance a policy of building high and dense within the city limits. But also, just as in the South-East and the Midlands, speculative builders have been compelled by land shortage and high land-cost to raise densities on the plots they have bought at increasing cost. In all these areas, there can be little doubt about the identity of the main beneficiary. It is the rural house-owner, often himself an exurbanite, who maintains his rural view and his rural way of life.

Perhaps the most strikingly different pattern from any of those so far described is found around some of the freestanding cities, such as Leicester. Here, relationships between city and county seem to have been easier. Land was not so scarce and builders had quite generous supplies of it. There have not been the same battles on questions of public overspill. Land prices have not escalated in the same way and densities have not been forced up to the same degree.

PLANNING, CHANGE AND THE *STATUS QUO*

This relative mildness of conflict in the smaller areas however, only underlines its greater severity elsewhere. And here indeed is the central theme, if there is one single central theme, which has emerged in this first Volume and which must be analysed in greater depth in the second. There is an essential conflict, indeed a whole set of related conflicts, relating to the use of land in those parts of rural England that have come under the shadow of large neighbouring urban areas. These conflicts first began to appear in the interwar period, when suburban growth began in earnest around the major conurbations and free-standing cities. The conflict expressed itself with greatest force around the greatest urban areas, where housing conditions were poorest and where the need for overspill solutions was most evident: Greater London, the West Midlands, South-East Lancashire, Merseyside. It was the counties bordering these conurbations where the greatest alarm was felt: Berkshire, Surrey, Warwickshire, Cheshire. That the gulf was greatest here can partly, no doubt, be explained by the scale of the problem and the remoteness of the parties. But in part, like so many features of English life, the roots go deep into the sociology of the Industrial Revolution: the traditional groups in the counties felt threatened by the forces of the industrial city. For a time, between 1940 and about 1950, they made common cause with the radical reformers who campaigned for planned urban dispersion as a preferable alternative to no plan at all. When that solution was seen to involve fundamental attack on the workings of the land market, it was abandoned. The compromise that was then reached, about the middle 1950s, was not fundamentally disturbed afterwards. It was a compromise that profoundly favoured the conservative interests (we use the word without party political connotations) in the countryside. Though the balance shifted somewhat towards a more positive urban dispersal policy again during the 1960s, the main emphasis throughout remained a negative one: urban growth was viewed as an unwanted phenomenon which should be tightly controlled if it could not be abolished.

The main theme underlying this attitude, as we have seen, is the undesirability of rapid or profound change. This is not surprising as a slogan for a group which was securely in possession and which felt a threat to the *status quo*. What is surprising is the extent to which, over a long period, it has proved generally acceptable as a consensus view among opinion leaders and opinion formers. The so-called costs of economic growth, which became so fashionable a theme of commentators in the late 1960s and early 1970s, was in reality nothing new for Britain at all, novel as it may have been for the much more growth-oriented society of North America. It had been a constant theme among those who set up the 1947 planning system; avoidance of change was seen as one of the objectives of that system. In the theory, this was countered by the need for radical, once-for-all changes in the distribution of population. But even this was conceived, as we have seen, within the framework of a society where the pace of change was very slow. No one was prepared for the reality of rapid change which obtained in the Britain of the late 1950s and much of the 1960s.

This change it must be remembered, has been slow compared with most other countries. The rise in the birth rate lasted only a decade, and the rate of natural increase never approached that in parts of continental Europe or in Canada, for instance; the rate of economic growth was notoriously slow. Yet it was rapid enough to lead to renewed doubts about the consequences. Policies to restrain population were canvassed when the rate of population growth was plummeting of its own accord. The costs of economic growth were urgently debated at a time when the rate of economic growth was virtually nil. That these things should happen is itself the most powerful testimony to the strength of pure emotion on the issue. But, it has to be stressed, it was emotion on the part of the decision makers and the opinion formers, who happened to be among the more affluent minority of the population. They in truth, had most to lose.

The consequence - it is difficult to avoid the conclusion – is that those in possession sought to preserve the *status quo*. This was easier because as possessors, they could manage the political system. Within the county system of local government, by definition the newcomers had no power at all. The main thrust of county planning policies was towards restraining urban growth. In the case of publicly sponsored schemes to create new and expanded towns, the reaction was often one of blank refusal. In the case of development plan control for speculative building, it was restraint. With blessing from the Ministry of Housing, which defended the policy on the grounds of husbanding scarce agricultural land, densities of new housebuilding were systematically increased. This trend was incidentally reinforced by the shortage of available building land in many parts of the main urban axial belt, which forced prices up and encouraged builders to economize on space to the greatest possible degree. At a time when average number of children per family appeared to be rising, and the number and the volume of possessions in the average household was certainly increasing drastically, the available space to accommodate them in and around the home was actually falling.

Whether around London or around Birmingham or around Manchester, the effects of these policies can be clearly seen. There is indeed a new archetypal suburbia of the 1960s and the 1970s, which is very distinctive and very different from that of the 1930s. Houses occur far less often in the familiar semidetached form of the interwar period, far more often in the form of terraces (town houses, in the estate agent's circumlocution). Front gardens are pocket sizes of lawn leading directly to the front pavement, without benefit of a wall or hedge; a North American import via cinema and television, but well suited to tight space standards. Back gardens too may be well nigh non-existent; they are replaced by yard space no bigger than that of the typical Lancashire mill street of the 1860s. There is garage space for a small car; a bigger one might bring problems. Inside, this house may well have a single cramped living room for all the communal purposes of the family – eating, watching television, reading, playing with the children. Space for special purposes, whether indoor games for children or a noisy Saturday night party for teenagers, is entirely missing. So, surprisingly, is even minimal storage space; the baby's pram, even the child's bicycle, may find its way into the living room or the kitchen for lack of any other space. Inside as out, the space standards of this house are little better than those of by-law housing built a century before: it has a small bathroom and more electric points and a small garage; that is about the measure of difference. It is almost certainly smaller, and has less space around it, than the corresponding house that a corresponding family would have bought in the 1930s. Most oddly of all, though it will have been bought by an owner who probably regards himself as superior to the average council tenant, it may well be built to standards inferior to those which are mandatory for new council housing.

Perhaps only a few yards from the new estate, at most perhaps a mile or two, the open countryside extends uninterruptedly. Here and there stand meticulously preserved villages or isolated cottages, long since deserted by their original agricultural owners and bought by the more fortunate citizens of exurbia. Occasionally too, a small market town has acquired a reputation as the centre of the local gentry, and has spawned a number of new housing estates of a quite different character; detached houses standing in generous grounds, with double garages and perhaps a hardstanding for the third family car. The people who bought these houses have paid for the privilege; for the land they were built on was expensive like all the rest. Having paid typically three times as much for their house as their less affluent neighbours, these new entrants to the countryside become vociferous opponents of any disturbance of their *status quo*.

Rural England was of course always a place of segregation and of social status, where the social hierarchy was finely but firmly drawn. By and large, it has remained so. The more prosperous members of the old county society, joined by selected newcomers from the cities, have sought to defend a way of life which they regarded as traditionally their right. The weapon they have used, and it has been a powerful one, is conservationist planning. The result has been to segregate the less affluent newcomers as firmly as ever the medieval cottagers were. Even the houses provided for them, by the combined agency of the private market and the development control system, bear more than a passing resemblance to a more sanitary version of the labourer's cottage of a century ago. Their owners are victims of the policy; and as long as they lack effective political power, they will remain so.

But they are not the people who suffer the most. At worst, they, and their equivalents in the new towns, enjoy less space than they might have obtained in the conditions of the 1930s. But the system has at least provided them with new houseroom, whether for sale or to rent, at a price they can afford. It has provided elementary planning which makes sure that (subject to local and temporary stresses and strains) their homes are matched with schools for their children, public services like gas and piped water and main drainage and electricity, and public transport services. It has provided them with a level of environment which often falls far short of the ideals of the garden city and new town pioneers, but which is a reasonably healthy and pleasant environment for family life and the rearing of children. The groups who really lose from the process, in fact, are those who are left behind. These are the people who, for a whole variety of reasons – lack of money, lack of credit-worthiness, lack of information, lack of opportunity, lack of political power and influence – have been unable to gain a foothold either in the suburban owner-occupier market, or in the public-sector housing system which embraces the new and expanding towns. They are the forgotten minority of the system: the true victims.

These are assertions and impressions, awaiting demonstration and illustration and proof. Volume Two of this study is designed to probe deeper into those relationships and these consequences. It opens by considering, in much greater detail than has been possible in this first Volume, the objectives of those who created the postwar system of planning. Then it examines, in a series of case studies, the actual operation of the development plan and development control system in the counties. It continues by examining systematically the role of the developer in the process, and goes on to look at the whole operation of housing policies in relation to planning. It looks at the policy of creating planned new communities, and at the related policy of trying to decentralize work and home together. Then, in three concluding chapters, it seeks to pass a general verdict on the whole complex of policies. It asks how well the policies in practice fulfilled their objectives, where they appeared to go wrong, and who have been the gainers and the losers. Finally, from the viewpoint of the new system of planning that is being ushered in by the 1968 Planning Act and the local government reform, it looks at prospects for the future.

INDEX

THE CONTAINMENT OF URBAN ENGLAND

VOLUME TWO

THE PLANNING SYSTEM

Objectives, Operations, Impacts

THE CONTAINMENT OF URBAN ENGLAND

BY

PETER HALL
HARRY GRACEY
ROY DREWETT
RAY THOMAS

ASSISTED BY

BOB PEACOCK, ANNE WHALLEY, CHRIS SMITH,
ANTHONY BECK AND WERNER HEIDEMAN

VOLUME TWO

THE PLANNING SYSTEM

Objectives, Operations, Impacts

PEP
12 Upper Belgrave Street, London

London
GEORGE ALLEN & UNWIN LTD

Beverly Hills
SAGE PUBLICATIONS INC

First published in 1973

ISBN 0 04 352041 3 (George Allen & Unwin Ltd)
ISBN 0 8039 0246 8 (Sage Publications Inc)

Library of Congress Catalog Card No. 73–77182

Printed in Great Britain
in 10 point Times Roman
by Alden & Mowbray Ltd
at the Alden Press, Oxford

To the memory of
John Madge

CONTENTS

VOLUME ONE URBAN AND METROPOLITAN GROWTH PROCESSES

CONTENTS

VOLUME TWO THE PLANNING SYSTEM: OBJECTIVES, OPERATIONS, IMPACTS

LIST OF TABLES (VOLUME TWO)

LIST OF TABLES

FIGURES

PREFACE

This present volume may be read as a self-contained entity. But it also forms the second half of a larger work, *The Containment of Urban England*, which represents the output of a five-year study at Political and Economic Planning (PEP) into the processes of urban growth in England after the Second World War and the impact of the postwar British land-use planning system upon those processes. The two volumes have different starting points and different foci of attention. But it is hoped that read together, they will illuminate and reinforce each other.

Those who have read the first volume, *Urban and Metropolitan Growth Processes or Megalopolis Denied*, will know that its central focus was the process of urban growth. It looked at definitions of urbanism and of urban growth, arrived at new frameworks for the analysis of these phenomena, and presented a uniform statistical picture of growth and change in 100 major urban areas of England and Wales for the period from the early 1930s to the early 1970s. Then it turned to a detailed analysis of five extended areas of complex urban development, located within the most heavily urbanized belt of England: the area we have termed Megalopolis England, though this turned out to be more a useful framework of analysis than a real phenomenon in a physical sense. It studied changes within these areas in land use, in migration patterns and in socio-economic segregation. Finally, it recounted in detail the postwar history of development in each of these five zones and the impact of planning policies and planning controls upon it. In these later chapters the theme of planning was explicitly introduced. The final chapter of Volume One attempted to sum up the main conclusions that have been learned both from the overall statistical analysis and the detailed accounts.

In this present volume, by way of contrast, the main focus is on the planning system and its interaction with other actors in the land development process. The volume centrally tries to answer three questions. First, what were the objectives of the rather sophisticated system of urban and regional planning which was set up in Britain shortly after the Second World War? Secondly, how in practice did the system operate, especially in so far as it involved complex interrelationships with developers and with clients such as industrialists and intending house owners? And thirdly, what have been some of the principal impacts of the system, intended and unintended: on the house building programme, on the housing and land markets, on patterns of journey to work? What, specifically, has been the contribution of the new towns and expanding towns programmes to the total pattern of urban development since the Second World War? Finally, what sort of judgement can be reached on the system in comparison with what might have existed without it? What policy options exist for the future in the light of knowledge of the recent past?

Thus the stance of the two volumes is different. Whereas Volume One was concerned with urban development and urban growth, Volume Two is principally concerned with the processes that bring about that development and growth – above all the planning process. Whereas Volume One was concerned first with statistical analysis of trends and then with historical dissection of events, Volume Two is principally concerned with systematic deep probing of the forces which bring about urban growth, and of their interrelationships. Whereas the main input into Volume One was first geographical and then historical, the main inputs into Volume Two are sociological, political and economic. Whereas Volume One reaches provisional conclusions about the ways the urban growth process has operated, it is left to the end of this present volume to make a considered summing-up of the contribution of the British land-use planning system in comparison with what might have existed in its place.

A NOTE ON AUTHORSHIP

Both this volume, and its companion, were produced by a team which worked for four years at Political and Economic Planning (PEP). Of this central team, one (Peter Hall) was part-time, the others (Ray Thomas, Harry Gracey and Roy Drewett) were full-time members. The team was assisted by a number of research assistants, the most important of whom are credited specifically on the title page and in the Acknowledgements of both volumes.

The great bulk of both volumes was drafted by individual team members, usually alone, occasionally in co-operation. In each case, the authorship is clearly shown in the contents list and at the beginning of each chapter. These chapters essentially represent the views of their authors, who bear responsibility for them individually. Certain of the concluding chapters of Volume Two, however, were drafted collectively after intensive team discussion; and these can be regarded as the work of the whole team. Both volumes were edited for final publication by Peter Hall.

ACKNOWLEDGEMENTS

This five-year study (1966–71) would have been impossible without the help of two institutions which provided nearly all the necessary financial support. Resources for the Future, Inc., first provided a grant to initiate the study, simultaneously with the start of their own parallel study of suburban land conversion in the Northeastern Urban Complex of the United States; and they provided a one year supplementary grant to bring the study to a conclusion. The main finance was provided by the Leverhulme Trust. PEP is very grateful to both the Leverhulme Trust and Resources for the Future.

Dr Marion Clawson of Resources for the Future, who initiated and directed the parallel study, has been a constant source of advice and encouragement to us during the five-year period of both studies.

We owe a great debt to the advisory group of eminent individuals who gave so many hours to reading successive drafts of the manuscript and to discussion of it in regular meetings, as well as to others who gave informal help in designing the research and in reading and commenting on the drafts. Many were central and local government officials who cannot be thanked by name. We are grateful to them all.

Our particular thanks go also to many individuals and institutions who gave without stint of their time and expertise to help us with difficult technical questions and to make material available to us. Particularly we want to thank Mr Pearson and Mr Rossi of the Ministry of Housing and Local Government (later Department of the Environment) Library, and Miss Whale and Mr Grove of the Ministry's Map Library, and Miss Munro who was instrumental in finding many other land use maps from Ministry files. Librarians at the British Museum and the London School of Economics Library also helped us by prompt and efficient service in our bibliographic explorations.

We owe a special debt to Dr Alice Coleman, Director of the Second Land Utilization Survey of Great Britain, for making freely available to us all published and unpublished sheets of the survey, and for giving research space to our assistants. Without her generous help the analysis of the survey would have been impossible. Similarly, we wish to express our thanks to county planning officers all over the country, who worked to make available the sheets of their original land use analyses made as part of the survey work for the first edition of the Development Plans for their areas. Their labours alone made it possible to reconstruct the land use pattern of urban England at the time the 1947 Planning System was set up.

We owe another debt to the planning officers and their staffs for co-operating so freely in our survey of the planning system recorded in Volume Two of our study. Similarly, we wish to thank all the developers who took part in our survey of developers' decision-making processes.

One development company should be mentioned by name: Messrs. Wates Limited, who made a small supplementary grant to permit the exhaustive work of bibliographic preparation on the philosophy of the planning system, which was the basis of Chapter One of Volume Two of the study. We are indebted to them for this help.

The main research officers, who worked on the project during the whole or principal time of the study, are properly shown on the title page of this Volume. Without their unstinting work, often involving tedious and repetitive calculations, much of the foundation of the study would have been lacking. Other research workers, who gave valuable help to the study for shorter periods, include: Jeannie Drake, Paddy Hughes, John MacMullen, Sylvia Kasch, Netta Bloom and Mike Bristow. A special debt is due to Mohammed Hegazi and Elizabeth Razowska, who performed much of the detailed analysis of land-use patterns.

The majority of the maps were drawn by Mrs Kathleen King, whose speed and accuracy, coupled with a rare ability to spot imperfections in original drafts and to suggest improvements, greatly eased our task. Mrs Eunice Wilson, of the London School of Economics drawing office, gave us many hours of help on the difficulties of interpreting the First Land Utilization Survey, on which she had worked. Mrs Wilson, and Mrs Jeanne Marie Stanton of the same office, also drew a whole series of supplementary maps for the study, which are incorporated in these volumes. We owe a great debt to all these valiant cartographic workers.

The secretarial team at PEP bore an exceptional burden during the five years of the study in typing and retyping manuscripts amounting in total to many millions of words, often under severe time constraints. They include Mrs Ann Eccles, Mrs Alex Morrison, Miss Elizabeth Green (to whom we owe a special debt), Mrs Elspeth Waddilove, Miss Stephanie Purcell and Miss Barbara Livermore. Their task, and ours, was greatly eased by the always efficient and helpful administrative staff at PEP.

Magda Hall and Francon Whelan were successively responsible for the exhausting work of checking and editing for press a manuscript of over half a million words. Sally Burningham undertook the equally onerous task of checking the proofs for press. We wish to put on record our thanks for their meticulous care.

Lastly the team, and PEP, have one sad debt to record. John Madge, who as Chief Consultant to PEP was convenor of the research team, died suddenly in 1968 in the middle of our work. We dedicate it to his memory as our only appropriate mark of his contribution.

PH
RT
HG
RD

THE STRUCTURE OF THIS WORK

The study has been written in two Volumes, each of which consists of four Parts. The first Volume concentrates on the actual processes of urban and metropolitan growth in England with which the planning system has had to contend since the Second World War. It deals incidentally with the planning system and its impacts. Its focus ranges from the Megalopolitan scale, through the metropolitan scale, to the local area scale, but with special emphasis on the first two. Much of it is descriptive, even in those places where it is heavily statistical. It aims to document what has happened, leaving detailed explanation and discussion to Volume Two. Volume Two then turns to focus on the planning system: its main objectives, the machinery and the people who operate it, the complex processes of interaction between the main agents of development, and the chief impacts. Much of its focus is either at a very particular or a very general scale. It is essentially concerned with exposition and explanation.

THE PREVIOUS VOLUME

The first Part of Volume One is a geographical and historical introduction to the whole study.

Chapter One gives an overview of the world pattern of urban growth, and focuses on the concept of the super-urban-agglomeration, or Megalopolis. It tentatively identifies one such concentration in England, and discusses some problems of scale and definition that arise in analysing trends within it.

Chapter Two describes the processes of urban growth in England from the Industrial Revolution to the Second World War, with particular reference to those features which contemporaries identified as calling for more effective planning: the crowded, unhealthy nineteenth-century city, the spreading suburbs of the interwar period, and the contrast between the prosperous South and Midlands, and the unprosperous North, in the 1930s.

Chapter Three runs parallel with Chapter Two, and describes the evolution of the planning movement from its nineteenth-century origins to the report of the Barlow Commission in 1940, the subsequent wartime reports and plans, and the legislation which set up the postwar planning system between 1945 and 1952.

Part Two takes us into the heart of the study. Its main focus is a detailed account, mainly from statistics, of geographical changes in urban England in the period approximately from 1931–66, a period that includes the great urban spread of the 1930s, and the operation of the planning system after the Second World War. This type of analysis has been often and well done by American demographers and geographers,[1] but has been less common in

[1] Donald Bogue, *The Structure of the Metropolitan Community*. University of Michigan, Ann Arbor (1949), Donald Bogue, 'Urbanism in the United States, 1950', *American Journal of Sociology*, 60 (1955), pp. 471–86, Amos K. Hawley,

Britain. It has three chief geographical frames of reference: 100 *Metropolitan Areas*, a functional concept of urbanization borrowed from the United States; *Megalopolis England*, a super-urban-agglomeration of sixty-three SMSAs; and five *Study Areas* within Megalopolis, composed of groups of metropolitan areas, for more detailed analysis of growth and change.

Chapter Four is a purely technical chapter introducing some of these concepts, and discussing problems of measurement and analysis. The general reader may skip it, except for its conclusions.

Chapter Five is in many ways the heart of Part Two. It is a detailed analysis from Census statistics, of growth and change in the 100 metropolitan areas of England and Wales. These are urban areas functionally defined in terms of commuting patterns around major employment centres. The analysis demonstrates not merely a pronounced growth trend in most of these areas, but also a notable tendency to internal decentralization of residential population and, latterly, employment.

Chapter Six, building on Chapter Five, asks whether a Megalopolis can meaningfully be identified in England. It concludes that such an area, taking a notably linear form along the main urban and industrial axis of England from the Sussex coast to Lancashire and Yorkshire, is a meaningful and useful focus for the study of urban growth and the impact of planning, though in a physical sense the operation of the planning system has so contributed to the containment of urban spread that the existence of Megalopolis has been denied. It ends by isolating five areas within Megalopolis for more detailed study.

Chapter Seven analyses population, employment and land-use changes within these five chosen study areas. It is an essential preliminary to the detailed history of urban growth, and the impact of the planning system on that growth, in the five study areas, which forms the subject matter of Part Three of our study.

Part Three, therefore, focuses on the five study areas. For each, it presents a detailed history of urban growth since the 1930s, and of the impact of the planning system on that growth after the Second World War. As far as possible, this history is taken from official sources: the plans, reports and studies which form the plan-making activity in each area. A deeper analysis of attitudes, actors and interrelationships is reserved until Volume Two, Part Two of the study.

Chapter Eight describes London's western fringes: the western suburbs of Greater London, developed rapidly during the 1930s, and the adjacent home counties of Buckinghamshire, Berkshire, Surrey and eastern Hampshire, together with the County Borough of Reading. This has been an area of exceptionally rapid urban growth both in interwar and postwar times, and of strenuous attempts by planning authorities to control it since the Second World War.

The Changing Shape of Metropolitan America: Deconcentration since 1920. Free Press, Glencoe (1956).

Chapter Nine looks at another area of rapid growth, though on a smaller scale: South Hampshire, developed around the two cities of Southampton and Portsmouth.

Chapter Ten considers the impact of a major provincial conurbation, Birmingham and the West Midlands, and the neighbouring city of Coventry, one of the most rapidly-growing large cities of England in the twentieth century, upon the neighbouring counties of Worcestershire and Warwickshire.

Chapter Eleven, on Leicester and Leicestershire, in contrast recounts the history of a freestanding city of moderate size and its relationships to its surrounding county.

Chapter Twelve returns to the impact of conurbation growth. In this case, North-West England, there are two major conurbations, with centres only thirty-five miles apart. They have had a profound impact upon the neighbouring counties of Lancashire and Cheshire.

Part Four consists only of Chapter Thirteen. It tries to summarize some of the main conclusions of Volume One and to provide a link forward to the analytic studies of interrelationships within the planning process, which form a major theme of Volume Two.

THE PRESENT VOLUME

In Volume Two there is a shift of focus to the planning system created between 1945 and 1952. Its object is a systematic analysis of the system in theory and in practice. It looks at the objectives of the system as conceived by those who set it up, and at the machinery created to serve the attainment of the objectives. It then shows how in practice the system worked as a complex series of interrelationships between different actors in the development process – planners of all kinds, developers, industrialists and home buyers. It then turns to look at some main effects of the system on land values, on house building, on commuting patterns, on social segregation, and on the creation of planned communities. Finally, in a series of three interlinked chapters, it attempts to give a tentative verdict on the system and its results.

Part One is an introduction to the analysis. Its aim is to introduce and describe the system.

Chapter One examines the objectives of the system as they evolved in the minds of those who helped create it, over a long period from about 1898 – the date of Howard's classic *Garden Cities of Tomorrow* – to 1947, the date of the historic Town and Country Planning Act.

Chapter Two describes the planning machinery set up under the 1947 Act and associated Acts. It looks at the operation of the local planning authority offices and at the interrelationships between different parts of the machinery. It acts as an introduction to the detailed studies of development control which follow in Part Two.

Part Two is one of the central sections of Volume Two. It describes and analyses the operation of the planning system in practice by successively focusing on the major agents or actors in what is, essentially, a complex process of interaction among planners of different kinds; developers of housing, and industrialists; and the clients who buy the houses in the new residential areas.

Chapter Three is the first of two chapters on the role of the planner. Dealing with the control of new employment (especially manufacturing industry), it looks particularly at interrelationships between the industrialist and two sorts of planner – the central government planner concerned with administering the scheme of central control over factory location, and the local authority planner.

Chapter Four deals with the parallel control over new residential development. It focuses on private developments by speculative builders for sale, and brings out the complex and delicate interrelationships between the local authority planners, the developers and their architects.

Chapter Five introduces yet another agent in the system, the buyers of the new homes provided by the developers. From a sample survey, it considers their motives for moving and for their selection of their new home; their experiences there, their degree of satisfaction with the move, and their future aspirations.

Chapter Six, finally, focuses on the residential developer. It considers his land-buying decisions and his subsequent construction processes. It brings out the fine financial calculations that he must make, and the critical role of land prices in the calculation. Thus it provides a direct bridge to Chapter Seven.

Part Three moves towards the final conclusions of the study. It consists of a series of chapters which describe the main effects of the planning system on the pattern of urban growth and on related phenomena. Some of these chapters range outside Megalopolis to draw on additional experience in other urban areas of Britain.

Chapter Seven takes up a theme already identified at the end of Chapter Six; the remarkable rise in land values since the Second World War, especially during the second half of the 1960s. It considers how far the planning control system itself was responsible, and how far the Land Commission affected the trend during its brief life.

Chapter Eight logically takes up the pattern of housebuilding in relation to migration and household formation. It finds that the density of occupation, measured in persons per room, has fallen between the 1930s and the 1960s. But in the medium density ranges, this is due to falling size of household rather than rising size of dwelling. The chapter also supports the idea that rising land values have contributed to higher house prices.

Chapter Nine analyses the relationships between home and workplace. It shows that as population has decentralized faster than employment, the length of journeys to work has almost certainly increased.

Chapter Ten turns to the phenomenon of the comprehensively planned communities – the new and expanding towns. It concludes that the new towns have succeeded in being self-contained communities as their planners intended, though many of the expanding towns have not. But even the new towns have not achieved social balance: they have failed to cater for enough of the poorer unskilled workers' families who – as Chapter Seven has shown – have remained behind in the urban cores.

Part Four, finally, contains the conclusions of the study. It is organized in three chapters.

Chapter Eleven tries to summarize the essential functions of the planning system set up after the Second World War. It concludes that the most important of these was the control or guidance of social change.

Chapter Twelve turns to some concrete results of the system. Based mainly on the findings of Chapters Seven to Eleven, it identifies some of the most important as physical urban containment; suburbanization, or the separation of home and workplace; and rising land values. It compares what might have occurred under possible alternative systems.

Chapter Thirteen, finally, considers the relationships between planning policies and a wide variety of policies in closely related fields such as economic development, agriculture, housing and transport. It does so both for the recent past – the period from the Second World War to 1970 – and the immediate future of the 1970s and 1980s.

Our study ends without positive policy recommendations, for such have not been our aim. Rather, we have sought to clarify the objectives set by those who operated the system, and to see how far these have been attained in practice. We have been especially concerned to look beyond the surface language of policies, to see underlying objectives. We have been concerned, too, to analyse in detail the interactions between the objectives of the planning system and the reality of the world that was being planned – a world that often seemed to change faster than the planning system could adapt. From this analysis, finally, we have tried to evaluate – not in the form of a rigorously quantified cost-benefit analysis, but in a more general way – the effect of the whole system on the process and the form of urban growth. In this way, we hope that we shall give indirect guidelines to policy-makers and administrators in the future. For though the 1947 system of planning that we describe has technically been subsumed by the 1968 system, essentially its foundations remain the same; and the same agents, the same personalities, interact within it.

PART ONE

THE SYSTEM IN CONCEPT: ITS AIMS AND MACHINERY

This volume focuses on the planning system created between 1945 and 1952. Its object is a close systematic analysis of the system in theory and in practice. It looks at the objectives of the system as conceived by those who set it up, and at the machinery created to serve the attainment of the objectives. Then it shows how in practice the system worked as a complex series of interrelationships between different actors in the development process – planners of all kinds, developers, industrialists, home buyers. It then turns to look at some main effects of the system: on land values, on house building, on commuting patterns, on social segregation and on the creation of planned communities. Lastly, in a series of three interlinked chapters, it attempts a tentative verdict on the system and its results.

Part One is an introduction to the analysis. Its aim is to introduce and describe the system.

Chapter One examines the objectives of the system as they evolved in the minds of those who helped create it, over a long period from about 1898 – the date of Howard's classic Garden Cities of Tomorrow *– to 1947, the date of the historic Town and Country Planning Act.*

Chapter Two describes the planning machinery set up under the 1947 Act and the associated Acts. It looks at the operation of the local planning authority offices and at the interrelationships between different parts of the machinery. It acts as an introduction to the detailed studies of development control which follow in Part Two.

CHAPTER ONE

THE 1947 PLANNING SYSTEM: OBJECTIVES

This chapter tries to penetrate to the objectives of the planners who set up and then operated the planning system of the 1947 Act. It finds that the system had a heavy bias towards design-based plans, in which objectives were often subsumed in physical forms; so that in consequence it is often difficult to distinguish the real objectives, and so to obtain any good measure of performance. It distinguishes three chief policy elements – urban containment, protection of rural land and the creation of self-contained and balanced communities – and tries to investigate the rationale behind them in writers from Ebenezer Howard (1898) to the Barlow, Scott, and Reith reports (1940–46). Lastly it investigates an alternative concept of planning developed out of the social sciences and applied in recent years to corporate management.

This chapter was compiled by Peter Hall from drafts by Harry Gracey, Peter Hall and Ray Thomas. Basic work on bibliographic preparation was done by Malcolm Moseley.

INTRODUCTION

In trying to reach a verdict on the performance of the British planning system in the period between the 1947 and the 1968 Planning Acts, it is first necessary to try to understand what the objectives of planning were. This might seem a simple question to answer, but it is not. In the first place, the objectives were by no means clearly spelt out in the plans themselves; it is often necessary to imply them from what is said, and in the second place, there may well have been other objectives, which were not written out anywhere, and which have to be implied in an even more indirect way. Therefore, in this chapter we cannot rely wholly, or even principally, on statements on the plans themselves. We shall need to go behind them to statements made in the course of their public business by leading planners, to the type of education they received and in turn gave new entrants to the profession, and to their objectives as implied in the type of plans they produced.

PLANNING AND PLANS

We first need to make a distinction which may seem either elementary or perverse: between *planning*, in the sense of the planning *process* or *method*, and the act of producing actual *plans*. There is an ambiguity here, and it is expressed in the Oxford Dictionary definition of the verb *to plan*:

> make a plan of (ground, existing building), design (building to be constructed, etc.), scheme, arrange beforehand (procedure, etc.).

There are in fact two quite separate meanings here. One refers to the act of producing a design in physical form, whether of an existing or of a projected object. The other refers to a *method* of arranging a sequence of action in advance. In shorthand, we can refer to the two meanings as *physical planning* and *general planning*.[1] Now, it should be clear that there is no necessary connection here. A plan in a physical sense may be produced without the need to draw up a carefully co-ordinated sequence of actions. Conversely, such a sequence can be drawn up without its having a physical expression at all. The first requires the skill of the draughtsman; the second requires quite special expertise about the thing being planned, plus some skill in sequential logic which now often goes under the technical name, systems analysis.

This has particular relevance for the study of the subject which used to be called town and country planning, which is sometimes called physical planning, and which is the subject matter of this chapter and indeed of this book. For throughout the history of the subject, we find profound confusion and even disagreement about these two meanings of planning. Melvin Webber has argued that:

> City planning has not yet adopted either the planning idea or the planning method. It has instead internationalized the concepts and methods of design from civil engineering and architecture.[2]

Planning, in Webber's understanding, is a word that should be reserved for the *process*: it involves explicit goal formulation, evaluation of alternative futures and alternative future courses of action, a reliance on feedback of outcomes and payoffs; it is an ideal, not ever attainable fully in practice. The art of *physical* plan-making, on the other hand, is better labelled *design*.[3]

Most observers who have troubled to make this distinction (whatever the terminology they have used) have concluded that British town planning has had a heavy *design* bias. Donald Foley, for instance, wrote of British planners:

> They viewed the metropolitan community as having a spatial, physical form that could be grasped and reduced to maplike graphic presentation. In line with this outlook, they viewed planning as an activity dedicated to establishing a scheme for a future physical-spatial form and to fostering

[1] Cf. Peter Hall, *Theory and Practice of Regional Planning*. Pemberton, London (1970), pp. 1–2.

[2] Melvin Webber, 'Permissive Planning', *Town Planning Review*, 39 (1968–9), p. 278.

[3] Ibid., p. 280.

such other development and control measures as would best ensure realising the desired future form for the community.[4]

Thus, in Foley's terminology, British planning has tended to be *unitary*, built round a single comprehensive physical design for the future:

The programme . . . stresses the primacy of striving toward a positively-stated future spatial form as a physical environmental goal product. The plan is characteristically presented for a hypothetical future point or period in time.[5]

Such as approach naturally leads towards an emphasis on a desired, *idealized future community*. Thomas Reiner, yet another American observer of European planning, has defined such a community:

. . . a mapped representation of the total urban environment . . . deduced from basic assumptions about the good life, but only occasionally are these explicitly stated.[6]

Characteristic of such ideal community planning is the fact that:

. . . much of planning has been involved with the means necessary to reach predetermined goals rather than with developing a methodology for evaluating alternative ends or with proposing such alternatives.[7]

And behind the thinking is the half-explicit concept of what Maurice Broady[8] has called 'architectural determinism':

. . . that in the first instance it is possible and worthwhile to manipulate the environment, that the good man is a reflection of a decent and healthy environment.[9]

To an important degree, this emphasis resulted from the early experience of rapid industrialization and urbanization in nineteenth-century Britain. Observers saw what appeared to be a very close connection between a poor environment and a poor life. They rapidly drew the conclusion that the nineteenth-century city should be rejected and that a new sort of physical community, capable of producing a more desirable life, should take its place. So the real order of the proposition was stood on its head: it was no longer necessary to ask what the good life was; it was that life produced by the good environment.[10]

[4] Donald Foley, *Controlling London's Growth: Planning The Great Wen 1940–60*. California U.P., Berkeley and Los Angeles (1963), p. 56.

[5] Ibid., p. 56.

[6] Thomas A. Reiner, *The Place of the Ideal Community in Urban Planning*. University of Pennsylvania Press, Philadelphia (1963), p. 15.

[7] Ibid., p. 16.

[8] Maurice Broady, *Planning for People*. National Council of Social Service, London (1968), p. 7.

[9] Reiner, op. cit., p. 18.

[10] The connection with Victorian industrialism is stressed by H. Myles Wright,

Central to the concept of the ideal community is the rejection of existing communities and existing social forms. In this sense, the ideal community movement is ideological in the sense coined by Karl Mannheim,[11] as Reiner points out.[12] Yet, Reiner goes on to emphasize, the main impact of ideal community thinking on British planning was through Ebenezer Howard and the Garden City movement; and in a world perspective, what distinguishes their ideas is their relative practicality and their firm rooting in social trends that could be harnessed and exploited.[13]

PLANNING FOR LIMITED OBJECTIVES

The concept of an ideal community found a ready response from professional planners who would have to design it. We shall see in the next chapter that as in other countries, the planning profession in Britain from the outset had a heavy design bias: an obsession with plan design, in the form of a physical blueprint, rather than with planning method. Not surprisingly, it also lacked any tradition of research into the social and economic environment which it sought to control; until the second half of the twentieth century, the social sciences occupied an insubstantial part of the training of the average professional planner. Together, these features had a critical result. The obsession with design led to the idea that cities and regions were working physical mechanisms whose performance could somehow be improved by a better design, as if a city were a sewer or a region were a highway. This idea of course had an important element of truth in it; but it was only one element among many. Consequently there was an obvious tendency to define the objectives of planning, as well as the end results, in terms of a very limited set of physical criteria. This was fortified by the lack of any basis in the social sciences in two ways. First, planning had no rigorous way of formulating and discussing objectives of a social character – whether these objectives were sociological, economic, psychological or geographical. Thus there was no way of systematically sifting out objectives and of considering their interrelationships; the whole complex process of arriving at goals tended to be by-passed. And because there were no rigorously defined goals, there could be no question of rigorously defined criteria for evaluating their achievement or non-achievement; if you do not know what you are trying to achieve, it is impossible to measure how far you have achieved it. Second, and relatedly, there was no systematic way of analysing the social environment within

---

'Planning Ideas – the Ideal, Worthwhile and the Practicable', *Journal of the Town Planning Institute*, 49 (1963), p. 351. Cf. also L. Benevolo, *The Origins of Modern Town Planning*, Routledge & Kegan Paul, London (1967), *passim*; and Ruth Glass, 'Urban Sociology in Great Britain: A Trend Report', in R. E. Pahl (ed.) *Readings in Urban Sociology*. Pergamon, Oxford (1968).

[11] Karl Mannheim, *Ideology and Utopia*. Kegan Paul, London (1936), Chapter 4, *passim*.

[12] Reiner, op. cit., p. 29.

[13] Ibid., pp. 42–43.

which planning decisions had to be made. This meant that the planner had no way of dealing adequately with the complexities of the economy or society as they evolved. He therefore had no way of monitoring the relationships between his plan proposals and reality, except for the crudest indices of physical change; still less had he any hope of predicting these interrelationships for the future, to provide a guide to planning strategies.

The net result was that the objectives of planning were reduced in practice to a very short and simple list of criteria, which were wholly or partially physical (or spatial) in character, and which had only the most indirect relevance to any index of welfare such as a social scientist might have tried to produce. Furthermore, these criteria tended to be set out as absolute objectives which must be attained, rather than as a set of objectives which might be achieved in greater or lesser degree. Once again, the analogy with physical design is clear: a plan, in the sense of physical design, is expected to be realized as a whole, because it is well known that a house without walls, or a sewer without connections, is an absurdity.

These main criteria may usefully be classified according to the scale at which they operate. One, the idea of *maintaining the existing regional balance*, is by definition a criterion which operates at the *national-regional* scale, that is at the scale of the relationship of the major regions to the whole country. It has only an indirect relationship to our theme of urban growth, albeit an important one. The most important criteria for us operate at the *regional-local* scale, often known as the *sub regional* or *city regional* scale; they essentially concern the pattern of land uses, activities and investments within a small region. Here we can distinguish three particularly important, interrelated objectives: *urban containment*, the most important; closely linked with it, *protection of the countryside and of natural resources*; and closely linked in turn with the first, the *creation of self-contained and balanced communities*. Two other objectives may be viewed as subsidiary; they are the *prevention of scattered development*, which may be viewed as an aspect of urban containment, and the *building up of strong service centres*. Lastly, at the local scale British planning has had two dominant objectives, not easily reconciled: the enhancement of *accessibility* to urban functions and services, and the maintenance and promotion of a *high level of physical and social environment*. These two objectives have found their reconciliation in a *preferred urban structure*, which combines three features: segregated and hierarchical land-use patterns, neighbourhood planning, and a preferred range of residential densities. In turn, these highly physical design features may be regarded virtually as more immediate objectives of planning; and they will be discussed as such.

The objectives then were highly specified and physical in form. But underlying them, it can be argued that there was a deeper and more general social objective, sometimes explicitly voiced, more often implicit in the statements of planners themselves: the control and guidance of change in the interest of social stability and continuity with the past. The planners and those who created the planning system have been engaged in implementing a basic value in society, which has to do with the comprehensive control of basic social forces, such as the changing distribution of population and employment in and between the regions of the country, in the interests of conserving its basic social structure. As such, it will be argued in the conclusions of this Volume, planning has some responsibility both for the social stability Britain has experienced since the Second World War in comparison to other Western countries, and also for the relative economic stagnation experienced during the same period in comparison to the other advanced countries of Europe and North America.

THE REGIONAL OBJECTIVE

The first of our list of objectives is arguably the most basic and important, because on it the success of the others will hinge. It is the objective of preserving a balance between different parts of the country in terms of economic growth and population change, through the mechanism of controlling and guiding the pattern of employment. Strictly speaking, of course, this is not an objective that has to do with urban growth. But as the Barlow Commission in 1940 first realized, in practice it is inseparable from the urban question: the notion of controlling the growth and spread of the great conurbations is inevitably associated with the idea of promoting the growth of those older industrial areas which are outside those conurbations. The difficulty is that this duality is too simple: not all these older industrial areas are outside the conurbations, and if the argument for controlling the growth of London is admitted, then so, presumably, should the argument for controlling the growth of Glasgow. Nevertheless, by and large the postwar generation of planners saw the two policies – regional balance and urban containment – as neatly complementing one another.

For our analysis, however, the significant fact is that whatever the soundness or otherwise of the regional balance objective, the job of securing it was outside the control of the professional town planners who were trying to contain urban growth. It was the Board of Trade which was the critical influence in this field. The 1947 Planning Act itself required that the possession of an Industrial Development Certificate granted by the Board should be a prerequisite for all but the smallest factory building. The IDC itself certifies that 'development can be carried out consistently with the proper distribution of industry'. The implication here is that there is a proper distribution of industry, that it can be discovered, and that the Board of Trade officials can secure it. There can be little doubt that this power, put in central government hands in order to achieve a national objective, has proved far more important in practice than the professional planner's power to give or refuse planning permission. And the local planner has shown little sign of wanting to interfere. The National Plan of 1965, and the subsequent work of the Regional Economic Planning Councils, was at first seen in purely economic terms; physical planners were little involved, and seemed to express genuine surprise when (as in the South-East, with the publication in 1967 of a physical Strategy) the work of the Council involved a land-use planning element. Professional planners, by and large, have accepted the current interregional policies which are being followed.

This view is defensible. It can be argued that strictly in land-use planning terms, it is a matter of indifference how population is distributed between regions – though clearly, as our analysis in Volume One shows, population growth will impinge most heavily on land where the percentage of urban population is already greatest. But in any event, few would deny that the distribution of population between regions is important in social and economic terms. Those who have argued for a policy of control in the interests of regional balance – we can call them the Celts – point to the loss of economic activity represented by higher unemployment and lower activity-rates in the peripheral regions, and to the costs of congestion in the big conurbations. Those who argue that the policy is a mistake – we can call them the Saxons – stress the dangers of restricting enterprise and the unique locational advantages of South-East England. The point here has already been made; it is that there is no simple duality between regional decline on the one hand, congestion on the other. Berkshire is arguably less congested than central Clydeside; the arguments for aiding Glasgow have to rest on the waste of human resources through unemployment and underemployment there, not on the economics of congestion. In other words, the argument here is a regional rather than an urban one.

THE OBJECTIVE OF CONTAINMENT

The professional planner, therefore, only came into his own at a more local level: at the level of organizing and guiding the physical growth of cities and towns within any one region. And even here, it can be argued that the professional planner was merely an executive officer, exercising powers under the 1947 Act to implement broad policy decisions that had already been determined in the forum of national debate, and expressed in policy documents such as the Barlow Commission Report or the Greater London Plan. The verdict applies also, in some measure, to the lay propagandists of the Town and Country Planning Association, whose views essentially dominated that national debate; by swaying the opinions of the Barlow Commission during the years 1937–40, they shaped critically the whole series of events that led to the passage of the 1947 Act.[14] Their justification, in turn, might have been that their beliefs about objectives were fully worked out, and even given operational form, by the pioneers of the movement many years before. Thus we find a considerable paradox, on which more than one observer commented at that time.[15] The central principles and objectives of urban and regional planning were developed in England around the turn of the century, at a

[14] On this influence, cf. Foley, op. cit., p. 44; and also D. Foley, 'Idea and Influence: The Town and Country Planning Association', *Journal of the American Institute of Planners*, 28 (1962), pp. 10–17.

[15] F. J. Osborn, *Green-Belt Cities*. Faber, London (1946), p. 24. F. J. Osborn,

time when the modern social sciences scarcely existed. They then remained in a more or less fixed mould for over forty years, during which they had little practical effect[16] but increasing intellectual influence, culminating in the Barlow Report of 1940. From that, the influence had a critical effect on the way the planning system was set up at the end of the Second World War, and on the general policy objectives of that system: planning, when it came to effective power in England, was working with ideas that were over forty-five years old.

But as the Town and Country Planning Association campaigners argued so zealously in the 1930s, they were such good ideas. Howard's treatise[17] is distinguished by his understanding of social and economic trends, his foresight for the future, his flexibility of mind, and above all, by the hard-headed practicality of his utopia. As his chief follower, F. J. Osborn, has said, the chief defect of the book is that like many great books, it is apparently too simple to be taken seriously. The truth is that the simplicity and directness of the style conceal great breadth and subtlety of thought. The thought is extremely compressed; complex notions are reduced to shorthand slogans. Nowhere is this more clearly seen than in Howard's famous diagram of the Three Magnets, (Figure 1.1).[18] For here, surely, is the definitive statement of objectives in English planning philosophy. Modern writers on planning would put it all much more theoretically, and much more ponderously. Consequently, they seldom recognized it for the definitive statement it is.

Two of the magnets in the diagram pose the advantages and disadvantages of town and country, respectively; the third shows how a new type of settlement, town–country, can combine the advantages without the disadvantages. The point is that when analysed and reduced to the abstractions of modern planning jargon, the diagram is saying that the two supreme objectives of planning are *accessibility to opportunities* and *environmental quality*. Essentially (to continue in the jargon) individuals and households make combined work and residential decisions; in doing so they trade off increasing accessibility versus decreasing environment, or vice-versa. Accessibility is to opportunities, which are listed in the town magnet. They may be economic (*high money wages*, *changes of employment*), social (*social opportunities*) and recreational (*places of amusement*). But competition to reach these opportunities leads to costs, both privately imposed (*high rents and prices*, *distant work*, *excessive hours*) and socially imposed (*army of unemployed*). There are also, Howard recognizes, some specifically urban forms of amenity which represent the

Overture to Planning. Faber, London (1942), p. 11. G. Pepler, 'Presidential Address', *Journal of the Town Planning Institute*, 36 (1949–50), p. 2.

[16] Only two garden cities were built: Letchworth (1902) and Welwyn (1920).

[17] Ebenezer Howard, *Tomorrow: A Peaceful Path to Real Reform*, Swan Sonnenschein, London (1898), subsequently republished (1901) by the same publisher under the better-known title *Garden Cities of Tomorrow*.

[18] It is a pity that this diagram, like the subsequent diagram of *Social Cities*, cannot be reproduced in the rich colour of the 1898 edition. Someone could do planning (and planners) a service by reproducing the originals.

social benefits of economies of scale (*well lit streets*). But they are far outweighed by the disamenities (or, in the latest jargon, the disutilities) which for the most part are socially imposed on the entire population: *closing out of nature, fogs and droughts, foul air, murky sky, costly drainage, isolation*

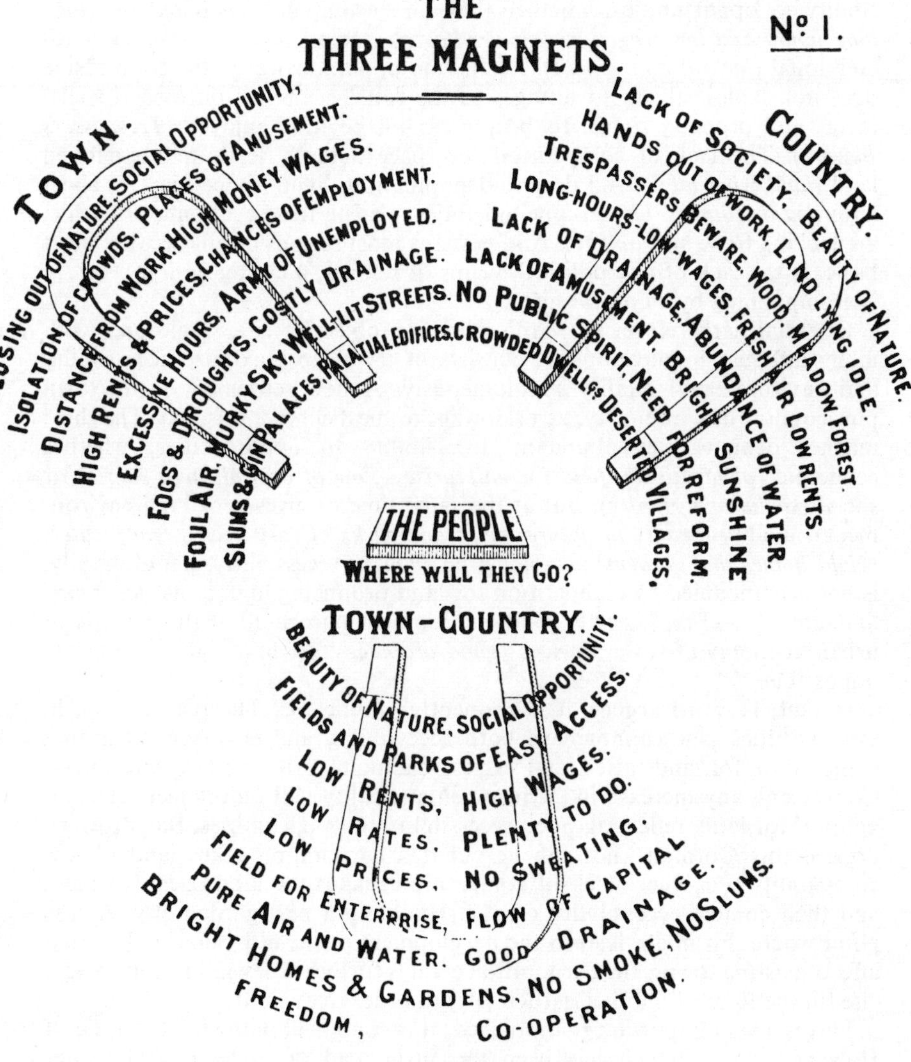

Figure 1.1 Howard's Three Magnets

of crowds. Though improved technology and management of the economy make some of these features seem less real today, Howard's first magnet still stands serious examination as a check-list of the benefits and costs of urban life.

The country, in contrast, offers benefits in terms of high environmental quality: *beauty of nature; wood, meadow and forest; fresh air; abundance of water; bright sunshine*. This is balanced by the countryside's lack of accessibility to opportunities, whether these are economic (*hands out of work*, *long hours and low wages*, *deserted villages*), social (*lack of society*), or recreational (*lack of amusement*). Furthermore, paradoxically, the countryside does not exploit all its advantages to the full, because of outmoded social forms and property rights. Its beauty cannot be fully enjoyed (*Trespassers Beware*). The lack of competition for space actually leads to abandoned land (*land lying idle*). And despite depopulation, living space remains short (*crowded dwellings*). Urban-type amenities, arising from economies of scale, are lacking (*lack of drainage*). And perhaps most serious of all, because most basic, is the lack of any political means of reform; a crying *need for reform* is accompanied by *no public spirit*.

Essentially, therefore, Howard's planning objective is a single one, with many different implications; it consists of trying to maximize accessibility and environmental quality simultaneously. A new settlement form, town plus country or garden city, can (Howard argues) achieve this feat. The third magnet demonstrates abundant accessibility to opportunities, whether economic (*plenty to do*, *field for enterprise – flow of capital*, *high wages*) or social (*social opportunity*). But at the same time, it gives very high environmental quality (*beauty of nature*, *fields and parks of easy access*, *pure water*, *bright homes and gardens*, *no smoke*, *no slums*). Accessibility, paradoxically, is not accompanied by competition for land producing high costs (*low rents*, *low rates*, *low prices*); nor is good environment purchased at the expense of urban economy-of-scale services (*good drainage*). At first sight, it appears impossible.

In fact, Howard argues, it is eminently practicable. The reason why, in existing cities, one cannot have both accessibility and environment is that competition for land raises land values, leading to a decline in environment. Conversely, any increase in environmental quality will reflect lack of competition for land, reflecting poor accessibility to opportunities. But, Howard argues, this Gordian knot can be cut if a corporation takes land of low accessibility (i.e. where lack of competition makes the land cheap to buy), and then confers accessibility on it by building a new garden city. At the point where this might lead to the development of the old vicious circle that affects existing towns, the corporation creates further accessibility somewhere else (in the form of another garden city) in order to avoid it.

This is a very important point indeed; it is contained in the final chapter of Howard's book, which has been too little read or understood by later commentators. Most people have understood that Howard preached the virtues of containment of cities in order to avoid the problems of congestion. This is true; but it is only a part of what Howard advocated. Central to his hypothesis is the concept, contained in his final chapter, of the social city;

a city which multiplies indefinitely, in a cell-like way, in order to distribute accessibility evenly and so prevent the imposition of the costs of accessibility. Later, in Chapter Eleven, we shall ask what Howard's suggestion would have meant in practice. At this point, it is merely important to recognize that Howard advocated containment only as an element in planning a city in a state of constant growth.

Later, in the 1920s and 1930s, that emphasis tended to be dropped. It is not difficult to see why. Howard wrote only twenty years after the high birth rates of mid-Victorian England had begun their long decline. As a Victorian, to him growth was the natural order of things. To his followers of the 1930s in the Town and Country Planning Association, in contrast, a general stagnation seemed to provide the framework for policy decisions. This meant that if growth were allowed to occur in one place, necessarily that implied a decline in another place.[19] The result was that Howard's ideas suffered a subtle yet profound transmogrification. Instead of being essentially a recipe for flexible planning, as their originator had intended, they were turned progressively into a fixed blueprint for the future: a design solution *par excellence*. Some of the most active propagandists of that period, indeed, positively argued that rapid change itself was bad, since it set up pressures which could not easily be accommodated in an orderly planned way.[20]

The changed environment was not the only reason, however, for the hardening of the garden-city concept. Partly, it reflected the influence of planners trained in architecture, who reinterpreted Howard's ideas in terms of blueprint planning. Abercrombie, certainly the most influential professional planner of the 1930s and 1940s, stated the objectives of planning quite simply in his textbook: Beauty, Health and Convenience – in that order.[21] In fact, Abercrombie was quite specific that urban containment was desirable on aesthetic grounds:

> The essence of the aesthetic of town and country planning consists in the frank recognition of these two elements, *town* and *country*, as representing opposite but complementary poles of influence. . . . With these two opposites constantly in view, a great deal of confused thinking and acting is washed away: the town should indeed be frankly artificial, urban; the country natural, rural.[22]

This was to be expected from a planner whose vision of his subject was that 'Planning is a conscious exercise of the powers of combination and design'.[23] But it is a long way indeed from Ebenezer Howard.

We have already noticed the long delay between publication of Howard's

[19] L. Dudley Stamp, 'Agriculture and Planning', *Journal of the Town Planning Institute*, 30 (1943–4), pp. 131–41.

[20] Cf. the standard planning textbook of the interwar years: Patrick Abercrombie, *Town and Country Planning*. T. Butterworth, London (1933), p. 25.

[21] Ibid., p. 104.

[22] Ibid., pp. 18–19. Almost the same point is made by L. Dudley Stamp, op. cit., p. 138.

[23] Abercrombie, op. cit., p. 12.

ideas in 1898, and their acceptance by the Barlow Commission in 1940. For a substantial part of that period, men who were convinced of the rightness of Howard's thesis were campaigning diligently to get them incorporated into policy. Perhaps the most influential, and least acknowledged, was Neville Chamberlain, who began to campaign for garden cities almost immediately on his return to Parliament in 1920, and who must be given the credit for having the Barlow Commission appointed in 1937.[24] During this long period of delay, it seems clear, ideas froze; and so did the very conception of the problem the ideas were supposed to solve. Thus when the Barlow Commission began to hear evidence, there was contradiction between the strictly factual evidence on conditions in the big cities, and the tenor of the argument of those who were arguing for containment.

Two examples of this may be useful. The Town and Country Planning Association's view was that large cities were unhealthy. It was repeated by F. J. Osborn in 1942, two years after publication of the Barlow Report, in a document originally published in 1918.[25] Yet the very long and careful memorandum, which the Registrar General put to the Commission, showed that mortality was by no means necessarily associated with urbanization; and recognized the international evidence which showed that cities could be as healthy as the countryside.[26] The Commission accepted the force of this argument, but nevertheless concluded that there were 'social' disadvantages to large towns.[27] Again, on transport, the Commission itself concluded that journeys to work were increasing in London,[28] but in fact the statistics of London Transport had shown no significant increase in longer journeys between 1921 and 1937.[29] It is hard to resist the conclusion that by the 1930s, Howard's forty-year old message had permeated to the extent that people accepted it emotionally, whether the evidence fitted or not. And this even applies to the august members of the Barlow Commission.

[24] On Chamberlain's role, see: K. Feiling, *The Life of Neville Chamberlain*, Macmillan, London (1946), especially pp. 54 and 307; and the Interim Report of the Committee appointed by the Minister of Health to consider and advise on principles to be followed in dealing with unhealthy areas, HMSO (1920), which Chamberlain chaired and which advocated garden cities. The decision to appoint the Barlow Commission was announced in March 1937, when Chamberlain was effectually Prime Minister. Earlier, as Minister of Health, he had taken the first decisive step towards the establishment of a London Green Belt. He had declared his belief in urban dispersal as early as 1915. Feiling, op. cit., p. 54.

[25] F. J. Osborn, *New Towns after the War*. Dent, London (1942), pp. 27–8.

[26] *Royal Commission on the Geographical Distribution of the Industrial Population, Minutes of Evidence*, 28th Day, 16 Nov. 1938, Evidence of Registrar General, paras 55–6. Cf. also the evidence of the Ministry of Health representative who admitted that large towns were not necessarily unhealthy: ibid., Q. 8051.

[27] *Royal Commission on the Distribution of the Industrial Population, Report*. Cmd 6153, HMSO, London, (1940), pp. 58–66.

[28] Ibid., p. 69.

[29] *Royal Commission Minutes*, op. cit., 12th Day, 15 Feb. 1938, Evidence of Frank Pick, Exhibit F, p. 372.

The objectives of planning, as they emerged from the report of the Barlow Commission in 1940, can be seen largely as a design solution which avoids certain disadvantages held to be inherent in the big city. These disadvantages were felt 'alike on the strategical, the social, and the economic side'.[30] On the economic side, though there were private benefits to employers through proximity to market, lower transport costs and available labour, these were counterweighted by the social disadvantages of high site-values, traffic congestion, long work-journeys which led to fatigue and hence loss of efficiency and output.[31] On the purely social side, there was the evidence about health (which the Commission admitted was unclear), about poor housing and about overcrowding as well as long journeys to work and traffic congestion.[32] Lastly there was evidence, which was presented in camera but which the Commission found convincing, that big cities presented a major strategic risk; in the fraught atmosphere of 1938 and 1939, this evidence may well have proved decisive.[33] But, it should be noted, the Commission's final conclusion was muted. There were disadvantages in 'many, if not in most of the great industrial concentrations'.[34] As we noted in Chapter Ten of Volume One, Birmingham had argued before the Commission that the West Midlands conurbation, and the City of Birmingham, did not suffer the deficiencies the Commission were investigating.[35] As a matter of fact, the Commission was only specific in one case: London, which presented a 'social, economic and strategical problem which demands immediate attention'.[36]

In its pure form, the idea of containment was peculiarly strong for the generation that created the 1947 planning system. Later, facts showed that many of the assumptions behind it could not fully be justified. It has been thought for example that Britain faced a period in which the level of population would stagnate. In fact population has continued to grow. It was also assumed that the high population densities of the inner areas of the cities were a social evil which only positive planning could combat. But later it became clear that population was decentralizing of its own accord – not as fast as postwar idealists would have liked, but certainly in ways which have made government intervention less necessary.

Other premises underlying the idea of containment have been modified by events. There was some agreement that the large tidal movement of people to and from work in places like central London was undesirable. But by the 1970s it seems less certain that this is forced upon people. For some, perhaps it is. But others are probably exercising a choice, and for them the objective is to improve the quality of the commuter ride – not necessarily to abolish it. Again, the tendency towards decentralization of employment in the 1960s

[30] *Royal Commission Report*, op. cit., p. 195.

[31] Ibid., p. 97.

[32] Ibid., pp. 58–70.

[33] Ibid., p. 103.

[34] Ibid., p. 195.

[35] See Vol. 1, pp. 509–10.

[36] *Royal Commission Report*, op. cit., p. 195.

– albeit more belated and less marked than the decentralization of homes – is altering the dimensions of the problem, above all round London.

Easy access to the countryside was yet another justification of the objective of urban containment. It was thought that urban man had particularly strong needs for fresh air and green fields. Peripheral suburbs were seen as barriers between the mass of population living near the centres of our major urban concentrations and the open countryside. But as the queues of cars leaving the major conurbations grew with the coming of any fine bank holiday weekend – many, perhaps most, on their way to the seaside, but not to the country – it became evident that the view taken on this point was too astigmatic. The problem was increasingly seen, again, as one of improving the quality of transport rather than as one of improving the distribution of land uses.

These changes in attitudes stem from a common cause. As compared with the interwar period, it is less possible to see most of the population as the victims of circumstance, who needed the hand of a beneficent planning authority to change the basic circumstances of their lives. Instead, there was an increasing tendency to think of people as free agents, making their own decisions in reasonably full knowledge of the likely results. This view seems to have reached its apogee about the middle 1960s. After that, one school of economists again began to stress the importance of externalities and spillovers – the costs which people's individual actions imposed on society as a whole, in the form of pollution of all kinds. Pollution, in this definition, was not just smoke in the sky or poison in the rivers. It was also the pollution of people *en masse* destroying the quality of what they all individually wanted to enjoy, whether on the Italian Riveria or in the English Lake District. In this way, at least in part, questions like outdoor recreation have come to be seen again as problems of arranging land use, as the policy of country parks shows.

PROTECTING THE LAND

By the time of Barlow, yet another consideration entered into the idea of containment. This was the need to save good agricultural land from unplanned urban growth. In a sense, this too dates back to Howard, and to the dark days of the agricultural depression of the 1890s, against which he wrote. But as the three magnets diagram showed, to Howard town and country were separate; their problems did not interconnect, though one set was a mirror image of the other. As Osborn has commented, Howard's ideas were upset by the Locomotive Act of 1896:

> What did the internal combustion engine and the electric motor do but vastly enlarge the noble company of carriage folk? The tram, the bus, the train, the tube, enabled millions to seek the eternally desired situation between town and country . . . the advocates of the garden city were overwhelmed by the new suburban rush.[37]

[37] Osborn (1946), op. cit., p. 38.

H. G. Wells in 1902 had been more percipient than Howard. His *Anticipations* portrayed an England in the late twentieth century, in which the diffusion of homes and jobs had caused the distinction between town and country to disappear. He gives an astonishingly accurate picture of the low-density exurbia now found at the edges of urban growth in the East Coast Megalopolis of North America.[38] It was the beginnings of this process which so alarmed observers in the 1930s.

Two main influences helped to identify this as an issue at that time; both were associated with dominant personalities in the great debate about urban containment. Patrick Abercrombie and a few others set up the Council for the Preservation of Rural England in 1925. It immediately began to wage a ceaseless war, under Abercrombie's chairmanship, against the invasion of the countryside by speculative building, and quickly built up a position as a force to be respected. What was interesting, in the CPRE's evidence to the Barlow Commission, was that the Council was by no means an advocate of pure urban-containment orthodoxy. Their representative actually told the Commission that in general, controlled peripheral development was preferable to a Green Belt and satellite towns; the danger of the Green Belt was that development would leapfrog it and start on the other side, threatening wider tracts of the countryside than before.[39] But since Abercrombie himself was an outspoken advocate of Green Belts, it is clear that at that time the Council did not by any means speak with one voice.[40]

The other new influence was the Land Utilisation Survey of Great Britain, and the personality of its director, the geographer, L. Dudley Stamp. As already outlined in Volume One, Chapter Four, the Survey started in 1930; by 1937 it was virtually complete, and Stamp was able for the first time to produce detailed estimates of the urban areas of the country, which have later been proved broadly accurate.[41] Stamp went on to produce estimates of the quality of the land, which were much used by a postwar generation of planners. He became one of the most tireless and outspoken critics of urban sprawl.

Abercrombie's influence on the conclusions of the Barlow Commission is clear; equally so is Stamp's influence on the conclusions of the Scott Committee on Land Use in Rural Areas, which reported in 1942.[42] Here, more clearly than before Barlow, a difference of opinion appeared among the rural preservationist movement. Both the Council for the Preservation

[38] H. G. Wells, *Anticipations of the Reaction of Mechanical and Scientific Progress upon Human Life and Thought*. Chapman, London (1902), pp. 60–63.

[39] *Royal Commission Minutes*, op. cit., 19th Day, 4 May 1938, Memorandum Paragraphs 27–8 and Q. 4769.

[40] Ibid., Q. 4861, where the witness admitted there was a conflict of interest on the CPRE Council.

[41] Cf. the examination by Robin Best in R. H. Best and J. T. Coppock, *The Changing Use of Land in Britain*. Faber, London (1962), p. 169.

[42] Ministry of Works and Planning, *Report of the Committee on Land Utilization in Rural Areas*. Cmd 6378, HMSO, London, (1943).

of Rural England and the Town and Country Planning Association were united in opposing urban sprawl into the countryside. But whereas the CPRE naturally stressed the protection of the countryside for the benefit of the countryside's inhabitants – that is, by and large for agriculture – the TCPA stressed the importance of decentralization of population into planned new towns:

> Agriculture and industrial productivity should be a main objective of town and country planning, but should subserve, and not have priority over good living conditions for all, which is the greatest of objectives.[43]

It was the Scott Committee's task to reconcile these differing objectives. In doing so, it can be said that they leant heavily in the CPRE's direction; and the dominant influence here was surely Stamp's. His hand for instance is clear in the famous paragraph which argues the Scott Committee's central doctrine of onus of proof:

> Where the land concerned is of a good agricultural quality and there is no dominant reason why there should be constructional development, the task of the Authority is simple – its answer will be 'No!' But in the case of some of the intermediate qualities of land, especially where pros and cons are at all easily balanced, or other sites are offered to the applicant, as alternatives. . . . it would be of very general assistance to all persons likely to want sites for construction as well as to the owner of the agricultural land, and the Minister of Agriculture himself, if it were common knowledge that agricultural sites would not be handed over unless a clear case of a national advantage was made out.[44]

As Wibberley has shown, postwar planning has never accepted this principle unreservedly. Yet successive postwar Ministry circulars stressed the need to avoid taking productive land for development where less productive land was available,[45] to consult with Provincial Land Commissioners, who had information on the land which the Ministry of Agriculture was prepared to see developed;[46] and to keep good agricultural land in food production and not take it for housing unless it was unavoidable.[47] One of these circulars is particularly interesting in its emphasis on saving land by higher densities. Admitting that the resultant saving in land was:

> . . . small, smaller than is usually realized by those who are concerned with the agricultural interest; but every acre matters[48]

it went on to call for an: 'ever present consciousness that land, even though its cost be low, is one of the nation's most valuable assets.'[49]

[43] F. J. Osborn (ed.) *Planning and the Countryside*. Faber, London (1942), p. 39.
[44] *Report, Utilization*, op. cit., p. 233.
[45] Ministry of Town and Country Planning, Circular 28/46, p. 1.
[46] Ministry of Town and Country Planning, Circular 99/50, p. 5.
[47] Ministry of Housing and Local Government, Circular 65/52, p. 4.
[48] Circular 99/50, op. cit., p. 8.
[49] Ibid., p. 8.

Here, in a sense, we find the purest statement of the views of the Scott Committee. The argument about protecting the countryside was essentially an argument about protecting agriculture as a priceless national asset, irrespective of the apparent exchange value of the land or of the produce from it. In other words, as Wibberley points out, it ignored the complex relationships between agricultural land and output. Increasing agricultural output may be associated with a diminishing use of land, as has occurred since the Second World War in England and as seems likely to continue being the case.[50] The Scott Committee, on the other hand, seem to have thought that the country would need all the land it could get; and Wibberley thinks that this was a reasonable attitude, perhaps, in 1942. Yet curiously, an eminent economist on the Scott Committee put the opposite case in an ably-argued minority report. Professor S. R. Dennison made precisely the point Wibberley put nearly two decades later: that a prosperous agriculture did not necessarily mean a large traditional agriculture; prosperity entailed efficiency, which might mean less workers per acre. Protection of the land would restrict the dispersion of industry into the countryside, which might help raise real incomes and so help pay for the expensive job of providing rural services to dispersed rural communities. In short, Dennison argued, the majority report ignored *how much* was to be paid for preserving amenity; and *who* was to pay this price.[51] The argument was striking and forceful; but it was ignored. However, it does allow us to identify the real nature of the Scott Committee's objectives.

Essentially, these objectives were not economic at all; it appears clear that the majority did not understand, or did not care to understand, the relatively elementary economic arguments that Dennison put to them. The objective was *social*: the preservation of a traditional way of life, and a traditional economy, *whatever the cost*. A subsidiary argument, perhaps, was *aesthetic*: there was a bonus in the preservation of a traditional countryside, for the benefit of town dweller and country dweller alike. But there could be no doubt that the main beneficiaries were the existing country dwellers; and that the price would be paid, in one way or another, by the townsmen who constituted 80 per cent of the population. This case was upheld by appealing to a 'national interest' which required the preservation of traditional farming patterns. Stamp, in particular, constantly referred to this concept of the national wellbeing as justifying the maintenance of traditional patterns:

> Whereas in the past the power of the purse of the individual has been almost the sole deciding factor, in the future it is the balance of a national interest which should be dominant. In view of the fact that land use in this country is the result of the action and interaction of a wide variety of factors there are usually very good reasons for the existing use of land and for this

[50] G. P. Wibberley, *Pressures on Britain's Land Resources*. Loughborough, Nottingham University School of Agriculture (1965), pp. 5–8.

[51] *Report, Utilization*, op. cit., pp. 105, 110–11, 113–14.

> reason if for no other the onus of proof should be upon the proposed change of uses. . . .[52]

It is hard to resist the conclusion that the objectives were not rational in a strict sense. They were mystical. In the special circumstances of a major war, that is perhaps understandable. But the effects were felt long after the war was over. The most important was to give the new planning system a pronounced preservationist bias. Those who operated the system in the counties accepted, in effect, the value judgements of the Scott Committee.

THE CHANGING GREEN BELT CONCEPT

The notion of urban containment, and the notion of rural preservation, come together in the concept of the green belt. In the history of the green belt idea, and in particular in its changing justification and changing form, we can find perhaps the most accurate idea of planning objectives as they were seen by the founders of the British planning system during the 1930s and 1940s.

There are several possible *objectives* of green belt policy. One is pure containment: the idea of stopping towns growing any larger. Another is to give adequate access to the countryside for recreation of townspeople. A third is the protectionist argument: to preserve agriculture and a rural way of life. The first two of these can be presented largely as giving advantages to townspeople; the third as a policy in the interests of countryfolk. There are also several different *forms* of green belt. At one extreme, a narrow green belt (perhaps even discontinuous) can be reserved to provide for the recreational use of the population and perhaps to provide some simple notion of containment. At the other extreme, the countryside can be preserved *in toto*, with urban development allowed at intervals against a green background. Between these two extremes are all forms of green belt which are wider than the narrow park reservation, yet less than the reservation of the whole countryside. The forms, necessarily, are associated with the justifications. A planner concerned with the recreational needs of townspeople will stress the park strip. A planner concerned with protection of a rural way of life will stress the preservation of the countryside as a whole.

The true inventor of the green belt in modern planning theory was of course Ebenezer Howard. And in his view, as we have already seen, there was no conflict between the needs of the countryside and the needs of the town. The disutilities of urban growth were imposed on the townspeople themselves; similarly the lack of accessibility of the countryside imposed cost on rural dwellers. A garden city policy resolved both problems simultaneously. In this reconciliation, the green belt simultaneously restricted the growth of any one urban unit, and provided the countryside with a ready urban market close at hand. But Howard's particular concept of the green belt should be

[52] L. Dudley Stamp, *The Land of Britain: Its Use and Misuse*. Longmans, London (1948), p. 432.

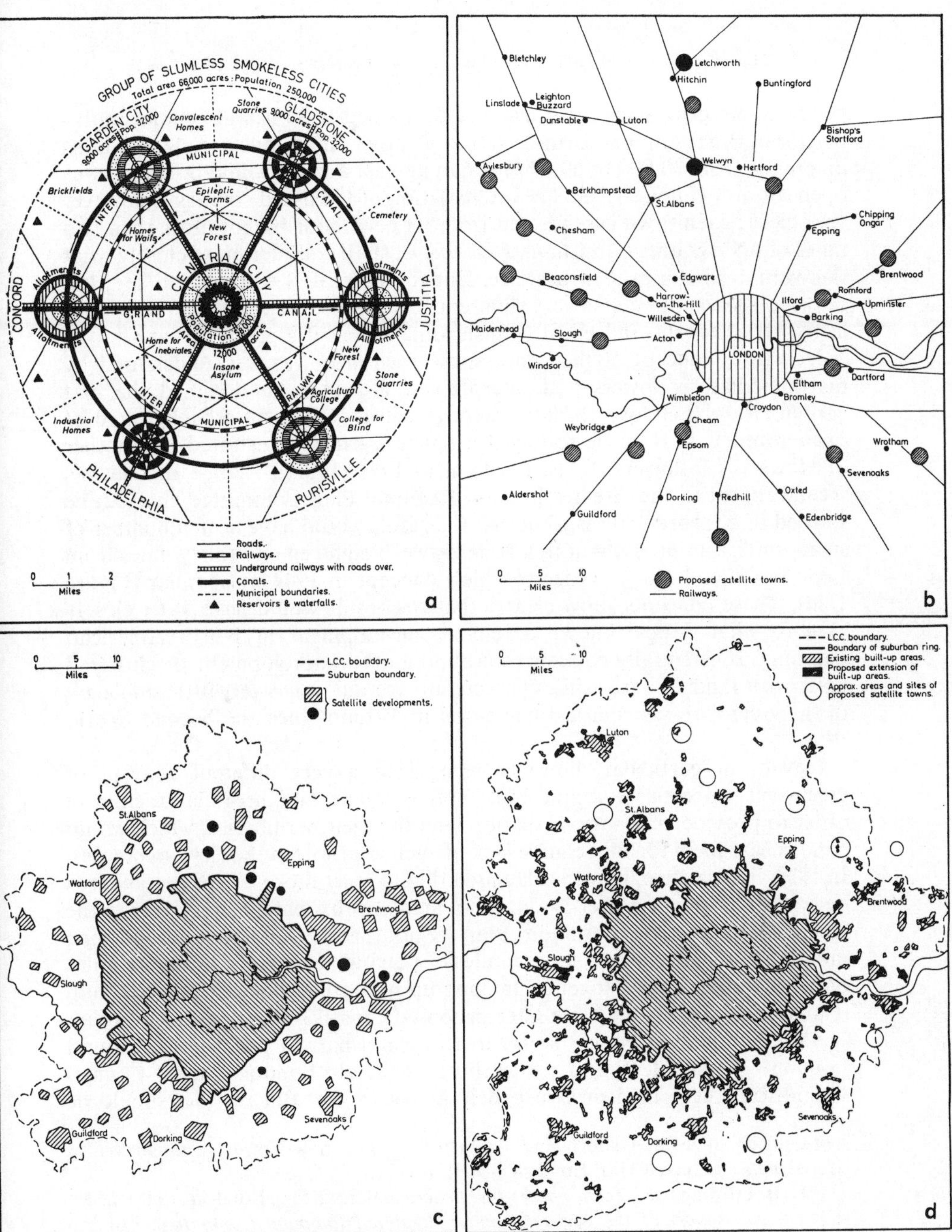

Figure 1.2 (a) Howard's Social Cities
(b) Purdom's Diagram of Satellite Cities
(c) Unwin's Diagram of Satellite Cities
(d) Abercrombie's Diagram of Satellite Cities

carefully noticed. Since his social city developed by constant cellular multiplication, the result was a whole series of rather small towns (ranging, in his diagrams, from 30,000 to 60,000 people) against a background of continuous open country (Figure 1.2a). The intercalation of town and country is however very close; each town is separated from its neighbour by not more than two miles of open country. In Chapter Eleven we shall consider more closely what this would have meant in practice. But for now, it is sufficient to say that Howard's Green Belt was very different from the concept as it is now popularly used. Perhaps, indeed, it is misleading to call it a green belt at all.

Howard's concept of the continuous green area was well understood by his immediate followers and interpreters. Unwin, who designed the first garden city of Letchworth, later described it as 'towns on a background of open country'.[53] Here he followed a concept earlier illustrated by another of Howard's followers, C. B. Purdom, in 1921 (Figure 1.2b).[54] In Unwin's second report to the Greater London Regional Plan Committee, in 1932, he showed in a theoretical diagram that the result would have been a number of small units, scattered about in a zone between eighteen and thirty miles from London (Figure 1.2c).[55] Abercrombie's concept in 1944 was similar (Figure 1.2d). These concepts show clearly that the result would have been closely akin to what is now known as cluster development in North American planning. It essentially consists of grouping urban development in clustered units with land of a park-like character all around; it has very little similarity to the green belt concept as understood in Britain since the Second World War.

Unwin, in particular, however recognized a very different concept of green belt—albeit as a second best. This was land bought by large cities in order to provide necessary recreation land for their peripheries, which would compensate them for the relative lack of such land within the city boundaries. In 1929, for instance, Unwin calculated that to meet the open-space standards he had laid down, Greater London (an area approximately equivalent to the Abercrombie Greater London Plan region, and containing about nine million people) needed 63 square miles of playing fields and 143 square miles of general open space, together making up more than one-tenth of the total land-area of the region.[56] He later proposed (in 1933) that land to make up this total should be bought so far as to form a narrow green girdle around London[57] (Figure 1.3); and it was this that the old London County Council sought to achieve in their Green Belt Act of 1938.[58] But the fact should be

[53] Quoted by F. J. Osborn and A. Whittick, *The New Towns: The Answer to Megalopolis*. Leonard Hill, London (1969), p. 134.

[54] C. B. Purdom (ed.) *Town Theory and Practice*. Benn Bros., London (1921), p. 32.

[55] *Second Report of the Greater London Regional Planning Committee*. London (1933), following p. 32.

[56] *First Report of the Greater London Regional Plan Committee*. London (1929), p. 16.

[57] *Second Report*, op. cit., p. 32.

[58] David Thomas, *London's Green Belt*. Faber, London (1970), pp. 80–3.

stressed that to Unwin, this was very much a second best; as a follower of Howard, he believed that all the land round satellite cities should be owned by those cities.

The pure Howard gospel, as preached by the Town and Country Planning Association, in effect involved a much greater degree of urban spread on a

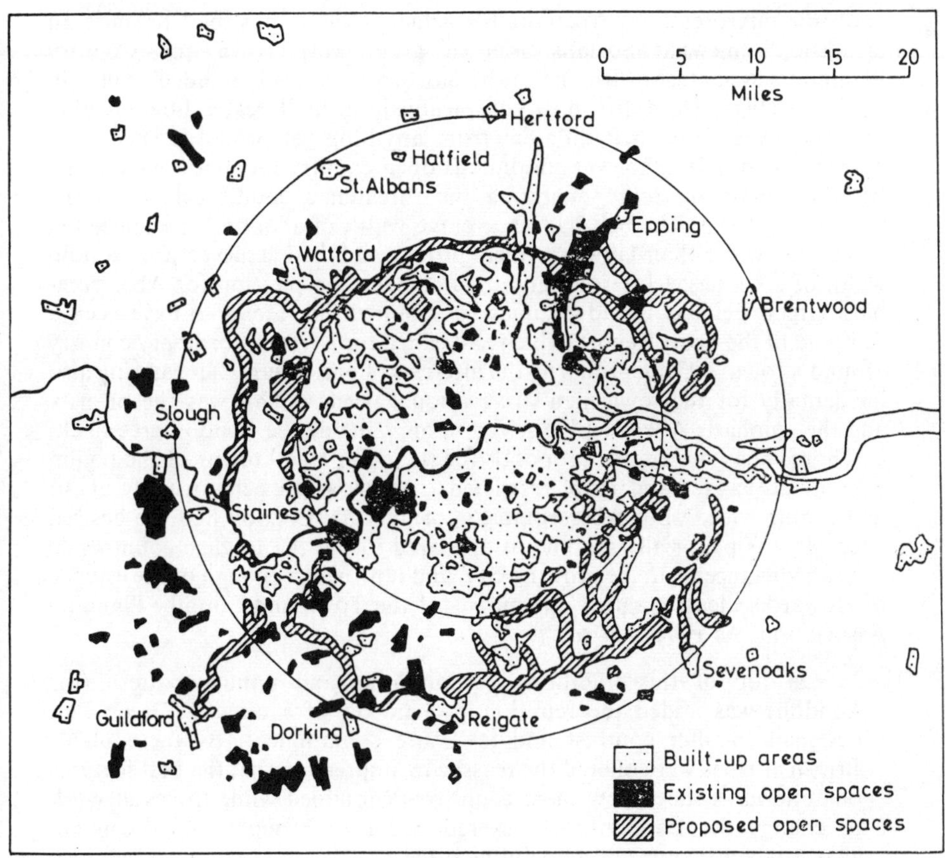

Figure 1.3 Unwin's Green Girdle

regional scale than even the pattern of unplanned sprawl of the 1930s – albeit that it was concentrated and limited at a smaller scale. This was the danger the Council for the Preservation of Rural England clearly saw at the time of the Barlow Commission.[59] Abercrombie's greatest achievement was perhaps to reconcile this conflict of interests, so as to unite the two sets of forces, and thus perhaps decide the issue. As Donald Foley has said:

[59] See above, p. 49, fn. 39.

> While the Green Belt concept had the support of those seeking outdoor recreational opportunities for London residents . . . the scales may well have been tipped by the sympathetic advocacy of a conservative class which has traditionally respected a country gentleman, landed-estate pattern of living combined with an elite responsibility for guardianship of the English countryside.[60]

In this interpretation, Abercrombie achieved the impossible: to unite an idealistic, somewhat Socialist-oriented group (the Town and Country Planning Association) with one of the most conservatively minded groups in English society. He did it most conspicuously in his Greater London Plan of 1944, by a green belt different from anything yet proposed: neither a narrow green girdle, nor yet continuous open countryside, but a wide green belt or *cordon sanitaire* separating the threatened countryside from the threatening town. The belt had an average width of about a little under ten miles – far wider than Unwin's green girdle which had achieved a maximum width of six miles.[61] Interestingly, the immediate inspiration for Abercrombie's Green Belt (as David Thomas has pointed out) seems to have been a footnote in the Scott Report, which had called for a tract of ordinary country around a town, serving primarily the interests of agriculture, but catering also incidentally for the townsmen's recreational needs.[62] This was the priority and the emphasis Abercrombie seized upon. Outside the London green belt, as Thomas has shown, his proposals for the other small towns of the region were much vaguer and more restricted: narrow green belts, usually about half a mile wide.[63] But Abercrombie's formula for London had the desired effect. It was pictorially graphic: it appeared to put the English countryside at a safe distance from the growing city, and it provided enough of the essence of Howard's ideas to satisfy the purists of the Town and Country Planning Association. As Foley has put it:

> . . . On top of this traditionally monolithic and unitary pattern (for London) was added the reinforcing character of a circular Green Belt designed to offer contrast and to assure containment. By these plans, British citizens were offered the reassuring impression that the best features of London as they knew them could be maintained while forces at work to change the London they revered could be brought under control. This was a welcome and hopeful message.[64]

Thus Abercrombie's green belt was essentially a masterly compromise, reflecting the idealism of the period in an inspirational design, and uniting all interests in its favour.[65] Though it was implemented in a slightly modified

[60] Foley (1963), op. cit., p. 45.
[61] Thomas, op. cit., pp. 79, 84.
[62] Ibid., p. 84.
[63] Ibid., p. 85.
[64] Foley (1963), op. cit., p. 45.
[65] The author is indebted to Lord Holford for this observation. For the atmos-

form by the new planning authorities around London after 1947, no progress was made on green belts around other large urban areas until the publication of the famous Ministry of Housing and Local Government Circular 42/55, which recommended planning authorities to consider establishing a Green Belt:

(*a*) to check the further growth of a large built-up area;
(*b*) to prevent neighbouring towns from merging into one another: or
(*c*) to preserve the special character of a town.[66]

In a later explanatory memorandum in answer to questions from the Town and Country Planning Association, the Minister agreed that the primary purpose of green belts was to set a limit to urban expansion and help preserve rural areas for the enjoyment of town dwellers; agriculture should be the principal land use but sports fields would be an appropriate element. Five to ten miles would be a useful guide as to width, though local circumstances would change the case. Perhaps most significantly, he agreed that in many cases green belts would involve the resettlement of overspill population and industry in new and expanded towns beyond the Belt.[67]

This last point was particularly significant. Immediately after publication of Circular 42/55, Lord Silkin (the ex-Minister responsible for the 1947 Planning Act) had declared his view that:

> If the Government and local authorities are not able or willing to stand up to the pressure from agricultural interests, will not the result of the Green Belt policy be to induce local authorities to increase substantially the density of development in an effort to house as many people as possible within their own boundaries? In this case, may not the result be that congestion and overcrowding will be as bad as, or even worse than, before and a new and greatly accentuated problem will have been created for future generations to solve, which will be even more intractable than the present one? . . . If that were to be the effect of Green Belts it might have been better not to have encouraged them at all.[68]

A successful green belt policy, Silkin declared, must be accompanied by decentralization of industry and population, which was not always possible.[69]

In the event, Silkin's words proved prophetic: the New Towns Act and the Town Development Act together did not provide enough capacity for overspill to proceed smoothly. Above all, this was true in the West Midlands and around Manchester, as we have seen in Chapters Ten and Twelve of

phere of the time and its effect, cf. the account of F. J. Osborn and A. Whittick, *The New Towns: the answer to Megalopolis*. Leonard Hill, London (1969), pp. 71–2.

66 Ministry of Housing and Local Government, Circular 42/55, 3 Aug. 1955, para. 3.

67 D. Sandys, 'Green Belts: Minister's Reply', *Town and Country Planning*, 24 (1956), p. 151.

68 Lewis Silkin, 'Green Belt Policy', *Municipal Journal*, 63 (1955), p. 2335.

69 Ibid.

Volume One. In his verdict on the Wythall Inquiry in the West Midlands, Peter Self wrote:

> It is in my view the central Government which was mainly to blame for the negative state of planning at the time of the Wythall Inquiry. The Government warmly recommended the implementation of restrictive Green Belts but it held aloof from the complex problems of urban dispersal which must be solved if such Green Belts are to be workable.[70]

The conclusion, Self wrote elsewhere, was a return to the principles of Howard and Unwin: 'Green Backcloth' was a better term than 'green belt'. More land needed to be available for development, related to more dispersed employment provided in the outer parts of the urban regions where increasing numbers would live.[71] Yet not long before this, the then Minister of Housing, Henry Brooke, had been emphasizing the danger of allowing too much development land outside the Green Belt.

> The very essence of a Green Belt is that it is a stopper. It may not all be very beautiful and it may not all be very green, but without it the town would never stop, and that is the case for preserving the circles of land around the town.[72]

There is clear conflict here, and it is the same conflict that had existed even in the 1930s, but that Abercrombie had concealed by his compromise. It is between a mainly negative view of the green belt, as a preserver of agricultural land and of a rural way of life, and a positive view which sees a green backcloth to a pattern of regional planning. It is historically appropriate that a Minister associated with the right wing of the Conservative Party, Duncan Sandys, should have been responsible for initiating the policy of the green belt as a negative weapon of containment; it is equally just that the Town and Country Planning Association should have found themselves in conflict with the policy on the grounds that it did not represent positive regional planning. The significant point perhaps is that the Planning Officer of a politically Conservative county facing large problems of urban growth, Gerald Smart, could record his professional belief in 1965 that the Green Belt policy had been created in a period when population growth was expected to be far more modest, and when no developed concept of city regional planning existed; and that the green belt:

> . . . as now officially understood, is out of date. It is in danger of forcing the preservation of an archaic settlement pattern when it should be shaping the manner of living and working of the twenty-first century.[73]

[70] P. Self in J. Long (ed.) *The Wythall Inquiry*. London, Town and Country Planning Association (1962).

[71] P. Self, 'Wise Use of Green Belts', *Town and Country Planning*, 30 (1962), pp. 166–8.

[72] Quoted by D. Heap, 'Green Belts and Open Spaces: The English Scene Today', *Journal of Planning and Property Law* (1961), p. 18.

[73] A. G. Smart, 'Green Belts: Is the Concept out of Date?' *Town and Country Planning*, 33 (1965), pp. 374–8.

The irony is that the planning vanguard, as represented by Self and Smart, were in effect calling for a return to the principles Ebenezer Howard had set out over sixty years before.

About the same time the then Minister of Housing, Richard Crossman, was making exactly the same comment about unexpected population growth. But his reaction was different: while he was prepared to defend the essential purpose of green belts (among which he numbered accessibility of open countryside to city dwellers and the protection of the rural way of life), he could not bring himself to a final decision on provisional green belts until after comprehensive regional studies of the need for development land. Essentially, therefore, Crossman was making the same point as his predecessor in an earlier Labour Government, Silkin, had made ten years earlier. The green belt policy made sense only if employed on behalf of the townsperson as well as the country dweller; and that meant that it had to be fitted into a total strategy for the development of the region – a strategy that had been conspicuously missing since the early postwar years.[74]

THE GARDEN CITY CONCEPT

The third essential element in British planning philosophy has been the belief in the creation of planned, new, self-contained and balanced communities[75] variously called garden cities, satellite towns and new towns. It is, of course, the essential counterpart to the policies of urban containment and rural protection we have outlined. But as with the other concepts, this concept has seen significant variations in interpretation since Ebenezer Howard first developed it in 1898.[76]

Howard himself was at pains to point out that he did not invent the idea of new towns, any more than he invented Green Belts. Edward Gibbon Wakefield had advocated planned movement of population before 1850, and James Silk Buckingham had developed the concept of a model city.[77] But perhaps the true originator of the new-town concept as an answer to the problems of urban growth was the economist Alfred Marshall, whose ideas Howard specifically acknowledged. And Marshall, as a good economist, had a very clear picture of the objective to be attained and the benefits to be achieved. There were, he argued: 'large classes of the population of London whose removal into the country would be in the long run economically advantageous.[78] Marshall was specific as to the reason. These would be

[74] R. H. S. Crossman, *Statement on Green Belts*, Ministry of Housing and Local Government Press Release, 14 Jan. 1965.

[75] Ray Thomas, *London's New Towns: A Study of Self-Contained and Balanced Communities*. PEP (1969). The essence of the argument is set out in Chapter Ten below.

[76] Howard, op. cit.

[77] Ibid., edn of 1946, p. 119.

[78] A. Marshall, 'The Housing of the London Poor. 1. Where to House Them', *Contemporary Review*, 45 (1884), p. 224.

workers not in service industries, but in those footloose manufacturing industries where 'the supply of labour is determined by the character of the population, and the demand follows the supply.'[79] Marshall here reminds us that he was the last English economist for many years who knew about (or cared about) the economics of location.[80] He had grasped that the costs of such industries partly reflected social costs (the remainder were paid by the community, in welfare services) and that these would be higher in large cities, as they then existed, than in smaller communities.[81] These points Howard specifically recognized.

Marshall, therefore, was clear about objectives. And, as we have already seen, so was Howard. The difficulty was that because the methods of social science were lacking, there was no way of quantifying the objectives or the benefits in a way that would guide planning decisions. Nor, in the next forty years up to the Barlow Commission and the 1947 Act, did subsequent disciples come forward to fill the gap. We can find statements of the case for garden cities; but in general, they repeat Howard's own arguments. Thus no one proves, or tries to prove, that garden cities would do what their proponents say they would do. And, of course, there is no quantified discussion of the pros and cons of different ways of building garden cities. Almost no information is forthcoming for instance on garden city size and spacing, of the effects of this on self-containment and interaction, and on the benefits and costs of such interaction. Yet these were critical practical questions as soon as a new-towns programme began to be a serious possibility.

The general case for new towns was made in similar terms by a number of writers in the 1920s and 1930s, including Raymond Unwin,[82] Thomas Sharp[83] and above all F. J. Osborn.[84] They mention advantages like the reduction of travelling time and cost, access to the countryside, supply of fresh foodstuffs, possibly cheaper public services (above all cheaper housing), more efficient operation of industry, a better unit for social life, and better public health. But few if any hard figures on any of these questions are to be found anywhere in the large body of literature before the Barlow Report – whose conclusions, as we have noticed, are in many respects tentative and unsatisfactory. The result is that the case for garden cities remained a largely intuitive one, unbacked by detailed evidence.

One immediate result was that criteria were lacking as to the best size and spacing of towns. Howard's logic here was simple in the extreme. In his view

[79] Ibid., p. 227.

[80] Cf. Peter Hall's introduction to P. Hall (ed.), *Von Thünen's Isolated State*. Pergamon, Oxford (1966).

[81] The argument is developed in Marshall's Memorandum to the Royal Commission on Local Taxation, Memoranda chiefly relating to the classification and incidence of Imperial and Local Taxes. C 9528, HMSO, London, (1899), *Parliamentary Papers*, 1899, 36, p. 124.

[82] In Purdom, op. cit., pp. 80–101.

[83] Thomas Sharp, *Town Planning*. Penguin, Harmondsworth (1940), pp, 69–71.

[84] Osborn (1946), op. cit., *passim*.

the size of the town was determined on environmental grounds: no citizen should have to walk more than about three-quarters of a mile to reach the open countryside – a journey of about fifteen minutes for an average healthy adult. Assuming a circular town for purely theoretical purposes, as Howard did, this suggests a town of about one and a half miles diameter. At the densities Howard proposed – which were high by modern standards[85] – 32,000 people could be accommodated in such a town; the corresponding figure today might be only half as many. But, as Lionel March has stressed,[86] that was not the end of the matter. As we have already noted, essential to Howard's concept was that such a unit was only part of a much larger unit – the Social City, which expanded by constant cellular multiplication. It is unfortunate for modern readers that later editions of Howard's book did not reproduce the whole of this concept (Figure 1.2a). The original has a central city of 58,000 surrounded by six garden cities of 32,000 giving a total population of exactly a quarter of a million – the same total as the modern 'giant' new city of Milton Keynes.[87] But as Reiner points out in a perceptive analysis, Social City had no limit;[88] it could expand indefinitely, to a million or more. Since the units within this giant city would have been very close together – not more than two miles apart, in Howard's prescription – the effect would have been quite unlike any settlement form we recognize today: it would have contained perhaps dozens of rather high-density clusters close together, separated by narrow agricultural belts.[89]

Most of Howard's followers did not diverge seriously from this prescription. Unwin in 1921 advocated a group of towns with between 50,000 and 100,000 people, with good communications to each other, and with one central city containing specialized facilities, which would afford nearly all the advantages hitherto offered by the large town.[90] Osborn in 1946 advocated units of 30,000 to 50,000 separated by two to three miles – that is, with distances of about six miles between centres – having a great deal of transfer and interchange between one centre and another, and with certain specialized services provided for a group of towns together.[91] He was specific that in the location of new towns, industrial considerations must come before agricultural ones:

> The siting of our new towns must be practicable from the point of view of urban industry, and this factor makes for grouping them as Social Cities and placing them within fairly easy reach of the bigger centres.[92]

[85] F. J. Osborn in Howard, op. cit., new edition, Faber, London (1946).

[86] Lionel March, 'Let's Build in Lines', *New Society*, 20 July 1967, pp. 55–7.

[87] Though more scattered.

[88] Reiner, op. cit., pp. 42–3.

[89] A near approach in actuality is the belt of mid-Hertfordshire containing Howard's original garden cities at Letchworth and Welwyn, and the new towns of Stevenage and Hatfield.

[90] In Purdom, op. cit., pp. 97–8.

[91] Osborn (1946), op. cit., p. 145.

[92] Ibid., p. 146.

Abercrombie's concept in his 1944 Greater London Plan (Fig. 1.2d) was more modest: a mere eight new towns, scattered around London, plus limited extensions of existing built-up areas. It was this more modest concept, with detailed modifications, that prevailed.

The Final Report of Lord Reith's Committee on New Towns, in July 1946, put an official view which was accepted and used in the planning of the first postwar generation of British new towns: the normal optimum range (as suggested by Osborn) should be 30,000 to 50,000, but with provision to go up to 60,000 and even 80,000 in exceptional cases. The lower limit would be set by the need to provide adequate shopping and cultural services, balanced industries and a balanced community; the upper limit by the need to put all homes within walking or cycling distance of jobs and shops, by the need for contact with the open countryside, by the importance of maintaining civic consciousness, and the need to maintain a coherent building labour-force.[93] But here, as elsewhere, there was no attempt at prediction or quantification. For instance, no one attempted to forecast how the amount of interaction between towns would vary according to their size and distance apart. For this was before the era of the modern transportation study, with its technique of forecasting journey patterns from the locations of workplaces and homes.

Therefore, none of the new-town advocates could be very specific or concrete on another central feature of new-town doctrine: the need to establish self-contained and balanced communities.[94] From Howard onward, the term was generally understood to mean communities which themselves provided the vast bulk of the services – job opportunities, social opportunities, entertainment and educational opportunities – which their inhabitants were reasonably likely to want; and which contained a population sufficiently mixed in terms of age, sex, social and educational background to approximate the wider national population. Most writers agreed for instance that a new town of 30,000 to 50,000 could provide a sufficient range of jobs, shops, schools and entertainment to satisfy most needs: the more specialized needs would be met by travel within Social City.[95] But social balance, besides being desirable in itself, would be necessary to guarantee provision of services. A working-class town, for instance, would not provide those services which the middle class might be expected to need. Only by achieving the social balance which larger towns tend to achieve by reason of their size, therefore, could the garden city prove competitive in its range of urban services. Here arose a difficulty, which Howard saw. If the inspiration for garden cities was to provide a better life for the most wretched in the great cities, as Marshall had argued, how to reconcile that with the need for social balance? This is a dilemma which has racked garden city planners ever since. It is extremely doubtful whether either Letchworth or Welwyn achieved complete social

[93] *Final Report of the New Towns Committee*. Cmd 6876, HMSO, London (1946), pp. 8–9.

[94] Ibid., pp. 12–13. This was in the Committee's terms of reference.

[95] Cf. Osborn (1946), op. cit., p. 146.

balance; their populations were conspicuously lacking in just those sections that Marshall wanted to help. And as Ray Thomas shows, the same verdict goes for the new towns set up around London since the Second World War.[96]

SCATTERATION VERSUS CONCENTRATION

Two further associated ideas can also be identified at the scale of city region planning. In a sense they can be regarded as subsidiary objectives, aspects of the general theme of urban containment and of rural protection. On the one hand, the system has continuously worked since 1947 to prevent low-density development in the form of ribbons of houses along roads which are otherwise inter-urban or rural in character, or isolated dwellings or small settlements widely distributed over the countryside. One important justification for this has been the costs of providing public services to such scattered developments: the postal and the telephone service, the educational system, the electricity boards and the milk roundsmen are all said to prefer compact developments to scattered ones. On this point, there is a variety of factual evidence. But it is important to sift it carefully, and in particular to consider the impact of scatteration at different scales. Lionel March for instance has defended ribbon development precisely on the ground, *inter alia*, that it economizes on the use of services that are already provided along existing country roads.[97] Threshold theory, imported from Poland, via the University of Edinburgh, has demonstrated that the problem of economizing on public-service provision is a complex one, depending on whether existing infrastructure is under-utilized or not.[98] Some types of public service can be provided in other ways because of technical or social change: calor gas replaces piped gas, the car and the supermarket replace the milk round. Nevertheless, for many public services with high linear unit costs – telephones, electricity, mail, piped water – the argument against scatteration remains strong.

Another closely related argument stresses the benefits of concentration rather than the costs of scatteration. It is the argument for building up a strong hierarchy of service centres so as to improve the general provision of services in an area. This argument may be particularly compelling in rural areas where the general population densities are low and the distances to big cities are great. It was used by the Cheshire planners in the immediate postwar period to justify the expansion of small market towns,[99] and by the East Anglia Planning Council in their 1968 Study.[100] It also may be used to justify

[96] Thomas, op. cit., pp. 416–27. This evidence is summarized in Chapter Ten.

[97] March, op. cit., pp. 75–7.

[98] J. Koslowski and J. T. Hughes, 'Urban Threshold Theory and Analysis', *Journal of the Town Planning Institute*, 53 (1967), pp. 55–60.

[99] Cf. Volume One, Chapter Twelve, of this study, p. 582.

[100] East Anglia Economic Planning Council, *East Anglia: A Study*. HMSO, London (1968), para. 127, p. 21.

the regrouping of population and the building up of new towns in areas of scattered mining or industrial development, as in postwar County Durham where the smaller villages were consciously allowed to die and a new town like Peterlee was built up to serve the scattered colliery villages around.

OBJECTIVES WITHIN THE TOWN: ACCESSIBILITY AND ENVIRONMENT

Some of the most important objectives of planning ideologists and planning professionals, therefore, have concerned the broad aims of planning within the region: the distribution of town and countryside, the pattern of urbanization, which is in fact the main theme of this study. But it is relevant finally also to ask about the objectives at a more intimate scale. Given the containment of big urban areas, the preservation of the countryside, the creation of self-contained and balanced communities, the prevention of scatteration and the strengthening of service centres, what sorts of objectives were finally to be pursued in the urban communities thus created? On this point, the public pronouncements of planners are notable for their bland generality. Lewis Keeble summarizes the objectives of town planning as the provision of the right amount of land for each use in the right place and on sites physically suitable for each use.[101] Josephine Reynolds writes that: '. . . the aim of town planning is to bring about an all-round improvement in the physical environment.'[102] And on matters of detail, the vagueness is hardly diminished. Nevertheless it can be observed that running through almost all the prescriptions are two basic objectives of planning at the scale of the town: improving environment and improving accessibility.

To improve environment, the traditional solution has been the physical separation of conflicting land uses. It is recommended that industries which are noisy, which produce unpleasant odours, which exude smoke or grit, or which generate large traffic volumes (either by their nature or by their degrees of concentration) should be segregated from residential land uses. It is recommended that different kinds of traffic flow should have their own circulation system, ranging from high-speed primary routes through local distributors and segregated pedestrian systems. To improve accessibility, the means are very varied. They range from provision of parking and the local improvement of traffic flow to planning the disposition of land uses.

The difficulty is that these objectives themselves conflict in many cases. Separation of land uses often makes access more difficult, as is clear in many of the immediate postwar new towns, where the segregation of industry into big peripheral estates has led to major traffic problems. Lower residential densities in the inner areas of cities, unless accompanied by the decentraliza-

[101] Lewis Keeble, 'Principles and Practice of Town and Country Planning', *Estates Gazette*, London (1969), p. 134.

[102] Josephine P. Reynolds, 'The Plan, The Changing Objectives of the Drawn Plan', in *Land Use in an Urban Environment*, special issue of *Town Planning Review*, 32 (1961–62), p. 151.

tion of employment, must lengthen the average length of the journey to work. Rising car ownership in the postwar era has raised the general level of accessibility to jobs and services, especially the more scattered ones, but only at the expense of increased traffic congestion in those areas or cities which are not structured for the private car – in particular, the radial approach roads to the city centres. The Buchanan Report, *Traffic in Towns*, still regarded by many planners as the most authoritative work on the topic, has virtually nothing to say about the complex interrelationships between land uses and transportation patterns.

At the level of the whole town, indeed, it can be argued that the solution to this problem has totally eluded the planner. The conflicts between different groups of the population are too great, the problems of reconciliation too complex, the power of the planner to affect the situation too limited. But within the residential areas, it is a different matter. In favourable circumstances, here the planner can be almost unconstrained, for there is often only one client – a large developer, a local authority or a new town development corporation. The site is sometimes quite undeveloped – a green drawing board with the potential inhabitants unaware of what is being done on their behalf. Here, the idea of the neighbourhood unit has come into its own as the means of reconciling accessibility with environment.

The origins of the neighbourhood unit go back to Yosman in 1916 and traces of the concept can be found in Ebenezer Howard's writings on the wards of his garden city. But Clarence Perry, working on the New York regional plan in the 1920s, was the godfather and main publicist. The idea is that residential areas should be developed in accordance with three main principles. First the unit should include basic community services: a primary school, shops, public open space and other communal facilities. Second, it should have fairly well-defined boundaries: invariably major roads, perhaps also open space, or industrial areas. And third, the unit should exclude through traffic – a notion that was taken even further in Clarence Stein's plan of the early 1930s for Radburn, New Jersey. This last is a feature which the neighbourhood shares with Sir Alker Tripp's precinct, developed in England in 1942,[103] and with Buchanan's environmental area which is essentially a rediscovery of Tripp's principle.[104] In all these schemes, physical amenity is reconciled with physical accessibility through the principle of separation and hierarchy. But the neighbourhood idea also contains another important element: the promotion of social amenity through the deliberate creation of a social unit, in which the inhabitants form a community identifying themselves with the locality. It is this idea that has often provoked fierce disagreement even within the planning profession, particularly in the 1960s. People, sociologists and others have argued, have very varied patterns of social activity and contact. They cannot be forced into the straightjacket of the neighbouring unit.

[103] Sir Alker Tripp, *Town Planning and Road Traffic*. Arnold, London (1942), pp. 75–9.

[104] *Traffic in Towns*. HMSO, London (1963), paras 100–1, pp. 41–2.

Even if the case for something like a neighbourhood unit is admitted on narrower grounds such as protection from traffic – above all for the small children who will walk to the primary school – it is perhaps only possible to think of achieving it quickly in a new development, whether in a new town or in an urban renewal project. In existing towns, where the physical fabric is more difficult to adapt, there is paradoxically a strong case in theory for the neighbourhood unit on traffic grounds, if only on the principle of the greatest good of the greatest number. But this means that some people – those on the traffic streets – will probably suffer actual deterioration of their conditions, and there is an obvious conflict of interest. It is significant that the only large-scale comprehensive experiment yet made along these lines in a British city – that in Barnsbury in North London – has provoked severe controversy among the residents of the area.

THE DENSITY ISSUE

There is one critical question which might have been expected to provide a clear set of objectives at the town scale, but which in fact has not. This is the question of the range and the distribution of residential densities. Some guidelines have come to be accepted largely as a matter of faith. On the one hand, as we have seen earlier, the objective of preserving land has led in effect to the establishment of minimum densities for the great majority of development. Twelve and even fifteen houses (36–46 people) to the net residential acre have been regarded as the norm, and Whitehall cost-yardsticks for public housing have been deliberately structured to achieve it. On the other hand it has been widely agreed that densities should not exceed a certain maximum, which varies somewhat from town to town but is usually in the range 100–200 people to the net residential acre. The justification here has been partly the costs of building high (which will be borne in part, if only in small part, by the local authority), partly the social problems said to be created for mothers with small children, and partly the possible congestion problems. Local authorities have responded to these constraints as a rule by preserving the traditional pyramidal structure of population densities typical of European cities: highest densities near (but not in) the centre, progressively lower densities towards the periphery. Their justification has been the high prices of land near the centre, the competition for space and the general shortage of housing there, and the problems of shifting low income workers too far from their city centre jobs. London has traditionally allowed densities of 200 to the acre near the centre, and in 1969 approval was announced for a development in Chelsea at 250 to the acre. Yet in other situations, densities like these would be quoted as evidence for the existence of slums which needed to be cleared. Latterly, there have been cases of exceptions to the general trend: cities have built high flats at their peripheries – Birmingham at Chelmsley Wood for instance – to make maximum use of the limited land left within their boundaries. But these are expedients rather than reflections of a conscious objective.

THE PHILOSOPHY OF BRITISH PLANNING: THE ELEMENTS IN CONCERT

These then were the main elements out of which British planning thought was classically composed. First, underlying the other objectives but regarded as largely outside the control of the practising planner, was the control of industrial location in the interests of regional balance. Then, central to the system, were the three basic objectives: urban containment, protection of the countryside, and the creation of planned self-contained and balanced communities. Associated with them were subsidiary aims related to the idea of containment: prevention of scatteration and enhancement of strong urban service centres, leading to a notion of the preferred size of urban settlement. Lastly, at the local scale, there were the objectives of promoting accessibility and environmental standards through neighbourhood planning, segregation of land uses and hierarchical transportation systems. Of course, as was said at the beginning of this long analysis, it is artificial and unreal to separate the elements in this way. They belonged in a total, inseparable package which, viewed as a whole, had an extraordinary intellectual and emotional impact on the thinking public. It is not difficult to see why. There was the statement of a problem (or rather a dual problem, for by the 1930s, the problem of urban growth had been coupled with that of regional depression). There was the statement of a total physical, design solution which would cope with the problem. The whole was couched in the language of general intellectual debate, without the interjection of jargon or complex quantification; it was an argument which any educated man could follow and accept. Its weaknesses in retrospect were precisely its strengths at the time. Perhaps nowhere had the total argument been more succinctly and more powerfully expressed than by its most able and persistent advocate, F. J. Osborn, in 1942, in describing the 'orthodoxy of policy' which the Barlow Commission report had at last succeeded in establishing:

> That the nation cannot tolerate any longer a drift of urban development which created depressed regions in some parts of the country and over-swollen cities in other parts. That prewar planning under the Town and Country Planning Acts was ineffective for the main purposes. That most great city centres are too congested and must be rebuilt on more open plans, their excess industry and population being offered better accommodation in 'decentralized' situations. That urban amenities should be protected by country belts around and between towns. That to provide for decentralization and for new industries, new towns and trading estates should be built, and selected existing towns, some of them in depressed regions, assisted in extension or revival. That local community activities should be more actively promoted in housing and planning. That the best land should be preserved for agriculture and scattered development discouraged and that there should be special National Park areas and coastal areas reserved from ordinary building. That there should be more diversification of industry in different parts of Britain. That regional

consciousness and regional administration should be fostered. That conscious design should be applied to development, and that to do these things a powerful central machinery of planning should be set up.[105]

The emotional impact of the package is critical; Abercrombie's plan for Greater London appeared at a highly emotional period, after five years of war, and at a time when it seemed certain at last that victory was near. In passing the verdict of history it is possible to comment on the lack of measurement to evaluate alternative plans. Such things were not what the thinking public required in 1944. Nevertheless, in this as in other respects, the curiously fraught origins of the British 1947 planning system provide much of the explanation for its subsequent limitations.[106]

The essential features of the philosophy, we have already argued, are that it presents an absolute design solution which is supposed to solve a particular problem of society; that the problem, and its solution, are presented in a general, verbal way, so that no precise statement of costs and benefits is possible; that in consequence, no measure of the solution in operation, as against other solutions, is possible, and that it proves difficult to test variations of the basic solution (for instance, variations in the scale and location of the design features). All these arose from a tradition of planning in which the broad outlines of new policies were determined as the result of popular debate among the educated general public, who were by definition laymen; and in which the implementation of policies was then entrusted to professional planners trained within a design tradition, whose concern was to provide a fixed physical solution to an agreed brief. Such a working method is perhaps allowable in a small-scale, simple society with limited technology and a very slow pace of change in the general environment within which planning takes place. It is certainly not appropriate to a large, complex nation with rather sophisticated technology – certainly among the most advanced in the world at the close of the Second World War – and with very rapid and unpredictable changes in the social, economic and demographic environment of planning. And the latter, of course, is a description of British society since the 1947 Planning Act.

SOME LIMITATIONS OF THE 1947 PHILOSOPHY

One of the most important intellectual changes to come over British planning, during the 1960s, was a more critical attitude to its basic methods. The source of this criticism may easily be traced; it is the social sciences, as applied in particular to the related area of management. Management, up to 1945, was based fundamentally on an engineering approach – the efficiency approach – similar in some ways to that which dominated planning. But after 1945,

105 Osborn, *Overture to Planning*, op. cit., p. 13.

106 The author is indebted to Lord Holford for this observation. For the atmosphere of the time and its effect, cf. the account of F. J. Osborn and A. Whittick, *The New Towns: The Answer to Megalopolis*. Leonard Hill, London (1969), pp. 71–2.

management education was rapidly influenced by the social sciences. Psychology contributed a science of human group behaviour; sociology, a science of social systems; politics, a science of decision making; operational research, a science of optimization. From about 1960 onwards, the experience gained in these areas began to influence planning. It provided an important and a serious critique of the existing methods.

The first important element in this criticism has been that planners have been vague about their objectives. In particular, they have tended to rely on basic value-judgements instead of principles that could be tested for absolute truth. Donald Foley, one of the first of a line of American critics of the British system, put it as follows:

> It characteristically builds around seemingly self-evident truths and values and, in turn, bestows a self-justifying tone to its main propositions and chains of reasoning. . . . While it may contain highly rational arguments, it is characteristically suprarational in its all-over spirit.[107]

There are of course good reasons why the objectives should have been put in highly generalized, all-embracing and absolute terms. As compared with industrial managers, planners have a wider range of objectives, and these may be contradictory. Some (and only some) of their basic goals might be: full employment, a healthy physical environment, a healthy social environment, participatory democracy and good design.[108] The range of the objectives immediately makes it obvious that they are difficult to compare.

British planning has sought to deal with this multiplicity of goals by ignoring it. Its method stems from a characteristic model of political organization, which Meyerson and Banfield have called *unitary*.[109] In it, decision-takers have an organismic view of the public interest; all other interests are subordinated to that of the social 'organism'. This is opposed to a *utilitarian* view, which would essentially consist of trying to compare and sum up individual pleasures and pains. A unitary concept of politics, Meyerson and Banfield conclude, is natural to upper- and upper middle-class people; the opposite view is held by lower- and lower middle-class people, who may find that the rough and tumble of party political machine politics gives them a better approximation to what they want.[110] It is small wonder, given the natural tendency to elite government in Britain, that the unitary view has prevailed.[111] Such an approach tends to an extremely lofty yet imprecise definition of the public good in terms of ends with infinite values, which are ideologically derived, and are characteristically presented in terms of the absolute virtue of

[107] Foley (1963), op. cit., p. 53.

[108] Melville C. Branch and Ira M. Robinson, 'Goals and Objectives in Civil Comprehensive Planning', *Town Planning Review*, 38 (1967–8), pp. 267–8.

[109] M. Meyerson and E. C. Banfield, *Politics, Planning and the Public Interest: The Case of Public Housing in Chicago*. The Free Press, Glencoe (1955), p. 289.

[110] Ibid., p. 292.

[111] Cf. Foley (1963), op. cit., p. 56.

a concrete set of policy measures.[112] Lord Reith, perhaps the most celebrated exponent of the unitary approach, gives a characteristic example of the method from a passage written in 1946:

> There are few in this country who would increase existing conurbations; there are few in this country who would not feel that the suburban sprawl of the past hundred years is deplorable from every point of view, and would still have been so even if it had been decently planned.[113]

A central feature of the approach, it will be seen, is the notion of a Rousseau-like general consensus among the whole of the nation as to values, coupled with an assurance that the policies advocated will automatically maximize these values. By definition, there is no room here for specifying values, alternative policies or measures of valuation. Nor, within the political system is there any room for what Foley calls the adaptive method,[114] which places its faith in a series of incremental decisions, adjusting constantly to the pressures and desires of different groups, through a sensitive political machine. The unitary approach, in this criticism, achieves the rare feat of being both non-rational and undemocratic.

There is yet another feature of the British approach to value formulation, which has already been noted. It is the concept that (as Dahl and Lindblom put it)[115] a particular set of large-scale changes will have a predictable outcome. This involves a belief in determinism for which there can be no empirical justification. Furthermore, in this case, the set of large-scale changes is defined completely in terms of physical or spatial arrangements, so that the determinism is of an environmental character, as Reiner puts it:

> . . . the confidence that the stage sets the play, that the most reasonable and efficient road to the better life is by means of reconstruction of the environment.[116]

Here in fact is a classic case of what Simon has described as the problem of identification in organizations; physical planners, simply because they are employed as such, define their objectives in terms of what they do, and furthermore assume that what they are doing must be effective.[117] In such a situation, each decision-maker regards himself as responsible for a particular area of competence and a particular set of values and beliefs; he assumes that other objectives, values, beliefs will be taken care of by some other group. By definition, then, resolution of the conflicting values will have to take place on

[112] Melvin Webber, 'Permissive Planning', *Town Planning Review*, 39 (1968–9), pp. 284, 288–9.

[113] J. G. Reith, 'New Towns: An Essay in Civilization', *Britain Today* (1946), p. 5.

[114] Foley (1963), op. cit., p. 56.

[115] R. A. Dahl and C. E. Lindblom, *Politics, Economics and Welfare*. Heyer & Bros., New York (1953), p. 86.

[116] Reiner, op. cit., p. 112.

[117] Herbert A. Simon, *Administrative Behaviour*. Macmillan, New York (1957) Chap. 10, *passim*.

the political plane.[118] But in a unitary political system, it may not take place at all. If well-to-do citizens dominate the planning system, either as politicians or as officials, they may totally neglect that there are social plans as well as physical plans, and that for achieving[119] certain objectives the social plans are more relevant. Physical planning may even work contrary to social planning objectives in important respects, as Gans has suggested.[120]

There are important implications here for the study of the British planning system. From the start as we have seen throughout the study, British planning has been based on a narrow physical concept and on an implicit belief in environmental determinism. There has been little explicit attempt to relate the physically-defined policy objectives – such as urban containment or the protection of rural land – to fundamental objectives related to the value systems of people; nor, by extension, has there been an attempt to relate to the value systems that might exist as the basis for other programmes – in housing, in transport, or in education, for example. Consequently a very wide variety of public programmes has been allowed to proceed simultaneously, without any systematic attempt to consider whether they were compatible. It seems clear, for instance, that the objective of urban containment has in practice proved inconsistent in some important ways with the objective of providing cheap owner-occupied housing. It may even have run counter to the objective of saving resources in transportation investment. Some, if not all, of these contradictions might have been avoided if there had been a clearer statement of objectives and their realization, in all policy programmes, from the start.

We shall need to bear this relationship – or lack of relationship – in mind in the chapters that follow. Finally, when we come to sum up, we shall first look (in Chapter Twelve) at the achievements of the physical planners in their own terms, and then (in Chapter Thirteen) at the wider relationships of physical planning policies with policies in related fields.

[118] C. E. Lindblom, 'The Handling of Norms in Policy Analysis' in M. Abramovitz *et al.*, *The Allocation of Economic Resources*. Stanford University Press, Stanford (1959), pp. 173–6.

[119] R. Walker, *The Planning Function in Urban Government*. Chicago University Press, Chicago (1950), p. 35.

[120] Herbert Gans, 'Planning: Social, Regional and Urban Planning', in David L. Sills (ed.), *International Encyclopedia of the Social Sciences*. Macmillan, New York (1968), pp. 12, 135.

CHAPTER TWO

THE 1947 PLANNING SYTSEM: THE PLAN-MAKING PROCESS

On the basis of the discussion of objectives in the previous chapter, the analysis now proceeds to the system in practice. Chapter Two is concerned with one of the main roles of the system: the making of development plans for county boroughs and counties, which was made mandatory by the 1947 Planning Act. It considers four dimensions or aspects of the plan-making process. First, and most directly related to the discussion of the objectives, is the conceptual basis of plan making; in particular, the concern with urban containment and with the creation of new communities. Second, there are the technical aspects of the administrative processes which governed the plan-making procedures. Third, there is the political dimension: in each county and county borough, the professional planning official is finally accountable to elected members and through them to the public. Lastly, there is the aspect of the profession itself, and, related to this, the nature of its training. The chapter concludes by isolating two different professional attitudes to planning in Britain, one interventionist and active, the other adaptive.

This chapter was written by Harry Gracey. Peter Hall contributed notes on the professional education of the planner.

INTRODUCTION

In Chapter One we saw how town and country land-use planning, and regional economic planning, were both introduced on a national scale in Britain in the decade following the Second World War. The programme of the planning movement, for controlling urban growth, redevelopment of existing cities, preservation of the countryside and the construction of new self-contained industrial cities, which had been advocated by the reformers for at least forty, and in some cases a hundred years, was incorporated in the recommendations of the various pre-and postwar government commissions. The Barlow Commission was perhaps most important because it recommended that the government undertake regional economic planning and national town and country land-use planning. The Uthwatt Commission recommended the means for a national programme of land-use planning in the nationalization of land development rights and the confiscation of profits from permitted changes of land use. The Scott Commission put forth the forceful and effective, if not entirely logical argument for preserving agricultural land from urban development almost at any cost, reinforcing the conservationist aspect of national land-use planning. The Reith Committee in 1945 recommended construction of the famous new towns to house Britain's population growth and the slum-clearance families from the large cities. This proposal for comprehensively planned new industrial communities, to be financed by the government and built by government appointed development corporations, was quickly taken up by the reformers in the planning movement, as a partial realization of the garden city programme for the construction of new industrial communities in the countryside, sufficiently far from the old cities and with sufficiently balanced populations to develop their own self-contained societies and economies. The planning Acts of Parliament of 1944 and more particularly 1947 created the comprehensive, compulsory national land-use planning system, assigning the responsibility for planning the use of all land in the country to the counties and county boroughs under the supervision of the National Government. The Distribution of Industry Act of 1945 was the first of a series of measures passed by Parliament to control the distribution of industrial activity among the regions of the country, attempting to severely limit new growth in the prosperous South-East and Midlands regions and induce new industrial growth to the declining outer regions in the North of England, Wales, Scotland and Northern Ireland. The New Towns Act of 1946 and the Town Development Act of 1952 gave the central government and the local governments, respectively, the power to build new communities, providing the authority and the financing to acquire the necessary land and construct new industrial towns or to greatly expand existing small industrial communities.

Perhaps as important as any of these Acts of Parliament to the shaping of postwar planning, was Duncan Sandys' Green Belt Circular from the Ministry of Housing in 1955, encouraging the counties to establish green belts around the major cities to prevent their further peripheral spread into the countryside. Taken together, these new policies of the government were seen by the reformers as implementing the three interrelated goals of the planning movement in Britain. They provided for the containment of the existing cities and, along with the housing reform, the internal redevelopment of the old cities. They required the preservation of the countryside and the conservation of agricultural land-planning and development activities throughout the country. And they started what was hoped would be a major national programme for the construction of new self-contained industrial communities at appropriate locations throughout the country. These government Acts, based on the Commissions' recommendations and derived from the planning movements, show that it had been decided at a national policy level that the cities ought not be allowed to grow any larger than they were, that regions should not be allowed to decline economically and their populations migrate to other regions if this could be prevented, and that any new growth in population or overspill from slum clearance in the old cities ought to be accommodated in comprehensively planned and constructed new towns built by various government corporations.

The basic land-use planning policies were exemplified in Patrick Abercrombie's Greater London Plan of 1944. Abercrombie, asked by the government to prepare a plan for the London region, broadly conceived, developed a classic application of the basic planning programme. He proposed that London be contained within its then built-up area, that a Green Belt of varying width be drawn around the entire built-up area, and that new towns be constructed at distances of between thirty and fifty miles from Charing Cross to house migrants from the city and families uprooted from slum-clearance areas, and accommodate new population growth. The Greater London Plan came to be taken as a model for city-region planning in Britain when city and county planning authorities were established to carry out comprehensive land-use planning under the 1947 Planning Act. The planners, taking up their new and unfamiliar tasks in cities and towns throughout the country, seemed to have assumed that the Abercrombie Plan could be applied to solve the problems of urban growth of any large city and not just the metropolis of London. City growth was often referred to as urban 'sprawl', revealing the basic spatial nature of the concern. The physical spread of cities and the uncontrolled consumption of land for urban use were assumed to be a unitary phenomenon which could be dealt with by a single well-conceived technique such as that Abercrombie seemed to provide.

The programme of regional economic planning was to foster industrial development in the declining areas of the North of England, Scotland, Wales and Northern Ireland through a combination of financial incentives for business to locate in those regions and a strict government control over the location and expansion of industry in the prosperous Midlands and South-East. Many different financial incentives were devised over the years beginning with the 1945 programme to subsidize new plant construction for industry in the development areas. Other subsidies added over the years included grants for the purchase of machinery and the training of workers, and some tax relief or deferred tax payments by the local authorities in the development areas. At the same time the government exercised ever closer control over the establishment and expansion of manufacturing industry in the prosperous areas of the South-East and the Midlands through the Board of Trade's Industrial Development Certificate (IDC) programme. Industries seeking to locate or expand in the prosperous regions had to obtain permission from the Board and be granted an IDC before they could proceed. The Board of course used its power to encourage industry to build in the development areas rather than in the prosperous regions, particularly if the proposed expansion would involve increased employment at the site. The overall purpose of the regional development programme was to stem the 'drift to the South', the movement of as many as 50,000 people a year from Scotland and the North, and many from Wales as well, to the more prosperous Midlands and South-East of England. Regional economic planning was a device by which the government sought to stem the tide of internal migration by providing new jobs in the declining regions from which the people were emigrating and curtailing the growth of new jobs in the regions to which they were immigrating. Like most modern migrations, the 'drift to the South' in Britain was a search for work on the part of the people involved, and the government, rather than accepting it as a contemporary demographic, or economic fact of life, sought to control it by getting new jobs back into the declining regions.

The drift to the South of England was also seen as contributing to the problems of urban sprawl around the large industrial cities by adding to their populations at a time when they were already growing and decentralizing from the centre of the cities. In most of England's Megalopolis, as identified in this report, economic planning and land-use planning were both being used to contain growth from their inception until the time of our study. The Board of Trade exercised strong control over the location and expansion of industry in almost all of Megalopolis. In Chapter Three on the development control process we will be concerned with the impact of the IDC programme on the development of industry in the study areas. In this chapter we want to examine some aspects of the process of land-use planning in the cities and counties of England's Megalopolis. This comprehensive, compulsory national programme of land-use planning is probably unique in the world with its three principal features of the use of every square foot of land in the country being planned for twenty years in advance, the nationalization of land development rights with the requirement that all changes of land use be approved by the local planning authority, and the provisions for the construction of comprehensively planned new and expanded industrial communities by the national and local governments.

The various studies of land-use planning in England's Megalopolis sought to identify and analyse important organizational and new-town construction aspects of the three operational dimensions of the system: planning, development control and new-town construction. In this chapter we will analyse the planning process in the local authorities, that is, the making of the statutory forward development plans by the local planners in the counties and the county boroughs. (In chapters which follow the development control process is analysed, both for industrial developments and for new residential development in Megalopolis. Other chapters in the present volume analyse the process of new town and expanded town-construction in some detail.)

The basic dimensions of the planning system having to do with the plan-making process which seem to be most problematic for the local planners include: the conceptual framework in which the system as a whole is conceived; some of the basic technical requirements of plan-making found in the laws and directives from the government; the political context of the planning process in the division of authority between the cities and the counties and the difference of interest which so often accompanies it; and the professional definition of the role of the planner and the function of planning in society. It is to these four dimensions of local authority land use plan-making – the conceptual, the technical, the political, and the professional – that we shall now turn our attention, showing how the system generated basic problems and how the planners came to deal with these and to advocate revision of the system.

THE CONCEPTUALIZATION OF TOWN AND COUNTRY PLANNING

In 1947 universal, compulsory town and country planning was created by assigning planning functions to the major political jurisdictions of the country, the administrative counties and county boroughs, to be carried out under the supervision of a ministry of the national government. Planning procedure was standardized across the country by the directives from the national Ministry. The result was that all cities and all counties were set to work drawing up the same sorts of basic city and county twenty-year Development Plans and submitting them to the Ministry for approval. In this way planning was standardized and bureaucratized as a function of local and national governments. The most influential plans of the time and those which became a model for planning in the country as a whole were undoubtedly those of Sir Patrick Abercrombie, especially his two London plans. The Greater London Plan, in particular, seems to have set the tone of city-region planning throughout the country. It contained all the prescribed features of planning from the movement, of which Abercrombie had been a leading participant for many years, including containment of city growth by a Green Belt drawn around the metropolis and the creation of a ring of new self-contained satellite cities in the countryside beyond the Green Belt, to which 'excess' city population and industry could be exported, making possible the redevelopment of the formerly congested areas of the city, and the development of efficient communication and transportation throughout the city. The Plan, which became a model for city-region planning across the country and embodied all the received wisdom of the planning movement, had been created specificially for the needs of London, the country's one metropolis. In practice, the division of the planning function between the cities and the counties meant that in most parts of the country the central cities were under one planning authority, while the suburbs and the hinterlands of the city were under another authority. One authority in an urban region was to draw up the plan for the city, while another was responsible for the plan for the suburbs and countryside of the region. The generators of urban growth, the cities, were separated for planning purposes from the receivers of urban growth, the counties, and the initial plan-making was carried on in terms of political administrative units rather than real urban units of the cities, their suburbs, and their functionally interrelated hinterlands. Boundaries of planning units cut right through the ecological units, in most of the urban regions of Britain.

Human ecologists who study the changing distribution of people and functions in urban space through time have come to distinguish two different processes involved in city growth, urbanization and metropolitanization, or the development of urban communities and the development of metropolitan communities. Their basic thesis is that the growth of urban agglomerations eventually brings a qualitative change in their form and function, referred to as the transition from an urban community to a metropolitan community. They point out that increasing the size of a social unit like the modern city does not result in the simple addition of more units of the same type; rather growth of population and increasing economic activity in cities creates increasing differentiation and specialization of urban people, activities and space.

Increase in the size of cities, then, leads to functional differentiation and specialization of space within the urban complex. As a city grows, areas acquire specialized economic, political and social functions. Suburbanization takes place along the lines of transportation leading out of the city. Agricultural specialization develops in the rural hinterland. This 'simple' ecological unit of the city, its suburbs, and its increasingly specialized rural hinterland is referred to as an urban community. Increasing size brings increasing complexity to the social unit. Continued economic and population growth will bring even greater differentiation and specialization of people, activities and space. Satellite cities develop in the urban hinterland with specialized manufacturing functions. Existing communities beyond the area of influence of the city begin to become specialized with regard to urban functions, becoming places of residence for the upper middle-class, for example, or recreation places for the urban population. The major city gradually becomes the central city of a much more complex ecological unit, the metropolitan community with a higher order of organization and a different sort of functional distribution of people, space and activities.

The implications of this theory for the type of comprehensive town and country planning introduced here in 1947 are clear, when we look at the organization and operation of the planning system. Organizationally, this system severed the city from its hinterland, as far as planning is concerned, when it made the administrative counties and the county boroughs separate and independent planning authorities. The growing suburbs of cities still in the process of urbanization were in the jurisdiction of the counties so these cities lost control of the areas where their growth would naturally go. Those with growth potential immediately set about trying to secure boundary extensions. Most failed, which is not surprising since they were fought tooth and nail by the counties, which did not want to lose any of the territory in their political jurisdiction. This meant that planning for cities could only be carried out jointly between independent local authorities. London, the one city which could be said to have entered the phase of metropolitanization, could be planned only through the co-operation of multitudes of local authorities, which were amalgamated in 1965 into the Greater London Council.

The programme involved containment of the cities in their current boundaries of Green Belts drawn tightly around them and the resettlement of urban populations in country villages and new towns in the countryside beyond the city boundaries, as Abercrombie had done for Greater London in his Plan of 1944. The administrative county planners drew Green Belts (or designated White Areas) on their development plans around the cities and used development control, in effect, to prevent further suburbanization. When it became evident that the population was indeed going to grow, they set about designating towns and villages in the county to receive this growth and drawing up town maps to plan for it. The city councils engaged in crash programmes of redevelopment in their borders to repair war damage, clear slums, and provide new housing for the population. They were prevented from expanding geographically by the Green Belts (which, with the exception of London's, were 'received' but never approved by the Ministry), and the counties' opposition to boundary extensions. In some cities, such as Nottingham, where the redevelopment programmes were highly successful, the result was the development of largely working-class cities filled up with new council houses, surrounded by Green Belts, beyond which the middle class would-be suburbanites were being settled in county towns, from which they had to commute across the Green Belt to work in the cities. City planners today often express metropolitan aspirations for their urban communities, desiring that they become centres of office employment, education and administration for the area, which means they are looking for the kind of employment which would attract white collar and professional workers who would in fact be forced to live in the country since suburbanization has been effectively prevented.

In terms of this model of urban growth, the standard planning programme of containment of city growth and the establishment of satellite cities in the hinterland was appropriate to the needs of a metropolitan community but not to an urban community. It could realistically be applied in the London region with some hope of success because London was in the process of metropolitanization. The London new towns have in fact been a highly successful development programme in terms of creating satellite cities for the metropolis, whereas in the other place where such a planning programme has been advocated for years, Birmingham, there was no new town satellite-city programme until 1963. In terms of the theory one would not be surprised at the success of a satellite-city building programme in the London metropolitan community or at the continued pressure for suburban development in urban communities.

Applied vigorously to other cities, still in the process of urbanization, the standard planning programme could only create distortions of the normal growth pattern as this is seen in the theory. The standard planning programme was based on a utopian vision taken from the planning movement, the vision of the garden city as the ideal community for modern man, which was made to appear feasible by the postwar population forecasts. When these forecasts were proved false by events, that is the population continued to grow and with it pressure for urban expansion, the utopian vision of the earlier advocates of planning became an ideology of the contemporary bureaucratic functionaries in planning. It served to justify all the man-years of planning work in development control in the Green Belts and White Areas around the cities, and production of all the town maps to plan the growth of towns in the countryside beyond. Today some of these Green Belts and White Areas are being considered by the planners for major urban expansion, in acknowledgement of the realities of urban growth pressures. Green Belts are being referred to by these planners as tools of planning technology rather than sacred items of planning ideology.

The planners in the cities and counties of England's Megalopolis very quickly realized they could not realistically plan land-use development without taking each other's plans into account. However, each of them was constrained by law to produce a separate Development Plan for its territory. Generally, by the time the official Development Plans were completed by the cities and counties of Megalopolis, the planners realized the futility of these separate individual efforts and began to look for ways of planning for urban regions across the local political boundaries. The political boundaries of the local authorities came to be regarded as administrative fictions as far as the planning function was concerned. In some cases the central government encouraged neighbouring local authorities to prepare joint advisory plans, and then to use these to guide development control in the separate political units. In other cases the local authorities themselves came together to produce joint advisory plans for urban regions. These plans could only have an advisory status because the statutory authority of planning remained in the local authorities. The new sub-regional plans are subject to approval by the local council in each of the authorities they cover, and technically must be adopted by the local councils before they can become instruments of development control. Political approval of the sub-regional plans has proved a drawn-out process, however, and planners are left with the old local plans as the statutory base of development control. Informal arrangements between local planning offices and the Ministry have filled the development control gap in some of the regions, however. The local planners, if they are committed to the sub-regional advisory plan, can use it as a development control instrument as long as the local council is willing to pass the decisions based upon it, and the central Ministry is willing to back up these decisions when the developers appeal against planning refusals. When the planners in the local authority and in the Ministry are committed to a sub-regional plan, decisions to refuse permission to develop land in contradiction to the provisions of the plan can be made to stick, providing they can be got through the local council.

By 1968 all of the local authorities in Megalopolis were engaged in some sort of sub-regional advisory planning with their neighbouring authorities. The planners felt that the sub-regional plans ought to provide the guidance for local planning, and were postponing drawing up new twenty-year Development Plans for their authorities until the sub-regional plans were completed and hopefully approved by the local councils. Local authority planning was coming to be seen as essentially sub-regional planning in these planning offices. In a few cases there has been what amounts to an unofficial merging of city and county planning offices through agreements among the planners to combine their efforts and drawing up a single comprehensive

Development Plan, assigning their staffs to different aspects of this single task. The central government has now recognized that the city region is the natural unit for land-use planning, and the Ministry of Housing, in its testimony to the Redcliffe–Maud Commission on the reorganization of local government, strongly urged making the city regions the new units of local government from the point of view of planning as well as other local government functions. If the local government boundaries are not changed in such a way as to make the local political boundaries coincide more closely with the functional urban units or city regions there will probably be more *de facto* merging of local authority planning efforts in regional and sub-regional land-use planning.

We have argued so far that planning was conceptualized in an unrealistic manner in the 1947 Act and subsequent planning legislation. By assigning planning to counties and cities separately, the legislation separated the cores of urban communities from their suburbs and hinterlands, placing these in different planning authorities because they were already in different political jurisdictions. By taking the Abercrombie Greater London Plan as the model for city-region planning the planners were being unrealistic themselves because the cities outside London were no more than urban communities at this time, in the process of suburbanization, while London was England's one metropolitan community, in the process of satellite-city generation. Of course it is quite possible that even if the framers of the early planning Acts had been familiar with the work of the human ecologists, from the 1920s on they would not have been able to set up the planning system except on the basis of the established political units of local government in the country. Administrative arguments might very well have taken the day from conceptual arguments even if the latter were entered in the early debates on the structure of the planning system. As it happened, local authority land-use planning in the 1940s followed the same development as it had done in the 1920s and 1930s. Individual local authorities who tried to plan under the early optional laws found they could not plan for the future land use in their territory without taking into account land-use development in neighbouring political jurisdictions. Neighbouring local authorities came together in many parts of Britain to make joint development plans.[1] There were quite a few regional advisory land-use plans drawn up by joint planning groups in existence in the late 1930s when the basic recommendations for the postwar planning system were being made in the important Commission Reports. This earlier experience with planning under the laws which left it optional to the local authorities seems to have been ignored, though, when the postwar planning system was drawn up. As has been seen, history did repeat itself quite closely, as the postwar local authorities found they had to take each other's plans into account in drawing up their own future development projections and began to consult with one another, form joint planning

[1] William Ashworth, *The Genesis of Modern British Town Planning*. Routledge & Kegan Paul, London (1954), p. 205.

groups and even have sub-regional plans drawn up for contiguous cities and counties.

TECHNICAL PROBLEMS OF THE PLANNING TASK

A Ministry of the central government is responsible for the supervision of town and country planning, which is carried out by the first-tier local authorities, the counties and county boroughs (cities), and by the Development Corporations appointed to build the new towns. Each county and county borough was required to appoint a qualified planning staff after 1947 which would have two tasks: (1) to prepare a Development Plan for land use in the local authority for the next twenty years, to be reviewed every five years; and (2) to exercise control of land development in the local authority in terms of this Plan once it has been approved by the Ministry. The Ministry itself has recruited a staff of professional planners and issued a series of bulletins and directives outlining the technology of survey, analysis and plan-making, and the standardized procedures to be used in development control. One of the most important Ministry directives is the famous Green Belt Circular sent out by the Minister in 1955 urging the local authorities to draw Green Belts around the cities as the most effective way of preventing their spread into the countryside. The administrative counties from one end of Megalopolis to the other followed this directive and drew Green Belts or designated White Areas on their original or revised plans.

Once a Development Plan has been approved by the Ministry, the local authority planners are required to exercise control of proposed development in terms of its provisions for land use in the city or county. All proposals to develop land, to change its use from that of 1947, have to be submitted to the local planning office for approval. Technically, the development of all land is now conditional on conformity to the provisions of the Development Plan through the approval of the local authority administering the Plan. An appeal mechanism was created whereby potential developers could appeal against local authority refusals and conditions on developments to the Ministry, which assigns one of the inspectors employed for this purpose to hear the case. The inspector hears the developer's and the planning authority's arguments in a quasi-legal procedure and reports the hearings, with his recommendations on the case, to the Minister. The final decision lies with the Minister, who acts with the professional advice of his staff, but within the context of political, and later economic, factors relevant for the case.

The Development Corporations appointed by the central government to build the famous new towns had the power of assembling the land within their designated areas through compulsory purchase. The new towns are financed by the national Treasury, which has kept the Development Corporations under very close fiscal control. In their original conception, the political control of the new towns was to revert to the local authorities in whose areas they were built after twenty years. The government has had second thoughts on this provision, however, and by the early 1960s four English new towns which had completed their planned population intake were controlled by a special government corporation created for this purpose. In 1952 an Act (The Town Development Act) was passed giving local authorities powers to plan very large comprehensive expansions of towns in their jurisdictions and finance their construction from local coffers, with some central government assistance. A number of these town expansions were underway in the late 1960s and early 1970s, being built by consortia of county, city, and urban district authorities which have created their own joint development corporations to supervise the projects.

Land-use planning after the war was based firmly on the ideology of urban containment inherited from the planning movement. Patrick Abercrombie's Greater London Plan of 1944 became the model planning exercise of the period, as it contained integrated programmes for preventing the further territorial spread of London by means of a Green Belt, reducing the population of the centre of the city through urban renewal and the moving of people and jobs to new satellite cities beyond the Green Belt, the new towns.[2] Postwar planning was also based on the assumption that there would be no significant population growth in the country and this made it seem quite feasible that cities could be 'contained' in their growth and that the expected magnitudes of suburban migration and 'overspill' from the cities could be accommodated in planned new developments. Abercrombie understood that if urban growth did occur it would bring change in the use of land and buildings in the cities and he thought this would lead to economically wasteful use and even obsolescence of the existing stock of buildings in the city.[3]

The exercise of town and country planning as it was conceived of at this time required the stability which would come from a lack of significant population growth in the country.

The county planners in Megalopolis generally have found the Development Plan task impossible to accomplish as it was specified by the Act due to the administrative procedures built into it, and fairly useless for the development control task once it was carried out, due to changes in land use which were necessitated by the unexpected population growth after the war. The unanticipated population increase and the changing land-use patterns thus engendered in cities and counties rendered most of the Development Plans obsolete, according to the planners, even before they were reviewed and given official approval by the Ministry. In some cases, they pointed out, it was as long as ten years between the surveys of employment, population and land use on which the Plans were based and the official approval of the Plan by the government. In many cases this meant that the conscientious authorities who were following the letter of official procedure were submitting a five-

[2] Patrick Abercrombie, *Greater London Plan 1944*. HMSO, London (1944), *passim*.

[3] Patrick Abercrombie and Herbert Jackson, *West Midlands Plan*, Interim Confidential Edition. Ministry of Town and Country Planning (1948), Vol. IV, para. IV.1 (pp. 10–13).

year review of their Plan to the Ministry before the original Plan had been given official approval. It also meant, of course, that by the time they came to use the Plan as the basis of their development control activities it was already outdated as a guide to local land use and development patterns.

The whole planning and development control task had to be adjusted to the inadequacies of the technical and administrative procedures and this was done informally through arrangements and understandings between the local authorities and the Ministry. The Ministry instructed the local authorities to exercise development control on the basis of the *submitted* Development Plan until such time as it could be reviewed and passed on by the Ministry staff. The Ministry, in turn, said it would back up the local planner's decisions on development control when they were based on the submitted plans. In reality, then, local planners drew up their Development Plans according to the specified procedures of the Ministry, and then began to exercise development control in terms of them as soon as the plan was sent off to the government. When developers appealed against planning refusals to the Ministry, it stood behind the local planners if it thought the decision had been right and if it was based upon the land-use provisions of the submitted local Development Plan.

Considering the nature of the task facing the local planners and the nature of the administrative procedures of the central government, the time schedules of the original town and country planning task seem wholly unrealistic. The local authorities on their side had to begin by recruiting a planning staff, who would then have to find the resources and develop the organization to conduct the research and draw up the local Development Plan. Trained staff were understandably scarce in 1947, and the demand for them great as every city and county had to develop a Plan. In some cases staff from the engineering or architecture department of the local authority had to be used, and this meant learning the task before actually carrying it out. The procedures and techniques for survey and plan-making had to be developed by the government and transmitted to the local planners, who then had to master them and put them into practice. The government, understandably nervous about this new activity being assigned to the local authorities, recruited a professional planning staff of its own to review all the Development Plans submitted by the local planners. Considering, then, that planning was a new activity in its 1947 form for most of the local authorities, and that the task had to be done twice, once by the local planners to create the Development Plan, and once by the Ministry planners to review it, the long delays in the process are easily explained.

What made the delays fatal to the purpose of the exercise – to provide a document to guide development in the local authority for the next twenty years – was the unanticipated increase in the population. It had been predicted that the population of Great Britain would grow from about forty-five million in 1945 to forty-seven million in 1951, and then drop back to forty-six million in the next decade. What happened was that the population increased to fifty million by 1951 and to fifty-four million by 1965. This population growth meant that in the areas where it was taking place there would be pressure on land for changing use patterns, so that by the time a local Plan had been prepared, the surveys on which it had been based were already out of date in the growth areas. Even in the place in Megalopolis where there was the smallest overall growth – Lancashire-North Cheshire, with a 1 per cent growth rate per decade – there was a massive suburban movement of the population from the major cities, which created intense demand for land for residential development south of the river Mersey. Planning had to contend not just with the relocation of families and business from the crowded centres of the large cities as it had been anticipated when the 1947 Act was drawn up, but with a wholly unanticipated natural increase of the population from the major cities, which created intense demand for land for residential development south of the river Mersey.

The goals of postwar planning – urban containment, preservation of the countryside and new-town development – required conditions of social stability, as Abercrombie realized, for their successful execution, and these did not obtain in Britain after the war. The population grew by natural increase far more than had been anticipated and England, like other countries experienced a baby boom in the 1950s. Prosperity came gradually to the country, bringing higher standards of living and rising standards of social welfare. The middle classes began to gain the money and the credit position to realize their goals of home ownership, and created the demand for new houses in the suburbs. Welfare standards in the country escalated with growing prosperity and the birth of the welfare state, and once again there was strong pressure by the social reformers and the city health officials to accelerate replacement of slum housing in the cities, and to up-grade the minimum housing standards. When one generation of slum houses was cleared, the housing of a later period was defined as unfit, classified as 'slum' by the city health officers, and the area designated for renewal. All this meant a constantly growing pressure for land for new housing, public and private, outside the boundaries of the old cities, which was far greater than anything anticipated by the framers of the Town and Country Planning Act of 1947.

Transportation changes also contributed significantly to the demand for new areas of development outside the cities. Postwar improvements in the railway service and the large increases in motor car ownership which came with prosperity made commuting easier between the suburban home and the city office or factory. Improvements in transportation thus facilitated the movement of population from the cities when this was not accompanied by the movement of employment as well, by giving the new suburban dwellers access to central city jobs.

Technological, economic and demographic changes which followed the Second World War in Britain conspired to render the assumptions upon which planning was based wholly inadequate and the task of the planners frustrating and difficult in the extreme. The necessary readjustment of planning goals and procedures was very slow in coming about, and city and county planners were left for twenty years to operate a system of planning inadequate to the real tasks of land-use development in the country. Any useful revision of the conceptualization of the task of planning would have to be based upon some more realistic assumptions about the economic, demographic and transportation trends which are causes of urban growth in modern industrial societies.

The Planning Act of 1968 incorporated many recommendations of the Planning Advisory Group for technical and procedural reforms of the planning system. It is an Act which attempts to rectify what has proved to be hamstringing administrative procedures and difficult or impossible technical requirements of the previous planning laws. In order to speed up the development control process a number of categories of final decisions on development applications are being devolved to local authorities. New types of city and county Development Plans are introduced, which are supposed to indicate overall land-use structure and general strategies for development in the county, giving a general indication of what development would be appropriate and where, but not specifying precisely where it ought to go and when it ought to take place. These detailed specifications of development are left for the Action Area Plans which under the new law are to be drawn up to guide proposed development in the cities and counties. While the city and county Development Plans will be filed with the Ministry, the local Action Area Plans will not necessarily have to be approved by the Ministry before the local planners can use them as development control instruments. Once again, however, changes in the procedures of planning have evoked timidity from the central government, and the new Act reserves to the government the power to designate which local authorities are ready to assume the responsibilities of the new planning, which give local planners greater autonomy in their work. The quality of the local planning staff will be the chief criterion according to the government, for deciding which authority is ready for the new type of planning. The local authorities, however, see no point in continuing with the old type of planning when they will eventually be told to prepare a new type of structure plan or county plan. Therefore, where the local planners are proceeding with work on new Development Plans, they define these in terms of the new strategy plans whether they have been given permission to do so or not. Most local planners in Megalopolis however, were not proposing new local authority plans in the late 1960s, because they felt that they must first get the results of the sub-regional studies now being conducted in most of Megalopolis, which brings us on to the next dimension of analysis: the problems caused by the designation of the local political authorities as the planning units in Great Britain.

A POLITICAL DIMENSION OF PLANNING

Planning is a function of local government, and even though the basic task and methods are prescribed by law, the work of local planners is strongly influenced by the local council's conception of the proper role of planning and the councilmen's aspirations with regard to their local areas. Chief planners and their deputies in the local authorities of Megalopolis speak of the need to 'educate' their local councils to their own professional conceptions of the planning task. At the same time the local councillors have their own ideas about how the local areas ought to develop and exert pressure on the planners to be guided by these ideas in their work. In the Megalopolis area of England it has generally been the case that the city councillors have aspired to growth and development for their communities, while the county councillors have sought to use planning to limit urban expansion as much as possible.

In the cities studied, planners have both allied themselves with the growth aspirations of the councillors and opposed them on planning grounds. Each city of even moderate size seems to aspire to the status of metropolitan centre for a region, the focus of commerce, administration and culture for the surrounding area. The councillors, for example, generally do not want to limit traffic in the cities, but rather to encourage it through provision of urban motorways and motorway standard access roads to the city centres. They seem to fear losing trade to outlying communities and the suburban shopping centre if customers cannot get close to city centre shops in their cars. The councillors want to encourage office development in the city to bring new employment and increase the city tax base, thus contributing to its growth in population, wealth and prestige. They look with favour at the establishment in the cities of educational institutions, medical facilities and cultural centres with museums and concert halls, to enhance and extend their metropolitan-centre role for the surrounding hinterland.

The planners in the cities of Megalopolis are generally concerned about the amount of traffic congestion these types of new development will bring and about the destruction of the historical town centres by road construction and redevelopment. Hence they tend to be conservative in their attitude towards city growth and development and to some extent to be in conflict with the goals of their political bosses. The responsibility for highway development has in most cities been left in the jurisdiction of the city engineer who is usually far more favourable to urban motorway construction than are the preservation-minded planners. It is also the case that in the city in Megalopolis which has carried out most urban reconstruction since the war, Birmingham, the entire planning function has been kept within the city engineer's department. However, until the general growth of population, planners have had to turn their hands to planning for growth and for land-use change which must accompany it in the cities. In this way they become willy-nilly allied with growth aspirations of the councilmen. They become concerned with organizing and rationalizing new development in the city, while at the same time preserving the historical sections of the city and its attractive traditional townscapes.

In the counties of Megalopolis, on the other hand, the leading councillors are mainly concerned with preserving the countryside and the attractive towns and villages from urban development. They were very much in favour of Green Belts and strongly supported them in the 1950s and 1960s as a powerful device for both containing the city territorially and conserving the traditional countryside. Though willing in some cases to tolerate the building of a few well-situated and well-designed homes in the county for the wealthy and the middle classes, these councillors were strongly opposed to any massive immigration from the city to the county or any extension of the city's boundaries around which the planners drew the Green Belts as tightly as possible. The county planners in Megalopolis often share the strong preservationist and conservationist sentiments of their county councillors and are sympathetic with their desire to keep new development to a minimum in the attractive areas of the county. At the same time, however, the planners are made aware of the need for new development to accommodate the population of the growing cities, which generally must be located outside the present built-up area of the city. In recent years in Megalopolis and other parts of Britain counties have been under growing pressure from the Ministry to release more land for residential development. The county planners have tried to resolve their dilemma by designating certain towns and villages to receive new development, often in the beginning by the negative criterion of those places which are considered not worth saving from new development because of their unattractiveness. In this way the county planners try to provide the need for new homes in the counties while preserving the rural amenities of the countryside. This compromise, though, has proved to be ultimately inadequate, and the cities have been able to gain permission of the Ministry to build or release land for housebuilding on their peripheries. Birmingham, for example, was building a new development for 60,000 on its border in Warwickshire at the end of the 1960s, and was planning smaller developments on its border with Worcestershire. Northampton was starting to build a new town on a site adjacent to the city in Northamptonshire. Woodley and Earley have grown up as extensive private suburban developments on the edge of Reading, as has Oadby on the border of Leicester.

The pressures of sheer population growth, of the suburban migration of the middle classes in search of homes and gardens (to be discussed in a later chapter), and the relocation of slum dwellers from areas of urban renewal, have all reinforced the aspirations of the cities for growth and development, and undercut the containment ideology of the planning movement which was built into the planning system by the 1947 Act and reinforced by the 1955 Green Belt Circular of the Minister. Most of the cities in Megalopolis had been attempting to get boundary extensions for many years in order to bring their suburbs within their borders. Few of these boundary extensions had been allowed, and as a consequence most new urban growth has had to take place in the counties. Once Green Belts were drawn around the cities, most new growth was forced out to places beyond the Green Belts. With the combined trends of urban redevelopment in the cities and the movement of the middle class to the suburbs, a definite trend has developed, in middle-sized cities like Nottingham and some larger cities, perhaps Birmingham, for the cities to become more working class in their composition while the new urban middle-class which works in the cities is being housed in towns and villages beyond the Green Belts in the counties. To the extent that the cities do achieve this metropolitan-centre aspiration they will accelerate this trend by bringing more white-collar and professional workers to work in the city who will have to find homes in the countryside beyond the Green Belts. Regardless of the results achieved, it can be said that the process of planning has been democratic, in the formal, representational sense of this term. Planning was assigned to the local political authorities and planners have worked within the political structure of the cities and the counties to implement the goals of the political leadership. City planners have planned for expansion and growth, and county planners have planned for containment of the city and preservation of the countryside. At the same time, of course, the planners have been under the influence of both the planning movement ideology and the supervision which the central government has exercised over their work. The county planning officers and their assistants have thus tried to, as they put it, 'educate the councilmen' to the need for planning and to what are considered good planning practices. City planners have pointed out the problems of congestion likely to accompany continued city growth and the county planners have reminded councillors of the need for land for new houses. But while the planners could argue, on the basis of their ideology and their statistics, with the local councillors, only the central government could coerce them into changing their programmes for development or control. In the cities the government could reduce reconstruction subsidies and institute control of new office development as it controlled new industrial development and in this way perhaps contain the growth ambitions of city councillors. In the country, the government could seek to free new land for urban development through creating a Land Commission and through granting applications for new development when the developer appealed against a local council refusal to the Ministry.

Planning, then, has been organized as it ought to be in a democratic political system. Planners have been government functionaries responsible to the elected local representatives of the governed and working within the framework of local political interests. This being the case (that is, if planning is already democratic in the sense of working according to the wishes of elected representatives in local government), it is necessary to question the functions of the new 'public participation in planning'. This effort in the late 1960s to bring more community groups into the planning process, to involve more local publics in the early stages of local plan-making, has been said to be aimed at democraticizing the planning process itself. It seems to imply that there are significant segments of the community, and legitimate interests in the community, which are not represented in representative local government in Britain if they cannot influence the local planning process through the normal political channels. If this is so, the logic of public participation would seem justified for all functions of local government.

It would be interesting to examine the public participation movement more closely than was possible in this study (because the field work was concluded just as that movement was getting underway) to see just what new interests the planners, and the others promoting public participation, thought would be brought into the planning process. Certainly, a serious programme of representation of a broad range of community groups and interests in the whole process of plan-making with the professional planners could put the professionals in a new strong political position as mediators and arbitrators of groups and interests in the community. This position might give the planners a greater leeway to apply their own professional criteria in the planning process. It would certainly enhance the potential power of professional planners as brokers of relevant interests in the local community.

A PROFESSIONAL DIMENSION OF PLANNING

The professional orientations of the planners in the cities and counties of Megalopolis are of particular interest to the future development of planning because they show what the planners would do with land-use development if they had a freer hand to apply their own criteria to the work. There is a chance that planners may acquire more power and influence in the planning process, through new developments such as public participation in planning, the reorganization of local government into city-region authorities, or the new administrative procedures for planning under the 1968 Act. The planners' orientations towards their task might give some notion of the directions in which they will try to take planning in the future.

The high-level planners interviewed in eighteen cities and counties of England's Megalopolis tended towards either a modest or an ambitious conception of the planning task, conceptions which were seen exemplified in their county planning and were perhaps most clearly illustrated in the sub-regional planning they were carrying out in parts of Megalopolis. The planners with the more modest conception of the planning task saw their role principally as one of guiding the urban growth processes already taking place in ways that would lead to more efficient, rational land-use patterns for cities or regions. These planners who thought of their job as guiding urban growth in the most felicitous directions, came mostly from the North of England and were working in county borough planning offices in Megalopolis. To them planning is a public activity which intervenes in the urban growth process, between the demographic, economic and technological forces causing urban growth and change in advanced societies and the resulting land-use patterns in cities and regions. The planners with the more ambitious conception of the planning task conceive that their role should be to determine the patterns of urban growth in a county or region. These planners who think they should decide where and how urban growth is to take place in the country come mainly from the South of England and are working in the administrative counties of Megalopolis. They would make the public activity of land-use planning the determinant of urban growth patterns, or at least an independent variable in the urban growth process, along with the forces of population growth, economic development, and technological innovation.

The planners who feel the role of planning is to guide urban development say they have to run as fast as they can just to bring some rational order to the development which is taking place in their cities. They are not interested in planning a visionary utopia for their cities, but rather in ordering patterns of growth and change which are occurring in ways which will make the development of the city as a whole more efficient and economical than it would be without any overall guidance from the public authority. Not that these planners disparage the visionary altogether; but in their pragmatic way they see utopias as possible sources of ideas which may occasionally be useful to them in their practical schemes for ordering urban growth.

The planners who think their role is to determine patterns of urban growth feel they are expected, as one put it, 'to be Solomons', all-wise in somehow knowing what the land-use patterns for the counties ought to be, and also all-powerful in seeing that these land-use patterns are realized. Planners with this more ambitious conception of the planning role definitely deny that planning must follow market forces or other trends in the society and simply try to rationalize them and make the development of urban regions more orderly than it would be otherwise. They believe that the planner's job is to decide on the basis of planning criteria what the patterns of urban development ought to be in his jurisdiction and produce a total plan, if not a utopian vision, of the correct form of development for the region. These plans will take account of economic, demographic and technological trends in the region, and of existing patterns of development, but the mark of these planners is the assertion that planning criteria ought to have at least equal status with these other factors; or even power for organizing them within the plan and thereby totally determining the urban growth patterns for the region.

The city planners were coping with strong pressures for growth, and change of land-use patterns in the cities. The local councillors, as we have seen favoured urban growth, as did the economic interests which these councillors often represented in the same cities. Most of the cities in Megalopolis had slum clearance and redevelopment programmes going on which called for new land-use patterns and transportation networks. There was strong pressure for office development and commercial development in many of the cities, and some cities, most notably Birmingham and Nottingham, have taken on large public-sponsored comprehensive developments of these kinds. Even in cities where the commercial-centre redevelopment was less comprehensive, as in Manchester and Leicester, there were strong pressures from the private and public spheres for new development and land-use change. The city planners' work did involve mostly organizing and rationalizing these pressures for growth and change in the cities in an effort to keep them functioning efficiently as total entities. The city planners were working with the private developers and the public developers – including the housing departments and the engineering departments of the city governments – in a continuing effort to co-ordinate their activities and bring orderly development to the city.

The administrative county planners in Megalopolis were also coping with strong pressures for urban development and land-use change in their jurisdictions. Private builders were seeking to build new houses in the countryside outside the cities, industrialists who could obtain Industrial Development Certificates from the Board of Trade were seeking land for expansion or relocation, and public authorities in the cities were looking for places to build housing for slum dwellers displaced by urban renewal. At the same time, as we have seen, the administrative county planners were under considerable political pressure from their county councils to hold back most kinds of new urban development in the countryside. These preservationist ideologies also gave them initially conservative attitudes towards new development. The county planners set to work to cope with new development pressure by controls, designating places where new development would be allowed, and closely supervising the new construction they achieved to see that it was carried out according to the plans they had approved. The county planners and the county councillors decided just how much and where they wanted new development in their administrative counties. They surveyed and classified all the communities in the county as to how much new development they ought to have and of what kind, such as public housing, private housing, commercial development. They made town maps to show where this new development was to be located in the community and in what period it could be built. They set the criteria for design, layout, and even materials to be used by developers in new residential or commercial development in the county. And they worked closely with the developers, public and private, to see that their planning criteria were incorporated in the developer's plans and carried out on the ground. The administrative county planners have been 'like Solomons' for fifteen to twenty years in directing the location of growth in their counties, though they have had no control over the sources of growth pressure, as these were in the cities and so beyond their jurisdiction.

Perhaps the best current illustrations of the modest and the ambitious conceptions of the planning function and the planners' role come from two sub-regional plans in Megalopolis. These plans are also interesting as indicating the directions planning might go in under these different conceptions of its task if local authorities were reorganized into city-regions in Britain. In any case, the new sub-regional plans for Leicester–Leicestershire, and for Nottinghamshire–Derbyshire, seem to be exceptionally clear illustrations of the two types of planning which the city and county planners in Megalopolis seem to subscribe to.

The sub-regional plan for Leicester and Leicestershire exhibits the northern pragmatic approach to the planning task. This plan proposes permitting new urban growth in the part of the county where the actual growth pressure is thought to be heaviest, on the periphery of Leicester, the region's medium-sized central city. The planners examined all parts of the sub-region and came to the conclusion that development pressure was heaviest on the periphery of Leicester and they recommended that this is where it ought to be allowed to take place. They then drew up suggested plans for guiding new development in the designated areas around Leicester. The planners were clearly using planning to organize and rationalize the growth trends already in existence in the sub-region. The development recommendations of the plan were based on the existing demand for land for urban growth, and on a logic that could be based on human ecology, that the natural suburbanization of a city the size of Leicester ought to be allowed to take place. The sub-regional plan proposed in effect that the natural growth tendencies of a city of this size in a region of this sort ought to be permitted, provided, of course, that they are carefully supervised by the public authority.

The new Nottinghamshire–Derbyshire sub-regional plan, on the other hand, is an illustration of the southern visionary approach to planning. This plan proposed that further growth of the region's twin central cities of Nottingham and Derby should not be permitted, even though it was known that the development pressure of the region was on the peripheries of these cities. Instead the sub-regional plan proposes that a new town should be built in and among the run-down industrial communities in the north in order to bring new population and industry to this declining part of the sub-region. Planning is to be used in this case to propose changing the direction of development in the region, turning it away from the prosperous parts where there is pressure for further growth and bringing the new development to the economically declining parts of the region. The sub-regional plan recommends strict limitations on any new development in and around Nottingham and Derby and strict enforcement of Green Belt control to prevent the expansion of these cities into the countryside. It recommends that significant new growth in the region be allowed only in the declining northern area, and that it be comprehensively planned and developed by a New Town Corporation. The report even goes so far in countering existing trends as to propose that some established industry in Derby and Nottingham be removed to the declining northern industrial area between Hucknall and Mansfield to help stimulate new growth there. The Nottinghamshire–Derbyshire study clearly advocates that planning be used to counteract the trends and pressures for urban development in the region; that public agencies be used to halt the existing trends of growth and decline in the region and to create a new pattern of urban development.

EDUCATIONAL AND PROFESSIONAL ATTITUDES

These very different attitudes undoubtedly stem, in part, from changing emphasis in the education of the planner in Britain. Historically, there can be no doubt, the emphasis was all on planning as design; the plan was seen as a physical blueprint showing an arrangement of buildings and of land uses. This resulted, as it did elsewhere, from the origins of planning; the new profession grew out of the existing skills of architecture, surveying and engineering, all of them design professions. Adshead and Abercrombie, the early pioneers of planning education at the universities of Liverpool and London, certainly had this view;[4] and the syllabus established at London

[4] William Holford, 'The Planning Schools: No. 2 University College, London', *Town Planning Review*, 20 (1949), p. 284.

remained unchanged in form for over thirty years to the end of the 1940s.[5] 'The Schuster Committee, investigating the problem in 1949–50 – just at the point when the newly-established planning offices were recruiting staff – found that senior posts were in almost every case held by engineers, architects or surveyors;[6] and a fuller examination a few years later by Peter Collison merely confirmed that the great majority of practising planners had first qualified as engineers.[7] Small wonder, then, that before the Schuster Committee, the Town Planning Institute should record its firm opinion that planning demanded: 'ability to prepare a plan (in the sense of something set out on a drawing board) as a necessary qualification.'[8]

The Schuster Committee in part rejected this view, declaring instead that 'planning is now primarily a social and economic activity limited but not determined by the technical possibilities of design.'[9] If this was the case there was a gap between ideal and reality; Lloyd Rodwin, a visiting American planner who wrote three years after the Schuster report, commented on British planning that

> the emphasis was on physical planning or practical professional routines. The planner was taught to think physically, visually, technically. He still does. He was only crudely familiar, if at all, with the nature and use of research and scientific method. He knew little of the thinking or the applicability of the social sciences, particularly economics and sociology.[10]

And the gap persisted; a decade later in 1965, Richard Crossman, then Minister for Planning, told Institute members:

> I am shocked that so little has been done in the way of research and the systematic collection of information. I want to see great changes in this field.[11]

Essentially the same criticism was voiced before the Institute by its President, Colin Buchanan, in 1963, and by a senior social scientist who had worked with Greater London planners in 1969:

> Many have taken the view that (1) there is no planning other than town planning, (2) there is no urban or indeed social research which is not town-planning research, (3) there are no urban research needs outside their particular sphere of activity. This has placed town planners at risk

[5] J. S. Allen, 'The Education of the Planner', *Journal of The Town Planning Institute*, 34 (1947–8), p. 31.

[6] Ministry of Town and Country Planning, *Report of the Committee on the Qualifications of Planners*. Cmd 8059, HMSO, London (1950), p. 25.

[7] P. Collison, 'Qualifications of Planning Officers', *Builder*, 187 (1954), p. 501.

[8] *Report of the Committee on the Qualifications of Planners*, op. cit., p. 35.

[9] Ibid., p. 69.

[10] Lloyd Rodwin, 'The Achilles Heel of British Town Planning', *Town Planning Review*, 24 (1953), p. 24.

[11] R. H. S. Crossman, 'Planning Policies of the Government', *Journal of the Town Planning Institute*, 51 (1965), p. 208.

of failing to use expertise and information already existing in other spheres and of failing to communicate their own research to other types of planners who might benefit from their work.[12]

There were distinct signs, in the regional and sub-regional plans of the late 1960s and early 1970s, that this criticism was losing its force as increasing numbers came into planning from the social sciences – above all geography, with its stress on the understanding of the way cities and regions actually worked. But as a criticism of the British planning profession during the period 1945–70, it seems fair. Associated with the emphasis on plan design rather than planning method, there was a lack of any real underpinning in the knowledge of the social and economic environment which planners sought to control. The obsession with design led to the idea that cities and regions were physical mechanisms whose performance could simply be improved by better design. The objectives, as well as the end results, of planning were defined in terms of a simple list of physical criteria; planning lacked a way of formulating and refining objectives of a social character. And because of the lack of clearly-defined objectives, there was a lack of criteria for evaluating their achievement or non-achievement. Parallel to this, there was a general lack of any systematic analysis of the economic and social environment, and the way in which it would respond to given actions by the planner.

All these strands resulted in a simple mechanistic view of planning, which tended to ignore the richness and complexity of the system which was planned, and which was therefore caught badly off-balance by unexpected developments, or reversals in trends, within that system. At the same time, in these planners' defence, it must be conceded that society's conception of their role was rather different in 1947 and 1948 from what it later became. As already noted, planning in the county boroughs, even in some of the biggest cities, was an outgrowth of the borough or city engineer's department, and often remained subordinate to it; as late as 1961, seventy-six out of eighty-three planning officers in county boroughs were also chief architect, engineer or surveyor – in some remarkable cases all three.[13] It naturally continued in a tradition of regulation and codification, which had evolved out of nineteenth-century public health preoccupations. Planning in the counties, on the other hand, was newly created in 1947; and it was here that the planning officer in the strict sense could come into his own. But it was here too that the prevailing view in 1947 gave the professional planner a much more positive, all-embracing role than he was subsequently to enjoy. The 1947 Act, it must be remembered, did not expect market forces to be very important in determining the future growth of urban England; the great majority of new development would take place in new planned communities, so that the professional planner would exercise complete control

[12] B. Benjamin, 'Statistics in Town Planning', *Journal of the Royal Statistical Society*, Series A, 132 (1969), p. 3.

[13] Gordon E. Cherry, 'The Town Planner and his Profession', *Journal of the Town Pianning Institute*, 48 (1962), p. 129.

from beginning to end, largely unhampered by other interests. In this view, there was less need to understand the system being planned, because there was less need to come to terms with it. It may have been a bad argument nevertheless; but it must have seemed more credible.

In fact, most county planners were almost immediately faced with a quite opposite situation; far from being in sole control, they were reduced to reacting to impulses coming from other agents in the development process. The only true exceptions were in those minority areas that retained the pure characteristics of the 1947 system: the planning of new and expanding towns. Here, planning teams could still exercise fairly complete autonomy, at least within cost and other limits laid down by other authorities. Whether in the field of housing, or open space, or town centre development, the initiative was theirs. The flow of families into the new housing developments, and of industry into the new factory estates, depended in practice on their decisions. Even in cases like these, planners learnt by painful experience that they needed to understand the social and economic systems they were interacting with; town centre development necessitated an understanding of retail geography and the psychology of crowds, the planning of residential neighbourhoods needs the contribution of social planners. But their capacity to manipulate the total situation, given this understanding, was almost unlimited.

Elsewhere, the ordinary plan-making and development control machines in the counties were faced with an acute dilemma. Because of the lack of understanding of social and economic forces, because of the absence of a research tradition, and because of sheer inexperience, there was very little feedback to the planner on the critical question: how far was he in control of the situation? How far, in other words, could he be confident in exercising his powers? If for instance there was a policy to restrict or control development in one area, what was the overall effect on development applications and approvals elsewhere? How far could control policies – for instance on the location of new industry – be circumvented by exploiting loopholes and exceptions in the control mechanisms? Questions like these could not be accurately answered, at least for a long time. In the absence of answers, the two philosophical positions of the planner's role remain unsubstantiated assertions.

TWO CONCEPTS OF PLANNING

The two different conceptions of the planner's role have quite different implications for the future development of planning in Britain. The more ambitious definition of the proper function of planning implies sustained government intervention in urban growth patterns, and especially in industrial location decision-making. It also implies massive government investment in community development on the new-town scale. It reasserts the social welfare conception of the purpose of planning, with the idea that planning ought not simply to follow and rationalize the work of the market forces in the economy and the resulting ecological trends in the city regions, but ought to promote some social values, such as the prevention of regional decline and resulting migration, to equal status in determining patterns of urbanization. The economic implications of the ambitious conception of the role of planning are complex, but in the beginning it probably involves some loss of industrial efficiency and investment and large government expenditures. This is not to say that it necessarily involves permanent economic loss; the new towns which were built after the war have shown a handsome return on investment for the Treasury and business seems to have prospered in them.

The more modest conception of the role of planning as guiding and rationalizing natural trends of urban growth allies this public activity with the demographic and ecological trends in regions. Provided these trends can be more or less accurately forecast, the pragmatic approach to planning will perhaps be more easily successful than the visionary approach; certainly it seems less risky on the surface anyway. However, the principal difficulty facing this approach is the problem of prediction; of anticipating the changes in urban growth pressure which will come with economic, demographic and technological developments in the future. Current development trends can be extrapolated a certain distance into the future, but at some point accumulative quantitive growth becomes quantitive change in new directions, and such points of change cannot yet be predicted.

PART TWO

THE SYSTEM IN PRACTICE: ACTORS AND THEIR INTER-RELATIONSHIPS

This part is one of the central sections of the book. It describes and analyses the operation of the planning system in practice by successively focusing on the major agents or actors in what is, essentially, a complex process of interaction among planners of different kinds; developers of housing and industrialists; and the clients who buy the houses in the new residential areas.

Chapter Three is the first of two chapters on the role of the planner. Dealing with the control of the location of new employment (especially manufacturing industry), it looks particularly at interrelationships between the industrialist and two sorts of planner – the central government planner concerned with administering the scheme of central control over factory location, and the local authority planner.

Chapter Four deals with the parallel control over residential development. It focuses on private developments by speculative builders for sale, and brings out the complex and delicate interrelationships between the local authority planners, the developers and their architects.

Chapter Five introduces yet another agent in the process: the buyers of the new homes provided by the developers. From a sample survey it considers their motives for moving and for their selection of their new home: their experiences there, their degree of satisfaction with the move and their future aspirations.

Chapter Six, finally, focuses on the residential developer. It considers his land-buying decisions and his subsequent construction processes. It brings out the fine financial calculations that he must make, and the critical role of land prices in the calculation. Thus it provides a direct bridge to Chapter Seven.

CHAPTER THREE

THE PLANNERS: CONTROL OF EMPLOYMENT

Chapter Three turns from plan-making – the subject of Chapter Two – to the creation of development control. After an introduction to this chapter and the next, which are both concerned with the general relationships between actors in the planning process, this chapter concentrates on a series of detailed case studies of planning decisions concerning manufacturing industry. Manufacturing is the main focus of interest because since 1945 it has been subject to comprehensive control at national as well as local planning levels, so that it offers opportunities for studying the complex relationships between the intending developer (the industrialist), the local planning officer and the central government official concerned with the implementation of national policies on location of industry. This chapter concludes that there is a clear pattern of success or failure in obtaining planning permission, related to the size of the firm and its geographical origin. Small local firms have the best chance of getting planning permission, followed in order by large local firms, large non-local firms and finally small non-local firms, which have the poorest chance. Large firms – even the great international corporations – find that they must co-operate with the government in locating some of their operations in the development areas if they wish to expand other activities in the South or Midlands.

This chapter was researched and written by Harry Gracey.

INTRODUCTION TO THE STUDY OF DECISION PROCESSES

The making of Development Plans for the local area and the exercise of development control in terms of the land-use provisions of the Plans are the two important activities assigned to the local authorities under the 1947 Planning Act. The Development Plans are comprehensive in that they show the projected use of all land in the local authority's boundaries for a twenty-year period. Development control is comprehensive in that practically any alteration in the use of land after 1947, including changes from one land use to another, alterations in the structure of existing buildings, and even the erection of signs on property must have the approval of the local planners. The only exceptions to this requirement are developments by central government departments, the New Town Corporations, and the Statutory Undertakings (the various gas, electricity and water boards throughout the country). These agencies, all of which are controlled ultimately by the central government, may legally build facilities where they want and when they want without the necessity of obtaining the approval of the local planners. Not all activities supervised by the central government are free from the local planners' authority – the British Airport Authority must get local planning permission to build or expand its airports – but by and large development control applies to private rather than public building in Britain. Development control by the local planners under supervision of the national Ministry is one of the ways in which the political system exercises control over the economic system in the modern British mixed economy.

In making Development Plans, the local planners seek to assign different forms of land use and development to different parts of the local authority's territory on the basis of their planning principles, and their ideas about which activities should be located where and at what point in time in the development of a region. The principles upon which development is thus located in time and space include assessments of economic location needs, as well as considerations of economy, amenity and efficiency in the functioning of urban communities.

At the same time, potential land developers make their own assessments of markets and production costs as a basis for deciding where to locate their activities in the cities and counties. All significant private development of land is done for commercial reasons: companies build factories, stores, and warehouses on the basis of market forecasts for their products; commercial estates are built by developers on the assumption that the buildings can be leased or sold to companies, and private home builders construct homes where they think there are families who will buy them. When a potential developer of land applies to the local authority for planning permission he is acting on the basis of his market calculations, which may or may not turn out to be accurate. The local planners respond to the developer's application on the basis of the provisions in their Development Plan, as amended over the years. The logic of the Plan meets the logic of the market in the exercise of the development control function in the local authorities. This relationship is illustrated in the abstract in Figure 3.1, which tries to encompass the influences acting upon the two sides of the relationship. The planners exercising development control are part of the political system, acting under its control and with its authority. Their actions are influenced by the goals of the political systems, local and national, in which they are implicated. These actions are also strongly influenced, at the national and local level, by the ideology and technology of planning, which have been incorporated into government in the various planning Acts passed since the war. The planning ideology and much of the technology is created and propagated in the 'planning world' which includes the overlapping social circles of the planning movement, the planning schools, and the planning profession. The private developers are part of the capitalist economic system, motivated by the search for profit and stimulated by competition to develop and expand their activities in the search for profit. Individual planners and developers, when they meet to consider a proposed new development, represent these two institutions, the political and the economic, and their two separate systems of logic, the plan and the market.

In any given case of development control the two logics of the plan and the market may coincide and development will be allowed to proceed. More often than not, however, the desires of the planners and the developers will conflict, especially in the parts of the country experiencing the unanticipated postwar population growth and suburban migration (and this includes most areas of England's Megalopolis). The market logic under which the developers act responds more quickly to the changes brought about by population

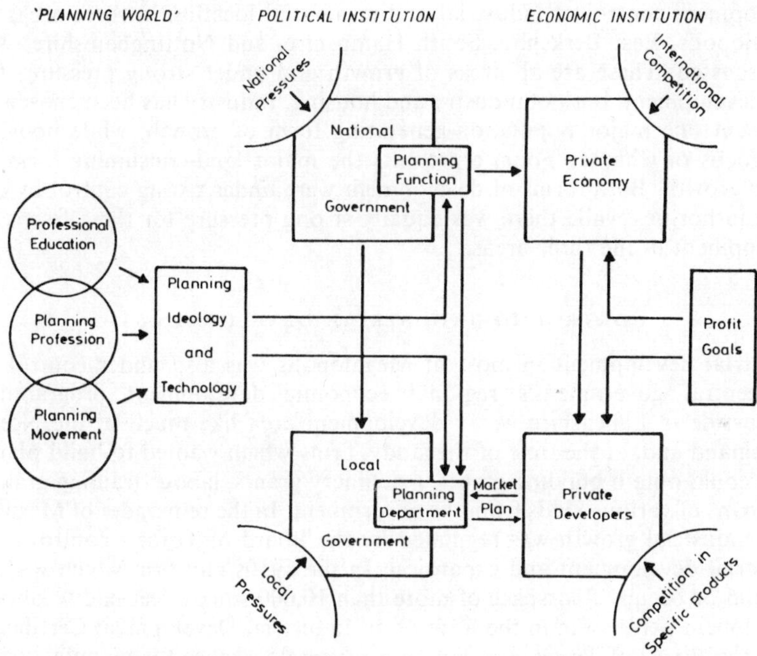

Figure 3.1 Model of Planning in Institutional Structure of Society

growth than does the planning logic under which the planners act. In areas where there is unanticipated growth, therefore, conflict between the planners and the businessmen can be expected to be the norm in the development control activity of the local authorities. This conflict will force changes in the actions and thinking of both parties: the planners can be expected to amend their Development Plans gradually to allow for more growth than was originally expected. Logically, it would be expected that developers might also amend their location and perhaps their investment activities in response to constant planning refusals for new development. An important question for research, therefore, which cannot be answered here, is to what extent businessmen have altered not only their decisions about where to locate their enterprises in Britain in response to the planning system, but more important for the economy as a whole, to what extent they have decided not to invest in economic activity as a result of negative development-control experiences. Planners, this study shows, are forced to revise their Development Plans to accommodate some of the new pressure for growth in their areas. Businessmen, it has also been found, are sometimes forced to devise intricate strategies and tactics for dealing with the recalcitrant local planners, and these failing, to alter their location plans for the activity in question, and even to change company investment policy.

In the remainder of the chapter the results of some forty case studies of development control of industrial and residential location in three areas of Megalopolis, East Berkshire, South Hampshire, and Nottinghamshire, will be discussed. These are all areas of growth and under strong pressures for new development, both of industry and housing. Industry has been chosen to represent one major population-generating form of growth, while housing (the focus of Chapter Four) represents the major land-consuming form of urban growth. Both forms of development were under strong control by the local authorities while there was equally strong pressure for these forms of development in the three areas.

CONTROL OF INDUSTRIAL DEVELOPMENT

Industrial development in most of Megalopolis was also under control of the central government's regional economic development programme. Merseyside in Lancashire was a development area like much of the North of England and, at the time of the study, firms which wanted to build plants there could obtain building grants, machinery grants, labour-training grants, and loans of various kinds from the government. In the remainder of Megalopolis industrial growth was regulated by the Board of Trade's control over industrial development and expansion. In the 1950s any firm which wished to build or occupy floorspace of more than 10,000 square feet had to obtain government permission in the form of an Industrial Development Certificate from the Board of Trade. The amount of new floorspace for manufacturing for which permission was required was gradually reduced, in the 1960s, to 5,000 square feet, and finally to 3,000 as the government attempted ever closer control of industrial development in the prosperous South-East and Midlands regions of England. Control of warehousing developments was also instituted because it was found that firms constructed buildings which they called warehouses but that manufacturing was later being carried on in them, or goods formerly stored in factory buildings were being moved to the new buildings in order to release new space for manufacturing in the factories. At the end of the 1960s it was necessary to obtain permission to build more than 5,000 square feet of warehouse floorspace. Government control of office floorspace had been instituted in much of Megalopolis, which meant that companies which wanted to have more than 3,000 square feet of office space attached to their factories had also to obtain a permit from the Board of Trade. All of these government controls on the floorspace of manufacturing and related activities is part of an effort to prevent the growth of manufacturing employment in the South-East and the Midlands, which of course is a complementary programme to the efforts to get new employment to the development areas in the North of England, Central Scotland, South Wales and Northern Ireland.

The industries studied were all attempting to locate or expand their operations in places where the Board of Trade sought to limit employment growth of all kinds. Additions to warehousing or manufacturing space of over 5,000 and 3,000 square feet respectively, or the building of office space in excess of 3,000 square feet, all required certificates of permission from the Board. All new buildings and changes in the use of most existing buildings for manufacturing purposes required the approval of the local planning authority in these areas as well. The planning controls sought to hold down the growth of employment and hence of population in these prosperous areas of the South-East and the Midlands. The industrialists with whom we talked had been determined to build or expand their businesses in the South-East or the Midlands, for economic or personal reasons, and consequently to conduct extensive searches for suitable buildings and where necessary conduct extensive negotiations with the national and local planners to get permission to build or expand their factories. The determination of these industrialists to locate or remain in the South-East or the Midlands was clearly as strong as the desire of the planners, especially at the national level, to send them to the development areas, in the North of England, or even to South Wales.

In the process of discovering the actual locations of newly-located industry in the South-East and the Midlands, the researcher is led typically to two kinds of sites, new industrial estates on the boundaries of county boroughs and urban districts, and disused airfields in the countryside controlled by the administrative counties. The reason for these kinds of locations for new and expanding industry becomes clear in talks with the industrialists and the city planners. The cities, as we have seen, are governed by councils which are at least not adverse to urban growth, and in most instances positively in favour of it. The councillors, usually representing local business and industry itself, are in favour of bringing more wealth-generating activities to their communities, and they want their planners to look with favour on requests from industry for location or expansion in the local authority. The new economic growth helps to increase the city tax-base and brings new income into the community, much of which will be spent with local merchants. The new economic activity also generates new population, and problems of providing housing and transportation, but these are problems which the business-minded councillors may think can be taken care of with the new wealth which development will bring the community.

Local planners tend to be less optimistic about handling these problems, as has been seen in the previous chapter, and sympathize with the Board of

Trade in its efforts to hold down economic development in most of Megalopolis. Without the new development, they may feel, there need not be new problems of housing and transportation or congestion in the city centre.

The pragmatic compromise which seems to have been worked out in the cities of Megalopolis is that a certain amount of land has been designated for industrial estates in the local Development Plans, and any industry which wants to establish itself or expand in the city must find accommodation in these estates. The estates in some cases have been comprehensively developed by a land development firm, and buildings are rented to industrial occupants. In such cases the developer will frequently have built the structures on the estates as 'warehouses' in order to circumvent the central government controls of factory building then in effect. The industrialists who come to occupy these buildings must then apply to the Board of Trade for permission to use them for manufacturing activities. The estate developer would have obtained local authority planning permission for putting up the buildings themselves, and the manufacturer who occupies them will have to prove to the local planners that he has Board of Trade permission, and submit applications to them if he wants to change the building structure in any way.

A representative case of this type is a small chemical products firm located on an industrial estate in a small city near London. Two local men founded the firm after the Second World War as a chemical research laboratory in a garage owned by one of the men. They specialized in consultant work, doing product research for chemical manufacturing firms. In a few years they moved to a laboratory which they built on some land owned by a friend in another part of the city. Here they gradually began to manufacture some of the products they were developing for the large chemical firms, including detergents, dyes, polish, adhesives and bleaches. In a few years the consulting and product development activities were split from the manufacturing activities, and Mr Smith, the Director of Manufacturing, took this activity to a small building of some 3,500 square feet on a local industrial estate. So far, the firm's activities were too small to be of interest to the planners from the Board of Trade, but each of its moves did require local authority planning approval. This was forthcoming, Mr Smith said, as each of its buildings conformed to the local building and zoning codes. The manufacturing end of the business continued to expand over the next five years, and eventually outgrew the small factory in which the firm was located. Mr Smith began to look for a new factory. He knew of a new industrial estate being built on the other side of town and went to a local estate agent who found him a building of 18,000 square feet of floorspace on this estate. This building was large enough to fall within the jurisdiction of the Industrial Development Certificate requirements of the Board of Trade, and since it had been built as a 'warehouse' by the developer, Mr Smith had to apply to the Board for a 'change of use' of the building to manufacturing. An inspector from the Board of Trade came out to the old plant and Mr Smith showed him the crowded conditions there, particularly the lack of space for using mechanical materials-handling devices, like fork-lift trucks, to handle the bulk supplies they were now receiving and producing. Smith also pointed out what was obvious, that there was no room for him to expand at this site, for his building was sandwiched between two others. Smith was asked to promise he would not employ more than his present labour force of twenty-five at the new site, and when he did he was given permission to change the use of his building on the new industrial estate and move his manufacturing activities into it.

Mr Smith said that the Board of Trade gave him no trouble in getting the IDC for his new factory once the need for more space had been established to their satisfaction. They did suggest he might move to sites in the development areas, South Wales, the North-East, and Scotland, as Smith recalled, and gave him brochures on these places. Mr Smith had no intention of moving out of his home city and paid no attention to these blandishments, including the 40 per cent building grant for his new factory which he thought he would qualify for in a development area. Local authority planning permission was readily obtained for the new factory once he had the IDC, Smith said. 'The local authority is only too keen to keep business in town,' he said. Mr Smith was born in the town, likes it there, and does not want to live or work anywhere else. He does not think his labour force, now numbering thirty, would want to leave the city and he does not want the trouble of building a new one. His five supervisors of the various product lines work closely together sharing the mechanical facilities of the plant and drawing up overall production plans. They all have their desks in the same office, and the easy relations among them enables the firm to function smoothly, or at all, Smith feels. Both goods and people are easily transported in and out of this city, which Smith considers ideally located with regard to both his suppliers and his customers. The company still works closely with the laboratory run by Mr Smith's ex-partner, which remains in the city. Together they present a research and manufacturing 'package' to their customers in the chemical industry. Finally, Mr Smith reports that the company's financing is still managed on overdrafts from the local bank, and he feels that this depends on his close relationship with the bank manager. They have lunch together regularly and Smith keeps the manager informed of the firm's activities. The manager helps Smith obtain his overdrafts, even at times when banks are ordered by the government to cut back on overdrafts. Until he has other kinds of financing, Smith feels his relationship with the local bank is crucial to the firm's continued operation. In the future, Smith thinks it is possible that the firm might expand, if it took up a particular product line for mass production and obtained finance for it in the form of a large sum of money from a firm of stockholders. In such a case, Smith said, he would consider setting up a separate manufacturing unit near their customers in the North of England, or in the Common Market.

The expansion experiences of Mr Smith's small chemical firm in a town near London are typical of many firms' experiences. These are cases in which expansion is allowed by the Board of Trade, which exacts the conveniently unenforceable promise of no additions to the firm's labour force on expansion and is permitted by the local planners, who do not want to lose local industry.

The experiences of firms locating or expanding in the countryside outside the towns and cities is something quite different. It is true that the administrative counties in Megalopolis had designated some industrial estates in their territories on the Development Plans drawn up after 1947. These designations were usually efforts to control and regulate developments already taking place at different places in the county prior to planning. The planners in the typical county in 1947 took some of the areas where industry was clustering and designated them for further industrial development, hoping to channel all new industrial growth onto them over the course of the next twenty years. Whenever the opportunity arose, the county planners also tried to get industry located elsewhere in the county to relocate to these designated industrial areas. Thus applications for expansion by industries located in 'non-conforming' areas would be rejected with the suggestion that the entire industry be moved to ample new quarters on one of the designated industrial areas. The industrial areas in the counties were also used, in co-operation with the cities, as sites to relocate manufacturing and warehousing activities uprooted by renewal projects in the city centres.

The search for the locations of new industry in the counties invariably led to disused airfields, where firms had stumbled upon land and buildings (hangars, control towers and service buildings) where they could engage in manufacturing activities without prior approval of the local or central government planners. The land and buildings were already zoned for non-residential use in the Development Plans, and there was nothing to prevent this from being put to manufacturing use or even establishing service trades there. Depending on what sorts of companies happened to find these geographical loop-holes in the land-use control system the airfields were developed in one of two ways after the Second World War. A few of the disused airfields in Megalopolis were taken over by single companies which turned them into major industrial developments for their own products, such as earth-moving equipment. Most of the airfields were found by a number of smaller companies, which set up shop in the existing hangars and control buildings or tore these down and built new factories of their own. A small airfield might have from six to twelve different manufacturing and service industries located on it by the late 1960s.

On one such airfield in the countryside not far from London we found half a dozen businesses in operation, including a lumber yard, an answering service, an electrical manufacturer, a metal manufacturer, and a plastic bottle manufacturing company. The plastic bottle company rented some hangars and the control tower, which had once belonged to Handley Page, and carried on one of the two largest plastic bottle manufacturing activities in the country. The company was started in the 1950s by a local man who founded a small factory, of some 10,000 square feet floorspace, on an industrial estate in the nearby city. Plastic bottles gained markets very rapidly at this time and the company attracted the interest of some large investors, who offered to underwrite a major expansion of the firm. There was talk of building a new facility on an estate in a development area in the North of

England at this time, but the decision was made to stay in the South because most of the firm's customers were in the South, and transportation is a very large part of the total cost of a product like empty plastic bottles. The company therefore looked around the local area, and found the hangars at the disused airfield. They rented 110,000 square feet of hangar space for manufacturing and storage, and refurbished the airfield control tower as the company's executive offices. Mr Thomas, the Director, said the company had been very fortunate to find a building with so much floorspace for manufacturing in the South-East. They would never have been able to get Board of Trade permission to build so much manufacturing floorspace in the South-East, or to increase their labour force tenfold, from twenty at the old location to about 200 on the airfield. Mr Thomas said an IDC from the Board of Trade had been unnecessary because the buildings were already scheduled for the category of light industrial use. Planning permission from the local authority was not necessary either, he said, as they were only altering the interior of buildings on land for which the local Development Plan showed no change of use from the existing light industrial (airfield) status. Finding the hangars was a stroke of good fortune for the company, Thomas said, for there was just no hope of finding facilities for manufacturing on this scale in any other way in the South-East or the Midlands, and getting Board of Trade permission to build 'is just not on', he said. 'The Midlands would have been the ideal spot, but the only real alternative was South Wales at the time', Thomas claimed. The firm moved to the airfield simply because the hangars were empty and could be converted for use without too great an expense. The company had since become very successful at plastic bottle manufacturing and at the time of the study had been sold at a good profit for the backers. Mr Thomas thought that the new owners might build a branch plant in the Liverpool-Manchester area to get the product closer to the northern customers, and perhaps also expand the operation on the airfield in the South-East.

The disused airfields in the South of England and the Midlands have provided an important means of industrial expansion in these regions where the Government has tried to control industrial growth so tightly. Another source of growth space in the counties of Megalopolis has been the industrial estates established before and during the Second World War on which companies have managed to continue operation, or in some cases expand or even locate new operations during the postwar planning period. The local authority planners, when drawing up their twenty-year Development Plans after 1947, designated some of these areas for industrial use, but others were included in areas designated for non-industrial use, such as residential or countryside preservation. The industries already located in these latter areas became, by the 'act of the planner's pen', non-conforming local land uses. They were usually single industries, small in size, located in what had become residential neighbourhoods or what remained rural areas. The planners could not require these companies to move once they had become technically non-conforming land uses when the local Development Plan was accepted by the Ministry.

What the local planners did was to very closely limit these companies' expansions at their 'non-conforming' sites and try to convince them to relocate entirely to the designated industrial estate in the county.

Two cases of firms which had become non-conforming land users on the Development Plans adopted in their counties after 1947, were studied. Both firms were in small, precision machinery manufacturing and had occupied abandoned farm buildings in the South-East of England after the Second World War. Their business had grown and they had expanded their operations, to nearby buildings in one case and to temporary buildings put up on the site in the other. These expansions had brought them into contact and conflict with the local planners. In the case of firm A, a rather large private housing development had grown up around its site, the land being zoned for housing in the county Development Plan. The county planners considered the firm as a non-conforming industrial use in what ought to be a residential district and would not give it permission to expand at this site. The company wanted to build a new factory to house all of its operations from the old buildings and the new temporary structures. The old buildings were inefficient, the company manager said, as they had discovered from the increase in productivity which came when workers were moved to the new temporary structures. These latter buildings, however, had been erected on the site without consent of the local planners, and so stood in permanent danger of a legal removal order should the county choose to take the matter to court. The company went to the Board of Trade and presented its needs for additional space to accommodate its growing production. An IDC for a factory of 20,000 square feet floorspace had been granted on the promise that the company would employ the same number of people in the new factory as it did in the old buildings. When the Company went to the local planners to get permission to put up the new building, it 'met with a blank wall', according to the director. He said that the local planners 'were flat against us' and suggested in no uncertain terms that they sell the land at their present site and build their new factory on one of the planner-designated industrial estates in the county. This the company might have done, for the price it could get for its present site from home developers would pay the cost of land on an industrial estate and probably the expenses of moving to the new site. It was afraid, however, that the move might lose the firm its highly-trained labour force, 'because it is mainly local women, very local, who are used to going home at noon to make their husband's lunches,' the manager said. Perhaps more important, the manager said, was the fact that the company could move into a new factory on its present site with hardly any interruption of production, whereas a move to another site, even one only a few miles away, would entail some interruption of production and delays in delivering orders to customers. The company was bidding for some rather large American orders at the time and needed to be able to guarantee delivery dates of the goods.

The other small precision metal-products firm, company B, established itself in some rural buildings located in an area which came to be designated for preservation in the rural state on the county Development Plan. The previous occupant of the buildings, who also had occupied them for a business use, had been refused permission to expand by the local planners and had turned over the site to the present company. Company B was given permission to use the land for industrial purposes for two years, and at the end of this period the local planners extended the use permission for another ten years. The company claimed the land had been used for industrial purposes so it was not applying for a change of land use. The local planners in return pointed out that the land was now legally designated for non-industrial use and the company was a non-conforming land use. However, the planners agreed that the company, with its small labour force and non-polluting form of industrial production, was causing no problems at its present location and could be permitted to continue operations there, until perhaps it was ready to relocate on an industrial estate. After eight more years at the rural site, company B applied for permission for permanent use of this land, on the grounds that it had a skilled local labour force which had been with it for many years and that it was causing no environmental problems even though located in a rural area. The county planners refused to give permission for permanent operation of the company at this site and the company appealed against this refusal to the Ministry of Housing and Local Government. A planning inquiry was never held, however, for the Ministry, the local planners and the company worked out a compromise by which Company B was given permission to operate at its present site for an additional two years (this was later extended to five years) and to build a new factory on one of the county-designated industrial estates, provided it moved all its production to the new factory at the end of the extension period. The planners were more lenient with company B than they had been with company A because, though both were non-conforming land uses, company B in the rural setting was not interfering with the development of a designated residential district, as was company A at its location. As one of the local planners put it, they were not trying to put local industry out of business in the county, they were just trying to eventually get it located in the proper places – by *their* planning standards, of course.

Certainly, though, much of the industry the planners found in existence in their cities and counties when they began to draw up Development Plans was much too large and well-established to think of trying to relocate, even if it might be better placed by planning standards. These industries the planners incorporated into the county Development Plans they drew up, designating their present sites as land for industrial use. Where these large industrial sites were fairly well-situated by planning standards for industrial growth the planners sometimes designated them as centres of industrial estates, and zoned the land around them for industrial use also. In other cases, where the planners thought no new growth ought to take place at the site they drew the industrial-use category line tightly around the existing factories and service buildings.

In one Midlands city, a tinplate firm had been situated in the city centre for over 100 years. Its large industrial site was zoned as industrial land-use in the city's post-1947 Development Plan, but the surrounding land was zoned for commercial use in this plan, the hope of the planners being that the area would gradually change from industrial to commercial use. In the 1960s the firm had developed some new products and new production processes which required much more space for production. The management felt they had to increase their industrial floorspace from their present 150,000 square feet to about 250,000 square feet. They also felt that the entire plant should be at one location to allow them to get the maximum advantage of long production lines. The company felt that it was well-located at the present with regard to suppliers, customers and transportation and it had a skilled, loyal local labour force. It also had a number of industrial linkages in the area with printers, designers, and other service industries. Management were convinced, the general manager reported, that 'it was *right* for the growth product to be based in this area', from the company's point of view. He seemed to want to emphasize particularly the good labour-relations the company had at its present location and the loyal labour force it had built up over the years here. This, he felt, would be sacrificed if the company moved to an industrial estate in a development area in the North-East or in Scotland or South Wales. For a couple of years the management looked around the local area for sites which would be suitable to them and acceptable to the planners. The city planners wanted to help them locate on an industrial estate in another part of the city, but there was not enough space there to meet the company's needs. Sufficient land was found adjacent to this estate and the planners were willing to change the designation of this land so the company could build there, but it was found that the land was too soft to bear the weight of the factories. Then the management found that a vehicle company was taking its operations out of an airfield in the county, where it had occupied several large hangars. The tinplate company was able to lease the 250,000 square feet of production floorspace in these buildings at the airfield, and it began moving its entire operation from the centre of the city to the airfield. Now it is in the process of selling its city centre site, which no longer has industrial-use rights, the planners having now designated the entire site for commercial use. The planners were glad to have the old factories finally removed from the centre of the city where they thought shops and offices ought to be located, but the city council were unhappy that the company had relocated outside the city boundaries, taking its tax base into the county.

One of the larger industries studied in the course of the research was a major metal fabricating company which had established an operation in some wartime munitions factories after the Second World War. The plants had been built by the Ministry of Supply between 1940 and 1945 in a quiet rural location in the South-East which also had good rail connections to the major industrial centres, undoubtedly for strategic reasons. A private company bought the complex, of twenty-three acres and close to 300,000 square feet of industrial floorspace, after the war, and in 1950 it applied for planning permission to use the buildings for 'storage and industrial use'. This permission was granted by the county council on the planners' recommendation, in order to legalize the development which took place on the site during the war. The site was then designated as a place for industrial land-use in the county Development Plan a few years later. The original owner, however, as soon as he received the planners' designation of the area for legal industrial use, put the site on the market, as he had no intention of using it himself. The metal fabricating company is located in a factory complex in one of the South-East's smaller industrial cities. It was looking for a site to set up production of a new product line, a site large enough to contain the total production of the new metal product, major commercial appliances, and yet close enough to the existing company site to be easily controlled from there. The company found that the munitions factory complex would be large enough to contain the whole of the projected commercial appliance lines and was able to purchase it at what it considered a bargain price from its owner. The company was, of course, only interested in a property with industrial-use permission, and this as we have seen had been obtained by the owner before he put the site on the market.

Once established in the munitions factory complex, the appliance manufacturer began a gradual but constant expansion of his manufacturing floorspace. All non-manufacturing facilities were gradually moved out of the factories, a strategy which was used by many companies in the study for increasing production space without applying for an IDC. Small outside buildings, requiring local planning authority approval but not Board of Trade permission, were built to house the heating plants, the gas meter buildings, toilets, offices and storage for raw materials or for finished products, and as each of these facilities was moved outside the factory building a few hundred more square feet of floorspace became available for manufacturing activities. After ten years of operation at this site, the company began to request permission for building additions to the factories and storage buildings which were only slightly over 2,000 square feet at a time and so did not require Board of Trade permission. The local planners granted permission for some of these extensions. Later, increases in export orders forced the company to seek major space expansions at the site. The company needed factory floor space and what it termed 'prestige office space' in order to impress foreign customers. One of the buildings on the site, a four-storey brick structure which would serve admirably for offices, was partially occupied by another company, a small electrical firm partly owned by the parent company of the appliance firm. No planning permission had ever been obtained for this company, which was producing its highly specialized electrical products in the building that the appliance company now wanted for its offices. The parent firm of the two companies applied to the Board of Trade for an Industrial Development Certificate for a 35,000 square-foot factory on the site, citing the need for more production facilities to meet new export orders. Because of the balance of payments problem, obtaining export orders had become a major argument used by companies to get government permission to expand industrial activities in the South-East and the Midlands. The Board of Trade granted the IDC to the parent company, which then applied for local planning permission to build a new factory on the site. The local planners were reluctant, however, because they were aware of the small electrical company on the premises and thought the parent company was trying to get it a factory of its own without actually coming right out and saying so, because the company really had no legal existence at the site. A factory of its own, on the other hand, would give it an actual existence and its location at this site would be a *fait accompli.* Thinking to deter this outcome, the local planners recommended to the council that the new factory be allowed only if the parent company agreed to give up the equivalent floorspace in manufacturing activity elsewhere on the site, so that 'floor space for industry should not be increased at this location.' The county council accepted this recommendation, and the company was forced to deliver a plan of the site and indicate 35,000 square feet of floorspace currently in manufacturing use which would be given up to other uses. They were required to 'relinquish all existing rights to use the designated land for industrial purposes' and not to claim any compensation from the council for this act.

The parent company of the electrical firm and the appliance company agreed to this condition which was attached to the permission to build the new factory they wanted for the electrical firm. The appliance company drew up a floor plan of its space at the site and indicated areas which were being used for storage and would continue to be so used after the new factory was built. In the accompanying letter to the planners the managers pointed out however that while the designated areas were now being used for storage, the storage space 'may be moved to other parts of the factory complex from time to time in the interests of efficient production'. The planners accepted this qualification which had the effect of making it impossible to enforce the agreement by the company to relinquish permanently over 30,000 square feet of manufacturing floorspace on the site. Once the county council gave permission for the new factory on the basis of this agreement, the electrical company began to deal directly with the planners on the details of construction at the site. After the factory was built and in operation, the electric company began to apply to the local planning authority for permission to build small out-buildings on the site, to house the heating plant, the gas meter house, a compressor house, and finally a 'small storage building of 4,000 square feet floorspace'. The process of the expansion of a successful firm in an area of closely-controlled industrial development was now underway with this company.

The simple chronology of events in the expansion of firms such as these companies at the industrial site in the countryside in the South-East, does not really show the complexity and intricacy of these expansion activities and the relations between the businessmen and the planners in particular. In this case the parent company and the appliance firm both maintained continuous relations with the planners in the county and the rural district in which the factory was located. The top planners and members of the county council were invited to meetings at the site and the management discussed the firm's growth and space problems at these times. The county officials were shown around the plants, had the manufacturing processes explained to them, and were shown the large new export orders on which the firm was working. The managers said they had a policy of trying to keep the county planners and the council members informed about the company's needs and activities. The relations between the company and the planners over a period of about fifteen years show clearly that while the company was required to conform to legal requirements of obtaining IDCs and local authority planning permission, its requests for expansion were given sympathetic consideration at the highest levels of planning authority where the officials were willing to accept the company's claims that they would not significantly increase employment with increases in manufacturing floorspace. In the middle levels of the planning authority, some accommodation had to be worked out between the official, county policy of discouraging industrial expansion in sites other than the county-designated industrial estates, and the fact of the appliance company's continuing expansion needs. Here at this level an intricate game of space chess came to be played between the middle-level planners in the county planning office and the middle level managers in the company, as the company is seen not to be increasing total floorspace as it builds new factories for its new production lines. The managers justified new buildings in part by claiming they were tearing down old buildings of similar floorspace, these often being wooden shacks which had been put to various odd uses on the site, mainly storage or office space. Then as they drove themselves out of office and storage space in this way, they came to the need for new offices and storage areas, for which it was possibly easier to obtain the governmental permission they received than it would be for manufacturing space in the South-East. The middle-level planners balked at the new factory they rightly thought was being built for the electrical company on the site, and hence the creation of the probably unenforceable formal space agreement on that occasion. The company was finally seeking permission to build a new factory complex on the remaining four acres of the site, which have been given over to playing fields. So far, the managing director reported, the Board of Trade has indicated that the firm will not be granted an IDC for this development, which would be a major industrial growth in the South-East, and the local planning authorities have said they would give permission only for additional warehouse or storage space, and only on the condition that the company obtain an IDC for the development. The manager feels that this response 'needs to be taken with a pinch of salt . . . it's only the first initial contact, and I think we'll get permission in the end'. The manager's confidence is based on the company's past success in getting the expansion it has wanted at this site.

It is interesting to note further that even a company so successful in getting industrial expansion in the South-East feels cramped by government industrial development controls. The appliance company, over the past fifteen years, has acquired rival firms in three other cities in Britain. Using the financial power of the huge parent firm, it has been buying out rivals in the commercial appliance industry. Now it would like to centralize all of its manufacturing in one place, in the interests of efficiency. The logical place, the company managers feel, for the company centralization is the site in the South-East. However, as one of their acquired firms is in the Liverpool area and another is in Glasgow, which are both regional economic development areas, the company sees no hope in centralizing this production in the South-East. The company's reasons for wanting to remain in the South-East, and for not wanting to go to the North or to Scotland, are the usual ones: it likes being close to international airports for the convenience of foreign customers; it is on a direct rail line to the ferry to the Continent for export orders; it feels it has a unique team of technically trained people in the South-East who would find other jobs there rather than move with the company to the North or Scotland; and it has very good labour relations generally in the South-East, which it does not feel could be easily achieved elsewhere in the country, certainly not in some of the development areas. The company men therefore say that the major effect of the government's planning policy has been to prevent the company from centralizing its production at this rural site in the South-East, or in their opinion, from expanding it significantly at this site. The present scattered location of their production facilities increases the costs of administration and the managers feel that the size and cost of managemen could be reduced significantly with centralization, thus increasing the competitiveness of the company in the international market, in which they have become heavily involved in the past twelve years. One wonders, in observing the company's facilities, however, if the government controls have not also contributed to the efficiency of manufacturing in the company by encouraging rationalization and automation of production so that more products can be produced at the South-East plant without significant increases in the labour force there. The company managers are reluctant to admit this influence of government policy restricting employment increases in industries in the South-East, but we feel it remains a possibility.

By no means all firms in our sample were so concerned to concentrate manufacturing operations in one area. Some of the larger firms, as the price of government permission to expand their facilities in the South-East and the Midlands, agreed to locate some operations in the development areas. The more usual attitude of these companies toward industrial location in the development areas was that these were places to send self-contained, highly routine manufacturing operations for products which were beyond the development stage and into that of mass production. Research and development were activities which were seen as properly located in the South-East or the Midlands, close to the large centres of technical labour supplies and specialized technical services. A good example of this attitude is found in a large and rapidly growing chemical firm in the South-East. The company was bombed out of London during the blitz, took refuge in the hills near the Welsh border in some farm buildings and after the war began looking around for a permanent site in the South-East.

The company found twenty acres in a rural area, which already had some factories on it, and moved its operations there in 1946. Since that time it has expanded its operations greatly, become affiliated with a large American chemical firm, and moved into many new product lines in chemicals, plastics, adhesives, fertilizers, and so on. The firm has gradually expanded on its site in the South-East, putting up new factories and warehouses over the years. The last expansion on this site was a factory building of about 20,000 square feet of floorspace. The company has bought out firms at three other locations in Britain and established factories on sites in two development areas. Since land is limited at the South-East site, the director said, the firm tries to locate new manufacturing operations elsewhere, especially in the development areas where it gets development grants and other financial incentives from the government. It wants to conserve space at the South-East site for administration and research and development, the director said. 'Since R and D is located here exclusively, we don't want to fill up the site with operations which could go somewhere else.' The factories at the development area sites are 'absolutely mechanized, simplified, large-scale batch production operations only', the director continued. He felt this was the sort of operation that ought to be located in the development areas, while the creative development and sales work is kept at the South-Eastern location.

The fact that the company has plants in development areas 'counts for us with the Board of Trade when we want to expand here', the director said. He continued: 'They know we aren't trying to expand here just for the fun of it'. The management is convinced that the fact that the company has plants in two development areas is a strong argument in their favour with the Board of Trade, when applying for permission to expand some operation in the South-East. The managers thought that this was an important reason for the fact that they had little trouble in getting permission to expand at their South-East site over the past twelve years.

There has been quite substantial industrial growth in the South-East and the Midlands since the 1950s when government and local authority planning controls sought to limit this kind of development in these rapidly-growing regions of the country. There is a great demand by firms for space to locate or expand industrial activity in the South-East, for reasons of access to markets, access to transportation by air, land and sea, industrial interconnections with other firms or branches in the region, the need for particular kinds of skilled labour and professional workers and services, and because of personal preferences of management for living in the South-East as opposed to other parts of Britain. In most of the smaller firms studied the directors are local people who started their companies in their home towns and do not want to move anywhere else. Firms engaged in modern advanced technology industry, including chemicals, electronics and metallurgy, prefer the South-East for their research and development activities and for manufacturing because of the skilled labour and professional services available in the area, as well as good international communications, for most of them are part of international companies and all are engaged in international trade. The large corporations prefer to have their headquarters and administrative activities in the London area for the same reasons. All these kinds of companies must therefore develop strategies and tactics for finding suitable sites and dealing with the planners, from the Board of Trade and the local authorities, in order to do business in the South-East.

Modern electronics firms, for example, have been developing in Berkshire to the west of London since the Second World War. This location was found to be useful for them for all the reasons given previously, which might be summarized as nearness to Heathrow Airport for the movement of people and goods, and closeness to London for the supply of highly trained and specialized labour. The establishment of the government's two atomic energy research sites in Berkshire after the war helped make the county a magnet for high-technology industry and services, and for technical labour. A number of small, highly specialized electronics and related firms have been established on industrial estates in Reading and Berkshire over the last twenty years, with the permission, of course, of the county borough or county planners. Trips through these estates bring one to many little firms making highly sophisticated electrical and electronic components – micro-switches, transistors, exotic metals for supersonic aircraft components, and so on.

Some major American electronic firms have also tried to establish themselves in Berkshire since the war, and these have been viewed with some misgivings by both the government Board of Trade planners, who would prefer perhaps to have them established in Scotland along with IBM and NCR, and the local government planners who are also trying to limit industrial growth especially in the county. These firms have not let themselves be deterred by the reluctance of the British planning system to let them into the Berkshire high-technology industrial region. They have, our studies show, moved operations into the region little by little over a period of time, first gaining a foothold perhaps in rented quarters in old buildings in the County Borough of Reading, then expanding their operations by bringing in new product lines and applying, now as local firms, for permission to occupy a factory building on a local industrial estate. In this way one American electronics firm had established manufacturing and sales activities in six different locations in Reading since 1960. The firm first moved into the area in order to 'establish a British presence' to support the sales of its products to the British government and industry.

The director of manufacturing for the firm said that the company has found that it can market and service its products in a foreign country from its American plants for a certain period of time, but that eventually its customers want to deal with a local branch of the company, in local currency. Its products are technologically very sophisticated and therefore dependent on adequate servicing and spare-part availability, he said. It was important for the company to be situated near an airport, the manager said, as many components were air-freighted from America to the British operation. The South-East of England was also a logical location because most of the company's customers were located here, including the communications industry, the computer companies, the research and development operations of many advanced technology companies, and the government agencies and research establishments requiring their product. The company found rented quarters in an old building in an industrial section of Reading in 1960 and established a small manufacturing and servicing operation there. In 1964 it purchased another old building in the city and converted it as its headquarters for European and African operations. It expanded its manufacturing operations to three more rented locations and then purchased five acres in a new industrial estate opened by the city and applied for an IDC to build 30,000 square foot of factory floorspace on this site. By this time it was a 'local firm' in the Reading area. It received the IDC, the manager said, because it had already established a presence in Reading, was in effect a 'Reading firm' and because it had agreed to build a production facility in a development area – and actually purchased a site in South Wales to show its good intentions. The company was holding on to its rented properties in the area and only gradually developing its new manufacturing facility as it expanded its total local production. The company, the manager reported, was entirely satisfied with the Reading location, feeling it was 'absolutely ideal for our business' in the British market. It would like to continue to expand its operation here, to service both the British and the Continental market, but in the hypothetical case in which it was prevented from further expansion here by the planners, it would consider moving the bulk of the operation to Brussels, in the European Common Market, where the company had already purchased property. It would always maintain a small presence in Britain, however, to service its sales here. In this way, the American electronics firms have added their presence to that of the British and some European companies in developing, quite without public plan or foresight, this major new high-technology industrial area in the South-East of England.

The industrial location desires of business and the land-use provisions of the local planners generally coincided in the relocation and establishment of local industry on the industrial estates in the county boroughs and counties of Megalopolis. These estates were designated for industrial location in the county Development Plans and the planners felt that what industrial development did take place in their areas ought to take place on these new estates. Local industries sometimes had to be strongly persuaded to go to these estates, especially those out in the counties, but probably more often local businessmen were happy to locate their enterprises in locations where they were assured of the planners' co-operation. Two examples of the happy coincidence of the interests of planners and developers occurred on a new housing estate that one of the cities in Megalopolis built in the countryside to accommodate the overspill from its redevelopment programmes. This was a huge council-housing estate by the standards of the time, some 20,000 homes being built on it. Provisions were made in the plan of the estate for two industrial estates, one on the edge of the estate which was built around some existing heavy industry, and one in the centre of the estate, which had no existing industry. The industrial area designated in the centre of the estate was planned specifically for light industry which would employ women. As this was a working-class estate the planners thought that as well as the men, many of the wives, and grown daughters too, would want work if it were available. They therefore planned for industry which would employ women, and planned its location in the centre of the estate so that women from a majority of the homes could comfortably walk to work in the factories here.

One of the companies which was attracted to the estate was a paper-products firm from London. Its sales had been growing over the years; it anticipated breaking into the African market soon and was looking for a site where it could build up to half a million square feet of production floorspace over the next ten to fifteen years. There was no room for such expansion at the London site, the manager said, and the firm began looking around for a site to relocate its entire operation. The manager contacted the Board of Trade about sites, and the Board tried to convince him to open a plant in Northern Ireland. When he said that this was too far in terms of shipping the products, sites in other development areas in the U.K. were suggested. The manager says that the company looked at sites all over the country but that it wanted to be in the South-East because he felt the company executives would not go to Glasgow or the North of England to live. Also the company was expected to export 35 per cent of its production at the new factory and for this reason wanted to stay near the southern ports. The company decided on the housing-estate industrial location because it wanted a good supply of female operatives and felt it would have almost an unlimited female labour force here in the middle of an estate of 20,000 families. Both the Board of Trade and the planners from the city who were managing the housing estate were happy to have the company come there, as it was a designated industrial site and the company would absorb some of the female labour, which the plants on the heavy industrial site at the edge of the estate could not use. After fifteen years on the site the company has doubled the employment it had had at the London plant, about quadrupled production, and built factory floorspace totalling about 300,000 square feet. The management felt that the site has been a good location in every way: the firm was still in the South-East; it was even closer to the docks; there were no problems finding workers, and the planners both in the Board of Trade and the local planning authority had been 'most helpful' at each stage of the company's expansion. The company had obtained Industrial Development Certificates for three major extensions of its original plant. However, according to the manager, after the last IDC the Board of Trade told the company not to bother to apply for another, as it would not be granted because there was no longer sufficient labour in the area for further industrial growth. The last extension was granted on condition that half the new space be used only for storage. The manager said that there is still room for increasing production in this plant, but production is expanding steadily and in five or six years the Company may need to build a new plant. The company would prefer it to be close to the present plant for management purposes, so it could be run from this factory, but they anticipate difficulties, the manager said, finding a site which in this area the planners would approve.

The other company which had located successfully on the industrial estate in the centre of this overspill council-housing estate was a specialized electric toy manufacturer which had been located in a small plant in a neighbouring town. Its expansion needs were different from the paper products company but the overspill estate location was equally ideal for it. The company had a highly skilled staff in its small plant when it was bought-out by a major toy manufacturer who saw a future in expanding the production and sales of the product over a hundred times in the next year or so. The manager said the new company was looking for a site where it could build a quarter of a million square feet of production floorspace over the next two or three years, which was close to the old factory so that it could keep the skilled workers as the core of its new labour force. And of course, the new company needed a large labour supply if it was to carry through expansion plans for the product. The housing-estate location proved ideal for its needs. This location, according to the manager, 'has near ideal conditions for our sort of manufacturing'. The company has made four expansions on the site, bringing its total manufacturing floorspace to over 200,000 square feet. At the time of the company's last application, the manager said, 'the Board of Trade began to get sticky'. In order to get the IDC, he went on, 'we had to promise not to increase our labour force beyond an agreed level, and to use most of the space for storage'. If the company does expand any further, he felt, it will have to be by building factories elsewhere or, more likely, by taking over other small companies and expanding their operations.

CONTROL OF COMMERCIAL AND OFFICE DEVELOPMENT

The building of shops and offices in the cities and towns, and even in the countryside is a matter of major concern to the local authority planners. Land is designated for commercial and office development in the twenty-year county Development Plans, and specific provision is made for shops, and for offices where this is appropriate, in the town maps and the neighbourhood plans drawn up to guide the developers of private residential estates. Of course, the city-centre redevelopment plans which have been drawn up for a number of cities in Megalopolis contain extensive provision for new and rebuilt shopping precincts and new office blocks. There are, as we shall see, a number of important considerations taken into account by the planners in their control of commercial and office development. The traffic which is generated, especially by commercial development, is a major planning problem which has become greatly exacerbated by widespread use of the motor car over the past twenty years. The preservation of historic areas and townscapes in the face of new development is another task taken on by the planners in their control of new commercial building. The out-of-town shopping centre idea which is so much in evidence in America has come to Britain in the wake of increasing car ownership and caused great concern among the local planners. City planners see the suburban shopping centre as a threat to the commercial viability of the heart of their city, and county planners often see it as a potential threat to the amenities of the countryside they are trying so hard to protect. We shall discuss one example of an out-of-town shopping centre development, and one case of a city-centre commercial redevelopment programme.

The shopping centre development was proposed in a south coast county. The developer had a large company which was surveying sites around many major urban areas in England. He claimed to have looked at over 200 possible sites before submitting planning applications for four of them. The development company fully expected to be refused planning permission by the local authorities involved, in view of the known opposition of local planners to this kind of development, and it had made application on those sites which it felt the Ministry would be most likely to allow it to develop on appeal. The southern-county site was a parcel of unused land on the main road at a crossroads just outside a major urban centre. The development company chose the site because it was maximally accessible by car, and had room for both a large shopping centre and the large car park which would be necessary to the success of the venture. It felt that out-of-town shopping centres could be commercially successful in many parts of the country and that only the opposition of the planning authorities stood in the way of large-scale developments of this kind.

The planners pointed out that the land was in the White Area of their county map, meaning it was scheduled for no change of use for the duration of the county Development Plan. It was valuable horticultural land, the planners claimed, even though it was not being used for this at the time. The planners felt that the owner might be holding it speculatively in a derelict state. Eighteen acres were purchased by the development company and an application submitted to develop it for two large stores and a number of small shops, along with parking space for 1,000 cars and a petrol filling station. The application was rejected by the local planning authority because it was outside the areas designated for commercial development on the county Development Plan. The developer appealed to the Ministry, arguing the existence of a demand for new shopping facilities in the area and pointing out the known congestion in the centres of the nearby cities. The planners argued in defence of the Plan, saying commercial development ought to go to the designated areas and pointing out that if this development were allowed, there would probably be great pressure for more commercial development on neighbouring White land. The shopping-centre development was allowed by the Ministry and a number of other applications for development permission were submitted for parcels of adjoining land.

The planners were very upset by the Ministry's decision. They felt that if the Ministry had approved their county Development Plan it ought not to approve deviations from it such as this development represented. 'It is an example of creeping development,' said the planner. 'It's not planning, it's letting things go. It's gradual expansion instead of planned development.' He pointed out that industry and other businesses were buying land adjacent to the shopping centre and requesting development permission. Some of these were local businesses who the planners knew needed room for expansion, or consolidation of their operations and the planners felt clearly uncomfortable about the prospects of refusing local interests the location advantages that the Ministry had allowed an outside commercial interest.

The planners also felt the shopping centre might compete with the city centre for the speciality shopping trade. They were in the process of developing a commercial development policy for the area which envisaged speciality shops developed in the town centre and everyday grocery shopping taking place in the high streets of the city's residential neighbourhoods. In this way they hoped to alleviate the congestion at the town centre and provide for the commercial viability of both the centre and the high street shopping districts. If the local merchants went along with this shopping development policy, then the planners felt obligated to protect their interests to some extent when exercising development control in reference to proposals such as the out-of-town shopping centre. The local planners felt that out-of-town shopping centres were thus a threat to their neat division of shopping into two types: speciality stores for the city centre, everyday provision stores for the neighbourhood's high streets. A number of strategically located suburban shopping centres might endanger the commercial viability of both types of local commercial districts, they felt. The local planners felt that it was their job, in other words, to protect both the Plan and the interests of the commercial establishments operating in accordance with the land-use provisions of the Plan. In the case of this development, the planners felt they had done their best to fulfil their responsibilities but that their efforts had been undermined by the Ministry.

In a prosperous Midlands city, where our second example of commercial development control comes from, private developers were submitting applications for planning permission for new shop developments in the city centre, and for conversions of old Victorian mansions just outside the centre to office use. The planning department decided that it ought to make an integrated Development Plan for the city centre to accommodate all this development. It commissioned a firm to do a forecast of shopping floorspace needs over the next twenty years, and another survey to forecast office space needs for the same period. As the planners state their purpose: 'We did not want to be "overshopped" in the centre.' They felt an obligation to existing centre businesses to protect their commercial viability. Also they 'did not want office development scattered down the main roads' but preferred to have it concentrated in the town centre. With the results of the surveys in hand, the planners set about designing a city-centre redevelopment project which would accommodate the new floorspace for shops and offices which would be commercially usable in the city, and also the development of new residential buildings to provide apartment housing in the centre of the city. The centre redevelopment plan called for city purchase of the most run-down part of the city centre, an area consisting mainly of old warehouses and a few factories, and redevelopment of the entire area in one integrated plan, leasing the new buildings to the private commercial interests.

With their integrated plan for city-centre redevelopment the planners hoped to provide for necessary commercial floorspace in the city centre, to protect the most desirable features of the central city area from piecemeal redevelopment, and to get rid of a visually and commercially undesirable area all at the same time. The integrated shopping, office and high-rise apartment development, located where they wanted it, would 'round-off' the city centre according to the planners, making it a well-defined and well-designed urban unit. The planners were quite concerned with preserving what they considered to be the most attractive areas of the old city centre from redevelopment and to preserve the views of the castle and the cathedral, the local landmarks, from being obscured by any new development in the centre. A small neighbourhood of old commercial buildings and narrow, winding streets was made an historic preservation area to prevent its redevelopment. Models were made of each new building proposed for the city centre and these were inserted in the appropriate place on a complete scale model of the existing city centre to assess their visual impact on the centre. A special periscope was used to assess the visual impact of these buildings from the street level on the scale model. Almost infinite care seemed to be taken by the planners to try to make sure the new development would add to the urban amenities of the city centre and not detract from any of its present desirable characteristics, while providing the floorspace which was needed for central city functions.

The city had purchased the land the planners wanted to redevelop in the city centre, and the department was working on designs to accommodate the various kinds of tenants expected in the buildings which would ultimately be constructed. The planners were very pleased that they had an opportunity to bring all the new 'proper city centre uses' together in the centre itself. Shopping would be kept in the city, especially they felt when the new ringway and feeder roads into the centre were completed. Office development would be prevented from straggling out along the roads leading to the residential areas by gradually converting the old mansions along these streets to commercial use. Some population could be kept in the city centre, provided the central government allocated funds to subsidise the high-rise apartment blocks the planners wanted to include in the redevelopment scheme. They knew, in other words, that there would be many problems to be overcome in realizing this scheme even after its acceptance by the city council and even after the land was purchased by the city. They saw this work as part of their job of caring for the city centre and promoting its proper development according to planning standards.

SUMMARY AND CONCLUSIONS

An interesting pattern has emerged from the small sample of industries studied, in which success or failure in obtaining planning permission is consistently related to size of firm and its place of origin. Briefly, small local firms have the best chance of getting planning approval to locate or expand in the local authority area. Large firms of local origin have the next best chance of government and local authority co-operation in expanding their activities. Often these are firms which were originally small local companies and have grown over the years with the co-operation of the planners. Large non-local firms come next in order of priority, and small, non-local originated companies have the smallest chance of success with industrial development control, probably because they lack the large company's resources for manipulating the planning system and exercising other forms of political influence. Quite large firms, and here the great international corporations come into the picture, find they must co-operate with the government by locating some operations in the development areas, if they want to get permission to go on expanding other activities in the South-East and the Midlands.

Small industries of local origin have for the most part had the easiest time getting themselves established and expanding their activities, providing they have not added significantly to the number of their employees. The Board of Trade has not tried to force these businesses to go to the development areas, though it has suggested such a move to them, and the local planners are sympathetic to their growth needs provided they are already located in appropriate places by planning standards. The local planners would like to have all these businesses on the industrial estates and many are willing to locate on them or move to them when they need more space for their manufacturing activities. On the other hand, a few of the small local businesses are located in areas which have been zoned for residential use or for countryside preservation and these have the most difficult time with the planners when they want to expand their activities. The local planners try to move these 'non-conforming' industrial uses to industrial estates, even if they have obtained permits from the Board of Trade to expand at their present location. These industries were often established before the Development Plans and the town maps were drawn up by the planners and their attempts to expand present pure cases of the conflict between planning logic and economic logic. The companies want to remain on their present sites and expand there because of the capital investment they have in buildings, the expenses and loss of production involved in moving, and in the case of those employing mainly women, in order to keep their present labour force. The planners on the other hand, contend that the companies ought to move out of the areas completely because it has been decided that these are to be zoned for residential and other non-industrial use on the basis of planning criteria.

The large firms in the sample which have developed locally are often located on sites with room for expansion, either older industrial sites or in the vast hangars of disused airfields. These companies maintain close relations with the local planners to keep them informed of changes in space needs in the plant. One very large firm, a branch of a national corporation, played an intricate game of space chess with its factory complex, constantly increasing factory and office floorspace and at the same time tearing down unusable buildings on its site so as to be seen to be maintaining the 'same' space usage.

It was also under considerable pressure to rationalize production and automatic production lines so that it could increase production without increasing its labour force. Both the Board of Trade and the local planners were very much concerned with preventing any significant increase in labour demand in the area, and the firm had to assure them that each 'reorganization' of production would not be accompanied by increased demands for labour.

Firms which are trying to move operations into the local areas of the South-East from the outside have a more difficult time than do local-based firms. These outsiders have no special claim for consideration from the local planners and no reason to expect sympathetic consideration in an area in which the government is trying to prevent the growth of employment. The large firms which had been successful in locating in the South-East from the outside in the last fifteen years, since planning had been in effect, achieved their goals with either a special support from the national government or by first becoming 'local' firms in the local authorities. The international oil corporation which established a refinery and ancillary facilities in the area was strongly backed by the Ministry of Power on grounds of national economic development and savings on the balance of trade. The three international electronics firms which were establishing themselves in the area were moving in very slowly. They first rented premises and set up small manufacturing operations in them. Then as the production grew they rented more separate facilities, and finally applied to the local authorities for permission to move all their operations into a single large plant in the interests of efficient production and administration. Over a period of eight to ten years these corporations were developing major operations through this kind of incremental development. The large international corporations were forced by the Board of Trade to build major expansions in the development areas, as at one time or another the government flatly refused to allow them to expand in the South-East. Once they had built significantly in development areas these firms used this fact in bargaining for expansions of their South-East operations. All of them wanted to keep administration and research and development in the South-East and as these grew they had to apply for permission to expand their plant and sometimes their labour force.

The firms in the sample, both large and small, regard development areas as places to send fully-developed and routine manufacturing operations. The directors of small firms said that if their markets grew and they had to increase production of particular products significantly, then they would consider setting up a manufacturing operation in one of the development areas. They would not move their headquarters or their experimental work to these places, but only completely routinized, and hopefully trouble-free units of production. The large international chemical corporation in the sample had the same attitude towards development-area location: when a new product was fully developed and its production process completely routinized, then it could be moved to a factory in a development area or a northern new town. The international car manufacturing corporation showed the same attitude towards development-area location. It would have preferred to have all of its operations in the South-East, but as this was made impossible by the government, it sent separate manufacturing operations to Merseyside and South Wales, and made service at these distant plants a prerequisite for promotion in the corporation's management structure in order to induce managers to these places.

Small firms which are not of local origin have the most difficult time of any type of firm in locating in the local authorities of the South-East. In fact, it is almost impossible for them to do so legally. A few have located in the study area simply by moving into the premises of larger firms, renting space on a short-term basis and never applying for planning permission. When the larger firm wants the space it has thus been renting out, it might apply for permission to build a new building itself, and then move the smaller firm into it. Short of some such tactics, there is little hope for the small non-local firm to get located in the areas studied because it has no claim on the local authority for any special consideration and has no backing from the national government to help it overcome local authority objections to new employment-generating development. The central government can only be expected to weigh in on the side of a firm in the interests of national economic development.

CHAPTER FOUR

THE PLANNERS: CONTROL OF NEW RESIDENTIAL DEVELOPMENT

This chapter considers some detailed case studies of relationships between developers and planners in proposed new residential developments on hitherto underdeveloped land. In some cases the planning application was finally successful, in others not, and the chapter analyses reasons for this. It concludes that planners have been generally successful in their objectives of organizing development in large units, in areas designated for development and imposing comprehensive plans for estate design. They have systematically discouraged small scale – especially individual – house developments. They have tried to educate developers, and a measure of understanding between planner and developer has come about over the years. The major problems have been the segregation of public urban renewal schemes in the cities from the new suburban private developers in the counties, and the failure to provide enough land in the plans to meet the demands for new housing. This last has caused the central government to intervene in the process of land allocation during the 1960s.

This chapter was researched and written by Harry Gracey.

INTRODUCTION

The control of residential development has been the largest single task for most of the local planners in Megalopolis since drawing up their county Development Plans in accordance with the 1947 Planning Act. This is not surprising for the planners in the cities and counties of the South-East, where there was a 12 per cent increase in population between 1950 and 1960, or in the Midlands, where the population grew by 6 per cent during this same period. Even in the North, however, where there was a very small overall population increase, suburban migration of city dwellers has created a huge demand for new homes in the suburban areas south of Liverpool and Manchester. In general, population growth and the heavy outward migration of families from the city centres has created a tremendous demand for new homes throughout Megalopolis over the past twenty years.

Fully half of the new homes constructed in Britain during the quarter of a century since the Second World War have been council houses, built by the local authorities in the cities and counties and allotted to families on their local housing lists. The planning authorities in the county boroughs and counties generally played a relatively minor role in the council-housing building programmes. This local government activity is usually the province of the engineering department or in some cases, a special housing department of the local authority, which in many cases had been building council houses for many years prior to the establishment of comprehensive, compulsory town and country planning in 1947. The planners have over the years been trying to gain influence in the council-house building programme in their local authority, and some have succeeded in getting planning criteria, such as neighbourhood design and provision of public facilities, taken into account in urban redevelopment and the construction of council estates in the counties.

The local planners do, however, have direct jurisdiction over private enterprise home-building in the territory of the local authority. No private builder can put up houses without prior permission of the local authority, and the planners in local government recommend to the local council whether or not to give permission for a new home development, as they do on all other kinds of new private development. Thus here, as in the study of industrial development control, we are examining mainly the location control exercised by the public authority over the private sector of the economy. Much more of this private home-building has taken place in the counties than in the cities of Megalopolis over the past twenty years, so most of our housing development control examples will come from the administrative counties. We shall, however, also look at examples of efforts of planners in the cities of Megalopolis to provide space for private home construction within the city boundaries and to exercise some influence in the slum-clearance and redevelopment programmes being carried out in their cities, in order to show some of the efforts planners are making to exercise control over house building in the public sector.

RESIDENTIAL DEVELOPMENT CONTROL

The twenty-year Development Plans, drawn up for the cities and counties after the 1947 Planning Act, and the various town and neighbourhood plans which were made following approval of the Development Plan, were the chief instruments by which the planners designated where residential development ought to go in their local authorities. In making these official Plans the planners had to decide in general, *what* sorts of development ought to go *where* in the local authority, and *when* it ought to be allowed to be built. New residential development was assigned very generally in the Development Plans to those areas in the county borough or county where it could be most appropriately located by planning criteria. It was much more specifically located on the town maps and neighbourhood plans, which showed what sort of residential development was to be allowed, in precisely what parts of cities and towns it could be built, and when it could be built. The type of residential development thought to be appropriate for a particular site was indicated by the population densities which were specified for new development on the more detailed town and neighbourhood plans. These detailed plans also showed the order in which the planners felt the residential sites in a particular place ought to be developed, and at what period in time they should be developed, based of course on their overall estimates of population growth for the local authority. These detailed plans were the chief instruments of control of private residential development in the local authorities of Megalopolis.

By 1970 the planners in the cities and counties of Megalopolis had been engaged in the control of new private residential development for over twenty years. During this time development control of private home building had gone far beyond the simple problem of locating new homes in the places designated on the plans, town maps, and neighbourhood plans of the local authorities. Ever closer control had been exercised over all details of site development which could contribute to the character of the new estate and to its impact on the surrounding area. Residential development control had become a process which was concerned not only with locating new home construction in its proper place by planning criteria, but also with supervising the layout and construction of the new private-housing estates, looking to the provision of public facilities such as schools and shops in the new developments, protecting the local amenities of the sites and of the communities in which they were located, and even with the details of the design, siting and materials of the individual houses on the estates. The planners in Megalopolis have developed standards of location, layout, design, and even materials to be used in the construction of new homes, and they consistently employ the planning process, and other local government controls, to force private home developers to conform to these standards.

Two constrasting examples of residential development control in the South illustrate the variety of concerns which the planners bring to this important activity and some of the means they use to achieve their ends, as well as the limits of their power in this area of public control. One of the proposed developments, located in the small city of Brookfield and carried out by a local firm, Hendersons Home Builders, is allowed and supervised by the planners while the other, proposed for the edge of a small town in the countryside by the London firm of Kensington Developments, is turned down by the planners and by the Minister on appeal. We shall first consider the successful proposal of Hendersons, then the unsuccessful effort of the Kensington builders.

Hendersons Home Builders is a small construction firm operating in the South of England which specializes in developing high-quality residential estates of from thirty to one hundred houses each, in the price range of seven to ten thousand pounds. Hendersons is interested in acquiring plots of land in the South, four to ten acres in size, which already have planning permission for residential development. In other words, they look for land on the market which is located in areas designated for residential development in the town or county maps of the local authorities in the South. Hendersons have built up a network of contacts over the years, with estate agents, architects, and solicitors, who know the sort of land they are interested in and let them know when a piece comes on the market. The company policy, the managing director explained, is to enter into contract to purchase land only after at least outline planning permission for residential development has been obtained. It is too small a firm, he said, to buy land not scheduled for residential development and hold it speculatively, as some of the larger home builders do. At the same time, Hendersons do not want to devote executive time to fighting planning appeals for the development of unscheduled sites in the South, because the success rate of such appeals is too low at the moment. The company's policy, then, is to take an option to buy land, obtain planning permission for residential development if the owner has not already done so, and then sign a contract to purchase the site.

The history of Hendersons' Ridge Road site in Brookfield began when a local solicitor, representing the owner of the land, told the developer that the local manor house, Fairview, and its five remaining acres of land was now for sale. The Ridge is the best residential neighbourhood in Brookfield and Fairview is located on 'a magnificent sloping site with many fine trees, a marvellous view, and catching the sun most of the day', according to a report by the local planning officer. The whole area is scheduled for residential development of fairly low-density, and therefore high price, on the local town plan which has just recently been approved by the County Council. The owner had obtained outline planning permission for house construction on his remaining five acres before putting this land on the market through his solicitor. Hendersons purchased the site and hired one of the best-known architects in the area to draw up a detailed plan for development of the site. The developer thought he could get more houses of the sort he was building onto the site than would be allowed with the densities provided in the local authority plan, and he instructed his architect to design a layout for fifty-four houses rather than the forty-eight which the planner's density would allow. The layout plan and house types which the developer's architect submitted to the local planning authority set off a controversy which lasted seven months.

The local area planners were very dissatisfied with the development proposed by Hendersons' architect and at the same time dismayed at the prospect of conflict with such a prestigious man in the field. They asked the County Council Planning Committee to withhold permission for the development, 'pending a tree preservation order on the site', while they organized for action on the proposal. The Committee of the Council told the developer, without granting or withholding permission, that: 'The best possible detailed layout will be required in view of the visual significance of this site and its existing landscape value.' This reply was requested by the planners and reflects their definite disapproval of the housing density, site layout and house designs submitted by the developer's architect.

The developer's architect had submitted a site plan which called for fifty-four semi-detached and terraced houses in the neo-Georgian style, to be built on two roads running parallel across the hillside. The local planners thought this was completely wrong for this site, and asked for support from the county planner's office and for the convening of the local Architects' Panel to review the developer's plan. The local area planner reported to the Panel: 'This is a unique site with a south-facing slope and excellent trees and calls for a special form of development.' He went on to criticize the developer's plan, saying:

> The submitted scheme adopts a form of expression more suited to a level site . . . the houses are poorly related to the ground and to one another . . . the houses are too close to the best trees. . . . No attempt has been made to make use of the avenue of trees along the existing drive.

One of the deputies from the county planner's office also criticized the developer's plan, reporting to the Architects' Panel:

> Intelligent use of the site using a rational building form would create an excellent environment here without recourse to unnecessary features and pretentious styling. . . . The site should be developed in high-density pockets of modern design buildings leaving space around the existing trees, rather than in parallel lines of terraced Georgian houses.

The planners thought that:

> The Georgian house type is out of place in this setting, which has an almost rural atmosphere . . . a modern design would give a more informal result in keeping with the setting.

The county Architects' Panel considered Ridge Road to be 'an important site with fine trees' and also reacted negatively to the developer's layout and house design. In their report they said: 'The submitted design of buildings requires a formal approach which is considered to be fundamentally unsuited to the slope of the ground and the preservation of the trees.' In their opinion: 'A more organic design is required here.' The local area planners were asked to meet with the developer's architect to 'discuss exploiting the site to better advantage.'

Hendersons were furious with the local planners for criticizing their architect's scheme for development of the Ridge Road site. The director said he placed 'greater reliance on our architects than on local authority critics,' and complained to the county's chief planner about what he called 'the humiliating state of relations between qualified and highly reputed architects and planners in this county'. He instructed the architect to negotiate with the local planners, but at the same time file an appeal with the Minister of Housing and Local Government to force the county to rule one way or the other on their detailed application. The director felt it would be difficult for the county actually to refuse them permission to develop on design grounds and noted that the law requires the planning authority either to grant or refuse planning permission within ninety days of the submission of an application for development. Clearly Hendersons felt their design was right for this site and completely disagreed with the planners' criticisms of their plan, including the density, house type and layout design.

After the first few meetings between the developer's architect and the local area planner, the architect brought in a revised plan for the site showing some modifications in house design and some change in the layout of houses on the site, as well as a reduction in the number of houses from fifty-four to fifty. Further meetings were held, some with a member of the county Architects' Panel present, in which the planners urged further modifications of the revised development scheme. The developer's architect eventually agreed to make further alterations in his house designs and estate layout, including regrouping some of the houses on the site, moving them further away from the best trees, and creating three public open spaces on the site in the vicinity of its largest trees, and eliminating two more houses from the scheme. This site plan, the result of seven months' negotiations and revisions, was submitted to the county Planning Committee and approved by them on the advice of the planners. Hendersons began construction and at the same time instructed the architect to apply for planning permission to build the last two houses they had given up on one of the three open spaces they had been forced to designate in the scheme to get planning permission. The director knew they would be refused by the local planners and he planned to appeal against this refusal to the Minister, who he thought would grant permission because the design was right for the site. 'There are limits to the degree that we can accommodate the foibles of the local planning authority,' he said.

The local planners were also dissatisfied with the outcome of this conflict with the developer. The local area planner felt he had got very little of what he wanted in the way of development on the Ridge Road site. 'We got the architect to break up one of his lines of terraced houses, and got some houses moved away from the best trees, and got some open spaces put into the design,' he said, 'and that was about all. Minor concessions but no basic changes.' In point of fact, however, the planners had succeeded in protecting the amenities of the site from their point of view, including its fine trees and landscape, and had caused the developer to make some important changes in his layout design as well as some minor changes in his house designs. The planners also watched the construction on the site very carefully to see that these agreements were actually followed through by the developer.

The development proposal submitted to the local planning authority by Kensington Developments presented quite a different set of development control problems. Kensington Developments is a London-based construction firm which works throughout the South-East on both commercial and residential developments. The firm undertakes designing, engineering and construction work on its projects and has a large staff in its London office. At the time of the study it was constructing custom-built factory buildings and doing some smaller commercial construction in cities in the south. A local landowner who the company had met in its work had recently purchased a forty-acre farm and he approached the owners of Kensington Developments with the proposal that the firm develop part of it for housing. The farm was located between two small villages in the countryside. The would-be partners in the development went to a local planning consultant, a man who had formerly worked for the county planning authority, and asked his advice on applying for permission to develop homes on some portion of the farm. The consultant pointed out that all the land was situated in the proposed local Green Belt. The county planners, he pointed out, relied upon the Green Belt as their major instrument of development control in the county outside the major towns and cities. He advised the developers that the only land they might get permission to develop was a parcel of about six acres which immediately adjoined one of the villages. New homes had recently been built on land inside the village boundary adjacent to this field, so that the field was bounded on two sides by development and on the other two by what are called natural boundaries: a hedge with small trees and a stream ran down one side, and the fourth side fronted on the main road. The consultant said that in the appeal they would have to make to the Minister after being refused by the local planning authority it could be argued that the field was a 'natural' part of the village. He also suggested that the Minister, and even the local planners, might be impressed by a high-quality modern design for the homes and the estate as a whole. He cited the case in a neighbouring county in which a developer had just recently been given permission by the Minister to build a whole village in an area designated as Green Belt and one of the strongest arguments in his favour against the local planning refusal was thought to be the imaginative modern design his architect had created for the whole village.

Kensington Developments hired a leading local architect as a consultant to their own design department with instructions to produce a high-quality site design and house designs for about one hundred homes, ranging in price from three to five thousand pounds. Conversations with estate agents in the area, and their own experiences there, had convinced the developers that there was a large market for houses and flats in this price range in this part of the countryside near the south coast. They also knew of a long-term Development Plan which had been carried out by the central government which predicted large population increases in the area in the near future. The developers probably had hopes of undertaking more such developments over the years as land now included in the Green Belt was released for development in accordance with provisions of this new master plan. They anticipated that the local planning authority would turn them down flat, on Green Belt grounds, and placed their hope in the appeal against this refusal which they planned to make to the Minister of Housing and Local Government.

The local planning authority was quite surprised, therefore, to receive Kensington Developments' application for planning permission on these six acres of Green Belt accompanied by a completely detailed site plan and complete detailed plans for each house type. 'One is puzzled,' the planners wrote in their report to the Planning Committee,

at the expenditure of time and effort in producing such detailed drawings

> for a site which is outside the village area designated for development and which has a history of planning refusals. Apart from the lack of drainage, visual amenity and possible highway and agricultural objections I feel it is especially important that the Green Belt between these two towns should be conserved, at least until the implications of the master plan are better known.

The county Planning Committee refused permission for the development on the grounds that 'it violates the Green Belt zoning regulations, is an undesirable extension of the neighbouring village, has no main drainage in the area' and on a number of technicalities of the actual layout design, including road widths, footpath locations, highway access and sight lines, and so on. The Green Belt, the planners explained, was the chief instrument of development control in the county, and with it they hoped to prevent any new development outside the existing settlements until the government and the local authorities had decided on a master plan for the development of the entire area. The planners were aware that there was heavy pressure for development in the county – they knew that Kensington Developments could find buyers for their proposed homes, and many more like them in the years to come. They used the Green Belt to oppose the present development in the countryside for the sake of comprehensively-planned development of the area in the future.

The developers were not surprised at the local planning refusal of their proposed new housing estate. They appealed immediately to the Ministry of Housing and Local Government and were granted an appeal hearing before a Ministry inspector. The developers hired a local solicitor and again engaged the local planning consultant to help develop their arguments. During the hearing the developers' solicitor argued their case basically on the grounds of known housing demand in the area, the relation of their site to the adjoining village development, and the high quality of their development design. He made a major point of the known demand for housing in this price range in this part of the county, saying that Kensington Developments were simply trying to provide for a known demand in the area, to give the people what they wanted. The solicitor argued that the field they wanted to develop was geographically an integral part of the village, bounded on two sides by streets of new houses recently built in the village with planning permission, and separated from the rest of the countryside by the hedgerow and the stream. This development, he argued, would make a natural rounding-out of the village and was hardly a significant incursion into the Green Belt. The solicitor also argued that his clients had gone to the trouble and expense of getting a leading architect to produce a very good design for the site development.

The area planning officer who testified for the county at the appeal hearing made a number of specific points in objection to this particular proposal, but argued basically against development generally in this part of the county at this time. The planner did not challenge the claim that there was a market for homes in this price range in the area at this time. Instead he argued that sufficient provision had been made for new housing development in a number of village maps the planners had drawn up for the small communities in this part of the county. Of course, none of these provided for a development of this size and many were used up already, to the point of only single-house infilling being permitted. He claimed the development was too large for an area without main drainage. He pointed out that the proposed development violated the Green Belt in a particularly sensitive part, the space between two small communities which the planners wanted to keep open in order to preserve their separate identities. The county's case against the development really rested, however, on the Green Belt and the proposed master plan for the area. They wanted to use the Green Belt to prevent any development at all in the county open spaces until the local authorities in the area and Whitehall had all decided on a new comprehensive plan for the development of this entire region of the south coast. The Ministry also wanted to preserve the area from new construction until the comprehensive master plan for future development had been agreed upon by the various governments. Kensington Developments' appeal was refused by the Minister and they were not permitted to build their housing estate on this land at this time.

It is ironic that the type of development which the planners wanted for the Brookview site on which Hendersons put up their neo-Georgian terraces, they were offered on a site they had to turn down because of its location outside the areas scheduled for present residential development in the county. It shows the basic characteristic of the planners' position in residential development control, that they are trying to shape the residential development in their cities and counties by an instrument of public action which allows them only to respond to the initiative of private developers once they have made their town maps and designated where they think new residential development ought to go, and when. The initiative for private development is then up to the builders who propose the new developments for their own economic reasons. The planners can only respond to what the builders propose and try to shape it to their own ideas of how residential development ought to be carried out in particular places at particular times, using the various legal powers and operating procedures of the agencies of local government. In a sense the examples of Hendersons' successful development and Kensington Developments' unsuccessful proposal are more characteristic of the early years of development control, when planners and developers were just learning to take each other's measure, than of the more recent times when they have come to know pretty much what to expect from each other. Today the planners know what sort of work to expect from the different home developers operating in their areas, and the home developers have a good idea of the kind of residential development the planners are hoping to see constructed in the different parts of the local authority. Each also has an idea of how far the other can be pushed, and by what tactics.

The planners' goals with regard to residential development in the counties are generally well known to the architects, estate agents and home builders operating in the local areas. The first goal, of course, is getting the development located in the right places in the county, according to planning criteria. This involves designating areas for residential development on the county Development Plan and the various town and village plans drawn up in the planning office, encouraging the proper kinds of residential development on the proper sites while discouraging the wrong kinds of housebuilding for specific sites, and preventing builders from putting up houses on land not designated for residential development. In the areas of the county which are designated for residential development the planners try to get the development carried out for entire estates at a time, rather than through the building of one or two homes at a time on individual plots of land. County planners all over Megalopolis seek to promote comprehensive residential development by major home-builders rather than individual house-building by owners of small plots of land in the areas designated for residential development. In a number of the cases studied during the research it could be clearly seen that the planners were using local government controls and regulations to discourage the small landowner from building one or two homes on his property and to encourage the large home-building firms to assemble large tracts of land and build comprehensively-planned housing estates, whatever the house type and price range of the homes being built. Not all planners, by any means, favoured modern house designs. More typical, but perhaps also extreme, was the county planner in the Midlands who boasted that no modern building had been permitted in his jurisdiction. Modern architecture he considered an abomination, at least in his county, and most new home-construction since the war had been done in imitation native stone. The large, comprehensively-planned estate built by a developer known to the local planners could be controlled more easily in the interest of planning goals than could individual house-building, it was generally felt. A number of examples in our study show how the planners achieved this goal in substantial new developments in a West Midlands county.

In the case of site A, the planners began receiving applications in 1950 from owners of small plots of land who wanted to build one house, for their own use or sale. The site was scheduled for residential development on the county's town map for the area, begun in 1960 after the neighbouring land had been developed. The entire area would house over 50,000 people when development was completed according to the county Development Plan, the planners having made the decision that a substantial portion of the county's expected population growth ought to be housed on this land. The county planners consistently turned down individual applications from landowners for building one or two homes on land in the area, in order to force these small landowners to sell out to the large home-developers who could put in a comprehensive development scheme of at least fifty to a hundred houses to the planning authority. The Ministry of Housing and Local Government allowed a few of these individual homes to be built, on appeals by the owners against the local planning refusals. This the planners felt was regrettable, but they continued to turn down the applications for permission to build one or two houses, giving as their reasons poor land drainage, poor highway access, lack of sewers, and most important of all to them, prejudice to the ultimate comprehensive development of the area that they hoped to see. Both local and national home development firms were quick to see the opportunities presented by these sites and a number of new estates were built or were in the process of being built at the time of the survey. The entire 1,000 or so acres of land scheduled for development were filled with new homes by 1970. The new development had come up to the borders of Site A on two sides by the late 1950s and the planners were hoping they could continue to discourage individual home-development until a large developer bought the site's forty acres and submitted a development plan for the whole. In 1958 a London home-builder took an option on the property and put in an application for the development of eighty homes on ten acres as the first of three stages in which he planned to develop the site. The planners compared his proposed layout with the road systems of the neighbouring tracts which had already been developed, and with a map on which they had made a tentative road plan for the entire area. On the basis of this comparison they recommended some changes in the developer's layout before he submitted a detailed development plan for their approval. Over a course of three years the home builder developed the entire site, designing and building on ten acres at a time. With each application the planners sought to see it aligned with surrounding development street systems and with their plan for the ultimate development of the area. Through twenty years of this kind of development control the planners supervised the development of an entire community the size of a new town, built by private developers. The entire development included a council estate which had already been situated in the area, and private homes built at an average of eight or nine homes to an acre, all in the medium price range.

The second example of development control in this county concerns the building of a prestige estate on fifty acres of wooded manor grounds in another part of the county. This land is also scheduled for residential use and the planners were ready to supervise the building of new housing-estates on it by the right developer for this prestige setting. The estate was zoned to a density of four to five houses to the acre which would mean homes in the price range of upwards of £9,000 each. The first effort at the development of prestige site B, as we shall call it, came from the owner of the estate himself. He applied for permission to build four to five houses per acre on nine acres of the estate. The planners recommended refusal of permission in their report on this application to the County Council, giving as their reasons surface drainage problems on the land, the absence of sewage disposal facilities in the area, and an unsatisfactory layout for the development, 'in as much as it does not relate to the comprehensive development of the area as a whole'. The owner submitted a few more applications for permission to build houses on different parts of the estate, only to have these turned down by the planning office for the same reasons. After these disappointments with the county authorities, the landowner agreed to sell the entire fifty acres to a well-known quality home developer in the area. This developer proposed developing the entire site according to a comprehensive plan, in ten stages over seven or eight years. He conferred extensively with the local planners to see what kind of development they thought was suitable here, and assured them of his intentions to 'use the best architects available' and to 'develop an estate worthy of a Civic Trust Design Award'. This developer's intentions and the local planners' hopes for the development of site B coincided perfectly, and the two worked closely together over almost a decade developing the site. Arrangements for solving the drainage and sewage disposal problems of the estate were made with the local rural district in which the site was located. A density of four houses to the acre was agreed upon by the planners and the developer. They also agreed that the natural features of the site would be retained as far as possible, including the land contours and the major trees. The developer produced layout designs which conformed to the natural features of the site and the planners watched carefully to see that these were followed and that the best trees on the estate were preserved during the construction period. The estate won two Civic Trust Design Awards for excellence in residential estate design and construction.

These two examples of sites A and B from a Midlands county show how the public authority, through the local planners, can be a strong positive force in the residential development of the county, even when the actual development is carried out by business firms for private profit. The planners can use the powers of local government to control the location, size, and even design of new private housing-estates in the counties. It is interesting to note also that the planners do not confine their supervision of private housing-estates to their location and construction. In the Midlands county at least they inspected the estates periodically after the homes had been sold and the new owners had moved in, to see that the design and tree-preservation regulations were being adhered to by the new owners. Having taken the trouble to supervise the design and construction of the estates according to their standards the planners felt it would not be right to let the home owners cut down trees in their front gardens or put up unsightly garden houses, or garages or fences on their property.

Residential development control in an East Midlands county provides a picture of firmly-established, smooth working relationships between planners and developers, and adds something to our understanding of the contribution the developer's architect can make to this relationship. In this county the proposed Green Belt was firmly established and generally accepted, by planners, developers and the public. The planners designated land for home building in 'village envelopes' in the Green Belt: land in and around established settlements which they hoped could provide all the new private homes needed in the area. With this development control instrument they hoped to preserve the countryside, conserve the attractive villages, and concentrate new home-development in areas where it was not a threat to either of these county amenities. As the planners produced town maps for each of the 'envelope villages' in the Green Belt, the home builders working in the county knew just where new development was to be allowed and at what densities, and therefore what priced homes could be economically constructed in which parts of the county. The planners here were just as reluctant as those in the South and the West Midlands to allow individual home-construction on single plots of land and so home-building firms have gradually bought up the land designated for home development in the villages and constructing new housing estates. Over the years the planners' preferences for estate layout and house design became known to the architects regularly employed by the home builders in the county. These demands of the planners are actually the cause of the developers hiring architects in the first place, in many cases.

A fairly typical case of home development in this county began with the submission by the developer's architect of an application for the development of seventy homes on eight and a half acres of land. The application was designated as 'phase I' of a larger project to develop about thirty acres of land zoned for residential building in one of the 'village envelopes' in the Green Belt. The architect submitted a very detailed layout scheme for the first phase and detailed drawings of the house types, with lists of materials and colours to be used in their construction. His layout called for the retention of three open spaces on the site, called children's play spaces, and for the retention of the remainder of an orchard currently on the site. A meeting was held with the local planners, who asked the architect to change the layout somewhat, to provide a public footpath through the site, to retain the large hedgerows on the site, and to change details for their proposed landscaping. The planners also asked for changes in some of the house designs, for which the architect requested a formal letter criticizing the designs, which he could show to the developer. The chief planner wrote a letter to the architect in which he praised various aspects of his house designs and severely criticized other aspects. He said he was happy that certain house designs used by the developer elsewhere were not used here: he referred to one house design as 'particularly interesting and suitable to the site', criticized another as 'really old hat', and made suggestions about the colour of bricks and tiles to be used, suggesting that simplicity was called for in this site and reminding the architect that 'red and brown are the south-county roof colours'. The architect later personally thanked the planner for his criticisms of the home designs wanted by the developer because they 'strengthen the architect's hand when he endeavours to improve design qualities on developer's estates'. The architect considered that he and the planners were working together to educate home developers to the importance of good design and that they were 'slowly winning' the campaign. Revised house designs were submitted to the planners by the architect, and further negotiations were carried on over these and over landscaping and tree planting on the estate.

Toward the end of the 1960s, when it became evident that the combination of population growth and suburban migration was creating an unexpected pressure for new land for private home-development, the central government was forced to inject itself strongly into the local development control process. The county Development Plans for Megalopolis, which were drawn up following the 1947 Planning Act, and subsequently revised where possible, simply had not provided sufficient land for new house construction. These plans were based on population growth projections which proved false and had not taken account of the increasing pressure of suburbanization around the cities. The prosperity which gradually returned to the country in the 1950s and 1960s brought increased demand for family home-ownership. The combination of land costs in the cities themselves, and the amount of land being taken for urban renewal projects in the cities made it increasingly difficult for families to find homes for sale in the cities, even if they wanted to remain urban dwellers when they became home owners. The new homes were being built on the estates in the towns and villages out in the counties, and this is where the families who wanted a home of their own to purchase had to go. The planners in the counties did try to accommodate many of these families in the new estates, but their county Development Plans did not provide nearly as much land for new residential development as these groups needed. Around the larger cities of Megalopolis there was also a shortage of land for new council housing, particularly for those cities with extensive urban renewal programmes for their central business districts and city-centre slums.

The central government, beginning in the mid-1960s, conducted a number of studies of population increase and suburban migration, and on the resulting need for land for new residential development in the future. The results of these studies showed that around the large cities, and especially in the Home Counties around London, twice as much land as was provided in the local county Development Plans would be required for new residential development over the next twenty years. The government took a number of actions on the basis of these future projections. It created the Land Commission to assemble tracts of land in suitable places and sell it to developers for private home-construction.* The Ministry of Housing and Local Government sent directives to the counties to prepare plans for accommodating as much as twice the population increase forecast in their existing plans. The Ministry also began to look at planning appeals from private developers in the light of these projections which forecast a far greater need for private home development than was provided for in the local Development Plans. Applications from home builders for permission to develop land which was not zoned for residential development in the county Development Plans or the local town maps, which were refused by the local planners and appealed to the Ministry, began to be examined there in the light of the unmet future development-needs for new homes in the counties.

The home builders in the South and the Midlands read the government reports forecasting the far larger than expected population increase and suburban migration, and saw that eventually far more land would have to be zoned for residential development. The larger firms began to look at likely parcels of land in the counties, where they thought development might be allowed on good planning principles, and to purchase or take options to

* The role of the Land Commission is analysed in detail in Chapter Seven.

purchase this land. New regional development plans, which the government encouraged or sponsored, became a kind of 'speculators' map since they indicated the parts of the counties which might be opened up for new residential development in the future. The developers began to look at the unoccupied land in the areas where they operated and speculate as to whether they might ultimately get permission from the Ministry to develop it, if they were likely to be refused in the first instance by the local planners.

One such home-building firm, a developer of small high-quality residential estates in the London area, acquired a farm in the commuter belt south of London. The developers thought that the central government might reasonably allow development on this site. They knew, however, from their contacts with the Ministry of Housing that the land was zoned as part of the Green Belt and the developers were sure proposals for home construction there would be rejected by the local planning authorities. However, they thought the central government might reasonably allow the development in the light of its new population estimates for the county. They were aware from their contacts with the Ministry of Housing planners that only an exceptionally good layout and house-design proposal would be acceptable to the Central government in overruling the local authorities and allowing the development. The developer's architect designed an entire 'village' of two thousand dwellings in a comprehensive, integrated layout plan. The plan, with detailed house designs, was submitted to the local planning authority, which, as expected, refused permission, on the grounds that the development was in the proposed Green Belt and not in an area zoned for new residential development. The developer's scheme received wide publicity because of its unusual nature as a design and the audacious manner in which he was challenging the local authority on the near-sacred principle of the maintenance of the Green Belt. The proposal did meet the criteria of the central government though, by providing for many homes which would be needed in the area and showing high-quality work in the design of the layout and of the various types of homes to be provided. The developer had also designed a shopping precinct in his plan, a couple of public parks, and land for elementary schools. Agreement had been reached with the Greater London Council for providing a neighbourhood of council houses on the estate. The central government overruled the local planning authority and allowed the developers to proceed with the project. This decision was carefully noted by home developers throughout the South and the Midlands (see our second example in this chapter) who saw it as clear evidence of the possibility of greatly increasing their operations in these rapidly-growing areas in the future. The local planning authorities also took note of this watershed planning decision by the central government, especially after they received requests from the Ministry of Housing to find land for new home-development which would accommodate the increased populations forecast for their areas. Some of the local planners seemed to be aware that a new era of residential construction and development control was upon them. In the more advanced county planning offices there began a search for new criteria for development control, perhaps coming from the social sciences, which could be used along with their standards of good layout and design, to help them plan the new residential communities and use their powers to guide the private home-builders in their developments. These planners are beginning to feel it takes more than good architecture and design to produce good communities, and to ask if the social sciences cannot help tell them what people need and want in their new communities.

The planners in the cities of Megalopolis had in a way already come to these problems of social design in their efforts to influence the urban renewal and council-house building programmes which constituted most or practically all of the new house-building in their jurisdiction. In the first place, the city planners saw clearly that the urban renewal programmes and very large council-house construction programmes in some of the cities were fixing the class structure of regions in what might be an undesirable manner. Since council houses are mainly occupied by the working class, and private homes are mainly purchased by the middle class, the cities were in effect redeveloping themselves as working-class communities and the counties were getting all the new middle-class families. The cities with the most ambitious urban renewal programmes were creating the greatest class segregation, for their housing or architecture departments were trying to get as much land in the city as they could to put up their new council estates. Most of the land available in the cities for new home construction was thus being taken by the public authorities for essentially working-class housing. As one city planner said, with the very great need for land to rehouse the working-class families from the various slum-clearance programmes in his city, it was felt in some quarters to be 'almost criminal' to suggest some of this land be put aside for private developers and middle-class estates. Even if some land were so put aside, this planner was doubtful that private developers would buy tracts on the edge of large council estates to put up private housing-estates. They would be afraid they might not be able to interest middle-class families in living in such locations.

Another problem arises for those cities whose councillors and planners have ambitions for them to become metropolitan administrative centres with a great deal of white-collar employment in office work, government work and so on. The administrative offices they hope to attract to the city will employ people who are for the most part forced to live outside the city, perhaps beyond the Green Belt, and to commute to the city to work. Most of the heads of households of families living on the new estates constructed in the 'village envelopes' of the Green Belt in the East Midlands county probably commute daily to work in the central city. At the same time the planners are wary of proposals for industrial development out in the county for they realize that much of the labour might have to commute to work from the working-class housing estates in the central city. The city council in another Midlands city, on the other hand, has taken the advice of the planners to provide for a large housing-estate on a large wasteland site which happens to be within the city's boundaries. This land is, in effect, being reserved for private home-development in the future, in part to assure the continuation of a middle-class population within the city's boundaries. Its slum-clearance problem is perhaps not as acute as that of the other city, but the planners have also managed to inject some sociological criteria into city land-use decision making.

Planners in at least one city in Megalopolis have also recently attempted to get social criteria as well as design and layout principles taken into account in the location and design of new council estates by their local housing or architecture departments. As one planner put it:

> we recognize the social malaise which afflicts the old council estates, and we're doing everything we can to get them to make social provisions on the new estates. The trouble is, it all costs money.

The department constructing the new council homes naturally wants to spend all the money allotted to it on houses, to get as many families relocated as possible with the funds they have. Any move to force them to make more spacious layouts, include more public areas at the expense of houses, or to spend money on public facilities outside the bare necessities will naturally be resisted. The planners in this case have applied to the central government for supplementary urban renewal funds to provide better layouts and more facilities which will promote a better social life on the new estates. At the same time they are working with the city Housing Department, which does the slum clearance and council-estate construction, to get provision for social facilities written into future renewal plans submitted to the central government for their approval. They want to develop 'urban renewal packages' which include adequate space and good design and provide for social facilities such as schools, welfare, shopping, medical care, youth activities, and public open space, to see if the government will support the creation of communities, or urban neighbourhoods rather than continue to finance 'dreary housing projects'. These city planners seek to inject some of the same kinds of thought on urban neighbourhood development into the development of council estates in the cities as the advanced county planners want to use in controlling private home development in the counties. In the case of city redevelopment, the cost of advanced design and social provision will have to be paid for by the public authorities, whereas in the counties the private home-owners must eventually pay the cost of any social amenities which the planners are able to get the developers to include in their new housing estates. Clearly, though, the more advanced planning authorities in the cities and the counties of Megalopolis are thinking seriously of the social requirements for good living on new estates. They are searching for sociological guidelines for the development of new estates, neighbourhoods and communities which they can incorporate into their residential development-control process in the future.

SUMMARY AND CONCLUSIONS

The planners generally try to organize new home-construction into fairly large units which can be comprehensively planned and developed and then exert their influence on the developer to make a comprehensive plan for the development which incorporates the planners' idea of proper estate design and layout. It is difficult to generalize about the criteria the planners apply to residential development control, but probably the most commonly used are the neighbourhood unit principle and some variation of the Radburn principle of pedestrian-vehicle segregation: two concepts relating respectively to the size and design of residential neighbourhoods which were developed in the United States in the 1920s and 1930s.

Housing redevelopment in the cities is carried out by the engineering, public works, architects or housing department of the local authorities in areas designated for clearance by the chief health officer. The housing which is defined as slum and in need of clearance changes over time as the city redevelopment programme progresses; for example, when all working-class homes built before 1890 are demolished and replaced, the goal becomes to clear the working-class quarters built before 1914. The planners have tried to bring themselves into the slum-clearance programmes in order to inject some principles of the neighbourhood design and provision of social facilities into the redevelopment programme to supplement the concern with sheer numbers of old houses replaced. The planners are becoming conscious of the fact that redevelopment, while it may replace homes does not replace community life in the slums, and are concerned about the social malaise which afflicts so many redevelopment areas. They are also conscious of the fact that the crash programmes for housing redevelopment in the cities are turning them into one-class communities, for the new council housing being built is occupied principally by the working class. The planners would like land to be provided for new middle-class housing in the cities, but point out that in most cases the local authority feels it cannot spare land from its slum redevelopment programme to give over to private house-developers, and the private builders are not particularly anxious to build estates for home owners next to huge council estates because they fear they will have difficulty in selling the houses. In the one city where there was land which could be spared for private development, the planners have drawn up a comprehensive plan for the entire area, which divides it into neighbourhood units designed around a modified Radburn plan of pedestrian and vehicle segregation.

Residential development control in the counties is concerned mainly with locating new private housing in the areas planned for expansion, and with supervising the developments so that they conform to the planners' standards for estate layout and house design. The county planners have by and large succeeded in getting new private residential construction located in the areas they have designated for expansion in their Development Plans and town maps. These are usually towns and villages, in the Green Belts and beyond them, which the planners do not like aesthetically and therefore consider not worth saving from new development. Much of the new home-building for private home-owners in the counties has consequently been carried out in the less attractive parts of the region; the developers would have preferred to build in other places in the first instance, but the planners feel the new development would have spoiled the beauty of the more attractive areas.

In the areas they have designated for residential development, the county planners have consistently tried to encourage comprehensive estate developments on larger tracts of land by the home-building firms and to discourage single-house developments on small plots (except for infilling between two other buildings already erected) by small landowners. They have used the planning and other local authority regulations to prevent the small landowner from erecting one or two houses on a lot where there is other land which could be developed in conjunction with this. Instead, they have by their opposition to small development encouraged the small landowner to sell his property to the estate builder, and they have actively encouraged the professional home-building firms to assemble tracts of land on which new residential estates can be planned and developed comprehensively, in neighbourhood units with social provisions, such as roads, pavements, stores, public open spaces, and land for primary schools. The planners then require the developer to submit a plan for the development of the tract as a whole, or for one neighbourhood at a time if it is particularly large, which they approve before giving final permission for the development. In this way the planners use local authority regulations to realize their ideas about the size, location, layout and design of new housing-estates built by the private developers. The planners further try to encourage work by developers whose architects they feel have higher standards of design and workmanship and greater concern for preserving attractive features of the local landscape. When a large developer whom the planners think does not use particularly good design or whom they feel does not care about the local amenities, has conformed to all the local government regulations and finally cannot be prevented from carrying out the development, the planners apply pressure at the design and development stage to try to move him in the direction of their goals for development in the area.

The local planners have worked very hard over the years to induce the professional builders to plan and develop land comprehensively and in conformity with the local character of the areas, including using the building materials and even house styles which the planners feel are appropriate to an area. The planners speak of their long efforts to educate the developers and their architects to these principles of estate layout and house design, which often include various versions of pedestrian and vehicle segregation on estates and the provision of social facilities where appropriate. Land agents and home developers have learned the planners' preferences over the years, and relations between planners and builders in residential tract development have become fairly straightforward, if not always smooth.

The county planners have largely succeeded in preventing new suburban growth around the large cities and in channelling new private home-building to the communities they have designated for expansion. They have also been largely successful in seeing that this new development is carried out comprehensively where there are large tracts designated for new development.

The major problem in new home-development is that demand for private homes far exceeds the supply of land designated for home construction in the county Development Plans and their town maps, due to the unanticipated growth of population and the new suburban migration pressures in most urban regions. The central government has now had to put strong pressure on the local planners in the counties to release more land around the growing cities, especially in the South-East and the Midlands, for new home construction. The Labour Government in 1967 created the Land Commission to facilitate the assembling of tracts of land for new house-development in the growing regions. Some of the basic planning ideology is being called into question because of the new population and suburban migration pressures; large new residential development is now being permitted on the periphery of cities such as Birmingham and Northampton, and the Home Counties around London are being pressured by the government to release twice as much land for residential development as has been allotted in the Development Plans. The cities, in other words, are turning to the central government to realize their goals of peripheral expansion in opposition to the preservationist ideology of the county planners. The central government, armed with its population and housing demand forecasts, is now over-ruling the county planners and permitting new urban expansion of the kind which has been resisted in the counties since the passing of the 1947 Planning Act. Central government intervention is made necessary by the facts of population growth and suburban migration and the traditional division of planning authority between the cities and the counties. If city regions were established as the new units of local government in Britain, then the city and its hinterland would be under a single planning authority; which ought to facilitate planning for the natural growth of cities. The central government had become convinced, by 1968, that city regions were the logical units for land-use planning.[1] The number of new sub-regional studies in areas of high population growth and movement indicates that city and county planners now realize also that there must be co-ordinated programmes for development of regions. It is likely that, in the event that the city region principle is not adequately recognized in the reform planned for the early 1970s, the sub-regional plans will become the instruments for guiding development in the cities' reorganization, and counties of Britain.

[1] *Royal Commission on Local Government in England, 1966–9, Written Evidence of the Ministry of Housing and Local Government.* HMSO, London (1967), paras 26–36, pp. 64–5.

CHAPTER FIVE

THE HOME SEEKERS: FAMILY RESIDENTIAL MOBILITY AND URBAN GROWTH

This chapter turns to the basic mechanism affecting the residential development decision process from the viewpoint of a different actor in the process – the resident. It presents the results of a sample survey of moves into new private developments in the five main study areas within Megalopolis. One main finding is that families are mainly motivated by house, job and financial reasons; the balance between these varies with age. In choosing a location families look mainly at house characteristics and prices, and the need for a reasonable work journey for the husband; the characteristics of the community, both physical and social, are important secondary factors. Changes in family life conditions seem to provide the main reason for mobility. These families see themselves as moving from cities to suburbs; many would like to move further into the country. But the desire for country living is secondary to employment and housing considerations in the choice of area.

This chapter was researched and written by Harry Gracey.

INTRODUCTION

Earlier chapters of this report have examined the patterns of growth and the changing distribution of population and economic activity in Megalopolis and the five metropolitan regions, as well as the physical expansion of their urban areas from the 1920s to the 1960s. In the preceding chapters we have looked at the operation of the comprehensive land-use planning system introduced in the 1940s and its influence on the urbanization process and patterns of urban growth. In the present chapter we shall examine the urban growth process from a somewhat different perspective, that of the families who are moving to the new residential estates in the counties of Megalopolis. We have selected fourteen new private estates in the five metropolitan study areas of Megalopolis and sampled a total of 867 families living on them. Each family in the sample was interviewed during the study and asked questions about its social and economic characteristics, its motives for residential mobility, the effects of mobility on various aspects of family life, and its hopes or plans for future residential mobility.

All of the families in this study are engaged in the process of voluntary residential mobility. They have chosen to purchase homes on new estates which the home developers are building on green-field sites, at the edges of cities and in the country towns and villages. These families typify the sections of society which provide the market for new privately-built homes in the countryside, hence the stimulus to the physical enlargement of urban areas. They represent the demand side of the private market for new homes in the countryside of Megalopolis, and are a major contributor *in toto* to the physical growth of settlements there. In our study we sought to find out *who* these families were, *why* they were moving, *what effect* this move was having on their lives, and *where* they would actually prefer to live. Later in this chapter we shall present findings from our survey which show the social and economic characteristics of these families; their reasons for leaving their former homes and for choosing their new places of residence, the consequences of the move for family social life, finances and travel to work, as well as personal satisfactions; and the family's future mobility desires and plans.

THE EXTENT OF RESIDENTIAL MOBILITY

The data presented in Volume One shows that there has been a considerable movement of population from the metropolitan cores to the rings in all the study areas, whether or not there has been an overall population growth in any given region as a whole. It has also been shown that residential use is by far the largest consumer of land in the physical expansion of cities, villages and towns in these regions. There has been a general outward migration in the five study areas, from the city and conurbation centres to the peripheries and into the country beyond. This outward migration of families accounts for the largest part of the conversion of land to urban use, consuming more land than industry, commerce, public services or recreation, in the physical spread of communities. This outward movement of population will be shown again in Chapter Nine on the boundary-crossing journeys to work; many of the people moving to the peripheries of cities and into the towns and villages around them continue to work in the city centres, so commuting is generally on the increase in Megalopolis. The result of these changes is that the political boundaries of the cities have become mere historical artifacts bearing less and less relation to the actual physical extent of the built-up urban area and the functional metropolitan area. J. B. Cullingworth has indeed referred to the 'obliteration of administrative boundaries'[1] between counties and county boroughs as representing real boundaries between physical or social urban units, through the continual development of land contiguous to the cities, but administratively in the counties. Since 1931 the population has been 80 per cent urban in Britain, yet the proportion of the national population living in the politically-defined county boroughs has fallen, from 42 per cent in 1921 to 36 per cent in 1961.[2] The pattern of this population growth, Cullingworth points out:

[1] J. B. Cullingworth, *Town and Country Planning in England & Wales.* Allen and Unwin, London (1967), p. 268.

[2] Ibid.

> . . . has produced large residential areas in the country districts adjacent to and physically indistinguishable from the county borough, and, at the same time, often unrelated to development in the rest of the county district.[3]

Cullingworth goes on to comment:

> the county boroughs regard this fringe growth as a good justification for boundary extensions; an argument which, not unnaturally, is seldom accepted by the counties.[4]

The study reported in this book, and others which have been carried out recently, show that many parts of the remainder of the counties not contiguous to the cities have also become functionally related to the cities – non-contiguous suburbs where people who continue to work in the cities come to live. In a recent study of a section of the Birmingham Green Belt, for example, David Gregory concludes that in spite of the fact that stringent Green Belt controls have been exercised on development for ten years, 'the district remains "rural" in name only' because the population filling villages and towns where development has been allowed is urban in terms of its origins, life style and its present place of work.[5] A recent study of migration trends in Britain as a whole, by Harold Lind, confirms this impression of outward movement of population on a national scale. He finds that two-thirds of the annual internal residential migration, fully 100,000 people a year, is moving out from the centres of conurbations and large cities to the periphery of the built-up areas and beyond into the country villages and towns.[6] This compares with his estimate of about 10,000 people a year who are migrating from rural areas to places classified as urban in Britain. Geoffrey Powell, in his study of growth in the London region, found evidence in the 1950s that young workers were being drawn to central London from all over the country:

> When they marry they make an initial home broadly within the County of London. As the family grows, the tendency is to move out into the suburbs and, later, possibly into the country beyond the suburbs. . . .[7]

Powell went on to say that:

> this migration cycle provides the basic mechanism for the expansion of London. . . . [and it] cannot be checked whilst the economic life of London remains as vigorous as it is today.[8]

[3] Ibid.

[4] Ibid.

[5] David Gregory, *Green Belts and Development Control*, University of Birmingham, Centre for Urban and Regional Studies Occasional Papers, No. 12. CURS, Birmingham (1970).

[6] Harold Lind, *Migration in Britain*. Unpublished MS., NIESR (1968).

[7] Geoffrey Powell, 'The Recent Development of Greater London', *The Advancement of Science*, 17 (1960), p. 81.

[8] Ibid.

SOME EXPLANATIONS OF RESIDENTIAL MOBILITY

The question is frequently raised as to the motives and desires of these families who are moving in such great numbers to new private estates outside the cities of Britain. What are the motives for residential mobility and why select these areas of new urban development? Of course families can only go where the planners allow developers to build, if they want a new house, but is this what they want? Some very simple explanations have traditionally been offered for family mobility behaviour in Britain. One of these is the hypothetical 'Search for Arcadia', according to which every family's ideal home is a house and garden in the country – though never more than five minutes from town. Home ownership and country living are the main motives for residential mobility in this popular theory. No one is going to deny that country living has traditionally been highly valued here, but it is not known how widespread this value is today, nor what part it actually plays in family mobility decisions. Nor is it known to what extent home ownership is a value in itself. If such values are widely diffused in the population and are also effective motives for residential mobility, we would predict strong pressures for development near the attractive villages in the countryside around the major cities and conurbations, and this is the kind of pressure county planners often report today. As we have seen, they usually resist this pressure as strongly as they can in order to preserve the beautiful areas of the countryside from the ravages of new development.

Another single factor explanation which has been offered for the outward movement of families from the conurbations is the fall in the cost of land as one goes outward from the city centres. This drop in land cost is reflected, it is said, in a regular decline of house prices as one moves out from the edges of the larger conurbations of London and Birmingham; the evidence is summarized in Chapter Eight. This fall in house prices tends to be more pronounced for new houses than for old houses on the market. It is argued that families seeking new homes are forced by the nature of the market to the fringes of the city and into the country unless their incomes are quite above average. This hypothesis assumes that family mobility is motivated by the desire to purchase homes, and especially new homes, or else that homes for sale are the only type of accommodation available to families who want to move, for whatever reason.

A study conducted in 1958 of a national sample of households found that 8 per cent of them had moved in the last year. Donnison reports that in a pilot study for this project: '. . . half of the households told an interviewer they would like to move', so he feels the households who do move during a year can be considered 'the winners of a race which many others run'.[9] What is this race for? Donnison reports that, 'Most moves were responding to changes in personal and family circumstances, and seeking better housing . . .' In terms of housing change, the survey shows the flow of move-

[9] David Donnison, 'The Movement of Households in England', *Journal of the Royal Statistical Society* (Series A), 124, (1961), p. 72.

ment to be, '. . . from furnished to unfurnished private housing, and from privately-rented housing into council housing and owner-occupied housing'.[10] The study found that movers as compared to non-movers include a significantly larger proportion of households where the head was in the administrative, professional, managerial or skilled manual occupations, which may help to explain why these families were successful in the contest for new homes. But occupation was related to moving in another way for this sample. Donnison reports that:

> Change of job was mentioned by 42 per cent of these housholds with heads in administrative, professional or proprietary jobs as the reason for moving, and by 11 per cent of households with heads in other occupations.[11]

Change of the husband's job, or a promotion or transfer, seems to be a major motive for mobility among the middle-class or white-collar workers, but not among the working-class or blue-collar employees.

Some recent sociological studies of new private estates have found the families living on them to be highly mobile, and their mobility is strongly associated with the husband's job. Bell, in his study of two new estates outside Swansea, and Broady, in his study of new estates just outside Basingstoke, both found that half of their families expected to move again, the great majority because of anticipated changes in the husband's job, including transfers and promotions.[12, 13] Bell divided his mobile families into two groups according to the geographical context of the husband's career. In one group, the families with a local base, the husband was making a career in a local business, often a family business, and residence on the suburban estate was perceived as part of the family's upward social mobility. They planned to move to a house by the sea in Gower eventually. These 'locals' are a minority of the mobile families. Their residential mobility parallels their social mobility and symbolizes their ascent, beginning with a residence in the city, moving up to a house on a new estate in the suburbs, and eventually acquiring a house in a high-status village by the sea.

In the majority of Bell's mobile families the husband was making a career in a national or international organization and expected to be transferred from one branch to another around the country, and perhaps end up in the head office in London towards the end of his career. The estate outside Swansea was just one of many stopping places for the families of these managers, administrators, technicians and professionals, on their way through careers in the corporations and the government. This kind of job mobility is characteristic of advanced economies generally, but is undoubtedly also stimulated by regional economic planning which encourages large corporations to scatter factory units about the country.

[10] Ibid., p. 65.

[11] Ibid., p. 62.

[12] Colin Bell, *Middle Class Families*. Routledge & Kegan Paul, London (1968).

[13] Maurice Broady, *The Sociological Aspects of Town Development*. A Report prepared for the Basingstoke Town Development Joint Committee, 1964.

Upward social mobility has also been found to be a stimulus to geographic mobility. People who are ascending the social ladder generally seem to move away from their places of origin. This is partly because their new jobs take them away, and partly because getting away helps them to rise by freeing them from potentially embarrassing associations. Birch, in his study of Glossop, found that:

> People who get ahead.... tend to become geographically as well as socially mobile, and to join the increasingly large class of professional and managerial workers who have not got any strong roots in any local community.[14]

Upward social mobility from the working class to the middle class is a structural trend of modern societies, reflecting the changing occupational pattern which is creating great numbers of new jobs which have middle status, such as those of clerks and technicians, and reducing the number of lesser-status jobs, such as unskilled workers. Upward social mobility and the geographical mobility associated with it are likely to continue and increase in the future.

The pressures toward suburbanization and interurban migration can be expected to continue, and perhaps to increase in the future since they are products of basic socio-economic trends and processes in modern Britain. Demographic, social and economic processes – including population increase, prosperity, the growth of large-scale organizations in business and government, the changing composition of the labour force which induces upward social mobility, and even success in bringing new economic activity to the development areas – are among the factors which promote residential mobility and the increasing consumption of land for urban residential purposes. Looking at the statistics and the sociological facts behind them, one cannot help but wonder how this social process is experienced by the people involved and to what extent it expresses their desires and preferences.

THE SURVEY OF FAMILY RESIDENTIAL MOBILITY

I The Sample Families

The families moving to the fourteen new urban developments in the five regions of Megalopolis are of course 'successful movers' in Donnison's terms and it is not surprising to find they come from the higher-status groups in society, at least judging by the occupations of the family heads. As is shown in Table 5.1 families with husbands in middle-class and upper middle-class occupations are much more strongly represented in our sample than they are in the population as a whole, and manual workers, especially unskilled manual workers, are much fewer in our sample than in the country altogether. The average family income is about £1,800 per year for our sample families in 1967, which is probably higher than the average for the country, but the

[14] A. M. Birch, *Small Town Politics*. Oxford University Press, London (1959), p. 35.

Table 5.1

OCCUPATIONAL STATUS GROUPS

	Heads of household samples of families (1968)	Socio-economic group, employed males in England and Wales (1961)
	per cent	
UM: Professionals, managers and employers (upper middle-class)	33	13
LM: Non-manual and self-employed workers (lower middle-class)	32	24
UW: Foremen and manual skilled workers (upper working-class)	21	32
LW: Semiskilled and unskilled workers (lower working-class)	4	23
AF: Armed Forces members	5	2
EI: Retired, other economically inactive	4	0
Other occupations	0	6
Total	100 (n = 867)	100

Source: Residential Mobility Survey; Census 1961, England and Wales, *Occupation Tables*, Table 28.

Table 5.2

FAMILY ANNUAL INCOME 1967

	All families	Socio-economic groups					
		UM	LM	UW	LW	AF	EI
	per cent	per cent					
Over £3,000	6	16	1	1	0	5	5
£2,001–3,000	25	43	25	10	0	19	6
£1,001–2,000	51	31	57	73	69	66	22
£1,000 or less	5	1	4	6	9	0	46
Refused	7	6	9	5	9	0	19
Don't know	5	4	5	5	13	11	3

Source: Residential Mobility Survey. (For explanation of abbreviations see Table 5.1.)

Census gives no information on family income, (Table 5.2). About 56 per cent of sample husbands have GCE O-level education and above, and fully a quarter have college or university degrees and professional qualifications

Table 5.3

EDUCATIONAL ATTAINMENT OF SAMPLE HUSBANDS

	All families	Socio-economic groups UM	LM	UW	LW	AF	EI
	per cent	per cent					
University degree	10	24	3	0	0	7	3
Teacher's certificate, other professional qualification	16	34	11	1	0	11	11
A-level GCE	11	11	16	8	0	5	0
O-level GCE	19	10	28	25	13	16	3
Apprenticeships	7	3	3	23	0	16	3
Others	5	5	5	6	3	11	5
None	22	10	23	30	66	23	30
Don't know	10	4	11	8	19	11	46

Source: Residential Mobility Survey. (For explanation of abbreviations, see Table 5.1.)

Table 5.4

RESIDENTIAL MOBILITY AND FAMILY LIFE-CYCLE POSITION

	First-married home	One other home	Two other homes	Three or more other homes
	per cent			
FLC Position:				
I No children	68	16	9	7
II Infant school children	61	25	9	5
III Primary school children	19	31	23	26
IV Secondary school children	12	38	15	35
V Secondary children, adults over 45 years old	10	27	17	43
VI Adults 45+, no children	19	26	23	29
Total families	31	30	18	21

Source: Residential Mobility Survey.

(Table 5.3). As shown in Table 5.4, these are a fairly mobile sample of families, for about 30 per cent have lived in two places since marriage, while almost 40 per cent have lived in three or more places. Table 5.4 shows mobility as related to the 'age' of the family as a unit, its position in the family life cycle and the age of the head of the household. Forty-three per cent of the families with heads over 45 years of age and with children in secondary school have lived in three or more different places since marriage, whereas only 5 per cent of the young couples with infants have been as mobile as this since marriage. The families in the sample will probably be experiencing considerable further residential mobility, as 61 per cent think it is likely or very likely that they

Table 5.5

RESIDENTS' CHARACTERIZATION OF THEIR COMMUNITIES

	Town	Suburbs	Country	Other
		per cent		
Old place	25	44	18	13*
New place	7	58	35	0
Desired future place	8	29	59	4**

* abroad, military base, etc.
** by the sea, overseas, etc.
Source: Residential Mobility Survey.

Table 5.6

REASONS FOR LEAVING FORMER COMMUNITY

	Order of importance		
	1st	2nd	3rd
		per cent	
Housing	45	26	17
Husband's job	28	9	3
Finances	6	11	6
Area's physical characteristics	8	13	11
Area's social characteristics	6	9	7
Community facilities	1	2	4
Others	3	1	1
None	0	28	52

Source: Residential Mobility Survey.

will move again. All the families perceive their mobility as being outward from the city to the suburbs and almost all of them expressed a desire for this kind of geographic mobility (Table 5.5).

II Reasons for Moving

The respondents gave a great variety of reasons for moving and these have been summarized in Tables 5.6 and 5.7. Separate questions were asked to find the reasons for *leaving the old community*, on the one hand, and reasons for *choosing the new community*, on the other. Housing is mentioned most often as the primary reason for leaving the old home (45 per cent) and choosing the new one (34 per cent) by the sample families. The desire for home ownership is very strong in the sample, with 20 per cent of the families considering it the most important reason for moving. While about half (55 per cent) of families had owned the home in their old community, 96 per cent own their present homes. There is also a significant change in house type with movement in the new community, as shown in Table 5.8. Just over 40 per cent

Table 5.7

REASONS FOR CHOOSING NEW COMMUNITY

	Order of importance				
	1st	2nd	3rd	4th	5th
	per cent				
Housing	34	30	28	21	16
Husband's job	23	11	10	5	3
Finances	20	16	8	6	4
Area's physical characteristics	12	24	27	21	20
Area's social characteristics	5	5	7	8	5
Community facilities	4	10	10	16	10
Others	1	1	*	*	*
None	0	3	9	22	41

Source: Residential Mobility Survey.

Table 5.8

TYPE OF ACCOMMODATION

	Former place	Present place
	per cent	
Flat (or maisonette)	21	2
Terraced house	12	2
Semidetached house	34	47
Bungalow	8	17
Detached house	9	33
Other (Shared house, etc.)	14	0

Source: Residential Mobility Survey.

had lived in detached or semidetached houses in the last community, while 80 per cent of the families have this type of housing in the new community. Monthly housing costs have increased on the average of one-third for the families with the last move, going up from an average of £16 in the last community to about £23 in the present place (Table 5.9). The type of accommodation achieved by families in the new community is significantly related to the status of the husband's occupation as Table 5.10 shows. High-status occupations and their higher salaries tend to give families access to detached houses, while those in lower-status and income brackets have to be satisfied with semidetached houses and bungalows.

The husband's job is the next most frequently mentioned main reason for leaving the old community (28 per cent) and for selecting the new place to live (23 per cent). Promotions, transfers, and change of job account for most of the 'job reasons' for leaving the old place, while accessibility to the husband's new position is the main 'job reason' involved in selecting the new home. The proportion of husbands in the sample who travel to work by car has increased with the last move from 67 per cent at the previous home to 81 per cent in the new place, so accessibility to jobs probably means good road systems for most families (Table 5.11). It is interesting to note that the

Table 5.9

MONTHLY HOUSING COSTS

Cost	Former place	Present place
	per cent	
Up to £9·49	19	7
£9·50 to £19·49	30	6
£19·50 to £29·49	22	32
£29·50 to £39·49	5	22
£39·50 and over	2	9
Don't know/refused	21	24
Average house cost	£16	£23

Source: Residential Mobility Survey.

Table 5.10

TYPE OF ACCOMMODATION BY SOCIO-ECONOMIC GROUPS OF FAMILIES IN NEW COMMUNITIES

	UM	LM	UW	LW	AF	EI
			per cent			
Detached houses	52	30	14	17	19	33
Semidetached	35	53	57	58	16	47
Bungalows	10	12	26	22	51	17
Others	3	4	3	3	11	4

Source: Residential Mobility Survey. (For abbreviations see Table 5.1, p. 152.)

average distance from work has increased for the husbands with the last move (Table 5.12) as did the average time taken to get to work (Table 5.13). This reflects the fact that a quicker journey to work for the husband is not the main reason for selecting the new place to live for the majority of the families in the sample.

Family financial circumstances are given by a small portion of the sample families (6 per cent) as the main reason for leaving the former community but by a larger portion (20 per cent) as the primary reason for choosing the new community. Financial reasons for leaving the old community are mixed, as some families are in a position to afford a more expensive home, though probably a majority of these would not mention finances as the primary reason for moving, while a small portion of the sample, 4 per cent, are couples going to retirement and looking for a smaller home, and some of

Table 5.11

CHANGE IN MODE OF TRAVEL TO WORK

Mode of travel		Former place	Present place
		per cent	
Car		67	81
Train or tube		9	7
Bus		7	4
Bike or motorcycle		7	4
Walk		5	3
Company transport		3	2
Other/Don't know		2	*
	Total	100	100
	n =	683	822

Base: Heads of households in employment, whose type of work does not require a particular form of transport, e.g. excluding sales representatives and vicars.
Source: Residential Mobility Survey.

Table 5.12

CHANGE IN DISTANCE OF JOB FROM HOME

Distance of trip		Former place	Present place
		per cent	
Under 6 miles		46	37
6–10 miles		23	23
11–20 miles		18	23
21–30 miles		6	9
Over 30 miles		5	8
Don't know		2	0
	Total	100	100
	n =	652	773

Source: Residential Mobility Survey.

these may very well have been experiencing a reduction of annual income. For the 20 per cent of our sample families who give finance as the main reason for choosing their new home, the majority find themselves in a tight housing market where they feel constrained to buy the house they can find and which they can afford, and all other desires about the place they wanted to live have to be secondary.

The physical and social characteristics of the area and the community facilities provided for the families, come into the family mobility decision-making as secondary reasons for leaving the former community and for choosing the new one. The attractiveness of the community's physical location, the layout of the estate, the types of people living there, and various social facilities available, such as stores, schools, and churches, are cited by only 21 per cent of the sample as the main reason for leaving their former community, but by 24 per cent of the sample as the second most important reason for leaving the old place (Table 5.6). In the choosing of a new place to live, only about 21 per cent of the sample families cite these community characteristics as the primary factor in selecting a new place, but 39 per cent consider them the second most important factors to take into consideration in choosing a new place to live (Table 5.7). The physical features the respondents are looking for in their new communities are country, secluded place, space and views, good estate layouts, and being close to towns. The social characteristics they are looking for in the new places include being near friends and relatives, having a higher class of people as neighbours, and being near other young families. The area facilities these families are looking for in their new community are mainly schools, shops, churches, good roads and public transportation.

Table 5.13

CHANGE IN TIME TAKEN TO GET TO WORK

Time of trip	Former place	Present place
	per cent	
Less than 6 minutes	10	5
6–10 minutes	17	14
11–19 minutes	12	13
20–29 minutes	17	23
30–59 minutes	29	32
1 hour or more	13	13
Don't know	2	*
Total	100	100
n =	652	773

Source: Residential Mobility Survey.

It seems clear that for the large majority of families on the new estates selected for this study, family needs and desires related to housing, and the husband's job and finances, are the primary motives in moving house, while physical or social characteristics of the community are secondary considerations in both the decision to leave the old home and the process of choosing a new place to live. *Family* reasons provide the principal push and pull forces of residential mobility, whereas *community* reasons are secondary considerations in both the decisions to leave the old community and in the selection of the new community.

III Response to Mobility

Most of the families in our sample express satisfaction with their last move: about three-quarters prefer the new community to the previous one, while 15 per cent prefer the former place and 6 per cent have no preference. This preference pattern does not vary with length of residence in the new community as Table 5.14 shows, for nearly as many who have lived in the new place less than a year prefer it as those who have lived there three years or more. Not surprisingly, nearly all the families (94 per cent) feel they had experienced some personal gains by moving to the new community. As Table 5.15 shows, 44 per cent of the families think they are living in a more attractive physical environment than previously while less than 20 per cent feel the new environment is less attractive than the old one. 24 per cent of families have ex-

Table 5.14

FAMILY PREFERENCE FOR PLACES OF RESIDENCE

Preference	Total	Length of residence in present place: Under 1 year	1–2 years	2–3 years	3–5 years	Over 5 years
	per cent			per cent		
Present place	76	76	75	74	78	74
Last place	15	14	17	18	13	12
No preference	6	6	5	5	7	7
Don't know	3	4	3	3	2	7
Total per cent	100	100	100	100	100	100
Number	753	126	194	132	184	117

Source: Residential Mobility Survey.

Table 5.15

PERCEIVED FAMILY GAINS AND LOSSES WITH LAST MOVE

Experiences	Gains	Losses
	per cent	
Physical environment	44	19
Housing	37	2
Personal emotional satisfactions	33	3
Family social life	31	24
Convenience – accessibility	18	19
Jobs, family finance	12	6
Other gains, losses	1	2
Don't know	1	1
No gains or losses reported	6	51

(n = 753)

Source: Residential Mobility Survey.

perienced losses in the quality of social life in the community as against 31 per cent who have experienced gains with the move to the new community. Slightly more families find community facilities less convenient or accessible in the new place than those who find them more convenient here than in their former community. Moving to the new community has thus brought 'mixed blessings' with it for the families in our sample. There are gains and losses in different areas of life for different families in the sample. Overall,

Table 5.16

TYPE OF SOCIAL ACTIVITY WITH FRIENDS IN OLD COMMUNITY AND NEW PLACE

	Former place	Present place
	per cent	
Home visits	55	57
Evenings out	37	32
Trips around town	32	31
Trips out of town	18	14
No close friends	18	26

Source: Residential Mobility Survey.

Table 5.17

FREQUENCY OF CONTACT WITH FRIENDS AND RELATIONS IN OLD COMMUNITY AND NEW PLACE

	Former place	Present place
	per cent	
3+ times a week	23	22
1 or 2 times a week	42	34
Once a fortnight	6	5
Once a month	4	7
Less frequently	7	5
No close friends	18	26

Source: Residential Mobility Survey.

the majority of families think they are better off in the new community, or are just making the best of this decision they have now to live with.

The families in the sample have experienced little change in the patterns of their social life with the move to the new community. They tend to engage in the same sorts of social activities here as in the former community. As Table 5.16 shows, they go out in the evenings with friends or relatives, pay visits or receive visitors in their home, go to town for shopping and on other activities with close friends and relatives and take short trips out of town, in both the old community and the new one. As would be expected, the families in the sample as whole report less contact with friends in the new community than they had at their previous homes as Table 5.17 shows. However, the longer families have lived in the new community the more friends they report having there, and the more often they report seeing them. Beginning with four or five friends or relatives in the first year in the new community, families show an average gain of one friend a year during their residence on the estate.

IV Future Mobility

The majority of families in our sample anticipate further residential mobility; about two-thirds think they will move again. Most of these families have a definite idea of the sort of place they want to live in, whether town, suburb or country, and about two-thirds think they will be able to move to the sort of place they desire. The majority, or 59 per cent of the families who think they will move again, want to live in the country (Table 5.5). Overall, then, the mobile families living on these new estates want to continue their movement out from the city and suburb to the country, and they think they will be able to do so in the future.

V Summary and Conclusions

The families in our samples seem to be motivated primarily by house, job and financial reasons in their decision to move. Younger families are seeking a home of their own to purchase. Some older families are seeking larger houses for their growing families and others are experiencing job mobility which forces them to move. The oldest families, those of retired people, are also seeking smaller homes which are easier to care for. In choosing a new place to live, the families in our samples seem mainly motivated by house characteristics and prices and a desire for a reasonable journey to work for the husband. They regard characteristics of the community, including its physical location and layout, its social composition, and its public facilities, as important secondary factors in selecting a place to live. For the majority of these voluntary movers, changes in family life – a new job or retirement, increase or decrease in family size and an increase or decrease in income – seem to provide the main motives for mobility, along with the values of owning a house of one's own. The fact that these families see themselves as moving out from urban centres, and would like to move further out in most cases where further mobility is anticipated, indicates that a value of country living also motivates their mobility. However, the data clearly indicate that country-living desires are secondary factors in choosing a new place to live while work journey, house types – larger for the growing families, smaller for the retired people – and house costs are the primary pull factors attracting these families to their new residences.

These residentially mobile families are very much a part of the British social scene today, and will continue to provide the demand for new housing in the future. They are moving primarily for two types of reasons: housing and jobs. New houses being built for sale are built in the suburbs or the countryside of the metropolitan areas, and these are the sorts of places the majority of the families want to live in. Job mobility will continue to increase as employing organizations, both public and private, become larger and their activities more scattered about the country. The need to provide land for this kind of urban growth is therefore not likely to decrease in the future, and with any significant rise in prosperity is likely to increase as more families find they have the financial ability to implement their desires to buy homes away from the city centres, and to get the cars they need to commute to work.

CHAPTER SIX

THE DEVELOPERS: DECISION PROCESSES

This chapter focuses on the development decision processes from the developer's end. It considers how he assembles land, how he buys it, and how the price of land is determined. It looks at the effect of planning decisions on land prices. Then it considers the factors affecting construction costs. It focuses finally again on the critical issue of rising land costs – the subject matter of chapter Seven.

This chapter was written by Roy Drewett.

INTRODUCTION

The conversion of land from a rural to an urban use involves a multiplicity of decisions and actions by individuals and organizations in both the public and the private sectors of the economy. One could focus attention upon a number of different facets and actors in this process. For example, one could try and establish the economic rationale of the original landowner in parting with his land; or study the space and locational preferences of the final consumer of the product, the householder; or consider the planner, who perceives a need for land designation in the wider context of relating different land uses and the need for servicing them; or examine the role of the financial intermediaries, whose function is vital at various stages in the land conversion process, providing financial backing to developer and consumer alike. The urban development process is the aggregate outcome of many decisions in a complex social-economic-political system, which will remain difficult to articulate and comprehend, unless a deeper understanding is achieved of the decisions determining it. The decision-making variables in land-use planning, industrial location and in residential mobility are considered in separate chapters of this study. In this chapter we focus in detail upon the residential developer,* whose role appears central in the urban growth process. He acts as link man for perceiving the social and economic determinants of housing demand and supply, and having purchased land he has to anticipate consumer needs and satisfy them. For an industry which is characteristically fragmented and dominated by the small family business

* The term 'developer' is used generically to signify builder or developer of residential property.

with low equity, this role is no mean entrepreneurial skill. Although in reality the consumer is also vulnerable, as he is forced to select within the range of what a developer builds.

In its very simplest terms the developer uses a number of factor inputs to convert land that was previously non-urban into marketable housing packages (Figure 6.1). This development process is continuously evolving in time and space and many decisions are made which pertain to the release of such a plot of land. Developers, financiers, estate agents and planners prepare the land for urban development. The speculator, industrialist and householder often enter as the final consumers. Except for obtaining permis-

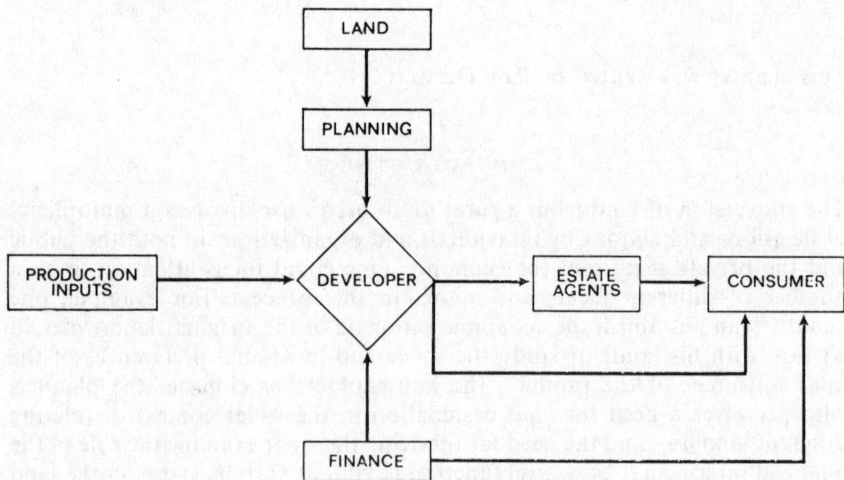

Figure 6.1 Interrelationship of Decision Agents in the Land Development Process

sion to develop, the process by which establishments are allocated to sites is basically a market-clearing solution. It is time that the planners understood this market process, for the physical land-use and environmental criteria used by them are frequently incompatible with the economic criteria used in location investment decisions by developers. Our understanding of these interrelationships between market, organizational and legislative forces remains unsatisfactory, and as expressed by Schofield in 1957:

> Certain attitudes, beliefs and subjective values concerning land have emerged from the social and economic environment in recent years that

have interacted with purely marketing considerations to modify and to some extent dominate market behaviour.[1]

For these reasons there remain a number of aspects of the land conversion process about which relatively little is known.

An attempt has been made by H. B. Fisher to conceive this process as a set of decision chains (Table 6.1). This descriptive model of the land development process helps to simplify the set of decision chains by identifying the stages of development along the top margin, with the key actors and decisions down the side margin.[2] It shows the sequence of development from a non-urban situation through the various conditions of urban shadow (where speculation and urban interests are rife) to planning application, land purchase and construction. These sequences will vary considerably both in detail and in the time taken for each stage, and overlaps occur and the order may change. As others have noted:

> Decision chains follow rational and fairly predictable sequences but on close examination *chance* considerations are found to enter into the process, with a randomizing effect serving to modify the sequence.[3]

THE SAMPLE OF DEVELOPERS

To analyse the decision chains more closely a survey of developers was made in three of the study areas described in Volume One, namely, the outer metropolitan areas centred on Berkshire; on the East Midlands; and on the Cheshire-Lancashire border near Manchester. These locations were chosen as representative of areas where the land conversion process was very active in recent years; they were stratified geographically so as to determine the extent of regional variations in the process. Interviews were held in depth with developers to probe their sequence of decisions from the initial stages of searching for land development to the final stage of selling the house to a consumer. The results of this survey form the substantive basis of this chapter and the next. A random sample of builders and developers was made, stratified by company size (measured by turnover in housing), from local lists of registered builders and from local advertisements. The resultant interviews were with a self-selected sample of those who agreed to co-operate. It is worth stressing that such competitive information of costing and returns on capital employed by a company is exceedingly difficult to obtain in a systematic way. The resultant sample consisted of twenty-eight companies who between them built a total of 22,000 housing units during 1970 which

[1] W. H. Schofield, 'The Land Market and Economic Development', *Journal of Farm Economics*, XXXIX (1957), 1500–1510.

[2] H. B. Fisher, 'Financial Intermediaries in the Development Decisions Process', unpublished Research Paper submitted to Centre for Urban & Regional Studies, University of North Carolina, 1966.

[3] T. G. Donnelly, F. S. Chapin, and S. F. Weiss, *A Probabilistic Model for Residential Growth*. Chapel Hill: Centre for Urban and Regional Studies (1964).

Table 6.1

THE LAND DEVELOPMENT PROCESS

Stages of development	Non-urban use	Non-urban use: under urban shadow	Urban interest	Active consideration (1) Planning permission	Active consideration (2) Purchase of land	Active development	Purchase of development
Description	In agriculture, or woodland, or other non-urban use. Possibly idle	Changed use: greater intensity of use, multiple use, recreation, idle	Decision agent recognizes land has potential for a time period	Agent contacts planning authority and/or government for development permission	Agent contacts another agent re possible land sale	Physical development of land	Purchase of property and occupation
Decisions	Opportunity costs lower than present use	Relative location change or pressure of opportunity costs	Decision to consider land	Decision to purchase land	Decision to purchase land	Decision to develop land	Decision to purchase

Decision agent	Landowners	Landowner, speculator, developer	Landowner, developer, speculator	Planner, developer, landowner, speculator	Developer, planner	Developer, planner	Consumer
Financial support	Unchanged	Agricultural Mortgage Corporation	Preliminary arrangement of financing	Preliminary arrangement of financing	Purchase of Raw Land Loan	Construction loan	Mortgage, local authority, broker
Land price	p_1	p_1	p_1	p_1	p_1	p_1	p_1
Improvements	—	p_2	p_2	p_2	p_2	p_2	p_2
Speculation	—	—	p_3	p_3	p_3	p_3	p_3
Community action	—	—	—	p_4	p_4	p_4	p_4
Construction	—	—	—	—	—	p_5	p_5
Appreciation	—	—	—	—	—	—	p_6
Total development cost	—	—	—	—	—	—	p_1 to p_6

represented approximately 12 per cent of the total housing completions for the whole country for that year. The structure of the sample survey of developers, classified by size groups, is shown below (Table 6.2). The survey was also used to collect data to analyse the behaviour of the *land market* during urbanization, particularly the market for residential land. The data provides values for p_1–p_6 in the cells for the bottom half of Table 6.1. The results of this analysis are presented in the next chapter.

Table 6.2

THE SAMPLE STRUCTURE OF THE DEVELOPERS INTERVIEWED IN THE SURVEY, CLASSIFIED BY TOTAL ANNUAL HOUSING-UNIT TURNOVER

Number of Housing Units built on average per year	Number of Companies interviewed
More than 1,000	6
500–1,000	6
100–500	12
Less than 100	4
Total: 22,000	28

Source: Developer Survey.

LAND ASSEMBLY PROCEDURES

Land is the developer's stock in trade; he is always looking for land and unless there are new technologies of developing floating sites at sea or of building residential blocks in mile-high columns, he will always be searching for sites, as there are no substitution effects upon the relative elasticities of demand for land. In the housing industry there is no substitution for land. It is not surprising to find, therefore, that the building industry is both financially and emotionally sensitive to the availability of land and changing land costs. The decision to buy land is considered the most important development decision; it is an investment decision and a locational decision, the combination of which will determine the likely marketing success of the project and thus the gross return on capital employed. Land assembly and purchase procedures therefore warrant a detailed enquiry. However, in addition to the price paid for land there are a great many others factors which will affect the final profit. These include: (*a*) the technical and management skill involved in construction; (*b*) marketing and advertising strategies; (*c*) a detailed knowledge of the planning process and the skill to deal with planning applications; (*d*) availability and cost of financing; and (*e*) availability of consumer credit.

In attempting to understand a developer's locational decisions, we must first turn to the procedures of land assembly. Developers have a number of alternatives available by which to search for land. Those chosen vary according to the size of the company and the relative difficulty of finding suitable sites. The most common method is for the developer to employ land scouts, or land hounds, who have to find sites and negotiate terms. Procedures and tactics in this very complex cloak and dagger exercise are many, but as a general rule the success of finding sites is achieved through developing contacts with local people. If a company is operating outside its region, then this contact is achieved by setting up regional sub-offices. Some of the most important methods of finding sites are: (*a*) *Lobbying*: The developer contacts local estate agents and surveyors and obtains particulars of sites if and when they become available. (*b*) *Saturation*: The developer would employ a small research team to study local development plans, feasibility studies, policy documents, etc., in order to identify any trends in development and likely future growth areas. Having identified areas of possible future development, the land negotiator would then approach the landowner and make direct personal contact to negotiate terms. (*c*) *Personal*: contact with local solicitors and building societies, who through their own contacts would introduce the developer to dealers in land personally. (*d*) *Contact with area planning officers*: who would be asked to indicate availability of land. The proviso here is that the company has established a friendly relationship with the officers and has established the company's good name on the type of development that it can offer. (*e*) *Auctions*: Many companies attend auctions to study the market for land but very few of the sample interviewed bought land by auction unless it was absolutely necessary. Reputable companies appeared to stop bidding at auctions at a set price and those exceeding this price were companies who were either very desperate for land, or new companies with small land stocks who were attempting to buy their way into the market. In this way, auctions tend to bid land prices higher. Established companies would not pay these higher prices, as they would consider that every site must yield its proper return. (*f*) Companies also obtain land through *landowners* contacting them directly. Developers usually prefer this arrangement, as the land is likely to be cheaper than land bought from agents. (*g*) Companies acquire land from *other companies*. These are either land stocks which are proving too expensive for other companies to carry, or through buying out companies which would appear to be going to the wall, and which own land stocks.

LAND PURCHASE DECISION

The skill in buying land lies with the ability of the negotiator in *assessing risk*, which basically means the value of the land in relation to the probability of selling houses. This is difficult to estimate because the decision must relate to future consumer choice. The potential cash flow from development is affected by a number of factors, which includes the land price element. The decision to purchase land is primarily an investment decision through a locational choice, in that as a factor input in the construction of a housing package it must yield a satisfactory return. The decision to buy and the likely success of the investment are influenced by a number of important considerations, all or in part determining the price to be paid for the land: (*a*) planning conditions (permissions, density, etc.); (*b*) estimated development costs on the site; (*c*) estimated type of housing demand and selling rates; (*d*) size of the site; and (*e*) type of contract with landowner.

Ideally a developer would conduct an econometric exercise of these expectations and cash flow amongst a number of alternative sites and select the optimum location. However, many builders would not have the expertise available to make such an assessment and because land has been so scarce, the luxury of a choice of sites is becoming rare. Therefore, the process of selection tends to be *ad hoc* in many ways and less systematic than one would expect. Rather than being optimum in character, it would only have to satisfy the developer in a number of limited criteria. It is interesting to note the similarity of this process with those in the United States:

> . . . the locational decision process emphasizes the *ad hoc* nature of the process in contrast to a systematic rational decision-making model. The process seldom seems to involve an explicit weighting of alternatives by developers. More typically, the developer selects the most favourable site on the basis of preliminary considerations, evaluates the feasibility of that site and either purchases the site or moves on to an evaluation of other sites in a similar manner.[4]

LAND PURCHASE: THE RESIDUAL APPROACH TO CALCULATING PRICE

Under normal marketing considerations, the price paid for land is calculated by a residual process. As the land is a derived demand from housing demand, then land prices relate to other fiscal decisions in housebuilding. As the supply of materials and labour are relatively elastic, the only inelasticity of supply occurs with the land. Given a perceived demand and selling rate the builder can then determine what he can afford for land, i.e. he implicitly tries a rent-theory approach which states that the price of the land is due to the demand for housing. This particular rent-theory approach will be examined in more detail in the next chapter which deals with the escalation of land prices and house prices during a period of falling demand. However, in normal economic conditions it appears that many builders use the residual approach to land pricing. A majority of the developers interviewed assessed their capacity to pay for land by this technique, although larger builders would achieve it in a systematic way, while many smaller builders worked on the basis of comparability, i.e. what worked elsewhere on the last site will work again. To illustrate the procedure let us consider Developer A, who was

[4] S. F. Weiss, J. E. Smith, E. J. Kaiser and K. B. Kenney, *Residential Developer Decisions.* Chapel Hill: Centre for Urban and Regional Studies (1966), p. 28.

a medium-sized builder in the late 1960s (750 housing units per year on average). The detailed schedule (Table 6.3) was used by him to make a preliminary economic assessment of each site under consideration using sketch layouts with types of houses likely to sell in that location. The company established building costs, site preparation costs etc., and from this it could

Table 6.3

RESIDUAL APPROACH USED BY DEVELOPER A IN ASSESSING THE LAND COST COMPONENT OF ALTERNATIVE SITES IN THE LATE 1960s

Preliminary economic assessment of alternatives				
	Site A	Site B	Site C	.....
Description/type	Semidetached 3 bedroom 850 sq. ft.	etc.	etc.	
Plot width	25 ft.			
Number of units	150			
Fixed costs				
Building costs	35			
Special fittings, central heating	2			
Site preparation and abnormals	2			
SET etc.	5			
Services, cost allowances, land replacement	5			
Total estimated building costs	49			
Roads, sewers, amenities	7			
Contingencies	2			
Legal/sales/advertising	3			
Total estimated costs	61			
Variable costs				
Land allowance	24			
Profit	15			
Total selling price	100			
Gross Return	Not known			

Source: Developer Survey.

arrive at a residual value for the land, assuming a constant profit level. This could be compared with similar estimates for other sites; the estimates would vary site by site and house type by house type, and by the various plot widths. Being a fairly large company, this firm was able to make a more systematic comparison of sites than was common with smaller builders. In this case, the company examined twenty sites before purchasing one. The estimates of fixed costs were based upon experience, and such an estimate for all above-ground costs would be accurate to within £50. The only difficulty that might

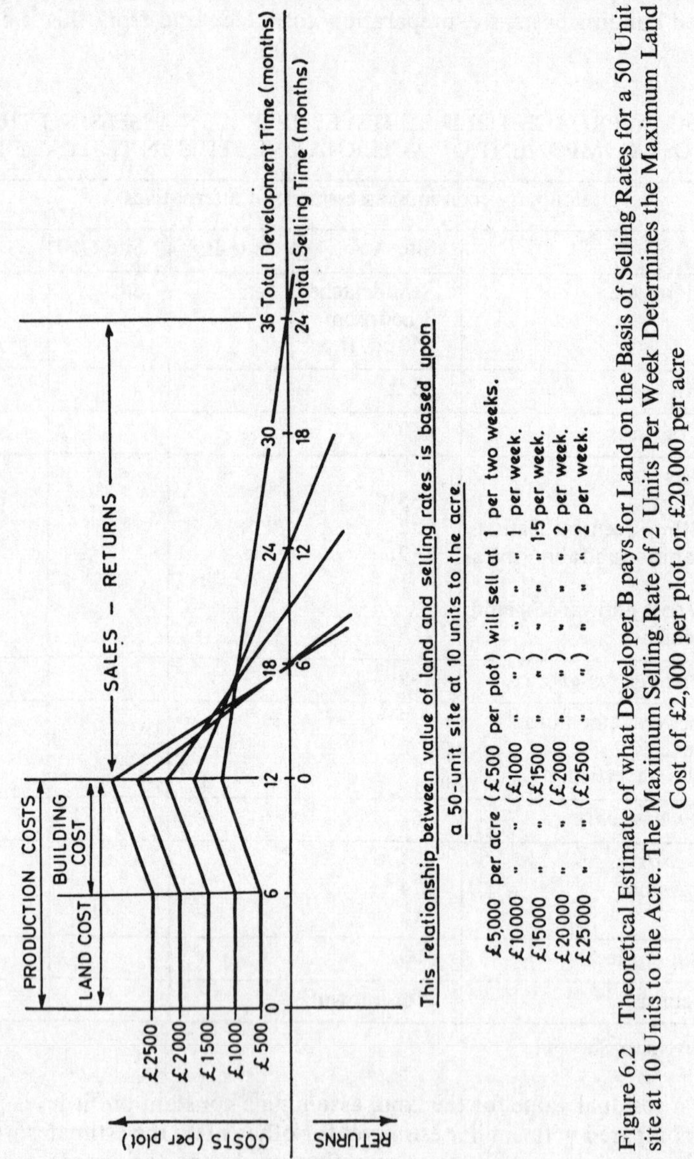

Figure 6.2 Theoretical Estimate of what Developer B pays for Land on the Basis of Selling Rates for a 50 Unit site at 10 Units to the Acre. The Maximum Selling Rate of 2 Units Per Week Determines the Maximum Land Cost of £2,000 per plot or £20,000 per acre

arise would be with the abnormals – the below-ground costs – which could be difficult to estimate, even with sample borings of the site having been made. Assuming a fixed profit proportion (in this case 15 per cent) which is related to the required gross return on capital employed, the residual proportion will equal that which is payable for the land, in this case 24 per cent of the total house price. A policy decision would then be made on whether the purchase price of the land would be charged to the consumer or the replacement cost of the land. This decision would be based on the current selling rates of houses and the present nature of the housing market. This example from an actual development is very typical of calculations made by many of those interviewed. The implications of a rising land-cost component on the remaining fixed and variable costs will be discussed later.

LAND PURCHASE: THE SELLING RATE APPROACH TO CALCULATING PRICE

A few companies, generally characterized by more dynamic and imaginative management, assess the price to be paid for land by assessing the likely selling rates of houses for a given size and type of site. The dominant consideration was not the price of land or other inputs but the speed of cash flow – i.e. capital turnover during the year. These firms considered they could always make a profit – the main problem was to get money in and out as fast as possible. They considered land the major element in their calculations, due to its price and holding costs, and therefore the biggest threat to cash flow.

The theoretical calculations indicate what percentage these companies would consider paying for land and this procedure is illustrated by the experience of Developer B in the late 1960s (Figure 6.2). It is based entirely on the rates of *selling* houses. The maximum selling rate for a site of 50 units would be two houses per week, with a two to one ratio of construction costs to land costs. With very cheap land the company experiences slow sales, i.e. one house in every fortnight, which would take nearly twenty-four months for all 50 houses to be sold. At £1,500 per plot the company can sell at one and a half houses per week and it would sell all the houses in about nine months. At £2,000 per plot it would sell in six months, but the company cannot sell any faster than this and therefore it would not be worth paying more for the land. Therefore, Developer B allows the ratio of land cost to construction cost to increase up to this limit, provided the company can sell houses at the required rate. The economic rationale on which this is based is that of turnover of the capital – the company turns over its capital three or four times a year if possible – which is the only way, as the management sees it, to combat rising land prices. *The selling rates per week therefore determine the ceiling price to be paid for land.* The company considered the present market had an artificial price; the extra land price should indicate a quicker demand though at the present time it did not.

SIZE OF SITE

Another important consideration, which is related to selling rates, is the size of the site. Larger sites were generally not attractive to builders in 1970 because of the high holding costs, due to high costs of credit. There was considerable evidence to show that the size of site used by builders in the past few years varied in relation to the current rates of credit. Whereas in 1965 a developer building 500 units a year would have been interested in 300-unit sites, in 1970 he was looking for 50-unit sites. This trend towards the use of smaller sites has created a dilemma for the planner, who in the later 1960s has tended to favour planning applications for larger sites in order that planning control be more effective with regard to layout and amenity standards. Only the very largest builders – those building more than 1,000 units a year – seemed to be interested in developing the larger sites at that time (1970). With current holding charges at nearly 10 per cent per annum, and cash flow from housing sales unlikely to occur for at least two years from the time of land purchase, it is clear that the size of a site is an important determinant on the likely profitability of any building project. Some builders have a rule of thumb about the size of sites, varying with increasing distance from their headquarters. With increasing distance, operational overheads increase, there are higher transfer costs, higher supervisory costs, and the need for more intensive controls, etc. Therefore, the company would need larger sites at a greater distance in order to compensate for these increasing costs. For example, one company tried to operate on 20-unit sites up to twenty miles in distance, on 40-unit sites at forty miles distance and on 60-unit sites at sixty miles distance. The size of sites and the number of building plots on them also relates to the size of *land stocks* held by a developer. In the short term all builders must have a stock of land. The minimum required is about two years' supply and except for the very large builders, no builder in the sample interviewed had more than three years' supply. A stock of land is vital to a development company to plan a continuity of operation (i.e. use of plant, labour, marketing arrangements, etc.) and to embark on a growing programme of planned investment. It was an interesting conclusion from the survey that the larger land stocks held by companies in the mid-1960s had been the salvation of the developer and house purchaser alike. Rather than make a profit on the land, many companies have charged the customer the price at which the land was bought. In other words, *cheap land* was being used by many builders during the worst period of land price escalation in the 1967–70 period. Some of the builders in Leicestershire, for example, became well-known in the industry for having over five years of land stocks, and they were then able to build and price houses for much less than they would have done if current land prices had been used. For this reason, several large national developers from other parts of the country have been forced to close regional offices and cease building in the area because their houses would not sell, purely for price reasons, reflecting their higher land-costs.

LAND PURCHASE TERMS

The purchase of land is achieved either through a direct sale at market value or from obtaining an option from the owner to buy at an agreed price within a stated number of years. The different methods depend upon: (*a*) the timing and need of landowner and builder; (*b*) the financial backing available; and (*c*) the status of the land regarding planning permission.

An option works on the basis that the *vendor* also wants a share of the profits if development occurs and the contract is usually conditional on that event. Many landowners like the arrangement, as they normally receive a non-returnable down-payment and the developer also has the incentive, and more expertise, in bringing the development to fruition. For the developer, it shields him from the worst effects of the market; he does not invest fully in a plot that may not be developable, and therefore minimizes his risk. His initial deposit is very low and his holding costs nil. In this way he can keep his equity moving, which is an important consideration in an industry where equity is characteristically small. Many developers would prefer a system of staged payments for land, by which they would pay, for example, one-third of the land price at the start of building, one-third halfway through the project, and one-third at completion. On the other hand, some landowners feel that with land in short supply they would prefer to have unconditional arrangements so they can take advantage of a quick sale, and therefore in recent years options have become increasingly difficult to arrange. This trend therefore makes the land purchase decision and the financial and related locational commitments of the decision even more critical than it was before 1966. The type of contract obtained and the price of land paid is determined fundamentally by the type of residential development that is permissible and, more emphatically, whether development is permissible at all.

PLANNING DECISIONS

The market for land is strongly influenced by the pattern of designations in the land Development Plan prepared by the local authority planning department and approved by the Department of the Environment. Local authorities have the power to approve applications in relation to the agreed plan and to set down such conditional arrangements as the authority deem appropriate to a particular location. These arrangements may pertain to such things as layout, density, amenity or access. Any deviation from the plan must have the approval of the Minister. It is in relation to: (*a*) obtaining planning permission to develop land, and (*b*) satisfying the conditions relating to that development, that friction occurs in the development process. It is this interface between the public and private sector that creates not only political attrition but also considerable delays (and costs) in land development. The basic cause of this friction is partly due to philosophical and ideological differences, but it also follows through each side having different environmental and economic perceptual experiences upon which decisions are made. The developer feels he knows what the market wants to buy; at least he will know what is currently selling and what the reactions of consumers are to his product. In short, his criteria are economic in character. The planner has wider altruistic considerations and responsibilities, many of which are intangible and relate to better environmental standards; he therefore frequently uses criteria which are non-economic. This is illustrated by builders who have refused to develop designated land because they felt houses would not sell due to the poor aspect of the site. The planner's role is also moderated by the philosophies and characteristics of the ultimate decision-making body, the *city* or *county council*. Planning decision-making is therefore a *political* decision, the criteria for which are not explicit but will reflect those vested interests whose lobbying can be made most effective. The landowning interests in the counties have been a major stumbling block to urban expansion in many parts of the country and this sector of society is both vocal and influential in using the political process. The planner is generally content to concur, but for very different reasons. As we saw in Chapter One, a philosophy of containment is part of planning heritage and education. The most likely group to benefit from peripheral growth are the new residents, yet these are obviously unorganized and silent, since they are not yet living in the area. In effect, their plight is exacerbated by the most recent suburban and ex-urban movers who form amenity societies to halt the process of further development, a process of which they were once part (i.e. to maintain the considerable benefits from the externalities of green-field sites). Therefore any demands of potential newcomers to the urban fringe can only be perceived and championed by the developer, who is in effect their only political voice. Many developers interviewed had attempted to develop friendly relations with planning departments and some had been quite successful. However, it would appear that the basic conflicts outlined above are the central cause of friction in the land development process. It could be argued that it may be a good thing if development is made difficult and slow, so that there is time to make a good development. This view would appear difficult to substantiate when one considers the arbitrary and inconsistent nature of planning approvals and refusals and the piecemeal nature of private development that is being allowed in many parts of the country.

PLANNING PERMISSION

As we have just seen, planning decisions affect developers in two main ways. First, there is the need to obtain planning *permission* to develop the land, which substantially affects the value of that land. Second, with the need for detailed negotiations with the planning department on such things as layout, density, or amenity, *delays* frequently occur which may cause a project to cross the narrow divide between viability and failure.

The availability or non-availability of land planning permission has probably caused more difficulty to the building industry than any other factor; there is great dissension; widely differing views are held on how much land is actually available. The problem appears to be due to varied interpretations of the word *available* and to the *time lag* that exists between land purchase and development, a peculiar characteristic of the house-building industry. Planners view availability as that amount of land designated as residential, less the amount that has been built upon in the interim. The building industry has always disputed this; it was supported by the survey of the Land Commission, whose estimates of what was available differed widely from those of local planning authorities. In parts of the Midlands the Land Commission estimates were one-seventh that of the local authority. In the Wilmslow (Cheshire) Enquiry the planning authority stated that a three-year supply of land was available in the Manchester area, i.e. 885 acres. A study conducted by local builders for the Enquiry showed that only 300 acres were actually available for immediate use. This study showed that three main factors affected land availability. First, some of the land was already in the hands of other developers. Some of it was no doubt held speculatively, but much of it was required for normal continuity in residential developers' building programmes. Second, some land was being withheld from the market by the landowners. Third, some of the land, although designated, was without the required services.

This latter problem is well illustrated by the South Hampshire interim policy plan which restricted growth for two years pending the publication of the South Hampshire Development Plan. However, the policy document did indicate the various sites that were available for development (totalling 280 acres) and classified them into three categories: 1, where development would be allowed subject to formal approval; 2, where development would be allowed where services were available, and 3, where development would be allowed after certain studies had been carried out. Two hundred and eighteen acres were classified in category 3, fifty-eight acres in category 2 and four acres in category 1. In other words, 4 acres were available in two years in the whole of the growth area of South Hampshire. Many other authorities in the country have also used the sub-regional study as a means of delaying land designation.

This resistance to land release, which was particularly noticeable with county authorities surrounding the large cities, resulted in artificial *scarcity* existing in the supply of land on the market and was undoubtedly a major factor in explaining the dramatic escalation in land prices in this country between 1960 and 1970, more noticeably after 1965.

PLANNING DELAYS

The price paid for land nearly always includes an estimate of the time required for surveying the site, designing the layout and making formal application to the planning authority for permission to start construction. Most developers were agreed that from the time of hearing of the land being available until obtaining planning permission to develop was a minimum of twenty weeks (Table 6.4). Four weeks are allowed, during which time preliminary appraisals are made of the site and the deal, and offers are made for the land. This is followed by an option on land purchase. Ten weeks are allowed for detailed surveys, road layouts and plans. Two weeks are then allowed during which the plan is submitted to the planning department for approval. Four weeks follow during which time the plan is considered by the planning department culminating in a full planning committee decision. The sequence varies from developer to developer; some developers apply for permission as soon as plans are available, while others plan the date of application very carefully, using modern management techniques such as critical path analysis, to keep their holding charges on the land to a minimum.

Most of those interviewed compared the present difficulties and time taken for completing the negotiations with the planners, with the previous decade. In the 1950s a developer could be under way in a little over a month after buying the land. Today, although the minimum would be twenty weeks, it is much more normal to spend between six and eighteen months in negotiation, although great variation occurs in planning attitudes, and hence in the delays

Table 6.4

THE SEQUENCE OF EVENTS AND TIME LAGS BETWEEN A LAND PURCHASE DECISION AND A PLANNING DEVELOPMENT DECISION

Preliminary economic assessment; land purchase decision	Detailed surveys, road layout and access. Preparation of detailed plans, elevations, amenity etc.	Submission to planning authority for approval	Consideration by planning authority and planning committee decision
4 weeks	10 weeks	2 weeks	4 weeks
Total time lag: 20 weeks			

Source: Developer Survey.

incurred, in different parts of the country. The main outcome for the developer is the effect on costings. For example, one developer bought a site for fifty houses for £80,000 (£1,600 per plot). The interest charges on this site in 1970 amounted to £700 per month. A six-month delay therefore would increase his costs by £4,200; a twelve-month delay by £8,400; and an eighteen-month delay by £12,600, (i.e. an increase of between £84 and £252 on each house price). Most developers considered that a planning clearance within nine months was good at this time.

Many of these delays result from the need to discuss density and layout. Planners are tending to favour large comprehensively-developed sites as these facilitate easier unitary control over development. Many builders would prefer to work this way also, but high land-prices and interest rates militate against using large sites and, as we have already seen, there is a general tendency towards the use of smaller sites. From a pure marketing standpoint this is no bad thing as new houses on small estates are easier to sell.

One particular planning concept was frequently raised during the interviews. This was the Radburn layout which some authorities have adopted and which they advocate strongly for developments over a certain size. Gloucestershire was one county mentioned more than most in this respect. The developers felt that the industry and the public shared a mutual dislike of such schemes and when the density was low the developers had great difficulty with their selling rates.

There has been a general attempt by planners to increase residential density during the last decade and most developers were in agreement with this policy, for certain types of property, as a means of absorbing part of the increases in land prices. The modern town house is an excellent example of how urban residential densities have been increased by agreement between planner and developer alike and made into a *marketable* scheme by careful design and subtle advertising. In effect nothing more than a terraced house with a small patio garden has become a residential vogue with the middle class in the mid-1960s.

When planning permission is refused the developer has the right to appeal through the public inquiry system to the Minister. Although this procedure can take many months, it was surprising to find how many developers were involved in planning appeals. The ratios of success in winning appeals varied between one in five and one in ten, but clearly this sort of success rate was sufficient to encourage developers to take advantage of this possible outlet. Little or no information is available on the real and opportunity costs of the public enquiry system – costs which would appear to be borne by the public at large either through housing costs or through the public purse.

DEVELOPMENT DECISIONS

As soon as planning permission is given developers will commence building at an early date; houses will be sold as soon as they are finished, frequently well before the rest of the estate is complete. This element of early cash flow is normally essential to the viability of the whole scheme. Having assembled the land parcel and obtained planning permission, the developer now has to combine the remaining factor inputs to produce the housing package. The development costs constitute approximately 60 per cent of the final house price and this decision on the use of materials and labour is very responsive to the demand for housing. The supply of labour and most materials is highly elastic, so that if the volume or amount used changes there is little or no change in price. Nationally-bargained wage rates influence the total industry and the costs of imports and import taxes likewise. The only scope open to the developer is to assess how well he is being served by his suppliers and modern techniques such as *vendor rating*[5] enable a developer to record his experience with respect to service, quality and price. The developer can then

[5] Peter Baily and David Farmer, *Purchasing Principles and Techniques*. Pitman, London (for Institute of Purchasing and Supply) (1968).

set this information down in a logical way and assign values to it (Table 6.5). Taking the three broad assessment categories and their sub-divisions, this Table illustrates the ways in which a developer can assess the quality of his service.

Table 6.5

VENDOR RATING: AN ASSESSMENT BY A DEVELOPER OF THE COSTS AND QUALITY OF HIS MATERIAL SUPPLIERS

A Service

1 Delivery – There are three aspects to delivery service:
(*a*) promptness: right time at right place;
(*b*) short lead-time (taking the average lead-time for any particular material as a marker);
(*c*) packaging: ease of handling.

2 Quantity – correct in accordance with order.

3 Security – if a supplier cannot take an order for material he has in his catalogue, he costs the customer money in searching for another supply. Capacity to absorb the customer's largest likely demand must be obtainable.

4 Pre/after sales – under this heading come such things as:
(*a*) well-designed catalogues that are easy to update;
(*b*) good technical information and advice;
(*c*) good information on stockholdings and forward availabilities;
(*d*) readily available information on research and development and new products;
(*e*) interest in helping to solve customers' problems.

B Quality

1 Supply to specification – the maintenance of consistent standards; low rejection rate.

2 Range – choice of qualities and specifications.

3 New products – capability to provide new materials as they come on the market.

4 Management – poor management by the supplier can jeopardize supplies and services. Good management can be seen in the efficient performance of the sales, warehouse factory and service areas. Failure to practise modern management techniques (e.g. work study, value engineering) would reduce score.

C Price

1 Competitiveness – willingness to negotiate. Consistent attention to possibilities of price reduction.

2 Credit – consistent and reasonable accommodation.

3 Discount – (discounts should be calculated on an annual basis to obtain comparability). Willingness to balance short credit against high discount.

4 Financial stability – A supplier must be financially sound or the customer may find himself with a broken contract.

Source: S. Robinson, 'Vendor Rating', *Faculty of Building Review*, Vol. IV (1969), No. 2, p. 34.

Having assessed the vendor rating in this way, the developer will base his reaction upon: (*a*) his buying policy, (*b*) number of competing suppliers, (*c*) the quantities being purchased. Taken together the developer is then able to obtain the very best service of supplies for himself.

THE ROLE OF THE BUILDERS' MERCHANT

It may well be that vendor rating is a waste of time for very small firms. The building industry is an immensely fragmented one and there are many difficulties of planning, co-ordination, organization and distribution of supplies. An efficient building organization requires a co-ordinated effort by many different people, including architects, engineers, quantity surveyors, contractors, specialists, etc. In the forefront of these are the designer and the contractors. There are others however who are less in the public eye, who make a real contribution to the distribution side of the industry. These are the builders' and plumbers' merchants who between them handle materials to a total value of around £500 million per year. When a developer is constructing an average three-bedroomed semidetached house, he has to co-ordinate about 500 different items from about eighty different manufacturers. These problems are overcome by using builders' and plumbers' merchants:

> Their functions are in no way diminished by the changes that are incurring in the market for building materials and components and on their past performance they are well-equipped to continue to serve the manufacturers and the construction industry and to perform the distribution functions economically and effectively.[6]

The builders' merchant also makes other useful contributions. It is the merchant who keeps abreast with developments. He is a source of technical data and cost information and gives advice and help for which there is no charge. The merchant also provides credit facilities to builders and contractors alike, and in the U.K. this amounts to approximately £90 million at any one time. This is a very important contribution to the building industry and should not be underestimated, particularly in an industry which is generally acknowledged to be under-capitalized. The builders' merchant, then, makes a contribution to stockholding, distribution, financing showrooms, giving information and advice, and providing credit facilities.

CONSTRUCTION COSTS AND RISING HOUSE PRICES

For most years during the 1960s, construction costs and labour costs have increased on average by 4·4 per cent per year; in real terms however, they have remained steady due to inflationary changes of the same proportion. In contrast, the changes in the total house-price have been quite dramatic,

[6] Quoted by V. J. Farstone, 'The Role of the Builder's Merchant', *Faculty of Building Review*, 4 (1969), p. 36.

with the price increasing on average by 8·6 per cent per year, (Figure 6.3). The trend between house prices and construction costs (including labour) was consistently divergent from 1962 until late 1968, (Figure 6.4). After that date and until early 1971, the gap between them narrowed due to the sudden increase in construction costs of 14 per cent during 1969.

Let us first examine in more detail the recent changes in construction costs and attempt to isolate what factors have influenced developers' decisions with respect to rising costs.

Most of the developers interviewed stressed that, except for the period early 1969–mid 1970, increases in construction costs have been approximately equal to changes in inflation. Of greater significance have been certain employment costs. These included: *(a)* Selective Employment Tax, and *(b)* paid-up holidays. The SET was payable by all developers from 1966 until

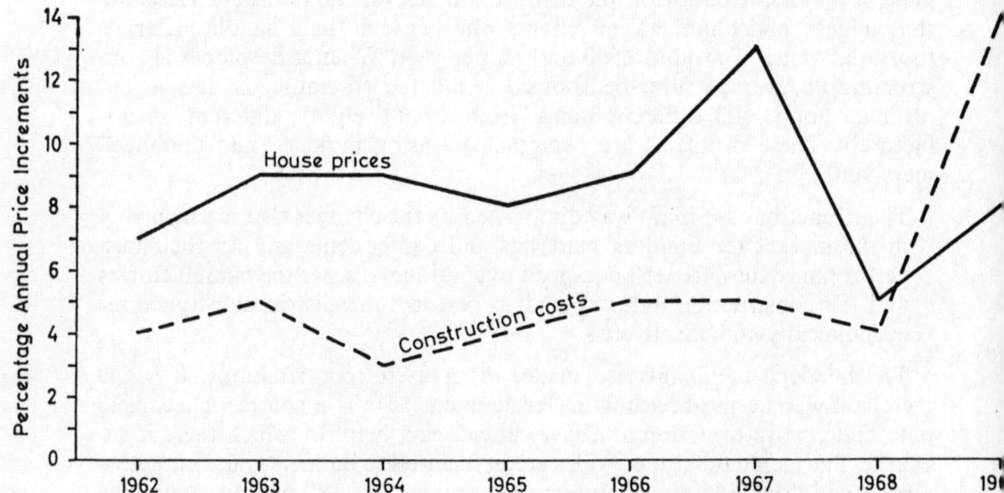

Figure 6.3 The Disparity between the Percentage Annual Price Increments of House Prices and Construction Costs, Great Britain 1962–1969

1973, and was greatly resented by the industry generally. Construction was classified as a non-manufacturing industry and therefore, as a *service* industry, was not eligible for any rebate and had to pay the tax in full. The actual amount of tax has varied over the years. In 1966 when it was introduced it came to £1.25 per man per week. This rose to £1.87½ in 1968 and to £2.40 in 1969. The effect of SET varied according to the type of labour contract used by the developer. Where sub-contracted labour was used, the tax was avoided and, in addition, this type of fixed-contract labour also meant that the developer only had to face the wage problem at intervals and were therefore shielded from the immediate effects of wage settlements. However, those companies fully employing their own labour paid the tax on the number of workers employed and they were forced to pass the amount of SET directly on to the customer. The amount varied according to the particular tax level operating at a given time. The interviews revealed some variation in the effect of SET on house prices, but the lowest effect was quoted as £150 on a £4,000 house in 1956 and up to £400 on a similar-sized property in 1970, the date of our survey. The average range of estimates was between £200–£300 per house. Far from encouraging labour mobility, the tax appears to have simply inflated house prices by between 5 and 10 per cent.

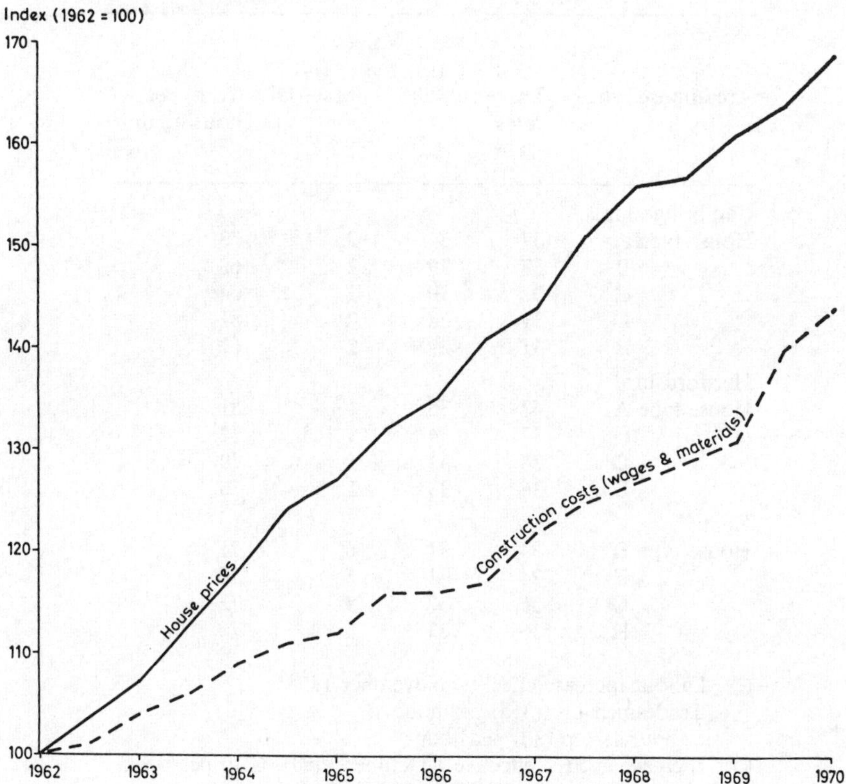

Figure 6.4 Indices of New House Prices and House Building Costs, Great Britain 1962–1970 (1962 = 100)

Another smaller influence upon construction costs was the effect of devaluation in 1967. It mainly affected the price of certain imported raw materials for which there is no likely substitution effect. The materials most affected were timber and copper. They were also further affected by the 50 per cent import duty which tied up much-needed capital at the dockside for six months.

Late in 1968 there were two increases in construction costs which affected total *unit* costs. Wage increases became effective and a 50 per cent increase occurred in SET (62½p per man per week). Developer C illustrated the effect of these increases on unit costs for three locations in Cambridgeshire, Hertfordshire, and Kent, for roughly equivalent house types (Table 6.6). This

Table 6.6

A BREAKDOWN OF INCREASING CONSTRUCTION COSTS EXPERIENCED BY DEVELOPER C (LATE 1968)

Area/house type	Values (i) Labour rates £	(ii) SET £	(iii) Material £	Total per housing unit £
Cambridgeshire				
House type A	37	34	2	73
B	32	29	2	63
C	32	30	2	64
D	31	28	2	61
E	31	29	2	62
Hertfordshire				
House type A	42	38	1	81
C	37	34	1	72
D	36	33	1	70
E	36	33	1	70
Kent				
House type B	34	31	6	71
F	34	31	5	70
G	35	32	5	72
H	36	33	5	70

(i) Labour increase effective November 1968:
Tradesmen 1½p (3½d) per hour
Labourers 1 p (3d) per hour

(ii) Increase in SET effective 1 October 1968 – 62½p per week

(iii) Material increases October 1968

Source: Developer Survey.

particular example of increasing costs illustrates how fixed costs have to be adjusted during a building programme. It is interesting to note that increasing material costs were minimal.

A year later in November 1969 more significant increases occurred. The company (Developer C), as a result, analysed the complete construction costs, including external works, roads and sewers, and the complete labour and materials content were extracted. The analysis assumes that the full increases would apply to all trades and would take effect immediately. With some companies this would not occur as sub-contractors work on a fixed-price basis. Therefore the full effect would be delayed in these cases. The increasing costs were three-fold: (*a*) increase in basic wage rates (Table 6.7); (*b*) increase in tool allowance averaging 7p per man per week; (*c*) increase in

Table 6.7

BUILDING INDUSTRY BASIC WAGE RATES AND NATIONALLY-BARGAINED WAGE INCREASES 1969–1971

	Craftsmen		Labourers	
	Per hour	Increase in rate	Per hour	Increase in rate
November 1969	40p	—	34p	—
February 1970	44p	4p	37p	3p
November 1970	46p	2p	39p	2p
June 1971	50p	4p	43p	4p

Source: Developer Survey.

Table 6.8

THE EFFECT OF INCREASED LABOUR COSTS UPON THE COSTS OF HOUSING 1969–1971

	Increasing labour costs. Averages for tradesmen and labourers	Increase in tool allowance	Increase in CITB levy	Total (cumulative)
		per cent		
November 1969	0	0	0	0
February 1970	11·1	0·5	2·4	14·0
November 1970	5·6	0	0	19·6
June 1971	10·4	0	0	29·0

Source: Developer Survey.

Construction Industry Training Board (CITB) levy to £25 per man per annum, an increase of 37p per week. When these increases are cumulated they result in a 14 per cent increase by February 1970, a 19·6 per cent increase by November 1970 and a 29·0 per cent by June 1971 (Table 6.8).

The company then applied these increased labour costs to all its production units. An example of this for house type C is shown in Table 6.9. Current increases for materials are also included. The increases fall into two groups:

house construction (labour, materials and other items); and roads and sewers (labour, material and plant). In both cases the increases are dominated by labour costs. For an 800 sq. ft three-bedroomed, semidetached house the effect was to raise the total unit-construction costs by £165, £254 and £382

Table 6.9

THE EFFECT OF INCREASED CONSTRUCTION COSTS FOR DEVELOPER C UPON A 800 SQ. FT SEMIDETACHED THREE-BEDROOMED HOUSE 1969–1971

	Costs per housing unit			
	November 1969 (£)	February 1970 (£)	November 1970 (£)	June 1971 (£)
A House Construction				
1 Labour				
House	594			
Externals	152			
On site costs	68			
Sub-total	814	+114 (14·0%)	+160 (19·6%)	+224 (29·0%)
2 Materials				
House	1068			
Externals	228			
Sub-total	11,296	+32 (2·5%)	+65 (5·0%)	+97 (7·5%)
3 *Items other than labour and materials*				
Plant, scaffold, NHBRC, maintenance, fuel, petty cash etc.	257	0	0	0
Sub-total	257			
Cumulative total	2,347	+146 (6·2%)	+225 (9·6%)	+341 (14·5%)
B Roads and Sewers				
1 Labour	105	+15 (14·0%)	+21 (19·6%)	+30 (29·0%)
2 Material	150	+4 (2·5%)	+8 (5·0%)	+11 (7·5%)
3 Plant etc.	45	0	0	0
Sub-total	300	+19	+29	+41
Cumulative total	2,647	+165 (6·2%)	+254 (9·6%)	+382 (14·4%)

Source: Developer Survey.

for the three time-periods between November 1969 and June 1971. This goes some way in explaining the rapid increases in national trends of construction costs plotted in Figure 6.3.

DEVELOPMENT DECISIONS AND CURRENT PROBLEMS

One fundamental question that remains unanswered so far is why house prices have increased more rapidly then construction costs, despite the wage increases (Figure 6.4). Using index numbers, with 1962 as the base year, it can be seen that construction costs had increased by only 31 per cent by 1969 and then rose more sharply to 45 per cent in 1970. Meanwhile, house prices had increased steadily – 61 per cent by 1969 and up again to 69 per cent in 1970.

Table 6.10

COMPARISON OF LABOUR AND RAW MATERIALS COSTS BETWEEN SPECULATIVE HOUSE-BUILDING IN THE U.S.A. AND SOUTH-EAST ENGLAND

Cost comparison	Cost ratio U.S.A.		South-East England
Labour			
Labourer	2	:	1
Painter	3	:	1
Carpenter	3	:	1
Plumber	4	:	1
Electrician	5	:	1
Raw materials			
Cement	3	:	2
Timber	1	:	1
Bricks	2	:	1

Source: A. G. Hollands, op. cit., p. 20.

A recent comparison by A. G. Hollands, between speculative house-building in the U.S.A. and in England, suggests an explanation.[7] The American house-builder generally uses good building land and builds at three or four to the acre. It would be rare for town houses to reach eight to the acre. Labour is usually sub-contracted. In the U.S.A., as compared with the U.K., labour costs some three and a half times as much and raw materials as much and more (Table 6.10), yet the final building costs per square foot for a comparable specification are *less*. The reason is the American use of mass-produced catalogue components which are both very much cheaper and generally a better product than those on the British market. For example,

[7] A. G. Hollands, 'Speculative Housing in America', *Faculty of Building Review*, 4 (1969), No. 2, pp. 15–22.

softwood roof trusses (10 per cent cheaper), staircases (25 per cent cheaper), joinery generally (25 per cent cheaper), aluminium windows (25 per cent cheaper), cookers, refrigerators, dishwashers (40 per cent cheaper), etc.

The cost comparison clearly illustrates why American house buyers are able to get much better value for their money then the equivalent consumer in England. The great difference is that lower cost of land, and savings on foundations and building costs, result in much more money being made available for fittings, finishing, air conditioning, higher-quality plumbing and electrical specification. Developments in Britain are usually at higher densities and often on more difficult sites, and therefore take longer to plan. This

Table 6.11

HOUSE DEVELOPMENT COST COMPARISON: FOR SELECTED EXAMPLES IN THE U.S.A. AND SOUTH-EAST ENGLAND

Inputs	U.S.A. per cent		South-East England per cent	
Raw land (unimproved)	4·5		23·0	
Building costs				
Foundations	3·5	65·0	6·5	54·0
Superstructure	23·0		21·0	
Mechanical trades	12·5		9·5	
Finish and fitting	26·0		17·0	
External, sewers, roads, drainage	13·0		15·0	
Overheads	3·5		5·5	
Sales and marketing	8·5		2·5	
Customers' legal fees	5·5		0	
Selling price	100·0		100·0	

Source: A. G. Hollands, op. cit., p. 22.

comparison was based on data from developers in New York, New Jersey, Maryland, Virginia, Washington, Tennessee, Texas and California, which were then compared with data from developments in the South-East of England. The American data varied from coast to coast and from south to north, but the firm conclusion was:

> land prices can only be really compared on a density basis, but whatever way you look at it, building land in America costs a mere fraction of land prices here.[8]

From this comparison, set out in Table 6.11, it is clear that although building costs and marketing costs are higher in the U.S.A., this is more than com-

[8] Ibid., p. 20.

Table 6.12

'HOUSE-BUILDING PROGRAMME: FACTORS HOLDING BACK YOUR CURRENT BUILDING PROGRAMME'

Federation of Registered Home Builders, Special Inquiry, August 1969

Government restrictions on bank lending Respondents: 1,143				Mortgage problems 1,131				Shortage of land 1,100				Planning permission delays 1,060				Lack of sewer facilities 1,009			
Crucial	Very important	Important	Negative	Crucial	Very important	Important	Negative	Crucial	Very important	Important	Negative	Crucial	Very important	Important	Negative	Crucial	Very important	Important	Negative
522	366	170	85	548	369	165	54	341	253	241	265	137	175	257	491	97	85	173	656
per cent				per cent				per cent				per cent				per cent			
45·7	32·0	14·9	7·4	48·5	32·6	14·6	4·7	31·0	23·0	21·9	24·1	12·9	16·5	24·3	40·3	9·6	8·2	15·6	65·0

Source: *House-Builder and Estate Developer*, November 1969, Vol. 29, No. 11.

pensated for by the significant differences in land costs (4·5 per cent of the total cost in the U.S.A. and 23 per cent in South-East England).

Can one then attribute the difference between the rates of change in construction costs and house prices – over 30 per cent for the period 1962–69 and 24 per cent for the period 1962–70 – to the residual factor input of land?

A survey of 1,143 members by the Federation of Registered House-Builders in August 1969 tried to assess the causes of a 'very serious position of firms at that time'. The response represented a cross section of the private house-building industry by both size of firm and location. It was found that the main problems were being faced by the small builders whose activities were virtually at a standstill. The survey (Table 6.12) revealed that financial backing was the most serious problem. The restrictions on bank lending for the builder and the lack of mortgages for the house buyer were classified by about 80 per cent of the respondents as either the most crucial or very important factor in holding back current building programmes. This factor also influences the capability of the developers to invest in land and although only 56 per cent thought that land *shortage* was crucial or very important, it is not possible (because the question was not raised) to detect whether the *cost* of land was a major factor. In comparison to the major fiscal and land problems, the builders did not consider planning permission and lack of services as particularly important. Obviously, as demand was slack the problems of *actual* development were not being faced; the main problem was to try not to go to the wall. All the factors in the survey were interrelated and there was no attempt to separate and weight them.

A specific example of house-cost changes for a comparable housing unit (Figure 6.5) illustrates the relative importance of changing unit costs between 1965 and 1970. Developer D was also interviewed in the survey. His house prices have risen between 19 per cent and 42 per cent in the five years. Other increases have been less, but this would be misleading as these houses have been built at higher densities to keep the land content down. It is also important to compare houses of similar floor area and standard of internal fittings. So what can explain this escalation in price? An analysis shows that profits, measured as a percentage of total selling costs, have remained fairly static. Other developers interviewed, on the other hand, were making considerable reductions in their profit margins in order to stay operational. In the example shown here from developer D (Figure 6.5) much of the blame for the purchase price-rise rests with a remarkable increase in *land costs*. In this case, they have increased by 74 per cent from £1,320 in 1965 to £2,290 per plot in 1970. As a percentage of the final house price this represents an increase from 16 per cent to nearly 21 per cent (which is actually quite low by South-East standards generally). Of the increase in house price, totalling £3,170, some 30 per cent was due to increases in land costs. In this example, the same specification of housing unit is used at both dates, the comparability ensuring an accurate assessment of changing land costs. It is worth stressing, however, that many developers did *not* hold their product constant. Rising

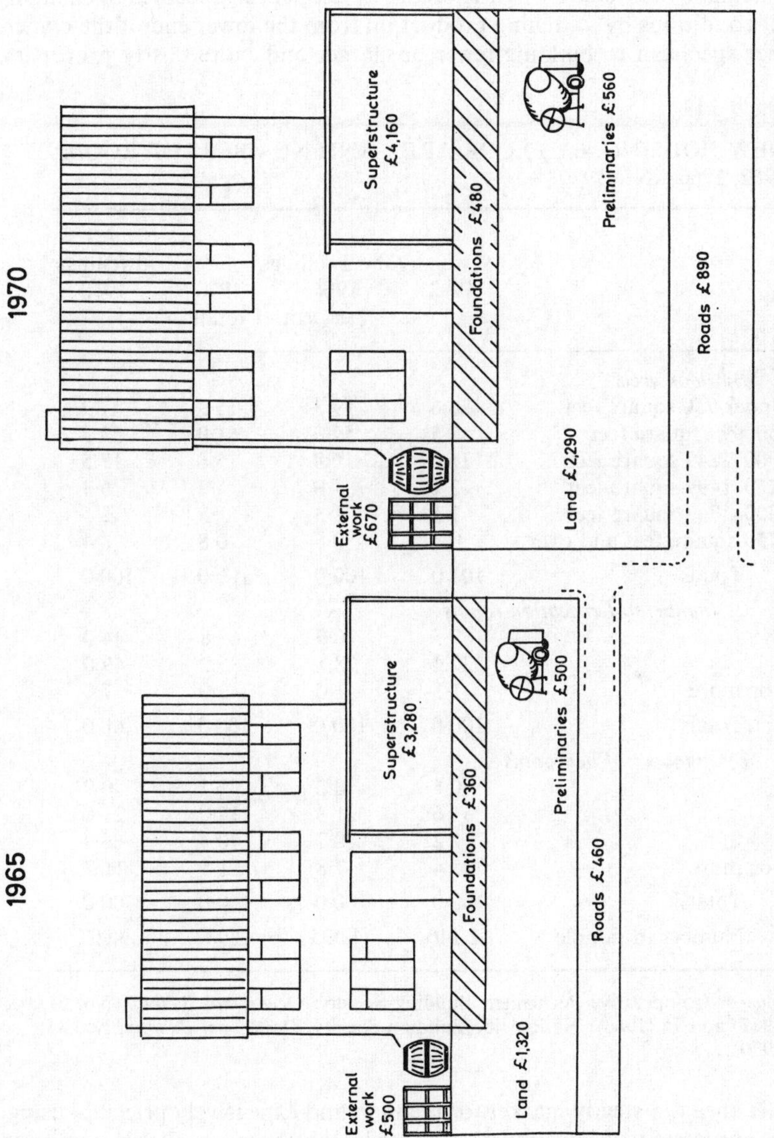

Figure 6.5 The Construction Costs of a Detached Four Bedroomed House with Double Garage in 1965 and in 1970

land-costs, and thus rising house-prices, pushed many developers into building at a higher plot-density together with a decrease in the actual house area, i.e. a decline in space standards both inside and outside the house. With consumer demand restricted by tighter credit, developers also reacted to changing market conditions by switching production from the lower end of the owner-occupier spectrum to building fewer but larger and more costly properties.

Table 6.13

NEW HOUSING, BY FLOOR AREA AND NUMBERS OF ROOMS 1962, 1966 AND 1970

	New dwellings			All dwellings
	1962	1966	1970	1970
		per cent of totals		
A By floor area				
Under 750 square feet	26·6	19·3	15·9	17·9
750–999 square feet	53·5	59·0	61·0	53·3
1000–1249 square feet	14·6	15·8	15·6	17·5
1250–1499 square feet	3·4	4·0	5·2	6·3
1500–1749 square feet	1·1	1·3	1·5	2·6
1750 square feet and over	0·8	0·6	0·8	2·4
Totals	100·0	100·0	100·0	100·0
B By numbers of reception rooms				
1	69·5	70·9	61·8	44·0
2	29·4	28·1	35·2	49·0
3 or more	1·1	1·0	3·0	7·0
Totals	100·0	100·0	100·0	100·0
C By numbers of bedrooms				
1	0·8	0·2	1·1	0·9
2	31·6	21·3	17·0	21·0
3	62·2	70·7	70·4	66·9
4 or more	5·4	7·8	11·5	11·2
Totals	100·0	100·0	100·0	100·0
Number in sample	2,140	4,095	2,980	9,907

Source: Co-operative Permanent Building Society, *Occasional Bulletin*, No. 51 (1962) and 75 (1966); Nationwide Building Society, *Occasional Bulletin*, No. 97 (1970).

There is always a steady market for medium and expensively priced housing.

This impression of lower space-standards, which was explicitly expressed by virtually all the developers interviewed, is further substantiated by a series of sample surveys of new houses mortgaged through the Nationwide Building Society (Table 6.13). This analysis for 1962, 1966 and 1970 shows there is a continuing and surprising increase in the proportion of new dwellings between 750–999 sq. ft. There was a static proportion of new dwellings between 1,000–1,249 sq. ft., the very size and type of dwelling one would expect to be expanding rapidly. There has been a slow but steady growth of property over 1,250 sq. ft.

The proportion of reception rooms is still dominated by one room but is increasing. However, it still remains well below the average number of reception rooms in existing dwellings. The number of bedrooms is also slowly increasing, the emphasis moving away from two to three bedrooms towards three to four. With this apparent shift towards more rooms but without a concomitant increase in floor area, the only conclusion must be a progressive fall in room size. An analysis of space standards based upon persons *per room* would therefore be very misleading.

Two important conclusions emerge. First, as society enters the last quarter of the twentieth century with an increasing emphasis on consumer demand and the need for *much more space* in the home, we are in a position where over 77 per cent of new houses in the private sector are being built at less than 1,000 sq. ft. Second, the average size of *new* dwellings, without exception, is smaller than the average size of *existing* dwellings.

CONCLUSION

The decisions made by developers of residential sites involve a wide range of expertise which extends from perceiving the correct demand for housing types, making locational decisions through land purchase, designing sites, dealing with the requirements of the planning process, arranging finance, assembling relevant building supplies, and house construction, to the final stage of selling and marketing. The interviews with developers have helped to unravel some of the elements in this complex process. One conclusion is clear. The industry is characteristically fragmented and undercapitalized. With so many small companies the dividing line between success and failure leaves little room for error and, as a result, builders frequently top the bankruptcy lists. With low equity, the industry is very sensitive to any slight changes in the value of its production inputs. During the past ten years the costs of two components in the production process have increased disproportionately in relation to other inputs. These are the cost of *credit* and the cost of *land*. The development process starts with a search for land and throughout this enquiry, the problems relating to the land component persist. Whether the developer is searching for land, purchasing land, arranging finance for land, obtaining planning permission to develop land, or paying the betterment levy to the Land Commission, the issues related to *land*, particularly the supply and cost of land, appear to create more decision-making problems for the developer than any other at the present time. For this reason, we turn in Chapter Seven to a detailed enquiry into land values and the functioning of the suburban land market, a market that deals in land being converted to urban use for the first time.

PART THREE

THE SYSTEM IN EFFECT: SOME IMPACTS

Moving towards the final conclusions of the study, Part Three consists of a series of chapters which describe the main effects of the planning system on the pattern of urban growth and on related phenomena. Some of these chapters range outside Megalopolis to draw on additional experience from other urban areas of Britain.

Chapter Seven takes up a theme already identified at the end of Chapter Six: the remarkable rise in land values since the Second World War, especially during the second half of the 1960s. It considers how far the planning control system itself was responsible, and how far the Land Commission affected the trend during its brief life.

Chapter Eight logically then takes up the pattern of house building in relation to migration and household formation. It finds that the density of occupation, measured in persons per room, has fallen between the 1930s and 1960s. But in the medium-density ranges, this is due to falling size of household rather than rising size of dwelling. It also reinforces the idea that rising land-values have contributed to higher house prices.

Chapter Nine analyses the relationships between home and workplace. It shows that as population has decentralized faster than employment, the length of journeys to work has almost certainly increased.

Chapter Ten turns to the phenomenon of the comprehensively planned communities – the new and expanding towns. It concludes that the new forms have succeeded in being self-contained communities as their planners intended, though many of the expanding towns have not. But even the new towns have not achieved social balance; they have failed to cater for enough of the poorer unskilled workers' families who – as Chapter Ten shows – have remained behind in the urban cores.

CHAPTER SEVEN

LAND VALUES AND THE SUBURBAN LAND MARKET

This chapter continues directly from the last, which concluded that in the 1960s rising land-values had been one of the main features of development prices. It first reviews the main academic approaches to the study of urban land values, which may be called the analytic, the statistical and the economic approaches to the problem. The conclusion from this review is that in an imperfect market where much depends on local circumstances, it is useful to take a behavioural approach through a study of actual land transactions in detail. The study is based on the sample of developers already described in Chapter Six. It concludes that in the 1960s, and especially between 1967 and 1970, land prices have risen faster than house prices, and have therefore formed an increasing proportion of the total costs of building. In some cases builders have reacted by raising densities. One explanation is that landowners are in a strong bargaining position: they commonly need not sell in the short term, while the developer must buy. But factors other than pure supply and demand enter the explanation, in particular the effects of legislation. In a detailed study of the operation and effects of the Land Commission's work between 1967 and 1970, the chapter concludes that the Commission's operations may actually have contributed to inflation rather than reducing it.

This chapter was written by Roy Drewett.

INTRODUCTION[1]

The problem relating to the cost and supply of land for urban development is probably the most fundamental and contentious issue facing planners and developers alike at the present time. Despite the economic and social implications of the problem, there has been surprisingly little interest shown in academic or planning research into the value of land, in transactions in land, and the utility of land as a factor of production. However, such market and legislative decision-making processes critically determine the temporal and spatial characteristics of the market for land. As Mills has tried to show

[1] An earlier version of this part of the chapter was published as: 'Land Values and Urban Growth' by Roy Drewett, in *Regional Forecasting*, edited by Michael Chisholm, Colston Papers No. 22 (1970), pp. 335–57.

theoretically,[2] it is the properties of production functions that are mainly responsible for city size and structure, the latter being understood as a set of market responses to opportunities for production and income. As we have seen in the previous chapter, such economic postulates used by residential developers are further influenced in the British context, where the decision-making process relating to land development occurs within a framework of legislative controls. In this chapter we will consider the effect of these legislative constraints on the supply of, and demand for, land during the urban growth process and attempt to identify and measure the social costs that may be attributed to private and public policy.

This objective is attained through a review of our understanding of land values and their determinants. It is followed by an analysis of actual case-studies of land development for residential purposes. The view is taken that only through carefully formulated behavioural analyses can we begin to understand the attitudes, beliefs and subjective values that influence decisions within the imperfect market structure that exists for land and housing. The expectations of land buyers and sellers are considered to be a vital element in explaining the recent escalation in land values and particular emphasis is given to the criteria used by the *supply* side of the market. There has been a distinct emphasis in most urban and sub-regional simulation and predictive models on the criteria of *demand* for land and housing, the supply side being taken as given. This assumption is questionable, as land designated for growth is not necessarily developed, while the development of white land has frequently been contested with some success. Therefore, the criteria of land designation, land supply, assembly of land parcels for development, and the market potential for selling houses, are all important determinants of the rural-to-urban land conversion process. The objectives and possible effects of planning permissions and the role of the Land Commission are discussed and the possible economic and social consequences of such public action evaluated.

LAND VALUES AND THE LAND MARKET

There is general agreement that in a free market urban land values reflect an exchange worth determined in accordance with rational economic behaviour, which allocates land to its most productive uses. The value of a site reflects an estimate of the benefit accruing by using that site.

> It is the use to which the land can be put at present or sometime in the future that conditions the market prices users are prepared to pay.[3]

For example, underdeveloped suburban land:

> . . . already taken out of other land uses, [which] obviously must derive

[2] E. S. Mills, 'An Aggregate Model of Resource Allocation in a Metropolitan Area', *American Economic Review*, 57 (1967), pp. 197–210.

[3] B. Goodall, 'Some Effects of Legislation and Land Values', *Regional Studies*, 4 (1970), pp. 11–23.

its value from the expectation of its latent development as urban land. An expected future income or value can be discounted back to its present worth or value. An interest rate or discount rate is required to do so.[4]

However, two important qualifications have emerged. First, the property market deals in rights and not in land.[5] It is vital to know something of the proprietary interests in land of the buyers and sellers, and the behaviour of all other active parties in the market. Second, the value of developed land can be visualized as residual. In other words, its value is equal to the difference between the capitalized income from the improvements and their replacement costs, minus depreciation. Hoyt[6] sums this up as follows:

> Land value is the capitalized value of the net income remaining after deducting from the joint land and building income, the operating expenses, interest and depreciation on the cost of building, real estate taxes and insurance.

Wendt[7] agrees that:

> Current urban land values represent the present value of the expected future net returns attributable to land.

and describes a simple model of the factors influencing these expected returns, i.e.

$$V = \left[\frac{f(P, Y, B, S, PI) - \Sigma(T + O + I + D)}{f(I, Q, \mathrm{G})} \right]$$

V = aggregate land value;
P = population;
Y = average income spent on urban services;
B = competitive pull of the urban area;
S = supply of competitive urban land;
PI = prospective investment in public improvements, e.g. parking;
T = sum of local property taxes;
O = operating costs;
I = interest on capital invested in present and future improvements;
D = depreciation allowances on present and future improvements;
Q = allowances for expected risk;
G = expectations concerning capital gains.

Most studies of land values have investigated the factors influencing these

[4] M. Clawson, 'Urban Sprawl and Speculation in Suburban Land', *Land Economics*, 38 (1962), pp. 99–111.

[5] D. R. Denman, 'Land in the Market', *Hobart Paper* No. 30, Institute of Economic Affairs, London (1964).

[6] H. Hoyt, 'Changing Patterns of Land Values', *Land Economics*, 36 (1960), pp. 109–17.

[7] P. F. Wendt, 'Theory of Urban Land Values', *Land Economics*, 33 (1957), pp. 228–240.

variables. There is no agreement as to which, if any, of these factors are actually operative in valuation. In fact, there are no rigid laws for the determination of land values:

> [They] are not so much a tangible reality in themselves but rather a symptom and reflection of uses in land, of what is happening, has happened and is tending to happen to land use.[8]

In understanding land values, the valuer must be aware of the conditions in the market and the structure and growth of urban areas.

In their survey of the problems of land-value determination Adams and Milgram, *et al.*[9] go further and claim:

> The capitalization of expected returns implies an underlying time path for land prices. Changes in the economy, for example, in interest rates, business conditions, the real estate market and construction activity, all affect land prices.

In addition to these economic and chance considerations, a further determinant operates and is particularly relevant to a study of land values in Britain; this is the role of national and local legislation. Goodall[10] argues that:

> The value of land depends today largely on public policy and is little influenced by any other action on the part of the owner.

This may well under-estimate the ingenuity of market forces and stake too strong a claim on the influence of public action. However, few would disagree with his further observation that:

> Any alterations to the framework within which the market mechanism functions will bring about change in the general equilibrium of prices . . . many of the more important changes in land values (either individual, aggregate or distributional patterns) are the result of changes in the legislative part of the framework within which those land values are determined.

Oppenheim[11] gives an example of a piece of land with two possible uses. If shops are to be erected to produce an income of £6,000 per annum, the value of this development (assuming a net return of 7 per cent) will be £85,000. However, if offices were permitted above the shops, the annual income may be £15,000, making the total value £200,000. The second case allows a higher price to be paid for land, even if initial costs are greater. This implies that the development permitted largely determines the price of the land. In practice,

[8] N. Lichfield, 'Economics of Planned Development', *Estates Gazette*, London (1956), Ch. 22.

[9] F. G. Adams, G. Milgram *et al.*, 'The Time Path of Undeveloped Land Prices during Urbanization: a Micro-Empirical Study', *Discussion Paper* No. 24, Department of Economics, University of Pennsylvania (1966), p. 2.

[10] B. Goodall, op. cit., p. 11.

[11] C. Oppenheim, 'Some Thoughts on Urban Land Values', in P. Hall (ed.), *Land Values: A Symposium*. Sweet and Maxwell, London (1966).

a developer would find it very difficult to make a countrywide survey of land values for different types of development. There cannot possibly be a conscious interpretation of all the factor influencing values. In particular, estimating future rent incomes is a hazardous occupation, in the light of changing costs, tastes, rates of interest and rates of growth.

The role of the land developer and the effects of public legislation will be considered later in this chapter, when an attempt will be made to measure their relative influences on the market for land. It is in the context of an imperfect market framework that land is converted to urban use. This framework consists of economic considerations of supply and demand and locational and institutional considerations. A number of different studies have been made to understand this process and they can be described as the analytical, statistical and economic approaches.[12] A brief outline of each approach is given to illustrate the need for more detailed theoretical and empirical research. A deeper understanding of the functioning of the land market during the urban growth process is required before any worthwhile predictive capability can be developed.

ANALYTICAL MODELS OF THE LAND MARKET

A number of equilibrium models have been developed to explain the workings of the urban land market – for example, Alonso,[13] Muth,[14] and Wingo[15] have hypothesized a market equilibrium which results in a spatial equilibrium.

Alonso[16] criticized the early writers on the land market for following the form rather than the logic of von Thünen. They failed to consider residential land users, whose main location criterion is satisfaction:

> A consumer, given his income and his pattern of tasks, will seek to balance the costs and bother of commuting against the advantages of cheaper land, with increasing distance from the city, and the satisfaction of more space for living.

Perhaps Alonso's major contribution is his consideration of the size of sites The prospective house owner moves by choice and exercises a space preference. With this in mind, Alonso developed a series of 'bid-rent curves'.[17]

[12] J. R. Drewett and C. J. Smith, 'Factors Affecting Land Prices: A Review of the Literature', *Working Paper* No. 6, *Urban Growth Study*, Political and Economic Planning (1970).

[13] W. Alonso, 'A Theory of the Urban Land Market', *Papers and Proceedings of the Regional Science Association*, 6 (1960), pp. 149–57.

[14] R. F. Muth, 'Economic Change and Rural-Urban Land Conversions', *Econometrica* (1961), pp. 1–23.

[15] L. Wingo, 'An Econometric Model of the Utilization of Urban Land for Residential Purposes', *Papers and Proceedings of the Regional Science Association*, 7 (1961), pp. 191–205.

[16] W. Alonso, op. cit., p. 149.

[17] W. Alonso, *Location and Land Use*. Harvard University Press, Cambridge, Mass. (1964).

Mohring (1961)[18] developed a theoretical model to show how transportation improvements affect land values and travel times. Land values are used as an expression of the value of travel times; in other words they represent the value drivers and occupants place on their time. The closer a site is to the centre, the lower its associated travel time and costs will be. Specifically, the difference in annual travel costs to the centre between a central lot (K_i) and a distant lot (K_j) will be:

$$2N(T_j - T_i)VT$$

where T_i and T_j are the travel times, N is the number of trips per year to the centre and VT is the value placed on travel times.

Muth has written a number of articles concerned with the land market, including discussions of the demand and supply functions of urban land and housing, the rates of substitution of production factors and the behaviour of land values. For example, Muth develops a von Thünen-type model of two competing industries locating on homogeneous land.[19] One industry produces food and the other housing: the problem is to determine which areas they will locate in and how the location changes with changes in demand and supply conditions.

This is a model of the conversion of rural land to urban uses – an equilibrium model, where land in the market goes to the use yielding the most rent. The most important conclusion is that the changes in land area used for housing will depend on the exponents of the production function: the size of the city (area), the price gradients (for both goods), and the elasticity of demand for the local agricultural good. For example, an increase in demand for houses would bring about increases in price and in rents paid for land. More land is required; this is taken from the agricultural industry, whose land supply and consequently output will be reduced. The price of agricultural goods must be bid up and higher prices will be paid for land. The aggregate effect is to increase the market price and central rents of both industries, and the land-use boundary moves away from the market centre. In a later article, Muth develops a theoretical model for a producer of a single, homogeneous good.[20] In a series of equations, he derives the industry's factor-demand schedule and explores some of its features. This is followed by a discussion of the industry's supply schedule. The model is then applied to the housing market. From his own work and that of others[21] he presents estimates of the elasticity of demand for land for the housing industry, and the industry's supply elasticity. Two major conclusions result from this work: 1. As Mohring[22] points out, the effect on land values of a transport

[18] H. Mohring, 'Land Values and Measurement of Highway Benefits', *Journal of Political Economy*, 69 (1961), pp. 236–249.

[19] R. F. Muth, op. cit., pp. 1–23.

[20] R. F. Muth, 'The Derived Demand Curve for a Productive Factor and the Industry Supply Curve', *Oxford Economic Papers*, 16 (1964), pp. 221–34.

[21] M. G. Reid, *Housing and Income*. University of Chicago Press, Chicago (1962).

[22] H. Mohring, op. cit., pp. 236–49.

improvement depends on whether the demand for urban land is elastic or inelastic. Muth estimates that demand for urban land by the housing industry is inelastic and with the elasticity of substitution also less than one, he argues that an improvement in the transport network would seem likely to lower total land values. Thus, the old problem of Haig, Ratcliffe and others has reappeared and been partially solved. 2. The theory also helps to explain why some cities have grown faster in their outer areas, and appear more spread-out, than others. Muth[23, 24] and Clark[25] have observed that urban gross population-densities tend to decrease at a roughly constant relative rate from the city centre, or exponentially. The explanation appears to be as follows: the elasticity of housing supply varies directly with distance from the city centre; as demand grows, the housing output in outer areas will grow at a faster rate than in the inner areas, so that the population increase will be more rapid, and the rate of density decline with distance will fall.

STATISTICAL MODELS OF LAND PRICE DETERMINATION

Numerous studies have examined the statistical relationship between land values and a number of independent variables. It has been common practice to relate price increases to macro- and micro-variables, some of which, as we will examine later, result directly from public action. In general, the macro- and micro-variables are economic in character.

MACRO-VARIABLES

It seems obvious that land prices will vary with such factors as inflation and population growth, but it is difficult to determine the nature of the relationship. Milgram[26] attempted to isolate four independent variables to act as surrogates for economic conditions. These were (*i*) average interest rates on new mortgages; (*ii*) personal incomes; (*iii*) housing starts in the region; and (*iv*) interest rates. The housing starts proved to be the only variable significant at the 95 per cent level and, with an r^2 value of only 0·26 the exercise was abandoned. In another study, Adams and Milgram *et al.*[27] regressed similar variables over time. Theory had suggested that the price of land suitable for development would tend to follow a time path determined by the future returns at the prevailing interest rate. They found, however:

[23] R. F. Muth, 'The Spatial Structure of the Housing Market', *Papers and Proceedings of the Regional Science Association*, 7 (1961), pp. 207–20.

[24] R. F. Muth, 'Urban Residential Land and Housing Markets', in H. S. Perloff and L. Wingo (eds) *Issues in Urban Economics*. Johns Hopkins, Baltimore (1968).

[25] C. Clark, 'Urban Population Densities', *Journal of the Royal Statistical Society*, Series A, 104 (1951), pp. 490–96.

[26] G. Milgram, *The City Expands*. Institute of Environmental Studies, University of Pennsylvania (1967).

[27] F. G. Adams, G. Milgram *et al.*, op. cit.

> . . . that adjustment of the time path occurs in accordance with changes in expectations, interest rates and holding costs. Market imperfections, short-term construction needs and stochastic elements also lead to a divergence of prices from the path.

Macro-variables affecting the course of land prices over time have been referred to implicitly and explicitly in many studies of the land market but are not often treated separately. Ellman[28] briefly touches on some of the macro-variables that could have an effect on land prices but merely lists them: Selective Employment Tax, devaluation, leasehold enfranchisement, mortgage famine, strikes, pay claims, capital gains tax, corporation tax, Green Belts and other planning activities. The problem here is that several of the variables could be acting at both the macro and micro level simultaneously. This is especially true of construction costs, servicing costs, general accessibility and general expectations. The works of Gottlieb[29] and Maisel[30] provide good examples of models in which the independent variables can be thought of as operating at several levels. Gottlieb found that relative lot supply had no influence on Federal Housing Administration (FHA) site values in the United States but was a major influence over lot values. Lots are purchased by speculators or would-be builders for ultimate use for building purposes. The site is a sub-divided lot prepared and ready for construction. Variations in income levels were significant for FHA and lot values. The speculative activity variables for growth rates over five years and levels of assessment (for property tax purposes) exerted little influence over FHA site values but an appreciable influence over lot values. The *per hectare* value of farm and real estates in surrounding areas was found to have almost no influence over either value.

Maisel constructs a dynamic model which satisfactorily explains the variance of urban land values in United States cities. He also explains the rapid rise in the prices of building sites since the war:

> Dynamic forces were assumed in our model to be represented by growth of income and population, changes in housing tastes and costs, and finally by the existing population density. Variables reflecting the differential distribution of jobs and houses appeared to have no relationship to variance or growth in the dependent variable.

With his comparative statics approach Maisel was able to consider the possible impact of expectations and normally (or artificially) induced lags in the adjustment of supply and demand. There is, at last, some attempt to measure speculative influence. A combination of this approach with the time path

[28] P. Ellman, *The Effect of the Land Commission on the Cost of Residential Building Sites*, Unpublished M.A. Thesis. University of Strathclyde (1969).

[29] M. Gottlieb, 'Influence on Value in Urban Land Markets; U.S.A. 1956–61', *Journal of Regional Science*, 6 (1965), pp. 1–16.

[30] S. J. Maisel, 'Price Movements of Building Sites in the United States. A Comparison Among Metropolitan Areas'. *Regional Science Association Papers*, 12 (1964), pp. 47–60.

analysis of Adams and Milgram *et al.*[31] might provide a better indication of the movement of prices in land through time.

MICRO-VARIABLES

In addition to the more general macro-variables, many of which reflect the economic climate of the country generally, there are other characteristics of a piece of land which will affect its value. Some of these variables are thought of as indices, with each index a function of several different variables. For example, a site's accessibility is a joint function of its proximity to different activities and the nature of the transportation system connecting it with these possible destinations. Similarly, the social and atmospheric conditions associated with the site affect its amenity indices. The accessibility of a site measured by distance or time cost incurred in travel to the central business district or other localities has been thought to play an important role in determining site rents. The theory is that urban land has a value over and above its rural use because it offers relatively easy access to desirable activities. Adams and Milgram *et al*[32] used four measures of accessibility in the time path analysis: (*i*) travel time to the central business district; (*ii*) distance in kilometres to a major road; (*iii*) dummy variables 1 for a property being on main artery and 0 for those elsewhere; and (*iv*) distance in kilometres to public transportation.

Cyamanski[33] advanced the hypothesis that the time-distance function to the major concentrations of nine urban functions was enough to explain most of the differences in urban land values. He calculated isopotential lines, i.e. the index of accessibility, from the following equation:

$$X = \sum_{j=1}^{n} \frac{W.L_j}{d_{ij}\alpha}$$

X = accessibility to all urban functions from a grid point
i = any one of the grid points
j = any one of the urban centres
d_{ij} = distance from any i to any j
L = index of the central functions of any one of the centres
W = weight parameter
α = distance parameter

Most studies have agreed that accessibility is the most important factor determining land values. Mohring[34] developed a model to show how transport improvement affects land rents and travel times. He demonstrates how this would affect spatial re-locations, but that the actual costs and benefits affect different groups of the population, depending on: (*i*) their locations *vis-à-vis* the improvements; and (*ii*) their status and income group.

[31] F. G. Adams and G. Milgram *et al.*, op. cit.
[32] Ibid., p. 14.
[33] S. Cyamanski, 'Effects of Public Investments on Urban Land Values', *Journal of American Institute of Planners*, 32 (1966), pp. 204–16.
[34] H. Mohring, op. cit., pp. 236–49.

However, Weiss, Donnelly and Kaiser[35] refer to other accessibility variables, such as distance to nearest elementary school, distance to play or recreation, and distance to shopping. These additional variables would seem important if we accept Stegman's[36] argument that: 'It is essential to break away from this confining notion that accessibility [to work] rules the location decision-making process'. Using data from a recently conducted national survey of housing preferences Stegman notes, among other things, that *neighbourhood quality* rather than accessibility to employment was a major concern in residential choice. We have little or no information on the effects of such preferences on the future market for urban land.

In addition to accessibility characteristics, there are other interdependencies and externalities which are important determinants of land values. These include plot characteristics, such as plot size, and the level of service provision, and local amenity value. Naturally, a site with a higher amenity level is more desirable and more valuable than one with fewer amenities. Amenity in this case is a highly subjective factor, reflecting the overall desirability of an area. Brigham[37] 'measured' amenity from the preferences of a sample of individuals. Such an index of amenity could no doubt be highly correlated with a number of variables such as: non-white proportion of the population; median family income of the area; level of overcrowding; mean temperature; smog levels; nature of the terrain; and so on. Similarly Weiss, Donnelly and Kaiser[38] included variables for residential amenity, dwelling density and proximity to areas of blight and non-white population, but none added significantly to the level of explanation. Cyamanski[39] attempted to measure the degree of blight of an area, using some eighty-two characteristics and a scale of one to four. The age of structures proved to be highly relevant in explaining land values. Clawson[40] included many such variables in his discussion of 'Externalities and Interdependencies'. These provide costs and benefits which have an effect on values but cannot be assessed against, or accredited to, their originator. For example, there are complementary land uses such as parks and residential areas; and non-complementary uses such as factories and houses.

Other micro-variables that have been identified include ownership characteristics, levels of land and property taxation, and certain historical factors.

[35] S. F. Weiss, T. G. Donnelly and E. J. Kaiser, *Land Value and Land Development Influence Factors: an Analytical Approach for Examining Policy Alternatives*. Centre for Urban and Regional Studies, University of North Carolina, Chapel Hill (1967).

[36] M. A. Stegman, 'Accessibility Models and Residential Location', *Journal of the American Institute of Planners*, 35 (1969), pp. 22–9.

[37] E. F. Brigham, 'The Determinants of Residential Land Values', *Land Economics*, 44 (1965), pp. 325–34.

[38] S. F. Weiss, T. G. Donnelly and E. J. Kaiser, op. cit., p. 232

[39] S. Cyamanski, op. cit., pp. 204–16.

[40] M. Clawson, *Suburban Land Conversion in the United States: An Economic and Governmental Process*. Resources for the Future. Johns Hopkins Press, Baltimore (1971), pp. 166–87.

As Brigham[41] notes: 'An historical factor is the employment of land in a way that is no longer suitable'. In this respect, it is the point of time at which development occurs which influences land prices.

Wendt[42] explained the difference in land values and growth trends between San Francisco and Oakland only in terms of historical factors:

> The historical comparison of economic and land value trends for these two cities emphasizes the importance of continuity, momentum and dominance as factors contributing to urban growth.

ECONOMIC ANALYSIS OF THE LAND MARKET: PRICE ELASTICITY OF DEMAND FOR HOUSING AND LAND

To understand the role of the land market as an input to the housing market, it is necessary to consider briefly the nature of the housing market. The demand for land is derived from housing demand which in turn is derived from household or consumer demand. The special characteristics of the housing market determine the interplay between the inputs, land being one.

For any product, the quantity purchased or consumed depends upon price, income and credit elasticities. However, little is known, and few estimates have been made of, the pure elasticity of demand for housing. Many studies have dealt with income or housing upon the quantity purchased. Reid[43] has estimated that the price elasticity of housing is not above 1·0 and is probably lower. Space requirements, location, family size, and stage of life cycle are important criteria in housing choice and are thought more important than pure price-quantity relationships in housing demand.

The peculiar nature of the housing market makes studies of demand unreliable. There is little turnover in stocks. The stocks held are large and the annual additions are small. For these and a number of other reasons, market information is imperfect and the lack of standardization in housing makes the measurement of demand difficult. People tend to occupy space for sentimental reasons and through inertia. They would not know the cost of equal or better housing elsewhere and the price they would receive for their own property is unknown and fluctuates. For these reasons, it is difficult to argue that present dwelling space for the majority represents a closely reasoned choice of cost or space and of quantity purchased or consumed.[44] It seems highly probable that pure price elasticity of demand for housing is overwhelmed by income and credit elasticities.

The income elasticity of demand for housing is relatively high (1·0 to 2·0), showing that quantity and expenditure are each responsive to changes in income. However, care needs to be taken in relating income changes to housing expenditures. It is necessary to distinguish between *actual* take-home income and the lower *basic* income (without overtime, bonuses, etc.). It is

[41] E. F. Brigham, op. cit., p. 330.

[42] P. F. Wendt, 'The Dynamics of Central City Land Values – San Francisco and Oakland 1950–1960', *Research Report 18*, Real Estate Program, University of California, Berkeley (1966), p. 46.

[43] M. G. Reid, op. cit.

[44] M. Clawson, op. cit., p. 114.

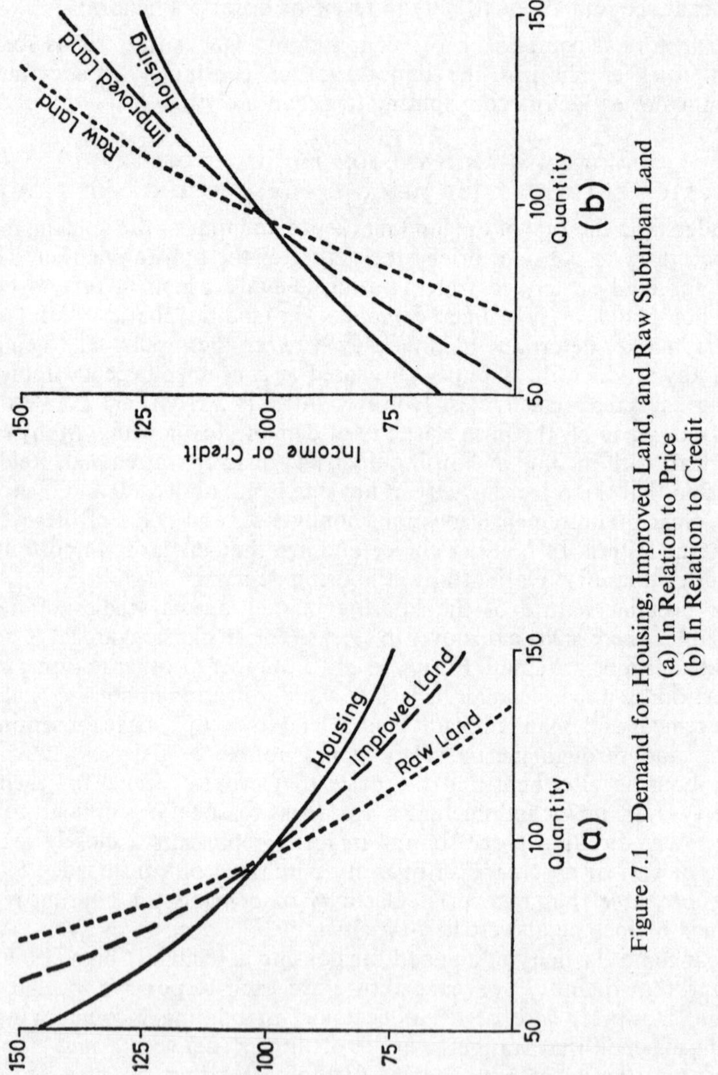

Figure 7.1 Demand for Housing, Improved Land, and Raw Suburban Land
(a) In Relation to Price
(b) In Relation to Credit

the latter income which determines a potential consumer's capacity to bid for a mortgage. This is particularly important at the present time when house prices are increasing faster than the increase in basic wages. Credit elasticity of demand for housing is moderately high. The cost of credit appears not to influence such purchases greatly; it is the ease of getting the loan that matters. Demand for housing is therefore sensitive to available credit, and particularly the size of the down-payment, and to a lesser extent on the prevailing interest rate.

We do not know the exact position and shape of price and income and credit demand curves for housing, nor do we know their elasticity exactly. However, it is possible to make estimates for these relationships on the basis of accepted economic theory of rent and make logical deductions as to the relative elasticity of demand for housing and for the land component.[45]

On deductive grounds, one may argue that the supply of other factors that must be combined with raw land to produce houses is relatively elastic. A major part of the construction cost is labour and materials and the cost of these does not vary greatly with short-term fluctuations in demand. It is the volume or amount that is the variable, the unit costs remaining fairly stable, with slow upward adjustments. Figures 7.1(a) and 7.1(b) show demand curves for housing, for improved lots and for raw suburban land, as summaries of Clawson's deductive argument. The elasticity of demand with respect to house prices is moderate, with the response in terms of quantity roughly half of the response to income or credit. The general shape of the curve seems reasonable in the light of such research as has been published. The land price demand curves are shown for improved and for raw land. They are progressively less elastic, reflecting the need to combine the land with other factors of production which are highly elastic.

Although the exact values of the elasticities are not known, the general relationship is reasonable. A significant relationship exists in that the demand for lots is less elastic than demand for housing and that the demand for raw land is even less elastic than the demand for improved lots. These deductions are inherent in neo-classical rent theory, and, although the precise relationship may vary, they show that the bulk of the *fluctuation in demand* for housing *falls upon the price of land.*

A BEHAVIOURAL APPROACH: THE CONCEPTUAL FRAMEWORK

The analytical and statistical studies already outlined are useful in identifying the many macro- and micro-variables that determine land values. Neo-classical rent theory also gives some indication of the price elasticities of demand for housing and land. There remain, however, several aspects of land value determination during the land conversion process about which relatively little is known. Whenever one has to attempt to answer a few apparently simple questions in the field of land values, one is made to realize that all one

[45] Ibid., p. 117.

can do is to scratch the surface of an immensely complex subject – a subject in which there are *remarkably few cut and dried facts and where, because of market forces, so much depends on the negotiating position between buyer and seller*. In view of this, and because so much also depends upon all the circumstances relating to a particular piece of land and to the market condition in a particular place at a given point in time, a behavioural approach was adopted through a detailed survey of actual transactions.

The descriptive model of the land development-process (Chapter Six), which was based upon a conception of a series of decision chains, was also used during the in-depth interviews with each developer to collect data to

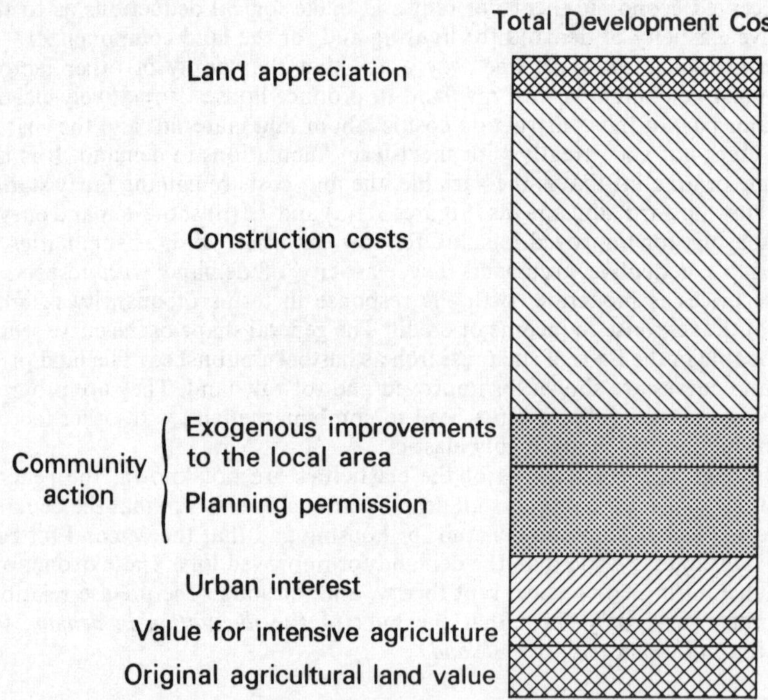

Figure 7.2 Price Increments in the Land Development Process

analyse the behaviour of the *land market* during urbanization, particularly the market for residential land. The data provided values for p_1 to p_6 in the cells at the bottom of Table 6.1 on page 167. The analysis of the land market is mainly of two kinds. First, the identification of the temporal and spatial variations in development costs for completed residential sites. Second, the analysis of the components of the complete site price – the opportunity costs for agriculture, speculation increment due to urban interest, increments due to community action (due both to exogenous improvements to the general area, such as services, and to the granting of planning permission for a specific site), and construction costs (Figure 7.2). This analysis, similar to the one completed by Schmid,[46] provides a deeper understanding of the role of the land market, a level of analysis which has not been undertaken in Britain

Table 7.1

AVERAGE PRICES AND SITE VALUES OF NEW HOUSES MORTGAGED TO THE NATIONWIDE BUILDING SOCIETY

	Average house price £	Average site price (inc. services) £	Site price as per cent of house price £
London and South-East			
April–June 1966	5,208	1,323	25·4
October–December 1966	5,223	1,336	25·6
April–June 1967	5,474	1,416	25·9
October–December 1967	5,482	1,554	28·3
April–June 1968	5,610	1,570	28·0
October–December 1968	5,688	1,555	27·3
April–June 1969	6,283	1,816	28·9
October–December 1969	5,894	1,673	28·4
Midlands			
April–June 1966	3,581	741	20·7
October–December 1966	3,750	768	20·5
April–June 1967	3,962	855	21·6
October–December 1967	4,130	893	21·6
April–June 1968	4,361	936	21·5
October–December 1968	4,398	981	22·3
April–June 1969	4,501	991	22·0
North-West			
October–December 1966	3,628	607	16·7
April–June 1967	3,710	607	16·4
October–December 1967	3,893	619	15·9
April–June 1968	4,093	691	16·9
October–December 1968	4,405	788	17·9
April–June 1969	4,398	762	17·3
October–December 1969	4,302	764	17·8

Source: Nationwide Building Society.

before. It helps to clarify the relationship between land costs and urban development, i.e. whether land costs act as a dependent or independent variable in the process, or act as both. The isolation of the component of

[46] A. Schmid, *Converting Land from Rural to Urban Use*. Resources for the Future. Johns Hopkins Press, Baltimore (1968).

price due to community action also facilitates the partial evaluation of the costs of economic and physical planning to the community.

The characteristics of the sample of developers interviewed and the geographical areas included have been described in detail in Chapter Six. It is worth stressing again that obtaining information which is competitive in nature from companies is extremely difficult on a systematic basis. There are some data available on a regional basis. The Nationwide Building Society releases quarterly data on house prices and site prices (Table 7.1)[47] and a

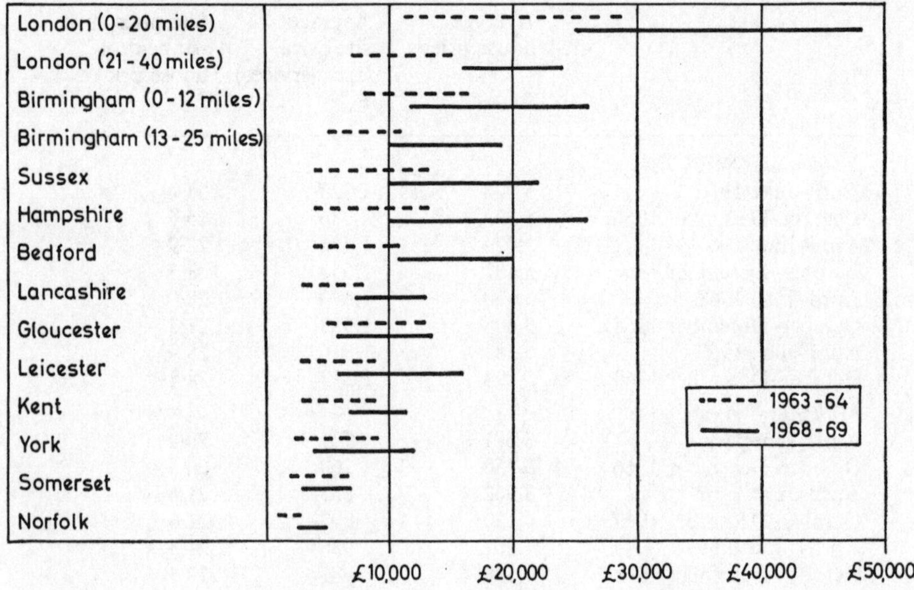

Figure 7.3 Typical Ranges of Residental Land Prices for 1963–1964 and 1968–1969

similar data set was published by the *Estates Gazette* (Figure 7.3).[48] Both data sets confirm the need for a regional classification. They confirm the following trend that land prices have increased steadily since 1963 and more rapidly after 1966, when the median value nearly doubled in many areas. This is reflected in the increasing proportion of land as a cost in the final house price. These trends are consistent throughout the country but in general are higher both absolutely and relatively in the South and South-East of the country, grading off through the Midlands towards the North-West. These general trends from published sources are confirmed by the data gathered from the *Developer Survey*. The transactions in suburban land for residential

[47] A wide range of data related to housing are available in the *Occasional Bulletin* compiled and published by the Nationwide Building Society, London.

[48] J. McAuslan, 'Residential Land Prices', *Estates Gazette*, 11 April 1970, pp. 13–14.

development which were made by the sample of developers are plotted (Figure 7.4) for the three survey areas. No attempt is made at this stage to make these data comparable by density or type of development; they are

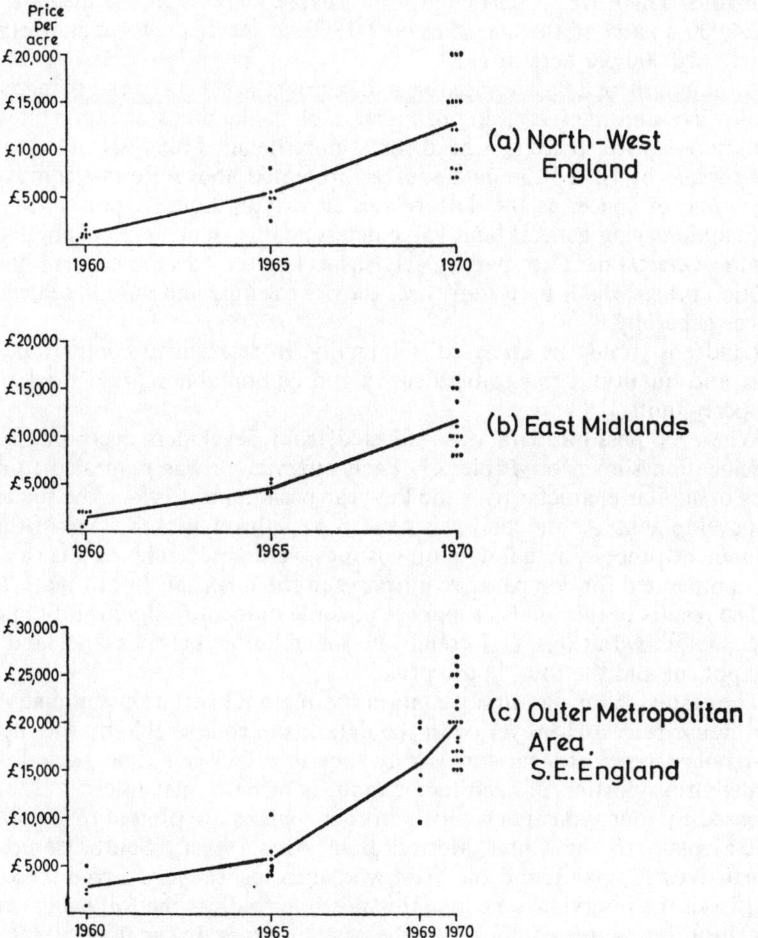

Figure 7.4 Transactions in Suburban Land for Residental Development: Price Changes 1960–1965–1970
(a) North-West England
(b) East Midlands
(c) Outer Metropolitan Area (West), South-East England

presented here as a global summary of the survey to illustrate the general trends in land prices. The transactions for the East Midlands and for North-West England are very similar; i.e. from around £1,000–£1,500 per acre in

1960, to £5,000 in 1965, and up to £11,500–£12,500 per acre in 1970. The most rapid increase occurred in the outer metropolitan area of the South-East. Prices were slightly higher but roughly equivalent in 1960 and 1965 with the other two regions; but between 1965 and 1970 the prices increased nearly four-fold. There was a particularly noticeable increase in the median value of £4,000 an acre in the one year 1969–1970, to reach a new median value of nearly £20,000 per acre in 1970.

Although these data are valuable and convey the general trend of increasing land prices and the increasing proportion of the land cost component in the final house price, there is a need for a more detailed analysis of costs on a *comparable* basis. All the data sources presented above are not comparable over time or space, as the data relates to varying house types, varing plot sizes and varying general land value determinants, such as accessibility. The *Estates Gazette* data are particularly suspect as they are based mainly upon auction prices which are usually near the price ceiling and unrepresentative of prices generally.

Land costs must be analysed, minimally, in relation to comparable sites (size and quality), comparable density and comparable market price of the property built.

Wherever possible data was collected from developers according to the specification shown on Table 6.1. Each interviewee was requested to select sites of similar character over the ten-year period and to trace the sequences of development. As the land was seen to pass through each stage of the development process, actual data on costings were noted. The results can then be summarized for comparative purposes in the form shown in Figure 7.2.

The results of this analysis make it possible to identify significant temporal and spatial variations and trends in the relation between the land cost component and the total house price.

The results from the survey confirm the regional variations in land values and house prices. However, with the data made comparable by site, density and house type, comparison is now possible between time periods. The changing proportion of each factor input is of particular interest. The data released by four typical developers in four regions are plotted in Figure 7.5. These relate to the Outer Metropolitan Area (West), South Hampshire, North-West England, and the West Midlands respectively. From these data and from the interview schedule, it is possible to draw the following general conclusions about the trends over the past ten years. In the majority of cases data were released by interviewers for 1960 and 1970, although in two cases used here additional data were made available for 1965.

First, and most important, the cost of land has risen out of all proportion as a percentage of the total house price. In the examples given in Figure 7.5 and 7.6(a) for North-West England, the increase occurred from 4 per cent in 1960 to 23 per cent in 1970; for the West Midlands, from 12·5 per cent in 1965 to 20·7 per cent in 1970; for South Hampshire, from 10·5 per cent in 1960 to 20·8 per cent in 1970; and finally in the Outer Metropolitan Area, to the West of London, from 12 per cent in 1960 to 30 per cent in 1970. These

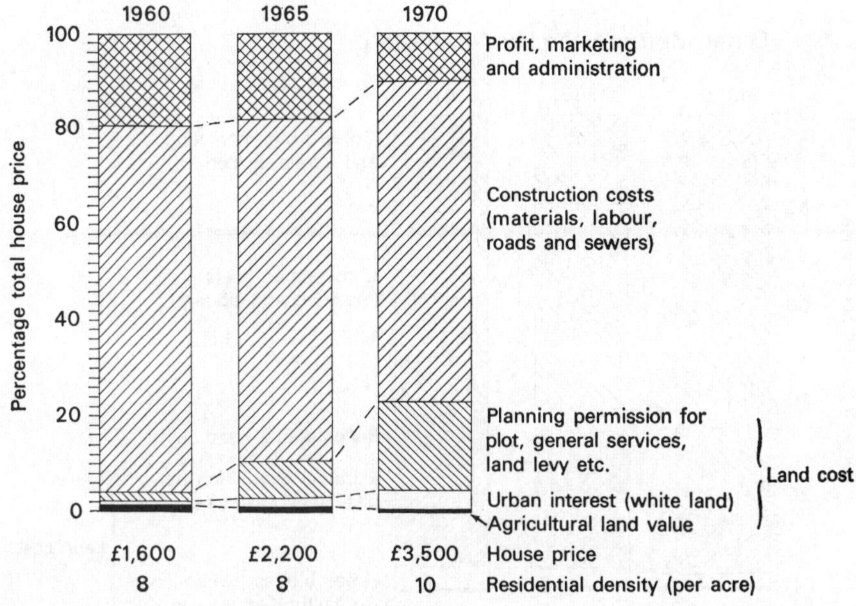

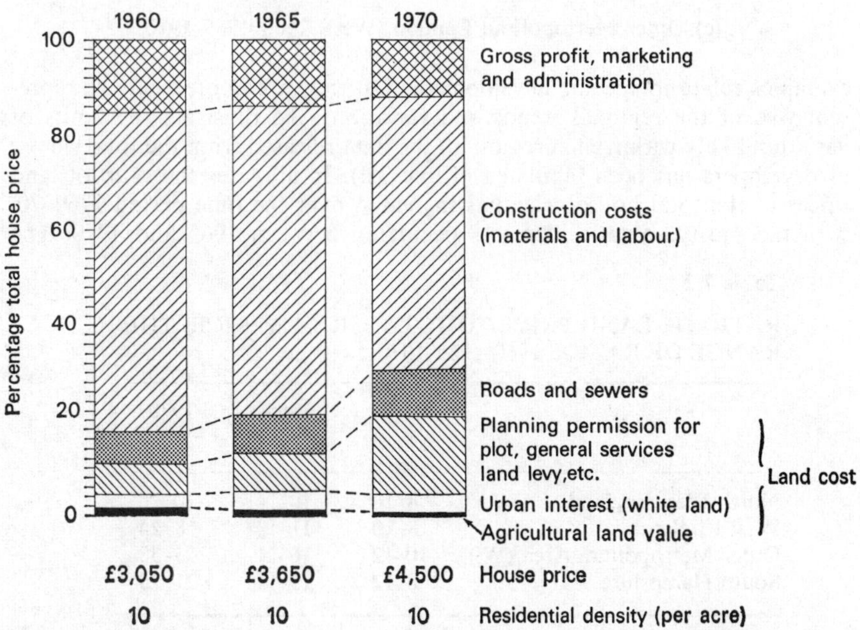

Figure 7.5 Cost Variations of Factor Inputs in a Housing Package
(a) North-West England 1960–1970
(b) South Hampshire 1960–1965–1970

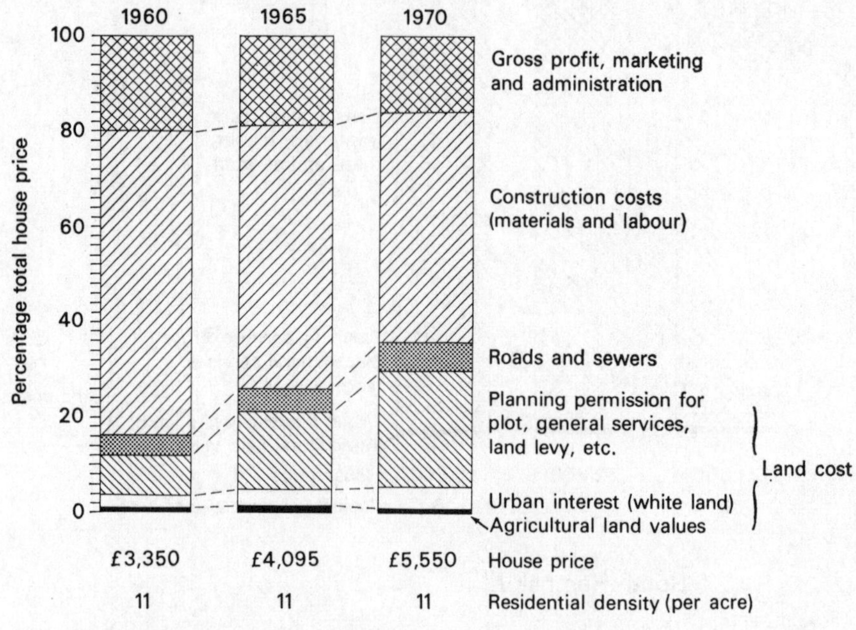

(c) Outer Metropolitan London (West) 1960–1965–1970

examples relate to specific developments but they are quoted here as representative of the regional trends and variations. To illustrate the limits of variation likely within each region all the data released from the total survey of developers has been tabulated (Table 7.2). In all cases the ratio of land prices to the total house price has increased over the time period 1960–70, with the most dramatic increases occurring between 1965 and 1970. The

Table 7.2

RATIO OF LAND PRICE TO TOTAL HOUSE PRICE: THE RANGE OF RATIOS 1960–1965–1970

	1960	1965 per cent	1970
North-West England	4–10	10–14	20–26
West Midlands	8–10	11–13	18–24
Outer Metropolitan Area (W.)	10–12	16–21	25–38
South Hampshire	8–12	13–14	21–25

Source: Developer Survey.

highest ratios are reached in the Outer Metropolitan Area of South-East England where ratios of over 30 per cent are quite common by 1970, and where the staggering figure of 38 per cent was reported as the upper limit. Although distinct *regional* variations existed in 1960, these differences outside London narrowed between 1960 and 1970 and the proportion of land price to total house price around the major urban areas of South Hampshire, the Midlands and the North-West was very similar by 1970, all occurring within the range of 18–26 per cent.

In the West Midlands example we are able to make a further comparison which specifically isolates the increasing costs due to an increase in land prices. This is only possible as the developer built the same property on two comparable sites which were purchased at different times; one was developed continuously at 1965 prices, the other site bought in 1970 was developed at 1970 prices. In Figure 7.6 the cost changes between 1965–1970 are made with the land cost held constant, i.e. at 1965 prices. The price increases of all factor inputs other than land, due to the 'passage of time', was £555 in five years – where the land costs had to be included the total increase was £1,200 in five years (Figure 7.5). As we have already detected (Figure 6.3), construction costs have risen at a slower rate than house prices. Construction costs have been increasing at about 5 per cent per year during the period 1960–69 and rather faster during 1970. This changing rate is equivalent to the changing inflationary value of purchasing power over the same time period; i.e. in absolute terms the value of the construction element in house building has remained constant. However, the developer survey illustrated that *relative* to the total house price the proportion of total development costs due to construction inputs (labour and materials) has declined during the ten-year period. Therefore, as profit margins have remained constant or in many cases decreased slightly over the period (a 10 per cent to 15 per cent gross return on capital employed would be a normal expectation in the building industry) one can *attribute the escalation in house prices to the residual factor input of land.* One further point needs emphasis. In several of the developments illustrated here, the residential density has increased from eight to ten dwellings per acre in North-West England and from eleven to thirteen in the West Midlands. It was the common practice by which builders offset the increases in land prices. This is why it is important to collect data by house plot and by acreage in order to measure the *real* increase in land costs which would otherwise be concealed.

THE DISTORTED LAND MARKET – TOWARDS AN EXPLANATION

The emphasis of this chapter lies with the individual housing plot or housing development. We are not addressing ourselves to the aggregate of land values in the urban system or the distributional pattern of such values. This is an important qualification as sites are not independent in the market; quite the reverse, and such externalities cause values to shift between sites. However, the simplifying assumptions adopted are necessary at this stage.

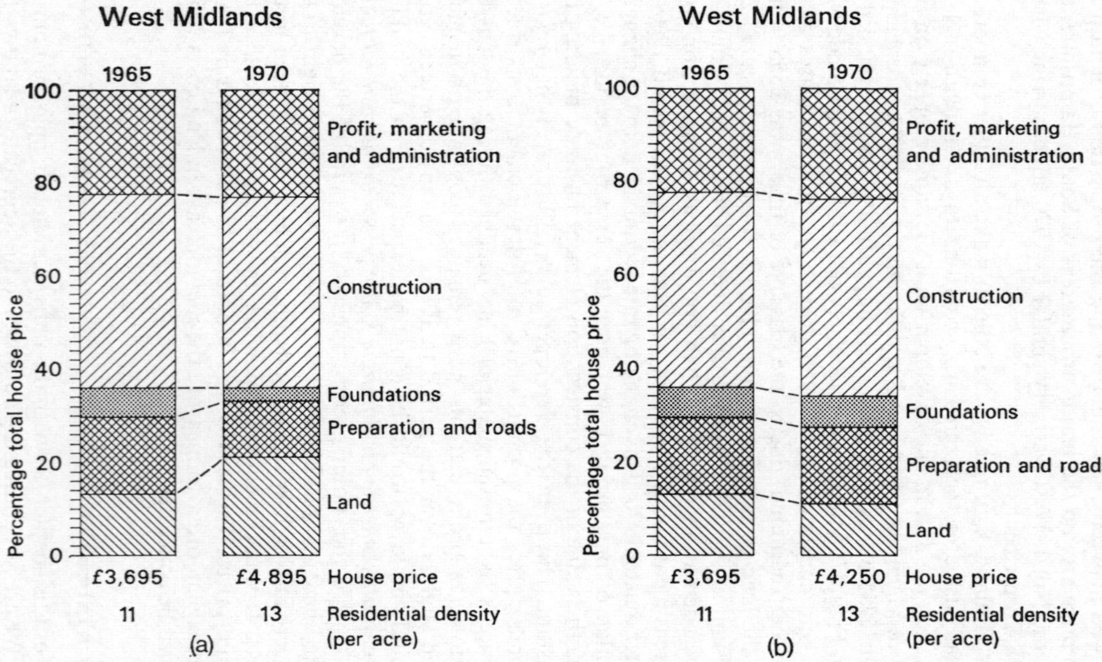

Figure 7.6 Cost Variations of Factor Inputs in a Housing Package for the Continuous Development of a Site, West Midlands 1965–1970:

(a) At Current Land Prices
(b) At Constant 1965 Land Prices

If the initial conceptualization of the development sequence is borne out, then any distortion in land values can be attributed either to market forces (speculation or 'hope-value' as it is called), or to legislative effects (national or local planning controls), or both. However, the survey revealed that two forms of *taxation* further complicated the land and housing market, namely the Betterment Levy imposed by the Land Commission, and Selective Employment Tax which seriously affected the house-building industry. The latter tax was considered as a fixed overhead by the industry at large and was added directly to the labour costs of construction. In effect, as we saw in Chapter Six, it was passed directly and in full to the consumer and increased the costs by £150–£400 per house. The effect of Betterment Levy on land prices will be examined later in this chapter.

The distorted land market may therefore be attributable to speculation, legislation and taxation. But in what proportions? Considerable difficulty arises in isolating such values which may be attributable to private decisions or public policy. Other determining factors, such as population changes, are not constant and in any given situation it may be extremely hazardous to suggest what proportion of an increase in land values, consequent upon an increase in demand, was brought about by legislation.[49] Although one cannot hold demand constant, the results of the survey indicate such similarity in change in many localities over a relatively short time span that other determinants would seem responsible; namely the nature of the land transactions, speculation, local planning control and the Betterment Levy.

A PRIVATE MARKET DECISIONS

(*i*) *The Nature of the Suburban Land Market*

In order to assess how the nature of the suburban land market influences the value for land it is necessary to consider briefly the criteria used by the supply side (landowner) and the demand side (builder or developer) of the land market.

A landowner expects to sell equal to or above a minimum price (his reservation price) and if the value drops below that price he will or need not sell, providing his expectations are reasonable and providing he is not financially extended. In the late 1960s this reservation price was often higher than what the market should pay because the landowner needed to recoup all or part of the 40 per cent Betterment Levy imposed by the Land Commission on all transactions which capitalized on a development value created by the community at large. The work of the Land Commission will be reviewed later in this chapter, but the effect of the tax on the land market would appear to have been at least twofold. First, through the uncertainty about the future of the Commission, land became more scarce as expectation of the levy being abolished increased and second, where land was transacted, then a proportion of the levy was reflected in higher land prices.

The land buyer is usually using the land as a factor input in a production process. The vital determinants in a builder's estimates of a development's

[49] B. Goodall, op. cit., p. 13.

viability are the residential density and the likely price of houses that will sell in a particular locality. These relationships determine what a builder can afford for land. Land is therefore a derived demand from housing demand and is a residual in the costing of the development (the residual approach to costing was described in Chapter Six). The builder can pick and choose sites but ultimately he is in a weaker position than the landowner in that he *must buy land* at some stage. A land stock of two or three years is the minimum required for the forward planning of a land development project. A builder usually borrows money for this purpose, incurring the carrying charges as part of the land cost, rather than using equity capital. With these considerations in mind it is not surprising to find that most builders and developers attempt to speculate in land, not so much to capitalize on land, but to enable them to use cheap land and retain a cash flow from sales of competitively priced housing.

These quite different negotiating positions of buyer and seller create an unusual demand and supply market relationship. The land buyer uses land as a stock-in-trade and at some stage he must buy land or go out of business. The landowner, on the other hand, views land differently; he may not want to use his land and with expectations high on a rising wave of value he need not sell. This is clearly illustrated by one landowner during the survey, when he remarked:

> I have, at the moment, no sensible alternative investment and, therefore, have no real need to sell. I would only be influenced to sell if I received a truly exceptional offer or found a project in which to invest the cash which would also be of practical use to myself and my family.

Here we are given the clue to the land price problem; with land in scarce supply and rising in value, land is viewed by its owners as a sensible form of investment comparable to stocks, paintings or *objets d'art*. As there is no tax on holding land, the disincentives of continued ownership are minimal.

(*ii*) *Speculation*

Speculative activity and its effect on the land market have been discussed at length by Clawson[50, 51] and by Harvey and Clark.[52] However, the precise role that speculation may have played in increasing land prices is not clear. The study of the American market by Schmid[53] estimates an average appreciation of land values above farm values in 1964 of between 892 per cent and 1,875 per cent and concluded that present prices are considerably higher than expectation about future increase of value. How are these expectations calculated? In theory they reflect the capitalized value of the land's economic rent and are determined by the expected return on investment in it and the structures placed upon it. The price depends upon estimates of this expected value, the expected time of development and the discount rate which is applied. However, holding land may not be rational investment policy, at

[50] M. Clawson, op. cit. [51] Ibid., p. 102.

[52] R. Harvey and W. A. Clark, 'The Nature and Economics of Urban Sprawl', *Land Economics*, 41 (1965), pp. 1–19. [53] A. Schmid, op. cit., p. 19.

least in all cases. The fact that the land is ultimately sold for much more than was paid for it is no evidence at all that it was a profitable deal; on the contrary, unless a great deal more is obtained the deal was probably a losing one.[54]

It would be reasonable to assume that the price for residential land should be expected to increase annually at the same rate as construction costs and wage rates. The fact that it does not but rises faster, poses the question: whether the difference between the inflation rate and the actual rate is the cost of maintaining a private market for land? The data and analysis do not permit answers to such a question, which is in part ideological. What can be said at this stage is that the speculative value of white land (not designated

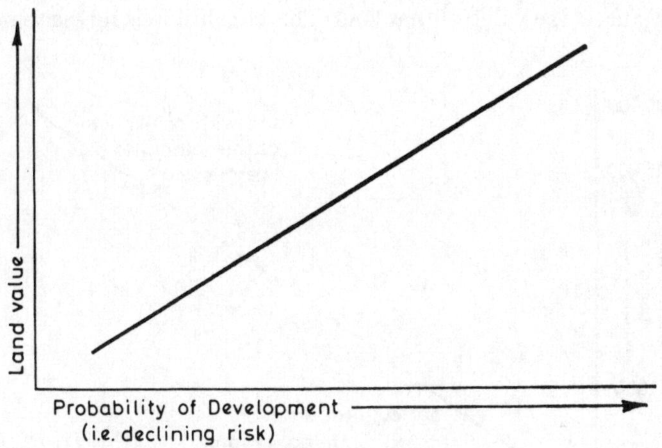

Figure 7.7 Theoretical Relationship between Land Value and the Probability of Development

for any use and not Green Belt) varies between one-fifth and one-tenth of the market value for land *with* planning permission. The appreciation of land values above farm values was between 200 per cent and 400 per cent. Ironically, when builders do own land speculatively, as many have done in the past, very few have passed on the full development value to the consumer, in order to keep the housing market active. This does not mean that they would not have passed on the full value if the housing market had been more buoyant. If there was a market for land related to a system where development control did not exist one would expect, in theory, that any increase in the value of the land would be a function of a declining risk in holding the land, i.e. with an increasing probability of development occurring (Figure 7.7).

However, one of the most interesting and unambiguous conclusions to emerge from the developer interviews was that such a speculator's charter, as it has been called, does not exist in Britain. Land values are certainly related to development potential but *there is no continuum of value*. In essence,

[54] M. Clawson, op. cit., p. 125.

there are *two markets* for suburban land in this country at the present time. First, the market for land which has planning permission or has a very high probability of gaining such permission, and second, the market for agricultural land or land without planning permission and with little likelihood of achieving it in the foreseeable future, i.e. within ten years or more (Figure 7.8).

B EFFECTS OF LEGISLATION

(*i*) *Planning Permission*

The effect of having to obtain planning permission upon the developers' decision-making process was outlined in Chapter Six. One major conclusion emerged; that the need to obtain *planning permission* to develop land substantially affects the value of that land. This conclusion is further emphasized

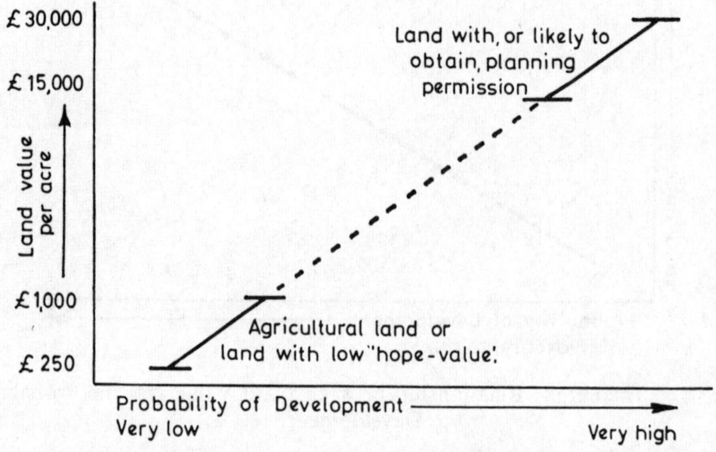

Figure 7.8 The Effect of the Probability of Development on the Value of Land

by the dichotomous nature of the land market which, in effect, classified land broadly into two categories reflecting the short-term probability of the land being developed (Figure 7.8), with vastly different values for land in each group. Despite the claim by many local authority planning departments that sufficient land is designated and available for development, there was little doubt in the minds of all our respondents in the survey that the cause of high land-values in Britain was largely attributable to a *scarcity* of *supply*. It was considered that the position of acute scarcity arose through two main factors which have resulted from *public policy decision*. At the national level there was the effect of taxation measures introduced with the Land Commission, and at the local level there was the effect of too little land being designated for residential development by the various local planning authorities.

A measure of these combined effects creating a scarcity of land supply is deducible from the four case studies outlined above (Figure 7.5 and 7.6(a)). For example, in North-West England one can estimate the value, due to the combined effects of national and local legislation, to be £250 per acre in 1960 and £6,500 per acre in 1970. Making allowance for inflation and devaluation, the difference remains at approximately £6,000 per acre or an additional burden of £600 per house for the potential purchaser. In the South-East (Outer Metropolitan Area) the effects were much greater; the difference being between £4,400 an acre in 1960 and over £18,000 an acre in 1970. Discounting for the effect of inflation and devaluation, the difference remains in excess of £11,000 an acre or an additional cost of exactly £1,000 for every house buyer.

The question now arises whether this interpretation of the land market distortion being caused by legislation is a valid one. Let us briefly consider the facts. During the period 1955–62 the demand for housing was increasing and the relationship between construction costs (labour and materials) and house prices was fairly constant. Therefore, land costs (the residual cost element) were increasing at approximately the same rate. This would be consistent with a rent theory of demand. Now let us consider these relationships for the period 1962–70. During this period, the demand for private housing, especially during the four years 1966–70 was constant or *declining*. Housing demand was affected by tighter credit and unsold new houses were not uncommon. Under these circumstances one would expect land prices to stabilize or decline. Quite to the contrary, the relationship between construction costs and house prices (Figure 6.4) was generally a divergent one due to a distorted land market: during the years 1967–70 land prices had *doubled* or more.

To understand how such an escalation could occur it is necessary to recall once again the differing negotiating positions of land owners and land buyers. Let us consider a hypothetical example of a land transaction that might well typify the market in land in the late 1960s. The expectation of the landowner may set a value on a piece of land at £10,000 per acre. It has been argued by F. Willey[55] that in the case of housing land it is the price that the houses themselves fetch which primarily determines the price which will be paid for the land on which the houses are put. Using such an estimate of the local housing market, the builder may set a limit on the piece of land, say £9,000 an acre. However, if the landowner is not financially extended, and given reasonable expectations of a future rise in value, coupled with uncertainty about future land taxation (all of which existed, real or apparent in the land-owner's mind) *he will not sell*. However, at some stage the builder *must buy* and *if all his competitors* are faced with the same level of land prices he will pay the additional £1,000 (as will his competitors). This increment in value resulted from a *scarcity of supply* of land. As we have observed this reduction in supply was caused by a combination of factors. In addition to the characteristics of the land market itself, the main reduction occurred

[55] F. Willey, *Parliamentary Debates* (*Hansard*), 808 (16 Dec. 1970), Col. 1412.

through the creation of a dual market in land with the need to obtain planning permission. The position was exacerbated by the existence of the Land Commission, since it temporarily reduced still further the amount of land available. As it is axiomatic in economics that price is determined by the interaction of supply and demand, the explanation of land price inflation during this period must lie in the *relative* rates of reduction in supply and demand. The inference being made is that the reduction in supply outpaced the reduction in demand after 1962; such a relative increase in demand interacts upon the reduced supply and puts up land prices.

(ii) The Land Commission

When Mr Peter Walker, Secretary of State for the Environment, addressed the House of Commons on 22 July 1970, yet another attempt by the State to control land prices and recoup betterment had come to an end. The announcement, that the Land Commission (Dissolution) Bill would soon be presented to parliament, meant that four Conservative Governments during this century had been forced to repeal land legislation introduced by either a Liberal or a Labour administration (in 1909, 1931, 1947 and 1967); all had attempted to enforce a system of land value taxing and all were subsequently seen to fail or prove administratively cumbersome. In place of the Land Commission, the Secretary of State made provision for development value realized from future land transactions to be dealt with through the normal system of taxation and capital gains. Betterment Levy was, therefore, not payable on chargeable acts after 22 July 1970, and the Commission's programme of land acquisition was brought to a halt and arrangements made for the orderly disposal of land in the Commission's possession.

The Government justified the need to repeal the legislation because, in their view, the Land Commission had failed to achieve two objectives: (*a*) to stabilize land prices, and (*b*) to aid land release in areas of acute shortage. The Government considered the availability of land for development essential to the stability of land prices and to the revival of the house-building industry.

Before attempting to assess the validity of these criticisms, a brief outline is given in the next section of the main features and objectives of the Land Commission and its powers.

THE ACT: THE CONTEXT

The Land Commission Act of 1967 was designed to achieve the objectives set out in the White Paper of September 1965.[56] These were clearly stated as:

(a) to secure that the right land was available at the right time for the implementation of national, regional and local plans;

(b) to secure that a substantial part of the development value created by

[56] *The Land Commission.* Cmnd 2771, HMSO, London (1965).

> the community returns to the community and that the burden of the cost of land for essential purposes was reduced.[57]

To fulfil the first objective, the Act gave the community powers to trade in land, including the power of compulsory purchase (acquisition). The collection of Betterment Levy was the means of achieving the second objective.

It is important to view this legislation historically. In 1947, the Central Land Board was set up to effect the principles of the 1947 Town and Country Planning Act. Hopefully, planning would be made more effective by solving the problems of compensation and betterment. Briefly, the Act stated that whenever development rights in land were created by planning permission, a charge was to be levied on developers. The Development Charge was equal to the increase in land value resulting from the permission, and was payable to the Central Land Board. It was thought that private land would change hands at existing use-value only (i.e. excluding development value). This also meant that no compensation was payable when restrictions were placed on land use. The cost of planning decisions would be reduced, and planning made easier. The Government argued that the loss of development value did not entitle owners to compensation. To avoid hardships, however, it did provide a sum of £300 million to pay claims based on 1947 value.

The 1947 Act had tried to make all land transactions public. The methods used, and the results obtained, help to explain the 1967 legislation. The Central Land Board had only limited powers of compulsory acquisition. In fact only thirty-five Compulsory Purchase Orders were made between 1948 and 1952; and furthermore, the Board was not able to carry out development. It could only dispose of the land to likely developers at a price sufficient to cover the cost of purchase and the Development Charge It is probably fair to say that the legislation stifled the private market in land. As McAuslan noted: 'it was found that the supply of land . . . was severely curtailed as owners were unwilling to sell land merely at existing use value'.[58]

The Central Land Board admitted (in its reports for the years 1949–50 and 1950–51) that: 'Sales at or near the existing use value are more the exception than the rule.'[59] At the same time, the Board's inadequate powers of compulsory purchase were insufficient to ensure the ready supply of development land.

The 1954 Act abolished the 1947 Development Rights Scheme and the Development Charge; the market was revived for private land dealing.[60] After 1954 land with the benefit of planning permission could be sold at higher prices than land subject to restriction. Local authorities could still buy land at current use-value with compulsory purchase orders. This was

[57] Ibid., para. 7.

[58] J. McAuslan, 'The Land Commission – past, present and future?', *Chartered Surveyor*, Vol. 102, No. 5, Nov. 1969, pp. 222–7.

[59] Annual Reports of the Central Land Board for 1948–56. HMSO, London (1949–56).

[60] 1954 Act.

unpopular as well as unfair to unfortunate owners. In 1959 market value was restored as a basis for compensation of compulsory acquisitions. The period 1959–67 has been called the heyday of the private sector. Prices rose and:

> The gap opened up by the 'unscrambling' provision of the 1954 Act – between the openmarket value of land with the benefit of planning permission and that of similar land on which development had been restricted by planning controls . . . was bound to be widened by the passage of time and rising prices.[61]

In view of what has been said, the Land Commission Act can be viewed as an attempt to redress the balance between the private and the public sector.[62]

THE ACT: ITS POWERS AND LIMITATIONS

All of the Commission's offices had a Lands Division and a Levy Division – responsible for the two main objectives of the Act.[63] These divisions derived their powers from Parts II and III of the Act respectively. As G. R. Chetwynd (Deputy Chairman, later to succeed as Chairman for a short period) has said:

> The Land Dealing and Levy provisions, though quite different in character, are really complementary. The levy might discourage land owners from bringing land on to the market for development, and shortage of land can lead to rising prices. It is, therefore, right that the power to collect levy on development value should be backed by powers to ensure the supply of land.[64]

McAuslan viewed the legislation the other way round:

> . . . the compulsory acquisition powers of the Commission were of primary importance and basic to the aims of this legislation and . . . the levy was merely a device to ensure, in theory, that free and compulsory sales proceed on the same basis.[65]

Put another way, it was the fear of levy reducing the supply of land, which made compulsory acquisition necessary. Some critics of the Land Commission were unhappy with this situation. P. H. Clark wrote: 'It seems an

[61] F. G. Pennance, 'Housing, Town Planning and the Land Commission', *Hobart Paper* No. 40, Institute of Economic Affairs, London (1967).

[62] P. Ellman, op. cit., p. 4.5.

[63] Betterment Levy collected went to the Exchequer. The Land Commission's own land transactions were financed out of the Land Trading Fund, which could be primed with Treasury loans of up to £45 million. In fact, by selling land at market value and buying at a price minus levy, the Commission made a profit of 40 per cent on its land deals. This went into the Land Trading Fund; in this way the Commission hoped to become self-supporting.

[64] G. R. Chetwynd, 'The Land Commission – Friend or Foe?', *Building Technology and Management*, 6 (1968), pp. 150–51.

[65] J. McAuslan, 'The Land Commission' op cit., p. 223.

unsatisfactory position when compulsion has to be used to get back to a situation which prevailed before its introduction'.[66]

LAND ACQUISITION

The Commission could only acquire land compulsorily in pursuit of objective (*a*). One of five conditions ensuring that the land was suitable for development, had to be satisfied. This parcel of land in question had to:

either

1 have planning permission in force for material development which had not been taken up in part or whole;

or

2 be zoned for a specific purpose in the current Development Plan or incorporated in proposals for the amendment of the Development Plan;

or

3 be designated as subject to compulsory acquisition in the current Development Plan;

or

4 be designated as the site of a new town;

or

5 be wholly or partly an area declared as a clearance area.

If no planning permission existed, the Commission could apply for permission itself. The Commission had to show some acceptable purpose for development, viz:

(*a*) for securing the carrying out at an early date of material development which the Commission felt ought to be carried out;
(*b*) for securing that land be developed as a whole;
(*c*) for making land available for development or used by a person or body of persons who could be authorized to acquire it compulsorily;
(*d*) for disposing of land on a concessionary Crownhold basis.

The first Chairman of the Land Commission, Sir Henry Wells, listed five types of land they might buy:

1 Land already allocated for development by a planning authority but which evidence showed might not have been put on the market for development. This land could be affected by the levy.
2 Conversely, land where the owner wished to develop immediately but no services were available and the local authority wanted to wait several years for development. In this case the Land Commission could help programming by buying from the landowner in advance and holding the land till it was needed.
3 Land not yet allocated but which the planning authority wished to

[66] P. H. Clark, 'Land Commission Doubts', *New Society*, 1 Dec. 1966.

see developed and would give planning permission. The planning judgement would be made by the local authority but the first approach might be made by the Land Commission, an owner, or developer or all three working together in partnership.

4 Land which threw up special or peculiar problems which could only be resolved by acquisition by the Commission, e.g.
(*a*) an area of fragmented ownership; or
(*b*) where the ownership was unknown;
(*c*) land straddling the boundaries of several local authorities which should be developed comprehensively. In this way the Commission could help regional planning;
(*d*) developed land, where acquisition was expensive for local authorities in terms of money and administrative resources. At the beginning of its career, the Commission could only envisage a pilot scheme or two in this field for several years to come.

5 Land on which the Commission hoped it could make most profits to build up the Land Trading Fund. This land was mainly in the counties surrounding old cities and was part of large new allocations for housing and industry not catered for by the new towns.

DISPOSAL OF LAND

The land purchased by the Commission did not have to be sold immediately – it could be serviced, improved, then disposed of by sale, lease or tenancy. Land disposal was normally for 'The best consideration in money or money's worth which could reasonably be obtained.'[67] The Commission could also dispose of land on special Crownhold terms, under which it reserves to itself future development rights in the land. Alternatively, the land could be disposed of on concessionary Crownhold terms at less than market value, for housing purposes. These powers were not in fact used.

BETTERMENT LEVY

One result of the 1954 Act had been a two-price system – the level of compensation was below the price obtained in the open market. To balance this situation, the Commission charged a levy on all transactions resulting in a realization of development value. Unlike the 1947 Act, the new legislation allowed the vendor to retain part of the development value. Levy was charged at 40 per cent. The purpose of this was to 'encourage the willing sale of land for development.'[68]

[67] Land Commission Act, S. 16(2).

[68] *Note*: Development value has been explained as 'any additional element of value which is realized from land over and above the value for its current use and which is attributable to the possibilities of putting the land, or some other land, to another and more profitable use. More precisely, it may be defined as the additional value derived from, or from the prospect of, the right to carry out material de-

Development value was realized when calculations revealed its presence whenever a 'chargeable act or event' occurred.[69] This event need not in fact have been a development (as in 1947) and was paid by the recipient of the development value, which may not have been the developer himself.

There were six cases of 'chargeable acts or events' (labelled A to F):[70,71]

A Sales and assignments of freeholds or other interests in land.
B Creation of tenancies.
C The commencement of development.
D The receipt of compensation for revocation or modification of planning permission.
E The grant or release of an easement of restrictive right.
F Any other event designated as chargeable under regulations made by the Minister.

THE 1947 AND 1967 LEGISLATION COMPARED

There were three main ways in which the financial provisions of the 1947 Act differed from those of the 1967 Act.

1 Powers of acquisition were different. The Central Land Board could only acquire compulsorily after failure to acquire by agreement; and this power was not to be used to enforce sale at existing use-value. The Land Commission had much wider powers. It also had special procedures to prevent delaying tactics, e.g. avoiding public enquiries; simplifying the serving of notices for Compulsory Purchase Orders; cutting lengthy conveyancing procedures; and so on.

2 The Central Land Board could not carry out development itself. The Commission could buy land in advance of need; assemble land for 'comprehensive development'; contribute to the provision of services if necessary and so on. It was anxious to act as a National Land Dealing Corporation – to achieve a rapid turnover of land by acting as a middleman.[72]

velopment. *Betterment Levy: an Explanatory Memorandum.* HMSO, London (1967), p. 72.

[69] The Land Commission Act, 1967.

[70] *Note*: 1 Betterment Levy was not to tax increases in current-use value of land – it was chargeable only on development value realized.

2 If developers bought land between the 1 August 1966, and 6 April 1967, they could have levy assessed under Schedule 5 of the Act; if they satisfied certain conditions, viz: (*a*) their main purpose was house building; (*b*) the developer owned the freehold or leasehold interests; (*c*) the developer was in business on 23 September 1965; (*d*) the project was begun ('started') by 6 October 1967. Schedule 5 assesses Net Development Value as Market Value minus Purchase Prices. Normally the builder will have paid Market Value, so Development will be nought.

[71] D. B. Evans, 'Betterment Levy – the Exemptions and Reliefs to House Builders', *Building Technology and Management*, 5 (1967), pp. 3–5, 16–18.

[72] F. Longdon, 'The Land Commission Act, 1967. Nationalisation or Rationalization: Taxation or Frustration'. *Estates Gazette*, 21 Oct. 1967.

3 The 40 per cent Betterment Levy appears to have represented a concession in comparison to the Development Charge. McAuslan questioned such a view:

> . . . bearing in mind that there is, on this occasion, no £300 million fund on which to claim and that the Commission's powers to acquire are, and will become, far in excess of those available to the Central Land Board, second thoughts on the subject are more than justified.[73]

The 1967 Act could have prevented some of the most permanent deterrents to developers. For example, after 1947 developers had to pay full market value and were also faced with a development charge. The 1967 legislation required levy to be paid by the vendor of land; not by the developer before he had recouped any profits.

THE OBJECTIVES OF THE LAND COMMISSION

It was continually stressed that the main purpose of the Land Commission was to act as a trader in land.[74] In this respect levy was simply a method of betterment collection and a means of financing land dealings. At other times, the Commission was described as an instrument in planning. Sir Henry Wells emphasized this role:

> . . . as a national body whose main function . . . is to acquire and dispose of land for development, we are in a better position than the individual local planning authorities to turn plans into reality.[75]

Similarly the Minister for Land and Natural Resources considered the Commission was to: 'introduce a new dynamic, positive element into planning.'[76]

There were a number of ways in which the Commission was to assist planning. These were:

1 Through consultation with planners about future acquisition and disposition of land, e.g. ensuring that tracts of land were planned comprehensively with a mixture of public and private development;

2 Through helping local authorities to acquire the land they urgently needed, in large estates, so that they could be developed in an orderly way, under one ownership. It was the Commission's hope to use their powers of instant conveyancing to speed up the acquisition process;

3 In the words of the Chairman, the Commission was to act as '. . . a

[73] J. McAuslan, 'The Land Commission', op. cit., p. 224.

[74] Sir Henry Wells, 'Functions of the Land Commission', *Architects Journal*, 5 Apr. 1967.

[75] Sir Henry Wells, 'The Land Commission – Planning for the Future', *Building Technology and Management*, 7 (1969), p. 3.

[76] F. Willey, reported in P. H. Clark, op. cit.

national property dealing company' to ensure that developers of all kinds, but in particular the small private house-builder, could get land where the demand was. The major concern was land for housing, especially in the pressure areas of the South-East, Midlands and North-West. Douglas Calverley, a member of the Commission, saw its role as:

> . . . loosening up the land market, not only buying land with permission, also buying land without permission and going to appeal if necessary.[77]

Using the funds accumulated from development value, the Commission was to help finance redevelopment. Calverley describes how the Commission could:

> . . . use levy funds to bridge the gap between cost and value . . . opening up a completely new idea of opportunity to the initiative, expertise and enterprise of the private developer.[78]

In particular, this was a reference to the 'twilight areas'.

G. R. Chetwynd, who was the successor-designate to Sir Henry Wells as Chairman of the Commission at its dissolution, described its main efforts as:

(*a*) providing land for private housing, especially in areas of most need. Sir Henry Wells also stated at intervals that it was important to keep small builders in the market;[79]
(*b*) achieving stability in land prices;
(*c*) acting as a catalyst to loosen up the market (through fear of Compulsory Purchase Orders);
(*d*) carrying out a detailed survey of land availability.[80]

SOME THEORETICAL IMPLICATIONS OF THE LAND COMMISSION'S OBJECTIVES

Pennance raised a number of questions about the Land Commission's objectives and economic efficiency.[81] First, price increases, whether steady or bumpy are:

> . . . the normal result of rising demand, resulting from rising incomes and wealth in the community and from the changes in preference they promote.[82]

Pennance regards any attempt to control price and provide land cheaply for planning authorities as economically inefficient. Such insulation, he argued, was unlikely to produce rational economic decisions on the best use of resources. Second, Pennance argued that the Commission could not possibly

77 D. Calverley, letter to *Estates Gazette*, 25 Nov. 1967.
78 Ibid.
79 *The Economist*, 1 Apr. 1967, or *Architect's Journal*, 5 Apr. 1967.
80 G. R. Chetwynd, op. cit., p. 151.
81 F. G. Pennance, op. cit.
82 Ibid., p. 29.

get more land on to the market unless it persuaded local authorities to release more land:

> If the current price is not high enough to bid more land from its existing uses, then either this represents an equilibrium situation, or the pressure of demand will bid land prices higher to secure additional supplies.[83]

Third, according to Pennance, providing land to small builders, and attempting to keep prices stable, involved some degree of subsidy. He wrote:

> It [the Commission] will in effect be using its powers to transfer land from relatively efficient to relatively inefficient builders with no benefit to ultimate consumers.[84]

Fourth, in Pennance's view, the Commission's role as a central agency or land bank was superfluous:

> . . . since land that is anywhere must be somewhere and held by someone, there has always been in existence a 'land bank' in the sense of a stock. It has always been possible to obtain releases from that bank on payment of the market price.[85]

PUBLIC REACTIONS TO THE WORK OF THE COMMISSION

Public reactions to the work of the Commission were generally critical and related to a number of different issues. These included the effect of the Betterment Levy on land prices, the uncertainty about the actual amount of levy payable, the witholding of land from the market, the failure of the Commission to fulfil its objectives, the threat of using white agricultural land for new housing, and whether the Commission was the right body to assess demand for land. These will be reviewed briefly.

The Land Commission was often cited as a cause of rising land prices, often the major cause. Ellman observed:

> There does, however, appear to be a genuine inflationary trend in operation where the price of housing land is concerned. Record prices for separate plots are being reached every year all over the country, but this trend was evident long before the advent of the Land Commission and was one reason why the Land Commission was established in the first place. The Land Commission, by bringing more land on the market would like to stabilize prices, but if it proves powerless to do so, at least the levy enables the community at large to share in the fortunes of the few who are lucky enough to own land with development value.[86]

Although there was considerable difficulty in isolating statistically any one

[83] Ibid., p. 32.
[84] Ibid., p. 33.
[85] Ibid., p. 34.
[86] P. Ellman, op. cit., p. 6.6.

factor, such as the impact of the levy on land prices, it has been shown that record prices for land were reached after 1967. Ellman also quotes many examples where Betterment Levy was passed on:

> By 1968, in all areas of demand, vendors definitely expected the current price to reimburse them for Betterment Levy, compared with prices ruling prior to the 1967 Act.[87]

In 1968, Mr Costain asked a number of pointed questions in Parliament.[88] He had heard of 20 per cent price increases since April 6th, 1967, and wanted to know what effect the levy had had. The Minister replied that the 1967 average increase of prices might even have been lower than for recent years. This can be explained because the conditions in the land market during the first year of the Commission's activities were characterized by a prolonged period of stagnation, largely as a result of restocking by builders before the first appointed day. However, by 1969, the *Estates Gazette* reported:

> The advent of the Land Commission has undoubtedly led to a sharp and distinct rise (over and above the normal increase due to inflation) in the market prices of residential land in these areas.... Transactions during the past year known to the firm, show that prices have increased by 25 to 50 per cent over the pre-Betterment Levy period.

The report continues that:

> The main cause is that potential vendors are doing one of two things. First, in view of the Conservatives' promise to abolish the levy, they refrain from seeking planning consent now for any improvements to their property. Second, if they already have planning consent, they try to obtain a higher price for their land sufficient to cover the cost to them of the Betterment Levy ... our view is that they are succeeding in selling their land at these higher prices, first because planning restrictions still exist and second because building land is scarce. Buyers are, therefore, forced to pay the high prices to get the land they want.[89]

These general comments were supported by reports from the regions. A report for Leicestershire in the *Estates Gazette*'s Survey of the 1969 Property Market claimed:

> There is evidence that less building land has come on to the market, owing, one can only presume, to the effect of the Land Commission Act, and the hope in the minds of potential vendors that a change in government may produce a change in levy provisions. Such parcels as have been offered have shown a trend towards higher prices.[90]

[87] Ibid., p. 6.29.

[88] *Estates Gazette*, 2 Mar. 1968.

[89] *Estates Gazette*, 31 May 1969; report by Strutt and Parker and Co., on sales of land in Essex and East Anglia.

[90] *Estates Gazette*, 31 Jan. 1970.

Or, for Hertfordshire:

> As yet there is no sign that the much-vaunted Land Commission Act has either produced cheaper land for residential development, or made more such land available . . . the converse is in fact the case . . . The cost of building land, allied to the numerous forms of taxation which now attend development, makes it extremely difficult for the small builder to offer houses at competitive figures.[91]

There was considerable amount of uncertainty about the actual amount of levy payable. Brackett and Hoyes voiced this criticism in the *Chartered Surveyor*.[92] They asked if the administrative arrangements for notifying transactions and determination of levy would be simplified, to prevent them from constraining market operations.

The Land Commission was criticized for failing to do its job properly. For example, an editorial comment in the *Estates Gazette* reported criticisms that the Commission was not collecting enough levy; that the Commission was not acquiring enough land; and that local authorities had complained that the Commission was buying land:

> They [authorities] see that the Commission is attempting to break the planning stranglehold and force more land onto the market when, they claim, services – such as drainage, electricity, water, schools, etc. – necessary to support development, are not available, and cannot be made available in time.[93]

The article concluded that:

> The Land Commission's position was untenable from the start. The time is overdue to bring to an end an unworkable scheme.[94]

Some alarm was also expressed in connection with the Commission's policy of looking towards white (agricultural) land to solve the housing problem. For example, the Country Landowners' Association objected that:

> . . . Nor can we stand idly by when vast acres of white land – highly productive agricultural land – are taken for development while there are still great acreages of industrial derelict land, a blot on the countryside, left completely unused and apparently without hope of reclamation.[95]

The *Estates Gazette* has also expressed doubts as to whether the Commission could assess the demand for land, when no land was available:

> . . . it is only if there is substantial allocation of land for development in many places at once that the market will show what the true requirements

[91] Ibid.

[92] W. R. Brackett and T. Hoyes, 'The Land Commission and the Property Market', *Chartered Surveyor* (1966), pp. 128–32.

[93] 'The Commission in Trouble', *Estates Gazette*, 12 Apr. 1969.

[94] Ibid.

[95] 'The Land Commission and Local Government', *Estates Gazette*, 30 Sept. 1967.

> are. If that happens, however, individuals, small builders, large builders and development companies will have all the land they need, and the Commission becomes wholly redundant. If it does not happen, even the Commission cannot buy one square inch of land.[96]

In the same editorial, the *Estates Gazette* stated that the Commission was not the right body to survey the demand and supply problem. The reasons were quoted as:

1 It had no research facilities or staff (it did employ consultants to look into the availability of land in certain areas, though).
2 It was a political body and could not be objective.
3 There was a grave doubt as to whether the job could be done by any organization.

Public reactions that were sympathetic to the work of the Commission were few and far between. Most of them have come from the Commission officials and members of the Labour Government in power at the time. For example, Sir Henry Wells was often quoted in defence of the Commission. In the *Estates Gazette* (June 1968) he replied to criticisms of the Commission's early record of two acres bought at a cost of £3 million and £1½ million collected in levy.[97] He claimed that there was no truth in allegations that the levy had generally raised land prices. The major cause was, he said, the shortage of land allocated by planning authorities in a time of peak housing demand. The few bits of land that were zoned for development in areas where there was a demand for housing were subject to fierce competition between developers and the price rises were inevitable. Wells maintained that the Commission was being blamed for something it had no control of: 'We have not, nor should we have, any powers to make planning decisions.'[98] The Minister had asked planning authorities in the South-East to release enough land for 35,000 new houses per year for the next seven years, but the response was not encouraging.

Lack of substantive evidence appears to be the major problem in assessing the Commission's performance; but Ellman wrote:

> While the Commission's record of land acquisition for this purpose (housing) is by no means spectacular, there is ample evidence that the Commission is taking its work seriously in this field . . .[99]

Ellman also pointed out that the major effect of the Commission would not be felt immediately after the Act, because of the stocks builders had acquired. Little land was coming on to the market at first, but eventually the situation was reportedly improving. Ellman, however, mentions a number of achievements of the Commission. By 1969 it was claimed to have brought 1,000

[96] 'One Year Old', *Estates Gazette*, 6 Apr. 1968.
[97] *Estates Gazette*, 15 June 1968.
[98] Ibid.
[99] P. Ellman, op. cit., p. 6.8.

acres on the market by its very presence. When the Commission showed an interest in the land, people were moved into selling to private developers.[100]

The restocking process in 1966 is mentioned by McAuslan. He mentioned that:

> . . . for every acre purchased by the Commission at least a further acre has come freely on to the market as a result of its searches.[101]

McAuslan also praised the Commission's role in the proposed development of 415 acres at Walderslade, Kent:

> The Commission, by virtue of its power and special advantages, seems to be well-suited to ensure the comprehensive development in the county Development Plans for at least ten years.[102]

Senior had a number of good things to say about the Land Commission.[103] He believed that the major advantage the Commission had was in powers of land assembly. In this way, the Commission could make possible the implementation by private enterprise of comprehensive plans for new development: 'and in so doing to smooth out the bumps in the building cycle'.[104] This, Senior argued, had made the Commission an integral part of development planning and control, irrespective of the Betterment Levy.

> It has justified its existence as a catalyst of co-operation between the public and private sectors of this system . . . In its capacity as an assembler of land ownerships, the Commission is, in fact, the vitally necessary but previously missing link between the other two functions contributing to the tripartite process of comprehensively planned development.[105]

Unfortunately, the isolated examples Senior provided cannot adequately justify these claims. He mentioned cases where the Commission was called in by county councils to buy up land from willing sellers, drain it and put in spine roads to an agreed comprehensive plan (e.g. a site near Woking, and another near Teeside of 1,000 acres). Senior claimed:

> In the north, this drill is now common form, to the general satisfaction of all parties. The authorities get comprehensively-planned development exactly the way they want it; the builders, large and small, get prepared sites on the scale they can afford, at current interest rates, to hold on borrowed capital, and the owners of land. . . . are well content to sell by agreement on the terms.[106]

[100] Ibid., p. 5.9.

[101] J. McAuslan, 'The Land Commission', op. cit., p. 225.

[102] Ibid., p. 226.

[103] D. Senior, 'The Land Commission', *Official Architecture and Planning*, 33 (1970), 349–53.

[104] Ibid., p. 350.

[105] Ibid.

[106] Ibid.

Unfortunately, such benefits and good feeling were not widespread. None of the builders interviewed in the Developer Survey (Table 6.2, page 168) claimed to have directly benefited from the Commission's intervention in the market. It is to these reactions by the developers interviewed and an analysis of the actual transactions made by the Commission that we now turn.

THE ACHIEVEMENTS OF THE LAND COMMISSION

Before attempting to assess the influence of the Land Commission from the developer's viewpoint, we will now try and specify precisely what the Land Commission actually did achieve in terms of land acquisition and tax raised through Betterment levy.

The total amount of land purchased during the lifetime of the Commission was 2,800 acres (Table 7.3). From these acquisitions only 338 acres were sold on the market. No land was acquired or sold during the first year; this was due to a number of factors. The Commission had to be created, recruit staff and develop a philosophy. The time-consuming task of surveying land availability had to be undertaken and estimates of demand made. Discussions had to be held with local authorities, and public enquiries further delayed the acquisition process. To criticize the Commission upon its first year's performance in land purchasing was clearly unjustified. During the following two years the land acquisition programme gathered momentum but at the time of the Commission's dissolution only 2,800 acres were actually purchased and most of this land was located in the North or in areas of slack demand. This explains why the average price paid by the Commission of nearly £4,000 per acre was so modest; it was during a time, as we have seen in an earlier section of this chapter, when the prices of residential sites in the main pressure areas from London to Birmingham and Manchester were in the range of £15,000 to £30,000 per acre.

In the South and South-East, the area of greatest pressure on land and the area which would have benefited most from land purchase, assembly and release by the Commission, only 286 acres were bought. One hundred and eighty-eight of these were surplus government requirements (an airfield) which were subsequently released for gravel working. Therefore, less than one hundred acres were acquired to supplement the needs of the whole area of greatest pressure. The picture was equally black in the Midlands, another area of great land development pressure. Here some one hundred and ninety-four acres were acquired and only *four acres* were released.

With the Betterment Levy, the Land Commission was more active at an early stage. After the appointed day, all chargeable acts were issued with a notice of assessment. The market was slow during the first year (Table 7.4), as builders had bought land ahead of time to avoid tax. During the first year £1·6 million of gross levy was assessed and this rose to £15·3 million in the second year and to £31·8 million during the third. Over the whole lifetime of the Commission, 47,310 notices were issued with the gross levy reaching £71 million. This figure gives some indication of how much *potential* reduction

Table 7.3

THE LAND ACQUISITION PROGRAMME OF THE LAND COMMISSION

Year 1 March–31 April	Land purchased (acres)	Value £ million	Land sold	Receipts £ million	Further purchase approved (acres)	Estimated value £ million	Land held
1967–68	0	0	0	0	1,500	5·7	0
1968–69	946	3·6	6·4	0·04	5,217	17·4	939
1969–70	1,267	4·6	312·0	0·60	9,273	41.6	1,888
1967–70	2,207*	8·2	318·4*	0·64	—	—	—

* During the period 1 April–22 July 1970 the Land Commission purchased a further 593 acres and sold a further 20 acres. During the life of the Commission the grand total of land purchased = 2,800 acres and total land stocks sold = 338 acres.

Source: The *Report* and *Accounts* of the Land Commission[107,108,109].

[107] *First Report and Accounts* of the Land Commission, Mar. 1968.

[108] *Second Report and Accounts* of the Land Commission, Mar. 1969.

[109] *Third Report and Accounts* of the Land Commission, Mar. 1970.

Table 7.4

THE ASSESSMENT AND COLLECTION OF BETTERMENT LEVY BY THE LAND COMMISSION

Year	1967–68	1968–69	1969–70	April 1970– July 1970	Grand total 1967–70
Levy					
Notices of assessment	3,449	15,390	18,178	10,293*	47,310*
Gross levy assessed and interest	£1,655,162	£15,273,143	£31,782,117	£22,289,578*	£71,000,000*
Receipts from assessed levy	£461,608	£8,103,058	£21,172,250	£17,263,024*	£47,000,000*

*Estimates of Assessment and levy

Source: Annual *Reports and Accounts* of the Land Commission, op. cit.

in aggregate land value was caused by the levy and how much capital gain was lost, in theory, by individual landowners.

The reaction by the developers interviewed to the role and effects of the Commission's work varied considerably in different parts of the country and by the size of the company. With respect to land prices, there was general agreement that the escalation in price was mainly due to *scarcity of supply*. The Land Commission had made no contribution to loosening up the market or to supplying land to these particular companies. There was no evidence of parcelling land and most of the respondents believed that such a 'drip-feed' principle of land release, even if it had been seen to operate, was the wrong way to tackle high and escalating land prices. In fact, in some cases, rather than be supplied with land, the Land Commission had issued Compulsory Purchase Orders on land already owned by the developer!

There was a general feeling that the Land Commission was just another force in the market which helped to push up prices through unfair competition, as the Land Commission did not have to pay the 40 per cent levy. The operation of the Commission tended further to exacerbate the shortage of land because draft notices on land which was approved for acquisition had the effect of freezing large areas of land. This is an important consideration as the land purchased lagged seriously behind the amount of land for which purchase had been approved (Table 7.3). Even though 5,217 acres were approved in 1968–69 only 1,261 were bought in 1969–70; some 9,273 acres were approved in 1969–70 but only 600 acres had been bought during the four months after March 1970.

With the Land Commission acting in a demand capacity, together with some land frozen by draft notices; and with landowners withdrawing land from the market on the reasonable expectation that the government would change and the Land Commission abolished (expectations which turned out to be correct) and also with some landowners attempting to recoup part of the levy, it was not surprising to find in practice that land prices increased rapidly during the period of the Commission's existence. There was plenty of evidence from the survey to substantiate the reports of land prices *doubling* in the three years, the fastest rate of growth in land prices for over two decades.

The Betterment Levy had one further unfortunate effect on the building industry; it militated against the developer holding and planning the development of large sites. Developers were discouraged as land was revalued for the Commission by the district valuer every two years. It is well known that a district valuer will value on the principle of 'comparables' whenever possible. This involves using the recent sale price of comparable sites nearby to assess the value, including auction prices which are notoriously high and near the price ceiling, for many reasons (see Chapter Six). This process of revaluation and its effects can be illustrated with the following example given by an interviewee. Land was bought in 1966 at a cost of £10,000 per acre; however the land was not used until 1970. The levy paid was assessed on its new value of £16,000. Having incurred £5,000 in interest charges, the levy increased the cost of the site well over and above its realistic market potential. However, the development proceeded with a higher land-cost element and so, in this case, the influence of the Land Commission was *inflationary*.

The small builders were particularly bitter about the Land Commission. They had initially welcomed the contribution the Land Commission was likely to make when it was introduced in 1967. At that time they felt it would help to maintain the present structure of the industry by helping the small builder assemble land at the right price. In this way the individuality of the industry would be retained. However, it did not take long for these small builders to become sceptical and finally very cynical about its role. Rather than a help to the industry it became viewed as a positive hindrance. The large builders, meanwhile, were less critical; in many ways they were content with rising prices and high land-costs. When prices are high, land is always available – at a price. The large builder with equity capital at hand was able to accumulate sufficient land stocks at a time when other builders were either selling land or certainly reducing the size of their land banks.

With rapidly increasing land prices and increasing land scarcity, the small and medium-sized builder appeared to have every reason to be critical of the Land Commission but it is not clear that the blame can be fairly placed on the shoulders of the Land Commission. There seems little doubt that *part* of the escalation in land prices was due to the Betterment Levy. There was also much *uncertainty* about the future of the Commission which further restricted the supply of land. Also, the contribution by the Commission to the supply of land in the areas of greatest need was modest to say the least. However, despite all these apparent shortcomings, it appears that the *Land Commission failed for other reasons*. In fact, the Commission found itself having to tackle the vast socio-economic and political problem of *land-use planning*, a task for which it was manifestly not conceived and certainly not equipped.

THE LAND COMMISSION AND THE PLANNING SYSTEM

At its inception, the Minister indicated to parliament that the Land Commission was to be an independent body, substantially exercising its own discretion and judgement. However, although no directive was issued the Minister wrote to the Commission outlining the policies which the Government of the day considered the Commission should follow. The Government indicated the scale of the Commission's operation and the priorities the Commission should observe. The Commission were asked to:

> . . . use their land acquisition powers to ensure that they did not lead to a shortage of land, particularly land for private-enterprise housing . . . they should make it their business to be aware of the pressure of demand for housing land particularly in London, the Home Counties, the West Midlands, and in North-West England, where the main pressures were, and to buy land to ensure a steady flow onto the market . . . they were also to

have regard in disposing of land to the need to ensure that house builders without stocks obtained enough to maintain or increase their output.[110]

Given this brief the Commission set about its business and during its early surveys in the first year discovered that *the shortage of land for immediate development was due to insufficient land being allocated in local authority Development Plans.* This was particularly true for the regions of pressure listed above. This view was substantiated by the considerable correspondence received at the Commission's Regional Offices from the medium and small building-firms who complained that they could not obtain enough land to maintain their house-building output.

In the South-East and the West Midlands, the Commission's survey revealed that in many areas available land was limited to only a few years' supply, and much of this land was unsuited to development, e.g. parcels too small, physical difficulties, etc. As a result, the Minister asked local planning authorities to allocate more land over the following few years, and to maintain contact with the Commission to ensure that the land was brought into early and orderly development. The first signs that such a policy of co-operation between the various authorities was not expected to succeed were hoisted as early as 1968 when the Commission claimed they would: '. . . have to take the initiative and if necessary seek a decision from the Minister on appeal'.[111] The Commission therefore viewed itself as an important addition to the planning machinery in a country where the planning system is primarily designed to *control* land use rather than promote the development of land use. Development Plans represent what the local planning authorities would like to see but until now their implementation has depended almost exclusively on the initiative and capacities of private developers.[112]

By the time the Commission published its second Annual Report[113] it recognized that its contribution to the steady flow of land on to the market had been modest but its explanation of the cause was now more pointed. It was: '*largely due to planning policies which are directed to the containment of urban growth and the preservation of open country*'.[114] The planning authorities had come forward with proposals which fell considerably short of the requirements put forward by the Ministry. The Commission did make the point that they did receive valuable help from many authorities but this was usually in the areas of least pressure. Where co-operation was not forthcoming, the Commission set about supplementing Development Plan proposals by finding land independently of the planning authorities and making it the subject for a planning application, seeking appeals to the Minister when necessary. Under such circumstances it is not surprising that the Commission's acquisition programme was slow. Yet it was mainly on

[110] *First Report*, op. cit., p. 3.
[111] *Second Report*, op. cit., p. 4.
[112] *First Report*, op. cit., p. 10.
[113] *Second Report*, op. cit.
[114] Ibid., p. 4.

these criteria that the work of the Commission was eventually judged and subsequently brought to a halt in 1970.

THE DEMISE OF THE LAND COMMISSION AND THE RETURN TO THE STATUS QUO

There is no doubt that the Land Commission failed to meet its objectives. On reflection, it now seems that it was doomed to failure from the outset. The collection of levy gave the Commission a stigma that carried over and and influenced its land acquisition activities. This suspicion, coupled with the uncertainty about its future, created an unfavourable image in the public mind. With a £45 million budget the Commission had little chance of making a serious contribution to the functioning of the British land market which had an estimated annual turnover of £1,200 million at 1967 prices[115] and with the Betterment Levy not being retained for land acquisition but sent to central Treasury funds, the Land Commission was further handicapped by low equity. In many ways the Commission reflected the general character of the building industry itself. Despite these shortcomings, the Commission was starting to gain some momentum during its fourth year of operation but its demise came finally through being the whipping boy for the scarcity of land which was mainly created by local planning authorities. The Land Commission's life of three years, three months and twenty two days was clearly an inadequate amount of time to tackle the tasks it had been set. It basically had *no chance to succeed.*

For the various reasons outlined above, the contribution by the Land Commission to land release was modest and in global terms was a failure. After the three years of its existence, the *basic problem of land supply remained.* The core of the problem was reflected in a speech in the House of Commons by Mr D. Howell in 1970,[116] when he observed:

> . . . the trouble is that the land that has to be found is not situated where the great housing need is. Birmingham is not in trouble in Birmingham, it must have land in Worcester, Gloucester and Shropshire. London is not in trouble because it does not have land in the middle of London, it is in the outer metropolitan areas that land has to be unfrozen.

Mr Peter Walker, who became Secretary of State for the Environment in the 1970 Conservative Government, agreed with the Opposition when he stated in the House: 'I believe that the release of land by local authorities is almost the most vital task in terms of the whole housing programme.'[117] This is the curious anomaly; both the previous Labour Government and the present Conservative Government diagnosed the problem correctly, but the

[115] B. Goodall, op. cit., p. 19.

[116] Denis Howell, Land Commission (Dissolution) Bill, *Parliamentary Debates* (*Hansard*), Vol. 808, No. 57 (16 Dec. 1970), col. 1465–1466.

[117] Peter Walker, *Parliamentary Debates* (*Hansard*), Vol. 804 (22 July 1970, col. 552).

incoming Government's prognosis was to scrap the only *type* of legislation likely to assess demand for land objectively and overcome the intransigence of many county planning authorities. Leaving the onus of land release in the hands of individual planning authorities was a return to the status quo of the early sixties which created the shortage in land that brought the need of a Land Commission into being. It seems totally unrealistic to expect local planning authorities, and county authorities in particular, to put national needs before local vested interests of their own free will, after resisting so strongly the recent work of the Land Commission. The Commission may no longer be with us but a new formula of land assembly and release, maybe under another name, will have to be instituted soon if the needs of the building industry and the housing programme are to be met.

THE ECONOMIC AND SOCIAL CONSEQUENCES OF RISING LAND PRICES

Much of this chapter has dealt with the concept of value in the land market. The trends in that market have been identified and the relative influences of private and public decisions examined. To conclude, we now turn briefly to the economic and social consequences to the developer and consumer alike of an escalation in land prices. Further reference to these effects will be made in the next Chapter.

How does the builder react to an increasing cost in one factor input of a production process? As we have identified in Chapter Six and in this chapter, the developer has a choice. First, he can increase the *house price* by some proportion and all the developers interviewed had done this. If this increase was at the same rate as inflation, the increase in price would not affect the consumer's purchasing position. But the increase was higher and therefore effective demand was reduced. Second, he can increase the residential *density* and give a smaller plot size for the same price. Third, he can reduce the *quality* of the housing package. There are no standards set down in the private market that are equivalent to the Parker Morris standards in the public sector. There are also no systematic data on the changing quality and quantity of housing in the private market. From the developer interviews it became clear that for a developer to remain competitive he had to cut costs and this translated itself into smaller rooms, poorer and cheaper fittings, less cupboard space and the removal of waste disposal units, refrigerators, washing machines etc., to that enticing category of the optional extra. In many instances, the much-vaunted and envied owner-occupier in the outer suburbs was *worse-off* in terms of *quantity* and *quality* in housing than tenants in new public authority property.

Developers also reviewed critically the trends in housing sales and made a number of decisions which had serious repercussions on housing *choice* in the market. Many developers started building flats instead of houses to keep plot costs down. Others diversified into the more lucrative sectors of the construction industry. Some switched their energy overseas and built vacation homes in Europe and the Caribbean. A much more serious effect occurred when many developers switched from building a wide range of housing by price to a narrower range; in effect that meant a change from cheaper to more expensive housing. This was done because the middle and upper sections of the housing market are much less sensitive to price changes than the lower part of the market. An increase of £250 on a £10,000 house is neither here nor there, but an increase of £250 on a £2,500 house is enough to seriously curtail demand. The developer, naturally wishing to maintain his cash flow from sales, therefore cut back on the number of houses being built in the lower range.

The real burden of rising land prices therefore seems to have been borne by those families at the *lower end of the private market*. If they were successful in purchasing a speculatively-built home, it was usually of poor quality and small in size. If they failed, and many families were unable to cope with the increase in house prices, what options were open to them? They could rent property, which is increasingly difficult to obtain; they could buy older property which was often substandard; they could share accommodation with other members of their family; or they could drop out of the private market altogether and increase the burden of demand for public housing.

The irony of this land and housing dilemma is that *planning decisions* are mainly creating the economic and social costs which are borne in the main by one sector of the private housing market, the sector whose price elasticity of demand is so high.

CHAPTER EIGHT

HOUSING TRENDS AND URBAN GROWTH

From a preliminary analysis of migration trends, this chapter focuses on the characteristics of the new houses built in urban England and Wales between 1945 and 1970 – their physical characteristics, their builders, the tenure system on which they are held. It looks at the unique characteristics of this market in order to understand how land and property prices are related. It looks in detail at the characteristics of property prices and at the effect of housing subsidies. Inflating land prices, it concludes, have been the main factor in the rise in house prices in the postwar period. But land prices also lead to higher densities – encouraged, in the case of local authority building, by the subsidy structure. Yet at the same time, higher living standards are causing people to demand more space – a fact which is underlined by an analysis of the sizes of dwellings, in terms of numbers of rooms, over time. This analysis also shows that the distribution of high and low densities of occupation has not changed much over time, despite great changes in the values themselves. It looks at the areas of crowding – which have become the same as the areas of highest density per acre, and are located in the inner areas of the conurbations. Lastly it considers the forces tending towards segregation in the housing market.

This chapter was written by Ray Thomas.

MIGRATION PATTERNS

At the turn of the century, as was pointed out in Chapter Two, Volume One, nearly four-fifths of Britain's population already lived in areas which were classified as urban. Unlike any other country Britain experienced most of its rural depopulation in the nineteenth century. As a result the dominant feature of the urban growth trends of the twentieth century – and those throughout the period of our study – is that of decentralization. Most people in Britain – rich and poor – live in towns and cities and have done so for a very long time. The process of urbanization is essentially one of an urban population moving to rural areas and taking with them an urban life style.

Farmers and agricultural workers in Britain may complain that they do not get an adequate share of the nation's wealth, but the fact is that Britain probably has less extensive rural poverty than any other country in the world simply because only a small proportion of the population live in truly rural areas. Neither does Britain have shanty towns at the periphery of the built-up areas of its major cities which are often the counterpart to large-scale rural poverty. Housing standards in areas of urban growth in Britain are set, and set effectively, by what is considered appropriate for an urban population, by governmental bodies composed of and representing an urban population. Only a small proportion of the population can afford to rent or buy a new house built to the standards which are generally considered as appropriate to the needs of the second half of the twentieth century. As a result, poverty in Britain, like employment, occurs mainly in older urban concentrations.

Table 8.1

NET MIGRATION IN ENGLAND AND WALES 1951–1961, BY URBAN/RURAL AGGREGATES

Area	Percentage change in population 1951–1961	Components of change (annual averages in thousands)	
		Natural increase	Net migration
Greater London Council area	−2·8	33·3	−56·1
Other conurbations	1·8	42·2	−27·3
Other urban areas with a population of 100,000 or more	2·8	28·5	−11·8
Urban areas with a population of 50,000 and less than 100,000	14·5	18·3	35·8
Urban areas with a population less than 50,000	9·2	30·8	49·0
Rural districts	10·4	41·9	44·0
England and Wales Total	5·4	197·5	40·6

Notes and Sources: The figures for migration are a residual obtained by subtraction, i.e. population growth minus births plus deaths. Net emigration is denoted by a negative sign. The figures for the conurbations and the England and Wales total are mid-year estimates of the home population taken from the Registrar General, *Quarterly Return for England and Wales*, 4th Quarter 1968, published June 1969. The other data are calculated from Table 7 of the *Age, Marital Condition and General Tables* of the 1961 Census, and they relate to the enumerated population at the time of the Censuses in April 1951 and 1961. The use of these slightly inconsistent sources means that the invididual figures do not add up to the total.

The migration trends within England and Wales are shown in Tables 8.1 and 8.2 on a fairly large scale. Table 8.1 compares the growth of population and the migration trends for urban areas of different size, and it reveals some remarkably close correlations. The population of inner London has of course been falling for many decades, but over 1951–61 the population of the conurbation itself began to fall. Net migration from the capital was much greater than the natural increase of the population. The population of the other conurbations in England and Wales stagnated – only the West Midlands conurbation gained significantly. Other urban areas with a population of

100,000 or more grew slowly in total population but lost heavily by migration. Over the whole decade nearly one million people moved out of the conurbations and other urban areas with a population of 100,000 or more. The London conurbation itself accounted for more than half of this total.

The main gainers of this outward movement of population in proportionate terms were towns with a population in the 50,000 to 100,000 range. The population of this group increased by more than 14·5 per cent in this decade. Twice as much population was gained by migration as by natural increase. But it should be remembered that at this scale the figures are much affected by ways in which the administrative boundaries are drawn. Towns in this group are generously bounded. The overall population density of these towns in 1961 was 8·1 persons per acre as compared with 13·1 persons per acre for urban areas in the 100,000 or more range, and 17·17 for the London conurbation. Population was also decentralizing in the urban concentrations with population in the 50,000 to 100,000 range, but most of the decentralization was occurring within their administrative boundaries. We have yet another example of the scale of the analysis affecting the apparent findings.

The major gainers from migration in absolute term were small towns with a population of less than 50,000. Over the decade this group gained nearly half a million population by migration – about 60 per cent more than they gained by natural increase. Interestingly enough most of the new towns fall into this category, giving another indication that their successful growth is partly attributable to the fact that they fitted in with the existing trends. But the population growth of the new towns was not of course of sufficient importance in statistical terms to affect the general pattern of change revealed by these figures.

Population growth was also very rapid in areas which were still labelled as rural. But the experience of rural districts probably varied more widely than any of the other groupings considered. Truly rural areas, situated twenty or more miles from a major city or forty or more miles from London, declined in population as agricultural productivity increased. Most of the growth took place in rural districts near to towns and cities, and a high proportion consisted of extensions of the built-up area of an existing town or city over its administrative boundary into the contiguous rural districts.

Table 8.2 shows the trends in a rather different kind of way with a breakdown by conurbation and region, and it also gives figures for the 1961–6 period. In the 1961–6 quinquennium both the natural increase in population and the net migration flows occurred at a faster rate than in the previous decade. Net migration from the London conurbation, for example, accelerated from an average of 56,000 per year to 81,000 per year. Net migration from the West Midlands conurbation accelerated from an average of 3,000 per year to nearly 12,000 per year.

The Table also shows how population was redistributing regionally. Only the North and the North-West lost consistently by migration over the fifteen-year period. And even in these regions the natural increase of population was greater than the net out-migration. In terms of proportionate rate of growth the fastest growing regions were East Anglia and the South-West. Over the 1961–6 period growth by migration in these regions exceeded the natural increase – a phenomenon which did not occur in any other regions.

But the most dramatic changes took place within the regions. The South-East, excluding London, was gaining population by migration at a rate of

Table 8.2

NET MIGRATION IN ENGLAND AND WALES 1951–1966, BY CONURBATIONS AND REGIONS

Conurbation and Region	1951–61		1961–66	
	Natural increase	Net migration	Natural increase	Net migration
	(thousands per year)			
South-East Region				
Greater London Council area	33·3	−56·1	52·3	−81·2
Remainder of South-East Region	33·1	102·7	57·9	103·1
Total South-East Region	66·4	46·5	110·2	22·0
West Midlands				
West Midlands conurbation	14·3	−2·9	21·1	−11·7
Remainder of West Midlands	13·3	8·8	20·0	18·3
Total West Midlands	27·6	5·9	41·1	6·6
North-West				
Merseyside conurbation	10·9	−11·1	12·1	−15·3
South-East Lancashire conurbation	7·5	−6·7	14·1	−8·5
Remainder of North-West	5·1	7·1	11·8	19·4
Total North-West	23·5	−10·7	38·0	−4·4
Yorkshire and Humberside				
West Yorkshire conurbation	4·4	−2·8	8·7	−3·1
Remainder of Yorkshire and Humberside	14·8	−5·7	19·1	3·3
Total Yorkshire and Humberside	19·2	−8·5	27·8	0·2
Other Regions				
East Midlands	16·0	6·6	23·7	8·2
East Anglia	6·5	3·8	8·7	9·8
South-West	10·5	8·3	16·9	22·9
North	19·4	−7·5	20·7	−7·1
Wales	8·4	−3·8	11·5	2·2
England and Wales	197·5	40·6	298·5	59·3

Source: The Registrar General, *Quarterly Return for England and Wales*, 4th Quarter 1968, published June 1969.

more than 100,000 per year. Although the North-West as a whole was losing by migration, the Merseyside and South-East Lancashire conurbations more than accounted for the total outflow. The gains by migration in the areas of the North-West outside the conurbations actually exceeded the natural increase. Even on the basis of these highly aggregated statistics it is clear that the biggest changes in population distribution are associated with centrifugal migration from the major urban concentrations rather than interregional moves.

Table 8.3

MIGRATION IN ENGLAND AND WALES 1961–1966

Migration flow	Thousands
Migrants within a local authority area	7,707
Migrants between local authority areas	6,848
All migrants within England and Wales	14,555
Population of England and Wales aged five years or over	43,122

Notes: Migrants in this Table refer to persons whose address in April 1961 was different from that in April 1966 when the Census was conducted. Many persons may have changed their address more than once during this five-year period. The figures for migrants exclude therefore children aged less than five years.

Source: Sample Census 1966, *Migration Summary Tables*, Part 1, Table 1B, and *Great Britain Summary Tables*, Table 2.

Table 8.4

MIGRATION IN ENGLAND AND WALES 1960–1961, BY DISTANCE OF MOVE

Migration flow	Thousands of migrants	Percentage of all migrants
Within a local authority area	1,151	52·1
Crossing local authority boundaries:		
Distance less than 5 miles	287	13·0
Distance 5–14 miles	286	12·9
Distance 15–39 miles	173	7·8
Distance more than 40 miles	311	14·1
All migrants within England and Wales	2,209	100·0

Notes: Excludes migrants from outside England and Wales. Distances are measured between the estimated population centroid of local authority areas and are therefore only approximately accurate.

Source: Census 1961, *Migration Tables*, Table 9.

These flows in terms of net migration merely summarize the end result of a myriad of individual moves of varying length, most of which are centrifugal to the old urban concentrations, but many of which are in the reverse direction. The figures give no indication of the magnitude of the gross flows or the length of moves. A complementary picture is given in Tables 8.3 and 8.4 which summarize data for England and Wales relating to the frequency and length of all moves.

In an age when people seem to be becoming ever more mobile in almost every way it may seem strange to draw attention to people's residential immobility. But the available evidence suggests the majority of the population do not move very often, and of those who do change their homes not many move very far. In 1966, as shown in Table 8.3, about two-thirds of the population of England and Wales were living at the same address as they lived five years earlier. Of the fourteen and a half million people who did move more than half still lived in the same local authority area as they did in 1961. This picture is confirmed by the figures given in Table 8.4 which relate to a single year, 1960–1. Again just over half of all migrants within England and Wales had moved from another address in the same local authority area. Nearly two thirds of moves were probably less than five miles in length. More than three-quarters were less than fifteen miles, and only one in about every seven was forty miles or more. If 1960–1 is typical, less than one in every hundred of the total population move a distance of more than forty miles every year.

These aggregative statistics give many clues as to the sort of person who moves into a new dwelling. Typically the head of the household was born and bred in a town or city. Typically he has moved from an older dwelling situated in one of the major concentrations. Typically he earns an above average income – otherwise he would not be able to afford the cost of a new dwelling built to as high, or higher standards, as the one he has vacated. Typically he has migrated only a short distance in an outward direction. And, quite often, as shown in Chapter Nine, he still migrates daily in the reverse direction back to a place of work in the town or city of origin. Let us next examine what sort of dwelling he moves into.

NEW DWELLINGS

Six million dwellings were constructed in England and Wales in the quarter of a century between the end of the Second World War and the end of the 1960s. Scarcely any houses were built during the war, but high priority was given to new homes immediately afterwards. In 1946 more than 70,000 temporary dwellings popularly known as 'prefabs' were built, as well as more than 50,000 permanent homes. The total level of output has increased at a fairly steady rate since and reached a temporary peak of 350,000 in 1968, falling to 282,000 by 1970. It was estimated that at the end of 1968 dwellings built since 1945 accounted for 37 per cent of the country's total stock.

But there is nothing exceptional about the levels of housing output achieved in the postwar years. The number of dwellings completed each year, for example, did not match the peak achieved in the 1930s until 1966. In terms of dwellings completed per head of population the level of output is still well below the levels of the prewar boom (Figure 8.1).

The dwellings built over this twenty-five year period can be divided into two distinct categories. Rather less than half have been built privately for owner occupiers. Just over half have been built by local authorities – new town development corporations, and housing associations – almost wholly

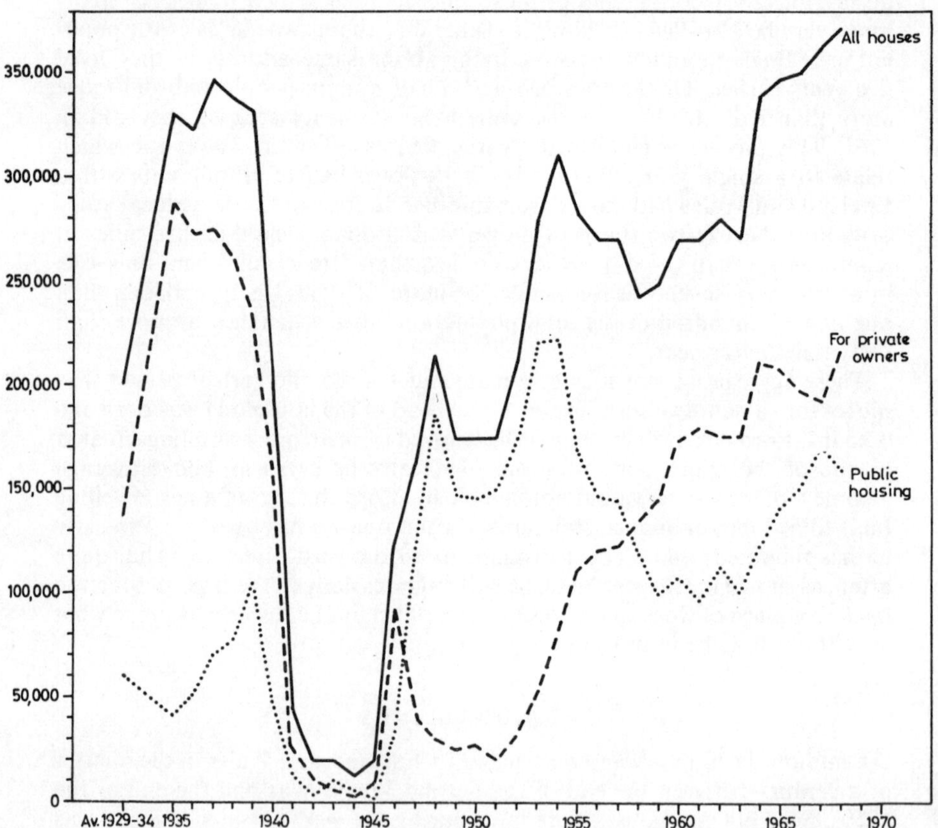

Figure 8.1 Dwellings Constructed in England and Wales 1929–1969

for renting. In the public sector the large majority of houses have been built by local authorities within their own administrative areas and for occupation by existing residents of that area. In the private sector a large proportion of houses have been built in small towns and villages, and at the periphery of larger urban concentrations, and have been offered for sale on the open market to whoever could afford to buy them.

The rates of construction of public and private housing have not been the same over this period. Up to 1957 more houses were built by the public sector in every year except 1946. Over this period less than one-third of houses were built for the owner occupier. In the period since 1957 the situation has been reversed. For every seven houses completed for the public sector about ten have been built for the owner occupier.

The price at which houses have been sold to owner occupiers has been determined by the market forces – as influenced by supply, demand, the availability of mortgages and central governmental taxation policy. But the rents at which public housing has been available have not been determined by the interplay of market forces. Virtually all new dwellings for rent have been directly subsidized by the central government. In some cases these houses have also been subsidized by the local authorities themselves out of the rates. And in most cases there has also been a cross subsidy by the local authorities of new houses from the rents obtained from older dwellings. (Local authorities charge rents for older dwellings which more than cover maintenance and the historic construction costs. The financial surplus earned on old dwellings is generally used to reduce the rent on new dwellings to a level which can be afforded by those on the housing waiting list.)

Just under a quarter of local authority and new town dwellings built over the period 1945–60 were flats, about half of which had two bedrooms. After 1960 the proportion of flats built was nearly one half and the average size of flats fell. The one-bedroomed and two-bedroomed categories during the 1960s each accounted for about four out of every ten local authority flats built. Typically one-bedroomed flats (for two persons) have a floor area of about 500 square feet. The floor area for a two-bedroomed flat is mostly in the 600–850 square feet range. The average construction costs in 1966 were £2,700 for all flats in two to four storey blocks (average floor area 680 square feet), and £3,700 for flats in blocks of five or more storeys (average area 690 square feet).

Seven out of every ten houses built by local authorities from 1945–60 had three bedrooms. Since 1960 the proportion has been about six in every ten. The proportion of two-bedroomed houses – about two in every ten – has remained unchanged, but the proportion of both one-bedroomed houses and houses with four or more bedrooms has increased slightly. The average floor area of three-bedroomed houses built in 1966 was 950 square feet, and the average cost of construction of £2,700 was just about the same as for the (much smaller) flats in blocks of two to four storeys.

Taking local authority flats and houses together the pattern of changes in size over recent years is more marked. Over 1945–60 nearly six out of every ten dwellings had three bedrooms. But after 1961 the proportion has been less than four out of every ten. The proportion of two-bedroomed dwellings – three out of every ten – has remained unchanged. But the proportion of one-bedroomed dwellings has increased sharply from one out of every ten to nearly three out of every ten.

The high proportion of flats built by local authorities in recent years is reflected in the levels of residential density. In 1966 a third of all tenders for local authorities which had new towns in England and Wales were for schemes at a net density of between eleven and sixteen dwellings to the acre, but only 8 per cent of dwellings were in schemes at densities lower than eleven dwellings to the acre, and the average number of dwellings to the acre for all schemes was eighteen.[1]

Table 8.5

DWELLINGS CONSTRUCTED FOR LOCAL AUTHORITIES AND FOR PRIVATE OWNERS IN ENGLAND AND WALES 1945–1968, BY TYPE OF BUILDING AND NUMBER OF BEDROOMS

Dwellings constructed, by type and number of bedrooms	Average 1945–60	1961	1966	1968
		(percentage of total)		
Local authority dwellings				
(i) by type:				
Flats	22·6	42·2	51·6	48·8
Houses	77·4	57·8	48·3	51·2
(ii) by number of bedrooms				
One bedroom	10·0	26·1	26·5	26·4
Two bedrooms	29·6	32·0	34·7	31·8
Three bedrooms	58·0	39·9	36·6	39·0
Four or more bedrooms	2·4	2·0	2·2	2·8
		(percentage of total)		
Dwellings for private owners				
(i) by type				
Flats	n.a.	8·5	9·0	7·0
Houses	n.a.	91·5	91·0	93·0
(ii) by number of bedrooms				
One bedroom	n.a.	1·8	2·0	1·7
Two bedrooms	n.a.	35·1	25·0	21·2
Three bedrooms	n.a.	59·6	67·3	70·0
Four or more bedrooms	n.a.	3·5	5·7	7·0

Notes: Local authorities in this Table includes New Town Development Corporations.

Source: Ministry of Housing and Local Government, *Housing Statistics.*

Information on dwellings built for private owners is not so plentiful. But at least since 1961 less than one in every ten have been flats. The proportion of dwellings with three bedrooms increased from six out of every ten in 1961 to seven out of every ten by 1968. The proportion of dwellings with less than three bedrooms has fallen over the last decade, and the proportion with four or more bedrooms has increased.

[1] See Ministry of Housing and Local Government (later Department of the Environment), *Housing Statistics*. HMSO, London, annually.

The available data suggests that there may well have been little difference in the average size of local authority and private dwellings constructed in the 1950s. But since then the average size of local authority dwellings has certainly fallen, and at least since 1961, the average number of bedrooms in dwellings built for owner occupiers has increased. In 1966 the average dwelling constructed for sale was at least half a bedroom larger than local authority dwellings. In terms of floor area, the average size of dwellings constructed for sale was probably about 900 square feet – modest indeed compared with North American standards, where the average house built for sale in 1967 had 1,480 square feet and one in four had more than 2,000 square feet, but generous compared with the average local authority dwelling at 770 square feet. Admittedly, the situation with the local authority house was just changing radically with the general introduction of Parker Morris standards. The average family house built according to these standards has a minimum of 960 square feet. This, ironically, is close to the 900 square feet recommended for local authority dwellings by the Tudor Walters Committee of 1918 and the Dudley committee of 1944. By 1970, it looked like being achieved at last.[2]

Little information is available on the density of dwellings built for sale. In the interwar period a high proportion of development took place at a net density of ten or twelve dwellings to the acre, in accordance with the recommendations of the Tudor Walters Committee. In the postwar period, as we shall presently describe, the price of land and official policy have both encouraged higher densities. It seems unlikely that the general level of densities is as low as before the war. On the other hand the fact that dwellings for sale are built at more decentralized locations than local authority dwellings means that it is unlikely that private dwellings are built at an average density as high as eighteen dwellings to the acre.

Although local authority dwellings are smaller than those built for sale, and although they are probably built at higher densities, there is little difference in the average cost. In 1968, for example, the estimated average cost of local authority dwellings constructed, including estimates of the cost of land, ancillary buildings, and site works, was £4,340. In the same year the average price of new dwellings mortgaged to building societies was only £4,447.[3]

Whey are the costs of building local authority houses so high? Is this a sign of inefficiency in the public sector or is it a reflection of high land costs? Have council tenants of new dwellings obtained better bargains than owner occupiers? If so why have more and more people become owner occupiers instead of putting pressure on local and national government for more local authority building?

To attempt to answer questions of this kind we need to analyse the way in

[2] See *Housing Statistics*, Tables on floor area and costs of construction, industrialized and traditional buildings; and Nationwide Building Society, *The Prospects for Housing*. The Society, London (1971), pp. 14–23, 52.

[3] See *Housing Statistics*, No. 14 Aug. 1969, Table 42 and Supplementary Table No. IV. HMSO, London (1969).

which the market for houses and land for residential development works and to describe how this market has been affected by both urban growth trends and governmental policies.

THE LAND MARKET

People talk about buying a house. For the house owner, or the potential house owner, it is the structure, the number of rooms, services like electricity, water and drainage which seem to be important. But in law, and in the market for property, it is not the building itself which is important as far as ownership is concerned. The crucial element is the property rights in land which ownership confers.

To talk of house ownership as being a matter of property rights in land may seem to be a case of unnecessary use of jargon. In fact some such phrase as 'property rights in land' is vital to an understanding of the way the housing market works. The factors which determine the supply of property rights in land are very different from those which determine the supply of bricks, mortar, labour and all the other inputs which go to make up a house.

The market for property rights in land is different from that of almost every other commodity partly because property rights in land are not physically transportable. Every other item which goes to make up a house and garden can be moved. Even land itself can be dug up and loaded on to the back of a lorry. But property rights in land are spatially specific. As a result, the supply of property rights in any locality is in many ways inflexible.

An increase in the demand for cars in London can be met by driving a batch down the M1 from Coventry. But an increase in the demand for property rights in land cannot be met so easily. If the supply is not available in London, or in Birmingham, the prospective purchaser must look elsewhere – to some more decentralized location.

The market for property rights in land is also different from that of almost any other commodity because of the abstract nature of property rights. The price of every other item which goes to make up a house, for example, is determined as much by the costs of production as by demand in the market. But, except in special circumstances such as reclamation, there are no costs associated with producing land. Land is truly God's gift to man – to be used, misused, or left vacant. The costs of producing property rights in land are usually little more than the lawyers' fees necessary to establish ownership and, since the 1947 Planning Act, the costs associated with obtaining planning permission. As a result the price of property rights in land is dominated by demand considerations, and is often quite arbitrarily related to the existing use of the land, or the size, nature, age, or condition of the buildings situated upon it.

Before the passing of the 1947 Planning Act the property rights in land which go to constitute home ownership could be created almost entirely at the discretion of the landowner. There was little need to get permission from any governmental authority in order to build houses on undeveloped land,

and then sell them. As a result the price of any particular piece of land for residential development was then rather indeterminate.

In the period between the two world wars a typical price for agricultural land was about £40 per acre, and there were plenty of owners willing to sell. But the price at which land was exchanged 'ripe for residential development' was typically about £200 per acre. Exactly which land was 'ripe for development' was mostly a matter of judgement on the part of builders, developers and dealers in land.

This situation led the Uthwatt Committee on Compensation and Betterment to popularize the doctrine of 'floating values'. It was recognized by the Committee that only a certain amount of land was required each year for new housing, and it was assumed (in that pre-inflationary era) that only a limited amount of money would be forthcoming from builders, developers, and dealers in land for residential development. The question was: which land would be bought? And the Committee concluded:

> Potential development value is by nature speculative. The hoped-for building may take place on the particular piece of land in question, or it may take place elsewhere; it may come within five years, or it may be twenty-five years or more before the turn of the particular piece of land to be built upon arrives. The present value at any time of the potential value of a piece of land is obtained by estimating whether and when development is likely to take place, including an estimate of the risk that other competing land may secure prior turn. If we assume a town gradually spreading outwards, where the fringe land on the north, south, east and west is all equally available for development, each of the owners of such fringe land to the north, south, east and west will claim equally that the next development will 'settle' on his land. Yet the average annual rate of development demand of past years may show that the quantum of demand is only enough to absorb the area of one side within such a period of the future as commands a present value.
>
> Potential value is necessarily a 'floating value', and it is impossible to predict with certainty where the 'float' will settle as sites are actually required for purposes of development.[4]

The 1947 Act was an attempt to fix these floating values. Development rights over land were nationalized. A fund was established to compensate those who lost development rights, and the idea was that henceforth land would be bought and sold at only its existing use-value. The weaknesses of the scheme soon became apparent. There was no incentive for owners to sell land for development, and after a few years the provisions of the 1947 Act relating to the price of land were removed by the 1953 and 1954 Planning Acts.

But the necessity for planning permission remained. And the price of any

[4] *Final Report of the Expert Committee on Compensation and Betterment* (Uthwatt Report). Cmd 6386, HMSO, London (1942).

particular piece of land no longer depends entirely upon whether the owner, a developer, or a speculator thinks that it is suitable or ripe for development. The price now depends mainly upon the nature of the planning permission which can be obtained. Planning permission in effect puts a price label on the land. The price still depends of course upon the locality; but also depends on the nature and density of the permitted development, or in other words, the kind of property rights in land which can be created.

The planning system has not ended the phenomenon called floating values by the Uthwatt Committee. Much land is bought and sold with an eye to residential development but without the price tag which a residential zoning gives. Which land of this kind is exchanged, and at what price, is as much in the hands of developers and dealers as it was before the 1947 Act. But it seems likely that most land for residential development is bought and sold after it has been zoned residential at a particular density and after outline planning permission has already been granted. One of the purely incidental benefits of the planning system is that it is now possible to compare more systematically than before the market price of land for residential development at different locations and intended for development at different densities (intended that is by the planning authority).

Although the sources of information on land prices are fragmentary there do appear to be a number of generalizations about the level of prices which can be made. Prices are highest in the most prosperous areas of the country around London and Birmingham and within these regions prices fall as distance from the centre increases. But the price also depends critically upon the level of permitted density. The greater the number of houses which can be built upon a site, the higher the price.

In the London and Birmingham regions these three variables – price, permitted density, and distance from the centre – were systematically brought together in a study made by P. A. Stone.[5] In the London region over 1960–2, Stone estimated that land situated at about twenty miles from the centre realized about £7,000 per acre with a permitted density of five houses to the acre, but nearly £30,000 per acre if the permitted density was forty dwellings to the acre. If the zoned density was twenty to the acre for a plot situated at five miles from the centre the price was about £28,000 per acre. But a plot with the same permitted density sixty miles from London realized only about £3,000 per acre (Table 8.6).

The study from which these figures are quoted showed a broadly similar pattern in the prices of land for residential development around Birmingham, although the influence of this city appeared to extend only to a radius of about twenty-five miles, not up to sixty miles as in the case of London. The study also investigated prices for a number of sites near the South Coast. Here again density appeared to be a crucial variable. The average price per acre ranged from about £4,000 for plots with a permitted density of five dwellings

[5] P. A. Stone, *The Price of Sites for Residential Building*, Building Research, Current Papers, Design Series No. 23 (1964). (Garston, Herts: Building Research Station.)

to the acre up to a little under £20,000 for sites with a permitted density of thirty dwellings to the acre.

Some of Stone's findings were corroborated in a later study by McAuslan.[6] The McAuslan study did not take into account density in the same systematic way, but it found that prices did fall with distance from the centres of the London and Birmingham regions. In the London region the median price for sites within twenty miles of the centre in 1968 was £40,300 per acre compared with the median price for the twenty-one–forty miles range of £18,000. The median price for sites situated within twelve miles of Birmingham was £20,000 as compared with £13,000 for sites in the thirteen–twenty-five miles range. McAuslan's study also covered prices in other parts of the country. Outside

Table 8.6

ESTIMATED AVERAGE PRICES PER ACRE FOR RESIDENTIAL BUILDING LAND 1960–1962

Region	Zoned density (dwellings per acre)					
	5	10	15	20	30	40
			£ thousand			
London						
5 miles from centre	12	17	23	28	39	50
10 miles from centre	10	14	19	23	32	41
20 miles from centre	7	10	13	16	22	28
40 miles from centre	3	4	6	7	10	13
60 miles from centre	1	2	3	3	5	6
Birmingham						
5 miles from centre	8	11	14	17	23	n.a.
10 miles from centre	6	8	11	13	18	n.a.
20 miles from centre	3	5	6	8	10	n.a.

Source: P. A. Stone, *The Price of Sites for Residential Development*. Building Research, Current Papers, Design Series No. 23, 1964.

the South-East and Midland regions prices were highest in the North-West, where the median value in 1968 was £9,300. Prices were lowest right outside Megalopolis. In Cornwall, Dorset, Devon and Somerset the median price was only £3,000 per acre (Table 8.7).

NEW AND OLD HOUSES

Once a house has been built upon a plot of land the market value of the property rights in land can only be conceptually distinguished from the value of the structure of the dwelling. But the market value of the site can be estimated on the basis of that of other undeveloped sites in the same locality. In other words the site can be treated as if the existing dwelling were demolished and the site cleared for redevelopment. Estimates of site value made in this way

[6] John McAuslan, 'Price Movements for Residential Land, 1965–69', *The Chartered Surveyor*, 102 (1969), 123–7.

usually include the value of site works – such as the provision of water and drainage – but otherwise the estimate of the site value approximates to the value of property rights in land which ownership of the dwelling confers.

Since 1966 the Nationwide Building Society has published such estimates of the value of sites of new houses (some of which were shown in Table 7.1, page 211). In 1966 the average value of sites of new houses mortgaged to the Society in Great Britain was £810, or 20 per cent of the average house price. By 1969 the average site value had risen to £1,040, or 21·5 per cent of

Table 8.7

MEDIAN PRICES FOR RESIDENTIAL BUILDING LAND 1968

Region	£ thousand per acre	£ thousand per plot
London		
0–20 miles from centre	40·3	2.8
21–40 miles from centre	18.0	2.6
Other parts of South-East		
South of London (Kent, Surrey and Sussex)	11·2	1·8
West and North (Beds., Bucks., Herts., Hants, Oxon.)	8·1	2·1
East and South (Wilts., Hants, Berks.)	13·0	2·0
Birmingham		
0–12 miles from centre	19·7	2·5
13–25 miles from centre	15·0	1·5
Other West Midlands		
Gloucester, Worcs., Staffs., Salop, Warwicks.	8·2	1·4
East Midlands		
Notts., Northants., Derby., Leics.	5·8	1·0
North-West		
Cheshire, Lancs., Yorks.	9·3	1·2
East Anglia	4·5	1·1
South-West	3·1	0·8

Source: John McAuslan, 'Price Movements for Residential Land, 1965–69', *Chartered Surveyor*, No. 102, No. 3, September 1969.

the average house price. The house estimates show considerable regional variation. The site value was highest in the South-East – average value £1,900 – and lowest in the North-East – average value £650.[7]

The Nationwide estimates are confined to the site values of new houses. But there does not appear to be any serious difficulty in estimating the site values for old houses. In a study made in 1963 by a professional body (the Rating and Valuation Association) estimates of site value were made for

[7] See: Nationwide (formerly Co-operative Permanent) Building Society, *Occasional Bulletin*.

every piece of land in Whitstable – a town of 20,000 population.[8] The Urban District of Whitstable at that time contained about 8,000 dwellings. The study estimated that the aggregate site values measured as a capital sum amounted to a little under £7 million, giving an average site value of a little under £1,000.

The RVA study of Whitstable is also of interest because the method of valuation was made quite explicit. Each site was of course treated as if it were vacant, and assumptions had to be made about the nature of the rights over property which would be permitted by the planning authority. In general the study envisaged: 'the most economic, the most financially advantageous, development possible'. But the purpose of the study was to establish site values as a possible basis for taxation, and the report pointed out that: 'It would produce an untenable position if a man's land were to be taxed on the basis of a development which he would not, in fact, be permitted to carry out'. The study therefore valued all land in accordance with the planning authorities' zoning for the site.

This information on site values – one set relating to new houses, and the other to a small town fifty miles from London – does not give anything like a representative picture of the general level of the market values of property rights in land. In particular these statistics do not give any indication of the value of property rights in land which go with the bulk of Britain's stock of older housing which is located in the conurbations and major cities. But we can get some indirect indications of the general level of market values for property rights in land, by comparing the market price of old with new housing.

In Britain we possess many carefully-maintained dwellings which date from the first half of the nineteenth century or earlier. But, as houses age, the costs of maintenance increase, and so do the costs of adapting them to present-day standards. Brickwork first needs repointing, then the bricks themselves become crumbly and a protective coat of pebbledash is often applied; but pebbledash doesn't weather very well and painting and repainting every few years becomes necessary in order to maintain a good appearance. Tile and slate roofs can be maintained, but sooner or later the high costs of maintenance demand complete renewal. By this time woodworm will have eaten away a portion of the timbers of the dwelling and eradication treatment at least is required. The various facilities and services provided in the original shell soon become worn out, outdated, or inadequate. Water tanks and pipes need replacement. A garage, central heating, ring main electricity supply, more lavatorial facilities; all these need to be added to our older dwellings to reach the standards set by the majority of houses built in recent years.

It is to be expected that the value of the structure of a house falls as its age increases. Indeed at some time in its life rebuilding becomes more economic than repair and maintenance. At this point of time the value of the old structure is zero.

[8] H. Mark Wilks, *Rating of Site Values – Report on a Pilot Survey at Whitstable*. Rating and Valuation Association, February 1964.

But the market price of the dwelling can be regarded as the sum of the value of the structure and the property rights in land which go with ownership. As the structure ages therefore, the value of the property rights in land form an ever increasing proportion of the market price of the complete

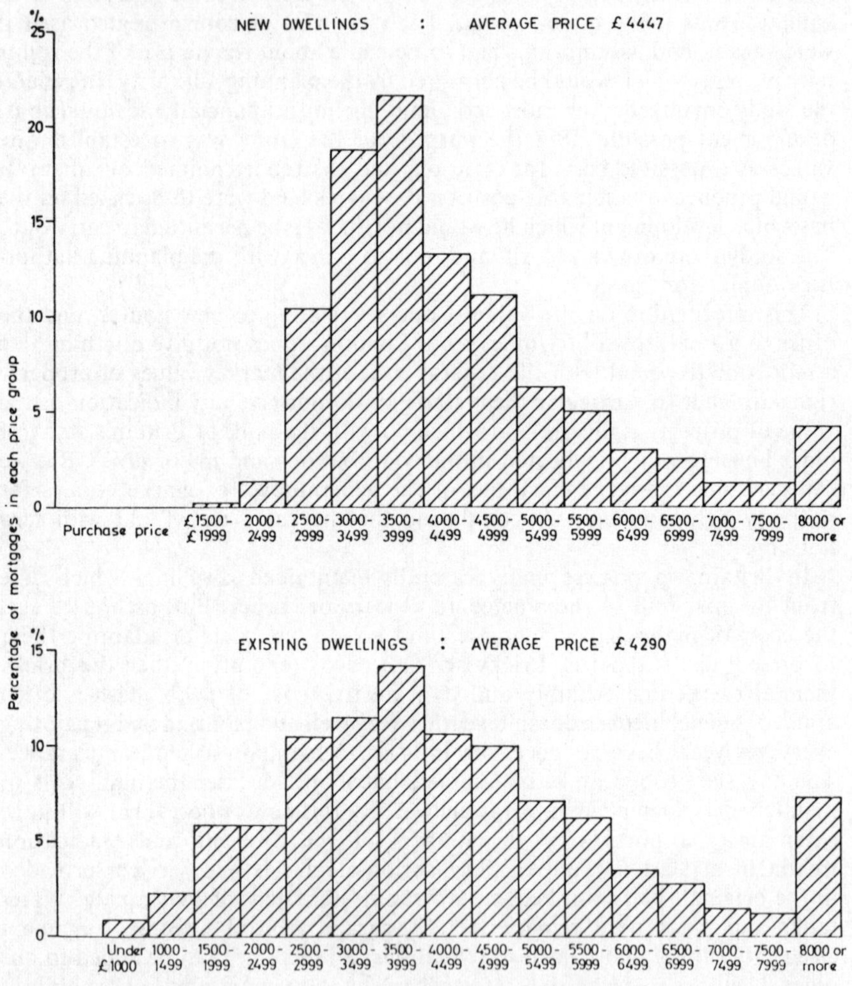

Figure 8.2 Price of New and Existing Houses Mortgaged to Building Societies in 1968

property. It is in theory possible to obtain an indication of the general level of market values in property rights by comparing the market value of new dwellings with older dwellings. We know from the Nationwide Building Society figures quoted above that the site values of new houses account for about a fifth of the market price. The question is, what proportion of the market value of old houses is accounted for by the property rights in land?

In fact there appears to be extraordinarily little difference between the price of new and old dwellings. In 1968 the average price of new houses mortgaged to building societies in Great Britain was £4,447 compared with an average price for existing dwellings of £4,290. The distribution of these dwellings by purchase price is shown in Figure 8.2. The range of price for existing dwellings is wider than that for new houses – a higher proportion of existing houses have both low and high prices. This is to some extent a reflection of the greater range of size of old houses. It is estimated, for example, that there are 1·5 million pre-1919 dwellings with seven or more rooms which account for nearly a quarter of the total stock of dwellings of this vintage. But only about 250,000 of the dwellings built since the war are of this size, and it seems likely that these larger dwellings only account for something like 5 per cent of houses currently being built.[9]

But there is no reason to suppose that the differences at the other end of the size scale are so large. There is probably not much difference between the proportion of new dwellings built for sale which have, say, four or fewer rooms than that for existing dwellings. If this is so, it is surprising that there are very few existing houses sold at a low price especially when regional variations are taken into account. In 1968 only about one in every nine existing houses sold for less than £3,000.

Some further light is thrown on the situation by the figures given in Table 8.8 which compare the price of a three-bedroomed semidetached house in different age groups in different parts of the country. The pattern revealed is complex, and there is some variation in the pattern in different parts of the country. It is worthwhile discussing the differences in some detail.

The variation seems most systematic in the South-East region. In the London conurbation the average price for a new house in 1968 was £6,940 which is £830 more than for houses built between 1945 and 1965, or £850 more than for those built in the interwar period, and about £1,250 more than houses built between 1919 and 1944. New houses are at a premium, but old houses hold their value very well. The fact that these prices, irrespective of the age of dwelling, are higher than those for houses in any other part of the region, or any other part of the country, confirms the findings of the Stone and McAuslan studies on the price of undeveloped sites, which were quoted in the previous section. The value of property rights in land in London is exceptionally high.

But in the rest of the South-East it appears that old houses depreciate at an even slower rate than they do in London. In urban areas in the South-East outside the conurbation the price of a new house is only about £750 above that of one built before 1919. In rural parts of the South-East the corresponding amount of depreciation is only about £500. In urban areas outside the conurbation the average price of a new house is actually below the level of those constructed between 1945 and 1965. In rural areas the

[9] See *Housing Statistics*, No. 14, Aug. 1969, Table III(g), p. 75.

Table 8.8

AVERAGE PRICES OF THREE-BEDROOM SEMIDETACHED HOUSES SOLD IN 1968, BY AGE AND AREA

Area	Age Group			
	New	1945–65	1919–44	Pre–1919
	£	£	£	£
South-East Region				
London conurbation	**(6,940)**	6,110	6,090	5,690
Other urban areas	4,960	**4,990**	4,730	4,200
Rural areas	4,910	**4,970**	(4,960)	(4,430)
West Midlands Region				
Conurbation	4,020	**4,220**	4,050	(3,710)
Other urban areas	3,490	**3,930**	3,490	(3,340)
Rural areas	3,770	**4,080**	(3,820)	(4,450)
North-West Region				
Conurbations	3,870	**3,980**	3,660	3,340
Other urban areas	3,330	**3,490**	3,400	(3,260)
Rural areas	(3,480)	3,680	(3,650)	**(3,750)**
East Midlands				
Urban areas	3,460	**3,530**	3,250	(2,720)
Rural areas	(3,430)	**3,580**	3,290	(3,360)
Yorkshire and Humberside				
Conurbation	3,130	3,320	3,190	**(3,390)**
Other urban areas	3,040	**3,560**	3,300	(3,120)
Rural areas	**3,490**	3,450	(2,950)	(3,210)
East Anglia				
Urban areas	**3,880**	3,850	(3,780)	(3,320)
Rural areas	(3,890)	**4,100**	(3,820)	(3,720)
South-West				
Urban areas	4,000	**4,160**	4,110	3,710
Rural areas	3,950	**4,150**	(3,750)	3,840
Northern Region				
Conurbation	4,000	**4,410**	4,000	(3,870)
Other urban areas	3,590	**3,700**	3,450	(3,140)
Rural areas	(3,510)	(3,810)	**(3,890)**	3,190
Wales				
Urban areas	3,520	**4,100**	3,930	(3,230)
Rural areas	**(3,730)**	3,690	(3,380)	(3,000)
Unweighted averages excluding London conurbation				
Conurbation	3,760	3,980	3,730	3,580
Other urban areas	3,700	3,920	3,720	3,340
Rural areas	3,800	3,950	3,720	3,670
England and Wales	3,750	3,940	3,720	3,520

Notes: The figures are based on a sample of approximately 35,000 owner-occupied houses.
Figures in brackets are liable to large sampling errors.
Bold figures are the age group with the highest price in a particular area.

Source: Ministry of Housing, *Housing Statistics*, Great Britain, No. 15, November 1969, Table 111.

average price of a new house is also below that of houses constructed in the interwar period.

In most other parts of the country the relative prices of houses of different age are more like those of the outer South-East region than for the London Conurbation. In general the price of new houses is about £200 less than that of houses built between 1945 and 1965. This difference may be partly a reflection of some of the temporary disadvantages of buying a new house. A new house has to be completely furnished and fitted with items like floor coverings and curtain rails. The garden often needs to be planted. In the case of existing houses basic fittings are often included, and the previous owner will usually have tidied up the grounds and carried out a bit of planting. These benefits could well be worth a premium of £200.

But in most parts of the country there is little difference between the price of a new house sold in 1968 and those built between the wars, and in general the average price of new houses is only between £100 and £300 more than a similar house built before 1919. The differences are not wholly systematic. In rural areas of the North-West and in the West Yorkshire conurbation for example, the average price of pre-1919 houses, admittedly on the basis of a limited sample, is actually above that of other age groups. In rural areas of Yorkshire and Humberside and in the towns and cities of East Anglia on the other hand the price of new houses, again on the basis of a limited sample, is higher than that for any other age group. But, in general, the price is little affected by age. Even houses which are more than fifty years old are on average only about 5 to 10 per cent cheaper than new houses.

A wide variety of factors contribute to the slow depreciation of house prices with age. It may be that many three-bedroomed houses built fifty years or more ago have larger rooms than new houses. Many of the old houses which actually come on to the market have been fairly extensively modernized. Some people may be especially attracted by ownership of an old house and be willing to pay a premium.

But it is unlikely that the slow rate of depreciation is explicable in terms of the values of the structure itself. The capitalized maintenance cost of an old house alone probably amounts to a sum greater than could be accounted for by the differences in average price shown in Table 8.8.[10] When the costs of obsolescence are taken into account as well there is little doubt that we must go beyond a consideration of structure alone to find out why old houses maintain their value so well.

The property rights in land associated with dwellings, being intangible in

[10] Little information is available on the way maintenance costs increase with age. Figures are published on the maintenance costs of local authority dwellings but there is considerable variation in the pattern by age. In 1967–8 the GLC expended about an average of £61 on maintenance of prewar dwellings as compared with £36 on those built between 1945 and 1964. But some local authorities actually spent less on the newer dwellings. No suitable aggregate figures are available. See Institute of Municipal Treasurers and Accountants, *Housing Maintenance and Management Statistics*, 1967–8, May 1969.

nature, are not affected by age and weather in the same way as the structure. The market value of the property rights depends mainly upon the location of the house and the size of the plot, and it seems likely that both of these factors have helped to keep up the price of old houses. Most old houses stand on sites which have high values because they are more accessible than new houses to urban facilities of all kinds; this is a reflection of the age of Britain's urban concentrations and the fact that population has decentralized from these concentrations faster than any other land use.

Some evidence illustrating the importance of this factor is given even in the highly aggregative statistics of Table 8.8. In the North and North-West as well as the South-East and Midlands the price of houses in the conurbations is fairly consistently above that of other parts of the region. The physical environment of these conurbations may not be exceptionally attractive but they are Britain's largest concentrations of employment and they are major distribution points for every kind of good and service.

The same factor may also be important at a much smaller scale. A house near the centre of a town of, say, 20,000 population is much more conveniently situated for accessibility to such things as shops and public transport than a house on the periphery of the same town which might be two miles from the centre. And it would be surprising if this difference in accessibility were not reflected in the market price.

But the fact that old houses nearly always occupy more accessible sites does not wholly explain their high price. The figures of Table 8.8 show, for example, that old houses in rural districts maintain their value rather better than houses in urban areas, or at least better than in urban areas outside the conurbations. It seems likely that the other factor in operation is the size of plot. There is no good evidence available on this point but it seems probable that semidetached houses built over forty or sixty or more years ago have larger gardens than those built in recent years. (We shall return to this point later in the chapter.)

It is difficult to generalize about the relative importance of these two factors of density and accessibility. Some old houses in and near city centres have maintained their value solely because of their accessible position. Some old houses in rural areas have maintained their value because of their large gardens. But perhaps most old houses maintain their value because in some combination of plot size and density they are better endowed than new houses.

HOUSING SUBSIDIES

It was estimated in 1961 that 90 per cent of households in this country could not afford to buy a new house out of income.[11] This calculation was based on the building societies' rule that outgoings on account of house ownership should not exceed a quarter of basic income (excluding overtime, bonuses and spare time earnings). Since 1961 new house prices have risen in line with

[11] Lionel Needleman, 'A Long-Term View of Housing', *National Institute Economic Review*, 18 (1961), p. 27.

incomes, and the rate of interest for mortgages has increased substantially. In 1971 it was just as true as it was in 1961 that only a small minority of the population could afford to become owners of new houses.

An apparently obvious solution for the majority of the population would be to buy an old house. But it is clear from the discussion of the preceding section that only a small proportion of old houses are actually bought at prices much below those of new houses. In the north of England it was possible in 1971 to purchase a two-up two-down terraced cottage for a price measured in terms of hundreds of pounds, and in old mining villages such a dwelling could be obtained for less than £100. But in all the prosperous areas of the country the market price of the meanest kind of structure was measured in terms of thousands of pounds rather than hundreds, and the price of any moderately spacious house in a reasonable state of repair in nearly all parts of the country was, as the figures quoted for the average price of three-bedroomed semidetached houses indicate, extraordinarily similar to that of a new house of comparable size.

One consequence of this situation is that the housing of every major sector of the community is subsidized in some way or other. A substantial but decreasing minority of the population who live in older houses are subsidized by their landlords through the operation of rent control which has existed since the First World War. A substantial but growing minority of the population are council tenants and are subsidized by the central government, by the local housing authorities, and are cross subsidized among themselves. The origins and workings of these kinds of subsidy have been described in some detail in a number of studies.[12] Our present concern is with the subsidies to owner occupiers who represent the most rapidly expanding sector of the housing market, who in recent years have come to be a near majority of the population. These subsidies to owner occupiers are important because they affect the operation of the largest sector of open-market housing.

The most well-known subsidy for the owner occupier is the full tax relief allowed on mortgage interest payments. Most owner occupiers in 1970 were paying tax on earned income at a rate of 41p in the pound. Since there is tax relief on two-ninths of earned income the effective marginal rate of tax was 32p in the pound – an effective reduction in cost of interest payment of 32 per cent. With a straight repayment mortgage, interest represents a high proportion of total mortgage payments in the early years and gradually tapers to nothing as the capital sum is repaid and the term of the mortgage expires. For a mortgage of this kind over 25 years, the effective reduction in the costs of home ownership through tax relief was 27 per cent in the first year's payments. The amount of tax relief gradually falls almost to zero as the mortgage expires (Table 8.9).

[12] See for example: A. A. Nevitt, *Housing, Taxation and Subsidies*. Nelson, London (1966). *Report of the Committee on Housing in Greater London* (Milner Holland Report). Cmnd 2605, HMSO, London (1965). A. J. Merrett and Allen Sykes, *Housing Finance and Development*. Longmans, Green and Co., London (1965).

The taxation system in Britain is described as progressive because the proportion of income taken by tax generally increases with the level of income. Subsidies for owner occupation are progressive in the same kind of way. Since the tax relief on mortgage interest payments is granted at the marginal rate of taxation, the subsidies increase with the income. Until 1967 those with low incomes who paid no tax could not get any tax relief. With the introduction of the *Option Mortgage Scheme* in 1967 the subsidy was extended in such a way that the relief for those with low incomes works out at only a little less than that afforded to those paying tax at the standard rate.

People with unearned income and people whose high earnings make them subject to surtax get more relief. For someone who paid tax at a marginal rate of 54p in the pound, for example in 1970, the tax relief worked out at 45 per cent of the payments in the first year of a twenty-five year mortgage

Table 8.9

TAX RELIEF ON MORTGAGE PAYMENTS ON £1,000 LOAN FOR TWENTY-FIVE YEARS AT 7⅝ PER CENT RATE OF INTEREST

(1968)	Repayments in: Year 1	Year 5	Total repayment over 25 years
Actual payments	93	93	2,325
Payment after tax relief			
Option mortgage	77	77	1,925
Marginal tax rate 23p in £	75	76	2,021
Marginal tax rate 32p in £	68	70	1,903
Marginal tax rate 41p in £	61	63	1,768
Marginal tax rate 54p in £	51	54	1,630
Tax relief as a percentage of payments			
Option mortgage	17	17	17
Tax rate 23p in £	19	18	13
Tax rate 32p in £	27	25	18
Tax rate 41p in £	34	32	24
Tax rate 54p in £	45	42	30

Source Consumers' Association, *Money Which?*, December 1968.

(assuming a 7⅝ per cent rate of interest) and totalled 30 per cent of the total payments made over the whole period of the loan. In the financial year of 1964–5 there were more than a quarter of a million surtax payers in England and Wales.

The total amount of tax relief on mortgage interest payments by owner occupiers has increased along with house prices and the rate of interest. In 1967–8 the total for Great Britain was £180 million and in 1968–9 the total was £202 millions. This last figure works out at an average of around £43·50 per owner-occupied dwelling (owned by a person enjoying tax relief) per year. The total amount of tax relief actually exceeds central government housing subsidies to local authorities, which in the years 1967–8 and 1968–9 added up to £117 and £137 millions respectively.[13]

The largest subsidy to the owner occupier is arguably the fact that since the abolition of Schedule A tax in 1963 he is not taxed on the imputed rent of his dwelling. If an individual invests, say, £5,000 in equities, he might well receive £400 per annum in dividends which would have been taxable as unearned income at a rate of 41p in the pound in 1970. But if the individual invests the same £5,000 in buying a house for his own occupation he does not have any tax on the return which takes the form of rent-free accommodation.

It is also arguable that to tax people for the benefits obtained through owning a house would be tantamount to a tax on wealth. If an owner is taxed to the imputed rent of a £4,000 bungalow, should not a man equally be taxed to the imputed enjoyment of ownership of a £4 million Botticelli? The question is tied up with attempts to make a distinction between capital and income. Ownership of any property confers a stream of benefits. Where these benefits take monetary form they are, in Britain, taxed. Where no payments are involved they are not taxed.

The problem also occurs in the measurement of national income. In general items are only included where payments are involved. The benefits of ownership of durable goods of all kinds are usually covered only at the point of time that they are actually purchased. It is assumed in effect that they are consumed instantly. The benefits obtained from use of a car bought last year, or the enjoyment of a park laid out in the last century, are not counted as part of this year's income. But the ownership of houses is far too important an item to be omitted because it is not marked by the signing of cheques for rent. If the imputed benefit from owner-occupied dwellings were not counted as part of national income, the national income statistics would show a fall as rented houses are bought and are thereby reckoned to be consumed. In 1967 the imputed rent of owner-occupied dwellings was estimated in the national income statistics at £812 millions.

The equity or otherwise of taxing people for the imputed rent of the dwelling they occupy goes a little beyond the main subject matter of this chapter. But some of the implications of the controversy have immediate relevance. The lack of such a tax is a powerful and direct encouragement to owner occupation. Payments by owner occupiers to mortgage companies might at first sight seem the equivalent in all respects to the rent paid by local authority tenants, and if the tax relief and central government subsidy is the same in each case it might appear that the financial position of the two kinds of households is identical. But the vital difference is that the payments to a mortgage company do acquire an asset. The owner occupier is an owner. He can sell his house at any time or leave it to his dependants when he dies. Most important, in an inflationary situation, he has invested his money in a form of asset which is appreciating in value every year. The purchase of a

[13] Minister for Planning and Land, Written Answer, 20 Dec. 1968, *Commons Hansard* (1968–9), Vol. 775, col. 511.

house to live in has proved in recent years to be the safest and most profitable form of investment that anyone could possibly make.

This situation has far-reaching consequences throughout the housing market. Since scarcely any houses are built for renting on the open market, the open market is defined in terms of what owner occupiers and potential owner occupiers can pay for housing. The cost of land for local authority dwellings, for example, is determined by the open market price; and the price of land on the open market is determined ultimately by what owner occupiers are willing and able to pay for houses.

The theory of welfare economics depends upon the assumption that the market price of a product is equivalent in some way to the value to individuals of that product. It is impossible to apply this theory in the field of housing and land. Every sector of the market is dominated by the influence of taxation policy, subsidy, and/or artificial control. The so-called open market, for example, is restricted to what is still in Britain a minority (mostly in the top half in income terms) who are fortunate enough to be owner occupiers. Favourable tax treatment means that there is a long queue of would be new entrants to this market. The prices of the cheapest dwellings for sale are determined by what the new entrants at the head of the queue can afford. But what buyers are willing to pay depends partly upon what financial advantages they see in becoming owner occupiers. If they are fully aware of the taxation position they may well be willing to pay a substantial premium for the privilege of joining the owner occupiers' band wagon.

To analyse the urban growth trends of recent years therefore, we need to consider a much wider range of factors than demand and supply, as these are usually conceived. We need to examine the variety of institutional influences on new house-building. We need to look closely at the ways in which governmental policies have interacted with the so called open market.

THE COST OF HOUSING

In retrospect the building boom of the 1930s may be seen as one of the most powerful influences on the principles and practice of planning in the postwar era. Many people reacted against a monotony of semidetached houses built at a density of ten or twelve to the acre. Many deplored the rate at which rural land was lost to urban uses. Many people disliked the way new estates took the form of ribbon development extending along, or adjacent to, the main traffic arteries. Many people perceived the weaknesses of an urban form in which a growing proportion of the population were coming to live further and further away from the main centres of employment.

But the 1930s was an era of cheap land and low interest rates. The large majority of the houses then built were well constructed and have stood the test of time. The number of new houses produced per head of population was greater than has since been achieved. Although since the 1930s income per head in Britain has nearly doubled, the proportion of the population

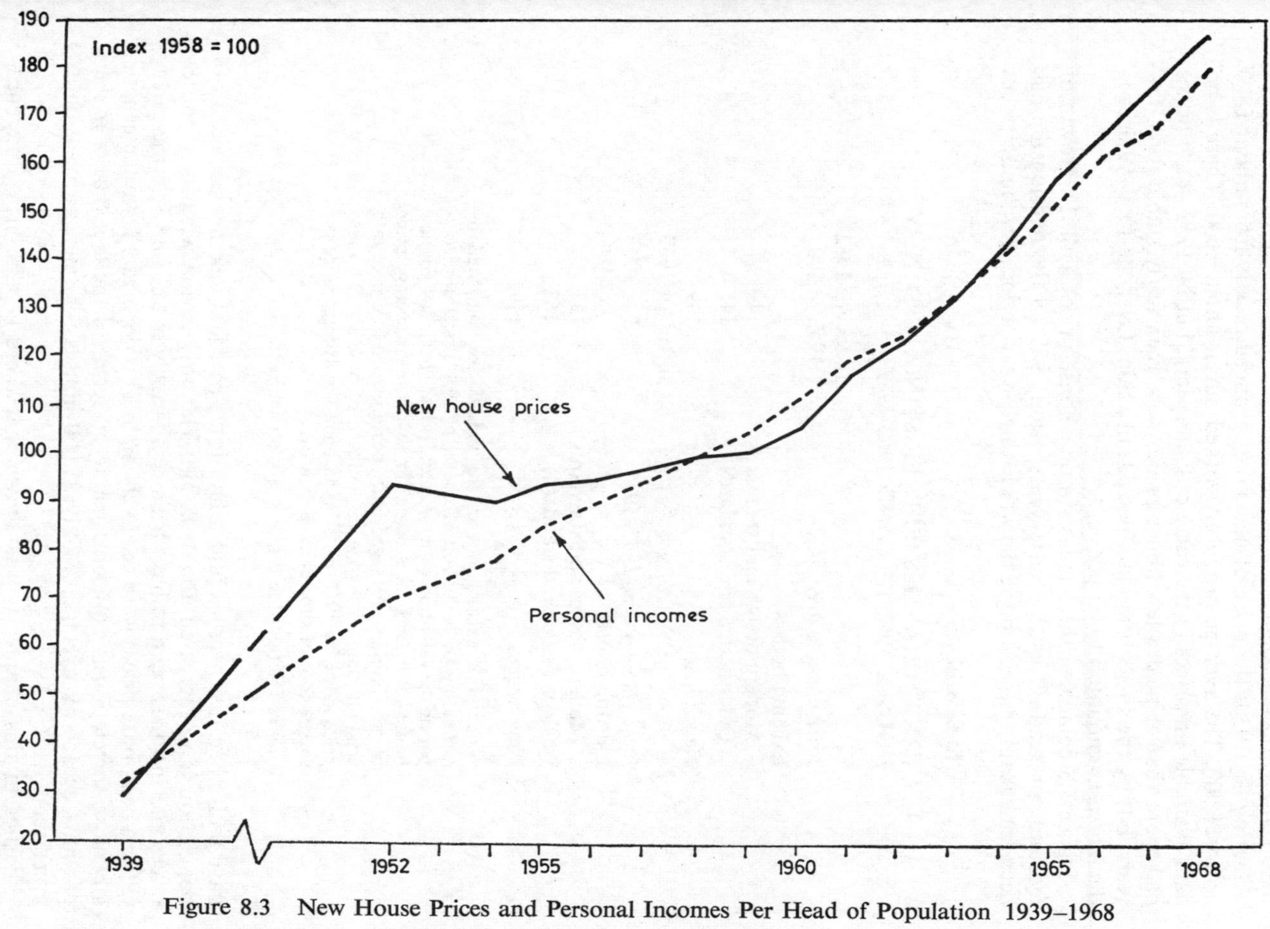

Figure 8.3 New House Prices and Personal Incomes Per Head of Population 1939–1968

who can afford to buy a new house does not seem to have increased and may have actually decreased.

During the 1930s the price of new houses ranged mostly from about £400 up to £1,000. The average probably worked out at about £600. There is no data available on prices in the early postwar years, but by 1952 house prices had more than tripled. New house prices were then fairly stable for a few years, but by the 1960s prices jumped ahead again. Over the 1959–69 decade the increase amounted to 75 per cent.

Figure 8.3 compares the increase in new house prices with the growth of incomes per head. Over the thirty-year period 1939–69 the relationship has been remarkably close. Taking the whole thirty-year period, new house prices

Table 8.10

PRICE CHANGES FOR EXISTING AND NEW HOUSES 1952–1962 AND 1962–1969

Price changes over 1952–62	Index for 1962 1952 = 100
Existing houses	
Modern design and standards	140
Older design and standards	147
New houses	149
Price changes over 1962–69	Index for 1969 1962 = 100
Existing houses	
Modern design and standards	153
Older design and standards	152
New houses	148

Notes: For existing houses the indices are computed by estimating the valuation of houses at 1939 prices and comparing the valuation with the actual price. The 'index' for new houses over 1952–62 is based simply upon the average price of new houses mortgaged and does not therefore take into account changes in size or standard of amenity. The new price index for 1962–69 is based upon the average price per square foot of superficial floor area.

Source: Nationwide Building Society indices.

have multiplied just over six and a half fold; personal incomes per head of population have increased about sixfold. The only period when new house prices and incomes seem to have been significantly out of line is in the early 1950s when house prices were relatively high. This departure from the generally close correlation is explicable mainly in terms of the fact that over the previous decade an average of only 25,000 houses for sale had been built every year.

Earlier in this chapter it was shown that there is very little difference between the price of old and new houses. It is not surprising therefore that existing house prices have increased as fast if not faster than those for new houses. Table 8.10 gives some figures on this topic for 1952–62 and 1962–9. In the earlier period prices of existing houses increased slightly less than new houses. But over the period 1962–9 the price of existing houses actually increased slightly more than new houses.

The parallelism of new and old house prices is nevertheless notable. In a period of rising incomes it might be expected that more and more people would be able to afford higher standards of amenity – more comfortable heating systems, better fitted kitchens with dishwashing and clothes-washing apparatus, bathrooms with bidets and showers, better sound insulation, landscaped gardens planted with at least semi-mature trees – and it might be expected that builders of new houses would attempt to cater for this demand. In fact people who have wanted amenities of these kinds have more often than not bought old houses (or simply retained their existing house) and have added such facilities (where this was possible) as they have been able to afford them. The relative price of old and new houses has not reflected rising housing standards. The standards of most new houses built in the 1960s seem to be very little different from those built 30 years earlier.

The markets for old and new houses do differ in some ways. The mortgage which can be obtained for an old house, for example, is generally a lower percentage of the valuation than that of a new house. But in most respects the markets for new and old houses are highly interrelated. The same sorts of factors have predominated in each case.

One reason why the standard of amenities of most new houses has not increased significantly over the past few decades is that the market of owner occupation has been extended to members of lower income groups. The proportion of the population who are owner occupiers has steadily increased. Most of the new entrants to the market have been satisfied enough to have a home of their own and have not also expected to get houses with large rooms, central heating, and Californian kitchens.

But the main reason why the standard of amenities of new houses has not increased is simply that a high proportion of potential purchasers has not been able to afford such luxuries. Although the proportion of owner occupiers has increased, the level of house prices has moved in parallel to that of incomes per head. As a result an ever increasing proportion of houses has been bought by people who could only just afford to become owner occupiers. The standards of accommodation of new houses built for sale have been determined by the need to sell to members of relatively low income groups.

This situation has produced some curious contrasts. Many new houses built for sale are below the standards, and below the costs, of new houses built by local authorities for rent. The fact that local authority housing is subsidized by the central government has actually led many observers to take the view that local authority housing standards should be reduced.

It seems more pertinent to ask why the prices of both old and new houses seem to be more closely related to incomes per head than any other variable. Some, but certainly not all, of the price rise of new houses can be explained in terms of construction costs. But this factor cannot explain the rise in price of old houses. Is it that the price of both old and new houses has little to do with costs? Is the price wholly determined by demand considerations?

There is little doubt, as we saw in Chapter Seven, that the inflation in the price of property rights in land has been the most potent component of rising house prices. There are many problems involved in attempting to measure the contribution of the rate of inflation of these rights. In the case of old houses, for example, it would be difficult to separate that part of the price rise which is attributable to the structure from that part which is attributable to the location and size of the plot upon which the structure is situated. But in the case of undeveloped land there are a number of indications of the rate of inflation.

The prospectus for Welwyn Garden City issued in 1919 claimed that land bought for housing in the London suburbs cost £700 to £2,000 per acre, and that land in the immediate vicinity of a railway station situated twenty-one miles from the centre of London realized £500 to £1,000 per acre. One of the main attractions of the new-town idea was that a large estate of land could be bought twenty miles from the centre at an agricultural land price rather than a residential price. In fact 2,400 acres were bought for Welwyn Garden City at an average price of £44 per acre.

It seems unlikely that there was much inflation of land prices throughout the interwar years. Indeed prices may actually have been falling. The Uthwatt Committee report, quoted earlier, talks of the average value of development rights as being £200 per acre without giving any indication of the location of such land.[14] The MacAuslan figures, also quoted in the land market section earlier in this chapter, for the median price paid in 1968 were £40,300 per acre for sites up to twenty-one miles from central London and £18,000 per acre for sites in the twenty-one–forty mile range. If these figures are anything like representative it seems that land prices have increased by a factor of twenty-fold or more since the prewar era. Mary Waugh's researches on metropolitan Kent also give a twenty-fold increase from 1939 to 1961; they show that site costs as a percentage of total costs rose from 10 per cent to 30 per cent over this time, and that in real terms the value of land on the urban fringe was lower in the 1930s than at any time in the century 1861–1961.[15]

There are both practical and theoretical difficulties in attempting to measure changes in land prices over such a long period. Apart from changes in the nature of property rights in land (which are the product of the planning legislation) there is the simple fact that land bought and sold in the two periods is a very different commodity. In general land sold in the 1930s, for example, is more accessible to the main concentrations of employment and central area facilities than land bought in the 1960s. In order to make an accurate comparison it would be desirable to compare the prices of the same

[14] *Report of the Expert Committee on Compensation and Betterment*, op. cit., p. 41.

[15] Mary Waugh, *Suburban Growth in North-West Kent 1861–1961*. Unpublished Ph.D. Dissertation, University of London (1968), pp. 208–12.

plots of land. But in practice nearly all the vacant sites actually on the market in the 1930s will have been covered by houses by the 1960s.

But the exact magnitude of the increase in land prices is not our immediate concern. More important in the present context are the implications of the changes in price for the resulting forms of urban development. To examine this topic we need to consider some of the other influences on the market for land.

THE PRESSURES FOR HIGHER DENSITIES

It is often said that good and successful planning should act in harmony with the underlying market forces. If so, the advocacy of high densities by many planners and architects, and by central government policy in recent years, can be regarded as an example of exceptionally prescient planning. As the price of land for residential development has increased so has building at higher densities become more economic.

But it would be an oversimplification to assume that land prices have inflated independently of planning policy. Zoning land at higher densities

Table 8.11

INDEX OF PRICES OF BUILDING LAND AND HOUSES 1939–1963

Year	Building sites		Houses
	Per foot frontage	Per acre	
1939	100	100	100
1959	323	792	333
1963 (mid)	526	1,615	437

Source: D. R. Denman, Land in the Market, *Hobart Paper No. 30*. Institute of Economic Affairs (1964), p. 15.

is in itself a factor of some importance in the inflationary spiral. Permitting more dwellings to the acre puts a higher price tag on the land. Planning and the market have interacted to produce the escalation of land prices.

Table 8.11 is reproduced from a study made by Dr D. R. Denman. According to these data residential land prices measured in per acre terms increased sixteenfold over the period 1939–63, but prices measured *per foot of frontage* increased only a little over fivefold. Denman's conclusions are worthy of full quotation:

> The exceptional price rise from 1939 to 1959 where land was sold by the acre was not reflected in a corresponding rise in the price of houses and house plots. The ratio of plot price to house price was the same in 1959 as it was in 1939. Where, then, small parcels of land were sold by the foot frontage, the length of frontage offered in 1959 would have been the same as in 1939. But it does not follow from this that the size of the plots

would have remained constant; the ratio between house price and price per foot frontage could remain constant if the plots were unchanged in width but shorter, so that the 'superficial area' was less. The constance in ratio between plot price and house price, in the face of a rise in acreage prices more than twice that of the increment in house prices, points to smaller plots and higher densities on the newly-developed housing estates, and of course to the erection of blocks of flats. Between 1959 and 1963 both frontages and plot sizes were squeezed into narrower dimensions and thus maintained the constant ratio between land price and house price. The steep rise in prices in land sold by the acre did not push house prices up proportionately at any time. What the higher prices in land have done is to reduce considerably the physical ratio between land and house premises. A house bought in 1939 was set in a more spacious garden and had more and larger rooms than the corresponding house of 1963.[16]

Corroborative evidence for the interaction of zoned densities and land price is also contained in the studies by Stone and MacAuslan quoted earlier. Stone's study found that in the London and Birmingham regions and in areas on the South Coast (after location within the region was taken into account) the price per acre was related to zoned density in the form:

$$Y = A + Bx$$

where Y = price per acre, x is the zoned density, and A and B are constants. Thus in the London region for sites situated twenty miles from the centre the price of sites zoned at ten dwellings to the acre averaged £10,000 per acre whereas in a similar location the price of land zoned at thirty dwellings to the acre averaged £22,000 per acre. In the Birmingham region at locations ten miles from the centre the corresponding prices were £8,000 and £18,000 per acre respectively. On the South Coast prices in the areas studied averaged £9,000 per acre for sites zoned at ten dwellings to the acre and £19,000 for sites zoned at thirty to the acre. MacAuslan's study is wholly consistent in that it shows much less variation in the price of land per plot than in the price per acre.

How much land is zoned at a particular density depends of course upon the local planning authority who may be influenced by a wide variety of local considerations. But the most common and general influences have been clearly expressed in central government policy. The old Ministry of Housing urged local planning authorities to zone at higher residential densities in order to maintain 'vital planning objectives such as the preservation of the countryside and the protection of good agricultural land'.[17] More specifically the Ministry stated:

Before the war there was little or no recognition of the need to be economi-

[16] D. R. Denman, 'Land in the Market', *Hobart Paper No. 30*. Institute of Economic Affairs, London (1964), p. 16.

[17] Ministry of Housing and Local Government, *Residential Areas – Higher Densities*, Planning Bulletin No. 2. HMSO, London (1962), p. 4.

cal in the use of land and maximum net densities of eight houses per acre or less were frequently imposed on new development. The consequences were suburbs sprawling around all the great cities. Today the need to avoid wasteful use of land is generally recognized yet the density policy of some local planning authorities has not changed.... Thirteen houses to the acre is a very modest density: it still allows about 3,000 square feet of land for each house and garden. Densities of... twenty dwellings to the acre are perfectly practicable with two-storey terrace housing and modest gardens. Densities of... thirty dwellings to the acre can be used to provide a good variety of housing types... in schemes covering several acres. Tall blocks of flats will become necessary at densities higher than this, but they need not predominate until densities of at least 140 persons to the acre are reached.[18]

The densities at which dwellings are actually built depends also upon negotiations between the developer and the planning authority at the stage when detailed planning permission is being sought. A private developer may seek to build at higher than the zoned density if he believes that it is in his financial interest to do so. If the proposed layout and design seem satisfactory to the planning authority there may be no particular reason to refuse permission. The developer is much more likely to press for higher density than lower. It is a rare situation for an area to be so exclusive in character that houses can be more profitably built at lower than the zoned density.

Where the local housing authority is the developer there are a number of factors which can lead to development at high densities. An authority engaged on slum clearance cannot usually rehouse all the inhabitants on the same site, but many of those displaced want to live as near as possible to their former homes. Most urban local authorites have long waiting lists for council houses (composed of their electors) and suffer from an acute shortage of land within their own boundaries. To help meet these demands local authorities have been obliged to acquire land in uses other than residential (and pay a premium for it) and to acquire land (such as Thamesmead, built on marshland in south-east London), which requires costly site works. Both the high cost of sites and the pressure of demand induce local authorities to increase densities.

The system of government subsidies for local authority housing have throughout the period of our study also encouraged building at higher densities. The Housing Act of 1946 raised existing subsidies for development on high-cost land to £41 per dwelling per year for sixty years for land costing £20,000 per acre, and introduced a new subsidy of £7 per year for flats of four storeys or more in which lifts were installed. (The expensive site subsidy encourages development of high-cost land and so is an indirect inducement to build at higher densities.) These subsidies were increased by the Housing Act of 1952. Under the 1956 Act subsidies for tall blocks of flats were increased, and a new expensive site subsidy was introduced at £60 per acre for

[18] Ibid.

land costing £5,000 per acre, and £34 per acre for each additional £1,000 per acre paid. The subsidies for tall blocks were again increased by the 1961 Housing Act.

The Housing Subsidies Act of 1967 provided for quite a new form of subsidy, which made good to local authorities the difference between loan charges on approved costs and the loan charges which would have been payable had local authorites been able to borrow at a 4 per cent rate of interest. The subsidy is 'open ended' in two senses. First the local authority is insulated against a high level of interest rates – in effect the government guarantees a loan at 4 per cent. Second the subsidy is payable on the approved costs of approved schemes. The subsidy is used to encourage higher construction standards and to help meet the cost of building at high densities. There are *Housing Cost Yardsticks* which lay down, for example, that an approved cost at a density of eighty dwellings to the acre is about 50 per cent greater than that of schemes at a density of twenty-five dwellings to the acre. The 1967 Act also retained both the supplementary subsidies for high flats and expensive sites.

Central government subsidies account for only a proportion of the total costs of local housing authorities and in purely economic terms they are only a limited incentive to build at high densities. The main pressure on local authorities – the desire to meet demand within its own boundaries – is without doubt the most important factor involved. But the system of subsidies, which is primarily designed to encourage local authorities to provide more houses, has also given an official stamp of approval to local authorities to build as many dwellings to the acre as is acceptable to members of the community who have little other choice on the housing market.

PEOPLE AND ROOMS

Population growth is not the only factor leading to the demand for more houses. Higher living standards are directly and indirectly a factor of equal importance increasing the demand for homes and for space within them. As incomes have risen so has the age fallen at which people marry and so have young couples less commonly been obliged to live with their parents. There has been an increase in the number of one- and two-generation households at the expense of what have actually come to be known as extended families composed of members of three generations. The number of separate households has for many decades been growing faster than population.

At the same time people have come to occupy more space within the home. This is partly the product of the growing number of households. People need space for cooking, eating, social activity, and sleeping, and they often prefer to have separate rooms for these activities whether the household consists of one person or six persons.

Higher living standards have also increasingly come to mean separate bedrooms for parents and children, separate bedrooms for children of different sexes, and even separate bedrooms for each member of the household.

Refrigerators, clothes and dishwashing machines, central heating boilers, record players, transistor radios and TV sets have all increased demand in the way of space as well as in the number of rooms. Further education has increased the desire for separate rooms for study.

Table 8.12

PROPORTION OF HOUSEHOLDS IN ENGLAND AND WALES LIVING AT SELECTED OCCUPANCY PATTERNS 1931, 1951 AND 1961

Occupancy pattern	1931	1951	1961
	(percentages of all households)		
Typical low occupancies (less than 0·5 persons per room)			
1 person in 5 rooms	0·7	1·7	2·7
1 person in 4 rooms	1·2	2·4	3·4
2 persons in 6 rooms	2·7	2·5	3·2
2 persons in 5 rooms	4·5	7·5[3]	9·3[1]
Sub-total low occupancies	9·1	14·1	18·6
Typical medium occupancies (0·5 to 0·8 persons per room)			
2 persons in 4 rooms	5·3[3]	7·8[2]	8·9[2]
2 persons in 3 rooms	3·8	5·0	4·4
3 persons in 5 rooms	5·8[2]	8·2[1]	8·4[3]
3 persons in 4 rooms	6·1[1]	7·3[4]	6·7[5]
4 persons in 6 rooms	2·8	2·1	2·7
4 persons in 5 rooms	5·1[4]	7·2[5]	8·0[4]
Sub-total medium occupancies	28·8	37·6	39·0
Typical high occupancies (1 person per room or more)			
2 persons in 2 rooms	3·2	3·2	1·9
3 persons in 3 rooms	3·8	4·0	2·6
3 persons in 2 rooms	2·5	1·7	0·6
4 persons in 4 rooms	5·0[5]	5·3	4·5
4 persons in 3 rooms	2·8	2·4	1·3
5 persons in 5 rooms	3·4	3·9	4·1
5 persons in 4 rooms	3·2	2·5	1·8
Sub-total high occupancies	23·8	23·1	16·7
Total all 17 occupancy patterns	61·7	74·8	74·3

Notes: The References [1–5] give the most frequent, the second most frequent, third most frequent etc., occupancy pattern in each year. The occupancy patterns were selected for inclusion in the Tables on the basis of frequency in 1931 and 1961. The rise in the total coverage of the 17 occupancy patterns over 1931–51 is associated with the declining average typical household.

Source: Censuses, 1931, 1951, 1961.

The most straightforward way of measuring the overall effect of these trends is in terms of occupancy rates – or the average number of persons per room. This measure does not take into account the falling size of household, or the size of rooms, or the age or condition of the dwelling. But it does provide an aggregative indication of the ways in which housing standards in the way of space within the home are changing.

In 1931 the average number of persons per room in England and Wales was 0·83. By 1951 the average occupancy rate had fallen to 0·74, and there was a further fall to 0·67 by 1961. Table 8.12 gives some indication of what these average changes have meant in terms of common occupancy-patterns. In 1931 less than one in every fifty households comprised one person living in four or five rooms. By 1961 one in every sixteen households were of these types. In 1931 two-person households occupying five or six rooms accounted for 7 per cent of all households. By 1961 two-person households with five or six rooms accounted for one in every eight of the total. In 1961 in fact the combination of two persons in a five-roomed dwelling was the most common single occupancy type. The children born in the 1930s had left home, leaving their parents alone in the three-bedroomed semidetached.

The changes at the other end of the scale have not been so dramatic. In 1931 the most common pattern of high occupancy rates comprised four-person households living in three or four rooms. In 1931 these types accounted for one in every thirteen households and a rather higher proportion of the total population. The proportion of households of these types had not changed significantly by 1951 but fell to one in every eighteen by 1961.

For the bulk of the population the main changes occurred in the medium occupancy ranges. In 1931 the most common single combination was three persons living in four rooms. By 1951 the most common combination was three persons living in five rooms. In 1931 the second most common occupancy type was three persons living in five rooms. By 1951 the second most common occupancy combination was two persons living in four rooms.

These falling occupancy rates are only to a slight degree attributable to an increase in the size of dwellings; in 1931 the average size of dwelling was 4·6 rooms and by 1961 the average size had increased only to 4·7 rooms. The main changes over the period are associated with a decline in the size of households. In 1931 the average household consisted of 3·8 persons; by 1961 the average size had fallen to 3·1 persons. What has happened is that the number of dwellings has increased by more than the number of households. A larger number of smaller households are distributed over a yet larger number of dwellings, and since the average size of dwellings has not changed, the average density of occupation in terms of persons per room has fallen substantially.

This pattern is one of the changes associated with the various kinds of housing 'subsidy' described earlier in the chapter. The tax relief for owner occupiers has made it easier for literally millions of people to purchase a home of their own. The various kinds of subsidy for council tenants have made it possible for millions of people to afford the rent of a council house or flat. Rent control and protection against eviction have made it possible for millions of people to retain their tenure on their private unfurnished dwelling. But these measures have also had their effects on the distribution of incomes and wealth, and most important in the present context, have had their effects on the way the stock of housing is shared out among the population.

Some indication of the redistributive effects of the conditions of the housing

Table 8.13

TRENDS IN CROWDING AND LOW OCCUPANCY 1931–1966

Group	1931	1951	1961	1966
	(average occupancy rates in persons per room)			
Most crowded tenth of households	2·176	1·684	1·443	1·237
Middle 30 per cent	0·815	0·725	0·632	0·565
The tenth of households with the lowest occupancy rates	0·298	0·265	0·247	0·195
Average all households	0·826	0·736	0·655	0·572
Ratio of average occupancy rates of most crowded tenth, and tenth of households with lowest occupancy rates, to those for middle 80 per cent				
Most crowded tenth	2·67	2·32	2·28	2·19
Tenth with lowest occupancy rates	0·35	0·37	0·39	0·36

Notes: Each Census includes a Table in the form of a matrix giving households classified by number of persons along one axis and dwellings classified by number of rooms along the other axis. From this Table occupancy rates in terms of persons per room for all households can be calculated. Using arithmetic class intervals the distribution of households (or population) in terms of occupancy rates is skewed in the direction of below-average occupancy rates, but if geometrical class intervals are used (which might seem more logical for a ratio measure such as persons per room) the distribution is skewed in the direction of above-average occupancy rates.

The distribution displays a kind of multi-modality which is the product of the fact that both persons and rooms are measured entirely in terms of whole numbers which are also small. In 1951, for example, there were more than two million households living at a density of one person per room (one person in one room, two persons in two rooms, etc.), but there were only a few hundred households living at a density of between 0·87 and 1·0 persons per room because the only way in which occupancy rates in this range could occur would involve exceptionally large households and dwellings, e.g. nine persons in ten rooms.

In the light of features of these kinds the analysis of the distribution was made mainly in terms of deciles. The average occupancy rates given in the Table relate to the tenth of households with the highest occupancy rates, the tenth of households with the lowest occupancy rates and the four-fifths of households in between. In several cases the occupancy rate which defines the range of one of these three categories falls within one of the modal rates: i.e. in 1966 less than one-tenth of households lived at more than one person per room, but the proportion of households living at a density of one person per room or more was greater than one tenth. It was assumed in cases of this kind (for the purpose of calculating the average occupancy rate for a particular decile group) that the smaller the size of dwelling for a given occupancy rate the higher the occupancy: i.e. one person in one room was ranked in fact as a higher occupancy rate than two persons in two rooms, which in turn was ranked as a higher occupancy rate than three persons in three rooms, and so on.

Source: Censuses, 1931, 1951, 1961, 1966.

market has already been given in Table 8.12 which shows how the proportion of households living at high densities of occupation has decreased and that at low densities of population has increased. But this Table is restricted to common occupancy-patterns, and it does not include the data available from the 1966 Census because of a major change in the way in which rooms were defined. A more precise indication of changes in the distribution of persons with respect to rooms is given in Table 8.13.

Table 8.13 has been constructed by ranking all the different occupancy patterns given in the Census in order of density of occupation. Thus in 1966 the highest occupancy rate recorded in the census is for two households (in the 10 per cent sample) consisting of nine people living in a single room. The lowest occupancy rate recorded is for 976 one-person households living in ten or more rooms. These are both extreme samples. A more representative picture of the distribution is given by separating out the top and bottom deciles. In 1966 the most crowded tenth of households lived at a density of occupation of one or more persons per room. The tenth of all households with the lowest occupancy rates lived at a density of one person to four or more rooms. Four-fifths of all households lived at a density of occupation of between one person per room and one person per four rooms.

A comparison between the average occupancy rates of the most crowded tenth, the middle 80 per cent, and the tenth with the lowest occupancy rates, provides a convenient method of examining changes in the distribution of the housing stock even over a long period. This method measures changes in the equity of the distribution in a way which is fairly independent of changes in nature of the population and in the nature of the definitions used in the Census. The method is only indirectly affected by the fall in average size of households, for example, or by the major change in the definition of a room introduced in 1966. (Prior to 1966 a kitchen was counted as a room only if it was regularly used for eating.)

In 1931 the most crowded tenth lived at an average density of occupation which was 2·7 times that of the middle 80 per cent. By 1966 the most crowded tenth lived at a density of occupation which was 2·2 times that of the middle 80 per cent. Most of this minor reduction in the inequality in the distribution of housing stock occurred over the period 1931–51. The large volume of public housing produced since 1951 does not appear to have made very much difference to the degree of inequality in the distribution.

The changes at the other end of the scale appear to have been even smaller. In 1931 the tenth with the lowest occupancy rates were living at a density of occupation equal to a little more than a third of that of the middle 80 per cent. By 1961 the difference between average occupancy rates of the tenth with the lowest occupancy rates and the middle 80 per cent had narrowed slightly, but there was a reversion to the 1931 difference by 1966. The change over 1961–6 may be more apparent than real in that it may have been affected by the change in the definition of rooms. (People living at low densities may be less likely to use the kitchen for eating than those living at average sorts of occupancy rates.)

It is often said that Britain has become a much more egalitarian society over the past generation or so. But there is little hard evidence which would support or contradict this view. The statistics on the distribution of incomes collected by the Commissioners of Inland Revenue provide supporting evidence, but some authorities argue that this evidence is misleading. The data on the distribution of population with respect to rooms, which was used to construct Table 8.13, provides what is perhaps the best single measure of changes in the distribution of one of the most important kinds of 'good' possessed or used by every member of the population. On the kind of breakdown given in this Table there is certainly no evidence of a massive redistribution in the direction of greater equality in the field of housing. Someone has to be at the bottom, but, relative to the average living conditions, it appears that those at the bottom are almost as badly off as they were before the war.

The conditions of the housing market, including the influence of the various kinds of governmental subsidy have, however, had a marked effect on the way housing is distributed in different tenure groups. The incidence of crowding is most marked among local authority and private unfurnished tenants. The crowded local authority tenants comprise mostly large families in average size dwellings. The crowded private tenants (a truly unsubsidized sector of the market) comprise small households in even smaller dwellings.

The pattern in 1966 is shown in Table 8.14. In that year there were 910,000 households which were tenants of local authorities living at a density of one or more persons per room. 23 per cent of all local authority households were crowded – according to this particular definition of crowding – and these 910,000 households accounted for 40 per cent of all crowding. The most common occupancy-patterns were four, five and six-person households in as many rooms, and six persons in five rooms.

The incidence of crowding among owner-occupied dwellings was only one-third as great as in local authority dwellings. The incidence of crowding was as high in private furnished dwellings as in local authority dwellings, but private furnished dwellings are the smallest tenure group and the crowding consisted mostly of one and two-person households living in as many rooms. Crowding in private unfurnished dwellings and in other tenure groups was below average and no particular occupancy pattern predominated.

In a sense these figures all understate the incidence and extent of crowding because they are given in terms of the proportion of households not persons. In some ways they also understate the contrast between local authority households and other tenure groups. Local authority households are the largest – an average of 3·3 persons as compared with 2·9 for all households. Thus although local authorities account for 40 per cent of crowding measured in terms of households, they account for more than 45 per cent of all persons living in crowded conditions.

Differences in the incidence and extent of crowding by tenure groups are fairly consistent with differences at the other end of the occupancy scale. On any measure most low occupancy occurs in owner-occupied and privately-rented unfurnished dwellings. There are 912,000 owner-occupied households and 514,000 private unfurnished households living at a density of one person

Table 8.14

SELECTED EXAMPLES OF CROWDING 1966, BY TENURE

Occupancy pattern	Tenure Group: Owner occupiers	Local authority tenants	Private unfurnished tenants	Private furnished tenants	Other and not stated	All tenures
			(thousands of households)			
1 person in 1 room	5	9	27	118	2	160
2 persons in 2 rooms	11	14	35	36	3	99
3 persons in 3 rooms	15	15	52	19	5	106
4 persons in 4 rooms	107	159	84	9	23	382
5 persons in 5 rooms	116	223	38	3	28	408
6 persons in 6 rooms	92	104	23	2	15	236
6 persons in 5 rooms	38	113	15	1	12	179
Sub-total seven occupancies	384	637	274	188	88	1,570
Total of all occupancy at one person per room or more	540	910	421	264	126	2,262
			(percentages)			
Proportion of households in tenure group living at one person per room or more	7·5	23·1	14·3	23·4	16·0	17·7
Proportion of all households living at one person per room or more by tenure	23·9	40·3	18·6	11·7	5·6	100·0

Notes: The examples given are the seven most common occupancy-patterns at one person per room or more among all occupancy patterns which are not always the most common occupancy-pattern within a particular tenure group.

Source: Census, 1966.

Table 8.15

SELECTED EXAMPLES OF LOW OCCUPANCY 1966, BY TENURE

Occupancy pattern	Tenure group					
	Owner occupier	Local authority tenure	Private unfurnished tenants	Private furnished tenants	Other and not stated	All tenures
			(thousands of households)			
1 person in 4 rooms	210	142	204	12	13	581
1 person in 5 rooms	203	81	128	5	12	429
1 person in 6 rooms	275	34	135	4	9	457
2 persons in 8 rooms	74	1	14	1	8	98
Sub-total four occupancies	762	258	481	22	42	1,565
Total all occupancies at 0·25 persons per room or less	912	261	514	24	58	1,769
			(percentages)			
Proportion of households in tenure group living at 0·25 per persons per room or less	12·7	6·6	17·5	4·6	7·4	11·5
Proportion of all households living at 0·25 persons per room or less by tenure group	51·6	14·7	29·1	1·4	3·3	100·0

Notes: The examples given are the four most common occupancy-patterns at 0·25 persons per room or less.

Source: Census, 1966.

to four or more rooms. In the case of private unfurnished dwellings this number is mostly a reflection of the high incidence of low occupancy, but in the case of owner occupiers the extent of low occupancy reflects both the size of this tenure group and an above-average incidence of low occupancy (Table 8.15).

The striking feature of this low occupancy is the extent to which it consists of one-person households. The typical case of low occupancy comprises a single owner-occupier living in six rooms. In 1966 there were 275,000 households of this character. It seems likely that the large majority of these households consists of an old person living alone. Thus it seems that low occupancy is not a reflection of inequality in the distribution of income, but rather the complex set of factors associated with growing old in a society in which most households span only one or two generations.

The interesting point which arises is that this problem, if it is a problem, does not occur with local authority dwellings on anything like the same scale. The incidence of low occupancy among local authority tenants, for example, is only half that among owner-occupied dwellings. Local authorities do build small dwellings specially suited to the needs of old people, and they are able to encourage or persuade people to move into them. But the private developer does not appear to have achieved any success in catering for this end of the market.

AREAS OF CROWDING

The distribution of persons with respect to rooms gives only a very partial picture of the ways in which the stock of housing is used. Occupancy rates measured in terms of persons per room give no indication of the size of rooms, or of the condition and standard of amenities of the dwelling in which these rooms are situated. The figures given in Table 8.13, above, may systematically understate the degree of inequality in the distribution of housing among the population at large.

The degree of inequality in the distribution of housing is particularly important at the lower end of the socio-economic scale because of the frequent coincidence of poor and overcrowded housing conditions with low incomes and poverty. It is often suggested that inadequate housing, especially if this is measured (as in this chapter) by means of a relative standard, is an inevitable reflection of inequalities in the economic and social fields. If this is so attempts to improve the stock of housing conditions of those with low incomes by housing or other land-use means alone are doomed to failure.

The geographical distribution of areas of crowding provides a number of indications of the nature and extent of inequality in the housing field, and the ways in which this is changing. It is to be expected that the incidence of crowding would be highest in two types of place – in low-income areas, and in areas where the demand for housing is high relative to supply. The implications of crowding in these two types of area are different. If areas of crowding, areas of poor old housing, and areas of poverty coincide, then it would seem that the degree of inequality shown in Table 8.13 understates the degree of inequality in the distribution of housing, and that crowding is simply a reflection of inequalities in the distribution of incomes and wealth. If on the other hand areas of crowding are different from low-income areas, then crowding can justifiably be regarded as a problem susceptible to land-use solutions which would either increase the supply of housing in the crowded areas, or help bring about in some way a reduction in the pressure of demand for housing in the crowded areas.

In 1931 the largest concentrations of crowding in England and Wales occurred in the northern mining areas and in inner London. In both County Durham and Northumberland 13 per cent of all households, containing 20 per cent of the population, lived at an occupancy rate of more than two persons per room. The corresponding figures for England and Wales were 3·9 per cent and 6·9 per cent respectively. The incidence of crowding in some London boroughs was even more severe. In Finsbury and Shoreditch for example 18 per cent of households lived at a density of more than two persons per room – more than four times the national average. But in most of the boroughs of inner London the proportion of crowded households was around twice the national average.

Other concentrations of crowding in 1931 occurred in the South-East Lancashire coalfield running from Widnes to Wigan, in the small mining towns of the West Riding of Yorkshire – like Skelmanthorpe, Southowran, and Heckmondwike – and in the Black Country towns between Birmingham and Wolverhampton, like Tipton and Wednesbury. All of these areas had two or more times the national average of households living at a density of more than two persons per room.

Crowding was not particularly extensive in Britain's cities other than London. Liverpool, Leeds, Hull and Sheffield had slightly above the national average of crowding. But in Birmingham, Bradford, Bristol, Manchester and Wolverhampton the proportion of households living at more than two persons per room was actually below the national average.

Thirty-five years later in 1966 the general level of crowding had been substantially reduced, the definition of what constitutes a room had been extended, and together these factors meant that the standard of crowding was very different. Whereas in 1931 3·9 per cent of households lived at a density of more than two persons per room, in 1966 only 5·4 per cent of households lived at a density of more than one person per room. But we can use this 1966 proportion in exactly the same way to measure the geographical distribution of crowding.

There is one striking point of similarity between the geographical distribution of crowding in 1931 and 1966. In 1966, just as in 1931, the inner London boroughs contained a high proportion of crowded households. The pattern in inner London had changed a little; the concentrations of crowding in what are now the London Boroughs of Tower Hamlets and Southwark is less marked than it was in 1931. But more generally crowding, measured by this relative standard, has become more extensive. In most of the inner London boroughs the incidence of crowding is actually higher relative to the national average than it was in 1931.

The main changes in the geographical pattern of crowding have occurred outside London. A few pockets of crowding still exist in towns in the North-East and in the West Riding of Yorkshire but in general crowding, even measured on this relative scale, has been substantially reduced. Instead crowding has increasingly come to be a big-city phenomenon.

In 1966 Liverpool and the adjacent areas of Bootle, Kirby, Huyton-with-Roby and Whiston all contained double the national average proportion of households living at a density of more than one person per room. Manchester had a 50 per cent higher share of households living at about this density. Birmingham, West Bromwich and Wolverhampton all had well above the national average of crowded households.

This association of crowding with big cities should not be exaggerated. Except in London and Liverpool the concentrations of crowding do not appear to be very extensive. In general, in fact, areas of crowding are less well-defined in 1966 than they were thirty-five years earlier. But there is no doubt about the general pattern of geographical change. In 1931, except in London, crowding was associated with areas where industry was declining and unemployment rates were high. In 1966 extensive areas of crowding were nearly all situated within easy distance to work of the major concentrations of employment in the central business districts of London, Liverpool, Manchester and Birmingham.

Crowding in the North has been relieved by the drift to the South. Instead of being associated mainly with low incomes and high levels of unemployment, crowding has come to be associated mainly with the pressure of demand for space in the large urban concentrations of Megalopolis England. The main concentrations of crowding, measured in terms of persons per room, have come to coincide with the most extensive areas of high density in terms of dwellings to the acre.

SOCIAL SEPARATION

The trends in the location of crowding together with the variations in the incidence and extent of crowding in different tenure groups illustrate, at a large scale, one half of one important aspect of the pattern of urban change. As we saw in our previous volume (Chapter Seven) there has been an incipient extension in Britain of some of the symptoms of what on the other side of the Atlantic would be called 'the urban problem'. In the inner areas of the major urban concentrations there has been a growth of most of the different ingredients of that complex and geographically intimate mixture of affluence and squalor, vitality and sordidness, which help to make most people's attitudes to the big city deeply ambivalent.

The problem is not primarily one of poverty. The income levels of those who live in crowded conditions in Britain's major cities may be low in comparison with those of their neighbours, but they are probably higher than in most small towns and rural areas. Neither is the problem primarily one of bad housing. Most of those living in crowded conditions in the cities are local authority tenants and their dwellings are maintained in good state of repair and are generally provided with a full range of amenities. Perhaps in Britain these are only symptoms, without any evidence of serious organic disorder.

But there is little doubt about one feature of the pattern of urban change. An increasing proportion of those who live in the inner areas of cities are local authority tenants. The cities still house a good proportion of the affluent and those who are relatively affluent because they have no dependents to support. But a decreasing proportion of the population of the cities comprises families with above-average incomes. The complementary half of this aspect of the pattern of urban change is that a disproportionate number of those who migrate centrifugally are owner occupiers, or become owner occupiers when they move out. As a result, social separation is occurring on an ever larger scale.

This concentric pattern of social separation is contrary to the trends in the location of employment which will be analysed in Chapter Nine. White-collar jobs are slow to decentralize, but a high proportion of white-collar workers are owner occupiers and have been in the vanguard of the outward movement. Blue-collar jobs have decentralized readily, yet blue-collar workers are more likely to be local authority tenants and so remain residents of the inner areas. Why are these trends so divergent?

To answer this question we must go back to the subject of housing subsidies and taxation. The favourable fiscal position of the owner occupier encourages everyone who can get a mortgage to buy a house. To a great extent increasing radial social separation is simply the product of the distribution of incomes and wealth, as abetted by the taxation system. Those who could afford to move out have done so.

An additional factor of considerable importance is not however a matter of income levels but is a product of the way mortgage companies work. Building Societies are geared to make loans to white-collar workers. White-collar workers get salaries. They know how much they will earn next year. They mostly get annual increments and they also know what at minimum they will be earning in five or more years' time. White-collar workers find it relatively easy to fill in a large and detailed form of application for a mortgage; dealing with forms is often part of their daily experience.

The position of the blue-collar worker is very different. His annual earnings are the sum of fifty weeks' wages and are uncertain because they depend upon the ups and downs of the economy and upon how much overtime is available; it is understandable that many mortgage companies do not give much weight to overtime earnings. There are no automatic annual increments for the manual workers – there is only the uncertain outcome of the next pay claim to look forward to. The manual worker himself, and the building societies, know also that the peak of his earning capacity will probably be passed before he reaches the age of forty.

HIGH PRICES AND HIGH DENSITY

The favourable fiscal position of the owner occupier, the inflationary trends, and the planning system have together shaped the pattern of housing development in postwar Britain. Each of these elements has played an interlocking role with the other two, but the interaction has been rather complex and rather different from the typical textbook examples of how markets function.

According to economic theory market prices are determined by the interaction of supply and demand. But in the housing market of postwar Britain prices have been largely determined by expectations. At the consuming end of the decision-making process is the potential purchaser of a new house. Next come all the intermediaries – mortgage companies, the land-use planners, the builders, speculators and so on. And at the other end of the decision-making process is the owner of land zoned with residential planning permission. Let us first consider just some of the influences on the actors at the two extremes.

The potential purchaser of a new house is in a rather more constrained position than the owner of residential land. Typically he needs somewhere to live fairly urgently, either because of a change in family circumstances or in workplace. Typically he is unlikely to be qualified even to get on the waiting list for a local authority dwelling, and the rent of any housing which might be available on the open market seems to him exorbitantly high in relation to house prices. He decides to buy. The potential purchaser can of course buy an old house, but he soon finds that there is little difference between the price of old and new houses and that it is much easier to get finance to purchase a new one. The question is how much should he pay?

If he asks a building society for advice they will tell him that they will lend about two and a half times his annual income, and they may well point out that a house is a very good investment. The potential purchaser would certainly be encouraged to take a long-term view. In taking this view he would be foolish to be dominated by considerations relevant to his immediate housing needs and present earnings. Given a persistently inflationary trend he can foresee that his earnings will increase by at least 5 per cent per annum and that the resale value of any house he might buy will appreciate at an even faster rate. Yet his mortgage outgoings would remain the same – subject only to changes in the rate of interest.

In this situation the price he is willing to pay is unlikely to be a matter mainly of present costs and benefits, but will be mainly a question of making the best investment – taking into account his circumstances and the likely inflationary trends. The market for housing has essentially been a market for the future. The typical house purchaser has been in the position of being best advised not to buy what he needed, but to buy almost the maximum he could afford.

The owner of land for residential development, at the other extreme, is naturally interested in getting the maximum price a developer will pay. But the owner of land is not constrained in the same way as the potential house purchaser. He may have no urgent needs to fulfil and there is no tax on idle land. Most important he is aware that he owns an asset whose value has a fairly easily ascertainable market value which will appreciate without any effort on his part. Moreover, judging from the trends, his land is appreciating faster than almost any other kind of asset, and at an annual rate which is usually much greater than the ruling rate of interest.

The trends in house and land prices are hardly surprising. For the past generation there has been a seller's market in residential property. House prices have been determined by the maximum which purchasers could afford. The level of money incomes has been both the constraint and mainspring of house prices.

Existing owner-occupiers have in a sense benefited from the inflation of prices. Their capital gain has made it easier for them to acquire a new house. But new aspirants to the status of owner occupation have suffered. It has not become any easier for members of low-income groups to purchase a house, and as interest rates have increased, house purchase for new entrants to the market has actually become more difficult.

Although housing has been predominantly a seller's market with a vigorous demand from existing owner occupiers and those with high incomes, at the lower end of the scale demand has been weak because of lack of capital and of borrowing power. Many developers have been constrained to reduce costs in order to cater for the low-income low-capital demand – which in numerical terms is of some importance. As a result many new houses built for sale are below the standard and below the cost of houses built by local authorities for rent.

The planning system has also translated this low-income low-capital demand into high-density development. Without a fairly effective planning system many developers would have chosen to build on more remote but lower-cost sites, and if this had occurred Britain would undoubtedly have experienced much of the scattered form of development characteristic of urban growth in the United States. But the planning system has more or less effectively determined which land is developed and put a price tag on it. The only course open to the developer catering for the mass market has been to economize on land costs by increasing densities.

These peculiar conditions of the housing market have also limited the amount of urban growth as well as its nature. The generally upward trend in house prices since 1964 for example has actually been accompanied by a slackening of demand. Instead of building 500,000 houses per year as the government expected and promised, new construction has actually fallen to around 350,000 houses per year. Because of, and in spite of, the inflation of land and house prices, builders have been unable to avoid reducing output for the mass market.

The influence of market forces has not been confined to the private sector of the housing market. The favourable fiscal position of the owner occupier has also had its effects on local authority construction. The local authority market for housing is heavily regulated, but governmental measures have only partly controlled the market for land; they have largely determined which land is developed, but not its price. The public and private markets for land are of course the same. Whether local authorities purchase on the open market, or use compulsory powers, they have, at least since the 1959 Act, paid open market prices. These prices have been determined in the ultimate by what owner occupiers have been willing to pay for a new house.

The favourable fiscal position of the owner occupier could be regarded as an open-ended subsidy of a very similar kind to that granted by the central government to local authorities. As incomes, house prices and interest rates have increased, so has the tax relief afforded for mortgage interest payments and the benefits associated with the lack of any tax on imputed rent, and these increases been translated into rising land prices. The cost of land has been the most potent factor pushing up the cost of local authority construction. There has been irresistible pressure to increase rents and for higher central government subsidies, but the expression as far as the physical pattern of urban growth is concerned has been the same as in the private sector. Local authorities, like private developers, have been under increasing pressure to build at high densities.

Soaring land prices have perhaps been the largest single influence on the pattern of urban growth in the postwar period, and they certainly represent the biggest single failure of the system of planning introduced with the 1947 Act. The creators of this system believed that they would be successful in nationalizing all development rights in land. The planners may have been inaccurate by a few percentage points in the predictions they accepted for the growth of population, but they were wrong in terms of thousands of percentage points as far as land prices were concerned.

The nationalization of property rights in land was an important part of the whole planning machinery. Cheap land would have made it easier for local authorities to build houses when and where they wanted. It would have made it easier for the land-use planners and private developers to co-operate fruitfully instead of being in a fairly continuous state of conflict. It would have made urban renewal vastly more economic. But when the last vestigial remains of the abortive attempts to nationalize property rights in land were formally removed by the 1959 Act, nothing else was produced as a substitute. The planning system was left to carry on as if nothing had happened.

It is arguable that as a result we have the worst in both public and private worlds. The private world has made the cost of new houses as high, relative to incomes, as they have ever been in Britain's history. The public world, dominated by the planning system, has ensured that most new housing construction has taken place at a density of development which seems anachronistic for an age in which every other household possesses a motor car.

CONCLUSIONS

Housing is a large and complex subject. The discursive treatment given in this long chapter is intended to focus attention on the ways in which the conditions of the housing market have shaped the pattern of urban growth, and the ways in which new construction has helped, and failed to help, solve Britain's housing problems. At this point the various threads of the argument are brought together in a summary diagnosis.

From the point of view of land use the most striking feature of the pattern of urban growth has been the relatively high density of new construction. Whereas new houses currently built in the United States, for example, are at an average density of about three to the acre, in this country the average density of development is probably well above twelve dwellings to the acre, and is certainly higher than the average level of the 1930s.

Central government policy, the planning system, and the price of land have all been factors working in the same direction to help produce these relatively-high levels of density. The economical use of land has limited losses for agricultural purposes, it has helped preserve the countryside against urban intrusion, and it has made it easier to create encircling Green Belts around Britain's major conurbations and cities. But the economical use of land has not made the construction of dwellings cheaper. Costs in the public sector at least have been substantially increased by the high-density policy. In the private sector the extent to which old houses, even in decentralized locations, have maintained their value suggests that many people are willing to pay what is in effect a heavy premium for the chance to live at low density.

The number and nature of new dwellings constructed has in general satisfied the main needs of the population. The falling size of household has been accommodated by an increase in the number of separate dwellings, and occupancy rates (persons per room) have fallen steadily. But the degree of inequality in the distribution of housing stock with respect to population has persisted.

Crowding (high-occupancy rates in terms of persons per room) has been substantially reduced as the average size of household has fallen. But when crowding is measured in terms of a relative standard (i.e. in comparison with *average* occupancy rates) the reduction in crowding in the postwar period has been only marginal. Most crowding occurs in local authority dwellings and consisted in 1966 mostly of five or six-person households living in as many or fewer rooms. But the incidence of crowding is highest in the private furnished sector – the major unsubsidized sector – where the model occupancy-pattern is one person in one room. The geographical pattern of crowding has changed significantly over recent decades. In 1931 most crowding, outside London, occurred in the poverty-stricken mining areas of Lancashire, Yorkshire, and the North-East of England. The extent of crowding in these mining areas had been substantially reduced by 1951 and has continued to fall since. But crowding (again measured in relative terms) has persisted in the inner areas of London, and has become more extensive in the Liverpool and Birmingham conurbations. Thus the highest occupancy rates have come to be concentrated in the very areas which are built up at the highest densities in terms of dwellings per acre.

At the other end of the scale the number of households living at low occupancy rates has increased steadily both in absolute and relative terms. Both the incidence and extent of low occupancy is heaviest in owner-occupied dwellings. The most common form of low occupancy is one person living in five rooms or more. In 1966 there were more than half a million owner occupiers living at these patterns of occupancy. The nature and extent of this low occupancy suggests that private new construction has failed dismally to provide an adequate number of small dwellings attractive to, and suitable for, old people.

These trends are all the product of the conditions of the housing market as influenced in particular by the planning system, by central government subsidy and taxation policy, and by the location of employment. The dominant factor has been the favourable fiscal position of the owner occupier. The tax relief on mortgage interest payments plus the lack of any tax on the imputed rent of an owner-occupied dwelling have together indiscriminately encouraged everyone who could get a mortgage to purchase a house.

As a result the price of new houses has for several decades moved more or less parallel to that of incomes per head. Part of this rise is attributable to construction costs, but the major element in the increase has been land prices. Perhaps the biggest single failure of the 1947 planning system is that it failed to check the rise in land prices, which has probably been the largest and most potent element of Britain's postwar inflation.

As well as encouraging higher densities the price of land has influenced both the nature and level of housing output. The private sector has catered for a growing proportion of the population. But a growing proportion of the potential market has consisted of marginal purchasers – people whose relatively low levels of income make it difficult for them to obtain a large enough mortgage. As a result the high price of housing has limited demand for new houses both in terms of quantity and quality. Lack of demand has restrained the growth of output. The low level of demand, in terms of the price which could be afforded, has encouraged the construction of dwellings to space and amenity standards below that of new local authority dwellings.

As land prices and interest rates have increased, so has the tax relief given to owner occupiers. The level of land prices on the open market, which is the product of the favourable fiscal position of the owner occupier, has also determined the price paid for housing land by local authorities. As well as encouraging higher densities the escalation of local authority land costs has pushed up the level of subsidies granted to local authority tenants.

Trends in the location of employment have also been a major influence on the housing market. The slow rate of decentralization of employment from the conurbations and major cities has helped to ensure that the price of most old houses has inflated as much as that of new houses. The high level of house prices means that the proportion of the population who can afford to buy out of income a house which is in good condition and provided with what is generally regarded as acceptable standards of domestic facilities is probably as low as at any period in Britain's history.

CHAPTER NINE

HOME AND WORKPLACE

This chapter systematically analyses some of the relationships between place of living and place of work, which have emerged implicitly in other chapters of the book. After a brief historical introduction, it looks first at densities of living and working and at changes in these densities – with special reference to Colin Clark's theory that densities pivot around a central value over time. It examines evidence for the mobility of employment, before going on to its main subject matter: examination of the evidence for the thesis that residential areas are becoming increasingly separated from traditional concentrations of employment. Through examination of commuting trends at different scales – town, conurbation, county and SMLA – it finds clear evidence for such a separation. It considers how far the separation of home and workplace is related to the socio-economic group of the worker in some major British conurbations, both at one point in time and in terms of changes over time. Lastly it considers an important distinction for the student of urban growth – between a dormitory suburb *and a* satellite *with employment of its own.*

This chapter was written by Ray Thomas. Sundry additional tabulations were made by Peter Hall.

INTRODUCTION

One of the earliest indications of urbanization is the establishment of centres of employment. Markets, from which originated many towns and cities, are characterized by the concentration of buyers and sellers in an area small enough to allow for the immediate exchange of information on prices. Manufacturing, the mainspring of nineteenth-century urban growth, is characterized by the division of labour according to specialized functions, usually under a single roof.

The counterpart of the growth of concentrations of employment of these kinds is the separation of home and workplace. It was at a very early stage of urban history that the majority of the population ceased to use the same buildings for sleeping as it did for work. It was also at a very early stage of urban history that dwellings – buildings which were designed to be used for such activities as eating and sleeping – became transformed into places of work. This displacement of residential land uses by employment land uses and land uses associated with employment, was for a century or more one of the main features of the urban growth process in all major towns and cities.

Employers wanted accessible sites. They needed to be near to their customers, to their suppliers, and to their labour force. The existing concentrations of population pointed to the most favourable locations – the crossroads, the exchange, the hub, the node, the core. As the level of employment in these central areas increased, so were houses built at the periphery.

It seems almost an academic question to ask why employers can nearly always outbid residents in the market for land and property. But the facts of the situation seem clear. Even the smallest employers can afford to pay more for the floorspace they need than the large majority of the population. Asking this question does however focus attention on another characteristic of the urban growth process. The residents displaced in the inner areas of towns and cities are not necessarily, or even usually, the same as those who occupy the new houses on the fringe. Those who are displaced are often the poorest members of the community who are unable to afford the cost of new dwellings or the travelling cost associated with suburban locations.

It is a fascinating intellectual exercise to consider what might have happened had a cheap and efficient means of personal transport been invented at an early stage of the Industrial Revolution. We would have to imagine something like the situation which eventually occurred in 1918 happening instead about a century earlier. At the end of the First World War the internal combustion and electric engines had already proved to be economical and fairly reliable means of motivation. By 1920 there were 75,000 licensed public road service vehicles in Britain[1] and London had an extensive underground railway network. 'Homes fit for heroes' was the slogan of the hour, and the Tudor Walters Committee decreed that these homes should be built at a density of ten or twelve to the acre. The towns and cities of Britain spread in this interval period at a rate unprecedented before or since.

If the urban growth trends of the nineteenth century had occurred with a background of this kind, the resultant pattern would have been very different. But it was cabs, omnibuses which were literally horse powered, and trains pulled by steam engines which created the urban structure. The technical inefficiency of these means of transport made their use too expensive for the majority of the population. It is estimated, for example, that in the 1850s there were 400,000 journeys every day in and out of the City of London made on foot, as compared with 88,000 by omnibus and only 62,000 by train.[2]

The nineteenth-century railway developments actually confirmed and strengthened the attraction to many employers of central areas. The central business districts of all Britain's major cities were delineated by the railway termini. Overall residential densities were reduced in and near these central

[1] An unknown proportion of these were taxis, not buses.

[2] According to John R. Kellett this is the first survey of traffic in London. See *The Impact of Railways on Victorian Cities*. Routledge and Kegan Paul, London (1969), pp. 45–6. It seems likely, because of differences in income levels, that the proportion of public transport passengers was lower in other cities.

districts as dwellings were displaced by businesses and by the railways themselves. But only a small proportion of the population was displaced, and only a small proportion of new migrants to the major urban concentration, could afford to live at low density at or near the urban/rural fringe and commute to the central areas. The large majority of the population were pushed out only to within walking distance of the centre, and as a consequence they were obliged to live in crowded conditions in what are nowadays mostly called the twilight areas.

As more efficient and cheaper forms of public transport developed in the first half of the twentieth century, these rings of high-density residential developments confirmed yet again the accessibility of central areas. The centrally located employer could still draw upon the labour market of the entire city, and there were few compensating advantages at suburban or exurban sites, or in small towns. The superior accessibility of central areas has only since the 1950s been jeopardized by the growth of private vehicle ownership, by the consequent spread of traffic congestion, and by the growth of air transport.

THE SEARCH FOR SPACE

The densities at which people live are generally lower than those at which people work. In and near city centres the contrast is particularly noticeable. But important manifestations of the difference also occur in the suburb, in the satellite, and at the urban/rural fringe. And the differences have a widespread influence on the prices of urban growth.

Some examples of high-density working and living are given in Table 9.1. The highest employment densities in Britain undoubtedly occur in the City of London. More than 350,000 people work in an area covering a little more than a square mile, with an overall density of 345 to the acre and densities rising locally to over 500 people to the acre. Densities almost as high are found in parts of the West End. The densities of employment in the central business districts of other major cities of Britain appear to be much lower, but the overall density of employment of even the generously-bounded central business district of a city the size of Leicester is well over 100 persons to the acre.

The highest residential densities are found in the rings surrounding the central business districts. In London they are notably higher than elsewhere – even than Glasgow, that archetypal representative of the high-density Scots city. The major provincial English cities, which were developed in the form of two-storey housing, have few wards where the population density rises above 100 to the acre – a fairly common density in inner London.

Many of the reasons for this difference between the space used by the employee at his workplace and at his home are associated with what seem to be fairly immutable differences in function. Buildings for working, and the land on which they are situated, serve fairly narrowly-defined purposes – few of which are exceptionally demanding in their space needs for land. In the case of offices, to take an extreme example, the floorspace provided by a site can be increased seemingly almost without limit by piling storey upon storey to make a tower block. The only major physical constraint is the provision of transport facilities such as car parking space to help people to get to the building, and lifts for internal circulation.

Table 9.1

SOME VERY HIGH URBAN DENSITIES

	per acre
(1) *Population* (Census, 1961)	
London	
(Westminster) Dolphin Ward	167·9
(Paddington) Harrow Road North Ward	146·5
(Westminster) Churchill Ward	141·5
(Paddington) Harrow Road South Ward	137·0
(Kensington) Golborne Ward	128·5
Birmingham	
Lozells Ward	72·8
Manchester	
Beswick Ward	70·3
Liverpool	
Netherfield Ward	104·9
St Domingo Ward	103·7
Glasgow	
Woodside Ward	116·3
Gorbals Ward	98·9
Townhead Ward	89·5
(2) *Employment* (Transportation Studies, 1964–68)	
London	
Zone 202 (City of London: East)	524·7
Zone 204 (City of London: West)	434·2
Zone 205 (Aldwych, Strand)	494·7
Zone 207 (Marylebone)	297·1
Zone 208 (Soho, Mayfair)	278·2
Birmingham	
Central Birmingham (District 1)	309·3
Manchester	
Manchester Central Area	168·1

Sources: Census of England and Wales and of Scotland, 1961, *County Volumes*. *London Traffic Survey*, Vol. 1 (1964). *West Midlands Transport Study*, Vol. 1 (1968). SELNEC *Transportation Study*, Working Paper No. 4 (1968).

There may not be large differences in the floorspace demanded by working and living, but in the space required around the building the differences are substantial. Residential areas are multi-purpose. They provide space for play and recreation, education, gardening, hobbies, worship, sunbathing, and even dying – just to mention some of the activities which can be fairly demanding in their space needs. And residential areas provide space for the worker's dependents, especially his children, as well as for the worker himself.

As living standards have risen the demand for space in and around the home has increased. Although the residential densities found near city centres are high, they have been gradually falling for a century or more.[3] Part of this fall, as already described, is attributable to displacement by other land uses. But the number of people living in wholly residential areas has also fallen as building and daylighting standards have been enforced, as people have been able to afford to pay for more space, and as their needs for recreational and educational needs outside but near to the home have been fulfilled.

The decline in residential densities has even occurred in smaller towns and suburban areas at some distance from the major city centres. Colin Clark has suggested that over a particular period of time residential densities tend towards a particular level. The population of areas above the *pivotal* level falls, while the populations of areas of growth approach the pivotal level. Some evidence to support this thesis is shown in Figure 9.1. The population of Hertfordshire to the north of London was growing faster than that of any other county in Britain over 1951–61, but the population of eleven of the fourteen wards in the county with the highest overall density of population in 1951, fell over the decade. The population of many other wards in the county increased, but none reached the density of that of the fourteen highest. The pivotal density worked out at about sixteen persons per acre, equivalent to a density of residents in employment of only six to seven persons per acre.

It would not make much sense to attempt to formulate some kind of pivot theory for employment densities. For one thing the space needs of different types of employment vary widely, and as a consequence different types of employment are distributed in very different ways in relation to city centres. Employment in city centres is predominantly in offices; though these centres also include the main concentrations of particular kinds of manufacturing – like newspaper printing. The density of factory employment, like that of nearly all other urban densities, is higher near city centres than in the suburbs. But the general pattern is much more decentralized than offices.

Another reason why it does not make sense to have a pivot theory for employment is that only in very recent years has the employment level in major city centres shown any sign of falling. Employment in central London, for example, has increased over the forty-year period 1921–61 by about 120 thousand or around 10 per cent. Only in the early 1960s was there the first indication of any decline. Although there is no comparable data for the period before 1961 for any other major city centre in Britain, it seems likely that in the past the pattern has been similar to that of central London. Employment levels have been fairly stable until the early 1960s. It seems unlikely that these falls in density in recent years are attributable to the need by employers for more space. What has happened is that central business districts have become

[3] The population of the City of London fell in the first decade of the 19th century.

less attractive to some employers because, for the first time, central areas of big cities have ceased to be the most accessible sites for many kinds of activity.

Many kinds of employment, other than in offices, certainly have decen-

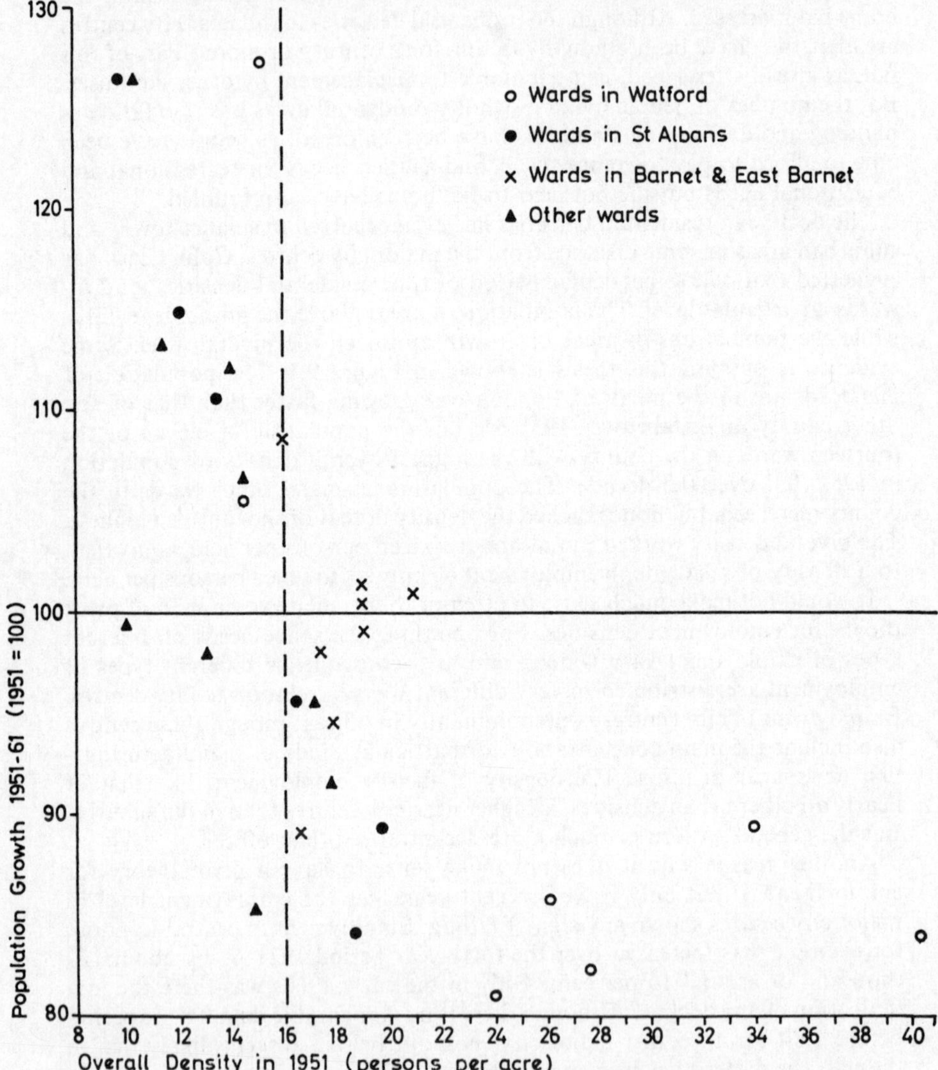

Figure 9.1 The Pivoting of Urban Densities in Hertfordshire 1951–1961

tralized in order to find more space. According to Kellet the large urban factory in the central district was an anachronism as early as the 1860s.[4]

[4] John R. Kellett, op. cit., p. 346.

Factories, shops, warehouses and other employment land uses have decentralized within the major cities and outside the major cities to towns and suburbs in the hinterland. Some of this movement is associated with the centrifugal movement of population. Shops, schools and most personal services are market-oriented to the location of their customers. But factories and warehouses have moved out as they have expanded to get new and more spacious sites.

Most forms of employment however, even at the most decentralized locations, use land more intensively than housing developments. Current plans for industrial trading estates usually allow for a site density of about fifty persons to the acre, and at these decentralized locations, this density is several times the comparable figure for workers in their homes.

A selective but precise picture for residential and a number of different employment land-uses is given in Table 9.2. These figures relate to Harlow

Table 9.2

EMPLOYMENT AND POPULATION SITE-DENSITIES IN HARLOW 1966

Employment and population type	Employment and population numbers	Site area acres	Density persons per acre
Offices and commerce	5,450	11·4	478
Shops	3,088	18·0	172
Manufacturing industry	15,099	310	48·6
Public buildings	1,718	83	20·7
Wholesale and storage	645	57	11·3
Education	1,869	312	6·1
Resident employed population	31,000	1,570	19·8

Notes: The site areas given exclude roads. Public buildings include hospitals and medical services and places of refreshment, entertainment, etc.

Source: W. S. Atkins and Partners, *Harlow Transportation Study*, 1969.

New Town and they may not all be typical of other areas of growth. But they do represent what are considered as acceptable and desirable standards.

In Harlow the site density of factory employment is two and a half times the site density of residents in employment. Shops and offices employ people at densities which are nine and twenty-three times, respectively, the comparable density of workers when they are sleeping. Only kinds of employment like education and warehouses consume more space per person than housing areas.

THE DECISION TO MOVE

Changing the place of residence is a normal part of the human life cycle. A young person often first moves away from the parental home with his first job into lodgings, a hostel, a bedsitter or a flat. For several years the young person is highly mobile residentially, and if it has not occurred already a second move is in any case likely to follow on marriage. A third is probable if and when there are children, and yet a fourth with the change in financial circumstances which occurs when the children themselves start work or with the change in space needs when they leave home.

There is no such cycle for the firm, or any other employment establishment. There are no general changes of circumstances, except growth, which automatically lead to consideration of a new location. In general, firms and organizations tend to stay wherever they were started.

The birthplace and natural location for most small independent employment establishments is near to existing centres of employment. These centres may provide the market for the establishment's output, they may provide the best supply of the specialized services or products which contribute to input, and they almost certainly help to provide the pool of suitable labour needed. Such small organizations benefit greatly from the external economies of scale afforded by central business districts and major concentrations of manufacturing employment. There is rarely any incentive to decentralize from locations of this kind.

The position of the larger firm is rather different. Its size gives a measure of independence from customers and suppliers, and the most important constraint on moving is the size of the labour force. The larger the firm, the larger is the catchment area for its employees, and the higher the proportion it can be sure of losing by any move of more than a small distance. A high proportion of 'moves' in fact are not moves in the full sense of the word – lock, stock and barrel – but are the opening up of a new branch or the setting up of a new functional specialization by establishment within the same firm. The only common factor which induces firms to move is growth.

For the manufacturing employment there is quite a lot of evidence available relevant to moves, and some of this is shown in Table 9.3. Over the period 1960–65 three quarters of Industrial Development Certificates granted in Britain related to extensions of existing factories. It is apparent that the large majority of firms prefer to expand on their existing locations rather than move or set up a branch factory. But it may be noted that these extensions to existing premises account for a significantly lower proportion of the amount of floorspace approved – 62 per cent – than the proportion of moves. Firms which did move or establish branches occupied factories which were larger than the extensions made by the non-moving firms. The figures also suggest that the larger the distance of the move, the larger the new premises.

Further evidence is provided by a study of industrial migration from north-west London.[5] D. E. Keeble concluded that in the case of about 85 per cent of all factories set up by north-west London firms over 1940–64, the move was the direct result of the growth of the individual firm. Keeble concluded that there is little space for industrial expansion in north-west London;

[5] D. E. Keeble, 'Industrial Migration from North-West London, 1940–64', *Urban Studies*, 2 (1965), 15–32.

expanding firms are unlikely to have room for extensions and the cost of vacant factories in the area is high (in 1964 it was 50p–62½p per square foot per year) compared with locations in other parts of the country. It is interesting to note that Keeble puts shortage of labour as a factor only third in importance in inducing moves.

There are no comparable sources of evidence relating to the moves by offices. This is partly the consequence of lack of data. Both the studies quoted on factory employment are based on data gathered by the central government as a by-product of the Factory Acts and of the planning controls on industrial location. No similar source existed for most other forms of employment until the passing of the Offices, Shops and Railway Premises Act of 1963 and the institution of the Official Development Permit system in 1964.

Table 9.3

INDUSTRIAL DEVELOPMENT CERTIFICATE APPROVED BUILDING IN GREAT BRITAIN 1960–1965*

	Number of IDCs	Percentage of total	Thousands of sq. ft.	Percentage of total
Buildings on new sites inter-area moves†	452	4·4	25,161	10·1
Buildings on new sites intra-area moves†	2,289	22·4	69,608	27·9
Extensions to existing premises	7,497	73·2	154,647	62·0
All Approvals	10,238	100·0	249,416	100·0

Notes: * During nearly all of this period IDC approval was required for all new industrial buildings of 5,000 sq. ft. or more. The figures given may account for only a small proportion of the total number of new industrial buildings and extensions, but they probably cover a high proportion of the total floor area built.

† These statistics are based on the division of Great Britain into 50 areas. The largest in terms of population is the Greater London Council area. See *Source* for details.

Source: R. S. Howard, *The Movement of Manufacturing Industry in the United Kingdom 1945–62*. Board of Trade, London, HMSO (1968).

But it may also be partly the consequence of fewer moves by offices. In terms of land requirements there is little constraint on the expansion of offices even in central areas. Office rents are certainly much higher in central London, and the central business districts of other major cities than they are in the suburbs or in small towns. But until the 1960s there was no indication that this rent differential had begun to bring about large-scale decentralization. Indeed the fall in employment in central business districts of recent years may be attributable entirely to a continued decline in non-office land uses.

MOBILITY AND SEPARATION

The metropolitan areas on which much of the analysis of Volume One was based were delineated in terms of the proportion of commuters from an encircling ring into a central core which is defined in terms of the high density of employment. This method of delineation proved to be extraordinarily realistic in areas which otherwise vary considerably in character and size. The usefulness of this approach draws attention to some of the factors which have created functional units of this kind. Historically, these metropolitan areas are the product of two fairly distinct trends – the growth of personal mobility and a trend towards the systematic separation of residential areas from the major concentrations of employment.

The first of these trends – increasing personal mobility – has received the greatest attention in recent years. Over the past two decades the number of cars on Britain's roads grew more than fivefold. This mobility explosion has given new opportunities to millions of people to live conveniently at some distance from their place of work, and it has lent new severity to the chronic road-congestion problems of our historic settlements.

The second of these trends – the growing separation of residential areas from the old concentrations of employment – is the main subject matter of this chapter. In recent years this trend has occurred more gradually than the changes in mobility. But it seems likely that the consequences have just as far-reaching implications.

This distinction between the trends in mobility and those of home and workplace separation may seem artificial. People move to the suburbs at some distance from their place of work in the city centre partly as a reflection of their growing mobility. At first sight it would appear that home and workplace separation is only an item to be subsumed under the heading of growing mobility.

Some observers in the U.S. (where the metropolitan-area idea originated) appear to deny the usefulness and validity of this distinction. These observers emphasize the interdependences which exist between all parts of the metropolitan area as much as those between core and ring. Dobriner, for example, writes:

> Two implications of the preceding discussion regarding the commuting pattern are central to our entire analysis of the suburbs. First, travelling regularly to work is not a peculiarly suburban pattern at all, but a phenomenon of complex societies – it is a characteristic of metropolitanism in particular but of American society in general; indeed, the commuting pattern is found all over the urban-industrial Western world. Second, the suburbanization of manufacturing, the growth of suburban shopping centres, the continued expansion of employing satellites, and similar developments, have created many jobs within the suburban zone. As a consequence, suburbanites are finding employment within the zone itself. The net result is a reduction in the number of commuters who travel into the central city core area, but an increase in the number of suburbanites who commute to work within the suburban zone. The traditional dependence of the suburb on the central city seems to be shifting toward a

greater economic interdependence of zones within the metropolitan area itself. Indeed, the number of central city residents commuting to the suburbs appears to be increasing.[6]

Other authorities, and in particular those professionally concerned with land-use planning, appear to have attached considerable importance to this distinction. Many planners in Britain, for example, have emphasized that one of the objectives of land-use planning should be to avoid massive one-way daily tidal movements of commuters. Perhaps the best short statement representing this point of view comes again from North America. Hans Blumenfeld seems to be the author of the aphorism about the objectives of regional planning as: 'to maximise the opportunity for commuting but minimize the need for commuting'.[7] The two halves of this aphorism correspond roughly to the distinction between mobility on the one hand, and home and workplace separation on the other.

The distinction can be looked at in terms of the factors which determine a particular choice of place of residence. We can classify the reasons why a person lives at a particular dwelling (and so undertakes a particular journey to work) under two headings. There are the personal and historical factors which are peculiar to the individual concerned, and there are the impersonal factors which are the product of the distribution of the stock of housing and the operation of market and other institutional forces.

A person may live at a particular address for a variety of personal reasons. He may have been born there. He may be specially attached to the neighbourhood because of the friendships he has formed. The person we are talking of may be a married woman who lives in a particular house simply because it was chosen by her husband and herself in the early years of their marriage when she did not go out to work. Most of the personal factors of this kind can be regarded as the present-day manifestation of past decisions. They are often the reasons for *not* moving. A high degree of personal mobility makes it possible for the journey to work to be only a minor consideration in choosing, for example, a new job and 'deciding' to live in the same place as before.

But we can also emphasize the impersonal considerations which determine where people live. At the time the decision is made the individual's choice is constrained by the availability of dwellings. Personal factors may seem to be the dominant considerations in any individual case, but individual choices are made in the context of a competitive situation for the supply of dwellings. Individuals certainly have choice, but the sum of their choices is the physical pattern of housing development.

The stock of housing can be distributed in different ways in relation to the distribution of employment. An interdispersion of homes and workplace

[6] William M. Dobriner, *Class in Suburbia*. Prentice Hall, Englewood Cliffs (1963), pp. 17–18. The confidence with which these assertions are made is surprising considering the paucity of U.S. data on changes in the pattern of commuting.

[7] Hans Blumenfeld, *The Modern Metropolis*. MIT Press, Cambridge, Mass. (1967), p. 46.

makes for a minimum of separation. The length of journeys to work in such a situation is mostly a reflection of people's willingness and ability to travel. But if there are large concentrations of employment, physically separate from extensive residential areas, then the length of journeys to work is a reflection of this separation, as well as that of people's mobility.

The distinction between mobility and separation can also be made in statistical terms. Consider, for example, the situation in the County Borough of Leicester in 1951. Already at that date Leicester was tightly bounded by its city limits. The population of the Borough was 285,000 and its area 17,000 acres, giving an overall population density of seventeen persons to the acre. There was little land left in the city for new development and there were many areas of high residential density which were losing population.

Like every other major city Leicester is an employment centre importing labour every day from the surrounding area. In 1951, 28,000 people travelled daily from places outside to work in the city. The flow in the other direction was a little under 8,000. The difference between these flows of 20,000 is a measure of what we shall call the *employment surplus* in Leicester. It is the net volume of commuting into the city, and is identical to the difference between the level of employment and the numbers of residents in employment in Leicester.

The size of Leicester's employment surplus is a fairly minimal measure of the extent of home and workplace separation between the city and its hinterland. We can therefore divide the total number of journeys crossing Leicester's boundary into two elements – the *imbalanced component* (or imbalance for short) of 20,000 which is identical to Leicester's employment surplus, and the *balanced component* (or balance for short) of 16,000 which consists of the whole of the daily flow from Leicester plus a conceptually equal flow in the reverse direction. The relative size of these two components can be regarded as measures of the relative importance of home and workplace separation on the one hand, and mobility on the other, in making for journeys to and from Leicester.

The size of the imbalanced component, because it reflects the spatial distribution of employment relative to population, is a matter of land use. Changes over time in the size of this component can be used to tell us things about what sort of buildings are being put up or pulled down in Leicester, and how the use of buildings is changing. But the size of the balanced component does not depend primarily upon the pattern of development. It depends mainly upon the cost and ease of travel in and out of Leicester and upon individual attitudes to the cost of travel and the time spent travelling.

Like all statistical classifications the distinction between the imbalanced and balanced components is based upon a fairly arbitrarily-drawn dividing line. The size of the imbalanced component was described as a fairly minimal measure of separation because only the aggregate number of jobs and residents in employment were considered. When we disaggregate by type of job and type of person we shall find that home and workplace separation is a more complex and important factor than the simple aggregative measure suggested. For example the separation of home and workplace for managers who work in the city, but live in small villages many miles away, is much greater than for the factory workers. But in disaggregating in this kind of way we would be involved in making much more complex statements about land use and mobility. For the moment we shall examine changes at the simplest level.

THE CREATION OF DORMITORIES

Let us stay with our Leicester example. A decade later, in 1961, the number of people travelling daily from places outside to work in Leicester had

Table 9.4

JOURNEYS TO WORK IN LEICESTER 1951 AND 1961

Type of journey etc.	1951	1961	Change 1951–61	
	thousands		thousands	percentage
Journeys crossing boundary				
Workers resident outside	28·5	46·9	18·4	65
Residents working outside	7·7	10·3	2·5	32
Imbalanced component	20·7	36·6	15·9	77
Balanced component	15·5	20·5	5·0	32
Total crossing journeys	36·2	57·1	20·9	58
Journeys within Leicester ('local' journeys)	138·6	129·7	−9·0	−7
Employment and population in Leicester				
Employment	167·1	176·5	9·4	6
Residents in employment	146·4	139·9	6·5	−4

Notes: The imbalanced *component* is a measure of Leicester's employment surplus which is defined as identical to the net daily inflow of commuters. The balanced component is the difference between the gross and net flows across Leicester's boundary and is identical to twice the daily outflow.

Totals, differences, and percentages have been calculated before rounding.

The figures for employment, residents in employment, and journeys local to Leicester, classify residents with no fixed workplace or with workplace not stated, as if they worked in Leicester.

Sources: Census, 1951, *Report on Usual Residence and Workplace*. Census, 1951, *Industry Tables*. Census, 1961, Workplace Tables.

increased by 18,000, but the flow in the reverse direction increased by less than 3,000. When the changes are re-expressed in terms of the imbalanced and balanced components (shown in Table 9.4) the contrast is even more marked. The separation of home and workplace, as measured by the imbalance between the levels of employment and population, has been the dominant factor in the growth of journeys crossing Leicester's boundary. The imbalance accounted for four-fifths of the total increase in crossing journeys. The balanced movement increased by just under a third in the ten years, while the imbalance increased by more than three-quarters.

Over this decade the urban concentration we call Leicester spilled over its administrative boundaries into the neighbouring urban and rural districts. But it has not spilled over evenly; some activities have spilled over more than others. Journeys to work have overspilled most – the number of journeys with both origins and destinations in Leicester had actually fallen. Leicester's resident population decreased by 12,000 and the city lost about 25,000 residents through migration over this decade. Of the three activities which we are presently considering, the overspill of employment was least. We do not have figures for *natural increase* or *migration* for employment as we do for population. But employment in Leicester increased by only 6 per cent over the decade; this is rather less than the national increase, so that it seems likely that there has been *some* decentralization of employment.

The result of these trends has been the creation of new dormitory suburbs in the hinterland of Leicester. These dormitory areas vary considerably in character. They include developments of a purely suburban type which appear to be nothing but an extension of the built-up area of Leicester. They include developments which are part of small satellite urban concentrations like Oadby and Wigston. And they include freestanding villages situated some miles away from the edge of the built-up area of Leicester. Many of these areas have historic centres and are provided with quite a variety of facilities like shops, and a certain amount of employment. But there is one characteristic which is shared by nearly all the areas situated in the ring of between say four and fourteen miles around Leicester. They have over this decade become more and more dormitory areas for the city itself.

The trends in and around Leicester are not atypical of those occurring in other parts of Britain over the 1951–61 decade, nor of the trends throughout the country before and after this ten-year period. There is decentralization of the resident population from every historic urban concentration. The density of nearly all dwellings built before the First World War already seem an anachronism to many families with such space-demanding possessions as children and motor cars. In addition there is the long-term trend of falling occupancy rates in terms of persons per room which is evidenced in the rates for all types of household.

But employment, even where it has decentralized, has not decentralized at as rapid a pace as the residential population. One of the main features of the urban growth trends over the last two decades, and probably over a much longer period as well, is the increasing radial separation of home and workplace.

This increasing separation occurs at different scales in urban concentrations of different size. The Greater London conurbation for example was a net daily importer of 100,000 workers as early as 1921. By 1961 the employment surplus had increased to more than 300,000, and there was a further increase of more than 30,000 over the five-year period 1961–6 (Table 9.5).

The balanced movement of journeys to work across the boundaries of the

London conurbation has also been increasing for a long time. But this movement is smaller in magnitude than the net inward flow. And the increases have been smaller in proportionate as well as absolute terms than the increase in the employment surplus: over 1951–61 for example, 137,000 or 80 per cent. In the same period the balanced component of crossing journeys (equal to twice the outward flow) increased by only about 20,000 or 12 per cent. The figures show that few people stay living in London if they have a job outside.

Table 9.5

JOURNEYS TO WORK IN LONDON CONURBATION 1921–1966

Type of journey etc.	1921	1951	1961*	1961*	1966*
			thousands		
Journeys crossing conurbation boundary					
Imbalanced component (net inward flow)	105	172	309	321	348
Balanced component	n.a.	142–56†	177	n.a.	223
Total crossing journeys	n.a.	314–28†	486	n.a.	570
Journeys within London	n.a.	3,866–73†	4,086	n.a.	3,864
Employment and population in the conurbation					
Employment	3,607	4,288	4,449	4,378	4,323
Residents in employment	3,502	4,116	4,140	4,057	3,975

Notes: * The first set of figures for 1961 relate to the conurbation as defined by the GRO prior to the creation of the Greater London Council. The second set, and the figures for 1966 relate to the GLC area. The 1961 figures are not adjusted for bias, nor are the 1966 figures adjusted for under-enumeration.

† The tabulations on which these figures are based do not include flows between local authority areas of less than 25 persons and it is therefore impossible to specify these figures exactly.

Sources: Census, 1951, *Report on Greater London and Five Other Conurbations* and *Industry Tables*. PEP, 'London's New Towns', *Planning* No. 510, Apr. 1961 and 1966, *Workplace Tables*.

The counterpart to the imbalance between employment and population in London as a whole is the imbalance in the rest of South-East England. As the employment surplus in London has increased so has the employment deficit in the surrounding region. For the 1966 Census the General Register Office delineated the Outer Metropolitan Area which forms an annulus about twenty miles thick around the Greater London Council area. Perhaps the most important single characteristic of this ring is that it is a dormitory for those who, because of their place of work can be called Londoners. In 1966 more than one in every six of the resident occupied population of the Outer Metropolitan Area commuted to London for work.

But by the time the Outer Metropolitan Area was delineated it was already becoming out of date. In 1966 there were nearly 450,000 daily journeys to work in London from other areas. Just under 400,000 of these came from the Outer Metropolitan Area. The remainder of just over 64,000 came from places beyond.

The county of Berkshire is fairly typical of the areas of rapid growth in the region surrounding London. Over the period 1951–66 the population of Berkshire increased from 403,000 to 568,000, more than 40 per cent. Most of this growth is attributable to London. Over the five-year period 1961–66, for example, the net migration flow from London to Berkshire amounted to 18,500. Employment has also decentralized from London to Berkshire. But the growth of employment was not quite as fast as population. The overall employment deficit in Berkshire increased from a little under 10,000 in 1951 to 22,000 in 1966.

The changes in the pattern of journeys to work associated with this rapid growth are shown in Table 9.6. All journeys with origins or destinations in the

Table 9.6

JOURNEYS TO WORK IN BERKSHIRE 1951, 1961 AND 1966

Type of journey etc.	1951	1961 thousands	1966	Change 1951–66 thousands	Change 1951–66 percentage
Journeys crossing local authority boundaries					
Imbalanced component	14·6	27·5	36·5	21·9	150·5
Balanced component	54·5	80·8	98·1	43·6	80·0
Total crossing journeys	69·0	108·2	134·5	65·5	94·9
Local journeys	127·7	145·3	159·2	31·4	24·6
Employment and population in Berkshire					
Employment	172·6	216·3	244·6	71·9	41·6
Residents in employment	182·3	229·9	266·8	84·5	46·4

Sources: As for Table 9.4.

county have been classified under one of three headings similar to those used in Tables 9.4 and 9.5. Journeys with both an origin and destination in the same local authority area are counted as *local* journeys. Journeys crossing one or more local authority boundary are divided into their imbalanced and balanced components. The imbalance is a measure of home and workplace separation in the county. The size of the balance is an indication of mobility.

In 1951 nearly two-thirds of all journeys with origins or destinations in the county began and ended in the same local authority area as they started. Berkshire was very much an area of self-contained towns and villages with only a small proportion of long-distance commuters. In view of the rapid growth of population it is perhaps surprising that fifteen years later more than half of journeys to work were still local in character. But in proportionate terms the growth of longer distance commuting has been dramatic. Over 1951–66 journeys crossing local authority boundaries in the county increased at nearly four times the rate of local journeys.

In 1951 only just over one-fifth of crossing journeys were attributable to the separation of places of employment from residential areas in the county. Although Berkshire was already a dormitory area for London, long-distance commuters represented only a small proportion of the total population, and otherwise there was a close balance between the levels of employment and population in the towns and villages of the county. Again, in view of the rapid growth of population, it is perhaps surprising that fifteen years later the separation of places of employment from residential areas still accounted for only a little over a quarter of crossing journeys. But in proportionate terms increasing separation of this kind has been dramatic. Over 1951–66 the imbalance between the levels of employment and population increased at nearly twice the rate of the balanced movement.

There are two quite distinct reasons for this growing imbalance. The most important element is the increase in the overall employment deficit in Berkshire. Over this fifteen-year period the county became more of a dormitory area for London – to the tune of 12,000 more residents in employment relative to the employment level. The smaller element is the growth of dormitory areas for the centres of employment in Berkshire itself. The employment which moved to or expanded in Berkshire is not all in the areas of rapid population growth. Much of it went to the existing employment centres. Employment recentralized rather than decentralized to the county. Employment in Reading for example increased by 17,000 over the fifteen-year period, but the resident population was already spilling over into the surrounding countryside and spawning new suburbs in the contiguous Rural Districts of Bradfield, Henley and Wokingham.

Let us look at the trends in an area of totally different character – the West Riding of Yorkshire (Table 9.7). This is a county containing several large cities which are fairly generously bounded by their administrative area. The West Riding is the only major urbanized area of Britain without any planned overspill schemes. Unlike Berkshire the West Riding is an area of only slow growth. Over 1951–66 employment in the county increased by only 4 per cent, not 40 per cent as in Berkshire. The West Riding is also a much larger county in every dimension. It covers an area of 2,800 square miles. It has a population of more than three and a half million. And it contains more than a hundred local authority areas.

The dominance of several large cities in the county – Leeds, Sheffield, Bradford, Huddersfield – and the fact that they are fairly generously bounded by their administrative areas means that a high proportion of journeys to work in the county are 'local' in the sense in which we have used the word. Many of the journeys lumped under this heading are relatively long in terms of time and distance. In 1951 nearly four-fifths of journeys in the county originated and ended in the same area. Over 1951–66 the number of journeys of this kind actually declined – by 63,000 or nearly 5 per cent.

By contrast the number of crossing journeys increased by 141,000 or more than a third. And as in Berkshire the rate of increase of the separation of places of employment from residential areas increased at nearly twice the rate of the balanced component of crossing journeys. All of this increase in the imbalance was attributable to the nine County Boroughs in the Riding. Leeds' employment surplus increased by 12,000, Sheffield's by 24,000. These

Table 9.7

JOURNEYS TO WORK IN THE WEST RIDING OF YORKSHIRE 1951, 1961 AND 1966

Type of journey etc.	1951	1961 thousands	1966	Change 1951–66 thousands	Change 1951–66 percentage
Journeys crossing local authority boundaries					
Imbalanced component	109	150	169	60	55·3
Balanced component	276	322	357	80	29·1
Total crossing journeys	385	472	526	141	36·5
Local journeys	1,317	1,284	1,254	−63	−4·8
Employment and population in the West Riding					
Employment	1,682	1,726	1,751	69	4·1
Residents in employment	1,672	1,707	1,726	54	3·2

Sources: As for Table 9.4.

two cities alone accounted for more than half of the county's total increase in the separation of home and workplace. The resident population of both of these cities has fallen, but the employment level in both has increased.

Let us change the scale of our analysis once more. One of the problems in using data for local authority areas is that the boundaries were mostly established many years ago and are now fairly arbitrarily drawn with respect to the concentrations of employment, population and patterns of journeys to work. We do have one set of boundaries which were not fixed mainly by administrative fiat, but were intended to encompass the very largest continuously built-up areas of Britain. We have already examined the journeys crossing the boundary of the London conurbation. Figure 9.2 presents some of the same data for the other four conurbations in our main areas of study. (We use the official names for these conurbations which have been carefully selected to avoid giving offence to the smaller local authority area which they include. In fact Merseyside is dominated by Liverpool, South-East

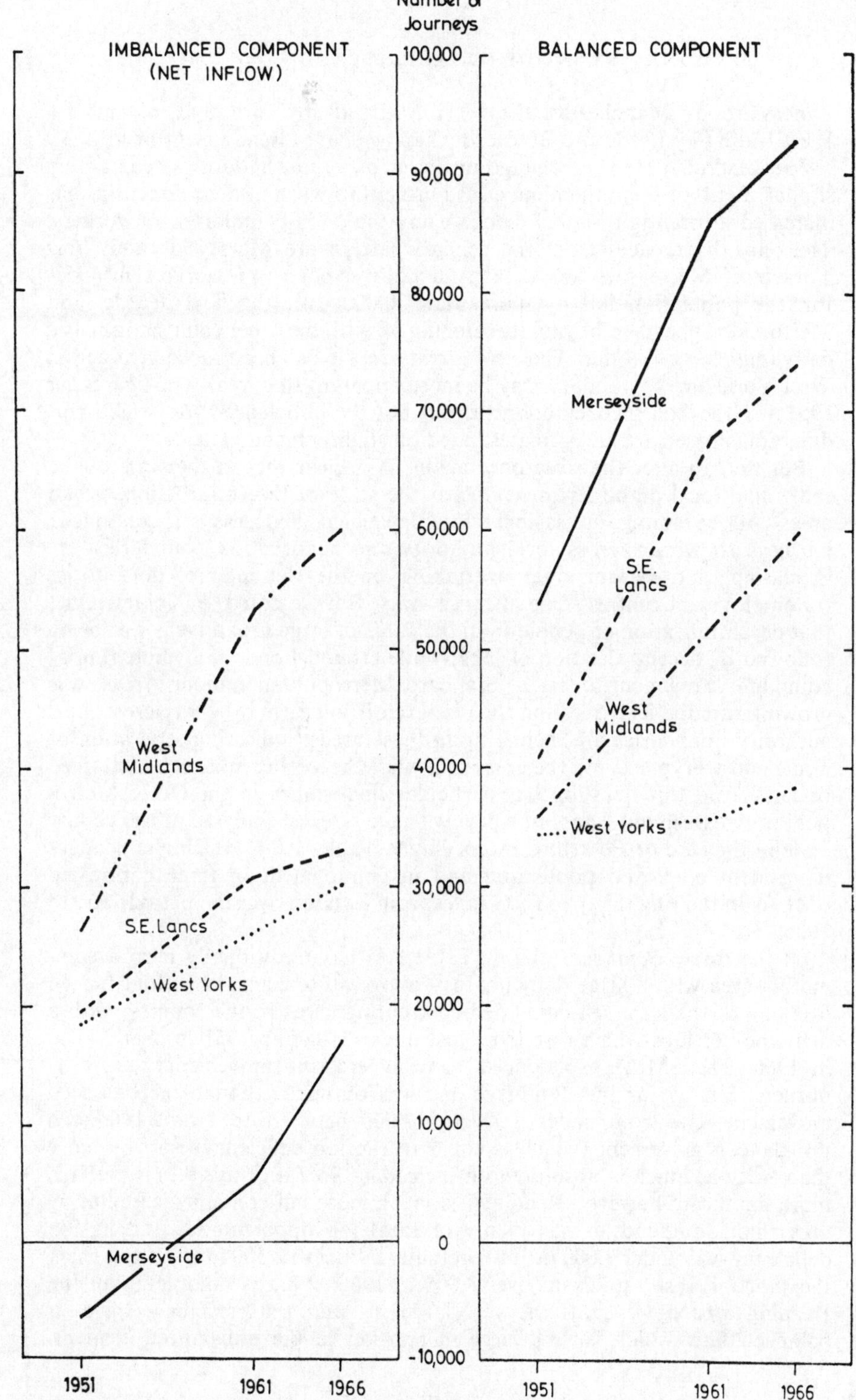

Figure 9.2 Journeys to Work Crossing the Conurbation Boundary in 1951, 1961 and 1966: Merseyside, South-East Lancashire, West Midlands and West Yorkshire

Lancashire by Manchester, the West Midlands by Birmingham, and the West Riding by Leeds and Bradford which we have already mentioned.)

The general pattern of change in these four conurbations is remarkably similar. In all of them the number of journeys to work in both directions has increased substantially. All of them are now major daily importers of workers. The only divergences from the general pattern are Merseyside and West Yorkshire. Merseyside was actually a daily exporter of workers in 1951. But the population fell by more than 30,000 over the next decade, and Merseyside appears to be rapidly catching up with the other conurbations as a daily importer of labour. The slow growth in the balanced movement across West Yorkshire's boundary may be more apparent than real. The figures for 1951 for the balanced component (but not the imbalanced) on which this diagram is based are all estimates based on slightly incomplete data.

But we can alter the scale once again. It is clear that at the scale of the individual local authority areas and at the scale of the conurbation, urban areas are becoming increasingly interdependent and less self-contained: journeys to work, across local authority and conurbation boundaries, are increasing, and certain areas are taking on the character of dormitories for employment centres some distance away. But we noted, in Volume One, that decentralization of people from the cores of large urban areas was being followed by decentralization of jobs; while around London, a whole ring of commuter catchment areas, or Standard Metropolitan Labour Areas, was growing rapidly. The question then is: even if journeys to work across local authority boundaries are increasing in these areas, indicating separation of home and workplace, are the areas as a whole becoming more self-contained or less? And this question has particular importance in the Outer Metropolitan Area around London, which we have already analysed at the county scale in the case of Berkshire. Accordingly, Tables 9.8–9.10 analyse changes in resident employed population and in employment in three contrasted SMLAs in the ring thirty to forty miles from London over the period 1951 to 1966.

Of the three, *Southend SMLA* (Table 9.8) has traditionally been a commuting area with a large daily net loss, above all to central London. Indeed it is one of the least self-contained commuting areas in the country, with a deficiency of jobs which rose from just under 21,000 in 1951 to over 33,000 in 1966. The SMLA experienced very big crossing movements across its borders, but by far the dominant one was outward; though the balanced movement rose from under 5,000 to 10,000 between 1951 and 1966, the unbalanced movement (which is equal to the job deficiency) rose by more than twice as much in absolute terms. *Reading SMLA* (Table 9.9) is perhaps more significant however. Reading is a much more self-contained commuting area than Southend; it has plenty of local job opportunities and its job deficiency was under 3,000 in 1951, actually falling to 2,500 in 1961. But then, the shortfall rose rapidly to over 8,000 in 1966. What is notable about the Reading area however, is the very large in- and out-movements give a balanced flow which is very large in relation to the unbalanced element.

And the increase in the balanced flow, over the fifteen-year period, was much bigger than the increase in the unbalanced flow. In this sense, Reading is intermediate between Southend and *Stevenage* (Table 9.10). The Stevenage SMLA clearly shows the effect of the establishment of a new town with its own range of job opportunities; of the three examples, it was the only

Table 9.8

SOUTHEND SMLA: RESIDENT LABOUR FORCE, EMPLOYMENT AND COMMUTING FLOWS 1951, 1961 AND 1966

	Resident labour force	Employment	Deficiency of employment	Total commuter movements*	of which: Balanced flow*	Unbalanced flow*
1951	82,706	61,737	20,969	25,633	4,664	20,969
1961	102,710	73,230	29,480	37,660	8,180	29,480
1966	118,640	84,970	33,670	43,670	10,000	33,670

Table 9.9

READING SMLA: RESIDENT LABOUR FORCE, EMPLOYMENT AND COMMUTING FLOWS 1951, 1961 AND 1966

	Resident labour force	Employment	Deficiency of employment	Total commuter movements*	of which: Balanced flow*	Unbalanced flow*
1951	93,296	90,314	2,982	14,732	11,750	2,982
1961	109,580	107,110	2,470	25,490	23,020	2,470
1966	129,690	121,430	8,260	32,260	24,000	8,260

Table 9.10

STEVENAGE SMLA: RESIDENT LABOUR FORCE, EMPLOYMENT AND COMMUTING FLOWS 1951, 1961 AND 1966

	Resident labour force	Employment	Deficiency of employment	Total commuter movements*	of which: Balanced flow*	Unbalanced flow*
1951	25,657	20,551	5,106	11,272	6,166	5,106
1961	45,810	39,270	6,540	17,920	11,380	6,540
1966	54,690	49,950	4,740	22,480	17,740	4,740

* Across the outer cordon of the Standard Metropolitan Labour Area; internal flows across local authority boundaries are ignored in these three tables.
Source: Censuses.

commuting area where the job deficiency actually declined over the period. What is remarkable though is that this was accompanied by a large increase – a doubling in fact – of total commuter movements in and out. The balanced flow was growing while the unbalanced flow was falling. Thus in net terms the establishment of the new town at Stevenage increased the self-sufficiency;

but in gross terms, as the new town grew it led both to more out-movements and more in-movements.

WHITE COLLAR AND BLUE COLLAR – A MOMENT OF TIME PICTURE

The aggregate pattern of journeys to work, and the changes in this pattern, which were described in the preceding section, conceal distinct sub-patterns of centrifugal migration. The dominant feature of these sub-patterns is that the degree and rate of decentralization is different for different types of worker and for different types of employment. A large proportion of the decentralization movement of residential population comprises white-collar workers. But the main decentralization movement of employment comprises jobs in factories. The major part of centripetal journeys to work – the imbalanced component – and increases in the number of journeys of this kind, consists of people going to work in offices.

The white-collar dormitory suburb is a familiar concept, and the growth of communities of this sort has long been associated with the successful search for space by those with above-average incomes. But it is oversimplification to think of the trends in urban growth as merely the reflection of inequalities in the distribution of income. The new dormitories are often white collar in their social composition, but they include members of below-average as well as members of above-average income groups, and the number of these communities is as much the product of the conditions of the housing market and of the location of employment, as it is of incomes and preferences.

Before we go on to analyse the ways in which this pattern is changing, let us take a snap shot at a particular point of time – 24 April 1966 – the date of the Census of population in that year. The date is appropriate for a picture of a society in a state of transition. At that time just a little under half of the households of England and Wales owned their own home and just a little under half possessed a private motor car.

Let us start with the 570,000 journeys which cross the London boundary every day. Table 9.11 summarizes some of the characteristics of these journeys. About one in every seven of the inward journeys originate in places outside the Outer Metropolitan Area which forms an annulus twenty miles in depth around Greater London itself. Four in every ten of the inward journeys originate in the OMA but have destinations in Central London fifteen or more miles away. Of all inward journeys, at least six in every ten are at least fifteen miles in length.

The relative importance for different socio-economic groups of the radial home and workplace separation on the one hand, and mobility on the other, can be measured by using the tools developed in the earlier sections of this chapter. Journeys crossing London's boundary can be divided into their imbalanced and balanced components for each group. In the case of London there is an employment surplus for every socio-economic group distinguished by the General Register Office, or, in other words, London is a net daily importer of every kind of labour. We can compare different socio-economic groups most easily by looking at the net inflow in proportionate terms. For this purpose *indices of home – workplace separation* have been computed by dividing the imbalance by the sum of employment and residents in employment in the conurbation, and expressing the result as a percentage (Figure 9.3).

These indices show that the degree of home and workplace separation for managerial and professional workers is greater than for any other social group and is nearly three times the average for all social groups. If anything these indices understate the contrast between managerial and professional workers and other socio-economic groups because they relate only to journeys

Table 9.11

SOME CHARACTERISTICS OF JOURNEYS TO WORK CROSSING LONDON'S BOUNDARY 1966

	Thousands of journeys
Geographical breakdown	
From outside Outer Metropolitan Area to GLC Area	64
From OMA to Central London	186
From OMA to GLC area excluding Central London	209
All inward journeys	459
All outward journeys	111
Breakdown by main means of transport	
Inward journeys	
by train	242
by bus	31
by private motor vehicle	173
by foot	5
other	8
Outward journeys	
by public transport	41
by private motor vehicle	62
by foot	3
other (including not stated)	5

Source: Census 1966.

crossing London's boundary. In fact, a higher proportion of managerial and professional people than any other group have the very longest journeys, travelling from places outside the Outer Metropolitan Area, and travelling to central London rather than the outer parts of the conurbation. The stereotype of the London commuter with *The Times* under the arm, a bowler on the head, and a tightly-rolled umbrella in the hand, may be sartorially dated. But it does capture a very important aspect of metropolitan life.

The degree of home and workplace separation is also above average for

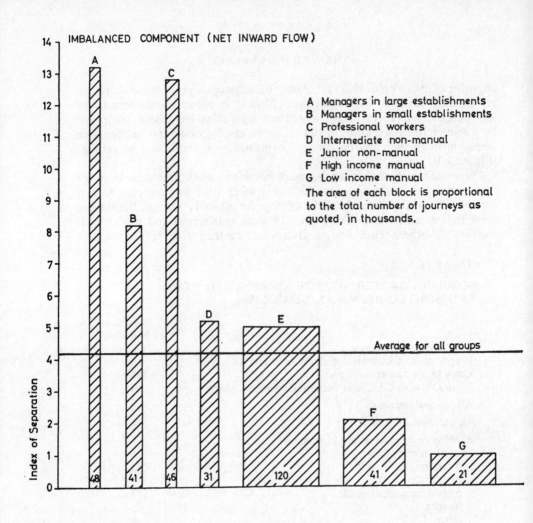

IMBALANCED COMPONENT (NET INWARD FLOW)

A Managers in large establishments
B Managers in small establishments
C Professional workers
D Intermediate non-manual
E Junior non-manual
F High income manual
G Low income manual

The area of each block is proportional to the total number of journeys as quoted, in thousands.

Average for all groups

Index of Separation

14 13 12 11 10 9 8 7 6 5 4 3 2 1 0

A 48 B 41 C 46 D 31 E 120 F 41 G 21

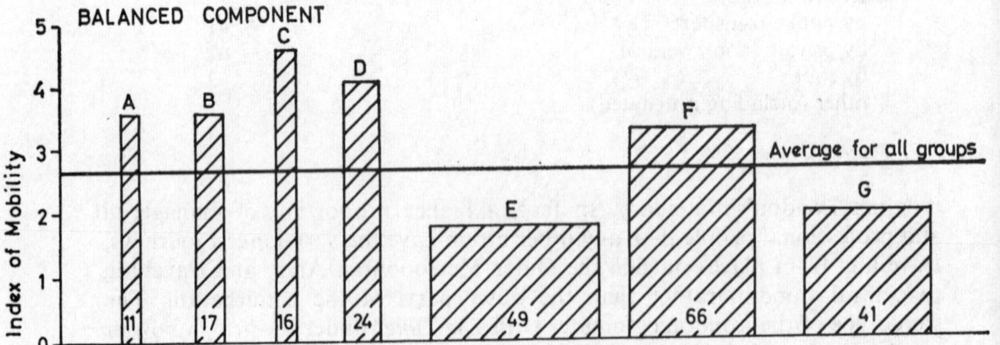

Figure 9.3 Journeys to Work Crossing Greater London Boundary in 1966, by Socio-Economic Group

other white-collar workers. And in numerical terms these low-income non-manual workers are more important than managers and professionals. The net inflow of low-income white-collar workers to London is just over 150,000 as compared with 134,000 for their high-income managerial and professional colleagues. There are more clerks, minor civil servants, secretaries and receptionists, cashiers and comptometer operators, shop assistants and shorthand typists, living outside and working inside London than the people who direct their work.

The degree of home and workplace separation is less than half the average for those whom we shall call *high-income manual workers* – skilled manual workers, foremen and supervisors, and own account workers (other than professional); and the separation is least for those who we shall call *low-income manual workers* – semi and unskilled manual, and personal service workers. London is a net daily importer of a little over 60,000 members of both of these groups of manual workers. Although the two groups account for half of employment in the capital, the net daily imports account for only one-sixth of the total.

There are both similarities and important differences between the composition of the net daily inward flow to London and the balanced movement across London's boundary. The most striking contrast is in the relative proportions of white-collar and manual workers. Manual workers account for only one sixth of the net flow to London, but they account for nearly one half of the flow in the other direction.

More light is thrown on the situation when we examine the size of the balanced component for each socio-economic group in proportionate terms. The relative volume of the balance of commuting across London's boundaries is shown in Figure 9.3 in terms of *indices of mobility* which are calculated in a similar way to the indices of separation in the upper part of the figure. Just as the degree of home and workplace separation is greatest for managerial, professional workers, and intermediate non-manual workers, so is the flow of journeys in the other direction greater for members of these groups than for any other. These earners of relatively-high incomes, it seems, tend to have longer journeys to work whether they live in London or outside.

The position of junior non-manual workers and high-income workers with regard to mobility are the reverse of their positions with regard to separation. The proportion of journeys to London by junior non-manual workers is above average, but the proportion of journeys from London is below average. The proportion of journeys to London by high-income manual workers is below average, but the proportion of journeys from London is above average.

These contrasts throw light on some of the fascinating interactions between urban structure and life style. It seems unlikely that those classified by the General Register Office as junior non-manual workers earn more than those whom we have labelled as high-income manual workers, and most of them probably earn much less. But the evidence presented here suggests that junior non-manual workers have the longer journeys, and a much higher proportion are centripetal in nature – from places outside the continuously built-up area of London into its core. Something like 100,000 of these white-collar workers spend £2 a week or more on a season ticket. A good proportion of the high-income manual workers probably spend about the same amount using their own vehicle for the journey to work.

Car ownership for low-income manual workers is lower than that for any other groups we distinguish in these diagrams (Table 9.12), and this fact

Table 9.12

HOME AND CAR OWNERSHIP IN ENGLAND AND WALES FOR SELECTED SOCIO-ECONOMIC GROUPS 1966

SEG No.	Socio-Economic Group of chief economic supporter	Number of households thousands	House ownership percentages	Car ownership percentages
1	Managers in large establishments	608	74·7	78·5
2	Managers in small establishments	943	70·6	78·2
3 and 4	Professional workers	586	75·3	82·9
5	Intermediate non-manual	550	65·0	62·2
6	Junior non-manual	1,976	53·8	46·8
8, 9 and 12	High-income manual	4,884	43·8	50·5
7, 10 and 11	Low-income manual	3,457	30·0	25·6
13–17	Other groups (mostly farmers and agricultural workers)	778	39·1	54·9
	Economically inactive	1,373	41·5	9·2
	All groups	15,359	46·7	49·2

Notes: The proportion of those in employment who are heads of households varies from one group to another mainly in accordance with the sex ratio. The proportion of those in employment who are female is highest for junior non-manual workers.

The figures for house ownership refer to the proportion of owner occupiers. Car ownership is measured in terms of the proportion of households owning one or more cars.

Source: Census, 1966.

is reflected in the low proportion of journeys from London as well as to London. But whereas the proportion of journeys to the capital is only one quarter of the average for all groups, the proportion of journeys from London is only a little below the average, and is actually a little above that for junior non-manual workers. Although there is a net inflow of low-income manual workers into London, the size of the inflow is lower relative to the outflow than for any other group. This is partly the reflection of the fact that in spite of the success of London's planned overspill schemes, as the GLC itself says: 'it was always the least fortunate members of the community who were left

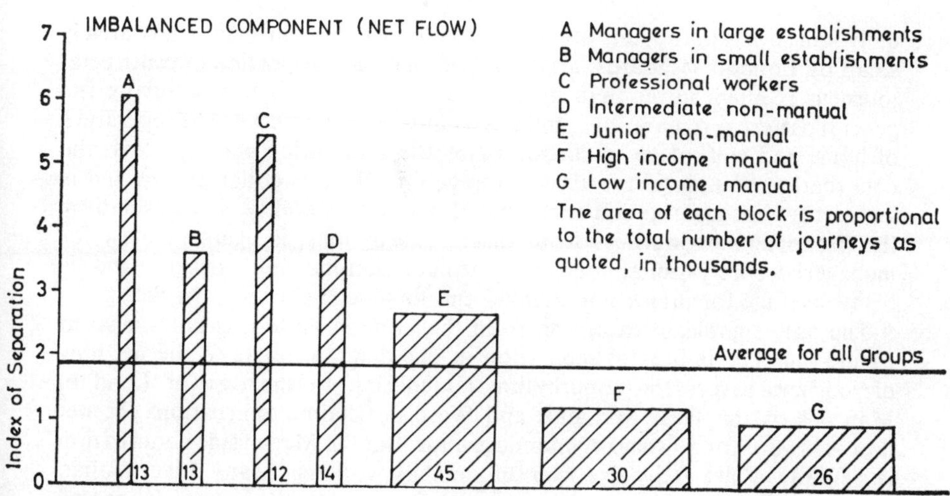

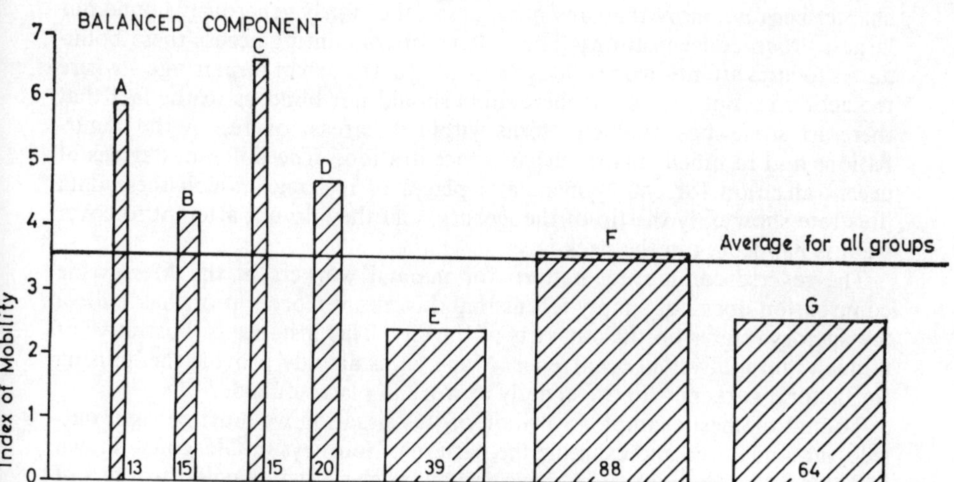

Figure 9.4 Journeys to Work Crossing Boundaries of Merseyside, South-East Lancashire, West Midlands and West Yorkshire Conurbations in 1966, by Socio-Economic Group

behind in the old centres'.[8] It is a point to which we shall return later in this chapter.

This pattern of living and working by members of different socio-economic groups is not something peculiar to the London conurbation. The number of

[8] Greater London Council, *Tomorrow's London – A Background to the Greater London Development Plan*. The Council, London (1969), p. 25.

daily journeys into the four other conurbations within our main study area is small by London standards, and in all of them the proportion of centripetal journeys is much lower than in the case of the capital. But otherwise the general pattern is remarkably similar – as shown by Figure 9.4. The separation of home and workplace, as illustrated by the commuting pattern across the conurbation boundaries, is above average for all white-collar groups and is greatest for managerial and professional workers. Mobility, as measured by the proportion of journeys from these conurbations, is again greatest for managerial, professional, and intermediate non-manual workers, and is below average for junior non-manual and low-income manual workers.

The only significant exception from the London pattern is not shown in Figure 9.4. The indices of separation in this diagram relate to the net flow of journeys across the conurbation boundaries. In the case of London, Manchester, the West Midlands and West Yorkshire conurbations the net flow is inward for all socio-economic groups. But the Merseyside conurbation is actually a net daily exporter of manual workers. Many Liverpudlian manual workers travel to work outside the city and outside the area delineated as the conurbation, to work in places like Kirkby to the east.

We have used the conurbations as units of analysis in this part of the chapter because, more than any other areas, they fairly generously bound our largest urban concentrations. The pattern of commuting across these boundaries focuses attention on what is happening at the urban rural fringe – where the action is. But the use of these units should not blind us to the fact that there are somewhat similar patterns within the areas covered by the conurbations and in much smaller urban concentrations. The different degrees of decentralization for employment and places of residence which these data illustrate show only the tip of the iceberg, and they do not attempt to cover what is happening in the pack ice.

The reverse commuting pattern for manual workers in the Merseyside conurbation does not simply tell us that Liverpool Corporation has built a few factory estates on the outskirts of the city. This instance is illustrative of a much more universal occurrence. Many cities already provide the housing for factory workers who travel daily to work in places outside.

To find the best example in Britain of this situation we must go right outside our study area and examine the pattern of journeys in Glasgow – shown in Table 9.13. Glasgow is a massive daily importer of white-collar workers of all kinds. The net inward flow of non-manual workers is more than 50,000. But there is a substantial flow in the other direction for all the major categories of manual workers. Glasgow's net exports of skilled, semiskilled and unskilled manual workers amount to more than 12,000. Most of this flow is composed of the low-income manual workers – the semi and unskilled.

The unusual and extreme situation of housing in Scotland has a lot to do with this commuting pattern. The problems of England's conurbations and major cities – old and substandard housing and low rents – are writ large in the Glasgow region. But a number of cities in England of varying size do have similar features in the commuting pattern. Manchester and Birmingham, for example, are large daily importers of every kind of labour except unskilled manual workers for whom the flow is in the other direction. Bradford, Bristol, Chester and Gloucester are all major employment centres but daily net exporters of semi and unskilled manual workers. Brighton and Hull are net exporters of all kinds of manual workers.

These net flows in and out of urban concentrations are the product of the location by type of employment and residential population. Most kinds of employment are more centralized than most kinds of people in their homes. But the general picture which emerges is that there is a fairly clear hierarchy by type of employment and by type of person in accordance with the degree

Table 9.13

EMPLOYMENT IMBALANCE IN GLASGOW 1966, BY SOCIO-ECONOMIC GROUP

SEG No.	Socio-economic Group	Imbalance thousands	Index of separation
1–4	Managerial and professional workers	+19·0	+24·3
5 and 6	Intermediate and junior non-manual workers	+33·7	+11·2
9	Skilled manual workers	−2·0	−0·9
10	Semiskilled manual workers	−6·6	−5·4
11	Unskilled manual workers	−3·9	−4·0
7, 8, 12–17	All other groups	+2·8	+3·7
	All groups	+43·0	+6·9

Notes: A positive sign indicates net inward commuting, a negative sign a net outward flow.

The breakdown given does not correspond to that of *high-income* and *low-income* manual workers as given in Figures 9.2 and 9.3 which include foremen and supervisors, own account workers, personal service workers. The net flow of commuting for all three of the latter groups is inward.

Source: Census, Scotland, 1966.

of decentralization and centralization. Table 9.14 sketches out such a hierarchy. For population it runs, going from most decentralized to least decentralized, almost in terms of descending income. But there seems to be a departure from this pattern in that white-collar workers tend to live at more decentralized locations than manual workers of similar income levels. The hierarchy for employment is more speculative. In general primary and extractive industries are most decentralized. Secondary industry is not so decentralized, and it seems likely that heavy manufacturing is generally more decentralized than light. Trading retail and wholesale is highly centralized. And there is little doubt that the most centralized employment of all is in the large office blocks which are the distinguishing feature of every central business district.

WHITE COLLAR AND BLUE COLLAR – THE TRENDS

Other things being equal the available evidence suggests that the price of land for residential building, and the price of houses for sale, decrease with distance from the centre of our major cities. In practice of course other things are never equal – especially in the case of housing. As distance from the centre increases the stock of housing gets newer, the gardens get bigger, and so does the general density of most kinds of non-housing development decrease.

The centrifugal decay of urban densities with distance from the centre is one of the most widely-observed urban phenomena. And it gives us the clue as to why house prices fall in the same kind of way. The closer to the centre,

Table 9.14

POPULATION AND EMPLOYMENT GROUPINGS IN ORDER OF DEGREE OF DECENTRALIZATION/CENTRALIZATION

	Population	Employment
Most decentralized	Professional workers	Extractive industry
	Managers in large establishments	Construction
	Managers in small establishments	Heavy manufacturing
	Intermediate non-manual workers	Vehicle manufacturing
	Junior non-manual workers	Engineering
	Foreman and supervisors manual	Light manufacturing
	Skilled manual workers	Shops
	Semiskilled manual workers	Warehouses
Least decentralized	Unskilled manual workers	Offices

the more accessible is a site to all kinds of urban facilities – jobs, shops, cinemas and churches, bingo halls and theatres. It is people's need to be near to amenities of these kinds which creates the unrequited demand for accommodation in all our major cities.

It might be expected from this pattern of development that those who earn the highest incomes would occupy residentially the more expensive sites in terms of cost per acre close to city centres. In fact this does not often happen. It is true that in most major cities there are exclusive residential areas close to the centre. But in general it is clear from the analysis already made that members of higher income groups tend to live at more decentralized locations. The curious paradox of urban structure is that most members of below-average wealth and income live on the most expensive land, and most of those with relatively high incomes live on cheaper land.

This paradox is mostly the product of the way in which housing is spatially distributed according to its age. The newer housing is on the periphery of the existing built-up area of the city or part of a village or town in the city's hinterland. The most accessible sites are already crowded with houses. Each wave of new housing is built on less accessible sites than the previous wave.

It is often asserted that those with few skills and below-average income need to live near to the core of our major urban concentrations because they can only afford short journeys to work and because they need choice in the labour market. But the only evidence usually cited to support this assertion is that those with low incomes do in fact live in the twilight areas near to city centres where there are plenty of jobs available. The argument is circular. But what can be asserted with confidence is that those with below-average incomes cannot afford to buy a new house, or a modern house, or even an old house which commands a good price because of its accessible position. In the areas near to our city centres rent-controlled privately-rented accommodation and subsidized local authority dwellings are the means by which those with below-average incomes maintain what are widely considered as acceptable housing standards.

Conversely the new houses at the urban/rural fringe are bought by those who can afford them – who are virtually all members of above-average income groups. Members of lower-income groups do get new houses rented from local authorities but these are usually built within the area covered by the local authority and they are generally not so dispersed geographically as houses built for sale. In general those with relatively high incomes pay a high proportion of their housing costs for the house itself. Those with below-average incomes pay indirectly a higher than average proportion of their housing costs for the land on which their dwelling is situated. This is not to say that those with relatively high incomes pay less for the land on which their house is situated than those with below-average incomes. The size of house plots increases with income. Those with relatively high incomes pay less in terms of costs per acre but as much, if not more, in terms of total land costs because they live at a lower density.

Factors of this kind have been in operation for many decades, and there is nothing new in the product – radial segregation of members of relatively high-income groups from those with below-average income. Such segregation is as old as the city itself. The major new influence is the increased scale at which such segregation occurs.

The static picture presented in the previous section illustrated the degree to which this segregation had influenced the pattern of journeys to work by 1966. We can get an impression of how the pattern has changed in recent years from the data presented in Figure 9.5 which relates to the aggregate of journeys to work crossing the conurbation boundary for Merseyside, South-East Lancashire, the West Midlands and West Yorkshire in 1961 and 1966. (These kinds of data are not available for 1951. The data for 1961 and 1966 are both on a 10 per cent sample basis; large numbers are necessary in order to say something significant about changes – hence the aggregation. This type of analysis could be extended to cover London, where it would be necessary to adjust for boundary changes. And it should be extended to examine

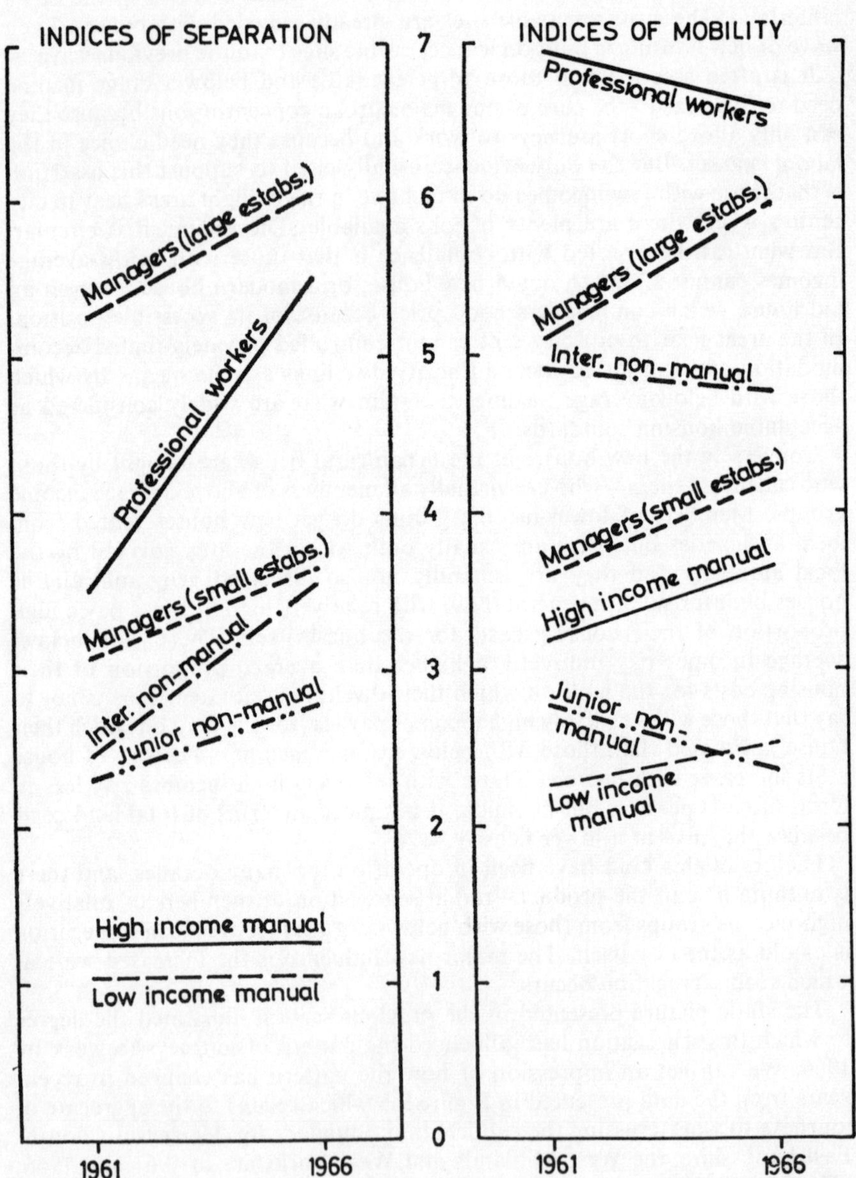

Figure 9.5 Trends in Home and Workplace Separation Measured across Boundaries of Merseyside, South-East Lancashire, West Midlands and West Yorkshire Conurbations in 1966, Disaggregated by Socio-Economic Group

changes in the pattern across the boundaries of the major cities outside the conurbation; but in this case aggregation would again be necessary in order to get significant differences.)

The most rapid change shown over 1961–66 is for professional workers. The net daily imports of professional workers into these four conurbations actually doubled in this five-year period. The radial home and workplace segregation also increased for all other white-collar groups, albeit not so dramatically. But there was no significant change as far as manual workers were concerned.

These differences can be viewed as being mostly the product of employment growth in the conurbations. The fastest-growing sector of employment in the conurbations over this period was that for professional workers. The total number of jobs increased from 95,000 to 117,000 which is the largest proportional increase for any social group. In general the employment level for all kinds of white-collar jobs in the conurbations increased, but that for manual jobs decreased.

The people appointed to these new white-collar jobs had to live somewhere. Most of the new stock of housing was built outside the conurbations, and it is hardly surprising, without even much consideration of the institutional factors in the housing market, that the radial separation of home and workplace increased most sharply for the fastest-growing groups.

But the detailed operation of these forces, making for the radial segregation of members of white-collar groups, is much affected by the housing policies followed by local authorities on the one hand, and the conditions of the market for mortgages on the other. The housing authorities of our major cities discriminate in the allocation of rented dwellings in favour of residents and in accordance with the length of time a person has been resident. There are often waiting lists for housing of several years duration. The result is that a large share of council housing is taken up by middle-aged and old people.

Mortgage companies tend to favour young couples. The younger a person, the longer the period over which the loan can be repaid. Mortgage companies do not take into account where a person comes from, nor the journey to work costs. Mortgage companies also favour the white-collar salary earner. This makes it easier for many households whose principal earner has an office job to get a mortage, than a household headed by a skilled manual worker who with overtime may be bringing home more money nearly every week.

The trends in journey to work mobility – as indicated by the proportion of journeys leaving the conurbations – are very different. The most startling changes are the apparent falls in 'mobility' for professional, intermediate non-manual, and junior non-manual workers. Again this is mostly the product of the trends in employment growth. The rapid expansion of jobs in the conurbations meant that residents in these groups had increased opportunities for employment relatively near to their homes. There is less need for them to travel outside for work.

The trends for managers provide an interesting contrast. The proportion of journeys leaving the conurbation has increased. This group is just as mobile in a real sense as any other white-collar group. But the difference is in the trends in employment locations. Although employment for managers in the conurbations has increased, the increase is much less in proportionate terms than for any other white-collar group. A lot of managerial jobs have decentralized, and many managers have kept their homes within the conurbations while travelling out to these decentralized locations.

There is nothing new in the major themes explored in this chapter. One of the main concerns of the fathers of the 1947 planning system was the growing separation of home and workplace. An associated concern was the spatial segregations of members of different social groups. These concerns were expressed in very direct form in the plans made for the new towns which form the subject matter of the next chapter.

CHAPTER TEN
THE PLANNED COMMUNITIES

This chapter examines the comprehensively-planned communities built under special legislation since the Second World War: the new towns and the expanding towns. It analyses the role of the new towns in relation to their size and siting, and tries to follow through the evolution of the concept of the new town over the quarter century after the Second World War. Then, mainly through a close analysis of the eight original Mark One new towns built to house London's overspill, it seeks to ask: how far did the new towns attain their stated objectives of being self-contained and balanced communities? The chapter then analyses the much more heterogeneous group of expanding towns built under the provisions of the 1952 Town Development Act, and reaches tentative conclusions about the success of the policy in relation to the objectives. Lastly the chapter isolates perhaps the most significant feature of the two programmes: their failure to provide more than a small minority of all the housing built in England and Wales in the postwar period. This, certainly, was not the intention of the founding fathers of British postwar planning.

This chapter was drafted by Peter Hall on the basis of earlier material by Ray Thomas and himself, with some additional material on the expanding towns.

INTRODUCTION

Most of the preceding chapters have concentrated on what has been called – for lack of a better name – the normal processes of planned development. By 'normal' we mean the most usual system of development that has taken place in England under the 1947 Planning System. As we have tried to stress, it essentially involves a complex interrelationship between three sets of actors involved in the development process: the planning authorities, the developers, and the people who will finally occupy the houses and flats that are built. None of these actors has anything like real power over the situation. The planning authorities, as we have noticed, have a limited set of powers to control physical development; they have much more limited control over the most basic forces that initiate the development pressures, in particular the growth of basic employment. And in the last resort, even their powers over physical growth are limited by political forces and by the developer's right of appeal through the inspector to the Minister. But the developer's power is similarly limited: on the one hand he must build to sell at a profit, and the costs of holding land make this a far less certain event than many laymen might suppose. This means that he must build where his public want to buy, and that may be by no means the same place as the planning authority is willing to see developed. Lastly, the public hold the purse strings – subject to control by the building societies and other mortgage agencies, of course. But, especially in the more rapidly-expanding parts of Megalopolis, their power is limited by escalating land prices. They may simply not be able to buy the house they want in the place they want at the price they can afford. Faced with this situation, because they are after all individual decision-units who cannot exert collective pressure, they will settle for the best they can. The situation more closely corresponds to the classic *laissez faire* model of price determination than to a monopolistic model. But it is far from a *laissez faire* situation that has prevailed in land development in Britain since the Second World War.

The point here is that there is an entirely different sort of development model. Though we describe the first as normal, because that is a description of historical fact, the intention of the Founding Fathers of the British planning system was fairly clear that this second type should be the normal type. We refer to the process of developing planned communities such as new towns and expanding towns. This present chapter seeks to isolate the central features which distinguish this development model from the first. It will identify the objectives of those who hoped to make this the normal mode of planning; and then seek to ask how far these objectives were realized in practice, in those developments – a small minority of the total – which were actually built under this system.

TYPES AND DEGREES OF PLANNING

We start with a basic difficulty of terminology. In what sense do we call these 'planned' communities? Are not all developments, since the historic 1947 Act, 'planned'? What is the essential difference?

To this there are several answers. The planned communities we are discussing here are essentially the new towns, built by Development Corporations under the 1946 New Towns Act, or the expanding towns built by agreement between exporting and importing authorities under the Town Development Act of 1952. At first sight it might seem that these two sets of machinery are very different. One deliberately tries to limit the role of local government in the development process, by giving the job of planning and building – in contradistinction to maintenance and provision of services – to special *ad hoc* Development Corporations, insulated to a remarkable degree from both central and local government pressures and comparable in many ways with the corporations set up to run the nationalized industries. The other deliberately encourages the maximum participation of local government in the actual development process, whether the planning and building is carried out by the exporting authority (an agency scheme) or by the importing country town (a nomination scheme). The role of the central government is essentially limited to subsidy for provision of infrastructure, such as roads and sewers, which are beyond the capacity of both authorities to supply. Yet despite these superficial differences, the essential features which distinguish these planned communities from other sorts of development are quite clear.

The first is the much more important role of the planner. Typically, both new town development corporations and the local authority offices responsible for expanding towns have big offices employing many qualified planners. These planners are responsible for almost every aspect of the development of the town. In conjunction with the Department of Trade and Industry, they exert a considerable influence on the basic industry that comes to the town. They plan – and up until recently, in most cases themselves build or contract – the residential areas. Whether area A or area B is the first to be developed, the density of housing, the relation to factories and offices – all this is something the planner will determine. There is not the same interaction between different actors as in the normal development process. Indeed, it can even be argued that in these towns the planner has taken over some of the functions of the intending resident. For the Industrial Selection Scheme, by which the offer of a house in a new town is linked to the possession or offer of a job there, in effect pre-selects the occupants of the housing, abolishing the role of the market altogether. Some new towns have even tried to extend this rule to owner-occupied housing by asking for first refusal if the occupant moves out. In the future, as the new towns try to achieve the government target of 50 per cent of new housing built for owner occupation, restrictive covenants of this sort may be increasingly difficult to achieve. But up to the time of writing, the degree of control has been extraordinarily effective.

This degree of control needs to be seen in relation to a second feature: the scale of the development involved. In the so-called normal development process, the planning office essentially works incrementally. Population estimates for the area are raised, some extra provision must be made, there is a possibility of a hundred or a score of new houses on the periphery of the town at a certain point, a developer already holds the land and is pressing for permission. The wider implications – on transport, on school demand, on the town centre – may be considered. But no one could honestly say that the small area-plan fitted into a logical and coherent grand design. With the new town or expanded town, it is very different. Here it is the grand design that is paramount, and adaptation that is sometimes difficult. Most of the early new towns, for instance, were designed for very specific final-target populations, according to quite rigid blueprints. When, in many cases, the time came to try to revise these targets to cope with unexpected regional population growth, in some cases this meant major reconsideration of the plan: Bracknell for instance had to scrap its town centre plans and start again. But nowhere, outside the new towns and some of the largest expanded towns, have developers sat down to plan communities of 50,000 and more people all at once. The result is, or should be, a greater measure of coherence in the town when it is built. New towns might not be able to avoid completely such everyday phenomena as traffic congestion or under-provision of services. But if their planners are doing their job properly and have the resources, they ought to be able to deal rather better with these things than can the hapless local authority planner in the ordinary town or county, faced with a series of reluctant piecemeal adaptations to the fact of unexpected growth.

The third element is simply the financial one. New towns and expanded towns are built on financial arrangements which are noticeably favourable compared to the normal run of development. In both cases, the development agency is entitled to buy the land at a price which excludes the rise in value brought about by the general growth of the town. Elsewhere, even local authorities developing municipal estates must pay the whole market value of the land. This distinction of course was not in the mind of those who drafted the 1947 Act. For them, all development rights were to be nationalized and all development values were to revert to the community. On all development land, the owner would receive only the agricultural value, having had compensation at some date after the 1947 Act for any lost development value he may have expected to get. In the case of commercial developments, the state would enjoy the development value; in the case of public developments, the municipality or new town corporation would have the land at its rural value. This logical but perhaps unworkable solution was abolished by the Conservative Government in 1953; then, because of the anomaly this created with regard to compulsory purchase by public authorities, in 1959 the basis of such compulsory purchase reverted to open market-value with the sole exception of the new and expanded towns. Hence the distinction – a very fortunate one for the new towns. But it is important to notice, in this respect as in others, that the new towns and the expanded towns are only being built according to rules which, in 1947, it was expected would be the normal and general ones.

THE NEW TOWNS[1]

Their common administrative and financial basis is, however, about the only thing all the new towns have in common. Their origins, their locations and their objectives are exceedingly diverse. All the towns to be discussed in this section of the chapter have been designated under the New Towns Act of 1946, and have therefore been planned and built (or are currently being planned and built) by specially appointed Development Corporations. There were

[1] Much of the material in this section is taken from Peter Hall, 'Geological and Geographical Factors in the Siting of New Towns in Great Britain', *Proceedings of the Association of Engineering Geologists Annual Conference*, Washington DC, 1970. The Association, University Park, Pennsylvania (1971).

twenty-one such towns in England, two in Wales and five in Scotland at the beginning of 1971 (Table 10.1): they housed 1,415,488 people, representing an addition of almost 700,000 to the 717,530 that had been living in them at the dates of their respective designations. Thus about one in every sixty of the British population lived in a new town; a respectable achievement after a quarter century of effort, though doubtless far from the original expectations of campaigners like Abercrombie or Osborn.

Our interest in this section is in the English and Welsh new towns, which are shown in detail in Table 10.2. Chronologically, according to the date of designation, they fall into two well-defined groups. The first, often known as the Mark One new towns, consists of eleven towns in England and one in Wales designated in a short period from November 1946 to April 1950. And with one exception, in turn this group may be divided into two clearly-defined sub-groups according to the purpose of the designation. The larger

Table 10.1

SUMMARY: NEW TOWNS IN GREAT BRITAIN 1970

	Population		
	Original	31 December 1970	Net growth
London ring	98,440	470,830	372,390
Others in England and Wales	575,990	759,958	183,968
England and Wales	674,430	1,230,788	556,358
Scotland	43,100	184,700	141,600
Great Britain	717,530	1,415,488	697,958

Source: *Town and Country Planning*, January 1971, pp. 46–7.

of these consists of the new towns that were intended to achieve the specific objective of Ebenezer Howard and the Garden City movement, that is the planned dispersal of population from overcrowded urban areas, which had been given semi-official approval by the Barlow Report of 1940. In England all the eight Mark One towns designated for this purpose were around London; they are shown in order of their designation in the Table. Three other towns of this period were set up for another purpose: to aid regional development policies in the development areas. Again in order of designation, they were Newton Aycliffe and Peterlee in County Durham and Cwmbran in Monmouthshire. All of them had an incidental purpose too: Newton Aycliffe and Cwmbran served existing industrial estates; Peterlee was intended to provide a better settlement structure, and improved housing conditions, for coal miners in the colliery villages of the East Durham coalfield. Finally, the new town of Corby in Northamptonshire was an anomaly in this or any other group. Located in a region distant from the problems either of the great conurbations or the development areas, it was established in order to provide housing and communal services for a large steelworks built shortly before the Second World War.

The second group marks a significant break in time. After 1950, no further new towns were designated in England and Wales for eleven years. The

Table 10.2

NEW TOWNS IN ENGLAND AND WALES 1971

	Date of designation	Original population	Target Population original	Target Population revised	Distance from conurbation city centre miles
		all populations in thousands			
1. Conurbation overspill towns					
1.1 Greater London					
Stevenage	1946	7	60	105	32
Crawley	1947	9	50	80	31
Hemel Hempstead	1947	21	80	—	25
Harlow	1947	4	60	90	25
Hatfield	1948	8	29	—	21
Welwyn Garden City	1948	18	36	50	23
Basildon	1949	25	50	133	29
Bracknell	1949	5	25	61	30
Milton Keynes	1967	40	250	—	49
Peterborough	1967	84	190	—	81
Northampton	1968	131	300	—	66
1.2 Birmingham – West Midlands					
Telford	1963	70	90	220	34
Redditch	1964	32	90	—	14
1.3 Merseyside					
Skelmersdale	1961	8	80	—	13
Runcorn	1964	28	100	—	14
1.4 Manchester					
Warrington	1968	122	200	—	18
Central Lancashire	1970	240	430	—	30
1.5 Tyneside					
Washington	1964	20	80	—	8
2. Development area towns					
Newton Aycliffe	1947	60	10	45	—
Peterlee	1948	200	30	—	—
Cwmbran	1949	12	55	—	—
Newtown	1967	6	11	—	—
3. Other towns					
Corby	1950	16	40	80	—

Sources: F. J. Osborn and Arnold Whittick, *The New Towns: Answer to Megalopolis*; Frank Schaffer, *The New Town Story*; *Town and Country Planning*, January 1971; Gazeteers.

Conservative Government of 1951 tried to put all its emphasis on the 1952 Town Development Act, and even announced in 1957 that no further new towns would be built. Only in 1961, with the increasingly clear realization that the expanding towns programme was not solving the problems of the conurbations rapidly enough, was this policy reversed. Eleven new towns were then designated in England and Wales between Skelmersdale (1961) and Central Lancashire (1970). With a special exception – Newtown, designated in 1967 to help solve the problems of the thinly-populated hill area of mid-Wales – all these towns were intended to solve the specific overspill problems of the major conurbations. Three were designated to take London overspill, in addition to the existing eight Mark One towns there: Milton Keynes, Peterborough and Northampton, all designated in 1967–8. Further north, new towns were designated for the first time to take overspill from the three biggest provincial conurbations. In the West Midlands Telford was designated (under the name Dawley) in 1963, and Redditch in 1964. For Merseyside, Skelmersdale was designated in 1961 and Runcorn in 1964. And somewhat belatedly, for Greater Manchester, Warrington was designated in 1968 and the Central Lancashire new town (Preston-Leyland-Chorley) in 1970. Finally, local problems of overspill from the Tyneside conurbation led to the designation of Washington (1964). Washington and the two Merseyside towns also incidentally served the objective of promoting a development area, and enjoyed all the special incentives applicable to such areas.

Of the twenty-one new towns in England, therefore, eighteen were intended specifically to provide for the orderly overspill of people from the conurbations; three of these additionally happened to be in development areas, as were two of the remaining three not associated with overspill schemes (Figure 10.1). But Table 10.2 shows that this broad uniformity of basic purpose was to be achieved in different ways, according to the date the town was designated and the region of the country. The distance of the town from the centre of its parent conurbation is set by two contradictory forces: the desire to keep the town as close as possible for good economic and social reasons, and the planner's desire to provide a physical and social separation. Because characteristically the Green Belts around the conurbations have widths averaging about ten miles, the resulting distance of the new town tends to be a function of the size of the parent conurbation. In the case of Greater London, the continuous built-up area had already reached a radius of twelve–fifteen miles by 1939 and has hardly increased since. Located beyond a Green Belt five–ten miles wide, the eight Mark One London new towns range in distance between twenty-one and thirty-two miles from the centre of London. Immediately after the Second World War, that seems to have been considered safely out of the commuting range of the metropolis; but during the 1950s and 1960s, of course, many commuters found homes in this belt. As a result, when in 1964 the official South-East Study suggested new planning guidelines for the region around London, it proposed further new towns at considerably greater distances – fifty to eighty miles away – in order to maintain functional separation from the capital.

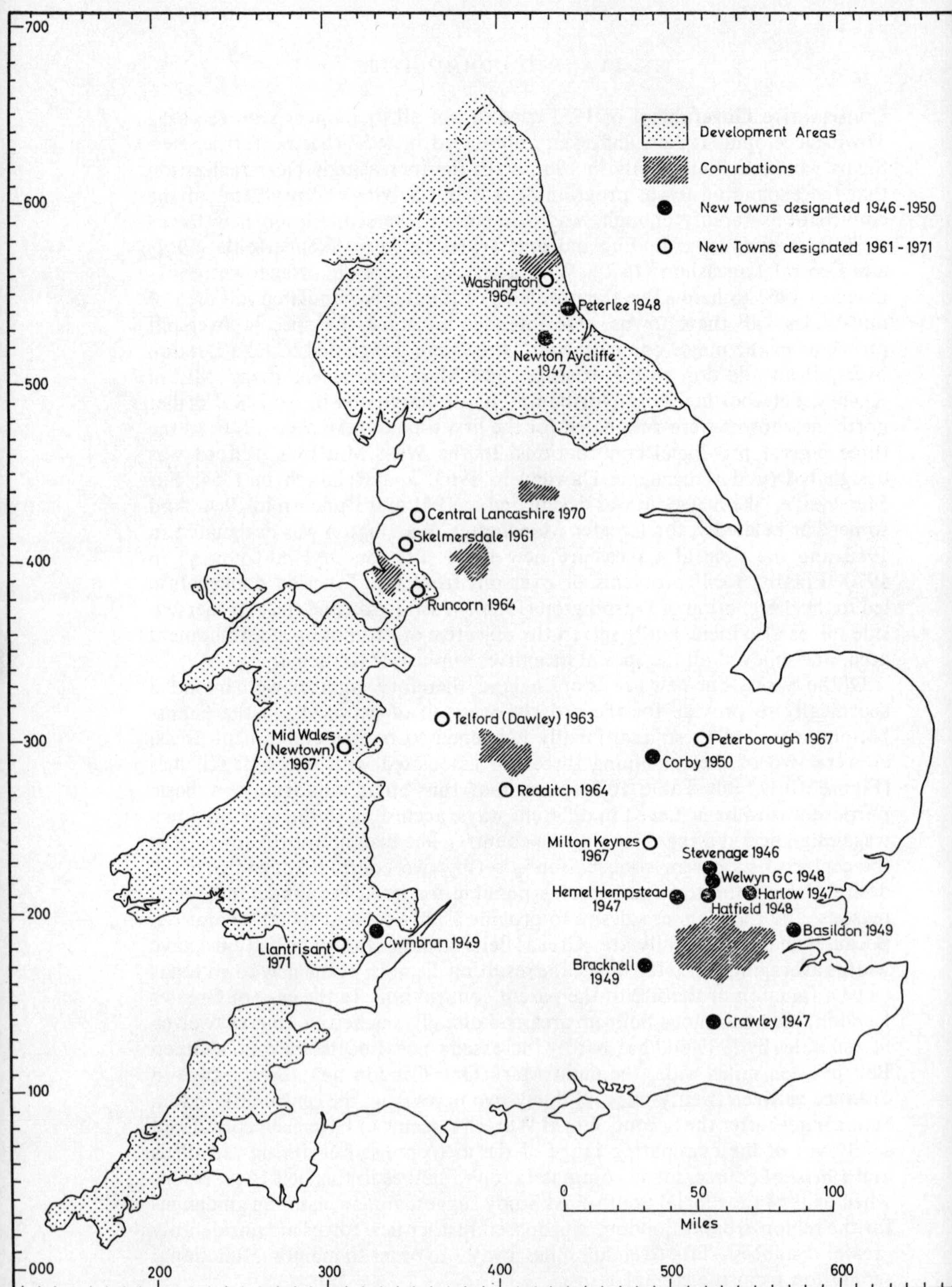

Figure 10.1 New Towns in England and Wales 1946–1970

Elsewhere, distances naturally tended to be shorter. But much depended on local geography. Some conurbations had little available building land nearby because of topography or existing urban development; others might have a much freer choice of sites. Thus, of the two new towns designated in the 1960s for the West Midlands, Redditch, was only fourteen miles from Birmingham; Telford, was thirty-four miles from central Birmingham though only nineteen miles from the edge of the conurbation at Wolverhampton. Merseyside is a compact conurbation surrounded by open land, and it was possible to find sites for new towns not far away: Skelmersdale is only thirteen miles, Runcorn fourteen miles, from central Liverpool. But in the more spread-out conurbation of South-East Lancashire – North-East Cheshire (Greater Manchester), with its closely neighbouring industrial towns, the possibilities were more limited and the new towns are accordingly more distant: Warrington is eighteen miles and central Lancashire thirty miles from central Manchester. In contrast again, the Tyneside conurbation has a linear form which offers open land close by, and it is no accident that Washington is the nearest of all the overspill new towns to its parent conurbation: only eight miles.

The chronology of new town development is important, too, when considering their sizes. The pioneers had recommended rather small garden cities: Howard had suggested units of 32,000 (though grouped into multi-centred units of 250,000 or more), and the Reith Committee had suggested a range between 30,000 and 50,000, with some latitude above or below. In the event the Mark One new towns were remarkably faithful to the Reith recommendations: all save two had target populations of between 25,000 and 60,000. (Of the exceptions, Newton Aycliffe with a target of 10,000 was a special case of redeveloping a wartime arms factory; Hemel Hempstead with 80,000 was already a flourishing market town.) The Mark One towns, in fact, differed far more in their existing populations at the time of designation than in their target populations; there were differences, therefore, in the amount of expansion involved. Very few were genuine green-field sites like Newton Aycliffe, whose 1948 population was only about sixty. Most were villages or small market towns with existing populations of between 5,000 and 10,000. And four – Hemel Hempstead, Welwyn Garden City, Basildon and Corby – had substantial populations of between 15,000 and 25,000 at the date of designation.

The Mark Two new towns of the 1960s show two striking breaks with this earlier tradition. There is a sharp increase in the size of the town, and a sharp increase in the size of the base population; they are of course associated. Whereas the typical Mark One new town might start with a population of 10,000 in a small town or village and build up to a target of 50,000, a typical new town of the 1960s is likely to start with an existing town of 100,000 and build up to 200,000 or 300,000. But generalization is more difficult, because the new towns of the 1960s are more diversified. Several of the new towns built for overspill from the provincial conurbations – Skelmersdale and Runcorn on Merseyside, Redditch for the West Midlands, Washington for Tyneside – followed the traditional formula but with modest increases in the planned target-populations to between 80,000 and 100,000. This reflected a fairly general belief by this time that a town of this size was needed to provide adequate levels of shopping and other services; and several of the older new towns had their original targets raised to about this level at the same time. But Northampton and Peterborough for London overspill and Warrington for Greater Manchester overspill, use a quite new formula: expansion of an existing large town (Peterborough 84,000, Northampton 131,000, Warrington 122,000) by a factor of about two, to populations of 190,000, 300,000 and 200,000 respectively. An even more radical version of this formula is central Lancashire: a large urbanized region containing several towns and a combined population of 240,000, to be expanded rapidly to a target of 430,000. During the 1960s, the concept of a new town has evolved first into the concept of a new town added to an old town, and then to the concept of a planned city region. But this last is not far removed from the idea of the Social City, first enunciated by Ebenezer Howard in 1898.

THE CONCEPT OF SELF-CONTAINMENT[2]

Some fashions in new-town building, then, have changed. But some have been more enduring. In particular, virtually all the new towns have been designated with the idea – to quote the words of the Reith Committee – that they should be: '. . . self-contained and balanced communities for working and living'. It is perhaps these two ideas – *self-containment* in terms of providing most of the needs of everyday living, including work and shops and other services, *balance* in terms of a mixture of different social and economic groups – which together distinguish the new towns from most other modern examples of consciously-planned developments. Interesting or inspired as they might be, Radburn in New Jersey and Vällingby or Farsta in Stockholm and Hampstead Garden Suburb could not claim self-containment as a virtue, nor could a distinguished early pointer to the new-town ideal, Barry Parker's Wythenshawe, designed outside Manchester in the 1930s. Wythenshawe was, and is, also far from being a balanced community. Like many less distinguished municipal housing estates of the period, it tends to be a one class – or, more accurately, a three or four socio-economic group – community. It is this threat of social polarization that the new towns were specifically intended to avoid.

Self-containment was clearly an objective of the pioneers of the Garden City movement, all the way back to Ebenezer Howard. A rich range of different sorts of employment, and of urban services, would be available without the need for costly and tiring journeys. Clearly, the ideal of self-containment is a matter of degree: the principle of the hierarchy of urban service levels is proof of that. And a development corporation cannot

[2] This section is based on Ray Thomas, *London's New Towns: A Study of Self-Contained and Balanced Communities*. PEP Broadsheet 510, London (1969), Chap. 3; detailed references will be found there.

guarantee it, or any given degree of it. What it can do is to create the conditions that make it possible and likely: like matching the population and employment levels. But self-containment depends in part on the other concept, that of balance. A full range of jobs – as the Reith Committee pointed out – should include head offices, administrative and research establishments, and sections of government departments. If there is a mixture of different social groups, that will create stronger pressure for jobs to be provided locally for those groups. But conversely, the existence of those jobs would be more likely to encourage to the town the sorts of people who did them. A wider range of people would also tend to encourage a wider range of shopping and other services, including education. So the two objectives were mutually reinforcing. But of course, social balance was desired for other reasons: for the economic strength which higher-income residents would bring, and the purely social advantages which were claimed for a mixed population. Previous public housing policies, it was claimed, had segregated the manual workers. But the experience of the existing garden cities of Letchworth and Welwyn showed that socially-balanced communities could work.

The new-town planners were in a strong position to ensure self-containment – or a high degree of it – because of their high degree of control over the twin levers of employment and housing. Admittedly, their control over employment was less than complete. Firms coming to the new towns, as to anywhere else, had to get an Industrial Development Certificate from the Board of Trade; big firms, in particular, might prefer to negotiate direct with the Board and once they had their IDC, there was little the Development Corporation could do but accept them. But in general, firms negotiated first with the Development Corporation because this increased their chances of getting the IDC. And the new towns soon became discriminating in the choice of firms, because they could afford to be. By the 1950s, government policy on industrial growth in the new towns was far from restrictive, so the Development Corporations tended to have plenty of applicants. They could afford to pick and choose.

Once the Development Corporation accepted a firm, it would provide housing for employees – a strong incentive for firms to migrate there. Existing employees would get housing priority in the new town, irrespective of previous need or location of previous home. But in addition, the new towns tried to relieve London's housing problems through the Industrial Selection Scheme. People on the London housing lists who were willing to move to a new town were kept on a special register, with details of their job skills. New town firms looking for workers were supposed to go to these registers first. This scheme worked well insofar as it was used. But it is not clear that all firms were keen on using the registers, or that London local authorities were keen on maintaining them. Only 10 per cent of those migrating from London to the new towns have gone through the ISS scheme, according to the Greater London Council. The great bulk of people seem to have come through word of mouth recommendation and their own initiative. But the procedures for allocating houses virtually guarantee that the vast majority of people living in the town also work there – at least initially. In the London new towns for instance it is generally possible to get housing only if there is first a job to go to. There have been exceptions to this policy from time to time in individual towns, both for housing to rent and housing for sale. But the great majority of all housing has gone to those with a job in the town – though there is no doubt that many Londoners would gladly have lived in these towns and commuted back to London jobs if they had been allowed to.

Nevertheless, it might be thought that the principle could not be held – at least after a time. Some of the town's workers might prefer to live in neighbouring towns or villages. Wives, sons, daughters might seek jobs that were

Table 10.3

INDICES OF COMMUTING INDEPENDENCE FOR LONDON'S NEW TOWNS 1951, 1961 AND 1966

Town	1951	1961	1966
	ratio of local to crossing journeys		
Harlow	1·42	2·04	2·05
Stevenage	0·92	2·29	2·03
Hemel Hempstead MB*	1·31	1·82	1·72
Crawley	0·98	1·59	1·58
Welwyn Garden City	1·12	1·09	1·12
Bracknell	0·90	1·13	1·02
Basildon	0·36	0·96	0·96
Hatfield RD†	0·65	0·63	0·66
Average (weighted)	0·85	1·33	1·33

Notes: * Some parts of Hemel Hempstead Municipal Borough, which include several factories, lie outside the designated area of the new town. The independence indices for the new town area are 0·80, 1·38 and 1·42 respectively, lower than for the MB.

† One of the main functions of Hatfield New Town was to provide housing for the de Havilland Aircraft Works (now Hawker Siddeley Aviation and Hawker Siddeley Dynamics) which lie outside the designated area. It seems preferable therefore to use figures relating to Hatfield Rural District, which includes the new town and the industrial centre it was designed to serve, although the RD also includes a substantial amount of other employment and population and covers a much wider area.

Source: Ray Thomas (1969), Table 4, p. 393.

not available in the town itself. Increased mobility arising from higher car ownership will allow people to widen their field of search both for jobs and homes. All these trends should tend to make the new towns less self-contained. But at the same time, if the town is still growing, the new arrivals will contribute to self-containment – at least for a time. The results of this tug of war may be gauged by comparing the growth of journeys within the new town with the growth of journeys to and from them.

For this purpose a special terminology is needed. It has already been used elsewhere in the book – especially in Chapter Five of Volume One and Chapter Nine of this Volume. Journeys within any local authority are *local journeys*. Journeys crossing local boundaries – the sum of those in and out – are known as *crossing journeys*. The ratio of local to crossing journeys is the *independence index*. Table 10.3 shows that the index of independence has increased in six of the eight London new towns between 1951 and 1966. The really dramatic change came about during the 1950s, as the arrival of new jobs caused a great increase in self-sufficiency. The larger of the towns – Harlow, Stevenage, Crawley and Hemel Hempstead – tend to be the most self-contained. And here, insofar as there is movement across the boundaries, it tends to be residents of other areas coming in to work – a product of a substantial employment surplus. Stevenage in 1966 for instance had 7,000 people coming in each day for work, against only 4,000 going out. Table 10.4,

Table 10.4

JOB RATIOS IN NEW TOWNS 1951, 1961 AND 1966

Town	1951	1961	1966
	ratio of employment to residents in employment as a percentage		
Bracknell	108	115	126
Basildon	37	82	107
Crawley	112	101	111
Hatfield RD	123	107	96
Harlow	98	86	97
Hemel Hempstead MB	101	96	97
Stevenage	124	109	112
Welwyn Garden City	124	125	122
Average (weighted)	100	100	107

Source: Ray Thomas (1969), Table 5, p. 396.

which shows the ratio of jobs to employed population in each town expressed as a percentage, indicates that six out of eight new towns in 1951, five out of eight in 1966, were net importers of labour in this way. Examined in detail, the relationships did not alter very much over the fifteen-year period. The most self-contained of the new towns also tend to have good balances of workers and jobs. But balance does not necessarily ensure self-containment, at any rate if the town is near London: the example of Hatfield shows that.

One good reason for the fact that the new towns have maintained their self-containment, or even enhanced it, is that in them the amount of women's employment – and therefore the percentage of female to all employment – has been rising. Everywhere, not just in the new towns, women tend to be less mobile than men for a variety of reasons – family ties, less accessibility to the car – being among the most important. As far as journeys to work by men are concerned, the new towns actually became a little less self-contained during the period under consideration. But these trends are not unique to the new towns. They lie in a distinctive area of the country – the Outer Metropolitan Area – which happens to have very high levels of car ownership and consequent possibilities of mobility in seeking for jobs. For this reason, comparisons between the new towns and other parts of the Outer Metropolitan Area are germane.

The first such comparison is with Berkshire – a county where movement patterns have already been studied extensively in the two volumes of this work, notably in Chapter Five of our first volume and in Chapter Nine of

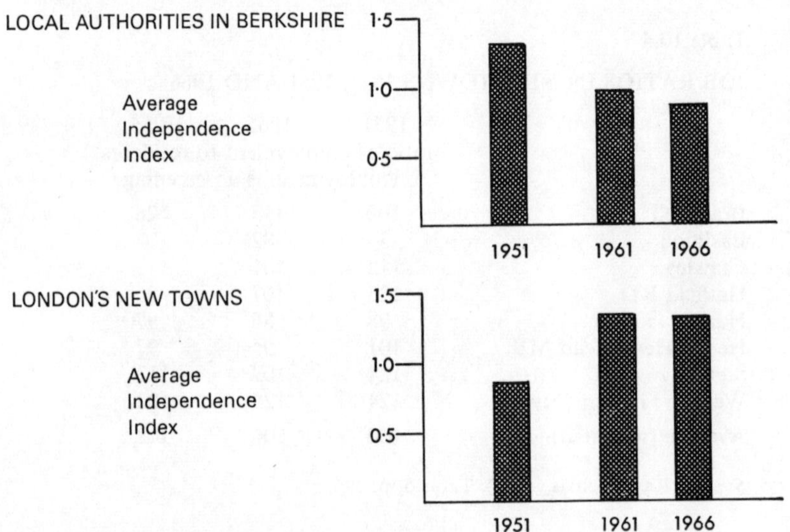

Figure 10.2 Indices of Commuting Independence for Local Authorities in Berkshire and London's New Towns in 1951, 1961 and 1966

this volume. During the period from 1945 to 1970 Berkshire has consistently been one of the fastest-growing English counties, though of course its rate of growth has been proportionately much slower than that of the new towns. Figure 10.2 shows that while in 1951 local authorities in Berkshire were on average more self-contained than the new towns, by 1966 their independence index had fallen to 0·82 while that for the new towns had risen to 1·33.

This comparison however is somewhat crude; it does not make full allowance for all the factors that help determine self-containment, such as rural or urban character or distance from London. To try to standardize for such factors, Figure 10.3 tries systematically to compare independence indices with distance from London, and Figure 10.4 to do the same for size

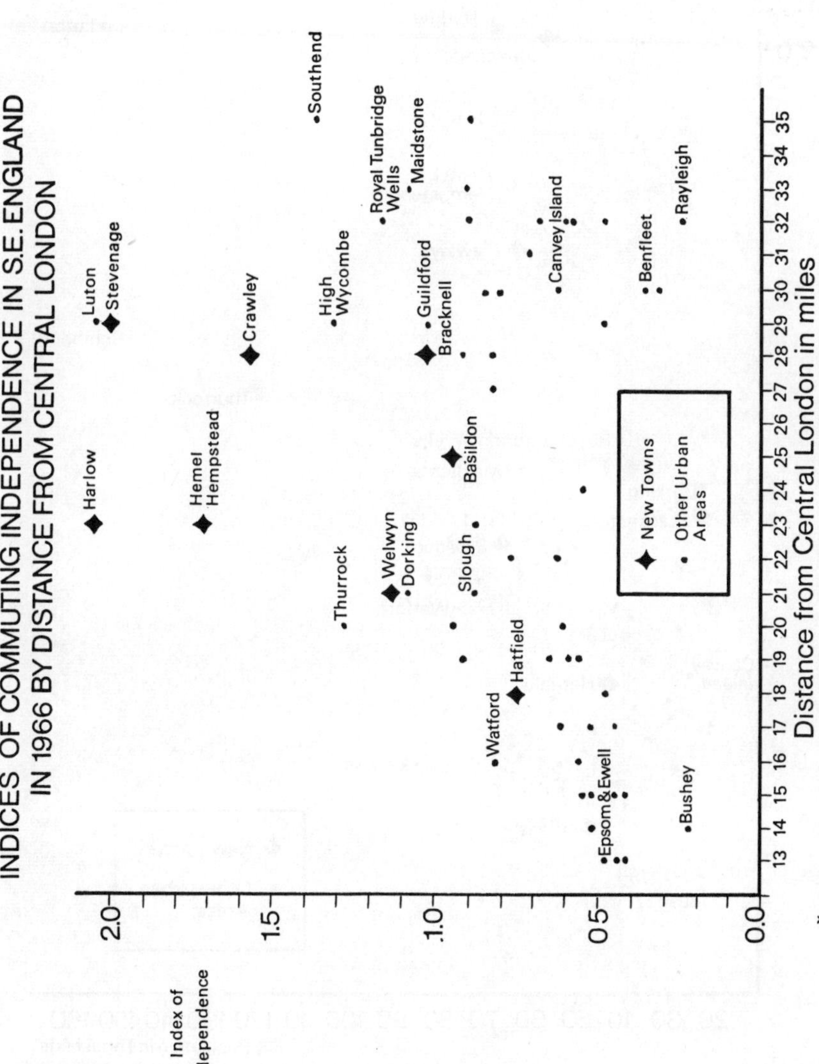

Figure 10.3 Indices of Commuting Independence in 1966 by Distance from Central London

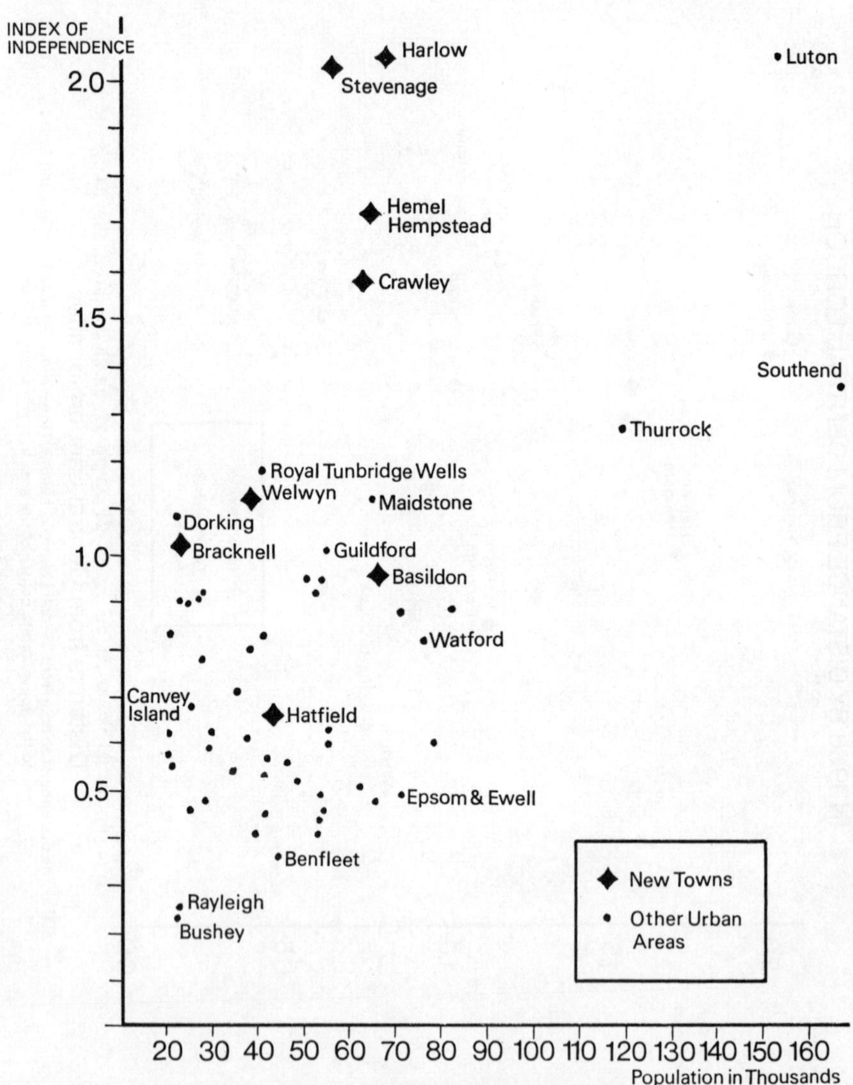

Figure 10.4 Indices of Commuting Independence for Towns within Thirty-Five Miles of London in 1966, by Size

of town. The new towns stand out startlingly. There are no towns within thirty-five miles of London and with a population of less than 150,000 which are as self-contained as Harlow, Stevenage, Hemel Hempstead or Crawley. Only a small proportion of towns are as self-contained as Basildon, Bracknell or Welwyn. The only new town comparable with other towns is Hatfield.

It might be thought that this distinction between the new towns and the others will disappear with time. But that is not entirely likely, because it

COMMUTING TO LONDON FROM THE NEW TOWNS IN 1951, 1961, 1966

COMMUTING TO INNER LONDON IN 1951 AND 1961

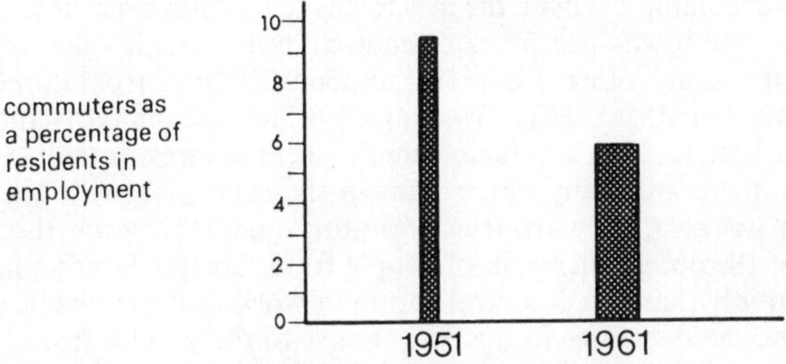

COMMUTING TO GREATER LONDON COUNCIL AREA IN 1961 AND 1966

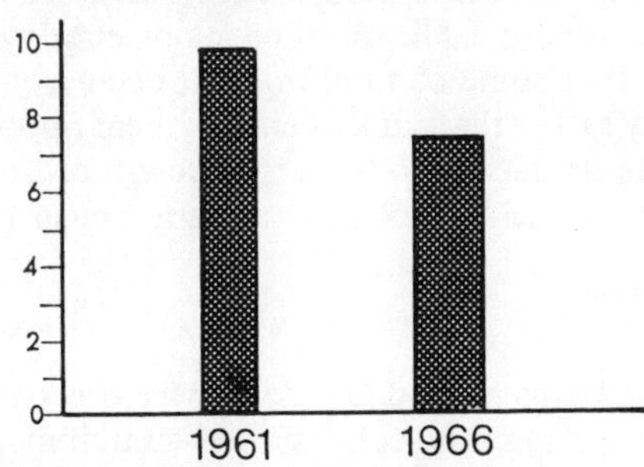

The area of the blocks is proportional to the total number of commuters

Figure 10.5 Commuting to London from the New Towns in 1951, 1961 and 1966

depends on the housing policies already described. Only in a new town do people find an agent (the Development Corporation, or, in the case of a completed town, the New Towns Commission) which helps them find a home in the same area as their place of work. Only in the new town can a person move rapidly to the top of a housing waiting list on the strength of having a job in the area. As long as these procedures are in operation, it seems likely that towns will remain relatively self-contained. It will, probably be modified somewhat: building by local authorities in the completed towns, and building for owner occupiership, is not likely to respect the home–work link to the same degree, if at all. So the new towns may tend to become more like other towns but never, perhaps, completely like them.

This discussion of independence has been conducted in very general terms. It has shown that the new towns are relatively independent, but that they do have an appreciable number of commuters both in and out. If a substantial proportion of this flow came from London, it would undermine one of the fundamental objectives of the London new towns. In fact, the evidence shows that the majority of the work journeys crossing new-town boundaries are short ones. Figure 10.5 shows that there has been a notable drop in the percentage of commuters from the new towns to London over the period 1951–66. Yet the new towns are by no means unique in their relation to London. There are many other places at similar distances from London – Luton, Chatham, Guildford, High Wycombe – which are similarly independent of London because they are major employment centres in their own right. To be sure, there are many other areas in the same ring with big surpluses of resident workers; they are true dormitory areas. They are the result of the fact that the decentralization of people from Greater London has proceeded more rapidly than the decentralization of work. But even while this has been going on, many centres in the ring twenty to forty miles from London – not just the new towns – have maintained their independence from the metropolis. What the new towns have done is to demonstrate the feasibility of the policy of moving work and homes out in step. The same policy could be applied, and is applying itself, to other major employment centres in the South-east. If after that some commuting still occurs, it is likely to represent increased mobility rather than lack of employment opportunities. If the aim of planning in the South-East is to limit the growth of London, the key is to decentralize jobs. The success of the new towns is a clear pointer to this policy.[3]

SOCIAL BALANCE[4]

The new towns around London, therefore, can be fairly said to have achieved one of their main objectives – self-containment. How far have they achieved the twin aim of social balance? Figure 10.6 attempts to provide an answer. It compares the socio-economic composition of the new towns with Greater London and with the country as a whole. Neither of these comparisons is completely satisfactory of course: Greater London has a specialized social and economic composition and the whole country includes many rural areas which are not proper subjects of comparison with the London new towns. But by taking both comparisons into account, some conclusion can be drawn. The most striking are the relative surplus of high-income manual workers

[3] This section is based on Ibid., Chap. 4.
[4] This section is based on Ibid., Chap. 5.

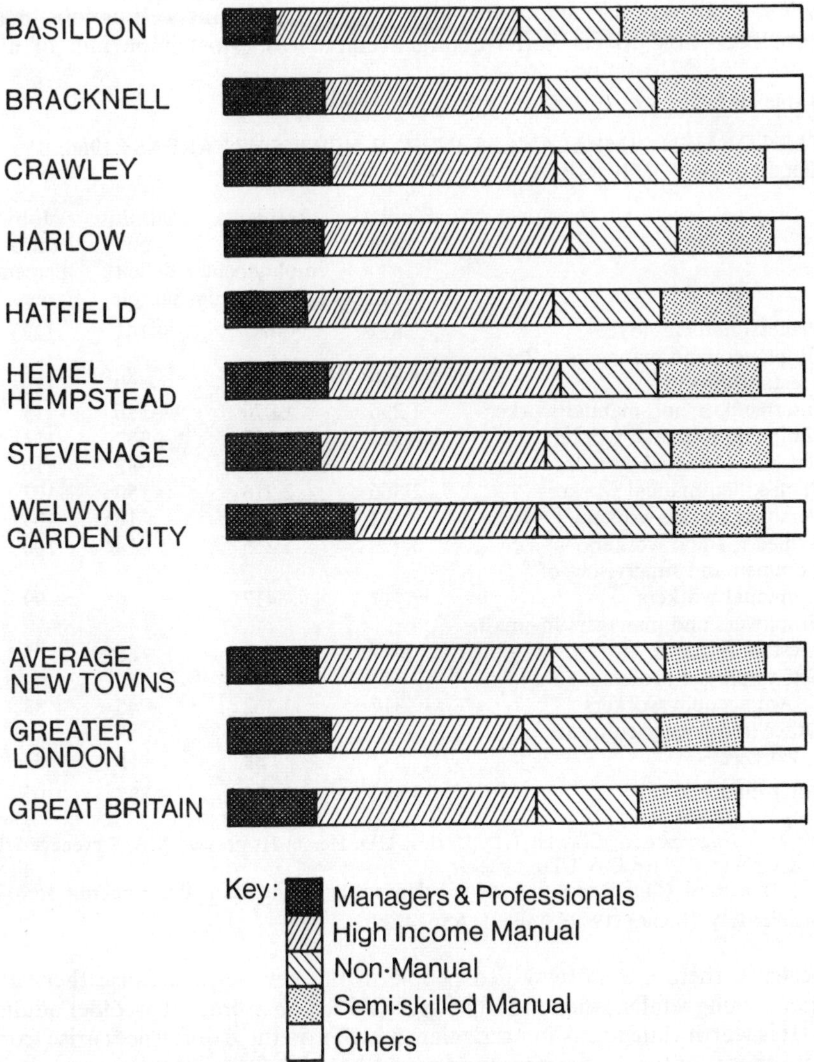

Figure 10.6 Social Composition of London's New Towns in 1966: Proportion of Adult Males by Socio-Economic Group

compared with London and (in the case of most of the towns) with Great Britain; and the corresponding well-marked deficit in the low-income group Other Workers. Some of the reasons for these differences must by now be obvious. The growth industries in the new towns tend to have high proportions of skilled (and also professional) workers; they have not encouraged low-income industries. The employee selection process may also have contributed: firms in the new towns, able to offer housing as well as jobs, may have been able to get better-qualified employees. Most important of all,

Table 10.5

EMPLOYMENT IMBALANCES IN FIVE NEW TOWN AREAS† 1966, BY SOCIO-ECONOMIC GROUP

	Employment	Residents in employment	Surplus or deficit‡	Job ratio percentage
	numbers in 10 per cent sample			
Professional employees	822	661	+161	122
Employers and managers in large establishments	548	458	+90	120
Intermediate non-manual workers	1,206	1,070	+136	113
Junior non-manual workers	3,525	3,193	+332	111
Unskilled manual workers	925	843	+82	110
Semiskilled manual workers	2,366	2,216	+150	107
Personal service workers	623	607	+16*	103
Skilled manual workers	3,279	3,265	+14*	100
Foremen and supervisors of manual workers	411	417	−6*	99
Employers and managers in small establishments	517	545	−28*	95
Self-employed professional and own account workers	317	362	−45	88
Other (mostly agricultural) workers	73	88	−15	83
All groups	14,612	13,725	+887	107

Notes: † Aggregate for Crawley UD, Harlow UD, Hemel Hempstead MB, Stevenage UD and Welwyn Garden City UD.

‡ An asterisk (*) indicates that the imbalance is not significantly different from zero.

Source: Ray Thomas (1969), Table 11A, p. 422.

perhaps, there are more skilled people in the new town because there are more young adults, who tend to be more skilled on average than older adults.

It is worthwhile to ask in particular: how far do these differences arise from job opportunities in the new towns, and how far from other factors – such as social choice? For this purpose, it is necessary to compare the skills of residents with the available job opportunities, and this is possible for only five of the eight London new towns. The results are shown in Table 10.5.

There are three striking conclusions. First, that in general there are more white-collar jobs in the new towns than there are white-collar residents. In other words, there is an inflow of white-collar commuters into these towns every day. The reason may well be straightforward: that top people prefer to live in a nearby village safely insulated, out of working hours, from their subordinates. But the rule seems to go for the more junior white-collar workers too. Second, that the higher-income manual workers are very well-balanced: there are just about as many jobs in these categories within the towns as there are resident workers to fill them. And third – perhaps the most significant conclusion – that the level of employment of the unskilled and the semiskilled is actually greater than the number of residents available to fill the jobs. The deficiency of workers amounted to no less than 2,000 in the five towns considered. It seems unlikely that low-income workers would have been reluctant to live in the new towns if they could; more likely that the housing allocation procedures, with their emphasis on nomination of key workers, actually discriminated against the lower-paid.

It looks then as if there may be some truth in the charge that the new towns do not make an adequate contribution to London's housing problems. The trouble seems to be that some members of the lower-income groups suffer from the housing policies followed by some of the Development Corporations and the New Towns Commission. The subject is complex and curiously ill-documented. But the main lines seem clear. In some new towns, there was a consciously discriminatory policy: a man must be nominated by his employer to get a house. Here, it is not surprising that there was discrimination in favour of the more skilled, high-paid employees. But even where this did not explicitly happen – in towns where there was an open-door policy, so that anyone with a job in the town could apply for a house – there was the basic difficulty that the low-income worker might not be able to afford the rent. By definition, the housing stock of the new towns in the early years was new; it was not easily possible to get an older dwelling at a lower rent. To have overcome this would have required a deliberately discriminatory rent policy in favour of the lower-paid worker. And this the new towns refused, or at least neglected, to do.

It seems then that the new towns around London were very successful in being self-contained and less successful in being socially balanced. They are the only English new towns, so far, built for overspill purposes which have had a long enough history to be analysed in this way. It will be 1981 before the oldest of the Mark Two new towns built for overspill from the big provincial conurbations, Skelmersdale, will be roughly as mature as the Mark One London new towns were at the Census of 1966. And the other English new towns of the 1946–50 period – Aycliffe, Peterlee and Corby – are in many ways so special that it would not be meaningful to analyse them in the same way. In general, the older new towns outside London have been successful in bringing about a balance between population and employment – just as the London new towns have been. They have also become more self-contained, in the sense of being more independent of commuting – again like the London new towns. They tend to have a conspicuously lower proportion of low-income groups than their immediately surrounding local areas.[5] Once again, it is the relative failure to provide for the least favoured groups – the poor and also the aged – which emerges as the most striking apparent failure of new-town policy.

The contribution of the new towns to a solution of housing problems, in fact, has been of a rather specialized kind. More than anything else they have helped young couples. They have helped the sort of people who, before the war, would mostly have taken up a privately-rented house. There have been few suitable dwellings of this kind available since 1945, and if these young couples had not gone to a new town most of them would have struggled to become owner occupiers or would have joined the long waiting lists for council houses within the conurbations. The new towns have added a new dimension to the housing market in this way. But the policy has not helped the old and the poor. This is perhaps not entirely the fault of the development corporations: frozen, or partially frozen rents in the conurbations have given little incentive to tenants to move in search of something better in a new town. But the development corporations have not gone out of their way to help the underprivileged either. For a long time, when the housing stock was still new and homogeneous, everyone – the craftsman and the labourer alike – got the same subsidy. Later, as the original housing aged, it became possible to introduce limited differentials. But it was not until the late 1960s that there were any substantial differentials related to income.

In defence of the development corporations it must be said that it would have been difficult to do everything at once. To make a substantial quantitative solution to the housing problem, the new towns had to be successful. To be successful, they had to attract industry and provide good housing. But to have helped the poor in the conurbations, they would have had to provide new housing at exceptionally low rents. They could have done this by building some housing at lower standards than those which were generally considered acceptable. Or they could have demanded even bigger government subsidies. But if they had done the first, they would have been accused of exporting slums to the countryside, and they would not have seemed such attractive places for living and working. And if they had demanded more subsidy, they would have weakened their negotiating position *vis-à-vis* the government on a score of other matters – especially approval of capital expenditure for social amenities – which would again have limited their growth. Probably, they were on the horns of an impossible dilemma. They chose to resolve it by going all out for growth and success. The problems of the poor were left to be resolved elsewhere – if at all.[6]

THE EXPANDING TOWNS

The expanding (or expanded) towns, developed under the 1952 Town Develop-

[5] Cf. Ray Thomas, *Aycliffe to Cumbernauld: A Study of Seven New Towns in their Regions*. PEP Broadsheet 516, London (1969), Chaps 1–3.

[6] The last three paras of this section were based on Ray Thomas, ibid., pp. 840–2.

ment Act, are a much more varied bunch than the new towns, as Table 10.6 and Figure 10.7 show. Whereas the new towns nearly all started with a quite uniform range of target sizes which have tended to be scaled upwards over time, there has never been such uniformity with the expanding towns: the

Table 10.6

TOWN EXPANSION (TOWN DEVELOPMENT ACT) SCHEMES IN ENGLAND AND WALES 1970

	Existing population 1961	Expansion target		Distance from conurbation centre miles
		Houses	Population*	
Greater London				
Andover B	16,985	6,000	18,000	66
Ashford UD	27,996	4,250	12,750	54
Aylesbury B	27,923	3,000	9,000	40
Banbury B	21,004	2,236	6,708	72
Basingstoke B	25,980	11,500	34,500	47
Bletchley UD	17,095	5,000	15,000	47
Bodmin B	6,214	500	1,500	234
Braintree and Bocking UD	20,600	1,200	3,600	43
Burnley CB	80,559	700	2,100	205
Bury St Edmunds B	21,179	3,000	9,000	75
Canvey Island UD	15,605	414	1,242	38
Frimley and Camberley UD	28,552	1,177	3,531	30
Gainsborough UD	17,278	1,000	3,000	148
Grantham B	25,048	500	1,500	110
Haverhill UD	5,445	4,500	13,500	56
Huntingdon and Godmanchester B	8,821	2,450	7,350	62
Kings Lynn B	27,536	3,500	10,500	98
Letchworth UD	25,511	1,500	4,500	37
Luton CB	131,583	1,000	3,000	32
Luton RD	36,462	3,896	11,688	32
Melford RD	13,317	750	2,250	60
Mildenhall RD	20,458	2,000	6,000	71
Peterborough B	62,340	300	900	81
Plymouth CB	204,409	300	900	211
St Neots UD	5,554	2,000	6,000	57
Sandy UD	3,963	700	2,100	49
Sudbury B	6,642	1,500	4,500	58
Swindon B	91,739	8,580	25,740	79
Thetford B	35,399	3,000	9,000	82
Wellingborough UD	30,583	10,000	30,000	68
Witham UD	9,459	3,000	9,000	40
Total – Greater London	1,041,239	89,453	268,359	Average: 77

	Existing population 1961	Expansion target Houses	Expansion target Population*	Distance from conurbation centre miles
Birmingham				
Aldridge-Brownhills UD	77,440	2,500	7,500	13
Banbury B	21,004	235	705	41
Cannock UD	42,191	500	1,500	17
Daventry B	5,860	5,275	15,825	37
Droitwich B	7,976	2,000	6,000	20
Leek UD	19,182	100	300	50
Lichfield B	14,087	1,200	3,600	16
Lichfield RD	39,935	500	1,500	16
Rugeley UD	13,017	300	900	25
Stafford B	47,806	750	2,250	27
Stafford RD	17,930	300	900	27
Tamworth B	13,646	6,500	19,500	15
Tutbury RD	17,597	60	180	33
Uttoxeter UD	8,185	200	600	34
Weston-super-Mare B	43,938	802	2,406	108
Total – Birmingham	389,794	21,222	63,666	Average: 32
Bristol				
Keynsham UD	15,152	642	1,926	5
Sodbury RD	44,884	136	408	12
Thornbury RD	30,679	500	1,500	13
Warmley RD	19,406	1,000	3,000	6
Total – Bristol	110,121	2,278	6,834	Average: 9
Liverpool				
Burnley CB	80,559	2,200	6,600	51
Ellesmere Port B	44,681	5,500	16,500	10
Widnes B	52,186	4,160	12,480	13
Winsford UD	12,760	6,666	19,998	33
Total – Liverpool	190,186	18,526	55,578	Average: 27
Manchester				
Burnley CB	80,559	2,700	8,100	24
Crewe B	53,195	4,000	12,000	34
Macclesfield B	37,644	1,250	3,750	18
Winsford UD	12,760	564	1,692	28
Total – Manchester	184,158	8,514	25,542	Average: 26
Newcastle upon Tyne				
Seaton Valley UD (Cramlington)	26,095	6,500	19,500	5
Longbenton UD (Killingworth)	46,530	4,017	12,051	9
Total – Newcastle upon Tyne	72,625	10,517	31,551	Average: 7

	Existing population 1961	Expansion target Houses	Expansion target Population*	Distance from conurbation centre miles
Salford				
Worsley UD	40,393	4,518	13,554	3
Total – Salford	40,393	4,518	13,554	Average: 3
Walsall				
Aldridge UD	77,440 (Aldridge UD and Brownhills UD)	215	645	4
Brownhills UD		229	687	6
Total – Walsall	77,440	444	1,332	Average: 5
Wolverhampton				
Cannock RD	42,191	400	1,200	8
Selsdon RD	36,981	1,546	4,638	5
Tettenhall UD	14,867	131	393	3
Wednesfield UD	33,048	2,450	7,350	3
Total – Wolverhampton	127,087	4,527	13,571	Average: 5

CB = County Borough, B = Municipal Borough, UD = Urban District, RD = Rural District

* Estimated on the basis that 1 dwelling contains 3 people. (The actual ratio for new towns in England and Wales from 1945 to 1970 was 3.1.)

Sources: *Town and Country Planning*, January 1971; Gazeteers.

scale of the operation depended too much on local circumstances, including the existing size of the town, its enthusiasm for rapid growth, and the needs of the conurbation or city authority. At one extreme, especially in the early days of the operation of the Act, there were plenty of penny-packet schemes involving 3,000 people or less – some of them 1,000 or less. At the other, schemes like those made between London and Basingstoke, London and Swindon, and London and Wellingborough are indistinguishable in scale, or eventual character, from new towns. The Swindon development, indeed, threatens to become one of the largest town developments of any kind in twentieth-century Britain, comparable in magnitude with new towns grafted on to old ones in places like Northampton and Peterborough.[7] But even taking these brave exceptions into account, the fact is that the average town-expansion scheme is far smaller than the average new-town scheme. Out of sixty-seven schemes shown in Table 10.6, twenty-eight or round about two in five were for less than 3,000 people. Fifty-one or almost exactly

[7] Useful material on Swindon includes: J. B. Cullingworth, 'The Swindon Social Survey: A Second Report on the Sociological Implications of Overspill', *Sociological Review*, N.S., 9 (1961), pp. 151–66; Kenneth Hudson, *An Awkward Size for a Town: A Study of Swindon at the 100,000 Mark*. David and Charles, Newton Abbot (1967) (especially useful); D. Ian Scargill, 'The Expanding Town of Swindon', *Town and Country Planning*, 35 (1967), pp. 111–14; and Michael Harloe, 'Swindon Expands', *Town and Country Planning*, 39 (1971), pp. 14–18.

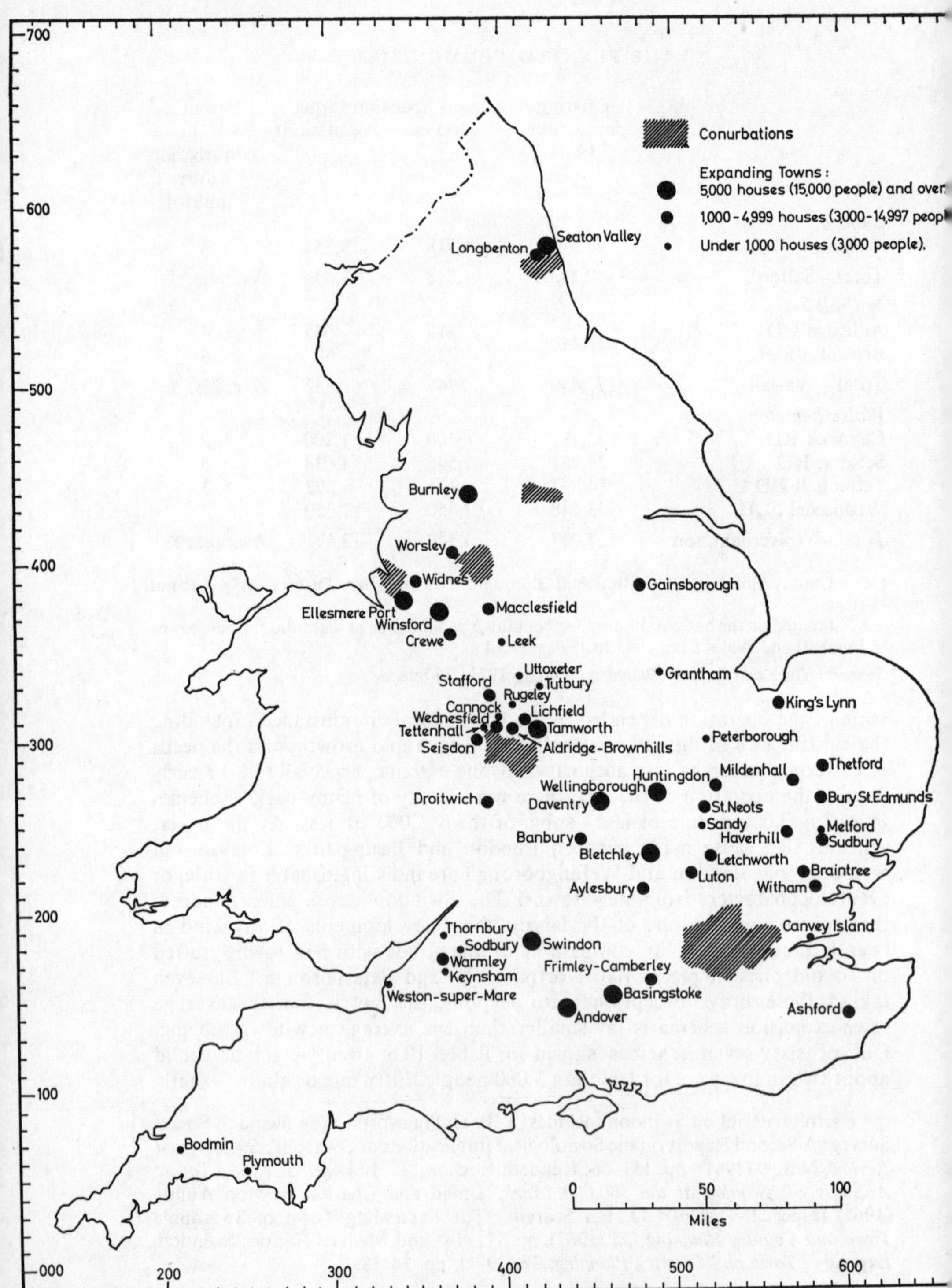

Figure 10.7 Town Development (Expanding town) Schemes 1952–1970

three-quarters were for less than 10,000. And it is noticeable that the bigger schemes tend to be those related to London overspill. Here, two-thirds of schemes involved more than 10,000 people and over a quarter involved more than 20,000. But elsewhere in the country, more than half the schemes were for less than 3,000 people and over three-quarters were for less than 10,000.

This distinction is explained to some extent by another feature illuminated in Table 10.6, on which the expanding towns also differ quite sharply from the new towns. Those new towns which were built to house overspill were located quite carefully in relation to their parent conurbations: far enough to be self-contained and physically separate, but near enough, in most cases, to attract industry and people. So there is a maximum and a minimum distance here: the Mark One new towns for London, and the provincial new towns of the 1960s, are almost all in the range between twelve and thirty-five miles from the conurbations from which they draw people. But the town expansion schemes do not seem to be subject to any such constraints. Out of the thirty-one London expanding town schemes, only three are in the distance range (under thirty-five miles) of the Mark One new towns; no less than sixteen, or almost exactly half, are more than sixty miles distant, and three are over two hundred miles away. It is clear from inspection that many of the London schemes involved fairly modest additions to population at quite considerable distances from the capital. And this needs to be coupled with the fact that very many of the towns or rural districts concerned had very small populations. For many Londoners, a move to an expanding town was a move to a small country town a long way from London – and often a long way from anywhere else of any size.

The experience in the provinces was different. Here, on average, the town development schemes were much nearer their parent conurbations – with rare exceptions like Birmingham's agreement with Weston-super-Mare. When account is taken of the physical spread of some of these conurbations, indeed, it is apparent that many of the schemes were only just beyond their boundaries. Half the Birmingham schemes were under thirty miles from the centre of the city: but since most of them were to the north, this meant that most of them were not more than six or seven miles from the conurbation edge. Walsall and Wolverhampton reached agreements with neighbouring local authorities; here, the Town Development Act was used for what was little more than council housing on the other side of the Borough boundary. The same goes for the scheme which Salford made with Worsley, or for the Bristol schemes. Though Newcastle's two developments in Northumberland fully justify their title as small local authority new towns, they too are within the conurbation (in one instance) or just outside it (in the other). Only in the case of Manchester and Liverpool did the schemes range more widely; and two of the Liverpool schemes were in the conurbation or adjacent to it. It is impossible to generalize about the size of these near-in provincial expansions. They range from the very small to the quite large.

The form and the impact of town development schemes, then, appear to have been quite different in different areas. Many of the London schemes took people sixty miles or more, to quite small and remote country towns which were being expanded by a modest amount. Axiomatically, jobs here had to go with the people; the possibilities of commuting back into the conurbation were virtually nil. The chief objection that can be raised against this formula is that it provides a very restricted range of jobs and of urban services at a time when the general tendency in planning is to think of bigger variety in both. But some of the bigger developments, such as those at Swindon or Basingstoke, are not open to this objection; they approximate to well-developed new towns. One or two of the bigger provincial schemes – the best example is Winsford in Cheshire – resemble these larger London schemes; but most are small-scale schemes which represent little more than house-building on the other side of the borough boundary. The important point is that these latter schemes are more than likely to result in commuting back into the conurbation to work. They are the very reverse of self-contained and balanced development. They have little in common, save their origin, with a development like Swindon or even a smaller, but still self-contained, development like Thetford.

The very diversity of the expanded towns reflects their genesis. Unlike the new towns, they did not arise from a careful process of selection of alternative sites. Rather, they arose from a series of separate initiatives. Though the exporting authorities might do their best to advertise the advantages of expansion – Birmingham had tentative negotiations with hundreds of places – finally the initiative lay with the country town; and there, as things stood, it frequently lay with a very few people or even with one dominant personality. The giant Swindon scheme, it is generally agreed, owed a great deal to the persistence of the town clerk. The same was certainly true at Thetford. This meant in effect that the places with a positive attitude to expansion managed to expand. There was no systematic examination of their suitability for the role; during the 1950s, when many of the agreements were made, the overspill problem for many of the conurbation authorities was so serious that they were glad to take what they could. The result was that many of the schemes are in somewhat remote places which had economic problems when they entered into negotiations. Swindon for instance was facing the threat of decline in its basic industry, railway engineering.[8] Thetford had been in decline for a long time when it made one of the earliest agreements with London under the Act.

Despite this lack of careful and systematic selection, the programmes seem to have worked better than it was reasonable to hope. People and jobs have moved, even to out-of-the-way places. One good reason was that there were solid material incentives. Workers, just as in the new towns, got well-designed housing relatively cheaply. They could move through the Industrial Selection Scheme, just as to a new town. Employers found that apart from

[8] Cf. Scargill, op. cit., p. 112; John Gretton, 'Out of London', *New Society*, 15 Apr. 1971, p. 621.

key workers who went with the factory and must be paid London rates, local wage-levels in small country towns were substantially lower than they had experienced in the conurbations; they are still much higher than the local agricultural rates, so there is no shortage of local workers looking for jobs.[9] Towns like Thetford and Haverhill and Huntingdon have probably acted as centres of rural regeneration, bringing additional prosperity to areas where the main problem was not so much structural employment as sheer low-wage levels. In other words, they have fulfilled a different role from the new towns – just as Abercrombie, or Chapman in Cheshire, apparently intended them to do at the end of the Second World War. The biggest objection is that these towns could not provide the same variety of jobs and services as the new towns: mainly because they were smaller, but also because they were so much more remote from other job opportunities.[10] But as target populations in many of these towns have tended to be revised upwards, that perhaps is an objection of diminishing force.

The biggest doubt, as Cullingworth and Dickinson recognized at the beginning of the 1960s,[11] does not so much concern these true country-town expansions. It concerns those schemes which represented short-distance overspill just over the town boundary, and which were so marked a feature around the provincial conurbations and cities. Taking into account all overspill schemes – not just those under the Town Development Act – Dickinson found in 1962 that 60 per cent of conurbation schemes were actually within the conurbations, while for towns outside the conurbations no less than three-quarters were within two miles of the town boundary. He concluded that these schemes were simply following a line of least resistance and that they would tend to repeat in the provincial conurbations the story of suburban sprawl round London in the 1930s. But he recognized a fact that has loomed large in the whole of the present study: that in most of the country, the solutions applicable to London were simply not typical. Much of provincial England, at least until well into the 1960s, simply does not seem to have recognized the Barlow Commission case for urban containment and the creation of self-contained and balanced communities. There are exceptions under the Town Development Act outside the South-East – Winsford is perhaps the most notable – but they are not common.

IDEAL AND REALITY

The new towns and the town expansions may individually have realized many of the objectives that were hoped for – the new towns, perhaps, more com-

[9] Gretton, ibid., p. 662.

[10] On the lack of job opportunities for qualified women in Swindon cf. Hudson, op. cit., pp. 85–6. And for the views of teenagers there on social provision, cf. ibid., Chap. 10.

[11] J. B. Cullingworth, *Housing Needs and Planning Policy*. Routledge, London (1960), especially Chap. 10; G. C. Dickinson, 'Overspill and Town Development in England and Wales, 1945 to 1971', *Town Planning Review*, 33 (1962–3), pp. 49–62.

pletely so than the expanded ones. But collectively, the overwhelming impression that emerges from a study of the planned developments is the gap between the ideals of the generation of 1940–7 which brought the postwar planning system into being, and the reality of the quarter century after the Second World War.

There seems to be little doubt, from the pronouncements of that time, that men like Abercrombie and Reith and Osborn intended the two programmes of planned developments, together, to make up by far the greater part of the total postwar housing programme. In Abercrombie's Greater London Plan, for instance, there was a total overspill population of 1,270,000 to be

Table 10.7

NEW TOWNS AND EXPANDING TOWNS: CONTRIBUTION TO THE TOTAL HOUSING PROGRAMME 1945–1970

	Total dwellings completed*	In new towns Number*	In new towns per cent of total	In expanding towns schemes Number†	In expanding towns schemes per cent of total
South-East region	2,231,835	125,596‡	5·6	41,445‡	1·8
Rest of England and Wales	4,266,123	56,363	1·3	26,896	0·6
Total England and Wales	6,497,958	181,959	2·8	68,341	1·1

Notes: New Town figures are from date of designation; include all dwellings built from that date. Expanding town figures include only dwellings built under the scheme.

* To 31 December 1971

† To 30 June 1971

‡ Includes all new towns and expanding towns serving Greater London overspill, whether or not in South-East region.

Source: *Housing Statistics*, Great Britain, No. 20, February 1971; *Town and Country Planning*, January 1971.

accommodated outside the conurbation. Abercrombie appears to have proposed that 125,000 of these should go into quasi-satellites next to the conurbation – a short-term expedient. 383,000 would go to new towns and no less than 525,000 to planned town expansions at up to 100 miles from London. Additionally, 19,000 would move spontaneously to the new towns. Only 214,000 of the total would be left to be housed outside the planned communities. Elsewhere, as in the West Midlands Plan, even though new towns did not appear, the broad intention was clearly the same. This was the ideal. As Table 10.7 shows, the postwar reality has been very different. Even in the South-East, only a little over 7 per cent of the total housing programme has gone into the new and expanded towns. In the rest of England and Wales, up to 1970, it was actually less than 2 per cent. Overall, just under 4 per cent of the total housing effort had gone into the planned communities.[12] It is an extraordinary discrepancy, and in Chapter Eleven, as we consider the alternatives that might have existed for urban growth in England since the Second World War, we shall want to focus on it.

[12] Table 13.2 of Volume One of this book has a more extended analysis of regional variations in the New Towns programme in the period 1945–69.

PART FOUR

TOWARDS A VERDICT

Part Four contains the conclusions of the study. It is organized in three chapters.

Chapter Eleven tries to summarize the essential functions of the planning system set up after the Second World War. It concludes that the most important of these was the control or guidance of social change.

Chapter Twelve turns to some concrete results of the system. Based mainly on the findings of Chapters 7–10, it identifies some of the most important as physical urban containment; suburbanization, or the separation of home and workplace; and rising land values. It compares what might have occurred under possible alternative systems.

Chapter Thirteen, finally, considers the relationships between planning policies and a wide variety of policies in closely-related fields such as economic development, agriculture, housing and transport. It does so both for the recent past – the period between the Second World War and 1970 – and the immediate future of the 1970s and 1980s. It ends by suggesting some unresolved questions for planning in this immediate future period.

CHAPTER ELEVEN

SOME FUNCTIONS OF THE BRITISH PLANNING SYSTEM

After an introduction outlining the different purposes of planning in different areas of the world, this chapter looks at the main problems which planning has had to deal with in post-1945 Britain, and focuses on the central function which the planning system has exercised: the control and guidance of change. It then studies the system of power which was responsible for translating the values of the planning system into action. Originally intended as a highly centralized system, planning after 1947 was in effect decentralized into local centres, represented by local authority planning offices. Lastly, the chapter considers whether, in trying to guide change, planning in postwar Britain has had the effect of limiting economic growth.

This chapter was written by Harry Gracey with certain additional material from Peter Hall.

INTRODUCTION

Planning in advanced industrial societies can be seen as a way of controlling and guiding the ubiquitous social changes which these societies experience, principally as a result of continued population growth, scientific discovery and technical innovation, and economic development. Through the process of planning, public agencies attempt to channel growth, and change and control its effects on society, in line with certain social values. The amount of planning for the control of social change and the values in terms of which the planning is exercised will vary from one modern industrial society to another. There is a great deal more public planning in the mixed economy of modern Britain than there is in the United States today, or than will probably exist for some time yet in the more comparable economies of Germany and Japan. Even activities which go under the same name, such as land-use planning or economic planning can have quite different meanings in these different national settings. Land-use zoning in the United States has traditionally been used to protect the money property values of land and the developments on it, while land-use planning in Britain has been an enterprise of much wider scope and social purpose, including as we have seen in this study, efforts to protect the countryside, preserve rural land, conserve natural resources, preserve the treasured villages and city townscapes from indiscriminate redevelopment and create comprehensively-planned and carefully located new urban developments. The greater planning effort in Britain is thus associated with the control of change in the interest of different social values.

In the underdeveloped countries of the world, on the other hand, planning is often used for the express purpose of bringing about social change in the form of the modernization of the nation. The use of planning to initiate social change can be seen today in many underdeveloped countries of the world in their efforts to move from a rural-agrarian society. The results of such planned change can be seen perhaps most spectacularly in the industrialization of the Soviet Union over the past sixty years. Even within the most highly-planned socialist societies, however, the content of the planning which is taking place, the ways in which the society is being moved towards the modern urban industrial type, do differ from country to country and these differences have been related in some cases to traditional values which predate socialism, or in the case of Yugoslavia, even the founding of the country itself. In modern Britain, with its mixed capitalist-socialist economy, some effort has been made to use planning to initiate change in the society and the economy. We are not here referring to the abortive National Plan of 1965 when the government attempted to set production goals for the private economy, which it did not control and therefore could not force to conform to its pattern for economic development. We are thinking rather of initiatives by the government to bring about social and economic change in areas in which it did have control or substantial influence, which would include the building of the famous new towns in the urban planning field, and such initiatives as the nuclear energy policy in the economic planning field.

In an advanced industrial society with a mixed economy, such as Britain has today, planning can then perhaps be used both to control the rate and direction of change which emanates from sources not under public control, such as the private sector of the economy, and to initiate new social and economic programmes for the nation. It is also perhaps at times difficult to tell how much of a public project is a response, and how much an initiative, on the part of the public authorities. The new towns, for example, are part of the planning response to the pressure of population growth and urban expansion which the country experienced following the Second World War. They are also a creative invention, a government initiative in the sense of being a unique way of responding to these problems, one which is being taken over and copied by other countries experiencing similar population pressures. Clearly, however, the planning which has formed the subject of this study has been principally a response to social changes stimulated by the growth of population, changes in technology, and developments in the economy; and it is these changes which the government has tried to control through the agencies of town and country land-use planning and regional economic planning. In this chapter we shall summarize the changes which the planning programmes sought to control in Britain, and identify some of the social values in terms of which these changes were organized and channelled through planning. We also want to speculate somewhat about the results of the planning effort as a whole, that is, its effects on the economy and the society we now live in.

CONTEMPORARY TRENDS OF CHANGE

The programmes of modern city and regional planning in Britain were drawn up in their essentials in the 1930s and 1940s when a number of government commissions brought in recommendations for planning policies and procedures and these were variously incorporated into law by the postwar Labour Government. The Barlow Commission on the distribution of the industrial population, the Scott Committee on the preservation of agricultural land, the Uthwatt Committee on compensation for nationalization of land development rights, and the Reith Committee on new towns, together proposed the essential elements of regional economic planning and national land-use planning which were implemented in Acts of Parliament passed from 1943 through to 1968.

In addition, Abercrombie's Greater London Plan which was published in 1944 set the pattern for land-use planning which was to be practised throughout the city regions of the country under the powers of land-use control which were granted to central and local governments by the great Planning Act of 1947.

The planning effort as a whole, as it has developed over this period, was initiated to deal with the consequences of economic, demographic, and technological changes being felt in the country at the time and still in evidence today. In summary form these changes are:

1 The decline of the traditional industries of the North of England, South Wales and Central Scotland, including most importantly, coal mining, shipbuilding and textiles;
2 The development of modern industry in the South-East of England and the Midlands, including machinery, automobiles, electrical and electronic industry, computers, chemicals, and a great variety of modern administrative and service industries;
3 The consequent decline of population in the North, Scotland and Wales and the continued rise of population, through migration and natural increase, in the South and the Midlands, the 'drift to the South' of people and jobs;
4 The increasing use of the motor car as a popular means of transportation, facilitating the dispersal of urban populations over wider areas. The development of rapid rail transportation, facilitating wider functional interconnections of urban areas with railway electrification and rapid inter-city services;
5 The continued growth and expansion of urban areas with suburban and exurban migration of urban populations and the growth of the national

population as a whole in a country already 80 per cent urban, resulting in the problem of urban sprawl into the countryside.

Planning, in both its regional economic form and its town and country land-use form, has been a general national effort to intervene in these basic processes of change in society. The goal of regional economic planning has been to achieve a regional balance of population and employment in the nation. The goal of land-use planning has been first of all to contain the physical spread of cities over the landscape of the country. The programme of regional economic planning has been to encourage modern industry to develop in the North of England, central Scotland and Wales and to limit its expansion as much as is practicable in the Midlands and the South-East of England. The programme of town and country planning has included Green Belts around the existing cities to halt their spread into the countryside, the designation of towns and villages in the countryside to receive the necessary urban development, and the construction of the comprehensively-planned new towns to organize both population and employment in new urban settings carefully situated in the countryside. Two basic value judgements are of course inherent in these planning programmes. The first is that new economic development ought to be spread over the country as a whole rather than being allowed to continue concentrating in the currently most prosperous areas. The second is that cities ought not to continue to expand physically, and new population ought to be accommodated in pre-planned expansions of smaller places, and in the new towns.

The planning programme sought to influence the spatial distribution of people and economic activity in the nation by intervening in those basic trends of change known as the 'drift to the South' and the 'urban sprawl' because these trends were thought to be undesirable for the nation.

What we would like to suggest here is that whether or not these specific trends were harmful in themselves, the control of change *per se*, through the two planning systems, has had consequences for the society and economy of Britain. Controlling social change or channelling its effects, as the planning system has tried to do, may have reduced both the disruptive results of rapid social change and the rate of economic growth in the society.

GENERAL VALUES UNDERLYING THE PLANNING PROGRAMME

It has been said that planning, in its regional economic and land-use forms is a conscious effort to control some basic trends of change in society in the interest of certain social values. We have identified some of the trends of change, and summarized some relevant ones in the concepts of the drift to the South and urban sprawl. But what are the social values in terms of which these trends were opposed and the reasons why they were judged to be undesirable for the nation? Some of these values, we would suggest, include social stability and harmony, public economy and safety, political power, the quality of urban life, and 'stewardship of the land'.

It is sometimes said, often by foreign observers, that the English at any rate dislike change itself, that non-change is a basic value in English life and that the élites try to find policies which avoid or prevent change. It is certainly true that continuity and stability are highly valued by the traditional élites in this society, and have been so for some time, at least since the Industrial Revolution disrupted the entire pattern of life in society. However it is probably not true that change itself is opposed, so much as there is a strong desire to control the effects of change, directing it in ways which preserve the traditional values of society. Rather than simple opposition to change, there is the control and organization of its effects in the interests of political stability, historical continuity and other traditional values.

To take just one example, the boundaries of local government have been altered to some extent, in response to changing settlement patterns, almost every decade since the mid-nineteenth century. The decision-making process by which they have been changed illustrates this attitude towards change, that it must be organized and controlled in the interests of maximum stability and continuity with the past. Royal or government commissions are appointed to recommend needed boundary changes, testimony is heard over a period of years, if need be from the interested parties, on-the-site observations are made of existing and proposed boundaries, and a series of judicious compromises are reached between the interests of the cities and the counties and other local government units. The function of the Royal Commission, which is technically appointed by the monarch and stands above partisan political interest, is to ascertain the national interest on any particular question it has been created to investigate, which it does by hearing testimony from persons and groups with any interest in the problem being investigated, before making recommendations to the government as to the most judicious resolution of the issue. The testimonies on the commissions, which sometimes take years to hear, serve two social functions. First, they force the commission to take account of a wide range of opinion with regard to the subject under study and encourage it to come up with proposals which accommodate as wide a range of interests as possible. Second, but just as important in the effort to maintain social stability and continuity in society, the hundreds or thousands of hours of commission hearings give the groups who think their interests may be affected a chance to be heard and to feel their interests will be taken into account in the making of the final recommendations. Furthermore, attendance at the hearings and reading of the testimony of other interested parties can give the various interest groups an indication of the range of interests involved in the issue and a realistic idea of how much of their own position they can expect to be adopted in any accommodation of interests which is reached.

The chance to be heard, to put one's case to the commissioners, in all probability also helps groups to accommodate themselves to the disappointment of not getting all they would want from any particular commission's recommendations. Having been heard perhaps helps interest groups to accommodate themselves to the changes which are recommended. Most may feel they have been fairly accommodated in the consensus-maintaining decision-making process, and the rest can perhaps feel they have had a fair hearing for their point of view. More importantly, the aftermath of bitterness and resentment which is bound to follow significant social change ought to be reduced measurably by such a decision-making process at the national level. Interest groups would be less likely to see themselves as the helpless victims of impersonal social forces, and resentment and bitterness which are bound to accompany social change may be kept to a minimum by this decision-making procedure. It might even be hypothesized, since we are clearly speculating here, that the whole commission process of organizing social change is less technically efficient than other kinds of decision-making processes might be, because of the time and money it takes, but socially effective in minimizing potentially disruptive frustration and anger and therefore highly functional in maintaining social consensus in society.

In addition the ultimate decision on a commission's recommendations for change is brought into the ordinary political arena; the recommendations are given to the government of the day which then decides what to do with them. Therefore, in deciding whether to implement by law any of the recommendations for change made by commissions, the government is constrained by public opinion to the extent of looking to the effect of these changes on its chances in the next election. Change as such is not opposed; rather this is an effort to organize and control it in such a way which maintains continuity and stability in society. What is opposed is disruptive change, change which might cause serious dislocation in the social system which might lead to disorganization and conflict in society.

The people who created the British planning systems also opposed those changes which they thought would bring public diseconomies. Public economy was one of the principal arguments made by the government for its regional economic planning programme. It was pointed out that if the large migrations continued from the depressed or declining areas to the more prosperous areas of the country, various governments would have the expense of creating the social infrastructure to support these populations. New schools, council houses, roads, hospitals and other public facilities would have to be built by central and local governments, in the Midlands and the South-East, to serve the new populations, whereas these were already in existence in the economically declining areas of the North, Scotland, and Wales from which these people were migrating. From this point of view the drift to the South entailed large public diseconomies in the form of new expenditures for duplicate facilities in the South. Thus this change in location of population and economic activity in the nation was opposed by the planning system partially on the grounds of saving unnecessary public expenditure.

In land-use planning we have also seen the argument of savings in public expenditure, and private expenditure too, made in opposing social change. Patrick Abercrombie, in his seminal Greater London Plan and in the plan he produced for the West Midlands, argued that allowing the continued growth of existing cities would lead to additional expenditures by government and by private investors as the use of different plots of land and of different buildings changed. He said specifically, in the West Midlands Plan, that urban expansion in the form of the continued growth of existing cities would lead to changes in land use in the cities and this would entail the expenses of converting land and buildings to new uses. He also felt that continued growth of existing cities would lead to a waste of urban resources in that some land and buildings in the city centres might be abandoned as, for example, some industry and perhaps shops moved further out into the suburbs where they would find land for expansion and perhaps be closer to the areas of new house-building and therefore population growth. Abercrombie and the early land-use planners who agreed with his thinking, did not seem to consider the possibility that the new economic activity generating urban growth and expansion might be creating sufficient total new wealth for the community and society to cover the costs of the land-use transformations it would also bring. In other words, granted that the urban expansion would be partly a result of industrial expansion and economic growth generally, the total wealth of the community and society would be increased by this activity, and this new wealth would probably pay for many of the costs which accompanied industrial growth. There might perhaps be a problem of transferring this new wealth from its producers, the economic enterprises, to the public agencies which must pay some of the costs of expansion in the provision of additional public services, but this would be a problem in the area of taxation rather than planning itself.

However, in an industrial society of only modest wealth, and one which was at the time still paying the costs of a terribly destructive war, the argument of public economy undoubtedly weighed heavily with decision-makers in the government. The prospects of significant economic expansion, sufficient to pay the costs of the public expenditures which would be caused by the drift to the South and continued expansion of existing cities, was perhaps not seen as a realistic possibility in a period which saw postwar reconstruction and urban slum clearance as two of its major social tasks.

Regional economic planning also had its political side in Britain, as seems the case in all Western European countries where it is practised. The depressed areas of the 1930s, which became the areas of economic decline in the 1950s, were of course areas of traditional Labour Party support. These were essentially the areas of nineteenth-century industrial development, in the North of England and South Wales in particular, where the workers of the Industrial Revolution founded the Labour Party and where it has had perhaps its most solid support since. The Labour Party, in power after the Second World War, could therefore be expected to use its powers to the benefit of the homelands of its supporters, in much the same way as the Gaullist Party in France, on the other side of the political spectrum, used its regional planning powers to support the peasant agricultural areas from which it derived some of its most solid support. In both cases an economic rationale is found for support of the political decision. In Britain these were economically declining areas, objectively speaking, and all that was needed to justify subsidizing their development from the central government Treasury was the judgement that there ought not to be in the country economically declining areas from which people migrated to areas of growth in search of jobs, a judgement which is expressed positively in the concept of the Barlow Commission's 'regional economic balance'.

Preferences for a certain quality of urban life are also clearly seen in the formulation and operation of the British planning system. The values of smallness, compactness, neatness and tidiness in settlement design, reflect these values in British life generally.

It has often been said that British town and country planning is anti-urban in outlook and the evidence cited is the opposition of those involved in planning to the growth and spread of existing cities. We have seen that this charge is true to the extent that urban is identified with the growth of large cities. However, those involved in the planning movement here have always rejected the charge of being anti-urban and in fact seem hurt and angered by the charge, especially when it is made by American observers who, they feel, do not really understand their position. British planners see urban in terms of density rather than size. Their preference, they would perhaps say, is for one type of urban settlement as opposed to another. The type they favour is the small, compact self-contained settlement exemplified in their eyes by the new towns. The new towns, as well as large cities, are considered urban settlements, and as we have seen, many British planners prefer the construction of these small, economically self-contained cities in the countryside to the continued growth of the larger cities.

The preference for small, comprehensively-planned communities generally built up of smaller, comprehensively-built neighbourhood units has been interpreted by some observers as a function of the British class structure. It has been suggested that a preference for small urban units is historically a result of the fear of the urban working class assembled *en masse* in the cities, with the potential for revolutionary organization. The population, it is pointed out, might be more easily controlled in small cities or towns than in huge urban conglomerates. Easy control of the urban masses in the industrial capitalist society is suggested to be one of the implicit goals of the planning movement's preference for small towns to big cities. This argument has good historical foundations and can be developed sociologically. Social control ought to be easier in small communities than in larger ones, or in smaller groups of any sort simply because small groups have a simpler social structure than large groups, given at least equal density of settlement as a measure of intensity of interaction. Small communities are less complex than larger ones. Increasing size usually means an increase in heterogeneity of the population, increasing complexity of social organization, and increasing creativity in many areas of life, including social deviance. Social control is more complex, and therefore more expensive in the large city than in the small place. Small places are simpler than large ones and therefore easier to keep orderly.

The small, comprehensively-planned community is a neat and tidy unit of urban life when compared with the great sprawling, dirty, congested city, and would appeal in Britain on these grounds. Neatness and tidiness are social values, things good in themselves and therefore goals to be striven for in social life. Even the smallness of these communities fits the British value system, which in direct contrast to the American, prefers smallness as opposed to largeness. Small, clearly-bounded towns are preferred to large cities whose suburbs straggle out across the countryside.

Of course, preventing the peripheral spread of the existing cities, and locating the new cities at carefully selected sites in the countryside, would clearly implement the values of preserving the countryside and conserving natural resources. The planning movement, the people who created the planning system, and the original creators of plans to implement these ideas were deeply committed to maintaining and preserving the traditional British countryside. This included the open country, of course, but also just as important in their minds, the old towns and villages, so long a treasured part of the English rural scene. One of the strongest values of the planning movement was and is the preservation of rural England, and it is of course the basic value of the high-status pressure group represented by the Council for the Preservation of Rural England. They all seek as strongly as they can to prevent urban development in the valued parts of the countryside, including the treasured towns and villages. In judging applications for permission to build new houses in rural villages and towns, county planners all over the country make the distinction between those villages which are as they say, 'worth saving' from new development, and those which can be 'let go' to new development because they are 'not worth saving'.

The conservation of natural resources, especially of high-quality agricultural land, was one of the basic values which the founders of the planning system sought to implement. An expert committee had reported on the conservation of agricultural land and it was recommended that this ought to be a major criterion for deciding if, and where, urban expansion would be allowed to take place. The Second World War put a fear into the governing group of Britain's strategic vulnerability, to the extent that she relied on imports for basic foods. There was also the balance of trade problem after the war and the consequent desire to reduce the national import bill in relation to the exports in order to achieve economic viability for the nation. The strongest possible arguments were therefore arrayed in support of the conservation of agricultural land, partly through the containment of urban growth and spread in Britain. The argument for the containment of cities in order to preserve high-quality agricultural land was not wholly convincing, as was pointed out in a minority dissent to the expert committee report.[1] However, it was employed compellingly by the founders of the planning system and was incorporated as a goal into all original county Development Plans drawn up under the 1947 Act. One suspects that the conservation of agricultural land argument for preventing urban spread was compelling in

[1] Ministry of Works and Planning, *Report of the Committee on Land Utilization in Rural Areas.* Cmd 6378, HMSO, London, 1943, pp. 105, 110–11, 113–114.

the operation of town and country planning partly because it complemented and supported the other goal of the preservation of the countryside, which had always been a basic value of the planning movement.

The maintenance of access to mineral deposits under the land was also one of the goals of the planning system when it was created. This was seen as part of the effort to conserve natural resources, preventing urban development in places where it would 'seal off' access to mineral deposits which might be profitably exploited in the future. The exploitation of such resources would also contribute to reducing the country's dependence on imports for basic commodities.

The land-use planning system may also be said to implement the traditional British value of the stewardship of the land, extending the sense of societal responsibility for the care and keeping of all the land in Britain. Land-use planning in Britain is perhaps unique in the world in its comprehensiveness, for as we have seen, theoretically the use of every square foot of land in the country is planned in some county or county borough Development Plan or supplement thereto. All of the Planning Acts of Parliament have been town and country planning Acts, showing that planning has always been seen as a concern for land use everywhere in the country, in the city and in the countryside. The land of Britain was seen by the founders of the planning movement, and is seen by the leading figures in the field today, as part of Britain's precious national heritage, to be conserved and tended with loving care by each generation and to be committed to the care of the next generation in the best possible condition.

Stewardship of the land, in its modern form as a basic value of those involved in planning and the planning movement, is a concern for the proper care and use of all the land in the country, urban and rural. Obviously an extension of traditional aristocratic values in society, it provides the ideology behind the power and responsibility of the contemporary land-use planners. Most of the values considered so far are manifestations of this (and of social responsibility assumed by the planners) – for example, concern for the preservation of cities, towns and countryside, conservation of resources and preference for small, compact units of urban settlement.

The civil servants in national and local government who together apply the value of stewardship of the land on a national scale in Britain, see themselves for the most part as bearing a heavy social responsibility. It is true that they often feel that they do not have sufficient authority to properly exercise this responsibility. But our study has clearly shown that conscientious city and county planners in Britain see themselves as responsible for the care and keeping of their land and settlements in their charge. Their attitude is paternalistic and often conservative with regard to the care of their charge, and this is certainly implied in the concept of stewardship, a pre-modern social value which was incorporated into the core of the planning-movement philosophy in the nineteenth century and transmitted from the movement to the planning system created in the second half of the twentieth century.

POWER IN THE PLANNING SYSTEM

The values, which have been identified in the last section, have to be translated into actions within the planning system by the exercise of power. It will already be apparent that in essence, the 1947 Planning System was élitist in its concept of power: it held that the values of society should be interpreted and guided by professional planners, monitored and controlled in the last resort by democratically accountable political power, but with a great deal of freedom not merely in day-to-day administration but also in the formulation of basic policies. Professional planners, as one of them remarked in an interview during our study, were expected to be Solomons: not merely omniscient, but omnipotent. It was assumed that with this disinterested guidance, differences of interest among different groups could be resolved. There was, in other words, an objective best solution which optimized everyone's own interests. Such a belief is perhaps understandable in the special circumstances of 1945, at the end of a major war with a considerable element of ideological unity throughout the whole nation. In practice it led to the notion that the whole nation should vote for a package of values, and then leave the professionals considerable freedom in their interpretation.

Such a set of beliefs seems essentially to demand a centrally organized system of planning, in which the values of society are interpreted by a national agency or agencies. And both the Barlow and the Uthwatt Reports talked in terms of a national planning authority, in which critical decisions on matters of location and of land use would be taken centrally. The Uthwatt Report, for instance, assumed that such a central authority would determine when land was required for urban development, and would then itself buy it compulsorily from its owner at existing use-value (the owner having been compensated for loss of development rights on the land). Later, in similar vein, the Reith Committee reports on the new towns recommended that they should be developed by Development Corporations free of the existing local government structure; the Dower and Hobhouse reports assumed that the national parks should be administered by an autonomous National Parks Commission. The Labour Government of 1945 accepted this logic for new towns but not for national parks, despite the protests of the national parks campaigners that this would make the whole programme ineffectual.

In fact, the compromise adopted in 1947 leant heavily towards the principle of local autonomy. The new towns, it is true, would be built by Development Corporations appointed direct by the Minister, as provided for in the 1946 Act before an effective local planning system existed. But otherwise, the 1947 Act relied on the strong powers given to the largest available local authorities – the county boroughs and counties. There was provision for co-ordination, both at national and regional level, through the requirement that all Development Plans and their revisions should be submitted to the Minister, who would be advised by regional offices; these last, in effect, would work on a continuous updating and monitoring of a regional plan. It is just possible that in a relatively static situation, such a system could have provided a delicate balance between local autonomy and central direction. But in the event, this proved impossible for two main reasons: the pace of change was much faster than had been imagined, and the central planning staff was not expanded rapidly enough to cope. (The regional organization of the Ministry, an important part of the apparatus, was in fact dismembered during the 1950s on economy grounds.) As a result, long delays occurred in the vetting and approval – or modification – of Development Plans. The vital central control proved steadily less effectual in monitoring changes in the situation and reacting to them.

This was compounded in turn by the obvious fact that the local government system was not at all well-structured for the task of planning on this scale. Already by 1947, the advisory regional plans had made it quite clear that the most important problems of planning – urban redevelopment, the reception of overspill, the conservation of the countryside – required cities and their surrounding countryside to be planned together: it was not for nothing that the 1947 Act was entitled the Town and Country Planning Act. The government, at about the time the Act was passed, was contemplating a fairly radical reconstruction of the existing local government system, which had been inherited from the late nineteenth century; but nothing came of the move. As a result, planning for urban growth in England passed largely to the new county planning offices; the city planning machines, which were largely at first offshoots of the existing engineer's department, were restricted mainly to problems of reconstruction and renewal. The consequence, an extraordinary one in retrospect considering the intentions of the founders of the system, was that the planning of the growth of the cities was entrusted to interests which, politically, were almost bound to be opposed to it.

All this, it is curious to note, is not very different in important respects from the situation in the postwar United States. There also, many people shared an anti-urban ethos, and had retreated to the far edge of suburbia in order to live in a setting of rural arcadia – even if they might work in the city. There also, these people successfully resisted further growth by restrictive zoning ordinances at one home or less to the acre. (This, in effect, was not very different from the effect of Green Belt restrictions in England.) There also, the cities were excluded from any political jurisdiction over their surrounding suburbs. There was however one outstanding difference. In America, most suburban communities were by no means averse to growth. Most encouraged development because of the additional tax base it brought. Their motivations were economic rather than social. But in England, as we have seen, the preservation of a way of life counted heavily above any economic considerations. Indeed, it might be said that the counties took a conscious decision to rank quality of life above economic growth – nearly a quarter-century before this problem of trade-off became a fashionable one.

This perhaps is not surprising. The counties were controlled politically, in most cases, by their more prosperous residents. To them, in many cases, the country was a place of consumption – even of conspicuous consumption – rather than of production. It was logical for them to try to defend a way of life against rapid change. What was surprising is that the wider community, represented by the central government, allowed them so successfully to do it. The reason has however been suggested. A system set up to achieve one set of purposes – broadly, the control of the pace and the direction of change in the interests of all – in practice too often became a system devoted to the restriction of all change in the interests of a specific group or groups. This was because the crucial central controls were lost, and because the whole system had no built-in mechanism for adapting to rapid changes from outside. Central government officials were well aware of this, as is shown by the appointment of the Planning Advisory Group in 1963, culminating in their report and the establishment of a more flexible system in the 1968 Planning Act. During the same time, far more effective central and regional monitoring machinery was recreated, so that by the end of the 1960s central government was again as strong in relation to local planning authorities as it had been at the end of the 1940s.

SOCIAL AND ECONOMIC EFFECTS OF PLANNING

Another crucial contemporary question which emerges when the planning function is placed in an institutional model of society is to what extent town and country planning has had a deterrent influence on national economic growth. Has local land-use planning and development control, as practised since 1947, made the total level of economic development less, even if more orderly and tidy, than it would have been without this form of political control? Planners have been acting the role of caretakers of the physical environment trying to keep everything neat and tidy, to put all development in its 'proper' place by their standards. In doing so they have prevented much development from taking place where the developers wanted it to be and, it is likely, prevented a certain amount of development from occurring at all, though it is impossible by the nature of the situation to determine how much investment has been deferred or sent abroad because of planning controls. The planners in areas of great development pressure realize their controls have prevented new development in many cases, and some are of the opinion that their work has held down the national level of economic growth. They have two different attitudes toward this result: those socialized in the field of economics think it is a scandal, while those who received their professional socialization in the town planning schools seem to consider it is a price the nation should be willing to pay for the benefits of order and stability which they feel their work has brought the country.

One might suggest the hypothesis that physical planning controls have effectively been part of a 'national trade-off' of economic growth for political stability over the past twenty years. Such a hypothesis finds some empirical and theoretical support. Empirically, there is the suggestion, in some current, on-going studies of developers' location decisions, of investment which has not been undertaken because businessmen could not locate their enterprises where they wanted them. Theoretically, since economic growth is one of the causes of urban growth, a strong and sustained effort to put a cap on urban expansion should reverberate back on economic activities and slow down the rate of economic expansion. How one evaluates such a result, however, depends on the value position from which one views it.

It is very difficult indeed to estimate the extent to which economic growth, rather than urban growth, has been influenced by planning in Britain. All that can be said from our studies of industry in the South-East is that there are apparently expansions and investments which would have been undertaken if there had been no planning restrictions, and that not all of these have been undertaken in the development areas. Some of this investment seems to be going to Europe, but certainly the Common Market has as much to do with European versus British location decisions, as do the British planning restrictions. Some of this investment has just not been made, or is not being made until planning restrictions are eased in the South-East or the individual firms find the ways around the rules to get themselves located in the South-East. Smaller businesses, as we have seen, have the most difficult time with the planning system if they are not local firms, and these are the firms which lack the resources in time and energy for contravening the planning restrictions. The evidence for these conclusions was presented in Chapter Three of the present volume.

Town and country planning has been seen as an effort to control national trends of development and change in the interest of some basic values. Here it was physical urban growth, the spread of cities into the countryside, which threatened traditional values with regard to the size and location of settlements, the physical urban structure of society. Ribbon development was extending fingers of urbanization into the country along the roads leading out of the major cities and towns. Peripheral growth was proceeding apace on the edge of urban areas all over the country. Even in the North, where total population was remaining static, there was a massive population shift going on with people moving from the city to the suburbs, following the normal pattern of urban and suburban development for cities of this size. In the South and the Midlands, where the economy and therefore the population was expanding, urban sprawl was even more marked, stimulated by overall population growth as well as suburban migration, and especially worrying to people identified with the goals of the planning movement. Such trends were another example of uncontrolled social change, and it was felt in governing circles that they ought to be controlled, again we can say, in the interests of certain social values. The free operation of the laws of urban development, leading to urbanization, suburbanization, and the development of metropolitan communities was to be controlled and organized to serve basic values held by certain portions of the society, and represented for the most part in the ideologies of the planning movement. These goals include preservation of both cities and the countryside, conservation of national resources, the achievement of public economies, and the preference for small, compact self-contained urban units as opposed to huge, sprawling cities.

We have shown that planning criteria have been developed and used to influence the location, size and even design of new development in Britain. Planning is an institutional force in society, with ideology, criteria of judgement, goals and powers of its own for influencing growth and change. The institution has been highly successful, in its own terms, in controlling land development and influencing the location of industry in Britain. The activities of the institution have probably influenced the development of society as a whole over the past and the slowing of the rate of change in the present. It has, at the same time, probably slowed the rate of economic growth in the society as a whole while contributing to the maintenance of stability. As is so often the case in contemporary societies, the socialists have used planning to implement traditional values which are often in opposition to the free play of the capitalist market forces. The paternalism and social responsibility which the planners, and their sometimes allies in the various conservationist groups, have exercised over the past thirty years, has undoubtedly contributed to the maintenance of historical continuity and social stability in contemporary British society. The valued civility of English life, so envied by the citizens of more chaotic modern nations, has been purchased at a price of some social and economic inefficiency which probably contributes to placing the country in a disadvantaged position among the other developed countries of the world. The effort to maintain continuity with the past and control the rate and direction of social change in the present by these societal housekeepers in the planning institution has surely left its mark upon the society. The job of implementing the equally valued but conflicting goals of social stability and economic growth in a mixed society remains the continuing task of the national decision-makers who control the future of the planning system in Britain. On their success in this effort depends the continued co-existence of prosperity and civility in modern Britain.

CHAPTER TWELVE

PLANNING AND URBAN GROWTH: TOWARDS A VERDICT

This chapter starts by isolating certain alternative models of urban growth which could be regarded as possibilities for the urban development of the period 1945–70. One is a continuation of the trends of the 1930s, without the interjection of the 1947 Planning System. Another is the ideal of decentralization of the urban overspill population into comprehensively-planned new and expanded towns. A third is an approximation to the actual process which has dominated urban growth in the postwar period – the peripheral growth of freestanding towns by the normal processes of development control. The chapter then goes on to show that the process of urbanization has included elements of all three models though it has been dominated by the third. Its outstanding features are urban containment, the development of suburban communities isolated from employment and other opportunities, and rises in land and property values – an unexpected effect of the system.

This chapter was written by Peter Hall, Ray Thomas and Roy Drewett.

INTRODUCTION

Against the background of the last chapter, it is now time to try to reach a tentative verdict on the operation of the planning system and its effect on urban growth in the quarter century following the Second World War. In this volume we have looked in detail at the objectives of those who operated the system, at the way the system worked to make plans and operate development control, at the effects on the housing industry, and at the programme of creating new communities. But in order to try to bring this material together into a set of conclusions, it is first necessary to pose two difficult questions. The first is: what alternatives might have existed to what happened? In other words, what would have happened if there had been no 1947 Planning System, or a different kind of system? The second, related question is: how far did the actual operation of the 1947 system in practice reflect the ideals and aspirations and objectives of those who created it? In other words, it may well be that there are two separate ideas: the ideal concept of planning as it existed in 1947, and the reality. In that case, the ideal concept would itself logically constitute one of the alternatives to be considered.

The question of alternatives can be approached in two ways. We have seen that the objectives of the 1947 system were all too often defined in terms of desired physical forms, expressed in end-state blueprint plans; and that there was a general lack of understanding of the relationships between physical plans and other policy measures (such as housing or transport policies) which might have clear physical effects. From this, it follows that alternatives to the 1947 system can be traced in two different dimensions. The first is in terms of different physical forms. The second would consist of different bundles of policy measures in a variety of fields, including physical planning, so as to realize stated social and economic goals. Policies of this type would have physical effects on development patterns; the patterns would constitute partial ways of achieving the objectives of the policies.

This distinction explains the form of our two concluding chapters. In this chapter we shall consider two ideal physical or design alternatives, each of which can be associated with a particular attitude to physical planning. One will consist of a non-plan attitude; here we assume that the 1947 system had never been brought into being, but that the trends of the 1930s had continued to operate unchecked in the postwar period. Another will consist of the ideal operation of the planning system, as it seems to have been imagined by the pioneers and evangelists who set it up. These will be contrasted with the system as it actually operated, and with the effects that were actually produced. After passing a provisional verdict on these alternatives, we shall proceed in the next chapter to a broader-based examination of policy alternatives. It should be stressed that the two chapters belong together and should be read together. They sum up the conclusions of our study.

A NON-PLAN ALTERNATIVE

The first idealized alternative to the 1947 Planning System would be no plan at all. But this is difficult to imagine as a reality. All developed societies have some planning, even if it is called by-law enforcement. Britain had some planning from the mid-nineteenth century, and by the 1930s it had a fairly elaborate system; it merely wanted in comprehensiveness. In posing a first alternative to the 1947 system, non-plan really means a continuation of the trends of the 1930s, which so alarmed the Barlow Commission and the Scott Committee.

There is a difficulty in setting up this alternative: our information, particularly about employment and transport patterns, is very scanty for the interwar period. What we can discover, however, is very different from the archetype which is often presented.

The information is most complete (or least incomplete) for London. Here, Westergaard showed that though the great suburban expansion of London was accompanied by an increase in the concentration of jobs at the centre, this central area actually had a smaller share of total conurbation jobs in 1951 than in 1921. The suburbs added population massively; they also added jobs, though less massively, and they actually reduced their deficiency of jobs. By 1951, 40 per cent of workers who lived in these suburbs actually found jobs in their own local authority area, compared with only 21 per cent who commuted to the centre. And parts of suburban Middlesex and Essex and Hertfordshire, where job opportunities had actually grown faster than residential population, were much more independent of central London jobs at the end of the interwar period than at the beginning. In these areas, the typical journey to work was a short one to the local factory zone. Physically, they might be part of London; functionally, they formed virtually self-contained towns.[1] This evidence powerfully confirmed Frank Pick's remarkable testimony to the Barlow Commission in 1937, which showed that in the interwar period the proportion of longer journeys in London, contrary to all belief, had not increased. The great majority of public transport journeys made on London Transport – 92·5 per cent in 1921, 95·8 per cent in 1937 – were under four miles.[2] It is true that some of the increase in longer-distance commuting would have gone to the main-line railways, so this picture is incomplete. Yet there were great extensions to the tube system in this period, so the static picture is quite remarkable. By the 1930s, half of all work journeys were crossing journeys from suburb to suburb, not radial journeys to the centre.[3]

All this suggested that suburban employment growth powerfully modified the functional geography of London in the 1920s and 1930s. And for the future, the changes might have been even more profound. Pick pointed out to the Barlow Commission that:

> . . . so far at any rate as the centrifugal movement of the population is concerned . . . London cannot become fully developed beyond a zone stretching roughly 12 to 15 miles from the centre.[4]

Any additional commuters would go further out along fast main lines, to places like Reigate, Hatfield or St Albans; but these would not coalesce into continuous suburbia. What might however modify the situation, Pick stressed, was further decentralization of industry, which might allow self-supporting satellite towns to develop round London, coalescing into a 'confluent pox': 'layering first industry and then residences . . . indefinitely, but that would not be London.'[5]

Pick was saying, in other words, that there was a distinction between the physical and the functional London. Functionally, London was to him the area economically dependent on central employment; and that could not extend continuously beyond the twelve to fifteen mile radius, at which point London might contain up to twelve million people. Beyond this, London

[1] J. H. Westergaard, 'Journeys to Work in the London Region,' *Town Planning Review*, 28 (1957), pp. 40–2.

[2] Royal Commission on the Geographical Distribution of the Industrial Population *Minutes of Evidence*, 12th Day (15 Feb. 1938), Exhibit F, p. 372.

[3] Ibid., Q. 3181.

[4] Ibid., p. 358.

[5] Ibid., Q. 3107.

might extend physically but it would not be a functional unit. Pick objected to this process, not on the grounds of the cost and time of the journey to work – since he could demonstrate convincingly that this was not likely to be the problem – but on social and even aesthetic grounds. He might even have foreseen, though he did not mention, another consideration: for the future, with the growth of mass car ownership, the layering of decentralized employment and housing would lead to greater reliance on the private car for cross-commuting, and a weakening of London Transport. This, more than anything, would have helped to fill any intervening spaces, and lead to continued suburban spread. Curiously, therefore, the Barlow Commission's logic was correct. They sought to restrain the growth of London by controls on factory employment, and have been criticized for ignoring the more rapid growth of tertiary jobs. But for shaping the growth of London in 1938, it was the distribution of decentralized factory jobs that was most critical.

There was, though, another factor already present in the geography of London. Raymond Unwin's proposed green girdle had been embodied in the LCC 1938 Green Belt Act. The Council found that it could soon acquire the land it needed under the Act;[6] almost without doubt, it would have been emboldened to extend the acquisition programme. Open space would have been bought, some of it in the form of linear parks, just outside the twelve–fifteen mile limits; there might have been radial extensions outwards to separate the towns, as suggested in Unwin's map.[7] The result would have been rather like the pattern in the outer New York City region on the New York side of the Hudson in the 1920s and 1930s: a conglomeration of communities separated by areas of parkland which were owned and managed by the community. Unwin's girdle would have done for London what Robert Moses' parks did for New York.

There was a last relevant point. The 1932 Act had positively encouraged local authorities to make local planning schemes, so as to guarantee good layout and separate different land uses. By the spring of 1939, nearly half the land in Britain was in schemes which were either approved or waiting approval; all areas which expected development on any scale were covered.[8] The general effect would not have been to stop development – that was not in general the aim – but to raise the standards of the development. In fact, as in zoning as practised in the United States, the effect might have been to increase space standards and reduce densities, so as to raise the quality of the area and reduce the cost of supplying expensive services (such as education). Though it cannot be proved, the effect might well have been the opposite of the effect of the 1947 system. In that sense, it might be said to have encouraged sprawl. But a low density is only one dimension of sprawl; the other, scatteration of development in small packets, would have been discouraged by

[6] David Thomas, *London's Green Belt*. Faber, London (1970), p. 81.

[7] Cf. the map in ibid., p. 79.

[8] Royal Commission on the Distribution of the Industrial Population, *Report*. Cmd 6153, HMSO, London (1940), p. 108.

the making of town planning schemes. And green-girdle parkland would also have worked to reduce scatter.

To sum up, if the trends of the 1930s had continued to operate around London, the result would have been by no means the same as the actual result observed during that period. Central London workers would have tended to seek homes in freestanding towns at considerable distances from London, where fast train services were available. Decentralized factory jobs would have led to coalescence of industrial towns, though that might have been met by special powers over location as recommended by the Barlow majority; it would not have led to long or costly commuter journeys. The use of town planning schemes would probably have lowered densities but reduced scatteration. Parkland reservations would have given a certain shape and limit to the growth of urban communities.

In many respects, these developments are not so different from what actually happened. Longer-distance commuting did transfer populations to the freestanding towns, and the Green Belt actually hastened the shift by truncating shorter-distance rail plans which penetrated the Belt. The decentralization of factory jobs proceeded apace. Residential development adhered mainly to existing towns where urban services were readily available. The town maps produced by the local planning authorities have often maintained the existing residential character of each area, as would have occurred with schemes made under the 1932 Act. The chief differences are obvious enough: the wide Green Belt and its extensions, the tight containment of the towns nearer London, the much higher building-densities, and the failure to buy more parkland under the 1938 Act, because it was felt that the Abercrombie Green Belt had made it unnecessary.

In the other conurbations, the situation was different. These urban areas were all much smaller than London; they had grown in different ways, and by the 1930s they functioned in very different ways from London. Even the bigger conurbations tended to be polycentric; growth took place from a number of nuclei, so there was nothing like the continuous mass of building that existed in London. Average journey lengths were much shorter and were easily handled by road-based public transport, first tram and then bus; rail transport was not very important (save locally), even for centripetal journeys. The bigger cities had developed big slum-clearance schemes, coupled with the development of extensive peripheral housing estates (Manchester's Wythenshawe, Liverpool's Speke, Birmingham's Erdington) which in several cases led to pressure for boundary extensions; but even from these developments journeys were still quite short, quick, and (aided by subsidies in some cases) remarkably cheap. As in London, the newer and faster-growing industries (engineering, electrical goods, vehicles, pharmaceuticals) were decentralizing out of cramped central city sites to peripheral locations; but they still found it necessary to be within the conurbations, close to public transport routes which would guarantee their labour supplies. Though neighbouring counties were sometimes worried about city growth (and there was bitterness over boundary extensions, as between Manchester and Cheshire over Wythenshawe), in general there was no feeling in these cities that peripheral growth was anything but normal. Certainly cities did not accept that urban growth should be restrained. These areas, to adopt the terminology used in Chapter Thirteen of Volume One and Chapter Two of this Volume, were still urbanizing – and suburbanizing – rather than acquiring a metropolitan character. Here was a very striking contrast with London.

It is therefore easy to predict that without a 1947-style planning system, this pattern of growth would have shown little change; for unlike London, these cities were not facing some critical breakpoint in their history. Home buyers would have continued to seek new houses at the periphery, and would have found commuting no great burden, even to the city centre; as car ownership spread, more of them would have sought more distant homes in villages and market towns beyond the conurbation edge, but they would almost certainly have constituted a minority. City housing authorities would have continued to build peripheral estates, at medium densities, to rehouse their slum dwellers; the bigger ones would have developed trading estates there for decentralized industry, on the lines of the developments which Liverpool introduced at Speke and Kirkby in the 1930s. The result would have been steady advance of the built-up areas of the city on a broad peripheral front; but precisely because it was broad, it would not have been very deep. David Gregory's interesting conjecture of the probable growth of the West Midlands conurbation without controls up to the mid-1960s, based on refusals of planning permission and reproduced as Figure 12.1,[9] shows a maximum advance of two–three miles over a ten-year period. These advances would have led to boundary conflicts between cities and counties, periodically resolved in the cities' favour. There would almost certainly have been extensive parkland purchases on the model of Unwin's green girdle for London: Birmingham's extensive purchases in the Lickey Hills, and Manchester's at Wythenshawe Park, were strong pointers in this direction. Densities would have been generally lower than between the wars, and certainly lower than those that actually obtained after the Second World War; this would have encouraged car commuting, putting a strain on subsidized bus services.[10]

Here again, the surprising point is that the 1947 Planning System represented a less sharp break with the past than might be supposed. The major provincial cities were unwilling (as with Birmingham) or apathetic about the whole notion of urban containment, which the Barlow Commission seems to have developed mainly to deal with the very different problem of London. The whole notion of trying to decentralize urban growth into planned self-contained communities, which had been developed for London, seemed much

[9] David Gregory, *Green Belts and Development Control*. University of Birmingham Centre for Urban and Regional Studies, Occasional Paper No. 12, CURS, Birmingham (1970), p. 30.

[10] Ray Thomas, *Journeys to Work*. PEP, London (1968), pp. 369–71. Clifford Sharp, *Problems of Urban Passenger Transport*. U.P., Leicester (1967), Chap. 1, *passim*.

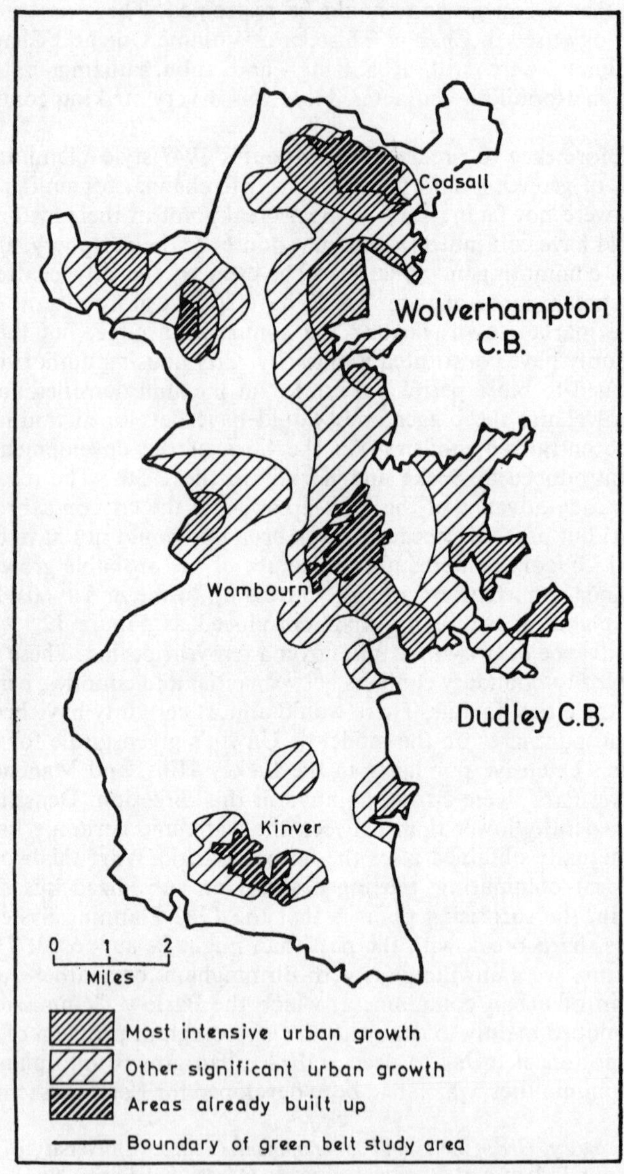

Figure 12.1 The Probable Development of the West Midlands Green Belt, West of Wolverhampton, in the Absence of Development Control
[*After David Gregory*]

less appropriate here and was much slower to gain acceptance, as witness the fact that none of the provincial English conurbations acquired a new town until 1961. The cities thus continued to grow peripherally, but came up against Green Belts drawn up by the counties, who used them as *cordons sanitaires*; in some cases, the counties seem to have been as unenthusiastic as the cities about planned communities. Since neither cities nor counties were notably warm about overspill policies – save perhaps the counties in the case of the more stagnant or depressed parts of their areas – the cities responded by raising densities in their redevelopment and rehousing schemes, with high-rise flats in the clearance areas and even (as at Birmingham) in peripheral estates; central government subsidies positively favoured these expensive schemes. Transport patterns remained broadly as in the 1930s, since industry remained in the conurbations and most journeys were radial. But car use rose, and even for central area work journeys Manchester, Liverpool and Birmingham had higher proportions of car users than London by the mid-1960s. Yet buses still carried the great majority of commuters;[11] there was little shift to rail, despite ambitious schemes for rail rapid transit in Manchester and Liverpool, which were unveiled in the late 1960s.

The most important difference which the 1947 system brought about, in all probability, was in the area of densities and land values. Had the trends of the 1930s continued, there would undoubtedly have been rising land-values around the conurbations and the cities, associated with the prospect of early urbanization. Indeed, as we shall suggest in Chapter Thirteen, the progress of inflation after the Second World War would almost certainly have speeded this process as compared with the trend of the 1930s. But with this difference: that virtually all land would have been open to development, so that rising values would not attach themselves to particular plots of land. The phenomenon of floating and shifting land values, to which the Uthwatt Committee devoted particular attention, would have continued to operate: the rise in value on any one plot would be limited by the fact that the potential development could be shifted to an adjacent plot. What the 1947 Act did, in practice, was to change all this. The Development Plans identified the areas that were to be developed: these were the plots which would attract all the rise in value. Thus, paradoxically, the Act created a mechanism for rapid inflation of land values, which in turn forced builders to economize on land by raising densities. We shall return to this point later in the chapter, when we come to look at the specific patterns associated with the 1947 system.

A GARDEN CITY ALTERNATIVE

At first sight, it might seem facetious to pose a garden city solution, based on the principles of Ebenezer Howard and Raymond Unwin and Patrick Abercrombie, as a second idealized alternative to the planning system that actually obtained in England after 1947. Most people automatically think of building garden cities, or new towns, as a central element of that system –

[11] Ray Thomas, op. cit., p. 367.

perhaps its greatest achievement. But in fact, the overall result has been far from the ideals which Howard and his followers stood for. As was shown in Chapter Ten, a small minority of all new urban development in postwar England has been in the new towns and expanding towns. The vast majority has been in the form of peripheral additions to existing towns, whether freestanding or in conurbations, under the normal processes of development control. The very fact that we can speak and write of these processes as normal illustrates the gap between ideal and reality. For Howard or Abercrombie, the normal situation would have been for the great bulk of new development to be channelled into self-contained, socially-balanced, comprehensively-planned communities.

That accepted, it is nevertheless difficult to envisage what a full-blooded garden city alternative would have looked like and worked like. The reason is that the pioneers themselves did not agree on that point. There are important differences between the visions of Howard, of Unwin and of Abercrombie on critical points. We saw in Chapter One that Howard saw his garden cities as small units – they were to be less than a mile in radius and the recommended size was 32,000 – which functioned as cells of a much larger functional whole, the Social City. Within Social City, high-speed transport systems would link each cell to the others; Howard imagined a railway, we might substitute a motorway. The units were set on a green background which was publicly owned and was used for a wide variety of semi-urban purposes (colleges, hospitals, children's homes) as well as agriculture, with a density of one person to each two and a half acres; the distance across the green area from one cell to the next was narrow, only two miles. In other words, Howard was suggesting a form of polycentric urban agglomeration of great size – in his example it had 250,000 people, but he stressed that it could grow without limit by cellular multiplication – not self-contained garden cities as most people understand them. The densities in the urban cells were to be relatively high when expressed in terms of people: eighty to the acre, about the same as the high-density Scottish new town of Cumbernauld. But that is an expression of the large family size when Howard wrote: expressed in terms of houses, the density is about fourteen persons to the residential acre, rather lower than the provision in new towns of the late 1960s in England. And Howard, it must be remembered, was writing at a time when average urban densities were much higher.

There are few pictures in existence of what Howard meant;[12] even his own diagram of the Social City (Figure 1.2) has never been fully reproduced in modern editions of his book, and it is doubtful whether many of his followers fully understood his vision in consequence. In fact, for a region like South-East England, the universal application of Howard's ideal would have resulted in a very widespread scatter of small towns a few miles apart: urban development much closer to London than Abercrombie's new towns of the 1944 Plan, for the Green Belt, in the sense of a *cordon sanitaire*, had no part in

[12] There is an interesting interpretation in C. B. Purdom, *Town Theory and Practice*. Benn Bros., London (1921), following p. 32.

Howard's thinking. But more important than the question of how his concept would have looked is the question of how it would have worked. Writing two years after the repeal of the Red Flag Act, Howard can have had no concept of the effect of the car on patterns of living and working; nor did he perceive that better education and training would raise people's levels of specialization and aspiration, causing them to seek ever bigger pools of labour where they could sell their services. He seems therefore to have overestimated the capacity of his small cells to provide for the employment needs of most people. But in Social City he provided a safeguard: a labour market for a quarter of a million people, or more, within ten minutes by rapid transport. Social City, in the twentieth century, would have been a place of much commuting. With no dominant employment centre and rather even residential densities, there would have been no great tidal movements of traffic; criss-cross traffic flows would have been rather evenly spread. Social City would have functioned as a dispersed city like Los Angeles – even though it would have looked very different. That may seem surprising, but it is because the nature of Howard's concept has been imperfectly understood.

Howard's followers modified this pure vision in important ways. Unwin, in his famous pamphlet, stressed that nothing was gained by overcrowding; he, and his follower Barry Parker, were responsible for the widespread belief that all garden cities should be designed at the moderately low density of twelve houses per acre. Parker, and then Abercrombie, somewhat raised the permissible size of the garden city, from 30,000 to 50,000 or even 60,000 – the limits accepted by the Reith Committee in 1945. Both Unwin and Abercrombie (Figure 1.2) accepted the Howardian principle of towns on a backcloth of open country – Unwin's green girdle, he made plain, should be regarded as a second best – but the notion of the Green Belt as a *cordon sanitaire* seems specifically to be Abercrombie's. Most important, though, Abercrombie introduced an important modification of Howard's pure vision of the Social City. Of a total population of 1,170,000 people moving in his Greater London Plan to new homes in the ring beyond the Green Belt, only 400,000 (just over one-third) would be housed in new towns. But of the other 770,000, some 425,000 would be housed in planned expansions of medium-sized towns, in what later became Town Development Act schemes. Abercrombie in other words re-interpreted the Social City concept to include a much greater element of planned expansions of existing towns. He was as firm as Howard that all these were to be public enterprise schemes; more than three-quarters of the 1,170,000 would be housed in this way, less than a quarter by private builders.[13] But he was much less specific than Howard about the central features of Social City – its capacity to function as a single unit for certain purposes. The individual garden cities, in his view as in Reith's, could and should function as self-contained communities in their own right.

Between the time of Howard's book and the time of Abercrombie's Plan,

[13] Peter Hall, *London 2000*. Faber, London (1969), Table 5, p. 87.

of course, an important change had occurred in some basic planning assumptions. Howard, a Victorian, assumed rapid and constant growth; Abercrombie assumed slow and controllable change. It was this, above all, that caused Howard to stress the constant cellular multiplication of Social City, and that caused Abercrombie to assume a once for all process of population transfer to new communities, followed by a long period when the pace of change was so slow as to be imperceptible. Change for Abercrombie, unless it was initiated by the planner, was itself pernicious because it led to what he called structural obsolescence within cities: buildings outworn prematurely, because occupied by new functions for which they were not designed. His ideal city, then, was not merely static in aggregate population and employment, but also in its internal patterns.[14] It was not conceived in terms of change and adaptation, but in terms of resistance to them.

Because of this basic difference, the fact is that it is more easily possible to imagine Howard's concept applied to the rapidly-changing conditions of post-1945 England, than Abercrombie's. Howard's vision would have meant a very even pattern of urbanization when viewed at the very coarse scale, but with intense clustering at the finer local scale. The density of housing in the residential areas would have been very similar to that achieved in new towns in the later 1960s, and because of this the residential areas would have doubtless looked very similar. A limited range of jobs would have been available in each small unit, suitable for those with modest skills and low mobility; others, having skills which needed to be sold in a wider job market, would use the excellent transport system to criss-cross patterns across Social City. How many people would have lived in this type of environment, and how many in more conventional suburbs, it is impossible to say; Howard merely supposed that his experiments would extend as rapidly as money was forthcoming. Abercrombie, on the other hand, firmly believed that the great majority of people would be housed in publicly-sponsored developments of this type, whether new or attached to existing towns. Probably, faced with a growing population he would have reverted back to Howard's solution of constant cellular multiplication. He might even have allowed that in these circumstances an increased proportion of the total growth should be accommodated in private enterprise developments outside his planned communities. But this is speculative.

As compared with what actually happened, therefore, the Howard-Abercrombie alternative would probably have put a much larger proportion of the total growth into comprehensively-planned communities where jobs and homes were consciously provided close to each other. These communities would have been small in size – smaller than many of the communities where rapid growth did in fact occur in regions like the South-East and the West Midlands after the Second World War – but might have been connected up by a rapid transport system. The great majority of people would have found jobs either very locally, or within a few miles. This speculation finds con-

[14] Cf. the evidence from Abercrombie and Jackson's West Midlands Plan presented in Chapter Ten, Volume One of this study, p. 516.

firmation in the fact that the eight new towns around London have a significantly higher degree of self-containment, in terms of commuting, than equivalent towns at equivalent distances from London.[15] But this difference should not be overstressed. Even outside the new towns, the great bulk of workers – even in the mobile Outer Metropolitan Area of the South-East – still live quite close to their work.[16] The patterns of Social City are not so very different from the actual patterns of living and working in the Outer Metropolitan Area of London in the 1960s.

Once again, the main difference between Social City and the actual situation is not so much in these macro-patterns of living and working, but rather in the area of land values and the local densities within the residential areas. It is no accident that much of Howard's book is devoted to a detailed account of how the community would buy and manage the land required for garden city building. What specifically distinguished Howard's argument from other visionary planning concepts was his hard-headed realization that if the community could find the necessary capital to start the venture, then it could obtain a very good bargain in time. It would purchase land at agricultural value, beyond the sphere of influence of the existing cities, and in effect create its own urban land values. The soundness of this argument has been amply demonstrated in the actual construction of new towns since the Second World War, as Chapter Ten showed. Howard's programme thus offered a way of escaping from the phenomenon of urban land cost inflation, even without elaborate control mechanisms such as the Uthwatt Committee suggested. However, once the garden cities programme became the officially sponsored new-towns programme, a problem of land acquisition and land cost might well have arisen; for however it was conceived, the official programme would almost certainly have involved compulsory purchase on a large scale. Given this, the community might have found itself paying landowners for the urban land values which were, in effect, being created in their entirety by the community's own actions. This would have been intolerable; so that some solution like the Uthwatt one, or the alternative preferred by the Labour Government in their 1947 Act, would probably have been a necessary concomitant of a new-towns programme.

In any event, it seems clear that the solution envisaged by Osborn, Abercrombie and many of their contemporaries involved virtual abolition of the old market economy in land which had been typical of the 1920s and the 1930s. Land development rights and land-value increments would be nationalized; profit from land development would pass to the community. Within this framework, the vast majority of development would take place in new towns or planned town expansions, developed by public agencies within the framework of regional plans. There could have been no inflation of land values under this solution, almost by definition. The price at which

[15] Ray Thomas, *London's New Towns: A Study of Self-Contained and Balanced Communities*. PEP, London (1969), p. 406.

[16] South-East Joint Planning Team, *Strategic Plan for the South-East*, *Studies*, Volume I, *Population and Employment*. HMSO, London (1971), pp. 239, 251–2.

houses were sold, or rented, would be fixed by the public agencies to reflect the costs of construction together with any system of subsidy that was adopted. In designing the layouts, the planners of these communities would not be constrained in any way by the price of land. The densities they adopted would be governed by their own and by society's notions of what was proper, together with the general policies concerning the need to save agricultural land. It is difficult to surmise how these might have operated in the postwar period. Howard's chief working planner, Unwin, had been the inventor of the phrase: 'Nothing gained by overcrowding'. But the impact of the Scott Report, together with fashions in planning, might have combined to raise densities somewhat in the 1950s. The important point is that this would have reflected public decisions, not market pressures.

THE ACTUAL PATTERN

When now we come to look at the actual pattern of development which has occurred around English conurbations and cities since the Second World War, we find that it corresponds to neither of these archetypes. Essentially, it is a hybrid of the two. Almost certainly the Labour Government, when it passed the 1947 Planning Act, thought that it was replacing the modified *laissez-faire* system of the 1930s by another system, where most of the initiative came from the state and from its agents, the local authorities and the new town Development Corporations. Under this prescription, as we just saw, the market was not required to work because it was strictly irrelevant. The intention, it seems, was to pass straight from a non-plan archetype to an Abercrombie-Howard archetype, where the great bulk of all development would be carried through by public agencies. Regional plans, followed by county Development Plans and the operation of development control within the framework of these plans, would be necessary to ensure the broad framework of land uses and activities, within which the work of these public agencies would be carried on. But it does not seem to have been assumed that development control machinery would ever be needed for more than a small minority of the total development.

In practice, as we have seen in the last chapter of Volume One and again in Chapter Ten, of this volume, the situation has been quite different. Ever since the mid-1950s, private enterprise speculative building for sale has become the general rule for new building in the countryside; the exception for new and expanding towns. The change happened to be associated with the arrival in power of the 1951 Conservative Government, which rapidly scrapped building licences and the financial provisions of the 1947 Act, all in a short period from 1951 to 1954. But this was more than a matter of party-political ideology: the intellectual tide against planning and control was running strongly after 1948, as witnessed by the 'bonfire of controls' in the latter days of the Labour Government. And the change happened to coincide with the unexpected rise in the birthrate from 1955 onwards, which might have compelled a change in emphasis even from a Labour Government. At any rate, it is notable that when Labour returned in 1964, it did not attempt to go back to the 1947 position.

The critical point, in other words, is that the so-called 1947 planning system – the central theme of this book – is really two systems. One was the system as imagined in theory, and as given legislative expression in the 1947 Act. The other was a very different system, as actually operated in the 1950s and the 1960s. It worked within the general framework set up by the 1947 Act (with some amendments, particularly on the financial side), but with quite different emphases from those intended by the founding fathers of the system. In particular, the elementary but important fact about this actual system is that it depends basically upon an interaction between the private developer and the public planners. The local authority professional planner, in this framework, is only one actor in a complex process. He first has to interact with the elected representatives in his own authority. While his own values of conservation and containment may coincide with those of the representatives, especially in the rural counties, in the cities they may come up against the representatives' desire for expansion of their economic and tax base. He has also to interact with the professional officials and representatives of neighbouring authorities, who may have different interests from his; the next-door city may for instance desire physical extension across the the county boundary, which he may resist because he thinks the area should be preserved as a Green Belt. He must interact with central government officials who take important policy decisions which affect his plans: decisions on employment location for instance, or on the line of a new motorway. Then, he will have complex interactions with the agents who actually initiate the development prices under the actual 1947 Planning System: the industrialist or office developer in the case of developments in the sector of employment, and the residential developer of the homes where these employees may live. The relationships here are often tortuous, ranging from outright hostility (with subterfuges on the part of developers to avoid the intentions of the planners) to quite warm co-operation in the interests of good development which will bring credit on the developer and the planning authority alike.

One of the oustanding features of this pattern of interaction is that the planning system is primarily designed to *control* land use rather than promote the development of land use. While it is true that a Development Plan represents what a planning authority would like to see, it can be argued that plan implementation depends almost exclusively upon the initiative and capabilities of private developers. This is true not only at the local authority level; the same criticism could be levied at the plans of regional councils or regional teams. The Strategic Plan for the South-East which was published in 1970 contains recommendations for urban development in a number of outer metropolitan areas but it is clear that no executive or legislative power is contemplated to back the plan. Even if co-operation is forthcoming by local authorities, the plan can only be implemented through an agreement being made between the planners and the private developers based on marketing criteria, as the developers will be faced at the end of the day with the problem of selling the development to the public. The urban development process can therefore be viewed as the aggregate outcome of many decisions in a complex socio-economic and political system which is partly controlled by local government, but often initiated and strongly influenced by the private sector.

Within this mixed-development structure, the local authority planning authority does wield several important legislative powers, the most important being the designation of land for urban development and the granting of permission which allows development to take place. The use of such powers must be viewed in the context of the values and objectives which characterize the philosophy of planners in Britain. Planning policies have been largely directed towards the containment of urban growth and the preservation of the open countryside. When the *power* to control is linked with a *desire* to control urban sprawl, one can start to appreciate why conflict arose between the interests of the individual house purchaser, the residential developer, the landowner, and the land-use planner.

The power to grant planning permission for a plot of land to be developed creates a *monopoly* position in the supply of land for private development; but this monopoly exists without the planning authority having a fiscal responsibility to provide land at a fair price. It is a useful analogy to consider the position of gas or electricity supply in the country. These services were established by Act of Parliament and the decisions of the power authorities are financially accountable, equivalent to the position of a public corporation. The planner is not accountable to anyone for the fiscal effects of planning decisions on the market for land. With the exception of having to provide and finance basic services, such as sewer lines and storm-water drainage, the remaining locational criteria used by planners are generally non-economic in character. Planning control, therefore, usually means *physical* control and the system has failed as a means of *fiscal* control. In this way the planning system has had a strong *inflationary* influence.

This inflationary spiral has been partly caused through a lack of fiscal responsibility but in addition through a failure by the planner to understand certain basic characteristics of the residential development industry. This manifests itself most vividly with the scarcity of land occurring through inadequate amounts of land being designated for urban development. Various planning authorities considered that an adequate amount of land was available. The developers and subsequently the Land Commission, which was formed by central government to tackle this very problem, strongly disputed these estimates. It is necessary to appreciate the need for a developer to have some land in stock. We are not referring to the large land-banks which are undoubtedly held speculatively by the relatively few big development companies in this country, but a land supply which is necessary to facilitate the continuity of a two or three years' building programme. To designate land on a drip-feed basis to meet the apparent immediate development needs was a principle that failed to recognize the minimum requirements of development decision-making. To make matters worse, some land was designated without regard to its suitability for housing development; when such sites were too difficult to develop for technical reasons, or where the site would make the marketing of private housing difficult, the land, although designated, was not developed.

One elementary but important fact about the actual system is that in at least two important ways, it was based on premises which proved to be completely unrealistic. First, as we have already stressed in Chapter Eleven, it was designed deliberately to control and limit change; yet extremely rapid change occurred in the external world it was supposed to control. Because of this, it proved in practice an inflexible system, and often a fairly ineffectual one. This ineffectuality was perhaps most marked in the case of the elaborate system of controls on employment, at both central and local government level; these seem to have been only partially successful in diverting employment growth from the faster-growing to the more stagnant or declining regions of the country. It was less marked in the case of residential development, where the local planner possessed fairly effective negative powers. And it is here that the policy of containment had some serious, and even unintended, consequences.

Secondly, the ideal system – from which the actual system evolved – seems to have been specifically designed to meet the problems of a very large urban area in process of becoming metropolitan in character; that is, an area like London, where population and employment growth could be guided outwards into a series of largely self-contained satellites. But this model was more or less inappropriate to the situation in many, if not all, of the provincial conurbations, such as Birmingham, Manchester or Merseyside, and completely inappropriate in the case of the freestanding cities. Here, the appropriate model was one of simple suburbanization; population growth was taking place at the edge of the physically built-up area, while much of the employment growth was taking place either at the same periphery or in the very centre of the agglomeration. The problem was that many, if not all, these areas were too small, and insufficiently evolved, to support a programme of large-scale development of independent satellites at some distance from the conurbation or city. Perhaps this provides a good reason why, in the provincial conurbations, no such policy was embarked on until the early 1960s, and then on a relatively modest scale compared with London, while there was no hint of a policy for the freestanding cities, even by the early 1970s.

THE MAIN RESULTS OF THE 1947 SYSTEM

Against this background, and keeping in mind the likely results of the two feasible alternatives to the system as it worked in practice, we can now try to sum up the chief impacts of the 1947 Planning System. There are three of them that seem unambiguous and certain; and it is perhaps curious that only one has come about through the direct and conscious actions of the local authority planners – and even that not wholly. This first feature is that the amount of land converted from rural to urban use has been minimized and compacted: urban growth has been *contained.* A second feature was hardly intended, but arose mainly from the attempts to cope willy-nilly with the unexpected and unwelcome population growth, coupled with the lack of really effective local planning powers over the location of employment; it is the growing separation of residential areas from the main centres of employment and other urban facilities or services. In a word, we can call it *suburbanization*; ironically, the reverse of what the ideal 1947 system was trying to achieve. A third feature has not been willed by anyone expect perhaps a small body of speculators, and indeed is a source of grave embarrassment to successive governments. It is neither physical nor specifically spatial; but it is the direct result of applying spatial policies of control without understanding of the consequences. It is the fact of *inflation* of land and property prices, at least since the late 1950s, on a scale never before witnessed in British history. This fact in turn has reacted on the behaviour of developers, who have reacted with their own form of containment, more severe in character then ever the plans originally intended. But the planning system has connived at it, and has perhaps not found it wholly unwelcome, for reasons which must be explored.

CONTAINMENT

The containment of urban growth has had various meanings; it has been achieved in various ways, and has had varied results. We have already noticed some of these in passing, in considering the two alternatives. Green Belts around the conurbations and larger freestanding cities stopped their further peripheral extension at increasingly low densities; this control was most severe around the biggest conurbations in the regions where rapid population growth was occurring, and least restrictive around the freestanding cities. Beyond the Green Belts, the county planners worked to concentrate new development in substantial pockets in small towns and villages; scattered development of all kinds, and small-scale or individual house-developments, were strongly discouraged. Usually, the permitted developments were in the less attractive parts of the counties which were regarded as not particularly worth preservation. Especially after 1960, densities in the typical residential development were kept up, aided and abetted in the late 1960s by rising land prices (which will be discussed below). The cities and conurbations responded to containment by building their public housing schemes, which were needed to cope with slum-clearance programmes and natural increase of their populations, at high densities with substantial proportions of high-rise flats. In this way they kept their populations within their boundaries, keeping the need for overspill to a minimum, and helping to maintain their rateable-value base. So the containment philosophy, though it doubtless appealed to the counties wishing to maintain their traditional rural ways of life, was also not entirely unattractive to the cities which were faced with the prospect of massive population losses – especially since the central government paid much of the bill in the form of special subsidies for the high-rise flats on expensive urban land.

It can be argued that though densities have been kept up, both in the new developments in the counties and in the redevelopment schemes within the conurbations and cities, they are yet low by the standards which were usual in the past. A density of thirteen houses to the net acre, which has become typical for new private estates in the counties by the 1960s, was low by the standards of the nineteenth century. But the fact is that such densities were high compared with similar developments in Britain in the interwar period, when eight or ten were much commoner. They are also high compared with some other industrially advanced countries with similar housing traditions to ours – above all the United States, Canada and Australia. Similarly, though the densities of urban redevelopment schemes in the cities – typically between 120 and 150 to the net acre – are low by the standards of the slums they replace, they are extraordinarily high compared with the twelve houses to the acre of the typical interwar peripheral city estate built to rehouse the same categories of people.

The containment of urban growth has not prevented the centrifugal movement of population from the historic centres. Urban concentrations of every size have increased their continuously built-up areas as new houses have been built at the periphery. Rates of growth have varied widely, but a large part of this variation is attributable to the existing urban structure. The growth, in terms of continuously built-up area, has been slowest for the largest cities which are hemmed in by Green Belts and by other towns (the population of these major concentrations has stagnated if it has not actually declined), and the fastest-growing places, in both area and population, have been towns and small cities situated in the hinterlands of these conurbations. Decentralization is perhaps too simple a word to summarize this pattern of growth; the decentralization of population has been the dominant pattern of change in urban concentrations of every different size. But, viewed on a large scale, the pattern manifests itself as the movement of population from major urban concentrations to smaller concentrations.

The containment of urban growth can be regarded as an outstanding success for the planning system in terms of its own objectives; for the outcome accords in many ways with the ideologies of the early postwar period. In fact containment is only partly the product of conscious planning. Containment is also the result of the failure of the planning system to react quickly enough to the persistently upward revisions in population projections in the 1950s and early 1960s. Containment reflects the power of the agricultural and rural preservationist interest groups. Containment has to some degree been achieved because of the reluctance of urban local authorities to lose population. But the most important single factor resulting from – and in turn, reinforcing – containment has been soaring land prices.

The 1947 Planning Act worked as a system of physical controls but failed lamentably as a system of fiscal controls. Since the repeal of the provisions of the 1947 Act concerned with development values, no effective measures have been taken to check the rise of land prices and the system of physical control which remained has actually served as a key component in the inflationary spiral. The system has been directly inflationary by putting a price tag on land zoned for residential development; and by making it expensive in terms of time and money for developers to get permission to build on land not zoned for development. Thus containment has been achieved partly at the cost of rising prices.

Faced with this charge, planning officials have tended to deny it. They have pointed to the fact that their Development Plans have made careful projections of the population and have provided sufficient housing land for the additional people expected in each area. Though population rose faster than they expected, they will say, they modified their plans as fast as they could to take account of the fact. To this there are two arguments. The first is that accurate population projection, at county level, is not realistic; a given regional population increase may go into this area or into that, depending on the availability of land and housing, and often the projections of planning authorities seem to have been designed to ensure that it went somewhere else. The second is the paradox that even if the planning authority scrupulously provides just the right amount of land for the expected increase, by definition it will not be enough. The Development Plan, in the words of an Australian report, will act as a speculator's guide. Land with planning permission, or likely planning permission, becomes a desirable item which will be traded at increasing prices, or hoarded. In order to prevent this the planning authorities would have had to have provided very much more land than they knew would be needed. And this, for obvious reasons, they were unwilling to do.

But the inflation in land prices has also been a cause of containment – in two distinct ways. First, the high cost of land has encouraged high-density development. Both private builders and local authorities have, through pressure of costs, squeezed in as many dwellings per acre as the planning authority would permit. Second, the high cost of both old and new dwellings, and since the late 1950s, exceptionally high interest rates, have constrained demand. In spite of growing affluence the proportion of the population able to buy a new house out of income has actually fallen. Urban growth has been contained partly by a failure to translate higher incomes into higher housing standards which more new construction might have permitted.

For those affected by the policies – the people who live in the resulting houses and flats – the effects have been complex. The social investigation reported in Chapter Five suggests strongly that containment, insofar as it diverted population growth from the urban periphery to small towns and villages in the counties, may actually have been in accord with what people wanted for themselves. For those in the high-density public housing schemes in the conurbations, there was greater accessibility to urban jobs and services, with a better possibility of running frequent and efficient public transport services to them. But few people can have appreciated higher densities, or high-rise living with children, for their own sakes.

From the point of view of the objectives of the pure 1947 Planning System, containment as it has operated in practice can hardly be judged a success. For an essential feature of the pure system was the creation of communities that were self-contained and balanced. But the new suburban communities of owner-occupied homes in the small towns and villages cater for a narrow spectrum of social classes. Coupled with the concentration of municipal housing in the cities, the result is the development of a new form of publicly-sanctioned, publicly-subsidized *apartheid* – as can be seen from the detailed analysis of Census statistics in Chapter Seven, Volume One.

SUBURBANIZATION

With few exceptions (like some of the new and expanded towns) the areas of recent population growth are all suburban in character. The new housing estates often contain a primary school, a neighbourhood shopping centre and a doctor's surgery. But they generally lack any other urban amenities and they are nearly all more distant from the major centres of employment, shopping, and cultural, educational and entertainment facilities than the housing estates of the interwar period or any earlier era.

Most forms of urban activity have decentralized to some extent, but the rate of decentralization has been much slower than for population. Differences in the pattern of movement are clearest in the case of employment. In London, for example, it was not until the 1960s that the level of employment in the centre began to fall. In many of Britain's other major cities there is still no evidence of any declines in the level of employment in the central business district, and the level of employment in other parts of the inner area (where the residential population is declining) continues to grow.

Yet there has been a substantial centrifugal movement of employment from the major cities. Even if these cities recorded absolute growth in employment, there was relative decentralization by the 1960s; growth in the suburbs was faster. But most of the employment growth has occurred within smaller cities and towns. Trends in the location of population can be summarized as decentralization. But the trends in employment location are more accurately described as recentralization. The result is an increasing radial separation of places of residence from places of employment at every scale of analysis: journeys to work, if anything, have become longer than would have occurred under the former *laissez-faire* situation. Separation of residential areas in this way has also occurred in relation to most other kinds of urban activity.

The process of suburbanization is in part a product of these planning policies which deliberately aimed at the containment of urban growth. The planning system did not succeed in counteracting the inexorable forces which have led to the decentralization of population. But it did slow down the rate of decentralization of most other forms of urban activity. Development Plans, consisting largely of a confirmation of the existing land-use pattern (or the pattern of a previous era), proved very effective in discouraging the decentralization of offices, shops, cinemas, theatres, hospitals, museums, concert halls and higher-educational establishments. The fragmentation of local government helped ensure this: county boroughs were unlikely, in making plans, to countenance decentralization action on their commercial tax base. Neither the Industrial Development Certificate (IDC) nor Office Development Permit (ODP) systems have been used to encourage decentralization except at an interregional scale. In only a handful of cases has planning permission been given for out-of-town shopping centres. Drive-in cinemas are still a transatlantic dream. Central government seems to have aided and abetted the cities in this, by subsidizing expensive urban road investments which ease the rising traffic congestion.

Yet it can hardly be argued that suburbanization is in accordance with the objectives of the particular planning system. It was assumed when this system was set up that planned developments, in the form of 'self-contained and balanced communities', would play a major role in the process of urban growth. In fact population growth (multiplied by higher incomes, increased leisure and rising car ownership – which are some of the factors which have made the centrifugal movement of population inexorable) has ensured that new and expanded towns have played a role, which, in statistical terms, is relatively minor.

Suburbanization has not then occurred as a result of any kind of conscious community intent. The particular form which suburban growth has taken in this country has largely been the result of the failure to adjust to changing circumstances. It is perhaps hardly surprising that planners' reactions to the trend polarize into two contrasting views. One school calls for a reaffirmation of the traditional objectives of 'self-contained and balanced communities' – perhaps modified in some way in the light of recent experience. The other school is in favour of completely scrubbing predetermined objectives and substituting a high degree of flexibility in the planning process.

Curiously, from the local politician's viewpoint, suburbanization may have been acceptable. If he represented the city, then as a result of the policy of containment there was a shortage of space. Given that, many local administrations saw two priorities in land allocation: first, particularly if they were Labour administrations, urban renewal for their working-class constituents (to whom they undoubtedly felt a special responsibility), if necessary at high densities to keep their rate contributions and reinforce the political base; and second, profitable central-area renewal, bringing valuable commercial values to reinforce the rate fund. If the politician represented the county, he may have been not entirely averse to new middle-class residents who brought additional rateable value and did not too seriously disturb the existing social order; but he is likely to have been very opposed to industry in the countryside, and (perhaps more surprisingly) to major commercial developments such as out-of-town shopping centres, which might generate new traffic pressures over wide areas. There seems, then, to have been a sort of unspoken and unwritten compact in many areas that the central city could keep much of the additional employment both in white-collar and blue-collar jobs, while the county took suitable white-collar residents.

For some groups of the population too, suburbanization may not have been intolerable. Our social survey, which was dominated by white-collar residents in new housing developments in the counties, showed a clear enthusiasm for country living, and an apparent willingness to tolerate work journeys which after the move were longer not merely in distance, but also in time. This in turn may have been influenced by the fact that after the move, four in five were travelling to work by car – a figure not far different from North American suburbanites, among whom a similar indifference to longer work-journeys (up to a certain point) has been observed. Perhaps one can merely make the comment which has been made in the United States: that the principal fault is not the fact of suburbanization, but the fact that substantial low-income groups are excluded from the chance of joining in it.

The chief problem from the suburban consumer's point of view may well be not the length but the difficulty of travel. Because many new jobs have been created in the city centres while new homes have been built outside them, there has been a big increase in radial journeys. At the same time, because the new residential areas have been scattered within the metropolitan area (though locally they are concentrated at fairly high densities), it has been difficult to support good public transport, and use of the car for the journey to work has risen dramatically. But radial journeys to congested city centres do not easily accommodate mass use of the car. The same goes, to a lesser degree, for any other sort of radial journey – for shopping, education, entertainment. Much of the rising congestion, and increasingly expensive and controversial urban surgery, in the centres of Britain's towns, can be attributed to the basic fact of suburbanization. Though it may benefit local interests in the short run, it certainly does not seem to bring anything for the consumer except difficulty and frustration. And in its effects on the historic urban fabric of many towns, it may have quite pernicious social consequences. There has been a tendency to wish this situation away, by imagining that it could be cured by a combination of expensive public works and restrictions on the use of the car. In effect, since it arises from patterns of living and working, it can be cured only by changing those patterns – which would mean decentralizing jobs, shopping, entertainment and the rest into the suburbs where the people increasingly live. There are signs, from the 1960s, that this may already be beginning to happen.

LAND AND PROPERTY PRICES

Existing data on increases in land and property prices are notoriously incomplete. But from the various pieces of evidence that exist, including the completely new data assembled for Chapter Seven of this volume, it is possible to build up a reasonably consistent picture. The increase in the price of land 'ripe for residential development' (in the late 1930s) or with planning permission for residential development (in the late 1960s) has probably been ten and twenty-fold. Yet during this period, the general price-level has only risen four times. During the 1960s alone, the price of land in selected developments in Megalopolis has risen between three and twelve times, according to the evidence presented in Chapter Seven. As a result, the proportion of land cost in the total final housing cost has risen from between 4 and 12 per cent, in 1960, to between 18 and 38 per cent, by 1970. On average, it can be said that while land was probably less than 10 per cent of the housing package in 1960, only ten years later it was 30 per cent. Much of this increase occurred after 1965. At the same time credit was increasingly scarce and costly, affecting the calculations of developer and consumer alike.

The rise in costs of housing, it should be stressed, cannot be explained by an increase in demand; during the latter half of the 1960s there was actually a fall in demand for new property, and the existence of unsold housing was not uncommon. In fact the explanation, which is a complex one, is to be found in the supply side of the industry. A number of inflationary factors, such as the cost of credit, the effect of Betterment Levy, SET and devaluation, all played a part. But the most important determinant was the scarcity of supply of building land, coupled with the costs of buying land and holding land. This was mainly caused – the fact was generally recognized by the Land Commission, developers, and the Secretary of State – by local authorities not designating enough land for urban development. The situation was made worse by a general uncertainty in the market about the future existence of the Land Commission. The general problem was therefore two-fold:

(*a*) inadequate development land available; and

(*b*) unprecedented escalation in land prices.

Further costs were incurred by the high interest rates that prevailed in the late 1960s. This increased the cost of land holdings which were often extended through delays in development caused by lengthy negotiation in obtaining planning permission.

During the period 1965–70 there was curiously little true speculation in land. The market for land polarized into two sections. First, land which had planning permission or a very good chance of getting it and second, land which had little likelihood of obtaining planning permission. The escalation in this latter category in value over alternative use-value was as low as 200–300 per cent. The escalation in value due to planning permission was as much as 100-fold.

The Labour Government attempted to solve the problem with the introduction of the Land Commission in 1967. This attempt to assemble land and release parcels to developers, particularly in areas of greatest land pressures, failed for a number of reasons. The Land Commission had too small a budget and too little time to have a real chance of success. In fact, it made the problem worse. It created uncertainty and suspicion in the market and through its operations contributed to the inflationary spiral. It made no contribution to land assembly. The work of the Land Commission was strongly resisted by the local authorities, particularly the counties. It was this persistent resistance to a systematic release of land by county authorities that eventually caused the demise of the Commission. With the end of the Commission the basic problem of land supply remains and the return to the position where local authorities make estimates of demand and release land accordingly, virtually guarantees the problem to be an enduring one for many years to come.

The effects of scarce land, expensive land, falling demand and tighter credit were felt by both producer and consumer. The developer responded in a number of ways to achieve a reduction in costs and maintain cash-flow, as was shown in Chapters Six and Seven of this volume. The developer started using smaller sites which meant slightly dearer land per plot, but which were less expensive in carrying charges than a larger site held for a longer period. From a marketing viewpoint, smaller sites were preferred by the home buyer. The planners were less happy; they preferred to deal with large comprehensively-developed sites which facilitated easier control over access, layout, amenity etc. With increasing land costs, the developer also started building at higher density, particularly for cheaper housing. For more expensive housing, the density remained the same (for marketing reasons) and the costs rose proportionately. In addition to smaller *plots*, costs were further cut by reducing the size of quality of the housing unit itself. For many owner occupiers the standard of housing was lower than that set down by the Parker Morris standards for rented local authority housing. It is a curious anomaly that contemporary society can lay down relatively high standards regarding the space and fittings in the public sector while private housing, which is approximately 65 per cent of the housing market, has no such standards. It is true that the NHBRC guarantees the basic foundations and superstructure of the house of its members, but in addition there are no further guarantees on standards and there are certainly no data in existence on what is currently built, by standards of size, space and quality. If it were not for their green-field sites, many of the 850 square feet bungaloid developments in exurbia could easily be confused with being the equivalent of late nineteenth-century industrial slums with their poor architecture, repetitive and unimaginative designs and totally inadequate space standards for a consumer society about to enter the last quarter of the twentieth century.

Faced with increasing costs and slow sales for smaller houses, many developers switched markets and concentrated on building medium and expensively-priced property. This was rather ironic as it was the more desirable property that was being given development permission in the counties surrounding the large cities and conurbations. The counties' development policy was very selective; they wished to maintain the existing character of the area and therefore the limited land release that was allowed permitted low-density, high-value development near villages and small towns. As a result the effective *choice* for families at the lower end of the market was reduced. The switch by developers to dearer housing was also caused by tighter control on mortgage lending between 1965–70. With house prices rising faster than *basic* income (total income less overtime, bonuses etc.), the competitive position of the lower-middle and working class, particularly first-home buyers, to obtain credit was seriously restricted.

The main effects of change in urban development would seem to focus on the *costs* and *quality* and *choice* (or lack of it) in housing. There appears to be a conscious trade-off decision between space standards and quality of housing on the one hand and the containment of urban growth and the preservation of open space on the other. The objectives of the planning system unwittingly reinforced the value system of the rural and exurban population, aided and abetted by various amenity societies; the decision not to locate the third London airport at Cublington is a good example of a government decision supposedly based upon so called 'environmental criteria'. In effect, the 'environment' became a respectable front for a very articulate and wealthy rural/exurban minority who were capable of raising over £¾ million to influence a decision to protect local vested interest. It is this sector of society who are most familiar with, and can use, the political process that has dominated the philosophy and decision-making in planning around most of our great cities and conurbations.

The objectives of the planning system result in various economic and social costs being created and borne by different sectors of society. At the present time, the lower end of the private housing market (both the groups who succeed in purchasing and those who fail) seems to be bearing a high burden of real or opportunity costs. In effect, this is a direct *redistribution* of *income*. Unfortunately, this transfer is in the wrong direction; in this case from the relatively less well-off house purchaser to the rural landowner. This is not to say that an individual landowner would not sell his land and realize his asset given the chance. The development control policies imposed by county authorities protect not only the landowning farmer but also the suburban, exurban and rural population from unselective development. Rather than contribute and be instrumental in achieving an egalitarian society, the current planning of land development has made matters worse.

Buyers at this lower end of the market, it is clear, have got a bad bargain in various ways. The house they buy in 1970 may well be on a smaller site than the equivalent house bought new in 1960 – or even, perhaps, in 1930. It is also less accessible to the main concentrations of urban facilities, including jobs, than the equivalent house of the 1930s. There is evidence from our surveys, already quoted earlier in this chapter, that families moving into suburbia are willing to pay the extra price of commuting (and by extension travel) to obtain urban services. But some premium must be payable to represent the loss of accessibility.

The evidence on space standards is not very clear because unlike local authorities or new towns, private developers are under no obligation to report the size of the houses they build. Census figures, which show not new houses but the whole housing stock, were analysed in Chapter Eight of this volume and show that for those living at medium ranges of occupancy, the average size of dwelling remained roughly constant between 1931 and 1966. Space standards apparently rose, but that was because the average household was becoming much smaller, while the average dwelling was not. On the trends of the late 1960s, which are our chief concern here, there is no evidence in 1970.

The consequences of this change in relative prices are perhaps most serious for the first-time house purchaser without a significant amount of capital who is obliged to take out a 90 per cent mortgage or the maximum mortgage available. In the 1930s young couples who had just purchased a house paid, say, 2–3 per cent of their income to their mortgage society for the intangible property rights in land which the construction of their dwelling had created. By 1970 to buy an equivalent house a first-time purchaser would probably have to pay between 10 and 40 per cent of his income for the corresponding property rights.

In practice the mortgage society rule that mortgage payments should not exceed 25 per cent of income has put an *equivalent* house beyond the pockets of most members of the community. First-time purchasers have cut their outgoings by the purchase of an old house (of the 1918–39 vintage) or a new property whose total land area is generally about two-thirds of that of houses of the 1918–39 vintage. First-time purchasers of new housing are typically paying about 5–10 per cent of their income for the privilege of occupying about 300 square yards of English soil. First time purchasers of an interwar dwelling are typically paying 10–20 per cent of their income for the right to occupy about 450 square yards. (These percentages exclude, of course, the payments made *for the cost or value* of the structure of the dwelling.)

One of the results of the high cost of residential land has already been mentioned; it has limited the number of people who have been able to afford to pay an 'open market' price or rent, and a large and complex system of housing subsidies has proved necessary in order to maintain reasonable housing standards. But the inflation of land prices has also had wider implications for the distribution of wealth and income. It has presented about half the population with a small but significant stake in Britain's stock of capital. A person who purchased a house in the interwar period, or has inherited one from his parents, has acquired an asset worth several thousand pounds without any effort. A new privileged class of property owner has been created. Those who have purchased for the first time in the 1950s and 1960s have been less privileged. Many of them have got a smaller house, with less space, then they would have obtained in the 1930s. Thus the paradox – stressed in Chapter Eight of this volume – that the prices of older houses have kept up so well in relation to new ones.

The other half of this country's population – those who have failed to join the owner-occupiers' bandwagon – are a diverse group. Many of them pay relatively low rents to local authorities or private landlords for satisfactory dwellings, and some no doubt pay rents which are well below what they could afford. But within this half of the population there are a substantial number who occupy substandard housing and who cannot afford to pay for anything better on the 'open market'. The high level of land prices may not have reduced substantially the affluence of the majority, but it has certainly intensified the housing problems of the under-privileged minority.

The wider consequences of the inflation in land and property prices have implications for the system of land planning. Instead of nationalizing development rights, the system has defined development rights more clearly. Any kind of action which limits these development rights in any way has become exorbitantly expensive to the public purse. As a result the only significant kind of comprehensive public planning which has taken place has been in the new and expanded towns (where development rights have been nationalized effectively). The rest of the planning system has steadily become more negative in character. It has become a matter of granting or refusing planning permission for development proposed by individual persons and developers who may be unwilling or unable to take into account the interests of other members of the community. The planning system has actually created a conflict situation where any degree of coincidence between the interests of the developer and those of the planning authority (acting in the name of the community) is fairly fortuitous. It is hardly surprising that the planning system has fallen into disrepute.

The crucial weakness of the postwar planning system then, has been the failure to control the price of land. This failure is partly attributable to lack of understanding of the way in which the property market works (which in turn is associated with the lack of statistical data on property transactions). Non-economists generally seem to believe that the price of land and property is the inevitable result of uncontrollable forces of demand and supply. In fact under a planning system, the supply of land on the open market depends upon conditions which are almost entirely created by governmental action. Unfortunately economists, who might appreciate this fact, do not often seem interested in town planning.

Cheaper land would without doubt mean more urban growth. More people would be able to afford new houses and many would choose to have larger gardens. The inescapable fact is that the majority of households now own a motor car. Many of them want to live in a house which will accommodate the children's toys, the junk, and the odd sailing boat, as well as the car. Many want a house which can be enlarged to provide room for dishwashing machines, clothes driers, deep freezers, colour TV sets, teenagers who want to play records or guitars, quiet spaces for reading or study of Open University courses. These demands cannot easily be met by a flat, a terraced house, or even semidetached houses built at densities of more than about twelve to the acre.

More houses and bigger gardens would upset quite a few unfounded prejudices about preserving the countryside for agriculture or for stockbroker/farmers. But it seems likely that the only serious problems relate to suburbanization. The suburbs are all right for households composed of adults able to drive a car and able to afford to run a car. But what of the needs of children, old people, the poor, the disabled and the disqualified? How will the urban needs of these members of the community be catered for in an age when the methods of distributing goods and services are becoming more and more dominated by the assumption that everyone has a car?

There is a paradox here, and it is perhaps the central paradox of planning for urban growth in England or in any advanced Western country. Cheap land, low density, big houses in big gardens, decentralization of many urban activities into suburban centres, free use of the car, would represent a life style which would satisfy many families. North American lack of planning has been better than English planning at providing for this life style. But at the same time, all these mutually reinforcing trends make it more and more difficult to provide adequate public transport services. Groups like the young, the old and the poor may become progressively disadvantaged.

The key word here is 'may'. We cannot be absolutely sure. In North American-style suburbia, for instance, it is by no means certain that the young suffer. When they are children they have the school bus, their bicycles (which are relatively safe to use in suburbia), their parents' car (or cars). Nor is it by any means axiomatic that the old suffer. Very many of them do not live in suburbia, which is basically a society devoted to rearing children; they are in Florida or in other senior citizens' townships. This may or may not be deplorable on other grounds; it does mean that many of them are not affected by the dependence of suburbia on the car. The poor are a different matter. Where they exist in a largely car-based society where public transport has deteriorated (as in the case of Watts in Los Angeles) they may suffer serious deprivation, made more glaring by the fact that the vast majority have access to opportunities – both economic and social – denied to them. How serious this problem is, and how serious it may be, cannot be answered here because it was not part of the subject matter of this study. It is the subject of a separate study on accessibility to urban opportunities, started in 1970 as a development from the present study by Political and Economic Planning.

THE EFFECT ON ECONOMIC GROWTH

There is a fourth possible effect of the planning system, on which it is impossible to be certain. This is that the system may have throttled back the rate of economic growth. Many planners in our detailed investigations reported that they thought this to be quite probable, but in the nature of the phenomenon it is impossible to arrive at a quantified estimate of the effect. If it has occurred to any extent, it may be regarded as a conscious trade-off made by a certain section of society who was in control of making the decision. But it is not clear that if the issue had been presented to the public in this way, they would have been enthusiastic about the sacrifice of economic growth. For by and large, the beneficial effects of planning have probably been larger for those sections of society who are better off; while conversely, the negative effects have mainly been borne by those in lower-income groups. We must now summarize these distributional effects.

GAINERS AND LOSERS

Containment, suburbanization and rises in land values are the main effects of the planning system, and they can be seen in operation throughout the whole of urban England – albeit with some important regional variations, as Chapter Thirteen of Volume One showed. The restraint of economic growth is a more arguable, less certain effect. What is significant is first, that most of these results were not intended by those who were responsible for setting up the system; and second, that they have had clear effects on the distribution of costs and benefits among different sections of the community. Economists and planners, especially in the United States, began to become interested in these distributional effects of planning during the 1960s. For planning may supply, or fail to supply, certain environmental qualities which can be described as impure public goods; that is, they cannot be provided by the market but they do not arise free of charge to all. Pure air and light, freedom from noise, contact with nature, safe places for the children to play – all these are examples of public goods that the planner may supply. In an age when such public goods seem to be increasingly in demand as standards of affluence rise, their distribution is a matter of considerable public concern.

When these effects are considered for different sections of the population in postwar Britain, the results are interesting. Among the ruralites, those who owned land and might have sold profitably, had they been able to offer it for development, have lost materially. But probably most inhabitants of the countryside – those ex-urbanites who essentially use it as a way of life rather than a way of work – have gained; by establishing a civilized British version of *apartheid*, planning has preserved their status quo. This group has probably gained more and lost less than any other; and it has been quick to seize on the implications of increased public participation in planning, so as to cement its position in planning conflicts. Significantly, it is a group which in socio-economic terms is higher, and in material terms is richer, than the average.

The new suburbanites, who have succeeded in buying homes in the new developments, are themselves a mixed group; but they tend by the very fact of owner occupation to belong to the upper income groups, or at least to exclude the least affluent one-quarter of all families. They have gained new, convenient and comfortable homes – many of them an improvement on their equivalents built in the interwar period, in matters like built-in central heating or garage space – and they have done so with a generous subsidy in the form of tax relief. This gain, paradoxically, has been greater for those in the upper income brackets. For the intending owner occupier at the margin of ability to obtain a mortgage, the benefits are much less evident. The financial bonus from tax relief is much smaller for him, and may even – until the 1967 mortgage option scheme – have been non-existent.

Where the suburbanites have lost most is in the form of land and house space. The rising cost of land during the 1960s, which can be directly attributed to planning restrictions and planning delays, drove the price of new housing up to some degree; but the main effect was cushioned by building more houses on each acre of land; a solution which was actively condoned by most planning authorities. As a result houses and gardens may be smaller in the 1970s than in the 1930s – let alone the 1950s. And though most new houses are probably an improvement on their predecessors a generation ago, there is considerable evidence that some at any rate of the new houses built in the late 1960s represented poorer standards, in matter of space and equipment than equivalent houses built a decade before. But what is interesting, again, is that it is the lower-income levels of the home-buying market that have been affected most. The rising cost of land becomes more and more significant, the lower the final selling cost of land. It is here that builders have had to save space and sacrifice finish or equipment. In this way, it is the less affluent house-owner who has paid the greatest price for containment.

Many suburbanites, as we saw, face increasingly long journeys into city centres – though a majority will probably work within a fairly restricted radius of a few miles of their homes. They probably are not very concerned about the long work journey; if the evidence from our survey is representative, they find it a price they willingly pay for the advantages of living in or near the country. And the effects are mitigated by the fact that so many of them use the car to get to work. But again, the effects will be most serious for the minority without cars – again, the less affluent members of the suburban community, who live in an environment where lack of a car may represent real hardship.

In many ways, the tenant in public housing – whether in the high-density, high-rise city blocks or in the single-family homes of the new and expanding towns – is more privileged. His home, especially if built after 1965, is likely to have standards of size and fittings which are unknown in the marginal privately-built house. He also enjoys a substantial subsidy, which may be far from closely related to his income; so that again, the better-off members of the group are likely to obtain the biggest advantage. But all members of this group lose the advantage of capital appreciation. And it can be argued that were it not for the phenomenon of containment, they would have enjoyed even higher housing standards. For more of them would have been housed, as so many were between the two world wars, in single-family housing at the peripheries of the cities, instead of in the high-rise structures which have been the typical postwar response to land shortages.

This last reservation, of course, does not apply to the public tenant in the new or expanding town. He enjoys a house which will be a superior version of the same sort of structure that was built in the better municipal estates of the 1930s. Though it may be built at a slightly higher density than the older house – typically, thirteen or fourteen to the acre against twelve for the older house – it probably compensates by its superior equipment and fittings, especially in the matter of winter heating. He also has accessibility to a wide range of employment near at hand – at any rate if he lives in the average new town or in one of the bigger expanding towns. If he lives in one of the smaller expanding towns, remote from any conurbation, the choice of employment – and also of shopping and other urban services – may well be inferior to what he has become used to in the conurbation he came from.

There can be little doubt about the identity of the group that has got the poorest bargain. It is the really depressed class in the housing market: the poorer members of the privately-rented housing sector, which is heavily concentrated in the older property in the core cities of the metropolitan areas. Throughout this study, we have made relatively little reference to this group;

for it has not been at all prominently involved in the processes we have been describing. It has, simply, been left out of the urban growth process to a very large degree. The reasons for that fact are only partly to be found in the operations of the planning system. They arise mainly from the effects of policies in other related areas – above all housing policies. And this helps illustrate the fact that in practice, there comes a point when it is no longer helpful to discuss the operation of planning policies in isolation from all these other related policy fields.

THE 1947 SYSTEM IN THEORY AND IN PRACTICE

Before we turn to these wider relationships, in Chapter Thirteen, this is a useful point to sum up some of the features of the 1947 Planning System as it actually operated, in comparison with the apparent intentions of those who were instrumental in setting it up. These conclusion are drawn from both this chapter and the previous chapter.

In the intentions of its founders, the planning system was clearly intended to control and guide both the pace and direction of change. In practice the system thus created was too inflexible to cope with an unexpectedly dynamic external world. That is one principal reason why, in the Planning Advisory Group report of 1965 and the Act of 1968, the whole process of plan making had to be profoundly modified. But the failure went deeper than that.

The idealized system was clearly meant to be centralized or unitary in character. It was intended to depend on the wisdom and impartiality of professionals, who would interpret the best interests of society as a whole. It seems to have been assumed that it was possible for such a golden mean to be discovered, and that every group in society would then accept it. In fact, from the beginning the decision was made to operate the system not through a single central authority, as some writers had suggested, but through local authorities. So instead of a central model, the system in practice operated through the conflict of local interests, with a stronger element of political intervention than ever seems to have been in the minds of the creators of the system. In particular, there was a clear potential clash of interests between the cities (and conurbations) on the one hand, and the counties on the other.

The idealized system bypassed the market altogether, most perfectly in the Uthwatt Committee recommendations of 1942. Here however was another case where right from the beginning, there was a compromise; the actual system kept the market in being but, in the original provision of the 1947 Act as interpreted in the regulations, it did not allow the market to work. When this was rectified by the abolition of the Development Charge, great fortunes were made by the owners of land because of the accident of it acquiring planning permission. Yet, in theory and in law, these values were strictly the creation of the community and should have been claimed for the community.

The idealized version relied on the massive creation of planned communities, designed and realized by strong comprehensive planning agencies;

other agents would come into the development process only in a subsidiary way. The actual system has relied on an interaction between the planner, who has a negative control (and some positive influences on design), and the developer, who must take the initiative on the basis of his understanding of the demands of the market. The result in practice has been a continuation of the interwar process of suburbanization, but the new suburbs have been pushed farther from the city centres than would have been the case in the absence of planning.

Overall, the idealized system obviously had a strong element of planning for the least fortunate; urban containment, and the creation of self-contained and balanced communities, were supposed specifically to help the less advantaged members of society. But in practice, the system seems almost systematically to have had the reverse effect: it is the most fortunate who have gained the most benefits from the operation of the system, while the least fortunate have gained very little.

Not all of this can be laid at the door of the local authority planners and their political masters – though a substantial part of it can be attributed directly to the operations of planning control. Other policies have interacted with planning to affect the welfare, or the lack of welfare, of different groups of the population. In the concluding chapter of our study, we turn to look at the interaction between physical planning and these related policy areas.

CHAPTER THIRTEEN

POLICY ALTERNATIVES – PAST AND FUTURE

This chapter concentrates upon policy alternatives in other fields which are closely related to physical planning – notably housing, land, local government, transport and industrial location. It shows that in the period from 1945 to 1970 the main lines of policy in these fields were by no means always consistent with the policies of physical planning. It considers the range of alternative policies that exists in each of these areas for the future. Then it asks what effect these different policies might have on the future pattern of urbanization. It concludes by returning to the central problem of the objectives of the total planning system, and by isolating some unresolved questions for planning in the 1970s and 1980s.

This chapter was written by Peter Hall with additional material by Ray Thomas and Roy Drewett.

INTRODUCTION

Physical planning controls are clearly not the only factor affecting urban growth. Controls over the location of different sorts of employment – or the lack of such controls – are basic in regulating the numbers of workers, and their families, seeking homes in any local area. The rate of inflation, which influences people's attitudes to investment, and taxation policies as applied to different types of housing, critically affect the progress of the market for owner-occupied housing. Transport policies, both for road and for rail travel, affect the cost of transport in relation to wages and salaries, and may introduce a differential according to whether the trip is by road or rail, over short distance or long. Though presumably subsidiary to land-planning control policies, agricultural subsidy policies affect the prosperity of the farmer and thus the firmness of his resolve to stay on the land. Rural electrification and water supply policies, not to say the provision of television relay stations, affect the attractiveness of rural life in relation to town life. These policies have been controlled or affected by many different agencies in England since the Second World War, and we should not expect that they would prove fully consistent with each other in their effects on the urban growth process.

HOUSING POLICIES

We concluded in the previous chapter that one main indirect effect of the planning system was to make building land scarce, and thus to cause its price to rise faster than prices or incomes generally; the main effect was to cause builders to economize on land, so that building densities per acre rose compared with the 1930s. Building costs also rose relative to other prices (gains in productivity in this labour intensive field have been smaller than in most other industries) and made their contribution to the final house price. But it has been the rise in land prices which has certainly made a bigger effect. The influence of these factors has been expressed partly in the cost of the new houses and partly in space standards. House prices have not even kept in line with other prices but have moved upwards as fast and sometimes faster than money incomes. The size of house plots has stagnated and reductions have been made in the size of rooms. The typical buyer of a new house in the 1970s is getting less for his money than his counterpart obtained in the 1950s – or the 1930s.

Paradoxically the inflationary trends in house prices have in many ways had the effect of increasing the demand for owner occupation. Everyone has become accustomed to the inflation in house prices, and many have justifiably seen investment in a home (or a more expensive home) as the best easily-available hedge against inflation. The capital gains made by existing owner occupiers have made it easier for them to buy a new home by reducing the proportion of the purchase price which they needed to borrow. Building societies have willingly accommodated to the inflationary trends. Their assets have over recent decades doubled every six years or so, and some observers have even suggested that building society activity has strengthened the inflationary pressure in the housing market.[1]

Building society interest rates have increased substantially over the postwar period as investors have adjusted to the inflationary trends. In the 1930s the rate of interest was only 4½ per cent. It was no higher than this in the early 1950s. By 1970 the rate had increased to 7⅝ per cent. But as far as the mortgagee is concerned the increase in interest rates has been cushioned by tax relief. Although the British taxation system has preserved its generally progressive structure, the tax relief in mortgage payments is one highly regressive element in the system. The higher the marginal rate which an individual pays, the greater the taxation relief on mortgage interest payments.

The tax remission on interest payments has often been described as a regressive form of taxation since it gives maximum relief to the richest; but it gives sizeable relief even to the middle-income groups, and as incomes rise due to inflation, pushing more groups into the higher-income tax brackets, the amount of the bonus that comes from owner occupiership increases noticeably. Table 13.1 has been based on the Nationwide (Co-operative)

[1] Mary Waugh, *Suburban Growth in North-West Kent, 1861–1961.* Unpublished Ph.D. thesis, University of London (1968), pp. 208–212.

Table 13.1

SALARIES, MORTGAGES, TAX AND TRAVEL 1952–1969

Year	Average price £	Interest rate per cent	80% mortgage annual payment £	Starting salary £	Tax rate	Tax remission £	Mortgage repayment after remission £	Payment (after remission) as % salary	Rail travel £	Rail travel as % salary	Mortgage + rail travel as % salary
1952	2,758	4½	146.55	1,000	47½	28.87½	117.67½	11·7	—	—	—
1953	2,498	4½	133.85	1,000	45	24.50	109.35	10·9	—	—	—
1954	2,588	4½	143.15	1,000	45	25.20	117.95	11·8	—	—	—
1955	2,649	5¼	154.70	1,150	42½	36.29	118.41	10·3	—	—	—
1956	2,692	5½	157.50	1,150	42½	38.22½	119.27½	10·4	—	—	—
1957	2,761	6	158.95	1,375	42½	43.77½	115.17½	8·4	—	—	—
1958	2,844	6	178.65	1,450	42½	45.05	133.60	9·2	—	—	—
1959	3,013	6	189.30	1,410	39	43.79	145.51	10·3	—	—	—
1960	3,312	6	208.05	1,460	39	48.05	160.00	10·9	—	—	—
1961	3,680	6	231.10	1,650	39	53.47½	177.62½	10·8	—	—	—
1962	3,900	6½	255.90	1,716	39	61.22½	194.67½	11·3	—	—	—
1963	4,340	6	280.55	1,839	39	64.71	215.84	11·7	56·80	3·1	14·8
1964	4,977	6	312.70	1,894	39	72.12½	240.57½	12·7	61·20	3·2	15·9
1965	5,079	6¾	341.35	1,951	41	87.86	253.49	13·0	61·20	3·1	16·1
1966	5,101	6¾	342.85	2,174	41	88.27½	254.57½	11·7	64·40	3·0	14·7
1967	5,584	7⅛	389.60	2,250	41	101.89	287.71	12·8	64·40	2·9	15·7
1968	5,744	7⅛	399.75	2,250	41	104.77½	294.97½	13·1	69·20	3·1	16·2
1969	5,983	7⅛	439.25	2,475	41	130.76	308.49	12·5	69·20	2·8	15·3

Source: Nationwide Building Society and British Rail.

figures of average new housing in the Southern region for each year from 1952 to 1969.[2] In each year the annual mortgage repayments for a new mortgage (at 80 per cent of purchase price) are calculated on the rate of interest ruling then. For purpose of comparison, a typical professional or managerial salary for a man in his late twenties or early thirties – the starting salary in the principal grade in the Civil Service – is also given, together with the tax relief which would be attracted on this salary for a married man with two children. The table shows clearly that as a percentage of salary, net mortgage repayments have stayed stable over the period 1952–69 – despite a remarkable rise in the absolute size of the annual repayment. But there has been an upward trend. From 1952–60 inclusive, the net mortgage repayments (after allowance for tax relief) averaged 10·4 per cent of gross income; from 1961–1969 inclusive, the average was 12·2 per cent. Since tax rates have not varied markedly over the period, save in the early 1950s when they were higher, these results would be little different if applied to the net income after tax (but before tax relief). Over the whole period, salary rose slightly more than house price: salary about two and a half times, house prices about two and a quarter times. Because of rising interest rates, gross mortgage repayments trebled; but the total tax relief available on these payments rose four and a half times. This is a measure of the degree to which tax policies cushioned the average middle-class buyer, over this period, against the rising cost of borrowing for owner occupiership. In addition, Schedule A tax on owner-occupied property was abolished in 1962–63; though for some years before this the net tax liability could usually be covered out of maintenance relief, so the effect of abolition was probably minimal. No wealth tax has been introduced; and the owner occupier was specifically excluded from liability to capital gains tax introduced in 1965.

We are forced to conclude, then, that housing policies have not been consistent with planning policies. The only time when there was some consistency, perhaps, was in the period of the 1945–51 Labour Government. Then, the attempt was made to push the bulk of the housing effort into the provision of public housing in comprehensively-planned communities; owner occupiership was discouraged. But since 1951, Conservative and Labour Governments alike have been wedded to the ideal of a property-owning democracy. They have encouraged this by favourable tax concessions even though they were repeatedly reminded that these had a regressive effect. Yet at the same time, these governments managed not at all to cure the problem of land shortage due to planning restrictions. Considerable progress has been achieved in that the proportion of owner occupiers has dramatically increased. But, as with the wish granted by the monkey's paw, the result – accompanied by a substantial decline in space standards – can hardly have accorded with the original ideal of a property-owning democracy.

The only major exception to the generally inconsistent pattern was the

[2] We are indebted to Mr R. H. Betman of the Nationwide Building Society for supplying figures of house prices and to Mr Charles W. Smith for the tax calculations.

Labour Government's setting up of the Land Commission in the Act of 1967. This Act did two main things. On the one hand, it imposed a differentially high tax on capital gains in land – the so called Betterment Levy. Like the earlier Development Charge imposed by Labour in 1947, in practice this levy was apparently added to the price that was paid for land. In other words, far from reducing the price of land, it further inflated it. But the other main element of the 1967 Act was intended to be more important in the long run. It was the setting up of the Land Commission as a land-buying agency on a large scale. The idea of the Commission was attacked on the grounds that it was nationalization by stealth, and that is no bad description. Had it survived twenty years or more, there seems little doubt that the Commission would have become a dominant influence in the land market, able to release land for development when shortages threatened, and able to fight recalcitrant authorities on questions of development permission. It might have loosened the Gordian knot that has constricted the planning and development process. But it survived a mere four years; not long enough to follow through its first major fight with a local planning authority. Later in this chapter we return in more detail to the land problem.

In relation to public housing, government policies have operated rather differently. Though the details of policy have varied the broad impact has remained consistent enough over the whole of the postwar period. Local authorities have been exhorted to save land. They have been encouraged to do so by special differential subsidies on expensive land and for high-rise building. (Though since the 1968 Housing Act the structure discourages very high flats, it still operates in favour of high-density schemes.) Local authorities which wanted to redevelop at lower densities, so as to avoid high-rise solutions, were firmly told during the 1950s that they were wrong and would not be encouraged. These subsidy schemes have represented a considerable burden on the public purse. They have meant, in effect, that a given quantity of public resources would produce fewer dwellings than if there had been a whole-hearted policy of encouraging lower-density development on cheaper land. But it must be said, in explanation, that the general effect of dear land – even more in the public than the private sector – was to encourage the crowding together of as many dwellings as possible on each acre. This was particularly evident after 1959, when local authorities were again compelled to pay market value for any site which they acquired compulsorily. The ironic result of this provision was that a local authority, in making a plan to develop public housing on an area, would automatically raise its market value and thus be liable to pay additional value which, in effect, it had created. Thus, not only in the case of inner area slum clearance or of comprehensive development schemes, but also in peripheral developments at the edge of the city, high density became the general rule.

LOCAL GOVERNMENT POLICIES

Logically, this takes us on to the question of local government reform. One good reason why local planning authorities have been so restrictive in interpreting the idea of containment is that they are fundamentally rural authorities, dominated in many cases by rural political interests. The politics of local goverment explain much of this. After the war the Labour Government tried, but failed, to introduce fundamental local government reform. The Conservative Governments of 1951–64 reformed London government but made only minor changes in the structure elsewhere. The fundamental nineteenth-century distinction, between cities and large towns (county boroughs) and rural areas (counties) was maintained. It was natural then for the counties to defend the interests of the countryman against the encroaching townsman. Green Belts became political weapons in what was seen as a fight against takeover attempts by the cities. And no one seriously accepted the idea of a central planning agency with powers to control land use and development, thus balancing urban and rural interests, as had been suggested by the Uthwatt Committee on Compensation and Betterment in 1942. The gainers were the existing rural interests. The losers were the new ruralites, actual or potential, seeking homes in the suburban fringes around the county boroughs. But by definition, since they were either not there or only newly arrived, they had little or no political voice in the county structure.

It is also true that the county boroughs have often been on the side of containment – but in a rather different way and for rather different reasons. They have not acted against the wishes of those able to buy homes in rural districts. But they have sought to preserve jobs for the electorate within their own area. They have also endeavoured to hang on to the valuable tax by which employment land uses contribute to the rates. And in many cases they have sought to preserve the electorate itself by the construction of council dwellings on cramped sites within their own boundaries, rather than enter into overspill agreements with small towns in their hinterland. Changes in the local government structure, which like that in London, maintain the urban/rural distinction, do nothing to reduce the motivation for policies of these kinds or their disadvantageous side effects.

It can therefore be argued that here again is a contradiction. The planning powers created in 1947 could only be wielded fairly by some agency big enough to encompass, and weigh up, both urban and rural interests: either a central national authority, or a local government unit based on the union of town and country. But in some of the most problematic areas we seem little further in achieving a structure of this kind in 1971 than we were in 1947.

The policies of the 1964–70 Labour Government can be seen as a two-armed attack on this problem. The Land Commission, in effect, was a sort of reserve central planning authority. The reform of local government, which began with the appointment of the parallel Royal Commissions for England and for Scotland in 1966, was quite specifically intended to supply city-region planning authorities which would span town and country. And though the recommendations of the two Commissions differed quite substantially when they were published in the summer of 1969, both were united in their determination to create large planning authorities which took in a wide area even around the largest conurbations.

This was particularly significant around the very largest urban areas. The previous Conservative Government had reformed London government on the basis of what can be described as a conurbation solution: a single authority for the continuously built-up area, with district authorities for subdivisions of that area. This was attacked, at the time the Greater London Council came into being, and the Labour Government were contemplating the wider reform, on the basis that effective planning demanded a city-region solution: a wider-based authority, covering not merely the built-up area, but the whole functional sphere of influence all around taking in the area over which London's overspill problems needed to be solved. When the Redcliffe–Maud Commission on Local Government in England reported in 1969, it recommended that London's boundaries be left as they were. But around Manchester and Liverpool and Birmingham it recommended wide metropolitan areas, taking in not merely the conurbation but the surrounding Green Belt and some freestanding towns (including new towns and expanding towns) beyond. Their Commission's proposed West Midlands metropolitan authority, for instance, would have been far bigger in area than the Greater London Council. (Though even then it would not have extended to take in Telford, one of the new towns for the region.) The proposals, predictably, filled the rural fringes around the conurbations with alarm and fury; particularly since they involved the disappearance of counties as important as Cheshire and Staffordshire, and the dismemberment of Warwickshire. Almost immediately, the Conservative Opposition announced that they favoured a conurbation-type solution on the lines of the London reform; and returned to power, this is the solution that they applied in their White Paper of February 1971.

It is particularly interesting to notice the impact of the Conservative solution on these critical areas, as opposed to the Redcliffe–Maud solution which, in its broad outlines, was the one accepted by the previous government. The Maud solution would have made the metropolitan authority responsible for the critical structure plan that determined the future growth of the whole area. Then it would have given detailed planning power – to exercise development control – to a district authority which in nearly every case was based on urban population within the conurbation itself. The net result would have been almost total submergence of the rural interest by the numerically dominant urban interest; and it was this which aroused the hostility of the rural district councils, when they campaigned against the recommendations with their symbol of the goose-stepping bureaucrat, R. E. Mote.[3] In the revised version of the reform, they gained almost everything they could have wished. The responsibility for making the structure plan for these fringe areas was transferred from the metropolitan authority to the county authority; and it is significant that around the conurbations, the boundaries of these authorities were so drawn that they remained funda-

[3] Peter Hall, 'The Country Fights Back and Wins', *New Society*, 12 Sept. 1970, pp. 491–4.

mentally rural in character. The responsibility for development control was given to county district authorities which could be as small as 40,000 population, so guaranteeing the dominance of the most local level of rural interest. Such a solution, it seems, could only buttress the rural areas in their determination to contain urban England ever more severely.

TRANSPORT POLICIES

As urban land economists have long stressed, land and housing costs are only one element in the equation for the buyer or renter of houseroom. The money costs and the time costs of travel also have to be taken into account. If transport costs fall in relation to incomes, or if technological improvements make it possible to travel further in the same time, we should expect that people will extend their possible commuting range. American studies, for instance, have suggested that the vast Interstate Highway Programme of the 1960s positively subsidized suburban living by making it much easier to travel longer distances from the major urban areas.[4] And the interesting point is that in Britain, as in the United States and other advanced countries, the cost of transport does not at all reflect pure market considerations – any more than the cost of houseroom does. It is subject to all sorts of distortions due to subsidies, overt and concealed. It would be surprising if, overall, these distortions did not affect urban growth patterns indirectly – even if, sometimes, the effects were by no means intended.

The biggest single change in the transport situation in recent decades has perhaps been beyond the power of any democratically elected government to influence. Coincident with the period of Britain's first serious attempt at land-use planning occurred a mobility explosion in the form of rising car ownership, the like of which will never be repeated. In 1947 less than one in every seven households had use of a private car. By the late 1960s more than half of all households possessed a car and about one in every fifteen possessed two or more cars.

Government influence on the growth of car ownership could perhaps have only been marginal. But the same cannot be said about the effects of this trend on the personal transport situation in general. The lack of any policies to deal with the problems associated with growing car ownership has meant that the effects have been very mixed for different sections of the population.

At the same time, in general, some forms of public transport in Britain have risen far less in the postwar period than the general cost of living, earnings or house prices. The season ticket index for the second class commuter from Woking to Waterloo, for instance, on a base where 1938 equalled 100, had risen only to 430 by 1969; from Orpington to Charing Cross it had risen even less, to 374. In the same period the average clerical or technical worker's salary had reached a level of 635; while house prices (for a modern second-hand house in the London area) had gone up to around 800. This general

[4] Marion Clawson, *Suburban Land Conversion in the United States: An Economic and Governmental Process*. Johns Hopkins U.P., Baltimore (1971), p. 40.

rule was also true of shorter periods in the interwar period: the 1963-based index for the Woking-Waterloo fare was only 119 by 1969, compared with 143 for salaries.[5] In the late 1960s it became evident that many London commuting services were failing to cover their true costs, and in 1970 it was announced that fares would rise so as to abolish the subsidy element progressively over a period of years. But overall, there seems no doubt that the medium-distance commuter has benefited greatly from a sharply falling real cost of travel; the very long-distance commuter, because of the operation of sharply tapered rates, and improvements such as electrification, has probably benefited even more.

The short-distance public transport commuter within the big urban agglomerations, in contrast, has almost certainly gained nothing; during the 1950s and 1960s, his position seems to have worsened. This is because he travels by buses, which have suffered from traffic congestion and rising labour costs. Thus bus fares in London rose much more than the general increase in retail prices during the period 1953–67; the index, deflated by the Index of Retail Prices, on a base of 100 in 1952, was already 156 by the mid-1960s.[6] The main sufferer, almost certainly, was the inner urban resident.

On motoring costs the evidence is not entirely consistent. The National Income Statistics basis of calculation of car running costs, based on a 1963 index base of 100, had reached 128 by 1967 and 134 by 1969, closely in line with the cost of petrol which was 134. But AA figures for the cost per mile of a 1,000 cc car, on an index where 1958 equalled 100, record only 118 by 1967 (Figure 13.1). What is certain, again, is that the real cost of motoring fell in relation to earnings and the general Index of Retail Prices.[7] Partly this represents a falling real cost of car purchase in relation to income, a product of increasing productivity in the car industry. Large numbers of second-hand cars, too, were beginning to enter the market in the 1960s, lowering the threshold at which car ownership was possible. Though the price of the road fund licence rose during the 1960s more rapidly than the general cost of living index or earnings, this of course was not a major element in total annual running costs; fuel costs rose more nearly in line with general costs of living, demonstrating the unwillingness or reluctance of successive governments to raise the general cost of motoring. Furthermore, though much of the proceeds from licence and fuel tax were diverted elsewhere, the rapidly-rising revenue from these sources helped to finance an accelerating road-building programme; and though this was highly selective in its geographical impact during the 1960s, in certain directions it made possible much longer-distance commuting by car into and out of the major cities. Partly, it is true, for the city centre commuter this was counterweighed by congestion and by

[5] We are indebted to Mr P. W. Glassborow of British Railways Southern Region for this information.

[6] Cf. Ray Thomas, *The Journey to Work*. PEP, London (1968), p. 373 and Fig. (ii), p. 374.

[7] For an analysis of the figures deflated by the price index, cf. ibid., Fig. (ii), p. 374.

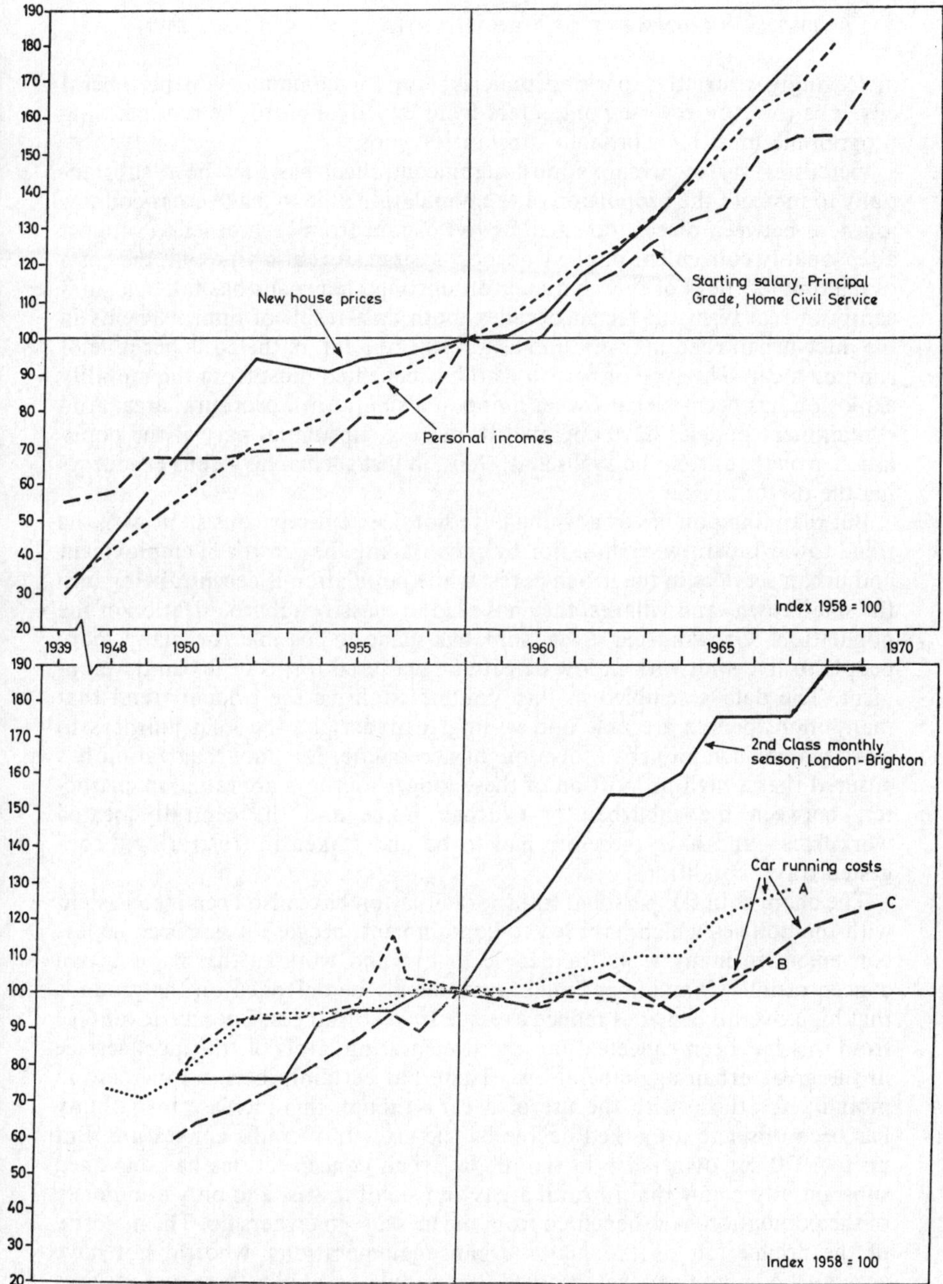

Figure 13.1 New House Prices, Incomes, Rail Fares, Driving Costs
A = National Income Basis
B = AA figures (weighted figures)
C = AA figures (1,000 cc car)

increasingly restrictive parking policies; but for commuters to peripheral city jobs (or even reverse commuters from city to suburb) the roadbuilding programme must have brought substantial gains.

Increasing car ownership's most significant effect has thus been substantially to increase the proportion of the population able to make cross-country journeys between places too small or too distant from each other to support a reasonably convenient public transport system. It is also true that the costs of making journeys of this character on uncongested roads has fallen significantly in real terms in recent decades, both as a result of improvements in the inter-urban road network and as a result of a fall in the costs per mile of running a car. The type of person who has benefited most from the mobility explosion has been the car owner living in a small town or a rural area. And containment policies have operated to place a substantial part of the population growth, during the 1950s and 1960s, in just such areas – thus encouraging the use of the car.

But planning policies as a whole have not been entirely consistent with the trend towards car ownership. For by encouraging the growth of employment and urban services in the urban cores, while population is decentralizing into the small towns and villages, they have led to massive suburbanization of the population. Growing car ownership has made it possible for many more people to live and work in low density or scattered forms of urban development. The data assembled in this Volume confirms the evident trend that many more people are able and willing to undertake the long journeys to work which such an urban form might necessitate. But suburbanization has ensured that a high proportion of these longer journeys are radial in character – between the suburban or exurban home and the centrally-located workplace – and have therefore had to be undertaken in frustratingly congested travel conditions.

The changes in the personal transport situation have also been inconsistent with the policies which have led to containment, because it has become less convenient in many ways for people to live and work in the major urban concentration. Containment might conceivably be defended on the grounds that high overall densities reduce average travel distances. But any advantage from this has been cancelled out by deteriorating levels of transport service in the great urban agglomerations. There has certainly been an increase in mobility for those with the use of a car – though this increase in mobility has been offset to a marked degree by the growth of traffic congestion. But up to 1970 car ownership in the major urban concentrations has remained substantially below that in rural areas and small towns, and only a minority of the population have benefited from the increase in ownership. The majority of the population of the major urban agglomerations, who do not have access to a motor car, has become less mobile as public transport services have become less frequent, as bus services have become more unreliable because of the growth of congestion, as the cost of fares has escalated at a rate roughly 50 per cent above the general rise in retail prices, and as the facilities available even for pedestrian movement have declined under the pressure generated by the attempt to accommodate the seemingly inexorable growth in the volume of vehicular traffic.

All in all, the broad drift of transport policies, though complex, is clear enough. Private transport costs, and some public transport costs (over longer distances) have fallen in relation to incomes; this has benefited the better-off members of the community more than poorer members (who tend to be neither car owners nor long-distance public transport commuters), and it must have encouraged dispersal of the population at increasing distances from employment. Falling private transport costs have been in accord with the basic planning policy of urban containment, which has dispersed new housing into small towns and villages where it is more difficult to support good public transport services. But they are not in accord with the trend to suburbanization which has been produced by the effects of the planning policies, because this has led to radial journeys into congested cities, even to their centres. Ironically, both a non-plan policy and a full-blooded new-towns policy would probably both have been better at dispersing employment and urban services; the first because there would have been no barriers to the process; the second because planned dispersal was the main objective of the policy. Both would therefore have been better in accord with the trend towards falling real private transport costs and higher car ownership. Rising public transport costs in some areas (especially short-distance bus journeys) have penalized that section of the population of the big urban agglomerations – still a majority in 1970 – which had no regular access to a private car. And they have reduced what could be claimed as a justification for containment: that by raising densities in the conurbations, it increased accessibility to urban jobs and services.

INDUSTRIAL LOCATION POLICIES

The policies we have considered so far have borne mainly on the decisions people make about the location of their homes. But the starting point of any such decision must be the location of the jobs of the working members of the household, and especially the main breadwinner. Our study of migration has confirmed what all such studies show anywhere: that in moving and home seeking, the most important basic factor is the location of the job. So policies affecting this location – or the lack of such policies – will clearly be critical for generating the forces of pressure for urban growth. And, as we stressed in the previous chapter, location policies by and large have been outside the sphere of competence of the local authority planner. He had to accept their implications, dealing with the consequences for residential growth and all the associated local authority and other services as best he could.

Here, notoriously, controls have been selectively and arbitrarily applied. The Barlow Commission, in its 1940 report, seems to have confused two meanings of the word industry, and so to have believed that the key to employment policy was the control of factory jobs; and this was the power that the government took in the Distribution of Industry Act 1945, which set up the Industrial Development Certificate system. Yet after the war, manufacturing employment stagnated and the whole net growth of employment went into the tertiary sector, which was left uncontrolled until the ban on London office building in November 1964. Even after office development was effectively regulated in the 1965 Act, which introduced the Office Development Permit to parallel the Industrial Development Certificate, a wide range of tertiary employment was left outside any control mechanism. And though much of this employment was doubtless of the local service type, some – especially the sectors of higher and further education, and scientific research – was certainly not. Ironically, much of this investment was directly or indirectly under the control of central government. Yet the development of scientific research was permitted or encouraged to concentrate disproportionately in London's West sector stretching to Winchester and to Oxford. And of the seven totally new universities founded in the early 1960s, only one – Stirling – was located in a development area. Yet this was at a time when Industrial Development Certificate policy was being applied to steer factory jobs out of South-East England, and into the development areas. Again, the policies were not consistent.

Even within the industrial sector, the operation of the policy was not always clear cut. Holmans has shown that in the South-East, only about one-third of the new factory industry during the 1950s could be accounted for by Industrial Development Certificate controls at all.[8] In the West Midlands, where factories provided a particularly large share of the total regional employment growth, the Board of Trade's main efforts were directed to persuading firms out of the region altogether and into distant development areas. Many firms preferred (as in the South-East) to expand in situ, making limited extensions each year which were outside the scope of control, doubling up within their premises, or buying up existing space which was again outside the Board's control. Thus there was very little overspill industry indeed to man in expanding or new towns beyond the regional Green Belt. The predictable result was that the overspill programme was slow to develop and that workers tended to commute back into the conurbation to find work, even from a new town as distant as Telford. This was a particularly important influence on the process of suburbanization, which we described in the last chapter. For if jobs were being retained in the conurbation while the physical growth of that same conurbation was being restrained, the sure result must be an increase in longer distance commuting across the Green Belt – a result which seems to have been an almost accidental effect of contradictory policies in different spheres.

LAND POLICIES

The supply and cost of land has been the Achilles heel in the residential development process. The cost of land has risen out of all proportion as a

[8] A. E. Holmans, 'Industrial Development Certificates and Control of the Growth of Employment in South-East England', *Urban Studies*, 1 (1964), p. 142.

percentage of the final house price. Our survey of developers showed that on average, for England the percentage has risen from between 4 and 12 per cent in 1960 to between 18 and 38 per cent in 1970. In the South-East, the average in 1970 was over 30 per cent. The factors determining this increase have been identified earlier in this study. It is worth stressing that through the scarcity of land, the continued ownership of land, because of its inflation, is now considered a sensible form of investment. The market relationship in land is an unusual demand/supply relationship even under normal economic circumstances, but the increasing problem of scarcity has made matters worse. Clearly, the price elasticity of demand for land is high, but in addition much also depends on the negotiating position between buyer and seller. The inequitable position has now arisen in the market where developers must buy land while landowners do not have to sell. This element of cost-push was particularly important during the life of the Land Commission when land was either withheld or inflated in value in response to the betterment taxation. Yet during the period following the end of betterment, land values have continued to increase at over 10 per cent per year. With no tax on holding land, the disincentives on holding land in order to realize an inflated asset are small.

The Land Commission was clearly an anomaly. It was no more than an extension of central government authority issued with a brief to tackle the inadequacies of local government procedures in releasing land. As we have seen earlier, the Land Commission failed either to stabilize prices or assemble land. When the end of the Commission was announced the Minister made provision for development value to be realized from future land transactions to be dealt with through the normal system of taxation and capital gains. The Commission was undoubtedly defeated through the intransigence of local authorities. However, the Minister further announced that the problems of land release could be handled by those same authorities and issued Circular 10/70 encouraging local authorities to make realistic assessments of land requirements and reassess the amount of land needed. The government therefore put its faith back in the local authorities to do a job that the Land Commission had started, but in which it had been defeated by those same authorities. As we have seen elsewhere in this study, the present local authority structure is totally inadequate to deal with the problem. Birmingham is not in trouble in Birmingham; it must have land in Worcestershire, Warwickshire and Staffordshire – areas over which the city has no jurisdiction and areas which have resisted urban expansion for so long. It is also of little comfort to expect the reorganization of local government boundaries to solve the problem; the new alignment of boundaries still manages to protect the areas of greatest pressure, particularly in London and the West Midlands.

The problem of land shortage and land cost has been identified in this study as perhaps the most serious contradiction in the 1947 Planning System as it actually operated. There is only one exception: the new towns, where a Development Corporation buys all the land that is needed for urban development at a price which reflects the fact that the public should not pay the speculative value of land if this arises from public action. But elsewhere, since 1959 even if it is clear that the value of land simply reflects the planner's decision that development should take place, even a public authority has had to pay full speculative market value.

This polarization of experience points to the crucial failure of the 1947 Planning System. The 1947 dream was to nationalize development rights in land. The rationale for this dream is easily defendable. The value of property rights depends mainly upon what economists call externalities. The value depends only partly upon what use can be made of a particular piece of land and rests much more on the uses which are made of adjacent land and other activities carried out in the surrounding area. Some of these externalities can, for example, be summarized by the word accessibility. The value of these externalities depends upon the quality of the transport network which serves the site and upon the range and variety of activities which the transport network makes accessible to the site.

The point is that the value of these externalities is created by the community. A plot of land is given value for housebuilding by the existence of the network of service facilities such as roads, sewers, water supply, by the existence of other houses in the locality, and by the availability of jobs, shops and schools in the area. This value is created by the public authorities responsible for providing the services and by the very existence of the private activities. It seems wholly inequitable that, since these values are created by other people, the profit should take the form of a windfall gain by the owner of the plot of land.

A non-plan solution would have allowed the value of these development rights to float freely – as they did in the 1930s. The developer would therefore have borne the costs of uncertainty. He would have to estimate whether or not the value of these externalities was sufficiently great to be realizable by a sale.

But the system which has existed since 1953 has suffered, from the point of view of the community, from the worst of both worlds. The individual owner, not the public authority, gained the profit. But the public authority did clearly define by zoning the property rights, and it published Development Plans long in advance which substantially reduced the uncertainties facing the developer in deciding whether or not to buy and build on a particular plot of land. The planners attempted to maximize the externalities. The developer attempted to take full advantage of the externalities. The ratepayer and taxpayer have met many of the real costs involved in the creation of externalities. But the value of the externalities created has been translated into market price which has been paid for by the consumer. The inevitable result has been that in a period of unprecedented affluence space standards have actually fallen.

In the new towns this sad sequence has been avoided by one simple provision. Development Corporations had the power to compulsorily purchase land at its existing use-value. Under the 1961 Land Compensation Act, an acquiring authority in a new or expanding town does not pay an increase in the value of the land if the increase is attributable to the scheme of development which gives rise to the need for the compulsory purchase.[9]

Without this provision the new towns, as we know them, would not exist. It would have been impossible for the Development Corporation to assemble the land without such exorbitant cost that the growth would have been stunted and the pattern of development distorted. It would have been impossible for the Development Corporation to achieve anything like a balance in the social composition of their populations.

With this provision the Development Corporations have succeeded in creating sets of assets whose value is so great as to be what is by some regarded as an embarrassment. Successive governments in recent years have urged the Development Corporations to substantially increase their sales of dwellings for owner occupation. Although the new towns represent a substantial investment of central government funds many of them have become financially profitable. The original intention was that the new town assets would on maturity be handed over to the local authority, but governments have refused to do this and some observers have attributed this refusal to the magnitude of the assets involved which would make the local authority too powerful.

The different price paid for land for development goes a long way to explain the dichotomy between comprehensive planning in the new towns and permissive planning elsewhere, but in 1947 it was believed that the same kind of rules of the game would operate everywhere. Why did the 1947 dream of nationalization of development rights work in the new towns but not in other places? Why was it accepted that a farmer in the designated area of a new town should get only £300 per acre for his land whilst the farmer on the fringe of a neighbouring town was able to realise £3,000, £6,000, or even more per acre?

One factor relevant to an attempt to answer this question is scale of operations involved. The Development Corporation buys land in terms of hundreds of acres and it is clear to all parties concerned that only the fact of designation as a new town would make it feasible to develop on that scale. The rules of the game are in accord with the obvious reality. Developers outside the new town generally operate on a much smaller scale. The land they buy in relatively small-sized plots at the periphery of the built-up area is fairly obviously ripe for development. The expectation of a residential land price is already there, and its status in this matter is usually confirmed by the Development Plan. It is significant that many of the larger house construction companies act much more like a Development Corporation. Instead of buying collections of small plots at the periphery, they go instead for large tracts more distant from the urban centres. They often buy land not zoned for residential development, years in advance, and are prepared to spend substantial funds on planning applications and appeals in order to get the required residential zoning. The total costs involved in operations of this kind in terms of interest

[9] Land Compensation Act 1961 (9 & 10 Eliz. 2, c.33,) S.5.

payments, extra expenditure on basic services for the more distant sites, design and legal charges, may well bring the costs per acre up to the level of land already approved by the planner as ready for development.

But there are no studies of substance which establish exactly why the 1947 dream of nationalizing development rights failed. It is usually said that the system gave no incentive for land owners to sell their land. The dream certainly failed to take into account the expectation of the owner of a small plot of land at the urban fringe who would prefer to withhold his land rather than sell it for its value as a piggery. It failed to take into account that a farmer could justifiably claim a substantial financial sweetener for a sale which would completely change his way of life. At a more basic level, the 1947 dream appears to have been an unrealistic denial of any role for the market in property rights in land. As Denman puts the matter:

> . . . the nationalization of land is likely to be or become a nominal affair. When land belongs to the community, lawyers may argue that a Minister of State or officials of his Department have custody (possession) but not ownership. What it amounts to is the *de facto* exercise by bureaucrats of the rights of property in what political convention calls the citizens' land. Property rights cannot be exercised by an indeterminate body of persons, the community, over the entire length and breadth of the country.[10]

Nationalization works in the new towns because the Development Corporations have a recognized claim to exercise power over property rights by virtue of the fact that they are both developers and principal purchasers. The county or county borough planning authority is rarely in a position to fulfil either of these roles.

WHO SHALL PAY? WHO SHALL PROFIT? WHO SHALL DECIDE?[11]

With these words, Melvin Webber initiated in Britain a new style of debate about the objectives and consequences of planning, which became common in the United States during the later 1960s. As we already noted in the previous Chapter, this approach takes a very different view of planning from that held by the founders of the postwar British system. Their approach was unitary; they assumed that the planner's objectives automatically represented the best interests of the entire community. The new approach, in contrast, recognizes what seems to have been the reality, as distinct from the idealized objective, of British planning in the postwar era: the fact that planning institutionalizes conflicts between different interest groups. Among these, the most important was the conflict between existing rural interests and urban interests, in particular between existing rural interests and urbanites aspiring to a rural life. The existing rural interests sought to limit and control

[10] D. R. Denman, 'Land in the Market', *Hobart Paper No. 3*, Institute of Economic Affairs (1964).

[11] Melvin Webber, 'Beyond the Industrial Age', *Town Planning Review*, 39 (1968–9), p. 195.

the amount of change. They would have found this easier in the rather static society which Britain presented between the two world wars. But the relative dynamism of postwar Britain, weak as it may have been compared with other nations, created gigantic strains in trying to impose the concept.

Recognizing this fact of conflict, the new approach seeks to identify the gainers and the losers from any system of planning, or from any particular planning act or proposals. At the end of the previous chapter, we already sought to make a provisional assessment of this sort with reference to the physical planning system. We shall now repeat the exercise, with reference to the wider effects of the interrelated policies which have been analysed in this chapter. Considering the whole range of policies – in housing, in transport, in land, in management of the economy – we shall ask who has benefited and who has paid the cost. And we shall also seek to discover how the decisions were made.

Those who have paid have been first, the aspirant rural or suburban dwellers. Families who sought rural life have had to settle for a suburban one – though they still aspire to the rural acres beyond. Suburbanites have been housed in homes that are smaller and meaner than their equivalents in the 1930s – an astonishing decline, when one considers the general advance in standards in the intervening period, and above all the wider range of increasingly bulky possessions that the average family owns. Since these homes will last a minimum of fifty to sixty years, this means that they will become functionally obsolescent long before the end of the twentieth century. The price has been paid, secondly, by all those public housing tenants in the great cities, who have been housed in high-density, high-rise developments because of the shortage of building land. These dwellings, to be sure, have been built to standards – of space and of interior fitting – which are superior to those of the poorer privately-built homes. But the general environment provided cannot be as satisfactory, for families with young children, as the typical council housing estate of the 1930s, when the great majority of families could be accommodated in houses with gardens. Here again, there has been an astonishing decline in the level of the environment available for large numbers of people, at a time when material standards were rapidly increasing in other areas.

There is a third group of those who have paid; those lower-income families who live in privately-rented housing in the big cities. Some of these private tenants, especially in London, are relatively affluent; they live in this type of accommodation because it suits them. But many are notably unaffluent; there is very clear statistical evidence of a substantial degree of mismatch between housing needs, in the form of low incomes or families with young children to support, and the provision of public-sector housing at low or subsidized rents. This question has not been examined until now in this study, because it was not our direct concern and because it is a result of housing policies rather than planning policies. But since this chapter is about housing policies among other matters, it may be worth while to summarize the evidence.

Official government housing statistics show that in 1968, both the median and the lower quartile incomes of households were markedly lower in privately-rented than in local authority housing (median £1,105 against £1,337; lower quartile £598 against £854). Partly this seems to be because privately-rented housing contains many old people with small pensions. But even for families with young children under five – the stage in the life cycle where out-payments are likely to be very considerable – the lower quartile income is lower for the privately-renting families (£1,018 against £1,040). Equally striking is the fact that this group has very little chance of entering the owner-occupier sector which accounts for so much of the new housing in the suburbs, the main focus of this book. One-quarter of privately-renting families with small children had family incomes under £1,018 in 1968; half had incomes under £1,252. Yet at this date, of families of the same type buying on mortgage, three-quarters had incomes above £1,287 and half had incomes above £1,562.[12]

This can be put another way. In 1968, the average price of all dwellings mortgaged by private owners in the United Kingdom was £4,344 and the average income of borrowers was £1,618, a ratio of 2·68. On this basis, a family with young children in privately-rented housing and with a household income of £1,018 (the lower quartile point) could afford a house costing £2,728. And the statistics show that in that year, less than 12 per cent of new mortgaged dwellings cost less than £3,000; the proportion costing less than £2,728 was probably much lower, between 5 and 10 per cent. The chances of such a family buying a house on mortgage were virtually non-existent. And one-quarter of all such families were worse off than this.[13]

Some further evidence on the point comes from Ruth Glass's study of housing in Camden, a typical inner urban area. Here, in 1967, only about 30 per cent of all households of semiskilled or unskilled workers were housed by the local authority. Forty-five per cent of households in unfurnished privately-rented dwellings, and 54 per cent of those in furnished privately-rented dwellings, earned less than £16 a week; 28 per cent in unfurnished, and 26 per cent in furnished, had less than £12 a week. Of this latter group, 45 per cent of the unfurnished tenants and no less than 78 per cent of the furnished tenants were paying more than one-third of their income on housing.[14]

Very different conclusions may be drawn by different observers from evidence like this. Thus Mrs Glass concludes that there is a need for more council building in big cities;[15] the Government, in their White Paper of July 1971, proposed putting private unfurnished tenants and council tenants on the same basis, by a common system of fair rents throughout the two

[12] Department of the Environment, Scottish Development Department, Welsh Office, *Housing Statistics, Great Britain*, No. 20, Feb. 1971. HMSO, London (1971), Supplementary Tables VI and VII.

[13] Ibid., Supplementary Table VII and Table 46.

[14] Ruth Glass, 'Housing in Camden', *Town Planning Review*, 41 (1970), Table 3, p. 37.

[15] Ibid., p. 25.

sectors.[16] What seems to be generally agreed is that privately-rented accommodation contains some of the most disadvantaged sections of the community. Not only do they pay more for accommodation; it is conspicuously poorer in quality, as every Census shows. Yet the process of suburban growth, through the agency of the private builder, has done almost nothing for them. More surprisingly, Chapter Ten of this volume demonstrated clearly that the new-towns programme had done relatively little for the low-income groups either. This seems to have been a combined failure of housing policies and planning policies. In the 1940s, idealists of the Abercrombie–Reith generation believed that the new towns would become socially-balanced communities which would do much to remedy the housing conditions of the poorest groups in the cities. Yet they have failed to house even a due proportion – let alone a more than due proportion. The poor, who happen in many cases to be the unskilled and less well-informed, do not find sufficient job opportunities in the new towns. And even if they get such jobs, they cannot afford new-town rents.

Another group that has paid, but less grieviously, is the new suburbanites. They experience the effects of the planning system – especially suburbanization, or the separation of homes from jobs and services. As a result they enjoy less accessibility to urban jobs and urban services, than if these jobs and services had decentralized at the same pace as the population. The intention of Reith and Abercrombie was that this co-ordination should happen. But as the programme of new community building was submerged under the programme of privately-built suburbia after 1950, it failed to happen. We should not exaggerate the amount of the price that has been paid here, of course. For one thing, there has been dispersion of jobs and services – albeit belatedly, as compared with the dispersion of people. Especially around London, jobs and services have recentralized in the medium-sized and small freestanding towns of the Home Counties. Here, the great majority of people enjoy short journeys to work, to shop, to obtain professional and public services; shorter, indeed, than many suburbanites in Greater London during the great building boom of the 1930s. And even the minority who make longer journeys may not pay an undue price. Their money costs of commuting, at least until the end of the 1960s, had been cushioned by taper rates and subsidies. Their time costs were less than proportionately greater because their services were faster than the short-distance commuter services, and had often been improved out of recognition by technical advances. Perhaps the greatest cost paid by these people, indeed, was the general traffic congestion in the hearts of cities, both large and small. The process of recentralization was actively encouraged by the county borough planning authorities, who saw it as a way of preserving the existing commercial strength of their towns. But as the numbers of shoppers grew with the general rise in population, as each of them on average made more (and more bulky) purchases, as more came to shop by car, the existing structure of the city centre became increasingly and obviously unable to cope.

[16] *Fair Deal for Housing*. Cmnd 4728, HMSO, London (1971), *passim*.

In the interests of preserving the commercial vitality of the city centres, local authorities everywhere found themselves committed to physical destruction on an unparalleled scale. The costs – which were supported by tax or rate subsidy – were often considerable. Yet at the end of the day, the resulting arrangements were still less convenient, more congested than if a completely new start had been made somewhere else. Here as elsewhere, the new town idealists had the answer. But it was never employed save in a handful of instances. Centres like Stevenage or Harlow are today among the rare examples in Britain of twentieth-century shopping centres built for the motor age.

Who then has profited? The inhabitants of the new and expanding towns, presumably, are one such group. Of course, the account is not all on one side of the ledger. The earlier inhabitants in particular suffered a poorer range of jobs, of shops and of urban services than in the conurbations they left behind. In some of the smaller and more isolated town expansions, that may continue to be the case for a long time. But the older new towns, by the early 1970s, were already approaching the same level of service provision as the older medium-sized county market towns. And apart from this, the new-town inhabitants enjoyed well-designed housing, and a general level of urban environment, which few speculatively-built developments could match. The only snag was that even here, space standards were still cramped and tending to become even more so.

Another group which has profited is very diverse in character. It comprises those fortunate enough to possess wealth in the form of property rights in land. The financial benefits which have been enjoyed by members of this group have to a considerable degree been created by the general inflation of the last thirty years. But the operation of the planning system has added significantly and substantially to these gains.

The largest gains have, of course, accrued to those with a major stake in the property market. The value of many small sites in or near city centres has, for example, multiplied enormously through the erection of blocks of offices. The profits from these developments are largely the product of the success of the containment policy coupled with the failure of the authorities concerned even to attempt seriously to influence the location of office employment until the mid-1960s. At the other extreme of the rural/urban continuum, the owners of tracts of land at the periphery of every built-up area (except the new and expanded towns) have had fortunes conferred upon them by the decision to allow residential development. The value of such land, which would be measured in terms of hundreds of pounds per acre for agricultural use has, without the necessity of any active contribution on the part of the owner, been given a price tag by the planning authority which has increased its price to levels measurable in terms of thousands of pounds per acre.

The redistribution of wealth which has resulted from gains of this kind has been highly inegalitarian in that it benefited only a tiny proportion of the population. But much of the redistribution of wealth arising from the inflation in property rights has benefited up to half of the population. In numerical terms the major beneficiaries have been the owner occupiers of private dwellings.

The gains to owner occupiers have not been evenly distributed. The earlier a household became an owner occupier the greater the gain. Those who were already owner occupiers before the war, and those who have inherited from their parents a house bought at that time or earlier, have seen the value of their property multiply by ten or twenty-fold. Those who purchased houses in the 1950s have seen the value of their property double every decade without any corresponding increase in their mortgage outgoings. Those who have purchased houses as recently as the 1970s can, under the existing planning and fiscal situations, confidently look forward to a continuation of these divergent trends in value and cost. These trends work out to the detriment of new households, and those of all ages who never manage to acquire sufficient capital or income to gain a foothold on the owner-occupier bandwagon.

The group which has profited most of all, though, is the existing rural inhabitants. By definition, most of them belonged to the category of older-established owner occupiers just discussed, and they benefited from inflation. But in addition they enjoyed the benefits of undisturbed enjoyment of the countryside. It should not be thought that all these people, or even a majority, are ancestral countrymen and countrywomen. Most villages of England contain few farmers. England lost its peasantry at the end of the Middle Ages; it employed only 5 per cent of its labour force in farming as long ago as 1900. The majority of English villagers, as S. W. E. Vince identified in 1952, are adventitious to the countryside.[17] They are either longer-distance commuters to the towns, or retired people; some may be part-time farmers, largely as a hobby. They tend to be prosperous and well organized, and they care a great deal about the countryside and the way of life it represents. They see the countryside as the repository of tradition and of stability in the face of change. They naturally wish to preserve this image, which makes them profoundly and instinctively conservative or conservationist – the two words, in this context, are synonymous. Conversely, they share a fear of the industrial town as an alien force – a belief that has a long ancestry, going back to the England of the Industrial Revolution and the Chartist riots. Their desire is to maintain as complete and as rigid a separation as possible between the two cultures. And they hold this belief sincerely, even though many of them may earn their living from the city. For them, there is an important distinction between the economic part of life, and the social or cultural part of it. Organized politically in the rural counties, and in the rural districts, they have been responsible for the successful policy of urban containment. The story of urban development in postwar England, essentially, is the story of their triumph.

[17] S. W. E. Vince, 'Reflections on the Structure and Distribution of Rural Population in England and Wales, 1921–31', *Transactions of the Institute of British Geographers*, 18 (1952), p. 54.

It has been a triumph achieved through power and influence. The final question 'who decides?', has a complex answer. In any democratic community there is a necessary conflict between a principle of centralism and a principle of local autonomy. The problem is on whose behalf does any government take decisions. If we said that the rich people could elect and pay taxes to one government and the poor to another, that would not seem equitable, and for central government (with minor exceptions such as the Channel Islands) we reject it. But local government, since income is distributed unevenly across the face of the country, will represent different balances among groups of people with different interests. Counties and rural districts are by definition responsible to their existing electorates, not to potential ones. They are not likely to give automatic weight to the interests of the urban poor, any more than the British electorate gives weight to the desires of poor Pakistanis to migrate to Britain, or the nineteenth-century electorate gave to the disenfranchized poor. It is a fact of political life that most groups do not act altruistically most of the time. Thus, within any political unit, it must be the centre that holds a balance between groups. The more power is fragmented geographically, the more difficult that is to achieve – as the experience of American federalism so clearly shows.

The original model posed for the development of urban England, by the idealists, was a highly centralist one. A beneficent central planning authority, acting on behalf of all the people, would take the important decisions. Mass movements of the people, from the cities to new planned communities, would be achieved by setting up Development Corporations responsible not to local communities but, at one remove, to the centre. The basic distribution of industry would similarly be determined centrally. The local planning authorities would only be faced with residual decisions. This philosophy aroused bitter opposition in rural England. It was not for nothing that the angry citizens of Stevenage renamed their railway station Silkingrad.

The philosophy was therefore scrapped and replaced by one which gave the real power to the ruralites to determine their own affairs. The division between town and country planning authorities was rigidly maintained. Further, new-town building was abandoned, and instead all faith was placed in the Town Development Act of 1952, which was based on voluntary agreements between urban and rural authorities. Struggles between urban and rural planners on major developments were invariably decided, after appeal, in the rural authorities' favour. The counties were positively encouraged to create Green Belts as *cordons sanitaires*.

This pure model associated with the Conservative Governments of the 1950s was modified after 1960. The Conservative Party itself started to give more attention to the interests of urban England. The Labour Government, after 1964, introduced a strong centralist institution in the Land Commission. It also embarked on the reform of local government in order to shift power once and for all away from the counties and towards the major urban areas. This attempt was frustrated by the election result in the summer of 1970. The counties will remain in control – perhaps for a very long time.

None of this was in the minds of the founding fathers of the planning system. They cared very much for the preservation and the conservation of rural England, to be sure. But that was only part of a total package of policies, to be enforced in the interests of all by beneficent central planning. It certainly was not the intention of the founders that people should live cramped lives in homes destined for premature slumdom, far from urban services or jobs; or that city dwellers should live in blank cliffs of flats, far from the ground, without access to playspace for their children. Somewhere along the way, a great ideal was lost, a system distorted and the great mass of the people betrayed.

ALTERNATIVE POLICIES FOR THE FUTURE

In considering what alternative policies might have been pursued in the past and might still be pursued in the future, it is best to be realistic. The consequences of some policies might be fascinating to trace as a theoretical exercise, but no one should assume that they are politically feasible. If governments had consistently pursued a deflationary or at least disinflationary policy after 1945, a situation like that in the 1930s would have obtained: people would have tended to speculate less in land and property, while landowners would have been more inclined to sell if they thought there were dangers of actual falls in value. Again, if agriculture were left without protection or without the generous subsidization which it has enjoyed since 1945, farmers would have been positively encouraged to sell their land for possible development, just as they did in the 1930s. But to posit policies like these, whether for Britain or any other European country in the post-1945 period, is not exactly realistic.

ALTERNATIVE HOUSING POLICIES

Variations in housing policy, on the other hand, might have been feasible and might still be so. Subsidies to owner occupiers could have been reduced, to encourage more people to rent; a unified housing policy could have been introduced, giving private landlords some of the same subsidy incentives as owner occupiers have enjoyed. On the other hand the owner-occupier subsidy element could have been increased, by extending its advantages to new groups not previously able to enter: this was the object of Labour's Option Mortgage Scheme of 1967, which in effect extended the benefits of the income tax concession to poorer families not paying enough tax to enjoy it, and it could be further increased by devices such as a 'balloon mortgage', part of which is repaid only on sale of the house. Most fundamentally of all, if there were ever a completely unified housing policy in which subsidies were attached to the family and its need, rather than to the particular type of housing occupied,[18]

[18] Adela Adam Nevitt, *Housing, Taxation and Subsidies*. Nelson, London (1966) pp. 54–169.

the result might well be a very large extension of demand for owner-occupied housing; for in a period of inflation, house ownership is advantageous to all. And this, in turn, would have given a strong impetus to further urban decentralization.

ALTERNATIVE LAND AND CREDIT POLICIES

There is no lack of possible alternative land and land finance policies, either. At one extreme, as the Uthwatt Committee recommended in 1942, there could be outright nationalization of development land outside existing urban areas, with compensation for lost development rights, and purchase at the point of development by a central planning authority at existing use-value.[19] This was a logically consistent policy in which the market in land would not be required to work at all. The Labour Government's Land Commission of 1967 was a watered-down version of the proposal; but even it could not command general political acceptance. So perhaps it is not realistic to think that the more radical Uthwatt proposal could. At the other extreme, it would be possible to return to a virtual non-plan situation, at least over wide tracts of the country. This would open up wide tracts of land for potential development, and allow development values to float freely – as they did in the 1930s – thus inhibiting the speculative withdrawal of development land from the market, and reducing development values generally. The Uthwatt solution and the non-plan solution in fact have this in common: that they both strike at the root cause of the planning-land value paradox. In the words of the West Australian McCarrey report, already quoted, a plan is a speculators' guide;[20] and when in addition it is a highly restrictive plan, the speculative gains are potentially very great. The only way to meet this difficulty is either to take the land out of the market, or weaken the force of planning, or to tax speculation.

This past possibility suggests a solution which has often been canvassed: site value rating, which would rate land on its site or position value, whether it were developed or not. It would have the opposite result to the present system, which levies no tax whatsoever on unimproved land, and thus charges the landowner nothing while he holds on to land, waiting for a land-hungry developer to make an offer. Under a planning system such as exists in Britain, site value rating (or call it a tax on land for development) would have to take account of planning permission or the lack of it. Land without permission would be taxed or rated as agricultural land (which, under present rules, means not at all). The tax would begin to bite only when the land was shown in the plan as potential development land. Even

[19] Expert Committee on Compensation and Betterment, *Final Report*. Cmd 6386, HMSO, London (1942), p. 32.

[20] *Land Taxation and Land Prices in Western Australia*, Report of a Committee appointed by the Premier of Western Australia on the Taxation of unimproved Land and on Land Prices, Part I. Government Printer, Perth (1968), p. 26.

a low rate of tax would then provide an incentive to sell. A high rate would make land hoarding an expensive business.[21]

A site value rating or land tax system would need to take account of the fact that some planning authorities zone land for residential development whether or not the land is suitable for this sort of development and whether or not the owner wants to develop it. In many cases there are genuine differences of view between the planner and the developer about whether a piece of land is suitable for development. This is one good reason for the paradox in many areas, that developers complain about lack of land while planning officers insist that there is five to ten years' supply. In these cases the owner should be able to serve a purchase notice on the planning authority, which would compel it to face up to the consequences of its policies.

It has to be admitted, though, that the change might make local authorities even more chary of zoning land for development – thus giving rise to a contradiction. In any event, the experience of the Betterment Levy and of Selective Employment Tax suggests that additional taxation might not inhibit large land-holdings and might push land prices up in proportion to the tax. And in those cases where the failure to develop is due to the inability of the local authority to provide the necessary servicing, because of squeezes on public spending, there could be an acute and embarrassing conflict between the person liable to taxation and the local authority. So it would be necessary to allow for this in any system that were devised, and it is simply difficult to see how this might be done.

In many ways, as suggested earlier in this chapter, the experience of the new town Development Corporations suggests that they would be an admirable model to follow. This is particularly so because the regional and sub-regional studies and plans of the late 1960s and early 1970s – studies like Leicester-Leicestershire, Nottingham-Derby, Coventry-Solihull-Warwickshire, the South-East Strategic Plan and South Hampshire – all lay stress on much larger-scale urban developments, over a long period, than has ever been normally the case before. In many ways, they are more akin to the scale of the new town than the relatively limited land releases planned by local authorities in the plans of the 1950s and early 1960s; and in one plan, that for the South-East, the proposed major growth zones are actually much bigger, as was stressed in Chapter Eight of this volume. Yet up to 1971, no land assembly procedures had been proposed in regional plans and no executive power existed to implement them. Extension of the Development Corporation concept to cover areas like these, as suggested by the South-East Planning Council in their comments on the Strategic Plan for the South-East, would appear to be an obvious and logical step. A less formal alternative version would be to create a local land board, including representatives of the local planning authority, the building industry, the district valuer, and consumer

[21] P. H. Clarke, 'Site Value Rating and the Record of Betterment' in Peter Hall (ed.) *Land Values*. Sweet and Maxwell for Acton Society Trust, London (1965), pp. 73–96.

organizations. Like a Development Corporation, this could buy land at a price which reflected the fact that increases in value would largely reflect general community action – though legislation would be necessary to ensure this. But in practice, the difference between this and the sort of Development Corporation created to handle major town expansions, such as the new towns at Peterborough, Northampton and Warrington, might not be very great.

Credit policies represent a closely related area where alternative policies merit close examination. The building industry and the home buyer are very susceptible to the vagaries of the economic climate which manifest themselves in the cost and availability of credit. Of particular importance is the *cost* of credit which affects the building industry and inflates development costs. However, it is not the cost of credit but the *availability* of credit which critically affects consumer demand. This is particularly important to first-home buyers. During 1967–70 many consumers armed with more than adequate down payments could not obtain the necessary credit. It seems curious that many basic commodities and industries are protected by government policies (such as farm subsidies) but no such policy exists to protect the home buyer from the worse effects of liquidity which are beyond his control. During such periods of economic stress it would be a great contribution if the government acted as guarantor to building societies or increased finance for housing through local authorities. This would even out the availability of credit and introduce *stability* in levels of construction and satisfy consumer needs in a basic commodity. Many families would have directly benefited during recent years from such alternative sources of financing.

ALTERNATIVE TRANSPORT POLICIES

Plenty of alternatives also exist in transport policies. Instead of building radial motorways into the centres of the cities – as in the case of the Aston Expressway in Birmingham, the Parkway in Bristol, or the M53 Mid-Wirral motorway and second Mersey Tunnel into Liverpool, all examples of roads under construction in the early 1970s – or instead of the costly inner city ring motorways proposed for London and other major cities, emphasis could be shifted to orbital motorways around the cities, giving good communication between different parts of the suburban rings. This is a policy that has been followed in the United States, with remarkable effects on land use and activity patterns in certain cities – Washington, Baltimore, Boston. Such outer ringways are under construction, or finished, around several British cities in 1971 – Bristol, Manchester – and others are planned for construction in the early 1970s, notably for London (the M25) and Birmingham (the M42). They would cost a good deal less to construct than inner city motorways and they would give good economic benefits; they would provide a relatively economic way of allowing people a wider range of home and job choices, and of encouraging people to find cheaper homes at some distance from the city centres. There might even be justification for encouraging subsidized production of a cheap car for suburbanites, rather than supporting an increasingly uneconomic public transport system in such areas.[22]

The opposite extreme to this policy would be to encourage better, high-speed, public transport systems along radial lines into the city centres, connecting suburban homes to city jobs. They might be express bus systems, using reserved facilities on motorways, or new or rehabilitated rail-based systems. In the late 1960s and early 1970s, for instance, both Manchester and Liverpool were proposing new rail-based rapid transit systems, while Tyneside was developing the idea of linking its existing rail tracks into a light railway system. Most of the systems being contemplated, it is noticeable, did not extend far beyond the conurbation boundaries. They seemed to represent better service for existing conurbation residents, at a time when conurbation populations were already on the decline. But since the boundaries of the new Passenger Transport Executives, established under the 1968 Transport Act, extend beyond the conurbation boundaries, there seems no reason why the new links should not also.

The 1968 Transport Act allows the possibility of 75 per cent central subsidy for approved investment infrastructure in new public transport schemes. And the Department of the Environment already pays the whole cost of national motorways – such as many of the orbital suburban motorways would be – or 75 per cent in the case of motorways serving more local purposes. Investments of this order, which are likely to run into millions of pounds for single projects, can have a large impact on the pattern of urban development, particularly by affecting the time costs of commuting: a new motorway may cut journey times by half or two-thirds depending on the congestion obtaining on the old road system, while new electric rail links can bring marked savings in time, regularity and comfort. But the money costs of a public transport service are increasingly likely to represent the true running costs; and here it seems that longer-distance commuters may pay increasingly more for their rides unless the philosophy is reversed.

ALTERNATIVE INDUSTRIAL LOCATION POLICIES

Industrial location policies, too, could be varied. Indeed, perhaps one of the most remarkable features of the postwar period in Britain has been the continued reliance on the control method of approach – the IDC, the ODP – despite the evidence that in many respects it was ineffective. During the 1960s and early 1970s there was increased enthusiasm for the ideal of a differential payroll tax on congested areas – however these might be defined – coupled with a negative tax, or subsidy, in uncongested or development areas.[23] This system might at first supplement, and then in time replace, the IDC-ODP system of controls. It would have the broad effect of raising the cost of immobile city centre activities. Those activities which had least need of a

[22] Norman Norton, 'Hop in a Car, not on a Bus', *The Guardian*, 17 Aug. 1970.

[23] The Labour Party, *Regional Planning Policy*. The Labour Party, London (1970), pp. 58–63.

city centre location, were most mobile, and were most sensitive to costs, would move most rapidly to uncongested locations. At that point, the precise effect would greatly depend on the relationship between the rate of tax (or subsidy) in overspill locations around the conurbations, *vis-à-vis* more distant development area locations. But one effect would be a more rapid decentralization of jobs from the conurbations to their suburban rings. The tax might not win much approval from the big city authorities such as Birmingham or the GLC – unless they got a share of the proceeds. For it would lead to a weakening of their rateable-value base, which they very much fear. But if congestion is regarded as a problem – albeit a difficult one to define operationally – the tax would be a way of meeting it. So would a system of charging for the use of scarce roadspace in congested cities at congested hours, the effects of which would be slightly more complex.

ALTERNATIVE POLICIES IN OTHER AREAS

There are a host of policies in other fields, which might have an effect on urban growth patterns. The resources allocated to inner urban slum schools, as against suburban schools coping with rapid population growth; clean air legislation and its enforcement; action to reduce the crime rate in certain inner city areas; the possible introduction of a negative income tax, giving poor people greater freedom to spend discretionary income, and facing them with the choice of what sort of housing they wanted to pay for, in what area and at what price;[24] all these, and many others, would have their impact. The argument here is that physical planners, in the period from 1945 to 1970, have all too seldom considered their own narrow range of policy objectives and policy instruments in relation to the wider framework of these programmes. By the early 1970s, with an increasing interest in comprehensive physical and social planning programmes in local authorities, it is at last possible that these barriers are breaking down. So it will be useful, finally, to consider some of the possible interactions between policy choices in these related fields, and the physical forms we discussed in the previous chapter.

POLICY ALTERNATIVES AND URBAN FORMS

Some of these policy choices are set out in Table 13.2 which has two halves. The first half (*Part A*) consists of alternative policy choices in a number of defined areas which are closely related to physical planning, such as general management of the economy, housing, transport, agriculture, and local government reform. Under several of the headings, one of the alternatives involves no change in the general policies pursued between 1945 and 1970, which are assumed to be reasonably consistent throughout that period despite changes of government and political philosophy. (In fact the shifts

[24] The Open Group, *Social Reform in a Centrifugal Society*. New Science Publications, London (1969), pp. 24–6.

Table 13.2

ALTERNATIVE POLICY OPTIONS AND URBAN FORMS

A POLICY OPTIONS

1 *Alternative ways of managing the economy*

1(*a*) Faster inflation.
1(*b*) About the same rate of inflation as in 1945–70.
1(*c*) Slower inflation, or disinflation, or deflation.

2 *Alternative agricultural policies*

2(*a*) More generous agricultural subsidies.
2(*b*) About the same rate of agricultural subsidies as in 1945–70.
2(*c*) Less generous agricultural subsidies, or none at all.

3 *Alternative housing policies*

3(*a*) More generous/easier entry mortgages.
3(*b*) About the same mortgage rates/ease of entry/housing subsidy as in 1945–70; subsidies of the same type as in 1945–70, i.e. attached to houses rather than people.
3(*c*) Less generous/harder entry mortgages.
3(*d*) A national home finance agency to provide easy mortgages underwritten by the State (in practice equals 3(*a*)).
3(*e*) Rationalization of the subsidy system to concentrate it more on those in hardship (low incomes, large families). Eliminate specific subsidies tied to types of housing, e.g. subsidies for high-density and/or expensive land.
3(*f*) Negative income tax to replace subsidies (in practice, effects similar to 3(*e*)).
3(*g*) Increase specific subsidies for high-density and/or expensive land.

4 *Alternative land policies*

4(*a*) Nationalize development rights; development through compulsory state purchase by central authority (the Uthwatt solution).
4(*b*) Nationalize development rights; development partly through private agencies paying Development Charge or Betterment Levy, partly through public agencies using compulsory purchase at a price below full market value (the 1947–53 and 1967–70 system).
4(*c*) Nationalize development rights; development partly through private agencies, but paying no charge or levy, partly through public agencies paying full market (i.e. development value) prices (the 1959–67 system; from 1953 to 1959 there was a mixture of 5(*b*) and 5(*c*)).
4(*d*) Do not nationalize (or denationalize) development rights, i.e. administrative non-plan (the pre-1939 system).

5 *Alternative transport policies*

5(*a*) Make public transport more attractive/cheaper through additional subsidies; leave private transport as it is, or make it more expensive (raise licence fees/ fuel tax/purchase tax on cars).
5(*b*) Proceed roughly as during 1945–70, i.e. some subsidy to public transport (hidden, through losses on public transport met by Treasury, up to 1968; thence social service subsidies to specific public transport operations).
5(*c*) Do not aid public transport but encourage spread of private vehicle ownership through lower purchase tax/licence fee/fuel tax, faster road construction, etc.
5(*d*) Devolve road construction from the Ministry of Transport to a roads Board

with the status of a nationalized industry; charges on road users to go to road construction (in effect similar to 5(*c*)).

5(*e*) Introduce a road pricing system which made travel on congested roads dearer, travel on uncongested roads cheaper, while keeping present level of charges on road users unchanged (the road pricing solution).

6 *Alternative technological policies*

6(*a*) Develop further industrialized, low-cost housing techniques, involving perhaps the modification of building bylaws.

6(*b*) Develop new methods of high-speed public transport, perhaps more 'individualized' than present to make them more competitive with private transport, with the help of state subsidies.

6(*c*) Develop cheaper cars which could be bought by a wider market, thus extending car ownership more rapidly than now forecast.

7 *Alternative administrative policies*

7(*a*) Reform local government along lines of Redcliffe–Maud recommendations of 1969: unitary authorities for most of England; metropolitan authorities for conurbations and their surrounding rural areas.

7(*b*) No reform; continue as in 1945–70.

7(*c*) Two–tier reform with some powers reserved to district authorities (as in the Senior memorandum of dissent to the Redcliffe–Maud report); metropolitan authorities restricted to the continuously built-up conurbations (c.f. the GLC boundaries).

7(*d*) Reform including a powerful tier of regional or provincial authorities, responsible for structure planning (effect similar to 7(*b*)).

8 *Alternative employment location policies*

8(*a*) Introduce a graded system of financial incentives and disincentives for location in different areas: a payroll tax in congested areas, subsidies to employers in uncongested or development areas.

8(*b*) Continue the 1945–70 system of controls (IDCs and ODPs).

8(*c*) Remove all controls; no incentives or disincentives.

B DESIGN ALTERNATIVES

1 *Peripheral growth of conurbations and major freestanding cities* (the *non-plan* situation of the 1930s) with:

1(*a*) Jobs concentrated at the centre and longer radial journeys.

1(*b*) Jobs dispersed at the periphery and local criss-cross journeys.

1(*c*) Any combination of 1(*a*) and 1(*b*).

1.1 Increasing dispersion of the peripheral development (scatter).

1.2 About the same degree of dispersion as in the 1930s.

1.3 Much closer concentration with high-density housing developments and very limited peripheral growth.

2 *Development of new towns or comprehensively-planned town expansions* (separately as in the Abercrombie prescription, or in groups as in the Howard prescription: the *garden city* ideal of the 1940s) with:

2(*a*) Jobs concentrated at the centre with short radial journeys. 2(*b*) Jobs dispersed at the periphery with short local journeys. 2(*c*) Any combination of 2(*a*) and 2(*b*).	2.1 Lower densities (less than 12 per acre). 2.2 Densities of 12–14 per acre. 2.3 High densities (15 + per acre).

3 *Peripheral growth of medium-sized or small freestanding towns*

3(*a*) Jobs concentrated at the centre with medium-distance radial journeys. 3(*b*) Jobs dispersed at the periphery with short criss-cross journeys. 3(*c*) Any combination of 3(*a*) and 3(*b*).	3.1 Low-density peripheral additions. 3.2 Medium-density peripheral additions (approximately 12 per acre). 3.3 High-density peripheral additions with much high-density renewal including high-rise structures.

have been less substantial than might at first be thought.) The second half of the Table (*Part B*) shows a number of alternative urban designs for accommodating urban growth, broken down into the most important elements: the distribution of jobs, the distribution of people and their homes, and the resulting urban form (which is very closely related to the distribution of people, because of the fact that residential and associated land uses are such a dominant part of the total urban fabric). Only the most likely combinations of people, jobs and urban forms are specified in the Table and in the analysis that follows.

Against this background, we can consider how the policy options in Part A of Table 13.2 relate to the feasible urban-form combinations set out in Part B of that Table. Figure 13.2 is an attempt to analyse these connexions systematically. Essentially, it is an attempt to combine deductive logic about the effects of policies with such empirical evidence as exists about their actual effects in the period 1945–70. Though it must be speculative and tentative, some perhaps significant conclusions emerge. One is obvious: that the policies of the recent past have had a specific intent, and on the whole have had specific results. Therefore, the alternative in most cases is to intensify the policy and the trends it produces, or to reverse them. But in a number of cases, it appears that whatever is done to alter policies, the same physical outcomes will result; the options are closed. In particular, two urban-form options, peripheral expansion of conurbations and large freestanding cities, and peripheral expansion of smaller freestanding towns close to conurbations or freestanding cities, emerge as by far the commonest outcomes from a very wide variety of choices in different fields. This is only confirmed by the history of urban development in Megalopolis since the Second World War, which has been of course dominated by growth in these two types of area. Only by means of a sharp and determined shift towards comprehensive centralized

A *Policy Options*

1 *Alternative ways of managing the economy*

1(*a*) Faster inflation
↓
Increased attractiveness of owner occupation
↓
Quicker flight from older rented property
↓
More homes bought wherever land available near work
↓
Peripheral growth of conurbations and freestanding towns

1(*b*) About the same as 1945–70
↓
Owner—occupation attraction
↓
Steady flight from older rented property
↓
Homes bought wherever land available near work
↓
Peripheral growth of conurbations and free-standing towns

1(*c*) Slower inflation
↓
Growth of owner occupation slowed down
↓
Movement from private rental sector slowed
↓
Public-sector housing list lengthens
↓
Pressure for public housing building land
↓
Development of peripheral (satellite) housing estates
↓
Overspill
↓
Development of new and expanding towns, comprehensively planned

2 *Alternative agricultural policies*

2(*a*) More generous subsidies
↓
Agricultural value rises further → Prestige of agriculture rises
↓
Building land scarcer, prices rise
↓
Builders respond by raising densities
↓
Higher densities in all options

2(*b*) About the same
↓
Agricultural value of land keeps up → Social prestige of agriculture rises
↓
Building land scarce, prices high
↓
Builders respond by raising densities
↓
Higher densities in all options

2(*c*) Less generous subsidies
↓
Agricultural value falls → Prestige falls
↓
Building land released, prices drop
↓
Builders respond by reducing densities
↓
Lower densities in all options

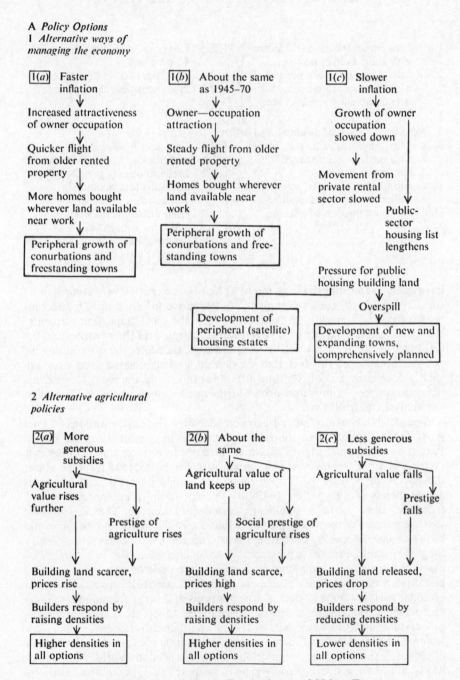

Figure 13.2 Alternative Policy Options and Urban Forms

3 *Alternative housing policies*

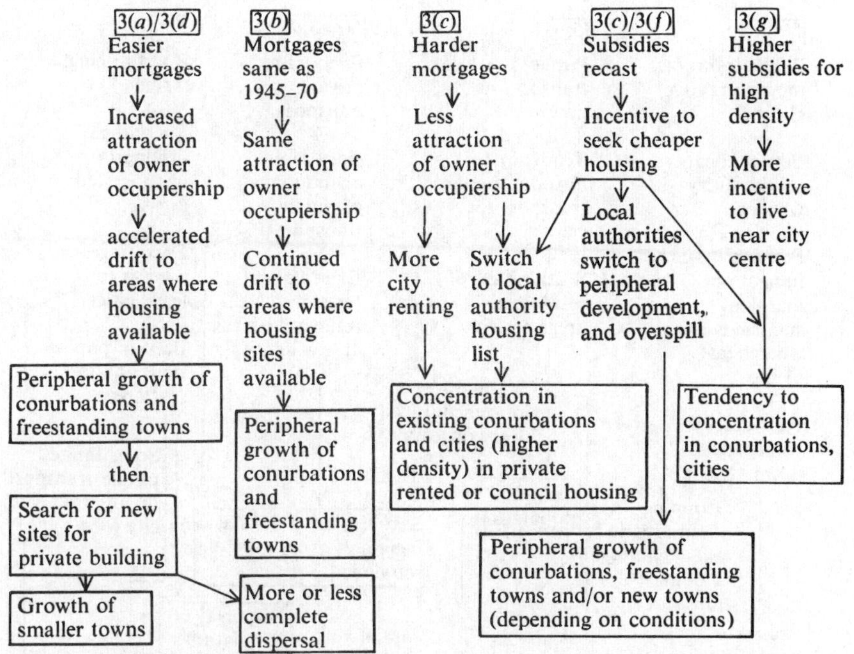

3(a)/3(d)
Easier mortgages
Increased attraction of owner occupiership
accelerated drift to areas where housing available
Peripheral growth of conurbations and freestanding towns
then
Search for new sites for private building
Growth of smaller towns
3(b)
Mortgages same as 1945–70
Same attraction of owner occupiership
Continued drift to areas where housing sites available
Peripheral growth of conurbations and freestanding towns
More or less complete dispersal
3(c)
Harder mortgages
Less attraction of owner occupiership
More city renting
Switch to local authority housing list
Concentration in existing conurbations and cities (higher density) in private rented or council housing
3(c)/3(f)
Subsidies recast
Incentive to seek cheaper housing
Local authorities switch to peripheral development, and overspill
Peripheral growth of conurbations, freestanding towns and/or new towns (depending on conditions)
3(g)
Higher subsidies for high density
More incentive to live near city centre
Tendency to concentration in conurbations, cities

4 *Alternative land policies*

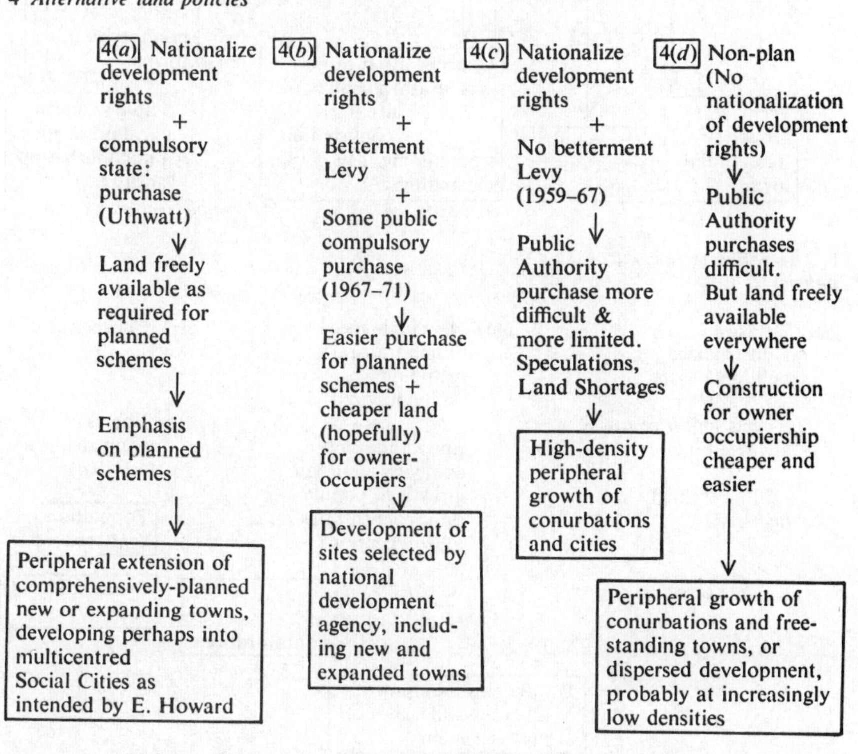

4(a) Nationalize development rights
+
compulsory state: purchase (Uthwatt)
Land freely available as required for planned schemes
Emphasis on planned schemes
Peripheral extension of comprehensively-planned new or expanding towns, developing perhaps into multicentred Social Cities as intended by E. Howard
4(b) Nationalize development rights
+
Betterment Levy
+
Some public compulsory purchase (1967–71)
Easier purchase for planned schemes + cheaper land (hopefully) for owner-occupiers
Development of sites selected by national development agency, including new and expanded towns
4(c) Nationalize development rights
+
No betterment Levy (1959–67)
Public Authority purchase more difficult & more limited. Speculations, Land Shortages
High-density peripheral growth of conurbations and cities
4(d) Non-plan (No nationalization of development rights)
Public Authority purchases difficult. But land freely available everywhere
Construction for owner occupiership cheaper and easier
Peripheral growth of conurbations and free-standing towns, or dispersed development, probably at increasingly low densities

5 *Alternative transport policies*

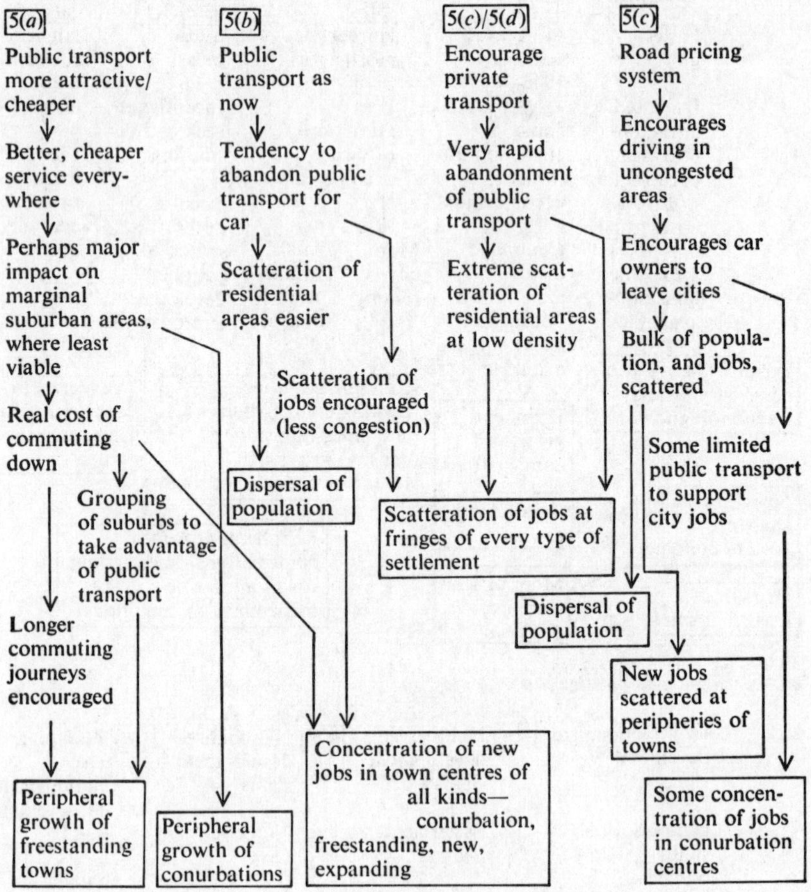

5(a)
Public transport more attractive/cheaper
Better, cheaper service everywhere
Perhaps major impact on marginal suburban areas, where least viable
Real cost of commuting down
Grouping of suburbs to take advantage of public transport
Longer commuting journeys encouraged
Peripheral growth of freestanding towns
Peripheral growth of conurbations
5(b)
Public transport as now
Tendency to abandon public transport for car
Scatteration of residential areas easier
Scatteration of jobs encouraged (less congestion)
Dispersal of population
Concentration of new jobs in town centres of all kinds—conurbation, freestanding, new, expanding
5(c)/5(d)
Encourage private transport
Very rapid abandonment of public transport
Extreme scatteration of residential areas at low density
Scatteration of jobs at fringes of every type of settlement
5(c)
Road pricing system
Encourages driving in uncongested areas
Encourages car owners to leave cities
Bulk of population, and jobs, scattered
Some limited public transport to support city jobs
Dispersal of population
New jobs scattered at peripheries of towns
Some concentration of jobs in conurbation centres

6 *Alternative technological policies*

6(a) Develop industrialized building
? Affects high-rise or low-rise building
(Till now chiefly high-rise)
Outcome ambiguous ????
6(b) New high-speed public transport, including 'individualized'
Encourages more compact suburban growth of population, concentrates on jobs in centres
Central job concentrations
Peripheral development of all types and scales of urban settlement
6(c) Cheaper cars
Effects equivalent to 5(c)/5(d)
Population scattered
Scatteration of jobs

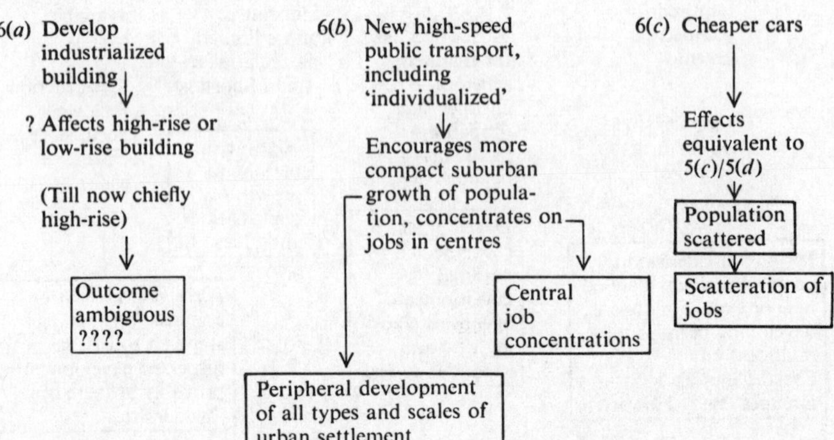

7 *Alternative administrative policies*

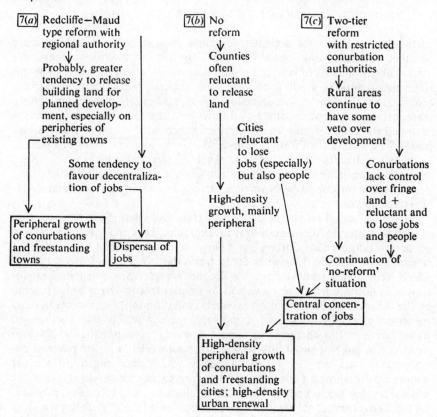

7(*a*) Redcliffe–Maud type reform with regional authority

Probably, greater tendency to release building land for planned development, especially on peripheries of existing towns

Some tendency to favour decentralization of jobs

Peripheral growth of conurbations and freestanding towns

Dispersal of jobs

7(*b*) No reform

Counties often reluctant to release land

Cities reluctant to lose jobs (especially) but also people

High-density growth, mainly peripheral

7(*c*) Two-tier reform with restricted conurbation authorities

Rural areas continue to have some veto over development

Conurbations lack control over fringe land + reluctant and to lose jobs and people

Continuation of 'no-reform' situation

Central concentration of jobs

High-density peripheral growth of conurbations and freestanding cities; high-density urban renewal

8 *Alternative employment location policies*

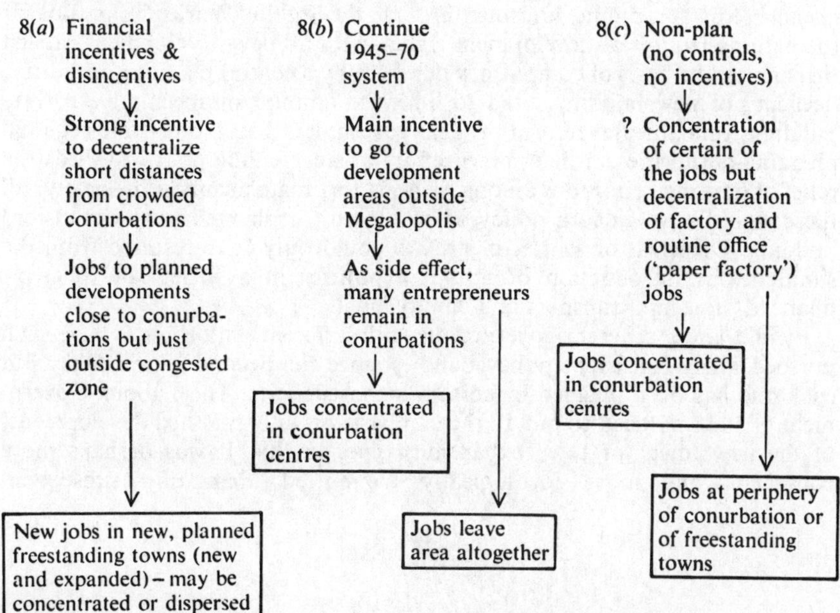

Strong incentive to decentralize short distances from crowded conurbations

8(b) Continue 1945–70 system
Main incentive to go to development areas outside Megalopolis
As side effect, many entrepreneurs remain in conurbations

Jobs leave area altogether

planning would there be a greater emphasis on new towns, or subsequently social cities which would be their natural outgrowth. And only by means of a virtual abandonment of controls would dispersal seem at all likely. Though some policy options would encourage higher-density redevelopment in cities, rental rather than owner-occupiership policy, and public rather than private transport, it is not physically possible to turn the main emphasis towards high-density renewal; the main population growth, and the main urban investment, will occur through peripheral extensions somewhere or other. It is these constraints which limit the range of physical outcomes to a very few, and make it likely that barring a major shift of policy, the bulk of the growth will continue to be housed in extensions to conurbations and major cities and towns.

Figure 13.2 emphasizes one other important fact: that there are a number of policy routes to the same physical outcome. They may well be used in concert to reinforce each other, but if they are used in conflict, this will result in confusion. The chart suggests for instance that the types of urban growth which have been strongest since the Second World War – peripheral expansion of conurbations/major cities and of smaller towns – have been fostered by the following different policy measures: inflation in the economy, making owner-occupiership attractive; a mortgage policy which also encouraged owner-occupiership through tax relief; a policy of nationalizing development rights but not providing strong powers to take land for planned developments such as new towns; a policy which encouraged private car ownership by allowing the cost of motoring to rise more slowly than the general level of prices and incomes; and a failure to carry through fundamental local government reform. An alternative form of urban growth on a large scale – new town, planned town expansions or planned city-regions, for example – would probably have required shifts in all or most of these policies. A slower rate of inflation, and less generous mortgage policies, especially cheap credit for public housing through the Public Works Loan Board; the nationalization of development rights, with all new development carried through on the basis of compulsory purchase by a central planning authority; licencing of new building, used to limit the amount of speculative private building; fundamental reform of local government based on strong regional planning authorities; a determined effort to steer public policy towards the relief of housing conditions among the least fortunate members of society: all these would have aided a policy of new town (or planned town-expansion) building. Dispersal or scatter of growth could only have resulted from the simultaneous introduction of non-plan policies in a variety of spheres – financial, housing, transport and employment.

By and large, different governments with different philosophies have each pursued fairly consistent policy bundles since the Second World War. But each one has been plagued by certain inconsistencies. The Labour Government of 1945–51 tried to put all the emphasis on fully-planned developments of the new town (or town expansion) type; in this, it was perhaps more consistent – and more ideologically committed – than any subsequent government. It tried hard to restrict inflation, it limited the spread of owner occupation by a rigidly-applied scheme of building licencing, it supported public housing through cheap credit, and it carried through financial provisions which in effect abolished the role of the market by making it unprofitable. But even here there were inconsistencies. The financial provisions in the 1947 Act, radical and unwelcome to many people as they were, lacked the pure logic of the Uthwatt Committee solution. They did not bypass the market, but made it function so badly that it almost stopped. And the nettle of local government reform was not grasped. The division between the cities and the counties was left as a source of future trouble.

In any case, as we have seen, the bundle of policies proved unacceptable to too many groups – landowners, potential owner-occupiers, big cities and counties bent on maintaining their freedom of action. The result was that after the Conservative return to power in 1951, the pure policy of building new and expanded towns was allowed to continue, but coupled with many reversals of policy which pointed in the opposite direction. Very quickly, the Conservatives abolished building licencing and welcomed the private builder back into business; they tried to restrict public house-building to slum-clearance schemes; they allowed inflation to proceed, and approved the continuation and extension of subsidies to owner occupiers through income tax relief. These policies made consistent sense; they encouraged speculative building on the pattern of the 1930s. But not quite; because the Conservative Government also encouraged urban containment through Green Belts, and showed no enthusiasm for a far-reaching local government reform that would have brought cities and their rural rings under the same planning machine. Development in this period, from 1951 to the early 1960s, therefore tended to take two forms: high-density, high-rise building for slum clearance and renewal in the cities, and speculative building at increasingly tighter densities in the suburbs. Ostensibly, the policy benefited the aspirant home owner. But more essentially, the free system thus created was bound to benefit most those who were in possession of the right cards at the beginning of the game. It benefited landowners who could make speculative gains, ruralites who resisted development, and county councils fighting urban encroachment. It did not benefit young couples seeking cheap owner-occupied housing, or builders wishing to build such housing, or cities looking for extra land to rehouse their slum dwellers. In a very true sense, it was conservative of existing rights. It mainly benefited those in possession.

It might have been expected that between 1964 and 1970 a Labour Government would have introduced a very different set of policy measures. But what is most significant, perhaps, is that once in office Labour made no attempt to return to the principles of 1945. It continued the subsidies to owner occupiers through tax relief, though confronted with evidence that this was regressive. It continued to give differential subsidies for building high and for using expensive city land, though in its 1969 Housing Act it modified the operation of the former. Despite some efforts, it allowed inflation to continue, further strengthening the case for owner occupiership. It made motoring a little more expensive, but built new motorways at an accelerating rate. It designated more new towns, thereby following a trend already set by the Conservatives when they reversed their policies after 1961. It operated industrial location controls more toughly again after a period of laxity in the 1950s, and introduced office location controls to accompany them. In two respects it made really fundamental innovations. It introduced the Land Commission, which might have fundamentally altered the balance of rural-urban power by acting as a strong development agency, able and willing to fight counties which were reluctant to allow development. And to the same end, it embarked on a fundamental local government reform with the avowed aim of uniting city and country. Any reform that did this was bound to represent a fundamental shift of power towards the urban interests that constitute 80 per cent of the population. But the particular form suggested by the Redcliffe–Maud Commission in 1969, and accepted by the Labour Government in 1970, was the most radical version: unitary authorities extending over the countryside, with no lower tier to represent more local interests, would shift the weight decidedly to the cities. What is finally interesting about these reforms, though, is that they were meant to achieve quite different objectives from those of the 1945 system. The mixed economy, and the market in land, were accepted. The pure Abercrombie vision survived, but it was still accompanied – as in 1951–64 – by acceptance of the reality of speculative development. The real intention of the Labour reforms was to make that development run faster and more smoothly.

By the return of the Conservative Government in 1970, the fate of the Land Commission was sealed; and the different formula for local government reform, unveiled in February 1971, naturally gave greater weight to the counties and the rural areas. Thus, a quarter of a century after the Second World War, the pattern of urban growth in England was still governed fundamentally by the uneasy compromise secured in the late 1940s and early 1950s. The pure vision of comprehensively-planned communities, represented by men like Abercrombie and Osborn, was allowed to survive as a minority movement. But the great bulk of development would still continue to be carried through as a result of interaction between developers, buyers and planners; and in this complex process, the negative element of conservation would continue to dominate. The essential contradiction – whereby a whole bundle of policies worked to encourage development, while another worked to inhibit it – would be allowed to remain, unresolved.

These contradictions have been evident in almost all places and at almost all times in postwar Britain. But there has been one significant set of exceptions to the prevailing pattern. The contradictions are not, for a variety of reasons, evident in Britain's new towns. There was no contradiction between declining space standards and the desire for owner occupation because owner occupation is only at minimal levels in the new towns. There may have been a conflict between the city and rural interests before designation of the new town, but after such designation such conflict was reduced to a minimum by placing effective power firmly in the hands of a Development Corporation with plenty of money to spend, controlled by non-elected appointees. The new towns may have their traffic problems, but they have already shown that they are much more capable of accommodating the private motor vehicle than historic towns and cities. In matters of industrial location the new towns have achieved a signal success in achieving a balance between the levels of employment and population.

The contrast between the trends in the new towns and the pattern of growth elsewhere is mostly the product of the differences in the role of the 'planner'. In most parts of Britain the planner has played a rather negative role. As outlined in Chapter Ten of this volume, the planner has merely responded to the initiative of others. The planner may have envisaged castles and cottages on his drawing board, but when it came to the crunch the outcome was determined largely by what private developers were able to sell, giving the fact of land shortage and high land prices. Only in the new towns was the planner free of this constraint. He himself was able to design and build neighbourhoods, shopping centres, factory estates, blocks of offices, parks and playgrounds. He has been able to experiment with new forms of housing and road layouts, and to use generous landscaping. Though he has been faced with cost constraints too, in the form of housing-cost yardsticks, they are not of the same order as those which have faced the private suburban builder. And this explains much of the difference in quality between the average new-town layout and the average suburban layout. Had land been more freely available, had its price not been bid up by artificial scarcity, he too would have had freedom to experiment.

EPILOGUE: FUTURE PROBLEMS AND PROSPECTS

This book has been about the experience of the past. At the time when it is finalized, there are already clear indications that in the 1970s and 1980s, the framework of planning will be very different from that which has been described and analysed in these pages. This new framework promises to settle at least some of the contradictions that have been examined in this chapter and the previous one. But certain important questions are still unresolved.

The first point to establish is that planning in England in the 1970s and the 1980s will be dominated by the same basic trends which were observed in Volume One of our study for the 1950s and 1960s: continued and rapid growth of metropolitan areas, coupled with a marked degree of decentralization from the cores to the rings, and even to the exurban areas outside the Standard Metropolitan Labour Areas but within commuting range of the cities. The absolute size of these movements will of course depend mainly on the rate of population growth in the country as a whole, which was falling throughout the second half of the 1960s as the birth rate declined. But the trend towards decentralization, not only of people but also of jobs, seems certain. Figure 13.3 shows an official population projection for economic sub-regions, with expected absolute population increases in the period 1968–

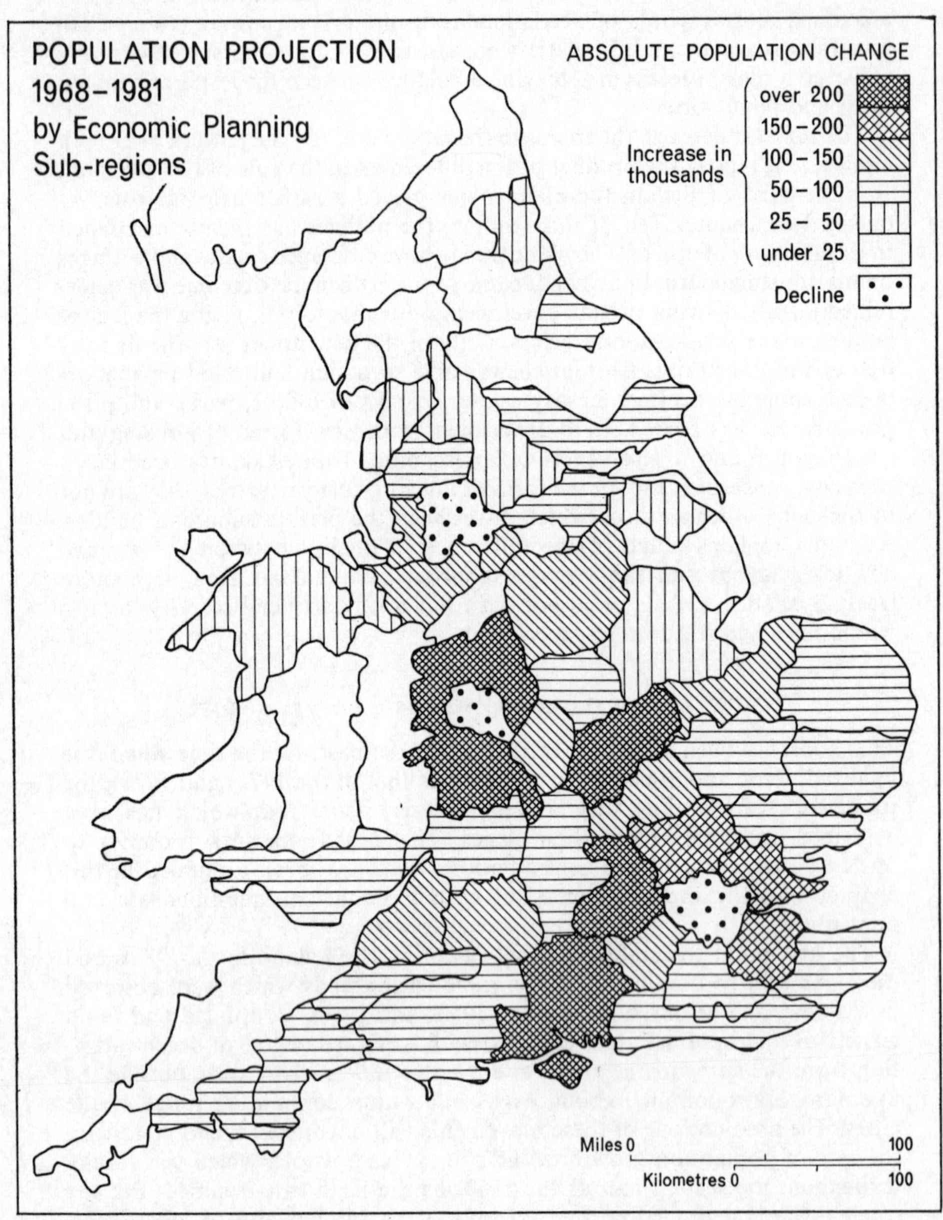

Figure 13.3 Population Projection 1968–1981, by Economic Planning Sub-Regions

81. It is dominated by expansions in county areas at some distance from the main conurbations. In particular, a belt of expansion stretches along the main axis of Megalopolis from the Home Counties to Birmingham and westwards to Southampton and Bristol. It was in these counties that many of the battles over urban expansion were fought in the 1950s and 1960s, and that the Land Commission experienced the biggest resistance to land release in the period 1967–70. Only three areas are expected to decline; they are based on the three major conurbations of Greater London, Greater Birmingham and Greater Manchester. It seems certain then that in the 1970s the same pressures will be felt in the same broad areas as in the 1950s and 1960s.

What will be different from the picture described and analysed in this book will be the machinery for dealing with the pressures. First, it seems certain that there will be a continuing process of preparing and revising strategic plans for standard (or economic planning) regions – or at least, those among the regions which experience the greatest urban growth problems. The machinery for producing these plans will probably be *ad hoc* and will vary somewhat from region to region. Most commonly, there will be a specially-constituted team drawing members both from central government departments (the Regional Planning Board) and local planning authorities, perhaps with some outside expertise. The plan will probably be commissioned jointly by the Regional Planning Council and the local Standing Conference of Local Planning Authorities, representing all the planning offices in the region. It will give what has been conspicuously lacking in the history described in this book: strong regional guidelines for development of the whole region, within which local planning authorities can set their structure plans.

This however still begs some questions. Unless the Crowther Committee on the Constitution reports to the contrary, and the government of the day accepts its report, these plans are not to be produced by a formal level of government, either central or local. Thus the teams that produce them will not be directly responsible to any elected, statutory body. The plans can therefore only be advisory, and would need to be accepted by all the constituent local authorities, and by the central government, before they could be made operational. But if agreement is forthcoming, then it will be without benefit of any approval by the general public; there is no machinery for consultation. So the machinery is cumbrous, and is certainly not very democratic. Nor is it very clear how conflicts of interest are to be resolved. It seems to be assumed that by working together, central and local government officials can reach some sort of agreement; and that by good diplomacy, the commissioning bodies can then be persuaded to give the agreement their blessing. This may put a premium on compromise solutions which disturb existing interests as little as possible.

The alternative would be some form of elected, democratically-accountable regional council to produce plans at this level. It would represent a new constitutional level in British government; and it might take various forms. A bicameral regional council, one chamber composed of elected representatives from constituent local councils, the other consisting of regional MPs, is one such proposal which was submitted to the Crowther Committee in 1971.[25] It has the obvious disadvantage of interposing yet another level of government into an already complex system, though it minimizes this by relying on indirect election. Yet without it, there remains a power and responsibility vacuum at this very important level of decision-taking.

Within the framework of the regional strategic plan, reformed local planning authorities will produce new-style structure plans for their areas, and then – within those – local and action area plans, as specified by the 1968 Act. The structure plans will be highly generalized in form and content, and they will of course cover wide areas. Here the crucial question is whether the boundaries of the new authorities will properly reflect the realities of planning problems. The theory of – and the main justification for – local government reform has been that by making local government boundaries correspond to city-regions, plan-making within each local authority can refer to a natural unit of economic and social interaction, which needs to be planned as a single unit. Over a large part of urban England, the structure of counties suggested by the White Paper of February 1971 may guarantee that this happens. Many of the units based on the bigger freestanding cities, such as Leicester, Nottingham, or Bristol, seem to correspond tolerably well to the city-region concept; these cities and their immediate rural hinterlands can henceforth be planned as a unit. But in some critical areas of the country – critical because they include some of the areas of rapid urban growth and stress which have been analysed in the study – there will be no such guarantee.

First, by cutting the areas of the so-called metropolitan counties back to the limits of the physically built-up conurbations, the reform perpetuates the split between city and countryside in precisely those places where it has proved to be most serious in the past. The essential conflict between the growth pressures of the conurbations, and the desire to protect and conserve the countryside, will thus not be resolved inside a single planning authority by a single set of representatives and officials, but will continue to be cemented into a clash of interests between neighbouring authorities. Thus, automatically, the task of resolving these conflicts will be sent up to the regional team, where it will underline the weaknesses of the *ad hoc* machinery which have just been outlined.

Second, by trying to preserve traditional county boundaries to the greatest possible extent, the reform continues divided responsibility for some of the most important growth areas of the country. This is most evident in South-East England, where one of the major growth areas identified in the 1970 Strategic Plan (Milton Keynes-Northampton) is divided between two county authorities, and another (Reading-Wokingham-Aldershot-Basingstoke) is divided among four. The ironic result is that almost certainly, as soon as they are set up the new authorities will have to set up *ad hoc* co-operative

[25] A Fabian Group. *People Participation and Government.* (Fabian Research Series, 293.) Fabian Society, London (1971), p. 23.

arrangements in order to produce their structure plans for these areas. It is reassuring that in the period before local government reform, all across the country local planning authorities are starting to co-operate on structure plan preparation in anticipation of it; so that it will not be difficult for them to continue in this co-operative mould after the day of reform. Yet even then, co-operation seems to be a second best; just as at the regional level, there will be no direct and effective democratic responsibility of those producing the plans.

Beyond this point, local plans have to be drawn up and development has to take place physically. It is here that some of the biggest doubts occur. From experience with the first major regional strategic plan – that for the South-East, which was published in 1970 – it seems likely that a general feature in the future will be for planned developments to be grouped in rather large discrete zones, on a larger scale than anything known in the 1945–70 system of planning. Thus major developments proposed in the South-East Plan, such as Reading-Wokingham-Aldershot-Basingstoke or South Essex, involve additions to population of half a million or more in thirty years in areas as much as three hundred square miles in extent – half the area of Greater London. In other words, these are much bigger than new-town developments. Yet no specific machinery is posed for acquiring the land and carrying through the expensive and difficult provision of infrastructure. It could be a task within the competence of a reformed local planning authority (or a group of them); but a Development Corporation, or something like it, would be a more effective agency because of its relative commercial freedom, though it would be less democratically accountable to local interests. In any event, the entire community (as represented by the regional planning team) has been responsible for the decision to develop at that spot – not the local authority; so, presumably, it is the whole community that should benefit from the resulting rise in land values. When the Development Corporation buys land for a new town at a price which does not reflect the rise in land value which its own actions have brought about, then it is merely saving money which otherwise it would have had to obtain from the general Treasury purse. So it is the whole community, finally, which benefits from this saving. The same should occur with the new developments.

There are, then, important doubts about the machinery of planning at every main level: regional, sub-regional, and local implementation. But even if the machinery were improved, it would not guarantee the result. From our study, two important conclusions have emerged for the future about the working methods of planning.

The first concerns the need for planning to be much more flexible and responsive to changes in the external environment it seeks to control. Nothing emerged more clearly from our study than the fact that too often between 1945 and 1970, the whole planning machinery failed to cope with changing events at anything like the necessary speed. Here, a more sensitive monitoring and information service is needed. But it should not merely record and act on events quickly; it should seek more actively to predict them, even over substantial periods into the future. Long-range technological and social forecasting, which has been adopted by a number of leading industrial corporations during the 1960s, is still very little employed in urban and regional planning. As a result most local authority planners have only a very dim idea of the world they may be planning for twenty-five years hence – only five years beyond the typical time horizon of their Development Plans.

If this is remedied, an important part of the predictive process will be prediction of the social environment: the world of those who are planned. The planner will need to know not merely about the numbers of people to be planned for in the future and their level of material affluence, but about their views of the world. Indeed, without this knowledge he will not even be able to make the mechanical projections successfully. Thus, basic population projections – one of the most important items for the planner – have been notoriously unreliable in the past because they failed to take account of changing popular attitudes to family-building. And, to give another example, it may prove very misleading to assume that as people become richer in the future they will own more cars, if the rising numbers of cars happen to produce a mass aversion to them and a new emphasis on public transport.

The second point proves to be closely related. It is the lack of, and the urgent need for, an explicit element in planning procedures for measuring the welfare impacts on different sections of the population. Some groups in our study proved to gain a great deal from planning policies and associated policies in related fields such as housing and transport. Other groups have lost; but the balance of gains and losses has often been surprisingly inequitable. There is an urgent need for procedures at all levels to incorporate an evaluation, not merely of aggregate benefit against cost to society as a whole, but of specific gains and losses to different groups. This incidentally will demand that physical plans be increasingly integrated with general plans for social development at both central and local government level.

In suggesting this, there is not intended to be any implication that there is any easy way of quantifying costs and benefits to different sections of the community. Real differences of opinion must occur on such matters as the weight to be put on the conservation of land, versus the need to provide adequate space standards; or the price to be paid in resources for the preservation and enhancement of amenity; or the value to be given to the interests of the present generation against the interests of future generations. These will remain, in part, subjective qualities, which can be resolved only through political processes. But insofar as these processes are bound to be imperfect because of apathy and ignorance on one hand, strong and well-organized pressure on the other, there is a strong case for not relying simply on public participation to secure equity; the result, paradoxically, might be more inequitable than paternalistic planning, even if it were nominally more democratic. Instead, or additionally, planners should try to improve survey methods so as to elucidate preference patterns even among those groups which do not prove vocal or well organized. This is particularly important, for many of the environmental qualities which planning tries to achieve are by definition not available now and so are difficult to conceive of, especially for disadvantaged sections of the population.

This does not mean that planning should remain merely passive, as a sort of predicting and surveying agency which examines people's wishes and predicts them into the future. Necessarily, planners will also take positive steps to suggest futures which will not be immediately apparent to many of the general population; for that is one thing that planners ought to be able to do well. Rather, they will have to maintain a delicate balance between the active and the passive roles. This will best be done if planners develop the method of forecasting in terms of alternative futures, the consequences of which can be traced as they affect different groups in the population. First steps towards this approach were being taken, in exercises like the South Hampshire Plan, at the beginning of the 1970s. But it is here that the greatest conceptual and technical advances will surely come.

INDEX

INDEX